A CLIMBER'S GUIDE TO THE

TETON RANGE

THIRD EDITION

A CLIMBER'S GUIDE TO THE
TETON RANGE

THIRD EDITION

Leigh N. Ortenburger
&
Reynold G. Jackson

THE
MOUNTAINEERS

Published by
The Mountaineers
1001 SW Klickitat Way, Suite 201
Seattle, WA 98134

First printing 1996, second printing 1998

Published simultaneously in Great Britain by Cordee, 3a DeMontfort Street, Leicester, England, LE1 7HD

Manufactured in the United States of America

Edited by Dana Fos
Maps by Irene Beardsley and Reynold G. Jackson
Cover design by Watson Graphics
Book design by Alice C. Merrill
Book layout by Virtual Design
Photo insert layout by Nancy Deahl
Typesetting by The Mountaineers Books

Cover photograph: Main image, *Spring sunrise lights up the Cathedral Group (Grand Teton, Mount Owen, Teewinot Mountain)*. Photo by Sandy Stewart. Inset, front, *Steve Rickert on first ascent of Emotional Rescue, north face of the Enclosure*. Photo by Reynold G. Jackson. Inset, back, *Stephen Koch following High Route on north face of the Enclosure*. Photo by Alex Lowe.
Frontispiece: *Paul Petzoldt on the first ascent of the East Prong, 1927*. Photo by Fritiof Fryxell.
Page 5: *Leigh Ortenburger on the summit of Mount Owen, 1948*. Self-portrait.

Library of Congress Cataloging-in-Publication Data
Ortenburger, Leigh N.
    A climber's guide to the Teton Range / Leigh N. Ortenburger & Reynold G. Jackson. — 3rd ed.
        p.   cm.
    Includes bibliographical references and index.
    ISBN 0-89886-480-1
    1. Rock climbing—Wyoming—Grand Teton National Park—Guidebooks.
2. Grand Teton National Park—Guidebooks. 3. Rock climbing—Teton Range (Wyo. and Idaho)—Guidebooks. 4. Teton Range (Wyo. and Idaho)—Guidebooks.
I. Jackson, Reynold G. II. Title.
GV199.42.W82G736   1996
917.87'55—dc20   96–19569
                                                                          CIP

For my friend

LEIGH

To other Teton climbers who are not forgotten

Fred Ayres	Bill Hooker
Walt Bailey	John Hudson
Allan Bard	John Jackson
Barry Bishop	Hans Kraus
Tim Bond	Juris Krisjansons
Jake Breitenbach	Fritz Lippman
Bill Buckingham	John Mendenhall
Hank Coulter	Craig Merrihue
Julie Culberson	Glen Milner
Don Decker	Tim Mutch
Dan Doody	Karl Pfiffner
Charles Dotter	Dick Pittman
Paul Driscoll	Tom Raymer
Dick Emerson	Patti Saurman
John Fonda	Dave Sowles
Fred Ford	Joe Stettner
Catherine Freer	Paul Stettner
Harry Frishman	Mugs Stump
Art Gilkey	Willi Unsoeld
Don Goodrich	Susan Walker
John Gottman	Fritz Wiessner
John Harlin	Jay Wilson
Gary Hemming	

And to the great pioneers

Albert R. Ellingwood
Fritiof Fryxell
Phil Smith
Robert Underhill

Contents

Foreword

In the early 1950s I received a call in Washington from a young man in California inquiring about any future plans for revisions of the 1947 Teton Climbing Guide. Was it to be revised? No. Was it to be reprinted? No. Was there any objection to someone else publishing a new guide? Certainly not. He anticipated being in D.C. in the near future—Could we get together and talk about it? By all means.

This was the beginning of a delightful 40-year friendship with Leigh Ortenburger, always stimulating and enlivening, at times a bit contentious, never acrimonious. Although the frequency of our contact fluctuated widely I was always careful to maintain a place on Leigh's list to whom he sent those magnificent Christmas cards he produced every year.

In the early 1980s when I established a *pied-à-terre* in Teton Basin and Jack was spending a lot of time there with me, we got into the habit of stopping off to see Leigh on our junkets to one place or another. It was during this time that we first became aware of the "Teton Magnum Opus," which was beginning to show glimmerings of light at the end of the tunnel. I'm sure that Renny, Irene, Carolyn, and Teresa plus a "cast of thousands" of whom I'm unaware didn't see much light in the tunnel, but then of course the "Pink Monster Edition" was the fun part of the project, and they have been faced with the dreary detailed drudgery of completion, tidy up, cross-check, and polish to an extent that would break the resolve of the most dedicated.

As Jack and I discussed the project with Leigh we were continuously flabbergasted by the extent to which he had gone in digging out leads, source materials, graphics, et cetera, which would never have occurred to others. He located and interviewed people whom everyone else was sure had been dead for decades. He found diaries, accounts, pictures, sketches, et cetera, in the most unlikely places, guided by some inner light unavailable to the average mortal. Naturally being grist for his mill from a bygone era we came in for many and vigorous interrogations. At one point we began fabricating outrageous situations and incidents but we didn't get away with it for long and it became easier to try to remember what Leigh wanted to know than to make up something better. Actually, it was surprising how often his poking and prodding fired a long-dormant synapse that provided some small facet that surprised everyone.

Well now it is completed, but to what end? Of course it is primarily a climbing guidebook but of course it is much more than that. Any researcher dealing with any aspect of the Teton mountains will discover in it a primary source of material and anyone not so using it will ultimately live to regret it.

What of those more closely aligned with the usual target for guidebooks?

If you are a hard man searching for the last unscrabbled overhanging crux pitch sandwiched between myriad intertwining routes on one of the big walls this is where you can figure it out. And good luck to you.

If, on the other hand, you are tired of waiting for them to install traffic control lights in Garnet Canyon and the Upper Saddle, be of good cheer. Leigh and Renny will point out all of the really beautiful smaller side canyons which you can have virtually to yourself with fewer visitors than in their heyday in the 1930s. Enjoy!

If you have achieved that inevitable stage where your legs operate much more effectively propped on your favorite hassock than they do on steep scree or boulder fields, and your hands have lost all the cunning that you so painfully taught them, except perhaps to dismantle one more twist-off bottle cap, do not despair. You have the whole gamut of climbing experience from Billy Owen on, to experience vicariously at any time, rate, and degree of difficulty you choose.

Truly there is something for everyone here. Don't be intimidated—go for it.

A word of warning. Don't procrastinate—we have it from an often reliable source that in keeping with the "wave of the future" the next 50-year revision of the Guide will be inscribed on a microchip to be implanted directly behind the location of the pocket in which a normal-sized guide is ordinarily carried.

Jack Durrance and Hank Coulter
January 1996

Acknowledgments

When I heard that Leigh Ortenburger was missing and it was feared that he had perished in the Oakland firestorm in 1991, my first thought was clearly that of denial. It was as if someone had told me that the Second Tower and the Molar Tooth had fallen off the Grand Teton, thereby altering forever the east ridge. As the truth of his loss began to sink in, I began to despair over the fact that this project might never reach completion. Writing this book had been, at Leigh's suggestion, a collaborative effort since 1985. With the driving force gone, it was at least a year before I could bring myself to sit down at the computer and go through the files.

All of this I have seen. Part of it I am.

This quote, from *The Aeneid* by Virgil, hung above Leigh's desk in Palo Alto and I thought about it often during those dark months after he died. Leigh was a mountaineer, historian, statistician, explorer, father, husband, and many other things. But he also kept track of and chronicled the climbing history of this range as no one ever has before or since. The reader, therefore, should realize that within these pages dwells much of a great man's spirit. I sincerely hope that along with that spirit a substantial bit of accurate climbing information will also be found.

I find myself in the unique position of being able to acknowledge certain individuals specifically for Leigh as well as many others who were known to both of us. This compilation of information over the past 30 years has been possible only through the generous assistance of hundreds of people. Leigh would perhaps begin by mentioning his debt to Henry Coulter and Merrill McLane, whose guidebook first inspired his own initial efforts. Richard Pownall also provided much of the original motivation toward a new climbing guide. As he mentioned in the 1965 edition, Leigh was indebted to Phil Smith, Joseph Hawkes, and Jack Fralick in connection with the 1940 handwritten manuscript of Phil Smith's revision of the 1932 book by Fritiof Fryxell, *The Teton Peaks and Their Ascents*. The foreword, by Jack Durrance and Hank Coulter, is not only greatly appreciated but also highly treasured. Sadly, shortly after its completion, Hank Coulter passed away.

We would especially like to thank *all* of the Jenny Lake rangers, past and present, as well as the many mountain guides that each of us has known over the years. At the risk of forgetting someone, this list must include the following individuals: Bill Alexander, Hooman Aprin, Peter Athans, Rich Baerwald, Jane Baldwin, Ralph Baldwin, Randy Benham, Michael Beiser, Scott Berkenfield, Wes Bunch, Andy Byerly, Dave Carman, John Carr, Andy Carson, Doug Chabot, Paul Cohee, Scott Cole, Greg Collins, Bill Conrod, Catherine Cullinane, Larry Detrick, Jim Dorward, Barb Eastman, Margo Erjavec, Nancy Feagin, Brent Finley, Tory Finley, Mike Friedman, Sherry Funke, Eric Gabriel, Paul Gagner, Jane Gallie, Scott Guenther, Keith Hadley, Randy Harrington, Susan Harrington, Chuck Harris, Pete Hart, Brents Hawkes, Gardner Heaton, Tim Hogan, Peter Hollis, Rex Hong, Paul Horton, Bob Irvine, Ken Jern, Lanny Johnson, Ron Johnson, Hans Johnstone, Jim Kanzler, Jason Keith, Tom Kimbrough, Stephen Koch, Leo and Helen Larson, Evelyn Lees, Peter Lev, Alex Lowe, Patricia MacDonald, Anne and Chas MacQuarrie, Mark Magnuson, Ron Matous, Tom Milligan, George Montopoli, Dean Moore, Goldie Morris, Don Mossman, Doyle Nelson, Mark Newcomb, Rod Newcomb, James L. Olson, Jim Olson, Richard Pampe, Rich Perch, Jim Phillips, Jay Pistono, Chuck Pratt, Kevin Pusey, Steve Quinlan, Al Read, Rick Reese, Steve Rickert, Mike Ruth, Jean Ruwitch, Kim Schmitz, Tom Sciolino, David Scroggins, Mattie Sheafor, Pete Sinclair, Jim Springer, Sean Sullivan, Herbert Swedlund, Jack Tackle, Ed Thompson, Gary Thorson, Ralph Tingey, Tim Toula, Bruce Tremper, Jack Turner, Krag Unsoeld, Mark Whiton, Jim Williams, Jed Williamson, Ted Wilson, Janet Wilts, Gary Wise, Jim Woodmencey, and Rick Wyatt.

We also wish to identify those who have made significant contributions to the book by providing material in their special areas of expertise: John C. Reed, Jr., for the geology section; Jim Woodmencey for the climatology section; Dan Burgette, Pete Armington, and Mark Magnuson on behalf of the National Park Service; and Tom Turiano for portions of the ice-climbing section and some assistance with the text in reference to the northern peaks. Much appreciation is extended to Jim Springer and Eldon S. Dye for their incredible artwork. We are very much indebted to the following individuals for taking the time to read the manuscript and to provide much-needed editorial comments: William Buckingham, David Dornan, Paul Horton, Robert Irvine, Ron Johnson, Tom Kimbrough, and Steve Rickert. Special thanks are due to Paul Horton for assistance and encouragement throughout the entire process. I also wish to thank George Montopoli for his endless computer help and Leslie Haning for her professional design contributions. We wish to recognize the following people for the outstanding photographs that they have provided: Hank Coulter, John Dietschy, Richard DuMais, Jack Durrance, Kenneth A. Henderson, David Jenkins, Lanny Johnson, Peter Lev, James L. Olson, Sandy Stewart, and Steve Walker. The darkroom talents of Jon Stuart were key to the final compilation of the historic and climbing photographs.

Without diminishing the important help of others, the following friends and contributors have been so generous with their time and assistance that they must be enumerated: Davey Agnew, Jim Beyer, Donnie Black, Beverly Boynton, Yvon Chouinard, Richard Collins, Barry Corbet, Bruce Crabtree, Dick DuMais, Dave Ellingson, Charlie Fowler, Matthew Goewert, Hal Gribble, Rick Horn, Jim Huidekoper, Raymond Jacquot, Peter Koedt, Juris Krisjansons, Norm Larson, Sam Lightner, Mark Limage, Rick Liu, George Lowe, Kent Lugbill, Callum Mackay, Rob Mahoney, Doug McLaren, John McMullen, Rick Medrick, Greg Miles, Stan Mish, Mike Munger, Sterling Neale, Mason Reid, Jim Roscoe, Chuck Schaap, Steve Shea, Joe Sottile, Steve Sullivan, Angus Thuermer, Buck Tilley, Ray White, and Tom Windle.

I also want to thank Irene Beardsley for her tireless efforts over the past four years. Without your dedication, Irene, this project could not have been completed. And to Dan Bloomberg, thanks for putting up with my difficulty in grasping the computer concepts that come so easily to you. Your help was invaluable!

I deeply thank my mother, Vivian, and my father, John, for instilling in me a love of mountains and of wild places. Many of the people mentioned above are those with whom I have ventured into the mountains over the years. The partnerships, adventures, epics, and climbs that we have had together account for some of the best experiences of my life and these are highly valued.

Finally, I wish to acknowledge the debt owed to my wife, Catherine, and my daughter, Jane. I have been consumed by the labor on this book over countless evenings and weekends for nearly a decade. Only they know how much time and effort have been expended and I thank them sincerely for their patience and understanding.

Since this book will be subject to revision in future years, it is very much the hope of the author that comments and corrections concerning the route descriptions, the climbing history, the difficulty ratings, the time information, and the bibliography will be sent to him at his home address (Box 35, Kelly, WY 83011) or via e-mail (rjackson@wyoming.com).

R.G.J.
Kelly, Wyoming
February 1996

It may be said that my father was a little crazy to ever have begun this guidebook. When he first started the project, he had only spent a few summers in the Tetons. More recently the difficulty has lain in the astonishing rate at which new routes continue to be put up in the mountains. He spent countless hours creating this work that is both an historic record and a reference for the next generation of climbers. Those who knew my father were well aware of his dedication to accuracy and his fascination with pondering the events of the past. In fact, he was so taken by the task that his fellow climbers have often wondered when, if ever, a new revision would emerge.

Eleven years ago, he and Renny Jackson decided to collaborate on a revised edition. This gave many of us renewed hope that such a revision might actually be possible. I know that his work with Renny was among the most rewarding of his life. He often spoke of his gratitude for the unique expertise that Renny brought to the project. They were a team that combined the benefits of youth and age, of present and past. And they shared a gentle sense of humor, a seriousness of demeanor, and a great love for the Teton Range. After my father's death, the task of completing this book was daunting. It seemed perhaps too large a task for those of us still living. I believe that it took a brave and determined heart to even consider the project. Renny Jackson took on that challenge and Irene Beardsley, my mother, worked with him as editorial assistant. Publication of this book would not have been possible without them, and I wish to thank them for their seemingly endless energy and efforts.

My father would be proud of the work that Renny and my mother have done. It is their gift to Teton climbers and to his memory. I can imagine how pleased he would be to know that the revision has finally been published, just as I can still see him hiking and climbing in the mountains that he so deeply loved.

Boulder Field / Moran Canyon

rock walking
the last place I
walked with you

rock walking
a new way to fly
with geologic consequences

gneiss and schist
are metamorphic footholds
between past and present
and I rock walk
this spider's dance
among my fears

rock walking
this one last time
I twist
and sway
and catch my balance
in the easy grace
of your memorized steps
from one boulder
to the next

Carolyn Ortenburger
Redwood City, California
March 27, 1996

Safety Notice

A guidebook is not a substitute for mountaineering skill, nor can it make climbing safe for those who do not apply sound judgment and practice the principles of safety.

Mountaineering and rock climbing involve risk, and those who engage in these forms of foolish activity must, either explicitly or implicitly, recognize this point. It is the purpose of skill to minimize, or eliminate, the consequences of this risk. Inexperienced climbers are urged to avail themselves of instruction in safe climbing techniques from mountain clubs, professional guides, or experienced friends before trying difficult ascents. No ascent is worth the deliberate risk of life. Do not attempt routes without proper equipment or beyond your abilities. Do not ignore the potential consequences of bad weather.

Steve Rickert on the South Buttress Right on Mount Moran (Photo: Lanny Johnson)

Introduction

Almost everyone who has done any mountain climbing in the United States sooner or later visits the Tetons and ascends one or more of the high peaks. These peaks rise steadily at a high angle, bristle with spires and pinnacles, and are topped by sharp summits. Whereas most other ranges are obscured by foothills, the Tetons rise abruptly as much as 7,000 feet from the flat plains of Jackson Hole and culminate in the 13,770-foot summit of the Grand Teton.

There is perhaps no climbing area in the country that can match the Tetons for general mountaineering of an alpine nature with excellent rock and moderate snow. This combination of characteristics provides an excellent training ground for the novice as well as the vast majority of climbers who simply seek enjoyable and challenging routes. There are also extremely difficult mixed alpine climbs that provide a testing ground for those who aspire to travel to the other great ranges of the world. From the large Himalayan expeditions of yesterday to the modern, alpine-style ascents of today, Teton climbers have played a key role in pioneering new routes throughout the world.

The Tetons are very accessible. Modern highways lead virtually to the foot of the peaks. The summit of the Grand Teton is little more than three horizontal miles from the nearest approach road. Every peak between Death Canyon on the south and Moran Canyon on the north can be climbed in one day from a campsite at Jenny Lake, although most of the higher and more distant peaks are seldom climbed in less than two days. And the climbing is enjoyable!

The prospect of the many high-angle routes on some of the finest rock for climbing has doubtlessly enticed many climbers from their home mountains. Nearly every grade of difficulty, from very easy to very difficult, is found in the Tetons. The Tetons have been more intensively climbed than any other range of equal size on the entire continent. As a result, almost every peak has at least six routes; the Grand Teton, the center of interest, now has 38 distinct routes and numerous variations to its summit. It should not be thought that the relatively small number of peaks allows one to "climb out" the range in a few weeks or even years. New routes remain to be explored, although on some peaks it may take a little research to find an unclimbed section. For those whose goals do not include the making of first ascents, there is an unlimited opportunity for hiking, on or off the 220-mile trail

system. The weather is usually pleasant, and during most of August one will find clear climbing days.

Not least among the attractions of the Tetons is the abundance of wildlife. Under the protection of the National Park Service (NPS), the moose, elk, deer, bear, marmots, and coneys have flourished and are often encountered by mountaineers. The birds, the flora, and the geology of the range are other features attractive to those interested in the natural scene. As a point of historical interest, the Grand Teton was well known to travellers in the early 19th century as an important landmark of the headwaters of the Columbia River. The Tetons were also a focal point for the fur-trapping business that prospered in the beaver-rich rivers and streams that surround the range.

Much of the first exploration of the wild areas of western America was carried out by fur trappers, whose stories and exploits have now become legendary. Whoever wishes to learn more of this fascinating era of American history will find a list of excellent historical accounts in the *General References* section. Also given there are references to the literature covering the flora, fauna, and geology of the Teton area. The geological aspects of the range are of such great importance and have such an intimate relation with the pursuit of climbing that a special section is devoted to this subject (see *Geology of the Teton Range*, later). To gain a broad and deep understanding of and appreciation for the Tetons, it is urged that the references in this latter section also be studied.

There has been intentional emphasis in this guide on the area between Death Canyon on the south and Moran Canyon to the north. It is this area of crystalline rock (with the exception of a very few crystalline peaks north of Moran Canyon) that has attracted the most attention from mountaineers. The easy sedimentary peaks that lie in the southern part of the range, along the divide between Jackson Hole and Teton Basin to the west, and those in the northern part of the range receive very little climbing traffic. However, they do remain worthwhile objectives for those with more moderate standards.

To minimize repeated geographical explanations in the main section on route descriptions, this guidebook assumes that the reader will also have in hand the U.S. Geological Survey (USGS) topographic map of Grand Teton National

Park. This map is essential to the understanding of the nomenclature and the directions and is remarkably accurate considering the extremely rugged terrain. Sixteen elevations absent from the published map have been used in this book; these figures were obtained from study of the manuscript of this map in the National Archives in Washington, D.C. Hence, the reader will occasionally find an elevation given, such as 11,644 feet for the Lower Saddle, which does not agree with that which one would deduce from the map, in this case 11,600+ feet. Little or no confusion will result because the feature whose elevation is given will always be identified by some means other than just its elevation.

There are primarily three categories of names that appear in this book. First are those that have official approval of the U.S. Board on Geographical Names; perhaps these should have been accorded a distinguishing mark, but readers in doubt concerning the status of a name can refer to the USGS map. If the name appears on the map, it has been officially approved; if it does not, then it is almost certainly unofficial (there are a very few names that have been approved but that do not appear on the map). There is a second, small category of names that appear on U.S. Forest Service (USFS) maps, in publications of various geologists who have studied the area, or on maps used by NPS rangers. Finally, there are a good many names that have been in more or less common usage by Teton climbers over the years. The authors have not seen fit to engage in any wholesale naming of peaks in the belief that this is a prerogative reserved for those who made the first ascent. Certainly there is nothing to be gained but confusion through efforts to change names that have already appeared in print, no matter how lofty the intention. In the absence of any overpowering reason to attach identifying names, perhaps our generation should leave to the next at least some peaks to name. The authors have also followed the practice of the Sierra Club in identifying peaks by their elevations (such as Peak 11,117) when no name has been given in the past. However, the following names have been attached by the authors: Murphy Peak, Two Elk Peak, Tukuarika Peak, Spalding Peak, Gilkey Tower, Bonney's Pinnacle, Pemmican Pillar, Fairshare Tower, Symmetry Crags, Ayres' Crags, Blockhouse, Unsoeld's Needle, Blackwelder Point, and Anniversary Peak. A climbing guidebook does not have space for the inclusion of the history of the nomenclature; this will have to appear separately.

Climbing History

The climbing history of the Teton Range is unusually long and complicated and space permits only a brief review. The first undisputed major ascent in the range was that of the Grand Teton on August 11, 1898, by William Owen, Franklin Spalding, John Shive, and Frank Peterson. The various attempts and claimed ascents of the Grand Teton, including the bitter controversy between Nathaniel P.

John Shive, Franklin Spalding, and Frank Peterson on the summit of the Grand Teton on the first certain ascent, August 11, 1898 (Photo: National Park Service, Grand Teton National Park; taken by William O. Owen)

Langford and Owen over the validity of the attempt or ascent in 1872 by Langford and James Stevenson, are discussed in the *Grand Teton* section.

Ten days after the ascent of the Grand Teton in 1898, the Bannon topographic party ascended Buck Mountain and saw the banner left by the Owen–Spalding party on the summit of the Grand Teton. This topographic party also climbed several of the easy peaks along the divide during their work, which culminated in the USGS Grand Teton quadrangle map. Although the 1898 ascent of the Grand Teton received considerable publicity, it seems to have had little influence in attracting other mountaineering visits, even though American mountaineers were active in other areas, notably the Canadian Rockies. During the summer of 1912, Professor Eliot Blackwelder, while studying the geology of the sedimentary strata, mostly on the west slope of the Tetons, made a few ascents of peaks on and west of the divide. The ascent of the north summit of Mount Moran in 1919 by LeRoy Jeffers was accorded more publicity than perhaps any other single Teton ascent. This climb motivated Dr. L. H. Hardy to make the first ascent of the higher summit, beating Jeffers by ten days when he returned to make the second ascent in 1922. The third ascent of the Grand Teton (the Owen–Spalding party climbed the peak twice) was made in 1923 by three youths from Montana—Quin Blackburn, Andy DePirro, and Dave DeLap—and was a remarkable early achievement. The modern era of climbing began in 1923 and 1924 with visits of Albert R. Ellingwood of Colorado and Paul Petzoldt of Idaho. Ellingwood in 1923 made the first ascents of the South and Middle Tetons and the fourth ascent of the Grand Teton. The next year he returned to pioneer the Northeast Ridge route on Mount Moran. Petzoldt's four ascents of the Grand Teton in 1924 marked the beginning of his lengthy career as a professional guide in the Teton Range.

The summers of 1925 and 1926 saw the first climbs of Phil Smith and Fritiof Fryxell, who during the next decade were to make much of the climbing history of the range. Fryxell's excellent account of the climbing history up to

Phil Smith, Robert L. M. Underhill, and Fritiof Fryxell on the summit of Mount Owen, July 16, 1930 (Photo: Kenneth Henderson)

1931 appears in his book *The Teton Peaks and Their Ascents*. Smith made the first ascents of Disappointment Peak and Mount Wister in 1925 and 1928, respectively. When the new Grand Teton National Park was established on February 26, 1929, Fryxell and Smith became the first members of the ranger staff. They started a systematic exploration of the range and placed summit registers on the prominent peaks. The completeness of the climbing records is due largely to their efforts. They initiated the practice of requiring climbers to check in with park authorities as a safety measure and to report all new routes and unusual climbs. In 1929 and 1930 they made first ascents of Teewinot Mountain, Nez Perce Peak, Mount St. John, and Symmetry Spire. Fryxell alone climbed Rockchuck Peak, Mount Woodring (Peak 11,585), Bivouac Peak, and Mount Hunt for the first time. The first climb of the Grand Teton by a route other than the Owen–Spalding route of 1898 was also made during the summer of 1929 when Robert Underhill and Kenneth Henderson, both with previous climbing experience in the Alps, successfully ascended the East Ridge. In 1930, with Fryxell and Smith, they climbed the summit knob of Mount Owen, which had balked three attempts in 1927 and one in 1928. Underhill and Henderson also climbed the spectacular Teepe Pillar in 1930.

The summer of 1931 was very important in the history of the Tetons. Glenn Exum, then in his teens, made his famous solo ascent of the ridge that now bears his name on the Grand Teton. Underhill and Fryxell in quick succession climbed the East Ridge of Nez Perce, the North Ridge of the Middle Teton, and the North Ridge of the Grand Teton. This last climb easily ranks as one of the great early climbs in this country. Underhill also pioneered the Underhill Ridge of the Grand Teton with Smith and the East Ridge of Mount Moran with Petzoldt. All five of these climbs by Underhill were made in one 12-day period. That summer Fryxell made the first climbs of Cloudveil Dome, East Horn, Storm Point, and Ice Point. Hans Wittich climbed the Dike route on Mount Moran and the Wittich Crack on the Grand Teton. Within the next three years the major first ascents were completed, chiefly as a result of the efforts of Fryxell and Smith, who climbed Rendezvous Peak, Rolling Thunder, Eagles Rest, Doane Peak, Ranger Peak, Veiled Peak, and Prospectors Mountain. Fred and Irene Ayres made their first visit to the park in 1932 and subsequently accomplished many first ascents, notably Rock of Ages and other pinnacles around Hanging Canyon, the West Horn, and Traverse Peak.

Inevitably, interest in the years after 1935 shifted to the making of new routes. Throughout the 1930s Petzoldt was guiding during the summers and made many important new climbs, such as the first ascents of Thor Peak; the North Face, West Couloir, of Buck Mountain; the West Ridge of Mount Moran; and the Koven route, West Ledges, and Northeast Snowfields of Mount Owen. In the same decade

Jack Durrance (Photo: Henry Coulter)

T. F. Murphy, the chief of the party assigned by the U.S. Geological Survey to map Grand Teton National Park, ascended a great number of vantage points in order to determine elevations and sketch the topography. In the course of the summers of 1934 and 1935, he climbed most of the peaks south of Buck Mountain, almost all the peaks of the divide, a few of the peaks west of Mount Moran, and many of the peaks bordering Webb Canyon. Hence, even though there are no written records of ascent, a climber visiting one of these lonesome peaks may find a cairn that was probably built by Murphy and his assistants, Mike Yokel, Jr., and Robert E. Brislawn.

In 1936, his first summer at the Tetons, Jack Durrance teamed with Paul and Eldon Petzoldt to make the first climb on the north face of the Grand Teton. Durrance's favorite routes were the ridges. With Henry Coulter and other Dartmouth climbers he made many new routes: the East Ridge of Disappointment Peak, the Durrance Ridge of Symmetry Spire, the North Face of Nez Perce, the Southwest

Ridge and Northwest Ridge of Mount Owen, the lower half of the Exum Ridge, the Southwest Ridge of the Enclosure, and the West Face of the Grand Teton. Many of Durrance's routes are genuine classics and, at the time they were pioneered, represented the highest caliber of American rock climbing.

In the last of the new climbing before World War II, Petzoldt in 1940 and 1941 led the now popular CMC route and the North Ridge of Mount Moran and the Petzoldt Ridge of the Grand Teton.

The war years, 1942–1945, mark a period of almost complete inactivity, because most of the mountaineers were in the service, many in the mountain troops. The years following have brought an enormous increase in the number of climbers visiting Grand Teton National Park, with a corresponding increase in the investigation of new routes and old routes that had been climbed only once. In the first decade after the war, new walls, ridges, and couloirs, purposely avoided by the prewar climber as being too difficult, were now sought out and explored for the first time with a competence matched rarely by earlier climbers. Several ascents now considered classics were successfully completed. The most important new routes and first ascents of this period include the North-Northwest Ridge of Buck Mountain, the West Chimney of the North Face of Mount Wister, the direct South Ridge of Nez Perce, the North Face of Cloudveil Dome, the Southeast Ridge of the Middle Teton, the West Face of the Exum Ridge and the direct finish on the North Face of the Grand Teton, the Red Sentinel, the Southwest Ridge of Disappointment Peak, the North Face and Northwest Ridge of Teewinot Mountain, the North Face and North Ridge of Mount Owen, the Southwest Ridge of Storm Point, the Direct Jensen Ridge of Symmetry Spire, the East Face of Thor Peak, and South Face I of Bivouac Peak. Nearly all of these were pioneered by a small group of active mountaineers including William Buckingham, Donald Decker, Richard Emerson, Art Gilkey, Paul Kenworthy, Robert Merriam, Leigh Ortenburger, Richard Pownall, and Willi Unsoeld. Many of these men served either as climbing guides or as seasonal climbing rangers.

The second postwar decade, from 1955 to 1964, provided a rapid advance in climbing ambition, courage, competence, and equipment. In step with rock-climbing progress throughout the United States, new routes required a high level of technical skill in free climbing and in pitoncraft. Fortunately there are, even now, few bolts in Teton rock. The use of direct aid or artificial climbing, which was a rarity in the Tetons prior to 1958, became an accepted practice and was required on many of the most difficult new routes. The most significant climbs of this era were made by Fred Beckey, William Buckingham, Yvon Chouinard, Barry Corbet, William Cropper, John Dietschy, David Dingman, David Dornan, John Gill, James Langford, Peter Lev, Frederick Medrick, Leigh Ortenburger, Richard

Al Read on the Great Traverse, South Buttress Right, Mount Moran (Photo: Peter Lev)

Pownall, Al Read, Royal Robbins, Pete Sinclair, Herb Swedlund, Willi Unsoeld, and Kenneth Weeks. In many instances the new climbs, often variations rather than routes, were made on less important, smaller faces and ridges because earlier efforts had preempted most of the larger, well-defined features leading to the summits. With the recent emphasis on rock climbing rather than general mountaineering, three important areas—the south ridges of Mount Moran, the south ridges of Disappointment Peak, and the buttresses in Death Canyon—have been extensively developed, although the routes in general do not lead to any summit. The easier sedimentary peaks of the north and south ends of the range, which remained untouched by previous climbers, were explored by Arthur J. Reyman, John C. Reed, Jr., Robert Stagner, and Leigh and Irene Ortenburger. A partial list of the more important climbs of this era includes the Raven, the Snaz, the Pillar of Death in

Death Canyon, the Wedge on Buck Mountain, the Direct North Face of Mount Wister, the Big Bluff of Nez Perce, the Robbins–Fitschen and Taylor routes on the Middle Teton, the Northwest Chimney and the Medrick–Ortenburger route on the north face of the Grand Teton, the Black Ice Couloir on the Enclosure, the North Face and Northeast Face of Teepe Pillar, the North Face of the Red Sentinel, the several north face and south ridge routes of Disappointment Peak, the Northwest Face of Teewinot, Serendipity Arête and Crescent Arête of Mount Owen, the three east face routes on Table Mountain, the east face of Yosemite Peak, the South Face of Ayres' Crag 5, the direct South Face of Symmetry Spire, and the several ridge and buttress routes and the North Face of Mount Moran.

In the Tetons, the years from 1965 to 1975 saw a continuation of the search for new routes which characterized the previous decade. New snow routes on Cloudveil Dome

William Buckingham (Photo: Richard DuMais)

(Zorro Snowfield), Moran (Sickle Couloir), and the South Teton (Southeast Couloir) proved notable. Ice climbing was sought and found in the infamous Run-Don't-Walk Couloir on Owen and the Hidden Couloir of Thor Peak. New mixed rock-and-ice climbs of major proportions were discovered or pieced together on the northwest flank of the Grand Teton, such as the combined Black Ice Couloir–West Face and the Lowe Route on the north face of the Enclosure.

The major activity, however, was centered in the rock work. New faces were found (Spalding Peak, South Face; Middle Teton, Briggs–Higbee Pillar on the north face; West Face of the Enclosure; Owen, Northwest Face; Crooked Thumb, direct North Face; Moran, West Buttress and North Buttress; Bivouac, South Face routes II and III), and untrodden ridges were climbed (Prospectors, upper North Ridge; Wister, Northwest Arête; Second Tower, South Ridge). The small pinnacle of the Red Sentinel yielded two new and difficult routes. A new pinnacle (McCain's Pillar) provided a difficult ascent. Some of the better climbs were but variations on previous routes (Nez Perce, Garnet Traverse on the direct South Ridge; Teewinot Mountain, Direct Buttress on the Northwest Ridge; Grand Teton, Italian Cracks). Other innovative climbs of this period included the South Buttress Central of Moran, and Simpleton's Pillar and the Southeast Chimney of the Grand Teton. Rock climbing crept forward slowly in this decade, with only a few new climbs in Death Canyon (Escape from Death, Widowmaker, Doomsday Dihedral), on Moran's No Escape Buttress, and on the Glacier Gulch Arêtes. A significant technical advance was made, however, with the first free ascent of the South Buttress Right, using a bypass of the main aid pitch. The major contributors of these climbs were Roger Briggs, Peter Cleveland, Jim Ericson, Art Higbee, John Hudson, Dave Ingalls, Ray Jacquot, Peter Koedt, Juris Krisjansons, George and David Lowe, Mike and Jeff Lowe, Leigh Ortenburger, Rick Reese, Don Storjohann, Ted Wilson, and Steve Wunsch.

The period through 1996 has seen important developments, many in novel directions with new emphasis. The existing Teton extremes of the climbing spectrum—both mixed alpine climbing and pure rock climbing—were explored and extended. The year 1977 saw the beginning of both types, with the new High Route on the north face of the Enclosure and new severe rock routes in Death Canyon (Yellow Jauntice) and on No Escape Buttress of Moran (No Survivors). The south face arena of Cloudveil Dome was opened that year (Cut Loose, Armed Robbery) and extended the following year (Silver Lining, Contemporary Comfort). But the explosion in rock climbing came with the frantic activity of 1978 and 1979 when seven new, very high standard routes were made on the same Death Canyon buttress that houses the now classic Snaz (Lot's Slot, Vas Deferens, Fallen Angel, Cottonmouth, August 11th Start, Caveat Emptor, Shattered). These remain today as some of the most difficult rock routes in the Tetons.

A number of additional rock-climbing routes were discovered in Stewart Draw on Buck Mountain (Peaches), in Leigh Canyon on No Escape Buttress (Direct Avoidance, Spreadeagle, Gin and Tonic), on buttresses and a pinnacle in Avalanche Canyon (Blind Man's Bluff, Abandoned Pinnacle), and on buttresses in Hanging Canyon (the three "bird" arêtes: Avocet, Ostrich, and Peregrine). A major objective, the free ascent of the original South Buttress Right on Moran, was finally achieved at 5.11. The proximity to Jenny Lake of the southwest ridge of Storm Point has resulted in several new variations on generally good rock in the vicinity of Guides' Wall. The most recent new climbs in Death Canyon (Aerial Boundaries, 1985; Sunshine Daydream, 1987) are two of the finer routes among the many in that area.

The Grand Teton yielded five more routes or variations on its broad eastern expanse (Horton East Face, Beyer East Face I and II, Keith-Eddy East Face, Otterbody Chimneys), and the golden rock of the direct East Ridge of Teewinot was also first climbed. A second major area for long routes of first-class climbing was extended on the huge diagonal west face of the south ridge of Mount Moran. To complement the Western Buttress (1969), the new West Dihedrals and Revolutionary Crest were added.

Perhaps the major accomplishment of recent times has been the emergence of the new, mixed, and very difficult routes on the north and west sides of the Grand Teton. In 1979 the Route Canal was established. The year 1980 saw two very difficult ice lines established on the north face of the Grand by the prolific alpinist Steve Shea. In 1981 two important climbs, Loki's Tower and the Visionquest Couloir, were completed. Alberich's Alley was added in 1982 to the other classic ice lines on the west sides of the Grand and Enclosure. The set was extended in 1991 with the impressive and improbable Lookin' For Trouble on the north face of the Enclosure. These alpine climbs, when added to the existing routes—North Ridge, West Face, Black Ice Couloir, Northwest Chimney, Emotional Rescue, Lowe Route, and High Route—provide an alpine climbing arena unmatched in the United States.

It was thought that the 1980s marked the end of an era that commenced over a century ago, the era of first ascents of unclimbed summits. The climbs of Art-and-Brent Pinnacle (1984), Mount Kimburger (1986), and the Zebra (1989) were believed to be the last of their kind within the thoroughly explored Teton Range. The discovery of as yet unknown peaks, pinnacles, spires, or simply high points will hopefully always await the next generation of mountaineers and explorers.

The return of truly alpine conditions to the Tetons brought on by generally poor weather during the summer of 1993 directed attention toward untravelled, ephemeral ice lines and major mixed climbs. The north chimney of Cloudveil Dome (Nimbus) was finally climbed, and the south-facing chute on the Second Tower was linked with the upper East Ridge of the Grand. The High Route on the Enclosure was done largely as a thin ice climb, and the Goodro–Shane route on the north face of the Grand was repeated in difficult late fall conditions.

Many climbers contributed to these most recent advances in Teton mountaineering and rock climbing, notably Jim Beyer, Dan Burgette, Yvon Chouinard, Jim Donini, Charlie Fowler, Paul Gagner, Keith Hadley, Paul Horton, Renny Jackson, Ron Johnson, Tom Kimbrough, Stephen Koch, Alex Lowe, Jeff Lowe, Greg Miles, George Montopoli, Mike Munger, Leigh Ortenburger, Steve Rickert, Steve Shea, Jim Springer, Mike Stern, Jack Tackle, Buck Tilley, Tom Turiano, Mark Whiton, Jim Woodmencey, and Steve Wunsch.

Even as these climbs of the past two decades were not anticipated, so the close of this century and the beginning of the next will very likely provide new climbs of a sort not easily imagined today. Many peaks have unexplored portions that should yield additional fine climbs. Ultimately, the current emphasis on "new climbs" will create a situation where the routes and variations are separated by only a few feet. It will be obvious then, and is seen to be true now, that the lasting value in Teton climbing is to be found in the long, classic alpine routes that lead to the major summits; for enjoyable and instructive mountaineering these routes have few peers in the United States. For major new climbs one will have to journey to Alaska or other countries where the peaks are larger and where the climbing has been less extensive.

The Great Alpine Climbs

Among American mountaineers who have not climbed extensively in the Tetons there is insufficient appreciation for what some consider to be the finest aspect of climbing in this range—the great alpine climbs. Casual acquaintance with the mountains does not suffice to understand these routes. Deeper exploration is required to bring the visitor into confrontation with a set of mountaineering challenges that are unmatched below the Canadian border. The virtues of these splendid climbs are acclaimed here to bring them to the attention of climbers from other areas. All of the routes assessed here are on the Grand Teton, lying between the two longest ridges on the mountain—the classic east ridge starting at the edge of the Teton Glacier and the northwest ridge rising from Cascade Canyon.

These climbs are distinguished in that they are all major ascents requiring a broad combination of mountaineering skills rather than specialized abilities in a single dimension. This breadth is imposed by nature—the mountain and the route. Great alpine climbs are those that entail serious climbing with a degree of commitment imposed by the altitude, the weather, the difficulty, and routefinding problems. A variety of terrain should be provided to the climber, including steep rock, glaciers, snow, and ice. The seven major routes discussed here satisfy these requirements and, when successfully ascended, should provide considerable satisfaction for the experienced mountaineer. Nature, however, while good, is seldom if ever perfect. The

Teton mountaineer will from time to time wish for less loose rock and more ice, but on almost all of these climbs will be found good rock and some mixed climbing. These great alpine climbs are recommended to mountaineers seeking Teton climbs to extend their experience, perhaps as training for larger climbs in the great ranges of the earth, the Himalaya, the Karakoram, and the Andes.

East Ridge: Perhaps the most remarkable aspect of this alpine ridge is that in 1929 it was the second route found to the summit. Although it was attempted several times in the 1920s, the exceptional skills of Robert Underhill and Kenneth Henderson, who were in fact trained in climbing in the Alps, were required to overcome the Molar Tooth, the first and main obstacle on the ridge. The standard East Ridge route is today not considered exceptionally difficult, but the two main towers, the Molar Tooth and the Second Tower, provide routefinding challenges. The initial section is but a scramble, but the original northern passage of the Molar Tooth requires one or two rappels with great exposure, followed by an icy climb with loose rock to reach the notch behind the tower. Today climbers know that the southern passage of the tower is faster and without the mental stress of the cold and shade of the north side. Either method requires careful route selection and immediately presents the climber with an interesting pitch up out of the notch. The slabs then are passed and interesting climbing will be found on the northern traverse of the Second Tower. For more enterprising climbers, one or both of these towers can be climbed en route, although this option is rarely done; it is recommended for those seeking a greater challenge than the normal route. Above the Second Tower, the East Ridge Snowfield stretches to the summit, providing a long, exhilarating finish to this classic route.

A complex ridge such as this contains a multitude of variations for passage along the ridge itself but especially for approach from the south or from the north. Some of these variations are major climbs and furnish alternatives well worth consideration. From the south there are three notable climbs up the south side of the Second Tower: Langford and Cropper (Grand Teton, East Ridge, 1957 variation), the Brimstone Chimney (1970), and the Tower Two Chute (1993). Two of these (1957 and 1993) have been used as climbs to the summit of the mountain. The steep snow couloir rising from Teepe Glacier to the giant boulder behind the Molar Tooth also offers a major alternative to the first 2,000 feet of the ridge. Among the numerous possibilities from the north are the Northeast Couloir, first climbed in an astonishing 6¾ hours by Hossack and MacGowan back in 1939, and the traverse from the standard North Face route by Sinclair and Ortenburger (1960).

North Face: This imposing wall, seen and admired by thousands and even millions of tourists, is *the* North Face in the United States. While there are certainly other north faces with greater notoriety in the Alps, the North Face of the Grand Teton is perhaps the best known mountain feature in this country. As a mountaineering objective, the face is not so highly rated by today's standards, but it was a clear object of fear some 40 or 50 years ago. In the early 1950s, a standard joking question among Teton climbers was, "When are you going up to do the North Face?" Sometimes with knowledge comes disrespect and even undeserved contempt, but the face remains a significant climb with many redeeming features. The glacier approach is still not completely trivial and necessitates bringing along ice-climbing gear. With good routefinding, the initial portion of the face is not difficult but is unfortunately somewhat subject to rockfall. There have been over the years remarkably few accidents from such acts of nature. The wet, slippery, and icy chimney giving access to the First Ledge has a bad reputation but perhaps should be viewed as one more of the great varieties of problems the seasoned mountaineer should know. The Pendulum Pitch high on the wall is a genuine classic of American mountaineering in the sense of its position, history, and difficulty. Except for one, all variations on the face funnel through this pitch. Pownall needed exceptional courage to attack this lead in 1948 via the pendulum, and Emerson's free lead of this pitch in 1953 was a *tour de force* for the time. See *Photos 114 and 115*. As a north face it will always be subject to serious consequences in the event of bad weather; climbers will need good judgment and adequate gear to cope with this possibility.

For those returning for a second climb on the face or just wishing for more than the normal route offers, there are several other routes that have been worked out over the years, especially among the Second, Third, and Fourth Ledges. Some of these are not easy. The major climb to the upper east ridge (Goodro–Shane, 1953) is icy and difficult and has been seldom repeated. The direct approach to the Second Ledge from the Grandstand (Medrick–Ortenburger, 1953) is another major route, which has yet to see a repeat ascent. The same is true of the three most recent climbs on the eastern portions of the wall (Myhre and Sommers, 1970; J. Lowe, 1972; Deuchler and Moerman, 1976). Additional prospects for the hard-ice climber are the very steep ice chutes on the lower eastern sections of the north face (J. Lowe and Fowler, 1979; Shea, 1980).

North Ridge: While the North Face is more widely known, it is the North Ridge of the Grand Teton that is the classic route in the range, climbed over six decades ago in 1931 by the pioneers Robert Underhill and Fritiof Fryxell. This was a truly exceptional undertaking for the time; at IV, 5.7, A0, it was then perhaps the hardest alpine climb in the United States. Equipment used for the climb was by today's standards primitive. Underhill used nailed boots and Fryxell had the impediment of leather-soled work boots. Pioneers earned their accolades. The old standard approach via the Teton Glacier from the east is a mountaineering task, replete with routefinding issues and noticeable danger from rockfall off the face above. In some years passage from the *bergschrund* of the glacier onto the rock presents a substantial problem. Even the climb up to the top of the Grandstand is not trivial. The ridge above is impressive, and the famous Chockstone Pitch has not been downgraded even by the current generation of rock specialists (free climbed by Fritz Wiessner at 5.8, perhaps the first climb in the United States at this difficulty). In bad or even slightly bad weather, this pitch and the two above are serious endeavors indeed. The North Ridge is not a climb to be undertaken in bad conditions. The slab pitch on the very corner of the ridge, when covered with *verglas*, is about as demanding of skill as climbing ever gets. The North Ridge is today regarded as a first-rate climb with near unanimity. With the discovery of the Valhalla Traverse in 1960, the approach from the west to the top of the Grandstand has come to be preferred to the more direct eastern approach, because the rockfall danger is reduced. And there is an important variation available for the second-time climber known as the Italian Cracks (Friedman and Woolen, 1971). A more extreme variation that has gained some popularity is to climb the North Ridge to the west end of the Second Ledge of the North Face and then veer out onto the face to finish the ascent with the final four pitches of that route. This combination produces a truly exceptional climb that will exercise the best.

West Face: This superb route, one of the greatest of the Teton climbs, was pioneered in 1940 by the outstanding team of Jack Durrance and Hank Coulter. Like the North Ridge ascent, this climb seems today to have been 10 or 20 years ahead of its time, going where man had not yet dared to venture. It was the first time the northwest aspect of the Grand Teton from Valhalla Canyon, named by these Dartmouth climbers, had been confronted by mountaineers. The initial problem of this west wall of the Grand is the approach to its base, because the rock portion begins at the upper lip of the main section of the Black Ice Couloir. Durrance solved this via the Rotten Yellow Chimney, an interesting if not solid feature of the mountain. The route attacks the center of the wall above, trying to follow the Great West Chimney, a major feature of the mountain. When icy overhangs forced the first climbers out on the left wall of the chimney, they found a brilliant solution, the difficult horizontal traverse back into the chimney above the chockstones. The West Face is a beautiful climb with continual interest even in good conditions. In early season, or after precipitation, the first pitches may be covered with *verglas*, making these leads truly desperate. Once on the summit, the climber feels the accomplishment of having gained a more complete understanding of this grand mountain.

As with the other major lines, several variations are available. Alternative methods of passing the upper chimney problems have been found, but some seem largely to provide escape routes, such as to the Owen–Spalding route or to the Upper Saddle. A significant exception is the diffi-

Hank Coulter exiting the West Face of the Grand Teton on the first ascent, 1940 (Photo: Jack Durrance)

cult rock-and-ice chute to the south of the main West Face line (Alberich's Alley). The foremost variation, however, which starts the climb by means of the lower section of the Black Ice Couloir, upgrades an already major route into the upper realm of Teton alpine climbs. While the normal West Face route does involve some ice, especially on the lower shelves, the lengthy initial ice of this variation dominates the climb and changes its character from one requiring mostly rock skills to one demanding extended competence on both rock and ice.

Other completely independent climbs of equal stature have been worked out near the north end of the west face. The first of these, and the second route on the Grand Teton out of Valhalla Canyon, discovered and entered the huge northwest chimney, one of the most conspicuous features of this side of the mountain (Dornan, L. Ortenburger, and I. Ortenburger, 1960). With the same initial approach as for the West Face, the wall guarding the chimney base was climbed and the climbers were soon enmeshed in its difficulties, including, as with the best of these alpine routes, a length of ice. The depth of this chimney combined with its aspect seems to imply that its inner portions have never seen the rays of the sun. It is indeed one of the coldest climbs on the mountain, so be prepared. The major variation of this route, found only nine days after the first ascent (Robbins, Fitschen, and Chouinard, 1960), combined the most difficult parts of this Northwest Chimney route with those of the West Face route, creating a climb of exceptional proportions. The final extreme in route combinations was the addition of the Black Ice start to this 1960 Northwest Chimney and West Face climb. By taking the ice to the base of the upper West Face route, and downclimbing the Rotten Yellow Chimney to the base of the Northwest Chimney route, Jackson and Kimbrough in 1980 created this formidable Teton alpine climb.

The last line worked out, Loki's Tower (Stern and Whiton, 1981) is at the far north edge of the west face, on the massive buttress between the north ridge and the northwest chimney. Involving vertical and at times unprotected rock leads, this extreme route is perhaps the most difficult of these west face climbs. The massive buttress is of the most solid Teton rock with very few cracks and weaknesses. The line ascended is certainly improbable to the untrained eye.

Black Ice Couloir: This narrow couloir has become perhaps the best-known ice climb in the country. It is again an example of a route whose initial climb exemplified unusual courage in the face of the unknown. Generations of climbers had peered down into the depths of the couloir from the Upper Saddle and had shaken their heads. It was something of a breakthrough in Teton climbing when the route was finally climbed in 1961 by Jacquot and Swedlund. The initial method of approach, the entire length of Valhalla Canyon and the rock wall below and left of the second icefield, surely contributed to the difficulties of the route. The Valhalla Traverse Ledge, combined with the short chimneys at its eastern end, is now virtually the only approach method used. The main icefields are substantial, but the veneer of ice in the upper narrow couloir is not thick, and so its extent varies according to season and from year to year. The ice-climbing conditions are also variable, ranging from mostly hard snow (early season), to wet, water-ridden snow on top of ice (in bad but warm weather), to hard, pure ice (late season). Rockfall, which discouraged early attempts, does occur from time to time, sometimes in large volume. Whether these are purely natural or the result of carelessness on the part of climbers on the Owen–Spalding route is not clear. Safety is increased by staying near the right edge of the ice, because the main line of rockfall is farther out on the face of the ice. The narrow crux pitch of this climb is indeed steep for a natural summertime formation; it is in the vicinity of 70° but is short and is passed in about 30 feet. A major alternative to this route is the even narrower Visionquest Couloir (Stern and Quinlan, 1981) that exits off to the right up the north side of the Enclosure from a point about halfway up the Black Ice. It involves a

Stephen Koch on the High Route, North Face of the Enclosure (Photo: Alex Lowe)

more difficult mixed start leading to an extended section of steep ice on a very interesting part of the mountain.

North Face of the Enclosure: The last bastion of the grand old mountain was the formidable north face of the Enclosure. Excepting the ice climb of the Enclosure Couloir on the west edge of this vertiginous face, no one had attempted or even ventured out in an exploratory foray in this direction until the two climbs of 1969. All four routes completed to this date are major undertakings on uncompromising lines, involving not only severe rock difficulties but significant ice climbing as well. Mixed climbs such as these are a rarity in the lower 48 states, and these four are among the finest. The Lowe Route (George Lowe and M. Lowe, 1969) follows a main chimney system that also serves as a drainage path for melting snow and ice above; when wet, as it always seems to be, strenuous acrobatics are needed to climb this route. The High Route, climbed eight years later

(Fowler and Glenn, 1977), follows a nearby but distinct line of weakness in this intimidating face, to the right of the Lowe Route. It also contains characteristics similar to those of its adjacent route—steep, hard, and usually wet, with ice climbing mixed in among the rock. Eight years after the first ascent of the High Route, on a day climb from the Lower Saddle, Emotional Rescue was put up on the blank-appearing wall to the left of the Lowe chimney system (Jackson and Rickert, 1985). The last word in improbable routes was discovered around the corner on the northern aspect of the buttress by Jim Beyer in 1991. Lookin' For Trouble was established by Beyer climbing solo over a two-day period, and it stands today as the most difficult route on the Grand Teton, displaying all the qualities of a great alpine climb. Difficult aid and 5.11 free climbing provide an indication of the maturity of modern techniques. Climbs such as these four provide accessible training for those who would venture into the highest ranges to try the most difficult routes.

Northwest Ridge: This multifaceted ridge extends for some 5,000 feet, from near the forks of Cascade Canyon over the top of the Enclosure to the summit of the Grand Teton. It is one of the longest such features in the range and was probably the first Grade V climb established in this country. While its difficulties do not properly place this ridge into the same class as the preceding routes, evaluations have been made mostly by climbers who do not trouble themselves with an ascent of the entire ridge. The initial half is long, time-consuming, and more or less flat, containing numerous subpeaks and pinnacles that are almost uniformly composed of loose rock. Some of these towers, however, do provide a noticeable defense when their passage is attempted, and at least one pinnacle has only recently been done free. This section and its miserable rock end abruptly at 11,200 feet, where the first steep section is encountered. This is the point where the Buck Mountain fault, from which the highest central Teton peaks were thrust, is crossed. After a dozen feet of very rotten yellow rock the climber is suddenly presented with the fine, precipitous crystalline rock expected on good Teton routes. On his early climb of this route (Durrance and Davis, 1938), Durrance made a lead up this section that remains impressive to this day. Higher, the route crosses the now much-travelled Valhalla Traverse Ledge and continues on respectably steep rock to the summit of the Enclosure. Beautiful, enjoyable climbing is found here on a portion of the finest golden Teton rock. It seems that no one who has made this climb fails to appreciate these qualities. This ridge is a very long and tiring climb if done in its entirety, and it perhaps has not yet been done in a single day.

One of the major attractions of this ridge today is a route on its north flank, the Enclosure Ice Couloir (Read, Lev, and Greig, 1962). This route has become perhaps the most popular ice climb in the range due to its numerous ice leads, its straightforward nature, and its ready accessibility via the Valhalla Traverse from the Lower Saddle. It has the serendipitous advantage of leading directly to the beginning of the final steep section of the Northwest Ridge, so those who persevere to the summit of the Enclosure can reap the rewards of both a trying ice climb and a most enjoyable rock climb at the top. This combination of rock and ice is very likely the best intermediate mixed climb in the Teton Range. Many of the slothful, however, do not leave sufficient time for this combination and must rappel down the back west side of the Enclosure to return to the Valhalla Traverse Ledge and the Saddle before dark. Get an early start and be rewarded.

Traverses

In a range such as the Tetons, where the difficulty is not excessive and the peaks are not immense, it is natural that some of the most pleasant mountaineering is to be found among the various traverses that combine the ascent of several peaks during a single day of relatively fast climbing. For the more difficult routes this is of course seldom possible, but the ridge traverses that combine more than one regular route are entirely feasible, even for those who do not customarily set speed records in the mountains. Some of the traverses that have been done are described here.

In the south end of the range several days can be spent on a series of traverses along the park boundary (Reyman, 1960), starting with the peaks on the northeast ridge of Rendezvous Peak and continuing west and north to the pass southwest of Buck Mountain where the "Skyline Trail" crosses the divide. Another interesting sedimentary traverse, which can be done in one long day, crosses the five peaks circling Open Canyon (Ortenburger, Melton, Monahan, and Dornan, 1960). Although a climb of Buck Mountain has been combined with that of Veiled Peak in one day (Irvin and Lowry, 1957), this latter small peak is more easily and naturally combined with Mount Wister (Unsoeld, Ortenburger, and Vogel, 1952). This combination is especially appropriate if a high camp is established for the climb of Wister, because in this case there will usually be adequate time for the extra ascent of Veiled Peak.

The principal area for high traverses, however, is the Garnet Canyon area. The most obvious combination is that of the South and Middle Tetons (Ellingwood, 1923). This traverse is easily accomplished using the regular routes on each, if the start is made from a camp in Garnet Canyon. The ridge from Cloudveil Dome to Gilkey Tower is a portion of the encircling ridge that provides worthwhile mountain scrambling (Fryxell and Hilding, 1931). If one is interested in major summits, one can climb Nez Perce, descend to the floor of the south fork of the canyon, climb the South Teton (Fryxell and Smith, 1930), and even include the Middle Teton (Goldthwaite, 1931); or, more thoroughly, one can traverse the entire ridge from the Middle Teton to Nez Perce (Ayres, 1932). The first traverse in the other direction as far as the South Teton was done a year later (Petzoldt and Hendricks, 1933). The traverse of the three Tetons is also a good day's climbing, making use of the North Ridge of the Middle Teton either for descent (south to north, Durrance and Butterworth, 1938) or for ascent (north to south, McLane and Snobble, 1946). The combination of the entire ridge from Nez Perce to the Grand Teton is a long and exhausting effort (Pownall and Brewer, 1950). The various pinnacles and towers in the Grand Teton area can obviously be combined into climbs by themselves or in combination with major routes on the larger peaks; in this category are the Enclosure, Pinnochio Pinnacle, Bonney's Pinnacle, Glencoe Spire, Teepe Pillar, Pemmican Pillar, Fair Share Tower, the Red Sentinel, Okie's Thorn, Molar Tooth, and Second Tower.

The classic ridge connecting Teewinot Mountain to Mount Owen provides an excellent day with continually impressive views (east to west, Edwards and McNeill, 1940); in the other direction, the traverse is more difficult and was first accomplished in 1963 (west to east, Steck, Long, and Evans). If the traverse is made from Teewinot to the Grand, one must ascend the difficult North Ridge of the Grand (Unsoeld, Pownall, and Schoening, 1959). This is now referred to as the Cathedral Traverse and is a fantastic day in the mountains. The Grand Traverse, from Nez Perce to Teewinot, a remarkable feat of endurance and route-finding, was completed in 1963 after years of discussion (Steck, Long, and Evans). Today the Grand Traverse is done in the opposite direction, from Teewinot to Nez Perce, and includes the climb of the North Ridge of the Grand instead of its descent by means of rappel. This ultimate of Teton traverses was recently done by Alex Lowe (climbing solo) in the astonishing time of 8 hours 40 minutes. On Teewinot, as on the Grand, some interest can be added to the climb by including some or all of its main pinnacles—Crooked Thumb, Idol, Worshipper—during the ascent, although the inclusion of the Thumb implies ascent (or possibly descent) of a north face route (Ortenburger and Buckingham, 1953). To the west of the Cathedral Group, the Wigwam divide, a line of easy peaks, forms the west boundary of Cascade Canyon and extends from the Wall to Littles Peak. A traverse of these peaks should not prove difficult but perhaps rather long for a single day.

In the St. John group are many opportunities to make a full day's climb of several of the relatively small peaks of that group. In recent years it seems that it is more normal to include Ice Point with the ascent of Storm Point than to climb either one by itself (Fryxell and Hilding, 1931). Symmetry Spire can be easily combined with Storm Point (E. Petzoldt, 1935). Storm Point and Ice Point, climbed by their regular routes, can be combined either with the regular route of Symmetry Spire (Sharples, Bedell, and Comey [all-female ascent], 1939) or with its Southwest Ridge route (Maxwell and Fix, 1948). Following an ascent of Symme-

try Spire one can also head west and climb as many of the Symmetry Crags as time and energy permit (Ayres, 1934). The five Ayres' Crags make a fine day of pinnacle climbing (Ortenburger and Roald Fryxell, 1953); the smaller pinnacles at the head of Hanging Canyon, from the Canine Tooth to the Jaw, require less energy (Robinson, Briggs, Crosby, and Brett, 1952). Although clearly any section of the ridge surrounding Hanging Canyon can be selected and traversed, the longest yet completed is that from Mount St. John to the Canine Tooth (Ortenburger and Hemming, 1954). Because the ascent of Rockchuck can be made in such short order, it has been the custom in recent years to traverse the ridge to Mount St. John in the same day (Ladd, Ladd, Pratt, Pratt, and Bartlett, 1946). The peaks between the Jaw and the crossing of the "Skyline Trail" over the Cascade–Paintbrush divide make an unusual and long day (Buckingham and Bierer, 1954; Buckingham and West 1958).

On the climb of Mount Moran one or both of the Horns can be included (west, Ayres, Creswell, and Ortenburger, 1951; east, Robinson, Briggs, and Brett, 1951); they provide outstanding views of the east face of the mountain. The entire west ridge of Moran from Thor Peak is a very long traverse along a high ridge which in places is very rotten (Petzoldt and Hartline, 1935). West of Moran a pleasant day's traverse consists of all of the peaks surrounding Cirque Lake (Ortenburger and Buckingham, 1953).

There is an almost unlimited number of traverses possible in the north end of the Teton Range, and indeed, here as in the south end, it would seem that the principal climbing interest is centered around these traverses because only in a few places is the climbing of technical difficulty. Only a few will be mentioned here; very extensive traverses in the untouched wilderness are possible and most enjoyable for those who derive pleasure from the mountains in ways that do not involve the surmounting of technical difficulties (Ortenburger, Ortenburger, Peterson, and Wilson, 1963). The complete Bivouac–Reynolds ridge involves many towers and much interesting scrambling, but the return from Raynolds Peak is a long proposition no matter how it is done (Fonda and Buckingham, 1955). The ridge linking Mount Robie (10,850+) with Eagles Rest Peak is fully as long but not as high or rugged as the Nez Perce-to-Teewinot ridge; it yields more than one high-level traverse—for example, Mount Robie to Ranger Peak, and Doane Peak to Eagles Rest Peak (Ortenburger and Ortenburger, 1957).

National Park Service Policy

Since the Teton Range lies almost entirely within the boundaries of Grand Teton National Park, climbing and camping in the Tetons are subject to regulations designed to protect the natural resources and promote safety. Park administrators are charged with the dual and difficult responsibility of overseeing valid recreational use by climbers and maintaining the protection of park resources. The NPS rangers directly in charge of the administration of the Teton backcountry are, for the most part, climbers themselves and understand that "freedom of the hills" is an integral part of being a mountaineer. But they also understand that reasonable backcountry regulations are essential to protect the park for future generations. Certain limitations become both unavoidable and understandable when one considers the horde of visitors that come to this outstandingly beautiful but compact mountain range each year. Of the nearly three million visitors to the park in 1988, almost 200,000 got out of their cars and hiked somewhere in the backcountry, almost 20,000 backcountry camping-nights were spent, and almost 3,000 attempted to climb the Grand Teton. Individually we may hike, camp, and climb without leaving apparent evidence of our passage, but collectively we can have a massive impact.

Resource Protection: Most NPS regulations are directed toward protecting park natural resources, especially in the backcountry. The portion of the mountain range that lies within Grand Teton National Park has been recommended to Congress by the National Park Service to be included in the National Wilderness Preservation System. Following NPS policy, the recommended wilderness is managed as if it were designated wilderness. The Teton canyons and mountainsides are generally in a healthy, natural condition, in part due to the regulations that have been enacted. Climbers especially should recognize their particular responsibility when visiting the Tetons, because they make up the primary visitor category that travels off-trail.

The primitive joy that a fire brings to a camping trip is appreciated by many, but the prohibition of campfires above 7,000 feet is an example of an indispensable beneficial regulation. The cumulative environmental impact of campers cutting wood, stripping branches from trees, and building multiple fire rings led in 1972 to the decision to ban all campfires in the high country. For cooking, bring a small backpacking stove. There are a few exceptions to this rule. Wood fires are permitted in the valley within the fire rings provided at all campgrounds and picnic areas. If they are built within the provided fire rings, wood fires are also permitted at the designated campsites on Jackson Lake, Bear Paw Lake, Trapper Lake, Leigh Lake, and Phelps Lake. With a permit obtainable at the visitor centers, one can also have a fire anywhere along the west shore of Jackson Lake between the water's edge and the high water line.

Those who go off-trail should appreciate that the vegetation and soils in the high country are extremely fragile and sensitive to the effects of boots and tents. Consider what the approach to the Grand Teton was like 50 years ago when it was climbed by only a half-dozen parties per year. The approach to the south buttress of Mount Moran today is an indication: there is just a hint of a path worn into the vegetation, compared to the deep trail from the Lower Saddle up toward the Black Dike on the Grand Teton. Alpine tundra grows very slowly—some studies suggest that it takes 300 to 500 years for a damaged tundra community to heal. If we are to preserve the beauty of the high country for future generations, we must not enlarge the human-impacted areas that exist today. If all climbers used only a single trail, the consequences would be greatly reduced.

Respect the native wildlife of the mountains. While it is fascinating to watch the bears, moose, deer, elk, and bighorn sheep from a distance, remember that these animals are trying to make a living in a sometimes harsh environment, so do not disturb them unnecessarily. Most of the animals are more interesting than troublesome or dangerous. In the troublesome category are the small varmints such as the ubiquitous marmots, who are quite willing to chew through the wall of an expensive tent to reach food carelessly left inside. Avoid this form of minor disaster by trying to cook outside the tent, always hanging your food from a tree or large boulder, or using a food storage locker if provided. In the potentially dangerous category are moose and bears. If common sense and caution are applied, one should have little trouble with either. One of the authors has spent some 40 years in these mountains with only one minor incident. For both moose and bear, beware of surprising a female with young, whom she will earnestly protect. Black bears constitute the main problem, and Teton climbers should obtain a copy of the NPS pamphlet describing strategy to avoid trouble in bear country. Apply the same rules about food and cooking as for smaller varmints. Many past bear incidents have occurred because of foolish behavior on the part of the hiker or climber. Grizzly bears are potentially a more serious problem and their range seems to be spreading south from the northern canyons.

Another less obvious form of danger lurks in the apparently clear water of the mountain lakes and streams. Several harmful organisms such as *Giardia* and *Campylobacter* may be transmitted through untreated water, causing intestinal disorders including severe diarrhea. Solutions to this problem are either to carry your water supply from approved sources in the valley (spigots and drinking fountains), apply some type of iodine-based treatment to mountain water in your canteen, boil the mountain water for at least five minutes, or use one of the commercially available water filters designed for backpacking.

To minimize our collective impact on the environment, all Teton climbers should follow these easy but important rules:

1. Use existing means of access. Walk on the single, main trail if there is one, and avoid creating new descent routes or approaches. Do not shortcut across switchbacks.
2. To avoid making a new trail when off-trail hiking, walk abreast and not in single file. Whenever possible, walk on rock or gravel, not on plants or soil.
3. Avoid creating new campsites by camping on existing ones. In pristine areas camp on durable sites such as

sand or gravel, thick duff or dry soils covered with grass or sedge.

4. Do not pollute streams by washing dishes or bathing in them.

5. When toilets are available, use them. Do not defecate within 200 feet of any water source. Bury your feces at least 6 inches below the soil's surface and burn or pack out toilet paper.

Camping and Climbing Regulations: In 1994 regulations that required registration for climbing, off-trail hiking, and over-snow travel away from plowed roads were deleted from the Code of Federal Regulations. It is hoped that this regulation change will be accompanied by a renewed commitment by climbers to take responsibility for their actions and the actions of their party while in the mountains. Make sure that someone (friend or family) has detailed knowledge of your plans and timetable. For those who have no one with whom to leave this information, a voluntary registration system is available. If you are going out overnight, you *must* obtain a backcountry permit. These are available at the visitor centers at Moose or Colter Bay and the Jenny Lake Ranger Station. The ranger station is open every day from Memorial Day until the end of September and is staffed by knowledgeable seasonal rangers whose responsibilities include patrolling the backcountry and the routes on the peaks, providing information on current climbing conditions, and performing the sometimes highly technical mountain rescues. These rangers can provide sound advice based on many years of experience in the range.

The following rules and regulations are similar to those that have been imposed elsewhere in the United States by climbers themselves and are included here as a reminder:

1. Do not disturb historic or archaeologically or environmentally sensitive areas.

2. Do not scar, chisel, glue holds onto, or otherwise deface the rock.

3. Leave fixed protection and anchors with great discretion.

4. Accept responsibility even for the impact of other climbers in the mountain environment by removing rotten slings and garbage from climbs, bivouac sites, and descent routes.

5. Motorized equipment (including power drills) is prohibited in the backcountry of the Grand Teton.

Maximum occupancy limits, defined either by designated campsites or by camping zones, have been specified for every canyon in the range to limit use to a level that the natural resources of soil, vegetation, and wildlife can sustain. Because of these quotas, camping permits for specific times and locations may not always be available during the busiest part of the summer because they are issued on a first-come, first-served basis.

Backcountry camping permits can be obtained no more than 24 hours in advance. It is also useful to remember that one-third of the backcountry camping permits in canyons with trails, and all the group campsites, can be reserved for a specified period in the summer, by writing to the backcountry Permits Office of Grand Teton National Park between January 1 and May 15 of the year (Grand Teton National Park, Attn.: Permits, P.O. Drawer 170, Moose, WY 83012; permits office, (307) 739-3309).

Backcountry camping areas that are heavily used either have designated campsites or are divided into zones, and limits have been set by the National Park Service for the number of people per night in each of the sites or zones. In popular Garnet Canyon, for example, three camping zones have been defined: Lower (which includes the Platforms and Meadows), North Fork (which includes the Caves, Moraine, and Lower Saddle), and the South Fork. Current policy allows two nights in any one zone and therefore six consecutive nights total within the canyon. An excellent informational sheet with complete details about Garnet Canyon camping is available from the National Park Service. For the pristine wilderness canyons—Leigh, Moran, Snowshoe, Waterfalls, Colter, Quartzite—camping regulations are minimal; there are no designated camping locations, but permits and no-trace camping techniques are required. Informational sheets are available for the other major canyons, which have similar limitations.

In general, camping parties are limited to two nights in any one zone (three nights on Jackson Lake), with a maximum of six nights out on any one particular trip. Camping parties are limited to six people in off-trail areas. Groups (7 to 12 maximum) must camp in designated group campsites. One exception to this last rule is that groups (12 climbers maximum) can get a permit for two nights on the Middle Teton moraine. For those who wish to enter the park from the west side of the range, camping permits can be obtained at the Targhee National Forest offices in either Driggs or Ashton, Idaho.

General Regulations: Because the seven major lakes along the base of the Teton Range provide an important avenue for mountaineering access, it is helpful to understand the boating regulations in the park. All boats must be registered. Park permits are obtainable for properly equipped vessels at the Moose and Colter Bay visitor centers and the Signal Mountain Ranger Station. Canoes, kayaks, and hand-propelled rafts are permitted on all the lakes along the front of the Teton Range. Rental canoes are available in Jackson or at Dornan's Store in Moose. Motor boats are allowed only on Jackson, Jenny (maximum 7.5 horsepower), and Phelps Lakes; they are prohibited elsewhere within the park. In addition, Wyoming State permits must be obtained for motorized boats. Rental boats are available for use on Jackson Lake at Signal Mountain Lodge and Colter Bay Marina.

For Jenny Lake, the Teton Boating concession also has rental boats available. Afternoon winds on Jackson Lake frequently make travel across the lake very rough. Hence, if at all possible, boating climbers should make the crossing early in the morning, although by early evening the lake often calms down and the crossing again becomes feasible. Allow about one hour for the crossing.

The only regular boat service in the park is provided by the Teton Boating concession on Jenny Lake. In the summer from mid-June through mid-September, these large boats (for a small charge) take passengers across the lake about every 20 minutes from 8 AM until 6 PM. This is extremely convenient for climbers headed for the Cascade Canyon region because it eliminates 2.2 miles of hiking.

The use of horses by climbers for approach to the mountains is rare these days, and park visitors should be aware that there is a substantial number of regulations regarding their use within the park. Anyone planning such use should write to the park for a set of these complex rules. In summary, horses are limited to designated trails, and even some of these are closed to stock. Parties travelling with stock must camp at the one of the seven horse campsites, and feed for stock must be carried because grazing is not permitted.

In the Teton backcountry the following are prohibited: picking or collecting wildflowers, pets, motorized equipment, wheeled vehicles (including bicycles), firearms, and explosive devices such as fireworks. Pets, such as dogs, are permitted only at locations where automobiles can be taken, and then they must be on leash. They cannot be taken on any trails or into the backcountry.

Accidents and Mountain Rescue: Mountaineering is a splendid sport that can bring many profound rewards to those who pursue it. It is also, however, an inherently risky activity both from the climber's standpoint and based on the fact that many objective dangers exist in the mountains. These include, but are not limited to, falling rock and ice, avalanches, lightning, and other forms of severe weather conditions. As a matter of fact, each year a number of accidents occur in Grand Teton National Park and the victims must be rescued. Both experienced and inexperienced climbers may find themselves in a position in which assistance is needed.

Some accidents requiring rescue are difficult to avoid; climbers may fall or be hit by rockfall or the weather may deteriorate. Skill and good judgment will minimize these dangers. Proper use of the ice axe, correct belaying techniques, adequate protection, good routefinding, and bad-weather gear are essential components of such good judgment. The avoidable accidents can commonly be traced to the lack of one or more of these factors. By far the most dangerous terrain in the Tetons are the snowfields. Inexperienced climbers are strongly urged to obtain instruction

Mountain Rescue on the Petzoldt Ridge, Grand Teton (Photo: Reynold G. Jackson)

and experience in ice-axe technique before venturing up or across the potentially hazardous snowfields, which are especially numerous in early and midseason.

The Jenny Lake rangers are a skilled, dedicated group who are willing to make every reasonable effort to rescue someone in need. However, climbers have a primary responsibility to do their best to extricate themselves out of their own predicament. In the event of an accident, depend first on yourself and your own party members. Practice self-rescue to the extent possible. Do not depend solely on the NPS rescue team, because many factors such as weather, darkness, or objective hazards to the rescue team itself may considerably delay or even prevent any rescue effort. In the high mountains, hypothermia is particularly dangerous following an accident; if symptoms appear, the victim should be helped immediately with dry clothing, a sleeping bag, and warm drinks, if these are available.

In the event of a life-threatening injury, however, efforts should be made to obtain assistance as rapidly as possible. This is almost always done either by notifying an adjacent party on the mountain who may be able to get word to the Jenny Lake Ranger Station (or the Moose Visitor Center) for help or by sending an extra party member down to the valley. Do not leave the victim alone unless absolutely necessary. When notified by such direct means the Jenny Lake rangers will attempt to take rapid and effective rescue action. Information needed by the rescue team includes time of the accident, exact location of the victim, nature of the injuries, equipment at the accident scene, number of persons there, and their plan of action (if any).

Of primary importance is an attitude that it is a personal responsibility to do your best to rescue yourself and that you *will* survive no matter what.

Route Descriptions

The route descriptions in this text have been placed into ten sections that are arranged geographically from south to north. They have been compiled from several different sources: the authors' own experience, accounts provided by friends who have climbed the route in question, accounts published in mountaineering journals, and mountaineering records maintained by the National Park Service. Considerable effort has been expended in an attempt to chronicle every route that has been done in the Teton Range. The description of how to get to the base of a particular climb has also been carefully researched. In some of the descriptions, information is meager due primarily to a lack of reliable data. Keep in mind that in many cases the first ascent has been the only ascent and that quite often the climb was done many years ago. Climbing terminology has changed over the years and a significant attempt has been made to update and standardize much of this terminology. Remember that the fine points of routefinding are left to the individual climber and that there is no substitute for this very necessary skill.

A chronology precedes the actual route descriptions to provide the reader with a concise climbing history of each individual peak. Following the chronology all of the known climbing routes on each peak have been assigned a number and arranged geographically in a counterclockwise fashion around each peak. The Grand Teton was used as the model for the rest of the peaks, beginning with the Owen–Spalding route. In the case of the Grand the Owen–Spalding was chosen because of its importance as well as being the standard route of ascent and descent on the mountain. To further assist the reader, a ☞ symbol is used to denote the "regular route," or the most commonly used route of ascent or descent.

The naming of a particular route has been left up to the first-ascent party; however, names have not been suggested in every case. If a name was not given one was assigned based on either the physical location of the route or, more simply, the names of the first-ascent party. The difficulty classification and first-ascent information then follow. The first-ascent data are based on extensive personal study and correspondence relating to the climbing history of the Teton peaks. This is a subject of some interest to climbers and deserves publication with accuracy, so any information regarding errors will be appreciated. In some cases, notably in the northern and southern ends of the range (where the peaks are easy but relatively remote), the party listed as having made the first ascent was very likely preceded by climbers currently unknown and unlisted in the records. The textual information that comprises the main body of the route description is of four types: (1) access to the route or, in some cases, to a group of routes, including where to park your car and the proper canyon for the approach; (2) approach considerations such as what trail to take, where to leave the trail, and how to recognize the start of the climb, including landmarks at the base and landmarks up above on the route; (3) special route considerations such as the seriousness of the climb or a particular pitch (protection and rockfall), the recommended method for making the climb (one day versus bivouac on route), special equipment recommendations, and escape possibilities, when known; and (4) descent from the top of the route or from the summit of the peak and the extent of rappelling (if any). At the end of the body of the description, time information and bibliographical references are given, if these are known. Only those bibliographical references that actually contain information significant for a prospective climber have been included. If a route has been climbed only once, these references are highly recommended for reading in addition to the descriptions given in this book.

The two other sources of information that are presented herein are the schematic route diagrams, or topos, and the photographs upon which route lines have been marked. In most cases where a topo is presented, text will accompany it. In this manner essential information about these climbs will be conveyed to the reader in a variety of formats. The written material should *in all cases* be consulted in addition to examining the topo. For many of the difficult new routes, no extended written description of the climbing route will be given; the topo serves to convey the route information. On page 62 is shown a key to the numerous symbols used on the topos. These have now become rather well standardized and should be familiar to climbers from various parts of the United States. The third method of assisting climbers is the photographs, which display climbing routes marked and labeled. These should also be examined by the prospective climber because they will help in the location of the start and the general line of the route. It should be noted that not all of the routes are marked on a particular photograph. The routes that are marked are based on good information or firsthand knowledge by one or both of the authors.

The term *early season* refers to the summer climbing period beginning about June 15 and lasting to about July 10. During this period the climbing in most of the couloirs and some of the canyons will be entirely on snow; glissading will be at its best, making fast descents possible on some peaks. Almost every route will require an ice axe for safety. The term *late season* refers to the period from about August 1 to September 15. By this time the snow is mostly gone so that climbing is generally less interesting, the glaciers will show bare ice, and during the daytime it will be hot in the sun. Most of the peaks will be accessible by at least one no-snow route.

The directions given in the route descriptions are in terms of the climber facing the summit of the peak. A peak has been arbitrarily defined within this text, with very few exceptions, as having five closed 50-foot contour lines. A systematic attempt has been made to use the following two sets of terms in order of decreasing size: saddle, col, and notch; and canyon, gully, couloir, chute, chimney, and crack. The terms used to describe other parts of a mountain are standard in mountaineering literature: arête, bench, chockstone, crag, face, ledge, moraine, needle, overhang, pinnacle, pitch, scree, shelf, slab, spire, and talus.

In some cases the elevation of a peak is followed by a T. This indicates that a spot elevation was determined by photogrammetric methods.

The prospective climber should also be aware of the inclusion of map information. An extensive and detailed set of topographic maps in the 7.5-Minute Series covering Grand Teton National Park are available. Published by the U.S. Geological Survey at a scale of 1:24,000 (2.64 inches per mile), a total of 16 of these quadrangle sheets is required to cover the entire range and its approaches. Most of these can be purchased at the Moose Visitor Center, the Jenny Lake Ranger Station, or mountaineering supply stores in the town of Jackson. The single large USGS sheet showing the entire park at a scale of 1:62,500 (ca. 1 inch per mile) remains available. An updated version of this map (privately printed) is also available on a water-resistant plastic base. The quadrangle sheet on which a peak appears will be listed alongside its entry in this book. Note that the abbreviation (prov.) after a map name indicates that the map is provisional.

Difficulty Ratings

The determination of the difficulty rating of a particular climb has always been a subject of considerable discussion among climbers. Many attempts have been made to devise a logical, easy-to-understand difficulty rating system that would be both universally accepted and then consistently used. Such a system has not yet appeared. Ultimately, any system by which climbs are categorized by difficulty relies on consensus—a foreign concept to most of us. The rating system described here is used in some form or another throughout this country and therefore should be familiar to most climbers using this text. Generally, the classifications given in the text have been made on the basis of good summertime conditions, and one should expect the difficulty to be much greater if the rock is wet, covered with snow, or icy. For little-known routes the estimation of difficulty hopefully will be a little on the high side in order to avoid misleading the inexperienced.

Grade: The first part of the rating system used in this book is a roman numeral from I to V, in ascending order of *overall difficulty*. It is applied only to an entire climb and never to individual moves or pitches within the climb. This overall difficulty is estimated by the consideration of many factors, including the following: the length of the route, measured by both time and distance; the average difficulty of all of the individual pitches; the difficulty of the hardest pitch; the ease of escape or retreat, if required; the extent to which adverse weather conditions may create problems; the various objective dangers of the route such as rockfall; and, somewhat more vaguely, the challenge or degree of commitment implied by the route. Most of the Teton routes are either Grade I or Grade II. It should be noted that some one-pitch climbs are listed herein as Grade I even though the single pitch may be very difficult.

I: These routes require little or no commitment in the sense of either time or difficulty. After leaving the approach trail, only a few hours are required for the climb, and retreat or escape is trivial. Little or no mountain experience is needed to undertake these routes. Single-pitch rock climbs, of whatever difficulty, are put into this category.

II: These are routes of moderate magnitude, usually requiring much of a day. They may involve some significant climbing, but escape or retreat routes are available. Some mountain experience may be needed to climb these routes safely.

III: For most climbers these routes require a full day, involve serious climbing difficulty, consist of several pitches, and require some commitment in the sense that escape or retreat will involve technical difficulties. Considerable mountaineering or rock-climbing skills and experience are needed for safe passage on these routes.

IV: All of these routes are long, requiring a full day of difficult climbing after a significant approach, have many difficult pitches, are committing in the sense that retreat is usually nearly as difficult and time-consuming as completing the route, and may be hazardous in bad weather conditions.

V: These routes will generally require more than a single day on the technical portion of the climb, have numerous very difficult pitches, and require considerable physical strength and stamina. Technical proficiency on both rock and ice may also be required, and these routes are roughly equivalent to two Grade IVs.

Class: The second part of the system used herein is represented by a series of numbers, in ascending order of difficulty, that attempt to describe the technically most difficult climbing move, series of moves, or section of climbing that one is likely to encounter during the climb.

1.0: Mountain hiking, on- or off-trail. (No use of hands.)

2.0: Easy scrambling with little exposure. Ice axe may be important for safety. (Occasional use of hands; some steepness of the terrain is implied; almost no one would feel that a rope is needed for safety.)

3.0: Scrambling with some exposure. Inexperienced climbers may want to be roped. Ice axe and knowledge of its use are important for safety. (Considerable use of hands; some may want to be roped; average attentive person can climb this level without fear of falling.)

4.0: Exposed climbing. Ice axe and knowledge of its use are essential for safe passage. (Many will want to be roped; an unsecured fall could result in serious injury or death.)

5.0: Exposed, serious climbing requiring application of technical rock-climbing skills. (Most will want to be roped; pitches of sufficient length to warrant some manner of intermediate protection during belayed climbing.)

At this point, because the range of difficulty becomes quite large, additional number(s) are placed after the decimal point to further describe the most difficult technical moves of a particular climb. The Yosemite Decimal System, as this scale of rating difficulty is now known, has become the widely accepted standard in this country and therefore will be used throughout this guide. Currently in the United States this scale extends from 5.0 to 5.14.

This difficulty ratings system was originally known as the Sierra–Wilts System and then somewhat later as the Southern California System. It was originally suggested by Royal Robbins as a means of classifying practice routes on Tahquitz Rock. The system was established by the joint efforts of Robbins, Don Wilson, and Chuck Wilts in the early 1950s.

In many climbing areas further subdivisions, especially within the upper range of difficulty levels, have been deemed necessary and lowercase letters (a–d) or symbols (+ or -) have been applied to the decimal ratings. In this guidebook a + or a - will be used and will equate to the letter grades as follows: **5.10-** = 5.10a/b; **5.10+** = 5.10c/d; **5.11-** = 5.11a/b; **5.11+** = 5.11c/d; and so on. The use of these symbols begins at the 5.9 level and **5.9+** simply indicates hard 5.9. If the decimal rating is simply **5.10** or **5.11**, for example, this means that information on the exact difficulty of the route is insufficient and therefore the rating could fall anywhere within that entire range. In one final attempt to convey information, the letter **R** will be attached to this portion of the difficulty rating in order to describe those climbs that have a significant runout section.

5.1: This general class covers the decimal ratings 5.0, 5.1, and 5.2 in this guide.

5.4: This general class covers the decimal ratings 5.3, 5.4, and 5.5 in this guide. Handholds are small, requiring skill and strength to climb. (Protection is important during belayed climbing of individual pitches.)

5.6–5.12+: Most of the technical rock climbs described in this guide fall into this range of difficulty ratings.

Aid: It will be noted that a number of climbs in this text are given an artificial-climbing difficulty rating. This is represented by the letter **A** followed by a number from 0 to 5, in ascending order of difficulty. This number indicates the difficulty of the hardest artificial or direct-aid pitch of the route. Because few of the routes in the Tetons involve artificial climbing, this part of the rating will be absent for most of the routes. While the lower levels of artificial climbing, such as A0, A1, and A2, can ordinarily be done using standard equipment, certain specialized equipment or techniques often will be required for the higher levels. This includes items such as hooks, copperheads, RURPs, knifeblades (KBs), tie-off loops, and so forth. Because some of the route descriptions contained herein are quite ancient and, in many cases, have had only one ascent, the prospective climber should be aware that some ratings are going to be wrong. Equipment has improved, techniques have progressed, and there have not been that many "new" aid climbs put up in the Tetons.

A0: This lowest of aid ratings indicates a situation that simply involves pulling up on a piece of protection. This is also known as "French free" in some areas.

A1: The best type of placement; often referred to as "bombproof" or "capable of holding a truck."

A2: Slightly harder to place and capable of holding less.

A3: More inventive techniques required for placement of protection and only capable of holding a short fall.

A4: Capable of holding only body weight.

A5: Several A4 placements in a row with big falls possible.

Ice: Because it is impossible to accurately describe the difficulty of a particular stretch of ice using the same system by which rock is described, a fourth designation is applied herein to climbs that are primarily ice. First of all, a **WI** or **AI** is placed at the front of this portion of the rating. The **WI** refers to ice climbs that are primarily seasonal in nature, that is, frozen waterfalls that usually melt out completely during the course of a year. These climbs are usually a winter phenomenon. **AI** refers to ice climbs that are usually present even during the summer months and includes the classic alpine gullies and couloirs. In this text a series of numbers from 1 to 5 are then assigned, once again denoting an ascending order of difficulty. The Scottish grading system, in which roman numerals were originally used to indicate overall ice difficulty, has in many areas evolved to this method of numeration with the hardest waterfall ice climbs currently in the 6–7 range. Additionally, the + symbol is used to further describe climbs that are at the uppermost end of a particular numerical ice grade. The following definitions will be used for the various categories of ice difficulty:

1: Glacier walking requiring the use of crampons and an ice axe.

2: Mountain routes for which basic knowledge of the use of ice tools and crampons is suggested. Most of these routes in the Tetons are on glaciers or moderately angled snow couloirs.

3: Most climbers would prefer to have two ice tools and place intermediate protection during the course of these climbs.

4: Vertical ice climbing is likely to be encountered at the crux of the route.

5: Significant sections of vertical ice climbing are to be expected on these routes.

Time Information

Time information is given at the end of the descriptive material for some of the routes. This information has been acquired through statistical study of the climbing (*ascent*) time records, listed in the cards filed after each ascent with Grand Teton National Park; the figures given, then, are neither an opinion of how much time *should* be required to make the ascent nor an estimate or guess of the required time. The figures accurately reflect the number of hours that have actually been required by those who have made the ascent in the past. In those cases in which a range of times is given—for example, 4½ to 6 hours—the meaning is that one-third of the past climbers have taken less than 4½ hours, one-third have taken between 4½ and 6 hours, and one-third have taken more than 6 hours. Hence, to use this information properly prospective climbers must estimate their own speed as being either fast (will require less than 4½ hours), medium (will require somewhere between 4½ and 6 hours), or slow (will require more than 6 hours). In those cases in which no range is indicated, the single median value of the time distribution is listed. The reason for omitting the time range information in some instances is that there have not been enough climbs of the route in question to provide a statistically valid estimate of this range. A single number—for example, 7¾ hours—means that half of the past climbers took less than 7¾ hours and half required more than 7¾ hours. Italic means that the listed time is based on only one or two recorded climbing times and, hence, is to be used with caution by the prospective climber. In all cases the climbing times are given with reference to the camping place. This time information has not been updated to any great degree during the last 15 years.

Climbing styles have changed, equipment and clothing have been vastly improved, and the Teton peaks are being climbed in a much more lightweight and fast manner than they ever have in the past.

Recommended Climbs

In any mountain range with the quantity and variety of known climbing routes as that found in the Tetons, there will develop among climbers with extensive experience in the range preferences for certain routes. These preferences may be based on many different things such as the view from the summit or the top of the climb, the relative solidity of the rock, the position and nature of the route, or the exhilarating nature of one or more of the pitches or of the entire climb. Some of the climbs listed in this section have been selected primarily because of their historical significance. Although these subjective preferences are somewhat intangible, a select few of these climbs are simply not to be missed and therefore have been given the symbol ☆. These are routes of the highest quality, true classics in every sense of the word. These *recommended climbs* have been grouped according to the type of terrain that one is most likely to encounter during the middle of a typical summer season. Additionally, the letter **M** has been placed after those climbs that require a combination of technical skill on ice, snow, and rock. All of the routes are mountaineering objectives that require good judgment and respect.

HIKING
1.0: Prospectors Mountain, Southwest Ridge
Static Peak, Southwest Ridge
The Wall, West Side
Table Mountain, West Slope ☆
Forellen Peak, Southwest Slope
2.0: Mount Woodring, Southwest Slope
Glacier Peak, North Ridge
Ranger Peak, Southeast Ridge

ROCK SCRAMBLING
3.0: Buck Mountain, East Face (**M**)
South Teton, South Ridge
Middle Teton, Southwest Couloir (**M**) ☆
The Enclosure, South Couloir ☆
St. John, South Couloir, East Ridge
East Horn, East Face
Bivouac Peak, East Ridge

EXPOSED ROCK CLIMBING
4.0: Buck Mountain, East Ridge (**M**) ☆
Mount Wister, Northeast Couloir to East Ridge (**M**)
Cloudveil Dome, East Ridge
Disappointment Peak, Southeast Ridge
Teewinot Mountain, East Face (**M**) ☆
Storm Point, Symmetry Couloir and Upper West Face
Ice Point, Northwest Ridge
Symmetry Spire, East Ridge

TECHNICAL ROCK CLIMBING

5.4: Grand Teton, Owen–Spalding ☆
Middle Teton, Chouinard Ridge
Grand Teton, Exum Ridge ☆
Mount Owen, Koven (**M**) ☆
Cube Point, East Ridge
Mount Moran, CMC ☆
West Horn, West Ridge
Cleaver Peak, North Peak, Northwest Chimney
Rolling Thunder, Northeast Ridge

5.6: Buck Mountain, Southeast Ridge, *var:* 1963
Middle Teton, North Ridge
Grand Teton, Underhill Ridge
Grand Teton, Petzoldt Ridge ☆
Grand Teton, Northeast Couloir (**M**)
Disappointment Peak, East Ridge ☆
Mount Owen, East Ridge (**M**)
Mount Owen, Northeast Snowfields (**M**)
Symmetry Spire, Durrance Ridge
Symmetry Spire, Southwest Ridge
West Horn, East Ridge

5.7: Nez Perce Peak, Direct South Ridge
Middle Teton, Southeast Ridge ☆
Grand Teton, East Ridge (**M**) ☆
Grand Teton, Stettner Couloir (**M**)
Grand Teton, Lower Exum Ridge ☆
Grand Teton, *var:* Direct Petzoldt–Exum Ridge ☆
Grand Teton, North Ridge, *var:* Italian Cracks (**M**)
The Enclosure, Enclosure Ice Couloir–Northwest Ridge (**M**) ☆
The Enclosure, Northwest Ridge
The Enclosure, Southwest Ridge
Teepe Pillar, Direct East Face
Red Sentinel, East Face and North Face
Table Mountain, East Face, South Buttress
Mount Owen, Serendipity Arête
Rock of Ages, Northwest Corner

5.8: Cloudveil Dome, Armed Robbery
Grand Teton, Beyer East Face II
Grand Teton, North Face, Direct Finish (**M**) ☆
Grand Teton, North Ridge (**M**) ☆
Grand Teton, North Ridge, North Face Direct Finish (**M**) ☆
Grand Teton, West Face (**M**) ☆
Grand Teton, Black Ice–West Face Combination (**M**) ☆
Grand Teton, Burgette Arête
Fairshare Tower, Corkscrew
Disappointment Peak, Irene's Arête ☆
Teewinot Mountain, Direct North Ridge
Teewinot Mountain, *var:* Teewinot Tunnel–Emerson's Chimney
Storm Point, Southwest Ridge, Guides' Wall

5.9: Death Canyon, Cathedral Rock, Snaz
Matternought Peak, Taminah Arête
Middle Teton, Whiton–Wiggins Dihedral
Grand Teton, Jackson–Rickert Crack
Grand Teton, It's Not A Chimney
Grand Teton, Beyer East Face I ☆
Grand Teton, Loki's Tower (**M**) ☆
Grand Teton, Northwest Chimney (free) (**M**) ☆
Grand Teton, Northwest Chimney, *var:* Jackson–Kimbrough Contortion (**M**) ☆
The Enclosure, North Face, High Route (**M**) ☆
Disappointment Peak, Open Book on Grunt Arête ☆
Disappointment Peak, Chouinard–Frost Chimney
Mount Owen, North Ridge (free)
East Cascade Buttresses, No Perches Necessary
Baxter's Pinnacle, South Ridge and Upper South Face
Leigh Canyon, No Escape Buttress, Direct South Face

5.10: Death Canyon, Cathedral Rock, Caveat Emptor I
Death Canyon, Cathedral Rock, Aerial Boundaries
Death Canyon, Cathedral Rock, Fallen Angel
Middle Teton, Briggs–Higbee Pillar
Middle Teton, Jackson–Woodmencey Dihedral
Grand Teton, Lower Exum Ridge, *var:* Gold Face
The Enclosure, South Face, Jim's Big Day
The Enclosure, North Face, Lowe Route (**M**) ☆
The Enclosure, North Face, Emotional Rescue *var:* Direct (**M**) ☆
Red Sentinel, Northwest Corner (free)
Mount Owen, Intrepidity Arête
Yosemite Peak, East Face, Chouinard
Cascade Canyon, Storm Point, Vieux Guide
Baxter's Pinnacle, East Face
Baxter's Pinnacle, North Face
Leigh Canyon, North Side Rock Climbs, No Escape Slabs
Mount Moran, South Buttress Central (free)

5.11: The Enclosure, North Face, Emotional Rescue (free) (**M**) ☆
Death Canyon, Cathedral Rock, Sunshine Daydream
Middle Teton, Direct East Buttress (free)
Cascade Canyon, Storm Point, Bat Attack Crack
Mount Moran, South Buttress Right (free) ☆

5.12: Mount Moran, Direct South Buttress (free) ☆

TECHNICAL ICE CLIMBING

AI2+: Middle Teton, Middle Teton Glacier
Mount Moran, Skillet Glacier

AI3: Middle Teton, Northwest Ice Couloir
The Enclosure, Enclosure Ice Couloir
Thor Peak, Hidden Couloir

AI3+: The Enclosure, Black Ice Couloir ☆
The Enclosure, Visionquest Couloir

AI4: The Enclosure, Black Ice Couloir, *var:* Alberich's Alley

WI4: Mount Owen, Run-Don't-Walk Couloir
WI5: Grand Teton, Route Canal
       Grand Teton, Grand North Couloir

Mountain Guides

For nearly 70 years professional mountain climbing guides, officially approved by the National Park Service, have been operating in Grand Teton National Park. In recent years the proportion of Teton climbers who use the guiding services has increased significantly, attesting to the current acceptability of this form of mountaineering. Climbing with guides provides inexperienced climbers, or those with no mountain experience at all, a mechanism to reach the high peaks and begin the mastery of the arts of rock climbing and snow-and-ice techniques. Climbers not sufficiently experienced to be confident in accepting the responsibility for the safety of their climbing party may well wish to utilize the guiding services.

Grand Teton National Park now provides two mountain guide and climbing concessions for those wishing professional instruction in mountaineering or rock climbing, or who wish to climb the Teton peaks. The two concessions are the Exum Mountain Guides, with an office at Jenny Lake, and the Jackson Hole Mountain Guides, with an office in Jackson. Both concessions are operated by guides with extensive experience and good safety records. The rates, which can be obtained either directly from the guides or from Grand Teton National Park (Moose, Wyoming 83012) are reasonable and have been approved by the government. The guides maintain established high camps at various points in the range and can supply most of the special equipment required for an ascent. The main seasons for the major peaks is in the months of July and August, but guiding service is usually available in June and September as well.

An important feature of these guiding services is the climbing instruction available in beginning, intermediate, or advanced climbing schools. Fundamentals of mountain hiking, roped climbing technique, principles of safe climbing, belaying, placement of protection (pitons, chocks, and other devices), rappelling, and snow-and-ice techniques are taught at convenient locations.

Climbing Equipment

In the Teton Range there is a tradeoff between having all the gear that you might wish to have and being able or willing to carry all the weight, as the approaches can often be several miles and 2,000 to 4,000 vertical feet from the valley to the base of what may be a relatively short rock climb.

An ice axe for safety on the snow and ice is an essential item on many of the routes for much of the summer, even on rock routes when the approach or descent involve a snow or ice slope. Skill with an ice axe is perhaps the single most important thing besides common sense that one can

carry into the mountains. Snow or ice conditions change considerably from year to year, and there is the usual decrease in snow as the summer progresses from spring to autumn. Hence, definite advice for specific times cannot be given in a book, but current information will be available at the Jenny Lake Ranger Station.

For the rock routes, a "standard Teton rack," if there is such a thing, would probably be similar to one used elsewhere in the mountainous regions of the country. The exact selection comes down to personal preference and no dogma will be given here. A suggestion might be as follows: camming devices, both three- and four-cam units in a size range from ½ to 3 inches; stoppers or hex nuts in a medium size range; a selection of small nuts or RPs; a number of slings (and quick draws), because Teton rock pitches tend to wander; and free carabiners.

If anything special in the way of protection is known to be needed for a route, it will be mentioned in the text. Such information will usually be a reference to the largest size of protection that is needed or to items of special emphasis. Pitons are rarely needed on the popular routes, but one may well wish to have some available on the major alpine routes. If the rock on such a route is iced or becomes iced while the climb is underway, a small selection (five to ten) of pitons of various sizes can provide an extra safety margin.

Climbing helmets are *strongly* recommended for Teton climbing routes. Many contain loose rock, fully capable of being unleashed by natural causes. On any climb where there may be another party higher on the route, any thinking, rational human being will wear a helmet. Both authors of this book have several friends who would not be alive today had they not been wearing a helmet when a rock came down. Indeed, both authors owe their lives to the critical protection that a good climbing helmet provided. Wear one.

Bouldering and Sport Climbing

Bouldering in the Teton Range is largely limited to a small number of glacial erratics that are scattered along the margin of the mountains on the valley floor. In addition to the bouldering, several excellent, bolt-protected sport-climbing areas are also available. For a much more thorough discussion of these, one can refer to *Jackson Hole—A Sport Climbing and Bouldering Guide,* by Joe Sottile. The individual route descriptions are excellent in this text and therefore only the locations will be mentioned here. The main areas are listed here from south to north. Information can also be obtained at the Jenny Lake Ranger Station, the American Alpine Club Climbers' Ranch, or mountaineering stores in Jackson or Moose.

The Tram: Several bolt-protected sport climbs are located high on Peak 10,450 (the one with the tram to its summit). After getting off on top, walk down to the vicinity of tower #5 where two famous couloirs (ski runs) take off toward the north. The first of these is known as Corbet's Couloir (named for Barry Corbet), and several climbs are located on both the eastern and western walls of the couloir. The second of the couloirs, S and S Couloir (named for Simms and Sands) is located immediately down to the east. A number of sport climbs are on the eastern wall of this couloir.

Blacktail Butte: This is the central of several steep-sided hills or buttes that rise out of the flat floor of Jackson Hole; it is located immediately east of the village of Moose. Many bolt-protected sport routes are located on the south-facing limestone cliffs at the northwest corner of the butte. They vary in difficulty from 5.10 to 5.13. A small parking area is located about 0.75 mile north of Moose Junction on US 26-89, on the east side of the road. The main cliff (80 feet high) and a smaller one to the west can be seen a short distance above the parking area. The stairway was completed in 1992 in an attempt to stabilize some of the erosional problems that stem from continued heavy use of this area. Please stay on the trail. It is also useful to remember that, because of its proximity to the road, Blacktail Butte attracts novice climbers, hikers and "rappellers." *Beware* of loose rock and *do not* knock anything down.

Taggart: Park at the Taggart Lake trailhead and follow the trail north for about 0.25 mile. This boulder is due west of the trail behind the horse corrals.

Climbers' Ranch: This large boulder is located up on a morainal ridge just west of the ranch.

Lupine Meadows: This collection of three boulders is about 0.5 mile up the trail from the Lupine Meadows parking area. Look for them on the west side of the trail just after crossing the bridge over the Glacier Gulch stream.

Jenny Lake: These four famous boulders were chronicled in the humorous *Guide to the Jenny Lake Boulders* (located at the Jenny Lake Ranger Station), by John Gill and Yvon Chouinard, which was written in 1958. From the south end of the Jenny Lake campground, walk north along the bike path that runs along the west side of the campsites. After a few hundred yards you will notice the steep, south-facing wall of Cut-Finger Rock. Falling Ant Slab is located just to the west overlooking Jenny Lake. Red Cross Rock is located to the northeast of Cut-Finger and sports the famous Gill Problem (B2) on its overhanging east side. Mount Fonda rounds out the group and is practically on the road just north of Red Cross. It is interesting to note that these boulders may have the distinction of being the first place in the country where gymnastic chalk was used. Richard Emerson, who was the first to climb on the boulders, was in the habit of using forest duff on his hands to improve his grip. John Gill, a former college gymnast, began using chalk on these boulders sometime during the 1950s.

String Lake and Leigh Lake: Although a number of smaller boulders are located on the moraines that surround these lakes, two large, top-roping boulders are of main interest. From the String Lake picnic area, walk north for 1.1 miles to the bridge over the outlet stream from Leigh Lake. The short portage from String Lake to Leigh Lake takes off to the north from here. The largest and perhaps most interesting boulder is located on Boulder Island in the south end of Leigh Lake. Some manner of conveyance across the water of the lake will be needed to reach the island. Once on the island, scrambling leads to the top from the east side. There are two bolt stations on top for top-roping the north and west sides. For the second boulder cross the bridge to the west across the Leigh Lake outlet stream and walk a couple hundred yards northwest toward Paintbrush Canyon. Look for a large boulder to the south that is somewhat hidden in the trees. Scrambling up the east side leads to the top.

Boulder Town: For this area park at the Cathedral Group Scenic Turnout on the Jenny Lake scenic loop road. These boulders are located on the moraine which is a few hundred yards north of the parking area. There are six major glacial erratics located in close proximity to one another with several top-rope and boulder problems with a wide range of difficulty levels.

Teton Canyon: From the town of Driggs on the west side of the range, drive up toward Grand Targhee Ski Resort. After nearly 6.0 miles turn off to the right where a sign points the way to Teton Canyon and Campground. Drive to the end of the road to the small parking area located at the trailhead. A short hike to the east puts one at the base of a few rock walls on the south-facing side of the canyon. The first of the these contain a bolt-protected 5.13 as well as a spectacular 5.11 roof for which one uses traditional protection. On the next major rock outcrop, known as the Grand Wall, there are also several other bolt-protected sport climbs.

Badger Creek: This area is on the west side of the range and is located about 3.0 miles north of Tetonia. A dirt road takes off to the north just past town and intersects the Badger Creek drainage after about 3.0 miles. Turn east and drive about 0.5 mile. The small outcrops of igneous rock will be seen rising a short distance above the road to the south.

Climatology

Jim Woodmencey, Meteorologist

The Tetons are big mountains, big enough to make their own weather, to hide some of the early signs of changing weather, and to keep the climber engaged with the mountain until the weather changes.

—David R. Brower, 1956,
from the publisher's foreword to the first edition of
A Climber's Guide to the Teton Range,
by Leigh Ortenburger

Every climb has its season. This is true in the Teton Range, as it is in most of the other great mountain ranges of the world. The seasonal fluctuations in the weather in the Tetons or, more comprehensively, the climate of this place, will have relevance to the choice, and perhaps ultimately the success, of your chosen climb. For instance mid-July, when temperatures in the valley are hitting 90°, is not the season to attempt to climb Run-Don't-Walk Couloir on Mount Owen. Or attempting to climb the Owen–Spalding on the Grand in January in a T-shirt and tennis shoes might be considered somewhat dim-witted. That's not to say that these two feats have not been tried, nor should you rule out the possibility of an anomalous record-breaking weather situation that could allow these ascents to be accomplished, in the aforementioned seasons, quite successfully.

Some knowledge of the climate of this area may assist you in the planning of certain routes in certain seasons. More specifically, an understanding of the seasonal weather patterns and the potential extremes of weather in these mountains will not only increase your chances for success, but also decrease your chances for getting into a dangerous and life-threatening situation. If nothing else, it should leave you with a greater respect for the power of these mountains and the weather in them.

It should be noted that the weather has played a role in precipitating a good portion of the search-and-rescue missions launched by the Jenny Lake rangers over the years. People get stuck in these mountains in bad weather, and often they can't get out on their own.

The Tetons lie in a climate zone classified as "alpine tundra," flanked by "alpine" valleys; therefore, one would expect an alpine environment to exist. That would neces-sarily denote some rather harsh weather, a good portion of the time, to produce such a climate. A region just doesn't qualify as "alpine" in the climate world with pleasant weather all the time. Alpine regions by definition are characterized by ample precipitation, which sustains the forests they contain, and cool summers. Alpine tundra regions, the peaks themselves, are classified as very cold and windy.

Regular visitors to the higher Tetons have experienced the strong winds of the Lower Saddle, they have descended through raging storms with the snow blowing sideways and the visibility near zero, and they have had to worry about hypothermia and frostbite as they made their way, as fast as possible, to the relative safety of the valley—not in the middle of winter, but right in the middle of July, supposedly the hottest and driest month of the year in the Tetons. If you have not experienced these conditions, it is because they are not the rule for that time of year but, rather, the exceptional conditions that can present themselves, at some point, almost every summer.

For the winter enthusiast, the Tetons have proven themselves time and again to have some of the harshest weather on the face of the earth, with -20° to -30°F temperatures at 12,000 feet, steady winds in excess of 120 miles per hour, and overnight snowstorms that raise the avalanche danger so high that retreat from some locations in the range would be ill-advised. On the other hand, there are those handful of days in the winter when it's so calm that you could light a match at the Lower Saddle, wearing a light shirt in 30°F temperatures, under cobalt-blue skies, in mid-January.

Timing of the weather is key to the success of any climb in this range, at any time of the year. To plan a trip here in July to climb the Grand by one of its classic routes is usu-ally a good choice, as July is the warmest and driest month of the year. Knowing whether the preceding winter or spring was wetter or drier than normal, and whether or not it has been snowing up high in the last two weeks, might be more pertinent and more timely information to have. The climate here, as in any location, is a collection of averages, patterns from 20 to 30 years of weather data. What's hap-pening this week can easily be way above or below what is considered normal.

With that caveat, you can still do some planning from a "monthly average" perspective. Also, the more time you have to spend here, the better the chances of hitting a particular season's "normal" conditions.

Normals

The climate station for Moose, Wyoming, is located behind Park Headquarters. This station represents the closest daily climatological station to the mountains (the latest data used for averages of temperature and precipita-

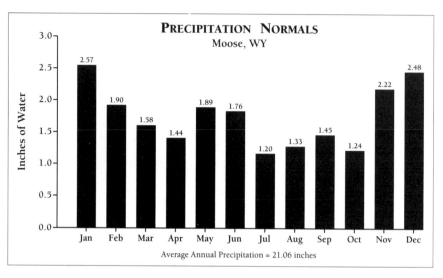

PRECIPITATION NORMALS
Moose, WY

Average Annual Precipitation = 21.06 inches

tion, from 1961 to 1990). This station's normals are quite a bit different from the normals seen in the town of Jackson, which is less than 15 miles farther south and 200 feet lower in elevation. There is no climate station in the mountains; however, the Jackson Hole Ski Area and the Avalanche Forecasting Lab there have over 20 years of weather data from the 9,000- to 9,500-foot elevation to compare to for the winter months only.

Wind data are more difficult to summarize because they contain both speed and direction and are very sensitive to the exact location where the measurement is taken. The best information on the mountain winds has been obtained at the Upper Rendezvous Station (10,300) at the Jackson Hole Ski Area near the south end of the range. These data show that summertime wind directions are predominately from the southwest and west, with a speed of over 20 miles per hour about 10% of the time, and an average speed of about 10 miles per hour.

It should be understood that on any given day there will be radical differences in the weather both linearly, from the south end of the range to the north end, and also vertically, from the valley floor to the ridge tops. In general, changes in the atmosphere will occur more rapidly in the vertical. Temperature, wind speed, and precipitation amounts and intensity can be significantly different, at the same time, between the valley floor and 11,000 feet. This is a consideration often disregarded or not inherently obvious to the uninitiated, as can be observed on any summer's day as people leave the trailhead in 70° weather in a T-shirt and shorts for a climb of a peak, with temperatures at 11,000 feet in the mid-30°s and wind-chill temperatures on top hovering at around 5° in a 30–mile per hour wind. Carrying the proper clothing with you for the changing conditions you may encounter is imperative most of the year.

The Seasons

Characterizing the seasons around Jackson Hole and the surrounding mountains is best put with the old adage, "There are nine months of winter and three months of bad skiing." Some years there are only a couple of weeks of bad skiing; others, we have up to four months where the skiing isn't very good! Still, there are a few observations to be made regarding each season, both from personal observation and from the climate data.

One can infer several things by perusing the climate data. First, it is a good assumption that the months with the most precipitation also have the greatest abundance of cloudy days, and conversely. Second, temperatures on a daily basis will fluctuate greatly, depending heavily on the amount of cloud cover each day. A clear night will produce much colder temperatures in the valley overnight than a cloudy one, even as a cloudy day will keep daytime high temperatures cooler than the averages shown. It would be reasonable in a given month to expect daytime temperatures to be plus or minus 10°F from the monthly averages. *Spring:* By the end of March winter is waning, and daytime high temperatures in the valley are well above freezing and up into the 40°s. On a sunny day, the season's first climbers can be found out on the south face of the Blacktail Butte practice rock at midday. In the mountains the snowpack is at its maximum; with a good freeze overnight, the spring skiing and climbing is at its best, and many of the peaks are skied right into the middle of May. By then the valley is getting muddy, and one must endure a mile or so of quagmire to get to the receding snow line. New snowstorms on the valley floor are still a possibility in the month of May. May is also the wettest spring month, and afternoon cloud buildup over the mountains is more commonplace.

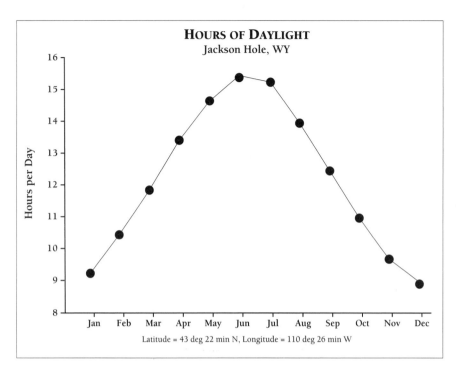

HOURS OF DAYLIGHT
Jackson Hole, WY

Hours per Day

Latitude = 43 deg 22 min N, Longitude = 110 deg 26 min W

October, but the frequency and reliability of these days from year to year are hit-and-miss. By November, winter has settled into at least the mountains, sometimes without enough snow to ski, but too much snow for casual walking.

Winter: The Tetons can have winterlike conditions almost any month of the year, but December and January are typified by a lot of snowfall and very few clear days. There are periods when high pressure builds over the northern Rockies and we can have a two-week drought, but more often than not it is hard to find a stretch of more than four or five days in a row in the winter months, December to February, without measurable precipitation in the valley. Keep in mind also that there are days when it is snowing up in the mountains and not snowing down to the valley floor, thus limiting the number of uncloudy days in the mountains even further. A comparison of the amount of snowfall in the mountains versus the valley shows that December and January are the snowiest months of the year and that during each of the four winter months, December through March, the snowfall at around 9,500 feet at the Jackson Hole Ski Area is almost consistently twice that of the valley floor station at Moose. Again, it should be stressed that it is possible in a given winter month to have more than twice the normal snowfall amount, or in dry years to receive half of the normal amount of snow.

Average Monthly Snowfall (in inches)

Month	Moose (6,450 ft)	Mountains (9,500 ft)
December	40	72
January	49	71
February	33	66
March	24	61

Data taken from Moose Climate Data, 1959–1980, and from Jackson Hole Ski Area, 1973–1992. These are the monthly averages for both locations. The extremes for both locations vary widely, and it should be understood that it is possible to have a given month with more than double the average snowfall shown or to have an entire month go by in the winter with less than half of the average amount of the total monthly snowfall.

Summer: By the first of June the snow line has retreated to well above the valley floor, afternoon thunderstorms over the mountains are beginning to show up more regularly, and the chances of long spells of wet weather dwindle toward the end of the month. June is the wettest of the three summer months, June, July, and August. July is normally the hottest and the driest month of the year in the range. An exception was the summer of 1993, when there were 3.29 inches of precipitation recorded at Moose for the month, and over 6 feet of snow fell that month at the Lower Saddle. This went on to become the coldest and wettest summer in Jackson Hole history. Thunderstorms and the danger of lightning, most often in the afternoon hours, are prevalent through the month of August. July and August are the months when the majority of the climbers are in the range, the weather is usually the most pleasant, the number of days with precipitation is lowest, and the hours of daylight are significantly longer than the rest of the year, an important consideration at this latitude.

Fall: The days become significantly shorter as you move through September. The weather can still remain quite nice, however, though with slightly cooler temperatures, even up high in the mountains. But one should be aware that September usually brings with it the first good snowstorm in the high mountains, and this can ice over even the south-facing routes on the major peaks. Typically, we will go through some nice stretches of fall or Indian summer weather into

Another wintertime weather phenomenon worth mentioning is the *inversion*. In the winter months, especially December through February, temperature inversions will set up during periods of high pressure or clear calm weather. An inversion, by definition, is when the air temperature rises with height; normally temperatures get colder as you go up in elevation. During an inversion the mountains are warmer, as the cold air drains to the valley floor. This is also, in general, the best time for winter ascents of the higher peaks. It can be brutally cold in the valley (-10° to -30°F) and at the same time, it can be a relatively pleasant 10° to 20°F up in the mountains.

For the sake of trivia, and the historic record of maximums and minimums, the hottest it has ever been in Moose in the summer is 93°F, and the coldest it has ever been in the park in the winter is -63°F. Those are the extremes of temperature and are certainly not approached on a regular basis.

Weather Sources

To the mountaineer, the weather forecast is a requisite item. You could say that without a forecast climbers would be negligent in their approach to these mountains. As Brower has said, these *are* big mountains and they *can* create their own weather. At the same time, not paying attention to the warning signs and not taking with you as much information about the weather as you can, before you go into these mountains, is not only reducing your chances for success, but possibly compromising your own personal safety.

There are several means by which to obtain weather forecasts for the Jackson Hole area. Local radio stations broadcast the weather for the valley, for the next 24 to 36 hours, almost every hour. TV stations from Idaho Falls, Pocatello, and Salt Lake City are available (it is suggested finding one that has a real meteorologist rather than a weatherman); unfortunately, they will concentrate more on the weather near their broadcast area. If cable TV is available, you can tune to *The Weather Channel* to see what's coming. The Jenny Lake Ranger Station usually will have the most current weather information for the mountains and also the most current conditions report on specific climbing routes.

In the winter, the Bridger–Teton National Forest Avalanche Hotline [(307) 733-2664] can be called for the latest avalanche hazard and mountain weather forecast; this is an invaluable resource in the Teton Range in the winter, from the first of December through early April.

Once in the mountains, an indispensable tool for updated weather information is a weather radio. This is a lightweight and simple means by which to hear what is going on in the atmosphere while you are out on an extended trip. This is a service provided nationwide by the National Weather Service 24 hours a day and can be received with a special radio or with any receiver with the proper frequency programmed in. (Many models are available from electronics stores and other sources for as low as $30.) The closest broadcast station to the Tetons is in Pocatello, Idaho (frequency 162.55 MHz), and can be received from many locations around the range, especially once you are up at the ridge crests.

Geology of the Teton Range

John C. Reed, Jr., Geologist
U.S. Geological Survey, Denver, Colorado

To the casual tourist or hiker, the geology of mountains is chiefly of academic interest, but to the mountaineer it is of vital concern. Geology determines the obstacles to be encountered and the strategy and tactics that must be used to overcome them. A variety of geologic factors must be weighed by the climber in selecting a route, in placing an anchor, or, indeed, with every move of a hand or foot. Thus, it is appropriate that a brief discussion of the geology of these mountains be included here.

The general architecture of the Teton Range is simpler than that of most of the other great alpine ranges of the world. The Teton peaks are sculptured from an enormous westward-tilted fault block of ancient metamorphic and igneous rocks that are part of the central core of the continent. These basement rocks were at one time completely covered by much younger sedimentary rocks that have since been stripped by erosion from the central part of the Teton block. The north-south–trending Teton fault, which marks the eastern edge of the Teton block, lies near the eastern foot of the range (see *Figure 1*). The eastern edge of the Teton block has been raised at least 8,000 feet during the last two million years at an average rate of almost 5 inches per century. This very rapid uplift (in geological terms) has resulted in tilted stream terraces in Jackson Hole, fresh fault scarps along the base of the range, and occasional earthquakes. There is every reason to believe that uplift will continue into the future, although the Teton fault has historically been ominously quiet. Maximum uplift along the fault has been in the segment between Death Canyon and Moran Canyon. To the north and south, the displacement diminishes and the Teton fault block disappears—southward beneath other fault blocks in the Snake River Range and northward beneath the lavas of the Yellowstone Plateau.

Figure 1. *Grand Teton and surrounding jagged peaks of the Cathedral Group stood above the ice that sculptured the lower slopes and produced the conspicuous U-shaped cross-section of Cascade Canyon. Jenny Lake is ponded behind the terminal moraine deposited by the glacier that moved down Cascade Canyon. The trace of the Teton fault lies just below the lowest rock outcrops on the lower slopes of Teewinot in the lower left portion of the photo.*

Other faults break the Teton block into smaller blocks. The Forellen Peak fault extends southeastward from near Survey Peak, through Forellen Peak to Ranger Peak; it is spectacularly exposed on the north side of Webb Canyon (see *Figure 2*), where basement rocks on the northeast side of the fault have been raised more than 2,000 feet above younger sedimentary rocks on the southwest side. The Buck Mountain fault, actually a zone of several closely spaced faults, passes through the saddle west of Buck Mountain and extends across the head of Avalanche Canyon, down the south fork of Cascade Canyon, and northward across Indian Paintbrush and Leigh Canyons into Moran Canyon (see *Figure 3*). These faults are marked by several-hundred-foot-wide zones of fractured, altered, and iron-stained rocks. Basement

Figure 2. *The Forellen fault northwest of Webb Canyon. Layers of light-colored Paleozoic sedimentary rocks southwest (left) of the fault are bent up against dark-colored Precambrian gneisses northeast of the fault. The fault trends northwest and dips 50–60° east. The thin, light gray layer capping the Precambrian rocks northeast of the fault is the Cambrian Flathead Sandstone. The same layer occurs nearly at the bottom of the canyon southwest of the fault, showing that the rocks on the northeast side of the fault have been raised at least 2,000 feet with respect to those on the southwest.*

rocks east of the Buck Mountain fault have been raised nearly 3,000 feet above younger sedimentary strata to the west, and sedimentary rocks near the fault have been bent steeply upward. The Buck Mountain fault parallels the segment of the Teton fault that has the greatest displacement, and all the loftiest peaks of the Teton Range have been carved from the uplifted wedge between these two faults.

As the Teton fault block rose, streams began carving deeper and deeper canyons. During the Ice Ages, valley glaciers flowed down the major canyons. The eastward-flowing glaciers advanced into Jackson Hole and at several times coalesced with great ice sheets that moved southward from the Yellowstone Plateau. Several separate glacial advances are recorded by overlapping layers of glacial till and outwash deposits in Jackson Hole. During one of the earliest, about 140,000 years ago, ice filled Jackson Hole to a depth of several thousand feet and extended several miles south of Jackson. During the last major advance, about 20,000 years ago, an ice sheet that extended southward from Yellowstone deposited the terminal moraine that forms the natural dam behind which Jackson Lake is now impounded. Valley glaciers issuing from Moran Canyon and

from canyons to the north flowed into this great piedmont ice sheet, but valley glaciers from the canyons to the south emerged onto the floor of Jackson Hole and formed the smaller terminal moraines that now enclose Leigh, Jenny, Bradley, Taggart, and Phelps Lakes.

During each ice advance, canyons were scoured and their floors and lower slopes rounded by glacial erosion. The projecting peaks and ridges were sharpened and the upper valley walls steepened by frost action, avalanches, and undercutting at their bases by the glaciers. During each interglacial stage, streams deepened the major canyons and their tributary valleys, while wind, rain, frost, and snow continued to erode the peaks. Because the streams and glaciers that flowed down the steep eastern face of the rising Teton fault block cut their canyons more rapidly than those that flowed down the gentler western slope, the drainage divide moved steadily westward. The present divide is not along the highest peaks, but several miles to the west, along the much lower ridge at the park boundary, and the deepest sections of the major canyons are not at the heads of these canyons but in the lower reaches where the canyons breach the chain of high peaks (see *Figure 1*).

Figure 3. *Mount Moran and the Cathedral Group from the southwest. Photograph was taken from over the head of Death Canyon. Layered Paleozoic sedimentary strata dip 15–20° west. The Buck Mountain fault tends north–south along the western flanks of the high peaks. Along it, the block of Precambrian rocks from which the high peaks east of the fault have been carved has been uplifted about 3,000 feet relative to the Precambrian rocks beneath the west-dipping sedimentary rocks west of the fault.*

All of the basement rocks are of Precambrian age—that is, they were formed at various times before 570 million years ago, the beginning of the Cambrian period. The oldest rocks in the range are layered gneisses that were formed by metamorphism of sedimentary and volcanic rocks at high temperatures and pressures, probably at depths of 10 to 20 kilometers in the earth's crust. The original sedimentary and volcanic rocks were probably deposited more than 2.7 billion years ago as parts of volcanic island chains like those that now fringe Southeast Asia. The gneisses were complexly folded, and about 2.5 billion years ago they were invaded by magmas that crystallized to form large masses and myriad dikes of granite. The youngest of the Precambrian rocks is dark diabase that forms several conspicuous, nearly vertical, east-west–trending dikes. These dikes, which are now known to be about 765 million years old, cut all of the other Precambrian rocks but were truncated by erosion before deposition of the Cambrian Flathead Sandstone (see *Figure 4*).

The layered gneisses are composed chiefly of various proportions of quartz, feldspar, biotite (black mica), muscovite (white mica), and hornblende (a dark green mineral forming prismatic crystals). Generally, the rocks are conspicuously layered. The layers, which are marked by differences in color and mineral content, range in thickness from a few inches to several feet. Layers of dark green to black amphibolite, a rock composed principally of hornblende and feldspar, are abundant in some places. Because the mica flakes and the prismatic hornblende crystals are arranged parallel to the layers, the rocks tend to split along these planes, forming smooth friction slabs on mountainsides parallel to the layering, as on the eastern slopes of Mount Moran. Slopes across the grain of the layering tend to be steeper, jagged, and more broken. The projecting edges of the harder layers commonly provide bucket holds, but holds are generally less sound than those on slopes parallel to layering, and loose rock is much more

Sedimentary rocks deposited during the Paleozoic era (between 570 and 245 million years ago) once blanketed all the basement rocks now exposed in the Teton Range. They still extend over wide areas at the northern and southern ends of the range and cover most of the western slope, but in the central part of the range they have been largely removed by erosion. All the higher peaks are sculptured in the older crystalline basement rocks. Small erosional remnants of the Flathead Sandstone of Cambrian age (about 540 million years old), the lowest of the Paleozoic deposits, are preserved on the summits of Mount Moran, Traverse Peak, Bivouac Peak, and Rolling Thunder Mountain. Other Paleozoic rocks form the ridge between Doane Peak and Ranger Peak and cap most of the minor peaks to the north and west. Layers of Paleozoic limestone and dolomite form impressive cliffs, such as those at the heads of Avalanche Canyon, Death Canyon, and the south fork of Cascade Canyon, in Alaska Basin, and on Rendezvous Mountain, but the areas of Paleozoic rocks are of little interest to the climber because of the unsound rock and the lack of challenging summits. It is to the basement rocks in the central peaks that mountaineers generally turn their attention.

of a hazard. In most parts of the range, layering in the gneisses and schists trends approximately north–south and slopes 30–60° eastward, so that east-facing slopes are generally parallel to the structure, while west, north, and south slopes cut across it at various angles.

Some of the gneiss is not conspicuously layered and resembles coarse-grained granite. It is shown as granite gneiss on the cross-sections. The biotite flakes are scattered uniformly through the rock but are aligned parallel to one another and form a foliation along which the rock splits more easily than it does across grains. The granite gneiss forms smooth slabs on slopes that parallel the foliation, as on some of the east slopes of Traverse Peak, Eagles Rest Peak, and Mount Moran. On slopes counter to the foliation, it forms precipitous cliffs and bold buttresses, as on the northwest face of Thor Peak and the southwest buttress of Mount Moran.

Figure 4. *The east face of Mount Moran. Most of the mountain is made up of granite gneiss and layered gneiss with layers that slope 40–60° eastward. Light streaks that slope gently north (right) are dikes of granite and pegmatite. The conspicuous black dike is overlain by a thin erosional remnant of Cambrian Flathead Sandstone (the smooth, light gray mound that caps the flat summit). Falling Ice Glacier and Skillet Glacier are two of the small active glaciers in the Teton Range.*

Layered gneiss and granite gneiss are the most widely exposed basement rocks north of Moran Canyon. Granite and pegmatite become increasingly abundant toward the center of the range, first as scattered dikes and small irregular masses, then as networks of dikes a few inches to several hundred feet thick laced irregularly through the gneiss and schist. The high peaks of the Cathedral Group and the upper reaches of Cascade Canyon are carved in a single mass of granite that locally contains abundant tabular blocks of layered gneiss, schist, and amphibolite, which range in length from a few inches to thousands of feet. Hundreds of these blocks, or inclusions, are magnificently exposed on the north wall of Cascade Canyon west of Ice Point, and on the north faces of Teewinot, Mount Owen, and the Grand Teton, where their darker colors contrast sharply with the predominantly lighter hues of the enclosing granite.

The granite (shown as Mount Owen Quartz Monsonite on the cross-sections) is a fine-grained, sugary-textured, white, light gray, or pink rock composed principally of smoky-gray, glassy quartz and pink or white feldspar and contains a few small scattered flakes of biotite and muscovite. Associated with it are abundant dikes and irregular masses of pegmatite, a rock that contains the same minerals as the granite but in which individual crystals are much larger. Many pegmatite dikes contain feldspar crystals as much as 2 feet in diameter, and some contain plates of silvery muscovite 6 inches across and blades of black biotite as much as 2 inches wide and 1 foot long. A few contain crystals of bright red garnet the size of baseballs. The pegmatite forms dikes and irregular masses, some of which pass gradationally into the granite, showing that the two rocks are intimately related.

Because of their lack of layering and foliation, the granite and pegmatite have no preferred direction of splitting and are therefore very solid and particularly resistant to erosion. Dikes of granite and pegmatite in the gneiss and schist project as ribs, ridges, and pinnacles that afford the beautiful and frequently very steep pitches that are among the great climbing features of the Teton Range. Prominent

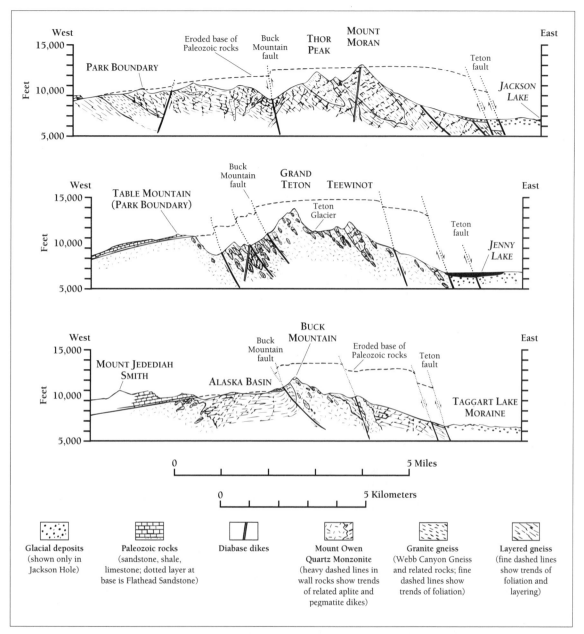

Geologic cross-sections of the Teton Range. *Lines of section are east-west. The northernmost section passes through Mount Moran, the central section through the Grand Teton, and the southern section through Buck Mountain. Heavy lines are faults. They are dotted where projected above the ground; arrows show relative direction of movement. Approximate position of the eroded base of the Paleozoic rocks is shown by a thin dashed line.*

examples are the dikes on the Exum Ridge, the upper ridges of Teewinot, and on Ice Point, Storm Point, and Cleaver Peak. Larger masses of granite and pegmatite form smooth friction slabs and enormous cliffs on which the climbing routes generally follow joints and fractures. On the lower walls of the canyons, where the rocks have most recently been scoured by glaciers, the granite and pegmatite are polished smooth, and tension techniques may be necessary on pitches of even moderate angle. Above the limit of glaciation, where the rocks have been continuously exposed and not planed smooth by moving ice, weathering has roughened the surface and commonly has formed pits, knobs, and gargoyles in the granite. Weathering has caused individual crystals in the pegmatite to stand out in relief, forming good holds and easy friction pitches. Inclusions of gneiss commonly form ledges and pits or projecting knobs, so that even high-angle faces may furnish relatively easy free climbing.

All of the Precambrian rocks are transected by planar fractures or joints, which control the orientation of faces and ledges and which furnish holds and cracks for anchors. Two sets of joints are conspicuous in most of the range. One group trends about north–south and slopes steeply west; the second group trends nearly east–west and is close to vertical. In the larger masses of granite and pegmatite, many joints trend north–south and slope eastward parallel to layering and foliation in the enclosing gneisses and schists.

About 765 million years ago, long after the granite and pegmatite were emplaced, but before the Paleozoic sedimentary rocks were deposited, several nearly vertical east-west–trending fractures developed in the Precambrian basement rocks, and molten rock welled up into them and crystallized to form the conspicuous black dikes now exposed on Mount Moran (see *Figure 4*), Grand Teton, and Middle Teton. The rock in these dikes is dark green to black diabase that closely resembles basalt in appearance and composition. The largest of these dikes, the one exposed on the east face of Mount Moran, ranges in thickness from 100 to 120 feet and has been traced westward for more than 7.0 miles to where it disappears beneath Paleozoic rocks northwest of Green Lakes Mountain. The other dikes are thinner and not as long: the one on Middle Teton is 20 to 40 feet thick, and the one on Grand Teton is 40 to 60 feet thick. The hot dike material baked and oxidized the adjacent rocks, commonly giving them a reddish color.

Where the dikes are more resistant to erosion than are the enclosing rocks, they project from the mountainside as walls or ribs, such as the rib formed by the upper part of the black dike on Mount Moran. Where the dikes are less resistant than the neighboring rocks, they form deep clefts and couloirs, as along the dike on the Middle Teton. The black dike that passes just above the Lower Saddle on the Grand Teton extends completely across the lower part of the south face of the mountain and eastward into Glacier Gulch. It forms the deep cleft that separates Teepe Pillar, Glencoe Spire, the Red Sentinel, and Disappointment Peak from the main mass of the Grand Teton. The gully along the dike furnishes an easy route from the head of Teepe Glacier into the Lower Saddle.

The present glaciers in the Teton Range are too small and scattered to present serious obstacles to the mountaineer. They are of interest chiefly as miniature working models of the great ice streams that once helped carve the present landscape. The modern glaciers are probably not remnants of the Ice Age glaciers—it is more likely that the earlier glaciers melted away and that the present ones formed within the last few thousand years. The Teton glaciers have retreated considerably since the latter part of the 19th century but now seem to have reached a temporary standstill. Photographs taken in 1898 by William Owen show that the Teton Glacier then extended 500 feet farther down the valley than it did in 1964 and was nearly 200 feet thicker. Ice in the central part of the Teton Glacier is moving down-valley at a rate of nearly 40 feet per year, but this advance is balanced by melting at the snout, so that the terminus has remained in about the same position since 1955. Ice movement in the glaciers is enough to open *bergschrunds* and a few impressive crevasses, so the snow-covered parts of the glaciers should not be treated too casually, as unwary climbers occasionally learn to their considerable dismay.

Because of the unusually sound character of most of the Precambrian rocks, talus is less extensive than in most other ranges in the Rocky Mountains. Many routes, however, do require considerable talus hopping. In spite of its obvious lack of other virtues, the talus does furnish the observant mountaineer with important clues to the character of the rock ahead. Small loose talus and fine scree warn of loose handholds and falling rock on the cliffs above; large stable talus blocks give promise of sound rock and good climbing.

Selected References

Bradley, F. H. "Report of Frank H. Bradley, Geologist of the Snake River Division." *Sixth Annual Report of the U.S. Geological Survey of the Territories etc., for the Year 1872,* edited by F. V. Hayden, pp. 189–271. Washington, D.C.: U.S. Government Printing Office, 1873.

Fryxell, Fritiof. *The Tetons, Interpretation of a Mountain Landscape.* Berkeley and Los Angeles: University of California Press, 1953, 77 pp.

Love, J. D., and J. C. Reed, Jr. *Creation of the Teton Landscape—The Geologic Story of Grand Teton National Park.* Moose, Wyoming: Grand Teton Natural History Association, 1968, 120 pp. Reprint, 1995.

Love, J. D., J. C. Reed, Jr., and Ann C. Christiansen. *Geologic Map of Grand Teton National Park, Wyoming.* U.S. Geological Survey Miscellaneous Investigations Series Map I-2031, scale 1:62,500, 1992.

Love, J. D., J. C. Reed, Jr., and R. L. Christiansen, with topography drawn by J. R. Stacey. *Geologic Block Diagram of the Teton Region.* U.S. Geological Survey Miscellaneous Investigations Series Map I-730, 1973. Reprint, Moose, Wyoming: Grand Teton Natural History Association, 1979.

Reed, J. C., Jr. *Observations on the Teton Glacier, Grand Teton National Park, Wyoming, 1965 and 1966.* U.S. Geological Survey Professional Paper 575-C, 1967, pp. 154–159.

Reed, J. C., Jr., and R. E. Zartman. "Geochronology of Precambrian Rocks of the Teton Range, Grand Teton National Park, Wyoming." *Geological Society of America Bulletin,* 84 (1973), pp. 561–582.

St. John, Orestes. "Report of Orestes St. John, Geologist of the Teton Division." *Eleventh Annual Report of the U.S. Geological and Geographical Survey of the Territories etc., for the Year 1877,* edited by F. V. Hayden, pp. 321–508. Washington, D.C.: U.S. Government Printing Office, 1879.

Steve Rickert on the first ascent of Emotional Rescue, North Face of the Enclosure (Photo: Reynold G. Jackson)

Canyons and Approaches

This section is intended to supplement, but not duplicate, the information regarding approaches to the peaks that can be found on the USGS topographic maps, on the maps published by Earthwalk Press, and in the excellent pamphlet *Teton Trails,* by Bryan Harry, published by the Grand Teton Natural History Association (Moose, Wyoming). Most of the maintained trails in the park are delineated on the maps, but some important ones have been omitted. The *Teton Trails* pamphlet contains much useful trail-hiking information but, because several important canyons and side canyons have no maintained trails, information on these canyons is also given in this section. The canyon descriptions are given from south to north.

In approaching the peaks the visiting mountaineer should appreciate that Teton climbing is so popular that very strict conservation measures must be taken if the natural beauty that now exists is not to be spoiled forever. All mountaineers must do their share to keep the mountains and canyons clean. Some Teton canyons, such as Garnet and Cascade Canyons, are more susceptible to damage than others simply because of the heavy volume of climbers and hikers. For example, between 1,500 and 2,000 climbers reach the summit of the Grand Teton each summer, and nearly all of these pass through Garnet Canyon both on the way up and on the way down. Each individual climber must leave *no* litter anywhere in the mountains. Indeed, leaving any sign of human passage in the true wilderness regions such as Snowshoe or Colter Canyon would be an act of desecration.

Granite Canyon

Prior to the completion of the aerial tram to the summit of Peak 10,450 (sometimes referred to erroneously as Rendezvous Mountain) at the Jackson Hole Ski Area in 1966, Granite Canyon was the domain of the horse packer, frequently from the west side of the divide, and was seldom entered by climbers. The sedimentary peaks surrounding the canyon were not then, and are not now, high on the priority list of Teton climbers. Since 1966, however, the ease of access provided by the tram both to the heights (10,450) and to the upper canyon have enormously increased the foot traffic in Granite Canyon. Peak 10,450 has even become one of the standard starting points for multiday trail

hikes on the Teton Crest Trail connecting to Cascade or Paintbrush Canyon. A favorite hike (12.0 miles) is now the trip from the top of the tram, down the back side on the Rendezvous Mountain trail, and back out Granite Canyon to the Granite Canyon trailhead. Because of the perceived danger to inexperienced hikers in early season, it is ski area policy not to allow access to the west side of Peak 10,450 from the top of the tram until it is mostly free of snow.

The mouth of the canyon is reached directly from the Granite Canyon trailhead, which is located on the Moose–Wilson road about 2.0 miles north of its junction with the short access road to Teton Village. The trail stays on the north side of Granite Creek past both the lower and the upper Granite Canyon patrol cabins, until finally crossing the stream in the north fork just below Marion Lake, one of the primary destinations in the canyon. The generally accurate 7.5-minute USGS quadrangle maps (Teton Village and Rendezvous Peak) for some reason fail to show the eight switchbacks on this trail. The drainage of the small side canyon immediately west of Peak 10,450 provides a speedy method of ascent to or descent from Peak 10,450, but crossing Granite Creek and the gigantic sedimentary boulders therein causes some difficulties. At the first junction on the trail the left fork is the Rendezvous Mountain trail, which leads south, up the upper south fork of the canyon, to the summit of the mountain. To reach the head of the south fork at the pass (9,960+) just northwest of Rendezvous Peak (10,927) involves nothing more than cross-country hiking.

The upper middle fork of the canyon is best reached via a cutoff trail connecting the Rendezvous Mountain trail with the Teton Crest Trail and leading to Marion Lake at the head of the north fork. Another approach used by both hikers and horse parties is via the Teton Crest Trail and Moose Creek Pass (9,085) on the divide. This trail originates at Highway 22, the Teton Pass road, goes up Phillips Canyon, over Phillips Pass (8,932) into upper Moose Canyon, and enters Granite Canyon at the Moose Creek divide.

The main trail in the north fork leads to the beautiful Marion Lake, a splendid camping area nestled just below the cliffs of the shelf below Housetop Mountain. Leading up to the lake the trail passes to the right of a curious natural bridge, located on the south side of the creek at 8,700 feet, just west of the junction with the Open Canyon trail. From

Marion Lake the Teton Crest Trail leads over a pass (9,560+) on north to Fox Creek Pass (9,560+) at the head of Death Canyon. To reach the Mount Hunt Divide (9,710), which provides the link with Open Canyon, take the right fork at the junction of the main north fork of the Granite Canyon trail with the Open Canyon trail. The secluded Indian Lake (9,805) lies high above the canyon at its north rim. It can be reached from the Open Canyon trail by hiking up the side canyon containing its outlet stream. Starting up this drainage from the floor of Granite Canyon is not recommended. The lake is perhaps most easily reached via the separate drainage immediately above and north of the upper Granite Canyon patrol cabin. Hike up to the head of this side stream, either from its intersection with the Open Canyon trail or directly from the cabin, and contour on a bench around to the right (east) to the lake.

The nature of the sedimentary rock in the southern and northern ends of the Teton Range is conducive to the formation of sinkholes and caves. Exercise some caution in cross-country hiking in such limestone terrain because some of these caves are simply and suddenly holes in the flat ground. A number of these are to be found on the slopes of Rendezvous Mountain and in Granite, Open, and Death Canyons. Two well-known caves, Wind Cave and Ice Cave, are found on the west slope of the range in Darby Canyon, as shown on the Mount Bannon quadrangle map. Some of these caves are very deep and entry and exit are difficult. Indeed, elsewhere in the range is one of the deepest, or perhaps *the* deepest, cave in the United States. While these natural features are, of course, of intriguing interest to climbers, details of the location of such formations are better presented in speleological journals and books since, to some extent, specialized equipment beyond that used in normal mountaineering is required to explore these formations safely.

Open Canyon

Open Canyon provides access to a half dozen of the highest peaks in the south end of the range. Although the peaks are sedimentary, an enjoyable day of ridge running is available to those who do not require vertical difficulty. The usual approach is from the Death Canyon trailhead via the Valley Trail, over the Phelps Lake Overlook, down to the junction with the Death Canyon trail near the west shore of Phelps Lake. Follow the left fork around the southwest side of the lake. Up on the lateral moraine take the right fork at the first of two junctions and hike into the canyon. At the point where the trail crosses the main Open Canyon stream, an important side stream, shown as intermittent on the map, comes down from the north, draining the major cirque lying below the upper northeast face of Prospectors Mountain. This drainage can be easily ascended or descended, and if the final ridge on the right (north) is gained

and climbed to the high point (10,560+), a route to or from Rimrock Lake can be put together.

The trail continues upcanyon to the vicinity of the forks, where it starts a steep uphill section to pass over the south rim of the canyon at the Mount Hunt Divide (9,710) and then drops into the upper portions of Granite Canyon. From the point (8,700) where the trail leaves the canyon floor to go up to the Mount Hunt ridge, it is easy to continue up the canyon in any direction. In early season the north-facing slope leading to the Mount Hunt Divide will be covered with snow, and an ice axe will be useful, perhaps essential. The beautiful alpine Coyote Lake (10,201) lies high at the head of the south fork. Even Indian Lake in Granite Canyon can be reached by crossing over the saddle (10,080+) west of Mount Hunt and contouring around the slopes to the lake.

Death Canyon

Death Canyon is a very long canyon with one of the oldest trails in the Teton Range running through it. Built in 1920–1921, it is one of the few trails that passes over the divide. To reach the Death Canyon trailhead from Park Headquarters at the village of Moose, drive south on the narrow and winding Moose–Wilson road for 3.1 miles and take the signed, paved turnoff road to the trailhead. From the parking area take the Death Canyon trail past the Phelps Lake Overlook at the top of the moraine that impounds the lake and, after two switchback corners (not to be counted in the following enumeration), drop down to the mouth of the canyon. The spectacular canyon is then entered, and the climber is soon flanked on both north and south by remarkable rock walls. A total of eight switchback corners (the quadrangle map shows only six) will be encountered on the trail in the canyon itself just before the Death Canyon patrol cabin is reached in the level region near the forks of the trail. The Omega Buttresses on the north wall of the canyon are approached from the vicinity of the second switchback corner. The main group of rock-climbing routes on Cathedral Rock is reached from the start of the first level section of the canyon before reaching the patrol cabin; leave the trail at the eighth switchback corner after entering the canyon.

The north fork trail rises in near-endless switchbacks, first to the Static Peak divide (10,180+) and then through No-Wood Basin to the Buck Mountain divide (10,480+). This north fork trail is heavily used by hikers going to or coming from the Teton Crest Trail in Alaska Basin on the west slope of the range. An alternative cross-country route to the Static Peak divide, directly from the east, is available. From the trail about halfway between the Death Canyon trailhead and the Phelps Lake Overlook, a small climbers' trail will be found leading off to the right, heading north toward Stewart Draw. After passing the stream draining the cirque east of the Static Peak divide, turn back left (south) and up into the main drainage leading to the cirque. At the upper end of the cirque below the divide an actual trail will be found. A second alternative, which provides a long glissade in early season, is the next large drainage south on the southern slopes of Albright Peak (Peak 10,552). This can be accessed by contouring around the west side of Albright Peak from the Static Peak divide.

The longer south fork trail continues at Fox Creek Pass (9,540+) via the Teton Crest Trail to Marion Lake at the head of Granite Canyon. From Fox Creek Pass the Teton Crest Trail can also be taken north along the Death Canyon Shelf to Mount Meek Pass (9,726), which provides a second method of entering or leaving Alaska Basin. A major southerly side canyon, commonly harboring mountain sheep, leads from the south fork to the remote Forget-me-not Lakes, high on the slopes of Prospectors Mountain. Another attractive side canyon, Connors Basin, leads north from the south fork and provides access to the divide between the seldom-climbed Peaks 10,300 and 11,086.

In a small cirque high on the south walls of Death Canyon is the isolated and beautiful Rimrock Lake. Do *not* visit this lake unless you are prepared to treat the fragile alpine environment surrounding the lake with the respect it deserves and requires. Great care must be taken with the tundra plants near the lake. To reach this lake from the Death Canyon trail, proceed past the patrol cabin (7,840) and across the bridge where the trail moves over to the south side of the main creek for the first time. The main drainage stream from the lake will be seen above, and to the right (west) is a smaller talus gully narrowing at the top and ending in a small cliff band. The left side of the main drainage stream can be followed to reach the lake, but roped climbing (5.4) will be required on the exposed and frequently wet slabs. A much better route ascends a slope with trees after crossing the bridge, heading toward the talus gully on the right, until near the top. It is then possible to turn left (east) with a brief section of rock scrambling onto a small ridge leading easily to the lake. In early and midseason the upper portion of this gully will contain moderate snow, requiring an ice axe for safety.

Stewart Draw

On the massive eastern expanse of Buck Mountain is Stewart Draw, which is more of a large stream drainage than a genuine canyon. It is given separate treatment here because it is an important access route, primarily to Buck Mountain, and its description requires some details. In the upper draw the trail is obvious, but the entire region around the base of Buck Mountain is confounded by obscure remnants of old horse trails dating from the days of the White Grass Ranch.

Start from the Death Canyon trailhead, following the Valley Trail west toward the Phelps Lake Overlook about 0.5

mile until, just before the third footbridge on the trail, a small subsidiary trail leads off to the north. Take this old trail into a large meadow, but do not continue all the way around the western edge of the meadow because the trail is easily lost. Instead, hike into the meadow for 100 yards along the trail, and then angle across the meadow aiming for the western edge of trees that extend into the meadow from the east; erratic boulders will be found here. Now follow due north along the edge of these trees, passing small fragments of old trails, and cross two small creeks, the second of which is marked by a large cairn on its south side. Continue north along the edge of the trees until two horse trails that join are encountered. Take this trail, now well defined, over a small ridge and into Stewart Draw, crossing the drainage stream near a huge boulder. At this point the buttress containing the Stewart Draw Rock Climbs rises above on the south side of the draw. Continue up into the canyon on this substantial trail past the old horse camp, staying mostly on the right (north) side of the creek, to the large cirque below Timberline Lake. One way to reach the lake is to take the large couloir that leads southwest from this cirque up the south flank of Static Peak and then traverse back to the right (north) onto the moraine that borders the lake on the east. If a two-day trip is desired, a camping spot can be found along the lakeshore or in the cirque below.

Avalanche Canyon

One of the major Teton canyons, Avalanche Canyon serves as an important and attractive route of approach to Buck Mountain, Mount Wister, Veiled Peak, South Teton, and, less commonly, Cloudveil Dome and Nez Perce. Adding to its appeal, this canyon seems to be the summer home of a good percentage of the moose in the park. Seldom does one enter the canyon without seeing one or more moose in the area around the forks. Outstanding high country campsites are found in the north fork of the canyon.

The preferred route into the canyon is around the north side of Taggart Lake on an unmaintained trail developed by the numerous climbers and hikers entering the canyon. (Note that if one attempts to gain the mouth of the canyon by hiking around the south side of Taggart Lake, an unpleasant swamp must be negotiated on the west shore of the lake [clearly shown on the map], just south of the stream from Avalanche Canyon.) From the Taggart Lake trailhead a few hundred yards south of the Taggart Creek bridge on the main highway, start up the trail and take the first right fork that soon crosses to the north side of the creek. Do not try the service road here because it dead-ends at a water tank. At the junction after 1.1 miles, take the Bradley Lake trail, the right fork, but only for 0.25 mile, and then move cross-country left (west) back down toward Taggart Lake and hike north on the trail near the shore of the lake toward the moraine separating Taggart and Bradley Lakes. (One can also stay on the Taggart Lake trail, the left fork, down to the lakeshore and then turn right on the trail to gain this same point, but this is longer.) On the open slope before reaching the top of the moraine (at the point where the trail crosses the 6,960-foot contour line and before reaching the first switchback corner), leave the main trail just above a large, fallen, dead tree on the left (west) side of the trail. A small but distinct trail will be found here heading west toward the canyon. This narrow trail stays on the north side of the creek, through some boggy areas, and past a very large isolated boulder (an interesting climbing problem!) near the forks of the canyon. The trail can be followed fairly easily all the way to the forks (about 2.0 miles west of Taggart Lake), where, depending on the destination, one can turn into either the north or south fork of the upper canyon.

South Fork: From the fork in Taggart Creek climb up toward the south fork of Avalanche Canyon on either side of the stream. Several campsites can be found along the shore of the shallow lake that lies just above the first headwall. Farther up the canyon there is considerable talus; feasible campsites are not numerous here but, with effort, can be found, even with water. At the west end of the canyon and under the southeast slopes of Veiled Peak are several high, grassy benches that will provide adequate, though windy, campsites with running water. The col (10,800+) between Veiled Peak and Mount Wister is easy to cross if one wishes to descend the north fork of the canyon. Another alternative exit is to ascend the slopes, covered with snow in early season, to the divide and the Teton Crest Trail in upper Alaska Basin.

North Fork: The climb up to the elegant Lake Taminah can be made either to the right or to the left of the splendid Shoshoko Falls. The initial headwall above the forks is, however, usually passed via the main talus slope descending from the north. The right (east) side of this slope is bounded by a small stream originating on the south slopes of Nez Perce. By following this streambed up a few hundred feet, one can avoid many of the bushes and contour easily over toward the falls. The upper end of the talus provides access to Lake Taminah by a nearly horizontal traverse. There are excellent campsites near the mouth of this lake. Do not attempt to pass the lake along its south shore. Use the north shore even though it appears to be somewhat longer. West of Lake Taminah and below the second headwall that leads to Snowdrift Lake is a meadow with deep grass. An enormous boulder will be found at the northwest corner of this meadow. Under it there is some space for a bivouac, but in early season the meadow and boulder may be wet and partially covered with snow.

Pass this second headwall on the right (north) up to one of the highest lakes in the park, Snowdrift Lake (10,006); it will have snow or ice on its shores until late in the season. In early season the snow on this headwall is steep enough to require the use of an ice axe for safety. The campsites among the *krummholz* near Snowdrift Lake are some of the finest in the park and care should be taken to leave this fragile alpine environment exactly as you found it. The saddle between Mount Wister and Veiled Peak can be easily gained directly from the east end of Snowdrift Lake. The base of the Wall at the west end of the canyon can readily be approached, and an easy hike to the north from the lake takes one to the small Kit Lake (10,320+), an above-timberline campsite. Exit from the canyon can be made by continuing easily to the north up over the saddle (10,560+) between the Wall and the South Teton and then joining the trail in the south fork of Cascade Canyon. This route can be reversed by hiking up the south fork of Cascade Canyon trail, taking the left fork to the Avalanche–Cascade divide, and descending into the uppermost portion of the north fork of Avalanche Canyon.

To descend the north fork from Lake Taminah follow the climbers' trail down toward the forks, edging east to meet the end of the main Avalanche Canyon trail. The extensive snowslides of the winter of 1985–1986 uprooted or knocked over many trees in this and almost every other canyon in the range, so avalanche debris will be encountered, hindering progress.

Garnet Canyon

Located in the center of the range, Garnet Canyon is the epicenter from which most of the Teton mountaineering activity radiates. It forms the principal approach to the three Tetons—South Teton, Middle Teton, Grand Teton—as well as many other central peaks, pinnacles, and rock climbs. Every summer a few thousand climbers camp at one of several sites in the canyon. Because of the impact of this volume, the National Park Service has placed limitations on the numbers of campers at these sites, and permits must be obtained. The Lower Saddle (11,600+) between the Middle Teton and the Grand Teton is considered by many to be the best camping area for climbs of the Grand Teton by standard routes. The advantages are a short summit day (2,200 feet) and commonly a colorful sunset; the disadvantages are a paucity of good campsites, little protection from the elements, and an almost continuous cold wind from the southwest. Other camping areas will be discussed below. The Garnet Canyon approach to the Lower Saddle is standard, but a completely different (and more difficult) route via Dartmouth Basin (see *Cascade Canyon*) can be used for either ascent or descent.

Access to Garnet Canyon begins at the Lupine Meadows trailhead, reached by driving about 0.25 mile south of the Jenny Lake campground, crossing the bridge on Cottonwood Creek, and continuing across Lupine Meadows to the parking area (6,732) at the beginning of the trail.

Garnet Canyon Campsites (Platforms, Meadows, Caves, Moraine, and Lower Saddle): Follow signs to the end of the maintained trail at the creek in Garnet Canyon. The overall water quality in Garnet Canyon has experienced an unfortunate decline during the past few years, which corresponds directly to increased use. It is advisable to drink selectively here and throughout the Teton Range for that matter. If starting from the American Alpine Club Climbers Ranch, a small trail up Burned Wagon Gulch is used to join the Garnet Canyon trail in the vicinity of the first junction. This climbers' trail begins immediately west of the bridge across Cottonwood Creek on the access road to the ranch, heads north and passes the Lucas-Fabian Homestead on the west, and turns due west up Burned Wagon Gulch. Proceed up this open valley, staying mostly on the right (north) side, and join the Garnet Canyon trail at or just below the first junction.

The flat area with trees just across the stream from the end of the trail is known as the Platforms (8,960) and it provides an excellent campsite; in the early years of the park there were tent platforms here used by trail crews. In early season this camping area will be covered with snow. The Platforms is a useful camping site for climbs of Nez Perce, Cloudveil Dome, South Teton, and Middle Teton or for rock climbs on Disappointment Peak. However, other sites higher in the canyon are equally suitable and are somewhat closer to the peaks. In an effort to minimize the erosion caused by random climbers' trails, the National Park Service has improved a climbers' trail (unmaintained) from the end of the maintained trail at the Platforms to the Lower Saddle. This trail starts some 30 feet north of Garnet Creek among large boulders, stays north of the creek, and can be easily followed through the next section, a boulder field, to the Meadows (9,200). Much of the area immediately east of the Middle Teton where the canyon forks was covered by morainal material from a landslide in 1951; after 40 years, it has recovered only some of its original features that led to the name, the Meadows, for this area. The vegetation in this area is fragile so use care not to disturb the plants and flowers. Recovery is very slow at these altitudes.

North Fork: The main features of the north fork of Garnet Canyon are the initial headwall (above the Meadows) containing Spalding Falls, the Petzoldt Caves (10,100), the Middle Teton Glacier moraine, the final headwall, and the Lower Saddle at the head of the canyon. *Note:* Described here is the standard route to the Lower Saddle as used in midseason or later; in early season a different route, described later, is strongly advised because of the danger inherent in the snow slopes above the Caves. Follow the NPS climbers' trail up from the Meadows, taking the steep switchbacks leading to the north up the talus to the right (east) of Spalding Falls, then through the trees, and finally back west to the Caves. This important campsite is just above the highest trees above Spalding Falls. Adequate protection from the weather is available for about six persons. In very early season considerable snow will be found here. The Caves are one of the three principal camping areas for the Grand Teton ascents, and those who wish to trade the rigors of Lower Saddle camping for a noticeably longer summit day (3,700 feet) will find the Caves a good compromise.

From the Caves take the NPS trail which then zigzags almost straight up the long slope above the Caves toward some scrub pines. When very near the base of Fairshare Tower that looms above, turn left (south) on the trail and make a nearly horizontal traverse to reach the lower end of the conspicuous Middle Teton Glacier moraine that runs down the center of the upper canyon floor from the Lower Saddle. Do not take the diagonal trails that will be seen traversing out to the left (south) from above the Caves. While slightly shorter than the NPS trail, these will involve, during much of the year, one or more traverses across dangerous snow slopes. These can and should be avoided by taking the trail straight above the Caves, as already described. On the moraine itself several camping sites will be found, and these are also suitable as alternatives to the Lower Saddle; they are not as attractive as the Caves, but they do provide a shorter summit day.

The narrow crest of the moraine is then followed to the upper headwall beneath the saddle. A fixed rope (the only one in the range) will be seen off to the right (north), leading up the usually wet slabs and cliff, providing assistance on this headwall. From the top of the fixed rope the trail traverses left (south) and up along the top of the headwall in order to reach the lowest portion of the saddle. *Use great caution* with the loose rubble in this area, as rocks kicked off here will go over the headwall and the chances are very good that other climbers will be just below. On the saddle itself, where small high-altitude tundra plants are found, use care to step on gravel or rocks in order to preserve the fragile and beautiful flowering plants. Stay on the designated trail. Early in the season the fixed rope may be covered by snow and ice; in this case, climb directly up the moderately steep snow couloir in the center of the headwall. This will require the careful use of the ice axe. For those experienced in the art of glissading, this couloir makes a fast route of descent from the Lower Saddle, but it is not recommended after the middle of the season when crevasses open up and boulders appear in the runout slope at the bottom of the couloir. As an alternative to following the crest of the moraine to the final headwall, walk along the flat glacier to the south of the moraine. This will not be as fast as the moraine crest except in early season when the glacier is covered with snow.

For early-season ascents, when the entire canyon is covered with snow down to the vicinity of the Platforms, the usual route up to the Caves and across the slope above to the lower end of the moraine is *not* recommended. Much or all of this long slope will be covered with snow and, taking the shortest line, many climbers erroneously make an upward, diagonal, and dangerous traverse on moderately steep snow to reach the moraine. Most of this snow slope has no runout and ends in the substantial cliff band, the lower headwall that contains Spalding Falls. Numerous serious, even fatal, accidents have occurred here. Experience with ice-axe self-arrest or with snow belaying is strongly recommended before attempting this section of the approach to the Lower Saddle. In early season, the preferred route is to climb from the west end of the Meadows directly up the moderately steep snow slopes next to the east cliffs of the Middle Teton to get past the first headwall and gain the Middle Teton Glacier moraine. This, too, will require knowledge in the use of the ice axe but has the advantage of being nearly straight up rather than diagonal. If one is ascending or descending this portion of the route early in the day before the sun has softened the surface, crampons will make the climbing easier and safer, but they are not really essential on this approach to the Lower Saddle. Careful kicking or cutting steps in the snow will suffice. When the snow is gone, this alternative near the Middle Teton is not recommended because the morainal material here is very loose.

South Fork: Little description is required for the route from the Meadows to the saddle (11,360+) between the Middle and South Tetons. Much of this section is an extended boulder and talus field. There are few routefinding problems, and the difficulty of the snow slopes is moderate; however, an ice axe is recommended, especially in early season. For those experienced in glissading, there are two steep snow couloirs near the Middle Teton. In late season a minimal climbers' trail beginning at the Meadows leads up toward the saddle at the head of the south fork. There are very few usable campsites in this fork of the canyon, but there are two or three grassy benches providing flat space as well as a small site at the saddle itself.

Glacier Gulch

Glacier Gulch separates Disappointment Peak from Teewinot Mountain and the Grand Teton from Mount Owen. It leads from the flats south of Lupine Meadows past the small Delta Lake to the Teton Glacier and ends at the sharp Gunsight Notch. For those who do not mind bushwhacking, the direct approach is interesting and wild; there are no trails, other than game trails, leading up this canyon. Delta Lake, gray-green from the glacial flour ground by the Teton Glacier, makes an agreeable and rarely visited camping place. The most commonly used approach into the canyon via Amphitheater Lake starts from the Lupine Meadows trailhead. Take the Garnet–Amphitheater trail to the first junction (with the trail that leads to Taggart Lake), and follow the right fork to the second junction, where the trail to Garnet Canyon turns left (south). Take the right (north) fork at this second junction. Surprise Lake is reached after 19 switchbacks. Three designated campsites are found a few hundred feet to the north, where a fine view of the Grand Teton and Mount Owen can be obtained. Continue another few minutes to Amphitheater Lake. To reach Delta Lake hike to the ridge crest just north of Surprise Lake, where a steep slope of grass and talus and scree will be seen curving directly down toward Delta Lake; a portion of this slope will be covered with snow in early and midseason. Another scheme to reach Delta Lake is to leave the main trail at the northern switchback corner where a large boulder is located. A faint trail will be seen leading to the west from this point. Some routefinding is involved and caution must be used, as this "trail" takes one over some cliff bands. However, it does provide more or less direct access to Delta Lake.

To reach the upper portion of Glacier Gulch and the Teton Glacier from Amphitheater Lake, continue on the trail to the col above and to the north of the lake. Follow this trail down the far (north) side for about 150 feet until it angles left (west) directly under the sheer north cliffs of Disappointment Peak. To make this traverse, several steep and dangerous snow slopes must be crossed (in late season these disappear and the traverse becomes very easy); one should not attempt to cross these slopes without an ice axe and experience in its use. Continue northwest for a few hundred yards, past the crest of the first moraine, to the bowl between the Grand Teton and Disappointment Peak. Climb north from this bowl, ascending the Teton Glacier terminal moraine at its left (west) edge which is next to the base of the east ridge of the Grand Teton. The glacier has receded considerably since the 1920s when it was possible to step down a few feet from the crest of the moraine onto the surface of the glacier. Now, however, a tricky little traverse to the left is necessary in order to reach the level of the glacier without losing too much altitude.

There is also an alternative direct approach up Glacier Gulch to Delta Lake and the glacier; this route is useful for descent back down to the valley. Leave the standard Garnet–Amphitheater trail shortly after leaving the Lupine Meadows trailhead to gain the crest of the moraine on the north side of the Glacier Gulch drainage. Wait until it is possible to see a more or less open route through the trees to reach this moraine; some bushwhacking will be necessary. A small game trail will be found along the morainal crest. Follow the crest west until it steepens and then cut left (south) into the gulch not far below Delta Lake. From Delta Lake, if one wants to reach the surface of the Teton Glacier, aim for the bowl on the left (south) side of its terminal moraine and proceed as in the standard approach described earlier. It is also possible to circle around the north side of the large terminal moraine and gain the glacier from that direction. Because the eastern approach to Gunsight Notch at the head of the canyon is protected by a steep, difficult, and dangerous (rockfall) chute, it is not feasible to pass out of the canyon by that route.

It is frequently desirable to return to a camp on the Teton Glacier or Surprise Lake from the Lower Saddle via the Black Dike, which cuts across the south side of the Grand Teton; this interesting and direct traverse is also occasionally used from Glacier Gulch to reach the Lower Saddle before an ascent of the Grand Teton. To take this Black Dike Traverse, ascend the long snow couloir leading southwest out of the bowl between Disappointment Peak and the Grand Teton; an ice axe is essential here. This couloir ends at the Dike Col between Pemmican Pillar and Okie's Thorn; the col is on the divide between Glacier Gulch and Garnet Canyon. To continue to the Lower Saddle, make an upward crossing of Teepe Glacier to Teepe Col, which separates Teepe Pillar from the southeastern cliffs of the Grand Teton. In late season the snow covering may disappear and this "glacier" (technically, just a snowfield) will show bare ice. The dike itself passes beneath the glacier and reappears at Teepe Col. Now follow the dike to the Lower Saddle, crossing over Glencoe Col on the way. In general, the loose rock encountered on this traverse is most stable at the extreme right (north) edge, immediately beneath the walls of the Grand Teton, and a faint trail can be found there. There are no great difficulties in this traverse, but it is a bit time-consuming, and an ice axe and the knowledge of how to use it are definitely recommended for safety. Early in the day, when the snow is frozen hard, crampons may be found useful on both Teepe Glacier and the Dike Col Couloir.

Cascade Canyon

Cascade Canyon is the central, largest, and best known canyon in the range containing the most heavily travelled trails. Lake Solitude, at the head of the north fork, is a principal tourist attraction. The Cascade Canyon south fork trail connects with the Death Canyon trail via Hurricane Pass (10,320+) and Alaska Basin, and the north fork trail joins the trail in Indian Paintbrush Canyon by way of the high Paintbrush Divide (10,560+). This system is known as the Teton Crest Trail. The Cascade Canyon trail provides, as described here, access to the Symmetry Couloir, the Teewinot–Owen cirque, and Dartmouth Basin. These in turn can be used to approach Teewinot, Mount Owen, the three Tetons, the peaks along the divide, and all the peaks and pinnacles on the ridge north of Cascade Canyon, such as Storm Point and Symmetry Spire. Valhalla Canyon, also accessed from Cascade Canyon, is discussed separately.

The spectacular Hidden Falls, near the beginning of the Cascade Canyon trail, can be reached in three ways. Most easily, from the boat dock at the south end of the Jenny Lake campground area take the boat across Jenny Lake and hike for 0.5 mile; or, from the same boat dock, hike (2.5 miles) around the south side of Jenny Lake via the trail past Moose Pond to the falls; or, third, start from String Lake, cross the bridge at the southern end of that lake, and hike (2.2 miles) around the north and northwest sides of Jenny Lake. The fastest route for climbers going farther west into the canyon is to use the horse trail. From the west shore boat dock on Jenny Lake immediately hike north 300 yards. Here the horse trail (marked) takes off to the west through the trees for 0.7 mile. After emerging from the last trees, the final upper section of the horse trail traverses horizontally south to join the level portion of the main Cascade Canyon trail above Hidden Falls. It is easy and fast going (4.5 miles from the boat dock) on this horizontal section of the trail to the forks.

Symmetry Couloir: About halfway along the upper horizontal section (above all of the switchbacks) of the horse trail, cross the stream that descends from the drainage between Storm Point and Symmetry Spire. A small climbers' trail starts right next to this streambed, leading west through the bushes and boulders toward the rocky cleft where the stream forms a waterfall in the cliff. Short of the cliff bear right past a small cascade into a secondary *cul-de-sac,* past a large chockstone or two, and exit up a short pitch on the left (west) side to gain the top of the cliff band that guards access to the main upper couloir between Symmetry Spire and Storm Point. Now move left (south) and up over ledges and slabs using a faint climbers' trail, staying away from the stream channel itself. This trail, if followed, leads through a short section of scrub pines near their left (south) edge up into the main Symmetry Couloir.

In early and midseason this couloir will contain moderately steep snow and has been the scene of many accidents, some fatal. The moats that open up are commonly in the main fall line and are especially dangerous. Beware. A rope combined with an ice axe and knowledge of how to use it for a self-arrest are basic for safety in this heavily travelled couloir. At the upper narrowing end of this couloir cross over to the right (some loose rock) into a shallow subsidiary couloir with a small watercourse. The Storm Point–Symmetry Spire saddle and the south routes on Symmetry Spire can now easily be reached.

Teewinot–Owen Cirque: The major cirque between Teewinot Mountain and Mount Owen provides access to the north, northwest, and west routes on Teewinot and the Crooked Thumb and to the northeast and north routes on Mount Owen. Climbers must expect some problems in crossing Cascade Creek, but with luck and some advance searching a log can often be located, permitting a dry passage. Inquiry at the Jenny Lake Ranger Station may yield information on the location of a suitable log. One suggestion is to hike west on the Cascade Canyon trail until past the point where the streams descending from the northeast snowfields of Mount Owen empty into the creek and then to cross where there is a very large boulder on the south side of the creek. Logs spanning the creek can sometimes be found in this area, but scouting the situation the day before the proposed ascent is recommended. Sometimes one must wade across the swift and cold creek, which, in early season when the water is high, can be difficult and dangerous. The bushwhacking up into the Teewinot–Owen cirque is not easy. Early routes used the left (east) side of the drainage into the Teewinot–Owen cirque, but most recent parties have hiked up through the trees on the right (west) side of the drainage. Either way scramble up the talus below the first snowfield. A campsite can be found in the lower reaches of the cirque beneath a very large boulder.

South Fork: At the head of the south fork of the canyon is a subsidiary trail leading to the saddle (10,560+) west of the South Teton; this provides climbers with a route into the north fork of Avalanche Canyon. The south fork of Cascade Canyon and Dartmouth Basin also offers climbers an interesting alternative to the customary Garnet Canyon approach to the Lower Saddle. About 1.0 mile south of the forks of the canyon, leave the trail and cross the creek; turn left (east) up the ravine leading toward Dartmouth Basin, which lies immediately west of the Lower Saddle. A small bit of bushwhacking is necessary, but after the initial waterfall is passed on the left (north) the going is easier. A beautiful, unspoiled grassy meadow for camping is passed at about 9,600 feet before the basin itself is reached. The west side of the Lower Saddle is protected by cliffs containing loose rock; these cliffs have been climbed (first by Frank Bradley in 1872) but are not recommended for either ascent or descent. The preferable route goes to the left (northeast) up a long, easy couloir that passes through the Black Dike and leads to the slopes north of the Lower Saddle. In early season this couloir will be filled with steep snow, requiring caution. To descend via this route from the Lower Saddle, climb toward the Grand Teton almost up to the Black Dike, then contour left (west) to a region of red rock, where the upper reaches of the couloir can be easily entered. There is loose rock in this couloir and caution should be exercised, especially if there is more than one party in it.

North Fork: The main trail provides complete access to this portion of the Teton backcountry. Camping is permitted in specified areas only and a permit is required.

Valhalla Canyon

Valhalla Canyon, a high canyon nestled between the northwest ridge of the Enclosure and the west faces of the Grand Teton and Mount Owen, is perhaps the most impressive and majestic in the park. Named with admirable sensitivity by the Dartmouth climbers in the 1930s, it is understood and entered only by mountaineers intent on one of the major routes on Mount Owen, the Grand Teton, or the Enclosure. This is a special place and may it ever be so. Entrance to the canyon is guarded by an arduous 2,000-foot climb up out of Cascade Canyon that requires crossing the cold Cascade Creek and bushwhacking.

Hike up the Cascade Canyon trail until the stream descending from Valhalla Canyon is in sight. The problem of crossing Cascade Creek remains, and because the existence and location of suitable logs spanning the creek are dependent on the year, the best recommendation is to make an inquiry at the Jenny Lake Ranger Station. In almost all years some manner of log can be found, usually near the woods 200 yards above the stream junction with Cascade Creek. If necessary, the main creek can be waded, but in early season this is not easy and is somewhat dangerous. Once on the brushy alluvial fan immediately below the entrance to Valhalla Canyon, head toward the main stream draining the canyon. A more or less adequate trail will be found close to the right (west) side of the stream, taking the climber up past the main cliff band guarding access to the upper canyon. Once past this section no difficulties will be found. Other routes used to pass this main cliff band include moving into the trees on the left (east) and climbing up and back to the right into the canyon (if properly done this can be good) and the use of the treed slope to the right (not so good). There are several fine campsites on the floor of the canyon, and the views of the faces and pinnacles above are very impressive. The upper section of the canyon consists of sloping talus, but one good campsite for two or three climbers has been constructed at about 11,000 feet. This site is located at the base of the first cliff (as one approaches from the floor of the canyon) immediately to the left (north) of the West Gunsight Couloir, the main snow couloir leading to Gunsight Notch between Mount Owen and the Grand Teton. Water is available at the West Gunsight Couloir.

The canyon was reached at least once from the south fork of Cascade Canyon by ascending to the crest of the northwest ridge of the Enclosure and then descending the loose rubble into the head of the canyon. This is, however, hardly the route of choice.

Because one of the principal uses of Valhalla Canyon is to approach the west or northwest routes on the Grand Teton or the north routes on the Enclosure, the discovery (on July 25, 1960, by Leigh and Irene Ortenburger) of a completely different route into the uppermost canyon via the Lower Saddle has proved to be both convenient and popular for experienced climbers. This access route, the Valhalla Traverse, requires only three to four hours, allowing one to camp at the Lower Saddle and return to the same camp after completing one of these climbs. This traverse is a serious undertaking, as even in the driest of conditions one can expect to find ice and wet rock. In certain sections the rock is of the poorest quality, and belay anchors and protection are difficult or impossible to obtain.

From the Lower Saddle it should be possible to see the large cairn constructed at a principal step on the crest of the southwest ridge of the Enclosure; for the convenience of others, such cairns should be maintained. Hike north up the main trail from the Saddle and veer off to the west (a small trail can be found) at a point about halfway to the Black Dike. Contour around and down into a gully of red rock. Follow a faint trail across this gully and around two small ridgelets and then up the final gully which leads to the cairn (mentioned earlier) on the southwest ridge of the Enclosure. From the cairn contour north along the very broad shelf leading across the west face of the Enclosure to the far (north) end of this shelf at the northwest ridge of the Enclosure. Some icy snow patches will usually be encountered on this shelf. A bivouac site will be found at the base of the steep wall at this corner; water is usually available at the snow patches. The crucial continuation of the Valhalla Traverse ledge system starts at this corner. Continue around the corner for 75 to 100 feet until a small ridgelet is encountered. The traverse becomes a very serious proposition from this point on. From this small ridgelet a small bowl can be seen immediately down and to the east. (In late season the climber will encounter in this bowl curious, yellow, muddy sand with the texture of wet cement; in early or late season the bowl will contain snow or even water ice.) Here the route splits depending on one's objective.

If one wishes to gain access to Valhalla Canyon itself or the west face of the Grandstand for routes such as the North Ridge, West Face, and Northwest Chimney of the Grand Teton, climb carefully down into this bowl. At the bottom of the bowl a narrowing, scree-and-ice–covered ramp will be seen descending down and to the east. Continue (with great caution) down along this ramp to its lower end, where an expanse of ice or snow must be crossed to gain the shelves leading toward the Grandstand. This snowfield (in late season this will be ice) is immediately beneath the Enclosure Ice Couloir and the fall line of the Black Ice Couloir on the north side of the Upper Saddle. *Beware of rockfall at this point.* Cross as rapidly as possible to the benches directly west of the Grandstand, where the selected ascent route can be started.

If the objective is to descend into Valhalla Canyon, proceed down to the end of the ramp mentioned above and then down and across the ice/snowfield beneath the Black Ice Couloir (rockfall hazard). Continue several hundred feet down toward a broad, relatively flat promontory. From the promontory, scramble down to the northeast into the West Gunsight Couloir, the snow chute that descends from Gunsight Notch. Take the snow chute or the rocks along its southern edge all the way down to the floor of the Valhalla Canyon. Note that a high bivouac site is located 200 feet to the north along the base of the wall that forms the northern boundary of the snow chute.

For other routes such as the Enclosure Ice Couloir, Black Ice Couloir, or north buttress routes on the Enclosure, a secondary exit from the small bowl mentioned earlier is taken. Traverse across the bowl maintaining elevation until considerably better rock on the other side of it is met. Continue around (still maintaining elevation) for two traversing pitches (5.4) to the west edge of the Enclosure Ice Couloir that leads back up and right to the northwest ridge. On the far (east) side of this ice couloir two small, diagonal shelves will be seen at the base of the Enclosure north face buttress, the major and most impressive feature rising above and to the east. The smaller (upper) of the two diagonal shelves leads right up to the base of the Lowe Route and High Route. If the objective is the Black Ice Couloir, cross the Enclosure Ice Couloir and continue up and left (on the larger and lower of the two shelves) around the base of the Enclosure north buttress for about 300 feet; this starts out loose but gets better and harder. The last ropelength (5.6) up this shelf brings one to the base of the main icefield of the Black Ice Couloir.

Hanging Canyon

Hanging Canyon, an attractive canyon conveniently located near Jenny Lake, is encircled by the many peaks and crags of the Symmetry Spire–Mount St. John group. It harbors three beautiful alpine lakes—Arrowhead Pool, Ramshead Lake, and Lake of the Crags—which themselves are worthwhile objectives. The usual approach into the canyon is from the boat dock on the west side of Jenny Lake. Take the Valley Trail north past the main stream draining Hanging Canyon. After entering the trees, pass two small bridges before turning left (northwest) on a small but distinct trail heading off through the trees toward the main open slope leading up into the canyon. The upper section of this unmaintained trail into Hanging Canyon ascends an easily eroded hillside. To minimize damage caused by random vertical trails, the National Park Service improved this trail. So stay on the existing NPS trail to prevent the creation of parallel ruts. At the top of this slope the trail swings left, crosses a small watercourse, and proceeds upward into the canyon, staying on the right (north) side of the stream and the lakes. In early season an ice axe will be useful for the snow that lingers in this area. Fine campsites will be found just east of Ramshead Lake among the charred skeletons of trees. Small campsites can be found at Lake of the Crags.

Although more tedious and involving some bushwhacking, another approach to the lakes is to contour into the canyon from the north. From the south String Lake trailhead, cross the bridge and follow the trail that swings around the west side of String Lake; this trail crosses an open slope on the east side of Mount St. John. Climb up this slope, using game trails, to and past Laurel Lake. A few hundred feet above Laurel Lake, traverse left (south) toward Hanging Canyon. Pass through a short section of bushes, across a boulder field, and continue on into the canyon, keeping below the cliffs of Mount St. John.

Paintbrush Canyon

The trail in the easily accessible Paintbrush Canyon forms the northern end of the Skyline or Teton Crest Trail system and provides easy access to the few peaks of this region. The beginning of the (Indian) Paintbrush Canyon trail is reached by driving to the north String Lake trailhead and taking the Valley Trail (on the east side of the lake) to the bridge at the north end of the lake. Cross the bridge and follow the main trail to the left to the first junction; the right fork at this junction is the Paintbrush Canyon trail. The trail in the upper portion of the canyon bifurcates, the right branch leading to the beautiful tarn, Holly Lake. There are fine campsites in designated locations near the lake. The upper stretches of the trail over the Paintbrush Divide (10,560+) into Cascade Canyon will be covered with snow until late season. Hence, during most of the summer, an ice axe will be needed to cross safely over to Lake Solitude. To reach the solitary Grizzly Bear Lake from Paintbrush Canyon, do not aim for the low point of the divide between Holly Lake and Grizzly Bear Lake because the north side of this saddle is ringed with cliffs. Instead, take the trail to a point (about 10,160+) above and west of this saddle, and from there descend easy slopes into the Grizzly Bear Cirque. The upper portions of Leigh Canyon are accessible from Paintbrush Canyon by descending from the Paintbrush Divide into Blister Basin to the northwest or by descending the drainage from Grizzly Bear Lake down to the floor of Leigh Canyon.

Leigh Canyon

Leigh Canyon is one of the longer Teton canyons, cutting almost straight through the range from Leigh Lake to the divide. Many important climbs, most notably the major routes on the south side of Mount Moran, start from Leigh Canyon. Because it is currently without trail, this canyon is not a common backpackers' destination. A very early horse trail once extended into the canyon, but almost all traces of it have been lost during the intervening 60 years. In more recent decades good foot and horse trails were constructed around both the southwest and northwest shores of Leigh Lake to reach the mouth of the canyon, but these, alas, have also been abandoned by the National Park Service. During the past 10 or 20 years the total lack of maintenance has rendered these valuable trails nearly useless for man or beast. The old trail around the southwest shore of the lake is nonexistent, totally blocked by large quantities of deadfall as well as the bogs.

As a result canoeing across Leigh Lake is currently the recommended method for those seeking entry into Leigh Canyon. Begin by putting the canoe (they can be rented in Jackson or in Moose) into String Lake at the north String Lake trailhead and paddling to the north end of the lake (about 1.0 mile). Make the short portage to Leigh Lake, and paddle the 2.5 miles to the mouth of the canyon to the two designated campsites (14A and 14B) located on the lakeshore on either side of the outlet of Leigh Creek. Depending on one's objectives, these campsites can be used as a base of operations in Leigh Canyon.

Without canoe but with noticeably more exertion, hike from the north String Lake trailhead along the Valley Trail on the east side of Leigh Lake, to the patrol cabin at the

north end of Leigh Lake. Beyond (west of) the cabin the remnants of the once-good trail, at times overgrown by lush vegetation, can usually, with effort, be followed to the two campsites at the mouth of the canyon.

The rather dense vegetation in initial sections of the canyon can be passed via a climbers' trail which starts directly upcanyon from Campsite 14B (the one on the north side of Leigh Creek outlet). This trail is relatively easy to follow except in sections where recent avalanche debris has covered it, requiring some detours. Once in the canyon, stay on the north side of the creek, at times using rocks in or alongside the creek itself. This beaten trail ends at the point where exit is made to the talus below the south buttress on Mount Moran. Campsites can be found in this region near the stream. The two shallow lakes, just beyond this point, should be passed on the north side. There seem to be no well-defined game trails from the lakes to the upper end of the canyon, but the travelling is not too difficult. Some fording of the stream is necessary to avoid the dense willow thickets and scrub pine. It will usually be found most expedient to stay near the stream before turning up at right angles into a desired side canyon.

The seldom-visited upper section of the canyon can also be reached by descending from the Paintbrush Canyon trail to Grizzly Bear Lake and then climbing down on the west side of the stream draining from the lake. This involves some bushwhacking. More easily, the upper canyon can be gained from the Paintbrush Divide by descending the isolated Blister Basin northwest down toward Mink Lake. This remote region can also be reached from Cascade Canyon and Lake Solitude by climbing Littles Peak, traversing north along the divide, and then descending into Leigh Canyon from the low saddle 0.5 mile north of the summit. Campsites can be found here and there along the upper canyon floor.

Moran Canyon

For Moran Canyon there are several approaches, none especially easy or short; which is selected depends on the starting point and whether one is aiming for the mouth or the head of the canyon. The passage up the length of Moran Canyon from Jackson Lake to the divide is recommended only for enterprising hikers and climbers, as the trail is easily lost; once the trail is lost the bushwhacking is difficult. In addition, some of the stream fords can be very tricky, especially during times of high water. And to gain the mouth of the canyon between Mount Moran and Bivouac Peak is more difficult now than in previous years due to lack of trail maintenance.

The traditional method is to hike from the north String Lake trailhead around the east shore of Leigh Lake to Bearpaw Lake, which is the end of the maintained Valley Trail. Continue north past Trapper Lake around the east side of Mount Moran to the mouth of Moran Canyon. This last portion (3.0 miles) of the approach is neither easy nor pleasant, because many years ago the National Park Service abandoned the maintenance of the once-good trail beyond Trapper Lake to Moran Creek. Winter avalanches have since left a broad area of flattened tree debris. No specific recommendation can be given to simplify this section since serious bushwhacking seems to be impossible to avoid. At times remnants of the old trail may be found. An alternative is to head cross-country toward the extreme south end of Bearpaw Bay on Jackson Lake from the end of the normal trail near the upper Bearpaw Lake. After a fairly short and moderate bushwhack to the lakeshore, the beach can be followed around to the mouth of the canyon. This route is longer than the direct route through the trees but has the advantage of little or no deadfall and the disadvantage of a slanting, sandy surface. Since the route up the canyon from its mouth is on the north side of Moran Creek, a final problem of the traditional foot approach from the south is the crossing of the creek. With luck a log may be found.

One can avoid the first portion of this hike by canoeing across Leigh Lake to the north shore and starting the hike from the Leigh Lake patrol cabin. This involves 3.1 miles of paddling plus the String Lake–Leigh Lake portage. The best approach to the mouth of Moran Canyon, however, is across Jackson Lake, via power boat or canoe (on a day without excessive wind from the west). Power boats can be rented at Colter Bay or Signal Mountain Lodge, or one can canoe (4.0 miles of paddling) from Spalding Bay. Debark on the north side of Moran Creek.

To proceed upcanyon stay mostly on the north side of the creek. Using keen observation one will find a game trail almost all the way to the forks of the canyon. One secret is to stay close to the creek and avoid the natural tendency at places to try to hike along the sidehill. With luck and a good eye, it is even possible to pick up faint traces of an old horse trail marked by partly overgrown blazes on trees and axe-cut deadfall. Most of the blazes are to be found on the upstream (west) side of the trees. Adding interest to the canyon are two old moldering log cabins, probably built by hunters, tuskers, or poachers from the Idaho side of the range. While not shown on the recent maps (it was clearly marked on the 1948 map), there is a substantial swamp before the forks of the canyon are reached. Getting past the swamp is a problem. There are faint traces of a trail along the north edge of the swamp, but it may well be simpler to wade directly through the swamp, regaining the trail on the same (north) side of the stream at the upper (western) end of the swamp. In very late or very dry season the swamp is dry and it becomes easy to walk through its waist-high grass.

The remote Cirque Lake (9,605), one of the larger alpine lakes in the park, is reached by bushwhacking up the west side of its outlet stream from the floor of the south fork of Moran Canyon. The cirque provides numerous wild and beautiful camping sites. An alternative approach is going from the upper south fork of Moran Canyon to the saddle between Maidenform and Cleaver Peaks and then dropping down 1,000 feet to the lake. Another route that has been used (sometimes in reverse for exit from Cirque Lake) is to hike into Leigh Canyon, scramble north up the interminable slope to the low point (10,000+) on the Leigh–Moran divide, and skirt west around the head of the unnamed canyon on the north side to the saddle (10,400+) southeast of the lake, where an easy descent leads to the destination.

South Fork: From the forks of Moran Creek, cross the north fork stream, and continue up the open canyon to timberline. For those interested in wildflowers the upper portions of the south fork provide an astonishing display. It is a beautiful place in early or midseason. Maidenform and Cleaver Peaks are directly accessible from the south fork, and one can easily pass over the saddle west of Maidenform Peak and drop down into the head of Leigh Canyon. This upper south fork area near the divide is most commonly reached, not by ascending Moran Canyon, but by hiking the Cascade Canyon trail to Lake Solitude, climbing over Littles Peak, continuing north along the divide, and then dropping down into the south fork over the Maidenform saddle. Another scheme, which requires less physical effort, involves the trails of the Targhee National Forest west of the divide. From Driggs, Idaho, drive to the trailhead on North Leigh Creek at the edge of the USFS wilderness area on the west slope of the Teton Range (see the Granite Basin quadrangle map). Take the Green Mountain trail to the basin above and beyond Green Lake, from which one can easily reach and cross the divide at the broad saddle (9,760+) due west of Cleaver Peak and drop into the south fork of Moran Canyon.

North Fork: Travel up the north fork of Moran Canyon is relatively easy on either side of the stream. The cirque holding lake (9,610), Ortenburger Lake, high above the north fork, is an uncommonly beautiful location that provides a reflection of the Cathedral Group in the waters of the lake. At the extreme head of the south branch of the north fork is another rarely visited lake (9,680+) with the western extension of the Mount Moran dike exposed on its eastern shore. Entry into the head of the north fork can be gained from the west slope in a manner similar to that described earlier for the south fork. From Green Lake continue east and then north along the pack trail for about 2.0 miles and cross the divide at one of the low points south of Green Lakes Mountain.

Another method of reaching the north fork is via Webb Canyon and the Lake 9,610 cirque. From the extreme southern end of Moose Basin in Webb Canyon, cross the saddle (10,320+) just east of Peak 10,880+ and drop into the upper end of the south fork of Snowshoe Canyon. Without losing much altitude one can skirt around the head of Snowshoe Canyon, cross the Snowshoe–Moran Canyon divide via the saddle (10,400+) on the southeast ridge of Doubtful Peak (10,852), and then drop down to Lake 9,610. This requires some scrambling, and an ice axe is required for safety on the snow slopes. This scheme of transit from Webb Canyon to Moran Canyon is commonly used in conjunction with the Littles Peak–Moran Canyon route by those who wish to make an extended north–south traverse of the range, for example, from Cascade Canyon (or farther south) to Webb Canyon and beyond.

Snowshoe Canyon

Based on experience accumulated through the years, it seems not unreasonable to claim that Snowshoe Canyon is indeed the most difficult of all the Teton canyons. The already enormous bushwhacking problems of ascending the canyon from the shores of Jackson Lake were exacerbated by the winter avalanches of 1985–1986, when new forested sections were smashed and deposited like jackstraws on the bottom of the canyon. Simply put, there is no easy or even moderate route up the canyon to the forks. Nevertheless, the upper two forks of the canyon are ideal alpine valleys with outstandingly beautiful small lakes. And several important but rarely climbed peaks, such as Rolling Thunder Mountain and the twin summits of Eagles Rest Peak, are accessible from Snowshoe Canyon. But serious and exasperating effort must be made to reach these prizes.

Forty years ago Snowshoe Canyon was the most northerly canyon readily reached by the trail that led from the north String Lake trailhead around the east side of Leigh Lake and Mount Moran all the way to the Moran Bay patrol cabin. Since the National Park Service abandoned maintenance of the trail section north of Trapper Lake, this approach is no longer feasible. The only reasonable approach to the mouth of the canyon is by boat across Jackson Lake. Power boats can be taken from Colter Bay or Signal Mountain Lodge or, if experienced, one can canoe (4.9 miles) from Spalding Bay. From the shore in the vicinity of the patrol cabin, strike northwest through the trees, cross North Moran Creek, and try to enter the canyon. The usual advice to stay mostly on the north side of the creek is perhaps valid but cannot be strongly advocated. Some crossings of the creek may prove useful. Essentially, brute force must be applied to reach the forks of the canyon, but at this point most of the troubles are over.

From the forks, travel up the north fork is now relatively easy although two headwalls must be passed before Talus Lake is reached. The first, 0.75 mile above the forks, is probably best negotiated on the southwest side of the stream. The first lake (9,120+) in this fork is a rare jewel, surrounded by cliffs, near-timberline trees, and hundreds of alpine flowers. Admire but do not disturb. Pass this first lake on the right (north) and continue easily to gain the rocky shore of Talus Lake (9,670). Small campsites can be found along the east edge of the lake. Webb Canyon and Moose Basin can be easily reached either via the pass (9,920+) north of Talus Lake or simply by going over the ridge west of the lake.

To penetrate into the south fork of Snowshoe Canyon, faint game trails can be followed mostly on the right (north) side of the stream until above the first step in the canyon. Avoid trying to stay close to the stream. Above about 8,000 feet the south fork opens up and there are no difficulties to the secondary branching at about 9,000 feet. Above and south of the south fork are three major cirques with several glaciers that have seldom been visited—interesting country to explore. Moran Canyon can be entered by climbing over the pass (10,400+) at the head of the south branch and down to Lake 9,610. Throughout most of the summer an ice axe will be desired to negotiate safely the snow slopes leading to this pass. Webb Canyon and Moose Basin are accessible via the north branch of the south fork using the pass (10,320+) just west of Peak 10,894. This pass is the major thoroughfare for those enterprising hikers or climbers who are making a north–south traverse of the range. From this pass by contouring high around the head of both forks of Snowshoe Canyon one can traverse from Webb Canyon into Moran Canyon, or conversely.

Dudley Lake, perched up on the south side of the canyon above the forks of the canyon, was first explored by (and named for) the early park ranger Dudley Hayden, in 1933. This remote lake provides a picturesque camping spot and so is a good but strenuous hiking objective. It is best reached by bushwhacking from the south fork stream up the wooded slopes northwest of the lake, rather than by following directly up the stream draining the lake.

Waterfalls Canyon

The trailless Waterfalls Canyon, while providing access to the most spectacular waterfalls in the park, is very difficult to approach on foot. The northern approach along the west shore of Jackson Lake from the vicinity of the lower Berry patrol cabin involves several miles of difficult bushwhacking and may not have been used since the winter expedition of Lt. G. C. Doane in 1876. The southern approach, starting at the end of the trail at Trapper Lake, is equally long and even more exhausting, because the area at the eastern base of Eagles Rest Peak, between the mouths of Snowshoe Canyon and Waterfalls Canyon, is an incredible mass of mosquitoes, deadfalls, and nearly impenetrable forest. Thus, the only reasonable method for reaching the mouth of the canyon is via boat across Jackson Lake. Leave the shore of the lake north of the mouth of the stream and bushwhack west and up through the region burnt by the fire of 1974; move west through the dead trees and small swamps, staying within 400 yards of the stream. Continue through meadows at about 7,200 feet to within a few hundred yards of the base of Columbine Cascade. Pass the cascade on the north, climbing up through some dense willow thickets to about 8,280 feet; then head diagonally upstream to the top of the cascade at 8,600 feet. The stream junction of the north and south forks is in a large bowl just below Wilderness Falls. A good campsite can be found here or at timberline near the relatively large lake (9,615) above the falls. This lake is most easily reached by climbing the slopes north of the falls, although with skillful routefinding and some moderate scrambling the falls can also be passed on the south. Easy slopes above this lake then lead to Ranger and Doane Peaks. The minuscule lake at 10,480+ feet high in the north fork can also be used for a campsite. The south fork of Waterfalls Canyon can be used to reach Anniversary Peak and the extensive ice and rock glacier below the northwest face of Eagles Rest Peak. The head of the north fork of Waterfalls Canyon can also be easily entered from the southeast corner of Moose Basin in Webb Canyon via the broad saddle (10,800+) just north of Doane Peak.

Quartzite Canyon

Little-known Quartzite Canyon, immediately east of Ranger Peak, is valuable as the approach to the remarkably beautiful cirque on the east side of Ranger Peak. Several names have been given to the canyon, the original, Quartzite Canyon, applied in 1942 by Fryxell and Horberg in *American Journal of Science* (240, pp. 385–393), a geological journal. More recently, "Osprey Canyon" and "Falcon Canyon" have been used since the original name fell into disuse. Jack Reed says it is known as Osprey Canyon by local fishermen.

The only recommended approach is via boat across Jackson Lake to the shore north of the mouth of the stream. From the lakeshore bushwhack up and west through heavy timber and swamps, passing an abandoned cabin (unusable) at about 7,240 feet. Continue through open woods and grassy meadows. At about 7,600 feet climb up brushy slopes on the north side of the stream for about 400 feet before traversing back to the left (west) to reach the stream again at about 8,500 feet. Continue on the north side to 9,000 feet (campsite available here) and cross the stream here; move across brushy talus slopes on the south side and up a rock step to a good campsite at the first lake at 9,720+ feet. There are several small lakes in the remainder of the canyon, which ends at the east slopes of Ranger Peak.

Colter Canyon

Seldom-explored Colter Canyon holds no great interest for climbers, because it does not provide easy or direct access to any major peak, but it may be of interest to enterprising hikers seeking the wilderness. Cross Jackson Lake by boat or canoe and leave the lakeshore about 0.5 mile north of the mouth of the stream. Climb steep, heavily wooded slopes to the crest of the morainal ridge east of the prominent bend in the stream. This section will be difficult going because of all the trees downed as a result of the fire of 1974. Follow the crest of this ridge north and then northwest into the open meadows at about 7,300 feet. Stay on the north side of the canyon, reentering heavy woods at 7,500 feet, and

follow game trails to open woods near timberline at about 8,500 feet. The upper canyon can be followed either south to Ranger Peak or north to Mount Robie.

Webb Canyon

Other than Berry Creek, Webb Canyon probably saw more early-day traffic than any canyon in the range. In the 1880s it became known as a haven for mountain sheep, and so was originally named Sheep Canyon. Because of this good fortune and relative ease of access, many big-game hunting parties were attracted to the canyon, some guided by Richard "Beaver Dick" Leigh in his last years. Two well-known parties, under the sponsorship of William Seward Webb, were in the canyon in 1896 and 1897. (These years are correct according to *Along the Ramparts of the Tetons: The Saga of Jackson Hole, Wyoming*, by Robert B. Betts.) The canyon was named in Webb's honor by the USGS team that was starting the mapping of the Grand Teton quadrangle at that time. Prior to the completion of the dam on Jackson Lake, access by horse from the east into Webb Canyon was immediate because the lake ended at the mouth of the canyon. Webb Canyon is by far the largest canyon of the range in terms of area, containing much scenic open high country as well as one of the major climax forests in the park on its southeast side. Moose Basin is the name given to the upper open portion of the canyon east of the divide and west of the main creek. Curiously, the creek in Webb Canyon is called Moose Creek. Most of the canyon is hidden from view as seen from the valley and so is not appreciated until one hikes into its upper reaches. It is one of the great wilderness resources of the park even if the climbing opportunities on the surrounding peaks are limited. Of geological interest as well, the striking display of the Owl Peak fault on the north side of the canyon attracts the eye even of the unobservant.

Webb Canyon and Moose Basin are approached by trail from the Berry Creek patrol cabin on the west side of Jackson Lake near the mouths of Berry Creek and Moose Creek. The patrol cabin can be reached on foot from the Grassy Lake Reservoir road, as described under *Berry Canyon*, but this is a long hike (about 7.5 miles). Far better is to take a boat or canoe across the lake (0.7 mile) from Fonda Point at the Lizard Creek campground. Either way the Webb Canyon trail moves south across Berry Creek only 300 yards west of the patrol cabin. This trail, maintained and easy to follow into Webb Canyon, has recently been reconstructed and now, contrary to the USGS map, lies north of the stream, so stream crossings are not required. At about 7,680 feet, the location of one of the original Webb camps, the trail starts up the slope past the Moose Basin patrol cabin and continues to the Moose Basin Divide (9,800+). Moose Basin is open meadow country and so is easy and very scenic ground for cross-country hiking.

Exit from (or entry into) the upper Webb Canyon is available to the north at the Moose Basin Divide into Owl Canyon; to the south into the south fork of Snowshoe Canyon via the pass (10,320+) west of Peak 10,880+; into the north fork of Snowshoe Canyon via one of two passes (9,920+ and 10,000+) north and west of Talus Lake; or to the west via the USFS trail that comes from the north fork of Bitch Creek over Nord Pass to the divide at the saddle (9,680+) between Moose Mountain and Peak 9,970. With somewhat more exertion one can also exit due east over the main ridge of Doane and Ranger Peaks into Waterfalls or Colter Canyon using one of the available high passes (10,800+ and 10,720+). The lower pass (10,480+) near the north end of this main ridge is feasible only if one deliberately ascends the long northwest–southeast valley; the ridge bounding this valley on the west contains much sharp and shattered rock.

Owl Canyon

The main Owl Creek trail in Owl Canyon is being maintained by the National Park Service, but the sometimes inadequate trail markings imply that use of the map is important. The main difficulty is caused by lack of bridges when stream crossings are encountered; this is especially notable in early season when the streams are high. The standard access is via the trail from the trailhead on the Grassy Lake Reservoir road west of Flagg Ranch. It is also easily reached via Jackson Lake from Fonda Point at the Lizard Creek campground. Canoe across (0.7 mile) to the vicinity of the lower Berry Creek patrol cabin near the lakeshore. At the patrol cabin the Berry Creek trail is acquired and followed west into and up the narrows of lower Berry Creek to the junction where the left branch is taken into Owl Canyon. The Owl Creek trail then leads south to the Moose Basin Divide (9,800+) where it joins the Webb Canyon trail. From upper Owl Canyon there is no trail connection to the saddle west of Forellen Peak where the upper Berry Creek trail ends.

If one is making a high traverse across the head of Owl Canyon from Webb Canyon to Berry Canyon or conversely, it is best not to drop all the way down into Owl Canyon. Instead, stay high and contour as much as possible around the open country at the head of Owl Canyon between the two passes. The best route involves passing near the summit of Point 9,682 just west of the Berry–Owl divide. Because of limestone formations on the final portion of the trail to the Moose Basin Divide, little drinking water will be found, since water from the melting snow disappears into crevices in the rock. Hence, there is some difficulty in locating a suitable campsite in the upper elevations away from the main streams.

Berry Canyon

Of all the canyons penetrating the Teton Range, Berry Canyon was probably the first to be explored by Western man. Originally a Native American route, it was one of the trails of the fur-trapper era and later was an early scene of big-game hunting. The original north boundary of Grand Teton National Park as established in 1929 did not include this region; it remained in USFS control until 1943, then became part of the Jackson Hole National Monument and was incorporated into the park with the rest of the monument in 1950. Because the peaks surrounding the canyon are unspectacular and largely sedimentary, Berry Canyon is of more interest to the backcountry hiker than to the mountaineer. The full Grand Teton National Park map (1:62,500) can be used here, but some may prefer the three new (1:24,000, 7.5-minute series, provisional edition, 1989) topographic sheets—Flagg Ranch, Survey Peak, and Hominy Peak. These are valuable since they are very detailed and show nearly all the trails. The earlier 15-minute sheets—Warm River Butte, Grassy Lake Reservoir, and Huckleberry Mountain—are now somewhat out-of-date and the displayed trails are no longer valid.

The most northerly in the range, Berry Canyon is accessible by many different trails. The principal method of approach is from the Grassy Lake Reservoir road that passes around the north end of the range. From the junction immediately north of Flagg Ranch on the main highway leading to the Yellowstone south entrance, take the Grassy Lake Reservoir road west. After about 4.0 miles the small Berry Creek trailhead parking area will be seen on the south side of the road. This trail leads south, skirts the swamps near the Snake River, and when the head of Jackson Lake is reached moves west over a small pass (7,000+) to drop into an unnamed drainage. Two junctions with trails leading south are passed and, after a second low pass (7,440+) is crossed, Berry Creek is finally entered. To pass the swampy main section of the canyon the trail stays on the north side until reaching the east base of Survey Peak. The upper Berry Creek patrol cabin, as shown on the map, was removed and a new larger structure was constructed in 1987 at the same location. The entire region to the north, including the minor peaks at the extreme north edge of the park, is covered with dense lodgepole pine, making cross-country travel difficult. The lower part of Owl Creek is available via the trail in the main Berry Canyon, which heads south shortly after crossing the low pass mentioned earlier. The divide north of Survey Peak can be gained by using the trail that heads north up the last drainage prior to reaching the base of Survey Peak. Two additional trails depart from this same area. One leads south to the Forellen Divide (8,840+), which is southwest of Forellen Peak. The other heads west over the divide at what is marked on the map as Jackass Pass (8,460); this is a misnomer because this location is very likely the historic Conant Pass, which is shown some 2.0 miles farther south on the map.

This upper portion of Berry Canyon can also be reached from the west, starting from Ashton, Idaho, via the Ashton–Flagg Ranch road and then the Jackass road, which heads toward Hominy Peak. With the establishment of the Jedediah Smith Wilderness Area in 1984 one can no longer drive all the way to Hominy Peak or beyond. From the Hominy trailhead, the USFS trail leads to Hominy Peak and along the narrow ridge connecting with the divide at Jackass Pass (5.2 miles).

An easier method of reaching the mouth of Berry Creek is via Jackson Lake. From Fonda Point at the Lizard Creek campground it is a short (0.7-mile) canoe trip across to the vicinity of the lower Berry Creek patrol cabin near the lakeshore. At the cabin the Berry Creek trail is acquired and can be followed either north to join the trail already described from the Ashton–Flagg Ranch road or west into and up the narrows of lower Berry Creek where one may branch north into Berry Canyon or farther west into Owl Creek.

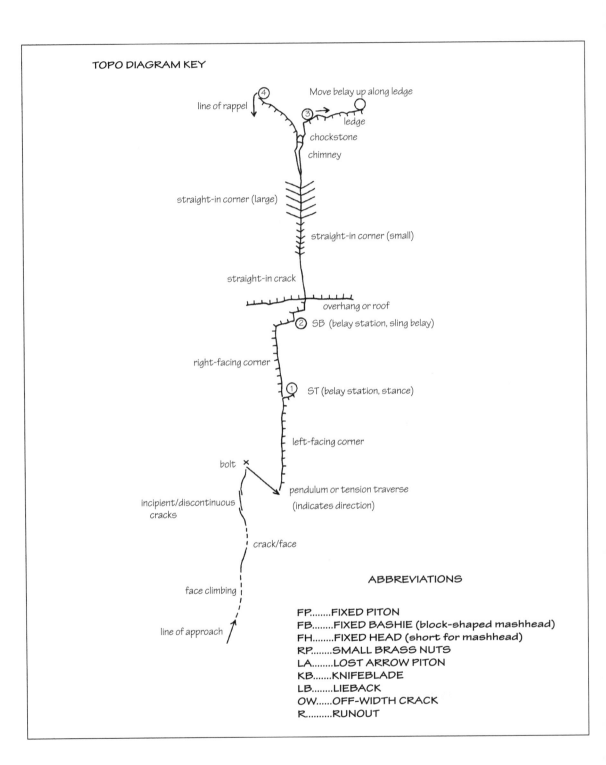

TOPO DIAGRAM KEY

Move belay up along ledge

line of rappel

ledge

chockstone

chimney

straight-in corner (large)

straight-in corner (small)

straight-in crack

overhang or roof

SB (belay station, sling belay)

right-facing corner

ST (belay station, stance)

left-facing corner

bolt

pendulum or tension traverse
(indicates direction)

incipient/discontinuous
cracks

crack/face

face climbing

line of approach

ABBREVIATIONS

FP........FIXED PITON
FB........FIXED BASHIE (block-shaped mashhead)
FH........FIXED HEAD (short for mashhead)
RP........SMALL BRASS NUTS
LA........LOST ARROW PITON
KB......KNIFEBLADE
LB........LIEBACK
OW......OFF-WIDTH CRACK
R..........RUNOUT

Routes on the Peaks

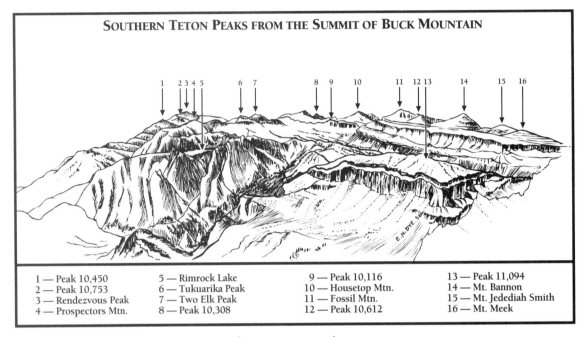

SOUTHERN TETON PEAKS FROM THE SUMMIT OF BUCK MOUNTAIN

1 — Peak 10,450	5 — Rimrock Lake	9 — Peak 10,116	13 — Peak 11,094
2 — Peak 10,753	6 — Tukuarika Peak	10 — Housetop Mtn.	14 — Mt. Bannon
3 — Rendezvous Peak	7 — Two Elk Peak	11 — Fossil Mtn.	15 — Mt. Jedediah Smith
4 — Prospectors Mtn.	8 — Peak 10,308	12 — Peak 10,612	16 — Mt. Meek

South of Death Canyon

PEAK 9,815   (1.6 mi WSW of Apres Vous Peak)

Map: Teton Village

Easily reached from almost any direction, this small, rounded peak lies on the boundary of the Jackson Hole Ski Area just northeast of Peak 10,450 where the aerial tram terminates. A high point on the same ridge about 1.6 miles farther to the northeast is Apres Vous Peak (8,426), which is reached by a chair lift from the ski area.

ROUTE 1. Northeast Ridge. I, 1.0. Probable first ascent in May or June 1934, by T. F. Murphy and Robert E. Brislawn. From the Teton Village parking area take the road, marked as a trail on the map, to Apres Vous Peak and follow the ridge to Peak 9,815. It starts immediately underneath the chair-lift cables.

PEAK 10,450   (2.7 mi NE of Rendezvous Peak)

Map: Teton Village

Innumerable visitors in both winter and summer reach this peak using the effortless aerial tram of the Jackson Hole Ski Area that terminates on this summit. Peak 10,450 provides a good viewpoint for the high peaks to the north and serves as a conveniently high starting point for hikes in Granite Canyon and climbs of other peaks in the southern portion of the Teton Range. There has been some confusion of names concerning this peak, which has no official name. The ski area sometimes erroneously refers to this single peak as Rendezvous Mountain or Rendezvous Peak. The name Rendezvous Mountain, strictly speaking, is the entire massif extending from the mouth of Granite Canyon on the northeast to Phillips Pass on the southwest. Peak 10,450 lies about midway along this ridge that comprises Rendezvous Mountain. Rendezvous Peak (10,927 feet) is a specific summit, the highest point of Rendezvous Mountain, and is discussed here.

CHRONOLOGY

Northeast Ridge: [probable] May or June 1934, T. F. Murphy, Robert E. Brislawn

Southwest Ridge: July 24, 1960, Arthur J. Reyman

ROUTE 1. Southwest Ridge. I, 1.0. First known ascent July 24, 1960, by Arthur J. Reyman, by a traverse from Peak 10,750. On the summit Reyman found a cairn but no record. The trail from Granite Canyon now ascends this ridge, although it is much more often used for descent than for ascent. In early season considerable snow will be encountered along this trail.

ROUTE 2. *Northeast Ridge.* I, 1.0. Probable first ascent in May or June 1934, by T. F. Murphy and Robert E. Brislawn. The saddle (9,520+) at the base of this broad ridge can be reached either from the northwest by bushwhacking up from the Granite Canyon trail or by hiking in from the southeast using the ski area road (marked as a trail on the map) most of the way. If approaching from Granite Canyon the main stream must be crossed, on a downed tree with luck.

JACKSON HOLE SKI AREA ROCK CLIMBS

Map: Teton Village

The eastern slope of the massive Rendezvous Mountain was largely unexplored before the study preceding the construction of the new Jackson Hole Ski Area. On June 21, 1961, Paul and Mike McCollister climbed this slope to the top of Peak 10,450. Four years of snow studies on this particular slope were done. The decision to commence ski lift construction followed a ski tour taken in the spring of 1963 by Paul McCollister and others. The winter of 1965–1966 was the first commercial season with three lifts operating. The aerial tram was completed on July 31, 1966, after 26 months of construction. The first examination of the fine cliffs of crystalline rock along the north side of Rock Springs Canyon was apparently carried out even before March 1967, when Rick Horn made a sequence of pioneering climbs with Steve Smith and Rod Dornan. These cliffs hold several fine rock-climbing routes, some still containing dirt and loose rock; additional cleaning would be useful.

Tram Buttresses (ca. 10,200)
(0.2 mi E of Peak 10,450)

The area of cliffs immediately below the Jackson Hole aerial tram tower #5 has received attention lately as a bit of a high-altitude sport-climbing crag. Unless the aerial tramway is used, however, the approach is much longer than most sport climbers want to deal with. The only drawback then is the expense of a tram ticket. At any rate, the setting is spectacular and the climbing is on steep dolomite featuring pockets and edges. From the summit of the mountain walk down to the east a short distance to either of the two famous couloirs on the north side of the peak. The first (and larger of the two) is Corbett's Couloir and is, perhaps, one of the most infamous ski runs in the country. The second, which is much narrower, is called the S and S Couloir and is just a short distance farther east. The climbs are bolted routes and are located on the upper, east-facing walls of either couloir. Development of these high-altitude crags included the following individuals: Richard and Kathryn Collins,

Greg Miles, James Burwick, Brents Hawkes, Jim Kanzler, and Mike Fischer.

Rock Springs Buttress (ca. 9,200)
(0.8 mi S of Peak 10,450)

ROUTE 1. *Rock Springs Buttress.* II, 5.4 to 5.10. See *Topos 1* and *2* and *Photos 1* and *2.* This fine crag is rather conspicuous as one approaches Teton Village along the road from the south. The buttress is located high on the southeast side of Rendezvous Mountain (on which the aerial tram is located), forming the north wall of Rock Springs Canyon. About ten routes have been done on this buttress. Although the rock is somewhat loose, the good quality routes are indicated on the topos and in the photographs. To approach the buttress, there are two primary options: (1) Take the tram to the top and walk down and east several hundred feet (vertically nearly 1,500 feet) to the top of the buttress where one can leave extra gear. Descend a faint trail and series of ledges on the west side of the westernmost buttress and select a route. (2) The approach can also be made from the bottom. After parking at Teton Village one can take the trail or the road leading up and south from the vicinity of tram tower #1. Contour around the ridge that forms the southern boundary of the ski area and use game trails to find the way up the beautiful Rock Springs Canyon drainage. For descent, one can either walk down the Rock Springs drainage or walk back up to the top of the buttress, then to the top of Peak 10,450, and ride the aerial tram back down to the valley.

PEAK 10,753   *(1.5 mi NNE of Rendezvous Peak)*

Map: Rendezvous Peak

This sedimentary peak is the first major summit along the ridge extending from the top of the aerial tram on Peak 10,450 south to Rendezvous Peak. A fine day of ridge running can be enjoyed by making the double traverse from the tram to Rendezvous Peak and back. An unofficial name, Cody Peak, has been applied by the nearby ski area. During the winter the Grand National Powder Eight Championships are held on its north slope. Three couloirs on this mountain have also become somewhat legendary among skiers. The "Once Is Enough" and "Twice Is Nice" Couloirs are located on the southeast side of the mountain, while the formidable "Central" couloir is on the north side.

ROUTE 1. *Southwest Ridge.* I, 2.0. First ascent July 24, 1960, by Arthur J. Reyman. The break in the west wall of this peak can be found by traversing north from the saddle between this peak and Peak 10,706. Once above the wall, follow the southwest ridge to the summit.

ROUTE 2. ☞*North Ridge.* I, 2.0. First descent July 24, 1960, by Arthur J. Reyman; first known ascent August 1968, by Leigh Ortenburger. Easily climbed, this route is part of the Rendezvous Mountain ridge traverse.

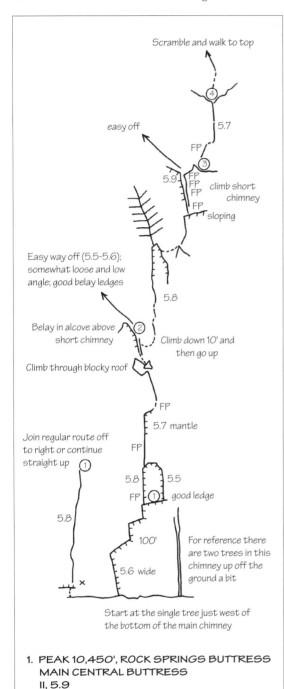

Scramble and walk to top

④

easy off   5.7

FP

③

5.9 FP
       FP   climb short
       FP   chimney
       FP
              sloping

Easy way off (5.5-5.6);
somewhat loose and low
angle; good belay ledges

                            5.8

Belay in alcove above   ②
short chimney   Climb down 10' and
                          then go up
Climb through blocky roof

                          FP

                          5.7 mantle

Join regular route off   FP
to right or continue
straight up   ①

     5.8   5.5
     FP   good ledge

5.8

              100'   For reference there
                        are two trees in this
     5.6 wide   chimney up off the
                        ground a bit
×

Start at the single tree just west of
the bottom of the main chimney

1. PEAK 10,450', ROCK SPRINGS BUTTRESS
   MAIN CENTRAL BUTTRESS
   II, 5.9

PEAK 10,706   *(1.0 mi NNE of Rendezvous Peak)*

Map: Rendezvous Peak

The normal approach to this peak is along the north ridge from Peak 10,753, but it can be easily reached from the extreme southern portion of Granite Canyon or directly from the east. The eastern approach, using the Fish Creek road north from the town of Wilson, has the complication of requiring permission to park a car, because the land along the road is in private ownership.

CHRONOLOGY

East Ridge: October 14, 1937, Arthur Rust, Nick Dietrich
Southwest Ridge: July 28, 1955, Gene Balaz, Redwood Fryxell (descent); July 24, 1960, Arthur J. Reyman (ascent)
North Ridge: July 24, 1960, Arthur J. Reyman (descent); August 1968, Leigh Ortenburger (ascent)

ROUTE 1. Southwest Ridge. I, 1.0. First descent July 28, 1955, by Gene Balaz and Redwood Fryxell; first ascent July 24, 1960, by Arthur J. Reyman. This easy route is used for traversing to or from Rendezvous Peak.
ROUTE 2. East Ridge. I, 1.0. First ascent October 14, 1937, by Arthur Rust and Nick Dietrich. Two hours of bushwhacking up the lower ridge take one to the final steeper east ridge leading directly to the summit. This ridge lies immediately south of Pinedale Canyon, an unofficial name given by local skiers.
ROUTE 3. ☞*North Ridge.* I, 1.0. First descent July 24, 1960, by Arthur J. Reyman; first known ascent August 1968, by Leigh Ortenburger. This ridge is used for the standard traverse from Peak 10,450, the top of the ski area tram, to Rendezvous Peak. It involves no difficulties.

RENDEZVOUS PEAK (10,927)

Map: Rendezvous Peak

Although this peak is neither inside nor on the boundary of Grand Teton National Park, it affords an excellent vantage point for most of the southwestern portion of the park. In addition, the terrain surrounding it is little travelled and offers features that contrast markedly with the usual climbing areas. Several approaches are possible, depending on the route to be used to reach the summit. From the west, the side road up Moose Creek from the main Jackson–Driggs Highway 22 leads to the trailhead. The Moose Creek trail then leads up the canyon past Moose Creek Meadows to the pass (9,085) that divides Moose and Granite Canyons. The upper portion of this trail can also be reached via Coal Creek, which holds the first main trail leaving the highway on the west side of Teton Pass. From the divide (9,197), at the head of Coal Creek, drop down Mesquite Creek to

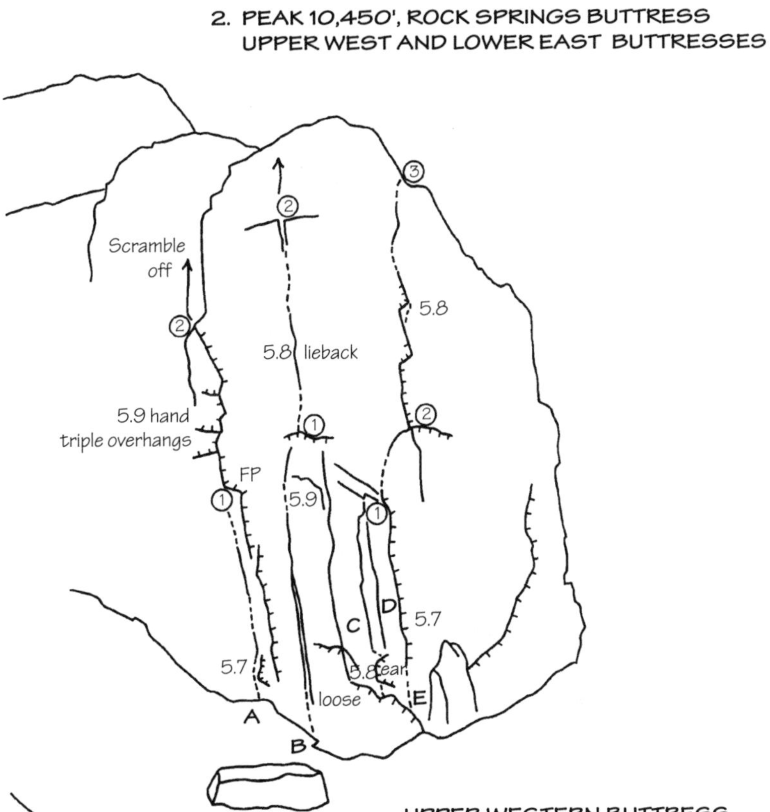

2. PEAK 10,450', ROCK SPRINGS BUTTRESS
UPPER WEST AND LOWER EAST BUTTRESSES

Scramble off

②

②

②

③

5.8

5.8 lieback

5.9 hand triple overhangs

①

②

FP

①

5.9

①

C   D   5.7

5.7   5.8 tear   E

loose

A

B

UPPER WESTERN BUTTRESS
A: 5.9; B: 5.9; C: 5.10+;
D: 5.11; E: 5.8

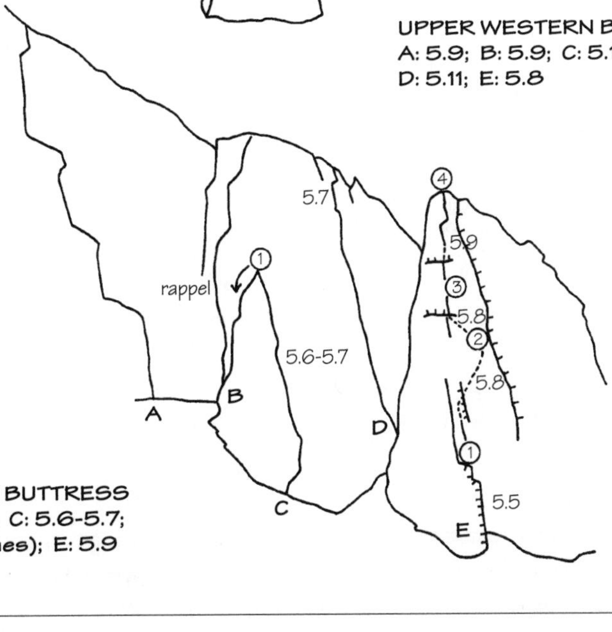

5.7

④

5.9

①

③

5.8

rappel

②

5.6-5.7

5.8

A   B

①

D

5.5

LOWER EASTERN BUTTRESS
A: 5.7; B: 5.6-5.7; C: 5.6-5.7;
D: 5.7 (three pitches); E: 5.9

C   E

Moose Creek Meadows. From the southeast, the road north from Wilson offers access to the direct east approach to Rendezvous Peak. This same road also leads to the mouth of Phillips Canyon. The Phillips Canyon trail begins here, crosses Phillips Pass southwest of Rendezvous Peak, and joins the Moose Creek trail about 2.0 miles south of the Moose–Granite divide. The shortest approach to Phillips Pass, however, starts from the gravel road that extends out to the Phillips Ridge from the north hairpin curve on the road over Teton Pass (Highway 22).

The complex structure of Rendezvous Peak requires some description. The upper portion consists of a northeast–southwest wedge, 0.3 mile long, with the summit near the southwest end. Four ridges support this wedge: the east ridge, which rises directly from Jackson Hole to the northeast end of the wedge; the south ridge, which is divided into three subridges south of the 10,332-foot southern subsummit; the west ridge, which splits into the broad west slope and the southwest ridge that descends to Phillips Pass after crossing Peak 10,053; and the north ridge, which also splits into a northwest ridge (which passes over Peak 10,277 before reaching the Moose–Granite pass) and the northeast ridge that continues over Peak 10,706. Some difficulty may be experienced in identifying the peaks and streams in this area. During most summers the long, horizontal snow crescent that lies just beneath the saddle between Peak 10,706 and the northeast end of the summit wedge of Rendezvous Peak serves as one identification point from the east.

Chronology

West Ridge: August 20, 1898, T. M. Bannon, George A. Buck
Southwest Ridge: August 4, 1933, Fritiof Fryxell, Leland Horberg
South Ridge: August 4, 1933, Fritiof Fryxell, Leland Horberg (descent)
Northwest Ridge: [probable] May or June 1934, T. F. Murphy, Robert E. Brislawn; July 28, 1955, Gene Balaz, Redwood Fryxell (descent)
East Ridge: June 23, 1941, Henry Coulter, Merrill McLane, Stewart Mockford
Northeast Ridge: July 28, 1955, Gene Balaz, Redwood Fryxell

ROUTE 1. West Ridge. I, 1.0. First ascent August 20, 1898, by topographer T. M. Bannon and his assistant George A. Buck. Rendezvous Peak was ascended by Bannon and Buck from the head of Moose Creek in order to establish a triangulation station known in the records of the U.S. Geological Survey as "Phillips Station." It is uncertain that this easy ridge was the route used, but it is most likely.
ROUTE 2. Southwest Ridge. I, 1.0. First ascent August 4, 1933, by Fritiof Fryxell and Leland Horberg. From Phillips

Pass, climb easily to the summit over the 10,053-foot southwest peak. *Time: 7½ hours* from the mouth of Phillips Canyon.
ROUTE 3. South Ridge. I, 1.0. First descent August 4, 1933, by Fritiof Fryxell and Leland Horberg. From the high saddle (10,160+) at the head of Jensen Canyon this ridge can be easily climbed. From the east one could hike all the way up Jensen Canyon to this saddle or approach from the west via the north fork of Phillips Canyon.
ROUTE 4. East Ridge. I, 2.0. First ascent June 23, 1941, by Henry Coulter, Merrill McLane, and Stewart Mockford. No difficulties will be encountered on this long ridge. *Time: 8 hours* from the base of the peak.
ROUTE 5. ☞Northeast Ridge. I, 2.0. First ascent July 28, 1955, by Gene Balaz and Redwood Fryxell. The long, bare saddle connecting Peak 10,706 to the northeastern summit of Rendezvous Peak is gained either directly from the east or from Peak 10,706, as was done by the first-ascent party. The southwestern, reddish summit is easily reached. *Time: 5½ hours* from the base of the ridge.
ROUTE 6. ☞Northwest Ridge. I, 3.0. Probable first ascent in May or June 1934, by T. F. Murphy and Robert E. Brislawn; first descent July 28, 1955, by Gene Balaz and Redwood Fryxell. To reach this ridge take the Rendezvous Mountain trail, either from the valley starting at the Granite Canyon trailhead or from the top of the aerial tram on Peak 10,450. Leave this trail where it crosses the south fork of Granite Creek, and head due south to the saddle separating Rendezvous Mountain from Peak 10,277. The upper portions of the canyon and the final ridge require some scrambling.

GRANITE CANYON, SOUTH SIDE ROCK CLIMBS

Map: Teton Village

At intervals along the south side of Granite Canyon are buttresses and small towers on which rock-climbing routes have been made. These are listed here from west to east.

Buchwald's Blister (ca. 8,400)
(1.35 mi WNW of Apres Vous Peak)

From the Granite Canyon trailhead take the trail upcanyon to a point about 50 yards past the eighth switchback corner on the trail. If the light is right, two pinnacles can be seen on the south side of the canyon above a long talus slope. The larger, Buchwald's Blister, can be recognized by a vertical yellow west face and smooth downsloping slabs on the north face. It appears on the map as a small 8,400-foot contour line circle about 0.2 mile east of Point 8,545.
ROUTE 1. West Couloir. I, 3.0. First ascent August 23, 1969, by T. Keith Liggett, Caryl E. Buchwald, and Philip S. Peterson. This west couloir is mostly a scramble to the notch between the wall and the summit of the pinnacle.
ROUTE 2. East Couloir. I, 1.0. First descent August 23, 1969, by T. Keith Liggett, Caryl E. Buchwald, and Philip S.

Peterson. This easy couloir descends to the east from the notch between the wall and the pinnacle.

ROUTE 3. North Face. I, 5.4. First ascent August 23, 1969, by T. Keith Liggett, Caryl E. Buchwald, and Philip S. Peterson. This route, consisting of one 130-foot lead, starts near the middle of the north face of the pinnacle and makes a traverse left to the small chimney, which is climbed to easier rock leading to the summit.

Phil's Pickle (ca. 8,400)
(1.35 mi WNW of Apres Vous Peak)

This, the smaller and more easterly of the two pinnacles seen from just past the eighth switchback corner on the Granite Canyon trail, has the appearance of a pickle.

ROUTE 1. Southeast Corner. I, 5.1. First ascent August 23, 1969, by T. Keith Liggett and Philip S. Peterson. This route ascends a small open book on the southeast corner of this 65-foot pinnacle.

Granite Central Buttresses (ca. 9,000)
(1.0 mi NW of Apres Vous Peak)

About halfway to the upper patrol cabin in Granite Canyon at 7,400 feet the trail reaches an open willow meadow, which is directly across the stream from large buttresses on the south side of the canyon. This section of willows is shortly beyond the sixth switchback corner in the trail. Two climbs have been made on the lower portion of the good rock of these buttresses between 7,600 and 8,000 feet.

CHRONOLOGY

The Hell You Say: August 8, 1980, Randy Harrington, Leo Larson
Lightning Crack: June 28, 1981, Rich Perch, John Carr

ROUTE 1. Lightning Crack. II, 5.10. First ascent June 28, 1981, by Rich Perch and John Carr. From the far (west) end of the aforementioned willows, one can look across to the south side of the canyon and back to the east and see on the more easterly (and northerly) of the two lower buttresses this easily recognized crack, which resembles a jagged lightning bolt, on a large west-facing slab. This crack leads directly to the crest of the buttress. After an initial pitch to reach the beginning of the crack, climb 40 feet up the offwidth 5.10 crack, which is to the left of a large left-facing corner.

ROUTE 2. The Hell You Say. II, 5.9. First ascent August 8, 1980, by Randy Harrington and Leo Larson. On the west face of the more westerly (and southerly) of the two lower buttresses, two large vertical cracks extend upward for some 150 feet. This route of three pitches ascends the right crack for two pitches to gain the beginning of a well-defined ramp leading up and right. The third lead goes up this ramp to its end where a short climb back left ends the route. Descent involves first ascending a prominent couloir to gain a complicated system of couloirs down to the northeast. Take a

normal rack with a couple of large nuts as well as camming devices.

Sharkshead Pinnacle (ca. 9,200)
(0.8 mi W of Apres Vous Peak)

This 500-foot buttress or pinnacle is a noticeable feature of Granite Canyon, the first prominent buttress protruding from the south wall of the canyon. It can be located on the map as the sharp arête extending north from Point 9,503, 0.8 mile west of Apres Vous Peak. The name is derived from the notch, which looks like a shark's head pointing upward when seen from the east. This shark's head is the identifying feature as one proceeds up the Granite Canyon trail. The couloirs that are located on either side of this buttress figure prominently in local skiers' lore and legend and are named "Milelong" and "Endless."

ROUTE 1. East Couloir and West Face. I, 3.0. First ascent August 24, 1969, by T. Keith Liggett and Philip S. Peterson, who found a tin can on the summit. Scramble up the east couloir to the notch separating the pinnacle from the mountain, and then climb around on the west face to the summit.

ROUTE 2. Givler's Arête. III, 5.9. First ascent August 25, 1979, by Keith Hadley and George Montopoli. This six-pitch route follows fairly closely the crest of the north arête of this pinnacle. From a ledge that is located about 100 feet to the west of the lowest point of the arête, climb up an easy chimney and belay on the east side of a block. The first pitch goes up a right-facing corner or large flake (4 to 5 inches to begin with, then 3 to 4 inches) and is the most difficult pitch on the route. The next pitch of 5.4 rock is followed by a more demanding 150-foot lead of 5.8 difficulty. Move the belay to the east approximately 30 feet to a tree where the fourth lead (100 feet) continues up and slightly left on 5.7 rock to a belay point very close to the crest of the arête on a slab. The next lead continues upward past a flake, followed by a stretch of unprotected 5.7 face climbing. Two sections of 5.8 are then encountered, the first being a thin left-facing corner and the second an exciting lieback. The final pitch of 70 feet is 5.6, and the climb finishes by scrambling up and across the summit ridge. This arête can be approached in a downhill fashion from the top of the tram by following the ridge down to Point 9,503 and then descending the east couloir to the base of the arête. Large devices are needed for protection on the first pitch.

Goat Rocks (ca. 7,600)   *(0.6 mi NE of Apres Vous Peak)*

This cliff is located on the map between 7,200 and 7,600 feet at the north end of the park boundary on the northeast ridge of Apres Vous Peak. Goat Rocks forms the eastern end of the north face of this peak.

ROUTE 1. North Side. I, 3.0. First ascent August 2, 1980, by Randy and Jan Harrington. Approach from the vicinity of Point 7,062 in lower Granite Canyon, as shown on the map. Three pitches were climbed on this route. While the rock is licheny and sometimes loose, the views from the route are good.

PEAK 10,277   *(0.7 mi N of Rendezvous Peak)*

Map: Rendezvous Peak

This grassy, roundtop peak with a broad, flower-covered northwest ridge is easily climbed from almost any direction.
ROUTE 1. Northwest Slope. I, 1.0. First ascent July 24, 1960, by Arthur J. Reyman. Walk up from the 9,085-foot pass crossed by the trail from Moose Creek into the middle fork of Granite Canyon.
ROUTE 2. Southeast Slope. I, 1.0. First descent July 24, 1960, by Arthur J. Reyman. Walk up from the saddle that connects with the Rendezvous Mountain ridge.

PEAK 9,925   *(1.8 mi SE of Housetop Mountain)*

Map: Rendezvous Peak

ROUTE 1. West Slope. I, 1.0. The Bannon topographic party placed a bench mark here in 1898. On July 22, 1960, Arthur J. Reyman climbed this tree-covered slope and found a 6-foot cairn on the summit.
ROUTE 2. Southeast Slope. I, 1.0. Probable first ascent July 26, 1931, by Leslie Shaw Henrie. Walk up to the northwest from the Moose–Granite pass (9,085).

PEAK 10,308   *(1.0 mi S of Housetop Mountain)*

Map: Rendezvous Peak

The northeast ridge of this sedimentary peak appears unsuitable for climbing, while the west slope probably provides the easiest access to the summit. The most convenient approach, however, is from Granite Canyon on the east.
ROUTE 1. South Ridge. I, 2.0. First ascent July 22, 1960, by Arthur J. Reyman. On the same day Reyman also reached Peak 10,315 (0.6 mile south-southwest) via the northeast slope and Point 10,240+ (0.4 mile southwest) via the east slope. From Point 10,240+ on the park boundary, a knife-edge ridge must be traversed to reach this peak.

PEAK 9,814   *(1.8 mi ESE of Housetop Mountain)*

Map: Rendezvous Peak

This small peak separating the middle and north forks of Granite Canyon is undistinguished except for one remarkable but seldom-noticed feature. On the lower sedimentary cliff band on the north side of this peak is a natural bridge, the opening of which measures approximately 60 by 30 feet. The width of this formation, which is perhaps the largest of its kind in the park, narrows to about 4 feet wide on top. This bridge is located at about 8,700 feet on the south side

of the north fork of Granite Creek, just past (west of) the junction of the Granite Canyon trail and the Open Canyon trail. It is apparently most easily seen in mid-afternoon when the sun shines behind it.
ROUTE 1. West Slope. I, 1.0. Probable first ascent in May or June 1934, by T. F. Murphy and Robert E. Brislawn; first known ascent July 23, 1960, by Arthur J. Reyman. Proceed from the Teton Crest Trail where it crosses the 9,280+-foot pass just west of the peak and south of Marion Lake.

HOUSETOP MOUNTAIN (10,537)

Map: Rendezvous Peak

Before 1931 this name was applied to the 10,916-foot peak, 2.5 miles to the northeast, that is now officially named Fossil Mountain. Following their mapping efforts in the 1960s, the U.S. Geological Survey abandoned a yellow surveying marker on the summit.
ROUTE 1. Southeast Ridge. I, 1.0. Probable first ascent in May or June 1934, by T. F. Murphy and Robert E. Brislawn. On July 22, 1960, Arthur J. Reyman climbed this route from the Game Creek trail and followed the divide to the summit, where an empty cairn was found. The ridge can also be reached from the high bench in Granite Canyon just east of the divide, using the Teton Crest Trail.

PEAK 10,116   *(0.8 mi ENE of Housetop Mountain)*

Map: Mount Bannon

Overlooking Marion Lake, this peak is protected on the north and the east by a serious sedimentary cliff band, which must be passed on the south. In late season the small lake on the high bench south of the peak becomes a mud flat without a water supply for camping.
ROUTE 1. Southwest Slope. I, 1.0. First known ascent July 23, 1960, by Arthur J. Reyman, who found an empty cairn on the summit. Leave the trail about 0.25 mile south of Marion Lake. Go south and west around the base of the cliffs at the west side of the lake. Easy flower-covered benches lead to the plateau above the cliffs; from there the remainder of the climb is easy.

SPEARHEAD PEAK (10,131)

Map: Mount Bannon

The northern aspect of this peak is quite imposing and resembles Devil's Tower in miniature. A walk completely around the base of the peak requires only 30 minutes and shows that the most interesting climbing lies on the northern half of the west face and on the north face proper. The best approach to Spearhead Peak is by the Death Canyon trail to Fox Creek Pass at the park boundary. Walk 0.5 mile south along the trail toward Marion Lake to the area west of Spearhead Peak. Considerable caution should be used in the cracks and chimneys on this peak because of the nature of the rock, which in the lower sections is Bighorn dolomite and at the summit is Gallatin limestone.

Of the high points to the east, Point 10,440+ (1.0 mile southeast of Spearhead Peak) has been reached by horseback, and Point 10,495 (1.3 miles east of Spearhead Peak) was first reached on July 12, 1960, by Arthur J. Reyman from the northwest. These two points enclose Indian Lake on the west and north.

ROUTE 1. ☞ South Ridge. I, 4.0. Probable first ascent in May or June 1934, by T. F. Murphy and Robert E. Brislawn; first known ascent either in 1941, by Alan and Judy Cameron, or on July 17, 1941, by Arthur J. Reyman. From the trail to the west, scramble up loose limestone blocks to the south side of the final tower. One 30-foot pitch on the southeast side of the ridge leads onto the summit area; a rope may be useful for protection on this final pitch. The holds are large, but many are loose.

ROUTE 2. North Face, East Chimney. I, 5.1. First ascent August 18, 1955, by Gene Balaz and Beatrice Burford. This route is a short, but delicate, 150-foot climb on which pitons or nuts are needed for protection.

ROUTE 3. In Search of. . . . I, 5.8. First ascent July 15, 1991, by Paul Horton and William Alexander. This one-pitch climb is on the southwest side of the peak and is 165 feet in length. The pitch begins with a 5.8 corner followed by a loose and blocky section of 5.4. After climbing a 5.4 chimney (no protection), traverse into a larger, easier chimney. At the top of this chimney step out to the left onto 5.6 face climbing that leads to the summit of the peak. Medium-size protection is suggested for this climb.

MOUNT HUNT (10,783)

Map: Grand Teton

This sedimentary peak shares a characteristic with a few other technically easy Teton peaks—a cairn of unknown origin was found on the summit in the course of the early systematic exploration of the range. An excellent view of the seldom-visited Coyote and Indian Lakes can be had from the summit. The peak was named for Wilson Price Hunt, leader of the overland Astorian expedition, which in the fall of 1811 entered Jackson Hole via Hoback Canyon and left via Teton Pass. On the 9,877-foot point on the east ridge of Mount Hunt, a triangulation station, "Picture Point No. 6," was established on September 3, 1946, by A. K. Andrews and J. Clark.

CHRONOLOGY

East Ridge: August 24, 1929, Fritiof Fryxell
West Ridge: [probable] June 27, 1934, T. F. Murphy, Robert E. Brislawn, Arthur Boles, Mike Yokel, Jr.;

July 31, 1936, Leland Horberg, LeRoy Brissman (descent)

ROUTE 1. West Ridge. I, 1.0. Probable first ascent June 27, 1934, by T. F. Murphy, Robert E. Brislawn, Arthur Boles, and Mike Yokel, Jr.; first descent July 31, 1936, by Leland Horberg and LeRoy Brissman. From the Death Canyon trailhead, follow the Valley Trail around the west shore of Phelps Lake to the cutoff to the Open Canyon trail. Take this trail up the canyon to the point where it turns left (south), toward the Mount Hunt Divide, away from the creek at 8,960 feet. Leave the trail here and continue up the canyon to the broad saddle between Mount Hunt and Two Elk Peak (the Open Canyon fault goes through this saddle). From here follow the easy ridge over the 10,560+-foot subpeak toward Mount Hunt. It would also be possible to skirt this subpeak around the north side to visit the small 10,000+-foot lake and then ascend the talus and scree to rejoin the west ridge of Mount Hunt. See *American Alpine Journal,* 12, no. 2 (1961), p. 374.

ROUTE 2. ☞ East Ridge. I, 2.0. First known ascent August 24, 1929, by Fritiof Fryxell, who found an empty cairn on the summit. From the Death Canyon trailhead (see *Death Canyon*) take the Open Canyon trail to the Mount Hunt Divide (9,710) between Open Canyon and Granite Canyon, just east of Mount Hunt. The cliff above this point can be avoided by continuing a short distance south along the trail before scrambling up to the summit. If one continues very far south, the route might more correctly be called the southeast slope. *Time: 6½ hours* from the Death Canyon trailhead. See *Appalachia,* 18, no. 3 (June 1931), pp. 209–232, illus.

TWO ELK PEAK (10,905) *(0.9 mi NW of Mount Hunt)*

Map: Grand Teton

This flat-topped summit, the south member of a double peak, lies at the head of Open Canyon and shows prominently from certain positions in Jackson Hole. The Open Canyon fault runs through the saddle between this peak and Mount Hunt; the throw, or amount of displacement of the fault, is about 2,800 feet. The name was given for the members of the first known ascent party, as seen from a distance.

CHRONOLOGY

Northwest Wall: July 12, 1960, David Dornan, Mark Melton, Mona Monahan, Leigh Ortenburger
Southeast Ridge: July 12, 1960, David Dornan, Mark Melton, Mona Monahan, Leigh Ortenburger (descent); June 9, 1967, R. Erickson, K. Eggart, M. Wischmayer (ascent)

North Chimney: June 14, 1974, John Kevin Fox,
Richard Day (descent)
West Ridge: August 20, 1995, Jim Springer

ROUTE 1. West Ridge. II, 5.4. First ascent August 20, 1995,
by Jim Springer. The crumbling gendarmes are generally
passed on the south, but some must be climbed over their
tops. This route is not recommended.
ROUTE 2. ☞Southeast Ridge. I, 1.0. First descent July 12,
1960, by David Dornan, Mark Melton, Mona Monahan, and
Leigh Ortenburger; first ascent June 9, 1967, by R. Erickson,
K. Eggart, and M. Wischmayer. Gain the saddle between
this peak and Mount Hunt either from Open Canyon or
from Granite Canyon; the broad ridge above leads to the
summit. This is the only easy route on this peak, which is
otherwise surrounded by sedimentary cliffs. See *American
Alpine Journal,* 12, no. 2 (1961), pp. 373–379.
ROUTE 3. North Chimney. I, 4.0. First descent June 14,
1974, by Richard Day and John Kevin Fox. From the col between this peak and Murphy Peak, traverse 200 feet around
to the right (west) side of Two Elk Peak, passing one chimney blocked by chockstones, to reach a recess in the cliffs.
Climb a 40-foot chimney at the left (north) corner of this
recess to the top of the first cliff band. The second band
above is climbed via an easier 20-foot chimney to the north
end of the summit plateau. Both chimneys are solid, but
there is much loose rock on the bench between the first and
second cliff bands.
ROUTE 4. Northwest Wall. I, 5.1. First ascent July 12, 1960,
by David Dornan, Mark Melton, Mona Monahan, and Leigh
Ortenburger. A 75-foot pitch on the rotten dolomite west-
northwest wall is necessary to pass the cliff band.

MURPHY PEAK (10,800+) *(1.0 mi NW of Mount Hunt)*

Map: Grand Teton
This peak is the more northerly of the pair of flat-topped
summits at the head of Open Canyon. It is named in honor
of the USGS topographer T.F. Murphy, who produced the
first Grand Teton National Park map (with 50-foot contour
intervals) in 1938, without the now-standard use of aerial
photogrammetry methods.
ROUTE 1. West Wall. I, 3.0. First ascent May or June 1934,
by T. F. Murphy and Robert E. Brislawn. Similar to Two Elk
Peak, Murphy Peak is ringed by cliffs, but a single break in
the western cliffs offers probably the only easy route. At the
extreme south end of the flat summit, a cairn containing a
nail but no note was found by a party in 1960; this cairn was
very likely built by the Murphy party while surveying the
southern part of the Teton Range. See *American Alpine Journal,* 12, no. 2 (1961), pp. 373–379.
ROUTE 2. West Chimney. I, 5.1. First ascent June 14, 1974,
by Richard Day and John Kevin Fox. About 200 feet south
of the main break in the western wall of this peak (see *Route

1)* is a broad chimney that also leads up through the wall.
Scramble up the chimney until it forks, then climb the left
fork to the bench above, from which one can continue easily
left (north) to the summit.

TUKUARIKA PEAK (10,988)
(0.9 mi NNW of Mount Hunt)

Map: Grand Teton
The second highest of the sedimentary peaks in the southern Teton Range, this peak is seldom climbed. While it
holds little technical interest, its summit provides a viewpoint from which one can appreciate the structure of
Prospectors Mountain, and both peaks can be climbed in
the same day from Open Canyon. Tukuarika is a Shoshone
name for the Sheepeater Indians, who commonly visited the
Teton region before the advent of the white man.

CHRONOLOGY

Northeast Ridge: July 12, 1960, David Dornan,
Mark Melton, Mona Monahan, Leigh
Ortenburger
West Ridge: July 12, 1960, David Dornan, Mark
Melton, Mona Monahan, Leigh Ortenburger (de-
scent)
South Side: August 24, 1969, Lyle Olson, Craig
Olson, Kirsten Olson, Kim Olson

ROUTE 1. West Ridge. I, 2.0. First descent July 12, 1960, by
David Dornan, Mark Melton, Mona Monahan, and Leigh
Ortenburger. There is a step on the lower portion of this
ridge that can be avoided by traversing left (north) to a
couloir. This couloir leads back onto the ridge, which is
then followed to the summit.
ROUTE 2. South Side. I, 2.0. First ascent August 24, 1969,
by Lyle Olson, Craig Olson, Kirsten Olson, and Kim Olson.
From Coyote Lake keep right (east) to avoid the cliff bands
that ring the southwestern end of the peak.
ROUTE 3. Northeast Ridge. I, 1.0. First ascent July 12, 1960,
by David Dornan, Mark Melton, Mona Monahan, and Leigh
Ortenburger. From the Open Canyon trail climb easily up
to the saddle between Prospectors Mountain and Tukuarika
Peak. Then follow the northeast ridge to the summit. See
American Alpine Journal, 12, no. 2 (1961), pp. 373–379.

PROSPECTORS MOUNTAIN (11,241)

Map: Grand Teton
The sedimentary capping on this large and bulky mountain,
the highest south of Death Canyon, has apparently prevented the development of the same level of interest that
climbers have shown for the crystalline peaks in the center
of the range. Yet Prospectors Mountain is an impressive
Teton peak, both for the view that its summit affords of the

range to the north, south, and west, and for the excellent exposures of crystalline rock on its north and northeast sides. These cliffs rise over 3,000 feet from the floor of Death Canyon and provide excellent climbing routes. The name commemorates the efforts of the early prospectors at the head of Death Canyon about 2.5 miles to the west. Rimrock Lake, which hangs in a small cirque on the upper northern slope of this mountain, is a place of remarkable but fragile alpine beauty, worthy of the effort required to reach it. Point 9,829, 1.4 miles to the west-northwest, was first reached via the southwest slope on July 20, 1960, by Arthur J. Reyman.

CHRONOLOGY

Southeast Slope: June 23, 1932, Phil Smith, Ray Cutter

East Ridge Couloir: [probable] June 23, 1932, Phil Smith, Ray Cutter (descent); [probable] June 22, 1934, Fritiof Fryxell (ascent)

Southwest Ridge: October 18, 1940, Allyn Hanks, Bennett Gale

Northwest Ridge: July 23, 1955, John Fonda, Gene Balaz, Robert Sellars

   var: **North Couloir:** June 14, 1974, Richard Day, John Kevin Fox

East Ridge, North Bastion: August 1, 1961, Stuart During, Dennis Wik

Upper Northeast Face I: August 28, 1963, Ted Vaill, John A. Thomas

Apocalypse Arête: July 14, 1964, William Buckingham, Ted Vaill

   var: July 7, 1989, Janet Wilts, Tom Vercolen

Upper North Ridge: July 12, 1966, Peter Cleveland, Ted Vaill

Apocalypse Couloir: June 18, 1978, Gregg Lawley, Owen Anderson

Northeast Couloir: July 1, 1983, Jim Woodmencey, Ed Thompson

Upper Northeast Face II: August, 1984, Yvon Chouinard, Rick Ridgeway

ROUTE 1. ☞*Southwest Ridge.* I, 1.0. First ascent October 18, 1940, by Allyn Hanks and Bennett Gale. See *Death Canyon* for directions to the Death Canyon trailhead. From there take the Valley Trail, then the Open Canyon trail, to a point at about 8,960+ feet, where it turns left (south), away from the main creek in Open Canyon. Continue up the northwest fork of the canyon to the saddle between Prospectors Mountain and Tukuarika Peak. From this saddle, which in mid-July is covered with beautiful alpine flowers, there is no difficulty in following the broad ridge directly to the summit of Prospectors Mountain. Little more than hiking is involved unless the season is so early that an ice axe is required for safety on the snow slope. See *American Alpine Journal,* 12, no. 2 (1961), pp. 373–379.

ROUTE 2. Southeast Slope. I, 1.0. First ascent June 23, 1932, by Phil Smith and Ray Cutter. After turning off the Open Canyon trail, at the same point as in *Route 1,* cross to the north side of the stream and scramble north up a broad ridge or a series of easy scree-filled couloirs, past grassy benches, to the center of three summit knolls. Before the construction of the trail up Open Canyon, the earlier ascents attacked the mountain from this more southeasterly direction. *Time: 6 hours* from the Death Canyon trailhead.

ROUTE 3. ☞*East Ridge Couloir.* II, 3.0. Probable first descent June 23, 1932, by Phil Smith and Ray Cutter; probable first ascent June 22, 1934, by Fritiof Fryxell. This route can easily be used for ascent, but it serves as the fastest and best route, by far, of descent from the summit of Prospectors Mountain. On the 7.5-minute quadrangle map, this couloir is clearly shown due east of the summit, with semipermanent snow in the upper section and a permanent stream in the lower section joining the main Open Canyon creek at the 8,000-foot contour line. From the summit descend about 0.25 mile along the plateau to the broad saddle connecting to the northeast summit before turning east down into the couloir. For those experienced with the use of an ice axe, this couloir in early season can be glissaded on unbroken snow all the way to the creek in Open Canyon. At no point is the couloir steep.

ROUTE 4. East Ridge, North Bastion. II, 4.0. First ascent August 1, 1961, by Dennis Wik and Stuart During. This climb appears to have been along the broad ridge that separates the east ridge couloir *(Route 3)* and the main upper northeast face. No information is available.

ROUTE 5. Upper Northeast Face I. II, 5.6. First ascent August 28, 1963, by Ted Vaill and John A. Thomas. Due east of the summit of Prospectors Mountain is one of the major features of the mountain—a large, wide couloir starting about 1.0 mile up the Open Canyon trail, leading northwest to a major cirque bounded on the west by the ridge above and east of Rimrock Lake. Northeast of this cirque is the ridge crest at the top of the main 3,000-foot northeast face, rising almost directly from the floor of Death Canyon. Above and southwest of the floor of the cirque is the 800-foot upper northeast face, where this route is located. The last 0.5 mile before the summit is a plateau of sedimentary rubble; the face itself, however, is of good crystalline rock.

Take the Valley Trail (see *Open Canyon*) around the west end of Phelps Lake to the top of the moraine south of the lake. Continue on the Open Canyon trail about 1.0 mile up the canyon, and then turn northwest up the wide couloir described above. Nearing the face, one can see a secondary, steep, snow-filled couloir bisecting the upper northeast face into two sections. The route begins at the top of an inverted "V" some 200 feet to the left (southeast) of this couloir and goes nearly directly up the face to its highest point. After scrambling to the top of the inverted "V," continue up to the left on slabs beneath an impressive overhanging wall (the

Yellow Garden Wall). Now work to the right and climb steep, slabby rock with good holds, past a smooth slab with small holds, and around an overhang (5.4) to the ledge above. A 5.1 open book, followed by three more leads of similar difficulty up and left, brings one to a small belay cave beneath a great overhang of the upper section of the Yellow Garden Wall. From the cave, ease around a corner to the right onto a ledge that leads diagonally up to a short grassy slope. The face above this slope is bounded on the left by a large vertical chockstone chimney and on the right by a rock chute leading to a window overlooking the bisecting couloir mentioned above. Climb the center of the face (5.6) to an open book, above which is a good belay stance under a small overhanging tower. The next lead goes around the tower on the left, up a smooth slab, and onto the top of the tower. After climbing another steep slab with beautiful holds, scramble up the last pitch on easy rock to the sedimentary summit plateau. Walk the final 0.5 mile to the summit cairn. See *American Alpine Journal,* 14, no. 1 (1964), p. 188.

ROUTE 6. Upper Northeast Face II. II, 5.8. First ascent August, 1984, by Yvon Chouinard and Rick Ridgeway. This route apparently lies to the right of Route 5 and ascends the buttress to the left of the snow couloir that cuts through this upper northeast face. Five pitches of good rock are involved.

ROUTE 7. Northeast Couloir. II, 5.1. First ascent July 1, 1983, by Jim Woodmencey and Ed Thompson. When Prospectors Mountain is viewed from the northeast, two distinct couloirs, steep and in early season snow-filled, will be seen leading toward the "Four Horsemen," the pinnacles between the top of Apocalypse Arête (Point 9,996) and the upper north ridge. The northeast couloir is the left (southerly) of the two, lying at the base of the main north face of the mountain. In early season (or winter), this route is largely a steep snow-and-ice climb, not pursued to the summit of the mountain. Descent from the ridge crest, the top of the climb, can be made down the back (west) side without difficulty.

ROUTE 8. Apocalypse Couloir. II, 4.0. First ascent June 18, 1978, by Gregg Lawley and Owen Anderson. This couloir is the right of the two that lead toward the Four Horsemen pinnacles on the ridge separating Point 9,996 from the upper north ridge of the mountain. The couloir parallels Apocalypse Arête on its left (south) side. In early season the first half of the climb is on steep snow. The remainder of the climb to the ridge crest is on rock of only scrambling difficulty.

ROUTE 9. Apocalypse Arête. II, 5.7. First ascent July 14, 1964, by William Buckingham and Ted Vaill. This long and sharp ridge forms the top of some of the facets of the north face of Prospectors Mountain and is bounded on the left (southeast) by a deep couloir. From the 8,000-foot contour to the 9,996-foot tower that forms the summit of the ridge, the primary orientation of this ridge is east–west; at this point the ridge turns abruptly southwest, past Point 10,560+ above and east of Rimrock Lake, to the summit of the mountain. The climb is started by leaving the trail at about the 7,600-foot level, crossing the stream, and scrambling up talus blocks to the base of the ridge. One could also reach the ridge by continuing on the trail to the Death Canyon patrol cabin and then contouring and bushwhacking east back to the base of the ridge.

The first third of the arête offers no difficulties and consists of 3.0 scrambling until a vertical-to-overhanging 200-foot step is reached. A direct attack on this step will probably require artificial climbing, so descend slightly to the left and traverse under the face of the step on ledges; then zigzag back about halfway up the step to a 4.0 pitch that leads to the top of the step. After another 3.0 interlude, a wall about 70 feet high will be met. Slightly to the right of the crest is a small dihedral with a loose flake above. Use a variety of techniques, including lieback and stemming, to climb this pitch (5.7); take great care with the flake, which is almost completely detached. Another section (2.0) leads to a third prominent steep step about two-thirds of the way up the ridge. Most of this step is not difficult (4.0), but the slightly overhanging top section is climbed via a 5.4 jam crack on small holds. Two towers are passed by 3.0 scrambling before the top of the arête is reached at 9,996 feet. The four pinnacles named the Four Horsemen, which suggested the name of this arête and which extend southwest toward the summit of Prospectors Mountain, begin at this point and can be seen on the map. The summit of the arête is the first of the Horsemen. The second is ascended easily by its northwest side whereas the third involves a 5.1 pitch on its south side. To descend from this third pinnacle, rappel from the large boulder on its summit. The fourth Horseman possesses a narrow summit flake, which is climbed, appropriately, à cheval. The first-ascent party descended to Death Canyon from this point in a couloir to the northwest.

Variation: II, 5.6. First ascent July 7, 1989, by Janet Wilts and Tom Vercolen. Instead of starting the route at the base of the ridge, begin around to the right on the north wall of the lower ridge by scrambling 100 feet up easy rock. The first short pitch starts from a block and goes up through trees and bushes to a ledge where a traverse left (20 feet) and up leads to a belay ledge. The second lead (150 feet) works up and left to an obvious crack (5.6) above which one angles left on a face, avoiding a right-facing open book. The next full pitch goes up the face above to the belay ledge from which 400 feet of scrambling up and left permit rejoining the main ridge route.

ROUTE 10. Upper North Ridge. II, 5.1. First ascent July 12, 1966, by Peter Cleveland and Ted Vaill. Apocalypse Arête (*Route 9*) leads to the most northerly point of Prospectors Mountain, Point 9,996, and ends after traversing four towers (the Four Horsemen) along the next flat section of the north ridge. The upper north ridge lies immediately above the far (south) end of this flat section; hence, one could climb Apocalypse Arête to approach this route. The first-ascent party, however, ascended the second couloir west of Apocalypse Arête to reach this point, the base of the next steep step of the ridge; this couloir lies well to the east of the outlet stream from Rimrock Lake. To reach the top of this steep step, climb slabs on the right (west) side of the face of the step. The top of this step is Point 10,560+, which can also be easily reached via its west ridge from Rimrock Lake or from the cirque to the east. The final section of the north ridge above, leading to the sedimentary cap, is a long knife-edge containing many towers. Stay on the crest, where interesting and exposed 5.1 climbing will be found travers-ing these towers, which are frequently rotten and loose. The two climbs of this route used different methods to pass the final tower. The first ascent bypassed it on the left (east) side traversing into a couloir, whereas the second ascent climbed out to the right (west) from the sharp notch preceding the tower to gain the saddle on the far side to reach the same couloir. If this route is combined with Apocalypse Arête, it will be a two-day climb or a very long one-day climb.

ROUTE 11. Northwest Ridge. I, 2.0. First ascent July 23, 1955, by John Fonda, Gene Balaz, and Robert Sellars. For directions to Rimrock Lake, see *Death Canyon.* Walk around the right (west) shore to the south end of this lake. Follow the talus slope and ledges up to the skyline saddle. Climb left (southeast) from this saddle to the summit knoll.

Variation: North Couloir. I, 3.0. First ascent June 14, 1974, by Richard Day and John Kevin Fox. From the south end of Rimrock Lake, instead of heading right up the talus slope and ledges to the northwest ridge, bear more left and climb a steep, narrow, snow couloir between two rock but-tresses. From the top of the couloir, join the upper northwest ridge and follow it to the summit knoll. In early season this provides a good and rapid descent route, pro-viding that one has knowledge of use of the ice axe for safety.

FOSSIL MOUNTAIN (10,916)

Map: Mount Bannon

This mountain presents the boldest outline of all the rounded peaks on the southern divide. It received its name from Fritiof Fryxell in 1930; previously it was known as Housetop Mountain, a name descriptive of its appearance.
ROUTE 1. Southwest Ridge. I, 2.0. First ascent July 9, 1933, by Leland Horberg and Frank Swenson. In May or June 1934, T. F. Murphy and Robert E. Brislawn also probably climbed this peak from the south.
ROUTE 2. ☞Southeast Side. I, 2.0. First ascent July 17, 1941, by Arthur J. Reyman. From Fox Creek Pass ascend the south cliff band to the upper bench; a small bit of

routefinding may be required. From here, the talus of the east slope leads to the south ridge, which is followed to the summit.

PEAK 10,612   *(0.7 mi S of Mount Bannon)*

Map: Mount Bannon

This unremarkable summit lies on the sedimentary divide above the Death Canyon Shelf between Fossil Mountain and Mount Bannon.
ROUTE 1. South Slope. I, 1.0. First ascent August 27, 1957, by William Edwards, Don Moser, and Robert Page, from the end of the road in Darby Canyon (see *Mount Jedediah Smith*).
ROUTE 2. North Slope. I, 1.0. First descent July 17 and first ascent July 18, 1960, by Arthur J. Reyman. Proceed from the upper bench above the Death Canyon Shelf.
ROUTE 3. East Slope. I, 1.0. First ascent July 21, 1960, by Arthur J. Reyman and two others.

MOUNT BANNON (10,966)

Map: Mount Bannon

The highest of the string of sedimentary peaks rising above the Death Canyon Shelf, this peak was named to honor the pioneer USGS topographer T. M. Bannon, who in 1897 undertook the intimidating task of preparing the first Grand Teton quadrangle map using traditional field methods of horse and plane table; the map, now out of print, was pub-lished in 1899.

CHRONOLOGY

East Slope: [probable] May or June 1934, T. F. Murphy, Robert E. Brislawn
South Slope: July 17, 1960, Arthur J. Reyman

ROUTE 1. South Slope. I, 1.0. First known ascent July 17, 1960, by Arthur J. Reyman, by a traverse from Peak 10,612. From the Teton Crest Trail on the Death Canyon Shelf, pass the sedimentary wall above via a talus slope to a ledge slop-ing for several hundred feet up and right (north) onto the upper bench. From there the route is easy.
ROUTE 2. East Slope. I, 2.0. Probable first ascent in May or June 1934, by T. F. Murphy and Robert E. Brislawn. On August 9, 1955, Hervey Voge, Harriet Parsons, William Hail, Nancy Slusser, Jerry Klein, Ed Nauer, Ralph Starr, William Moser, Roger Kuhn, Virginia Romain, Ben Cummings, Jean Atchinson, and John Gerstle climbed this route from the trail on the Death Canyon Shelf (about 9,500 feet) via a notch in the cliff wall, which is seen on the map due east of the peak. They found an empty 4-foot cairn on the summit. *Time: 3 hours* from the Death Can-yon Shelf.

MOUNT JEDEDIAH SMITH (10,610)

Map: Mount Bannon

This unimpressive peak on the divide scarcely does justice to this extraordinary man, who was one of the greatest of the trapper-explorers of the American West. After the passage of the Astorians in 1811 and 1812, Jedediah Smith rediscovered Jackson Hole in 1824, entering via the Hoback River and exiting through Conant Pass.

ROUTE 1. Southwest Slope. I, 1.0. First known ascent August 27, 1957, by William Edwards, Don Moser, and Robert Page. This party found a cairn on the summit containing a penny but no record. Start from the end of the road in Darby Canyon (8.3 miles from the entrance at the highway, 3.0 miles south of Driggs).

ROUTE 2. East Slope. I, 1.0. First descent July 17, 1960, by Arthur J. Reyman. First ascent September 20, 1960, by Al Read and Ann MacFarlane. Use the same approach as for *Mount Meek, Route 1.*

MOUNT MEEK (10,681)

Map: Mount Bannon

Towering above the popular Mount Meek Pass between the Death Canyon Shelf and Alaska Basin, this sedimentary peak was named for the renowned mountain man, Joe Meek, who visited Jackson Hole in 1835, 1839, and 1840, the final year of the romantic fur trappers' era.

ROUTE 1. Southwest Slope. I, 2.0. Probable first ascent in May or June 1934, by T. F. Murphy and Robert E. Brislawn. On July 17, 1960, Arthur J. Reyman climbed this route and found an empty cairn on the summit. From the Death Canyon trail at 8,400 feet scramble up to the Death Canyon Shelf, taking a route just left (south) of the stream southeast of Mount Meek. From the shelf south of Mount Meek Pass a steep chute will be found, which provides a break in the Mount Meek cliff band and allows access to the upper bench. The ascent is easy from this upper bench. When used for descent this route requires some routefinding skills.

ROUTE 2. Northeast Couloir. I, 4.0. First ascent July 21, 1995, by Jim Springer. From Mount Meek Pass traverse 200 yards to the northwest along the base of the cliffs. Then ascend the 600-foot, 40–50° snow couloir. This route is suggested as an early-season climb.

PEAK 10,300   *(0.8 mi E of Mount Meek)*

Map: Grand Teton

Of little mountaineering importance, this small peak forms the east boundary of Mount Meek Pass on the divide.

ROUTE 1. Southeast Corner. I, 1.0. First known ascent July 19, 1960, by Arthur J. Reyman, who found an empty cairn on the summit. The approach to the summit mass is easy from all sides, but the final buttress is most easily climbed from the southeast.

PEAK 11,094   *(1.0 mi WSW of Buck Mountain)*

Map: Grand Teton

This conspicuous sedimentary peak, the highest on the divide south of Buck Mountain, has received remarkably little attention, considering its proximity to the Teton Crest Trail.

ROUTE 1. West Ridge. I, 2.0. First ascent August 30, 1958, by Howard R. (Bob) Stagner, who found an empty cairn on the summit. This ridge can be attained at several places, even though it is guarded on the north by a cliff band. The peak can be approached via the Teton Crest Trail or the Alaska Basin Trail to Alaska Basin or, from the west, via the trail up the south fork of Teton Canyon to Alaska Basin.

ROUTE 2. Northeast Couloir. I, 3.0. First ascent September 15, 1963, by Charles Satterfield and Bruce Morley. From the Buck Mountain divide on the Alaska Basin Trail, climb the first couloir, which is rotten, left (east) of the nose of the northeast ridge cliff.

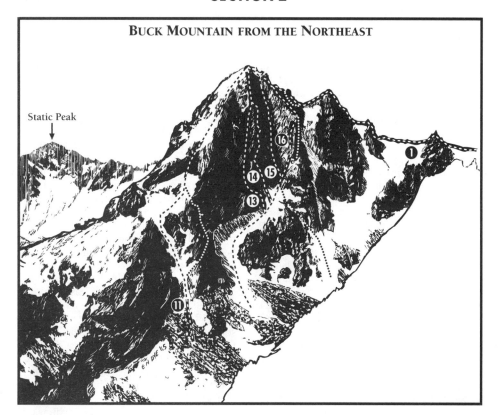

BUCK MOUNTAIN FROM THE NORTHEAST

Static Peak

Death Canyon to Avalanche Canyon

DEATH CANYON, SOUTH SIDE ROCK CLIMBS

Map: Grand Teton

The remarkable exposure of crystalline rock on the south wall of Death Canyon, constituting the north face of Prospectors Mountain, offers several difficult climbs on steep, dark-colored rock that in some sections has the impediment of needing cleaning. These routes are listed from west to east.

CHRONOLOGY

Poop-Out Pinnacle: Summer 1963, Rick Medrick, Peter Lev

Raven Crack: August 3, 1964, Yvon Chouinard, Mort Hempel

Northeast Face: June 25, 1973, Eric Bjornstad, Robert Degles

Yellow Jauntice: June 30, 1977, Mike Munger, Kent Lugbill

Predator: July 1987, Jack Tackle, Jim Donini

Black Diamond: August 13, 1987, Yvon Chouinard, Lynn Hill, Russ Raffa, Sandy Stewart

Carson-Whiton: August 17, 1990, Andy Carson, Mark Whiton

ROUTE 1. Poop-Out Pinnacle. II, 5.1. First ascent summer 1963, by Rick Medrick and Peter Lev. This small pinnacle is located halfway up the north face of Point 9,996, the culmination of Apocalypse Arête. One pitch was climbed on the north ridge.

ROUTE 2. Northeast Face. IV, 5.7. First ascent June 25, 1973, by Eric Bjornstad and Robert Degles. See *Photo 3*. This long climb was made from a bivouac on the south side of the creek in Death Canyon after the usual approach via the trail from the Death Canyon trailhead. The route ascends a line of weakness between two prominent couloirs on the lower northeast face. The eastern of these couloirs is the Raven

Crack (see *Route 3*), while the western one is the Northeast Couloir (see *Prospectors Mountain, Route 7*) leading due west to the south end of the horizontal section of Apocalypse Arête. While the line more or less leads up toward a large, yellow, triangular-shaped wall (clearly discernible from the Death Canyon trail below), the lower portion of the climb is characterized by bushes, trees, and mossy chimneys. After exiting from this vertical jungle, high-angle, clean, but often fractured and loose rock is found, containing blank areas that are passed by traversing a few feet right or left. Ascent is primarily by chimneys, liebacks, and jams, sometimes requiring large pitons, nowadays nuts, to protect. The route ends on the ridge leading east from Point 10,560+, which forms the north edge of the subsidiary canyon just below the upper northeast face of Prospectors Mountain. Descent is easily made down this subcanyon to the mouth of Open Canyon at 7,600 feet. *Time: 12 hours.*

ROUTE 3. Raven Crack. IV, 5.9. First ascent August 3, 1964, by Yvon Chouinard and Mort Hempel. See *Photo 3.* This route is in the long black crack or chimney in the middle of the dark south wall of Death Canyon. This chimney begins near the base of Apocalypse Arête (see *Prospectors Mountain, Route 9*) and, in short, the route goes directly up to its end. Approach via the Death Canyon trail to a point about 0.25 mile west of the base of Sentinel Turret and scramble up a talus slope to the base of a large wet couloir near the base of the wall. The waterfall in the couloir is passed on the right (west) side via exposed 4.0 climbing. At the top of the waterfall, traverse left onto ledges (3.0), then diagonal up and right to a chimney (3.0), which leads to a grass slope marking the beginning of the climb. The first pitch is 140 feet (4.0) to a belay ledge. Next ascend a crack for 15 feet; then traverse right to another crack and follow it for 100 feet to a ledge at the end of the lead. Ascend the chimney above the ledge and climb, with small 5.6 face holds, to the right of the overhang at the top. From here a jam crack leads to a belay ledge. The fourth pitch goes up and then right for 10 feet to another crack that takes one to a ledge at the base of a large overhang. The next pitch is the crux of the route (5.9). Traverse left, then back diagonally to the right. When possible, climb the overhang onto a face with small holds. Climb the detached flake above, carefully using downward pressure. From the top of the flake climb through the "funnel," a squeeze chimney, to a ledge; bypass an overhang on the right (5.7) and make a belay in the chimney above. Now climb right out of the chimney and follow a ledge that traverses right; after the ledge peters out, continue via face climbing diagonally right to the "Waldorf-Raven," an enormous grassy ledge. The next lead starts at the extreme left end of this ledge on 4.0 rock, then a slanting chimney is climbed, using face holds (5.7) on the right wall, up to a grassy belay ledge. The pitch above follows a jam crack to the next belay ledge at the base of a chimney. The final lead ascends this chimney, which narrows to a lieback crack, to

an enormous tree-covered ledge that traverses across the entire wall. If one does not wish to continue to the summit of the mountain, walk left (east) along the ledge to an open area where a large couloir, the one farthest south, descends to the talus slope below.

ROUTE 4. Predator. IV, 5.11, A2. First ascent July 1987, by Jim Donini and Jack Tackle. See *Photo 3.* This route takes a line very close to the crest that forms the left (east) edge of the Raven Crack or couloir. After crossing the creek in Death Canyon proceed up the main large talus cone at the base of the north cliffs of Prospectors Mountain. The initial task is to reach the major horizontal bench or ledge system that extends all across the face, about one-third of the way up from the talus. Take the snow couloir up and right (west) to a point where one lead of horizontal 3rd-class scrambling permits exit back to the left (east) onto the broken wall below the bench. Two leads of steep rock (5.8 and 5.7), continuing back to the east, take one to the easier rock at the upper end of Prospectors Falls, allowing easy access to the bench. Scramble up the beginning of the Raven Crack past a chockstone to the first of the upper nine pitches of the route. After one lead of 5.6, exit left onto the difficult rock of this route, which is just left (east) of the Raven Crack. One lead (5.10) is followed by a severe left-facing corner (5.11). The next lead (5.10) continues in this corner, but some aid (A2) is needed to pass a dirt-filled crack. A jog to the right at the end of this lead brings one to the start of the fifth pitch, again in a steep corner (5.9), to and past a ledge. Move left and up past a tree to the belay point. The next lead goes up a face (5.8) and cuts back right to a crack, which is then climbed. The final three leads of similar difficulty continue upward in this same line, exiting onto the top of the wall. The first-ascent party descended by means of ten rappels down the face to the east of the route, to and past the bench to the talus cone. An alternate descent is to hike down the drainage on the back (south) side of the top of the climb. This drainage is easily followed using game trails to hit the Open Canyon trail at 7,600 feet.

ROUTE 5. Carson–Whiton. III, 5.9. First ascent August 17, 1990, by Andy Carson and Mark Whiton. See *Photo 3.* Very little information is available about this climb, which begins in the couloir immediately west of Prospectors Falls in an area of white rock. After the first three leads, cut back to the east toward the Raven Crack to a chimney that is followed to a bench. Follow the bench back to the west and climb a very steep face for three pitches (5.9, 5.7, and 5.7). Protection is poor in this section. Traverse west for two pitches across an easy ledge to a point where 5.9 climbing leads around a corner. Another 5.9 pitch finishes the climb.

ROUTE 6. Yellow Jauntice. III, 5.10. First ascent June 30, 1977, by Mike Munger and Kent Lugbill. The south wall of Death Canyon, seen before the trail reaches the level section of the canyon, rises from about the 7,300-foot level and ends as the north edge of a major cirque (see *Prospectors*

Mountain, Route 5) that drains southeast into Open Canyon. The distinct Apocalypse Arête rises toward the southwest from the top of the large triangular talus cone at the base of this face. The upper portion of this talus, and more especially the couloir behind (south of) Apocalypse Arête, will harbor snow well into midseason. The face above the talus, to the south of and somewhat east of Apocalypse Arête contains three main chimneys or large corners separating sections of dark-colored, nearly vertical rock. This route ascends a yellow or white crack system on the easternmost of these dark walls; this relatively small crack system diagonals upward slightly from right to left. A large tree ledge or bench cutting across the entire face (about one-third of the distance up) diagonals slightly from lower left to upper right and ends in the Northeast Couloir (see *Prospectors Mountain, Route 7*).

Starting from the talus, or snow, the initial section below the large tree bench is a climb up broken and somewhat rotten rock and ledges with more difficult climbing in the upper part before reaching the tree bench. The first pitch is steep and like a jungle with rotten rock until some ledges are reached. Next, a moderate right-facing dihedral, past some trees, brings one to the crux pitch with an overhanging section. The first half of the third lead goes up a chimney and then up an easier right-facing dihedral to the right of the overhanging section. Now climb down and left under the roof and then up and right via a crack above to a sloping belay stance (5.10). Rope drag on this pitch suggests dividing it into two short leads. The next two pitches proceed up and right out of the crack system, switching from one dihedral to another, ending left at a belay on a large ledge. The sixth lead goes up and left in a crack and along a down-pointing flake to its top, then left and up onto the left edge of a large platform (difficult). The next pitch traverses right and then up a fist crack past a ledge. The final lead involves diagonal climbing via finger cracks to the summit block where a cairn will be found. This is a hard climb to a distinct summit, which can be discerned as such from the highway. Unfortunately the protection for the difficult climbing is relatively poor.

ROUTE 7. Black Diamond. II, 5.10. First ascent August 13, 1987, by Yvon Chouinard, Lynn Hill, Russ Raffa, and Sandy Stewart. This route ascends the first major formation on the left (south) side, as one enters Death Canyon. A fairly smooth face will be seen up and left, containing a left-leaning yellow dihedral that is the landmark for the route. From the talus below the face, scramble right up an ascending ramp to its end, which is still a bit left of the dihedral. From this point climb a moderate (5.6) pitch to a large pine tree. Scramble another 200 feet to the base of the upper wall, where the route stops wandering and becomes a good rock climb. The first lead is a 5.7 runout. The next lead, also a runout (5.10), goes under and just left of the yellow dihedral. The third long (160 feet) pitch goes up the dihedral

(5.10). Now continue straight up for another ropelength (5.8). The final fifth pitch wanders right up through overhangs (5.7); finish by following a ramp and ledges out to the right and top out. Descent is made down to the east.

POINT 9,840+   *(2.1 mi SW of Buck Mountain)*

Map: Grand Teton

ROUTE 1. The Lost World Plateau. II, 5.8. First ascent August 28, 1992, by Paul Horton and Brent Bishop. Point 9,840+ is the obvious, plateaulike formation located on the north side of Death Canyon slightly more than 1.0 mile west of the patrol cabin. Its south face is split by a large dihedral/chimney system that is prominent when viewed from the trail below. This route ascends this system in six pitches.

Boulder fields and gullies lead to the base of the dihedral, which is scrambled for a few hundred feet. A broad ledge marks the start of the technical climbing on the steeper cliff above. The route follows the obvious system with occasional wanderings onto the right-hand face. It consists of generally easy 5th-class climbing with a few 5.7 or 5.8 sections. A standard rack will suffice, but the face and chimney pitch near the top is difficult to protect.

The summit area is a wooded, granitic prominence at the end of a grassy limestone spur. It is an unusual place that is cut by deep chimneys and couloirs. To descend, downclimb into gullies lying due west and follow them down through cliff bands to the grassy slopes above the trail.

MOXIE TOWER (9,360+)   *(1.35 mi SW of Buck Mountain)*

Map: Grand Teton

This considerable tower is the largest of three that lie on the prominent buttress that separates the central and westerly of the three streams descending from the north down into Death Canyon near the patrol cabin. Overlooked for decades because it is usually not easily seen, Moxie Tower is readily visible from the valley given correct lighting conditions. Even the map neglects this tower, as no closed contour is depicted on the Grand Teton quadrangle sheet.

ROUTE 1. Southeast Corner. II, 5.8. First ascent September 25, 1987, by Andy Carson and Paul Horton. Approach via Death Canyon and take the Alaska Basin Trail up from the Death Canyon patrol cabin to the fifth switchback corner. Leave the trail here and head left into the drainage of the central of the three streams. Cross the stream and climb toward the largest of the towers. The first ropelength on the east side of the south face of 5.8 difficulty provides access to the next section, about 200 feet of 3rd-class scrambling along the crest of the south ridge. The second pitch of 100 feet, also 5.8 on the east side of the crest, leads to the belay for the final full ropelength on moderate rock (5.6), which ends only 30 feet short of the summit. Descent involves two rappels down the northwest side of the tower into the next drainage to the west, which is easily descended to the Death Canyon trail just west of the patrol cabin.

ROUTE 2. Northeast Ridge. II, 5.6. First ascent August 1, 1994, by Jim Dorward and Randy Benham. Approach in a similar fashion as for *Route 1.* Then scramble to the prominent northeast corner. Climb along the crest for two and a half ropelengths over easy, lichen-covered rock. Two overhanging sections are bypassed on the right. The descent involves downclimbing to a point located 50 feet above the col separating the tower from the next buttress to the north, where a short rappel is necessary.

DEATH CANYON, NORTH SIDE ROCK CLIMBS

Map: Grand Teton

This group of climbs located on the northern walls of lower Death Canyon constitutes the most concentrated collection of difficult rock climbs in the Teton Range. If rock climbs rather than mountaineering objectives are sought, this section of Death Canyon is certainly the place. Many of these climbs share a common approach and also a common descent route, simplifying the descriptions. While some loose rock will be encountered, especially on the less heavily climbed routes, in general the rock is excellent and steep. All of these routes have a relatively short approach via the Death Canyon trail from the Death Canyon trailhead. The topos delineate the recommended climbs and the routes are also shown in the section of photographs. These routes are listed from west to east.

Cathedral Rock (9,440+)   *(2.0 mi S of Buck Mountain)*

Cathedral Rock is the name given to the major large buttress on the north side of Death Canyon that forms the lower portion of the southwest ridge of Peak 10,552, officially known as Albright Peak. Its eastern edge is the steep chute or gully that bounds Sentinel Turret on the west. Cathedral Rock, the last formation on the north before the canyon opens out into the flat area near the patrol cabin, lies directly across the canyon from Apocalypse Arête.

CHRONOLOGY

Pillar of Death: July 19, 1964, Rick Medrick, Dave Dornan
  var: August 17, 1976, Eric Engberg, Stephen Angelini
The Snaz: August 4, 1964, Yvon Chouinard, Mort Hempel
  var: **Cousin Leroy:** August 31, 1987, Dave Insley, Dan Barto
  var: **Cousin Leroy's Uncle:** June 10, 1994, Tom Kimbrough, Beverly Boynton

Escape from Death: July 5, 1967, Rick Reese, Ted Wilson, Mike Ermarth
Widowmaker: August 18, 1969, Kevin Donald, Jim Erickson
Lot's Slot: July 16, 1978, Mike Munger, Buck Tilley
Vas Deferens: July 18, 1978, Jim Beyer, Buck Tilley
  var: **August 11th Start:** August 11, 1978, Buck Tilley, Bill Danford
Fallen Angel: July 18, 1978, Yvon Chouinard, Mike Munger
Cottonmouth: July 25, 1978, Mike Munger, Buck Tilley
Schmitz-Kanzler Dihedral: [probable] 1979, Jim Kanzler, Kim Schmitz
Shattered: July 4, 1979, Jim Beyer, Buck Tilley
Caveat Emptor: July 9, 1979, Jim Beyer, Buck Tilley
  var: July 24, 1979, George Montopoli, Mike Munger
Alpine Cow: late 1970s, Mike Munger and others
Aerial Boundaries: September, 1985, Greg Miles, Mike Fisher, Jeff Bjornsen, Tom Vajda
  var: **FNG:** July 16, 1995, Eric Gabriel, Bill Culbreath
Sunshine Daydream: September 2, 1987, Charlie Fowler, Alison Sheets
Walker: July 10, 1994, Pike Howard, Eric Busch

ROUTE 1. The Widowmaker. III, 5.8. First ascent August 18, 1969, by Kevin Donald and Jim Erickson. See *Topo 3.* This route starts in the prominent dihedral on the west face of Cathedral Rock, the massive rock buttress on the north side of Death Canyon, and follows it to the top. For the approach, take the Death Canyon trail to the point where the level part of the upper canyon is entered. Scramble up the talus slope of the Snaz descent route and continue up the gully to the point where the easy Snaz descent chimneys are visible. This route is in the prominent west-facing dihedral that starts above the top of the descent gully. The first two pitches go nearly straight up first in a squeeze chimney and then along a right-facing corner (both 5.7) ending on a belay ledge. Move the belay to a large block about 50 feet up and left to the beginning of the next lead, which is a 5.7 lieback up a long right-facing corner to a sloping belay ledge. Now continue up over a white chockstone (5.8) along a right-facing corner. The fifth lead passes some large, loose blocks between right- and left-facing corners and ends with a small 5.8 crack. The route ends with a final easier lead up and slightly left. Some loose rock requiring caution will be found on these last pitches. For the descent scramble up to the south to the regular Snaz descent (see *Route 9*).

ROUTE 2. Aerial Boundaries. II, 5.10. First ascent September 1985, by Greg Miles, Mike Fisher, Jeff Bjornsen, and Tom Vajda. See *Topo 4* and *Photo 4.* This is a recommended

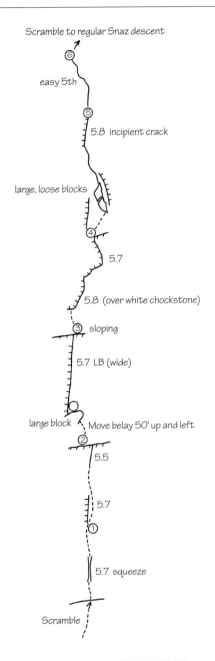

Scramble to regular Snaz descent

⑥

easy 5th

⑤

5.8 incipient crack

large, loose blocks

④

5.7

5.8 (over white chockstone)

③ sloping

5.7 LB (wide)

large block   Move belay 50' up and left

②

5.5

5.7

①

5.7 squeeze

Scramble

**3. ALBRIGHT PEAK, CATHEDRAL ROCK
THE WIDOWMAKER
III, 5.8**

climb characterized by difficult climbing right off the ground. For the approach take the Death Canyon trail to the level part of the upper canyon. Scramble up the talus slope and then up and east to the southwest corner of the Snaz buttress. The flakes of the first pitch can be seen on the yellow wall above. The complexity of the route is best presented in the topo. While none of the five leads of this fine route are easy, the first and third are most difficult. For protection take a standard rack to 4 inches. There are two alternatives for the descent. The first involves simply scrambling and walking several hundred feet up to the regular Snaz descent. Otherwise, scramble up just above the top of the last pitch to a large ledge that slants down and to the west. Follow the ledge downward (some scrambling toward the end) and do two 75-foot rappels from trees to get to the Snaz descent gully (see *Route 9*).

Variation: FNG. II, 5.10-. First ascent July 16, 1995, by Eric Gabriel and Bill Culbreath. See *Topo 5* and *Photo 4*. These guys were lost but nevertheless found a good climb! At the top of the third pitch one can either finish with the two last leads of *Route 2* or, as presented in the topo, do the 5.9+ finger crack.

ROUTE 3. Escape from Death. II, 5.9. First ascent July 5, 1967, by Rick Reese, Ted Wilson, and Mike Ermarth. See *Topo 5* and *Photo 4*. As viewed to the east a few hundred feet downcanyon from the Death Canyon patrol cabin, the southwest ridge of Cathedral Rock is seen in profile. This route begins at the base of the ridge in a large prominent chimney in light gray rock. It is an enjoyable one-day climb on good rock with good protection. For the approach, take the Death Canyon trail, continuing beyond the southwest ridge of the main buttress until the steep polished-rock chimney at the beginning of the climb is visible. The base of this chimney is located just below and to the east of the base of the first pitch of Aerial Boundaries. The first lead goes directly up this chimney onto the belay ledge. Move the belay up and left for the next pitch, which goes up the 5.7 face above. The fourth lead continues up and passes left under an overhanging wall to the belay at the base of a prominent wide crack. The final pitch goes up this difficult crack (5.9) onto the ledge above. The descent is the same as for the Snaz (see *Route 9*), using the lower descent ledge, which involves two rappels to reach the scree leading back to the trail.

ROUTE 4. Vas Deferens. IV, 5.9R. First ascent July 18, 1978, by Jim Beyer and Buck Tilley. See *Topo 6* and *Photo 5*. This route and Lot's Slot (see *Route 5*) are both identified in their upper section by a very large left-facing corner that forms the right (east) edge of a large amphitheater. Both start in the very broken rock of a prominent chimney system, the Slot. The initial portion of this route, as originally climbed and shown on the topo, can be replaced by the *August 11th Start variation* (next) and this is recommended. The approach is the

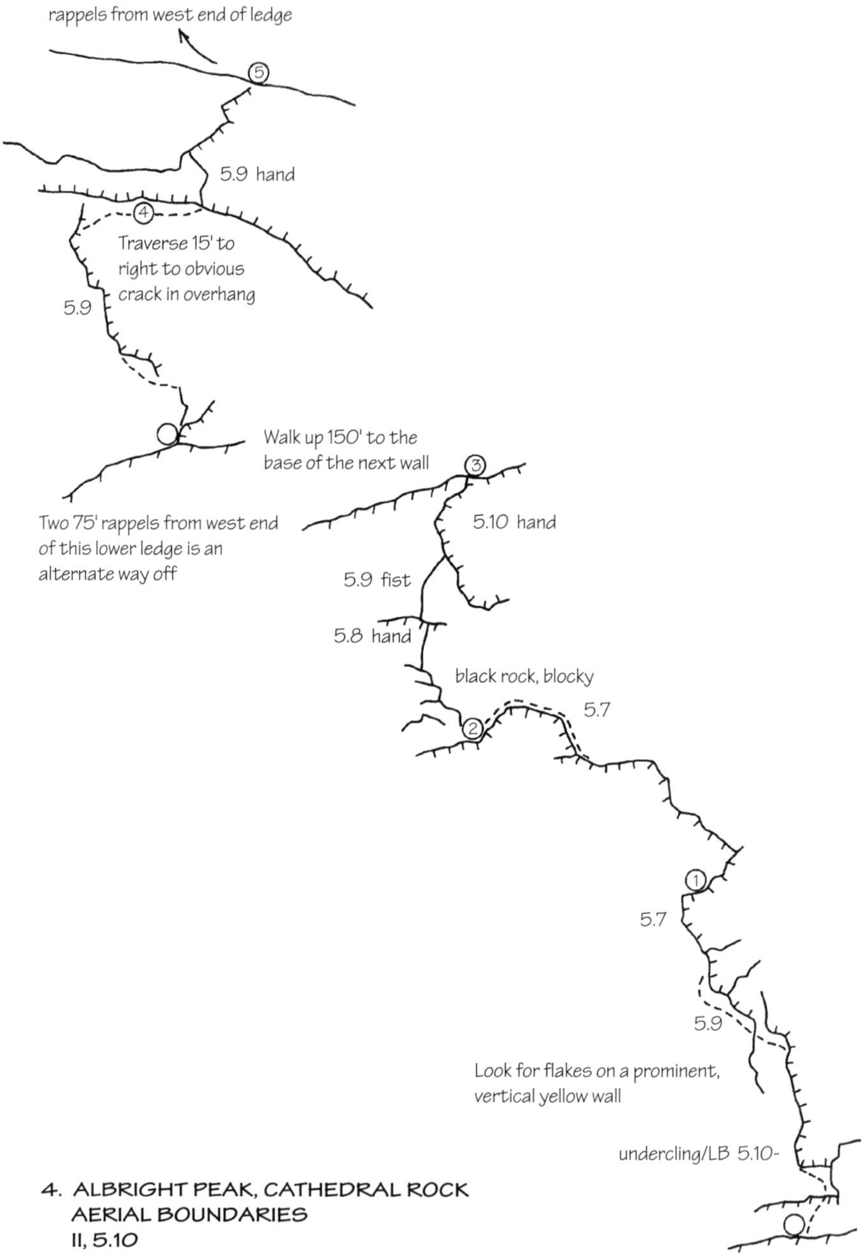

rappels from west end of ledge

⑤

5.9 hand

④

Traverse 15' to
right to obvious
crack in overhang

5.9

Walk up 150' to the
base of the next wall

③

5.10 hand

Two 75' rappels from west end
of this lower ledge is an
alternate way off

5.9 fist

5.8 hand

black rock, blocky

② 5.7

5.7

①

5.7

5.9

Look for flakes on a prominent,
vertical yellow wall

undercling/LB 5.10-

4. ALBRIGHT PEAK, CATHEDRAL ROCK
   AERIAL BOUNDARIES
   II, 5.10

5. ALBRIGHT PEAK, CATHEDRAL ROCK
A. AERIAL BOUNDARIES, VARIATION: FNG, II, 5.10
B. ESCAPE FROM DEATH, II, 5.9

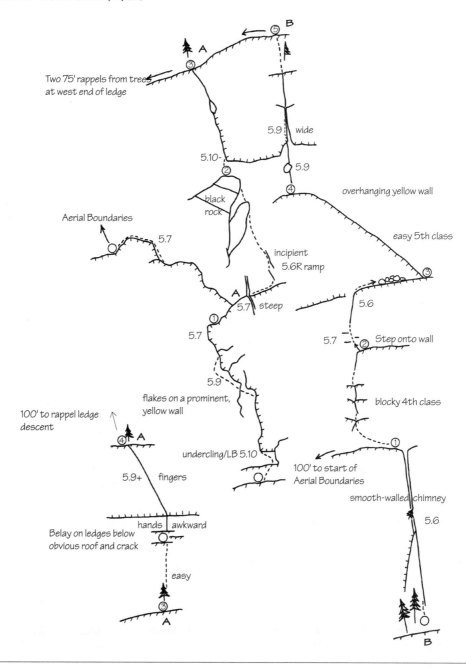

Two 75' rappels from trees at west end of ledge

5.9 wide

5.10-

black rock

5.9

overhanging yellow wall

Aerial Boundaries

5.7

easy 5th class

incipient 5.6R ramp

5.7 steep

5.6

5.7

5.7 Step onto wall

5.9

blocky 4th class

flakes on a prominent, yellow wall

100' to rappel ledge descent

undercling/LB 5.10

100' to start of Aerial Boundaries

5.9+ fingers

smooth-walled chimney

5.6

hands awkward

Belay on ledges below obvious roof and crack

easy

same as for the Snaz, but Vas Deferens starts about 150 feet to the west, immediately left of the Slot. The route is best understood from the topo. At the end of the third lead, move up and left across the face below the huge overhanging arches, instead of continuing up the Slot. The seventh lead involves an unprotected 5.9 face traverse. Exit is made off to the left of the overhangs. A standard rack to 3½ inches with small nuts suffices for protection. The descent is the same as for the Snaz (see *Route 9*).

Variation: August 11th Start. IV, 5.9. First ascent August 11, 1978, by Buck Tilley and Bill Danford. See *Topo 6* and *Photo 5*. This worthwhile variation of three good pitches leads into the upper portion of Vas Deferens or Lot's Slot, by either of which the climb may be finished. It starts about 100 feet to the left of Lot's Slot. The topo shows these pitches, which end on the same ledge as the third pitch of Lot's Slot.

ROUTE 5. *Lot's Slot.* IV, 5.10. First ascent July 16, 1978, by Mike Munger and Buck Tilley. See *Topo 6* and *Photo 5*. This route was the first of the new lines established on the buttress to the left of the Snaz. Lot's Slot and Vas Deferens (see *Route 4*) have the same first three pitches up a prominent chimney system, whose upper section is marked by a very large left-facing corner forming the right (east) edge of a large amphitheater. The topo presents the details of this route, which starts in the chimney system, the Slot, in very broken rock and continues for eight leads directly up this system, passing to the right of the set of overhanging arches. Climbers should be aware that the pitch out of the alcove is *very* serious, loose, and runout 5.9! The approach as well as the descent is the same as for the Snaz (see *Route 9,* later), but the route begins about 150 feet to the left (west).

ROUTE 6. *Cottonmouth.* IV, 5.10+R. First ascent July 25, 1978, by Mike Munger and Buck Tilley. See *Topo 7* and *Photo 5*. This route shares the same start as Lot's Slot and Vas Deferens (see earlier), immediately to the left of the large chimney system, the Slot. The details of this seven-pitch route are shown on the topo. This difficult route is committing with marginal protection on the crux pitch. For protection, in addition to a standard rack, take many small nuts and RPs. The descent is the same as for the Snaz.

ROUTE 7. *Alpine Cow.* IV, 5.11+ (unfinished). This difficult and as-yet unfinished climb was accomplished primarily by Mike Munger during a series of attempts during the 1970s. The climb was pushed to its current high point by Sandy Stewart in 1987 with Eric Reynolds. See *Topo 8* and *Photo 5*. This climb is located east of Cottonmouth and has the same approach as Caveat Emptor. After the first three pitches one can traverse over to Caveat Emptor and finish via the upper pitches of that climb. This is a good alternative start. The fourth pitch has been climbed two different ways. Mike Munger led the intimidating roof at the large chimney/offwidth to the left of the belay shown on the topo. Very awkward moves left under the roof and then steep

liebacking lead to the belay for the fifth pitch (5.11+). Stewart climbed the overhang to the right; start under a small, square hold over the lip. From that hold reach left and stand up (5.11). Two shallow KBs are clipped, then move left to a thin seam (5.9). After clipping another KB ascend the seam up to the double bolt belay stance (5.11). The route has been pushed only 30 to 40 feet farther out under a gray roof (5.10). The current high point ends in a rotten quartz wall.

ROUTE 8. *Caveat Emptor.* IV, 5.10-. First complete ascent July 9, 1979, by Jim Beyer and Buck Tilley. The section of Cathedral Rock between the Snaz and Cottonmouth has an extensive history of attempts, partial climbs, and unfinished routes. On July 5, 1974, Jim Donini, John Bragg, and Steve Wunsch climbed the first four pitches of the final Caveat Emptor route but then joined the Snaz at the top of its third pitch. An unfinished line, Alpine Cow, which has the same start as the current Caveat but heads straight up to a left-curving arch instead of angling right, was first attempted on July 1, 1977, by Mike Munger and Ron Matous. On June 12, 1977, Matous and Keith Hadley climbed two additional pitches in the general vicinity of Caveat. In 1979 Beyer and Tilley added the current beginning (the first pitch of Alpine Cow) and ending pitches of Caveat, making the first ascent of the entire route and giving the initial route name, High Tension Eliminate. The second ascent apparently was made on July 24, 1979, by Munger and George Montopoli, who provided a more direct variation on the first pitch, in order to separate the Cow from Caveat. The following year, on June 24, 1980, Rich Perch and Sandy Stewart made the third ascent of the complete route and applied the current name Caveat Emptor (Latin for "Let the Buyer Beware"). A second attempt on Alpine Cow by Munger and Jim Donini on July 27, 1980, left the line still unfinished. Munger returned on August 17, 1980, with Gordon Brooks and Charlie Gunn to attempt yet another (unfinished) line between the Cow and Cottonmouth.

Caveat Emptor, an outstanding rock climb, is one of the finest in Death Canyon, and highly recommended; it involves five pitches at the 5.10- level. See *Topo 9* and *Photo 5*. Caveat and the Snaz share the same first pitch. From the large ledge at the top of this pitch scramble up and west to the base of a left-leaning chimney, where the difficult climbing begins. The second lead starts up the chimney to a fixed pin, traverses right (5.10-), then continues straight up (5.9) to a right-facing corner; climb this corner and diagonal right to the belay at the base of a large pillar. The next excellent pitch ascends by means of finger locks and liebacks (5.9) to an overhang that is passed on the right (5.10-), then continues up the crack above to a comfortable belay ledge in dark rock (165 feet). The topo shows the two alternatives for the next pitch; both end up at the same place after a short distance. The fifth pitch climbs an overhanging hand crack (5.10-), followed by a left-leaning ramp or

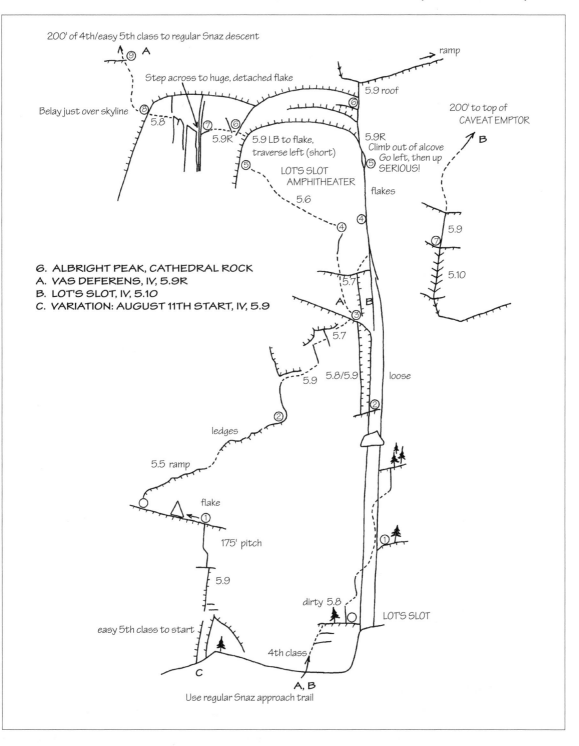

200' of 4th/easy 5th class to regular Snaz descent

⑨ A

ramp

Step across to huge, detached flake

5.9 roof

⑥

Belay just over skyline ⑧

200' to top of
CAVEAT EMPTOR

5.8

B

⑦ ⑥
5.9R

5.9 LB to flake,
traverse left (short)

5.9R
Climb out of alcove
Go left, then up
SERIOUS!

⑤

⑤

LOT'S SLOT
AMPHITHEATER

flakes

5.6

⑦ 5.9

④ ④

5.10

6. ALBRIGHT PEAK, CATHEDRAL ROCK
A. VAS DEFERENS, IV, 5.9R
B. LOT'S SLOT, IV, 5.10
C. VARIATION: AUGUST 11TH START, IV, 5.9

5.7

A B

③

5.7

5.9 5.8/5.9

loose

② ②

ledges

5.5 ramp

flake

△
①

175' pitch

5.9

dirty 5.8

①

LOT'S SLOT

easy 5th class to start

4th class

C

A, B

Use regular Snaz approach trail

200-300' of easy 5th class to regular Snaz descent

5.8

Belay on sloping ledge ⑥

5.8 — large, shallow
dihedral (160')

5.9

⑤

incipient 5.8

5.10+R

④

5.10

5.9 LB, White Dihedral

③

5.9 black rock bands

large, detached flake

②

Wander up low-angle area

①

dirty 5.8

4th class   LOT'S SLOT

Use regular Snaz approach trail

**7. ALBRIGHT PEAK, CATHEDRAL ROCK
  COTTONMOUTH
  IV, 5.10+R**

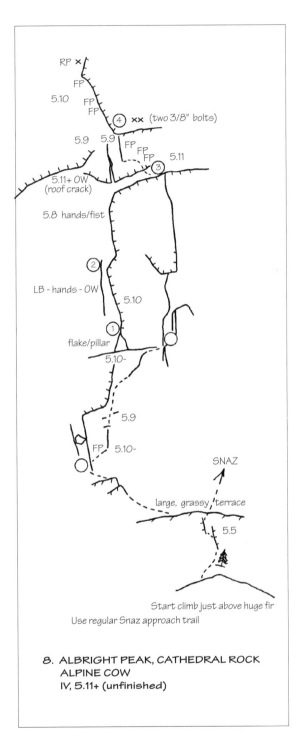

RP ✕

FP

5.10   FP
                FP
                    ④ ✕✕ (two 3/8" bolts)

5.9   5.9   FP
                    FP
                        FP   5.11
                             ③

5.11+ OW
(roof crack)

5.8 hands/fist

②

LB - hands - OW

5.10

①

flake/pillar

5.10-

5.9

FP   5.10-

SNAZ

large, grassy, terrace

5.5

Start climb just above huge fir

Use regular Snaz approach trail

**8. ALBRIGHT PEAK, CATHEDRAL ROCK
  ALPINE COW
  IV, 5.11+ (unfinished)**

corner, through a small overhang (5.10-) and then up to a small belay ledge. The sixth lead (crux) begins by face climbing up and left to a fixed pin not more than 10 feet above the belay. Continue up on steep rock past a series of small holes (one of which used to hold a bashie for protection on this formidable pitch), move left, then right to gain a small ledge (alternative belay). Proceed up and left via 5.8R face climbing to a good belay ledge at the base of a ramp. This pitch is not easy to protect, but it can be done by skillful placements. The final easier lead finishes past a large flake and on and up the left-leaning ramp. Fourth and easy 5th class for 300 feet leads to the standard Snaz descent (see *Route 9*). For protection take a standard rack of nuts, including RPs and camming devices, with extra pieces in the 2- to 3½-inch range.

Variation: IV, 5.10. First ascent July 24, 1979, by Mike Munger and George Montopoli. This variation started from the base of the cliff to the right (east) of the ramp of the regular start to the route. Climb directly upward on very difficult and poorly protected rock to join the upper end of the normal first lead of Caveat Emptor.

ROUTE 9. The Snaz. IV, 5.9. First ascent August 4, 1964, by Yvon Chouinard and Mort Hempel. See *Topo 10* and *Photos 5* and *6*. This rock route is one of the most popular of the difficult Teton climbs and has become something of a classic route. A sustained route, all free, it contains beautiful rock that can be well protected. To approach the Snaz, take the Death Canyon trail past the last switchback before entering the first level section of the canyon where the patrol cabin is located. From here one can look back to the Snaz buttress and see its west side and much of the descent route. Leave the trail at the east end of this last, small switchback; this is the eighth switchback corner after entering Death Canyon proper. After some scrambling immediately off the main trail, find a climbers' trail leading off and east along a large bench to the huge tree at the beginning of the climb.

In general, the route follows the obvious dihedral that cuts up the center of the face of Cathedral Rock but occasionally goes slightly right or left to avoid overhangs. The nine pitches of the Snaz are delineated in the topo. At the end of the ninth lead, the angle eases considerably and the character of the climb changes abruptly. There is no summit to this climb, but one must continue on upward in order to gain the standard Snaz descent route, which is now used as an exit from most of the other routes on Cathedral Rock. Beyond the last pitch of the Snaz about 300 feet of 4th-class climbing is required to reach the broad tree-covered bench from which the descent trail leads off to the west. Use caution with this section because it is very slippery when wet. Contour around to the west past the southwest corner of the buttress, then downclimb easy chimneys on the west side to the scree gully that leads down to the main Death Canyon trail. If you take the lower bench option, two rappels

will be necessary to get to this gully. For protection take a standard rack to 4 inches.

Variation: Cousin Leroy. IV, 5.9. First ascent August 31, 1987, by Dave Insley and Dan Barto. See *Topo 11* and *Photo 6*. This variation provides three pitches of an alternative ending to the Snaz. Climb the Snaz past the roof of the seventh pitch to the belay ledge. Instead of continuing upward for the eighth lead, move right on the ledge 75 feet past a large block and set up a belay just around a prow at a stance with shallow cracks. Face climbing (5.6) then leads up to a brown flake. A 5.9 lieback takes one to the top of the flake from which a hand/fist crack is then climbed (5.9) to the base of a chimney. Climb the 5.6 chimney to its top (wide protection), where a 5.9 move out and right provides an escape to a 5.6 crack. This 140-foot final pitch leads to a tree at the top of the climb. Some 300 feet of easier (4th-class) climbing leads to the standard Snaz descent route. For protection, TCUs are very helpful as well as other devices to 4 inches.

Variation: Cousin Leroy's Uncle. IV, 5.10+. First ascent June 10, 1994, by Tom Kimbrough and Beverly Boynton. See *Topo 10*. This one-pitch variation simply provides an alternative finish for the Snaz. From the ledge at the base of the final pitch of the Snaz, climb a corner that leads up to a series of stepped roofs (5.10+). The pitch finishes in a chimney that has a chockstone in it.

ROUTE 10. Sunshine Daydream. IV, 5.11. First ascent September 2, 1987, by Charlie Fowler and Alison Sheets. See *Topo 12* and *Photos 5* and *6*. This severe route is on the "golden face" to the right of the Snaz, starting at the top of the second pitch of the standard route. The topo shows two ways of starting this climb; the alternative start that was discovered on the second ascent is described as follows. From the bolt anchor belay station (at the top of third pitch of the Snaz) climb out and to the right (5.8) through intimidating terrain beneath a small overhang and around the corner to a 5.8 crack that leads up and left to a belay stance (2½- to 3½-inch protection needed for anchors). From the belay climb up to a bolt (¼ inch) and then face climb (5.10-) past it for 10 feet to a horizontal band that is then traversed to the east to a steep, thin crack. Climb the crack until it ends (5.10+) and then go left to another crack that leads to a nice big ledge. Easy climbing leads up and left to a belay under a thin finger crack. Climb the finger crack (5.11) and proceed up wide cracks to a belay that is just below a large, partially detached flake. The next pitch is long and varied. Follow a crack system immediately left of the flake, and at its top exit left (5.10) to a small ledge. Proceed past a small overhang and an easier wide section above until you are at the base of an offwidth. Climb the offwidth (5.8) to the belay. The final pitch joins the Snaz descent after easy climbing and some scrambling. This serious route is a recommended climb. For protection take a regular rack with two sets of TCUs and other camming devices to 4 inches.

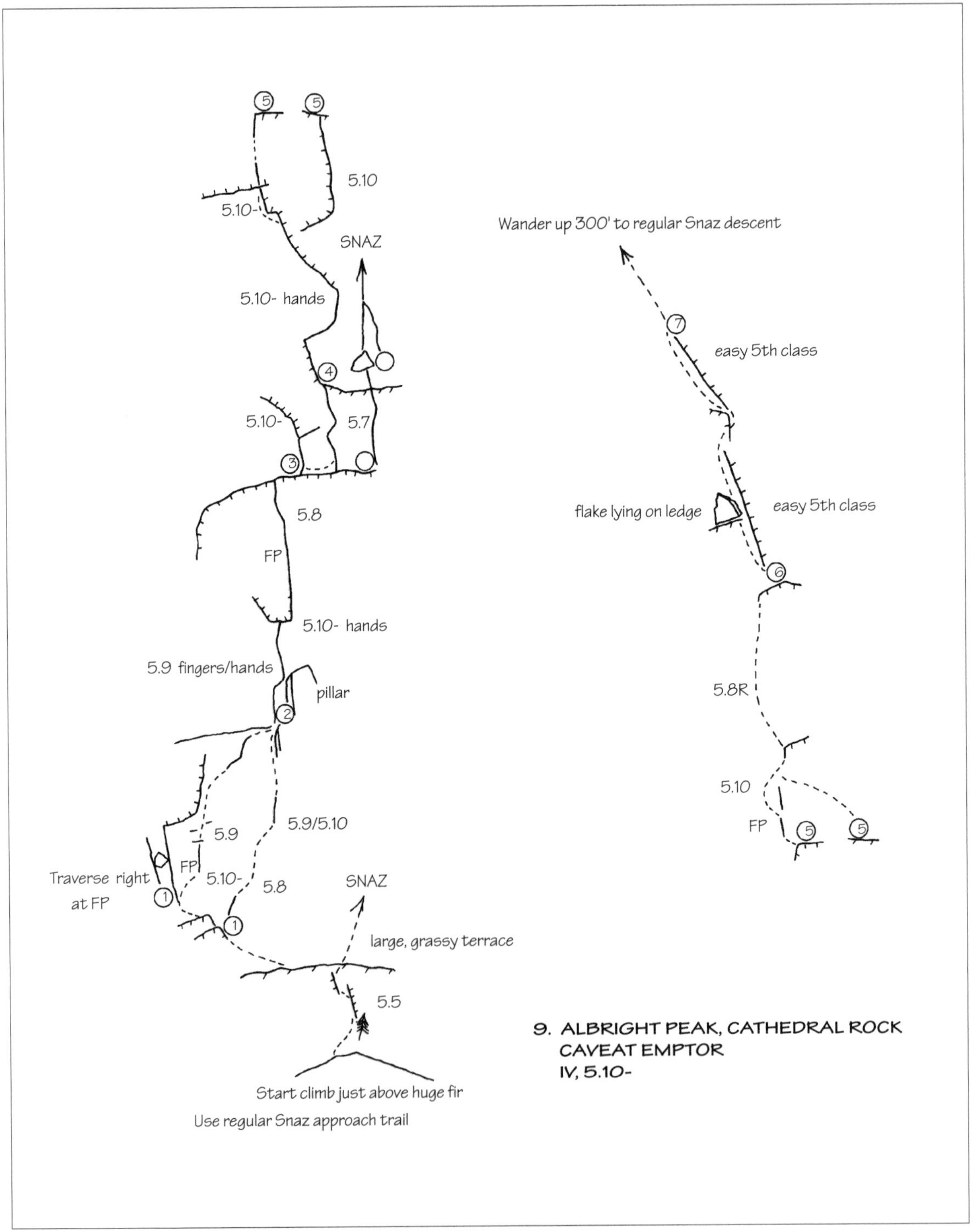

5.10

5.10-

5.10- hands

SNAZ

5.10-   5.7

4

5.8

3

FP

5.10- hands

5.9 fingers/hands

pillar

5.9   5.9/5.10

2

FP

Traverse right   5.10-   5.8   SNAZ
at FP
1

large, grassy terrace

5.5

Start climb just above huge fir

Use regular Snaz approach trail

Wander up 300' to regular Snaz descent

7   easy 5th class

flake lying on ledge   easy 5th class

6

5.8R

5.10

FP   5   5

**9. ALBRIGHT PEAK, CATHEDRAL ROCK
CAVEAT EMPTOR
IV, 5.10-**

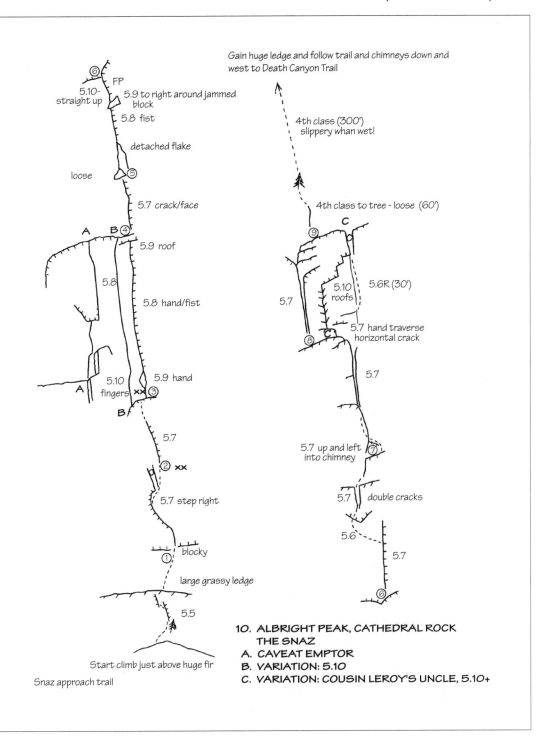

Gain huge ledge and follow trail and chimneys down and west to Death Canyon Trail

FP

5.10-straight up

5.9 to right around jammed block

5.8 fist

detached flake

loose

4th class (300')
slippery whan wet!

5.7 crack/face

4th class to tree - loose (60')

A   B ④

5.9 roof

5.8

5.8 hand/fist

C

5.10 roofs

5.6R (30')

5.7

5.7 hand traverse horizontal crack

5.10 fingers A

5.9 hand

xx ③

B

5.7

5.7

5.7 up and left into chimney

② xx

5.7 step right

5.7 double cracks

5.6

① blocky

large grassy ledge

5.7

5.5

Start climb just above huge fir

Snaz approach trail

10. ALBRIGHT PEAK, CATHEDRAL ROCK
    THE SNAZ
A. CAVEAT EMPTOR
B. VARIATION: 5.10
C. VARIATION: COUSIN LEROY'S UNCLE, 5.10+

ROUTE 11. *Shattered*. IV, 5.10. First ascent July 4, 1979, by Jim Beyer and Buck Tilley. The exact location of this route is not known; hence, it is not marked on photographs within this text. Refer to *Photo 6* for the general area of the climb. This difficult route, between the Snaz and Fallen Angel, starts in a crack system about 30 feet to the right (east) of the Snaz. (An unfinished line, Judgement Day, by Buck Tilley and Jim Beyer, lies slightly farther to the right.) This route unfortunately contains sufficient loose rock as to be not recommended by the first-ascent party. From the grass-covered ledge at the base of the second pitch of the Snaz move 30 feet to the right onto a small buttress. The first lead (150 feet) involves face climbing straight up across small ledges to a belay on a sloping ledge. The next pitch starts up and left on a short ramp, then moves up the face above past a small black roof (5.9), and finishes by moving back right and up onto a sloping belay ledge that diagonals up and left. Now climb up the left-diagonaling hand crack (5.10) and belay from above a small pedestal that lies at the beginning of a rotten chimney. The fourth lead moves up and left on the face to gain a face crack that leads up and slightly right past a block (5.10-) to the next belay ledge. Move right on this ledge and then climb a chimney, dihedrals, and a face for a long ropelength; from the base of this chimney a ramp will be seen leading diagonally left over to the Snaz. The sixth pitch goes up an inside corner and then up and right along a left-facing corner. The next lead goes up a shallow gully to a chimney, and after passing a chockstone exits onto a belay at the beginning of another gully. The final pitch goes up and left in this gully to a point from which the standard Snaz descent can be made. The last four pitches contain very loose rock, hence the name of the route.
ROUTE 12. *Schmitz–Kanzler Dihedral*. IV, 5.10. Probable first ascent June 1979, by Kim Schmitz and Jim Kanzler.

Gain huge ledge and follow trail and chimneys down and west to Death Canyon Trail

Join regular Snaz descent

5.6
5.9 exit right from chimney

5.6

5.9 hand
5.7 hand/fist

5.7

5.9 LB

5.6

5.7

block

Belay around corner at stance with shallow cracks

5.7 up and left into chimney

Prow

5.7   double cracks

5.6   5.7

Snaz

11. ALBRIGHT PEAK, CATHEDRAL ROCK
THE SNAZ, VARIATION: COUSIN LEROY
IV, 5.9

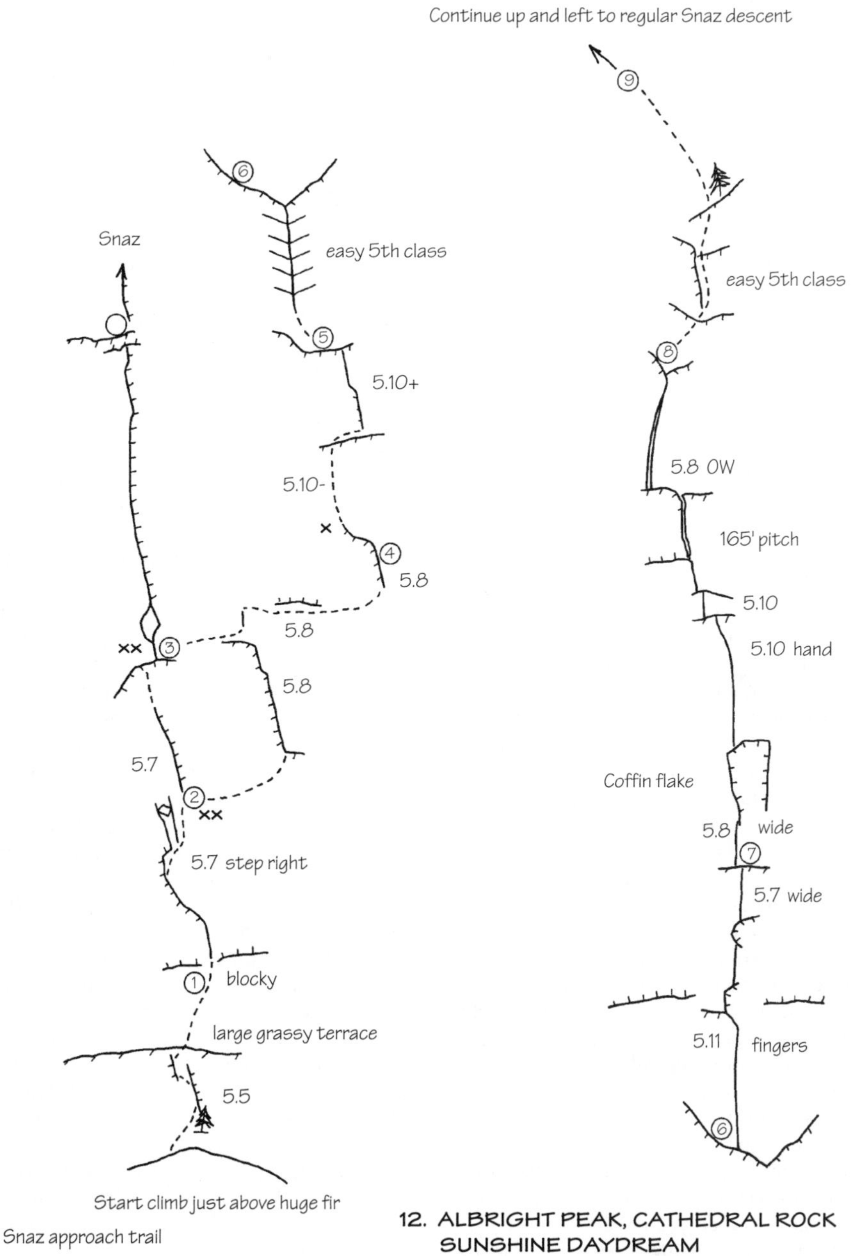

Continue up and left to regular Snaz descent

⑨

Snaz

⑥

easy 5th class

easy 5th class

⑧

⑤

5.10+

5.8 OW

5.10-

165' pitch

×

5.10

④

5.8

5.10 hand

5.8

×× ③

5.8

Coffin flake

5.7

5.8 wide

② ××

⑦

5.7 step right

5.7 wide

① blocky

large grassy terrace

5.11 fingers

5.5

⑥

Start climb just above huge fir

12. ALBRIGHT PEAK, CATHEDRAL ROCK

Snaz approach trail

SUNSHINE DAYDREAM

IV, 5.11

See *Photo 6*. This route goes up an extensive corner system to the left (west) of the Fallen Angel and comes out of the left (west) side of a small tower. The first lead is up a rotten squeeze chimney. The route above consists of corners, faces, and a chimney or two; there are about nine pitches on the route. For protection take a standard rack and a good supply of camming devices. Descent is via the standard Snaz descent route.

ROUTE 13. *Fallen Angel*. IV, 5.10+. First ascent July 18, 1978, by Yvon Chouinard and Mike Munger. See *Topo 13* and *Photos 5* and *6*. This route is committing and the routefinding is difficult. The beginning of the climb is on a gravelly 3rd-class ramp about 300 feet to the right (east) of the Snaz. The details of this complicated route are shown in the topo. The descent is via the standard Snaz descent, except that from the top of this climb one must first scramble several hundred feet up and to the west to a point above the top of the Snaz. For protection, take a standard rack to 4 inches with many small nuts.

ROUTE 14. *Pillar of Death*. III, 5.8, A2. First ascent July 19, 1964, by Rick Medrick and David Dornan. See *Photo 6*. The Pillar of Death is the prominent buttress or pillar of rock on the right (east) side of Cathedral Rock; this side is bounded on the right by the steep gully that separates Sentinel Turret from Cathedral Rock. This was the second climb done on this impressive buttress. To reach the base of the climb follow the Death Canyon trail to a point on the USGS map where the trail crosses the 7,360-foot contour line, just past (west of) Sentinel Turret. A long scramble up loose, broken rock leads to the base of the pillar. The route itself starts on the left (west) of the crest just past a small pine tree in the broken rock of a 5.6 chimney system. When possible, diagonal up to the right and end the first lead beneath a short overhang. The next pitch goes over the overhang and proceeds diagonally to the right on a moderate, but rotten, ledge to a somewhat insecure belay beneath an apparently blank wall. The third lead, difficult (5.8) and exposed, is the crux of the climb. Traverse 80 feet farther to the right with poor protection, then diagonal upward over rock of doubtful quality. At the end of this lead make a series of delicate steps, up and to the right, in order to reach the good ledge 20 feet above. Now climb off the belay ledge to the right; with a piton or two for aid, pass several small overhangs to reach a large open book chimney for a good belay stance. The fifth lead (5.6) ascends the wide chimney above, via the crack on the right, to an exit at a difficult step; from here climb onto a broad sloping ledge. Walk around the corner to the left and up to the far (west) end of the ledge, where the next lead ascends easy rock to a good belay in a short chimney beneath a large overhanging chockstone. The seventh pitch leads out of this chimney, passing the chockstone on the right, then crossing over to the left and up an easy overhang onto a wide ledge at the base of a gully. The final

two leads ascend to the top of this gully and then traverse right to the top of the pillar. To descend, scramble to the top of the rock below the upper face and traverse high around to the left (west) on a ledge system that eventually provides access to the Alaska Basin Trail; this is probably the standard Snaz descent route. Except for the third pitch, this route is on generally good rock with good protection, but nearly every pitch has a difficult section.

Variation: III, 5.9. First ascent August 17, 1976, by Eric Engberg and Stephen Angelini. While this climb was believed by the first-ascent party to be in the vicinity of the Pillar of Death, the location is not known and may have been on the southwest side of Sentinel Turret. Evidence of previous ascent was found during the first three and a half pitches in the form of rappel slings and two pitons at the end of the second pitch. The main clue regarding the location of the route is the profile of rock on the north skyline. After entering Death Canyon a profile in the form of a triangular nose protruding from a vertical wall is seen. This profile forms the left wall of a dihedral. The route follows a system of cracks that leads to and through this dihedral. The first pitch (150 feet, 5.4) goes up a system of small ledges to a grass-covered ledge for a belay at a pine tree. The next lead avoids the grungy corner above the tree by climbing the face (5.6) to the right to a ledge. The third ropelength moves left to a left-leaning, right-facing corner. Climb this (5.7) to its top, exiting left and then moving back right to a belay on sloping rock. The fourth pitch (90 feet) goes up and slightly right to an awkward, narrow, rounded chimney. A difficult (5.8) offwidth jam crack above leads to a flake system in a slot that extends to an insecure belay below an overhanging V-shaped slot. The next lead traverses out 20 feet on the left wall on loose rock around the corner. Continue this rising traverse 40 feet to the left (5.6) to a jam crack formed by the inside corner of the rock profile mentioned at the beginning. After 60 feet up this jam crack (5.8) a good belay stance will be found. The final pitch (70 feet) goes up the rightmost of two cracks for 40 feet to an overhanging finish (5.9) where one exits slightly left. The last 30 feet is face climbing to a large sloping ledge that was believed to be the southwest shoulder of Sentinel Turret. From this high point it appeared that there were two additional easy pitches to a prominent triangular point followed by more difficult climbing. Thus, it appears that this was an incomplete route. Descent was made by walking down and left, where two rappels, with slings in place, took them to a gully. Several more slings were found in place in the gully. This might have been the standard Snaz descent couloir or the couloir separating Cathedral Rock from Sentinel Turret.

ROUTE 15. *Walker*. II, 5.10-. First ascent July 10, 1994, by Pike Howard and Eric Busch. This climb is the first known route on the uppermost cliff of Cathedral Rock. It starts

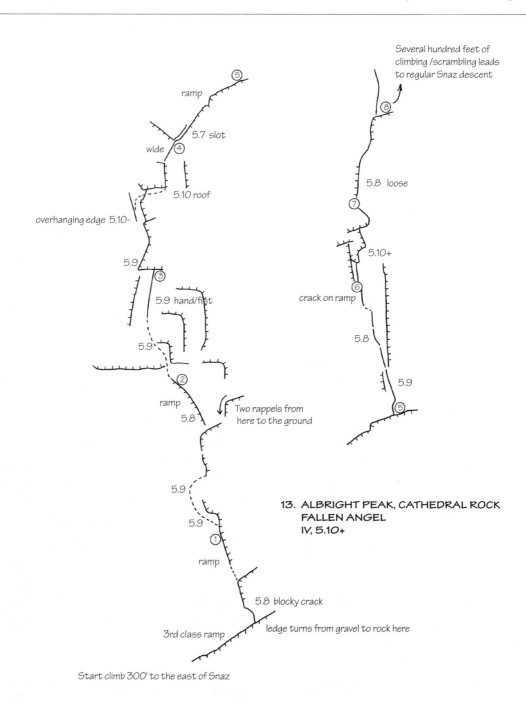

Several hundred feet of climbing /scrambling leads to regular Snaz descent

⑧

ramp

⑤

5.7 slot

wide ④

5.10 roof

overhanging edge 5.10-

5.8 loose

⑦

5.10+

5.9

③

⑥

5.9 hand/fist

crack on ramp

5.9

5.8

②

ramp

Two rappels from here to the ground

5.8

5.9

⑤

5.9

**13. ALBRIGHT PEAK, CATHEDRAL ROCK
FALLEN ANGEL
IV, 5.10+**

5.9

①

ramp

5.8 blocky crack

3rd class ramp

ledge turns from gravel to rock here

Start climb 300' to the east of Snaz

from the huge upper ledge that most of the preceding routes finish on. For the first pitch look for a left-facing corner (5.8+) with a loose block situated off slightly to the east. Ascend this, proceed up past two ledges with trees on them to the base of a shallow corner with a finger crack in it, and belay. Climb the corner (5.8) and continue up past three more ledges to an obvious, splitter-type hand crack located just to the right of a rock pillar and some loose blocks. From the top of the crack, face climb (5.7) to the belay. Another shallow corner requiring thin protection (5.9) is then encountered, followed by a 5.7 chimney. This third pitch ends with a 10-foot hand crack (5.9+). Many variations are possible for the finish of the climb. (*Note:* The first-ascent party used a 200-foot rope on their climb.)

Sentinel Turret (7,800+)   *(2.1 mi S of Buck Mountain)*

As one enters Death Canyon on the trail, and even from various places in the valley, a steep conspicuous buttress that culminates in a separate but flat summit block is seen about halfway up the wall on the north side of the canyon. On the map Sentinel Turret is easily identified as the only place where the 7,600- and 8,000-foot contour lines overlap. This appropriately named buttress or tower was the first rock climb explored in Death Canyon. It is separated from Cathedral Rock, the larger formation to the west, by a steep couloir guarded by a cliff band at its base. The broad Sentinel Gully is shown on the map as the westerly of the two streams descending from the north into the Death Canyon creek near the mouth of the canyon. This major drainage defines the east face of Sentinel Turret and separates it from Omega Buttresses, which lie immediately to the east. Sentinel Turret suffers from inadequate information regarding the exact location of its various routes and variations; only the East Ledges (*Route 3*) are well identified. However, because considerable detail on these routes is available, the descriptions are included below even though the locations of the climbs remain uncertain. Perhaps these descriptions will motivate research leading to their rediscovery.

CHRONOLOGY

South Face: August 3, 1959, Yvon Chouinard, Bob Kamps
> *var:* August 16, 1967, Jim Erickson, Sheldon Smith
> *var:* July 20, 1969, Mike and Jane Yokell
> *var:* **Doomsday Dihedral:** July 11, 1970, Jim Erickson, Dave Erickson
> *var:* **Black Chimney:** August 1975, David Lowe, Leigh Ortenburger
> *var:* **Beeline:** September 3, 1975, Jim Beyer, Jerry Cantor; July 1979, Jim Beyer, Misa Geisey (first free ascent)
> *var:* **That Sushi Thing:** summer 1986, Jason Keith, Greg Marin

East Ledges: August 3, 1959, Yvon Chouinard, Bob Kamps (descent); August 26, 1964, Ted Vaill, Brad Merry (ascent)
Southwest Ridge: June 21, 1964, Jeff Foott, Chuck Satterfield, Peter Koedt, Steve Miller
> *var:* June 27, 1964, Chuck Satterfield, Barry Corbet

ROUTE 1. *Southwest Ridge.* II, 5.6. First ascent June 21, 1964, by Jeff Foott, Chuck Satterfield, Peter Koedt, and Steve Miller. This route lies to the left (west) of the standard South Face route. Five pitches were climbed to reach from the west the col that separates Sentinel Turret from Harrington Spire and the upper mountain.

Variation: II, 5.6. First ascent June 27, 1964, by Chuck Satterfield and Barry Corbet. This line, similar to that climbed six days earlier, also leads to the col between Sentinel Turret and Harrington Spire but ascends an open book, containing rotten rock, to the right (south) of the earlier line but still to the left of the South Face route.

ROUTE 2. *South Face.* III, 5.8. First ascent August 3, 1959, by Yvon Chouinard and Robert Kamps. See *Topo 14.* This high-angle rock climb on the lower south ridge or face is in principal the primary route on this tower. Experience over the past 30 years shows, however, that it is uncommonly difficult to find; few parties claim to have located the original line. The topo shows only one of the possible south face variations. A description closer to the original route will be presented here. From the Death Canyon trailhead hike up the Death Canyon trail (see *Death Canyon*) toward the prominent tower on the north side of the canyon entrance. Leave the trail at the first talus slope past Sentinel Turret, after passing a section of slabs just off the trail, then walk back east to the upper cliff band. Continue up to the apex of a small grassy slope where a triangular alcove will be found with a wide left-leaning crack rising from its top. About 100 feet above, a perfect vertical 50-foot dihedral will be seen. Climb the crack to the large horizontal ledge below the dihedral. Move right on the ledge about 50 feet and climb a prominent broken crack system (5.7) for a ropelength. Do *not* go right after this pitch even though there is a ledge that permits such a lead. Continue up one more pitch in this crack system to easier ground. From this point an easy two-pitch variation is possible by continuing up a right-facing corner to big ledges where a long traverse leads right (east) to the top of the slab pitch described below. The proper and more difficult route, however, makes an unobvious traverse at this point right all the way to the right skyline. The slabs above, which form the crux pitch (5.8) on the right skyline, are now climbed for 100 feet to a tree ledge. The final two leads (5.7) continue on thin cracks and a knobby face to the summit. The easy descent route (see *Route 3*) is into Sentinel Gully, the drainage to the east that leads down to the Death Canyon trail. Make a 75-

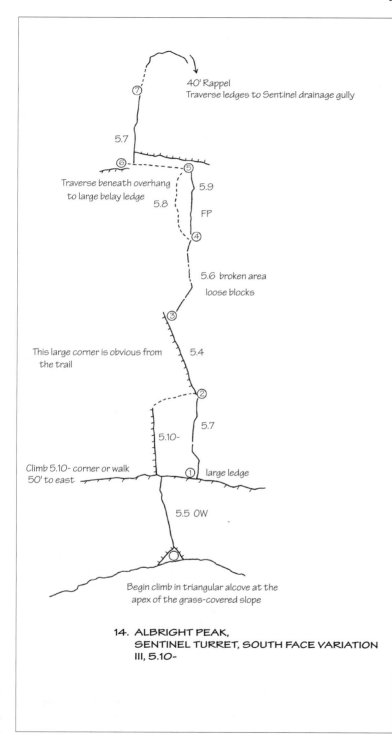

40' Rappel
Traverse ledges to Sentinel drainage gully

5.7

Traverse beneath overhang
to large belay ledge

5.9

5.8

FP

5.6 broken area
loose blocks

This large corner is obvious from
the trail

5.4

5.7

5.10-

Climb 5.10- corner or walk
50' to east

large ledge

5.5 OW

Begin climb in triangular alcove at the
apex of the grass-covered slope

**14. ALBRIGHT PEAK,
SENTINEL TURRET, SOUTH FACE VARIATION
III, 5.10-**

or 100-foot rappel onto ledges that can be contoured to the north into the bottom of the gully; a second rappel may be desired. It should be mentioned that some climbs of Sentinel Turret have been made using this gully as the approach to the middle of this route, coming in from the east around to the main crack system.

Variation: That Sushi Thing. III, 5.10-. This variation was named by Alan Hunt on a failed attempt during the summer of 1985. The first complete ascent was made by Jason Keith and Greg Marin in summer 1986. The climb starts near the base of the regular Sentinel Turret route *(Route 2),* if one is able to decipher that particular mystery. A full ropelength of crack and face climbing (5.8) leads to the large ledge just below and west of the clean dihedral visible from the trail below. The next pitch ascends a good, clean crack (5.7 to 5.8) and the clean dihedral to a belay from which the Chouinard route leads up and to the right. Climb up and left toward a short arête and then back to a 5.8 corner. Continue through a 5.8 overhang followed by a traverse left to a 5.10- roof and right-facing corner to the belay. Face climbing then leads past a large block (5.7) to a large ramp. Rejoin the South Face route and continue to the top.

Variation: II, 5.9, A2. First ascent August 16, 1967, by Jim Erickson and Sheldon Smith. This variation leads rather directly from the base to the upper part of the standard 1959 route on the Sentinel Turret and lies to the right (east) of Doomsday Dihedral (described later); however, the actual starting point is not clearly defined. Climb two or three pitches up toward a prominent open book, described as a clean, square-cut, right-facing, 120-foot dihedral. A short blank wall (5.9) then leads to the start of the dihedral, which was nailed using a thin A2 crack in the back. Thirty more feet up the left wall then completes this crux pitch. Four additional pitches along the same general line connect the top of the dihedral to the upper end of the traverse ramp on the 1959 route; at this point the original route is joined for the final three or four leads to the summit.

Variation: III, 5.8. First ascent July 20, 1969, by Mike and Jane Yokell. This incomplete variation of uncertain location apparently followed, or at least crossed, a previous climb or two, as evidenced by old iron that was encountered in two places. Proceed along the Death Canyon trail to a section of low angle slabs and scramble up past trees to an inside corner with bushes, ending on a large grassy ledge at the base of a 70° face. The first lead (5.6) goes up this face, just left of a chimney or inside corner for 135 feet to a large tree ledge (20 feet wide). The next ropelength ascends the face above (5.7) to a left-leaning ramp, ending in a difficult unprotected corner (5.8) for a belay on a 4-inch ledge. Twenty feet of 5.4 from the left end of this small ledge permit moving the belay to a more substantial 5-foot ledge above. The next long pitch moves 8 feet left to an overhang (5.7), which is passed to gain access to a vertical crack and chimney system. Climb this system and belay from the top of a 10-foot flake. Continue up the chimney, passing an overhang (5.7), into the inside corner above. Thirty feet of easier climbing (5.2) on the same line takes one up to a large grassy bench for the next belay. Similar climbing for 120 feet leads to the crest of the southwest ridge at another large grassy ledge where an old ring piton may be found. The final lead starts up a short face to a left-slanting crack that is passed on the left onto an overhanging corner. Climb this corner onto a face and traverse back to the right to an inside corner with a crack. Climb the crack on the left side of the corner (5.9), past an old 1-inch angle piton, to exit left onto a belay ledge (3 feet wide, 4 feet long). This placed the 1969 party at the base of a short but very difficult face about 70 feet below the summit; time did not permit completing the route to the summit.

Variation: Doomsday Dihedral. IV, 5.9. First ascent July 11, 1970, by Jim Erickson and Dave Erickson. The major feature of this relatively long but uncertain route is a large white dihedral near the left (west) edge of the south face of Sentinel Turret. This Doomsday Dihedral is located about 400 feet above the base of the face, and a crack system can be seen leading up to the dihedral. Unfortunately, directions to reach the start of this climb are unavailable. The first pitch (5.4) goes up a 150-foot chimney to a ledge near a tree. The next lead (5.7) aims right of the dihedral on face climbing to a ledge just below two parallel left-angling cracks, which are easily seen from below. Now climb the left-hand crack (5.7), up past a bulge to a ledge just right of a large slab. The fourth short pitch (5.9) goes upward for 50 feet in a jam crack to a poor belay stance from a piton. Now traverse left (5.6) on rotten rock for 30 feet around a corner to a belay point. The sixth lead, after an additional 30-foot traverse left, reaches the dihedral, which is climbed on difficult, rotten rock (5.9) with poor protection for 50

feet. The final lead of this variation, again on poor rock, now goes up the right-hand crack above, over a roof (5.9), and ends on a ledge, roughly on the southwest ridge of Sentinel Turret. Four more leads of lesser difficulty on the ridge, where old iron from a previous party was found, are required to reach the summit. This climb is dangerous due to the rotten and sometimes poorly protected rock and contains only two enjoyable pitches; hence, it cannot be recommended.

Variation: Beeline. III, 5.8, A1 or III, 5.9. First ascent September 3, 1975, by Jim Beyer and Jerry Cantor; first free ascent July 1979, by Jim Beyer and Misa Geisey. This eight-pitch variation starts to the left (west) of the standard Sentinel Turret route but the location of its beginning is uncertain. After an initial ropelength of moderate rock (5.5) to a ledge, the second pitch moves up a face and past a crack (5.6) to a belay. The third lead goes up a groove of similar difficulty slightly to the right to the base of a prominent white open book or right-facing corner. This open book, the main feature of this variation, is climbed for one lead but is abandoned out to the left on the fifth pitch. Move left past a small right-facing corner to a second such corner and up past an overhang on the left using hand-and-fist technique (5.9) to somewhat easier face climbing and a belay. The sixth lead moves right up past a large flake to the base of an easy ramp that is followed left out to its end. Now climb back right over loose rock (5.6) to the belay for the final lead, a 4th-class pitch to a tree at the end of the climb.

Variation: Black Chimney. III, 5.9. First ascent August 1975, by David Lowe and Leigh Ortenburger. This variation ignores the admonition given in the main description and goes right at the end of the second pitch. Move right for 140 feet along a diagonal crack and ledge to large, loose, black boulders at the beginning of a vertical open chimney. The lead up this black chimney is difficult (5.9) and ends on a ledge with trees on the ridge crest. The final leads of the standard route lie somewhere above.

ROUTE 3. East Ledges. II, 5.1. First descent August 3, 1959, by Yvon Chouinard and Bob Kamps; first ascent August 26, 1964, by Ted Vaill and Brad Merry, and also apparently the route of September 7, 1964, by Chuck Satterfield, David Allen, Ron Weber, and Kathy Fauerbach. The eastern aspect of Sentinel Turret is approached out of the major drainage to the east, Sentinel Gully, which separates the Turret from Omega Buttresses. This large gully is recognized as the second stream crossing as one proceeds west along the trail after entering Death Canyon. Scramble up this gully, at places somewhat unpleasant, until one can cut back left (south) on horizontal ledges to a point about 75 feet below the notch separating Sentinel Turret from the rest of the mountain above (Albright Peak). This notch also separates the small sharp pinnacle, Harrington Spire. One pitch of roped climbing is required to gain the notch from which the summit of the Turret is easily reached.

Harrington Spire (7,800+) *(2.1 mi S of Buck Mountain)*

In the notch separating Sentinel Turret from the upper ridge that eventually leads to Albright Peak is a distinct pinnacle, which apparently remained unclimbed during the first 30 years of climbing Sentinel Turret.

ROUTE 1. East Face. II, 5.7. First ascent August 20, 1988, by Randy Harrington and Evan Kaplan. From Sentinel Gully use the same approach toward the notch between this pinnacle and Sentinel Turret, taking the large ledge out to the left (south) to reach the base of the 75-foot crack system that is used in *Sentinel Turret, Route 3.* Instead of climbing directly up to the notch, start 10 feet to the right and climb a crack for about 60 feet. At the point where the crack ends, make a traverse to the right (5.7) for 10 feet to a point where one can scramble up and right to the spire, whose summit is attained by a mantle move.

Found Arrow Spire (ca. 7,500)

(2.1 mi S of Buck Mountain)

This pinnacle is located on the east flank of Sentinel Turret about 300 feet below the summit. A prominent horizontal band of white rock cuts across both the pinnacle and the Turret.

ROUTE 1. South and East Faces. I, 5.1. First ascent August 26, 1964, by Ted Vaill and Brad Merry. From the Death Canyon trail, ascend Sentinel Gully, the talus couloir just east of Sentinel Turret, to a point where it is possible to traverse back to Found Arrow Spire on wide ledges. The Spire overhangs on all sides, but a moderate route was found from the notch to the west, between the Spire and the face of the Turret. The single-pitch climb begins on the overhanging face above the notch in a wide crack; after 15 feet move out to the right to the corner of the exposed south face and follow up and right to a small platform. The 1-yard-square summit is then easily reached from the east. Descent is made by rappel from a piton into the notch.

Omega Buttresses (ca. 9,120+)

(2.1 mi S of Buck Mountain)

Immediately to the east of Sentinel Turret is a large drainage, Sentinel Gully, shown on the map as an intermittent stream that enters the main creek in Death Canyon from the north just below the 6,800-foot level. Farther east another (the only other) larger, open gully descends toward the southeast to the mouth of the canyon where its seasonal stream ends just above the Valley Trail bridge across the Death Canyon creek. The name, Omega Buttresses, has been applied to the entire wild collection of cliffs, walls, and towers that lies between these two major gullies. To specify route locations it is useful to divide these buttresses into three sections, as defined here. Over the years since 1964, numerous rock climbs have been made in this general area and many of these routes remain little known. Some of the routes described here still have unresolved locations but, because their descriptions are available, have been included in the hope of motivating research into their whereabouts. The enterprising climber of today may well encounter old iron in unlikely places. One cause of the confusion regarding these routes is the omission of a major switchback on the Death Canyon trail from the Grand Teton quadrangle map. It is to be found between the 7,200-foot contour line legend on the east and the intermittent stream from Sentinel Gully on the west. It extends from about 6,800 to 7,000 feet. To the extent possible, the routes below are listed from west to east.

Omega Buttresses (Western)

This is the major portion of the buttresses, extending from Sentinel Gully on the west to Ship's Prow Pillar on the east. See *Photos 7* and *8.* This western section is marked by a central, deep, V-shaped indentation bounded by very steep and smooth facets composed of alternating layers of light- and dark-colored rock. The right (east) facet is cut by a conspicuous continuous diagonal crack or narrow chimney.

CHRONOLOGY

Chimney of Death: July 22, 1968, Andy Cox, Mike Yokell

Swizzle Stick: August 7, 1971, Dave Erickson, David Smith, Joseph Bowman

Trapezoid Chimney: June 5, 1975, Mike Yager, Tom Huckin

Splooge: June 28, 1976, Kelly Elder, Matthew Childs

South Buttress: July 3, 1976, Gordon Brooks, Charlie Gunn, Jim Schubert

Cathy's Corner: August 19, 1986, Cathy Pollack, Rhys Harriman

ROUTE 1. Cathy's Corner. II, 5.7. First ascent August 19, 1986, Cathy Pollack and Rhys Harriman. This four-pitch climb enters the central V-shaped indentation of the western section and ascends the chimney to its left (west) edge. Approach from the Death Canyon trail and head toward the base of the V. Considerable scrambling among the trees and slabs is required to reach the area below the V. The initial lead (5.4) goes up into the V and gains the beginning of the left chimney. The next two leads (5.6 and 5.7) follow straight up this chimney. The final face if continued directly would be much more difficult, so an exit traverse is made up and to the right (5.6). To descend, a couloir, presumably the one that separates the western and central buttresses, was utilized but some rappelling was required.

ROUTE 2. Chimney of Death. II, 5.8. First ascent July 22, 1968, by Andy Cox and Mike Yokell. Although the exact location remains uncertain, this climb was originally stated to be on the first major buttress east of Sentinel Turret, which is the western section of Omega Buttresses. Approach from the first large boulder field past the second switchback corner on the trail in Death Canyon proper; go straight up the boulder field to the base of the rock. Scramble one ropelength up and then left until under a prominent left-facing open book. The first lead (5.4) proceeds 30 feet up the book past a corner and then makes a 50-foot traverse left to a piton belay at a corner. The next pitch of 80 feet goes straight up the face above, past a ceiling and the wall above to two solid trees. Scramble up and right 30 feet to a dead tree stump for belay under an obvious wall. The long third lead (5.7) goes straight up the wall to the right of the stump for 100 feet to a left-facing open book. Climb the book for 20 feet, then 10 feet up a chimney followed by a 10-foot traverse to another belay tree. The next pitch of 140 feet goes more easily up and left to a solid belay tree in a chimney under a left-facing wall. Now climb 30 feet up the wall to a bench, where one turns left up a difficult wall with a vertical 20-foot jam crack; a boulder for belay will be found after another 20 feet. The sixth pitch starts with a 30-foot lieback in a left-facing open book toward the prominent chimney or open book (Chimney of Death), which leads for the next four leads all the way to the crest. The next 300 feet up the chimney involves moderate climbing past bulges and chockstones to reach a large roof in the chimney. The ninth lead (5.8) passes this roof by an 8-foot traverse to the right and then involves a hand traverse back left into the chimney, which is followed to the crest. The final pitch goes up the crest to the summit of the buttress.

ROUTE 3. *Swizzle Stick.* II, 5.6. First ascent August 7, 1971, by Joe Bowman, Dave Erickson, and Dave Smith. Little is known about this route, originally stated to be on the first buttress to the right (east) of Sentinel Turret. From the base of the face several hundred feet of scrambling (3.0) and climbing leads to a ledge below the steep part of the face. From this ledge the route follows a prominent crack leading up and angling slightly right. Apparently four pitches are involved with the most difficult moves (5.6) on the first and fourth leads.

ROUTE 4. *Splooge.* I, 5.7. First ascent June 28, 1976, by Kelly Elder and Matthew Childs. This very short climb is on the lowest slabs just above the main trail below the western buttress section. The route starts in a left-facing corner and moves right out onto the face from the top of the corner. The second short lead moves on up the slabby face. Descent was off to the west.

ROUTE 5. *South Buttress.* II, 5.7. First ascent July 3, 1976, by Gordon Brooks, Charley Gunn, and Jim Schubert. This climb is on the south face of the west section of Omega Buttresses, ascending the conspicuous diagonal narrow chimney on the right (east) facet of the face. This chimney is the first break in the layered wall to the right of the central indentation of the face. From the trail, scramble several hundred feet up ledges from the northeast side of Sentinel Gully. The base of the large chimney with trees at the bottom will be approached from the left. From a belay alcove above two trees near the base of this chimney traverse up and to the right, heading toward a prominent horn (5.7). Move 40 feet above the horn to the belay ledge, which is in the diagonal chimney that is followed for the next two leads. The second pitch continues up this chimney through a V notch in a roof to a thin ledge for the second belay stance. Here a second chimney with several chockstones parallels and joins the main diagonal chimney. A smaller vertical chimney with a chockstone about even with this ledge is now on the left. The next lead moves up partly on the face to the right of this chimney, partly in the chimney until access is gained onto the smooth face to the right. Now make a long traverse (5.7) out to the right on the clean face under a prominent arch (a series of roofs), then through a break in the arch and up past a 5.7 ceiling on loose blocks to reach the easy ground at the end of this third lead; a fixed piton was found on the traverse by the first-ascent party. The route ends at the top of the right shoulder of the face, a crest with trees. Descent is via ledges leading north to a gully and then a scramble down to the trail.

ROUTE 6. *Trapezoid Chimney.* II, 5.7. First ascent June 5, 1975, by Mike Yager and Tom Huckin. While the identification is not certain, it appears that this route, originally called Trapezoid Tower, follows one of the chimney systems of the western section of Omega Buttresses. The tower of this route was described as the westernmost of three towers to the east of Sentinel Turret. The summit of the tower was described as an anvil-like formation having a large indentation and roof halfway up its southeast ridge. It was also described as presenting a reddish south face, bounded by two nearly vertical, but slightly diverging cracks or chimneys that give the face a trapezoidal shape. This route ascends the rightmost of these two chimneys. Thus, it appears that this climb utilized the next steep chimney to the right (east) of that taken by the South Buttress (*Route 5*). From the highest point directly below the tower, proceed upward via 4.0 scrambling to a broad ledge where a solitary spruce (the largest tree in the vicinity) will be found. The first ropelength goes directly up a narrow crack system (5.4) containing one 5.7 mantle. An easy scramble then takes one to the base of the chimney, described above as the rightmost of the two defining the trapezoid; this chimney is followed for the remainder of the route. The next ropelength ascends a short wall to the right, connecting with the chimney 20 feet up and ending at a belay alcove. The following lead passes a large, loose chockstone flake (5.6); use caution here. A ropelength of scrambling ends at a *cul-de-sac* caused by a narrowing of the chimney. The route ascends the short, vertical 5.7 wall to the left before angling back to the top of the overhang. The top is then reached by easy scrambling. The South Buttress route probably intersects this line in the course of the last difficult pitch prior to the scrambling. The route cannot be recommended because of the loose rock encountered.

Omega Buttresses (Central)

The central section consists of the flatiron-like tower, named Omega Tower in 1964, and the climbs on either side. The name was given during the first climb on these buttresses in response to the inadvertent destruction of an expensive wristwatch, a token of Barry Corbet's membership in the 1963 American Mount Everest Expedition. In more recent years this tower has become known as Ship's Prow Pillar. This section is isolated on both sides by very steep couloirs containing loose rock and trees; these angle up to the northwest and can be found on the map. To assist in identification of Ship's Prow: From the middle of the long switchback after the second switchback corner in Death Canyon one can observe on the right (east) edge of the cliffs above a pointed pillar resembling a flatiron or the prow of a ship and bounded on the left (west) by two conspicuous, sharp-edged left-facing corners. The right dihedral, capped by a large black roof with a white vein of rock in it, is the Dihedral of Horrors (*Route 4*). The south face of the pillar to the right of these dihedrals is steep to overhanging, with another black roof, lower than the one capping the dihedral, on its right (east) side.

CHRONOLOGY

Omega Tower: August 11, 1964, Barry Corbet, Rick Medrick
   var: **D.C.D.:** August 1977, Charlie Fowler, Dennis Grabnegger, Kent Lugbill
Dihedral of Horrors: August 18, 1967, John Behrens, Peter Avenali; September 1981, Bev Boynton, Bob Graham (first free ascent)
Ship's Prow Pillar, Man-o-War: July 12, 1970, Thomas Dunwiddie, Roger Zimmerman
Cardiac Arêtes: August 9, 1981, Rich Perch, Randy Harrington
Whiton's Corner: September 4, 1983, Mark and Diane Whiton
Annals of Time: August 19, 1984, Keith Cattabriga, Dale Dawson
   var: **Lycra:** August 1987, Jay Pistono, Keith Cattabriga, Bob Stevenson
   var: **No Question:** June 25, 1993, Steve Sullivan, Mark Berry
Right Parallel Crack: July 1987, Rhys Harriman, Tim Quinlan
That's Ridiculous: July 29, 1993, Janet Wilts, Robert Irvine

ROUTE 1. *Annals of Time.* II, 5.9. First ascent August 19, 1984, by Keith Cattabriga and Dale Dawson. See *Topo 15* and *Photos 7* and *8*. On the face to the left (northwest) of the conspicuous left-facing corners mentioned earlier are two parallel cracks in an otherwise unbroken wall. This three-pitch route goes up the left of these parallel cracks.

Approach from midway along the long section of trail between the second and third switchback corners in Death Canyon, well before crossing the stream from Sentinel Gully. The climb starts with a left-facing corner (5.7). The next pitch continues up and right through some blocky terrain (5.7) to the base of the crack that can be seen from far below. This last pitch is of good quality and passes through two 5.9 roofs in its 120-foot length. The route ends on the shallow col that separates Ship's Prow from the upper mountain. For descent a 150-foot rappel from the large tree at the top of Ship's Prow deposits one in the gully immediately to the east. Scramble back down this gully to the trail.

Variation: No Question. II, 5.9+. First ascent June 25, 1993, by Steve Sullivan and Mark Berry. See *Topo 15.* This 90-foot, left-facing corner adds one pitch of climbing to *Route 1.* At the point where the approach gully narrows, move out and right and undercling around a block to get to the base of the corner.

Variation: Lycra. II, 5.10-. First ascent August 1987, by Jay Pistono, Keith Cattabriga, and Bob Stevenson. See *Topo 15.* On the next to last lead, instead of moving right and up on 5.7 rock, go straight up a crack on thin holds. Many small wires and RPs protect this pitch.

ROUTE 2. *Right Parallel Crack.* II, 5.9. First ascent July 1987, by Rhys Harriman and Tim Quinlan. See *Topo 15* and *Photo 7.* This crack is approached in the same manner as the left parallel crack (Annals of Time), but unfortunately it is an unpleasant climb, both rotten and hard.

ROUTE 3. *Whiton's Corner.* II, 5.8. First ascent September 4, 1983, by Mark and Diane Whiton. Immediately to the right of the two parallel cracks (*Routes 1* and *2*) is a corner that is approached in the same manner as the cracks. From the base of the Right Parallel Crack make a short traverse to the right and down a bit to get access to this corner. One long lead up the corner leads to the same shallow col.

ROUTE 4. *Dihedral of Horrors.* II, 5.8, A3, or II, 5.9. First ascent August 18, 1967, by John Behrens and Peter Avenali; first free ascent September 1981, by Bev Boynton and Bob Graham. See *Topo 15* and *Photo 7.* The first (rightmost) of the two vertical left-facing corners at the west edge of the south face of Ship's Prow Pillar is the Dihedral of Horrors. It is capped by a huge, flat, black-rock roof, the Diamond Roof, which is cut by a vein of white rock. The topo shows the free version of what originally was an aid route. Follow the Death Canyon trail past the two switchback corners in the canyon proper to the talus slope from which Ship's Prow Pillar is readily visible. The dihedral in the layered rock of the upper Pillar above will be obvious.

Hike up the steep talus, and then go right up a gully for several hundred feet until there is a choice between a grassy gully on the right and a couloir of good rock on the left. Take the couloir (3.0), which eventually narrows to a width of about 3 feet. Climb this narrow portion for 15 feet until

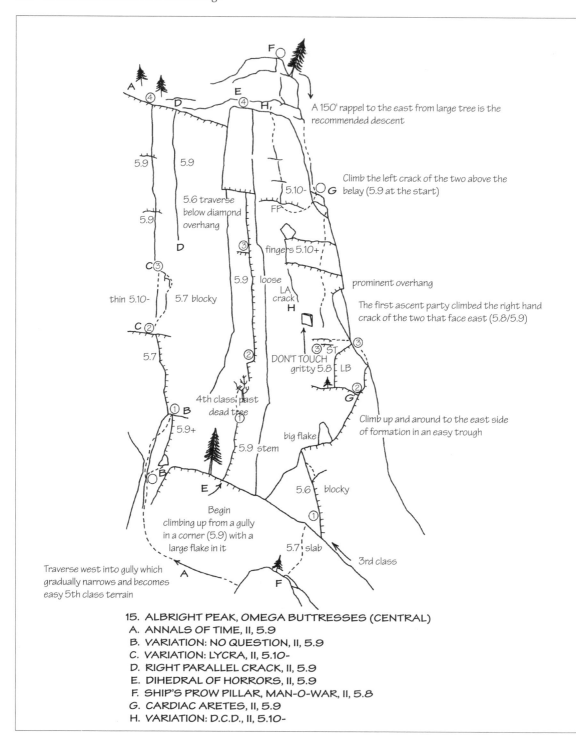

A 150' rappel to the east from large tree is the recommended descent

Climb the left crack of the two above the belay (5.9 at the start)

5.9

5.9

5.6 traverse below diamond overhang

5.9

5.10- G

D

FP

fingers 5.10+

C③

5.9 loose

thin 5.10-   5.7 blocky

LA crack

H

prominent overhang

The first ascent party climbed the right hand crack of the two that face east (5.8/5.9)

C ②

5.7

②

③ ST

③

DON'T TOUCH gritty 5.8 LB

② G

4th class past dead tree

① B

5.9+

big flake

Climb up and around to the east side of formation in an easy trough

B

5.9 stem

E

5.6 blocky

①

Begin climbing up from a gully in a corner (5.9) with a large flake in it

5.7 slab

3rd class

Traverse west into gully which gradually narrows and becomes easy 5th class terrain

A

F

15. ALBRIGHT PEAK, OMEGA BUTTRESSES (CENTRAL)
A. ANNALS OF TIME, II, 5.9
B. VARIATION: NO QUESTION, II, 5.9
C. VARIATION: LYCRA, II, 5.10-
D. RIGHT PARALLEL CRACK, II, 5.9
E. DIHEDRAL OF HORRORS, II, 5.9
F. SHIP'S PROW PILLAR, MAN-O-WAR, II, 5.8
G. CARDIAC ARETES, II, 5.9
H. VARIATION: D.C.D., II, 5.10-

it becomes possible to traverse right to a large bench. This bench has a large, living tree on it and is also the bench from which one can begin the Annals of Time climb. Dihedral of Horrors starts just to the east of the tree. Climb up using the left-facing corner (5.9) and face holds until it is possible to traverse west around the corner to a crack that leads up to the belay ledge at the base of the main dihedral. The next pitch is on gradually steepening rock beginning with liebacks for the first 10 feet, a 5.8 bulge and then finishing with a few 5.9 moves to a small, downsloping belay stance. From the stance climb up to the diamond-shaped roof (5.9 move) and then make an unlikely traverse beneath it to the right on 5.6 holds to the face around the corner. Watch out for rope drag here and continue up for 20 feet in an easy crack to complete the climb. From there a 150-foot rappel can be made to the grassy benches leading to the original grassy gully extending down to the original talus slope. This climb has been recommended for its short approach and its overall scenic location. Expect some loose and gritty rock, however.

ROUTE 5. *Omega Tower.* II, 5.8, A1. First ascent August 11, 1964, by Barry Corbet and Rick Medrick. This was the original climb in the area east of Sentinel Turret, made on a Guides' Day outing. It is clear that Omega Tower, named at the time, is the same as Ship's Prow Pillar, but the exact location of this 1964 route is uncertain. It is thought to be located immediately to the right of the descent gully from the routes on Ship's Prow Pillar. From the trail at the entrance to Death Canyon (below the 7,000-foot level), a flatiron-like tower, the second of three, can be seen up to the right (north) on the eastern fringe of the rock. This route ascends the short, steep face of the "small flatiron-like" tower, which must be Ship's Prow Pillar. Scramble to the highest point of 3.0 rock at the base of the face. About 10 feet out to the right on a diagonal ledge the belayer can be anchored. Now traverse 15 feet up and left along a narrow ledge to a vertical lieback crack that can be climbed with good holds to a large ledge on the right corner of the face. Next traverse left around a corner onto the center of the face where 20 feet of delicate 5.8 face climbing with excellent protection bring one to a good belay ledge. The second lead of this short route requires great care in passing around and up a very loose flake to a short wall leading to the bottom of an overhang. A good crack in the middle of the overhang can be climbed with aid to the easy rock above that leads to the top of the tower.

Variation: D.C.D. II, 5.10. First ascent August 1977, by Charlie Fowler, Dennis Grabnegger, and Kent Lugbill. See *Topo 15.* This two-pitch variation is known only through a rudimentary topo. The location is uncertain but it is tentatively identified on *Topo 15* as traversing left from the sloping ledge at the top of the fourth pitch of Cardiac Arêtes to a fixed piton at a 5.10 overhang. The original description indicates that the first lead from this point is a 50-foot perfect hand jam crack (5.10), which starts as right-facing,

continues with the midsection left-facing, and ends as a right-facing crack or corner, past a small overhang, to a second sloping ledge for the belay point. The second pitch of 150 feet is again up a crack (5.6), past a small overhang or two, to the top of the climb. The summit of Omega Tower, with cairn, lies off to the left from the top of this D.C.D. (Death Canyon Direct) route. Descent can be made via rappel from a tree which is off to the right, back down to the initial gully.

ROUTE 6. *Cardiac Arêtes.* II, 5.9. First ascent August 9, 1981, by Rich Perch and Randy Harrington. See *Topo 15* and *Photo 7.* While at least two climbs preceded this ascent, this route has the advantage of being well known and its details are presented in the topo. Cardiac Arêtes, a two-lead variation on the previous Man-O-War route, takes a line out on the south face of the buttress on steep, predominantly good rock with adequate protection. In addition to the five pitches shown on the topo there are two more (5.8) along the arête ending at the notch separating the summit. The approach is via the Death Canyon trail to the second switchback corner in the canyon. Scramble some 500 feet to the trees at the base of the buttress to begin the climb. Beware of the loose flake on the fourth pitch.

ROUTE 7. *Ship's Prow Pillar, Man-o-War.* II, 5.8. First ascent July 12, 1970, by Thomas Dunwiddie and Roger Zimmerman. See *Topo 15* and *Photo 8.* This climb goes up the east face of the central Omega Buttress. Approach via a scramble up the talus to the base of the buttress from the second switchback corner on the Death Canyon trail in the canyon proper and approach the pillar from the right (east). The first pitch is recognizable as a nice moderate-angle slab. The first lead goes up and along the sharp right edge of the slab to a large chockstone capping the break between the slab and the right wall. Now face climb (5.7) on the left to a small grassy spot above. The next pitch starts from the meadow in a lieback (5.7) up flakes on the right side. Follow the corner-crack directly up past a few bulges to reach another grassy ledge for the belay. The third lead takes a 6-inch crack in the inside corner above the belay ledge to a large prominent flake. Pass the flake to the right to an easy trough leading up and right, through a narrow and steep bulge in the trough to reach a low-angle slab that faces southeast. Climb to the top of the slab to the base of a steep east-facing wall, below the black roof on the east side of the south face mentioned earlier. On the next pitch, the crux of the route (5.8), pass the overhang using the rightmost of two cracks to the right of the overhang; this crack is better described as a tight dihedral with only a thin crack in the back. In this dihedral use face holds on the right, until a good horizontal hold in a crack on the left permits passing the difficult bulge at the top of the dihedral. The final long lead (5.7) follows the crack above to the top, passing three bulges or overhangs on the left, right, and left, in that order. The pitch ends with easier rock. All leads were a full 150 feet, except for the crux, and are well protected on excellent rock. The descent is located in the gully to the east.

ROUTE 8. *That's Ridiculous.* I, 5.9. First ascent July 29, 1993, by Janet Wilts and Robert Irvine. This climb is located on the south face of a small pinnacle located southeast of Ship's Prow. Use the same approach and, at the same elevation that one would traverse west to the base of the Ship's Prow routes, go east to the base of this climb. Begin by climbing the right crack on the south face just left of an overhang. The crack widens to offwidth size; climb past a ledge and a bulge to the belay (145 feet). The next pitch ascends the sharp hand crack to the left and then around on the west side of the arête. Face climbing takes one back to the east side and the top of the climb.

Omega Buttresses (Eastern)

The large eastern section of Omega Buttresses lies to the east of Ship's Prow Pillar and is separated from it by a substantial steep couloir.

ROUTE 1. *Sherm's Crack.* I, 5.9. First ascent June 19, 1976, by Sherm Wilson, Don Hultz, and Mo Donohue. Sherm's Crack is on the buttress to the east of Ship's Prow Pillar. From the right place on the Death Canyon trail, one can see a steep, orange slab with a crack up the middle. Approach from the second switchback corner on the trail in the canyon proper and scramble up to the base of the crack. The route consists of one pitch up the difficult crack.

ROUTE 2. *Donini's Crack.* II, 5.10. First complete ascent July 26, 1976, by Rich Perch and Jay Wilson; an incomplete attempt had been made in June or early July 1976, by Jim Donini. Approach as for Sherm's Crack (*Route 1*). Climb the one pitch up Sherm's Crack and then wander on ledges up to a right-leaning crack. The next lead goes up through an overhang, a 5.10 roof. The route ends with a mixture of climbing, scrambling, and roofs, including some 5.9 rock. From the top the descent is over to the left and down the gully just east of Ship's Prow Pillar.

ROUTE 3. *Crack of Dawn.* III, 5.10. First ascent August 20, 1987, by Yvon Chouinard and Sandy Stewart. This climb is on the first major rock formation on the north side of Death Canyon. Take the trail into Death Canyon to the point where the first stream crosses the trail. Hike up the streambed to the base of the buttress. The first pitch is an obvious 1½- to 2-inch perfect jam crack (5.8) on a vertical wall. The next lead, directly above on an indistinct prow, goes up to and over a short overhang, where one moves left back onto the prow (5.9); this is a runout lead on crumbly rock. The third pitch is difficult (5.9) and continuous up a red rock wall, followed by another lead over a 5.9 overhang. After a fifth pitch on enjoyable 5.7 rock, the final short lead on the last wall goes straight up cracks (5.8), finishing off to the right on 5.10 moves. The descent from this route is via scrambling off to the right.

Ticky-Tacky Pinnacles (ca. 8,160+)
(2.1 mi S of Buck Mountain)

These two small pinnacles lie on the eastern fringe of the various cliffs on the north side of Death Canyon and are separated from Ship's Prow Pillar by a broad col with a tree. A good view of the pinnacles can be obtained by traversing left (west) out from this col. The name was applied after ticks were unintentionally found on the higher pinnacle by the first-ascent party. The second pinnacle (Tacky) has a prominent 6-foot S-shaped crack on its west face.

ROUTE 1. *West Side.* I, 5.6. First ascent July 4, 1964, by Bill and Julie Briggs. From the second switchback corner on the trail in Death Canyon continue on the trail 40 yards to a talus slope. Ascend this talus slope 150 feet to a buttress that blocks access to a large couloir. Pass this buttress on the left up to a large chockstone and cave. Gain the couloir by passing the chockstone on the right. Directly above on the left side of the couloir is Ship's Prow Pillar. Continue up the couloir for a few hundred feet to the col separating Ticky-Tacky Pinnacles from the pillar. Take ledges out onto the west face of the first pinnacle (Ticky). At the end of the ledges a 10-foot hand traverse takes one to easier ground below the notch between the two pinnacles.

ALBRIGHT PEAK (PEAK 10,552)
(0.9 mi S of Static Peak)

Map: Grand Teton

This peak along with its neighbor to the north, Static Peak, forms a high and elongated extension of the southeast ridge of Buck Mountain, adding to its apparent bulk. The upper 1,000 feet of the peak are easy from all directions, but on the south the Pleistocene glacial action formed Death Canyon, leaving the lower 2,000 feet carved into steep walls of predominately good crystalline rock, yielding the excellent routes that are now described under *Death Canyon, North Side Rock Climbs.* The Alaska Basin Trail provides easy access to the summit of this peak, as does its eastern slope. The peak was officially recognized as Albright Peak in 1993 during the celebration associated with the fiftieth anniversary of the creation of the Jackson Hole National Monument by Franklin D. Roosevelt. This act of preservation culminated the work and dedication of such visionaries as Horace M. Albright and John D. Rockefeller, Jr.

CHRONOLOGY

North Ridge: [probable] June 1934, T. F. Murphy, Robert E. Brislawn

East Slope: July 6, 1960, William and Harriette Wallace

Southwest Ridge: August 18, 1975, Leigh Ortenburger, John Whitesel

ROUTE 1. *Southwest Ridge*. II, 5.6. First ascent August 18, 1975, by Leigh Ortenburger and John Whitesel. The summit pyramid of Albright Peak (Peak 10,552) extends in a modest ridge to the southwest for about 0.75 mile, where it ends as the top of Cathedral Rock, before it drops precipitously, forming the north wall of Death Canyon. The rock climbs of Cathedral Rock all have used the west ledges and gully for their descent route back into Death Canyon, rather than continuing along the upper southwest ridge to the summit of Peak 10,552. This route attained the upper ridge at its extreme southwest point (9,440+) from the east. Take the Death Canyon trail to the second stream crossing, the one from the large drainage, Sentinel Gully, which separates Sentinel Turret from Omega Buttresses. Follow the East Ledges route on Sentinel Turret (see *Sentinel Turret, Route 3*) to the notch separating the Turret from the ridge above. Pass the pinnacle in the notch and climb one or two pitches up to the north out of the notch. The next portion of the route involves scrambling, with occasional roped climbing depending on the exact route chosen, to reach the extreme southwest point described above. From this point to the summit of Peak 10,552, there are no serious difficulties, although some scrambling requiring care is involved in passing a rocky portion of the ridge crest.

ROUTE 2. *East Slope*. I, 1.0. First ascent July 6, 1960, by William and Harriette Wallace. The open eastern slope of this peak offers no difficulty to the experienced cross-country hiker. This slope is most directly approached via a bushwhack up from the Phelps Lake Overlook, the initial high point on the Death Canyon trail. It can also be reached from the drainage east of Albright Peak and south of Stewart Draw.

ROUTE 3. ☞*North Ridge*. I, 1.0. Probable first ascent in June 1934 by T. F. Murphy and Robert E. Brislawn. First known ascent June 1957, by Howard R. Stagner, Jr., Tom Haggart, David Chaterfield, and Fred Fish. The obvious approach to this peak is via the Alaska Basin Trail in Death Canyon, which leads to the saddle between this peak and Static Peak. The short ridge above, leading south directly to the summit, is not difficult.

STATIC PEAK (11,303)

Map: Grand Teton

This high but minor summit is frequently and easily climbed from the Static Peak divide (10,160+) and is an excellent objective for hikers of the Alaska Basin Trail. A small dying glacier lies at the base of the steep and crumbly north face of this peak, immediately south of Timberline Lake. A triangulation station was established on the summit of Static Peak in 1946 by Curtis LeFever of the U.S. Coast and Geodetic Survey.

Southwest Ridge: [probable] June 1934, T. F. Murphy, Robert E. Brislawn
North Ridge: August 10, 1953, Paul Burgess, Alan Williamson (descent)
East Ridge: June 6, 1961, Mike Petrilak, Scott Arighi, Joan Oosterwyk, Irma Ireland, D. Jan Black
North Face: June 19, 1971, Jeb Schenck, Bob Stevenson

ROUTE 1. ☞*Southwest Ridge*. I, 1.0. Probable first ascent in June 1934, by T. F. Murphy and Robert E. Brislawn. Almost all the ascents of this peak have been made from the Alaska Basin Trail, which mounts the southwest ridge of Static Peak to within 500 feet of the summit. *Time: 40 minutes* from the Alaska Basin Trail; *6½ hours* from the Death Canyon trailhead.

ROUTE 2. *East Ridge*. I, 1.0. First recorded ascent June 6, 1961, by Mike Petrilak, Scott Arighi, Joan Oosterwyk, Irma Ireland, and D. Jan Black. Approach from upper Stewart Draw. There is some loose rock on this ridge, but no difficulties.

ROUTE 3. *North Face*. II, 5.4. First ascent June 19, 1971, by Jeb Schenck and Bob Stevenson. Approach via Stewart Draw and Timberline Lake and take the steep snow leading to the base of the north face. This face is generally loose and rotten except for the dihedral used for this ascent. The route goes up this dihedral where the rock is reasonably sound for a few feet on either side.

ROUTE 4. *North Ridge*. II, 5.1. First descent August 10, 1953, by Paul Burgess and Alan Williamson. No information is available, but the rock on this ridge is likely to be unsound.

PEAK 10,696   *(0.8 mi E of Buck Mountain)*

Map: Grand Teton

This rounded forepeak of Buck Mountain provides the northern counterpart to Static Peak on the south. It is seldom climbed because Buck Mountain provides the primary objective of climbers in this part of the range. This peak and its northeast extension over Point 9,975 have the same effect as Static and Albright Peaks, in making Buck Mountain appear from the valley to be more massive than it really is. When one looks up at this area from the valley floor, a very large avalanche path will be seen immediately south of Point 9,975. Flanking the slide path on the south is a triangular face just in front of Peak 10,696. The name "25-Short" (referring to the number of feet that Point 9,975 is shy of 10,000) has been applied to the slopes north and east of Point 9,975. Its neighbor to the south, the large triangular face already mentioned, is widely known as "Maverick Ridge." These two areas are frequented by skiers throughout the winter months. The skiing potential of "25-Short" was first noticed by residents of Beaver Creek in the early 1950s and then later again by Barry Corbet in the early 1960s. Accessed today from either the Taggart Lake trailhead or the vicinity of the old Whitegrass Ranch, these two areas may be the most frequented sections of the Teton backcountry during the winter.

ROUTE 1. West Ridge. I, 4.0. Probable first ascent June 1934, by T. F. Murphy and Robert E. Brislawn; first recorded ascent June 6, 1961, by David Grant, Lucille Grant, Tom Wepfer, David Murray, and Paul Weinstein, who found an empty cairn on the summit. From Timberline Lake (see *Buck Mountain, Route 8*) proceed to the saddle separating this peak from Buck. The first portion of the ridge is steep and contains some loose rock; this can be climbed directly or bypassed on the north. Bypass the small gendarmes above and to the right (south); then climb the summit block via a short 4.0 pitch.

ROUTE 2. East Ridge. I, 1.0. First ascent July 10, 1966, by Thomas Gagnon, Douglas Curr, Gene Eckman, and Robert Andrews. Approach can be made directly from the east up from the Valley Trail or from the vicinity of Taggart Lake, using game trails to timberline, and then along the northeast ridge over Point 9,975 to the summit.

STEWART DRAW, SOUTH SIDE ROCK CLIMBS (CA. 9,000)

Map: Grand Teton

The standard approach for the regular route on Buck Mountain is from the Death Canyon trailhead up through Stewart Draw, the small steep canyon on the east slope. A rock buttress rising from the south side of this canyon provides a relatively attractive area for rock climbing, because the approach is conveniently short. The routes are listed from west to east.

ROUTE 1. Peaches. II, 5.8. First ascent June 28, 1980, by Yvon Chouinard and Kathryn Collins. See *Topo 16.* Approach via the trail into Stewart Draw (see *Buck Mountain*). About halfway up this small canyon, a prominent wall will be seen on the south side of the drainage, where this climb is located. This route starts just left of an overhang at the base of the buttress. The technical details of this route are presented in the topo. In some places on this route the rock is loose and protection is at times scarce. Descent is easily made to the northwest to the base of the climb.

  Variation: Cash for Less. II, 5.10-. First ascent July 1987, by Paul Gagner and Jim Woodmencey. See *Topo 16.* This variation, on the golden rock face to the left of Peaches, required two bolts for protection in addition to two fixed pitons. It consists of a single, difficult pitch.

ROUTE 2. Spigolo Nero. II, 5.7. First ascent July 1980, by Yvon Chouinard and Kathryn Collins. This route is to the left (east) of the more popular Peaches. The first lead passes an overhang (5.7) on the left. Two more pitches lead to the final section, consisting of cracks.

ROUTE 3. Larson Ridge. II, 5.8. First ascent July 18, 1980, by Leo Larson and Randy Harrington. See *Topo 16.* The approach and descent for this route are the same as for Peaches. This five-pitch route follows the left (east) ridge of the steep wall of the Peaches buttress and contains similar interesting climbing, although there is some loose rock and lichens. The climbing begins immediately to the right of the left (east) ridge at the base of the buttress, on gray rock left of a group of large boulders. Parallel the ridge up past a 5.8 overhang, tending right on a fractured wall, past a large roof, until one can turn upward in an overhanging lieback (5.8) to gain the ridge to the left. The second lead (150 feet) proceeds up the ridge on slabs, past a 5.8 overhang and a second smaller overhang to the belay. Two pitches of easier climbing on the ridge crest lead to the final short 5.7 pitch on poor rock on the summit pinnacle.

BUCK MOUNTAIN (11,938)

Map: Grand Teton

The first ascent of this major peak was made by the topographer T. M. Bannon and his recorder, George A. Buck, ten days after the Owen–Spalding party climbed the Grand Teton in 1898. On the summit they built a large cairn for use as a triangulation point known as "Buck Station," doubtlessly named after Bannon's recorder. In more recent years, the name "Alpenglow" has been suggested, after the appearance of its north face in the evening from the vicinity of Jenny Lake; but the name "Buck" retains the official sanction of the U.S. Board on Geographic Names. The southernmost of the crystalline peaks, Buck Mountain is also the highest peak south of the Garnet Canyon group and therefore its summit offers an excellent and unusual view of the rest of the range. It is a fine objective for the mountaineer. In the early part of this century, Buck Mountain may have been climbed by local ranchers, but no records were left. From the east, which is the usual route, the ascent is not hard but, from any other direction, varying degrees of difficulty will be met. Several fine climbs have been worked out on the north side while much of the south remains unexplored. The high basin just below the south cliffs of Buck Mountain is traversed by the Skyline Trail and has come to be known in recent years as "No-Wood Basin."

To approach the eastern routes on the peak via Stewart Draw start from the Death Canyon trailhead. This entire region is confounded by obscure remnants of old horse trails dating from days of the White Grass Ranch. Follow the Valley Trail west toward the Phelps Lake Overlook about

16. **STEWART DRAW, SOUTH SIDE ROCK CLIMBS**
A. **LARSON RIDGE, II, 5.8**
B. **PEACHES, II, 5.8**
C. **VARIATION: CASH FOR LESS, II, 5.10-**

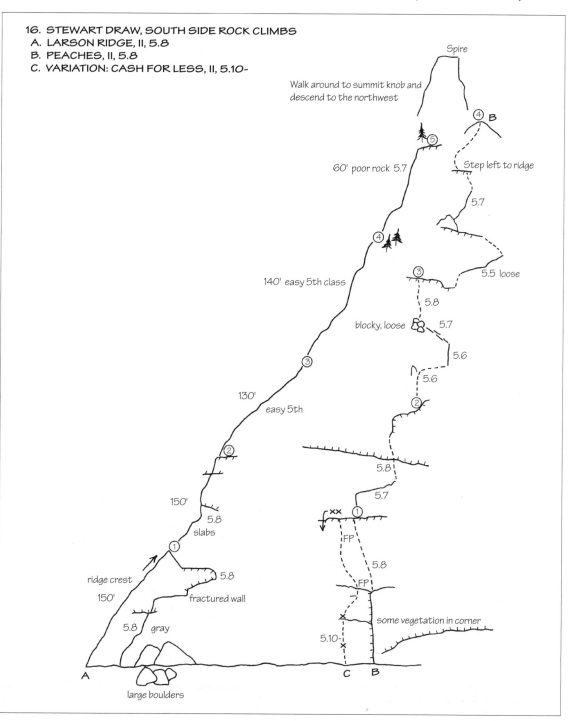

Spire

Walk around to summit knob and
descend to the northwest

④ B

⑤

60' poor rock 5.7

Step left to ridge

5.7

④

5.5 loose

140' easy 5th class

③

5.8

blocky, loose   5.7

5.6

5.6

③

②

130'

easy 5th

②

5.8

5.7

150'

xx ①

5.8   ↓

slabs   FP

①   5.8

ridge crest

150'   5.8   FP

fractured wall

5.8   gray   x   some vegetation in corner

5.10-   x

A   C   B

large boulders

0.75 mile until, just before the third footbridge on the trail, a small subsidiary trail leads off to the north. Take this old trail into a large meadow, but do not continue all the way around the western edge of the meadow because the trail is easily lost. Instead, hike into the meadow for 100 yards along the trail and then angle across the meadow aiming for the western edge of trees that extend into the meadow from the east; erratic boulders will be found here. Now follow due north along the edge of these trees passing small fragments of old trails, and cross two small creeks, the second of which is marked by a large cairn on its south side. Continue north along the edge of the trees until two horse trails that join are encountered. Take this trail, now well defined, over a small ridge and into Stewart Draw, crossing the drainage stream near a huge boulder. Follow this substantial trail up the canyon past the old horse camp, staying mostly on the right (north) side of the creek, to the large cirque below Timberline Lake. One way to reach the lake is to take the large couloir that leads southwest from this cirque up the south flank of Static Peak and then traverse back to the right (north) onto the moraine that borders the lake on the east. If a two-day trip is desired, a camping spot can be found along the lakeshore or in the cirque below.

The approach for the southern routes also starts from the Death Canyon trailhead and takes the Death Canyon and Alaska Basin trails to No-Wood Basin. For the north face routes, approach via the south fork of Avalanche Canyon.

CHRONOLOGY

East Face: August 21, 1898, T. M. Bannon, George A. Buck

Northeast Chimney: August 15, 1931, Fritiof Fryxell
   var: August 17, 1949, William Primak, Edmund Lowe, Reinhold Mankau
   var: **Sowles:** August 12, 1962, David Sowles, Robert Brooke, Sherman Lehman

East Ridge: August 23, 1934, Ernest Scheef, Heinz Recker

South Couloir: September 17, 1934, Floyd Wilson, Felix Bloch
   var: August 17, 1956, John Fonda, Marilyn Domer, Frank Pitman

Southeast Ridge: October 6, 1935, Phil Smith, Malcolm Smith
   var: August 1, 1953, Rainer, Beth, Peter, and David Schickele
   var: August 3, 1962, Don Monk, Les Wilson, George Wallerstein, John Post
   var: September 15, 1963, Chuck Satterfield, Bruce Morley

Northeast Couloir: July 2, 1937, Donald Grant, Robert Grant

North Face, West Couloir: July 16, 1940, Paul Petzoldt, Elizabeth Cowles (Partridge) (ascent); June 14, 1946, Dick Pownall, Albert Boursault (descent)

Southeast Couloir: August 29, 1940, John and Elizabeth Buck

North Face, East Couloir: July 17, 1941, Fred Ayres, Alan Cameron, Judy Cameron

West Ridge: August 27, 1935, Phil Smith, Herman Petzoldt, Walcott Watson (attempt); August 11, 1953, Leigh Ortenburger, Steve Jervis, Mary Sylvander (descent); July 16, 1957, John Dietschy, David Dingman, James Langford, Karl Pfiffner (ascent)

North-Northwest Ridge: July 23, 1954, Richard Emerson, Donald Decker, William Clayton
   var: **The Wedge:** August 2, 1961, David Dornan, Peter Lev, Herb Swedlund
   var: **The Free Wedge:** August 14, 1993, Greg Miles, Mark Limage

North Central Ridge: August 23, 1959, Barry Corbet, Rick Medrick, Sterling Neale

West Summit, South Face: July 28, 1964, Rick Medrick, Dean Moore

Southwest Couloir: July 26, 1980, Randy Harrington

West Summit, South Ridge: June 28, 1981, Yvon Chouinard, Juris Krisjansons

North Face, The Buck Sanction: August 6, 1992, Tom Turiano, Stephen Koch

ROUTE 1. West Ridge. II, 5.7. First descent August 11, 1953, by Leigh Ortenburger, Steve Jervis, and Mary Sylvander; first ascent July 16, 1957, by John Dietschy, David Dingman, James Langford, and Karl Pfiffner; attempted on August 27, 1935, by Phil Smith, Herman Petzoldt, and Walcott Watson. This is the ridge that forms the southwest boundary of the south fork of Avalanche Canyon. The best approach is probably via the "Skyline Trail," although the ridge can be reached more directly via the south fork of Avalanche Canyon. In addition to its west summit, Buck Mountain has another lower subsidiary west peak. The beginning of this ridge involves little more than uphill walking, but one rotten overhanging corner pitch is required to reach the easy scramble to the top of the west peak. Between the west peak and the west summit is a large gendarme with a smooth south face. Two pitches up a steep shelf on the west face of this obstacle lead to a third rather difficult pitch up and right (south) around the top of the gendarme. From the notch behind this tower, moderate climbing brings one to the west summit. The only remaining difficulty now is a short, overhanging pitch just past the col between the west summit and the main east summit

(5.7). The rotten rock encountered makes this route somewhat hazardous. *Time: 6½ hours* from the "Skyline Trail." See *American Alpine Journal,* 9, no. 2 (1954), pp. 147–149; 10, no. 2 (1958), pp. 85–88.

ROUTE 2. Southwest Couloir. II, 5.7. First ascent July 26, 1980, by Randy Harrington. See *Photo 9.* From the extensive talus slope lying at the base of the west peak, this southwest couloir slants up to the right toward the col which separates the west peak of Buck Mountain from the upper west ridge. Scramble up this couloir until directly beneath the gendarme on the west ridge (see *Route 1*), where a secondary open couloir is taken easily to the right (east). Ascend this couloir until its right fork steepens, then turn directly up, or slightly left (west) to the ridge just behind (east of) the gendarme. From this point the upper West Ridge route is joined, staying slightly on the north side, and is followed to the summit. The most difficult pitch on this route is the short, overhanging lead at the notch between the west summit and the main summit.

ROUTE 3. West Summit, South Face. II, 5.8. First ascent July 28, 1964, by Rick Medrick and Dean Moore. See *Photo 9.* This face, or buttress, which is approached by Death Canyon and the "Skyline Trail," leads to the west summit of Buck Mountain. The beginning of the climb, amid loose rock, is in the gully in the lower right edge of the face. Climb about 120 feet up a diagonal ledge to the left until the ledge ends at the beginning of a sloping chimney. After ascending this easy chimney for 15 feet, the second lead passes the steep wall above via a 15-foot overhanging jam crack (5.8); this crack seems to be the only break in the wall. Above this crack traverse to the left until it is possible to climb around and over a number of blocks to a ledge that leads back to the right to the belay point. The third lead ascends easy overhangs on the right, reaching, via 4.0 rock, a good belay at the start of the upper half of the face. From this position the face appears formidable. The next pitch is well protected and easier than it appears. First traverse left for 40 feet, then around some blocks for 30 feet, and finish by climbing up and to the right past blocks and flakes to a good ledge. The fifth lead traverses up and around a corner to the right before continuing for 100 feet to a good belay below an overhang. The last pitch goes over this overhang onto a ledge and then proceeds to the right to the bottom of a corner. This corner is readily climbed via small holds on the left face and the crack in the corner. This section can be well protected, and one exits easily to the right over the overhang at the top of the crack. Scrambling then leads to the west summit; the main summit can be reached as in *Route 1.* This route is an interesting problem in routefinding, and care should be taken with the considerable quantity of loose rock on the ledges. The climb can be compared to that of the southwest ridge of Symmetry Spire.

ROUTE 4. West Summit, South Ridge. II, 5.8. First ascent June 28, 1981, by Yvon Chouinard and Juris Krisjansons. See *Photo 9.* This route lies to the right (south) of *Route 3* but still avoids the initial section of this well-defined ridge. Climb the right-hand portion of the south (or southwest) face of the west summit to gain the crest of the south ridge at the lowest convenient point. The ridge is then followed all the way to the west summit, from which one takes the west ridge to the summit of the mountain.

ROUTE 5. South Couloir. II, 5.7. First ascent September 17, 1934, by Floyd Wilson and Felix Bloch. See *Photo 9.* The south couloir runs diagonally up the south face to the notch that separates the sharp west summit (ca. 11,800) from the higher east summit. From the Skyline Trail south of Buck, climb the shallow couloir. Pass on the right (east) a short cliff near the bottom of the couloir to reach the notch in the summit ridge (the same notch is reached from the north by *Route 13*). The west summit can now be reached very easily; but to attain the main summit on the right (east), one must surmount a short, overhanging pitch on the ridge crest (5.7). The 1934 party found a cairn of unknown origin on the west summit. *Time: 8½ hours* from the Death Canyon trailhead.

Variation: II, 5.4. First ascent August 17, 1956, by John Fonda, Marilyn Domer, and Frank Pitman. This party apparently avoided the 5.7 pitch out of the notch on the ridge crest, by turning straight up the wall shortly before reaching the notch at the upper end of the couloir. This took them directly to the summit.

ROUTE 6. Southeast Ridge. II, 4.0. First ascent October 6, 1935, by Phil Smith and Malcolm Smith. See *Photo 10.* The southeast ridge of Buck Mountain rises from the saddle connecting Static Peak with Buck Mountain. Although the original climb was in 1935, the standard route on this pleasant ridge is the following *1963 variation.* The lower portion of the southeast ridge of Buck Mountain contains a large, distinct tower, separated from the upper portion of the ridge by a small notch. There are couloirs on both sides, north and south, leading to this notch. This route easily ascends the couloir on the north side from the vicinity of Timberline Lake, usually approached via Stewart Draw. One could also approach over the Buck–Static saddle from the Alaska Basin Trail and No-Wood Basin on the south. After reaching the notch, the only difficulty on the upper ridge is a row of overhangs about two-thirds of the way up the ridge. Pass these on the left (south or west), and then scramble to the summit. The 1935 party may well have used, in part, the ridge to the left (south) of the main southeast ridge; this ridge begins below the notch and blends into the main ridge about 300 feet above the notch.

Variation: II, 5.1. First ascent August 1, 1953, by Rainer, Beth, Peter, and David Schickele. See *Photo 9.* The southeast ridge can also be reached by the easy couloir on the south side of the ridge. This couloir leads to the notch behind the initial tower on the ridge. The ridge can probably be reached at several places near or above this notch. The approach for this variation is from the Skyline Trail in Death Canyon.

Variation: II, 5.4. First ascent August 3, 1962, by Don Monk, Les Wilson, George Wallerstein, and John Post. See *Photo 9.* The couloir, leading from the south to the notch on the southeast ridge, is bounded on the left (west) by a ridge subsidiary to the main southeast ridge. This variation ascends the subsidiary ridge, or face, staying well left of the couloir. After meeting the main southeast ridge about 300 feet above the notch, the climbing becomes easier.

Variation: II, 5.6. First ascent September 15, 1963, by Chuck Satterfield and Bruce Morley. See *Photos 9* and *10.* From Timberline Lake, scramble up to the saddle between Static Peak and Buck Mountain, where this ridge route begins; in early season an ice axe will be needed to reach this saddle. The first section of this ridge forms a large tower with a distinct, separate summit. The initial portion of the variation uses the south ridge of this tower, the first arête left (south) of the Buck–Static saddle. From the saddle three leads of (5.4) climbing up the crest or slightly to the left of the crest lead to the summit of this tower. Descend about 30 feet to the east and contour around to reach the notch where the upper ridge begins. This upper section is not difficult, bypassing some overhangs on the left (south and west), before the final scramble to the summit. This is a pleasant but short climb on good rock, offering an alternative to the standard East Face or East Ridge route.

ROUTE 7. *Southeast Couloir.* II, 5.1. First ascent August 29, 1940, by John and Elizabeth Buck. West-southwest of Timberline Lake is the saddle separating Static Peak from Buck Mountain. Rising from this saddle is the southeast ridge of Buck, which includes a large, distinct tower. This southeast ridge effectively separates the east and south faces of Buck, so that a different approach is usually used for these two faces. The main cliff band, below the upper east face of Buck Mountain, rises directly above and west of Timberline Lake and is separated from the southeast ridge by the steep and narrow southeast couloir. Because the beginning of the couloir is almost at the same level as the Buck–Static saddle, one can approach this route from No-Wood Basin on the south side of Buck and traverse from the saddle over to the bottom of the couloir, as was done by the first-ascent party. This apparently was the first time the east side of the mountain had been reached in this way. More directly, one can ascend the talus slope above Timberline Lake and then climb the couloir. The top opens out onto the upper east face, where *Route 6* can then be easily followed to the summit. In early season steep snow will be encountered on this route, requiring knowledge of the use of the ice axe.

ROUTE 8. ☞*East Face.* II, 3.0. First ascent August 21, 1898, by T. M. Bannon and George A. Buck; on May 29, 1961, Barry Corbet, Elliot Goss, and Anne LaFarge ascended this route on skis. See *Photo 10.* This pleasant climb is the popular and standard route to reach the summit of this major Teton peak. Both the approach and the summit view are scenic and the time required for the ascent is not excessive, all combining to make an enjoyable day in the mountains. From the Timberline Lake cirque pass the steep cliffs rising above on the right (north), then make a long upward traverse to the left over moderate snow (early season) back to the center of the face. More slabs and grassy ledges with some snow patches (depending on the season) then lead to the summit. As cliff bands lurk below their lower edges, use great caution in traversing these snow patches. In early season the climbing will be almost entirely on snow from the cirque to the summit. *Time: 6¼ to 7 hours* from the Death Canyon trailhead. See *Appalachia,* 18, no. 3 (June 1931), pp. 209–232, illus.

ROUTE 9. *East Ridge.* II, 4.0. First ascent August 23, 1934, by Ernest Scheef and Heinz Recker. See *Photos 10* and *11.* This enjoyable ridge climb uses the same approach to Timberline Lake as *Route 6,* but is slightly more difficult. From the cirque at the lake, after passing the initial cliff band on the right, traverse farther right (north) to the crest of the east ridge and follow it to the summit. In places the ridge is sharp and exposed, providing excellent views down the north face. See *Appalachia,* 18, no. 3 (June 1931), pp. 209–232, illus.

ROUTE 10. *Northeast Couloir.* II, 3.0. First ascent July 2, 1937, by Donald Grant and Robert Grant. This is the easiest route from Avalanche Canyon. Climb directly up from the small, shallow lake in the lower south fork of Avalanche Canyon toward the very broad talus bench that lies below the north face of Peak 10,696. Follow this bench up and right (west) over huge talus boulders to the saddle between Peak 10,696 and Buck Mountain. From this point one can either stay on the crest and climb the east ridge or make an upward traverse to the left (south) and complete the ascent via the regular East Face route. *Time: 6 hours* from the south fork of Avalanche Canyon.

ROUTE 11. *Northeast Chimney.* II, 4.0. First ascent August 15, 1931, by Fritiof Fryxell. See *Photo 11.* Proceed up Avalanche Canyon to the vicinity of the shallow lake just above the first headwall in the south fork. Easily visible up the canyon is a large talus cone and couloir east of the talus leading to the bench below the north face. This talus cone is west of the slope that leads to the main saddle between Peak 10,696 and Buck Mountain. Ascend this cone and steep couloir for a few hundred feet until it opens out into a bowllike snowfield just below and north of the east ridge. Turn right (west) up the snowfield or slabs, depending on the season, to a wide, steep 200-foot chimney. From the top of this chimney traverse left onto the crest of the east ridge and follow this ridge to the summit. In early season or even midseason, this enjoyable climb will be largely on snow. But in late season the lower snow chute develops crevasses with overhanging upper lips, forcing one onto the rock, which is steep, very wet, and downsloping. The upper chimney will be bare, with some ice and chockstones exposed. See *Appalachia*, 19, no. 1 (June 1932), pp. 86–96.

Variation: II, 4.0. First ascent August 17, 1949, by Edmund Lowe, William Primak, and Reinhold Mankau. Instead of climbing directly up the couloir from the top of the talus cone, cut over to the right (west) and attain the crest of the ridge, which juts out at right angles to the north face. Follow this ridge to the bowllike snowfield to rejoin the main route. See *Chicago Mountaineering Club Newsletter*, 3, no. 6 (August 1949), pp. 25–26.

Variation: Sowles. II, 5.7. First ascent August 12, 1962, by David Sowles, Robert Brooke, and Sherman Lehman. See *Photo 11*. This moderately difficult climb also reaches the bowllike snowfield via the subridge used by the 1949 party; but the crest of this subridge is gained from the west, not the east. Use the same approach as in *Route 13* to the bench below the north face. Instead of following this bench (covered with snow in early season) out to the right (west), climb the 400-foot wall above and immediately east of the east end of this bench. The top of this wall is the subridge referred to above. Because of the loose rock encountered on the climb this variation is not recommended.

ROUTE 12. North Face, The Buck Sanction. III, 5.8+. First ascent August 6, 1992, by Tom Turiano and Stephen Koch. See *Photos 11* and *12*. This climb of nine pitches ascends the uncharted wall that is located on the eastern sector of the north face. From the scree slope below the face, begin the first of two pitches (4th class) that slant upward to the west to get to the bottom of *Route 13*. The second pitch consists of some loose 5.5 to 5.6 climbing (chimneys). Next, climb (3rd class) east over to the large ledge that cuts across the face for two ropelengths (spectacular), passing beneath some black dihedrals. The objective for the finish of the route is to intersect the large, curving chimney that cuts across this upper section of the face at its top. The fifth pitch consists of 5.7 face climbing to a belay on a sloping ledge. Pitch number six ascends a nice 5.8 crack to a belay near a block. Face climb (5.7) left over to a left-facing corner and then back right on knobs to a belay ledge. Then traverse over to a scary flake and then up to a short, left-facing corner. From the top of the corner, 5.6 face climbing leads to a ledge near the large chimney system mentioned earlier. The final pitch ascends the last portion of this chimney and joins the East Ridge route.

ROUTE 13. North Face, East Couloir. II, 5.4. First ascent July 17, 1941, by Fred Ayres, Alan Cameron, and Judy Cameron. See *Photo 12*. This is the more easterly of the two large couloirs that cut the north face of Buck Mountain. The problem of this route is to get into the couloir, which at its lower end dwindles down to a crack in a nearly vertical face. Lying below the entire north face of Buck is a broad, usually snow-covered bench where this route starts. Approach

via the south fork of Avalanche Canyon, then up the snow slope to the left (east) end of the bench, and then across the bench (usually covered with snow) until about 200 feet west of the crack, which is the lower continuation of the east couloir. A delicate, 100-foot horizontal traverse back to the left (east) leads to a flake that brings one to a wide ledge. Then make an upward traverse to the right (west); a ropelength leaves one among downsloping slabs. Climb another 50 feet of interesting rock, up and back to the left, to the easy ground of the couloir itself. Once in the couloir, climb either on its right (west) side or cross over to the right and proceed directly up the more difficult north central ridge to the summit. *Time: 10½ hours* from the south fork of Avalanche Canyon. See *American Alpine Journal*, 5, no. 2 (1944), pp. 220–232, illus.; *Appalachia*, 24, no. 2 (December 1942), pp. 199–208, illus.

ROUTE 14. North Central Ridge. III, 5.7, A1, or III, 5.8. First ascent August 23, 1959, by Barry Corbet, Rick Medrick, and Sterling Neale. See *Photo 12*. The north face of Buck Mountain is cut by two steep and very large couloirs; the summit lies at the apex of the distinct ridge that separates these couloirs. This route ascends this central ridge which rises from the broad bench (commonly covered with snow) at the base of the north face. Approach this bench as in *Route 13*. Climb the snow on the bench to near its highest point. The ascent of the wall immediately above, which truncates the lower end of the north central ridge, provides the principal difficulty of the route. Immediately after leaving the snow, traverse approximately 150 feet to the right (west) past two right-facing corners; two face-climbing pitches (5.7) then take one to an area of ledge systems and easier ground. Then climb 200 feet of 3rd-class ground up and east to the point at which the ridge becomes well defined. From here to the summit the route along the ridge crest is straightforward 3.0 climbing, with the exception of one 10-foot section, which required aid on the first ascent but has since been done free (5.8). This north face route is perhaps the best route on this peak. *Time: 10 hours* from the south fork of Avalanche Canyon.

ROUTE 15. North Face, West Couloir. II, 5.7. First ascent July 16, 1940, by Paul Petzoldt and Elizabeth Cowles (Partridge); first descent June 14, 1946, by Dick Pownall and Albert Boursault. See *Photos 11* and *12*. The north face of Buck is cut by two steep, prominent couloirs; this route ascends the westerly of these two broad but steep couloirs. To reach the beginning of this couloir one can approach the broad bench lying below the main north face from the east (see *Route 13*), continuing west across to the couloir. Or more directly, one can angle left up easy rock to the right (west) end of the bench and gain access to the couloir. Ascend the open couloir above, avoiding the loose rock, mainly on the left (east) side of the couloir, by climbing up the right wall of the couloir. Ice is likely to be encountered on this route, except in late season. Almost immediately after one reaches the summit ridge, there is a short, over-hanging pitch; once past this pitch, the ridge can be easily followed eastward to the summit. *Time: 5 hours* from the south fork of Avalanche Canyon. See *Trail and Timberline,* no. 353 (May 1948), pp. 67–70, illus.

ROUTE 16. North-Northwest Ridge. III, 5.7. First ascent July 23, 1954, by Richard Emerson, Donald Decker, and William Clayton. See *Photos 11* and *12.* This ridge leads to the west summit of Buck; hence, it is the first ridge west of the central north ridge, which leads to the main summit. It forms the west boundary to the couloir of *Route 15.* From the south fork of Avalanche Canyon two approaches are possible. One can either climb onto the snow bench at its eastern end (as in *Route 13*) and traverse all the way over to the base of the north-northwest ridge or, better, scramble up the easy rock angling to the west end of this bench, which is the beginning of the ridge. The route now progresses for three ropelengths up the extreme east corner of the trian-gular face, the "Wedge," which forms the lower portion of the north-northwest ridge. Climb a chimney that opens out onto an exposed platform at the top of a detached flake. The next pitch is the key to the climb. On the first ascent a rope was thrown over a small flake about 10 feet up, which gave the leader an upper belay for the difficult face lead diago-nally left up to the flake. Walk out to the right on the small flake, then traverse left back around the corner of the face on a downsloping ledge about 4 feet above. On the corner above, climb the steep and exposed rock for 40 feet before making a delicate and difficult 30-foot traverse left into a large chimney. It is recommended that this be made in two leads; otherwise, there will be considerable friction on the rope. Now climb upward, edging right (north) to the 5-foot-square platform at the very top of the triangular face.

The way is now clear, up the sharp arête leading toward the west summit. A cockscomb formation higher up on the arête is bypassed on the left (east) by descending a few feet. Unless one particularly wants to visit the west summit, it is better, at a point level with the sharp notch separating the west summit from the higher east summit, to traverse left off the ridge into this notch. Then climb the 5.7 overhang-ing pitch up out of the notch and proceed easily over to the summit of Buck Mountain. This is a long route and an early start is recommended if it is planned to leave Avalanche Canyon before dark. *Route 8* is probably the most suitable route for descent back into Avalanche Canyon. *Time: 10¾ hours* from the south fork of Avalanche Canyon.

Variation: The Wedge. IV, 5.6, A4. First ascent August 2, 1961, by Herb Swedlund, David Dornan, and Peter Lev. See *Photo 12.* This climb was a significant achievement in the Tetons at the time because it involved extensive aid climbing at a very difficult standard on a high, alpine wall. Swedlund compared the climb to that of Mount Conness in the Sierra, whose elegant west face he had climbed in 1959 with Warren Harding and Glen Denny. The lower 300-foot, wedge-shaped section of the north-northwest ridge is essen-tially vertical. There have been few repeats of this route since the first ascent. Take the large slanting ledge that ends under the "Wedge" to the base of a corner on the left side of the face. Climb a pitch up this corner to an aid lead that starts by nailing up under a roof. Then drop down to a slab until it is possible to pendulum around the corner to the right (west). Less difficult climbing then leads to a belay stance just right of the center of the face. The next lead of about 80 feet involves some difficulty in the placing of pi-tons for aid up noncontinuous crack patterns, which lead slightly to the left on vertical or overhanging rock. From a bolt, belay the next 60-foot lead, which works up and slightly right, and then from another bolt traverse left (east) off the face using poor pitons, including at least one knifeblade. The original climb of this severe route required two days and the placement of about 50 pitons; all of the belays on the face were from slings. See *American Alpine Journal,* 13, no. 1 (1962), pp. 216–220.

Variation: The Free Wedge. IV, 5.11 (unfinished). First ascent August 14, 1993, by Greg Miles and Mark Limage. See *Topo 17.* This variation marks the first real attempt to free climb this alpine wall and it may, in fact, differ slightly from the 1961 ascent. Although this climb was pushed free just beyond the top of the third pitch and remains unfin-ished, it stands as a significant achievement and will therefore be listed here. Begin with easy face climbing (5.6 to 5.7) up and into a right-facing corner system on the left side of the face. The climbing increases in difficulty in the corner (5.10) to a fixed piton under a small roof. Traverse down and right on small holds (5.10+) to the only real ledge on the face and belay at the base of another right-facing corner. For the second pitch steep liebacking and jamming (5.10-) lead to a belay stance inside a chimney. The third pitch goes up and right on small face holds (5.11) to a very steep, gently arching crack system (5.10) that ends at a small roof where a bolt was found. Two pitons now back the bolt up. Another bolt (stud) and fixed piton were visible in a crack system that angled up and left off the face. This attempt ended at this point, however, because of a large, loose block over which one must climb to finish the route. Take protection to 3½ inches with extras in the 2- to 3-inch category. Small wired nuts are also suggested.

BUCK MOUNTAIN, WEST PEAK (11,600+)

Map: Grand Teton

This peak, seldom climbed for its own sake, must be tra-versed in order to climb the complete west ridge of Buck Mountain, starting from the divide.

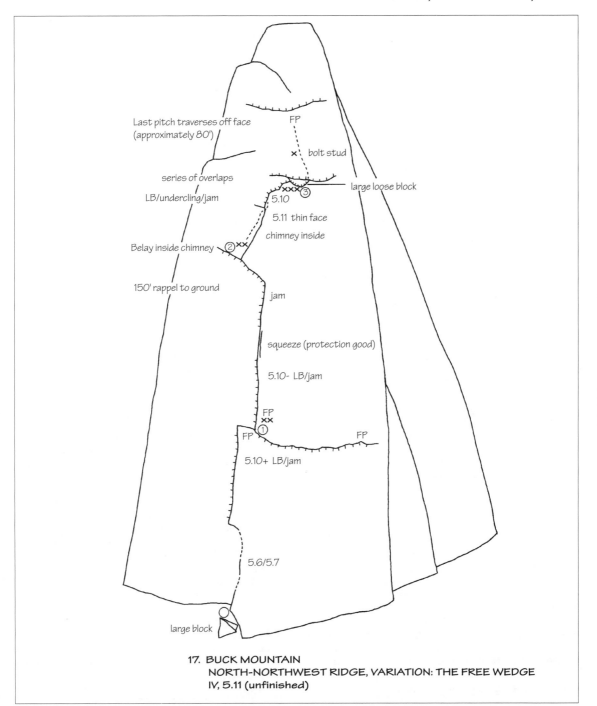

Last pitch traverses off face
(approximately 80')

FP

× bolt stud

series of overlaps

LB/undercling/jam

large loose block

③

5.10

5.11 thin face

chimney inside

Belay inside chimney

②

150' rappel to ground

jam

squeeze (protection good)

5.10- LB/jam

FP
××
①

FP   FP

5.10+ LB/jam

5.6/5.7

large block

17. BUCK MOUNTAIN
NORTH-NORTHWEST RIDGE, VARIATION: THE FREE WEDGE
IV, 5.11 (unfinished)

Northwest Ridge: August 21, 1921, Roland W. Brown, Sr., Roland W. Brown, Jr., Melba Brown, Carvel Brown, Hattie Robinson, Phebe Robinson

North Couloir: June 26, 1977, Paul Horton, James Alto

South Couloir: June 26, 1977, Paul Horton, James Alto (descent)

ROUTE 1. South Couloir. II, 3.0. First descent June 26, 1977, by Paul Horton and James Alto. See *Photo 9*. This talus-filled gully leads from the bench south of the peak to the notch just east of the summit; it contains one 15-foot cliff band. It is but a scramble from the notch to the top.

ROUTE 2. North Couloir. II, 5.1. First ascent June 26, 1977, by Paul Horton and James Alto. See *Photo 12*. From the south fork of Avalanche Canyon scramble for 500 feet up the lower portion of this couloir. In early season moderate-angle snow climbing for six ropelengths takes one to the notch east of the summit from which the top is easily attained. The angle of the snow is not as steep as it appears from below. Rock on the sides of the couloir is poor and, because the sun hits this slope early in the day, the snow may be unpleasantly soft.

ROUTE 3. Northwest Ridge. I, 4.0. First ascent August 21, 1921, by Roland W. Brown, Sr., Roland W. Brown, Jr., Melba Brown, Carvel Brown, Hattie Robinson, and Phebe Robinson. This very early Teton ascent made by local citizens from Teton Basin is unusual in that the record of the climb was found intact in 1957, and so has not been lost to history as were other similar climbs of the period. There are few difficulties on this ridge, but the rock is loose.

VEILED PEAK (11,330)

Map: Grand Teton

The outstanding characteristic of this small peak is the spectacular view of Mount Wister from the summit. Veiled Peak does have a prominent feature, however, in its sharp but rotten north ridge, which rises 1,300 feet from the shores of Snowdrift Lake. The cirque immediately northwest of the peak harbors a significant but seldom-visited glacier. The summit of the peak, situated nearly but not exactly on the hydrographic divide between Avalanche Canyon and Alaska Basin, is easily approached from the "Skyline Trail." In addition, both forks of Avalanche Canyon and the south fork of Cascade Canyon provide suitable approaches. The first ascent was the result of Avalanche Canyon being used as a shortcut from the Cascade Canyon trail workers' camp to Park Headquarters at Beaver Creek. The easily distinguished Buck Mountain fault crosses the foot of the west ridge.

Northeast Ledges: September 18, 1932, Phil Smith, Walcott Watson

West Ridge: July 17, 1940, Paul Petzoldt, Elizabeth Cowles (Partridge)

East Ridge: July 13, 1940, William Plumley, Harold Plumley, William Fralick, Jack Fralick (partial); August 27, 1952, Willi Unsoeld, Leigh Ortenburger, Beatrice Vogel (complete)

Southeast Flank: August 3, 1954, Martin Benham, Jeanne Price

North Ridge: June 18, 1960, William Echo, Dean Millsap

    var: **The Duck:** June 18, 1960, William Echo, Dean Millsap

South Ridge: August 17, 1963, William Buckingham, Margaret Pevear

    var: **Direct Buttress:** September 24, 1971, John Bousman, Dave Reed

ROUTE 1. West Ridge. I, 5.1. First ascent July 17, 1940, by Paul Petzoldt and Elizabeth Cowles (Partridge). Because this party reported the climb as less difficult than others have reported, it is likely that the ridge was not followed directly. There is a couloir south of the true west ridge that has been used as a route of ascent. It is also possible to traverse out to the north when confronted by the difficulties of the crest of the west ridge.

ROUTE 2. South Ridge. II, 5.6. First ascent August 17, 1963, by William Buckingham and Margaret Pevear. See *Photo 14*. This distinct ridge of excellent rock can be approached either via the south fork of Avalanche Canyon or from the Skyline Trail via Death Canyon. The ridge is reached from the left (west) via a couloir of loose rock. Follow the couloir to a notch formed by a rotten dike. (The steep, rotten section of the ridge, culminating in the gendarme that forms the south side of the notch, is thus avoided.) The first pitch is an easy 75-foot corner just left (west) of the crest. Scramble up to an overhanging tower, which can be passed by descending slightly to the left and then climbing the west face of this tower. To avoid use of aid on the 100-foot tower above, traverse right on a shelf for 70 feet, past two prominent chimneys (these will probably go) to the high-angle face just right of the second chimney. The lead up this face brings one to the crest of the ridge just beyond the top of the tower. Climb a pitch just 10 feet to the right (east) of the crest to the beginning of the sixth pitch. Work up about 70 feet, then cross the crest back to the left. After a few feet exit left onto a ledge, then up to the belay stance on the crest. The final pitch passes over two easy towers to the summit. See *American Alpine Journal*, 14, no. 1 (1964), p. 188.

Variation: Direct Buttress. II, 5.6. First ascent September 24, 1971, by John Bousman and Dave Reed. This variation adds four pitches by starting at the base of the initial buttress that the normal South Ridge route avoided.

ROUTE 3. Southeast Flank. II, 4.0. First ascent August 3, 1954, by Martin Benham and Jeanne Price. See *Photo 14.* From Alaska Basin one can cross along the base of the south ridge to gain access to the southeast flank of Veiled Peak. Once past the south ridge, relatively straightforward scrambling, staying clear of both adjacent ridges, then leads to the summit.

ROUTE 4. East Ridge. II, 5.7. First complete ascent August 27, 1952, by Willi Unsoeld, Leigh Ortenburger, and Beatrice Vogel; on July 13, 1940, William and Harold Plumley, Jack and William Fralick, all of the Chicago Mountaineering Club, climbed the southeast slope to the small notch in this east ridge and then continued up most of the ridge above before traversing right across the north ledges to gain the summit by the uppermost west ridge. See *Photo 14.* The complete east ridge is a straightforward climb up a well-defined crest. If one stays precisely on the ridge, one 5.7 friction pitch will be encountered about three-quarters of the way up. However, at several points one can leave the crest of the ridge to the right (north) and find easier climbing. *Time: 1½ hours* from the summit of Mount Wister. See *American Alpine Journal,* 8, no. 3 (1953), pp. 542–545.

ROUTE 5. ☞Northeast Ledges. I, 3.0. First ascent September 18, 1932, by Phil Smith and Walcott Watson. See *Photo 15.* From Snowdrift Lake either work directly up the northeast slope or first gain the saddle (10,800+) between Veiled Peak and Mount Wister and then cut out onto the northeast face at almost any point west of the saddle. The summit can be reached by scrambling up ledges.

ROUTE 6. North Ridge. II, 5.1. First ascent June 18, 1960, by William Echo and Dean Millsap. From Snowdrift Lake this ridge can be climbed directly to the summit past several pinnacles of dubious quality.

Variation: The Duck. II, 5.7. First ascent June 18, 1960, by William Echo and Dean Millsap. This is the first pinnacle (10,960+) north of the summit of Veiled Peak. The party (Mark Chapman and Andy Kegley, July 10, 1976) who made the third ascent of the "Duck" reported the climb to be four pitches starting on the east face slabs: two easy 5th-class leads to a steep 5.7 pitch on a south-facing wall just left of an alcove, finishing with one exposed 4th-class lead to its summit.

AVALANCHE CANYON (SOUTH FORK), NORTH SIDE ROCK CLIMBS

Map: Grand Teton

Located partway up the south fork of Avalanche Canyon, on the southwest side of Mount Wister, is a steep buttress of excellent rock that is approximately 300 feet high. The name "Fracture Line Buttress" has been applied to this formation by its discoverers. This buttress is situated directly across from the north face of Buck Mountain and slightly upcanyon from the small lake in the south fork.

ROUTE 1. I, 5.10. First ascent August 13, 1993, by Greg Miles and Mark Limage. There is a large, downsloping ledge from which these climbs begin at the base of the buttress. Scramble up onto this ledge. When looking at the buttress this two-pitch route is located just right of a prominent wide crack that curves up and slightly right. Climb a corner to a roof that is surmounted by a traverse to the right via jugs and a pocket. Traverse back to the left on the lip of the roof and then climb up and over a bulge to a horizontal crack that leads left to a belay. Continue up one more pitch to the top or walk left and downclimb to the base.

ROUTE 2. I, 5.11. First ascent August 13, 1993, by Greg Miles and Mark Limage. This climb is located near the right edge of the buttress and to the right (east) of the first route. Begin by climbing up to the large ledge from the east, heading for the large overhang at the eastern edge of the buttress (5.10-). Above the overhang is an obvious thin, clean-looking crack leading out from the apex of the roof. Lieback and undercling out and over the roof (5.11) straight up to where the crack splits. The right crack is finger to hand size while the left involves liebacking up flakes. A 150-foot rappel at the top of the pitch leads back to the large ledge at the base.

MOUNT WISTER (11,490)

Map: Grand Teton

This peak was named after Owen Wister, the famous author of *The Virginian,* who visited Jackson Hole several times before 1900 and later had a summer home there. As viewed from the valley, Mount Wister is not a prominent peak. This reticence, combined with the lack of a maintained trail up Avalanche Canyon, perhaps explains why it has been somewhat neglected by mountaineers. Nonetheless, this important Teton peak does provide interesting climbing, especially on the north face where there are now four distinct routes. From the summit impressive views can be obtained of the northern aspect of Buck Mountain and the southern walls of the Garnet Canyon peaks. Wister has three distinct summits, of which the easternmost is the highest. The central peak is usually bypassed by most parties, but the western peak must be traversed by climbers of *Routes 1, 8, 9, 10,* and *11.*

CHRONOLOGY

Northeast Couloir: September 23, 1928, Phil Smith, Oliver Zierlein

var: September 23, 1928, Phil Smith, Oliver
   Zierlein (descent); August 4, 1950, Gerald
   and Ted Brandon, Don Zastrow, Finn
   Brunevold (ascent)
West Ridge: August 23, 1929, Fritiof Fryxell
Southeast Couloir: June 27, 1931, Phil Smith
   var: July 6, 1935, Malcolm Smith
Southwest Ridge: August 16, 1931, Fritiof Fryxell
Northwest Face: August 16, 1931, Fritiof Fryxell
   (descent); July 19, 1960, Charles and Cora Sand-
   ers (ascent)
South Couloir: July 5, 1936, Fred Ayres, William
   and Harold Plumley (descent); July 19, 1936,
   Fred and Irene Ayres, Margaret Smith (ascent)
North Face, West Chimney: August 27, 1952, Willi
   Unsoeld, Leigh Ortenburger, Beatrice Vogel
   var: July 20, 1960, Ray Jacquot, J. Orren
   Church
North Face, East Chimney: August 22, 1956, James
   T. Smith, Bill Hoy (partial); September 9, 1957,
   William Pope, Mary Kay Pottinger (complete)
Direct North Face: July 20, 1961, Layton Kor, Gary
   Cole
Northwest Arête: August 30, 1966, John Hudson,
   Frank Sarnquist
Northwest Couloir: August 26, 1968, William
   Chadwick, Wallace Hunter

ROUTE 1. West Ridge. II, 5.4. First ascent August 23, 1929,
by Fritiof Fryxell. The saddle between Mount Wister and
Veiled Peak, which is the starting point for this climb, can be
approached in four different ways. The two most direct ways
are via the south fork and the north fork (shorter) of Avalanche Canyon, as the saddle is attained quite easily from
either direction. Another possibility is via the south fork of
Cascade Canyon, which joins the north fork of Avalanche
Canyon at the saddle (10,560+) between the South Teton and
the Wall. A fourth possibility is via the Skyline Trail to Alaska
Basin, then over the divide into the south fork of Avalanche
Canyon. The route above the saddle is fairly obvious. The
ridge can be followed either slightly to the right (south) or
slightly to the left (north) of the crest. The western summit
of Wister will be reached first and must be traversed in order
to get to the higher summit to the east. The center peak is
usually bypassed via ledges on its north side but can also be
passed on the south. *Time: 4 hours* from Snowdrift Lake. See
Appalachia, 18, no. 3 (June 1931), pp. 209–232, illus.

ROUTE 2. Southwest Ridge. I, 4.0. First ascent August 16,
1931, by Fritiof Fryxell. The upper south side of Mount
Wister contains three ridges, each leading to one of the
three summits; two well-defined couloirs separate these
ridges. A broken cliff band supporting scattered trees guards
the approach to these couloirs and ridges. Take the talus-
filled south fork of Avalanche Canyon up to near its west
end, past the 10,000-foot level, veering right above the
single *krummholz* and grass area, as if heading toward the
saddle west of Mount Wister. Gain the western of the three
ridges from the west, and climb the ridge along the right
(east) side of its crest. The climbing becomes increasingly
interesting toward the summit. The first-ascent route
crossed over into the next couloir or chimney to the right
(east) when about 300 feet below the summit. Before reaching the notch and about 50 feet below the summit, climb a
narrow vertical chimney with chockstones, using stemming
to gain the summit. This route differs from *Route 3* in that
one ascends farther west to the uppermost section of the
canyon before turning up the mountain. *Time: 4½ hours*
from the south fork of Avalanche Canyon. See *Appalachia*,
19, no. 1 (June 1932), pp. 86–96.

ROUTE 3. South Couloir. II, 4.0. First descent July 5, 1936,
by Fred Ayres and William and Harold Plumley; first ascent
July 19, 1936, by Fred and Irene Ayres and Margaret Smith.
This route ascends the large couloir leading from the south
fork of Avalanche Canyon to the notch immediately west of
the summit. The beginning of this route can be recognized
from below as a bare talus cone, leading to a steep watercourse break in the initial cliff band. This is the last (farthest
west) talus before reaching the *krummholz* and grass area,
which begins at about 10,000 feet. Some scrambling to pass
the initial cliff band is required. Three leads of 4.0 climbing
will be found.

ROUTE 4. Southeast Couloir. I, 3.0. First ascent June 27,
1931, by Phil Smith. The southeast side of Mount Wister is
composed of a complex series of broken cliff bands and
shallow couloirs; several routes are possible. Take the south
fork of Avalanche Canyon to about 9,600 feet; do not start
up the mountain too soon. The correct couloir leads to the
main col, east of the summit, that separates Peak 10,960+
from Mount Wister. The lower part of this couloir appears
as an indentation in the talus slope, just at the left (west)
edge of the section containing trees. Once past the initial
cliff band, where the couloir narrows, no difficulty will be
encountered until the east ridge col is reached. Follow the
delightful east ridge to the summit . *Time: 4½ hours* from the
south fork of Avalanche Canyon. See *Appalachia*, 19, no. 1
(June 1932), pp. 86–96.

Variation: II, 4.0. First ascent July 6, 1935, by Malcolm
Smith. Instead of taking the main southeast couloir that
ends at the east ridge col, start as in *Route 3* to the open
upper talus slope past the initial cliff band. Then, instead of
entering the upper south couloir, climb up and slightly right
(east) to the base of the broken face above. Ascend this face,
using one of the shallow couloirs that leads upward to join
the east ridge just short of the summit.

ROUTE 5. Northeast Couloir. II, 4.0. First ascent September
23, 1928, by Phil Smith and Oliver Zierlein. See *Photo 15*.

A conspicuous couloir rises from the north fork of Avalanche Canyon just below the headwall leading to Lake Taminah. Climb this couloir to the east ridge, which is followed to the summit. Near the ridge crest the couloir narrows to a wide chimney and the climbing becomes more difficult. This route has perhaps not been used since the first ascent because the easier *1928 variation* (described next) was discovered on the descent.

☞*Variation:* II, 4.0. First descent September 23, 1928, by Phil Smith and Oliver Zierlein; first ascent August 4, 1950, by Gerald and Ted Brandon, Don Zastrow, and Finn Brunevold. See *Photo 15.* This variation, a northeast approach to the upper east ridge, is the most straightforward method of reaching the summit of Mount Wister; it has the advantage of leading directly to the summit, without having to climb over or around either of the other two lower summits. From Lake Taminah cross the outlet stream and turn left (south) up into a small snow-filled cirque that contains the apparent remains of a small glacier at the northwest foot of Peak 10,960+. Ascend the loose talus and scree slope that leads to the broad col in the east ridge, between the summit and Peak 10,960+. In early season and midseason this entire slope will be covered with snow, an advantage over the loose rubble encountered later in the season; however, an ice axe will be essential. Once the crest is reached, turn right (west) and scramble up along the left (south) edge of the fine east ridge to the summit. See *Appalachia,* 18, no. 3 (June 1931), pp. 209–232, illus.

ROUTE 6. *North Face, East Chimney.* III, 5.6. First ascent September 9, 1957, by William Pope and Mary Kay Pottinger. See *Photo 15.* This prominent chimney marks the left (east) edge of the steep and slabby north face of Mount Wister. See *Avalanche Canyon* for the approach to a campsite in the north fork. Ascend the talus that leads to the base of the north face, and gain the beginning of the chimney either directly or (easier) from the east via a fairly obvious ledge. Two or three pitches, which include some scrambling up the lower section of the chimney, bring one to the steeper, upper section. Since the chimney is often wet, climb the first pitch on either the right or left wall. Both have apparently been used, but the right is perhaps preferable. Pass a small bulge; then go into and up the chimney. On the next pitch (120 feet) pass a large chockstone by climbing in behind it. On the third pitch (80 feet) one encounters a chockstone that can be surmounted by stemming over it on the outside. Next is a lead up loose rock to a roof, which can be passed by careful climbing on the right wall up and out of the chimney. At this point the angle eases considerably, enabling one to scramble up the slabs to a point on the east ridge a couple of hundred feet short of the summit. Although the rock is somewhat loose, this is an enjoyable, well-protected climb.

ROUTE 7. *Direct North Face.* III, 5.7, A2. First ascent July 20, 1961, by Layton Kor and Gary Cole. See *Photo 15.* This climb starts on the face to the right (west) of the initial chimney of *Route 8* and crosses it before reaching the upper part of the slabby north face. The first pitch diagonals up and right toward the corner of the chimney, where a jam crack leads up to the second ledge of *Route 8.* Starting at the corner of the chimney, climb a difficult jam and ledge system over a small roof to bypass the more obvious chimney. One easy ropelength leads to an obvious traverse left (30 feet) on a 10-foot ledge. After the disappearance of the ledge, climb down a 5-foot crack and continue the traverse diagonally left. The next lead (130 feet) ends at a belay from an 8-foot ledge. Again traverse diagonally left (east), past a flake (a piton should be found here), to the base of a small roof. A good belay stance will be found behind the huge boulder at the top of this roof. The next pitch of 60 feet above the boulder required aid in order to pass the small roof. Now traverse right (west) on a wide, grassy ramp for 10 feet before angling left up a smooth slab to the base of a third small roof, which is at the edge of the left (east) corner of the face. Two ropelengths bring one to the easy climbing at the base of the final north summit arête. Most of this arête can be climbed directly on the crest. The difficult section of the arête is near the top in a chimney on the right side of the crest. From midway up this chimney, traverse right to a 4-inch jam crack up the face to an obvious hole. Climb straight up out of this hole, past a small overhang; then, scramble up boulders to the summit, only 50 feet away. See *American Alpine Journal,* 13, no. 1 (1962), pp. 216–220.

ROUTE 8. *North Face, West Chimney.* II, 5.6. First ascent August 27, 1952, by Willi Unsoeld, Leigh Ortenburger, and Beatrice Vogel; a previous attempt stopped by a storm was made on August 27, 1946, by Ray Van Aken, Wallace Degen, John Montgomery, Eugene Paul, and Don Woods. See *Photo 15.* The problem of this interesting route is to get into the great chimney at the right (west) edge of the smooth north face. There are two grassy ledges on the lower part of the main north face, and from the higher ledge one can easily get into the chimney itself. A small chimney, roughly in the middle of the face, gives access to the first of these grassy ledges. The first pitch is the hardest of the route. Climb out of the small chimney to the right (west) past an awkward overhang to a good belay spot. Continue upward for two pitches to the first grassy ledge. From here, two more pitches lead up and to the right (west) to the second ledge. Climb easily into the great chimney and scramble a few hundred feet up to the crest of the west ridge, which will be attained just west of the west peak. Then follow *Route 1* to the summit. *Time: 5½ hours from Lake Taminah.* See *American Alpine Journal,* 8, no. 3 (1953), pp. 542–545.

Variation: II, 5.6. First ascent July 20, 1960, by Ray Jacquot and J. Orren Church. Instead of continuing upward to intersect the west ridge, a more direct route to the summit cuts left (east) near the top of the chimney onto the upper portion of the north face; the summit is then reached from the north.

ROUTE 9. *Northwest Arête.* IV, 5.9. First ascent August 30, 1966, by John Hudson and Frank Sarnquist. See *Photo 15.* This route is on the well-defined ridge between the west chimney on the north face *(Route 8)* and the prominent northwest snow couloir *(Route 10)* at the extreme west side of the face. It forms the right (west) edge of the north face proper. This long ridge, about 1,800 feet, contains ten or more pitches of fairly sustained climbing on excellent rock with good protection; there are variations possible on the ridge, however, and the exact route will depend on the line taken. The climb begins from a small grassy ledge at the base of the ridge below a very prominent crack about 50 to 60 feet to the left (east) of the northwest snow couloir. Climb to and directly up the left-facing corner (5.9) to a belay near a cave. The second pitch consists of an awkward and dirty 5.8 chimney. The base of the first major gendarme on the ridge is then reached after three or four leads interspersed with scrambling. The steep wall above is passed via a 5.8 jam crack for 50 feet. Scramble to and then climb a chimney on the left side of the gendarme, exiting through a keyhole. Slabs and scrambling bring one to the shoulder below the second pseudotower on the ridge. This shoulder or tower is passed in two leads by climbing up and right and then regaining the crest at the first possible crack; depending on the choice of routes in this section 5.7 difficulties may be encountered. Scramble up the ridge until it steepens. The steep wall above can be attacked via a sequence of two cracks (40 feet and 50 feet, 5.8) or one can traverse farther right around to the west side where a 5.4 crack brings one back to the ridge at a small notch onto a broad ledge. The final pitch can be taken either to the left, where a difficult (5.7) mantle and slabs are found, or to the right (4.0). Scrambling (4.0 or 5.1) then takes one to the base of the west summit, where *Route 1* is joined. At least one party has reported a steep, 5.9+ finger crack on the next-to-last pitch and then a steep corner followed by a few A1 moves to yet another finger crack on the final lead. Be prepared for a long, adventurous day.

ROUTE 10. *Northwest Couloir.* II, 5.7, A1. First ascent August 26, 1968, by William Chadwick and Wallace Hunter. See *Photo 15.* This is the large snow couloir that bounds the west edge of the north face of Wister. At its base is one of the finest talus cones in the range. From the meadow in Avalanche Canyon west of Lake Taminah, ascend the talus (or snow) cone leading to the entrance of the couloir. Conditions in the couloir will depend on the season. In early season two snow pitches bring one to a prominent overhang that is passed on the left (5.7, A1). The next 500 to 600 feet of snow climbing may contain ice patches in late season.

Climb another 200 feet to the point where the couloir splits. Continue up the narrowing couloir and then traverse right off to the west ridge and follow *Route 1* to the summit.

ROUTE 11. *Northwest Face.* II, 5.1 to 5.7. First descent August 16, 1931, by Fritiof Fryxell; first ascent July 19, 1960, by Charles and Cora Sanders. There are several lines of varying difficulty on the northwest face of Mount Wister, which lies between the west ridge and the ridge that forms the western edge of the northwest couloir; sooner or later all these lines join the upper west ridge. A portion of this face contains smooth, sound rock. From Snowdrift Lake scramble more or less directly up toward the (west) summit until reaching a break in the ridge west of the northwest couloir. The first-ascent party traversed south onto the upper west ridge after ascending a narrow chimney. In early season, the small gully or chimney that forms the upper continuation of the northwest couloir can be followed, mostly on snow, to gain the upper west ridge. Or one can cross this gully and ascend five pitches of crack and face climbing to gain the uppermost west ridge at the top of the northwest arête. In early season the lower portion of this face is a moderate-angle snowfield.

PEAK 10,960+   *(0.3 mi E of Mount Wister)*

Map: Grand Teton

Rarely climbed, this peak consists of a group of three pinnacles on the east ridge of Mount Wister. The most recent quadrangle map shows that the highest pinnacle is sufficiently separated from Wister to deserve "peak" status. The unofficial name, Wanda Pinnacle, was given by the second-ascent party in 1955. The most westerly of the three pinnacles is the most difficult.

ROUTE 1. *West Ridge.* I, 5.1. First recorded ascent August 4, 1954, by Dick Long, Tim Bond, and Mike Schoeman. This tower probably had been ascended at an earlier date— a piton that was not placed by the 1954 party was found in 1955. The climb begins at the broad col that separates this pinnacle from the main east summit of Mount Wister. The rock is somewhat loose.

ROUTE 2. *South Ridge.* II, 5.6. First ascent July 10, 1994, by Paul Horton and Ryan Hokanson. This route ascends the south ridge on the central and highest of the group of pinnacles on the east ridge of Mount Wister. From the south fork of Avalanche Canyon, work up to the emergence of this ridge from the broken slopes. An initial roped pitch is followed by several hundred feet of scrambling. Three pitches of cracks and slabs on excellent rock that stay generally right of the ridge crest bring one to 3.0 climbing that leads to the summit. The peculiarly shaped western pinnacle was also climbed via a 5.6 pitch of good rock on the east face.

NESSMUK SPIRE (9,600+)

(1.1 mi ENE of Buck Mountain)

Map: Grand Teton

This minor summit, or buttress, is located 0.3 mile north-northeast of Peak 10,696 and is shown on the map as an isolated contour of 9,600 feet.

ROUTE 1. East Face. I, 5.4. First ascent August 31, 1971, by Robert Weinreb and Barry Voight. Ascend the south fork of Avalanche Canyon past the small lake (sometimes a swamp or even dry), following the stream up toward the bench below the north face of Peak 10,696. On the right (west), just before reaching this bench, is the east face of Nessmuk Spire.

BROKEN ARROW SPIRE (8,640+)

(1.6 mi E of Mount Wister)

Map: Grand Teton

This distinct pinnacle lies on the south side of Avalanche Canyon, about 0.3 mile east of the forks of the canyon. It is separated from the remainder of the mountain above by large gullies on both the east and west sides but has only a small notch. It can be seen from the valley if the light is just right. The name Abandoned Pinnacle was also applied to this tower in 1979.

ROUTE 1. West Ridge. I, 5.4. First ascent August 7, 1968, by Paul J. Myhre and Eric Stern. This moderate route was climbed using four nuts.

ROUTE 2. Alone. II, 5.9. First ascent July 7, 1979, by Mike Munger. This route starts in a right-facing corner (5.4) between two dead trees at the base of the north face of the spire, leading past a sticker-bush patch to another dead tree. Traverse left toward a grassy crack that angles up and right. Climb a finger crack (5.9) to the right of the grassy crack, until one can traverse into the main crack at a bush, then proceed up this 4-inch crack to a belay stance at its top. The next lead is difficult (5.9) straight up but can be climbed on easier rock (5.5) slightly to the left to a stance below an overhang. Climb this overhang (5.9) and then a finger crack (5.8) above, just right of a second overhang, to a ledge. The next pitch goes left, past a 5.9 overhang, and up a right-facing corner to a tree at a belay ledge. The final lead is 4th class, past trees, ending at a tree left of and near the summit.

ROUTE 3. Lost. II, 5.10. First ascent July 13, 1979, by Mike Munger and Buck Tilley. This route lies to the right of *Route 2.* Take the same start, through the sticker-bush patch to the dead tree. Instead of traversing left here, climb the 5.8 right-facing corner that slants up and right from the tree for a full ropelength to a belay ledge. The final section below the ledge is a difficult headwall (5.10). The second lead moves left up over an overhang (5.9) and up a left-facing corner

(5.7) to a belay just above a detached flake. The next pitch (5.8) goes up and left into a corner left of a roof to the same ledge that was reached on *Route 2* after the second overhang. From this ledge, instead of traversing left, one can climb a 5.6 broken corner to the next belay ledge and then take easier rock (5.4) straight up toward the summit.

AVALANCHE CANYON, NORTH SIDE ROCK CLIMBS (10,480+)

Map: Grand Teton

Rising directly above and north of the east end of Lake Taminah in Avalanche Canyon is a set of buttresses containing excellent rock. These buttresses have the advantage of a relatively short approach and can be seen from the valley in morning or evening light.

ROUTE 1. Flying Buttress, Good for the Soul. II, 5.7. First ascent June 18, 1993, by Tom LoHuis and William Stanley. See *Photo 13.* Separated from and west of the main, central buttress (see *Route 2*) is a flying buttress upon which this climb is located. The main feature of the route, a prominent, right-facing corner, is obvious from below. The route begins 30 feet to the west of several pine trees, and the first pitch goes up the blocky face heading for a ledge below three left-facing flakes. Climb any one of the flakes to a shallow, left-facing corner and continue for 30 more feet until the main right-facing corner is in sight. The second pitch works up the leftmost crack in the main corner until one can step right into a crack that skirts a small overhanging block (below a large roof). Climb left to the slot in the roof and jam on up (5.7), belaying 25 feet higher in a shallow corner. Ascend this corner to a small, left-facing ramp that ends in a short, overhanging corner (5.7). After passing this obstacle, take the straightest line up to the flat ridge crest and belay. The fourth lead ascends a short headwall containing a jammed block. Work to the right around this block and run the rope out to a belay. From here the summit is easily reached. Descend the gully to the west back down to the base of the climb.

ROUTE 2. Blind Man's Bluff. III, 5.9. First ascent August 26, 1978, by Rich Perch, Yvon Chouinard, and Kent Lugbill. See *Photo 13.* This route ascends the central buttress, which is about 700 feet high. The climb starts on the left part of the face of the buttress, but right (east) of the obvious gully that separates a flying buttress on the left from the main central section of the buttress. Scramble up a few hundred feet of 3rd- and 4th-class rock and scree to reach the steep section. After an initial 5.7 pitch, the next lead involves a short traverse left, followed by 5.9 climbing up a left-facing corner. The third lead passes over a small overhang to reach a ramp that diagonals down from left to right, across the face of the buttress. Another 5.7 pitch above this ramp leads to a pedestal-ledge. The final 5.8 lead from the left end of this ledge goes up a beautiful straight-in crack, from the top of which the summit is easily reached. This is a good crack and overhang climb on golden Teton rock.

ROUTE 3. *Lugbill-White*. III, 5.9. First ascent late August 1978, by Kent Lugbill and Wendy White. This route follows the right (east) edge of the same central buttress as in *Route 1*. While this route also contains about the same amount of climbing including two good pitches (5.8 and 5.9), it is not as continuous because the steep rock is broken by low-angle sections.

ROUTE 4. *Yukon Jack Arête*. II, 5.7. First ascent July 29, 1979, by George Montopoli and Bob Howard. See *Photo 13*. From the talus slope below Lake Taminah this sharp arête will be seen 1,000 feet above a gully that is identifiable by a huge block that obstructs the passage. A dihedral can be seen on the right side of this arête from low in the talus slope. Proceed to Lake Taminah, then traverse easily along the trees below the cliffs to the north into the gully (which lies east of these cliffs) above the huge block. Start the climb for 60 feet on the left side of the dihedral. The next pitch (5.7) goes up this fine dihedral through white quartz rock. The final lead goes up to a ramp leading left into an open book containing the crux overhang (5.7).

MATTERNOUGHT PEAK (11,360+)

(0.3 mi SE of South Teton)

Map: Grand Teton

This peak is the prominent point above and northwest of Lake Taminah and about 0.3 mile southeast of the South Teton. It is surprising that the peak was overlooked for so many years, but the first-ascent party did find a Band-Aid can with no note on the summit. A well-defined col separates Matternought Peak from Gilkey Tower on the South Teton–Cloudveil Dome ridge.

CHRONOLOGY

East Couloir and East Ridge: July 25, 1960, George Hurley, Jean Tuomi

West Couloir, North Ridge: July 25, 1960, George Hurley, Jean Tuomi (descent); August 16, 1972, Leigh and Irene Ortenburger (ascent)

Taminah Arête: August 29, 1976, Kent Lugbill, Jim Tate

var: July 12, 1979, Norm Larson, Dick Olmstead

Dem Bones: July 1994, William Alexander, Mason Reid

ROUTE 1. *West Couloir, North Ridge*. II, 4.0. First descent July 25, 1960, by George Hurley and Jean Tuomi; first ascent August 16, 1972, by Leigh and Irene Ortenburger. The cirque between Matternought Peak and the South Teton harbors an interesting small glacier and can be reached by contouring into the cirque from the east end of Snowdrift Lake or by climbing directly up from the meadow west of Lake Taminah. In either case the north col separating Matternought Peak from the South Teton–Cloudveil Dome ridge is easily attained via the western couloir. A short climb, bearing slightly left, is then required to reach the summit. For descent this route can be used without rappel, but it is a tricky downclimb.

ROUTE 2. *Taminah Arête*. III, 5.9. First ascent August 29, 1976, by Kent Lugbill and Jim Tate. See *Topo 18* and *Photos 16* and *25*. From the west end of Lake Taminah one can see the top of this long and spectacular ridge, and the climbing matches the appearance. Ascend the talus slope diagonally to the northwest and angle up through a break in the first rock step. Traverse west beneath huge overhanging arches in the next rock step that eventually leads to the toe of the arête. A more straightforward approach can be made from Snowdrift Lake, where a simple traverse on tree-covered ledges allows access to the base of the arête. Scramble up over easy blocky rock on the east side of the arête to the base of the first pitch that goes up the orange rock wall above. There are at least two options for getting started on this ridge, but the route basically stays right on the ridge crest, providing considerable exposure down the sheer west face at times. The first pitch on the arête can be taken either up the face or in a chimney on the right (east). Follow the ridge (containing cracks in orange rock) to a 5.9 left-facing corner and beyond to a section of fine cracks forming a geometric pattern (also 5.9) to the belay. Climb along the ridge crest over blocks for 100 feet (5.5). The next lead is quite spectacular if one stays on or near the edge of the arête. This face contains numerous huge quartz crystals that provide steep and exciting climbing, easier than might be expected (5.6), for nearly 160 feet. Protection for the first 20 feet of the next pitch (5.7) is nonexistent as one ascends golden knobs just east of the crest. This fourth pitch ends at a sharp notch at which point 200 feet of 4th-class climbing leads to the final pitches. From the top of the sixth pitch, 400 feet of scrambling leads to the summit of Matternought Peak. Descent from the summit can be made, using *Route 3*, down the east ridge and the couloir leading back down to Avalanche Canyon. The descent route from the summit is treacherous, especially when wet, because it involves downclimbing slabs and some rotten rock. Take care! The solid, enjoyable rock with the exceptional quartz knob pitch makes this an excellent climb. Protection consists of a regular rack including RPs. (*Note:* This route has now been done in conjunction with *Sunrise Ridge* on *Gilkey Tower*—a combination that provides a great day in the mountains.)

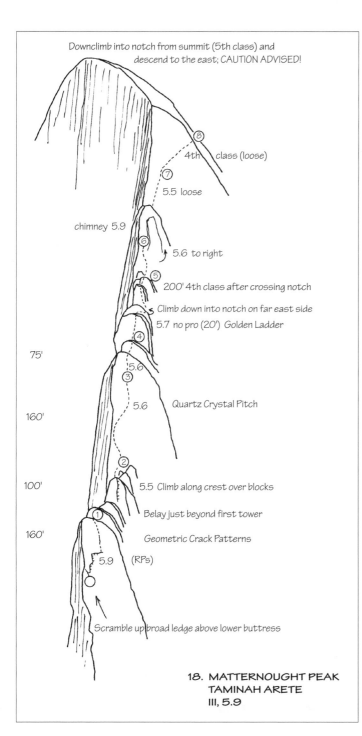

Downclimb into notch from summit (5th class) and
descend to the east; CAUTION ADVISED!

⑧

4th   class (loose)

⑦

5.5 loose

chimney 5.9

⑥

5.6 to right

⑤

200' 4th class after crossing notch

Climb down into notch on far east side

5.7 no pro (20') Golden Ladder

④

75'

5.6

③

5.6   Quartz Crystal Pitch

160'

②

100'   5.5 Climb along crest over blocks

Belay just beyond first tower

Geometric Crack Patterns

160'   ①

5.9   (RPs)

Scramble up broad ledge above lower buttress

**18. MATTERNOUGHT PEAK
TAMINAH ARETE
III, 5.9**

Variation: III, 5.8. First ascent July 12, 1979, by Norm Larson and Dick Olmstead. See *Photo 16.* From Lake Taminah, take the gully leading toward the west side of the main south buttress of Matternought Peak; as one approaches this buttress, it is seen to have a triangular south face. Climb the west side of the buttress, which is steep in the bottom section. This variation contains a total of five pitches of which two were 5.8 in difficulty. The rock on this variation is solid.

ROUTE 3. Dem Bones. III, 5.10. First ascent July 1994, by William Alexander and Mason Reid. See *Topo 19* and *Photos 16* and *25.* This is an interesting route that the first-ascent party claims "is as good as Guides' Wall." Proceed up Avalanche Canyon to Lake Taminah and then continue up the grassy slope past Blind Man's Bluff to the large triangular face that is on the southeast side of Matternought Peak. Allow approximately four hours for this approach. The details of the route are best presented in the topo, but to find the start climb up a 3.0 gully to a point just to the left of the biggest roof near the bottom of the southeast face (10,140 feet). From the top of the seventh pitch scramble around the corner, then continue across slabs to a descent gully. One could also continue up the ridge crest to the summit of Matternought Peak. This is a recommended climb in an outstanding setting.

ROUTE 4. East Couloir and East Ridge. II, 5.1. First recorded ascent July 25, 1960, by George Hurley and Jean Tuomi. From the north fork of Avalanche Canyon along the north shore of Lake Taminah, proceed up the considerable talus slope toward the cirque under the south side of Spalding Peak and Cloudveil Dome. Matternought Peak lies just west of this cirque. Take the east couloir to its intersection with the moderate east ridge. Some wet slabs, which may hold snow, will be met before reaching the col in the east ridge. Use care in this section. Once on the ridge two roped pitches will be found, followed by scrambling to the summit. For descent a 100-foot rappel will be needed by most climbers to reach the east ridge col. See *American Alpine Journal,* 12, no. 2 (1961), pp. 373–377.

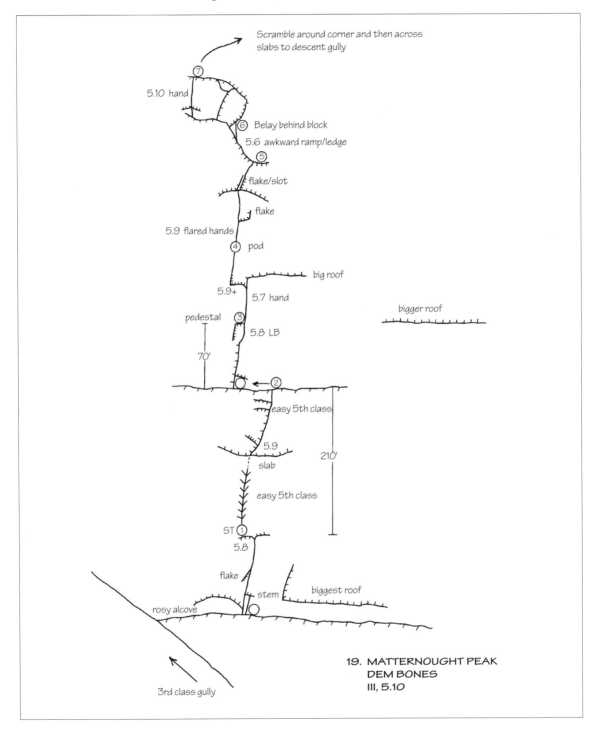

Scramble around corner and then across slabs to descent gully

⑦

5.10 hand

⑥ Belay behind block

5.6 awkward ramp/ledge

⑤

flake/slot

flake

5.9 flared hands

④ pod

big roof

bigger roof

5.9+   5.7 hand

pedestal   ③

5.8 LB

70'

② ←

easy 5th class

5.9

210'

slab

easy 5th class

ST ①

5.8

flake

stem   biggest roof

rosy alcove

3rd class gully

19. MATTERNOUGHT PEAK
DEM BONES
III, 5.10

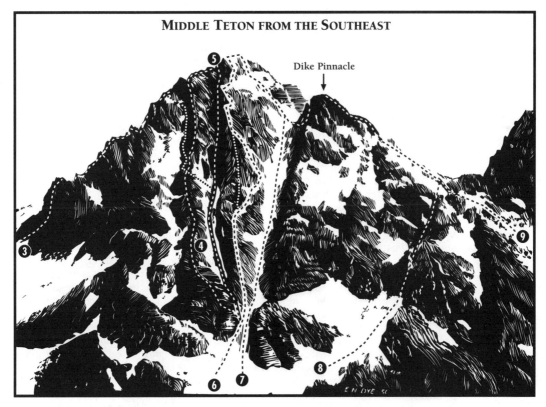

MIDDLE TETON FROM THE SOUTHEAST

Dike Pinnacle

Garnet Canyon Peaks

SHADOW PEAK (10,725)

Map: Grand Teton

This attractive small peak, while infrequently climbed, is a common sight for all those who traverse into Garnet Canyon along the trail. Shadow Peak lies out on the eastern margin of the Teton Range, protruding from the southeastern base of Nez Perce Peak. The name was given because the steep north face is almost never in the sunlight. The high cirque just north of the peak is a beautiful and relatively wild place, compared to the heavily travelled Garnet Canyon. Shadow Peak consists of a long ridge with many points of nearly equal elevation, and the true summit is not easily found by the casual climber. Most parties that have climbed the peak have reached only a few of the high points. The only certain way of reaching the summit is to climb them all, and this has seldom been done.

CHRONOLOGY

East Ridge: June 26, 1927, Phil Smith, Dorothea Marston

   var: **Day-of-Rest Pinnacle:** August 17, 1949, Ray Van Aken, George B. Harr, Christine Cole

Northwest Couloir: September 1, 1941, Judy Cameron (descent); June 21, 1955, John and Jean Fonda (ascent)

North Face: July 24, 1950, Robert and Doris Merriam, Leigh Ortenburger

West Ridge: July 20, 1955, John Lowry, George Ewing

Southeast Face: September 3, 1963, Ted Vaill, Hank Janes

Reese-Wilson: July 12, 1967, Rick Reese, Ted Wilson

   var: September 23, 1979, Rich Troy, Tom Newman

ROUTE 1. West Ridge. II, 5.1. First ascent July 20, 1955, by John Lowry and George Ewing; first descent August 27, 1960, by Ronald Gibbs and Thomas Smyth. From the Platforms in Garnet Canyon ascend the right (west) talus cone leading up to the bench above the south walls of the canyon. From this bench enter the cirque between Shadow Peak and the east ridge of Nez Perce. Contour around in a southwesterly direction to the col separating the two peaks. Start climbing eastward along the summit ridge. The first large tower, the most difficult one, is climbed via an 80-foot lead up jam cracks on its southwest face. The highest point is either the third tower east of the col or the second, depending on how the count is made. After gaining the summit, one can continue the west-to-east traverse, but steep western faces of more towers will be encountered. The "Knight," a spectacular monolith about 15 feet high, is reached during the course of the eastward scramble along the ridge crest. It was climbed for the first time by Lowry and Ewing by using small holds on its west face.

ROUTE 2. Southeast Face. II, 5.6. First ascent September 3, 1963, by Ted Vaill and Hank Janes. From a point about 1.3 miles up Avalanche Canyon, ascend the large couloir with an intermittent stream on the southeast slope of Shadow Peak. About three-quarters of the way up the couloir, cut diagonally up and left (northwest) to the base of the southeast face. This face guards the direct southeast approach to the eastern portion of the Shadow Peak ridge; the couloir below the right (east) edge of this face leads to the main col in the east ridge, described in *Route 3*. Near the center of the face scramble 200 feet up a couloir (filled with loose rock) to a shallow cave, where water will usually be found. Climb directly up the 5.1 face above the cave. The second pitch goes around to the right and up a vertical 25-foot wall (5.4) to a 4-foot ledge. From this ledge ascend a 5.6 open book formed by the face itself and a smooth, square pillar on the right. Once above this pitch scramble some 300 feet up and west to the summit ridge; work west along this ridge to the summit or, if time or perseverance is unavailable, to the highest convenient point. The Day-of-Rest Pinnacle (see *Route 3 variation*) will be east of the point at which the summit ridge is reached. See *American Alpine Journal,* 14, no. 1 (1964), p. 188.

ROUTE 3. ☞*East Ridge.* I, 4.0. First ascent June 26, 1927, by Phil Smith and Dorothea Marston. The long, tree-covered ridge leading toward Shadow Peak from Bradley Lake is easily ascended to the high point (10,160+) east-northeast of the main summit ridge. This point overlooks the cirque that is north of Shadow Peak and east of Nez Perce. Descend to the col in the east ridge, where the significant climbing begins. Above the col climb the ridge for a couple of ropelengths, generally staying left (south) of the crest. To reach the true summit of Shadow Peak most easily, contour around the south side of the walls guarding the first high point, the Day-of-Rest Pinnacle (see *Variation*),

and then continue west to the summit. Two or three rappels down the steep west faces of the intervening towers may be desired by parties making the complete traverse to the highest point.

Variation: Day-of-Rest Pinnacle. II, 4.0. First ascent August 17, 1949, by Ray Van Aken, George Harr, and Christine Cole. This party reached the main col in the east ridge of Shadow Peak from the cirque to the north (see *Route 1*). To gain this col, ascend the snow couloir leading east out of the cirque; an ice axe is recommended. Follow the ridge to a rotten gendarme; make a small detour off the ridge to the left (south), and continue along the south side of the ridge crest to the summit of the first tower, the Day-of-Rest Pinnacle. The highest point of Shadow Peak, which lies well to the west, was not reached by the party making this variation. It is possible to descend either north or south (easier) off the ridge crest, thus bypassing the steep west face of this pinnacle, before continuing west toward the true summit. *Time: 6 hours* from Jenny Lake; *4⅔ hours* from the Platforms.

ROUTE 4. North Face. II, 5.6, A1. First ascent July 24, 1950, by Robert and Doris Merriam and Leigh Ortenburger. See *Photo 17*. To reach this route, take the same approach as for *Route 1* to the cirque just below this face. A short snow tongue leads up to the face almost directly below the summit of the Day-of-Rest Pinnacle. From the east end of this snow tongue, scramble about 150 feet up and slightly left to the base of the first pitch. Climb 30 feet up to the right (west) to an overhanging flake and then back to the left another 30 feet to a belay position on a downsloping 3-foot ledge. A crack leads up from the east end of this ledge, which required aid on the first ascent. About 30 feet up this crack a large loose slab will be encountered. The next pitch is a tricky, horizontal traverse back to the right (west) for about 40 feet. A series of chimneys then leads left (east) up to the notch between the rotten gendarme on the east ridge and the summit.

Instead of climbing out on the east side of the peak (which one can do easily), traverse right (west) along a wide, horizontal ledge, back onto the north face. Climb directly up to the summit from this ledge. Some loose rock will be found on this last section. The final pitch comes out on the Day-of-Rest Pinnacle, which is the culmination of the north face. The highest point of Shadow Peak lies to the west. *Time: 10 hours* from Jenny Lake. See *American Alpine Journal,* 9, no. 2 (1955), pp. 147–149.

ROUTE 5. Reese–Wilson. III, 5.7. First ascent July 12, 1967, by Rick Reese and Ted Wilson. See *Photo 17*. This distinct north face route starts from the same point as *Route 4,* the eastern end of the snow tongue below the main north face. Instead of climbing up and left, this route goes directly up the nose of the face for a few feet and then cuts back right on an upward traverse for about 200 feet to a very large flake that forms a chimney. Just left of this flake climb straight up the short and very steep wall (5.7), and continue on easier rock, which is steep and has no cracks, for 170 feet (5.4), ending at a poor belay spot that offers no means of anchoring. The next pitch is up a large depression in the face for about 110 feet to the base of a steep overhanging wall. Cut right (west) here up along a ledge (5.5) to complete the route onto the summit ridge. A total of six leads are involved in this route. The rock on the north face of Shadow Peak cannot be recommended due to poor protection and an abundance of loose rocks and flakes.

Variation: III, 5.7. First ascent September 23, 1979, by Rich Troy and Tom Newman. See *Photo 17.* This variation, while similar to the 1967 route, starts from the western of the two snow tongues or ramps below the north face. Take the ramp out (east) for about 100 feet and then turn directly upward until the summit ridge is reached. Five pitches of consistent difficulty are climbed, with much rotten rock being the main problem. The ridge crest is reached immediately to the right of the Knight, mentioned in *Route 1.*

ROUTE 6. ☞*Northwest Couloir.* II, 5.1. First ascent June 21, 1955, by John and Jean Fonda. See *Photo 17.* Ascend the cirque between Shadow Peak and Nez Perce toward the col separating the two peaks, as in *Route 1,* until this northwest couloir can be seen in its entirety. It is easily recognized as the large snow tongue (in early or midseason) or distinct rotten couloir (late season) that leads to the summit ridge, just west of the main north face (*Route 4*). Ascend this couloir to a point short of the vertical wall at its head where ledges lead right (west) onto the summit ridge crest. The ridge is reached east of the true summit, so scramble west to the highest point.

NEZ PERCE PEAK (11,901)

Map: Grand Teton

This peak, with the exception of Shadow Peak, marks the end of what is actually the long east ridge of the South Teton. Nez Perce is a prominent sight from Jenny Lake, where its outline in the early years of the park suggested to some the name "Howling Dog." The official name comes directly from the Nez Perce (pronounced "nay pursay") tribe of Indians who hunted in the region near the Teton Range. Nez Perce consists of five peaks—East Peak, East Summit, main summit, West Summit, and West Peak. Deep notches detach the East Peak and East Summit, but only a shallow col distinguishes the West Summit from the main summit. The West Peak is separated by a conspicuous squarish notch. The two intersecting couloirs that bound the north face are distinctive features of this peak. They are called the "Hourglass Couloirs." The northwest side of the peak is the only side that offers easy access to the summit. The sharp west ridge has several small pinnacles, the highest of which apparently was not climbed (5.1) until August 15, 1952, by Richard Irvin. The lower south side of the peak is still little explored, as few have found the courage to abandon the accessible Garnet Canyon for the less convenient Avalanche Canyon. The view from the summit is one of the better ones in the park, showing not only the Garnet Canyon group but also the peaks to the south. Nez Perce is not an exceptionally long climb from the valley and, with an early start, even the more difficult routes can be done in a day. See *Garnet Canyon* for the approach.

CHRONOLOGY

Northwest Couloirs: July 5, 1930, Fritiof Fryxell, Phil Smith
> *var:* **South Couloir Approach:** June 30, 1934, Hans Fuhrer, Alfred Roovers
> *var:* July 19, 1951, Whitney Borland, John Spradley, Robert Ellingwood, Alfred Bush, Charles Pavlick, Barbara Weber, Sayre Rodman, Erwin Jaggi
> *var:* August 14, 1952, Willi Unsoeld, Don Kirkpatrick

East Ridge: July 12, 1931, Robert Underhill, Fritiof Fryxell; August 9, 1940, Jack Durrance, Henry Coulter (descent)
> *var:* **East Hourglass Couloir:** July 4, 1933, Paul Petzoldt, Sterling Hendricks
> *var:* **Southeast Couloir:** August 19, 1936, Fred and Irene Ayres, Allan Cameron
> *var:* **East Summit Bypass:** September 9, 1938, John B. Buck, Raymond Creekmore, Donald Grant, O. O. Heard, William Kemper
> *var:* **East Summit, South Face:** August 24, 1945, Joseph Stettner, John Speck
> *var:* **East Summit, Southeast Face:** July 15, 1949, Jim Harrang, Robert Brooke, Pete Brown
> *var:* **East Peak, North Face:** September 4, 1951, Tony Soler, Art Lembeck, Ray Moore
> *var:* **Hernando's Hideaway:** July 4, 1954, F. Keith Spencer, Richard Becker
> *var:* **Upper Southeast Chimney:** August 9, 1959, William Glosser, Pat Purdy, Jay Edwards, Peg Fowler
> *var:* **East Hourglass Ridge:** July 9, 1962, Steve Derenzo, Peter Gardiner, Richard Goldstone, Frank Knight

Southeast Face: July 21, 1935, Malcolm Smith

North Face: July 27, 1940, Jack Durrance, Fred Ayres, Henry Coulter (attempt); August 9, 1940, Jack Durrance, Henry Coulter
> *var:* **West Hourglass Couloir:** August 11, 1942, Orrin Bonney, Ernest Guild; August 16, 1951, Ed Keller, Bill Sloan, Bob Borbridge (descent)

Direct South Ridge: July 3, 1954, Robert Merriam, William Buckingham, W. Edward Clark

var: **Lower Ridge:** July 18, 1964, Peter and
    Rosanne Cleveland
var: early July 1966, Paul Ledoux, Jr., William
    Schipel
var: **Garnet Traverse:** August 10, 1967, Jack
    Weicker, Leigh Ortenburger
var: **Southwest Couloir:** July 3, 1987, Bob Gra-
    ham, Jack Bellorado
var: June 29, 1989, Keith Schultz, Jack
    Tcholske
  South Face: August 1, 1955, W. V. Graham and
    Mary Ann Matthews
  Southeast Couloir: September 3, 1960, Lloyd
    Arnesen, Victor Wylie
  South-Southwest Ridge: August 13, 1970, Leigh
    and Irene Ortenburger, David Coward
  Chief Joseph Buttress: July 31, 1988, Tom Turiano,
    Dan Powers

ROUTE 1. *South-Southwest Ridge.* III, 5.6. First ascent August 13, 1970, by Leigh and Irene Ortenburger, and David Coward. See *Photo 19.* This ridge lies immediately west of the direct south ridge (*Route 2*) and leads to the West Summit about 100 feet west of the main summit. Use the same approach as for *Route 2* from the Platforms in Garnet Canyon up into the cirque between Shadow Peak and Nez Perce. Traverse westward past the base of the direct south ridge and turn up the first gully leading north. Avoid the vertical beginning of this south-southwest ridge by climbing the large obvious chimney on the west flank of this ridge. After three straightforward pitches, the chimney culminates in an overhang, which is passed by a 20-foot awkward pitch (5.6) on the left (west) side. The fifth lead, up a narrow chimney and out on the exposed face to the right, leads to the crest of the ridge. From this point it appears possible to attack the remainder of the ridge directly on the ridge crest to the West Summit. This party, however, continued on easier 4.0 and 5.1 rock for a few hundred feet on the right (east) side of the crest, to the shallow col between the West Summit and the main summit. This is an enjoyable climb on good rock.

ROUTE 2. *Direct South Ridge.* III, 5.7. First ascent July 3, 1954, by Robert Merriam, William Buckingham, and W. Edward Clark. See *Topo 20* and *Photos 19* and *20.* This route is generally considered to be the finest available on this peak. Of the various ridges on the south side of Nez Perce Peak, this is the one that leads directly to the summit. To approach this ridge take the Garnet Canyon trail from the Lupine Meadows trailhead to the Platforms. Suitable camping areas for this route are the Platforms or the Garnet Meadows areas. Two major couloirs (either snow slopes or talus slopes, depending on the season) will be seen leading to gaps in the cliffs above the Platforms. Either of these can

be used (the easterly is perhaps the easier) to gain entry into the cirque between Shadow Peak and Nez Perce. From the col at the head of the couloir, contour to the south along the bench that leads to the upper cirque, which is bounded by the north face of Shadow Peak and the southeast face of Nez Perce. From the upper end of the cirque, two cols—the main one and a smaller one up and to the north—will be seen. Scramble up the gully to the upper col, where a traverse 200 feet farther to the west and up leads to the start of the route. (If additional climbing is desired, it is also possible to pass through the lower col to the base of the ridge, which leads to the higher col. Two or three pitches, the first of which is 5.6, take one to the top of the tower, which is separated from Nez Perce by the higher col. A short rappel is then required to descend to the col and proceed as already described.)

The first pitch is up an 80-foot chimney (5.7) on the right side of the crest. Another 500 feet of climbing near the crest brings one to a point just below a small pinnacle, which is easily passed on the right (east) side. After the short lieback crux pitch out of the notch behind the pinnacle, there is a 200-foot section of scrambling and contouring right (north) up to a steep massive buttress. Continue traversing around to the right on an obvious ledge for about 200 feet; then scramble 40 feet up to the beginning of a 120-foot lead straight up on steep rock. After another ropelength, one can turn left, back onto the difficult crest of the ridge, which can be followed for the next 100 feet. Scramble about 300 feet along a level section to a short wall. Climb directly up this wall and scramble the remaining 150 feet to the summit. This is an excellent and enjoyable climb on predominantly good rock (a rarity for Nez Perce). For descent use the regular Northwest Couloirs (*Route 9*). *Time: 7½ hours* from Garnet Canyon. See *American Alpine Journal,* 9, no. 2 (1955), pp. 147–149; *Dartmouth Mountaineering Club Journal,* 1957, p. 28, illus.

Variation: Lower Ridge. III, 5.7. First ascent July 18, 1964, by Peter and Rosanne Cleveland. The upper south ridge was reached from Lake Taminah in Avalanche Canyon by climbing the lower stepped section of the ridge. This adds considerably to the length of the climb.

Variation: III, 5.7. First ascent early July 1966, by Paul Ledoux, Jr., and William Schipel. This variation starts just left (west) of the initial 80-foot chimney of the standard route. Climb a short distance up to a ramp system that slants sharply up and left across the face. Follow this ramp system for six ropelengths until it turns around a corner and stops. Just short of this corner are two obvious vertical cracks in the wall above. Climb the right crack for four leads to reach the small pinnacle of the standard route, which is then followed to the summit. This variation, apparently all on the left (west) side of the ridge crest, contains fine climbing on excellent rock and is a good alternative, especially if the 80-foot chimney is wet.

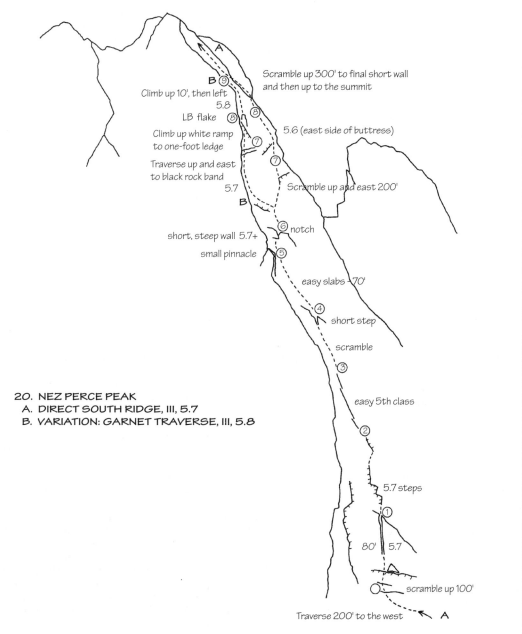

Scramble up 300' to final short wall
and then up to the summit

Climb up 10', then left
5.8
LB flake

Climb up white ramp
to one-foot ledge

Traverse up and east
to black rock band
5.7

5.6 (east side of buttress)

Scramble up and east 200'

short, steep wall 5.7+

small pinnacle

notch

easy slabs ~70'

short step

scramble

easy 5th class

20. NEZ PERCE PEAK
A. DIRECT SOUTH RIDGE, III, 5.7
B. VARIATION: GARNET TRAVERSE, III, 5.8

5.7 steps

80'   5.7

scramble up 100'

Traverse 200' to the west

Approach via Shadow Peak cirque and ascend
gully leading to the higher of two cols that
separate Shadow Peak from Nez Perce

Variation: Garnet Traverse. III, 5.8. First ascent August 10, 1967, by Jack Weicker and Leigh Ortenburger. See *Topo 20* and *Photos 19* and *20*. This significant variation goes directly up the "steep, massive buttress" referred to in the description of the original Direct South Ridge route. Climb directly upward to the left corner of the buttress. Make a somewhat tricky traverse across the face to the right and up to a black rock band, where it is possible to climb back left again to a white ramp leading to a 1-foot ledge below a large flake. Belay either from the base or top of this flake, which is climbed using lieback technique. Climb the face 10 feet above the top of the flake and then make a very delicate friction traverse left out to the extreme corner, where holds leading upward will be found. A single garnet crystal provides the crucial foothold on this traverse. This direct and consistently steep variation contains excellent rock.

Variation: Southwest Couloir. III, 5.7. First ascent July 3, 1987, by Bob Graham and Jack Bellorado. This variation follows the standard Direct South Ridge route, described in the preceding *Variation,* to the base of the "steep, massive buttress." From this point a rappel is made into the southwest couloir at a point about two-thirds of the way up from the bottom. The couloir is followed to the shallow col that separates the West Summit from the main summit. The summit is then easily reached. The couloir itself is wet, uninteresting, and of 5.6 difficulty.

Variation: III, 5.10-. First ascent June 29, 1989, by Keith Schultz and Jack Tcholske. It is unclear precisely where this variation is; however, it is an alternative to the first pitch. It is located just left of a chimney (perhaps the 80-foot 5.7 chimney of the normal route) and begins with a left-leaning, left-facing 5.9 corner. This is followed by an overhang and a 5.8, right-facing corner. Climb past another roof and the pitch finishes with a 5.10- crack.

ROUTE 3. *South Face.* III, 5.7. First ascent August 1, 1955, by W. V. Graham and Mary Ann Matthews. This route ascends the face that lies immediately east of the south ridge and west of the southeast ridge that connects with Shadow Peak. The approach is the same as for *Route 2.* The first section is not difficult and consists just of scrambling for about 500 feet, directly up the face to a very large grassy (or snow-covered) ledge. Ascend some 250 feet of 4.0 friction slabs to a large ledge covered with loose rock. About 30 feet above this ledge is a belay spot; from here climb a short distance and then traverse to the right (northeast) for 100 feet to an obvious belay spot below a nearly vertical wall. The 80 feet directly above the belay are difficult because only small holds are available. Two more difficult pitches follow to a point about 100 feet left (southwest) and 60 feet above the notch between the East Summit and the main summit. The final three or four leads of this route bring the climber to the crest of the east ridge, about 150 feet east of the summit. See *American Alpine Journal,* 12, no. 1 (1960), pp. 125–127.

ROUTE 4. *Southeast Couloir.* III, 5.6, A1. First ascent September 3, 1960, by Lloyd Arnesen and Victor Wylie. This route ascends the couloir that separates the direct south ridge from the southeast ridge that connects Nez Perce with Shadow Peak. Follow *Route 2* from the trail in Garnet Canyon up to the higher col on the Shadow Peak–Nez Perce ridge. Instead of traversing west from this col for 200 feet over to the beginning of the direct south ridge, descend slightly into the couloir on the far (west) side of the col and scramble north up this first couloir to the large chimney where the climb begins. The first short pitch of about 70 feet on steep rock and some talus leads to a belay spot at an overhang. This is turned on the left with a short bit of aid, followed by friction climbing to the next belay stance. The next 200 feet consist of broken talus. A moderate 40-foot rock section continues up the couloir to a point from which one can traverse left and up over a series of easy ledges to a prominent notch. A good belay will be found 30 feet above the notch. The next section angles up and left toward the south ridge but stays away from that crest in reaching the summit from the southeast. In this upper portion of the climb, there is some intermingling with *Route 3,* the South Face.

ROUTE 5. *Southeast Face.* II, 5.1. First ascent July 21, 1935, by Malcolm Smith. See *Photo 20.* There are probably several alternative routes on this face, and it is not clear exactly where the parties who have climbed it have gone; the following route description is that given by Smith. From the cirque between the base of the east ridge of Nez Perce and Shadow Peak, ascend into the bowl that is south of the east ridge and east of the southeast face of Nez Perce. The right (north) edge of this face is bounded by a steep and dangerous couloir that descends from the notch above the East Summit. The left (south) edge of this face is bounded by the southeast ridge of Nez Perce that rises from the higher notch reached as one traverses over toward the beginning of the Direct South Ridge route (see *Route 2*). The southeast ridge culminates at a small tower, separated by a small notch from the upper southeast face of the mountain. This route begins near the south edge of the face, in a shallow couloir. A short distance above the starting point, traverse right without losing any altitude, across smooth, steeply sloping rock to a point in the middle of the southeast face, just above a snow patch that is present most of the summer. It is also possible to reach this point directly from below, and probably even from the right. After reaching this point, a series of ledges and steep broken cliffs can be followed without great difficulty to the summit. This is an enjoyable climb on good rock.

ROUTE 6. *East Ridge.* II, 5.4. First ascent July 12, 1931, by Robert Underhill and Fritiof Fryxell; first descent (north traverse of East Summit) August 9, 1940, by Jack Durrance and Henry Coulter. This route has achieved some popularity because of its accessibility from the Garnet Canyon trail. From the Platforms, follow a climbers' trail that leads up to a small notch on the bench above the south walls of Garnet Canyon, at the edge of the cirque between Shadow Peak and Nez Perce. From the meadows on the bench, two broad shelves with scattered trees angle up, from right to left, to meet the east ridge. Take the upper shelf all the way to the ridge, where two ropelengths lead to the top of a small pinnacle; behind and to the south is a deep chimney (Hernando's Hideaway). From the small notch behind this pinnacle climb a jam crack (20 feet) on the north side and then move back onto the ridge. It is then just a scramble to the top of the East Peak. To reach the first notch, which is just below, downclimb about 60 feet slightly on the south side of the ridge to the first rappel point. Now either make one long rappel (150 feet) or two rappels (100 feet and 50 feet), or downclimb slightly on the north side to reach the second rappel point.

From the notch there are two possibilities: (1) Climb directly up and out of the notch on the west side. The first short pitch bears left on small holds. This pitch is followed by a traverse up and right for one or two ropelengths to ledges on the north side. At the first convenient point turn left and up onto the crest of the ridge again. The difficulty will depend on the exact route selected to get past this steep section of the ridge. Then scramble to the East Summit. (2) From the notch, contour right (north) for about 150 feet to a shallow chimney that leads upward and back toward the ridge. About six ropelengths bring one to the crest of the ridge above the steep section.

From the East Summit, either make a 120-foot rappel (entirely free) to the second notch between the East Summit and the true summit or climb partway down the north side before rappelling 60 feet to the notch. The downclimb is not easy to find. Old slings will be found at both rappel sites. Another more difficult possibility is to downclimb all the way to the notch. From the notch scramble the remainder of the ridge westward to the summit. *Time: 6½ to 9 hours from Garnet Canyon; 8 to 11½ hours from Jenny Lake.* See *American Alpine Journal,* 5, no. 2 (1944), pp. 220–232, illus.; *Appalachia,* 18, no. 4 (December 1931), pp. 388–408, illus.; *Chicago Mountaineering Club Newsletter,* 2, no. 6 (July–December 1948), pp. 2–3; *Trail and Timberline,* no. 447 (March 1956), pp. 47–48.

Variation: East Hourglass Couloir. II, 5.4. First ascent July 4, 1933, by Paul Petzoldt and Sterling Hendricks. See *Photo 21.* This climb starts from the apex of the talus cone that forms the bottom half of the Hourglass below the north face. Follow the left (east) couloir, sometimes using the rock on the left (east) edge, straight to the notch between the East Peak and the East Summit. This route is not especially recommended because of danger from loose and falling rock. In early season the snow in the couloir is quite steep.

Variation: Southeast Couloir. II, 5.4. First ascent August 19, 1936, by Fred and Irene Ayres and Alan Cameron. On this route the notch between the East Peak and the East Summit is reached via the southeast couloir. From the Shadow Peak cirque continue around and south past the base of the east ridge of Nez Perce on grass and scree ledges to the large southeast couloir, which extends from the cirque up to the notch. Some loose rock should be expected in this couloir, formed from a line of weakness in the rock formations. On the north face this same line continues as the East Hourglass Couloir. From the notch continue up the regular East Ridge route.

Variation: East Summit Bypass. II, 5.6. First ascent September 9, 1938, by John B. Buck, Raymond Creekmore, Donald Grant, O. O. Heard, and William Kemper. On this variation the East Summit is bypassed completely. From the notch between the East Peak and the East Summit, a series of ledges, chimneys, and flakes takes one completely around the north face of the East Summit to the very steep snow (in early season) leading to the notch between the East Summit and the true summit. This traverse is on poor and loose rock with some danger from falling objects (ice, rocks).

Variation: East Summit, South Face. II, 5.7. First ascent August 24, 1945, by Joseph Stettner and John Speck. This difficult and exposed variation on the upper south face of the East Summit can be started either by traversing up and left (south) out of the notch between the East Peak and the East Summit or by climbing partway up the southeast couloir described earlier. In either case, gain the broad, yet steeply inclined shelf that parallels the ridge crest about halfway up the south face of the East Summit. Some easy roped climbing will be required to reach the upper, west end of this ledge. From here directly ascend the steep, difficult, and very exposed face above, climbing just to the left (west) of an overhanging nose. See *The Iowa Climber,* 2, no. 2 (Summer 1948), p. 70, illus.

Variation: East Summit, Southeast Face. II, 5.6. First ascent July 15, 1949, by Jim Harrang, Robert Brooke, and Pete Brown. From the Shadow Peak cirque traverse south around the base of the East Peak to the southeast couloir leading to the notch between the East Peak and the East Summit. Scramble up this rock-filled couloir for about 200 feet, until one can easily exit left (west) onto the large slanting shelf, as described in the *East Summit, South Face variation,* earlier. Proceed up (west) along this shelf past one buttress to the base of a steep, obvious 40-foot chimney leading north up toward the ridge crest. To reach the top of the East Summit from the top of this chimney, bear left (diagonally) up a series of cracks and flakes for about four pitches.

Variation: East Peak, North Face. II, 5.6. First ascent September 4, 1951, by Tony Soler, Art Lembeck, and Ray Moore. This route goes directly up the very steep north face of the East Peak from the broad bench that cuts across the face about halfway from the canyon floor to the top of the East Peak. The approach to the broad bench is described in the *East Hourglass Ridge variation,* later. Little information is available on this route. It involves some 4th-class climbing with at least three pitches that are 5th class.

Variation: Hernando's Hideaway. II, 5.4. First ascent July 4, 1954, by F. Keith Spencer and Richard Becker. Follow the standard approach past the base of the east ridge to its southeast side. Here a prominent, deep chimney system, several hundred feet long, leads to the ridge east of the East Peak and isolates the small pinnacle mentioned in the main description of *Route 6.* A short bit of climbing past an overhang leads into the lower portion of this chimney. The first two pitches require stemming before the chimney opens up a bit. Chockstones fill the upper narrower portion. The final pitch that brings one out onto the east ridge is less difficult. This splendid chimney was originally described as "undesirable, narrow, deep, dark, wet, and slimy."

Variation: Upper Southeast Chimney. II, 5.4. First ascent August 9, 1959, by William Glosser, Pat Purdy, Jay Edwards, and Peg Fowler. Follow the standard approach past the base of the east ridge to the bowl at the base of the southeast face of Nez Perce. From the northwest corner of the bowl climb directly up the chimney (or small couloir) at the extreme right (north) edge of the southeast face, using mainly the left side of the chimney. This chimney leads to the notch between the main summit and the East Summit. This route cannot be recommended due to the considerable danger of falling rock.

Variation: East Hourglass Ridge. II, 5.4. First ascent July 9, 1962, by Steve Derenzo, Peter Gardiner, Richard Goldstone, and Frank Knight. See *Photo 21.* The left (east) border of the East Hourglass Couloir is a distinct ridge that begins at the intersection of the Hourglass Couloirs and leads to the top of the East Peak of Nez Perce. This ridge is divided into two sections by the broad bench that cuts across the north face of the East Peak about halfway from the floor of Garnet Canyon to the summit. This variation ascends the upper portion of the ridge. The initial task is to gain the broad bench, which holds a small, permanent snowfield, or perhaps glacier, below the north face of the East Peak. Take the standard approach from the Platforms to the grassy meadow on the initial bench just above the south walls of Garnet Canyon. Proceed southwest to the low-angle slabs that form the east end of the broad bench. Climb these slabs, near the right edge of a small chute, to an obvious ledge leading right (north). From the end of this ledge one can bushwhack west onto the broad open bench. Continue easily west to the base of the complex of chutes leading up to the crest of the East Hourglass Ridge. Take the middle chute to the sharp notch between a pointed gendarme and the large buttress on the left (south). From the notch angle left (east) on broken rock about 60 feet to some steep, shallow chimneys. Climb straight up for 30 feet to a sloping ledge that angles right toward the very exposed northwest corner of the buttress. Continue beyond the end of the ledge, past

an awkward niche, to a groove in the light-colored rock that leads to the top of the buttress. Four ropelengths take one to the top of the East Peak.

ROUTE 7. Chief Joseph Buttress. III, 5.10-. First ascent July 31, 1988, by Tom Turiano and Dan Powers. See *Topo 21.* This route ascends the buttress on the north face of the East Peak, rising directly from the small snowfield or pocket glacier on the broad bench at the base of the face. Approach the bench from the Garnet Canyon trail as described in *Route 6, East Hourglass Ridge variation.* Walk west along this bench to the west side of the pocket glacier. Scramble up talus and scree to the 3rd-class grassy ramp that diagonals up and back to the left (east). Refer to the topo for the technical details of the route. For protection take a regular rack to 3 inches.

ROUTE 8. North Face. III, 5.6. First ascent August 9, 1940, by Jack Durrance and Henry Coulter; previous attempt turned back by storm on July 27, 1940, by Jack Durrance, Henry Coulter, and Fred Ayres. See *Photo 21.* This is the broken face that rises directly to the summit from the intersection point of the two Hourglass Couloirs. From the Platforms proceed well into the Meadows of Garnet Canyon before turning south up the long talus cone that forms the lower half of the Hourglass. The route starts at the top of the talus where the two Hourglass Couloirs cross. Scramble up about 200 feet onto a wide ledge. Above this ledge is the first pitch of climbing, an obvious jam crack in the middle of the 30-foot face above. From the ledge above this pitch, climb 15 feet up the left corner of the face above to a stance on the corner itself; then traverse left on a delicate friction ledge into an easy chimney. From the comfortable ledge at the top of this chimney, continue up in a large chimney leading to the right (west). After two long pitches, the chimney peters out at a point somewhat west of the summit. Start edging left (east) until beneath a vertical section which can be climbed on excellent holds. From the top of this section, scramble out on the summit ridge very near the summit. This description is only one of the many variations that have been climbed on this large face. In general, the more direct the route to the summit, the more difficult it will be. *Time: 7 to 9½ hours* from Garnet Canyon.

Variation: West Hourglass Couloir. II, 4.0. First ascent August 11, 1942, by Orrin Bonney and Ernest Guild. See *Photo 21.* Starting from top of the talus cone below the intersection of the two Hourglass Couloirs, this variation follows directly up the right (west) couloir, sometimes using its right wall. During most of the season the couloir will be snow filled. From the top of the couloir, angle back left toward the summit, which is now somewhat to the east. As an option, there are at least three places, half to three-quarters of the way up the couloir, where one can cut left (east) out onto the north face from the couloir. In early season this couloir provides a fast descent via glissade for experienced climbers.

SECTION 1: SOUTH OF DEATH CANYON

1. Peak 10,450 (South Aspect), Rock Springs Buttress (Western and Central)

Upper West Buttress
A-E. (See Topo #2)

Main Central Buttress
F. (See Topo #1)
G. Chimney, 5.7

H. 5.8
I. Descent route from tram

2. Peak 10,450 (South Aspect), Rock Springs Buttress (Eastern)
Lower Eastern Buttress
A-E. (See Topo #2)

3. Prospectors Mountain (North Aspect), Lower Northeast Face
Death Canyon, South Side Rock Climbs

A. Northeast Face
B. Predator
C. Raven Crack
D. Carson–Whiton

4. Albright Peak (Southwest Aspect), Cathedral Rock
Death Canyon, North Side Rock Climbs
A. Aerial Boundaries   B. Escape From Death (last pitch)

5. Albright Peak (South Aspect), Cathedral Rock
Death Canyon, North Side Rock Climbs

A. Vas Deferens
B. Vas Deferens; *var:* August 11th Start
C. Lot's Slot

D. Cottonmouth
E. Alpine Cow
F. Caveat Emptor

G. The Snaz
H. Sunshine Daydream
I. Fallen Angel

6. Albright Peak (South Aspect), Cathedral Rock
Death Canyon, North Side Rock Climbs

A. The Snaz
B. The Snaz; *var:* Cousin Leroy
C. Sunshine Daydream

D. Schmitz-Kanzler Dihedral
E. Fallen Angel
F. Pillar of Death

7. **Albright Peak (South Aspect), Omega Buttresses (Western and Central)**
Death Canyon, North Side Rock Climbs

A. Omega Buttresses (Western)
B. Annals of Time

C. Right Parallel Crack
D. Dihedral of Horrors

E. Cardiac Arêtes

8. Albright Peak (South Aspect—Aerial), Omega Buttresses (Western and Central)

Death Canyon, North Side Rock Climbs

A. Omega Buttresses (Western)

B. Omega Buttresses (Central), Ship's Prow Pillar

C. Ship's Prow Pillar (approach)

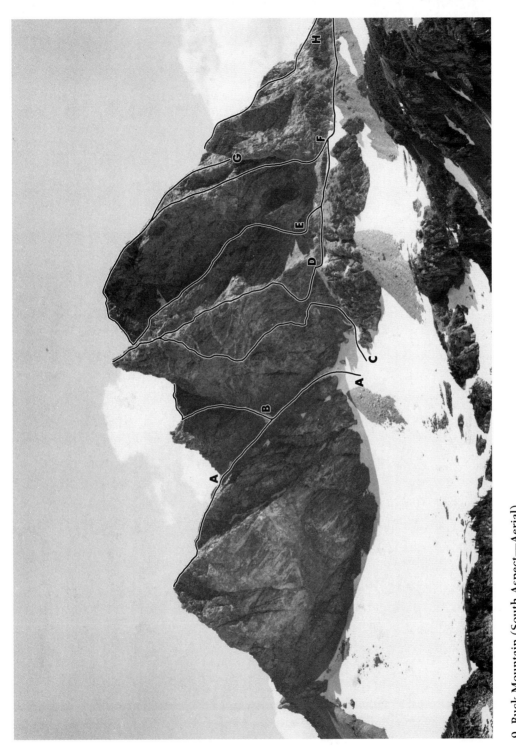

9. **Buck Mountain (South Aspect—Aerial)**
   A. West Peak, South Couloir
   B. Southwest Couloir
   C. West Summit, South Face
   D. West Summit, South Ridge
   E. South Couloir
   F. Southeast Ridge; *var.* 1962
   G. Southeast Ridge
   H. Southeast Ridge; *var.* 1963

10. Buck Mountain (East Aspect—Aerial)

A. Southeast Ridge; *var.* 1963

B. Southeast Ridge

C. East Face

D. East Ridge

11. Buck Mountain (Northeast Aspect—Aerial)

A. East Ridge
B. Northeast Chimney
C. Northeast Chimney; *var:* Sowles

D. North Face, The Buck Sanction
E. North Face, West Couloir
F. North-Northwest Ridge

12. Buck Mountain (North Aspect—Aerial)

A. North Face, The Buck Sanction
B. North Face, East Couloir
C. North Central Ridge

D. North Face, West Couloir
E. North-Northwest Ridge

F. North-Northwest Ridge; *var:* The Wedge
G. West Peak, North Couloir

13. Avalanche Canyon (South Aspect—Aerial)
North Side Rock Climbs

A Flying Buttress, Good For The Soul　　　B. Blind Man's Bluff　　　C. Yukon Jack Arête

14. Veiled Peak (South Aspect—Aerial)

A. South Ridge
B. Southeast Flank

C. East Ridge (1940)
D. East Ridge (1952)

15. **Mount Wister and Veiled Peak (North Aspect—Aerial)**

A. Northeast Couloir; *var:* 1928
B. North Face, East Chimney
C. Direct North Face

D. North Face, West Chimney
E. Northwest Arête

F. Northwest Couloir
G. Veiled Peak, Northeast Ledges

16. Matternought Peak and Cloudveil Dome (South Aspect—Aerial)

A. Taminah Arête; *var:* 1979   B. Taminah Arête   C. Dem Bones

17. Shadow Peak (North Aspect)

A. North Face
B. Reese-Wilson

C. Reese-Wilson; *var:* 1979
D. Northwest Couloir

18. Nez Perce Peak (Northwest Aspect)
    A. Northwest Couloirs   B. Descent rappel point (optional)

19. Nez Perce Peak (Southwest Aspect)

A. South-Southwest Ridge

B. Direct South Ridge

C. Direct South Ridge; *var:* Garnet Traverse

20. Nez Perce Peak (South Aspect—Aerial)

A. Direct South Ridge; *var:* Garnet Traverse   C. Southeast Face
B. Direct South Ridge

21. Nez Perce Peak (North Aspect)
A. East Ridge; *var:* East Hourglass Ridge
B. East Ridge; *var:* East Hourglass Couloir
C. North Face
D. North Face; *var:* West Hourglass Couloir
E. Northwest Couloirs

22. Cloudveil Dome (South Aspect—Aerial)

A. Matthews South Face
B. Contemporary Comfort; *var: Miss Demeanor*
C. Armed Robbery
D. Silver Lining
E. WFR
F. Cut Loose; Chouinard-Black (approximate)
G. Cut Loose; Buckingham-Fryxell (approximate)

23. Cloudveil Dome (Northeast Aspect)

24. South Teton (Southwest Aspect—Aerial)

25. South Teton (Southeast Aspect—Aerial)
A. Matternought Peak, Taminah Arête

B. Matternought Peak, Dem Bones

26. South Teton (North Aspect—Aerial)
A. East Ridge
B. Northwest Couloir

27. Middle Teton (Southwest Aspect) *James L. Olson*
A. Southwest Couloir

28. Middle Teton (South Aspect)

    A. Chouinard Ridge   C. Ellingwood Couloir

    B. Southeast Ridge   D. Dike Pinnacle

29. Middle Teton (Southeast Aspect)
A. South Couloir
B. Southeast Ridge

C. Ellingwood Couloir

30. Middle Teton (East Aspect—Aerial)

Garnet Canyon, West Side Rock Climbs

A. Direct East Buttress   B. Middle Teton Glacier

31. Middle Teton (Northeast Aspect)
    A. Middle Teton Glacier
    B. Taylor
    C. Robbins-Fitschen

    D. Briggs-Higbee Pillar
    E. Goodrich Chimney
    F. Northwest Ice Couloir

32. Middle Teton (North Aspect)

A. Taylor
B. Robbins-Fitschen
C. Whiton-Wiggins Dihedral

D. Jackson-Woodmencey Dihedral
E. Goodrich Chimney
F. Approach from behind Bonney's Pinnacle

33. Middle Teton (West Aspect—Aerial)
A. North Ridge   B. Northwest Ice Couloir

34. Grand Teton, Mount Owen and Teewinot Mountain (Southeast Aspect—Aerial)

36. Grand Teton, Wall Street Ledge on the Exum Ridge

35. Glenn Exum on the Exum Ridge, 1951   *Leigh Ortenburger*

37. Grand Teton (West Aspect)

A. Owen-Spalding
B. Wittich Crack
C. Collins-Hume
D. Emerson Chimney

38. Grand Teton (Southwest Aspect—Aerial)

A. Upper Saddle
B. Pownall-Gilkey

C. Jackson-Rickert Crack
D. West Face of the Exum Ridge
E. Exum Ridge

39. Grand Teton and Middle Teton (Southwest Aspect—Aerial) *George A. Grant, National Park Service*

40. Grand Teton (South Aspect—Aerial)

A. Exum Ridge
B. Lower Exum Ridge
C. Lower Exum Ridge; *var:* Gold Face
D. It's Not a Chimney
E. Burgette Arête

F. Beckey Couloir
G. Petzoldt Ridge; *var:* Direct
H. Petzoldt Ridge
I. Buckingham Buttress
J. Stettner Couloir

K. Underhill Ridge
L. Underhill Ridge; *var:* Direct
M. Otterbody Chimneys
N. East Ridge

41. The Enclosure and Grand Teton (South Aspect)

A. South Face, Jim's Big Day
B. Owen-Spalding
C. The Needle
D. Upper Saddle
E. Approach to Exum Ridge via Wall Street

42. Grand Teton, Underhill Ridge (Southwest Aspect)

A. Stettner Couloir
B. Underhill Ridge
C. Underhill Ridge; *var:* Direct

43. Grand Teton (East Aspect)

A. Teepe Pillar
B. Lev
C. Beyer East Face I
D. Keith-Eddy East Face
E. Southeast Chimney
F. Beyer East Face II
G. Horton East Face
H. Smith Outerbody

44. Grand Teton, Lower North Face (North Aspect)

A. East Ridge
B. East Ridge; *var:* King-Fitch, 1977
C. Route Canal
D. East Ridge; *var:* North Molar Tooth Couloir
E. Northeast Couloir

F. Northeast Couloir; *var:* Sinclair-Ortenburger, 1962
G. Northeast Buttress
H. Northeast Buttress; *var:* Little Wing
I. Grand North Couloir

45. Grand Teton (North Aspect)

A. East Ridge
B. Route Canal
C. East Ridge; *var:* North Molar Tooth Couloir
D. Northeast Couloir
E. Northeast Buttress; *var:* Little Wing
F. Northeast Buttress

G. Grand North Couloir
H. Northeast Couloir; *var:* Sinclair-Ortenburger, 1962
I. Simpleton's Pillar
J. Goodro-Shane
K. North Face; *var:* Direct Finish
L. Medrick-Ortenburger

46. Grand Teton (North-northwest Aspect—Aerial)
- A. North Face; *var:* Direct Finish
- B. North Ridge; *var:* American Cracks
- C. North Ridge; *var:* Italian Cracks
- D. North Ridge
- E. Loki's Tower

47. Enclosure (North-northwest Aspect—Aerial)

A. Black Ice Couloir; *var:* Alberich's Alley
B. Black Ice Couloir
C. Visionquest Couloir
D. Lookin' For Trouble
E. North Face, High Route
F. Enclosure Ice Couloir
G. Rhinelander-Jordan
H. Valhalla Traverse Ledge
I. Valhalla Traverse Ledge (Black Ice Couloir approach)

48. Grand Teton and the Enclosure (Northwest Aspect)

A. Valhalla Traverse Ledge
B. Valhalla Traverse Ledge (West Grandstand approach)
C. Northwest Chimney

D. Valhalla Traverse Ledge (Black Ice Couloir approach)
E. The Enclosure, North Face, Lowe Route

49. Grand Teton and the Enclosure (Northwest Aspect—Aerial)

A. Valhalla Traverse Ledge
B. Valhalla Traverse Ledge (West Grandstand approach)
C. Valhalla Traverse Ledge (Black Ice Couloir approach)
D. Loki's Tower
E. Northwest Chimney
F. Northwest Chimney; *var:* West Face Finish
G. West Face

H. Owen-Spalding
I. The Enclosure, North Face, Emotional Rescue; *var:* Direct
J. The Enclosure, North Face, Emotional Rescue
K. The Enclosure, North Face, High Route
L. The Enclosure, Northwest Ridge
   var: Kimbrough-Olson Crack

50. Grand Teton and the Enclosure (Northwest Aspect—Aerial)

A. Valhalla Traverse Ledge
B. Valhalla Traverse Ledge (West Grandstand approach)
C. Grand Teton, West Face
D. Valhalla Traverse Ledge (Black Ice Couloir approach)
E. The Enclosure, Northwest Ridge; var: Kimbrough-Olson Crack
F. The Enclosure, West Face

51. Second Tower (West Aspect)

52. Teepe Pillar (East Aspect)
    A. Underhill-Henderson
    B. Direct East Face
    C. Northeast Face

53. Second Tower (South Aspect)
   A. Otterbody Chimneys

54. Fairshare Tower (Southeast Aspect)
Garnet Canyon, North Side Rock Climbs

A. Corkscrew
B. Corkscrew; *var:* F.N.G.

C. Watchtower, Direct South Ridge
D. Disappointment Peak, Southwest Ridge

55. Red Sentinel (East Aspect)
A. East Face and North Face

56. Upper Garnet Canyon (East Aspect)

A. Upper Meadows
B. Spalding Falls
C. Caves

D. Middle Teton Glacier moraine
E. Lower Saddle Headwall
F. Lower Saddle

57. Disappointment Peak (West Aspect)
   A. West Face
   B. Great West Chimney
   C. West Side Story

58. Disappointment Peak (Southwest Aspect)

A. West Buttress
B. Great West Chimney
C. West Side Story
D. Whiton-Wiggins
E. Whiton-Wiggins; *var:* Sacco-Vanzetti Memorial
F. Jern-Wiggins

59. Disappointment Peak (Southeast Aspect—Aerial)

A. Fairshare Tower, Corkscrew
B. Watchtower, Direct South Ridge
C. Southwest Ridge
D. Caves Arête
E. Irene's Arête
F. Beelzebub Arête
G. Delicate Arête
H. South Central Buttress
I. Grunt Arête

J. Open Book
K. Almost Arête; *var:* Gray Slab
L. Almost Arête
M. Satisfaction Crack
N. Satisfaction Buttress
O. Fifth Column
P. Fifth Column; *var:* The Knob
Q. Lance's Arête
R. Hidden Arête

S. Lake Ledges
T. Snow Couloir
U. East Ridge
V. The Caves
W. Garnet Canyon Trail
X. Surprise Lake outlet stream
Y. Teton Glacier terminal moraine
Z. Disappointment Peak (summit)

60. Disappointment Peak (South Aspect)
A. Caves Arête   B. Irene's Arête

61. Disappointment Peak (South Aspect)
    A. Delicate Arête
    B. South Central Buttress; *var:* Dietschy-Langford, 1957
    C. South Central Buttress

62. Disappointment Peak (South Aspect)
   A. Open Book

63. Disappointment Peak (Southwest Aspect)

  A. Almost Arête; *var:* Gray Slab
  B. Almost Arête; *var:* Carson-Evangelista, 1980
  C. Almost Arête
  D. Almost Arête; *var:* Almost Overhanging
  E. Satisfaction Crack
  F. Satisfaction Arête
  G. Satisfaction Buttress

64. Disappointment Peak (North Aspect)
A. Snow Couloir
B. East Ridge
C. Upper North Face approach

65. Disappointment Peak (Northeast Aspect—Aerial)

A. Lake Ledges
B. East Ridge

C. Pownall-Unsoeld North Face
D. Chouinard-Frost Chimney

E. Kimbrough-Rickert
F. Direct North Face

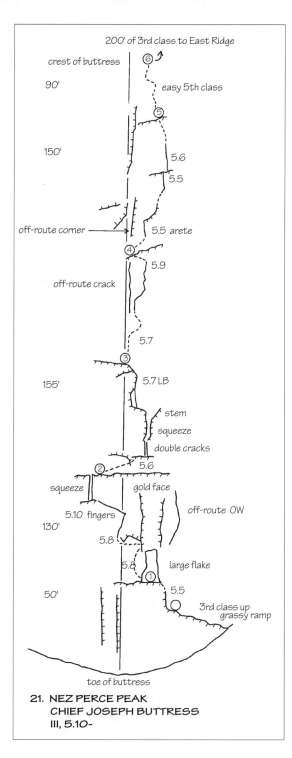

200' of 3rd class to East Ridge

crest of buttress   ⑥↗

90'

easy 5th class

⑤

150'

5.6

5.5

off-route corner ──→   5.5 arete

④

5.9

off-route crack

5.7

③

155'   5.7 LB

stem

squeeze

double cracks

②····   5.6

squeeze   gold face

5.10 fingers   off-route OW

130'

5.8

5.8   large flake

①

50'   5.5

○ 3rd class up
grassy ramp

toe of buttress

**21. NEZ PERCE PEAK
CHIEF JOSEPH BUTTRESS
III, 5.10−**

ROUTE 9. ☞*Northwest Couloirs.* II, 4.0. First ascent July 5, 1930, by Fritiof Fryxell and Phil Smith. See *Photos 18* and *21.* From the Lupine Meadows trailhead, take the Garnet Canyon trail to its end at the Platforms. Continue upcanyon to the Meadows, the relatively flat bouldery area just east of the Middle Teton. From here climb talus or snow, depending on the season, toward the col between Nez Perce and Cloudveil Dome. The route lies on the flank of the west ridge, well north of the crest, so do not continue all the way to the col. Beyond the lower cliffs of Nez Perce, there are several shallow couloirs leading southeast. All of them can be climbed, but one of the central ones is easier although a bit difficult to find. There is much loose and unpleasant rock in this part of the climb. Scramble up broken ledges, traversing left (north), toward the slabs that lead out northward from the squarish notch between the West Summit and the small West Peak. This notch will now be a hundred yards or so off to the right. The usual route crosses these slabs and then traverses left (north) before turning up a series of cracks and chimneys that lead back toward the ridge west of the summit. Continue east along the narrow arête that connects this ridge with the true summit. If there is a choice, this route on Nez Perce is recommended for early season, because much of the loose rubble will be covered with snow.

To descend from the summit, follow the arête leading west and downclimb the north side of the ridge past the West Summit (this section is sometimes rappelled) to the main rappel point where many old slings will be found. A 60-foot rappel (partly free) can be made from this point down to the squarish notch mentioned earlier; however, it is also a simple matter to downclimb carefully back around above the slabs. In early season the lower descent is facilitated by the long snow slope, which is excellent for those experienced in glissading. *Time: 4¼ to 6 hours* from Garnet Canyon; *6⅓ to 7½ hours* from Jenny Lake. See *Appalachia,* 18, no. 4 (December 1931), pp. 388–408, illus.; *Chicago Mountaineering Club Newsletter,* 2, no. 6 (July–December 1948), pp. 2–3; 5, no. 1 (January 1951), p. 5.

Variation: South Couloir Approach. II, 4.0. First ascent June 30, 1934, by Hans Fuhrer and Alfred Roovers. Although it has rarely been done, it is possible to reach the ridge between Cloudveil Dome and Nez Perce from the south by hiking up Avalanche Canyon and turning north up the large talus cone just below Shoshoko Falls. This party reached the west ridge of Nez Perce at a point east of the main col that lies close to Cloudveil Dome. By adroit selection of the proper southern couloir, one can attain the ridge at a secondary col about 0.2 mile west of the summit. From the ridge cut left (north) onto the northwest ledges and join the regular *Route 9* just below the slabs.

Variation: II, 4.0. First ascent July 19, 1951, by Whitney Borland, John Spradley, Robert Ellingwood, Alfred Bush, Charles Pavlick, Barbara Weber, Sayre Rodman, and Erwin

Jaggi. From the squarish notch between the West Summit and the West Peak, it is possible to traverse left (first north, then east) all the way over to the east ridge above the East Summit and then finish the climb on the upper easy portions of that ridge (see *Route 6*).

   Variation: II, 5.6. First ascent August 14, 1952, by Willi Unsoeld and Don Kirkpatrick. It is possible to climb a difficult crack directly up out of the squarish notch on the west ridge of Nez Perce, which was already described. After a single lead, the rappel slings are passed, and one can then climb on the north side to the West Summit where the arête is followed to the top.

GARNET CANYON, SOUTH SIDE ROCK CLIMBS (CA. 9,600)

Map: Grand Teton

The conspicuous walls on the south and north sides of the lower section of Garnet Canyon contain some excellent rock and many climbs have been worked out on these cliffs. These routes do not lead to the summit of any peak. The southern routes are described in this section.

ROUTE 1. Big Bluff. III, 5.6, A5. First ascent August 12, 1960, by Royal Robbins and Joe Fitschen. The ascent of this impressive overhang, rising directly above and south of the Platforms, illustrated, at the time, state-of-the-art Yosemite aid techniques. Starting from the gully to the west of the overhang, ascend easy ledges to the broad terrace under the 150-foot overhang. Begin near the left side of the overhang and climb diagonally to the right, up a steep red flake, to a bolt on a sloping ledge. Now traverse horizontally 30 feet and then upward to a quartzlike rock formation where a bolt hole should be found (a bolt was placed but fell out after it was used). This pitch is extremely difficult. The route now angles generally up to the left to the top edge of the overhang. Use caution with the large, loose flake that is met during the climb. Most of the climb is artificial; many pitons and three bolts were used on the first ascent. See *American Alpine Journal,* 12, no. 2 (1961), pp. 373–377; *Sierra Club Bulletin,* 46, no. 8 (October 1961), pp. 53–54.

ROUTE 2. Lemon Crack. III, 5.9, A3. First ascent August 1, 1969, by Peter Cleveland and Mike Yokell. This overhanging route, on the same cliff as *Route 1,* generally diagonals from left (east) to right (west). Start the climb at a cave with a large roof, beneath a white face characterized by a lemon-shaped block about 20 feet high. The first lead of 70 feet uses aid (A3) over the initial roof and then up the "lemon," ending with 30 feet free (5.8) to a large ledge with grass. Next drop down to the right, traverse around a corner, and diagonal up and right (5.9) past the tip of a tree (which grows from the ground up to this point) onto a belay ledge at the end of 90 feet. The third pitch (5.6) is a 60-foot traverse right on ledges and then up to a large belay ledge

just below an open book. The next lead (5.7) avoids this open book by traversing right and up (30 feet) to a large sloping ledge for the belay below an overhanging open book that diagonals off to the left. The fifth pitch (90 feet) uses aid to ascend the open book, mantling onto a sloping ledge on the left. At this point a very difficult tension traverse to the right permits access to a good ledge, from which one can walk around the corner to the belay position. The sixth lead is long (140 feet), consists of 5.7 climbing, and bypasses an overhanging band on the left. The final pitch is up easy rock to the top of the cliff. The climb is continuously interesting, containing a surprising amount of free climbing for a face that overhangs slightly from bottom to top.

CLOUDVEIL DOME (12,026)

Map: Grand Teton

On the long east ridge of the South Teton leading down toward Nez Perce Peak, Cloudveil Dome is but one of the several high points and pinnacles. Although it is not sufficiently separated from the upper portion of this ridge to be considered a separate peak, Cloudveil Dome was named before the first ascent because of its prominence when viewed from Jackson Hole and has become a standard Teton mountaineering objective. Even though the regular routes offer little difficulty to the experienced climber, the climb of Cloudveil Dome is nevertheless a worthwhile undertaking because its rounded summit provides a fine viewpoint for many of the peaks surrounding Garnet Canyon. All of the routes on the peak can be approached via Garnet Canyon and will require a full day from the valley; however, it is more pleasant to start from a camp at the Platforms or the Garnet Canyon Meadows. The climbs of the south face routes can also reasonably utilize the straightforward Avalanche Canyon approach.

CHRONOLOGY

East Ridge: July 21, 1931, Fritiof Fryxell, Anderson Hilding

West Ridge: July 21, 1931, Fritiof Fryxell, Anderson Hilding (descent); August 5, 1932, Fred D. Ayres (ascent)

North Face: August 22, 1950, Richard Pownall, N. Paul Kenworthy

 var: August 1, 1961, Jim Greig, Fred Wright

 var: **Nimbus:** July 1993, Alex Lowe, Stephen Koch (first ascent)

Matthews South Face: July 31, 1955, W. V. Graham and Mary Ann Matthews

Cut Loose: August 2, 1977, Yvon Chouinard, Rick Black

Armed Robbery: August 15, 1978, Mike Munger, Rick Liu

Contemporary Comfort: September 2, 1978,
Charlie Fowler, Bill Feiges
   var: **Miss Demeanor:** July 23, 1986, Paul
      Duval, Beverly Boynton
Silver Lining: July 12, 1979, Mike Munger, Bill
   Nicholson
WFR: July 11, 1990, Jim Dorward, Steve Rickert

ROUTE 1. West Ridge. II, 3.0. First descent July 21, 1931, by Fritiof Fryxell and Anderson Hilding; first ascent August 5, 1932, by Fred D. Ayres. This route is used exclusively for making the traverse from the South Teton (or from Cloudveil Dome to the South Teton). The ridge itself is but a scramble and offers no difficulties. *Time: 4 hours* from the summit of the South Teton.

ROUTE 2. Matthews South Face. II, 5.6, A1. First ascent July 31, 1955, by W. V. Graham and Mary Ann Matthews. See *Topo 22* and *Photo 22.* See *Avalanche Canyon* for the approach to Lake Taminah. From the east end of the lake, ascend the talus gully up toward the south face of Cloudveil Dome, which contains a considerable expanse of high-angle rock where several routes have now been climbed. At the base of the south face is a broad bench formed in a band of crumbly red rock that cuts horizontally across the south ridges of Nez Perce, Cloudveil Dome, and the South Teton. Two parallel cracks or ledges diagonal steeply up and to the left (west) across the south face above the bench. Ascend the lower crack or ramp up and across the south face, to a point on the west side of the face where the crack peters out. From here, go around the corner and then directly up for about four pitches to a broad ledge that leads right (east) to the higher of the two cracks. Climb this crack back to the west, arriving at the summit ridge just west of the summit. *Time: 6¾ hours* from Avalanche Canyon. See *American Alpine Journal,* 10, no. 1 (1956), pp. 116–119.

ROUTE 3. Contemporary Comfort. IV, 5.10. First ascent September 2, 1978, by Charlie Fowler and Bill Feiges. See *Photo 22,* although the route is not marked on it. This imperfectly known route apparently takes a line similar to the lower portion of Armed Robbery (*Route 4*) to reach the Matthews ramp and then follows this ramp out farther to the west, arching out up and left. When the crack thins out, a 5.10 pitch is climbed to reach a steep dihedral leading upward. Fourth-class climbing back to the right then provides access to the upper diagonal ramp. From here the line leads more or less directly up to the summit, perhaps along a line similar to that of Silver Lining (*Route 5*). This route may differ from *Routes 4* and *5* only in the section between the two ramps.

   Variation: Miss Demeanor. III, 5.9. First ascent July 23, 1986, by Paul Duval and Beverly Boynton. See *Topo 22* and *Photo 22.* This is a short two-pitch climb, which is reached by continuing up the Matthews ramp at the base of the hard climbing on Armed Robbery. It may well be identical to Contemporary Comfort (*Route 3*).

ROUTE 4. Armed Robbery. IV, 5.8. First ascent August 15, 1978, by Mike Munger and Rick Liu. This is a good climb, and it appears to be the finest of those so far completed on this face. See *Topo 22* and *Photo 22.* The Garnet Canyon approach is usually used for this climb. Take the Garnet Canyon trail from the Lupine Meadows trailhead. Proceed west past the Meadows in Garnet Canyon and into the south fork, heading to the col just east of Cloudveil Dome. Extra gear can be left here at the col because the descent route returns down the east ridge to this point. From the col drop down to the south and look for a red (dike rock) gully with much loose rock. Climb down into this gully until it is possible to scramble around and onto the broad bench at the base of the south face of Cloudveil Dome. This route proceeds roughly directly up the south face toward the summit from the bench. Instead of following the Matthews ramp across the face, three pitches ascend the face below and to the left, gaining the ramp about one-third of the way along its extent. The first pitch (140 feet) from the bench proceeds up a wall (5.6) west of a left-facing corner to a belay ledge. The second lead (5.6) goes up a left-facing corner, passing a horn on the right, up past a small ledge to another belay ledge. The final pitch (150 feet) onto the Matthews ramp is easier.

   Now move the belay up the ramp (about 150 feet) and onto a ledge (with an overhang above) below the two obvious cracks that are on either side of the central pillar on this upper section of the wall. Climb blocks (5.7) up to the upper right edge of the overhang and then traverse left (west) to the left-hand crack system (5.8 serious). The right side of the pillar is the Silver Lining route (*Route 5*). At the top of the very enjoyable crack system the upper of the two ramps that cut across the face will be intersected. A quick escape can be made on easier ground generally following this ramp up and to the west. The first-ascent party continued more or less straight up for three pitches, finishing very close to the summit.

ROUTE 5. Silver Lining. IV, 5.10. First ascent July 12, 1979, by Mike Munger and Bill Nicholson. See *Topo 22* and *Photo 22.* Use the same approach as for Armed Robbery (*Route 4*), and follow the first three pitches of that route to the Matthews ramp. Climb up past the right edge of the large overhang (5.10) and up the right side of the pillar (two pitches, 5.10 and 5.9). From the top of the pillar climb up and right to a belay on to the upper of the two main parallel ledges or ramps that diagonal steeply up across the south face from lower right (east) to upper left (west). The sixth lead goes up a thin, left-facing corner (5.10) to a belay just below an overhang. Climb a slot in the middle of the overhang to pass it and continue in the crack to the end of the lead. One more pitch of easier climbing brings one to the right (east) end of a grassy

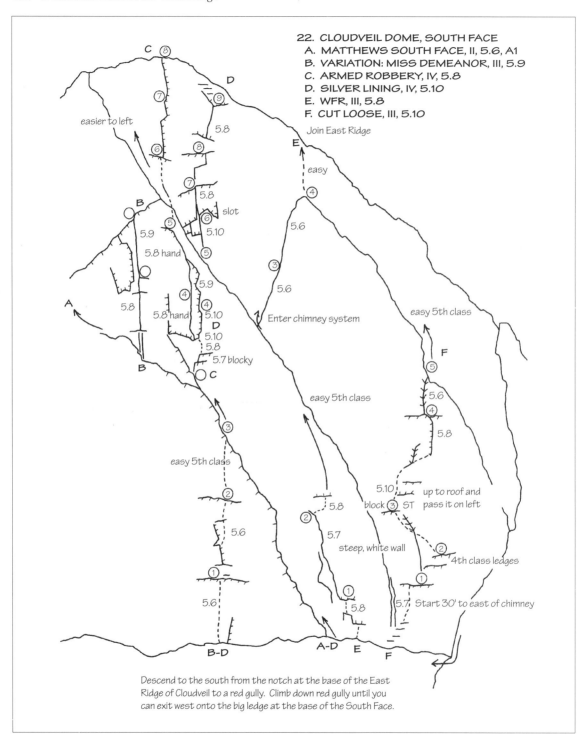

22. CLOUDVEIL DOME, SOUTH FACE
A. MATTHEWS SOUTH FACE, II, 5.6, A1
B. VARIATION: MISS DEMEANOR, III, 5.9
C. ARMED ROBBERY, IV, 5.8
D. SILVER LINING, IV, 5.10
E. WFR, III, 5.8
F. CUT LOOSE, III, 5.10

C ⑧

D

⑦

⑨

easier to left

5.8

Join East Ridge

⑥ E

⑧

easy

⑦ ④

B ⑥ slot

5.8

⑤ 5.10

5.9

5.6

5.8 hand ⑤

③

⑤ 5.9

④ 5.6

A 5.8 ④ easy 5th class

5.8 hand 5.10

D F

5.10 ⑤

5.8

B ⑤ 5.6

C 5.7 blocky ④

5.8

③

easy 5th class

easy 5th class

⑤ ③ ST 5.10 up to roof and
5.10 block ③ ST pass it on left

② ②

5.8

② ④th class ledges

5.6 5.7

steep, white wall ②

① ①

5.6 ① 5.7 Start 30' to east of chimney
5.8

B-D A-D E F

Descend to the south from the notch at the base of the East
Ridge of Cloudveil to a red gully. Climb down red gully until you
can exit west onto the big ledge at the base of the South Face.

ledge. Exit from this ledge at its right edge, up past an over-hang (5.8) and up a crack angling slightly off to the right, to the end of this final lead above yet another overhang. The remainder of the route to the summit, now to the west, is not difficult. This climb is more difficult than Armed Robbery and is recommended although it has not yet had many as-cents. For protection bring a wide range, including many small nuts and some up to 5 inches.

ROUTE 6. WFR. III, 5.8. First ascent July 11, 1990, by Jim Dorward and Steve Rickert. See *Topo 22* and *Photo 22*. Once again, use the same approach as for *Route 4*. Immediately right (east) of the ramp that curves up to the left and the upper section of the face, there is an obvious crack system leading up the middle of a triangular buttress. The first three pitches ascend this crack system. At the top of the crack a delicate traverse right with little protection brings one to a ramp that is followed for 30 feet to the crest of the buttress. A deep chimney can now be seen leading up and to the right behind the southeast section of the face. Ascend this chim-ney for two pitches, topping out near the east ridge. Scramble up and left 50 feet to the ridge, which can be fol-lowed to the summit. Protection devices to 3½ inches are suggested for this route.

ROUTE 7. Cut Loose. III, 5.10. First ascent August 2, 1977, by Yvon Chouinard and Rick Black. See *Topo 22* and *Photo 22*. As is not uncommon in the Tetons, there are probably several variations available on this face. The topo shows the Chouinard–Black line whereas the following description is probably a variation on this line. The first three climbs on this easterly portion of the south face of Cloudveil Dome may well have been distinct lines. On August 30, 1954, William Buckingham and Roald Fryxell made the first of these difficult climbs, but their route is uncertain. The as-cent of August 2, 1977, is the route described here. On August 13, 1977, Mike Munger and Charlie Fowler made what was reported as the second ascent of Cut Loose, but their description suggests that it was not the same climb. Use the same approach as for Armed Robbery (*Route 4*) to reach the bench at the base of the south face of Cloudveil Dome. The route starts on the broken face about 30 feet to the right (east) of the chimney that forms the bottom of the upper (right-hand) of the two parallel crack or ledge sys-tems that diagonal across the south face. The first 150 feet on the face (5.7) leads to a large ledge at the base of a steep white wall containing two cracks. Climb the right-hand crack until it becomes a left-facing dihedral. Here traverse out to the left for 20 feet to a belay ledge. The third pitch ascends a steep face (5.9) to a roof that is passed on the left (5.10). Above the roof, traverse right to a belay stance, beyond which there are two alternatives for the next 140-foot pitch. One can climb the very difficult corner (5.10) directly above the belay to a point a short distance above its top and then traverse right into a right-facing dihedral (5.8), which is followed to a large ledge. Or, easier, one can

traverse straight right from the belay over to the beginning of the left-facing dihedral. The final lead is easier (5.6), staying left on the steep wall, and takes one to a narrow ridge, which is then followed, ending about 300 feet east of the summit. In places, protection is somewhat difficult to place on this route, but the rock is excellent.

ROUTE 8. ☞East Ridge. II, 4.0. First ascent July 21, 1931, by Fritiof Fryxell and Anderson Hilding. From the Garnet Canyon Meadows, ascend a talus and scree slope (better when it is covered with snow in early season) to the col just east of Cloudveil Dome. Turn west at the col and proceed up the ridge. Only two pitches will be encountered, both slightly to the right (north) of the ridge crest; the remain-der is enjoyable scrambling over good rock. From the col one can also swing left (south) of the ridge crest and follow broad ledges to the edge of the south face. Make an exposed move (5.1) up and left (west), past a sharp, detached flake, and then turn back right (east) to regain the crest a few ropelengths east of the summit. *Time: 4 to 5 hours* from Garnet Canyon; *7 to 8 hours* from Jenny Lake. See *Appala-chia*, 18, no. 4 (December 1931), pp. 388–408, illus.; *Trail and Timberline*, no. 408 (December 1952), pp. 179–180.

ROUTE 9. North Face. III, 5.6. First ascent August 22, 1950, by Richard Pownall and N. Paul Kenworthy. See *Photo 23*. The lower portion of Cloudveil Dome that faces directly north is vertical, almost overhanging; the upper, narrow portion faces northeast, slanting steeply upward from lower left (east) to up-per right (west). This route goes up a section of the lower north face and then ascends the northeast face toward the summit. From the south fork of Garnet Canyon ascend the steep snow leading directly toward the gray slabs at the base of the eastern part of the north face, which can be readily recognized by the branched intrusions of light rock in the face. Cross the *bergschrund* onto the rock and climb with care about 150 feet up these downsloping slabs (some loose rock here) before traversing left (east) to the base of a very steep 25-foot chim-ney near the left edge of the face. Ascend this difficult chimney, passing an overhang, to a belay. After two or three ropelengths of climbing above this chimney, climb up to the right (west), making an exposed traverse across a steep, plate-like slab pitch. Climb to the beginning of the long, narrow northeast face. The first steep part of this section is climbed at the left (south) edge. The upper part of the lower angle leads more easily to the top shoulder of the main north face. From here one can scramble to the summit dome. See *Ameri-can Alpine Journal*, 8, no. 1 (1951), pp. 176–181.

Variation: III, 5.8, A1. First ascent August 1, 1961, by Jim Greig and Fred Wright. This variation provides a more direct route to the base of the upper slanting portion of the northeast face. From the topmost snow below the face, climb the initial slabs as in the preceding route. Now instead of traversing left (east) to reach the steep chimney (as in the 1950 route), climb the prominent gray ramp that angles up to the right to about 25 feet below its top. A downsloping ledge goes back left (east) from this point across a steep face. Step onto this ledge, climb a 6-foot loose flake, and from the top of the flake cross the steep face to the left on small holds to an overhanging crack. Ascend this crack using aid and make a short traverse left (east) to the base of a rotten chimney, which is then climbed. The angle of the large chimney above this one is not excessive; from the top of this second chimney the original route is rejoined at the beginning of the upper northeast face. Some of the leads on this variation are long (140 feet).

Variation: Nimbus. III, 5.9, WI5, A1. Attempted February 1986, by Dave Carman and Norm Larson, at which time the name Mare's Tail was applied. First ascent July 1993, by Alex Lowe and Stephen Koch. This is listed as a variation simply because the initial three pitches of *Route 9* may have been utilized as a way to begin the climb. Climb up the snow slopes below the eastern section of the north face until an area of loose, slabby rock is encountered. Proceed up this portion of the climb on easy 5th-class rock toward the beginnings of an ice/snow gully. The second pitch ascended this gully and exited via a steep, icy wall (5.8). The third pitch started with a 5.8 corner and finished with 60 feet of vertical ice to a hanging belay on a slab. Pitch number four was the crux with 5.9, A1, climbing to exit to an ice pillar. At this point the chimney system opened up into a snow-and-ice gully for the fifth and final pitch. Easy scrambling on wet rock then leads to the shoulder of the east ridge, which provides a straightforward descent route. The climb was attempted a number of times before this successful ascent and is another fine example of a very temporary route.

SPALDING PEAK (12,240+)
(0.25 mi W of Cloudveil Dome)

Map: Grand Teton

This is the first peak west of Cloudveil Dome on the long Cloudveil Dome–South Teton ridge. Although it is higher than Cloudveil Dome, Spalding Peak is rarely an isolated and deliberate objective. It is just one of the high points that must be crossed during the relatively popular traverse of this fine ridge.

CHRONOLOGY

East Ridge: July 21, 1931, Fritiof Fryxell, Anderson Hilding (ascent); August 5, 1932, Fred D. Ayres (descent)

West Ridge: July 21, 1931, Fritiof Fryxell, Anderson Hilding (descent); August 5, 1932, Fred D. Ayres (ascent)

North Snowfield: June 29, 1934, Herman Eberitzsch, Emil Papplau

Zorro Snowfield: August 5, 1964, Ray Jacquot, J. Hallein, M. Ihne

South Face: July 14, 1966, Dick Williams, John Hudson

Northeast Ridge: October 15, 1976, John Kevin Fox, Roger Mellen

ROUTE 1. ☞*West Ridge.* II, 4.0. First descent July 21, 1931, by Fritiof Fryxell and Anderson Hilding; first ascent August 5, 1932, by Fred D. Ayres. This short ridge separating Spalding Peak and Gilkey Tower is exposed 4th class. Ordinarily, the well-defined col between these two peaks is reached only during the course of a traverse from the South Teton to Cloudveil Dome, or *vice versa*. An ascent of the west ridge of Spalding Peak normally involves first climbing Gilkey Tower and descending its east ridge to this col. However, during the course of a slightly less-than-pure traverse from the South Teton to Cloudveil Dome, this col can also be reached from the snowfield below the Icecream Cone, across the north face of Gilkey Tower (about halfway up) on a very broad talus ledge. From the col follow the ridge to the summit.

ROUTE 2. South Face. III, 5.7, A2. First ascent July 14, 1966, by Dick Williams and John Hudson. The south face of Spalding Peak is well defined, bounded on both sides, east and west, by sharp couloirs or chutes, which slant up from right (east) to left (west). Near the center of the face, a third prominent chute cuts upward at the same angle. A direct approach to this face is up the very long talus slope from the east end of Lake Taminah in Avalanche Canyon. The preferable approach is from Garnet Canyon, up and over the Cloudveil–Nez Perce saddle, down the easy couloir about 300 feet to the distinctive reddish rock band that marks the dike that passes from east to west along the south margins of the Nez Perce–South Teton ridge. Follow this reddish rock band west to a ramp sloping downward to the west to reach the top of a talus slope. The route starts at the base of the central chute, climbing generally on the left (west) side on 4.0 or 5.1 rock for about 300 feet to large scree ledges. Scramble 40 feet up broken rock until a 5.4 traverse on blocks to the right leads to the base of an obvious dihedral. Climb the dihedral 30 feet to its top and exit on aid in a diagonal crack leading around a corner. The next pitch continues up to gain the base of a second steep dihedral. Climb this dihedral to an overhanging section where a hand traverse (5.7) leads up to broken ledges slanting up and left. Traverse left for 300 feet to a ridge crest. Climb the ridge and finish by a scramble up a gully and ridge to the summit.

ROUTE 3. ☞*East Ridge.* II, 3.0. First ascent July 21, 1931, by Fritiof Fryxell and Anderson Hilding. From the summit of Cloudveil Dome descend west a short distance to the broad col separating Cloudveil Dome from Spalding Peak. From the col scramble easily up a long ridge a few hundred feet to the summit. See *Appalachia*, 18, no. 4 (December 1931), pp. 308–408, illus.

ROUTE 4. Zorro Snowfield. II, 4.0. First ascent August 5, 1964, by Ray Jacquot, J. Hallein, and M. Ihne. The Zorro Snowfield on the northeast side of Spalding Peak, seen from the vicinity of the Garnet Canyon Meadows as Z-shaped in early or midseason, is the most conspicuous feature of this mountain. The lower right end of the Z is reached by scrambling from the main snowfield above the first headwall in the south fork of Garnet Canyon. The zigzag snowfield is then followed to reach the saddle between Spalding Peak and Cloudveil Dome; from the saddle one can turn either west to Spalding Peak or east to Cloudveil Dome. The snowfield is quite exposed, with numerous cliff bands lurking below it.

ROUTE 5. Northeast Ridge. II, 5.4. First ascent October 15, 1976, by John Kevin Fox and Roger Mellen. This ridge separates the region of the Zorro Snowfield, which leads to the broad col east of Spalding Peak, from the main north snowfield of Spalding Peak. Proceed into the south fork of Garnet Canyon past the initial two small headwalls to the upper talus field (or snowfield in early season) that leads to the South Teton–Middle Teton saddle. Scramble back toward the northeast ridge, staying left (east) of the lower snout of the north snowfield of Spalding Peak. Gain the ridge crest at an obvious bench; this is the upper right corner of the Z of the Zorro Snowfield. The serrated ridge above contains several moderate roped pitches, ending on the east ridge of the peak a short distance from the summit. This is a pleasant climb with the difficulty depending on how closely the crest is followed.

ROUTE 6. North Snowfield. II, 4.0. First ascent June 29, 1934, by Herman Eberitzsch and Emil Papplau. Use the same approach as for the Northeast Ridge *(Route 5).* From the upper portion of the south fork of Garnet Canyon, climb directly to the lower snout of this snowfield, which lies directly below and north of the summit of Spalding Peak. The route is a straightforward but steep snow climb leading to the col just west of the summit.

GILKEY TOWER (12,320+)
(0.3 mi W of Cloudveil Dome)

Map: Grand Teton

This is the sharp peak midway along the long Cloudveil Dome–South Teton ridge. Similar to Spalding Peak, Gilkey Tower is normally ascended only when making this ridge traverse. This Teton peak was named in memory of the Teton guide Art Gilkey, who lost his life in the 1953 attempt on K2, the second highest mountain in the world.

CHRONOLOGY

East Face: July 21, 1931, Fritiof Fryxell, Anderson Hilding (ascent); August 5, 1932, Fred D. Ayres (descent)

West Ridge: July 21, 1931, Fritiof Fryxell, Anderson Hilding (descent); August 5, 1932, Fred D. Ayres (ascent)

North Face: August 15, 1955, Dick Bonker, Tom McCalla

Northeast Snowfield: September 7, 1964, Howard Wignall, Dennis Wignall

Sunrise Ridge: August 16, 1972, Leigh and Irene Ortenburger

ROUTE 1. ☞West Ridge. II, 4.0. First descent July 21, 1931, by Fritiof Fryxell and Anderson Hilding; first ascent August 5, 1932, by Fred D. Ayres. This route, which starts from the col separating Gilkey Tower from the Icecream Cone, is used when making the traverse from the South Teton to Cloudveil Dome. The col can be reached along the ridge by making a genuine traverse of the Icecream Cone, up its west face and down its east face to the col. However, much more commonly, the col is gained from the South Teton by traversing along the top edge of the snowfield (icefield in midseason to late season, crampons useful) around and under the north face of the Icecream Cone. The small towers at the beginning of this ridge near the col are usually bypassed during the Cloudveil Dome–South Teton traverse. A party in 1962 found records on these towers dating from 1932.

ROUTE 2. Sunrise Ridge. II, 5.4. First ascent August 16, 1972, by Leigh and Irene Ortenburger. This distinct and pleasant south ridge rises to Gilkey Tower from the col that separates Matternought Peak from the Nez Perce–South Teton ridge. The first portion of the ridge is a tower, whose summit is reached after three leads (5.4), the last of which goes right around an overhanging bulge. From the top of this tower climb an easy chimney onto the crest of the ridge between Gilkey Tower and the Icecream Cone. Follow this to the summit.

ROUTE 3. ☞East Face. II, 3.0. First ascent July 21, 1931, by Fritiof Fryxell and Anderson Hilding. From the col that separates Spalding Peak from Gilkey Tower, enjoyable climbing brings one to the summit of Gilkey Tower, after an encounter with a small pinnacle just short of the summit. See *Spalding Peak* for methods of reaching this col; it is usually attained during the traverse from Cloudveil Dome to the South Teton.

ROUTE 4. Northeast Snowfield. II, 4.0. First ascent September 7, 1964, by Howard Wignall and Dennis Wignall. This is the same snowfield as described above in *Spalding Peak, Route 6.* Follow that route to the col just east of Gilkey Tower. From the col turn right and follow the East Face *(Route 3)* to the summit.

ROUTE 5. North Face. II, 5.4. First ascent August 15, 1955, by Dick Bonker and Tom McCalla. This seldom-climbed, long route starts from the prominent snowfield lying at the base of the face and leads directly up to the center of the main overhang on the north face. The overhang can be passed by climbing the shallow chimney in its center. A large horizontal bench will be passed about halfway up this face.

ICECREAM CONE (12,400+)
(0.1 mi E of the South Teton)

Map: Grand Teton

This distinct, well-named conical peak is the first one east of the South Teton. Even though it is but a small tower, it provides the finest climb of the Cloudveil Dome-to-South Teton traverse.

CHRONOLOGY

East Face: August 5, 1932, Fred D. Ayres
West Face: August 1, 1940, William Shand, Benjamin Ferris

ROUTE 1. West Face. II, 5.6. First ascent August 1, 1940, by William Shand and Benjamin Ferris. This route, which is seldom climbed, ascends one of the chimneys on the steep west face, a few feet north of the actual notch separating the Icecream Cone from the South Teton. To descend by this route most climbers will find a rappel (75 feet) convenient.
ROUTE 2. ☞East Face. II, 3.0. First ascent August 5, 1932, by Fred D. Ayres. This broken face provides the only easy route to the summit. The col separating Gilkey Tower from the Icecream Cone, where this route begins, is usually reached during the east-to-west traverse from Cloudveil Dome to the South Teton. When making this ridge traverse from west to east, it is customary, but less than pure, to use this route to climb the Icecream Cone, through the expedient of reaching this col from the South Teton by traversing east along the top edge of the snowfield (icefield in midseason to late season, crampons useful) around and under the north face of the Icecream Cone.

SOUTH TETON (12,514)

Map: Grand Teton

The South Teton, one of the famous "Trois Tetons" of 19th century history, is but the fifth highest peak in the range. Although the South Teton is not easily visible from Jackson Hole, it is prominent from Teton Basin to the west. It is one of the easiest of the major summits to reach and in the early days was frequently climbed. The regular route (*Route 7*, later) is approached from Garnet Canyon and begins at the saddle between the Middle Teton and the South Teton. The South Teton can be climbed from the valley in one day, as is true of most of the peaks accessible from Garnet Canyon, but a camp at the Platforms or higher is recommended if one wishes a leisurely trip. Other approaches to this high peak are the south fork of Cascade Canyon and Avalanche Canyon.

CHRONOLOGY

Northwest Couloir: August 29, 1923, Albert R. Ellingwood, Eleanor Davis (Ehrman)

West Ridge: August 21, 1924, Paul Petzoldt
North Face: July 5, 1930, Fritiof Fryxell, Phil Smith (partial); July 19, 1957, Yvon Chouinard, William Mason (complete)
East Ridge: August 5, 1932, Fred D. Ayres (descent); July 3, 1933, Paul Petzoldt, Sterling Hendricks (ascent)
   var: July 19, 1940, William and Harold Plumley, Jack and William Fralick
   var: August 24, 1962, Edward F., John, and Lawrence Little
South Ridge: July 2, 1955, W. V. Graham and Mary Ann Matthews
North Chimney: June 25, 1973, Harvey Gould, Robert Goren
Southeast Couloir: August 1, 1973, Jim Olson, Tom Watson

ROUTE 1. West Ridge. II, 4.0. First ascent August 21, 1924, by Paul Petzoldt. This route is only slightly more difficult than the normal route, *Route 7*. The best approach is via the south fork of Cascade Canyon to the saddle (10,560+) between the South Teton and the Wall; an unmaintained but good side trail leads from the main Teton Crest Trail below the Schoolroom Glacier to this broad saddle. However, the north fork of Avalanche Canyon can also readily be used to gain this saddle. From the saddle proceed up the broad ridge. The upper part of the west ridge is the most difficult and can be avoided by cutting horizontally left (north), when one is halfway up the ridge, toward the couloir that provides access to the main north slope. Some steep, loose scree will be encountered on this traverse. This couloir is the primary break in the rotten cliffs that protect the Middle–South Teton saddle from the west; it leads to a shoulder on the ridge above the saddle and on the edge of the north slope. Another alternative, which also evades the upper west ridge, crosses to the right (south) about halfway up the ridge and enters a broad couloir that leads up the southwest face. From the top of this couloir scramble among the boulders of the summit ridge to the north slope. Once on the north slope by either scheme, proceed to the couloir of *Route 7*. This route cannot be recommended because of an abundance of very rotten rock. See *Appalachia*, 18, no. 3 (June 1931), pp. 209–232, illus.
ROUTE 2. South Ridge. II, 3.0. First ascent July 2, 1955, by W. V. Graham and Mary Ann Matthews. See *Avalanche Canyon* for the approach and possible campsites. It would also be possible, but less direct, to approach via the south fork of Cascade Canyon and descend 400 feet into the north fork of Avalanche Canyon to the beginning of the ridge. The lower portion of the south side of the South Teton is composed of two main ridges, separated by a steep, narrow, snow-filled couloir. Both ridges contain several subridges. The two ridges and the couloir converge just above a promi-

nent notch in the mountain (about 800 feet below the summit). This notch was formed by the weathering out of the major reddish dike that runs east and west along the south side of Nez Perce to the base of the southwest face of the South Teton; the dike disappears when it intersects the main Buck Mountain fault, which is easily distinguished along the lower portion of the southwest and west faces of the South Teton.

From the flat area just east of Snowdrift Lake, scramble up toward the western ridge of the two main ridges. It is easiest to bypass the initial buttresses (and gendarmes) of the ridge and stay slightly to the left (west) side of this ridge as far as the dike notch, which is marked by the uppermost snow in the adjacent couloir. From the notch one can climb directly up, or traverse out to the right to gain the uppermost rock of the eastern south ridge, and ascend that to the final, unified south ridge. Either way, this section contains the principal problems of the route, partly due to some sections of poor rock. This upper ridge leads directly to the summit without difficulty. *Time: 4½ hours* from Avalanche Canyon.

ROUTE 3. Southeast Couloir. II, 5.4. First ascent August 1, 1973, by Jim Olson and Tom Watson. This prominent snow couloir, easily seen from the highway southeast of the South Teton, cuts directly up the southeast slope of the South Teton, ending on the south ridge about 200 feet below the summit. From the vicinity of Snowdrift Lake, gain the high cirque below the south faces of Gilkey Tower and the Icecream Cone, and reach the broad snowfield at the upper end. From this snowfield turn left (west) and upward to the base of the couloir, which consists of about nine leads of snow climbing. About two-thirds of the way up this couloir, a short rock wall capped by a large chockstone presents the principal difficulty on the route; it is passed on the left. The final three snow leads become increasingly steep, ending with a very steep cornice section at the top. Some rockfall may be encountered, but belay positions and protection are good. In some years and seasons a couple of ropelengths of ice may be encountered. This is a good climb; crampons are recommended.

ROUTE 4. East Ridge. II, 4.0. First descent August 5, 1932, by Fred D. Ayres; first ascent July 3, 1933, by Paul Petzoldt and Sterling Hendricks. See *Photo 26*. The first climbs of this route were made as part of the traverse from the South Teton to Cloudveil Dome, or conversely. In the course of this traverse, descend from the various pinnacles west of Gilkey Tower to the snowfield that lies at the north base of the Icecream Cone. Then, contour along the top edge of the snowfield and climb a short couloir to the col between the Icecream Cone and the South Teton. In late season, and in some years in midseason, this snowfield becomes ice, making crampons necessary. Or, this col can also be reached by first climbing the Icecream Cone and then rappelling down the west face of the Icecream Cone directly to the col. From the col climb the loose rock of the ridge to the summit, staying, for the most part, on the right (north) side.

Variation: II, 4.0. First ascent July 19, 1940, by William and Harold Plumley and Jack and William Fralick. A large snowfield extends down into the south fork of Garnet Canyon from beneath the north faces of the Icecream Cone and the South Teton and west of Gilkey Tower. This snowfield provides access to the col between the Icecream Cone and the South Teton, from which the east ridge can be followed to the summit. This variation is more interesting than *Route 7* for those wishing some experience on snow, but knowledge of the ice axe is essential. In late season, and in some years even in midseason, the upper portion of this snowfield becomes ice, and crampons are necessary. *Time: 4½ hours* from Garnet Canyon.

Variation: II, 4.0. First ascent August 24, 1962, by Edward F., John, and Lawrence Little. From the summit ridge of the South Teton, a spur of broken rock extends down to the northeast toward Garnet Canyon. This small ridge forms the right (west) boundary of the snowfield that reaches the col between the Icecream Cone and the South Teton. It provides a climb longer than *Route 4, 5,* or 7 but is of only modest difficulty. After climbing to a point somewhat above the level of the col, cross to the left (southeast) and reach the summit via the upper portion of the east ridge.

ROUTE 5. North Face. II, 5.6. First partial ascent July 5, 1930, by Fritiof Fryxell and Phil Smith; first complete ascent July 19, 1957, by Yvon Chouinard and William Mason. Because of icy conditions, the pioneer 1930 party was forced to contour left (east) to the east ridge and finish the climb to the summit by that route. From the bottom of the center of the face, climb directly up for about seven ropelengths on good but wet rock (possibly dry in late season). The last pitch is the hardest and it brings one out on the summit ridge only 100 feet east of the summit. This is a short but enjoyable climb. *Time: 5½ hours* from Garnet Canyon. See *Appalachia*, 18, no. 3 (June 1931), pp. 209–232, illus.

ROUTE 6. North Chimney. II, 5.1. First ascent June 25, 1973, by Harvey Gould and Robert Goren. The main north face of the South Teton is bounded on the right (west) by a very narrow and moderately steep couloir that diagonals up to the right from the top of a snow tongue extending up from the main snowfield below the face. This couloir or chute ends on the summit ridge only a short distance west of the summit boulders. Approach via the south fork of Garnet Canyon, but turn up onto the initial snowfield well before reaching the Middle–South Teton saddle. In early season the couloir is a snow climb, starting at about 30° and steepening to 45° near its top.

ROUTE 7. ☞Northwest Couloir. II, 4.0. First ascent August 29, 1923, by Albert R. Ellingwood and Eleanor Davis (Ehrman). See *Photo 26*. This regular route has become a popular Teton climb to one of the major summits of the range. From the saddle between the Middle Teton and the South Teton, climb the talus slope and the ridge of the South Teton heading toward the snowfield that protects this couloir, which lies on the north flank of the northwest ridge. The shallow couloir is easily seen from the saddle. With luck, something of a climbers' trail will be found in this section of talus. Cross the snowfield near its top edge to gain the short upper couloir, which leads onto the summit ridge only 100 feet west of the summit. A little scrambling over large boulders brings one to the top. While this is not a difficult climb, an ice axe and rope are recommended for the inexperienced for the snowfield crossing; even in late season, at least one stretch of moderately steep snow must usually be crossed in order to reach the upper couloir. *Time: 50 to 90 minutes* from the saddle; *4 to 5½ hours* from Garnet Canyon; *6½ to 9¼ hours* from Jenny Lake. See *Appalachia,* 18, no. 3 (June 1931), pp. 209–232, illus.

GARNET CANYON, WEST SIDE ROCK CLIMBS (10,480+)

Map: Grand Teton

At the extreme lower end of the east ridge of the Middle Teton, just to the right of the black dike, is a major buttress, separated from the remainder of the ridge by two steep narrow couloirs, one on the north and the other on the south. The slabby rock of this buttress is exceptionally clean, smooth, and steep, providing tremendous exposure. *ROUTE 1. Line of Lees' Resistance.* III, 5.10R. First ascent June 30, 1986, by David Koch and Evelyn Lees. See *Topo 23.* This climb starts just left of the lowest point of the buttress. The first lead ends at a ledge after a long section (140 feet) of face climbing (5.5), including fingertip liebacks. From the ledge climb a 5.7 crack and at its top exit right (5.9) to a small overhang. Once past the overhang, climb the 5.8 crack above to a large sloping ledge and belay at a fixed piton. The third lead, the crux at 5.10R, involves fingertip liebacks. From the belay stance traverse left to a big flake and then continue up to a ledge. The fifth pitch is easier and consists of 5.6 climbing up to a small ledge just below a large, square-cut overhang. The last lead of 100 feet involves lieback and undercling techniques (5.8), angling up and slightly right. Above, 3rd-class climbing leads to the "summit" of this buttress, which is separated from the remainder of the ridge above by steep and narrow couloirs descending both to the north and to the south. For descent it is suggested that the couloir to the north be used, as the one to the south requires a 150-foot rappel. In midseason to late season it is fairly straightforward to downclimb the northern couloir. However, loose and gritty rock will be encountered. A large rack, ranging from brass nuts to #3 camming devices, seems necessary to provide adequate protection on this exposed route.

ROUTE 2. Direct East Buttress. IV, 5.9, A2, or IV, 5.11-. First ascent July 19, 1989, by Tom Turiano and Matthew Goewert; first free ascent July 21, 1992, by Renny Jackson and Kevin Moore. See *Topo 23* and *Photo 30.* This route is twice as long as *Route 1,* but both routes share the fourth and fifth pitches. Start at the base of the buttress on low-angle slabs from a small black ledge where a fixed piton will be found. The details of the route are best presented in the topo. It is probably best to belay at the two bolts after climbing the first 5.9 pitch; this is a hanging belay, however. Climb past a small overhang and then continue out and right to the beginning of a small ramp, where a fixed piton will be found. Continue up the ramp to the left to its end where a tricky step down and left will have to be negotiated. Climb the steep section above via a 5.9 crack and step up onto a large sloping ledge. A 5.5 traverse to the south on this ledge places one at the belay at the base of the crux pitch. The thin crack above was aided during the first ascent, using tied-off ½- to ¾-inch pitons for approximately 60 feet. After reaching the alcove at the top of the crack continue up to a belay at two fixed pitons. The next two pitches are the same as in *Route 1.* The descent to the notch behind the "summit" of the buttress is easily made, and the exit moves up the short wall to the west are 5.8+ and unprotected. The next section involves walking up some loose scree and this detracts only slightly from the route's overall quality. From a belay situated next to a large flake ascend a crack up and over a bulge (5.7). The astonishing old fixed pitons found at the top of the bulge are of unknown provenance. The next lead in behind a huge flake, continuously difficult, is one of the most interesting of this route. Climb up the crack behind the flake (5.8 and 5.9 lieback) until it narrows to a nasty offwidth and then move out and left (5.9+). Finish by climbing up a crack on the outside face of the giant flake. The final pitch, a 5.7 crack, emerges on the top of the buttress. For descent, a route can be worked out on the southeast side of the Middle Teton, using the second couloir east of the Ellingwood Couloir. Two rappels, one wet, are required. For protection take a wide selection including RPs and camming devices to 3½ inches. A double set of small TCUs is useful for the crux finger crack. This climb is highly recommended.

MIDDLE TETON (12,804)

Map: Grand Teton

Many people consider the Middle Teton, third highest of the Teton peaks, to be one of the most interesting mountains of the range. Its structure is complex and harbors numerous routes, although only two, the Southwest Couloir and the North Ridge, are often climbed. With very few exceptions these are also virtually the only routes used for descent. The complexity of ridges and couloirs, especially on the south

23. GARNET CANYON, WEST SIDE ROCK CLIMBS
A. LINE OF LEES' RESISTANCE, III, 5.10R
B. DIRECT EAST BUTTRESS, IV, 5.11-

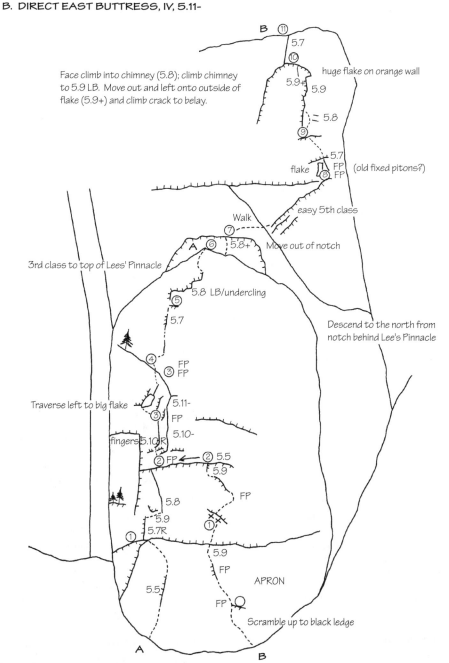

Face climb into chimney (5.8); climb chimney to 5.9 LB. Move out and left onto outside of flake (5.9+) and climb crack to belay.

huge flake on orange wall

flake   (old fixed pitons?)

easy 5th class

Walk

Move out of notch

3rd class to top of Lees' Pinnacle

5.8 LB/undercling

Descend to the north from notch behind Lee's Pinnacle

Traverse left to big flake

fingers 5.10R

Scramble up to black ledge

APRON

side of the mountain, has made the early climbing history very difficult to resolve; the first ascent of some routes as reported in the chronology may in fact have been made in previous years.

The Middle Teton is one of but two peaks in the range that afford genuine glacier routes to the summit. At the southwest base of the mountain is Icefloe Lake (10,652), the highest lake in the Teton Range. A black diabase dike forms a prominent part of the peak. Starting at the base of the east ridge, it follows this long ridge part of the way to the Dike Pinnacle, then veers off to the north to intersect the north ridge in a sharp notch before disappearing down the northwest side of the mountain. The high point on the north side of this dike notch is the North Peak; it was first climbed on July 5, 1940, by Paul Petzoldt and Elizabeth Cowles (Partridge). The Dike Pinnacle is the distinct subpeak (12,200+) on the crest of the east ridge; the col separating this pinnacle from the summit is reached from the north by the upper tongue of the Middle Teton Glacier and from the south by the Ellingwood Couloir. In addition, there are two distinct summits of the Middle Teton. The north summit is a few feet higher than the south summit, but from the couloir of the regular route it is impossible to tell which is higher. Both the Dike Pinnacle and the south summit of the Middle Teton were first reached on August 28, 1929, by Fritiof Fryxell and Phil Smith.

From the summit an excellent view is obtained of the entire south side of the Grand Teton; hence, the Middle Teton can be recommended as a warmup for those planning to ascend one of the south ridges of the Grand. The northern aspect of the mountain, between the Middle Teton Glacier and the northwest couloir, contains a considerable expanse of some of the finest solid Teton rock. The standard approach for climbing the Middle Teton is via Garnet Canyon, and the mountain has been only rarely climbed by any other approach. Doubtlessly, any of the routes can be climbed in one long day from the valley, but it is convenient to establish a high camp in Garnet Canyon.

CHRONOLOGY

Ellingwood Couloir: August 29, 1923, Albert R. Ellingwood (ascent)
Southwest Couloir: July 16, 1927, H. O., Morris, and Irven Christensen
    var: July 15, 1967, Rod McCally, John Harkness
Southeast Couloir: August 28, 1929, Fritiof Fryxell, Phil Smith
South Couloir: August 28, 1929, Fritiof Fryxell, Phil Smith (descent)
    var: [probable] July 3, 1959, Curt Butler
North Ridge: July 17, 1931, Robert Underhill, Fritiof Fryxell (ascent); July 4, 1933, Paul

Petzoldt, Sterling Hendricks (descent)
    var: July 5, 1940, Paul Petzoldt, Elizabeth Cowles (Partridge)
Northeast Face: August 24, 1936, Fritz Wiessner, William House, Elizabeth Woolsey
Northwest Slope: [possible] August 27, 1939, Stanley Grites, Frank Garbocz, Adam Koj; [probable] July 16, 1940, W. Heidholm; [certain] September 6, 1954, William Hooker, Peter Ludwig, Peter Luster, Craig Merrihue
Shand-Ferris: August 1, 1940, William Shand, Benjamin Ferris
Southwest Ridge: August 8, 1940, Jack Durrance, Henry Coulter
Middle Teton Glacier: August 4, 1944, Sterling Hendricks, Paul Bradt
Southeast Ridge: August 15, 1954, William Buckingham, Virgil Day
    var: July 7, 1961, Herb Swedlund, Peter Geiser
    var: July 9, 1994, Peter Lenz, Cory Pollock
Dike: September 14, 1954, Richard Irvin, Floyd Burnette
    var: September 15, 1935, Malcolm Smith, Newell Rohrer, Francis Neimann
West Ridge: August 4, 1955, William Buckingham, Mary Lou Nohr
Goodrich Chimney: September 4, 1955, Don Goodrich, John Reppy
Chouinard Ridge: July 2, 1957, Yvon Chouinard, Kenneth Weeks
Robbins-Fitschen: July 30, 1960, Royal Robbins, Joe Fitschen
Northwest Ice Couloir: June 16, 1961, Peter Lev, Jim Greig
Taylor: August 26, 1961, Royal Robbins, Jane Taylor
Briggs-Higbee Pillar: July 8, 1974, Roger Briggs, Art Higbee
Whiton-Wiggins Dihedral: September 20, 1981, Earl Wiggins, Mark Whiton
Jackson-Woodmencey Dihedral: June 25, 1988, Renny Jackson, Jim Woodmencey

ROUTE 1. West Ridge. II, 5.4. First ascent August 4, 1955, by William Buckingham and Mary Lou Nohr. The long west ridge of the Middle Teton separates Icefloe Lake on the south from the residual glacier (or icefield) in upper Dartmouth Basin, the neglected canyon on the west side of the popular Lower Saddle. The lower section of this ridge turns north-northwest at Point 11,256 and forms the western rim of Dartmouth Basin and the eastern boundary of the south fork of Cascade Canyon. In its entirety it is 2.6 miles long, one of the longer continuous ridges in the range. To start this route, hike up the south Cascade Canyon trail about 1.5 miles past the forks; then cross the stream and bushwhack up the gully to the broad col (9,600+) at the base of the first step of the west ridge of the Middle Teton. Scramble up the ridge to the first tower. Keep directly on the ridge over several black towers, across a flat brushy area; then climb the ridge to the high point marked by the 10,720-foot contour. Descend to the col to the east and climb steep rotten rock over several small towers. Climb the next large tower and descend to the east to the beginning of the rotten-red-pinnacles section of the ridge next to the main mass of the Middle Teton. At this point the first-ascent party descended about 200 feet and bypassed these pinnacles on the south in order to reach the steep cliffs of the main mass of the mountain. These cliffs are climbed in four pitches up a steep and difficult chimney just south of the crest of the west ridge. Another possibility is to climb back to the ridge crest at the notch separating the last pinnacle from the mountain and then climb directly up the ridge. The last portion of the ridge lies back at a more gentle angle and is easily followed to the summit. See *American Alpine Journal*, 10, no. 1 (1956), pp. 116–119.

ROUTE 2. ☞*Southwest Couloir*. II, 3.0. First ascent July 16, 1927, by H. O., Morris, and Irven Christensen, after climbing the South Teton earlier the same day. See *Photo 27*. This is the very popular regular route used by most parties and is approached via the south fork of Garnet Canyon. To avoid getting lost in one of the many south couloirs, climb *all the way* to the saddle between the Middle Teton and the South Teton until Icefloe Lake can be seen below; then, and only then, turn north up the largest and most obvious couloir visible from the saddle. There is no difficulty in the lower sections of the couloir. However, if the climb is made in early season or early in the day, crampons may prove useful in the steeper snow of the upper sections. An ice axe and, more importantly, the knowledge of how to use it, will be needed. Considerations such as these may lead some parties to turn out of the couloir in order to avoid the snow. One can do this at many different places, but in general it is best not to turn out until relatively high in the couloir. In a dry or late season something approximating a small trail will be found up this couloir, as this is a very popular climb. But because the route is so popular, use *great* caution with the loose rocks because other climbers may be below. On approaching the notch between the north and south summits, keep in mind that the left (north) summit is higher. About 100 feet below the notch climb to the left and hit the west ridge a short distance from the summit. Follow the ridge easily to the airy summit. As a variation, use the right (south) side of the couloir in order to avoid some of the steep upper sections. However, do not follow this too far because the summit lies on the opposite (north) side of the couloir. On the descent it is advisable to go all the way down to the saddle before turning east down the canyon, because the snowfield northeast of the saddle is steep in early season. *Time: 4½ to 6 hours* from Garnet Canyon; *6½ to 8 hours*

from Jenny Lake. See *Appalachia*, 18, no. 3 (June 1931), pp. 209–232, illus.; 19, no. 1 (June 1932), pp. 86–96.

Variation: II, 5.1. First recorded ascent July 15, 1967, by Rod McCally and John Harkness. This variation attains the saddle between the South Teton and the Middle Teton directly from the west. In the early years of the park this variation may well have been done by more than one exploring party. From Icefloe Lake, which is infrequently used as a campsite, this variation provides a direct start to the standard Southwest Couloir route on the Middle Teton. However, this climb is explicitly *not* recommended because considerable dangerous and rotten rock will be encountered, even though the absolute difficulty is not severe.

ROUTE 3. *Southwest Ridge*. III, 5.6, A1. First complete ascent August 8, 1940, by Jack Durrance and Henry Coulter. Previous climbs on this ridge include a partial descent on July 17, 1931, by Robert Underhill and Fritiof Fryxell, and a probable partial ascent on August 24, 1937, by H. K. and Elizabeth Hartline. This ridge, which might also be called a series of indistinct towers, forms the right (east) boundary of the Southwest Couloir route. The difficulty of this climb, like some others in the park, depends on how closely the crest of the ridge is followed. Ascend the south fork of Garnet Canyon to the saddle between the South Teton and the Middle Teton. The large, easily identified first tower, which marks the beginning of the ridge, can be bypassed on the west by gaining the crest of the ridge at one of several different points from the regular southwest couloir. On the original ascent, however, this difficult tower was climbed, using pitons for aid, via the overhanging crack on the very steep face, slightly on the west side of the tower.

Climb three 60-foot pitches from the notch behind this tower; then scramble to a short, overhanging step in the ridge, and climb this on its exposed south side. Three hundred feet of moderate climbing then leads one past the junction of a subsidiary ridge from the east and to the base of a large massive tower. Some steep climbing is then required to get onto the higher of the two wide ledges that slope upward to the left. Follow this ledge back to the left until it crosses the ridge crest. Then, either climb the ridge directly or follow the ledge on around to the left, where it is a simple matter to regain the crest. Follow the ridge past several indistinct towers to a tower at the end, which is separated from the vertical southwest face of the south summit by a distinct notch. Descend to this notch and cut left (north) and up to the main (north) summit. *Time: 10 hours* from Garnet Canyon. See *American Alpine Journal*, 4, no. 2 (1941), pp. 304–306.

ROUTE 4. *Chouinard Ridge*. II, 5.4. First ascent July 2, 1957, by Yvon Chouinard and Kenneth Weeks. See *Photo 28*. This is the somewhat jumbled ridge immediately west of the south couloir and is approached in the same manner. It contains good rock and is an enjoyable climb. Ascend the south fork of Garnet Canyon until it becomes possible to see the entire Ellingwood Couloir leading to the col between the Dike Pinnacle and the main summit of the Middle Teton; then climb (on snow until late season) the bottom section of the Ellingwood Couloir to the point where it is split into two branches by the southeast ridge. The left (west) branch is the broad and open beginning of the south couloir. Cross over to the rock at the beginning of the Chouinard Ridge, which is on the left (west) side of this snow couloir. The first seven ropelengths on this ridge are easy 5th-class climbing, and then an inside corner (difficult when wet) must be passed. A few more easy pitches then lead to a break in the ridge, which in early season is filled with snow. Climb a chimney above the snow patch to a small cave; then leave the cave on the left to reach another cave directly above. Now, traverse to the right to regain the ridge crest; follow it to the point where it joins the Southwest Ridge (*Route 3*) near its final tower. From this tower it is but a short distance to the summit. See *American Alpine Journal*, 12, no. 1 (1960), pp. 125–127.

ROUTE 5. South Couloir. II, 4.0. First descent August 28, 1929, by Fritiof Fryxell and Phil Smith. See *Photo 29*. The exact history of the climbs on the south side of the Middle Teton between the southeast and southwest ridges is confused because the topography is ill defined and the nomenclature for this region has only recently been clarified. The climbing is not, in general, difficult, and there are many route possibilities. The south couloir is the couloir immediately west of the southeast ridge; it leads northwest to the small notch that separates the top of the southwest ridge from the sharp south summit of the Middle Teton. The left (western) boundary of this couloir is the fairly well-defined Chouinard Ridge (see *Route 4*), which parallels the southeast ridge and terminates on the southwest ridge near its final tower. It is not known for certain when or if this south couloir has been ascended. Perhaps the lower part of the route of the 1923 party was in this couloir; a similar uncertainty applies to several parties in the 1930s and 1940s.

Use the same approach as for the Chouinard Ridge (*Route 4*). The southeast ridge always sharply defines the right (east) edge of the south couloir; once the beginning of the couloir is reached, there is little routefinding difficulty. The upper part of the couloir is rather narrow and steep and ultimately leads below and past the vertical southwest and west faces of the south summit of the Middle Teton. Pass the notch between the north and south summits and proceed to the north summit.

Variation: II, 4.0. Probable first ascent July 3, 1959, by Curt Butler. This variation leaves the couloir about halfway up, at the point where there is a break in the Chouinard Ridge on the left (west). In early season the snow in the south couloir extends all the way to the crest of the Chouinard Ridge. Cross this ridge into the next shallow couloir and follow it to the crest of the southwest ridge; then proceed along that ridge to the summit (see *Route 3*).

ROUTE 6. Southeast Ridge. III, 5.7. First complete ascent August 15, 1954, by William Buckingham and Virgil Day. See *Topo 24* and *Photos 28* and *29*. This major ridge of excellent rock forms the left (west) edge of the prominent Ellingwood Couloir and leads directly to the south summit of the Middle Teton. It is one of the most enjoyable of the moderate rock routes out of Garnet Canyon. The difficulty depends on exactly which variation is chosen from among the several possible. Take the Garnet Canyon trail from the Lupine Meadows trailhead to the Platforms. Proceed past the Garnet Canyon Meadows and up into the south fork of the canyon. The southeast ridge can be seen rising from the junction of the Ellingwood Couloir and the south couloir, which is on the west side of the southeast ridge. From this point (halfway up the south fork of Garnet Canyon) turn right and climb a talus and scree cone (covered with snow in early or midseason, requiring an ice axe) leading to the bottom of the Ellingwood Couloir and the beginning of the ridge. One can avoid the crest of the ridge entirely by climbing the right (east) side of the ridge, which would be the left (west) side of the couloir, until near the Dike Pinnacle Col. Then turn up and left to gain the ridge crest near the base of the south summit.

However, the standard Southeast Ridge route begins with 700 feet of 2.0 and 3.0 scrambling up the crest to a steep, smooth buttress. From the eastern edge of the buttress climb four ropelengths up and generally left (west). The difficulty ranges from 5.7 to 5.8 depending on the line taken, and the climbing consists mainly of cracks, corners, and slabs. Move the belay into the notch for the climb of the small tower on the ridge (5.7 out of the notch). Once atop the tower, the belay can then be moved onto chockstones located in the chimney behind it to the north. Proceed up 4.0 and 5.1 slabs for two pitches. Walk north on the large ledge below the final headwall to the base of some easy chimneys. Climb these for a ropelength (5.1) to another ledge. Easy broken rock then brings one to the top of the south summit. A one-rope rappel can be done from the north side of the south summit. This provides access to the easy eastern slabs and the true summit of the peak. Because this southeast ridge is broad, many variations are possible, especially in the upper portions and in the lower section leading to the buttress.

Variation: III, 5.7, A1, or III, 5.8. First ascent July 7, 1961, by Herbert Swedlund and Peter Geiser; lines of similar difficulty were taken on August 1, 1962, by Ants Leemets and Raivo Puusemp, and on August 16, 1964, by Peter Cleveland and Peter Crane. See *Photos 28* and *29*. Instead of bypassing on the right the "steep, smooth buttress" mentioned earlier in the standard Southeast Ridge route, there are two ways, originally with the use of aid, to climb the buttress directly. The first pitch begins at the base of the buttress and ascends a series of steep slabs. The wall above is then climbed to a 5.7 jam crack. The third pitch traverses

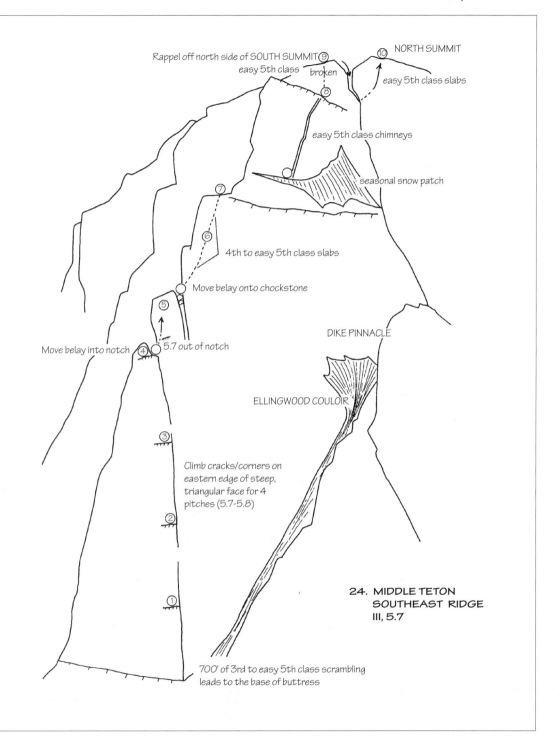

Rappel off north side of SOUTH SUMMIT ⑨

NORTH SUMMIT ⑩

easy 5th class   broken

easy 5th class slabs

easy 5th class chimneys

⑧

seasonal snow patch

⑦

⑥

4th to easy 5th class slabs

Move belay onto chockstone

⑤

DIKE PINNACLE

Move belay into notch ④ 5.7 out of notch

ELLINGWOOD COULOIR

③

Climb cracks/corners on
eastern edge of steep,
triangular face for 4
pitches (5.7-5.8)

②

**24. MIDDLE TETON
SOUTHEAST RIDGE
III, 5.7**

①

700' of 3rd to easy 5th class scrambling
leads to the base of buttress

right for 5 feet to a vertical crack in the wall, which is climbed (A1) up and over a small overhang to rejoin the standard route. An alternative direct variation on this buttress lies somewhat to the left (southwest) and, after passing an overhang (A3) at the end of the first long lead, stays near the left edge of the buttress and reaches a gunsight notch after another three or four leads. One pitch beyond this notch places the climber on easier ground.

Variation: III, 5.9. First ascent July 9, 1994, by Peter Lenz and Cory Pollock. This variation apparently ascends the final headwall of the south summit in a more direct fashion than the original route. From the large ledge located below the final headwall, climb a 5.8 dihedral for 120 feet that then leads into a deep chimney system and belay. Proceed up the chimney past some loose blocks and belay under a chockstone after 75 feet (5.9 face). The final 75 feet of the chimney are then climbed (5.9) to a blocky ledge, after which easy climbing leads to the south summit. Include protection to 4 inches.

ROUTE 7. Ellingwood Couloir. II, 5.1. First ascent August 29, 1923, by Albert R. Ellingwood; Eleanor Davis (Ehrman) and E. W. Harnden stopped a few minutes below the summit during a brief storm in which Ellingwood went on to the summit alone. See *Photos 28* and *29.* Because it is likely that the 1923 party used only the upper portions of this couloir, the first complete ascent may have been made many years later; one probable ascent was on August 5, 1934, by Glenn Exum, James Cooley, and Macauley Smith. In late season this couloir will be a rock climb up slabs, with isolated patches of ice in a few chimneys. In early season, however, the slabs are covered, and this route becomes a rather steep, pure snow-and-ice climb, requiring careful use of the ice axe. In general, this route is slightly on the left (west) side of the couloir. From the col climb to the summit as described in *Route 8.* See *Appalachia,* 18, no. 3 (June 1931), pp. 209–232, illus.

ROUTE 8. Southeast Couloir. II, 5.4. First ascent August 28, 1929, by Fritiof Fryxell and Phil Smith. During this climb first ascents of both the Dike Pinnacle and the south summit of the Middle Teton were also made. Ascend the south fork of Garnet Canyon until the large Ellingwood Couloir, which leads to the col between the Dike Pinnacle and the summit of the Middle Teton, is clearly visible. Take the next (rather poorly defined) couloir to the east. After the first 200 feet in this narrow couloir, which starts from a snow bench, either cut left (west) to gain the left fork, a shallow couloir leading to the ridge crest, or continue in the indistinct right fork of the couloir directly to the east ridge. From the ridge it is a scramble to the summit of the Dike Pinnacle.

Fortunately, the traverse to the summit of the Middle Teton, while a bit complex, is not as terrifying as the view might indicate. From the summit of the Dike Pinnacle, climb (some may prefer to rappel the last part) on loose, steep rock down to the notch between the Dike Pinnacle and a large gendarme. From this notch it is apparently possible to descend a couple hundred feet down the gully to the south in order to pass this gendarme and then climb back up to the snow col on the far side. It is more straightforward, however, to traverse around the south side of the gendarme remaining about the same level as the notch, to a point from which a 60-foot rappel puts one near the snow col that separates the gendarme from the main summit mass of the Middle Teton. The slabby east face of the Middle Teton, which is now directly above this snow col, can be climbed either on the right (north) or left (south) of the snow couloir that descends from the notch between the south and north summits of the mountain. In early season very steep snow must be expected in the couloir itself. The most direct route is probably slightly to the left of this couloir, which is partially blocked by a large chockstone not far below the notch between the two summits. Once above this point, easy rocks on the right (north) of the couloir lead to the summit, which is gained from the east. See *Appalachia,* 18, no. 3 (June 1931), pp. 209–232, illus.; *Sierra Club Bulletin,* 16, no. 1 (February 1931), pp. 47–54, illus. (The marked photograph in this latter article is incorrect with respect to the route of ascent.)

ROUTE 9. Dike. IV, 5.6. The history of this route is perhaps as unusual as any in the park. In 1929 Fryxell and Smith (see *Route 8*) attained the east ridge from the south and included the upper two-thirds of this route, including the Dike Pinnacle. On September 15, 1935, Malcolm Smith, Newell Rohrer, and Francis Neimann climbed a major portion of the route but avoided most of the lower dike by attaining the crest from the northeast, via a prominent chimney. On July 20, 1940, Jack Durrance, Joseph Hawkes, and Margaret Smith made the first climb of the lower dike, but a broken ice axe prevented their continuing past the Dike Pinnacle to the main summit. On September 4, 1940, Durrance returned with Henry Coulter, James Huidekoper, and Herbert Weiner to attempt the complete ascent but a storm intervened after they had climbed the lower dike. In the early 1950s several ascents were made via the dike to the summit of the Dike Pinnacle, but none of these parties persevered to the main summit. On September 10, 1954, Craig Merrihue, William Hooker, Peter Luster, and Peter Ludwig climbed the lower dike, bypassed the Dike Pinnacle, and then continued to the summit. It appears that the first complete ascent that included all three essential features—the lower dike, the Dike Pinnacle, and the main summit—was made on September 14, 1954, by Richard Irvin and Floyd Burnette. This route is the longest and one of the most interesting on the Middle Teton; some parties report as many as 22 roped pitches. This is the only route that ascends the entire east ridge.

From the Meadows at the forks of Garnet Canyon, climb the talus or snow to the base of the black dike, which provides the means for surmounting the first steep section of the ridge. The first few pitches on the dike itself are of relatively high angle, but the rock is fairly solid and generally better than one might expect. Within the first several pitches there is little opportunity to leave the dike, and routefinding is minimal because the dike is less than 40 feet wide. After several ropelengths there are two alternatives: one can remain on the dike itself and climb perhaps the most difficult portion of the route, or one can avoid this difficult section by climbing the easier rock to the left (south). Either way, the uppermost portion of the east ridge, where the angle eases off, will be reached and only scrambling is necessary to reach the summit of the Dike Pinnacle. The dike itself, however, veers off to the north some distance east of the Dike Pinnacle, passes beneath the upper Middle Teton Glacier, emerges, and cuts through the north ridge forming a conspicuous sharp notch. Hence, one must leave the dike before attaining the summit of the Dike Pinnacle. From there, follow Route 8 to the main summit of the Middle Teton.

Because many or even most parties, for one reason or another, do not continue to the summit of the Middle Teton from the summit of the Dike Pinnacle, suggestions on a descent route from the summit of the Dike Pinnacle are perhaps worthwhile. If ice axes are carried, the eastern tongue of the Middle Teton Glacier on the north can be quickly descended on snow in early season from the point where it reaches the crest of the east ridge; in late season, however, ice will be encountered on this descent route. Otherwise, from the same point on the ridge, one can descend to the south, or slightly southeast, for some 500 feet into the distinct couloir east of *Route 8*. Follow this large couloir all the way to a large, grassy bench some 600 feet above the canyon floor; two short rappels may be required to pass two chockstones. Contour west along this bench for about 1,000 feet to a wide gully that leads down to the canyon floor. *Time: 9 hours* from Garnet Canyon. See *Harvard Mountaineering,* 12 (May 1955), pp. 57–58.

Variation: III, 5.4, A1. First ascent September 15, 1935, by Malcolm Smith, Newell Rohrer, and Francis Neimann. The most easterly buttress of the Middle Teton extends a few hundred feet east of the beginning of the dike. This buttress is almost separated from the remainder of the east ridge of the mountain by two steep chutes, one from the south, very near the base of the dike, and one from the north. After ascending the talus or snow from the floor of Garnet Canyon directly to the easternmost point of this buttress, bear right along the base of the cliffs until naturally directed into the north chute, which begins as an open couloir. The upper end narrows considerably and is blocked by a large chockstone. Pass the chockstone on the right and traverse left to the small notch between the east buttress and the remainder of the ridge. The first 15 feet out of the notch required a shoulder stand on this early first ascent (5.8+). Above this steep, smooth pitch, climb up and left to the dike where the main route is joined.

ROUTE 10. Shand–Ferris. III, 5.4. First ascent August 1, 1940, by William Shand and Benjamin Ferris; this party did not continue to the summit but ended their climb at the Dike Pinnacle. One of the most prominent features of the Middle Teton, when viewed from the northeast (for example, from Disappointment Peak), is the large buttress that projects northward from the east ridge into the north fork of Garnet Canyon. This route utilizes the sloping east face of this buttress to gain access to the crest of the east ridge. The most direct approach to this route from the Garnet Canyon Meadows is to ascend the slope just under the east cliffs of the Middle Teton. In this way one is led naturally toward the east face of the buttress. One can also contour in to this same point from the trail above the Petzoldt Caves. The slabby face above, with its abundance of loose rock, can very likely be climbed in several ways. It appears that one could either proceed upward to the crest of the buttress and then follow it south to the point where it intersects the east ridge, or climb in or near the chimney at the extreme left (south) edge of the face. The first alternative on this face is probably easier. The difficulty will undoubtedly depend on the exact route selected. From the crest of the east ridge, which is reached above the difficult climbing of the Dike route (see *Route 9*), proceed as in *Route 8*.

ROUTE 11. Middle Teton Glacier. III, AI2+, 5.4. First ascent August 4, 1944, by Sterling Hendricks and Paul Bradt (complete); August 13, 1933, by W. T. Allemann (partial ascent, left branch to the east ridge of the Dike Pinnacle). See *Photos 30* and *31*. On the north side of this peak the broad Middle Teton Glacier extends all the way up to the Dike Pinnacle, where it splits; the left (east) section leads to the east ridge and the right to the snow col between the Dike Pinnacle and the true summit. This route is recommended as an early-season climb because crampons can then be worn all the way to the summit. From the Caves follow the usual route to the Middle Teton Glacier. The standard climb of this route ascends the glacier to just below the Dike Pinnacle. Then traverse right (west) into the steep snow couloir leading to the snow col between the Dike Pinnacle and the true summit. The *bergschrund* at the lower end of this couloir is passed on the left. Proceed up to the col, keeping on the left side of the couloir all the way. In late season, and sometimes in the middle of the season, the surface of the upper couloir above the *bergschrund* will be hard snow or ice. From the col follow *Route 8* to the summit. In late season on the lower glacier several crevasses open up and the snow cover disappears. It is possible to avoid the steep upper snow-and-ice couloir by the simple expedient of following the eastern section of the Middle Teton Glacier onto the east ridge. This minimizes the difficulties of reaching the ridge, but then one must climb over the Dike Pinnacle (not trivial) to the main summit, as in *Route 8*. *Time: 6 hours* from the Caves.

ROUTE 12. Northeast Face. II, 5.4, A1. First ascent August 24, 1936, by Fritz Wiessner, William House, and Elizabeth Woolsey. Ascend the Middle Teton Glacier as in *Route 11* toward the col between the Dike Pinnacle and the summit of the Middle Teton. Just below the mouth of the steep snow-and-ice couloir that leads to this col, ascend a crack in the rocks to the right (west) for about 100 feet to more difficult ground. A shoulder stand was used to pass this area of smooth rock and loose debris on the first ascent. Easier climbing leads to the broad grassy ledge (in early season this may be covered with snow) about halfway up the face. From here climb a series of cracks diagonally up and left (south) to a rotten rock couloir, which is the continuation of the dike from the east ridge. Cross the treacherous couloir at about the same altitude as the Dike Pinnacle and continue up and left (south) across smooth slabs to the main narrow couloir descending from the notch between the south and main summits. Ascend this couloir to the easy rocks below and immediately east of the summit. Scramble to the top.

ROUTE 13. Taylor. IV, 5.9, A4. First ascent August 26, 1961, by Royal Robbins and Jane Taylor. See *Photos 31* and *32*. This difficult climb is located near the eastern edge of the north face of the Middle Teton. Climb the Middle Teton Glacier to the beginning of the prominent ledge that slants steeply upward to the right (west), across the eastern portion of the north face. This ledge meets the glacier below the main *bergschrund.* The first three pitches ascend this ledge to a 25-foot-wide sloping grassy area. The overhanging wall above is broken on the right by a right-angle corner, and the difficult climbing begins here. Ascend this A2 corner and then follow a second crack (A3) up an overhanging white face. The sixth lead again ascends an A2 overhanging crack until a pendulum becomes necessary around a bulge and into a recess to the right (west). From the recess, an aid pitch (A4) up yet another overhanging crack brings one to some ledges, the second of which provides a convenient belay spot. The eighth pitch (A1 and 5.6) follows various cracks on the face above and eventually leads up to the right (west) to a steep ledge from which one can belay. Now, move right and up a gully, past two overhangs to another steep ledge; the first overhang (5.9) was wet on the first ascent. Climb this ledge and turn a third overhang on the right. For the tenth lead, ascend directly for 60 feet to a broad, sloping, rocky ledge, utilizing either a strenuous jam crack or a poorly protected face. This brings one out on the easy upper portions of the mountain east of the north ridge; from here, scramble to the summit. Parties attempting this route should have a comprehensive rack, including knifeblades and RURPs. See *American Alpine Journal,* 13, no. 1 (1962), pp. 216–220; *Sierra Club Bulletin,* 46, no. 8 (October 1961), pp. 53–54.

ROUTE 14. Robbins–Fitschen. IV, 5.10-, A1. First ascent July 30, 1960, by Royal Robbins and Joe Fitschen. See *Photos 31* and *32*. Ascend the Middle Teton Glacier to the bottom of the easternmost of the prominent chimneys on the north face of the Middle Teton. Climb 500 feet up a series of cracks and blocks on the right side of the lower extension of the chimney to the ledge at the beginning of the 500-foot wall right of the wet chimney. Using aid, climb the vertical crack about 25 feet to the right of the chimney. The last pitch on the wall angles steeply upward to the right, passing the final overhangs on the right by difficult free climbing (5.10-). From the top of the wall there is no great problem in reaching the summit from east of the north ridge. See *American Alpine Journal,* 12, no. 2 (1961), pp. 373–377; *Sierra Club Bulletin,* 46, no. 8 (October 1961), pp. 53–54.

ROUTE 15. Whiton–Wiggins Dihedral. III, 5.9. First ascent September 20, 1981, by Earl Wiggins and Mark Whiton. See *Topo 25* and *Photo 32*. This fine route on the excellent rock that characterizes the north side of the Middle Teton is steep and of sustained technical difficulty. Belay points are comfortable and protection is good. This route apparently is the same as the Briggs-Higbee Pillar for the second and third pitches. The start of the climb, however, is below and well left of the two dihedrals described under *Route 16.* It is reached in the same manner as described later, but the traverse eastward is continued for an additional 100 feet or so. This first pitch begins in a left-facing corner and then moves through an overhang (5.9) to gain a belay near but left of the bottom of the left dihedral, as described in *Route 16.* Climb the next two pitches of the Briggs-Higbee Pillar to the sloping belay under the final overhanging headwall. For the fourth lead bear right (west) and up to a belay past this headwall. The final lead continues right to gain the uppermost section of the Goodrich Chimney, at which point the top of the face is reached and the easier slabs and snow can be taken to the summit.

ROUTE 16. Briggs–Higbee Pillar. III, 5.10. First ascent July 8, 1974, by Roger Briggs and Art Higbee. See *Topo 25* and *Photo 31*. This route on the scenic and alpine north face of the Middle Teton lies well left (east) of the North Ridge route, but to the right (west) of the Robbins–Fitschen route. The short approach from the Lower Saddle is the same as that for the North Ridge, up to the sharp notch behind (south of) Bonney's Pinnacle. Climb up and left (east) out of the notch for 150 to 200 feet to a large ledge on which one can traverse, not always easily, east across the entire north face. In early season a snow couloir leading down to the Middle Teton Glacier will be crossed in the course of this scramble; an ice axe is useful in this section. Descend and traverse east past two major chimney systems (5.6) (the second of which is the Goodrich Chimney) until it is possible to climb toward the dihedrals that mark the central portion of the north face. Two dihedrals, the left one right-facing and the right one left-facing, are now directly above. The first lead of this route starts from a large ledge at the base of the right dihedral and then angles left using a lieback and thin crack to a small stance at the base of the left dihe-

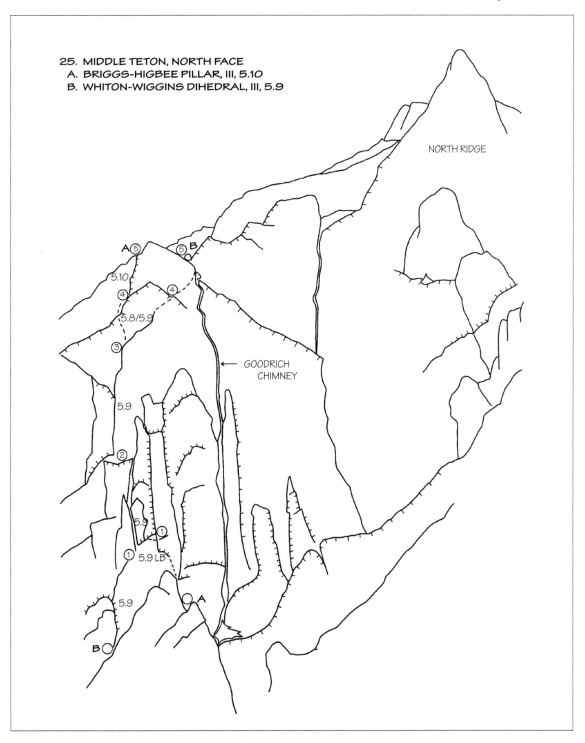

25. MIDDLE TETON, NORTH FACE
   A. BRIGGS-HIGBEE PILLAR, III, 5.10
   B. WHITON-WIGGINS DIHEDRAL, III, 5.9

NORTH RIDGE

A⑤   ⑤B

5.10

④   ④

5.8/5.9

③

GOODRICH
CHIMNEY

5.9

②

5.9   ①

① 5.9 LB

5.9   A◯

B◯

dral. Instead of continuing up the dihedral for the second pitch, climb up and left to the base of an overhang just left of the bottom of the dihedral. Climb an overhanging crack (5.9) for 30 feet to a ledge and continue on to a belay ledge another 20 feet higher and 10 feet to the left. The third lead (130 feet) follows the corner above for 30 feet and then ascends a steep, right-angling crack for 10 feet (5.9) before traversing right to a ledge; easier rock is then followed up and left to the belay. The next pitch goes up (100 feet) to the base of the final overhanging headwall (5.9) and then continues up and left under the headwall to a sloping belay stance at the base of an overhanging corner. The final fifth lead climbs this corner (5.10). Once above this point easier slabs and snow (in early season) lead to the summit, or the upper part of the North Ridge route can be taken.

ROUTE 17. *Jackson–Woodmencey Dihedral.* III, 5.10-. First ascent June 25, 1988, by Renny Jackson and Jim Woodmencey. See *Topo 26* and *Photo 32.* This route on the excellent rock of the north face of the Middle Teton attacks directly the leftmost (right-facing) of the two dihedrals described under *Route 16.* The first pitch is the same as *Route 16,* involving a face climb to a small overhang where a lieback (5.9) is taken around its left edge. The second lead goes directly up the right-facing dihedral above, using crack climbing and stemming techniques (5.8). At the top of this corner, exit out left and face climb into a perfect belay alcove on top of a large block. The next lead on easier rock (5.6) takes one to a comfortable belay ledge. The final lead of this route is the same as the last pitch of the Robbins–Fitschen route. Move up and left around a flake (5.8) and then stem up and left to a sloping ledge. Stem past a fixed pin (5.10-) using finger locks and step around the corner, where easier climbing is found leading in a short distance to the top of the climb. One can then continue to the summit using easier slabs and snow.

ROUTE 18. *Goodrich Chimney.* II, 5.6. First ascent September 4, 1955, by Donald Goodrich and John Reppy. See *Photos 31* and *32.* This is the second prominent chimney left (east) of the north ridge of the Middle Teton, as seen from the Lower Saddle. Scramble and traverse up and toward the east from the notch behind Bonney's Pinnacle (see *Route 19*) to the base of the second chimney system. The route goes directly up this chimney system for about six pitches; the last pitch out of the chimney and onto the slabs of the upper northeast face is difficult because of ice. For this reason, this route is recommended only for late season when wetness and ice will be at a minimum. From the top of the chimney one can scramble to the north peak where *Route 19* is joined. *Time: 6½ hours* from the Caves. See *American Alpine Journal,* 10, no. 1 (1956), pp. 116–119.

ROUTE 19. *North Ridge.* II, 5.6. First ascent July 17, 1931, by Robert Underhill and Fritiof Fryxell; first descent July 4, 1933, by Paul Petzoldt and Sterling Hendricks. See *Photo 33.* From the Lower Saddle between the Middle Teton and the Grand Teton, climb toward the base of the north ridge. Two large pinnacles that provide interesting scrambling will be met. Traverse the first, Pinocchio Pinnacle, on the west and the second (higher) one, Bonney's Pinnacle, on the east. On the far side (south) of the second pinnacle is a notch formed by the erosion of a small diabase dike. It is not difficult to climb out of this notch. Head toward an obvious ledge leading around on the left side of the ridge. Traverse along this ledge for perhaps 50 feet before going back to the right on another ledge for 60 feet to the "Room," a cavernous indentation in the ridge. It is possible to climb up and left out of the Room, but the more obvious way is via a shelf leading diagonally up and around the corner to the right. An even easier route, however, is to descend a few feet to some ledges below and to the right. One can then traverse right (west) along these ledges to the left edge of the northwest gully. Now head toward the notch formed by the black dike, keeping on the right side of the north ridge, staying in or near the northwest gully, and using a series of small connecting ledges and cracks. When the dike is reached, walk left (east) up its crumbling slope to the sharp notch it forms with the north ridge. Climb directly out of this notch, either using the face directly above or climbing large, somewhat loose blocks slightly to the right (west). This pitch is the most difficult portion of the North Ridge route. Easy ledges and slabs then lead up and around (east) to the summit. To descend by this route, it is convenient to rappel into the dike notch. *Time: 4½ hours* from the Lower Saddle; *6¾ to 8½ hours* from Garnet Canyon. See *Appalachia,* 19, no. 1 (June 1932), pp. 86–96; *Chicago Mountaineering Club Newsletter,* 2, no. 6 (July–December 1948), p. 6.

Variation: II, 5.6. First ascent July 5, 1940, by Paul Petzoldt and Elizabeth Cowles (Partridge). The standard North Ridge route described above bypasses the North Peak. This variation includes, one way or another, the summit of the North Peak on the way to the main summit. The difficulty of the climb (5.6 to 5.9) will vary depending on the exact line chosen. Only a short distance after cutting right (west) out of the Room, turn back left toward the ridge crest and a small notch. Cross over to the left (east) side of the ridge and climb a series of ledges on the upper northeast face of the north peak. After 200 to 300 feet the angle eases off, and one can continue easily to the North Peak summit, reaching it from the east. From this summit, climb partway down to the southeast and then rappel into the dike notch in order to reach the main summit.

Another possibility after leaving the Room is to stay on the right (west) side of the ridge, keeping very near the crest. On the smooth, downsloping slabs on the west face of the north peak, traverse back and forth up the horizontal and vertical cracks.

A third possibility is to climb ledges and cracks up and left from the notch behind Bonney's Pinnacle, staying east of the Room but near the crest of the north ridge on pre-

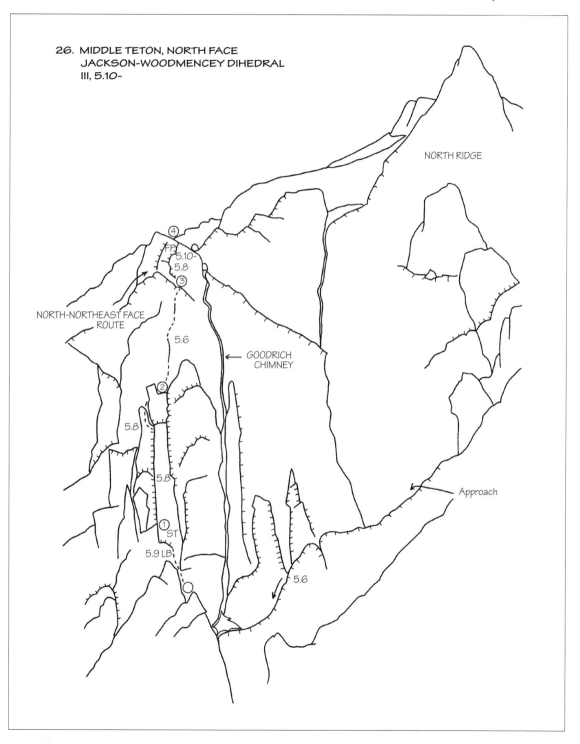

26. MIDDLE TETON, NORTH FACE
   JACKSON-WOODMENCEY DIHEDRAL
   III, 5.10-

NORTH RIDGE

④

FP
5.10-
5.8

③

NORTH-NORTHEAST FACE
ROUTE

5.6

← GOODRICH
CHIMNEY

②

5.8

5.8

Approach

① ST

5.9 LB

5.6

dominately excellent rock. Several pitches of enjoyable climbing will be found in this section, before striking the ledge of the upper northeast face, mentioned earlier.

ROUTE 20. Northwest Ice Couloir. III, AI3, 5.6. First ascent June 16, 1961, by Peter Lev and James Greig. See *Photos 31* and *33*. See *Route 19* for the approach from the Lower Saddle to the sharp dike notch behind (south of) Bonney's Pinnacle. Climb the wall on the far side of this notch and traverse right (west) into this northwest couloir. Climb more or less straight up this couloir, which ends on the west ridge a very short distance from the summit. The climb varies from a snow route in early season to perhaps the easiest of the classic Teton ice routes during midseason to late season. The angle of the couloir approaches 50° near the top. See *American Alpine Journal,* 13, no. 1 (1962), pp. 216–220.

Variation: III, AI4, 5.6. First ascent unknown. This variation provides a much more difficult start to the original climb. Approach the base of Pinocchio Pinnacle via the trail that wanders upward from the Lower Saddle. One can traverse easily out on a promontory to the southwest from which an impressive view of this variation can be obtained. Careful scrambling (4th class) down a chimney/gully to the southeast provides a reasonable entry into the couloir. The serious climbing is 80 to 100 feet in length and is AI4 in difficulty. From the top of this steep ice another 60 to 80 feet of climbing leads to the point where one would normally enter the couloir on *Route 20*.

ROUTE 21. Northwest Slope. II, 5.1. Possible first ascent August 27, 1939, by Stanley Grites, Frank Garbocz, and Adam Koj; or September 6, 1954, by William Hooker, Peter Ludwig, Peter Luster, and Craig Merrihue. See *Route 19* for the approach from the Lower Saddle to the sharp dike notch behind (south of) Bonney's Pinnacle. Surmount the wall on the far side of this notch and traverse right (west) into the prominent northwest gully, as in *Route 20*. Now pursue a diagonal course up and right (west) toward the west ridge, which can be reached at various points and then followed directly and easily to the summit. This diagonal course crosses the northwest ice couloir, which until late season is snow or ice filled, requiring the use of an ice axe.

Once on the far (west) side, the ill-defined ridge that forms the right (west) boundary of the couloir can be crossed in several places.

BONNEY'S PINNACLE (12,160+)
(0.15 mi N of Mount Teton)

Map: Grand Teton

This pinnacle is the higher of the two at the base of the north ridge of the Middle Teton. It is passed but not often climbed by those intent upon the north ridge of the Middle Teton.

ROUTE 1. East Face and South Ridge. I, 4.0. First known ascent August 11, 1948, by Orrin and Roger Bonney, who found a cairn containing a decomposed and illegible record. From the Lower Saddle traverse Pinocchio Pinnacle on the west, go through the notch between the two pinnacles, and climb easily the east and south sides of this small tower.

PINOCCHIO PINNACLE (12,160+)
(0.15 mi N of Mount Teton)

Map: Grand Teton

This, the lower of the two pinnacles at the base of the north ridge of the Middle Teton, is named after its profile as seen from the summit of Bonney's Pinnacle. These two pinnacles, which provide interesting climbing and an excellent view of the south side of the Grand Teton, are a worthwhile excursion from the Lower Saddle if one has the energy and an hour to spare.

ROUTE 1. East Face. I, 4.0. First ascent July 17, 1951, by Robert Merriam, William Whitfield, and Bertha Howald. From the Lower Saddle, traverse around the west side of this pinnacle to the notch between it and Bonney's Pinnacle. The face is a short climb.

ROUTE 2. North Face. I, 5.1. First ascent July 31, 1960, by Kellen Staley and William Echo. Approach from the Lower Saddle directly to the base of the north face. Climb about two-thirds of the face before angling left (east) to the northeast ridge. The final pitch to the summit is the most difficult.

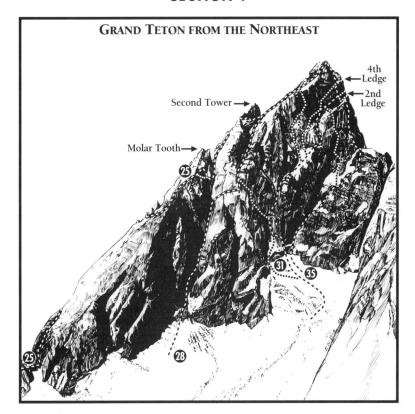

GRAND TETON FROM THE NORTHEAST

4th Ledge

2nd Ledge

Second Tower →

Molar Tooth →

Grand Teton and the Enclosure

GRAND TETON (13,770)

Map: Grand Teton

The Grand Teton is not only the highest peak in the range but also the high point of climbing activity. From any approach to the range, the Grand Teton towers above the lesser peaks and beckons the climber almost irresistibly. In more than 100 years of climbing on the Grand, routes to its summit have been found that will satisfy anyone's taste. From the Owen–Spalding route to the direct North Face route almost all degrees of difficulty can be found, but even on the easiest routes knowledge of the use of the rope is required for safety.

The structure of this highest peak in the Teton Range is complex. On the south (slightly west of south) the Grand Teton is bounded by the broad but windy Lower Saddle

(11,600+), which separates it from the Middle Teton. The much sharper Gunsight Notch (12,160+) on the north isolates its neighbor, Mount Owen. The Teton Glacier lies at the foot of the steep and renowned north face, with the southern portion of its terminal moraine at the base of the very long and pinnacled east ridge, which descends directly down into Glacier Gulch. The slabby upper southeast face of the mountain harbors, through most normal seasons, both the East Ridge Snowfield (above) and the Otterbody Snowfield (below), named over 60 years ago for its remarkable resemblance to the animal. The contracted form of the name, Otterbody, has been used in recent years although originally it was "Otter's Body." Below the steep rock of the southeast face is the Teepe "Glacier," a prominent snowfield in Garnet Canyon, just south of the east ridge. Teepe Glacier melted almost completely away during at least two summers of record (1931 and 1988), so strictly speaking it is not a true glacier, even though in late season ice climbing will be encountered on this snowfield.

Teepe Pillar and Glencoe Spire, two major pinnacles towering above the north fork of Garnet Canyon, are separated from the upper mountain by the Black Dike, which cuts across the southern portion of the Grand Teton at about 12,000 feet. The three distinct major ridges on the south—Exum, Petzoldt, and Underhill, named for pioneer Teton mountaineers of the 1930s—all rise from this very conspicuous dike. The first two are separated by the Beckey Couloir (rock) in the lower part and by the Ford Couloir (snow) in the upper part; the narrow Stettner Couloir separates the latter two. Above the Lower Saddle two large couloirs or gullies extend upward for 1,500 feet to the Upper Saddle (13,160+), which lies at the base of the upper western cliff band and separates the summit of the Grand from that of the Enclosure, a name now applied to the entire western spur (13,280+) of the mountain. Originally this name was applied more narrowly to describe only the circular man-made structure on the summit of this subpeak. The Enclosure itself is supported by a southwest ridge, which extends down into Dartmouth Basin, and a very long northwest ridge with origins in Cascade Canyon some 5,600 feet below. A small glacier or snowfield (rarely visited) lurks at the base of the west face of the Enclosure. The impressive northern aspect of the Enclosure rises vertically above the upper south end of Valhalla Canyon and is separated from the Grand Teton by the well-known Black Ice Couloir, which terminates at the Upper Saddle. The west wall of the Grand extends from the Black Ice Couloir north to the north ridge, which reaches from the Grandstand, above Gunsight Notch, up to the summit.

The Grand Teton has a long and sometimes turbulent history. Only a very brief outline can be given within these pages. The Grand, Middle, and South Tetons were the famous "Trois Tetons," well-known landmarks to the early fur trappers and others who journeyed through this section of the United States during the first half of the 19th century. Richard "Beaver Dick" Leigh, guide for the 1872 Hayden expedition, is quoted by Nathaniel P. Langford in his 1873 article in *Scribner's Monthly* as saying that one of these "mountain men," Michaud, attempted the ascent of the Grand Teton in 1843. The identity of Michaud remains uncertain, although he may have been Michaud LeClaire, who served as a messenger for the Hudson's Bay Company, carrying dispatches from Fort Hall (near present-day Pocatello, Idaho) to Montreal, Canada. Langford also places a Michaud LeClair as operating a toll bridge across the Smith Fork of Bear River in 1862. It is possible that the curious rock structure, the Enclosure, found on the summit of the high west spur of the Grand Teton, was constructed by Michaud during the course of his attempt, but it is more likely that it was built by Native Americans long before 1843.

The next known attempt was made by 14 members of the 1872 Hayden Survey (properly, the U.S. Geological Survey of the Territories), which was conducting an official exploration of the Teton–Yellowstone region. Two of the 14, Langford and James Stevenson, claimed to have reached the summit via an ice cliff from the Upper Saddle on July 29, 1872. Three other members of the expedition had reached the Lower Saddle: Frank Bradley, a geologist, stopped at the saddle to await the arrival of the mercurial barometer carried by Rush Taggart, assistant geologist; while two 17-year-old boys, Sidford Hamp and Charles Spencer, continued some distance above the Lower Saddle but stopped short of the Upper Saddle. There is no question that Langford and Stevenson reached the Upper Saddle and the Enclosure, because Langford wrote in his article the first description of the Enclosure. The question of whether or not they continued to the summit forms the basis of the famous and continuing controversy over the first ascent of the Grand Teton.

Five years later an attempt was made by four (perhaps only three) members of the Hayden Survey party in July 1877. Thomas Cooper, Stephen Kubel, Peter Pollack, and Louis McKean reached the Lower Saddle from the west and continued toward the Upper Saddle for several hundred feet. At this point Pollack and McKean apparently stopped while Cooper and Kubel continued a considerable distance farther. The various accounts of this climb differ, and it is not certain whether or not they reached the Upper Saddle and the Enclosure.

In 1878 it would seem that only sheer chance prevented a successful ascent of the Grand Teton when a third Hayden Survey party approached the peak. James Eccles, a member of the Alpine Club (London), together with his Chamonix guide Michel Payot, accompanied the Hayden expedition to the Teton–Yellowstone region; they were slated to attempt the peak with the triangulator A. D. Wilson and his assistant, Harry Yount (and perhaps also A. C. Ladd) on August 20. Eccles and Payot were detained at the last minute by a necessary search for two mules who strayed from their camp in the Hoback, and they were unable to join Wilson. If they had, it seems probable that they would have reached the summit, as Payot was a professional guide and Eccles an experienced mountaineer. The previous summer, on July 31, 1877, Eccles and Payot had made the first ascent of a south face route on Mont Blanc in the Alps. As it was, Wilson's party reached the Enclosure, and Wilson actually took a series of readings with his heavy surveying instruments set up on that airy site. By extraordinary chance, 97 years later in 1975, a metal matchbox, with "A. D. Wilson" inscribed in his own handwriting, was discovered by Leigh Ortenburger in a crack in the rocks at the summit of the Enclosure. Wilson was perhaps the most experienced climber in the survey at that time, having climbed many of the higher peaks of the United States, including Mount

Rainier, and he was much chagrined to have failed to reach the summit. In 1880 another well-to-do, itinerant Englishman and member of the Alpine Club, William Baillie-Grohman, while passing through Jackson Hole during a hunting expedition, explored the environs of the Grand Teton and reached the Lower Saddle in a desultory attempt from a low camp.

In 1891 William O. Owen made the first of his several unsuccessful attempts to scale the Grand Teton. With his wife, Emma Matilda, and Mathew B. Dawson and wife Jennie Dawson, Owen apparently reached a point somewhere between the Lower and Upper Saddles via the couloir from Dartmouth Basin. The second claimed ascent of the Grand Teton was that of Captain Charles Kieffer, Private Logan Newell, and a third man, probably Private John Rhyan, about September 10, 1893. The only evidence for this ascent is a letter from Kieffer to Owen on April 3, 1899, which was first discovered by the author among Owen's papers at the University of Wyoming. In the absence of other verification the cautious historian should entertain at least some skepticism. However, a careful check of Kieffer's military records shows that he was stationed at Fort Yellowstone during the summer of 1893 and, hence, presumably did have the opportunity to make the ascent. It is of interest to note that if Kieffer's drawing, which accompanies his letter, is to be taken literally, it shows his route to have been the Exum Ridge! In his letter Kieffer also indicated that he returned in 1895 but failed because "the gradual snow field . . . had fallen and left a steep jump off that we could not climb." Owen returned in 1897 with Frank Petersen and made several unsuccessful attempts from different directions, one in the couloir descending to Teepe Glacier from above the Second Tower; he was nearly killed during a glissade on the glacier below. Finally, on August 11, 1898, a party of six sponsored by the Rocky Mountain Club (Denver) started toward the Grand Teton from a camp in the cirque north of Shadow Peak. At the Lower Saddle Thomas Cooper, veteran of the 1877 attempt, decided not to continue and Hugh McDerment elected to go no farther at the Upper Saddle; the remaining four, Franklin Spalding, Owen, Petersen, and John Shive, continued to the summit, with Spalding largely responsible for leading and finding the route. This was the first *certain* ascent of the Grand Teton. Two days later Spalding, Petersen, and Shive returned to the summit to build a cairn and leave their names chiseled in the summit boulder while Owen obtained photographs from the Enclosure. The site of Owen's camp in the cirque between Shadow Peak and Nez Perce, along with a cache of 27 very heavy eyebolt "pitons" discarded in 1898, was found by the author in August 1969. One of these pitons, still solid, can be found even today in a boulder at this 1898 campsite. On July 6, 1984, the only piton actually emplaced by Owen on the Grand Teton was found by Rich Perch and Dan Burgette in the lower end of the Stettner Couloir. Others had been found abandoned on the rocks in 1934 on the upper Owen–Spalding route and in 1948 at the start of the Pownall–Gilkey route.

The now famous controversy between Owen and Langford broke out immediately after Owen's publication of a full-page article in the *New York Herald* shortly after the 1898 ascent, and it continues to the present day. There is insufficient space in this volume for a complete analysis of the evidence on the two sides of this acrimonious dispute. One of the authors has made an exhaustive search for information relating to this controversy and has now accumulated an extensive collection of information, published and unpublished. An unbiased presentation of the evidence must await the completion of a separate volume on the history of the exploration of the Teton Range. In the past Hiram Chittenden, renowned historian, Fritiof Fryxell, eminent geologist and authority on the Hayden surveys, and Francis Farquhar, authority on American mountaineering history, have all contributed to the available information and its interpretation. In recent years, however, several additional papers have been uncovered by the author that throw new light on certain aspects of the controversy. These include Owen's personal scrapbooks and the original manuscript for Langford's article in *Scribner's Monthly*. Because historical "proof" is extremely unlikely to be forthcoming for either side of the argument, perhaps the best way of regarding the problem, short of a detailed analysis of the probabilities, is to state that in 1872 Langford and Stevenson may have climbed the Grand Teton, in 1893 Kieffer, Newell, and Rhyan may have climbed it, and in 1898 Spalding, Owen, Petersen, and Shive definitely did succeed in reaching the summit.

The summit of the Grand Teton was not visited again for 25 years. This lack of attention is truly astonishing, as wide notice was given to the 1898 ascent and there was much climbing activity in the United States and Canada during the intervening quarter century. The modern era began on August 25, 1923, when a remarkable climb of the Grand Teton was made by three students from Montana State College. Quin Blackburn, the leader (who later served in the Antarctic with Richard E. Byrd), David DeLap, and Andy DePirro made the ascent and descent via the Owen–Spalding route in one day with no rope! Two days later Albert Ellingwood and Eleanor Davis (Ehrman) repeated the ascent. This was the first ascent by a woman. Paul Petzoldt began his extensive climbing and guiding career with an ascent of the Grand Teton in 1924, and in the years since the Grand Teton has become one of the most popular peaks in the country. It ranks as one of the finest mountaineering objectives in the United States.

This reputation is certainly deserved. A wide variety of problems will be encountered on the many faces and ridges of this complex mountain. Today one has a choice of some 90 routes and variations to the summit, with 18 more available on the adjacent Enclosure. Enjoyable ridge scrambling, high-angle rock walls, moderate snowfields, glaciers, and steep ice chutes are all to be found on this varied peak. A set of outstanding mountaineering routes, described in the introduction as the great alpine climbs, sets the Grand Teton apart from and above the lesser peaks of the range. From the summit almost every other peak in the range, with the notable exception of Mount Owen, can be seen. (To see Mount Owen one must descend a short distance down the north ridge.) The peak that retains greatest prominence from this viewpoint is Teewinot Mountain, its sharp pinnacles silhouetted against the flat plains of Jackson Hole. The Wind River Range forms the eastern horizon, and one can easily pick out flat-topped Gannett Peak, the highest in Wyoming. To the north one can see well into Yellowstone National Park and beyond, probably to Pilot, Index, and Granite Peaks. To the west Idaho is beautiful with its cultivated fields and rolling hills, but the western horizon is too distant for positive identification of the peaks.

It is emphasized that early-season climbs will usually entail greater, and frequently much greater, difficulties than are described here. Under such conditions, which may also arise as a result of a severe storm in any season, snow and ice can be expected on any route on the Grand Teton. A moderate climb, such as the Owen–Spalding route, can be extremely difficult if severely iced. Ice axe and crampons may become essential for the climb. Because the snow and ice vary from year to year, climbers should always inquire at the Jenny Lake Ranger Station for current conditions before setting out on a climb. Adequate preparation, skill, and equipment must be at hand for an ascent of the Grand Teton.

The usual rule is to allow two full days for the ascent and descent of the Grand Teton; this holds for every route. It is possible, though not commonly done, for a fast party to make the round trip in less than 24 hours. Even such long routes as the East Ridge and the North Ridge have been done in one day. Depending on the route, a high camp can be established at the Lower Saddle, in Garnet Canyon, at Surprise Lake, on the Teton Glacier, in Valhalla Canyon, or in Dartmouth Basin. The only route that can be recommended as offering an expeditious means of descent from the summit is the Owen–Spalding route; probably fewer than 50 descents have been made by other routes. A worthwhile and recommended 15-minute side trip from the Upper Saddle to the summit of the Enclosure (this is easier than it appears) will yield an excellent view of the entire west face of the Grand Teton.

Since the 1956 edition of this guidebook was published, a curious problem has arisen concerning the nomenclature of the couloirs on the south side of the mountain. In 1955 when the guidebook was in preparation, correspondence with Joseph Stettner suggested that their 1941 ascent of the Grand Teton had been made via the couloir between the Petzoldt and Underhill Ridges. That couloir was therefore named the Stettner Couloir, and the next one to the west, the Beckey Couloir, separating the Exum and Petzoldt Ridges, was named in recognition of the presumed first ascent of that couloir in 1948 by Fred Beckey, W. V. Graham Matthews, and Ralph Widrig. After publication of the guidebook in 1956, Jack Fralick, a longtime climbing friend of the Stettner brothers, indicated that he believed that the 1941 ascent had been via the Beckey Couloir based on his examination of a movie made during the climb. A reexamination of this movie in 1989 verified Fralick's belief, with the result that the long-standing names, Beckey Couloir and Stettner Couloir, are now seen to have been incorrectly applied for the past 35 years. While this error is lamentable, it seems that to attempt a change in names at this late date would be unwise and would result in considerable confusion. So, for better or worse, the original names will be retained.

The original speed record of 5 hours 22 minutes for the round trip from the Lupine Meadows trailhead to the summit and return was set on August 17, 1939, by John Holyoke and Joseph Hawkes. This record has been broken four times in recent years: Jock Glidden on August 12, 1973, in 4 hours 11 minutes, with no shortcutting; Bryce Thatcher on August 26, 1981, in 3 hours 47 minutes 4 seconds, with no rappel; Creighton King on August 10, 1983, in 3 hours 30 minutes 39 seconds, with no shortcutting; and Bryce Thatcher again on August 26, 1983, in 3 hours 6 minutes 25 seconds, with no rappel. Over the years the actual "trail" in Garnet Canyon has varied, so these times may not be exactly comparable. The unofficial "trail" past the end of the maintained trail, which terminates at the Platforms, was constructed in the summer of 1977. In 1939 and 1973 there was no trail.

Other events of note that have taken place on the Grand Teton include the first ski descent on June 16, 1971, by Bill Briggs and Robbie Garrett. As a variation, on June 11, 1982, Rick Wyatt successfully descended on skis using pin bindings and cross-country boots. Although illegal, the speediest descent to date was completed via parapente on September 19, 1987, by Jim Olson from just below the summit on the top part of the Buckingham Buttress and Underhill Ridge. The most recent series of escapades began with the first snowboard descent of the Grand on June 9, 1989, by Stephen Koch. Then, during the spring of 1994, major portions of the Black Ice Couloir were descended on snowboard (Koch) and on skis (Mark Newcomb), with both climbers alternating belaying one another. The Enclosure Couloir was descended in a similar fashion by Alex Lowe and Andrew McClain shortly afterward.

For the approach and campsites for *Routes 1* through *23,* see *Garnet Canyon;* for *Routes 24* through *34,* see *Glacier Gulch;* for *Routes 34* through *37,* see *Valhalla Canyon. Routes 34* through *37* can also be approached via Garnet Canyon.

CHRONOLOGY

Owen-Spalding: August 11, 1898, William Owen, Franklin Spalding, Frank Petersen, John Shive

  var: **Collins-Hume:** July 16, 1994, Greg Collins, David Hume

East Ridge: July 22, 1929, Robert Underhill, Kenneth Henderson (ascent); August 2, 1935, Paul Petzoldt, William Loomis (descent)

  var: **Southern Traverse:** August 12, 1935, Paul Petzoldt, Glenn Exum, Elizabeth Cowles (Partridge)

  var: **South Molar Tooth Couloir:** July 28, 1936, Paul Petzoldt, Karl Keuffel, James Monroe

  var: July 28, 1936, Paul Petzoldt, Karl Keuffel, James Monroe

  var: September 7, 1955, Leigh Ortenburger, Irene Beardsley

  var: August 11, 1957, James Langford, William Cropper

  var: **Molar Tooth, Tricky Traverse:** July 9, 1972, Robert Irvine, Jim Olson, David Lowe

  var: July 25, 1977, Jon King, Chuck Fitch

  var: **North Molar Tooth Couloir:** January 31, 1984, Alex Lowe

Wittich Crack: June 27, 1931, Hans Wittich, Walter Becker, Rudolph Weidner

Pownall-Gilkey: [probable] June 27, 1931, Hans Wittich, Walter Becker, Rudolph Weidner (descent); August 1948, Richard Pownall, Art Gilkey (ascent)

  var: September 2, 1993, Greg Collins, Colby Coombs

Exum Ridge: July 15, 1931, Glenn Exum (ascent); August 24, 1936, Jack Durrance, Ethel Mae Hill (descent)

Underhill Ridge: July 15, 1931, Robert Underhill, Phil Smith, Francis Truslow; September 5, 1937, Paul Petzoldt, Phil Smith, William House (descent)

  var: **Direct:** August 30, 1953, William Buckingham, Steve Smale, Ann Blackenburg, Charles Browning, Jack Hilberry

  var: **Wilson Crack:** September 2, 1965, Ted Wilson, Rick Reese

North Ridge: July 19, 1931, Robert Underhill, Fritiof Fryxell (ascent); first free ascent August 30, 1936, Fritz Wiessner, William House, Percy Olton, Beckett Howorth; July 6, 1933, Paul Petzoldt, Sterling Hendricks (descent, top half); September 3, 1955, Willi and Jolene Unsoeld (descent, bottom half)

  var: **East Gunsight Approach:** circa August 22, 1936, Fritz Wiessner, Paul Petzoldt, Brad Gilman, Beckett Howorth, Bill House, Elizabeth Woolsey

  var: **West Gunsight Approach:** August 6, 1940, Jack Durrance, Henry Coulter, Merrill McLane, Chap Cranmer

  var: **Valhalla Approach:** July 31, 1960, Pete Sinclair, Jake Breitenbach, Leigh and Irene Ortenburger

  var: **Italian Cracks:** August 19, 1971, Howard Friedman, Peter Wollan

  var: **Chockstone Bypass:** August 10, 1974, Jim McCarthy, Gerald Barnard

  var: **American Cracks:** July 7, 1988, Mike Colacino, Calvin Hebert

  var: **Odette-Sherner:** August 7, 1994, Chuck Odette, Jim Sherner

Stettner Couloir: [probable] July 30, 1933, Sam Younger, Albert Strube (descent); June 30, 1964, Charles Schaeffer, Bob Schaeffer, Mark Fielding, Curtis Stout (on snow, left fork); August 17, 1969, Leigh Ortenburger, Jennifer Ronsiek (on rock, right fork)

Petzoldt-Loomis Otterbody: August 2, 1935, Paul Petzoldt, William Loomis (ascent); September 10, 1936, Paul Stettner, Art Lehnebach (descent)

  var: August 6, 1961, J. Gordon Edwards, Kenneth Proctor

North Face: August 25, 1936, Jack Durrance, Paul and Eldon Petzoldt

  var: August 14, 1941, Paul and Bernice Petzoldt, Glenn Exum, Hans Kraus

  var: August 13, 1949, Richard Pownall, Ray Garner, Art Gilkey

  var: **Direct Finish:** July 24, 1953, Richard Emerson, Willi Unsoeld, Leigh Ortenburger

  var: July 9, 1954, William Buckingham, Fred Ford

  var: August 24, 1955, Willi Unsoeld, Frank Ewing

  var: September 2, 1955, Willi and Jolene Unsoeld

  var: **Upper Saddle Start:** July 31, 1960, William Echo, John Waage, Keith Staley, Dean Millsap

  var: **North Ridge Start:** August 11, 1976, Jim Donini, Rick Black, Michael Cole (from 1931 North Ridge route); July 20, 1977, George Montopoli, Ralph Baldwin (from Italian Cracks Route)

Lower Exum Ridge: September 1, 1936, Jack Durrance, Kenneth Henderson

  var: **Thin Man:** September 4, 1957, Charles

Plummer, Sterling Neale, Sam Silverstein
var: September 2, 1959, Frederick Medrick, Thomas Marshall
var: **Direct Start:** August 1986, Jim Williams, Robin Moore
var: **Gold Face:** June 27, 1988, Renny Jackson, Jim Woodmencey
var: **Direxum:** June 25, 1990, Carl Haiss, Joe Miller
var: August 27, 1990, Mark Whiton, John Berry
Smith Otterbody: September 5, 1937, Phil Smith, Paul Petzoldt, William House
Beckey Couloir: September 10, 1937, Joseph and Paul Stettner (descent); August 31, 1941, Joseph and Paul Stettner (ascent)
Northeast Couloir: August 8, 1939, Jack Hossack, George MacGowan
var: August 24, 1962, Leon Sinclair, Leigh Ortenburger
var: June 25–26, 1990, Todd Cozzens, James Earl
West Face: August 14, 1940, Jack Durrance, Henry Coulter
var: **Direct West Chimney:** August 13, 1960, Tom and William Spencer
var: **Traverse to Owen-Spalding:** August 10, 1966, Robert Irvine, Mike Ermarth, Rick Reese
var: **Black Ice–West Face Combination:** July 23, 1967, George Lowe, Mike Lowe
var: **Traverse to Upper Saddle:** February 2–4, 1971, George and David Lowe, Greg and Jeff Lowe
var: **Direct Approach:** August 28, 1973, Jim Olson, Doyle Nelson
var: **Tilley-Nicholson Traverse:** July 20, 1978, Buck Tilley, William Nicholson
var: **Neutron Burn:** August 7, 1989, Jon Patterson, Pete Keane
Petzoldt Ridge: July 14, 1941, Paul Petzoldt, Elizabeth Cowles (Partridge), Mary Merrick, Fred Wulsin, Jr.
var: **Direct:** August 30, 1953, Willi Unsoeld, LaRee Munns, James and Rodney Shirley, Austin Flint
var: **Petzoldt-to-Exum Traverse:** August 31, 1954, Robert Brooke, Tom McCormack
var: **Double Overhang:** June 25, 1986, George Montopoli, Leo Larson
Emerson Chimney: August 16, 1948, Richard Emerson, Pat Harison
Goodro-Shane: August 9, 1953, Harold Goodro, Jim Shane
var: July 2, 1961, Tom Spencer, Ron Perla

West Face of Exum Ridge: July 23, 1954, Richard Pownall, Robert Merriam
var: July 14, 1981, Yvon Chouinard, Cullen Frishman, Naoe Sakashita
Buckingham Buttress: August 19, 1955, William Buckingham, Richard Hill, Ray Secoy
var: **Ortenburger Arête:** July 1991, Brent Finley, Susan Harrington, Leigh Ortenburger
Lev: July 12, 1960, Peter Lev, James Greig, William Glosser, David Laing; first free ascent July 30, 1988, Renny Jackson, Richard Perch, Steve Rickert, Leigh Ortenburger
var: **Jackson-Woodmencey:** summer 1988, Renny Jackson, Jim Woodmencey
Northwest Couloir: July 26, 1960, David Dornan, Leigh and Irene Ortenburger
var: **West Face Finish:** August 4, 1960, Royal Robbins, Joe Fitschen, Yvon Chouinard
var: **Jackson-Kimbrough Contortion:** August 9, 1980, Renny Jackson, Tom Kimbrough
var: **Hummingbird Wall:** August 1990, Beverly Boynton, Ted Kerasote
Medrick-Ortenburger: August 14–15, 1963, Frederick Medrick, Leigh Ortenburger
Northeast Buttress: August 24–25, 1970, Paul Myhre, Dale Sommers; first free ascent about July 30, 1978, Jon King, Charles Foster
var: **Little Wing:** July 16–17, 1976, Tom Deuchler, Dave Moerman
Simpleton's Pillar: June 16–17, 1972, Jeff Lowe
Southeast Chimney: August 5, 1973, David Lowe, Leigh Ortenburger
Horton East Face: August 14, 1977, W. D. Horton, Paul Horton, Robert Snyder
Grand North Couloir: about August 1, 1978, Jon King, Charles Foster (mostly rock); June 6, 1980, Steve Shea (mostly ice)
Route Canal: June 17, 1979, Jeff Lowe, Charlie Fowler
Beyer East Face I: July 14, 1979, Jim Beyer
Otterbody Chimneys: September 14, 1979, Kim Schmitz
No Name Gully: 1979 or 1980, Steve Shea
Loki's Tower: August 2, 1981, Mark Whiton, Michael Stern
var: July 17, 1984, Renny Jackson, Steve Rickert
Beyer East Face II: August 15, 1981, Jim Beyer, Dan Grandusky
Jackson-Rickert Crack: June 20, 1986, Renny Jackson, Steve Rickert
Burgette Arête: July 26, 1988, Dan Burgette, Jim Springer

It's Not a Chimney: September 6, 1989, Jim
Dorward, Dan Burgette
    var: **It Is (Too) a Chimney:** September 1990,
Ralph Cooley, Jerry Johnson, Tony Jones
Keith–Eddy East Face: August 17, 1991, Jason
Keith, David Eddy

ROUTE 1. ☞Owen–Spalding. II, 5.4. First ascent August 11,
1898, by William Owen, Franklin Spalding, Frank Petersen,
and John Shive. See *Topo 27* and *Photos 37, 41, 49,* and *50.*
This famous route goes from the Lower Saddle (11,600+)
between the Middle Teton and the Grand Teton to the
Upper Saddle (13,160+) between the Enclosure and the
Grand Teton, then out onto the west face and up to the
summit. When conditions are good, this traditional route
remains the easiest way to reach the top of the mountain;
when iced, however, this route can be extremely difficult.
For the approach to the Lower Saddle, see *Garnet Canyon.*
The terrain between the Lower Saddle and the Upper Saddle
can be negotiated in several ways but is not difficult climbing; a climbers' trail will be found covering much of it.
Nevertheless, some climbing parties may, depending on
conditions, wish to use a rope for safety before reaching the
Upper Saddle. The major difficulties of the route lie above
the Upper Saddle.

Take the trail leading upward (north) from the Lower
Saddle to and past the Black Dike. Avoid trampling the fragile alpine vegetation. Immediately beyond the dike is a large
smooth-faced tower called the "Needle." Do not go to the
right (east) side of the Needle and try to ascend the large
eastern couloir (known as the Wall Street couloir) that lies
at the base of the walls of the Exum Ridge; it contains steep
sections and much loose rock, and there are problems in
exiting from the upper end. Instead, proceed up along the
left (west) of the Needle on ledges and sections of "trail."
The area west of the Needle and east of the Southwest Ridge
is composed of two separate couloirs. The most westerly of
these curves down and west as it drops steeply into
Dartmouth Basin. The couloir immediately west of the
Needle extends with only minor breaks all the way to the
Upper Saddle. The two couloirs are separated by a curious
knob or small tower, and in early season both will contain
nearly continuous snow. During the winter or spring getting
to the Upper Saddle can be a straightforward snow climb
weaving up the two couloirs. During the main summer
climbing season the best route stays on the left (west) flank
of the ridge that extends from the Needle to near the Upper
Saddle. The one described here was worked out by Glenn
Exum during his years as a guide.

Continue around the Needle to the large chimney (with
chockstone), which is the first break in its west wall. Just
past this chimney climb abruptly up and right across a small
face back into the chimney above the chockstone. Continue
easily up and right (100 feet) to a wide outlook ledge. Turn

to the north here and find the "Eye of the Needle," a tunnel
that leads under an enormous boulder. One can squeeze
through this tunnel, exiting onto a small ledge (frequently
icy) at the far (north) end. If the tunnel is blocked by snow
in early season, climb over the top and back down to the
ledge. Follow this small ledge north past an exposed corner,
known as the "Belly-Roll-Almost," into the gully that is the
upper extension of the initial chockstone chimney. Continue up and left (north) to the edge of this gully. From here
to the Upper Saddle one can simply take the path of least
resistance along the west side of the main ridge, which will
be on the right leading from the Needle to near the Upper
Saddle. The best but intricate scheme involves climbing
onto the crest of the main ridge above at a section of black
rock, staying on the right (east) side of the crest for 200 feet,
and then crossing back (west) into the upper main couloir
to reach the Upper Saddle.

An impressive view can be obtained by looking down
the north side of the Upper Saddle at the steep Black Ice
Couloir. A little scrambling is required to reach the relatively flat area just under the west cliffs of the Grand Teton.
This area is slightly above and east of the lowest point of the
Upper Saddle. The standard descent rappel point is at the
top of the cliffs above. Caution should be exercised here
because the scree is treacherously loose and a slip could
entail serious consequences. If there is a party above the
rappel point, beware; they are likely to knock down loose
rocks.

Several routes diverge from this point on the west side
of the Grand Teton. The Owen–Spalding route leads left
(north) and most parties rope up before starting out on the
scree ledge leading out of sight to the north. The first obstacle on this ledge is a very large detached flake known as
the "Belly-Roll," which one can easily pass on the outside
by using the excellent handholds along the top edge. Proceed a few feet farther along the ledge to the famous
"Crawl," or "Cooning Place." This is a very exposed ledge,
perhaps 18 inches wide, directly under an overhang. The
time-honored method used by the first-ascent party is to
crawl on one's stomach along this ledge, as the overhang
prevents standing or even going on hands and knees. However, there are enough footholds a few feet down on the face
below this ledge for one to use the edge of the ledge for
handholds and simply walk along on the outside. Neither
method is difficult but the exposure is exhilarating. On the
far (north) side of the Crawl, continue easily along the ledge
for about 10 feet. (To avoid becoming enmeshed in the
difficulties of the Great West Chimney, do not traverse too
far north here.) The "Double Chimney," which is the crux
of the route, is about 15 feet up and 15 feet to the left of this
point. (This name has been retained, although it is now
inappropriate, since the huge flake that divided the chimney into two parts collapsed against the north wall in the
summer of 1951.) Climb this chimney (5.5) to a good be-

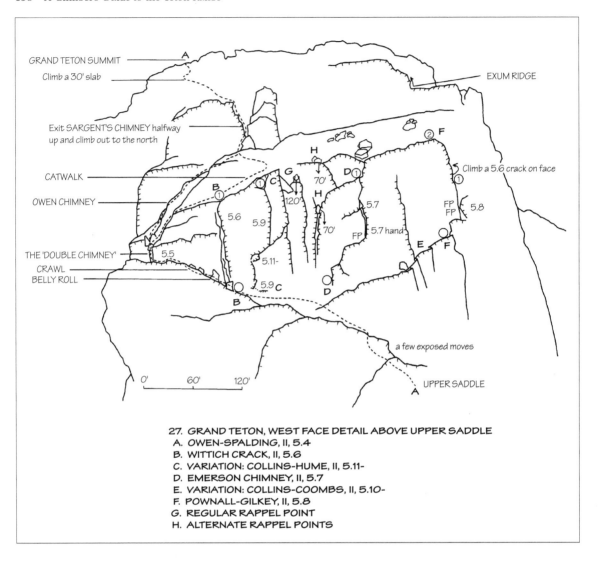

GRAND TETON SUMMIT

Climb a 30' slab

EXUM RIDGE

Exit SARGENT'S CHIMNEY halfway
up and climb out to the north

CATWALK

OWEN CHIMNEY

Climb a 5.6 crack on face

THE 'DOUBLE CHIMNEY'

CRAWL

BELLY ROLL

a few exposed moves

UPPER SADDLE

0'   60'   120'

27. GRAND TETON, WEST FACE DETAIL ABOVE UPPER SADDLE
A. OWEN-SPALDING, II, 5.4
B. WITTICH CRACK, II, 5.6
C. VARIATION: COLLINS-HUME, II, 5.11-
D. EMERSON CHIMNEY, II, 5.7
E. VARIATION: COLLINS-COOMBS, II, 5.10-
F. POWNALL-GILKEY, II, 5.8
G. REGULAR RAPPEL POINT
H. ALTERNATE RAPPEL POINTS

lay at the large sloping ledge at the base of the next feature, the Owen Chimney.

To pass the next section there is a choice. Most obvious is the large Owen Chimney, which starts almost directly above and angles slightly up to the right. A jam crack on the right side of this chimney is sometimes ice-free when the main chimney is iced. The more commonly used alternative from the top of the Double Chimney is the "Catwalk," an easy but very exposed 150-foot series of ascending slabs leading due south toward a point of rock on which a cairn can be seen. (Before continuing the ascent, the climber can observe the descent rappel route from the south end of these Catwalk slabs, where one can see on the opposite side of a 30-foot-wide, rotten chute the mass of sling rope used for rappelling [120 feet] to the Upper Saddle. *Note:* At this elevation, on the west side of the Grand Teton, there is a broad, sloping bench that extends from the Exum Ridge all the way north to the Great West Chimney.) From the south end of the Catwalk climb north and east a short distance (60 feet) up to the huge chimney system that is the obvious break in the wall above. This chimney system (known as Sargent's Chimney) is climbed on the left (north) side, although the right branch will also go. From the top of this chimney proceed upward and slightly to the left (north) for about 200 feet until one encounters a 30-foot, 45° slab. Above this slab traverse a short distance to the right (south); then scramble left up to the summit about 75 feet above.

On the descent do *not* climb directly down the west face. Keep in mind that in reaching the summit it was necessary to bear left (north) several times; hence, on the descent it will also be necessary to bear slightly left (south). The 120-foot rappel from near the south end of the Catwalk will take one all the way down to the Upper Saddle. This rappel (requiring two ropes) eliminates the lower part (Catwalk, Double Chimney, Crawl, and Belly Roll) of the Owen–Spalding route and is today used more often than the traditional downclimb. It is a most spectacular rappel, as the last 60 feet are free. (This rappel was discovered on August 18, 1948, by Richard Pownall, Ralph Johnson, and Jim Harrang; the first rappel into the Upper Saddle was made earlier, on July 20, 1948, by Richard Emerson and Fred Golomb, who utilized a point somewhat to the south.)

If escape is urgently needed and conditions do not permit downclimbing the Owen–Spalding route and there is but one rope available, two schemes are available. Instead of descending all the way to the standard rappel point, cut left (south) when about 20 or 30 feet above the rappel point, crossing the small buttress above the standard rappel point to gain another single-rope rappel point. Slings will be found here. This rappel goes down into the chimney immediately south of the regular 120-foot rappel. Look for a large chockstone from which another single rope rappel will take one to the Upper Saddle. If the first anchor point is not found, it is possible to use the main rappel anchor and diagonal into the chimney on the right to the chockstone.

Below the Upper Saddle, use the same route as that used for ascent, but remember to go right (west) a short distance before turning down into the main couloir, or else one may get into the Wall Street couloir. Because of loose rock and steep sections, this large eastern couloir immediately west of the walls of the Exum Ridge is *not* recommended for descent. Remember also that the Eye of the Needle, the key to an easy descent, is found on the right (west) side of the ridge that extends from near the Upper Saddle down to the Needle. After descending about 300 feet in the main couloir, cross the ridge to the left (east), descend 200 feet farther, and cross back to the right (west) to the black rock. From near the ridge crest one should be able to see the Eye of the Needle. If the route is missed, one can continue down the main couloir to the right (west), but some unpleasant cliff bands and steep, hazardous snow will be met before moving back left toward the Black Dike to gain the Lower Saddle. *Time: 3¾ to 4¾ hours* from the Lower Saddle; *5¾ to 7 hours* from the Petzoldt Caves; *6 to 7½ hours* from Garnet Canyon; *8½ to 10 hours* from Jenny Lake.

See *Alpine Journal,* 19, no. 145 (August 1899), pp. 536–543, illus.; *American Alpine Journal,* 3, no. 3 (1939), pp. 304–309, illus.; *Appalachia,* 18, no. 3 (June 1931), pp. 209–232, illus.; 22, no. 4 (December 1939), pp. 533, 535; *Chicago Mountaineering Club Newsletter,* 2, no. 6 (July–December 1948), p. 6; *Die Alpen,* 5 (1929), pp. 330–336, illus.; *Mazama,* 13, no. 12 (December 1931), pp. 63–71, illus.; 19, no. 12 (December 1937), pp. 12–16, illus.; *Outdoor Life,* 54, no. 3 (1924), pp. 181–186, illus.; *Outing,* 38, no. 3 (1901), pp. 302–307, illus.; *Princeton Alumni Weekly,* 28, no. 24 (1928), pp. 711–718, illus.; 920–921; 29, no. 24 (1929), pp. 756–763, illus.; *Scribner's Monthly,* 6, no. 2 (1873), pp. 129–157, illus.; *Sierra Club Bulletin,* 12, no. 4 (1927), pp. 356–364, illus.; *Summit* 3, no. 8 (August 1957), pp. 10–11, 21, illus.; 6, no. 6 (June 1960), p. 24; 7, no. 10 (October 1961), pp. 18–21, illus.; *Trail and Timberline,* no. 71 (August 1924), pp. 9–10, illus.; no. 83 (August 1925), pp. 1–8, illus.; no. 179 (September 1933), pp. 123–125, illus.; no. 389 (May 1951), pp. 58–60, illus.

Variation: Collins–Hume. II, 5.11-. First ascent July 16, 1994, by Greg Collins and David Hume. See *Topo 27 and Photo 37.* This is essentially a one-pitch variation to Route 1. It is also a fine rock climb on excellent rock. From the Upper Saddle just to the north of the big chimney and regular rappel, climb up and left up to a right-facing corner. Then traverse south and go up and over an overhang that is difficult (5.11-) and hard to protect (while hanging on!). Continue up to the prominent gray corner seen from below and finish the pitch right at the south end of the Catwalk.

ROUTE 2. Wittich Crack. II, 5.6. First ascent June 27, 1931, by Hans Wittich, Walter Becker, and Rudolph Weidner. See *Topo 27* and *Photo 37.* This remarkable but short (140-foot) route suffered the misfortune of being lost for 24 years and was then misidentified for another 8 years. Thus, the ascent of this route was not repeated until 1963. The Wittich Crack is not as subject to ice as the first Double Chimney of the Owen–Spalding route; hence, it is recommended as an alternate when the Owen–Spalding is severely iced. In addition, the excellent rock makes this route worthwhile for its own sake, but it is more difficult than the Owen–Spalding when both are dry. Proceed to the Upper Saddle and continue north toward the Belly Roll (see *Route 1*). About 10 or 15 feet south of the large block of the Belly Roll, there is an obvious crack system leading directly upward through the vertical wall. Ascend this crack system to an alcove beneath a large overhang. Pass this overhang on its left (north) side by face holds and hand jams (5.6) and pull out onto the slabs in the middle of the Catwalk. Reach the summit via *Route 1.* See *Appalachia,* 19, no. 1 (June 1932), pp. 86–96; *The Nature Friend,* 25, no. 7 (July 1947), pp. 5–11.

ROUTE 3. Emerson Chimney. II, 5.7. First ascent August 16, 1948, by Richard Emerson and Pat Harison (Emerson). See *Topo 27* and *Photo 37.* From the Upper Saddle the cliff band above and to the east is seen to be broken by three major chimney systems. The one on the north, vertical and usually wet, leads to a cave beneath a huge boulder a few feet north of the main rappel point. The central deep chimney, commonly containing ice, lies immediately to the right (south) of the line of the standard rappel. Fifty feet farther to the right is the third chimney system, the Emerson Chimney, cutting up through two bands of black rock to the bench at the top of the cliff band. From the Upper Saddle, climb up and right on broken rock to a flake at the base of the chimney. After passing the initial difficulties of getting into the chimney, a fixed piton (an Army horizontal) will be found halfway up this lead. At the top, where the chimney becomes an overhang, climb left and up (5.7) onto the bench. This bench is isolated from the main large bench, which extends across the southwest and west faces of the Grand Teton from the Exum Ridge to the Great West Chimney. One must climb a diagonal "Crawl" ledge up and left (north) to join the upper Owen–Spalding route or blocks up and right (south) to join the upper Exum Ridge route.

ROUTE 4. *Pownall–Gilkey.* II, 5.8. Probable first descent June 27, 1931, by Hans Wittich, Walter Becker, and Rudolph Weidner; first ascent August 1948, by Richard Pownall and Art Gilkey. See *Topo 27* and *Photo 38.* Proceed to the Upper Saddle as in *Route 1,* the Owen–Spalding route. Traverse right (south) from the Upper Saddle out to the end of a gradually steepening and narrowing ledge system. At the end of this ledge a block will be found with a thin crack on its left edge. Climb this crack to the top of the block and then continue up the crack system (5.8) via hand jams to a large ledge. The second pitch goes up an easier crack (5.6) to the broad bench extending across the southwest face of the Grand Teton. At this point one can traverse directly to the Exum Ridge route or the Owen–Spalding route. It is more interesting, however, to continue across the bench and up a fine, large chimney that leads to the uppermost mountain before joining one of the aforementioned routes. This route faces southwest on a high-angle smooth wall and, hence, offers an alternative to the Owen–Spalding route in early season or just after a storm. It is significantly more difficult, however, and the crux may be complicated by running water because the route drains a portion of the large bench above. *Time: 7 hours* from the Lower Saddle. See *American Alpine Journal,* 8, no. 1 (1951), p. 180.

Variation: II, 5.10-. First ascent September 2, 1993, by Greg Collins and Colby Coombs. See *Topo 27.* This one-pitch variation to the regular Pownall–Gilkey route ascends the finger crack on the striped wall to the north. The pitch is 150 feet in length and said to be of very high quality with excellent protection.

ROUTE 5. *Jackson–Rickert Crack.* III, 5.9. First ascent June 20, 1986, by Renny Jackson and Steve Rickert. See *Topo 28* and *Photo 38.* In the upper west face of the Exum Ridge is a wide, zigzag crack in an apparently vertical wall. It is, perhaps, the most prominent feature of that face when viewed from the Lower Saddle. This climb ascends this crack, which starts just above the beginning of *Route 6.* From the Lower Saddle use the same approach as for the West Face of the Exum Ridge (*Route 6*) to the large open corner of this 1954 route. This route of six pitches has approximately the same start but moves left onto much more difficult ground after the first lead. The three key leads involve 5.7, 5.8, and 5.9 climbing, the last being the crux offwidth. This route joins the Exum Ridge route at the beginning of the V pitch.

ROUTE 6. *West Face of the Exum Ridge.* III, 5.8. First ascent July 23, 1954, by Richard Pownall and Robert Merriam. See *Topo 28* and *Photo 38.* Much of what is seen of the Grand Teton from the Lower Saddle is the west face of the Exum Ridge, rising above the (right-hand) gully that leads to the Upper Saddle. While much of this face is sheer, it is broken in a few places. This route ascends the main vertical break in the upper portion of the wall, a very large, open corner system. From the Lower Saddle proceed as in *Route 7,* crossing the ridge of the Needle into the gully immediately west of the Exum Ridge. Instead of continuing on out to Wall Street, scramble north up the gully some 300 feet until directly below the dihedral in the face above. Begin by scrambling up and right for 40 to 50 feet to the start of the main corner. Climb a short, wide 5.8 crack and then run the rope out to a belay on a ledge. The second pitch is 4.0. Proceed up the main dihedral for a ropelength (5.6 to 5.7) and belay at the base of the upper chimney. The fourth pitch ascends a right-facing corner (5.7). Face climbing (5.7) out and left on the next lead provides an escape from the main dihedral.

Zigzag steeply up to the left (north) from this point, and gain considerable altitude. At one point it is possible to climb straight upward and join the Exum Ridge, but because this face lies below the crest of the ridge one must continue angling left (north) under a sheer wall in order to climb the entire face. An offsize flake (5.7) leads up and left to a large ledge that cuts back to the right (south) across the wall. Instead, move the belay to the north and climb a chimney with a chockstone in it (5.7) that once again leads to a ledge. Traverse right about 60 feet on this ledge to a finger crack leading directly up the wall above. Climb 40 feet up to the end of this crack (5.8), then make a delicate and exposed 30-foot traverse to the right (south) to join the Exum Ridge route at the middle of the V pitch. To locate this point from below: the rock that appears to be the highest point on the Grand Teton, when seen from the Lower Saddle, is actually the top of this V pitch, some 100 feet above the point referred to above. *Time: 10¼ hours* from Garnet Canyon. See *American Alpine Journal,* 9, no. 2 (1955), pp. 147–149.

Variation: III, 5.8. July 14, 1981. First ascent by Yvon Chouinard, Cullen Frishman, and Naoe Sakashita. This significant variation is at present little known and only a general description can be provided. Proceed as in the regular Exum Ridge route to the beginning of Wall Street. This variation starts in the huge chimney system that rises di-

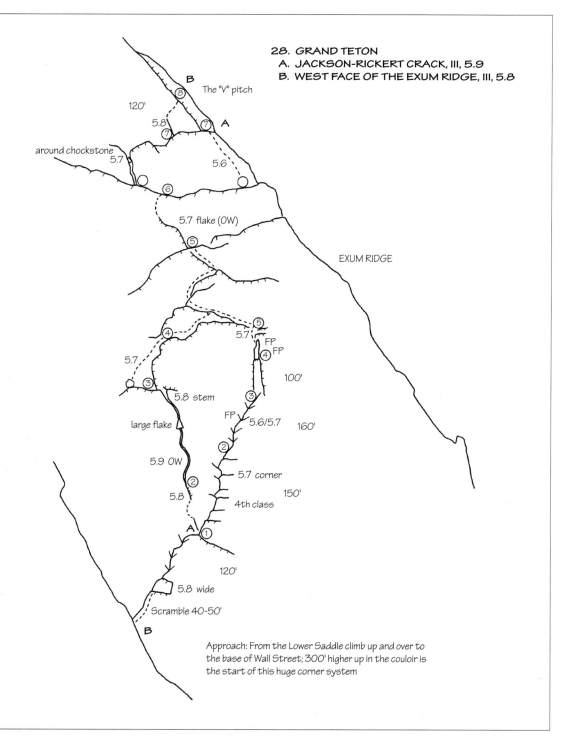

28. GRAND TETON
A. JACKSON-RICKERT CRACK, III, 5.9
B. WEST FACE OF THE EXUM RIDGE, III, 5.8

The "V" pitch

120'

5.8

around chockstone
5.7

5.6

5.7 flake (OW)

EXUM RIDGE

5.7

5.7

FP
FP

100'

5.7

5.8 stem

FP

large flake

5.6/5.7   160'

5.9 OW

5.7 corner

5.8

150'

4th class

120'

5.8 wide

Scramble 40-50'

B

Approach: From the Lower Saddle climb up and over to
the base of Wall Street; 300' higher up in the couloir is
the start of this huge corner system

rectly above the beginning of Wall Street. To avoid the ridge crest the variation repeatedly angles left (north) in a sequence of chimneys, cracks, and ledges. It may have crossed the very large right-facing corner of the 1954 route described earlier. The Exum Ridge route was not rejoined until rather high up on the ridge, but the exact location is uncertain.

ROUTE 7. ☞*Exum Ridge*. II, 5.5. First ascent July 15, 1931, by Glenn Exum; first partial descent July 25, 1933, by Stephen Koelz; first complete descent August 24, 1936, by Jack Durrance and Ethel Mae Hill, the first of three such descents by Durrance that summer. See *Photos 36, 38, 40, and 41*. It is interesting for the climber of today to contemplate the spectacular leap that Glenn Exum made from the end of Wall Street over to the large boulder on the other side and what was perhaps going through his mind as he psyched up for this maneuver. It is also interesting to note that Paul Petzoldt soloed the Exum Ridge on the same day as Exum for the second ascent after guiding two clients to the summit via the Owen–Spalding. Petzoldt used a more traditional means of ascent as he traversed across the Wall Street section. On the third ascent of the route by Paul Petzoldt, Theodore Koven, and Gustav Koven one week after Exum's daring solo climb, a haversack containing a can of beans, a can opener, and notepaper dated 1921 were found on the Wall Street ledge, signifying a surprising early attempt, probably by Teton Basin residents (see *Buck Mountain, West Peak, Route 3*).

Over the past half-century this outstanding ridge has acquired a tradition as the route of choice to the summit of the Grand Teton for the thousands who have travelled to this corner of Wyoming. For more than a generation the Exum Ridge route has been the most popular route to the summit of the Grand Teton. The combination of ready access, southern exposure, and moderate but exciting climbing with excellent rock on a line leading directly to the summit ensures its continued popularity. Although the Owen–Spalding route is a simpler climb and is recommended for those with less mountaineering experience, the Exum Ridge route has excellent rock and (in good weather) will be in sunshine once Wall Street has been passed. The Exum Ridge route is also not as subject to severe icing as the Owen–Spalding route. Two disadvantages are the length of the route and the relative difficulty of descending in bad conditions from partway up the climb; after passing Wall Street it is almost easier to continue to the summit than to descend. Three methods of escape from various points along the ridge will be described later, however.

Take the trail leading upward (north) from the Lower Saddle to and past the Black Dike. Avoid trampling the fragile alpine vegetation. Immediately beyond the dike is a large, smooth-faced tower called the "Needle." Proceed up along the left (west) wall of the Needle on ledges and sections of "trail." A large chimney (with chockstones), the first break

in the west wall of the Needle, will be seen rising above to the east. Just past this chimney climb abruptly up and right across a small face back into the chimney above the chockstone. Continue easily up and right (100 feet) to a wide outlook ledge. Turn to the north here and find the "Eye of the Needle," a tunnel that leads under an enormous boulder. One can squeeze through this tunnel exiting onto a small ledge (frequently icy) at the far (north) end. If the tunnel is blocked by snow in early season, climb over the top and back down to the ledge. Follow this small ledge north past an exposed corner, known as the "Belly-Roll-Almost," into the gully that is the upper extension of the initial chockstone chimney. Continue up in this gradually steepening gully for 150 feet to the small notch on the crest of the ridge that extends from the Needle toward the Upper Saddle. From this notch, the huge Wall Street ledge can be seen across the wide gully, which has come to be known as the Wall Street couloir. See *Photo 36*. This ledge was named by Petzoldt, during one of his early guided ascents, for a client who was a "Wall Street banker" by profession.

A descending traverse along ledges and chimneys leads across this gully to the lower left end of Wall Street. Take the huge Wall Street ledge out to its right (south) end and rope up and set the belay. The exposed gap to the boulder ledge on the ridge crest is passed either by balancing around on the narrow extreme end of the Wall Street ledge or by using the ledge for handholds. In good weather welcome sunshine should be found here.

Two ropelengths now lead to the wall of the first large tower. The initial 60 feet are the Golden Stair, solid, knobby, golden Teton rock; the remainder is scrambling along on almost horizontal rock. At the tower turn right (east) for 150 feet up a chimney and over blocks to the base of a wide, steep gully known as the Wind Tunnel. A jam crack (frequently wet or icy) provides access to the gully. Climb either the right or left edge of this gully for the next ropelength (150 feet). A second ropelength goes slightly right and then back left, ending near the crest. The boulder ledge at the base of the Friction Pitch, now out of sight almost directly above, can be reached by going either right or left from this point. The left alternative, the traditional route, involves a slanting chimney on the west side of the crest followed by a short face and crack onto the boulder ledge. The right alternative, more commonly used in recent years, uses a double crack system near the right edge of the ridge crest to gain the same ledge in one long lead. The ridge itself here is fairly broad, and the use of the word "crest" refers simply to the high point between the left and right edges of that ridge.

From the boulder ledge climb the Friction Pitch. This lead, the most difficult of the route, goes almost directly up from the boulder ledge for 120 feet, on relatively smooth and unbroken rock. Climb directly above the belay for 15 feet and then slightly left to two large black knobs, then up and slightly right (30 feet) to gain a shallow groove leading to the belay. Little protection is available in the course of this lead; fortunately, the difficult (5.5) friction move is only about 25 feet above the belayer. From the top of the Friction Pitch scramble up and right across the top of a black-rock gully to a very small notch (sometimes filled with snow). Continue scrambling for two pitches near the ridge crest until it is convenient to cross over to the left (west) side of the crest to the base of the "V" (also known as the "Open Book"), a large, left-facing corner at the top edge of the west face of the Exum Ridge. Climb the "V" (150 feet) and finish the pitch on a broad bench across which one can walk to the next tower, just west of the crest in an area of black rock. A left-leaning crack (often wet or icy) is then ascended. Now move back right to the crest and the next tower, which is climbed near its prow by means of a short jam crack (5.5). At the top of the crack follow the horizontal ridge crest to the base of the summit block. From here traverse right (east) along the top edge of the southeast snowfield. The summit is attained by easy blocks from the southeast.

If caught by a storm partway up the ridge, one can descend the route to a point just above the Golden Stair where a rappel (60 feet) can be made directly down onto the end of Wall Street. A second escape, somewhat difficult and exposed, is available between the Friction Pitch and the "V"; a ledge system, beginning with an exposed step-around on loose blocks, on the west face of the ridge starts at a small notch about 150 feet above the top of the Friction Pitch. Follow this ledge, up and down, for about 300 feet past more loose blocks to the lower end of the broad bench leading toward the standard descent rappel on the Owen–Spalding route. If higher on the ridge, a third, easy method of escape, from the top of the V pitch, is to make a horizontal traverse left (northwest) across the broad bench to reach the Owen–Spalding route and the standard descent rappel.

Variations: There are so many small variations available on this ridge that it is possible to make two or three ascents and scarcely touch the same rock twice. These will not be detailed here, but a few major variations must be mentioned. The inexperienced climber should appreciate that this multiplicity of variations implies that, should the exact route described here be lost, there is little cause for concern because almost any upward course will, sooner or later, place you on the summit.

The Friction Pitch can be avoided by two methods. On the pitch below traverse even farther to the right (east) into a gully parallel to it. There is loose rock and sometimes ice in this gully, so it is not highly recommended. Once in the gully, climb to the black-rock area at the top of the Friction Pitch. Or take the "Puff-n-Grunt Chimney," which is actually a difficult (5.6 to 5.7) corner between the Friction Pitch and the gully already mentioned. Some difficulty will be experienced in getting to this corner from the starting ledge.

When the "V" is iced, one can simply keep on the right (east) side of the ridge and climb an extensive system of cracks in the slabs to the horizontal section above. Finally, at the summit block a very interesting and worthwhile variation can be used. Instead of traversing right (east) underneath the summit block, cut left (west) 50 feet before climbing up into the cleft between the summit block and a detached rock mass leaning against it. Then scale the west side of the summit block to its knife-edge crest and ride this arête, known as the "Horse," for 180 feet to the summit. *Time: 5 to 6 hours from the Lower Saddle; 6¾ to 7¾ hours from the Caves; 7 to 9 hours from Garnet Canyon; 9¼ to 11 hours from Jenny Lake.* See *Appalachia,* 19, no. 1 (June 1932), pp. 86–96; *Chicago Mountaineering Club Newsletter,* 2, no. 2 (May–November 1946), pp. 17–18; 5, no. 6 (December 1951), p. 16; 10, no. 1 (February 1956), pp. 10–11; 15, no. 1 (February 1961), pp. 4–7; *Trail and Timberline,* no. 447 (March 1956), pp. 47–48; no. 491 (November 1959), pp. 169, 171.

ROUTE 8. Lower Exum Ridge. III, 5.7. First ascent (to the summit) September 1, 1936, by Jack Durrance and Kenneth Henderson; second ascent (to Wall Street) in 1938 by Jack Durrance and Andrew McNair. See *Topo 29* and *Photo 40.* This notable climb, one of the most impressive of the early Durrance routes, goes up the lower segment of the Exum Ridge from the Black Dike to the end of Wall Street. This section is steeper and much more difficult than the rest of the ridge above. Durrance considered it his best route in the Tetons. It is an excellent choice for climbers seeking good difficult rock on the Grand Teton and is especially suitable as an early-season climb because it is south-facing with few ledges to hold snow. An ice axe, however, is recommended for early-season ascents. In addition, the weather, which almost always comes in from the southwest or west, can be easily monitored as the climb progresses.

Before starting out for this route, it is useful to pick out the major landmarks from the Lower Saddle. The first of these is the initial 120-foot chimney, which starts at the top of the first step of the ridge; from the Saddle, this chimney has the appearance of a large left-facing corner. Note the large ledge diagonaling from the beginning of the chimney down to the right past the apex of the Black Dike at the base of the Exum Ridge. For the easiest approach, gain this ledge near the foot of the Petzoldt Ridge and scramble diagonally left (west) back to the base of the chimney. The lowest section of the ridge below can also be climbed more directly to this point. Once in the chimney climb over the first chockstone and behind the second; traverse out on the wall to the right (south) for a few exposed feet, then back into the chimney just beneath the large chockstone that blocks the top. The left wall yields a route past this obstacle to the wide ledge (with cairn) at the top of the second step. (This chimney can be avoided by walking right [east] along the ledge at the top of the first step until somewhat right [east]

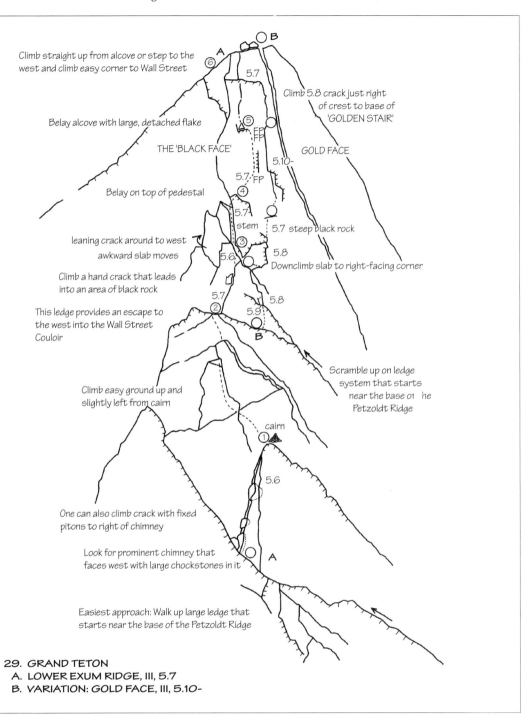

Climb straight up from alcove or step to the
west and climb easy corner to Wall Street

⑥   A   ○ B

5.7

Climb 5.8 crack just right
of crest to base of
'GOLDEN STAIR'

Belay alcove with large, detached flake

⑤   FP
      FP

THE 'BLACK FACE'   GOLD FACE

5.10-

5.7 FP

Belay on top of pedestal   ④

5.7

stem   5.7 steep black rock

leaning crack around to west →   ③
awkward slab moves   5.8

5.6   Downclimb slab to right-facing corner

Climb a hand crack that leads
into an area of black rock

5.7   5.8

This ledge provides an escape to   ②   5.9
the west into the Wall Street   B
Couloir

Scramble up on ledge
system that starts
near the base of the
Petzoldt Ridge

Climb easy ground up and
slightly left from cairn

cairn

①

5.6

One can also climb crack with fixed
pitons to right of chimney

Look for prominent chimney that   ○   A
faces west with large chockstones in it

Easiest approach: Walk up large ledge that
starts near the base of the Petzoldt Ridge

29. GRAND TETON
A. LOWER EXUM RIDGE, III, 5.7
B. VARIATION: GOLD FACE, III, 5.10-

of the crest. The face above can then be climbed to complete this chimney alternative.)

From the top of the second step scramble left (west) up to the crest of the ridge. Another ropelength (5.6) on the left (west) flank of the ridge brings one to the top of the third step. An easier alternative to this direct method of reaching the third step is to traverse 100 feet or more around to the right (east) to the obvious slabs that angle left, back up to the ridge crest at the third step.

At this point it is possible to exit from the ridge by traversing left (west) along a broken, black-rock ledge into the gully west of the Exum Ridge at the beginning of Wall Street. However, it is the steeper section above that leads to the end of Wall Street and provides the best climbing. Climb a short steep pitch just left (west) of the crest; drop down a few feet to a belay cave, then continue up and left to a sloping ledge and a second belay cave. This can be done as one long lead. Work up a small chimney that leads up and left around a corner. The lower lip of this chimney levels off into a ledge. Just before meeting the black rock, turn straight up until almost even with the notch behind the last tower on the ridge below Wall Street; this stubby tower is the top of the fourth step and it is common to belay on top of it. It is now necessary to descend right (south) a few feet to the 20-foot chimney by which the notch is reached. The 80° "Black Face" above this notch is the crux of the climb and is a single long lead. First climb 10 feet above the belay, and then traverse up and right (east) toward a loose flake in the middle of the face. Next, go almost straight up and slightly left via a 5.6 crack to a belay stance in an alcove at the upper left (west) edge of the face. This face, a beautiful example of high-angle climbing with adequate holds, contains many suitable cracks for protection, but the ledges are narrow and the angle is constant. From the alcove at the top of the face, move left (west) to an easy left-facing corner that leads to the boulder ledge at the end of Wall Street. *Time: 9 hours* from the Caves. See *Appalachia,* 21, no. 2 (December 1936), pp. 268, 271, illus.; *Dartmouth Mountaineering Club Journal,* 1957, pp. 24–25; 1958, pp. 31–34.

Variation: Thin Man. III, 5.7. First ascent September 4, 1957, by Charles Plummer, Sterling Neale, and Samuel Silverstein. This variation starts from the third step of the Lower Exum Ridge. Instead of traversing left (west) from the third step, climb straight up the face to a cave from which the first belay can be made. From here ascend to the right and up the face for about 15 feet; then continue diagonally right around a black overhang to a steep crack, at the top of which is the second belay stance. The 30-foot jam crack above leads directly to the base of the Black Face.

Variation: III, 5.7. First ascent September 2, 1959, by Frederick Medrick and Thomas Marshall. From the alcove at the top of the Black Face it is possible to continue directly up the ridge, reaching the boulder ledge at the end of Wall Street slightly from the east. This involves face climbing and a well-protected 5.7 crack.

Variation: Direct Start. III, 5.8. First ascent August 1986, by Jim Williams and Robin Moore. From the Black Dike scramble to the standard beginning of the route, but instead of heading diagonally up and left along the easy ledge, go downhill to the east to the base of the buttress. Climb from the lowest point up small corners and cracks. Three pitches lead to the large ledge at the top of the second pitch of the standard route. Some loose rock will be found on the second pitch.

Variation: Direxum. III, 5.9. First ascent June 25, 1990, by Carl Haiss and Joe Miller. This variation may, in fact, be nearly the same as the preceding one. It is two pitches in length and intersects the regular Lower Exum at the top of the main chimney at the bottom. Begin just above the Black Dike to the right of a large flake. Face climbing leads up and right to a right-facing corner (5.9) in pink rock. Continue on up and left on easy 5th-class ground or climb a crack (5.9, then 5.8 offwidth) to the large ledge by which one can traverse to the chimney on the regular route. The second pitch ascends the south face of the slab that forms this chimney. It consists primarily of 5.7 face climbing with a short 5.9 crack in the middle.

Variation: Gold Face. III, 5.10-. First ascent June 27, 1988, by Renny Jackson and Jim Woodmencey. See *Topo 29* and *Photo 40.* This difficult variation of four pitches goes up a section of very steep, golden rock out to the right (east) of the Black Face of the standard Lower Exum Ridge. The climb is approached on the right side of the Exum Ridge in the same manner as in *Route 9,* using the middle ramp from the Black Dike up west to the beginning of the Petzoldt–Fralick Chimney. Continue on past (west of) the chimney along the upward-sloping ledge system until just short of the crest of the Lower Exum Ridge, as shown on the topo; some exposed scrambling is involved. The first lead goes up a 5.9 face to and past a ledge and into a crack that angles slightly up and left onto a slab for the belay. Now downclimb the slab to gain a right-facing corner that is climbed past the right end of a roof to and up a steep black-rock face to a belay ledge. The third long lead is the crux of this variation, going up to and passing the left end of an overhang and then straight up the Gold Face on small holds (5.10-). The final lead ascends a 5.8 crack just to the right of the ridge crest and gains the boulder ledge at the end of Wall Street from the southeast. An alternative approach for this variation would be to climb the standard Lower Exum Ridge route to the end of the second pitch and downclimb the ledge to the start of the first of the four leads of this variation.

Variation: III, 5.10. First ascent August 27, 1990, by Mark Whiton and John Berry. This difficult, two-pitch variation ascends cracks just left of *Route 9* on the eastern facet of the Exum Ridge. Presumably one climbs *Route 9* until just below the main chockstone. From this point traverse up and left to the base of an obvious, vertical crack system. This hand- to finger-size crack passes through two bulges (first 5.10-, second 5.10) and ends at a stance in black rock after a full 160 feet. The second pitch goes straight on up the 5.7 hand crack above for 100 feet.

ROUTE 9. It's Not a Chimney. III, 5.9. First ascent September 6, 1989, by Jim Dorward and Dan Burgette; attempted on July 26, 1939, by Paul Petzoldt and Jack Fralick. See *Topo 30* and *Photo 40*. The main feature of this route is the conspicuous long chimney system that parallels the lower Exum Ridge on the right (east), terminating just above the Golden Stair on the upper Exum Ridge route. This Petzoldt–Fralick Chimney lies between the Beckey Couloir and the crest of the Exum Ridge. From the Black Dike, at the foot of the buttress that extends between the bases of the Lower Exum Ridge and the Petzoldt Ridge, there are three large ramps that slant up to the left (west). The lower left ramp is the easy approach to the lower Exum Ridge (see *Route 8*), and the upper right one is the start of the Beckey Couloir. This route takes the middle of the three ramps (5.1) and angles for 170 feet up to the southwest corner of the buttress. From a point just beyond and left of a large flake, climb a short crack system over a bulge (5.8) and then right up a 40-foot dihedral, finishing back to the left to a belay ledge. A 100-foot traverse left across the drainage and slabs now takes one into the base of the Beckey Couloir and the beginning of the large Petzoldt–Fralick Chimney, which is bounded on the right by the Burgette Arête and on the left by the Lower Exum Ridge. The first lead up the chimney is over a black-rock section (5.8) to easier ground. The next pitch continues up the chimney for another 120 feet (5.6) to a belay stance below the chockstone pitch; this probably marked the high point of the 1939 attempt, as a piton and carabiner were found at the base of the chockstone in 1989. Now climb a crack system in the chimney and exit left around the chockstone (5.6). The final difficult lead (5.9) follows a crack system on the face to the left of the chimney proper and traverses right (5.7) back into the chimney near the top of the pitch. This pitch is consistently difficult, but the rock is good and there are good cracks for protection. One can now easily (4.0) traverse left (west) from the top of the chimney onto the Exum Ridge at a point above the Golden Stair. Follow the Exum Ridge route to the summit. A suggested rack should include a full set of wired stoppers and protection to 3½ inches.

Variation: It Is (Too) a Chimney. III, 5.9. First ascent September 1990 by Ralph Cooley, Jerry Johnson and Tony Jones. See *Topo 30*. Climb It's Not a Chimney to the obvious first chockstone and belay in the alcove above it. From this point on the chimney is very steep and angles slightly to the east. The width varies from about 1 to 5 feet for the rest of its length. Proceed up the chimney, beginning on the right-hand wall. The entire distance from the belay to the second chockstone is consistently steep and difficult (5.9) and is the crux. The angle then eases, and a good belay can be found after climbing over the third chockstone (5.6). Fourth-class climbing leads up and west where the Exum is joined just above the Golden Stair. Bring protection to 2 inches for this climb.

ROUTE 10. Burgette Arête. III, 5.8. First ascent July 26, 1988, by Dan Burgette and Jim Springer. See *Topo 30* and *Photo 40*. This route ascends the buttress or arête that bounds the Petzoldt–Fralick Chimney on the right (east); this chimney and the arête lie on the right (east) side of the Lower Exum Ridge. Follow *Route 9* from the Black Dike to the beginning of the Petzoldt–Fralick Chimney; the initial section is identical for both routes. Instead of climbing the chimney, the first of five pitches moves right and across (5.6) onto the crest of the arête, short of the Beckey Couloir. The next lead goes up an inside corner (5.7) to the belay. Now cut right across a face into and up another dihedral just right of the crest. The fourth pitch moves back left onto and up the face of the crest where the protection is thin. A final lead (4.0) of easier rock takes one to the Exum Ridge at a point above the Golden Stair.

ROUTE 11. Beckey Couloir. II, 5.4. First descent September 10, 1937, by Joseph and Paul Stettner, after making the fourth ascent of the north ridge; first ascent August 31, 1941, by Joseph and Paul Stettner; second ascent June 29, 1948, by Fred Beckey, W. V. Graham Matthews, and Ralph Widrig. See *Photo 40*. This broad couloir separates the Exum Ridge from the Petzoldt Ridge. A most unusual aspect of the 1941 ascent was that it started from the floor of the north fork of Garnet Canyon and reached the Black Dike directly via the steep broken face to the right (east) of the small but spectacular waterfall that drains the couloir; this waterfall is just west of Glencoe Spire. The normal start is from the Black Dike at the base of the Petzoldt Ridge on the large ramp that diagonals up and left (west) into the beginning of the couloir. Climb the steep but sound rock of the couloir to the notch behind the main tower of the Petzoldt Ridge. The couloir is wide and offers a considerable expanse of rock up which many variations are possible. In early season the couloir is filled with snow and ice. From the notch the route is the same as *Route 12*. See *American Alpine Journal*, 7, no. 2 (1949), pp. 221–222; *Appalachia*, 23, no. 1 (June 1940), pp. 101–103, illus.; 27, no. 2 (December 1948), pp. 227–229.

ROUTE 12. Petzoldt Ridge. III, 5.6. First ascent July 14, 1941, by Paul Petzoldt, Elizabeth Cowles (Partridge), Mary Merrick, and Frederick Wulsin, Jr. See *Photo 40*. This important ridge, which lies between the Underhill Ridge and the Exum Ridge, contains some of the most enjoyable rock in the park, very steep but with enough knobs to prevent excessive difficulty. The Petzoldt Ridge is one of the recommended routes on the Grand Teton. More than one line is

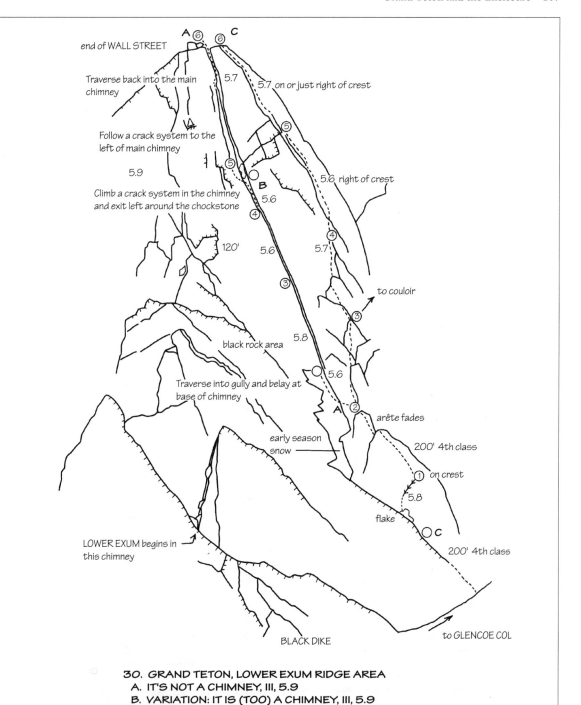

end of WALL STREET

Traverse back into the main
chimney

5.7

5.7 on or just right of crest

Follow a crack system to the
left of main chimney

5.9

Climb a crack system in the chimney
and exit left around the chockstone

5.6 right of crest

B

5.6

120'   5.6   5.7

5.8

to couloir

black rock area

Traverse into gully and belay at
base of chimney

5.6

arête fades

early season
snow

200' 4th class

on crest

5.8

flake

C

LOWER EXUM begins in
this chimney

200' 4th class

BLACK DIKE

to GLENCOE COL

30. GRAND TETON, LOWER EXUM RIDGE AREA
A. IT'S NOT A CHIMNEY, III, 5.9
B. VARIATION: IT IS (TOO) A CHIMNEY, III, 5.9
C. BURGETTE ARETE, III, 5.8

possible, however, so the difficulty will depend on the exact route followed; the topo shows only one of these lines. An ice axe is needed for ascents during most of the summer because moderately steep snow will be found in the Ford Couloir, which extends above the final tower on the ridge proper.

Traverse the Black Dike from either the Lower Saddle or Teepe Glacier to the snow couloir just west of the Underhill Ridge. Most of the ascents of the Petzoldt Ridge have been made by climbing up this couloir for approximately 100 feet before turning left (west) onto the rock. The following description is one of many possible variations.

Climb one ropelength to a small black-rock area with good holds. From the top of this black-rock area, climb right to a series of slabs leading to a left-facing corner system. A chimney leads out of this corner system and onto the easier climbing above. After two ropelengths, climb left onto an exposed and steeper pitch nearly on the left corner of the ridge. Ascend another ropelength to a high point on the ridge and descend 10 feet to some broad ledges. From here climb either the ridge itself or a chute to the right to reach a belay beneath a short chimney. Above the chimney a short scramble leads to the top of the main tower of the ridge.

Although a few parties have climbed down to the notch, a 50-foot rappel is recommended. From the notch, follow the Ford Couloir, the snow couloir leading toward the summit, for about two ropelengths before traversing when convenient to the right onto the upper Buckingham Buttress, the next rock ridge to the east. Because the crest of this buttress is attained well above its steep initial section, this rock ridge is easily followed to the summit block. Early in the season this last 500 feet will be on snow. *Time: 7½ to 8½ hours* from the Lower Saddle. See *Dartmouth Mountaineering Club Journal,* 1956, pp. 34–38; *Trail and Timberline,* no. 354 (June 1948), pp. 79–83, illus.

Variation: Direct. III, 5.7. First ascent August 30, 1953, by Willi Unsoeld, LaRee Munns, James and Rodney Shirley, and Austin Flint. See *Topo 31* and *Photo 40*. This major variation starts at the base of the ridge at the Black Dike and then goes directly up the nose of the ridge instead of along its right (east) side. It is longer and more difficult than the preceding usual route and has the advantage of leading past the "Window," an interesting and prominent feature of the Petzoldt Ridge.

Approach from the Lower Saddle as for the standard Petzoldt Ridge except that one starts upward on the rock before crossing the final snow chute (from the Stettner Couloir) that guards access to Glencoe Col. Climb moderate red rock at the toe of the ridge for about 200 feet to reach a ledge, where the steeper and more difficult climbing begins. The first pitch above this ledge is left and up into a steep slot, past some fixed pitons. The belay is found up and left (west) after a short chimney. The next lead goes on steep face climbing around the left (west) end of a black over-

hang. A third ropelength of crack and face climbing ends at the Window, where one can climb over it (5.6) or go through the Window (from east to west) onto easy ledges ending with a short, awkward crack that takes one back onto the crest. The following lead on excellent rock stays slightly right (east) of the crest, while the next goes directly up on the knife-edge crest. A final pitch then takes one to the top of the main tower of the ridge. This route, combined with the regular Exum Ridge route, is perhaps the finest of the routes available from the south.

Variation: Petzoldt-to-Exum Traverse. III, 5.6. First ascent August 31, 1954, by Robert Brooke and Tom McCormack; first descent August 9, 1980, by Bruce Coulter. For those desiring more climbing on this route, immediately after rappelling into the main notch on the Petzoldt Ridge, cut left (west) up a diagonal ledge to the beginning of the gully that parallels the first large tower of the Exum Ridge on the right (east). Then follow *Route 7* to the summit. This combination gives about twice as much rock climbing as is found on either *Route 7* or *12* by itself, and because none of it is excessively difficult it is recommended for those seeking a long, enjoyable climb. This option also provides an emergency retreat route from the Petzoldt Ridge off the mountain; once the Exum Ridge route is joined, climb down to the top of the Golden Stair, where a 60-foot rappel takes one to the end of the Wall Street ledge. *Time: 10½ hours* from the Lower Saddle. See *Stanford Alpine Club Journal,* 1955, pp. 48–50.

Variation: Double Overhang. III, 5.9. First ascent June 25, 1986, by George Montopoli and Leo Larson. From the belay stance at the end of the first difficult pitch of the *Direct variation,* instead of moving left (west) past a black overhang and fixed pin, move right 10 feet to the base of the major dihedral. Climb directly up this dihedral, over two difficult overhangs to gain its upper section. The standard *Direct variation* is then rejoined at the end of this single lead.

ROUTE 13. Buckingham Buttress. III, 5.6. First ascent August 19, 1955, by William Buckingham, Richard Hill, and Ray Secoy. See *Photo 40*. This buttress or ridge begins between the forks at the top of the Stettner Couloir. A significant problem of this route is that one must first climb most of another route just to reach the beginning of the climb. The first ascent was made, after an ascent of the Petzoldt Ridge *(Route 12),* by a descent (down to the east) of about 250 feet from the main notch of that ridge. Approach can also be made by climbing the Stettner Couloir *(Route 14)* to its forks. A short vertical pitch must be climbed to get onto the face of the ridge. Three hundred feet of very steep cracks and chimneys near the middle of the broad ridge leads to a small notch on the left (west) side of the ridge. At this point traverse a short distance alongside a large flake out onto the west face of the ridge. Now climb a long but easy chimney and traverse back out onto the south face of the ridge on a good series of ledges that peters

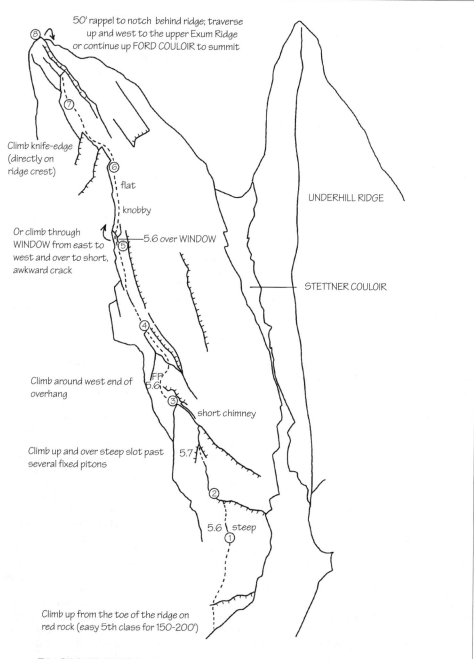

50' rappel to notch behind ridge; traverse
up and west to the upper Exum Ridge
or continue up FORD COULOIR to summit

⑧

⑦

Climb knife-edge
(directly on
ridge crest)

⑥

flat

knobby

UNDERHILL RIDGE

Or climb through
WINDOW from east to
west and over to short,
awkward crack

⑤ — 5.6 over WINDOW

STETTNER COULOIR

④

Climb around west end of
overhang

FP
5.6

③

short chimney

Climb up and over steep slot past
several fixed pitons

5.7

②

5.6   steep

①

Climb up from the toe of the ridge on
red rock (easy 5th class for 150-200')

31. GRAND TETON
PETZOLDT RIDGE, VARIATION: DIRECT
III, 5.7

out below a large ceiling-type overhang. Make a delicate step to the opposite wall of the chimney, which ends at the ceiling. Then climb 100 feet of high-angle, knobby rock to the more nearly horizontal section of this ridge. From here in late season the climb to the summit is an easy scramble or in early season an exhilarating snow climb.

Variation: Ortenburger Arête. III, 5.10-. First ascent July 1991, by Brent Finley, Susan Harrington, and Leigh Ortenburger. Of the nearly 90 first ascents, new routes, and variations that he pioneered in the Tetons, this was Leigh Ortenburger's final climb. It is located on the east side of *Route 13* and directly across from the top of the Underhill Ridge. Begin by climbing in a groove for one ropelength until a roof is encountered. From the belay beneath the roof, move out and left (west) via 5.10- face climbing and then continue up on easier ground to finish the pitch. An additional lead takes one to the top of the buttress, from which one can continue scrambling to the summit.

ROUTE 14. Stettner Couloir. II, 5.7. Probable first descent July 30, 1933, by Sam Younger and Albert Strube, an apparent mistake when the Owen–Spalding route could not be found; first ascent on snow June 30, 1964, by Charles Schaeffer, Bob Schaeffer, Mark Fielding, and Curtis Stout, who exited via the left fork; first ascent on rock August 17, 1969, by Leigh Ortenburger and Jennifer Ronsiek, who exited via the right fork. See *Photos 40* and *42*. This is the steep and narrow couloir that separates the Petzoldt Ridge from the Underhill Ridge. In early season the ascent can be made as a pure snow-and-ice climb and in late season it will be almost pure rock, whereas in midseason it will be mixed.

From the dike, which can be reached easily from the Lower Saddle or from Teepe Glacier, enter the couloir and start up the snow. Up to the point where the couloir splits, it is, through most of the season, hard snow with an occasional ice step; there will be some danger from rockfall. Crampons are recommended. As an early-season climb careful consideration must be given to the snow conditions because avalanches sweeping this couloir are standard following a significant snowfall or as the sun warms things up during the day. The right fork, which is usually an ice couloir, steepens considerably and leads to the small col at the top of the Underhill Ridge. In early season this right fork has been primarily a snow climb, but the exit at the top will require two pitches of rock climbing. During some seasons a 40-foot vertical pillar of ice forms up over the chockstone near the top of the right fork. This provides a difficult (WI4+, first climbed by Steve Shea and David Breashears in 1978) exit to the top of the Underhill Ridge. The 1964 route goes up the left (west) fork and reaches the main notch of the Petzoldt Ridge over moderate slabs, which may be covered with snow in early season. Follow *Route 12* to the summit.

In late season the nature of the climb is completely different. After one ropelength on the residual snow up to an alcove on the right (east) side, the floor of the couloir becomes a waterfall, with steep, wet, polished sides. Only a single crack system will be found on the right (east) wall of the couloir, leading to the bowl at the forks. Climb 100 feet up this crack system to a ledge at the base of a dihedral. Move right and up the continuation of the original crack system, ending the lead with a V chimney that narrows at its top. A belay will be found just below large flakes in the chimney above. The fourth lead, after passing these flakes to a large ledge, involves a 70-foot jam crack (5.7), the crux of this route. Exit from this crack, using the wall to the right, onto a comfortable belay ledge. An easy horizontal traverse now takes one to the bowl. Now take the right fork, partly on residual snow, for three ropelengths to a stance just below the right (east) edge of the largest of the three chockstones that cap this fork of the couloir. Climb black rock out to the right and then back left into the room below the uppermost chockstone. A very small tunnel permits exit from this room onto a short slope leading to the notch behind the top of the Underhill Ridge, which is then followed to the summit. See *American Alpine Journal,* 2, no. 2 (1934), pp. 254–255.

ROUTE 15. Underhill Ridge. II, 5.6. First ascent July 15, 1931, by Robert Underhill, Phil Smith, and Francis Truslow; first descent (using rappels on the west side) September 5, 1937, by Phil Smith, Paul Petzoldt, and William House. Underhill attempted this ridge on July 18, 1930, with Kenneth Henderson on the same day as their successful first ascent of Teepe Pillar, but they were stopped by a violent thunderstorm. See *Topo 32* and *Photos 40* and *42*. This route ascends the easternmost and shortest of the three major south ridges of the Grand Teton. The Underhill Ridge forms the right skyline ridge of the Grand Teton as seen from the Lower Saddle, and the route starts from the highest point of the Black Dike, which cuts across the south side of the mountain. This highest point is Glencoe Col between the Underhill Ridge and Glencoe Spire. Because the route is located on the west side of the ridge crest, it dries out more slowly than the Petzoldt or Exum Ridge routes; in general it is a colder climb. An ice axe is recommended for early-season ascents of this ridge.

From the col climb 50 feet north up easy rocks, then traverse horizontally to the right of the red slabs until the wall of the first tower is met. A series of cracks angles up (west) and left (south) 120 feet to the top of the slabs. Continue west for 200 feet on easier rock to the prominent ledge system that leads around to the left (west) side of the tower. From near the end of this ledge climb a 40-foot chimney to a broad ledge. A very difficult chimney (probably the one Underhill climbed on the first ascent) leads directly up from this broad ledge. Instead of using this chimney, go around the corner to the left (north) where an easier chimney leads upward. At the top of this chimney an overhang forces the climber out onto the right wall on very small

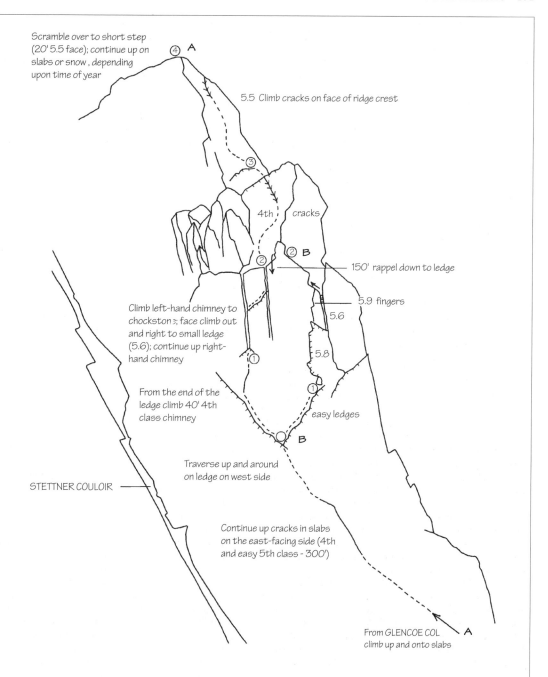

Scramble over to short step (20' 5.5 face); continue up on slabs or snow, depending upon time of year

5.5 Climb cracks on face of ridge crest

④ A

③

4th   cracks

② B

②

150' rappel down to ledge

5.9 fingers

5.6

Climb left-hand chimney to chockston ੨; face climb out and right to small ledge (5.6); continue up right-hand chimney

5.8

①

①

From the end of the ledge climb 40' 4th class chimney

easy ledges

B

Traverse up and around on ledge on west side

STETTNER COULOIR

Continue up cracks in slabs on the east-facing side (4th and easy 5th class - 300')

From GLENCOE COL climb up and onto slabs

A

32. GRAND TETON
  A. UNDERHILL RIDGE, II, 5.6
  B. VARIATION: DIRECT, III, 5.8

holds. With a handhold on the right edge swing onto a small ledge, from which the Underhill Chimney is regained for the belay. The next lead brings one back to the ridge crest.

Traverse around to the right (east) and then up to the steep, black face of the main tower. A good crack system in the middle of this face allows enjoyable climbing to the knife-edge top of the tower, which is then followed to the shallow col marking the end of the Underhill Ridge. From this notch, which is approximately even with the end of Wall Street on the Exum Ridge route, a short pitch (5.5) is required to pass the steep beginning of the slabs of this upper southeast face. In early season one can then ascend the moderate snow slope toward the summit block or, later, scramble up and left across the "seemingly endless" slabs to the rocky upper Buckingham Buttress that leads to the summit block. Then make a slight traverse to the left (west) and finish the climb by the easy top portion of the Exum Ridge route. *Time: 5¼ hours* from the Lower Saddle. See *American Alpine Journal*, 8, no. 3 (1953), pp. 542–545; *Canadian Alpine Journal*, 20 (1931), pp. 72–86, illus.; *Sierra Club Bulletin*, 42, no. 6 (June 1957), pp. 62–63.

Variation: Direct. III, 5.8. First ascent August 30, 1953, by William Buckingham, Steve Smale, Ann Blackenburg, Charles Browning, and Jack Hilberry. See *Topo 32* and *Photos 40* and *42*. From the Lower Saddle a conspicuous, white, angular pinnacle is seen on the skyline on the lower section of the Underhill Ridge. This variation goes up the spectacular chimney that separates this pinnacle from the remainder of the ridge. Follow the preceding route to the south end of the main ledge, which leads around the left (west) side of the ridge. Instead of traversing along this ledge, climb 30 feet up and to the right on broken black rock to the base of the chimney separating the pinnacle from the ridge. The first portion of the chimney overhangs slightly and is most easily climbed out to the left via a 5.8 finger crack in a left-facing corner. At the top of the corner traverse right and into the chimney (5.6) or continue up a nice crack system on the face to the left (5.9). Climb up to the notch and then onto the knife-edge at the left. One can then climb the next step in the ridge to rejoin the route given above at the face of the main tower.

Variation: Wilson Crack. III, 5.9. First ascent September 2, 1965, by Ted Wilson and Rick Reese. This variation of about three pitches provides a different and much more difficult start for the Underhill Ridge. Instead of proceeding to Glencoe Col, climb the snow of the Stettner Couloir a short distance until a wide crack bending to the right can be seen in the (eastern) wall above. Moderate climbing brings one to this crack, which is climbed with difficulty (5.9) past a bulge in its upper part. The standard route is joined at the main ledge system leading around the west side of the ridge.

ROUTE 16. Lev. III, 5.6, A1, or III, 5.8. First ascent July 12, 1960, by Peter Lev, James Greig, William Glosser, and David Laing; first free ascent July 30, 1988, by Renny Jackson, Rich Perch, Steve Rickert, and Leigh Ortenburger. See *Topo 33* and *Photo 43*. Immediately to the right (east) of the first tower on the Underhill Ridge is a huge, extensive chimney system marked by a very prominent branch that leads due west back onto the ridge. This route ascends the excellent rock to the east of this huge chimney. It is best viewed from the vicinity of Teepe Col. As in *Route 15*, scramble from Glencoe Col up the easy red-rock section toward the base of the wall of the initial tower on the ridge. Instead of turning left (west) as in the regular Underhill Ridge route, descend on the scree shelf down to the right (100 feet) to the chimney-crack system on the right of the initial tower. Two pitches up enjoyable rock lead into the section where the chimney splits and widens. The larger branch continues back left (west) toward the crest of the ridge at the notch behind the first tower of the ridge.

The Lev route ascends the left edge of the right (north and east) portion of the chimney system. The third pitch ends in an alcove (a fixed angle piton will be found here) just above a large and loose chockstone. Climb out right under a small roof onto the small ridge or face above, which leads to a well-defined 3-foot ledge. The ledge is at the base of a short, very steep 20-foot wall that is broken by a vertical crack. Climb this 5.8 crack (originally aided) onto easier ground above, leading to a wide ledge holding a large boulder, just beneath a huge overhanging section of gray rock. From this point an extension of the original chimney system can be seen over to the right (north) leading steeply up toward an overhang; this contains the last pitch of *Route 18*. Instead, take the easier stepped ramp leading up and out to the left (south). After about 80 feet on this ramp turn up and slightly right in a crack leading to a belay ledge. A final short crack in a left-facing corner takes one from this ledge onto easier rock leading onto the crest of the Underhill Ridge at the base of its final tower; that route is joined at this point. A distinct but more difficult line can be maintained all the way to the top of the ridge by climbing cracks (5.7) on the extreme right edge of the face past another fixed angle piton for the sixth lead. From the top of the Underhill Ridge, proceed to the summit as in *Route 15*. This climb is characterized by good rock and is quite enjoyable.

Variation: Jackson–Woodmencey. III, 5.9+. First ascent summer 1988, by Renny Jackson and Jim Woodmencey. See *Topo 33* and *Photo 43*. This climb was conceived as an exploratory probe of the prominent wide cracks on the east side of the Underhill Ridge above the first tower. Approach as in *Route 16* and climb the initial 200 feet of that route into the huge main chimney system. Continue up, passing a chockstone around its left side, and belay at the base of a very clean left-facing corner. Climb the corner and belay (5.9). The probe into the wide crack on the left was unsuccessful. Instead, a traverse (5.9+) was then made via flakes to the final pitch of *Route 16*. A more direct

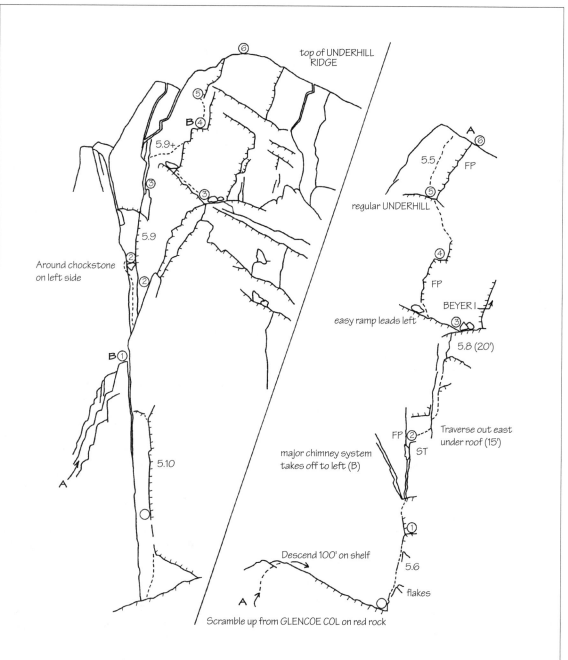

top of UNDERHILL RIDGE

5.9+

B ④

③

5.9

Around chockstone on left side

②

②

B ①

A

5.10

⑥

A ⑥

5.5

FP

regular UNDERHILL

⑤

④

FP

easy ramp leads left

BEYER I

③

5.8 (20')

FP ②

ST

Traverse out east under roof (15')

major chimney system takes off to left (B)

①

5.6

Descend 100' on shelf

flakes

A

Scramble up from GLENCOE COL on red rock

33. GRAND TETON
A. LEV, III, 5.8
B. JACKSON-WOODMENCEY, III, 5.9+

start was done by Keith Cattabriga in 1994, in which two more pitches on the initial portion of the east side of the face were climbed (the second pitch was a 5.10 left-facing corner).

ROUTE 17. *Southeast Chimney.* III, 5.9. First ascent August 5, 1973, by David Lowe and Leigh Ortenburger. See *Photo 43.* The southeast chimney is a significant feature of this side of the mountain. Extending for over 300 feet, it lies near the center of the east face of the Underhill Ridge and ends near the shallow notch that separates the final tower of the ridge from the main slabs of the upper southeast face. It is characterized by a broad, right-facing wall in the lower half and an equally large left-facing wall in the upper half. This route has the same start as the Lev route on the east side of the Underhill Ridge. From Glencoe Col follow *Route 16* to the section where the huge chimney system on the east side of the Underhill Ridge splits and opens out. Climb the first leads of that route on interesting rock to gain the wide ledge beneath the huge, overhanging, gray-rock area (see *Route 16*). This ledge is unique on the Grand Teton, being the common intersection point for four routes: Lev, Southeast Chimney, Beyer East Face I, and Keith-Eddy East Face.

Go horizontally right for one easy ropelength along the base of the wall, past the base of the right-facing corner of the upper Beyer East Face I route to a belay position among some blocks. Continue this traverse right to reach the southeast chimney itself at the right edge of this wall. Climb the first 50 feet of the chimney either on the inside or outside. The strenuous and awkward crux pitch is the narrowing section of the chimney containing two smooth flakes, one of which protrudes from the chimney. This lead is difficult (5.9) because the face to the right of the chimney is smooth and the left wall is vertical. Once past these flakes, continue to a belay point in the same chimney, which now forms the right edge of a slabby face. The third lead of the chimney begins by either climbing directly upward or partially using the slabs to the left. This is followed by 60 feet of easy climbing on the right side of the chimney to some 5.7 cracks. Finally, by stemming one can reach a belay in a small alcove. The steep section of the narrow chimney above goes at 5.7 as well. The exit from the chimney involves the use of some small holds and a splendid lieback in the crack to which the chimney has now dwindled. Scramble easily up to the notch on the main Underhill Ridge, where the usual southeast slabs are followed to the summit of the mountain. The rock on this route is excellent.

ROUTE 18. *Beyer East Face I.* III, 5.9. First ascent July 14, 1979, by Jim Beyer. See *Topo 34* and *Photo 43.* This important climb is an excellent route in the same class as, and perhaps even better than, the Lower Exum Ridge. The steep rock section is not extensive but is of high quality. The beginning of this route is approached from the snow at the top of Teepe Glacier. From the upper edge of the glacier,

bear up and left to reach the first objective, the lower of two small snow patches that lie on the slabs above Teepe Glacier and below and somewhat to the left (south) of the Otterbody Snowfield. This same general area is also quite easily approached from the Lower Saddle by scrambling around to the northeast from Teepe Col, where the Black Dike separates Teepe Pillar from the Grand Teton. Scramble left along the outer edge of this lower snowfield (a scree slope in late season) and beyond on easy broken rock toward the huge, right-facing dihedral (usually wet and/or icy) in the main wall above. At the bottom of this dihedral is a large ceiling or arch cut back in to the left (south).

The first pitch (150 feet) leads onto the main steep face out and around to the left on the outside of the dihedral. Begin by climbing up a small right-facing corner. After 20 feet a few moves of 5.9 permit an exit out and to the left to a small ledge. Then ascend a 5.8 crack to a belay stance. The second pitch is probably one of the nicest crack pitches in the range. Climb up to the small overhang directly above the belay and undercling and lieback out to a small stance at the base of the crack. The 120-foot hand-and-fist crack above (5.8) eventually leads to a comfortable belay ledge with some loose flakes on it. A short pitch puts one on a large ledge just above and to the left (south). Climb out and right again to a flake and then up to a large easy ramp (5.4) that leads left (south) to the wide ledge with boulders beneath the huge, overhanging, gray-rock area described under *Routes 16 and 17.*

This ledge is the common intersection point for four routes: Lev, Southeast Chimney, Beyer East Face I, and Keith–Eddy East Face. At this ledge the Beyer route crosses the Southeast Chimney route (which here traverses horizontally right [north]) and continues up into a very large (150 feet) open-book formation at the right edge of the gray wall. This spectacular open book is the crux of this Beyer route, starting with cracks (5.6) that turn into a right-facing 5.8 corner. Halfway up the corner a few moves of 5.9 out and up the right side of a small overhang lead to the scenic finish of this pitch. The view looking down to the valley floor framed by the spires of Teepe Pillar and the great towers of the east ridge is well worth the climb. The top of this pitch places one at the edge of more downsloping slabs, where the first of the layered black rock of the upper Underhill Ridge is encountered. Climb easily up and left past a small roof and around a corner to gain the crest of the Underhill Ridge, just below its final black-face tower. From this point the regular Underhill Ridge (*Route 15*) is followed to the summit. For protection, take a standard rack with perhaps some 4-inch pieces for the wide crack.

ROUTE 19. *Keith–Eddy East Face.* III, 5.10-. First ascent August 17, 1991, by Jason Keith and David Eddy. The name "Ritual de lo Habitual" was applied by the first ascensionists. See *Topo 35* and *Photo 43.* Use the same approach as in *Route 18* to the base of the huge, right-facing corner

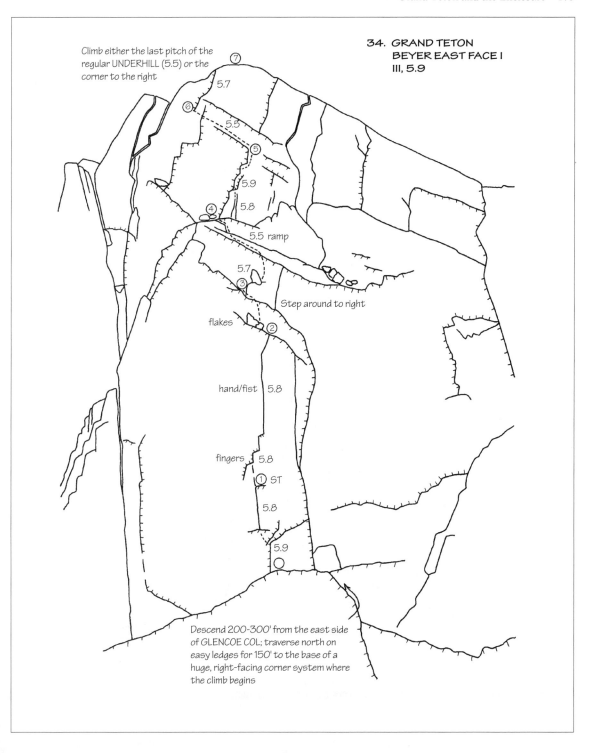

Climb either the last pitch of the regular UNDERHILL (5.5) or the corner to the right

34. GRAND TETON BEYER EAST FACE I
III, 5.9

⑦

5.7

⑥

5.5

⑤

5.9

5.8

④

5.5 ramp

5.7

③

Step around to right

flakes

②

hand/fist   5.8

fingers   5.8

① ST

5.8

5.9

Descend 200-300' from the east side of GLENCOE COL; traverse north on easy ledges for 150' to the base of a huge, right-facing corner system where the climb begins

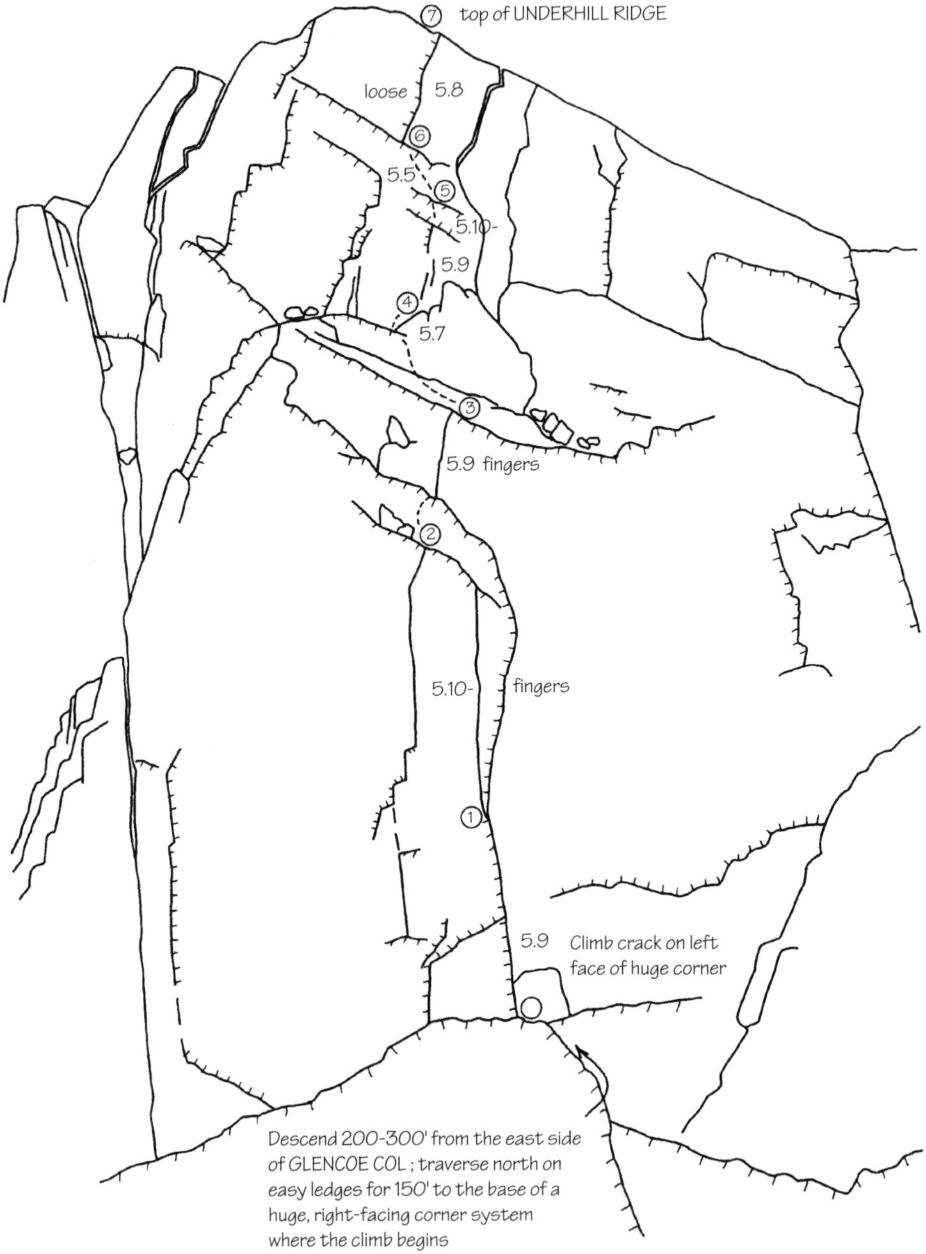

⑦ top of UNDERHILL RIDGE

loose 5.8

⑥

5.5

⑤

5.10-

5.9

④

5.7

③

5.9 fingers

②

5.10- fingers

①

5.9 Climb crack on left
face of huge corner

Descend 200-300' from the east side
of GLENCOE COL ; traverse north on
easy ledges for 150' to the base of a
huge, right-facing corner system
where the climb begins

35. GRAND TETON
KEITH-EDDY EAST FACE
III, 5.10-

system. The first pitch begins by climbing on the face of this corner for 100 feet (5.9). Exit to the left and belay at the base of a finger crack a short distance to the north of the hand-and-fist crack of the preceding route. The second pitch ascends this finger crack for 100 feet (5.10-). From the top of the crack climb up off the ledge past some flakes and then step right and climb a 5.9 finger crack to a large, sloping ramp. From this point many different exit options are available because three other routes are in the general vicinity. The distinctly separate finish of this route goes up just left of the finish of the Southeast Chimney route. Climb out of a blocky gully using a 5.7 flake/crack, which then leads to a short 5.10- section. From the ramp at the top of this pitch this route finishes with a right-facing 5.8 corner that is somewhat loose.

ROUTE 20. *Beyer East Face II*. III, 5.8. First ascent August 15, 1981, by Jim Beyer and Dan Grandusky; attempted August 25, 1969, by Rick Reese, Leigh Ortenburger, Burt Janis, and Sherm Beacham. See *Topo 36* and *Photo 43*. This difficult route lies between the Beyer East Face I (*Route 18*) and the Horton East Face (*Route 21*). It is important that dry conditions be sought for this climb because melting snow on slabs in the middle of this route will provide, at best, unpleasant conditions. This route follows a completely distinct line from the lower of the two small snow patches above Teepe Glacier to the col separating the top of the Underhill Ridge from the upper southeast slabs of the Grand Teton. For the approach to this initial snow patch, see *Route 18*. From the upper edge of this snow patch (scree slope in late season, when this route is best done), start by climbing up the initial short, blocky section and to a belay stance below a pair of parallel cracks that angle up from left to right. A long black roof looms above and left of these cracks. Climb the cracks (5.7), which eventually lead to a left-facing corner, and belay at a small stance near the right edge of the long roof. The second pitch continues up the corner system (which becomes a hand traverse) leading off to the right. Climb partway along this ramp and then cut back up a 5.6 face, angling left to reach a right-facing corner. The third lead goes up this corner and then steps around to the left (5.8) to gain the slabby middle portion of this route. Run out the rope up a shallow gully in these slabs to a large ledge. The next full ropelength takes one to another big ledge at the top of the slabs at the base of the final steep section. The fifth pitch is an outstanding 5.7 lead with good protection. Start in a left-facing corner and angle right to climb a steep finger crack on the outside edge of a rib. The final lead continues up a right-facing corner, moves easily right across slabs, and proceeds up the final rocks to the col at the top of the Underhill Ridge. Follow the upper Underhill Ridge to the summit.

ROUTE 21. *Horton East Face*. III, 5.7. First ascent August 14, 1977, by W. D. Horton, Paul Horton, and Robert Snyder. See *Photo 43*. This route connects the lower end of the Smith Otterbody chimney system (*Route 22*) with the "front feet" of the Otterbody Snowfield. The rock on this route is generally sound, but it is important to make this climb in dry conditions, either late in the season or in a dry year. For the approach to the slabs at the beginning of the Smith Otterbody route, see *Route 22*. Climb one long pitch up the Smith route. From the belay, leave the Smith line and follow corners up and left for 100 feet to a comfortable ledge beneath a headwall. To pass this wall the next lead follows the narrowing ledge left (south) to its end, where a few face moves up a slab lead up to a belay (150 feet, 5.7). Third- and 4th-class climbing leads up and right on ledges up and into the main feature of the route, the huge left-facing corner system below the "head and front feet" of the Otterbody Snowfield. One easy pitch up the left face of this corner takes one to a belay below another headwall. The crux pitch (5.7) above goes a short way up the wall, then traverses into a small open book in the right-hand wall with face climbing above to enter the crack at the back of the book and then up to a belay ledge. A right-leading chimney in the wall above has a tricky start but becomes easier and leads onto the rubble at the edge of the snowfield, where *Route 22* is joined.

ROUTE 22. *Smith Otterbody*. III, 5.6. First ascent September 5, 1937, by Phil Smith, Paul Petzoldt, and William House. In late July or early August 1930, Phil Smith and Robert Underhill attempted this route but were stopped by ice on the rock. See *Photo 43*. This route ascends the prominent chimney system that is the only major break in the wall above Teepe Glacier and below the Otterbody Snowfield. This very large chimney leads toward the "hind feet" of the Otterbody Snowfield and serves as a principal drainage path for the melting snow. Hence, this route should be attempted only in late season and very early in the day, before the sun's warmth melts the snow above, if reasonably pleasant conditions are desired.

The approach to the base of the chimney can be made either directly up Teepe Glacier from the vicinity of the Caves (crampons are useful) or, better, from the Lower Saddle. From the Saddle take the usual traverse along the Black Dike to Teepe Col, overlooking Teepe Glacier. From the col one can scramble along a system of ledges above the top edge of the glacier all the way to the slabs below the chimney. A series of tricky slabs leads to the base of the vertical section of the chimney system; these slabs are exposed to some danger from falling rock. After the initial pitches, a chimney with an overhang must be passed. In early and midseason, this overhang is an icy waterfall. Above this section, using the rock parallel to and on the right of the original chimney, climb about 200 feet to the Otterbody Snowfield. The snowfield will be reached somewhat north of the "hind feet."

Climb diagonally back toward the left (south) using ledges on the outside of the snowfield or, if necessary, along

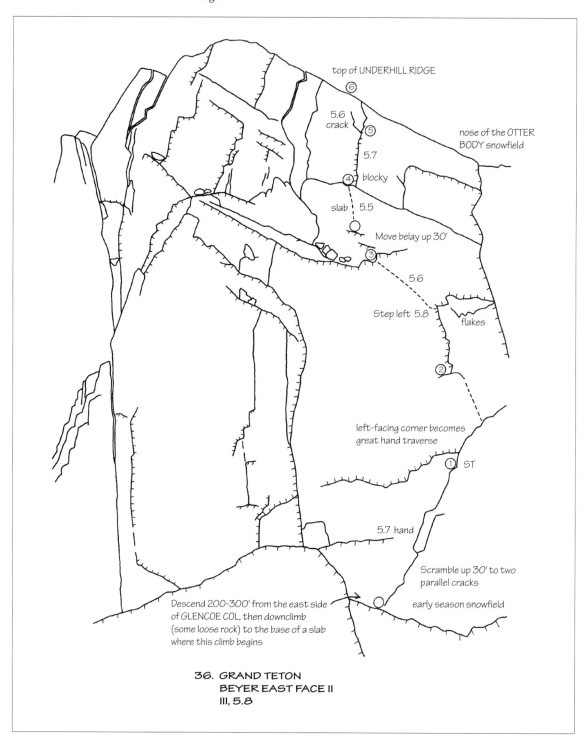

top of UNDERHILL RIDGE

⑥

5.6
crack

⑤

5.7

nose of the OTTER
BODY snowfield

④ blocky

slab | 5.5

Move belay up 30'

③

5.6

Step left 5.8

flakes

②

left-facing corner becomes
great hand traverse

① ST

5.7 hand

Scramble up 30' to two
parallel cracks

Descend 200-300' from the east side
of GLENCOE COL, then downclimb
(some loose rock) to the base of a slab
where this climb begins

early season snowfield

36. GRAND TETON
    BEYER EAST FACE II
    III, 5.8

the rather steep snowfield itself. The original method of exit from the snowfield is to kick steps up the snow to the "shoulder" of the Otterbody where a break in the wall, a wide chimney, leads to the slabby, partially snow-covered, upper southeast face of the Grand Teton. The second method requires proceeding to the "nose" of the Otterbody, from which one can climb to the shallow col separating the top of the Underhill Ridge from the upper southeast face. In late season, when this route is presumably being climbed, great expanses of slabs are exposed on this upper southeast face. Many paths can be threaded upward, but perhaps the easiest heads almost due west toward the ridge that forms the upper extension of the Buckingham Buttress. Slightly more difficult, but more direct, is a route well out on the southeast face, over slabs and snow, all the way to the summit block. Or, by making a substantial detour, one can cross over to the right (north) and join the East Ridge route (see *Route 25*). *Time: 8½ hours* from the Caves. See *Canadian Alpine Journal*, 20 (1931), pp. 72–86, illus.

ROUTE 23. *Petzoldt–Loomis Otterbody*. III, 5.1. First ascent August 2, 1935, by Paul Petzoldt and William Loomis; first descent (and second ascent) September 10, 1936, by Paul Stettner and Art Lehnebach. Although Petzoldt ranks this as one of the easiest routes on the Grand Teton, this is perhaps true only in good conditions and only for a small party of experienced mountaineers adept at routefinding and snow climbing. Also, there is substantial danger from rockfall, which is significantly increased during wet, warm weather. Climb directly up Teepe Glacier (ice axe and crampons recommended) as rapidly as possible. Leave the snow at its upper right (northwest) corner and gain the rocks just to the right (east) of the large couloir that comes down from above the Second Tower on the east ridge of the Grand Teton. Work up these scree-covered ledges (somewhat rotten), crossing left (west) into the upper, wet portion of the couloir. Ascend and ultimately cross the couloir to the left (southwest) onto the slabs on the outside of the Otterbody Snowfield. Traverse left (south) on these slabs below the snowfield, past the "hind legs" of the Otterbody; then kick or cut steps to the wide chimney leading up from the "shoulder" of the Otterbody. After a few pitches in this chimney, one will emerge onto the main, upper southeast face of the Grand Teton at the point where the chimney opens out to the left (west). In early season this will be mainly a large snowfield; in late season the underlying slabs will be exposed. For the three options to reach the summit from this point, see *Route 22*. *Time: 5¼ hours* from the Caves. See *Appalachia*, 20, no. 7 (November 1935), p. 420.

Variation: III, 5.1. First ascent August 6, 1961, by J. Gordon Edwards and Kenneth Proctor. This variation, a better alternate route to the "tail" of the Otterbody, follows the left (west) side of the couloir. Because it reduces the danger of rockfall, it is recommended in preference to the original route. Leave the snow about 25 feet to the left (west) of the couloir that comes down from above the Second Tower on the east ridge of the Grand Teton. Climb the slabs that angle up to the right (northeast), but stay well out of the couloir until about two-thirds of the way to the large snow patch high in the couloir. At the steepest part of the couloir climb over to the right (east) side; the stream that drains the snow patch must be crossed just below a 10-foot waterfall. After a short climb up the east side to the snow patch, cross quickly back to the left (south and west); from this point it is but a short scramble up slabs to the "tail" of the Otterbody Snowfield. See *Chicago Mountaineering Club Newsletter,* 15, no. 5 (December 1961), pp. 1–3.

Variation: III, 5.1. First ascent August 6, 1961, by J. Gordon Edwards and Kenneth Proctor. Since this party observed a rock avalanche in the wide chimney leading above the "shoulder" of the Otterbody onto the upper southeast face, they were motivated to pursue a different exit from the Otterbody. Instead of climbing up the snow to the top of the "shoulder," continue to the "nose" of the Otterbody. From here climb a series of narrow ledges to the shallow col separating the final tower on the Underhill Ridge from the upper southeast face. For routes to the summit from here, see *Route 22*.

ROUTE 24. *Otterbody Chimneys*. III, 5.7, WI3–4. First ascent September 14, 1979, by Kim Schmitz. See *Photos 40* and *53*. Rising from the upper right (north) corner of Teepe Glacier is a long, steep couloir-chimney system formed between the vertical southwest walls of the Second Tower and the main southeast face of the Grand Teton below the East Ridge Snowfield. The lower several hundred feet forms the initial broken rock of the Petzoldt–Loomis Otterbody route (*Route 23*). This route ascends the very steep upper portion of the same chimney system directly to the crest of the east ridge just above the Second Tower. Due to the rotten nature of this upper section, this climb should not be undertaken except in very cold conditions, such as winter, during which the rock is frozen in place by ice and crampons can be worn. Approach this route via Teepe Glacier in the same manner as *Route 23*. Climb several hundred feet to an easy section of snow at the extreme right end of the Otterbody "tail," leading toward the final, very steep, poorly protected chimney below the ridge. A total of six leads of mixed ice and rock, with sections of thin snow over rotten rock as well as vertical ice will be found on this route. In summer conditions this upper section will be heinous with much loose rock, mud, and running water. Once the crest of the east ridge is reached, proceed to the summit as in *Route 25*.

ROUTE 25. *East Ridge*. III, 5.7. First ascent July 22, 1929, by Robert Underhill and Kenneth Henderson; first descent August 2, 1935, by Paul Petzoldt and William Loomis (six rappels). As seen from Jackson Hole, the east ridge of the Grand Teton is the most obvious and enticing route to the summit of the mountain. The relatively easy beginning of the ridge led to a long sequence of early attempts. The early climb by Edmond Kelly and Richard W. G. Welling on August 21, 1894, may have been on this ridge but the information regarding their route is vague and their high point is unknown; they did "proceed to one of the high peaks," possibly the Molar Tooth, before turning back. The ridge attracted the attention of Franklin Spalding after his 1898 ascent of the Grand Teton. He wrote in 1899, "If I ever have a chance to try the mountain again, I would like to make the attempt from the east side." In September 1907, William Stroud attempted the peak from Jenny Lake, again reaching an uncertain high point, probably on the east ridge, which he claimed to be "80 to 100 feet from the top."

Paul Petzoldt, age 16, attempted the ridge with Ralph Herron on his first visit to the range on July 23, 1924, but they were defeated on the passage of the Molar Tooth and, lacking equipment, narrowly escaped with their lives. Petzoldt and Herron returned, along with Harold Criger and Melvin Whitehead, for another attempt on July 27, 1925. This attempt also failed after Herron sustained serious injury in a fall held by a rope. On August 31, 1926, Phil Smith, with William Gilman, Melvin Nevitt, and George Behen (and two dogs), attempted the peak, probably via the east ridge. Four years after their successful fourth ascent of the Grand Teton in 1923, Albert R. Ellingwood and Eleanor Davis returned to try the east ridge with Colorado Springs climbers Robert Ormes and Eleanor Bartlett. This effort was also stymied by the Molar Tooth, although they may have reached the top of this imposing tower. About August 24, 1928, two European mountaineers, Ulrich Wieland and Fredi Luce, tried the east ridge, but failed after a serious effort. The problem of the Molar Tooth was finally solved (as the logician and philosopher Underhill would have liked for it to be stated) on July 22, 1929, when Robert L. M. Underhill and Kenneth Henderson succeeded in passing it on the north and then continued to the summit. The next attempt, on July 7, 1934, by Fred Ohlendorff and Helmut Leese, ended in spectacular tragedy with one of their bodies being recovered on Teepe Glacier and the other on the Teton Glacier. During the second successful ascent on August 21, 1934, by Fritiof Fryxell and Fred Ayres, two cairns, one containing a faded fragment of coarse-weave cloth, were found about 20 feet below and south of the notch separating the gendarme from the Second Tower. Henderson and Underhill disclaimed responsibility for the cairns, and the condition of the cloth suggested that it much antedated even the 1929 first ascent. The identity of the early climber to this very high point on the Grand Teton remains unknown—a lingering mystery.

This fine ridge, the first new route on the mountain after the discovery of the Owen–Spalding route in 1898, remains today a significant mountaineering objective. See *Photos 40, 44,* and *45.* The variety of rock, the interesting routefinding problems, the snowfield near the summit, and

the absence of extreme difficulty make this 4,000-foot ridge one of the most satisfying climbs on the Grand Teton. The length of the route, however, necessitates an early start and efficient climbing. The two major towers on the east ridge, the Molar Tooth and the Second Tower, still form critical barriers, and much of the following route description concerns their passage. Supplementary details related to this route will be found separately under *Molar Tooth* and *Second Tower.* The ascent of one of these towers in the course of an East Ridge climb adds considerably to the interest, length, and difficulty of the route.

From Amphitheater Lake take the usual route underneath the north face of Disappointment Peak toward the Teton Glacier (see *Glacier Gulch*). The southern arm of the terminal moraine of the Teton Glacier offers the primary access to the base of the East Ridge route, as the climb begins only 50 feet south of the moraine crest. Scramble up the first 2,000 feet well left (south) of the crest of the east ridge. The smooth yellow walls of the first tower, the Molar Tooth, loom above. This tower blocked several early attempts to scale the Grand Teton and even today is a formidable obstacle if the route is lost; see *Molar Tooth.* The original East Ridge route, described here, bypasses this tower on the north, but the southern traverse (see the *Southern Traverse variation*) is now the much preferred alternative.

Scramble to the bowl, which is 300 feet below and just east of the Molar Tooth; the bowl is bounded on the north by the crest of the east ridge. Climb to the right (north) to gain the narrow crest of the ridge at a point just west of the first gendarmes on the crest. Proceed along the ridge crest to the northeast corner of the Molar Tooth. The objective now is to reach the main notch separating the Molar Tooth from the upper portions of the east ridge. Climb down the steep and exposed north side of the Molar Tooth about 50 to 100 feet, depending on the amount of snow present, until it is possible to make a 60-foot diagonal rappel down and across an ice gully to a small ledge on the far (west) side of the gully. From this ledge scramble right (west) for perhaps 100 feet (exposed and loose) over to the rotten yellow couloir that leads up to the main notch. This section may be partially covered by snow and ice. Two leads, either directly up the bottom (loose rock) or up the left (east) side (also loose) of the yellow couloir, then take one to the notch.

The first short pitch directly up out of the notch is difficult (5.7) and may require aid if it is wet. For the next few hundred feet belay positions are scarce, but the climbing of the series of slabs leading up to near the Second Tower is not difficult. From the top of the short pitch out of the notch, bear slightly right up some easy slabs to a chimney leading to an alcove about 130 feet above the notch. Climb right (north) out of this alcove and up one step to the beginning of about 300 feet of slabs. Angle slightly left (south) for several ropelengths in order to reach a break in the small ridge that descends to the south from the gendarme preceding the Second Tower. From the far (west) side of this small ridge ascend north up the gully (snow filled in early season), which leads to the sharp notch between the gendarme and the Second Tower.

To reach the far (west) side of the Second Tower, traverse around its north side on adequate ledges. About halfway around the tower descend about 10 feet and pass behind a very large upright flake. Then climb a 40-foot chimney (5.6) filled with many flakes. Once up this chimney, one can easily reach the notch between the Second Tower and the Grand Teton. Wet scree-covered slabs (covered with snow in early season) lead up to the East Ridge Snowfield, which is climbed along its right (north) edge. Extreme caution should be exercised while climbing these hazardous slabs, because belay positions are either poor or nonexistent and the exposure considerable. In late season the rock to the right (north) of the snowfield, along the edge of the great north face, provides a route to the summit block. During the rest of the season, an ice axe is required in order to negotiate the East Ridge Snowfield with safety; crampons are convenient.

From the top of the snowfield there are four ways to attack the summit block. The first is the traditional route and is the most difficult and direct, whereas the fourth is more commonly used. (1) Reach the summit directly from the east via the large chimney in the center of the summit block. Climb an 80-foot blocky section to the chimney pitch. This pitch consists of four short subchimneys yielding some of the most enjoyable climbing of the route, but one must pass a number of old tin cans from earlier days. (2) Contour around to the left below the summit block and join the top part of the Exum Ridge route (see *Route 7*). The second ascent of the ridge (in one day), on August 21, 1934, by Fritiof Fryxell and Fred Ayres, used this alternative. (3) It is possible to contour around the right (north) side of the summit block along an interesting ledge system at the extreme top of the north face, emerging at the upper end of the "V" (see *Route 31, 1953 variation*). One awkward and strenuous chimney must then be climbed to reach the last blocks leading to the summit. This alternative was first climbed August 12, 1935, by Paul Petzoldt, Glenn Exum, and Elizabeth Cowles (Partridge) during the third ascent of the ridge. (4) In the right (north) half of the summit block is a prominent chimney that comes out on the north ridge only 100 feet below the summit. Once on the ridge, weave in and out of the boulders to the summit. *Time: 10¾ to 13 hours* from Amphitheater Lake. See *Alpine Journal,* 42, no. 241 (November 1930), pp. 267–277, illus.; *American Alpine Journal,* 1, no. 2 (1930), pp. 138–139, illus.; 5, no. 2 (1944), pp. 220–232, illus.; *Appalachia,* 18, no. 3 (June 1931), pp. 209–232, illus.; 23, no. 4 (December 1941), p. 534; *Canadian Alpine Journal,* 18 (1929), pp. 96–97, illus.; *Mazama,* 31, no. 13 (December 1949), pp. 20–23, illus.; *Trail and Timberline,*

no. 141 (July 1930), pp. 5–7, illus.; no. 205 (November 1935), pp. 126–131, illus.; no. 237 (August 1938), pp. 87–89, illus.; no. 415 (July 1953), pp. 95–97, illus.

Variation: Southern Traverse. III, 5.7. First ascent August 12, 1935, by Paul Petzoldt, Glenn Exum, and Elizabeth Cowles (Partridge). This route, the southern traverse of the Molar Tooth, was discovered but not climbed by Petzoldt and Ralph Herron in 1924 on their first attempt to climb the Grand Teton. When approaching the Molar Tooth from the lower portion of the east ridge, bear left (south) and avoid the crest of the ridge, which leads to the northeast corner of the Tooth. From the bowl below the Tooth head for the broken chimney located approximately 300 feet south of a prominent 200-foot smooth-walled chimney; this latter chimney has only been descended by rappel. Climb up and left (south) past the bottom of the broken chimney. Proceed up on the left side of the chimney for a ropelength until it is possible to cut right around a corner to an obvious ledge that allows entry into the upper narrow section of the chimney. This is climbed without difficulty to the window in the sharp ridge crest that overlooks the great couloir leading north from Teepe Glacier to the main notch between the Molar Tooth and the Grand Teton. After descending about 100 feet on rotten and broken rock, climb the great couloir to rejoin the usual northern traverse route at the main notch. Depending on the season, steep snow and even ice may be involved; some have found crampons useful here. Pass the enormous chockstone that completely blocks the couloir just short of the notch by climbing the steep wall on the right (east). Depending on conditions this climbing can be quite difficult with either wet or *verglas*-covered rock. The chockstone may well be the largest in the Teton Range. The notch is then attained after 70 feet of scrambling over scree or steep snow depending on the time of year. See *Chicago Mountaineering Club Newsletter,* 2, no. 5 (January–July 1948), pp. 5–7; *Trail and Timberline,* no. 205 (November 1935), pp. 126–131, illus.

Variation: South Molar Tooth Couloir. III, 5.7. First ascent July 28, 1936, by Paul Petzoldt, Karl Keuffel, and James Monroe. From the right (east) edge of Teepe Glacier ascend the great couloir leading to the notch behind the Molar Tooth on the east ridge of the Grand Teton. For most of the summer this couloir will be filled with very steep snow. In late season it will no doubt contain steep, loose rock. Pass the same enormous chockstone mentioned in the preceding 1935 variation and join the main East Ridge route at the notch.

Variation: III, 5.4. First ascent July 28, 1936, by Paul Petzoldt, Karl Keuffel, and James Monroe. This seldom-climbed variation starts at the Molar Tooth and does not rejoin the regular upper East Ridge route until it reaches the sharp notch between the Second Tower and the gendarme immediately to the east. From the window in the south ridge of the Molar Tooth (see the *1935 Southern Traverse* *variation,* earlier) descend the rotten chute to the great couloir leading from Teepe Glacier to the notch between the Molar Tooth and the upper portions of the east ridge. Instead of following this couloir up to the enormous chockstone, cross the couloir and climb a rotten chute on the other (west) side to gain the obvious ledge system leading horizontally left (south) out to the crest of the skyline ridge (this is the south ridge of the gendarme that precedes the Second Tower). The high ledges are most suitable for getting around the corner at the ridge crest and into the next couloir, which runs up the south face of the Second Tower. A neat horizontal ledge leads from the corner into this scree-and rock-filled couloir. Scramble up this loose material to the steep rock at the head of the couloir. It is apparently possible to climb directly up this rock on the left (west) if one wants to climb the Second Tower *en route* to the summit of the Grand Teton; see *Second Tower, Route 2.* Otherwise, cut right (east) from the head of the couloir up a short chimney. From the top of this chimney walk up the snow (rock in late season) to the sharp notch between the gendarme and the Second Tower, and follow the regular East Ridge route to the summit. This variation is not as difficult as the usual route, but it contains more loose rock and requires some routefinding skill.

Variation: III, 5.7. First ascent September 7, 1955, by Leigh Ortenburger and Irene Beardsley. This intriguing variation starts from Dike Col, goes over the top of Okie's Thorn, and joins the southern traverse *(1935 Southern Traverse variation)* at the window in the south ridge crest of the Molar Tooth. From Dike Col climb Okie's Thorn by *Route 1.* This will be the most difficult part of the climb. Climb a short distance down the southwest ridge and make a 120-foot rappel to the black schist slabs on the west face of the Thorn, about even with the very sharp notch between the Thorn and the Grand Teton. This notch, formed by the weathering away of a rotten red dike, is only about 7 feet wide. On the first ascent of this variation a Tyrolean traverse was arranged across this obstacle. Do not descend the chute leading west onto Teepe Glacier; it is exceedingly rotten and dangerous, perhaps the worst such place in the park.

On the Grand side of this notch a wide ledge leads left (west) for about 100 feet. The wall above this ledge is almost vertical but not difficult, having many large holds. After about three ropelengths, angle right to gain the east side of the ridge (the south ridge of the Molar Tooth) in order to join the southern traverse of the Molar Tooth. Ascend the first chimney (counting from the south), which leads up to the crest of the south ridge of the Molar Tooth. For the route to the summit see the *1935 Southern Traverse variation,* earlier.

Variation: III, 5.6. First ascent August 11, 1957, by James Langford and William Cropper. A large couloir or gully descends the south face of the Second Tower onto the right (north) margin of Teepe Glacier. This gully is bounded

on the left (west) by the true south ridge of the Second Tower and on the right by the south ridge of the distinct large gendarme just east of the Second Tower. This variation starts from Teepe Glacier and reaches the usual East Ridge route, utilizing this south ridge of the gendarme. The chief obstacle is an 800-foot vertical section of smooth, gray rock, which is passed by following a diagonal, high-angle, 300-foot shelf leading from left to right (west to east) across the crest. The end of this shelf brings the climber to several hundred feet of easier climbing; the remainder of the ridge is climbed mostly on the right (east) side close to the crest until the usual East Ridge route is joined at the notch between the gendarme and the Second Tower. See *American Alpine Journal,* 11, no. 1 (1958), pp. 85–88.

Variation: Molar Tooth, Tricky Traverse. III, 5.7. First ascent July 9, 1972, by Robert Irvine, David Lowe, and Jim Olson. See *Topo 37.* This variation provides a relatively slick method of passing the Molar Tooth in the course of an East Ridge climb and can provide a drier alternative to the sometimes unpleasant wall to the right of the giant chockstone mentioned earlier. From the window notch on the south ridge of the Tooth, gained as in the *1935 Southern Traverse variation,* follow an obvious 5.7 crack system leading up and left around a corner to a large ramp. Take this ramp to its left (north) end and then climb up a wide crack (5.7) to a ledge slanting up to the left. From the left end of this ledge traverse across a short, steep face up to a broken rock area at a corner of the ridge. From here an easy, horizontal lead goes across a scree ledge to the top of the giant chockstone just below the main notch behind the Molar Tooth. This notch is then easily reached. Some loose rock will be encountered on this variation.

Variation: III, 5.7. First ascent July 25, 1977, by Jon King and Chuck Fitch. See *Photo 44.* This variation provides a much more difficult start to the standard East Ridge route. Take the regular approach from Surprise Lake out onto the Teton Glacier (see *Glacier Gulch*). Shortly after descending from the crest of the moraine down onto the glacier, look up at the eastern end of the north face of the Grand Teton. A broad but vertical rock buttress will be seen between the first (easternmost) of two gullies that lead from the glacier back onto the east ridge. This buttress lies well to the east of the large northeast couloir. A broad, smooth, 45° ramp, ascending this buttress from lower left to upper right, forms the beginning of this variation. After gaining the ramp from the glacier, climb only a short distance before turning directly up the wall above the ramp. The difficulty is about 5.6 or 5.7, and passage of some overhangs is involved. Once the east ridge is reached, join the standard route to continue to the summit.

Variation: North Molar Tooth Couloir. III, WI3+, 5.8. First ascent January 31, 1984, by Alex Lowe. See *Photos 44* and *45.* This significant variation, one of the few new climbs in the range first done in the winter, attains the notch be-

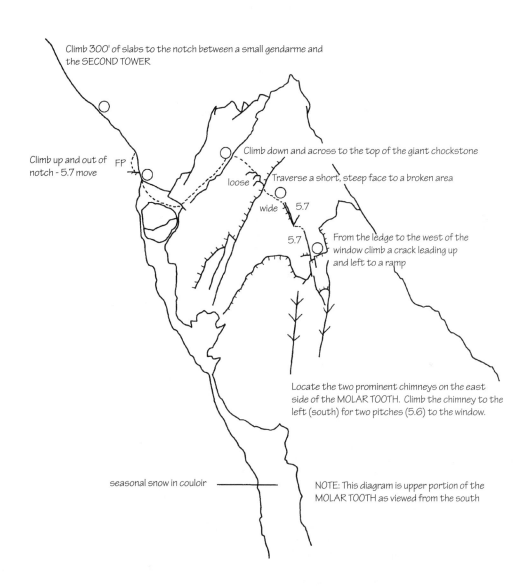

Climb 300' of slabs to the notch between a small gendarme and the SECOND TOWER

Climb up and out of notch - 5.7 move   FP

Climb down and across to the top of the giant chockstone

loose

Traverse a short, steep face to a broken area

wide   5.7

5.7

From the ledge to the west of the window climb a crack leading up and left to a ramp

Locate the two prominent chimneys on the east side of the MOLAR TOOTH. Climb the chimney to the left (south) for two pitches (5.6) to the window.

seasonal snow in couloir

NOTE: This diagram is upper portion of the MOLAR TOOTH as viewed from the south

37. GRAND TETON
EAST RIDGE, MOLAR TOOTH AREA, VARIATION: TRICKY TRAVERSE
III, 5.7

hind the Molar Tooth directly from the north. The climb begins with the first several hundred feet, about six pitches, of *Route 28, Northeast Couloir.* During the first ascent this involved climbing rock steps and some sections of good, but thin, water ice. At the point where *Route 28* moves right out onto the slabs leading to the Second Tower Couloir, this variation continues up the main steep couloir that descends from the Molar Tooth notch. Four difficult pitches of rock are then climbed, along with about 200 feet of water ice, which reached 70° for 50 feet or more. This route is most suitable for climbing when there is sufficient snow and ice to cement in place the loose rock of this couloir. Even in winter some loose rock was encountered although the rock was predominantly sound.

ROUTE 26. No Name Gully. III, WI4+, 5.7. First ascent 1979 or 1980, by Steve Shea. This very steep gully rises from the Teton Glacier about 200 feet east of the northeast couloir. It is separated from both branches of the northeast couloir (including the Route Canal, *Route 27,* described next) by a substantial rock ridge or buttress. The gully commonly contains two waterfalls that must be passed. From the Teton Glacier climb the steep snow apron leading to the first of these waterfalls. This pitch is difficult, but an easier section leads to the second waterfall. Once past this obstacle, climb several ropelengths to the top of the route, a notch behind a very sharp needle on the east ridge of the Grand Teton. In early season most of this route can be described as an ice course.

ROUTE 27. Route Canal. IV, WI5, 5.9. First ascent June 17, 1979, by Jeff Lowe and Charlie Fowler. This difficult ice route reaches the crest of the east ridge from the north at a small notch just east of the Molar Tooth, utilizing the narrow and nearly vertical chute that forms the left (east) branch of the northeast couloir (see *Route 28*) of the Grand Teton. See *Photos 44* and *45.* Approach this route from Amphitheater Lake via the Teton Glacier to the base of the northeast couloir. Several hundred feet of steep snow in the main couloir lead to a point where one can climb up and left to the beginning of this route. This is a serious climb of six pitches that includes vertical ice, 5.9 rock, and difficult mixed ground. The route usually comes into shape in the spring (or less often in the fall) when there is sufficient meltwater in this chimney system that then freezes and forms the climb.

ROUTE 28. Northeast Couloir. IV, 5.6. First ascent August 8, 1939, by Jack Hossack and George MacGowan; the fast time of the first-ascent party, 6¾ hours from the Teton Glacier, is noteworthy. See *Photos 44* and *45.* This remarkable and long route, largely on the north face of the mountain, does not join the regular East Ridge route until the notch above the Second Tower. Evidence easily observed on the Teton Glacier at the base of the couloir shows that hazardous rockfall occurs in this couloir. Select a day for the climb when there is no party on the East Ridge route. This route

is perhaps best viewed as an early-season climb when it is largely snow and ice and overnight low temperatures are well below freezing. As is the case with many of the couloir routes in the Tetons, during warm periods or when precipitation is likely, this route becomes a veritable bowling alley.

Take the usual route from Amphitheater Lake to Teton Glacier (see *Glacier Gulch*), walking toward the north edge of the glacier in order to be certain of selecting the right couloir. The correct couloir leads to the notch separating the Molar Tooth from the Grand Teton. The *bergschrund* is crossed near its left (east) edge. Usually a snow tongue will extend some distance up the couloir. Quickly climb either up the snow or up the rocks on the left (east) edge of the snow tongue to the point where the couloir forks. Continue another 300 or 400 feet up the right (west) branch of the couloir. In early season some steep ice may be encountered in this section. A great deal of rock debris will be found on the ledges in this area. At an obvious point, one or two leads above a snow patch, traverse out on the right (northwest) wall of the couloir on good ledges. Climb and scramble out to a shoulder from which the couloir descending from the notch above the Second Tower can be reached. Snow and steep ice will be found in the bottom of this Second Tower Couloir, and usually it cannot be avoided. In late season, however, it is possible to climb the rock on the right side of the couloir all the way to the notch; parts of this are steep, but, for the most part, just scrambling is required. Follow the East Ridge route (see *Route 25*), which is intersected just above the Second Tower, to the summit. See *The Mountaineer,* 32, no. 1 (December 1939), pp. 25–26, illus.

Variation: IV, 5.8. First ascent August 24, 1962, by Leon Sinclair and Leigh Ortenburger. See *Photos 44* and *45.* This variation reaches the bottom of the Second Tower Couloir of the Northeast Couloir route from the west by starting the climb on the regular North Face route. The lower northeast couloir and its rockfall problems are entirely avoided. See *Route 31* for the approach and beginning of the North Face route. Climb the first four pitches of the North Face route, up the left-slanting chimney to the point where one would begin the "obvious traverse...to the right toward the First Ledge." At this point, turn left and climb up to the left (east) on broken rock for three leads or so. The problem ahead is to get around the obvious corner at the east edge of the north face and into the Second Tower Couloir. A small ice chute protects this corner, and one must climb a pitch up the right (west) side of the chute before crossing it. The final lead crosses this narrow chute and goes up and around the very exposed corner into a short but smooth-walled dihedral (5.8). Were it not for this pitch, this variation would be the least difficult (technically, at least) of all those that approach the summit of the Grand Teton from the north. Once in the Second Tower Couloir, proceed as in the regular Northeast Couloir route. See *American Alpine Journal,* 14, no. 1 (1964), pp. 185–186.

Variation: IV, AI4, 5.7. First ascent June 25–26, 1990, by Todd Cozzens and James Earl. This variation is quite similar to the preceding one. Proceed as described to the area of the ice chute. This party rappelled 20 feet into the chute, which was then followed for three pitches. At that point one is about 75 feet from the bottom of the upper portion of the Northeast Couloir route, by which this route finishes.

ROUTE 29. *Northeast Buttress.* IV, 5.8, A4, or IV, 5.10+. First ascent August 24–25, 1970, by Paul Myhre and Dale Sommers; first free ascent about July 30, 1978, by Jon King and Charles Foster. See *Photos 44* and *45.* This route ascends the entire buttress immediately to the right (west) of the lower two-thirds of the northeast couloir. This buttress is bounded on the right (west) by a prominent ice chute, the Grand North Couloir, a major feature of the lower north face. The approach to the buttress is made via the Teton Glacier, heading toward the steep, conical snow slope below the *bergschrund* at the base of the northeast couloir. Gain the rock from the lower right (west) side of this snow slope, well below the entry into the couloir, on a wide ledge system leading diagonally out to the right in dark-colored rock. This ledge system ends about 30 feet short of the steep ice chute, referred to earlier, on the right side of the buttress. From here a large system of flakes (5.7) leads up to a narrow ledge after 75 feet. The next pitch goes up and right with some aid (5.8, A2) to a small ramp that continues diagonally up and right to a belay ledge. The crux of this route is a 5- to 8-foot ceiling, which was climbed using aid to traverse up and right on the first ascent. This was accomplished using tied-off 2- to 3-inch bongs in reportedly poor rock. Continue on aid above the ceiling to the right on broken but steep rock to a wide, high-angle ramp (5.8) that takes one through a small overhang to the bottom of the prominent chimney that is visible from the glacier. On the first ascent a bivouac was made at this point. Two pitches in the chimney then lead to a very slick wall, which is avoided by scrambling right into the chute on the right of the buttress and then back left (5.8) and up a short wall to return to the face of the buttress. One more pitch (5.6) then leads to the top of the buttress where the normal Northeast Couloir route is joined as it traverses right on slabs to gain the couloir descending from the Second Tower.

Variation: Little Wing. IV, 5.8. First ascent July 16–17, 1976, by Tom Deuchler and Dave Moerman. See *Photos 44* and *45.* This variation ascends the upper half of the same northeast buttress described earlier. This buttress contains three prominent, smooth ramps slanting up and right. This climb begins in the northeast couloir, ascending the steep snow for a few hundred feet to the base of the second ramp. Two pitches of 5.6 face or slab climbing lead to a large ledge at the top west end of the ramp. From the outside edge of the ramp, two moderate pitches on rotten rock provide access to the base of the large chimney near the right edge of the buttress; this chimney is easily seen from the glacier below and forms the upper part of *Route 29.* This 1976 variation apparently joins the Northeast Buttress route at about this point, and both proceed in slightly different ways to the top of the buttress to join *Route 28.* The rock on this variation varies from poor to excellent, making it difficult to obtain adequate belay anchors.

ROUTE 30. *Grand North Couloir.* IV, WI5, 5.8. First ascent about August 1, 1978, by Jon King and Charles Foster (mostly on rock); June 6, 1980, by Steve Shea (mostly on ice). *Note:* This route is also commonly referred to as Shea's Chute, even though Shea's ascent was two years after the 1978 climb. See *Photos 44* and *45.* This formidable couloir or chute is immediately to the right (west) of the northeast buttress, described in *Route 29.* In midseason or late season its ascent will be a mixed climb, involving both rock and ice. In early season it is a major ice climb, ranking with the Route Canal as one of the most difficult ice climbs in the range. This chute has important similarities with the Run-Don't-Walk Couloir on Mount Owen in that one must wait for exactly the right conditions for the climb. An extremely early start is recommended to minimize the objective hazard from falling rock and ice. The approach is via the Teton Glacier, across the *bergschrund,* and up a relatively low-angle gully leading to the base of the chute. Climb this lower section (5.6 to 5.7) and gain access to the chute itself. The climb contains five or six pitches, entirely on ice up the frozen waterfall of the chute, which rises in a series of vertical tiers. After the first four or five pitches the angle in the chute eases somewhat, but the final ice lead is again very steep. The route ends as one emerges out of the chute onto the broad slabby apron where the Northeast Couloir route (*Route 28*) traverses right to gain the couloir leading up toward the Second Tower. In midseason or late season, when more rock is exposed, this will be a very difficult mixed climb.

ROUTE 31. *North Face.* IV, 5.6. The north face of the Grand Teton—the most famous north face in the United States—has a long history that begins on July 6, 1933, when Paul Petzoldt and Sterling Hendricks descended about 1,000 feet down the north ridge of the mountain and explored the north face in the vicinity of the Second Ledge. This exploration led Petzoldt to think that there was probably a feasible route up the north side. The first actual climb on the face was made by Paul Petzoldt, Jack Durrance, and Eldon Petzoldt, on August 25, 1936. They left very early in the morning from the valley in order to sneak past another strong team camped at Amphitheater Lake, who they knew were up there for the same climb. When they reached the Third Ledge, the hour was late and a short rappel was made to the Second Ledge. They traversed this ledge to the north ridge which was then followed to the summit. The team that had been given the slip included Fritz Wiessner, Bill House, and Betty Woolsey. House and Wiessner had earlier in the summer made the impressive first ascent of the south face of Mount Waddington, which was undoubtedly the hardest climb in North America at the time. After realizing that Durrance's group had done the North Face, Wiessner turned his attention to the North Ridge and managed its first free ascent.

On August 14, 1941, this climb with one important variation was repeated by Paul and Bernice Petzoldt, Glenn Exum, and Hans Kraus. Both these early climbs, however, avoided the upper portion of the face. In 1946 Ray Garner, with Jim Smith and Kirk Smith, attempted the face but retreated from a point above the First Ledge. The direct route that includes the upper portion was finally climbed on August 13, 1949, by the strong party of Ray Garner, Richard Pownall, and Art Gilkey. The final step in the evolution of the now-classical direct North Face route was made on July 24, 1953, by Richard Emerson, Willi Unsoeld, and Leigh Ortenburger. The Pendulum Pitch, previously pioneered by Pownall, was climbed free and the delicate traverse into the "V" at the very top of the face was led for the first time. On July 21, 1963, Tom Cochrane made a solo ascent of this standard route. On December 28, 1992, Alex Lowe soloed the complete North Face route in an astonishing 20-hour day from the valley floor to the summit and back. The following descriptions are presented chronologically, but the reader should note that the standard North Face route follows the main description to the Third Ledge, the *1949 variation* to the Fourth Ledge, and the *1953 Direct Finish variation,* the Traverse-into-the-V finish, to the summit. See *Topo 38* and *Photos 45* and *46.* While the north face has lost some of its attraction over the years, it remains a worthwhile mountaineering objective, involving a variety of terrain including glacier ice, wet chimneys, and rock climbing on an impressive, exposed face. There is significant rockfall hazard on this route, mostly in the region below the First Ledge. The length of the climb requires relatively fast climbing to avoid benightment.

Four schemes have been used to climb this face: (1) from the valley in one day; (2) from a camp at Surprise Lake; (3) from a camp on the Teton Glacier; and (4) using a planned bivouac on the First Ledge. Each of these has its advantages and disadvantages. The best method will depend on the speed and experience of the party, the condition of the *bergschrund,* and the time of year.

From Amphitheater Lake take the usual route out to the Teton Glacier (see *Glacier Gulch*) and climb onto the upper section of the glacier, passing the crevassed section on the right (north). Bare ice is commonly encountered in this region. From the upper glacier two chimneys can be seen on the bottom part of the face. Avoid the right (west) vertical chimney containing rotten yellow rock; this truly bad chimney leads straight up the face from the bottom of the Grandstand and is not to be climbed. The initial section of the North Face route ascends the left-slanting chimney on the left (east); this chimney can be reached in various ways, depending on the manner in which the *bergschrund* is passed. The *bergschrund* presents a significant problem on this route and considerable time can be lost in its passage; crampons will be useful. A major but rarely used variant to gain the base of this chimney and bypass the entire upper glacier is to take the wide but tricky ledge that diagonals up (from left to right) along the base of the face on the left (south) of the icefall.

Once the left-slanting chimney is reached, climb several ropelengths up it until it is possible to see an obvious traverse on easy ledges and slabs up to the right toward the First Ledge. To reach the ledge, climb the large chimney that goes back into the wall on the left (south) edge of the steep beginning of the ledge. This chimney is 5.6 in difficulty; in some years it is icy. An unpleasant feature of this chimney (unique in the Tetons, fortunately) is the accumulation of bird (or bat, perhaps) droppings through which one must climb. Exit to the right at the top of this chimney onto the First Ledge. If a bivouac is planned on the First Ledge, a good place is at its lower end about 100 feet above the end of the chimney. A suitable cave will be found here.

Scramble to the west end of the First Ledge and make a 120-foot high-angle lead (5.6) up a shallow chimney, then another up a friction face to the Second Ledge. Avoid the large, ice-filled chimney a few feet to the west of the shallow chimney. If desired, it is now possible to traverse out to the right on the Second Ledge all the way to the north ridge, but a slippery section of water-covered slabs below the small snow patch on the Second Ledge must be negotiated. To continue the North Face route, proceed out on the Second Ledge for only two or three ropelengths and then climb up and slightly right directly onto the Third Ledge. Traverse right (west) up the Third Ledge until about 300 feet from the north ridge. An obvious rappel point will be found near the base of the Pendulum Pitch, which ascends a right-facing corner in the steep wall above. Rappel 110 feet down onto the Second Ledge, which is then easily followed a short distance out to the north ridge. For the remainder of this original North Face route to the summit, see *Route 35.*

In the event one is seeking escape from the face because of time considerations or bad weather, this 1936 route, rather than any of the following variations, is the quick and easy solution, because from the point where the Second Ledge meets the north ridge one can contour easily around the mountain to the Upper Saddle. From the north ridge, a short, ice-filled gully must be crossed just west of the ridge (more properly called "corner") in order to reach the main, broad ledge leading around the west face of the Grand Teton. Follow the ledge to the Great West Chimney where a few moves around the outside of a chockstone lead down (about 15 feet) into and across the chimney to the Crawl of the Owen–Spalding route. It is assumed that descent to the Lower Saddle from this point would be well known to any-

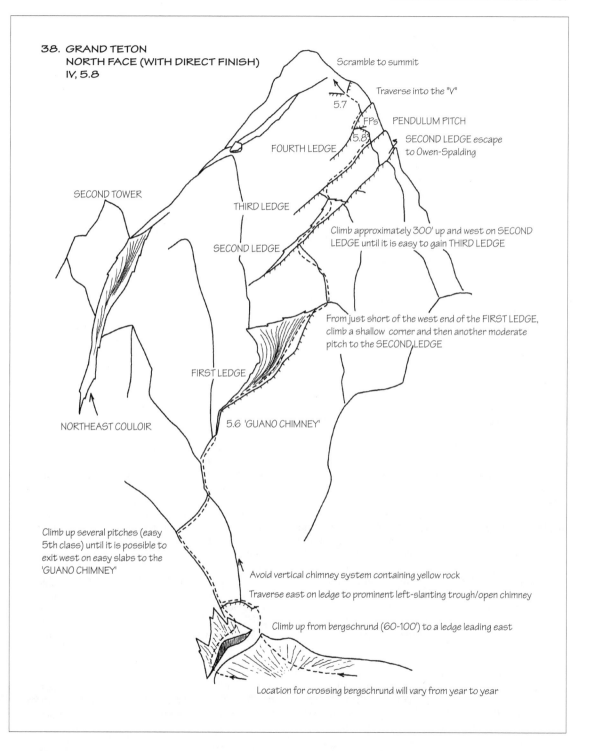

38. GRAND TETON
NORTH FACE (WITH DIRECT FINISH)
IV, 5.8

Scramble to summit

Traverse into the "V"

5.7

FPs

PENDULUM PITCH

5.8

SECOND LEDGE escape
to Owen-Spalding

FOURTH LEDGE

SECOND TOWER

THIRD LEDGE

Climb approximately 300' up and west on SECOND
LEDGE until it is easy to gain THIRD LEDGE

SECOND LEDGE

From just short of the west end of the FIRST LEDGE,
climb a shallow corner and then another moderate
pitch to the SECOND LEDGE

FIRST LEDGE

NORTHEAST COULOIR

5.6 'GUANO CHIMNEY'

Climb up several pitches (easy
5th class) until it is possible to
exit west on easy slabs to the
'GUANO CHIMNEY'

Avoid vertical chimney system containing yellow rock

Traverse east on ledge to prominent left-slanting trough/open chimney

Climb up from bergschrund (60-100') to a ledge leading east

Location for crossing bergschrund will vary from year to year one attempting the North Face route. To return to the Teton Glacier or to Surprise Lake to retrieve one's camp, the Black Dike Traverse along the south side of the Grand Teton (see *Glacier Gulch*) has traditionally been used, but this involves some steep snow in crossing the Stettner Couloir, descending Teepe Glacier, and descending from Dike Col down to the Teton Glacier. To return to Surprise Lake one can take the Garnet Canyon trail down to the Surprise Lake outlet and scramble back up that route to reach the lake. See *American Alpine Journal*, 3, no. 1 (1937), pp. 105–106; *Appalachia*, 21, no. 2 (December 1936), p. 268; 21, no. 3 (June 1937), pp. 425–426, illus.; *Dartmouth Mountaineering Club Journal*, 1961, pp. 40–48, illus.

Variation: IV, 5.6. First ascent August 14, 1941, by Paul and Bernice Petzoldt, Glenn Exum, and Hans Kraus. See *Topo 38*. Instead of going all the way out to the west end of the First Ledge, climb straight up the snow on this ledge and start working up the broken rock leading to the left (east) end of the Second Ledge. This is the easiest method of reaching the Second Ledge.

Variation: IV, 5.7, A1, or IV, 5.8. First ascent August 13, 1949, by Richard Pownall, Ray Garner, and Art Gilkey; first free ascent July 24, 1953, by Richard Emerson, Willi Unsoeld, and Leigh Ortenburger. See *Topo 38* and *Photos 45* and *46*. This direct variation ascends the upper portion of the north face above the Third Ledge. Proceed out (west) along the Third Ledge until about 300 feet from the north ridge. Do not turn up from the Third Ledge too soon; the proper place is almost the last feasible route.

The pitch directly above, the famous Pendulum Pitch, is one of the two most difficult on the route and is significantly more difficult than those preceding it. Climb up a right-facing corner (5.7) for 60 feet until it is possible to traverse out and left on a downsloping, narrowing ledge. The climb then moves left (east) on this ledge, around the corner (5.8) where the ledge inverts, and up to a black alcove at the beginning of the Fourth Ledge. In early season and midseason these final rocks will usually be wet, making the last few feet difficult. A number of fixed pitons will be passed on this pitch. Beware of the sharp crack at the corner, which presents a rope-jamming hazard.

Now traverse 120 feet up the Fourth Ledge to the right (west); the north ridge is now only about 50 feet away. Climb a chimney only a few feet from the crest of the north ridge. From the top of this chimney a blocky section leads to the summit. See *American Alpine Journal*, 8, no. 1 (1951), pp. 61–70; *University of Wyoming Outing Club Journal*, 1959–1960, pp. 64–70, illus.

Variation: Direct Finish. IV, 5.8. First ascent July 24, 1953, by Richard Emerson, Willi Unsoeld, and Leigh Ortenburger. See *Topo 38* and *Photos 45* and *46*. This variation leads into the V gully at the very top of the face. At the end of the 120-foot lead up the Fourth Ledge, traverse back to the left (east) and then turn upward in a small right-facing corner. At this point one is only about 30 feet west of the bottom of the "V." Make a delicate friction traverse across a 75° face in order to finish the climb. Once in the gully, scramble up blocks and chimneys to the summit. *Time: 8 to 11½ hours* from the upper Teton Glacier; *10½ to 13½ hours* from Amphitheater Lake. See *American Alpine Journal*, 1954, pp. 172–184, illus.; *Dartmouth Mountaineering Club Journal*, 1958, pp. 17, 47, illus.; *Sierra Club Bulletin*, 39, no. 6 (June 1954), pp. 27–33.

Variation: IV, 5.7. First ascent July 9, 1954, by William Buckingham and Fred Ford. It is possible to reach the north ridge by traversing out on the Third Ledge. Near the ridge this ledge inverts and becomes a horizontal chimney just large enough to crawl along. It is necessary to pass on the outside of a boulder in this chimney where the exposure is considerable.

Variation: IV, 5.7. First ascent August 24, 1955, by Willi Unsoeld and Frank Ewing. Reach the Second Ledge from the First Ledge via the *1941 variation*, described earlier. From a point just above the lower of the two snowfields, which remain on the Second Ledge throughout most of the summer (this point can also be identified as being directly above the west end of the First Ledge), climb the deep chimney that forms the extreme left (east) end of the Third Ledge. This chimney soon turns up to the right to join the main portion of the Third Ledge.

Variation: IV, 5.8, A2. First ascent September 2, 1955, by Willi and Jolene Unsoeld. This is the only known alternative to Pownall's Pendulum Pitch for reaching the Fourth Ledge from the Third. The eastern extension of the Fourth Ledge has the same property as the western extension of the Third Ledge—it inverts, becoming a ceiling instead of a ledge. There are three such inversions on this variation. When the Third Ledge is reached, cross it instead of walking out to the right (west). A very steep and difficult pitch leads to the Fourth Ledge at a point about 15 feet to the right (west) of the first large inversion. After 40 feet the Fourth Ledge terminates in an abrupt wall; the ledge is reduced to a sharply ascending crack in an otherwise smooth wall. This difficult crack was climbed by the use of an aid sling as a foothold for a long upward step across a smooth section. The two inversions in the remaining 150 feet leading to the intersection of the Pendulum Pitch and the Fourth Ledge are passed by very delicate traverses out on the face proper. See *American Alpine Journal*, 10, no. 1 (1956), pp. 116–119.

Variation: Upper Saddle Start. III, 5.8. First ascent July 31, 1960, by William Echo, John Waage, Keith Staley, and Dean Millsap. This enterprising party accessed the upper pitches of the direct North Face route from a standard camp on the Lower Saddle. Follow the Owen–Spalding route to the Upper Saddle and take the ledge system all the way out to the north ridge from the Crawl. Small difficulties will be met in crossing the Great West Chimney and in passing the final icy gully just before reaching the north corner at the end of the Second Ledge. From the west end of the Second Ledge two large dihedrals about 80 feet apart, leading up to the west end of the Third Ledge, will be seen above. Climb the 90-foot shallow black-rock chimney (5.7) that lies between these two dihedrals. Once on the Third Ledge, traverse about 20 feet back to the left (east) to the base of the Pendulum Pitch and join the upper North Face route at this point.

Variation: North Ridge Start. IV, 5.8. First ascent August 11, 1976, by Jim Donini, Rick Black, and Michael Cole using the standard 1931 North Ridge route, and on July 20, 1977, by George Montopoli and Ralph Baldwin using Route 35, Italian Cracks variation (which was named by this party). The difficult climbing of the 1953 direct North Face route can be effectively doubled by the devious method of using one of the North Ridge variations to gain the Second Ledge. In addition to increasing the magnitude of either route, this variation also provides two additional advantages. It bypasses the less pleasant portions of the standard North Face route below the First Ledge and is relatively clear of snow and ice. It also provides access to the upper direct North Face from the Lower Saddle via the Valhalla Traverse, a rather remarkable sequence. Directly above the point on the Second Ledge where the "Slab Pitch" comes out, one can reach the Third Ledge by simply climbing the black-rock area mentioned in the previous route.

ROUTE 32. Simpleton's Pillar. IV, 5.9. June 16–17, 1972, by Jeff Lowe. See Photo 45. This interesting and seldom-climbed route uses the normal start for the standard North Face route to gain the left-slanting chimney on the lower face. Instead of cutting back right (west) from this chimney system to gain the First Ledge, as in the normal route, continue up and left in this steep, snow- and ice-filled couloir. In early season ice will force the climber to use the outer lip of the couloir. Follow the couloir for a few hundred feet, until it is possible to leave it, not far from its end, via the lower of two right-leaning dihedrals. (A descent bolt, dating from repeated attempts [1959–1970] by Ray Jacquot on a still uncompleted route, will be found along the couloir near the base of these dihedrals.) Climb this dihedral to its top and then up a short but steep wall above. Continue up the broken wall above, reaching a left-trending crack system that leads up to near the top of the buttress or pillar. Follow up this crack system until it rounds the left corner of the buttress and becomes a ledge. Once around this corner easier climbing up and right takes one onto the east ridge at the hump near the snowfield.

ROUTE 33. Goodro–Shane. IV, 5.8, A1. First ascent August 9, 1953, by Harold Goodro and Jim Shane. See Photo 45. The point of departure for this route is the First Ledge on the north face. Instead of traversing this ledge to its west end, stay on the left (east) edge of the snow and continue straight up. Climb 100 feet up a chimney to a smooth 12-foot wall.

This very exposed pitch, the most difficult on the climb, required the leader to stand on the outstretched hands of his second man. From the top of this pitch move slightly to the right where a series of small ledges and terraces leads upward for about 300 feet. Continue up and to the right (west); some ice patches must be crossed. Then climb right up a steep, loose ridge for about 150 feet until one can cut left (east) into a shallow couloir filled with very loose rock. This couloir leads directly to the enormous boulder that is perched at the edge of the east ridge and hangs over the north face. Gain the east ridge and follow that route to the summit. See American Alpine Journal, 9, no. 2 (1955), pp. 147–149.

Variation: IV, 5.8. First ascent July 2, 1961, by Tom Spencer and Ron Perla. This variation also utilizes the large indentation near the eastern edge of the upper north face. It is possible to enter this indentation from the beginning of the Second Ledge instead of attacking it directly from the First Ledge, as was done in 1953. Use the Route 31, 1941 variation to reach the east end of the Second Ledge. A short distance up this ledge a high-angle crack leads slightly left (east) and up the wall above the ledge for about 100 feet to an excellent belay stance; this pitch was reported to be very strenuous with protection difficult to obtain. Midway in the next lead, which continues up the same crack, is a sequence of (5.8) moves onto a block and then up off the block, in order to make a traverse left (east) to the second excellent belay position. Make a short lead up and right to the easy slabs that meet the Goodro–Shane route in a gully in the aforementioned indentation. This ice gully can be followed up to the east ridge, or, after 20 feet, one can climb up and left, hand traversing a difficult slab. This avoids further climbing in the gully and gives access to a series of easy slabs that lead to the east ridge.

ROUTE 34. Medrick–Ortenburger. IV, 5.8, A2. First ascent August 14–15, 1963, by Frederick Medrick and Leigh Ortenburger. See Photo 45. This major route of ten pitches avoids the First Ledge completely by ascending the face directly to the middle of the Second Ledge. Below the western half of the Second Ledge are three huge, parallel chimney systems. This route ascends the easternmost of the three; the American Cracks variation ascends the westernmost chimney. From the upper glacier above the icefall, climb onto the slabs of the Grandstand as in Route 35, staying near the wall on the south edge. Approximately halfway to the top of the Grandstand, a small buttress forces one away from the wall. This route begins at the top of this buttress, which is gained from the right (north). The first ropelength leads back slightly to the left (east) over somewhat rotten rock to a prominent black cave, usually wet. The second lead traverses left (east) from this cave, past some loose gray rocks and around a corner to the beginning of a large shelf that angles steeply up and back to the right. Climb this shelf for about 50 feet, then out to the right edge and up a short vertical wall (5.8) to the end of this 150-foot lead. The next pitch continues up and right on good rock over two overhangs (5.6 and 5.7). The fourth pitch angles back to the left toward a wet, narrow chimney leading toward the base of two of the huge chimneys already mentioned—the eastern one and the central one. This 80-foot pitch past loose, yellow blocks perched on the ledges, is unpleasant. Go another 60 feet. Just short of the wet, narrow chimney turn up and right onto a large shelf that angles up to the right; this shelf more or less parallels the first such shelf mentioned above.

Proceed about 30 feet up this shelf, climb an A2 crack in the 20-foot wall directly above the shelf, then continue back to the left (east) to the start of a clearly defined 50-foot chimney containing ice and loose flakes. From this point it is possible to reach either the eastern or central huge chimney. Climb the 50-foot chimney, past loose rocks that are a hazard to the belayer, to the eastern chimney. Considerable ice will be found in the bottom of this chimney, so crampons are useful here. If not available, the eighth lead must be made on wet and icy rocks up the left (east) side of the chimney, using aid to reach a belay point about 30 feet below the first major chockstone. The ninth pitch attacks the wet slab-wall that forms the right (west) side of the chimney. An incredible flake with no visible means of support hangs on the upper part of this pitch. This flake may last for many ascents if climbers are careful not to dislodge it. From the belay position, climb an A1 crack on the left edge of this slab-wall and step across to the lower end of the flake. Climb to the top of this flake, then across to the right onto the wall itself. An adequate belay position out of the confines of the chimney will be found 20 feet above.

The last lead is long, 150 feet, and ascends the easier rock slightly back to the left to the Second Ledge of the standard North Face route, which is followed to the summit. This approach to the Second Ledge is considerably more direct than the standard route and approximately doubles the difficult climbing of the north face. Much loose rock must be passed in the course of the climb. When combined with the upper part of the direct North Face route (Pendulum Pitch and the Traverse-into-the-V Pitch), this is one of the more difficult routes on the Grand Teton. See *American Alpine Journal,* 14, no. 1 (1964), pp. 186–188, illus.

ROUTE 35. *North Ridge.* IV, 5.8. First ascent July 19, 1931, by Robert Underhill and Fritiof Fryxell. *(Note:* The rating of this climb on the first ascent was IV, 5.7, A0, because various tactics were employed. Fryxell stated, "[A]fter we were both roped securely to these [pitons], Underhill mounted to my shoulders and, using the upper ring, launched an offensive." On August 30, 1936, the route was repeated by Fritz Wiessner, William House, Percy Olton, and Beckett Howorth. The Chockstone Pitch was free climbed by Wiessner on his second attempt "by spreading across in front of it and edging up and over the sloping outer margin." These are excerpted from Fryxell and Smith's *Mountaineering in the Tetons: The Pioneer Period 1898–1940.)* First descent (upper half, summit to Second Ledge) July 6, 1933, by Paul Petzoldt and Sterling Hendricks, (lower half, Second Ledge to the Teton Glacier) September 3, 1955, by Willi and Jolene Unsoeld. See *Topo 39* and *Photo 46.* Even though pioneered over 60 years ago, the North Ridge of the Grand Teton remains today one of the great classic mountaineering routes in the range, a tribute to the vision and skill of the first-ascent party. At the time of its first ascent, this route was perhaps the most difficult climb in the country. This route, which averages over 63° for 1,200 feet, is better described as the intersection of two high-angle faces than as a ridge; a more accurate name, preferred by Fryxell, would be "North Corner." Three alternative approaches can be used to reach the top of the Grandstand, where the upper portion of this route begins; see the *1940* and *1960 variations* listed below. The recommended approach is described under the *1960 variation.* The original approach, described below, is directly from the east, up the Teton Glacier, then onto the east ledges and slabs of the Grandstand. While this option is very scenic, some danger from rockfall from the north face make the *1960 variation* from the west preferable. For those who wish to bivouac on the climb, there is a reasonable spot for four on top of the Grandstand, but it is quite often windy at this exposed location.

Proceed to the Teton Glacier (see *Glacier Gulch*) and climb to the upper glacier, passing the crevassed section on the right (north). Cross the *bergschrund* or *randkluft,* as the case may be, somewhere near the bottom corner of the north face and the Grandstand. The difficulty of getting started up the Grandstand varies with the year and the snow conditions; in some years this will be a difficult and time-consuming proposition. There is some danger from falling rocks during the ascent of the Grandstand. Climb to the top of the Grandstand either next to the wall on the left (south) edge or via a zigzag on ledges out on the Grandstand.

From the top of the Grandstand proceed up and south to a large block for the first belay. Climb behind the block and then out and left (5.7) past a few old fixed pins on steep rock for 20 feet or so. Continue angling up and left to a steep gully. Ascend the gully and belay just below an abrupt step. The next pitch continues up and right over steep black rock (5.7) to the belay at the base of the famous Chockstone Chimney. The final portion of this lead often involves climbing a small ice sheet to the bottom of the chimney. Climb up the first part of the Chockstone Pitch on gradually steepening rock until it is possible to swing into the subsidiary chimney on the left (5.8) and then gain the top of the main chockstone. One can also climb up and over the chockstone using hand jams and then stem across to the opposite wall (5.8). The next lead is an enjoyable large chimney (5.7) in an area of black rock and it brings one to the 80-foot slab

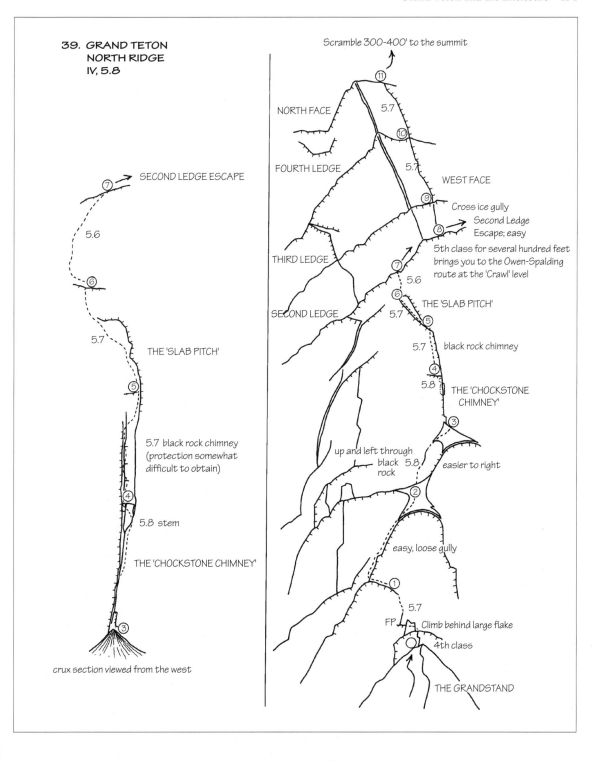

39. GRAND TETON
NORTH RIDGE
IV, 5.8

Scramble 300-400' to the summit

NORTH FACE

5.7

FOURTH LEDGE

5.7

WEST FACE

Cross ice gully
Second Ledge
Escape; easy

5th class for several hundred feet
brings you to the Owen-Spalding
route at the 'Crawl' level

SECOND LEDGE ESCAPE

5.6

THIRD LEDGE

5.6

THE 'SLAB PITCH'

5.7

SECOND LEDGE

5.7

5.7   black rock chimney

5.7

THE 'SLAB PITCH'

5.8

THE 'CHOCKSTONE
CHIMNEY'

up and left through
black   5.8
rock

easier to right

5.7 black rock chimney
(protection somewhat
difficult to obtain)

5.8 stem

easy, loose gully

THE 'CHOCKSTONE CHIMNEY'

5.7

FP   Climb behind large flake

4th class

crux section viewed from the west

THE GRANDSTAND

pitch. This slab pitch can be extremely difficult when coated with ice, so consider weather conditions carefully before attempting this climb. Climb up and then to the left across the slab (5.7) to the very exposed corner of the ridge and then continue up and right to the west side of the ridge. This point marks the west end of the Second Ledge of the north face. Three possibilities for the completion of the climb are now present: (1) Two obvious chimneys of moderate difficulty lead up just to the right (west) of the ridge crest to a point where the Fourth Ledge on the north face joins the north ridge. If this alternative (the most direct) is chosen, the remaining fairly difficult pitch ascends a 25-foot face just to the right of the crest. Above this pitch, easy scrambling leads to the summit. (2) One can avoid the upper ridge by traversing right (south) toward the Great West Chimney and from there scrambling quickly to the summit. (3) If it is late or the weather is bad, a fast descent can be made without going to the summit, by making a traverse almost horizontally south all the way over to the Owen–Spalding route. It may prove easier to climb about 100 feet before making a slightly descending traverse past the Great West Chimney to the Crawl of the Owen–Spalding route.

The classic North Ridge route can also be expanded in a major way by combining it with the final pitches of the direct North Face route, adding a great finish to what is already an outstanding route. This is described under the *1976 variation* of the North Face route. If the original North Ridge is not in good condition due to recent precipitation, the *1971 Italian Cracks variation* below is an excellent alternative to the chimneys of the standard route, because they are less of a major drainage and are generally drier. *Time: 12 to 13½ hours* from Amphitheater Lake. See *American Alpine Journal*, 1, no. 4 (1932), pp. 465–469, illus.; 9, no. 1 (1954), pp. 172–184, illus.; *Appalachia*, 21, no. 2 (December 1936), pp. 216–224, illus.; *Canadian Alpine Journal*, 1931, pp. 72–86, illus.; *Harvard Mountaineering*, 16 (May 1963), pp. 82–83; *Trail and Timberline*, no. 354 (June 1948), pp. 79–83, illus.

Variation: East Gunsight Approach. IV, 5.8, A1. First ascent circa August 22, 1936, by Fritz Wiessner, Paul Petzoldt, Brad Gilman, Beckett Howorth, Bill House, and Elizabeth Woolsey. Instead of gaining the Grandstand at its base, this party attempted to reach the Gunsight Notch directly from the east, via the gully from the upper Teton Glacier. About 200 feet above the upper glacier the gully is blocked by an enormous chockstone, which required a three-person shoulder stand (Woolsey on Wiessner on House) to pass. The rock above becomes looser, wetter, and steeper until the gully narrows to a width of 4 feet and 30 feet of vertical ice are encountered. At this point make a delicate traverse left across the south wall of the gully and around the corner onto the Grandstand where two difficult chimneys are then climbed. The top of the Grandstand is now easily reached.

Variation: West Gunsight Approach. IV, 5.8. First ascent August 6, 1940, by Jack Durrance, Henry Coulter, Merrill McLane, and Chap Cranmer. The top of the Grandstand can be reached by first ascending the west Gunsight Couloir out of Valhalla Canyon and then climbing up and left (southeast) out of Gunsight Notch to gain the Grandstand, which is then followed up to its top. Apparently, this party encountered difficult, rotten rock during the course of the climb directly up from the south side of the notch.

If one is traversing to the Grand from Mount Owen, then the top of the Grandstand can be gained using a different and better option out of Gunsight Notch. From the notch climb down to the left (east) on ledges for about 100 feet to the base of a crack system that leans to the right slightly, leading to a small notch. Ascend this crack (5.7) for 80 feet on excellent rock up to the notch. Scramble for 400 feet to the top of the Grandstand.

Variation: Valhalla Approach. IV, 5.8. First ascent July 31, 1960, by Jake Breitenbach, Pete Sinclair, and Leigh and Irene Ortenburger. See *Photos 47, 48, 49,* and *50*. The top of the Grandstand can be reached directly from Valhalla Canyon or, in combination with the Valhalla Traverse, from the Lower Saddle. This approach from the west side provides the currently recommended start to the North Ridge climb. Although it misses the alpine aspect of glacier travel involved in the standard eastern approach, climbing in the upper Valhalla drainage with the imposing west face of the Grand looming above is certainly a worthwhile alternative. It permits access to the beginning of the north ridge from Garnet Canyon, which has also increased the popularity of the classic North Ridge route.

From Valhalla Canyon it will be seen that the First Shelf of the West Face route leads directly to the top of the Grandstand. If starting from Valhalla, proceed as in *Route 38* toward the wall protecting access to the Second Shelf. The aim here is to get to the lower (west) end of the First Shelf. Most often, when conditions are the driest, this will require climbing a pitch of rock that is, at least, wet and about 5.6 in difficulty. This pitch will be in an area of black rock. The amount and difficulty of ice and wet rock encountered on the shelf proper will depend on the year and the season; an ice axe will commonly be required. If attempted in early season, crampons will be useful, if not quite necessary. Climb eastward up the shelf staying well out to the left (north) on the dry rock. With good routefinding little more than scrambling is required to attain the top of the Grandstand. Some loose rock will be encountered, but there is little danger from falling rock once past the area below the Black Ice Couloir. If the Valhalla Traverse from the Lower Saddle is used, one will exit from the traverse ledge after climbing down the ramp (often covered with snow) located just below the west end of the First Shelf; hence, this is a very efficient approach to the North Ridge route. See *American Alpine Journal*, 12, no. 2 (1961), pp. 373–377.

Variation: Italian Cracks. IV, 5.7. First ascent August 19, 1971, by Howard Friedman and Peter Wollan. See *Topo 40* and *Photo 46*. This important variation of the original North Ridge route lies around the corner and out on the north face, providing an excellent alternative for the famous Chockstone Pitch. Since it is a crack climb, however, the character of the North Ridge route is then completely changed. If one has climbed the original route, this variation on good rock is a recommended option for the second time. Climb the first two pitches of the original route up from the top of the Grandstand to a large belay ledge. Now move out left (east) along this ledge to the base of a crack in the wall above. Three pitches, almost straight up a sequence of cracks, now lead to the Second Ledge. The first lead of 150 feet includes the passage of a small overhang (5.7) just below the next belay ledge. Face climbing (5.7) up and to the right of a second short overhang makes up the second pitch. The third shorter pitch (70 feet) is easier face climbing onto the Second Ledge. Traverse right on the ledge to rejoin the standard North Ridge route at the corner.

Variation: Chockstone Bypass. IV, 5.7. First ascent August 10, 1974, by Jim McCarthy and Gerald Barnard. This variation bypasses the famous chockstone of the classic North Ridge route. From the belay point at the base of the chockstone chimney, traverse right 50 feet, stepping around a corner, to a large ledge below a steep 100-foot wall. Climb straight up from this ledge, first on blocks, then face climbing to a short curving 5.7 crack leading onto a slab. At the top of this lead the slab gives access to a ledge that can be taken back left (east) to rejoin the standard route, above the chockstone.

Variation: American Cracks. IV, 5.9. First ascent July 7, 1988, by Mike Colacino and Calvin Hebert. See *Topo 40* and *Photo 46*. This variation ascends the lower right portion of the north face, providing a new and difficult method of reaching the Second Ledge from the Grandstand. This crack system lies to the east of the Italian Cracks. From a large block 20 feet above the top of the Grandstand, a long ropelength (165 feet) diagonals up and left (5.7) to the gully leading to the regular North Ridge route. Descend from the belay point 10 feet and make a traverse horizontally left for 100 feet on a 4th-class ledge. Belay from a ramp, leading up and right from the end of this traverse. The next lead is short but difficult, starting directly up a dihedral (5.8) below a hanging flake to get into the 5.9 wide hand crack above; after 70 feet a good belay will be found. A second lead (5.7) of 100 feet up this same hand crack leads onto a huge ledge (with block), the same ledge from which the Italian Cracks start only a few feet to the right (west). From the block move left and down to a dihedral that is climbed to a belay on the next large ledge. The next long lead (5.9), the crux

of this variation, is a large chimney that curves slightly to the right; this is the westernmost of the three chimneys described under *Route 34*. Halfway up this difficult chimney is a set of platelike chockstones that must be passed. From the belay to the top of this chimney, one more easier lead up and then back left takes one onto the Second Ledge. Follow this out to the north ridge and rejoin *Route 35*.

Variation: Odette–Sherner. IV, 5.10+. First ascent August 7, 1994, by Chuck Odette and Jim Sherner. This variation of three pitches ascends the dark crack system between the classic North Ridge and the Italian Cracks. The first pitch was 5.10 in difficulty; the second was 5.10+; the third was 5.8 to 5.9. The second pitch was described as being "loose and dangerous" with a "huge death-flake on it."

ROUTE 36. Loki's Tower. IV, 5.9+. First ascent August 2, 1981, by Mark Whiton and Michael Stern. See *Topo 41* and *Photos 46* and *49*. This improbable and difficult route was discovered on the massive solid buttress between the north ridge and the northwest chimney. Routefinding on this somewhat featureless buttress is difficult. From the Lower Saddle use the standard Valhalla Traverse Ledge to gain the lowest of the three shelves leading up and onto the west face of the Grandstand. This route begins at the top of this First Shelf with two pitches of climbing (5.6) to the left (east) of the ramp that leads to the crux pitch of the Northwest Chimney route. The third lead passes a small overhang up into a corner with a 5.8 hand crack, followed by a 5.9 right-facing shallow corner, from the top of which face climbing leads left onto a belay ledge. The next difficult lead of steep and delicate face climbing (5.9+) followed by a vertical 5.9 straight-in corner is the crux pitch of the route with only marginal protection. The next pitch is strenuous face climbing (5.9) past two small overhangs. The sixth lead goes up and somewhat right to a belay at a ledge that is below and to the right (west) of the base of the Chockstone Chimney of the North Ridge route. The two final leads (5.7) of this route go directly up, via face climbing and cracks, to the top of the tower or buttress. From this point the Northwest Chimney route is joined at the exit from the Black Rock Bowl. The set of icy chimneys of that route is now readily at hand and is climbed for two long pitches leading upward to the extension of the Second Ledge of the north face.

Variation: IV, 5.9+. First ascent July 17, 1984, by Renny Jackson and Steve Rickert. See *Topo 41*. This variation of five pitches provides a distinct start to Loki's Tower and includes a spectacular traverse. Use the same approach as earlier to gain the base of the tower or buttress. The first pitch begins to the right of the lower extension of the northwest chimney with a 5.9 mantle into a right-facing corner (5.8) and up to the belay near the chimney extension. Two ropelengths along the right side of the ramp (5.6) bring one to the ice of the Northwest Chimney immediately below the crux of that route. An unlikely exit to the left (north) up and

Scramble to
summit

A ⑩

5.7 chimney

NORTH FACE

5.7

⑨

Traverse into "V"

WEST FACE

5.7 chimney

PENDULUM
PITCH

⑧ FP FP

SECOND LEDGE
escape to Owen-Spalding

5.8

FOURTH LEDGE

⑦

5.7
black
rock

⑥

B

5.5

THIRD LEDGE

70'

easy 5th
class

⑤

5.7

120'

ITALIAN CRACKS

plates 5.9

④

5.7

5.5

5.8

150'

AMERICAN CRACKS

5.9

5.6

corner 5.7

③

②

5.7

easy, loose gully

5.9

hanging
flake 5.8

B

①

150'

5.7

FP

Climb behind large flake

4th class

THE GRANDSTAND

A

**40. GRAND TETON
      NORTH RIDGE
   A. VARIATION: ITALIAN CRACKS (with DIRECT NORTH FACE finish), IV, 5.8
   B. VARIATION: AMERICAN CRACKS, IV, 5.9**

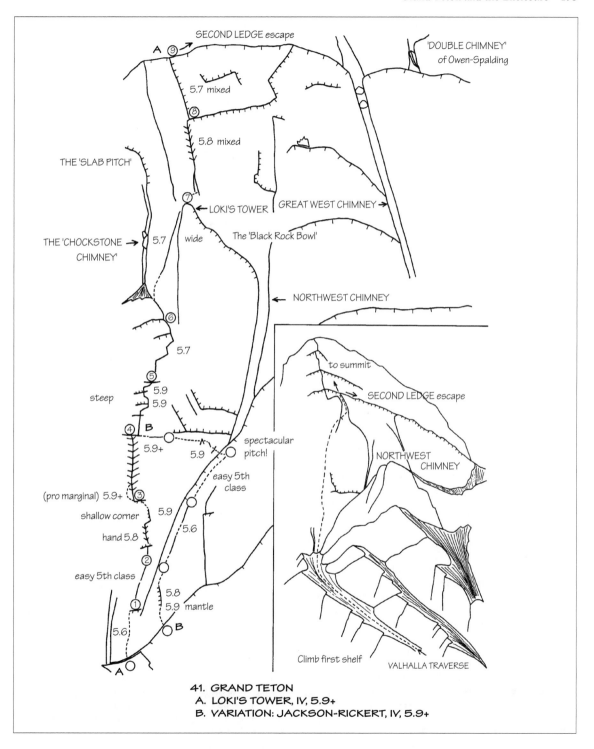

SECOND LEDGE escape

A ⑨

'DOUBLE CHIMNEY'
of Owen-Spalding

5.7 mixed

⑧

5.8 mixed

THE 'SLAB PITCH'

⑦ ← LOKI'S TOWER   GREAT WEST CHIMNEY →

THE 'CHOCKSTONE → 5.7   wide
CHIMNEY'

The 'Black Rock Bowl'

← NORTHWEST CHIMNEY

⑥

5.7

⑤   5.9

steep   5.9

to summit

SECOND LEDGE escape

④ B   ○
5.9+   5.9   ○ spectacular
pitch!

NORTHWEST
CHIMNEY

easy 5th
class

(pro marginal) 5.9+ ③
shallow corner   5.9
hand 5.8   ○ 5.6

easy 5th class   ②   ○

5.8
①   5.9 mantle

5.6 ○ B

Climb first shelf   VALHALLA TRAVERSE

A ○

41. GRAND TETON
   A. LOKI'S TOWER, IV, 5.9+
   B. VARIATION: JACKSON-RICKERT, IV, 5.9+

across the blank-looking wall is largely face climbing (5.9) on small holds followed by a difficult hand traverse to gain the ledge at the end of the crux pitch of the main route on the buttress. This is a most spectacular lead, initially under a line of overhangs, on the best solid Teton rock.

ROUTE 37. Northwest Chimney. IV, 5.8, A1, or IV, 5.9. First ascent July 26, 1960, by David Dornan and Leigh and Irene Ortenburger; first free ascent August 4, 1960, by Royal Robbins, Joe Fitschen, and Yvon Chouinard; attempted July 15, 1957, by Fred Ayres and Leigh and Irene Ortenburger. See *Topo 42* and *Photos 48* and *49*. This large chimney, lying between the north ridge and the Great West Chimney, is perhaps the most conspicuous feature of the Grand Teton when viewed from the northwest. Because of its orientation, this is a dark and cold climb where the sun is never seen. Crampons are useful because of the mixed nature of the climbing. This route can be combined with two other Valhalla climbs to create what is perhaps one of the finest of all the alpine routes in the Tetons, the Jackson–Kimbrough Contortion (see later).

On the first ascent this climb was approached from Cascade Canyon into Valhalla Canyon. The recommended, modern approach for this climb is the Valhalla Traverse Ledge from the Lower Saddle (see *Valhalla Canyon*). This approach is much the same as that of the West Face (*Route 38*) to the far (east) end of the Second Shelf. To the left of the Rotten Yellow Chimney (of the West Face route) two cracks are seen in the massive section of rock that separates the end of this shelf from the bottom of the chimney proper. This route begins in the left-hand crack. Climb this wide crack (5.8), which often contains ice-cold running water. From the end of this first 120-foot lead, climb one more ropelength up somewhat easier steep slabs to a perch along the right side of the 40-foot-wide sheet of ice in the bottom of the chimney. Cross the ice to a spot suitable for belaying the next pitch, which goes directly up the nearly vertical beginning of the chimney proper. Aid was used originally on the first portion of this pitch, although it has now been done free (5.9). Some loose rock will be encountered in this lead. Continue up still difficult rock (a nasty 5.8 flared chimney) until above the large chockstone seen from below. Now climb the 80 feet of ice above this chockstone to reach the steep section of the chimney above. A final lead past a 5.7 overhang ends where the chimney opens out into the Black Rock Bowl. With some difficulty a belay stance can be found in the bowl. Above this point the chimney overhangs and then disappears in the smooth west face. So traverse left (north) in the black rock to a crack or chimney system (often containing ice) near the extreme left (north) edge of the west face. After two leads directly up these cracks there is a wide scree bench that leads from the end of the second ledge of the north face all the way over to the Crawl of the Owen–Spalding route. The West Face route also leads to this same bench 150 feet to the right (south).

There are many possible routes from the bench to the summit. The one closest to the left is normally used by climbers of the North Ridge and is perhaps the most logical extension for this Northwest Chimney route. Or it is possible to walk south along this bench several yards to the easier, blocky area (which lies well north of the Owen–Spalding route) normally used by climbers of the West Face route. It is also possible to follow this bench south past the Great West Chimney all the way over to the Crawl of the Owen–Spalding route and finish the climb by that route. If time does not permit continuing to the summit of the Grand Teton and an escape is needed, this same scheme can be used to reach and then descend the initial portion of the Owen–Spalding route to the Upper Saddle. See *American Alpine Journal,* 12, no. 2 (1961), pp. 373–377.

Variation: West Face Finish. IV, 5.9. First ascent August 4, 1960, by Royal Robbins, Joe Fitschen, and Yvon Chouinard. See *Topo 42* and *Photo 49*. From the Black Rock Bowl traverse right instead of left and up to the flake at the beginning of the first of the two difficult pitches of the West Face route. Two leads of 5.7 face and crack climbing are involved to reach the flake. Use the West Face for the remainder of the ascent. This fine variation combines the most difficult portions of these two routes. See *Sierra Club Bulletin,* 46, no. 8 (October 1961), pp. 53–54.

Variation: Jackson–Kimbrough Contortion. V, 5.9, AI3. First ascent August 9, 1980, by Renny Jackson and Tom Kimbrough. This devious variation combines parts of three routes to create an extended alpine limb. Begin by climbing the 1967 *Black Ice–West Face variation* (see later) to the base of the rock of the West Face route. Then invert the West Face approach by traversing left (north) along the upper edge of the ice to the top of the Rotten Yellow Chimney. Climb or rappel down this chimney and traverse over to the beginning of the Northwest Chimney route. Climb the *1960 variation* that connects with the upper difficult portion of the West Face and finish the climb by that route. This combination produces the longest climb of all of the variations on the west side of the Grand Teton.

Variation: Hummingbird Wall. IV, 5.10-. First ascent August 1990, by Beverly Boynton and Ted Kerasote. See *Topo 42*. After some consideration it is thought that this route ascends the right-hand of the two cracks mentioned earlier at the beginning of *Route 37*. Three pitches were climbed from the base of the Rotten Yellow Chimney up to the main ledge that divides the West Face into two sections. The first pitch was a 5.9 crack for 80 feet (an old fixed piton was passed near the start), the second (somewhat lichen covered) consisted of a 5.10- hand and finger crack for 100 feet. From an alcove at the top of the second pitch climb up and right over 5.8 to 5.9 terrain to the large ledge. The regular West Face route was then joined and followed to the summit.

ROUTE 38. West Face. IV, 5.8. First ascent August 14, 1940, by Jack Durrance and Henry Coulter. See *Topo 43* and *Pho-*

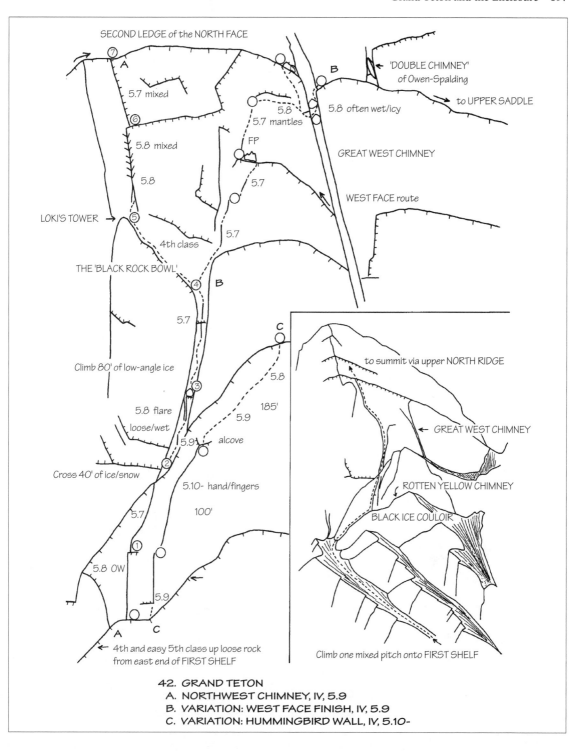

SECOND LEDGE of the NORTH FACE

'DOUBLE CHIMNEY' of Owen-Spalding

to UPPER SADDLE

5.7 mixed

A

5.8 often wet/icy

5.8

5.7 mantles

FP

GREAT WEST CHIMNEY

5.8 mixed

5.8

5.7

WEST FACE route

LOKI'S TOWER

4th class

5.7

THE 'BLACK ROCK BOWL'

B

5.7

Climb 80' of low-angle ice

to summit via upper NORTH RIDGE

C

5.8

185'

GREAT WEST CHIMNEY

5.8 flare

5.9

loose/wet

5.9

alcove

ROTTEN YELLOW CHIMNEY

Cross 40' of ice/snow

BLACK ICE COULOIR

5.10- hand/fingers

5.7

100'

5.8 OW

5.9

A

C

← 4th and easy 5th class up loose rock
from east end of FIRST SHELF

Climb one mixed pitch onto FIRST SHELF

42. GRAND TETON
   A. NORTHWEST CHIMNEY, IV, 5.9
   B. VARIATION: WEST FACE FINISH, IV, 5.9
   C. VARIATION: HUMMINGBIRD WALL, IV, 5.10-

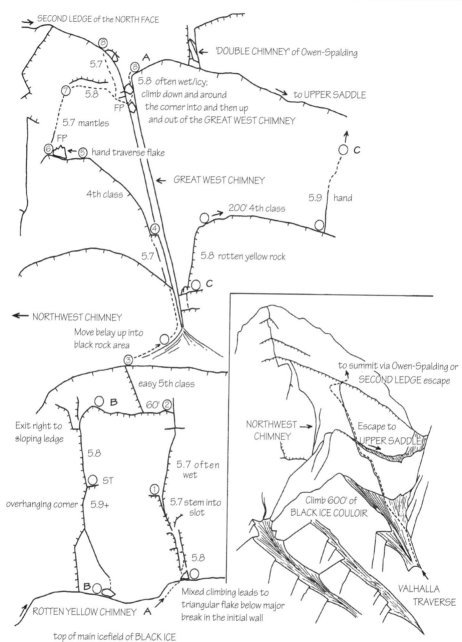

SECOND LEDGE of the NORTH FACE

'DOUBLE CHIMNEY' of Owen-Spalding

⑧
5.7

A
⑧
5.8 often wet/icy; climb down and around the corner into and then up and out of the GREAT WEST CHIMNEY

to UPPER SADDLE

⑦   5.8
FP

5.7 mantles

FP
⑥ ← ⑤ hand traverse flake

C

← GREAT WEST CHIMNEY

4th class

5.9   hand

200' 4th class

④

5.7   5.8 rotten yellow rock

C

← NORTHWEST CHIMNEY

Move belay up into black rock area

③

to summit via Owen-Spalding or SECOND LEDGE escape

easy 5th class

B   60' ②

Exit right to sloping ledge

NORTHWEST → CHIMNEY

Escape to UPPER SADDLE

5.8

5.7 often wet

ST

①

overhanging corner   5.9+   5.7 stem into slot

Climb 600' of BLACK ICE COULOIR

5.8

B

ROTTEN YELLOW CHIMNEY   A

Mixed climbing leads to triangular flake below major break in the initial wall

VALHALLA TRAVERSE

top of main icefield of BLACK ICE

43. GRAND TETON, WEST FACE
A. VARIATION: BLACK ICE-WEST FACE COMBINATION, IV, AI3, 5.8
B. VARIATION: NEUTRON BURN, IV, 5.9+
C. VARIATION: TILLEY-NICHOLSON TRAVERSE, IV, 5.9

tos 49 and *50*. This splendid route, the first of the Valhalla climbs of the Grand Teton, is a recommended climb; it is probably the finest of the early major routes on the mountain. The original approach is via Cascade Canyon into Valhalla Canyon (see *Valhalla Canyon*), one of the wilder and least travelled canyons in the park. From the upper reaches of this canyon, three distinct diagonal shelves will be seen extending across the bottom part of the west face of the Grandstand. The initial climbing and routefinding task is to gain the upper (eastern) end of the Second Shelf where the Rotten Yellow Chimney begins. Depending on the year and season, the climbing encountered getting to and up these shelves can include anything from pure ice, to iced rock, to wet rock, and, on rare occasions, dry rock. The main route described below is appropriate when the Cascade–Valhalla Canyon approach is used. In recent years, however, the standard approach to this route has been from the Lower Saddle via the Valhalla Traverse Ledge (see *Valhalla Canyon*) to the lower end of the First Shelf, at which point the original route is joined. The *1973 variation* provides a good route to gain the upper end of the Second Shelf.

From the upper portion of Valhalla Canyon, climb partway up the snow couloir that descends from Gunsight Notch between Mount Owen and the Grand Teton. To the right (south) of the couloir is what appears from below to be a roundtop rock tower; it is, in fact, only a broad buttress extending in a northwest direction from the wide bench above. Exit from the snow couloir on an easy system of ledges leading around the left (northeast) side of this buttress. Continue up easy ledges and slabs bearing slightly right (south) in order to connect with the black rock at the lower end of the three conspicuous shelves; this black rock can be seen from the floor of Valhalla Canyon. The rock runs along the bottom of the first two shelves and affords a route from the First to the Second Shelf. Some routefinding skill will be useful here.

After gaining the Second Shelf, climb left (east) and up several ropelengths of wet friction slabs and ice patches to the upper end of the shelf. A second band of black rock connecting the second and third shelves will be found here. From the east end of the Second Shelf, climb the Rotten Yellow Chimney leading south and up to the Third (uppermost) Shelf, which is actually the edge of the main icefield of the Black Ice Couloir (see *The Enclosure, Route 5*). This brings one to a ledge at the top of this icefield (a bivouac site has been constructed here). Traverse right (south) for perhaps 200 feet, first on this ledge and later along the top edge of the icefield, to a crack that is the second major break in the smooth wall above. A huge triangular flake sits at the base of this crack, which is the start of the main upper part of the West Face route. Not infrequently this initial crack will be wet or covered with *verglas*, greatly increasing its difficulty.

Climb this difficult crack (5.8) and continue up chimneys and ledges to the broad scree-covered ledge that is just below the level of the Upper Saddle. Once on the broad ledge traverse to the right (south) for about 100 feet to the left edge of the Great West Chimney. From here, a long ropelength up the left (north) wall of the Great West Chimney leads to the last ledge beneath a 100-foot smooth wall. Climb along this last ledge, which extends out north to a large flake. Go past this flake, traversing left (north) on its outside to a small belay ledge beneath a slightly overhanging wall. Climb about 30 feet straight up this wall via two 5.7 mantles before traversing back to the right (south) on very small holds to a 2-foot downsloping ledge for the belay. Now traverse directly back to the right (south), across a vertical face on small holds (5.8), in order to gain an adequate ledge around the corner. From this ledge a further traverse can be made right into the Great West Chimney, or, better, face climb (5.7) directly up to another broad bench. If the chimney is entered, an exit out and to the right (south) between two large chockstones will have to be made. This bench is the extension of the Second Ledge of the north face and connects on the south with the Crawl of the Owen–Spalding route. From this bench a series of easier ledges, chimneys, and cracks leads up the left side of the chimney to the summit. If time does not permit continuing to the summit of the Grand Teton after the conclusion of the difficult climbing, traverse south to the Owen–Spalding route. *Time: 13¼ hours* from Valhalla Canyon. See *American Alpine Journal*, 4, no. 2 (1941), pp. 234–238, illus.; 9, no. 1 (1954), pp. 172–184, illus.

Variation: *Direct West Chimney.* IV, 5.8, A1. First ascent August 13, 1960, by Tom and William Spencer. Instead of making the detour out to the left (north) and then back into the Great West Chimney, it is possible to climb straight up the chimney, using aid to pass the first large chockstone. Ice, chockstone, wet rock, poor protection, and a waterfall combine to make this an undesirable substitute for the original Durrance route.

Variation: *Black Ice–West Face Combination.* IV, AI3, 5.8. First ascent July 23, 1967, by George Lowe and Mike Lowe. See *Topo 43* and *Photos 47* and *49*. This superb combination joins in a natural way two of the finest Teton routes. The result is one of the great alpine climbs of the range. Approach from the Lower Saddle via the Valhalla Traverse Ledge around the north side of the Enclosure to the start of the Black Ice Couloir route (see *The Enclosure, Route 5*). Climb the initial 600 feet of ice (55°), angling slightly left on the main icefield to reach the huge triangular flake at the start of the rock of the upper West Face route. Out on the center of this icefield one is totally exposed to whatever rockfall occurs. In the event of bad weather or lateness of the hour, there are two alternatives to completing the entire long West Face route. One can simply complete the normal Black Ice Couloir up to the Upper Saddle. This option should take somewhat less time, and it has the advantage that the difficulty of ice is not greatly increased by new snow, while rock climbing may become enormously more difficult. The second option is the *1971 variation* described below; it, too, is not an easy option because it involves some serious climbing including more ice.

Variation: Traverse to Upper Saddle. IV, AI3, 5.7. First ascent February 2–4, 1971, by George and David Lowe and Jeff and Greg Lowe. From the broad scree ledge at the end of the third lead of the West Face route, it is possible, but not easy, to reach the Upper Saddle directly. A horizontal traverse from the extreme south end of this ledge or bench leads to a final section of ice and difficult rock guarding access to the north edge of the Upper Saddle. About three leads are involved in this variation, which is useful if an escape from the standard West Face route is required.

Variation: Direct Approach. IV, 5.8. First ascent August 28, 1973, by Doyle Nelson and Jim Olson. See *Photos 47* and *49.* This variation bypasses completely the climbing up the Second Shelf, climbing instead the First Shelf out to its far (east) end before turning up and right (south) to join the original route near the base of the Rotten Yellow Chimney. This is the preferred method of approach to the face if the lower portion of the Black Ice Couloir is not used. From the broad buttress at the start of the original route described earlier, a section of black rock can be seen cutting across the base of the first two diagonal shelves on the lower portion of the West Face route. Use this black rock to gain the lower end of the First Shelf or lower shelf. Climb or scramble up this shelf staying, if possible, out on ledges to the left (north) of the ice that, through most of the season, occupies the right portion of the shelf. In early or wet seasons one may have to climb directly up this icefield close to the right wall, which separates the First from the Second Shelf. After several hundred feet up the shelf, near its end, a second area of black rock is reached where the terrain steepens. Ledges in this section permit a traverse back to an area of steep cracks and chimneys in the right wall; a section of ice will probably have to be crossed here. One ropelength up an easy chimney system takes one to the Second Shelf and the Rotten Yellow Chimney. This variation offers a relatively quick method to reach this chimney, is less subject to rockfall than the lower end of the Second Shelf, and affords an expedient descent route in bad weather.

Variation: Tilley–Nicholson Traverse. IV, 5.9. First ascent July 20, 1978, by Buck Tilley and Bill Nicholson. See *Topo 43.* This difficult variation departs from the standard West Face route at the large scree ledge in the middle of the route. From this ledge, start from flakes up and to the right (south) of the Great West Chimney. Climb one pitch up a rotten, yellow, left-facing corner (5.8) to a ledge system on which a traverse 200 feet to the right can be made to an alcove about even with the Upper Saddle. From here climb a 5.9 hand crack and the face above it that leads onto the talus of the saddle.

Variation: Neutron Burn. IV, 5.9+. First ascent August 7, 1989, by Jon Patterson and Pete Keane. See *Topo 43.* From the ledge that runs along the top of the icefield (see main description, earlier), this surprising variation provides a two-pitch alternative to the upper West Face route. From the top of the Rotten Yellow Chimney proceed along the ledge south to a very large detached flake where this variation begins. Move up and left to a right-facing corner (overhanging), which is climbed (5.9+) onto a small ledge for the first belay. The second pitch continues up this corner (5.8) and exits to the right onto a sloping ledge for the second belay stance. Now make an easy traverse right to join the standard West Face route.

THE ENCLOSURE (13,280+)
(0.17 mi W of Grand Teton)

Map: Grand Teton

The western spur of the Grand Teton, the second highest point in the Teton Range, holds a curious man-made structure within a few feet of its summit. Discovered in the course of the controversial attempt to climb the Grand Teton on July 29, 1872, it was originally described as an "enclosure" by Langford in his now-famous 1873 article in *Scribner's Monthly.* According to Albert R. Ellingwood, who visited in 1923 when the site was in a near-pristine condition, this enclosure consisted of an elliptical arrangement of flat rocks placed on edge 7 by 9 feet across and 3 feet high. Even today one can see the remnants of the original circular arrangement, after a half-century of disturbance by a multitude of mountaineers. Speculation regarding the origin of this structure revolves around two alternatives: (1) built by Michaud, the only white man reported to have made an attempt to scale the Grand Teton prior to 1872; and (2) built by one or more Native Americans at a time ancient or recent (19th century), perhaps as a part of their "visionquest" ceremony. The latter possibility seems more probable. Regardless of its origin, the name has in the last half-century come to be applied to the entire peak, not just to the structure on the summit.

The depth of the Upper Saddle that separates the Enclosure from the Grand Teton is insufficient to qualify this western spur as a "peak." In this guidebook, its route descriptions have nevertheless been separated from those of the Grand Teton. Most of the 13 routes described here were not intended as routes to the top of the Grand Teton, although a few parties have continued to the summit via the Owen–Spalding route. Exceptions are the two Durrance routes, the Northwest Ridge and the Southwest Ridge, which were continued to the summit of the Grand Teton during their first ascents. When adverse conditions prevail, the Enclosure does serve as an alternative, easier summit when one has intended to climb the Grand Teton.

Thus, from most points of view the separation seems reasonable.

An ascent of the Enclosure is a worthwhile and recommended side trip during the course of an ascent or descent of its larger neighbor, the Grand Teton. From the Upper Saddle it requires only 15 minutes to scramble to its summit where one will be fully repaid with a spectacular view of the entire west face of the Grand Teton, extending from the Exum Ridge to the north ridge. Moreover, the unique summit structure is the only remaining prehistoric man-made structure to be found in the range.

CHRONOLOGY

South Couloir: July 29, 1872, James Stevenson, Nathaniel Langford

Northwest Ridge: August 8–10, 1938, Jack Durrance, Mike Davis

  var: **Kimbrough-Olson Crack:** July 21, 1976, Tom Kimbrough, Jim Olson

  var: **Jackson-Johnson:** August 17, 1994, Renny Jackson, Ron Johnson

Southwest Ridge: July 29, 1940, Jack Durrance, Henry Coulter, Fred Ayres

Black Ice Couloir: July 29, 1961, Ray Jacquot, Herb Swedlund

  var: **Alberich's Alley:** July 22, 1982, Renny Jackson, Peter Hollis

Enclosure Ice Couloir: July 22, 1962, Al Read, Peter Lev, James Greig

West Face: August 13, 1965, Leigh Ortenburger, John Whitesel

  var: **Right Edge:** August 1980, Kent Lugbill, Phil Pearl

North Face, Lowe Route: August 22, 1969, George Lowe, Mike Lowe; first free ascent August 5, 1977, Jim Donini, Rick Black

North Face, High Route: August 8, 1977, Charlie Fowler, Steve Glenn

Visionquest Couloir: August 10, 1981, Michael Stern, Steve Quinlan

North Face, Emotional Rescue: July 26, 1985, Renny Jackson, Steve Rickert; first free ascent about August 1, 1988, Alex Lowe, Jim Olson

  var: **Direct:** August 16, 1988, by Renny Jackson, Jim Woodmencey, Steve Rickert

South Face, Jim's Big Day: August 3, 1989, Jim Woodmencey, Renny Jackson

Lookin' For Trouble: July 4–5, 1991, Jim Beyer

Rhinelander-Jordan: April 16, 1994, Travis Jordan, Marcus Rhinelander

ROUTE 1. West Face. III, 5.7, A1. First ascent August 13, 1965, by Leigh Ortenburger and John Whitesel. See *Topo 44*

and *Photo 50.* The major portion of this face, which is bounded by the northwest and southwest ridges, lies above the main Valhalla Traverse ledge system, which could be used for approach to the middle of this route. The complete climb, however, begins in the lower reaches of Dartmouth Basin using the west ridge of the Enclosure to reach the Valhalla Traverse Ledge. This ridge lies south of the main stream draining the small icefield or glacier that nestles at the base of the lower west face of the Enclosure; it is separated from the lower extension of the southwest ridge by a rotten rock gully. Climb this ridge directly via a 5.4 chimney near the right edge of the initial broken face. Three towers will be encountered along this ridge, the latter two being bypassed on the south. Easy slabs are reached, leading onto the main upper west slope of the Enclosure at the Valhalla Traverse Ledge somewhat north of the southwest ridge. Looking up, one will see the next objective, a significant chimney with a large black chockstone in the middle of the upper vertical section of the face. The next 500 feet is ascended, mostly scrambling with considerable caution up a connecting series of ledges, slabs, and chimneys near the middle of the face; some rockfall may be encountered. Various routes can be found in this section with difficulty up to 5.6. Two small snowfields can be utilized or avoided, as desired, while following ledges generally covered with rocks and scree.

The difficult climbing commences on the vertical wall above the final scree ledge that leads left (north) toward the col behind the Great Tower of the northwest ridge. The chimney with the black chockstone is on the right (south) side of a small buttress projecting from the base of the face above. Traverse right on a ledge along the base of the face past the small buttress. Belay in the alcove on the right (south) side of the buttress, and climb the difficult chimney past the chockstone using a combination of techniques (5.7, A1). Continue up and slightly left (north) in a second chimney of similar difficulty to a stance below and to the right of an obvious hand traverse. Make this traverse (strenuous) 15 feet left to a second stance where an easier 40-foot section of free climbing leads to the base of an open book with cracks in its left wall. This short pitch is climbed using aid to a belay on the large scree-covered ledge at the top of the vertical portion of the west face of the Enclosure. The upper section of the face above, much of it composed of black rock, lies back at a more reasonable angle. The final chimney, now just above, is seen to be capped by a large black-bottomed chockstone. Climb one ropelength up to the right, then cut back into the chimney about 20 feet below the chockstone. Continue up the chimney and exit to the left to reach the final easy rock leading to the summit ridge. Scramble up to the square notch just right of the summit. Some difficulties will be found gaining the top of this notch. This entire route from the Valhalla Traverse

44. THE ENCLOSURE
     VALHALLA TRAVERSE-WEST FACE DIAGRAM
     (Refer to Canyons and Approaches, Valhalla Canyon, pp. 54–55)
 1. Corner of Northwest Ridge of the Grand (just past small bivouac sites)
 2. Continue around from corner until a small ridgelet is encountered.
 3. Ridgelet (shattered rock)
 4. Ice-filled bowl (early and late season)
 5. Narrowing, scree- and ice-covered ramp descends to the east.
 6. Gain bottom of First Ramp here (one pitch 5.6 rock) to access west side of Grandstand.
 7. Stay high and traverse across bowl to get to the Enclosure and Black Ice Couloirs.
 8. Climb 200-300 feet of rock (5.6 near the end) to the bottom of the Black Ice Couloir.
 9. Black Ice Couloir
10. Upper Saddle

Ledge in general stays in the middle of the face, never close to either of the bounding ridges.

Variation: Right Edge. III, 5.8. First ascent August 1980, by Kent Lugbill and Phil Pearl. This variation lies to the right (south) of the preceding main route and emerges onto the upper southwest ridge. Start from the Valhalla Traverse Ledge and climb and scramble easily up toward a prominent chimney in the right edge of the west face of the Enclosure. A total of four pitches are climbed to attain the southwest ridge crest. The second lead is the 5.8 chimney.

ROUTE 2. *Southwest Ridge.* III, 5.7. First ascent July 29, 1940, by Jack Durrance, Fred Ayres, and Henry Coulter. See *Topo 45.* This long route contains some excellent rock with many interesting features and is a very enjoyable climb. The ridge begins at about 9,600 feet in the lower reaches of Dartmouth Basin and forms the north rim of the basin. The first 2,200 feet are just scrambling. Because the Lower Saddle is a standard focal point for Teton climbing, it is perhaps the best starting point for this route. On the other hand, the approach from Cascade Canyon will reveal new vistas, and the lower Dartmouth Basin makes an excellent, beautiful, and wild camping site. Traces of previous human passage are rare, a stark contrast with the heavily travelled Garnet Canyon.

From the Lower Saddle one can see the horizontal section of the ridge about 500 feet below the Lower Saddle. Hike up the crest of the Lower Saddle until just short of the Black Dike, then contour left (northwest) toward the section of red rock that is immediately south of the Black Dike. Here descend an easy, loose-rock couloir below the cliffs that protect the southwest ridge, then continue west along the base of these cliffs, ultimately reaching the crest of the southwest ridge at the horizontal section. The first 1,000 feet of climbing on the ridge involve no serious difficulties, but the scrambling is interesting, especially if an effort is made to stay on the crest. This type of climbing ends abruptly at the second horizontal section where the Valhalla Traverse Ledge, leading to Valhalla Canyon, crosses the ridge. The cairn that marks this traverse can be seen from the Lower Saddle. Scramble on the left (north) side of the crest to pass the short, but steeper, portion above. The top of the slope above this step in the ridge meets directly the first major tower of the ridge several hundred feet above the Valhalla Traverse. Climb on the last boulder and start the roped climbing by stepping across to the rock on the right (south) side of the tower. Continue up and around the south side of this tower on a Wall Street–like shelf to a giant flake. Climb in behind this flake back to the left (north) to reach the main south wall of the tower. The short wall above and to the east is climbed by a 5.6 jam crack. The Wall Street–like ledge continues above this wall to an alcove below a small overhang at the end of the second pitch. The next lead goes up a small chimney for about 10 feet, then around the corner out to the right (south). Continue to the end of this

ropelength on the same ledge system from which this pitch started. The fourth pitch is up and around the corner to the right into a section of broken rock. The last 30 feet of the lead goes back up to the ridge crest in a classic 16-inch chimney; the first three and a half leads are all on the south side or edge of the first tower.

Now scramble for some 200 feet along the crest to a sharp, black-rock notch; this notch is not visible from the Lower Saddle. From the notch it is apparently possible to pass the wall above by going left (north) on ledges to an unattractive chimney. The best route here is to lead directly from the notch horizontally (south) across the vertical red-rock wall. This is a spectacular yet easy lead (5.4). After 80 feet one passes around the corner to a black-rock alcove for belaying. Climb out of the alcove via a jam crack into an easier section of broken rock. The third major tower, or step, in the ridge is reached by scrambling and is passed by the first obvious chimney on the left (north) side of the tower. This step, with its prominent overhang on the south and west faces, is perhaps the most obvious one when seen from the Lower Saddle. Two pitches up this chimney suffice to regain the crest. The two final steps in the ridge, the fourth and fifth, are climbed directly without great difficulty. The summit of the Enclosure is then easily reached.

ROUTE 3. *South Face, Jim's Big Day.* III, 5.10-. First ascent August 3, 1989, by Jim Woodmencey and Renny Jackson. See *Topo 46* and *Photo 41.* From the Lower Saddle the upper portion of the southwest ridge of the Enclosure has the appearance of a smooth slab with a large overhang at its top. This six-pitch route ascends the middle of the slab and escapes through the left side of the overhang. This is one of the most spectacular and scenic rock pitches in the range. As in the Owen–Spalding route, proceed from the Lower Saddle to the base of the Needle, and then turn off to the left toward the southwest ridge. Pass below the small rock knob that is seen up and to the left of the couloir (snow in early season) that goes up along the west side of the Needle. Cross the gully on the far (west) side to gain the section of good gray rock. The first pitch is a short lead (5.8) up onto a ledge system that heads west easily toward the southwest ridge. Move the belay 70 feet farther along this ledge system to the base of a wall with a vertical crack system that leads up the right (east) edge of a large slab toward the right edge of the main overhang. The next lead (140 feet) starts on a face (5.8) and passes a small overhang to a series of cracks leading to a belay ledge. This initial section can evidently be avoided by easier climbing up and around to the left (west). The third long lead (160 feet) goes straight up the wall, just left of a left-facing corner to a belay at the beginning of a second left-facing corner. Now climb this short corner (60 feet, 5.8) to a belay for the next major lead, at the right edge of the large overhang. This fifth pitch is severe, angling out to the left (west) using a crack just below the overhang and heading toward the small ledge on the skyline ridge crest at

200-300' of scrambling and easy 5th class
brings one to the top of the SOUTHWEST RIDGE

⑫ easy 5th class

JIM'S BIG DAY
overhang

5.6

⑪

5.7 wide

large flake

5.7

5.7 wide

⑩ big broken ledge

5.4 large black blocks

5.4

to roof pitch of JIM'S
BIG DAY

5.4

⑨

5.4

⑧

5.6 blocks, chimneys

loose/wet 5.10 →

⑦

large scree ledge

easy 5th class

⑥

5.4 red rock wall

Scramble 100' to
black rock notch

⑤

friction 5.7

④

**45. THE ENCLOSURE
SOUTHWEST RIDGE
III, 5.7**

Scramble 100' to crest

5.6

5.9

③

5.8

5.7

wide

5.7

brown slab

off-route ramp

flake

5.4

⑤ 5.6

② ST

5.6

5.7 hand

5.7 stem/squeeze

finger traverse
triangular pillar

SMOOTH
ORANGE
WALL

5.6

5.9 hand

① large flake

140'

LB/fingers

5.7

5.9+ fingers

Scramble up and north from
VALHALLA TRAVERSE cairn

Scramble up from large cairn
on VALHALLA TRAVERSE to
last boulder and step right

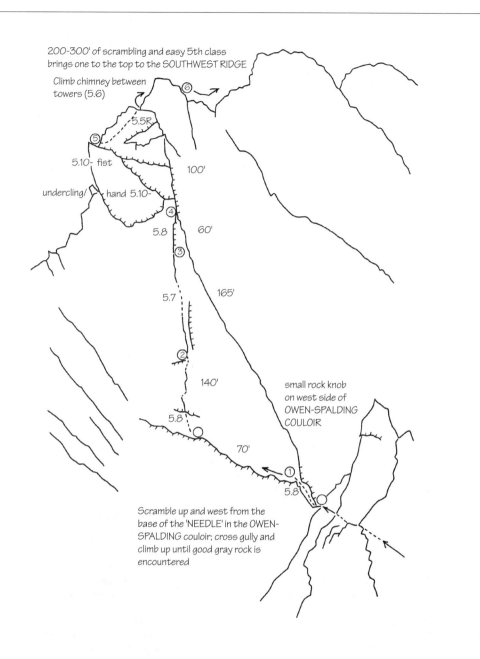

200-300' of scrambling and easy 5th class
brings one to the top to the SOUTHWEST RIDGE

Climb chimney between
towers (5.6)

⑥

5.5R

⑤

5.10- fist   100'

undercling/   hand 5.10-

④

5.8   60'

③

5.7   165'

②

140'

small rock knob
on west side of
OWEN-SPALDING
COULOIR

5.8

70'

①

5.8

Scramble up and west from the
base of the 'NEEDLE' in the OWEN-
SPALDING couloir; cross gully and
climb up until good gray rock is
encountered

46. THE ENCLOSURE, SOUTH FACE
JIM'S BIG DAY
III, 5.10-

the top of the overhang. This strenuous crack starts as a hand and undercling problem and ends as a fist crack; the rock is excellent. From the small ledge, face climb out and right up the slab (no protection, 5.5) to the ridge crest. Then finish by climbing a chimney between the last towers of the southwest ridge and scramble to the top of the Enclosure.
ROUTE 4. ☞ *South Couloir.* II, 3.0. First ascent July 29, 1872, by James Stevenson and Nathaniel Langford. From the Lower Saddle of the Grand Teton the Enclosure is seen to harbor on its south slope a large couloir, snow-filled during much of the season, extending from Dartmouth Basin below the Lower Saddle to the Upper Saddle. This couloir can be entered from the rocks above the Black Dike and below the Needle and climbed directly toward the Upper Saddle. This, however, is not recommended because in early season the snow in the couloir is steep with no runout, and hence dangerous, and in late season, steep, loose rock will be encountered. The better alternative is to use the Owen–Spalding route until only about 100 vertical feet short of the Upper Saddle. Instead of continuing all the way to the Saddle, turn up and left (northwest) and scramble in easy boulders and chutes on the southeast side of the Enclosure to the summit. If ascending this route during a descent from the Grand Teton, remember that the ascent of the Enclosure does not start at the Upper Saddle because there is a vertical rock step in the connecting ridge. Descend from the Upper Saddle about 100 feet to the southwest, along what has become almost a trail in the standard Owen–Spalding descent, until around the south side of the vertical step, and then scramble up the southeast side to the summit.
ROUTE 5. *Black Ice Couloir.* IV, AI3+, 5.7. First ascent July 29, 1961, by Raymond Jacquot and Herbert Swedlund. See *Photos 47, 48, 49* and *50.* This relatively long and, for the most part, narrow couloir, which sharply separates the Enclosure from the west face of the Grand Teton, has in the past 30 years become the best known of the Teton ice climbs, an American classic. This sweep of ice curves upward for 1,200 feet along the eastern edge of the imposing north buttress of the Enclosure. The Black Ice Couloir proper, where current climbing interest centers, consists of the upper two of four icefields on this part of the mountain. The lowest ice is found just above the floor of Valhalla Canyon and extends up toward the broad bench at the east end of the Valhalla Traverse Ledge. The second section consists of an easy ice slope and the rock walls above that guard the entrance to the main third icefield. The final fourth section is the steepest, narrowing considerably before meeting the Upper Saddle. The most difficult climbing is in this final section. The nature of the ascent depends on the time of year and conditions; in early season a portion of the couloir may have a snow cover, but crampons will always be desired.

The history of ice climbing in the Teton Range very nearly begins with the ascent of the Black Ice Couloir. In earlier years little pure ice climbing had been done, other

than what was normally required on the Teton Glacier to reach the base of the north face or north ridge of the Grand Teton. Numerous climbers had peered down into the upper reaches of the Black Ice Couloir from the Upper Saddle, but it was long believed that the couloir was too dangerous to be considered seriously as a climbing route. The first attempt, on July 7, 1958, seemed to verify this opinion: Kenneth Weeks, Yvon Chouinard, and Frank Garneau started at the very bottom but retreated from just above the first section because of a significant fall of rock and ice fragments. A second attempt on June 26, 1961, by Fred Beckey and Charlie Bell also failed.

The successful climb by Jacquot and Swedlund, credited with the first ascent in 1961, bypassed a considerable portion of the ice, entered the couloir halfway up the main or third icefield, and completed the final crux section to reach the Upper Saddle from the north for the first time. Their route started from the right (west) end of the Second Shelf of the West Face of the Grand Teton (see *Grand Teton, Route 38,* earlier) and moved up and east along this shelf for about 500 feet on wet slabs and ice patches past some smooth yellow buttresses to an area of black rock. Two moderate rock pitches up and back to the right (west) then led onto the Third Shelf, which is the edge of the main third icefield. The second ascent, on August 18, 1963, by Kenneth Weeks and Jim May, followed this line of the first ascent. When George Lowe and Mike Lowe pioneered the *Black Ice–West Face variation* (see *Grand Teton, Route 38,* earlier) on July 23, 1967, they were the first to link together the first three icefields, entering the main icefield near its base. The modern approach into the very bottom of the third (main) icefield from the Valhalla Traverse was first done on August 10, 1968, by Leigh Ortenburger and Rick Reese. One year later on July 22, 1969, George Lowe and Yvon Chouinard climbed the couloir in its entirety, all four icefields, from the floor of Valhalla Canyon. Note that this lower approach is not recommended because the climber is at risk from objective hazards for a greater period of time. The more modern route, which enters at the very beginning of the main icefield, is given in the main description that follows. On one occasion, the base of the main (third) icefield was reached by rappelling from the Upper Saddle, a novel and devious scheme to start the climb.

The current standard approach to this route is as follows. Take the Valhalla Traverse Ledge (see *Valhalla Canyon*) to the corner of the northwest ridge of the Enclosure. A faint trail continues down along the ledge for a short distance until a small ridge that forms the right (west) edge of a small bowl is met. Traverse across this bowl for a ropelength, maintaining elevation; the rock is very rotten in this area. Continue traversing for another ropelength, again maintaining elevation, to the west edge of the Enclosure Ice Couloir. On the far (east) side of this ice couloir two small, diagonal shelves will be seen at the base of the impressive

Enclosure north buttress. The object now is to traverse up and around the base of this buttress to the lower of these two diagonal shelves. Climb for two pitches up this shelf, with the final 20 feet being the most difficult (5.7), to the start of the ice climbing at the base of the main icefield.

The number of leads on the ice is about eight, depending on how it is climbed. The angle of the ice in the main icefield is about 50°. Belay anchors for this section are usually found in the fractured rock along the right (west) edge of the ice; most of these belays can be established under overhangs or in niches and so are somewhat protected from rockfall. Climb to the narrow upper couloir leading to the Upper Saddle from the upper right corner of the main icefield. At the crux in this section the couloir narrows considerably and steepens to 70° but only for 20 feet or so. Climbers venturing into this couloir should recognize the considerable danger from rockfall, both natural and that which is initiated by climbers on the Owen–Spalding route. Timing and speed can minimize these dangers. The climb should begin at a very early hour; the Upper Saddle should be reached before the sun strikes the west and northwest faces of the Grand Teton. The lower portion, where most of the rockfall is funnelled, should be climbed as rapidly as possible. For protection on the ice, ice screws are required and in addition to the usual rack, pitons may be found useful in the poor rock along the main icefield. See *American Alpine Journal*, 13, no. 1 (1962), pp. 216–220.

Variation: Alberich's Alley. IV, AI4, 5.9. First ascent July 22, 1982, by Peter Hollis and Renny Jackson. See *Photo 47.* This major variation starts, as in the *Grand Teton, Route 38, Black Ice–West Face variation*, at the base of the main icefield of the Black Ice Couloir. However, instead of climbing the icefield up and left toward the rock of the upper West Face route, this variation heads toward the regular Black Ice crux and ascends a thin ice runnel to the left (east) of the upper Black Ice Couloir; this runnel or ice chute is in the first chimney system to the right (south) of the West Face route.

The initial lead goes up the narrow ice chute, which becomes vertical for a 20-foot section, to reach a chockstone in the chimney. Climb in behind this chockstone and continue up and slightly left on very steep ice and rock (5.9) toward the giant jammed chockstone. Climb from under this huge boulder on thin ice out to the left to gain the southern end of the main bench that cuts across the middle of the West Face route. Take the *Grand Teton, Route 38, Traverse to Upper Saddle variation,* from this bench out to the right to the Upper Saddle or climb directly up, past another chockstone, and exit in an ice chute that leads to a point located 100 feet to the east of the Black Ice finish. A total of 600 feet of climbing are involved from the beginning of the narrow ice runnel to the Upper Saddle. This is a good technical climb.

ROUTE 6. **Visionquest Couloir.** IV, AI3+, 5.8. First ascent August 10, 1981, by Michael Stern and Stephen Quinlan.

See *Photo 47.* Directly across the Black Ice Couloir from the West Face route on the Grand Teton is the Visionquest Couloir, a narrow ice gully that provides 600 feet of excellent climbing. Take the Black Ice Couloir (*Route 5*) for about 600 feet to the top of the main (third) icefield and cut right (west) into the steep initial chimney of the couloir. The first two ropelengths are the most difficult, consisting initially of 40 feet of mixed rock and ice runnels (5.8), followed by a narrow ribbon of steep 60° ice. This narrow section leads to a wide ice sheet at about 55°. The second 300 feet ascends the left margin of this ice slope, continuing to a large chockstone jammed in the gully. Climb around this chockstone on the right and continue up, partly on ice, bearing right (west) winding around to the northwest ridge just below the summit. Gain the summit from the west. Once the initial couloir has been entered from the Black Ice Couloir, the route is difficult to lose. This is an excellent climb and is slightly more difficult than the standard Black Ice Couloir route. Conditions should be carefully selected for the climb; major rockfalls have been observed in this chute.

ROUTE 7. **Lookin' for Trouble.** V, 5.11, A3. First ascent July 4–5, 1991, by Jim Beyer, solo. This impressive route, the hardest thus far completed on the Grand Teton or Enclosure, was an exceptional *tour-de-force* by this talented climber from Colorado. No bolts were placed on the first ascent. Approach this imposing wall via the Valhalla Traverse, passing the Enclosure Couloir and then continuing up and around toward the beginning of the Black Ice Couloir. The route begins just around the prow from Emotional Rescue on the northeast facet of the wall. Look for two ramps that slant up and right (west), the lower one being white and the upper one black. After 30 feet of mixed climbing, stiff (5.10+) face climbing leads up and right to the black ramp to get started on the first pitch. See *Topo 47* and *Photo 47* for the somewhat complex route description from this point on. Note that sling belays were used on the first, second, third, and fifth pitches. On the first ascent the initial three pitches were climbed during the first day with pitch number one taking about 6½ hours. A bivouac was made at the base of the climb after leaving fixed ropes to the top of the third pitch. The climb was then completed the next day to the summit of the Enclosure in 14 hours, with the fourth pitch taking the longest (five to six hours). This route joins Emotional Rescue at the base of the eighth pitch and then follows that line to the top. For protection Beyer used two complete sets of Friends, two sets of TCUs, three sets of wired nuts (many small), a few pitons, and copperheads. Note that in the topo *FH* refers to "fixed head."

ROUTE 8. **North Face, Emotional Rescue.** IV, 5.10-, A2, or IV, 5.11. First ascent July 26, 1985, by Renny Jackson and Steve Rickert; first free ascent about August 1, 1988, by Alex Lowe and Jim Olson. See *Topo 48* and *Photo 49*. On the north side of the Enclosure, between the Black Ice Couloir and the

Enclosure Ice Couloir, is a huge buttress of massive excellent yellow Teton rock. The formidable lower portion rises vertically from the junction of the two couloirs, with major faces on its eastern, northern, and western exposures. This climb is located on a line to the left of the earlier Lowe and High Routes near the left-hand prow of the northwest facet of the buttress. It starts at the upper of the two diagonal ramps used for entry into the Black Ice Couloir. Because there are natural lines of drainage on this face, this route should be climbed in conditions as dry as possible; with any ice, it would be very difficult. A total of 12 pitches are required, with 8 on the initial steep buttress. Use the Valhalla Traverse from the Lower Saddle to the Enclosure Ice Couloir, then angle up and left to near the northern margin of the face of the buttress. The initial double cracks pitch rises directly above. The details of the route are shown on *Topo 48*. Note that hanging belays are needed at the end of the second, third, and fifth pitches. The Lowe Route, described later, is intersected in the sixth pitch; the two routes, however, have distinct finishes, as is shown on the topos. For protection, take a standard rack to 3½ inches with RPs and small wireds.

Variation: Direct. IV, 5.10-. First ascent August 16, 1988, by Renny Jackson, Jim Woodmencey, and Steve Rickert. See *Topo 48* and *Photo 49*. This variation follows the drainage line of this part of the face, while the original Emotional Rescue route avoids it to the right. Consequently, very dry conditions are needed for this variation. From the belay at the end of the third lead, face climb out from the left side of the overhang to gain a 5.9 crack. This crack is then followed to a belay under a double overhang. Pass the double overhang above (5.10-) on the right, then move left to another 5.9 crack leading up to a belay ledge. The third lead passes another overhang by following a 5.8 hand traverse to the right and then goes up a 5.7 right-facing corner at the top of which the original route is rejoined at the end of its seventh pitch.

ROUTE 9. North Face, Lowe Route. IV, 5.9, A2, or IV, 5.10. First ascent August 22, 1969, by George Lowe and Mike Lowe; first free ascent August 5, 1977, by Jim Donini and Rick Black. The first four pitches had been climbed earlier on the first attempt on August 6, 1969, by George Lowe, Jack Turner, and Leigh Ortenburger. See *Topo 49* and *Photo 48*. This pioneer route, the first established on the impressive north face of the Enclosure, was, in its day, probably the most difficult route on either the Grand Teton or the Enclosure. A mixed climb like the other two routes on this face of the Enclosure, it follows in part a major drainage, so climbers are advised to try for conditions as dry as possible. The initial attempt approached this climb from Valhalla Canyon, which added a considerable amount of climbing to a very serious and strenuous route; the first-ascent party used the standard Valhalla Traverse from the Lower Saddle.

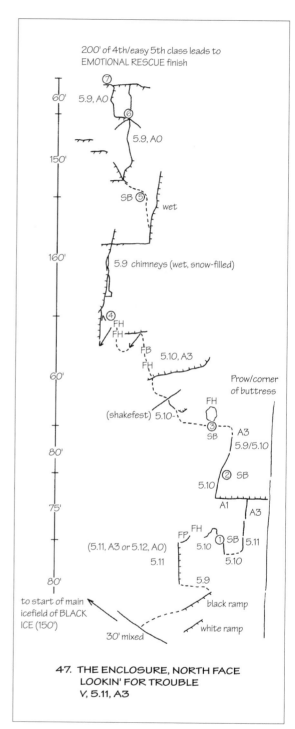

47. THE ENCLOSURE, NORTH FACE
LOOKIN' FOR TROUBLE
V, 5.11, A3

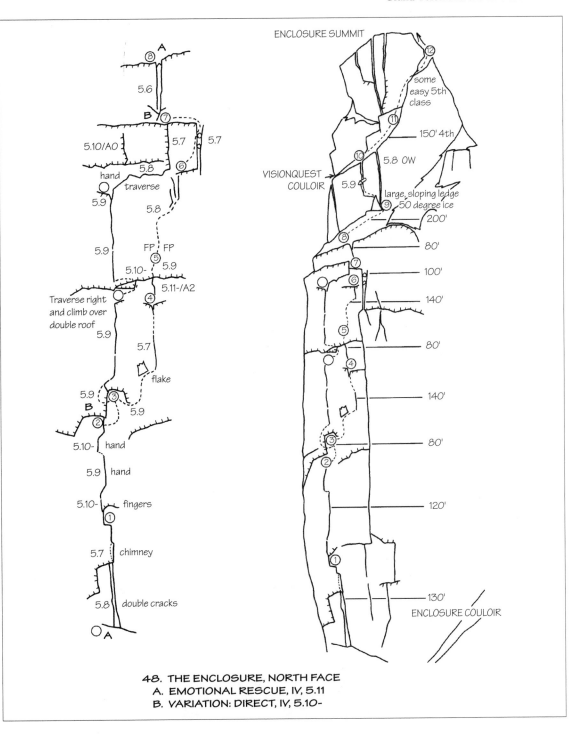

48. THE ENCLOSURE, NORTH FACE
A. EMOTIONAL RESCUE, IV, 5.11
B. VARIATION: DIRECT, IV, 5.10-

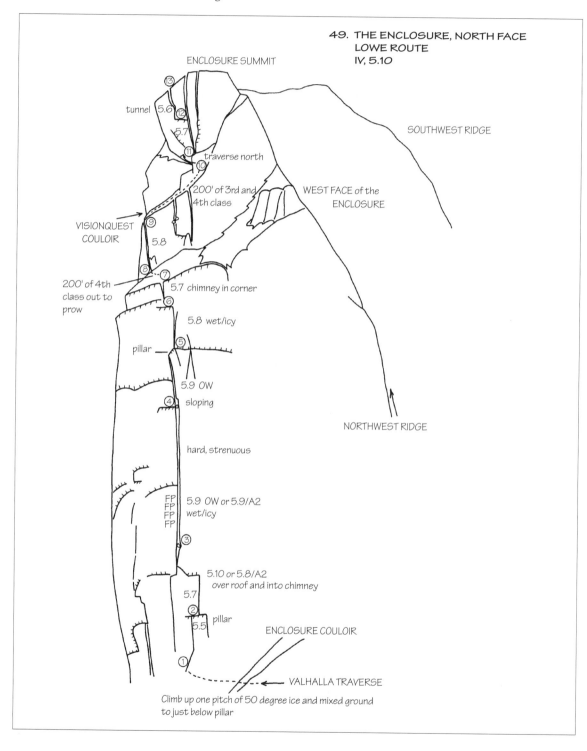

49. THE ENCLOSURE, NORTH FACE
LOWE ROUTE
IV, 5.10

ENCLOSURE SUMMIT

⑬

tunnel 5.6 ⑫

5.7   SOUTHWEST RIDGE

⑪
⑩ traverse north

200' of 3rd and   WEST FACE of the
4th class   ENCLOSURE

VISIONQUEST   ⑨
COULOIR
5.8

⑧ ⑦
200' of 4th
class out to   5.7 chimney in corner
prow   ⑥

5.8 wet/icy

pillar   ⑤

5.9 OW

⑭ sloping

NORTHWEST RIDGE

hard, strenuous

FP   5.9 OW or 5.9/A2
FP   wet/icy
FP
FP
⑬

5.10 or 5.8/A2
over roof and into chimney
5.7

⑫ pillar
5.5

ENCLOSURE COULOIR

①

VALHALLA TRAVERSE

Climb up one pitch of 50 degree ice and mixed ground
to just below pillar

After reaching the Enclosure Ice Couloir on the Valhalla Traverse, climb at least one pitch of ice before traversing up toward this crack and chimney system, the most obvious line on the face. The details of the route are shown on *Topo 49*. The top of the main buttress is reached at the end of the seventh lead. The final section to the summit was attacked directly via the leftmost (eastern) of three chimneys that penetrate the summit block. A tunnel in this chimney provides a neat ending to an outstanding mountaineering route. Take a small piton selection, plus a standard rack with many small nuts and other protection to 5 inches.

ROUTE 10. *North Face, High Route*. IV, 5.9. First ascent August 8, 1977, by Charlie Fowler and Steve Glenn. See *Topo 50* and *Photos 47* and *49*. This route ascends the crack and chimney system at the intersection of the main north buttress of the Enclosure with the northwest ridge of the Grand Teton. The High Route, which stays completely to the right (west) of the earlier Lowe Route, is in the same category of mountaineering difficulty as the two other routes (Lowe and Emotional Rescue) on the north face of the Enclosure. Mixed climbing including 50° ice is involved, and this route is perhaps more prone to icing and wetness than the other two. The Valhalla Traverse from the Lower Saddle is the recommended approach to the bottom of the Enclosure Ice Couloir. The first-ascent party began by climbing up and right from near the start of the Lowe Route (see earlier), but it is also possible to climb about two pitches of ice in the Enclosure Ice Couloir and then cut left to the start of the route. The details of the route are shown on *Topo 50*. Similar to the other two routes, eight difficult pitches are required to reach the top of the main buttress. At this point the same downsloping ledge crossed by the Lowe Route and the Emotional Rescue route is reached but not crossed. Instead, it is followed out to the right (west) for four pitches past a 150-foot ice apron to reach the crest of the northwest ridge. During very dry seasons most of this ice melts away, and what remains can be avoided by climbing along the side of it. From the northwest ridge some 300 feet of scrambling up the upper west face of the Enclosure leads to the summit. For protection take a standard rack to 3½ inches.

ROUTE 11. *Enclosure Ice Couloir*. IV, AI3, 5.7 (to summit of the Enclosure), or **III, AI3, 5.6** (with rappel descent). First ascent July 22, 1962, by Al Read, Peter Lev, and James Greig. See *Photo 47*. On the north side of the Enclosure is a prominent ice couloir diagonaling up to the right (west) to meet the northwest ridge at the notch that separates the first great tower of the steep section of the ridge from the upper ridge. The route has become one of the three most popular ice climbs in the range. This broad couloir, conspicuous from the summit of Mount Owen, begins at the east end of the Valhalla Traverse Ledge on the north face of the Enclosure. The standard and recommended approach (also that of the first-ascent party) is from the Lower Saddle via the Valhalla Traverse (see *Vallhalla Canyon*). Proceed

along the Valhalla Traverse Ledge only about halfway along the north side of the Enclosure. Instead of following the ledge downward along its narrow continuation, climb eastward horizontally or slightly upward in an area of broken rock and ledges. Continue around the corner to the left (east) and into the ice couloir about 200 feet above its beginning. If approaching from Cascade and Valhalla Canyons (rarely done), one can climb diagonally up and right (west) across the second icefield (see *Route 5*) onto the rocks just above and left of the extreme bottom end of this ice couloir. These rocks, while not pleasant, lead to the lower reaches of the couloir and the start of the ice climb. In early season the ice in the couloir may continue down into a narrow chimney that can be climbed.

The angle of the ice in the couloir is about 50° and during early season it can be snow climbing, for the most part. Ice screws are useful for belaying. Some falling ice blocks and rocks must be expected, but the danger is less than in the Black Ice Couloir. Depending on ropelength and choice of belay stances, six or seven pitches of climbing are involved in this route. Once the notch is reached, follow the upper Northwest Ridge (see *Route 13*) to the summit of the Enclosure. This excellent mixed route is highly recommended. If a shorter climb is desired or if the hour is late, descent can be made via rappel down the west face of the Enclosure to regain the Valhalla Traverse Ledge. Start by climbing down from the col in a gully to the south for approximately 200 feet, until the first of the rappel stations can be seen. See *American Alpine Journal*, 13, no. 2 (1963), pp. 487–489.

ROUTE 12. *Rhinelander–Jordan*. III, WI3+, 5.6, A1. First ascent April 16, 1994, by Travis Jordan and Marcus Rhinelander. This is another one of the Teton ice lines whose existence is somewhat fleeting. See *Photo 47*. On the first ascent this route was discovered accidentally; it probably exists as an ice line only during brief time periods in the early spring. To find the start of the climb, proceed around the Valhalla Traverse Ledge to the section that descends steeply down from the bowl located just around the corner from the northwest ridge. Traverse across this bowl and stay high near the base of the steep rock. At about the point where one turns the corner and catches a glimpse of the Enclosure Couloir, two parallel cracks can be seen going up to the south. Climb the left crack (5.6) to a ledge and then on up past a fixed piton to a belay on the left at the base of a slabby area. Proceed up the slabs to the base of the first ice pitch. Steep ice will be encountered on this lead and the belay is located in an alcove. Continue up the gully and belay in another alcove located on the left. The fifth pitch contained an overhanging chockstone that required aid to pass. Three more mixed pitches bring one to an unusual keyhole finish and the top of the climb. *Route 13* can then be used to get to the summit of the Enclosure. This combination is an excellent alpine Grade IV.

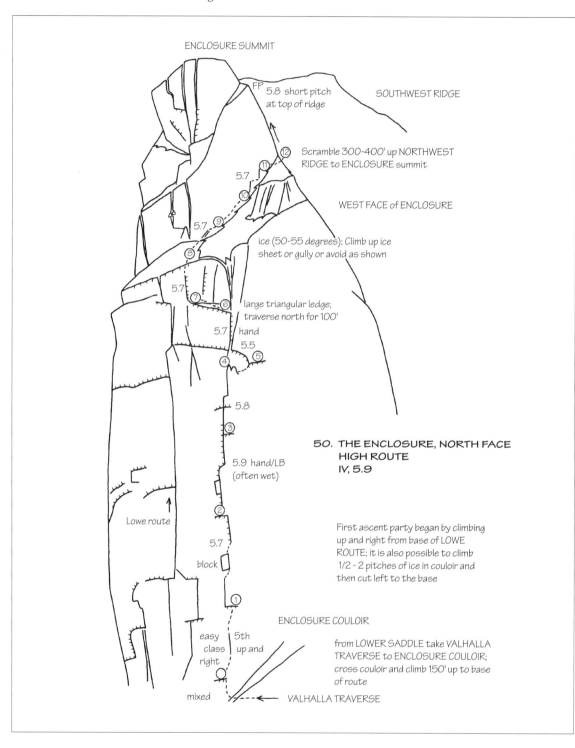

ENCLOSURE SUMMIT

FP 5.8 short pitch
at top of ridge

SOUTHWEST RIDGE

⑫ Scramble 300-400' up NORTHWEST
⑪   RIDGE to ENCLOSURE summit
5.7
⑩

WEST FACE of ENCLOSURE

5.7 ⑨

ice (50-55 degrees); Climb up ice
sheet or gully or avoid as shown

⑧

5.7 ⑦ ⑥ large triangular ledge;
              traverse north for 100'

5.7 hand
5.5
④   ⑤

5.8

③

5.9 hand/LB
(often wet)

**50. THE ENCLOSURE, NORTH FACE
HIGH ROUTE
IV, 5.9**

②

Lowe route

First ascent party began by climbing
up and right from base of LOWE
ROUTE; it is also possible to climb
1/2 - 2 pitches of ice in couloir and
then cut left to the base

5.7

block

①

ENCLOSURE COULOIR

easy | 5th
class | up and
right

from LOWER SADDLE take VALHALLA
TRAVERSE to ENCLOSURE COULOIR;
cross couloir and climb 150' up to base
of route

mixed ← VALHALLA TRAVERSE

ROUTE 13. Northwest Ridge. V, 5.7. First ascent August 8–10, 1938, by Jack Durrance and Michael Davis. See *Topo 51* for upper section. This ridge, one of the major features of the Grand Teton, has the misfortune of ending at the Enclosure; to reach the summit of the Grand Teton, as was done on the first ascent, one must descend to the Upper Saddle before continuing. The ridge contains three distinct sections that, if done in their entirety, produce the longest climb in the park. The initial part is the longest, a roughly horizontal section rising from Cascade Canyon, containing several subpeaks, towers, and pinnacles, before ending at the southwest corner of Valhalla Canyon where a fault cuts across the ridge at a vertical step. This fault divides the poor rock of this lower, initial section from the high-quality rock of the upper two-thirds of the ridge. The second section marks the beginning of the difficult climbing, rising steeply to meet first a talus slope and then a long section of low-angle, downsloping slabs that ends at the corner of the north end of the Valhalla Traverse Ledge. The final section, which rises abruptly above the traverse ledge, holds much excellent rock providing enjoyable but not excessively difficult climbing. The major tower on this section is separated by a notch, at the head of the Enclosure Ice Couloir, from the uppermost ridge, which ends not at the summit but, instead, veers off to meet the southwest ridge 150 feet below the summit. This final section has gained some popularity as another fine climb available from the Lower Saddle, using the Valhalla Traverse Ledge. The following description is for the complete ridge; if taking the traverse ledge, use the part of the description given in the third and fourth paragraphs below.

Follow the Cascade Canyon trail to a point just below the forks. Cross Cascade Creek and bushwhack directly up the north slope of the first and lowest tower on the ridge. Follow a large shelf up to the right-hand (northwest) ridge of the tower. From the end of this shelf a near-vertical pitch up solid rock leads to an awkward chimney. Above this, scramble to the summit of the first tower, Peak 10,405. The second tower, Peak 10,640+, is climbed from the col to the south by a shelf or large, left-facing corner system leading up and left for two pitches. A steep downclimb leads to the col between the second and third towers. The third tower is climbed directly from this col, traversing left (east) out on a diagonal ledge to a band of black rock that allows a traverse back to the right on a small ledge. This gives access to a second ledge leading left toward the summit of the tower.

There is little or no notch behind this tower, and mere scrambling takes one past two small gendarmes to the Rabbit Ears. The first "ear," the more northerly one, overhangs on all four sides and is one of the more difficult pinnacles in the park. The first three ascents of this ridge bypassed this "ear." For details, see *Rabbit Ears.* The second, or south, "ear" is much easier. The tower, or step, south of the Rabbit Ears must be contoured on the west side in order to reach the col beyond. The remainder of the horizontal section of the ridge involves indistinct towers and steps of no great difficulty.

The notch at the base of the initially steep second section of the ridge (at the south end of the horizontal section) contains rotten rock, and a small rotten red pinnacle rises directly above. A fault passes through this notch, and the character of the rock changes abruptly. This fault extends from Valhalla Canyon around the base of the west side of the Enclosure, ending at the lower, western extension of the Black Dike on the south side of the Grand Teton. Climb directly up the pinnacle from the notch to a belay position below a large flake. Above the flake is a 10-foot overhang with a steep, short face below. With protection in place climb to the right-hand edge of the overhang, where it narrows. A handhold will be found on the face above the overhang, and this allows the passage of this 5.7 pitch. Steep but easy solid rock then leads directly above to the 300-foot talus slope. A cliff band above this slope can be climbed directly at its left (north) corner up chimneys to the slabs above. Or, from the upper right corner of this talus slope, two 60-foot pitches up cracks lead to easy scrambling up the scree-covered slabs for about 500 feet. The slabs end at the Lower Saddle–Valhalla Traverse Ledge, which lies at the base of the first Great Tower on the steep third section of the northwest ridge. If the entire northwest ridge is addressed as a two-day climb, this large ledge provides a good bivouac site, because water can be found (except for late season) 100 yards to the right (south) of the ridge, and a small site has been constructed.

The west face of the Great Tower above is marked by two sections of black rock that are about one-quarter and halfway up the tower. Start the tower at the first reasonable crack (it has the appearance of a lieback crack) south of the north corner of the ridge. The first 20 feet of this lead is difficult, but the angle eases, and after another 60 to 80 feet climb slightly to the left. This pitch ends with a short lieback and easier black rock. Then scramble for three ropelengths over excellent rock. Ultimately, as high as possible, a traverse must be made up and around the right edge of the face into a shallow gully that leads back toward the crest. This gully should be reached only about 50 feet short of its top. Ascend the left side of the gully to the top, cross to the right, climb a short chimney, and traverse around the south side of the tower to a long, large crack or chimney that leads to the crest of the ridge at the col behind the tower. This is the same col that is reached from the other (north) side via the Enclosure Ice Couloir. Attaining the summit of the Great Tower, a solid yellow monolith, is part of the complete Northwest Ridge route, so scramble back to the tower, which is climbed by its south face. There apparently is no rappel anchor at the top of this tower.

The col at the base of the second tower (actually a buttress) is easily reached after negotiating the descent from

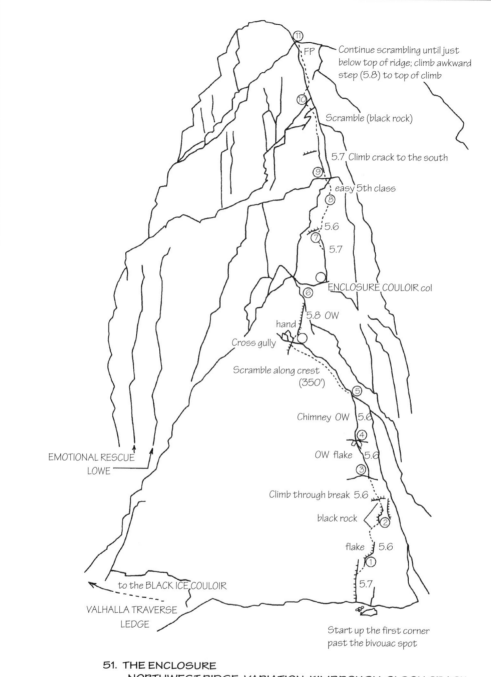

Continue scrambling until just
below top of ridge; climb awkward
step (5.8) to top of climb

FP

Scramble (black rock)

5.7 Climb crack to the south

easy 5th class

5.6

5.7

ENCLOSURE COULOIR col

5.8 OW

hand

Cross gully

Scramble along crest
(350')

Chimney OW 5.6

OW flake 5.6

Climb through break 5.6

black rock

flake 5.6

5.7

EMOTIONAL RESCUE
LOWE

to the BLACK ICE COULOIR

VALHALLA TRAVERSE
LEDGE

Start up the first corner
past the bivouac spot

51. THE ENCLOSURE
    NORTHWEST RIDGE, VARIATION: KIMBROUGH-OLSON CRACK
    IV, 5.8

the Great Tower. The first two ascents passed this buttress on the right, traversing beneath the overhanging face to a difficult water-worn crack that was ascended to reach the ridge behind the buttress. The better alternative is to climb it directly, up the obvious ledge and crack that slants up and left from the base of the buttress. The rock here is outstanding. One lead up along this crack (5.7) and the face just to the left places the party beneath an overhang. Pass this overhang on the right, using beautiful holds, and ascend the short face above to easier ground, which again leads to the crest behind the buttress; this overhang can also be passed on the left. The third tower, just a step in the ridge, is climbed by the crack system on the right side of the face. A tricky horizontal step leads to an awkward overhang; exit to the right onto easier rock. Then scramble to the black-rock region just beneath the summit of the Enclosure. The northwest ridge does not lead directly to the summit but ends at the southwest ridge, about 150 feet below the top. Before reaching the southwest ridge it is advisable to traverse left under a yellow wall to a black-rock talus slope leading to the crest of the southwest ridge just below and south of the summit of the Enclosure. Alternatively, scramble up to the final wall, where 5.8 moves on good rock lead around to the right of a fixed piton and the top of the climb. It is then but a short walk to the true summit of the Enclosure. See *American Alpine Journal*, 3, no. 3 (1939), pp. 364–365, illus.; *Dartmouth Mountaineering Club Journal*, 1938, pp. 29–36.

Variation: Kimbrough–Olson Crack. IV, 5.8. First ascent July 21, 1976, by Tom Kimbrough and Jim Olson. See *Topo 51* and *Photos 49* and *50*. From the Valhalla Traverse Ledge, instead of using the first crack to the right (south) of the corner of the ridge, this five-pitch variation takes the first corner around to the left (north) of the bivouac spot. Climb this vertical right-facing corner (5.7) to an easier right-trending flake. The second lead goes up this flake (5.6) onto face climbing on black rock to a belay at the beginning of a second flake, which forms a right-facing corner. The next pitch ascends the edge of this flake and continues up a steep, black-rock face (5.6) through a break in the wall. From the belay ledge, go for two leads straight up an offwidth flake past some large flakes, and end with an offwidth chimney. The angle eases here and simple scrambling up and slightly left for 300 feet leads to a shallow gully that diagonals up from right to left. At the gully the main route can be rejoined around on the right (south) side of the Great Tower. It is possible, however, to continue up in a hand crack that then leads to a 5.8 offwidth to gain the main route at a higher level.

Variation: Jackson–Johnson. IV, 5.8. First ascent August 17, 1994, by Renny Jackson and Ron Johnson. This is a two-pitch variation to *Route 13* that is on excellent rock located on the south side of the ridge. From the col at the top of the Enclosure Couloir, climb down the gully to the south (as if going down to the rappel; *see* Route 11) approximately 100 feet until it is possible to scramble up and left to the base of an amazing wide crack (would require cleaning) that is visible from the Valhalla Traverse far below. Two pitches (5.8) were then climbed up the right-facing corner system to the east of the crack. *Route 13* is joined and followed to the summit of the Enclosure.

DISAPPOINTMENT PEAK FROM THE SOUTHEAST

Garnet Canyon to Glacier Gulch

Glencoe Spire (CA. 12,320)

(0.3 mi S of Grand Teton)

Map: Grand Teton

This spire, one of two large towers on the south flank of the Grand Teton, lies due west of Teepe Pillar and is about the same altitude. The name is derived from the home town of the members of the first-ascent party. In the early days of the park, this spire was known as the "Red Sentinel," and the col, formed by the weathering out of the Black Dike between this spire and the Grand Teton, was "Sentinel Col." The switch in names is probably due to Hans Kraus, who in 1941 started his attempts on the pinnacle that is now known as the Red Sentinel. From Teepe Col, Glencoe Spire appears difficult but is actually a short, easy climb up from Glencoe Col at the base of the Underhill Ridge. The south face extends for almost 1,000 feet from the moraines of the Middle Teton Glacier. This face is flanked on the left (west) during most of the season by a waterfall draining the Stettner Couloir of the Grand Teton and on the right (east) by a steep, rotten gully separating Glencoe Spire from Teepe Pillar.

CHRONOLOGY

North and West Faces: July 25, 1947, Jack Lewis, Haldon Smith

South Face: July 29, 1959, William Buckingham, Bea Vogel

Glencoe-Teepe Gully: August 6, 1963, Dallas Kloke, Mike Killien

Direct North Face: August 11, 1967, Dave Foster, Ray Palmer

Direct South Face: August 28, 1974, Michel DeRoy, Alain Henault *var:* September 8, 1988, Paul Horton, Brent Bishop

ROUTE 1. South Face. II, 5.6. First ascent July 29, 1959, by William Buckingham and Bea Vogel. Below (south of) the Black Dike that cuts across the south side of the Grand Teton is a wall extending from Teepe Pillar to the Lower Saddle and forming the north rim of the uppermost north fork of Garnet Canyon. At the base of this wall below the Petzoldt Ridge is a small, nearly circular basin marked by black stains from a small waterfall draining the Beckey and Stettner Couloirs. This route begins at the right (east) side of this basin on the western part of the south ridge of Glencoe Spire. One can start either from the Lower Saddle or from the Caves.

From the Lower Saddle descend to the basin, cross the stream, and climb several hundred feet out of the basin up a series of black, loose chimneys on the right (east) side to the small terrace on the south face proper. From here 250 feet of easy chimneys and slabs leads to the base of the large slab below the "prow." Climb about 80 feet up the slab to the base of the prow. The next pitch zigzags upward with the initial zig to the right along the top edge of the slab and then a zag back to the left to a belay platform. The next pitch is long and steep and goes almost directly up the wall. It begins slightly left of the crest, traverses under an overhang to just right of the crest, and ends with a short jam crack that leads to a belay position in a pile of boulders on a sloping ledge. Climb through one of the breaks in the overhanging wall above for 150 feet to a broad ledge beneath the final steep wall. At the right edge of this ledge, climb 40 feet up a distinct black chimney and then traverse 60 feet left on a sloping ledge. After another 80 feet up the steep wall (good holds), a short eastward scramble leads to the summit. See *American Alpine Journal,* 12, no. 1 (1960), pp. 125–127.

ROUTE 2. Direct South Face. III, 5.9. First ascent August 28, 1974, by Michel DeRoy and Alain Henault. This fine route of ten pitches starts from the very bottom of the south face and follows a line distinct from the 1959 route. At the base of the face a corner is seen as the main break in the initial wall. Climb the crack (5.6) 15 feet left (west) of the corner for 75 feet until one can traverse horizontally back into the corner, gaining a big scree ledge for the belay. The next lead (5.7) starts in the center of the face 20 feet left (west) of an obvious corner, goes diagonally left, and passes a small overhang. The third ropelength (5.7) slants up and right onto the wall with two liebacks, just to the right of the obvious corner that contains loose rock and a large black crack. The next two pitches are easier, continuing the previous line for 30 feet, then proceeding up to the top of the large obvious gully above to a large crack. The sixth lead traverses left (west) on easy slabs at the base of the wall, to reach an obvious crack under the summit block. The next pitch of 75 feet is the most dif-

ficult (5.9); it starts on the wall 20 feet left of this crack and joins the crack after 60 feet and a small traverse. Now follow the crack upward for about 60 feet and then continue up to and left along the base of the summit block. The final pitch leads easily onto the summit. The rock on this route is in general solid, and the climb is clean, except for the scree ledge and the main lower gully.

Variation: III, 5.9. First ascent September 8, 1988, by Paul Horton and Brent Bishop. The upper portion of this variation is apparently the same as *Route 2.* A prominent chimney will be seen at the right (east) side of the upper portion of the face, above a big ramp that bisects the face. The continuation of this chimney is a gully that continues down from the ramp to the base of the face. Begin by scrambling up from below toward a ridge that is to the right (east) of this gully. The first three pitches ascend this ridge via easy 5th-class climbing and some 5.6 up and to the left (west) until the gully is intersected. Third- and 4th-class climbing then leads up the gully for another ropelength. Next, climb onto and across the ramp for a pitch until just below the prominent crack or corner previously mentioned. Continue up *Route 2* to the summit.

ROUTE 3. Glencoe–Teepe Gully. II, 5,4. First ascent (in conjunction with an ascent of Glencoe Spire) August 6, 1963, by Dallas Kloke and Mike Killien. The gully itself had been climbed four years earlier as part of an ascent of Teepe Pillar; see *Teepe Pillar, Route 2.* This gully, located between Glencoe Spire and Teepe Pillar, was ascended to the Black Dike, where the regular North and West Faces route (*Route 5*) was then taken to the summit. Not unexpectedly the party reported the gully to be "very rotten, rockfall danger extreme." This is a gully to avoid, although it may yield a reasonable ice climb if all the rocks are frozen in place.

ROUTE 4. Direct North Face. II, 5.6. First ascent August 11, 1967, by Dave Foster and Ray Palmer. From directly at the top of Glencoe Col climb 10 feet up and left on an easy ledge to the base of a left-facing open book, which is then climbed for 40 feet to a broad ledge. Continue past an overhang and up a wide chimney for 70 feet to another ledge. Thirty feet of easy climbing up yet another wide chimney leads to the north summit. After a short descent to the notch, the main summit is then easily reached.

ROUTE 5. ☞ North and West Faces. I, 5.1. First ascent July 25, 1947, by Jack Lewis and Haldon Smith. Glencoe Col, between this spire and the Grand Teton, can be reached either by traversing the Black Dike from the Lower Saddle or from Teepe Glacier. About 50 feet down to the right (west) from the col, climb a wide vertical chimney on the otherwise smooth north face. Scramble up a small gully in the west face to a small notch in the south ridge only a few feet from the summit. Descent can be made from the summit directly down to the col in two single-rope rappels. *Time: 1½ hours* from the Lower Saddle.

TEEPE PILLAR (12,266)

Map: Grand Teton

This major pinnacle, separated by the Black Dike from the southeast side of the Grand Teton, is the largest and most prominent of those that surround the peak. Teepe Pillar was named for Theodore Teepe, who was killed on August 4, 1925, while descending Teepe Glacier after a successful ascent of the Grand Teton. In recent years it has become a popular short climb, because from the west it can be ascended in less than one hour. The view from the airy summit shows the southeast face of the Grand Teton at very close range. Teepe Pillar can be approached from the Lower Saddle, from the Caves in Garnet Canyon, or from Amphitheater Lake via Dike Col.

CHRONOLOGY

Underhill-Henderson: July 18, 1930, by Robert Underhill, Kenneth Henderson

West Ridge: August 5, 1941, Hans Kraus, Susanne Kruger-Simon
    var: July 1970, Ray Jacquot, Henry Siracusian

Direct East Face: August 27, 1952, Robert Merriam, Steve Jervis, Chris Marshall

Southwest Ridge: August 1, 1956, David Dornan, David Anderson

South Ridge: August 10, 1957, Willi and Jolene Unsoeld, Norman Lee

North Face: July 21, 1958, Yvon Chouinard, Kenneth Weeks

Glencoe-Teepe Gully: July 5, 1959, Tim Bond, Richard Pittman

Northeast Face: August 24, 1961, Royal Robbins, Jane Taylor

South Face: August 10, 1978, David Beneman, Steven Winnett

ROUTE 1. ☞West Ridge. II, 5.4. First ascent August 5, 1941, by Hans Kraus and Susanne Kruger-Simon. This is a short but pleasant route to an airy summit. It is best climbed as a secondary ascent from the Lower Saddle or the Caves, rather than as a separate endeavor all the way from the valley. Although the route name has become fixed as the west ridge, strictly speaking it is the northwest ridge. The route, the most popular one on the pinnacle, starts from the high col formed by the weathering out of the Black Dike, which separates the Pillar from the Grand Teton. This col can be reached either from the Lower Saddle (easy) by traversing the Black Dike or by climbing up Teepe Glacier. From the col the route appears fearsome but is much easier than it appears. The first ropelength is up the jam cracks just right of the left (north) edge of the ridge. Continue up the ridge another ropelength or two until it is possible to traverse right over to the south ridge, which is then followed to the summit. In all, only four short pitches are required to reach the summit from the col. Descent from any of the other routes on the Pillar is via the West Ridge. Four rappels are commonly done using a doubled 50-meter rope. *Time: 6 hours* from Garnet Canyon. See *American Alpine Journal,* 10, no. 1 (1956), pp. 116–119; *Appalachia,* 24, no. 4 (December 1943), pp. 528–530; *Dartmouth Mountaineering Club Journal,* 1956, pp. 34–38.

Variation: II, 5.6. First ascent July 1970, by Ray Jacquot and Henry Siracusian. This one-pitch variation starts the West Ridge route from the col with a 40-foot traverse down and left onto the north face to a steep jam crack. Climb this crack, which widens into a chimney, exiting at the top of the first pitch of the regular West Ridge route.

ROUTE 2. Glencoe–Teepe Gully. II, 5.4. First ascent July 5, 1959, by Tim Bond and Richard Pittman. The steep south couloir separating Glencoe Spire from Teepe Pillar has two branches. This variation ascends the right (east) branch, which contains loose, rotten rock, and snow and ice (in early season), to Teepe Col from which the standard Kraus route is climbed. This alternative approach to the Black Dike and Teepe Col is unpleasant, hazardous, and not recommended.

ROUTE 3. South Face. II, 5.8. First ascent August 10, 1978, by David Beneman and Steven Winnett. The exact location of this climb is uncertain. In general terms, starting from the moraines, scramble up a talus slope to a chimney that leads onto a rock plateau. Continue upward until it steepens, and then take a narrow ledge all the way around to the left to Teepe Col. This ledge cuts diagonally across the large west-southwest face of Teepe Pillar. Because the face above overhangs, the climb occasionally becomes a crawl along a "tunnel." This traverse contains several difficult places (5.8), with the crux move near the end of the traverse. From the col the regular West Ridge route is taken to the summit.

ROUTE 4. Southwest Ridge. II, 5.6. First ascent August 1, 1956, by David Anderson and David Dornan. Approach from the Caves and start around and up the couloir just west of the Pillar. From a point well below Teepe Col climb two 5.6 pitches in order to reach the south ridge above. Once on the ridge the remainder of the route to the summit is enjoyable 4.0 climbing.

ROUTE 5. South Ridge. III, 5.8. First ascent August 10, 1957, by Willi and Jolene Unsoeld and Norman Lee. This ridge is most conveniently approached from the Caves. The route follows the extreme southeast edge of the large, triangular south face, utilizing small ledges that overhang the south face. After four leads, the third being the most difficult, the climbing eases off somewhat and eventually joins and follows the Underhill–Henderson route to the summit. *Time: 8¾ hours* from the Caves. See *American Alpine Journal,* 11, no. 1 (1958), pp. 85–88.

ROUTE 6. Underhill–Henderson. II, 5.4, A1, or II, 5.7. First ascent July 18, 1930, by Robert Underhill and Kenneth Henderson. See *Photo 52*. This climb starts at the base of the east face. Two intersecting chimneys cut the east face, one leading right toward the summit and the other leading left to the south ridge. To reach the grassy ledge at the base of the left (south) chimney, climb about 150 feet up a slab. From a ledge at the top of the slab climb 30 feet up to the large overhang at the base of the chimney. The first-ascent party used a shoulder stand on the south wall of the chimney in order to pass this overhang, but a few moves of 5.7 now suffice. Small holds then permit a traverse back into the chimney above the overhang. The next overhang, some 40 feet farther up the chimney, is easily passed on the right (north). Pass the large chockstone above by climbing on the south wall. Sixty feet of easy climbing leads to the south ridge. Follow this about 300 feet to the summit. *Time: 5¾ hours* from the Caves. See *Appalachia*, 18, no. 3 (June 1931), pp. 209–232, illus.; *Canadian Alpine Journal*, 19 (1930), pp. 84–91, illus.

ROUTE 7. Direct East Face. II, 5.7. First partial ascent August 21, 1938, by Bert Jensen, William Rice, William Bigelow, and Harry Kornberg; first complete ascent August 27, 1952, by Robert Merriam, Steve Jervis, and Chris Marshall. See *Photo 52*. The 1938 second ascent of Teepe Pillar did not follow the 1930 route exactly but utilized a portion of the east face and eventually cut left onto the south ridge and face. This direct route of 1952 follows the right (north) of the two major intersecting chimney systems on the east face; it leads almost directly to the summit. This is a fine climb on good rock.

From the base of the Pillar climb to the common base of the two main east chimney systems. A large chimney will be encountered leading onto a wide ledge. An exposed traverse to the left (south) can be made from here into the chimney of *Route 6*. For this Direct East Face route, however, continue nearly straight up on enjoyable rock, staying slightly to the right (north) of the main east chimney. The natural line leads to the foot of the double-crack pitch (5.7). From the top of this crux lead, move left (south) over a small overhang to a broken area affording a good belay position. After passing a small nose, keep to the right (north) of the main vertical chimney on the east face of Teepe Pillar, and continue all the way to the bottom of the final chimney with a chockstone at its top. This chimney is just left (south) of the large, smooth, overhanging face near the top of the Pillar. Climb this chimney and emerge onto the rock above, which leads easily to the summit. See *American Alpine Journal*, 3, no. 3 (1939), pp. 361–365.

ROUTE 8. Northeast Face. IV, 5.1, A3. First ascent August 24, 1961, by Royal Robbins and Jane Taylor. See *Photo 52*. This route lies between the Direct East Face route and the North Face route. From the right edge of the east shoulder, climb diagonally up to the right over easy rock to a right-angle recess, which is directly below a huge roof on the east ridge. Ascend this recess for about 100 feet, and then diagonal off to the right to a steep, sloping ledge leading up to the right. Follow this ledge to its end; then cut back left for 30 feet up to a second sloping ledge, where the difficult climbing begins. Traverse right to piton cracks in a smooth face. Proceed directly up using aid pitons (the last 30 feet are free) to a sharp orange overhang. Pass this overhang on the right, and turn a corner into a recess containing two black overhangs. Ascend this recess, and exit to the right above. Now follow a depression up to the right to a small notch, beyond which is a ledge connecting with the North Face route. From the notch, move left and then up a face, using aid in the cracks. Above these cracks, face climbing leads to a broad, sloping ledge. From this ledge, turn a corner to the left and climb two easier east face pitches to the summit. See *American Alpine Journal*, 13, no. 1 (1962), pp. 216–220; *Sierra Club Bulletin*, 46, no. 8 (October 1961), pp. 53–54.

ROUTE 9. North Face. III, 5.8. First ascent July 21, 1958, by Yvon Chouinard and Kenneth Weeks. From Teepe Col, at the base of the Kraus route, easily descend diagonally left (east) and out onto the north face to a difficult overhanging block. This is about 100 feet above Teepe Glacier. Descend a few feet from the top of this block and then climb around a difficult corner to a belay ledge 4 feet above. Now climb directly above this ledge, following an obvious ledge that slants up to the right. The next pitch continues a little farther on the ledge before striking vertically upward and slightly back to the left until a traverse to the left becomes obvious. This traverse starts on a 2-inch ledge that disappears; continue to a belay spot. The next-to-last pitch goes up from the belay spot on broken blocks until a very comfortable belay ledge with loose rocks is reached. Here one is directly below the conspicuous open book, which is the main feature of the upper north face. Climb the corner until an exit onto the overhanging face to the right is necessary. This leads directly to the summit. This somewhat intricate route is not recommended because of the broken and loose nature of the rock. See *American Alpine Journal*, 11, no. 2 (1959), pp. 307–309; *Sierra Club Bulletin*, 46, no. 8 (October 1961), pp. 53–54.

SECOND TOWER (12,960+)

(0.2 mi E of the Grand Teton)

Map: Grand Teton

This is the higher of the two main towers on the long east ridge of the Grand Teton; it rises at the lower edge of the East Ridge Snowfield. The west and southwest faces are sheer, and there is no possibility of bypassing the Second Tower on the south without extensive rappelling. The Second Tower is preceded on the east by a large gendarme that was first climbed on July 29, 1941, by Norman Dyhrenfurth, James Ramsey Ullman, and Donald Gardner.

North Chimney: July 18, 1951, Richard Irvin, John Mowat, Nick Clinch, Leigh Ortenburger

Southeast Face: August 19, 1956, Barry Corbet, Gerry Cabaniss

South Ridge, Brimstone Chimney: August 2, 1970, David Ingalls, Scott Brim

Tower Two Chute: June 14, 1993, Renny Jackson, Ron Johnson

ROUTE 1. South Ridge, Brimstone Chimney. III, 5.8, A1. First ascent August 2, 1970, by David Ingalls and Scott Brim. This is the lower of the two main chimneys, which might be described as large left-facing dihedrals, on the left (southwest) side of the south ridge of the Second Tower. The general route should be studied from the upper edge of the Teepe Glacier, and will be seen as a large, reddish corner, containing the narrowing chimney. From the top of Teepe Glacier, climb the lower portion of the Petzoldt–Loomis Couloir (*Grand Teton, Route 23*), using slabs on its left side until past the initial steep section. Traverse for two pitches across and right to the left side of the south ridge of the Second Tower. Climb another 150 feet diagonally up and right on broken, dirt-covered rock to the small gully leading to the base of the reddish corner. Climb the corner (5.8) and its right wall for 80 feet to a belay stance above a bulge. The next pitch continues up the corner, exiting with one move of aid. Climb up and right through a boulder field to a 150 foot, 5.4 pitch that goes up and left in a large crack breaking the low-angle slabs. Finish by climbing out and up to the right to the 3rd-class upper end of the ridge above. From this point the Southeast Face, *Route 3*, can be taken to the summit of the Second Tower. The East Ridge of the Grand Teton (*Grand Teton, Route 25*) could be joined by a short traverse to the right (east). A regular hardware assortment will suffice, but there are several cracks in the 1- to 1½-inch category.

ROUTE 2. Tower Two Chute. IV, WI4, 5.9, A1. First ascent June 14, 1993, by Renny Jackson and Ron Johnson. This route is very rarely in shape and its existence is fleeting. On the southern side of the tower two prominent ridges rise from the upper section of Teepe Glacier. These ridges flank a steep chute that provides a convenient path for the considerable meltwater that then freezes and forms the climb. Nine pitches of mixed climbing were encountered, the quality and difficulty of which will certainly vary from year to year. This climb joins the East Ridge route at the small eastern notch where one normally begins the northern traverse of the Second Tower.

ROUTE 3. Southeast Face. III, 5.4. First ascent August 19, 1956, by Barry Corbet and Gerry Cabaniss. On an ascent of the East Ridge route of the Grand Teton, when one reaches the south ridge of the gendarme just east of the Second Tower, instead of climbing up to the notch between it and the Tower, descend a few feet and scramble around the corner to the left into the small bowl on the southeast side of the Tower. The steep face above is broken by cracks and ledges and is climbed more or less directly to the traverse left of *Route 4* to the south ridge. Follow the knife-edge south ridge to the summit. See *Dartmouth Mountaineering Club Journal*, 1957, pp. 22–23, 50–51.

ROUTE 4. North Chimney. III, 5.6. First ascent July 18, 1951, by Richard Irvin, John Mowat, Nick Clinch, and Leigh Ortenburger. When one traverses around the north side of the Second Tower (see *Grand Teton, Route 25*), a shallow chimney will be seen leading up to a small notch east of the summit. Climb this chimney to the notch. Then traverse left (south) and up a steep series of ledges and slabs to the knife-edge south ridge, and follow it to the summit. One of the more difficult problems of this climb is getting off the Tower. Climb down for about 100 feet to the last small ledge on the west side (facing the Grand). A spectacular double-rope rappel deposits one at the notch that separates the Tower from the Grand.

MOLAR TOOTH (12,320+)

(0.35 mi E of the Grand Teton)

Map: Grand Teton

This unsymmetrical tower on the east ridge of the Grand Teton is actually one of the major features of the peak. Historically, the Molar Tooth is also important, having stopped several early attempts to reach the summit of the Grand Teton. Additional information regarding the Molar Tooth is given in *Grand Teton, Route 25, Southern Traverse* and *Molar Tooth, Tricky Traverse* variations. Although directly in the path of the East Ridge route, it has been climbed very seldom. The actual summit is a shaky stack of boulders.

The Tooth is also a significant obstacle for those descending the east ridge of the Grand Teton. Perhaps the fastest method of passing the Molar Tooth on descent is to climb from the main notch up and to the southeast for about 100 feet, reaching easily a notch in the upper south ridge of the Tooth. Two 150-foot rappels down the east face from this notch end the difficult part of this descent route.

Northeast Cracks: [probable] early August 1927, Albert R. Ellingwood, Eleanor Davis, Robert Ormes, Eleanor Bartlett; August 4, 1939, Norman Dyhrenfurth, Elpenor Ohle

Southwest Ledges: August 4, 1939, Norman Dyhrenfurth, Elpenor Ohle (descent)

South Ridge: June 23, 1955, Richard Long, Leigh Ortenburger, Donald Monk

East Chimney: August 8, 1955, William Briggs, Yves Erickson

Direct South Face: September 1, 1971, Gordon Parham, Terry Grainger

ROUTE 1. *Southwest Ledges.* II, 5.1. First descent August 4, 1939, by Norman Dyhrenfurth and Elpenor Ohle. This route starts from the main notch separating the Molar Tooth from the Grand Teton. See *Grand Teton, Route 25,* for the north and south approaches to this notch. Climb up and to the right (south) from the notch onto a series of ledges and chimneys leading to a small notch between the two summits of the Molar Tooth. The route is hard to find but is not difficult. This route is the best method of descent from the Tooth, if one wishes to continue from its summit up the east ridge of the Grand Teton.

ROUTE 2. *Direct South Face.* III, 5.7. First ascent September 1, 1971, by Gordon Parham and Terry Grainger. This route starts from Teepe Glacier and ascends the main snow (and chockstone) couloir descending from the notch behind the Tooth. In late season one can scramble up this couloir to the third talus- and scree-covered platform; in early season this platform will be covered with snow. From the platform, face climb for two pitches up and left to a good ledge. An easy crack leads up and left to a headwall that blocks progress. Here make a step-around to the left onto a narrow ledge. From the end of the ledge a broken chimney is climbed to the next belay ledge. The next pitch goes up a dihedral and squeeze chimney, then cuts back left. Face climbing then leads to the crux pitch, an overhanging crack that takes one to the ridge between the two small summits. Scramble to the eastern, true summit.

ROUTE 3. *South Ridge.* III, 5.7, A2. First ascent June 23, 1955, by Richard Long, Leigh Ortenburger, and Donald Monk. See *Grand Teton, Route 25, Southern Traverse variation,* for the route to the window notch in the south ridge of the Molar Tooth. From this sharp notch, climb directly up the ridge for 120 feet. Continue 60 feet up and slightly right (east) on easier rock to the knife-edge ridge crest. The next 80-foot pitch is difficult. Climb about 20 feet up a slab to a point where it is just possible to slither around the corner to the left (south) onto a small exposed ledge. At the end of this ledge climb upward and then left using aid. Regain the crest and walk to the base of a small chute (snow in early season) that leads up to the very small notch between the two summits. The base of this chute is the top of the 200-foot vertical, smooth-walled chimney referred to in *Grand Teton, Route 25.* From this small notch it is but a short distance to the summit.

ROUTE 4. *East Chimney.* II, 5.7. First ascent August 8, 1955, by William Briggs and Yves Erickson. Climb the first 2,000 feet of the east ridge of the Grand Teton as in *Grand Teton, Route 25, Southern Traverse variation.* Keep left (south) of the ridge crest. As the Molar Tooth is approached, two large chimneys with a common base will be seen in its east face. The left (south) vertical chimney ends at a horizontal step in the south ridge, and the right (north) one diagonals up to the right to meet a band of black rock 150 feet below the summit of the Tooth. Climb the wet slabs leading to the base of the right (north) chimney. The first lead goes straight up the chimney. The second lead is on the right (north) wall of the chimney and passes an overhang. Then scramble to the well-defined ledge leading back to the left (south). Walk left on this ledge and up to the base of the small chimney or jam crack that leads to the highest small notch in the south ridge, just short of the summit of the Molar Tooth. The 115-foot lead up the face to the left (south) of this crack is 5.7. From the crest of the ridge it is an easy scramble up to the shaky summit from the south and west. See *American Alpine Journal,* 10, no. 1 (1956), pp. 116–119.

ROUTE 5. *Northeast Cracks.* III, 5.6. Probable first ascent in early August 1927, by Albert R. Ellingwood, Eleanor Davis, Eleanor Bartlett, and Robert Ormes; definitely ascended August 4, 1939, by Norman Dyhrenfurth and Elpenor Ohle. For a description of the route up to the base of the northeast corner of the Molar Tooth, see *Grand Teton, Route 25.* From this point climb the chimney that slants up and right; then proceed out on a face until it is possible to work left onto easier rocks and up to a belay position. The first lead is of 5.6 difficulty. On the second pitch climb up and right (west, 4.0) to a place from which scrambling leads to the notch between the two small summits of the Tooth. The eastern summit, which is the higher of the two, is easily reached from the notch. Two 150-foot rappels from the notch suffice to descend this route.

OKIE'S THORN (11,840+)

(0.4 mi SE of the Grand Teton)

Map: Grand Teton

This sharp pinnacle, although providing one of the better pinnacle climbs in the park, is little known, perhaps due to its inconspicuous position on the southeast flank of the Grand Teton. The southeast ridge provides a good route. The name is derived from the fact that Willi Unsoeld nabbed the first ascent from Leigh Ortenburger, who had told him of the spire's existence. Ortenburger was born in Norman, Oklahoma. Additional information regarding Okie's Thorn is given in *Grand Teton, Route 25, 1955 variation.*

CHRONOLOGY

Northeast Face: September 5, 1953, Willi Unsoeld
Southeast Ridge: August 29, 1954, William Buckingham, George Houghton, James Butler

ROUTE 1. ☞*Southeast Ridge.* II, 5.6. First ascent August 29, 1954, by William Buckingham, George Houghton, and James Butler. This ridge, leading directly up the Thorn from Dike Col, is the most obvious route on the pinnacle. The pinnacle, however, is usually difficult to distinguish from the rock mass behind it when viewed from this angle. The first two ropelengths from the col require little more than scrambling. The south face, now above and left, is a steep, smooth wall cut only by a few cracks. The east face, to the right, is also relatively smooth but it lies back at a slightly more gentle angle. Climb this face for 50 feet on small, rounded holds to a point where a short traverse can be made into the small chimney that separates the south and east faces. This short chimney leads easily to a broad, sloping ledge. After another ropelength make a delicate traverse left (south) around a corner and across a smooth face to the easy ledges of the upper south face. From this point one can either climb right and up, reaching the summit from the east, or else cut left (west) over to the southwest ridge and follow it to the summit. The cracks out on the south face are of excellent quality and numerous difficult (5.9 to 5.10) variations are possible.

The descent of this pinnacle is by no means simple. Probably the only method that can be recommended is to rappel back down the southeast ridge to Dike Col. Four double-rope rappels are necessary to get off the climb. This pinnacle gets climbed very rarely, so check the anchors carefully before descent. The narrow, steep, and extremely rotten couloir descending west from the notch should be avoided at all costs. The couloir descending to the east, although not so steep, is very nearly as dangerous because of rockfall and is also not recommended.

ROUTE 2. Northeast Face. II, 5.4. First ascent September 5, 1953, by Willi and Jolene Unsoeld and Stanley Bishoprick (Willi ascended the final pitch alone). From Amphitheater Lake follow the usual route toward Dike Col; about 300 feet below the col, cut right and head directly for the sharp notch between the Thorn and the Grand. Use the more southerly of the two large prominent chimneys. As the notch is neared, turn onto the wall left (south) of the large chimney, and climb a 30-foot chimney to a sharp cleft formed by the separation of a large flake from the main wall. Ascend this flake, then span the gap (about 5 feet) and climb a shallow groove in the delicate wall opposite, to the ample ledges above. At this point it is possible to turn left (south) and reach the Southeast Ridge (*Route 1*) after 120 feet. To reach the notch, however, move right (north) and up over loose and rotten rock. From the notch climb 8 feet up *on the Grand side;* then bridge across and swing over onto the Thorn. One ropelength to the right, first across the slabs of the west face of the Thorn and finally up some steep walls, places one on the southwest ridge. Climb one ropelength up this distinct ridge to the summit.

PEMMICAN PILLAR (11,520+)
(0.25 mi E of Teepe Pillar)

Map: Grand Teton

This is the first pinnacle east of Dike Col on the ridge connecting Disappointment Peak with the Grand Teton.

ROUTE 1. West Side. I, 3.0. First ascent August 23, 1936, by Fred and Irene Ayres and Kenneth Henderson. This is a straightforward climb from Dike Col.

ROUTE 2. East Ridge. I, 3.0. First ascent July 19, 1951, by Richard Irvin and Leigh Ortenburger. This ridge involves only scrambling and is ordinarily used only for a traverse to or from Fairshare Tower.

FAIRSHARE TOWER (11,520+)
(0.3 mi E of Teepe Pillar)

Map: Grand Teton

This is the central of the three towers on the ridge between Dike Col and Disappointment Peak. All three—the Red Sentinel, Fairshare Tower, and Pemmican Pillar—present impressive north faces when viewed from the usual Amphitheater Lake–Teton Glacier route. The south ridge of this tower contains a broad, easy saddle that separates the Watchtower, a subpeak, from the upper ridge and main summit. This saddle provides an easy route to pass from the vicinity of Teepe Glacier over into the couloirs leading to the Red Sentinel. The Jackson Hole Mountain Guides utilize the west buttress of the Watchtower for short instructional ascents. The nonsummit rock climbs on the south side of this tower are described under *Garnet Canyon, North Side Rock Climbs.*

CHRONOLOGY

West Ridge: July 19, 1951, Leigh Ortenburger, Richard Irvin

East Ridge: July 21, 1951, Nick Clinch, Peter Robinson

South Ridge: July 9, 1957, John Dietschy, Irene Ortenburger

ROUTE 1. West Ridge. I, 3.0. First ascent July 19, 1951, by Leigh Ortenburger and Richard Irvin. From the summit of Pemmican Pillar it is an easy scramble to the summit of Fairshare Tower.

ROUTE 2. South Ridge. II, 5.1. First ascent July 9, 1957, by John Dietschy and Irene Ortenburger. As seen from the Caves, the double southern end of this ridge appears as two vertical buttresses. The first of 12 pitches commenced on good rock at the right edge of the eastern buttress, which lies just to the left (west) of the gully leading to the Red Sentinel. Stay on the east side of this south buttress until the ridge crest is reached just past the main south tower (the Watchtower) of this ridge. Then follow the crest to the broad saddle and on to the summit. A shorter version of this route can be obtained by approaching the ridge from the snout of Teepe Glacier to this saddle; this leaves a climb of 500 feet to the summit. Descent is normally made to the west over the top of Pemmican Pillar down to Dike Col. The rock on this ridge is excellent and escape into the gully on the right is possible from almost any point along the climb. See *American Alpine Journal*, 11, no. 1 (1958), pp. 85–88.

ROUTE 3. East Ridge. I, 3.0. First ascent July 21, 1951, by Nick Clinch and Peter Robinson. Start from the notch between the Red Sentinel and Fairshare Tower. This notch is reached from the south via the usual couloir approach to the Red Sentinel, immediately west of Disappointment Peak.

RED SENTINEL (11,200+)
(0.1 mi W of Disappointment Peak)

Map: Grand Teton

This remarkable, chisellike pinnacle lies on the ridge connecting Disappointment Peak with the Grand Teton. Of the four pinnacles on this ridge, the Red Sentinel is the most easterly, lying directly under the west face of Disappointment Peak. The most spectacular view of the Sentinel is the one obtained by looking straight down from the summit of Disappointment. There has been a change of names since the early 1930s when the highest col on the Black Dike (now known as Glencoe Col) was known as Sentinel Col and Glencoe Spire was known as the Red Sentinel. The first attempt to climb this sharp pinnacle was on August 6, 1941, by Hans Kraus and Susan Simon; they reached a point on the northwest ridge only 30 feet below the summit. Kraus returned six years later on August 12, 1947, with Donald Brown, Adolf Snow, and Haldon Smith, but was again stopped after 20 feet of aid climbing on the northwest ridge by the last 30 feet, "no cracks, no holds."

CHRONOLOGY

East Face and North Face: July 11, 1950, Robert Merriam, Richard Pownall, Michael Brewer, Leigh Ortenburger

North Face: August 22, 1956, Barry Corbet, Gerry Cabaniss

Northwest Corner: August 8, 1966, David Ingalls, Greg Joiner

Southwest Dihedral: July 27, 1968, David Ingalls, Roy Kligfield, Charles Bookman

ROUTE 1. Southwest Dihedral. II, 5.7, A3. First ascent July 27, 1968, by Dave Ingalls, Roy Kligfield, and Charles Bookman. Approach this three-pitch route from the Caves, as in *Route 2*, until the overhanging corner is seen on the southwest side of the Red Sentinel. The route can be started by climbing (5.6) to a belay stance in a cave or, better, by working around the left shoulder to the north face so that this cave can be entered from the rear. The first difficult lead works horizontally right from the cave on balance holds to a vertical aid crack that leads up into the dihedral. Continue up the dihedral for 20 feet to a sling

belay. The final lead (A3) continues up the dihedral and onto the exposed face above, which is climbed via unprotected 5.7 to the ridge. Once the ridge is attained, easier climbing leads to the summit.

ROUTE 2. ☞East Face and North Face. II, 5.7. First ascent July 11, 1950, by Robert Merriam, Richard Pownall, Michael Brewer, and Leigh Ortenburger. See *Topo 52* and *Photo 55*. From Garnet Canyon take the large talus couloir next to the west face of Disappointment Peak to reach the notch to the east of the pinnacle. During much of this approach the Sentinel itself will not be visible. It is also possible, but more difficult, to approach the Sentinel from the north, but steep snow will be encountered. From this col, the jam crack leading up the center of the east face is obvious. Climb this crack for 60 feet to its end, where a delicate friction traverse right leads to the northeast corner. Belay the next pitch at this corner. From the corner, face climb out onto the edge of the sheer north face up to a secure position behind a flake. Early in the season these ledges may be damp, if not actually wet. Then go *à cheval* up the sharp ridge to the small summit. The cracks on the north face are thin, requiring small nuts. For descent two ropes are required for the rappel to the northwest col. *Time: 3½ hours* from the Caves. See *American Alpine Journal*, 8, no. 1 (1951), pp. 176–181; *Dartmouth Mountaineering Club Journal*, 1957, pp. 22–23, 28, 50–51; *Harvard Mountaineering*, 12 (May 1955), pp. 57–58.

ROUTE 3. North Face. II, 5.8. First ascent August 22, 1956, by Barry Corbet and Gerry Cabaniss. See *Photo 67*. The first-ascent party apparently approached this route from Amphitheater Lake by the usual route, around the bottom of the north face of Disappointment Peak and up to the subsidiary glacier at the bases of the Red Sentinel, Fairshare Tower, and Pemmican Pillar. They then ascended the steep snow to the base of the north face of the Sentinel. A more logical approach is that of *Routes 1* and *2*. Starting 20 feet east of the chimney that forms the northwest corner of the Sentinel, climb up and left (east) until the crest of a small nose is reached. Climbing up this nose and then back to the right leads to a comfortable ledge containing a large belay boulder. From this boulder proceed upward to a wide ledge that permits a hand traverse left to an obvious 6-inch shelf. Traverse left again on sloping ledges that ultimately peter out about 8 feet from the flake of *Route 2*. This gap is difficult. From the flake, *Route 2* is joined and followed to the summit. *Time: 9 hours* from Jenny Lake. See *Dartmouth Mountaineering Club Journal*, 1957, pp. 22–23, 28, 50–51.

ROUTE 4. Northwest Corner. II, 5.8, A2, or II, 5.10-. First ascent August 8, 1966, by Dave Ingalls and Greg Joiner; first free ascent June 26, 1988, by Renny Jackson and Jim Woodmencey. See *Topo 52*. Approach via the Caves in Garnet Canyon and access the chimney that forms the northwest corner of the Red Sentinel from the west. Climb

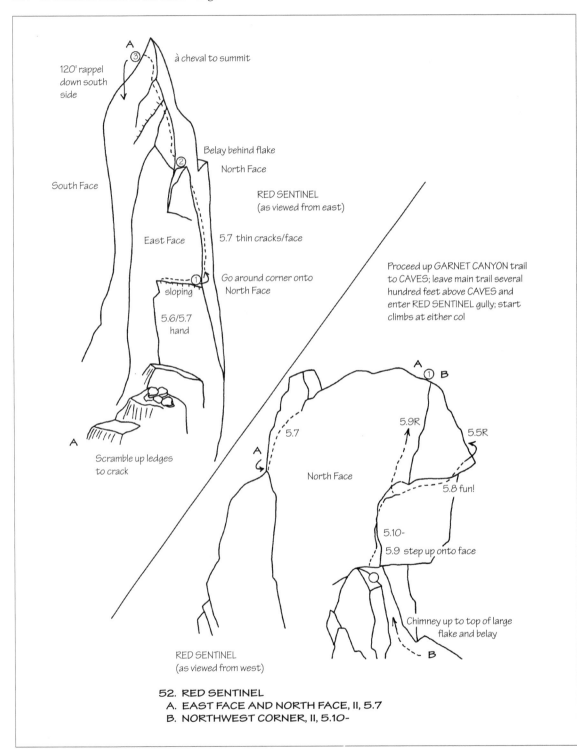

à cheval to summit

120' rappel
down south
side

Belay behind flake

North Face

South Face

RED SENTINEL
(as viewed from east)

East Face   5.7 thin cracks/face

Go around corner onto
sloping   North Face

Proceed up GARNET CANYON trail
to CAVES; leave main trail several
hundred feet above CAVES and
enter RED SENTINEL gully; start
climbs at either col

5.6/5.7
hand

A   B

5.9R
5.5R

A   5.7

5.8 fun!

North Face

5.10-

5.9 step up onto face

Scramble up ledges
to crack

A

Chimney up to top of large
flake and belay

B

RED SENTINEL
(as viewed from west)

52. RED SENTINEL
   A. EAST FACE AND NORTH FACE, II, 5.7
   B. NORTHWEST CORNER, II, 5.10-

the back of this chimney up and onto the top of the enormous flake that forms the north wall of the chimney and belay. Using small holds make the tenuous step up and onto the exposed face and climb up to a flake with a ring angle on its right edge. Turn the corner around to the right and climb a 1-inch crack (5.10-) to an adequate ledge. At this point there are two options for finishing the pitch. The first-ascent party climbed up 15 feet of rounded slabs to a small ledge and then continued up the right edge of the north face to the summit. This option involves runout face climbing (5.8) on small holds and angles to the right edge of the formation when possible. For the second alternative proceed out and right (south) on an airy, 40-foot traverse to the southwest edge of the Sentinel (5.8). Once around the corner climb the unprotected face (5.5) above to the summit. For protection take RPs and a selection of wired nuts and camming devices to 2½ inches.

DISAPPOINTMENT PEAK (11,618)

Map: Grand Teton

Disappointment Peak is unique in the Tetons in that it harbors two delightful lakes, Surprise and Amphitheater, high on its east slopes. The peak is ringed by cliffs on the south, west, and north; only the eastern approach is gradual, and even there the glacial action that formed Amphitheater Lake left a considerable headwall between the lake and the summit plateau, a remnant of an ancient peneplain surface. The trail to Amphitheater Lake, constructed in 1923 by J. G. (Gibb) Scott and Homer Richards as a commercial venture to allow guided trips onto the Teton Glacier, was much used in the 1920s because it was almost the only trail that penetrated the mountains. Because of the existence of this "Glacier Trail," Amphitheater Lake was used as the starting point for several early climbs of the Grand Teton. It was more than ten years later that the Garnet Canyon trail was completed.

The members of the first-ascent party were unfamiliar with the topography of the Grand Teton area and had thought that they might be able to reach the summit of the Grand Teton by climbing directly from Amphitheater Lake. Upon reaching Disappointment Peak and seeing the great gap between them and the Grand Teton, they attempted, but failed, to traverse farther toward their objective; Phil Smith and Walter Harvey named the peak on their return. Disappointment Peak has proved popular as a relatively easy, readily accessible peak with a spectacular view. This summit view is truly remarkable, showing all of the peaks and pinnacles surrounding Garnet Canyon and Glacier Gulch, the heart of the Tetons, to great advantage. By peering over the edge to the west, the impressive, slender splinter of the Red Sentinel is seen from an unusual angle. Easy access via the Garnet Canyon trail to the southern routes and via the Amphitheater Lake trail to the eastern and northern routes contributes to the popularity of this peak.

In recent years, the numerous southern ridges, and to a lesser extent the north face, have been the scene of considerable rock-climbing activity, because they provide a large selection of high-angle rock routes. The nonsummit rock climbs out of Garnet Canyon are described separately under *Garnet Canyon, North Side Rock Climbs.*

CHRONOLOGY

Lake Ledges: August 20, 1925, Phil Smith, Walter Harvey

Snow Couloir: August 20, 1925, Phil Smith, Walter Harvey (descent)

Southwest Couloir: July 14, 1926, Norman Clyde, Ernest Dawson, Alice Carter, Julie Mortimer, J. C. Downing

Southeast Ridge: [probable] August 12, 1935, Perry Gilbert

East Ridge: September 2, 1937, Jack Durrance, George Sheldon, Percy Rideout

West Face: August 14, 1947, Hans Kraus, Donald Brown

Merriam Couloir: July 17, 1950, Robert and Doris Merriam

　　var: July 30, 1973, Robert Fenichel, Richard Schmitz

Southwest Ridge: July 9, 1952, Robert Merriam, Richard Emerson

　　var: July 5, 1957, Art Gran, Robert Chambers, Paul Calcaterra

Northwest Shelf: August 20, 1925, Phil Smith, Walter Harvey (partial descent); August 11, 1953, Robert Brooke, Rob Day (complete descent)

Direct North Face: August 4, 1955, John Dietschy, William Cropper

Northwest Crack: August 15, 1955, John Dietschy, William Cropper

Pownall-Unsoeld North Face: July 27, 1956, Richard Pownall, Willi Unsoeld; first free ascent August 6, 1979, Mike Munger, Bill Feiges

East Chimney: September 5, 1956, Harvey Carter, Robert Beck

Gran: July 5, 1962, Art Gran, John Hudson

Chouinard-Frost Chimney: August 13, 1962, Yvon Chouinard, Tom Frost; first free ascent August 19, 1970, Dave Ingalls, Dave Loeks

　　var: August 3, 1994, Tom Kimbrough, Andy Byerly

Great West Chimney: July 17, 1964, Richard Goldstone, Raymond Schrag, Fred Pfahler

No Name Couloir: August 20, 1973, Randy Jamieson, Dave Alvestad

West Arête: July 17, 1979, Jim Beyer, JoAnne Urioste

West Buttress: September 24, 1986, Ken Jern, Jay Pistono

Kimbrough-Rickert: August 1994, Tom Kimbrough, Steve Rickert

ROUTE 1. West Face. II, 5.4. First ascent August 14, 1947, by Hans Kraus and Donald Brown. See *Photo 57.* This impressive face has the pleasant characteristic of appearing more difficult than it is. The route is recommended to those seeking a steep, enjoyable rock route that is easily accessible from the Caves. The route starts from the col between the Red Sentinel and Disappointment Peak. This col is most easily approached from the south via the talus couloir directly above the Caves. If approached from the north, steep snow and some loose rock will be encountered. This route involves only four pitches but is moderately high angled and exposed. Start from the col, climbing easy downsloping black slabs and ledges. Now diagonal up and slightly right (south) over steep rock that continues for two more ropelengths. There are, in general, several variations available on each pitch, and the difficulty will depend on which is chosen. The fourth lead is up a chimney to black slabs located below the crest. To maximize the climbing make a deliberate traverse back to the left on this lead. The edge of the summit plateau will be reached about 200 feet south of the summit. To descend, take the Southwest Couloir (*Route 6*) directly back to the Caves.

ROUTE 2. West Arête. II, 5.9. First ascent July 17, 1979, by Jim Beyer and JoAnne Urioste. See *Topo 53.* This route, which might better be described as a face climb rather than an arête, can be climbed in various ways in the lower portion, but the options all lead into the one difficult pitch near the top. Approach via the Garnet Canyon trail to the Caves, then ascend the Red Sentinel Gully at the base of the west face of Disappointment Peak to the start of the route about 300 feet south of the col. The first pitch is straight up a crack. Next, continue up a right-facing corner, past two overhangs. This is followed by a face-climbing pitch that ends with a 5.5 chimney onto the belay ledge. Move right and up through an overhang, passing a second overhang on the right to gain a right-facing corner (5.7); the lead ends with a left-facing corner to the belay. The fifth lead is the crux pitch, a 5.9 hand crack leading past a white flake, up onto a ramp angling up and right. One final pitch of easier climbing exits onto the summit ridge about 600 feet south of the top. For protection take a rack up to 3 inches with many small wired nuts. For descent back to the Caves use the Southwest Couloir (*Route 6*).

ROUTE 3. West Buttress. II, 5.7. First ascent September 24, 1986, by Ken Jern and Jay Pistono. See *Photo 58.* This route is on the left (north) portion of the wall that forms the left (north) boundary of the Great West Chimney (see *Route 4*). From the Caves proceed north up the Red Sentinel Gully at the base of the west walls of Disappointment Peak. Pass the Great West Chimney and the massive wall on its left (north) side. Near the left edge of this wall turn up and climb on

good rock for the first of four pitches. The top of this route emerges onto the uppermost plateau just below the final summit blocks.

ROUTE 4. Great West Chimney. II, 5.4. First ascent July 17, 1964, by Richard Goldstone, Raymond Schrag, and Fred Pfahler. See *Photos 57* and *58.* About halfway between the southwest ridge of Disappointment Peak and the notch at the Red Sentinel is a huge right-facing corner, the major feature of the western aspect of the mountain. An identifying feature of this corner is the dark-colored rock that forms the lower half of the left (north) face of the corner. The Great West Chimney is in the corner itself. The approach to the base of the chimney is from the Caves via the Red Sentinel Gully. The climbing up the chimney is not difficult, skirting overhangs and chockstones out on the right (south), but some loose rock will be encountered. The top of the chimney emerges onto the summit plateau at the north end of the horizontal step in the southwest ridge.

ROUTE 5. Southwest Ridge. II, 5.6. First ascent July 9, 1952, by Robert Merriam and Richard Emerson. See *Photos 54* and *59.* This ridge is better described as the broad indistinct corner where the west and south faces intersect. It is the westernmost of the myriad south ridges and faces of Disappointment Peak and it rises in two sections. The first section rises about 800 feet to the flat shoulder formed by the summit plateau, and the second section extends another 300 feet from this plateau to the summit. From the Caves a talus hike of about 30 minutes brings one to the base of the ridge. A multitude of routes on this broad but very steep ridge can be climbed, but there almost always seem to be ample good holds. During the approach an initial face with western exposure will be seen rising about 200 feet, giving access to the south face of the ridge. Climb broken rock on this face until a Wall Street–like ledge is reached. Follow this ledge back onto the crest. Climb about 30 feet out onto the west face until a V chimney offers a route up over a short overhang. Traverse a bit farther left and follow an upward-sloping ledge back to the crest. The remainder of this first section is enjoyable and not difficult staying near the crest. Easier climbing can be found out to the right (east) on the south face. Most of the alternatives on this upper part seem to converge to a chimney (5.6) with an old fixed piton.

Once reached, the summit plateau offers an easy route to the summit; one can detour out to the right (east) and approach the summit from that direction. The proper route, however, continues on the upper south face as close to the west face as possible. The angle decreases after the first pitch in this section and the climbing is easy. Given good weather, this high-angle route is in the sunshine most of the day, and the predominantly good rock assures a pleasant climb. *Time: 6¼ hours from the Caves.* See *American Alpine Journal,* 9, no. 2 (1955), pp. 147–149.

Variation: II, 5.6. First ascent July 5, 1957, by Art Gran, Robert Chambers, and Paul Calcaterra. Most of this varia-

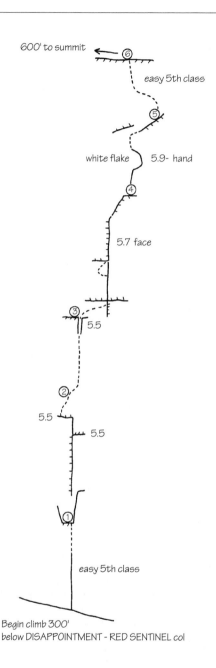

600' to summit ← ⑥

easy 5th class

⑤

white flake   5.9- hand

④

5.7 face

③
5.5

②

5.5

5.5

①

easy 5th class

Begin climb 300'
below DISAPPOINTMENT - RED SENTINEL col

**53. DISAPPOINTMENT PEAK
WEST ARETE
II, 5.9**

tion lies on the west face of the southwest ridge. Start on the crest of the ridge; then bear up and left to an exposed traverse leading onto the west face above the overhangs. Follow this traverse for about 180 feet to a slight break leading upward and follow the break for 140 feet to a ceiling. Pass this obstacle 30 feet to the left. Sixty feet above, an obvious traverse leads back to the crest of the plateau. Only one pitch now remains before the summit plateau is reached.

ROUTE 6. ☞*Southwest Couloir.* I, 4.0. First descent and ascent July 14, 1926, by Norman Clyde, Ernest Dawson, Alice Carter, Julie Mortimer, and J. C. Downing. Although the first use of this route to reach the Lower Saddle and the Grand Teton from a camp at Amphitheater Lake was somewhat by accident, this couloir does provide the easiest route from Garnet Canyon to the summit of Disappointment Peak. From the vicinity of the Caves (see *Garnet Canyon*) a very large couloir leads northeast up to the summit plateau of Disappointment Peak. The first large chockstone is easily passed, but the second requires some scrambling on the right (south). From the plateau it is little more than a walk to the summit. As a descent route this couloir is simple and fast down to the Caves. When the upper chockstone is reached, cross a rib into a subsidiary smaller couloir to the left (south) and scramble down to a steep 20-foot wall, which can be downclimbed, or rappelled with a single rope, to regain the main couloir. *Time: 2¾ hours from the Caves.* See *Sierra Club Bulletin,* 12, no. 4 (1927), pp. 356–364, illus.

ROUTE 7. Merriam Couloir. II, 5.1. First ascent July 17, 1950, by Robert and Doris Merriam. The couloir, which separates the South Central Buttress from Grunt Arête, provides a moderate yet interesting route to the summit of Disappointment Peak for those camped at the Platforms. Start the climb a short distance up the canyon from the Platforms. Some 4.0 climbing is required to pass the initial cliff band below the couloir. Ascend the short talus section and enter the moderately steep couloir proper. After about 250 feet the couloir narrows to a steep chimney, blocked by chockstones at two levels. The original ascent apparently continued to the top of the couloir, where a sloping slab provides an interesting lieback exit onto the southeast ridge. The summit can be reached after a long walk.

Variation: II, 5.6. First ascent July 30, 1973, by Robert Fenichel and Richard Schmitz. When confronted by the chockstones, move left (west) around the corner for 200 feet to the base of a brick-red wall. Climb this wall to a point in its upper left end that is near a chimney, then follow a steep fingertip crack up and right until one can scramble left into a large couloir. Ascend this couloir for several hundred feet to its end at a tight chimney. Scramble up and right to near the top of an open chimney in black rock. The next pitch traverses straight left on chicken heads around the corner, then farther left (5.6) across a steep face back into the original tight chimney for the belay. Climb the remainder of the chimney onto the southeast ridge.

ROUTE 8. No Name Couloir. II, 4.0. First ascent August 20, 1973, by Randy Jamieson and Dave Alvestad. This climb, stated simply as the gully west of the Surprise Lake outlet stream, apparently ascended the couloir separating Almost Arête on the east from Grunt Arête on the west. Leave the Garnet Canyon trail as it crosses the broad talus slope west of the Surprise Lake outlet stream and head for this gully. The lower portion of the gully appears easy, with perhaps some scrambling required to exit at the top onto the southeast ridge.

ROUTE 9. ☞Southeast Ridge. II, 4.0. Probable first ascent August 12, 1935, by Perry W. Gilbert. This long ridge, which bounds Surprise Lake and Amphitheater Lake on the south, provides the most straightforward route to the summit of Disappointment Peak from the east. From the Lupine Meadows trailhead take the trail to Amphitheater Lake. Cross the outlet stream from the lake and hike up grassy slopes, covered with snow in early season, to the saddle in the ridge south of the lake. Contour north along the base of the cliffs, which form the west side of the saddle, to a large, wide chimney seen from below to be blocked by two giant chockstones. Climb this chimney, passing the first by means of a tunnel, an uncommon feature. The second chockstone is turned via easy rock on the left (south). The gully above is then easily followed up to the eastern extension of the summit plateau. Proceed west to the summit along the flat ridge top, passing the various towers on this ridge, which are the "summits" of the more easterly southern ridges rising from Garnet Canyon. Note that if the ridge crest itself, which lies south of the wide chimney, is followed from the initial saddle, several pitches of greater difficulty will be encountered. On descent, a trail will be found leading from the low point of the summit plateau through the low, wind-deformed trees to the head of the aforementioned gully. This is followed down to the large chockstones. Remember that the ridge crest itself is more difficult and if followed will require some rappelling.

ROUTE 10. ☞Lake Ledges. II, 4.0. First ascent August 20, 1925, by Phil Smith and Walter Harvey. See Photos 59 and 65. From Amphitheater Lake a prominent snow couloir leads in a southwest direction up to the summit plateau. To the left (east) of this couloir a series of ledges and short cliffs leads to the ridge extending east from the southern edge of this plateau. These can be climbed in many places, and so the difficulty of the route will depend on the routefinding ability of the party climbing it. Some of the alternatives are moderately difficult. Once the plateau is reached, hike west and north to the summit blocks, which require a bit of scrambling. A 5.1 pitch must be climbed if these blocks are attacked directly from the southeast. Time: 2 to 4 hours from Amphitheater Lake; 6½ to 7½ hours from Jenny Lake.

ROUTE 11. Snow Couloir. II, 4.0. First descent August 20, 1925, by Phil Smith and Walter Harvey; first ascent uncertain. See Photos 59 and 64. The long snow couloir leading southwest from Amphitheater Lake up to the summit plateau is also referred to as the Spoon Couloir because of its distinctive shape. In early season it is a long moderately steep snow climb all the way from Amphitheater Lake to the plateau.

ROUTE 12. East Chimney. II, 5.7. First ascent September 5, 1956, by Harvey T. Carter and Robert Beck. Above Amphitheater Lake a band of slabby cliffs extends from the Snow Couloir (Route 11) on the south to the East Ridge (Route 13) on the north, effectively blocking access to the upper plateau of Disappointment Peak. The left (southern) section of this band is a nearly blank wall with vertical water stains. The right section, about 200 to 300 feet high, is more broken with cracks, ledges, and chimneys. Two chimney or open book formations cut up through the lower portion of this right section. This East Chimney route goes up the left (south) of these two chimney systems. In early season a small snow patch lies below and slightly left of this chimney. Scramble up a series of easy blocks and ledges for 150 feet to the base of the first section of the chimney. The first long lead goes directly up the chimney or inside corner, past two small overhangs (5.6) to easier ground, ending at a comfortable ledge with a very small tree. A fixed piton will be found a few feet above this tree. From the belay move right and then left across slabs to a small alcove, then out right to reach the main wide crack of the chimney. This long pitch begins with an awkward 5.7 bulge and ends on the large tree-, grass-, and talus-covered shelf that extends from the east ridge all the way south along the top of the main cliff band to the southeast ridge. One can walk south along this shelf and reach the summit plateau by one short pitch near the south end of the shelf. The original climb of this route, however, apparently continued up near the north end of the rock above. The rock on this route is good and solid. See American Alpine Journal, 11, no. 1 (1958), p. 84.

ROUTE 13. East Ridge. II, 5.6. First ascent September 2, 1937, by Jack Durrance, George Sheldon, and Percy Rideout. See Topo 54 and Photos 59, 64, and 65. This is a short, enjoyable climb on excellent rock leading to one of the finest viewpoints in the range, the summit of Disappointment Peak. For approach take the trail to Surprise and Amphitheater Lakes from the Lupine Meadows trailhead. From Amphitheater Lake hike north to the col overlooking Glacier Gulch and then follow the ridge left (west) through the trees to the start of the climb. The difficulty of this route can be varied, depending on how closely the crest of the ridge is followed. The initial short rock step is passed by a single pitch of easy climbing to reach the horizontal section leading to the base of the long steep section of the ridge. A lead of face climbing is followed by a second, which ends in a right-facing corner that takes one to a belay ledge. Two more

DISAPPOINTMENT summit plateau

⑥

easier   5.6

5.7

to North Face

FP

FP

⑤

5.5

5.7 crack/stem
move to left   ④

③

30'   crack

②

5.4

5.6   bulge

Walk along horizontal
section of ridge (150')   → to North Face routes

①

5.4

easier left of crest

**54. DISAPPOINTMENT PEAK
EAST RIDGE
II, 5.6**

pitches continue with crack and face climbing to gain the left edge of a ledge. The final lead, the most difficult, goes up a vertical face past two fixed pitons to the final ledge where one emerges onto the edge of the summit plateau of the peak. Now above the steep portion of the ridge, one can easily follow the somewhat jagged ridge to the summit. For descent take the Southeast Ridge (*Route 9*) or the Lake Ledges (*Route 10*). One should avoid the steep, east-facing Snow Couloir (*Route 11*) unless one has an ice axe and is knowledgeable in its use. *Time: 3 to 4 hours* from Amphitheater Lake; *6¾ to 9 hours* from Jenny Lake.

ROUTE 14. Pownall–Unsoeld North Face. III, 5.8, A2, or III, 5.10+. First ascent July 27, 1956, by Richard Pownall and Willi Unsoeld; first free ascent August 6, 1979, by Mike Munger and Bill Feiges, at which time the name Pin Time was applied. See *Topo 55* and *Photos 65* and *66*. Because of loose rock, scary traverses, and the degree to which the final pitch is vegetated, this route is best left to the true aficionado of the obscure. The north face of Disappointment Peak is divided horizontally by a broad shelf or bench that cuts across the eastern half of the face about halfway up from the bottom; this shelf blends into the face about halfway across. See *Photo 64*. This severe route diagonals from left to right up the indented eastern portion of the north face above this broad shelf. Climb to the top of the first step of the east ridge (*Route 13*). Two diagonal ramps, which are the major features of this route, should be visible from the top of this step. To find the base of the climb, traverse out across the shelf until just past a large overhang that usually has water dripping inside it. The first pitch begins just to the east of a second overhang (containing freshly fallen rock) in a nice finger crack that one must step up into. After about 30 feet of climbing, this crack begins to flare. At this point one is forced to exit right across a short section of face climbing (5.9) that leads to a right-facing corner. Follow the corner (10 feet) up and then onto a ledge that leads back left (east) past an old piton to a step that must be climbed (5.8) to allow access to the beginning of the first ramp. This ramp will be followed up and right for about 200 feet. A good belay ledge will be found at the east end of this first ramp beneath a chimney that slants off and to the right. Climb the chimney and a nice crack to the left of it for about 40 feet until it is possible to traverse left across a short section of face climbing (5.9). Then climb up and left to a prow, around which can be seen a 6-inch-wide, 20-foot-long ledge that goes out to the east. Proceed out across this ledge, the "Plank," without protection to its eastern end, where an exciting 5.8 move permits access to the second of the two ramps. Continue up the ramp (5.10, RPs useful) until the difficulty eases off and belay. The remainder of the ramp is much easier (5.6). The last lead (5.10+) up a vertical right-facing corner and cracks to the right is strenuous and the difficulties are compounded by the fact that the corner is

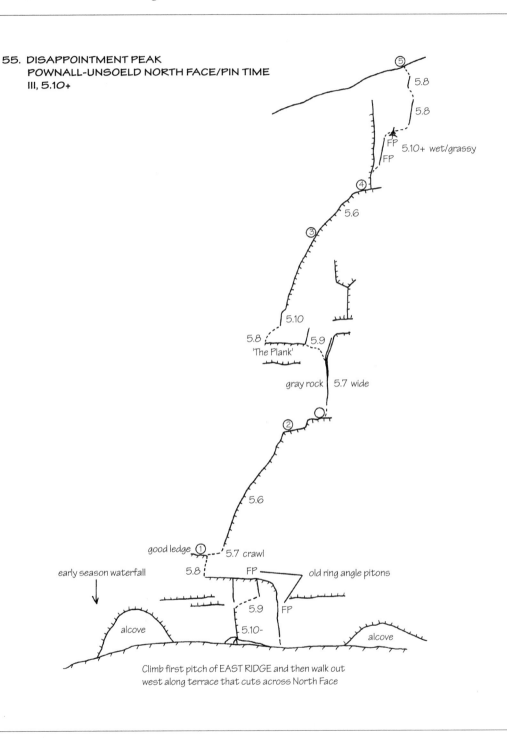

55. DISAPPOINTMENT PEAK
POWNALL-UNSOELD NORTH FACE/PIN TIME
III, 5.10+

⑤

5.8

5.8

FP
FP   5.10+ wet/grassy

④

5.6

③

5.10

5.8   5.9
'The Plank'

gray rock 5.7 wide

②

good ledge ①   5.7 crawl

early season waterfall   5.8   FP   old ring angle pitons

5.9   FP

5.10-

alcove   alcove

Climb first pitch of EAST RIDGE and then walk out
west along terrace that cuts across North Face

vegetated and the cracks dirt filled. Near the top, exit to the right near a small pine and continue up right-facing corners to the top of the climb. The first-ascent party used aid on the first and last pitches. As with any of these north face routes it is suggested that one seek conditions that are as dry as possible. See *American Alpine Journal,* 10, no. 2 (1957), p. 148.

ROUTE 15. *Chouinard–Frost Chimney.* IV, 5.9, A3, or IV, 5.9. First ascent August 13, 1962, by Yvon Chouinard and Tom Frost; first free ascent August 19, 1970, by Dave Ingalls and Dave Loeks. See *Topo 56* and *Photos 64, 65* and *66.* The eastern portion of the north face of Disappointment Peak is a massive wall broken about halfway up by a broad horizontal shelf that extends west from the east ridge. This long and severe route starts at the base of this wall and follows a prominent chimney up to this shelf about 450 feet above. The route then continues up the face, curving to the right (west) before reaching the crest of the east ridge. For the approach, take the Surprise and Amphitheater Lakes trail from the Lupine Meadows trailhead past Amphitheater Lake to the col to the north that overlooks Glacier Gulch. For the complete route descend to the base of the north face and start the climb at a point 600 feet west of the old cables (no longer there) on the lower portion of the face. An alternative start is to climb the first 150 feet of the East Ridge (*Route 13*) up from the col north of Amphitheater Lake and then to traverse out on the aforementioned horizontal shelf. This start avoids the first three or four pitches of the climb and is recommended because the lower section is reported to be quite unpleasant.

The climb starts in a large, low-angle, loose chimney up to the first chockstone, which is passed on the right (5.9) to a belay stance. The second pitch continues up this chimney, passing the second chockstone on slabs on the right (5.9), then back left; or one can climb over it. An easy lead then takes one to a large terrace. Scrambling then permits access to the main horizontal shelf, where the best climbing on the route begins in the chimney-crack in the wall above. With a 50-meter rope only two leads are required to reach the upper end of this chimney, which curves gently to the right. The first of these, a full ropelength, passes a chockstone via 5.9 hands on its right side and goes up through a 5.8 squeeze section to a belay stance above the next chockstone. The second continues more easily (5.6) up the chimney, curving right to a stance on a ledge just right of the end of the chimney. The next pitch continues up and right in steep and difficult cracks (5.9) onto a ramp that is followed past some blocks, ending with a traverse right (5.8) for 50 feet. The fourth lead goes up a large left-facing corner (5.9) that curves left and becomes an overhang before turning right again to the belay stance. Now climb a crack upward until one can work back left on easy ledges to a short 5.9 move up to the next belay ledge. The final pitch is easier, mostly scrambling, up and left onto the east

ridge at the edge of the summit plateau. An alternate last pitch was done in 1994 (Byerly–Kimbrough). Just after the preceding 5.9 move, face climb (5.9) up and left toward a left-facing corner that provides a 5.9+ finish for the route. Climb this route only in late season or when there is no chance of its being wet. For protection take a standard rack to 4 inches. For descent, use the Southeast Ridge (*Route 9*) or the Lake Ledges (*Route 10*). See *American Alpine Journal,* 13, no. 2 (1963), pp. 487–489.

ROUTE 16. *Kimbrough–Rickert.* III, 5.10-. First ascent August 1994, by Tom Kimbrough and Steve Rickert. See *Photos 64, 65* and *66.* This route follows a line of weakness located just to the east of the main large chimney system on the north face. Access to the route is gained via the ledge that cuts across the north face, so approach in the same way as for *Routes 14* and *15.* Just past *Route 15* climbing is required (two to three pitches, 5.7) to continue farther along to the base of this route located at the bottom of the aforementioned chimney system. Begin by climbing up into the main drainage and then traverse up and east for over two pitches (5.6), heading for an arch in an area of black rock. The third pitch consists of a 5.10- finger crack that leads up and left from near the bottom of the arch to a belay ledge. Now follow a big chimney or gully up and right for two pitches (5.4). Near the top of the second of these pitches, 5.9 face climbing permits access to a large ledge system. Traverse up and east on the ledge until a big, left-facing corner appears. Climb the corner (5.7) and belay where one can see a wild hand traverse leading to the east once again. For the seventh pitch, begin with this wild hand traverse (5.9 to 5.10-) over to a right-facing corner and then continue up and into a steep, left-facing corner (5.9), belaying beneath an overhang. Climb this overhang (5.9) up and onto the summit plateau.

ROUTE 17. *Direct North Face.* III, 5.8. First ascent August 4, 1955, by John Dietschy and William Cropper. See *Photos 65* and *66.* This difficult route goes up the right (west) portion of the main north face between two overhanging bulges. The face climbing on the first, third, and fourth pitches is superb. The base of the north face is reached in the usual manner from Amphitheater Lake. The approach to this route is then via the snow below the Red Sentinel. After leaving the snow (at the point indicated on the photograph), scramble back eastward for a few hundred feet. The first three pitches lead upward over broken cliffs toward the ceiling-type overhang that can be seen above. From a comfortable ledge just below the overhang, the smooth outside wall to the left looks promising, but there are no cracks for protection. Hence, the overhang must be attacked directly. Climb the back wall beneath the overhang for 25 feet, then traverse a few feet to the left until immediately below the horizontal 5-foot ceiling of the overhang. Now make a hand traverse on a flake, which is detached from the ceiling, out to the lip of the overhang. Once established out

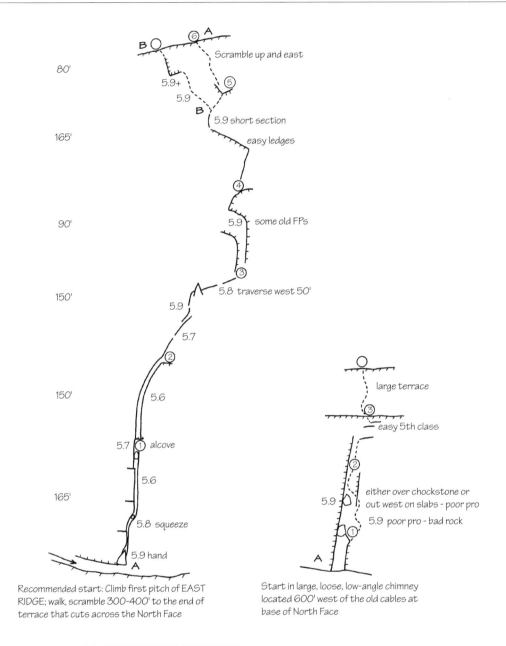

80'

B ⃝   ⑥ A

Scramble up and east

5.9+
5.9
B
5.9 short section

165'

easy ledges

④

90'

5.9 some old FPs

③

150'

5.8 traverse west 50'

5.9

5.7

②

150'

5.6

5.7 ① alcove

5.6

165'

5.8 squeeze

5.9 hand
A

large terrace

③

easy 5th class

②

5.9 either over chockstone or
out west on slabs - poor pro

5.9 poor pro - bad rock

①

A

Recommended start: Climb first pitch of EAST
RIDGE; walk, scramble 300-400' to the end of
terrace that cuts across the North Face

Start in large, loose, low-angle chimney
located 600' west of the old cables at
base of North Face

56. DISAPPOINTMENT PEAK
A. CHOUINARD-FROST CHIMNEY, IV, 5.9
B. VARIATION: BYERLY-KIMBROUGH, IV, 5.9+

on the face above the overhang, make a very thin traverse (5.8) to the left (east) before climbing upward to a good belay stance on a downsloping ledge below a second overhang. Two short pitches slightly to the right place one on a 10-inch ledge at the base of a very shallow gully bordered on the left by a 130-foot crack and on the right (west) by a steep chimney. The chimney is not recommended because of its steepness and its wet moss. The next lead up a 130-foot lieback crack is 5.6 and provides access to a broken ledge from which it is just a scramble to the east ridge and the summit.

An unexpected alternative start for this route is via the main horizontal shelf that divides the north face of Disappointment Peak. From the east ridge follow this shelf west, past both *Route 14* and *Route 15* to the point where this Direct North Face route intersects the western extension of the shelf. The final portion of this horizontal traverse involves some significant climbing. *Time: 8 hours* from Amphitheater Lake. See *American Alpine Journal*, 10, no. 1 (1956), pp. 116–119.

ROUTE 18. Northwest Crack. II, 5.4. First ascent August 15, 1955, by William Cropper and John Dietschy. See *Photos 66* and *67*. On the western portion of the north face of Disappointment Peak are three main shelves that angle left (east) up to the east ridge. The lower right (west) end of the lowest of the three shelves dwindles down to a crack in a steep wall. Approach this route from Amphitheater Lake or Glacier Gulch, leaving the steep snow below the Red Sentinel–Disappointment Peak notch at the base of this crack. If this crack is wet, make two short leads on the wall to the right (west) before traversing back left into the crack. Climb the next three ropelengths up the crack, sometimes using the wall to the left. The crack narrows to about 10 inches on the last pitch, and wedged chockstones must be used for holds. To reach the wide shelf above, climb right (west) out of the top of the crack. Scramble up the shelf to the east ridge, reaching the summit via the easy summit plateau. *Time: 7 hours* from Amphitheater Lake. See *American Alpine Journal*, 10, no. 1 (1956), pp. 116–119.

ROUTE 19. Gran. II, 5.8. First ascent July 5, 1962, by Art Gran and John Hudson. This route lies between the Northwest Crack (*Route 18*) and the Northwest Shelf (*Route 20*) using the central of the three ledge and chimney systems that slant from lower right to upper left to meet the east ridge. See *Photo 67*. Approach via the standard route from Amphitheater Lake out toward the Teton Glacier until west of the main north face of Disappointment Peak. Ascend the couloir (loose rock and steep snow) up toward the notch separating the Red Sentinel from the west face of Disappointment Peak. This route ascends the ledge that starts about 250 feet below this notch. Walk out left (east) on the ledge and scramble up a short wall to a higher ledge at the base of a large, steep open book. Climb the left wall for about 20 feet to a ledge where it is possible to enter the open

book and reach a second ledge. Ascend a crack in the right wall, cross to the left well up past chockstones, and then step left around a corner to a belay ledge. The next pitch traverses left (east) and up and over a difficult bulge. The chockstone ceiling above is passed on the right to a ledge that is reached after 90 feet. Now climb and scramble up to the east for about 170 feet until the ledge ends. A final scramble up to the right below the ridge leads to a small notch in the crest of the east ridge. Follow the ridge to the summit. See *American Alpine Journal*, 13, no. 2 (1963), pp. 487–489.

ROUTE 20. Northwest Shelf. II, 5.1. Partial descent August 20, 1925, by Phil Smith and Walter Harvey; first complete descent August 11, 1953, by Robert Brooke and Rob Day. See *Photo 67*. As a means of ascent, this route should be approached from Garnet Canyon up to the notch between the Red Sentinel and the west face of Disappointment Peak. On the western portion of the north face of Disappointment Peak are three main shelves that angle up to the left (east) to meet the long east ridge. From the notch a narrow ledge leads out on the north face to connect with the highest of these shelves. It may be necessary to descend slightly to reach the ledge. One can climb the shelf with no great difficulty by keeping to the right, next to the wall. The series of ledges and short faces that form the shelf are connected by a rotten chimney, which can be climbed. The shelf comes out on the east ridge at the first prominent notch east (about 200 feet) of the summit.

GARNET CANYON, NORTH SIDE ROCK CLIMBS

Map: Grand Teton

Fairshare Tower (11,520+)   (0.3 mi E of Teepe Pillar)

The precipitous southern extremity of Fairshare Tower is divided by a very steep, narrow chimney into a large buttress on the right (east) and a narrow, high-angle arête on the left. Most of this rock is of good quality. The following nonsummit routes lead to the Watchtower, a prominent pinnacle at the upper end of the south ridge of Fairshare Tower.

CHRONOLOGY

Watchtower, Direct South Ridge: August 2, 1958, John Gill, Bill Mason

Watchtower, North Ridge: July 9, 1957, John Dietschy, Irene Ortenburger (descent)

Corkscrew: July 25, 1969, Steve Wunsch, Diana Hunter

    var: F.N.G.: 1991, Bill Alexander, John Carr

Watchtower, West Arête: July 9, 1975, Bob Crawford, Kurt Mendenhall

ROUTE 1. Watchtower, West Arête. II, 5.9. First ascent July 9, 1975, by Bob Crawford and Kurt Mendenhall. The exact location of this five-pitch route is uncertain, but it lies on an arête, separated from the west side of the Watchtower by a snow gully. *Note:* The two cracks on the west side of the formation, directly below the summit, are both gritty and difficult. The left crack is most likely solid 5.11, while the one on the right goes at 5.10+. The initial lead of 100 feet, up a 100-foot 5.8 face, is followed by an easier lead (5.6) of 130 feet up the same line. At this point make a 45-foot traverse (5.7) to the right to ledges, from which a 90-foot lead turns directly upward. At the belay two cracks diverge upward, one angling right and the other slightly left. Take the left crack, 5.9 offwidth, for 120 feet onto the ridge crest, which is then followed easily back to the right to the summit of the Watchtower.

ROUTE 2. Corkscrew. II, 5.8. First ascent July 25, 1969, by Steve Wunsch and Diana Hunter. See *Topo 57* and *Photos 54 and 59.* This six-pitch route is one of the better rock climbs in Garnet Canyon because it is readily accessible, not subject to the weather problems of higher routes, and has relatively easy retreat options. The approach is from the Garnet Canyon trail above the Caves. Proceed up the switchbacks and leave the trail where it begins the long horizontal traverse toward the outlet stream from Teepe Glacier. The Fairshare Tower south ridge is a short distance from the trail. This route lies on the arête left (west) of the very steep, narrow chimney that splits the end of this ridge. It starts on the south side of the arête just right of center and then angles up slightly left for the next five pitches, ending on the west face of the arête. The first lead goes up and right from the bottom of the arête, past a small left-facing corner, to a large belay ledge in the main left-facing dihedral. From the ledge climb the dihedral to an exit onto low-angle slabs to the left. The third pitch ascends a jam crack (5.6) on the south face to a stance at the corner of the arête; go around onto the west face and continue up steep cracks on the left (west) side of the arête to a square-cut belay ledge. A short 5.8 section is then required to reach a chimney up and left, which is then climbed (5.7) to a notch behind a tower. The final pitch is easier climbing upward until one can scramble off the arête to the west. For protection take a standard rack up to 3 inches.

Variation: FNG II, 5.8+. First ascent 1991 by Bill Alexander and John Carr. See *Topo 57* and *Photo 54.* Proceed as in *Route 2* up from the Garnet Canyon trail to the base of the Watchtower, up and east of the start of the Corkscrew. The first pitch ascends a 5.8 right-facing dihedral that is somewhat tricky to protect. From the top of this dihedral climb a bulge via a hand crack (5.8) to a belay on a terrace. Face climbing (5.7+) leads up to a short offwidth with a chockstone at the bottom of it. Climb the offwidth (5.8+) and then continue up into a left-facing corner via 5.8 hands to a belay on another series of terraces. Move the belay up

and left (west) and then face climb (5.8) to intersect the upper part of the Corkscrew route.

ROUTE 3. Watchtower, Direct South Ridge. II, 5.8. First ascent August 2, 1958, by John Gill and Bill Mason. See *Photos 54 and 59.* The Watchtower is the only large tower on the south ridge of Fairshare Tower. The difficulty of this route depends on its directness; easier climbing can usually be found to the right (east) of the ridge crest. Start the climb from the upper corner of a gigantic gray boulder that is located just right (east) of the steep, narrow chimney that splits the end of the ridge. After one ropelength in a prominent chimney near the crest of the ridge, diagonal left and pass under a small roof to a 30-foot open chimney adjacent to the crest. Climb a pitch up the center of a slabby face and then move around a corner to the left into an open chimney on the crest. The roof and the difficult overhang above the roof are both climbed directly. Next climb a 50-foot crack on the right side of the crest. After some easier climbing to a small overhang, the final pitch containing an overhanging flake goes directly up the crest. Scramble to the summit.

ROUTE 4. Watchtower, North Ridge. II, 4.0. First descent July 9, 1957, by John Dietschy and Irene Ortenburger. This narrow ridge is the natural route on this pinnacle and can be climbed without difficulty from the broad saddle that connects with the main summit of Fairshare Tower. It can be gained either from the east or from the west.

Disappointment Peak (11,618)

The numerous southern ridges of Disappointment Peak were the first scene of nonsummit rock-climbing activity in the Tetons. The very convenient location of these ridges above the heavily used Garnet Canyon trail explains the early attention accorded this center of high-angle rock. While, as is usual in the mountains, not all of the rock on every ridge is solid, many of these routes contain excellent rock, and some of the best rock climbs in the Tetons are to be found here. A characteristic of some of the routes, however, is that the ridge or buttress is not well-defined and contains more than a single line, and its difficulty depends on exactly how closely the crest is followed. These nonsummit routes in Garnet Canyon are listed in order from west to east.

CHRONOLOGY

Satisfaction Arête: August 20, 1955, Richard
   Pownall, Allen Steck
Satisfaction Crack: August 19, 1956, John Gill,
   Gene Davant, Tom Clohessy
South Central Buttress: June 29, 1957, William and
   Evelyn Cropper, James Langford
      var: July 22, 1957, John Dietschy, James
         Langford
      var: **Direct East Corner:** August 5, 1958, John
         Gill, Bill Mason

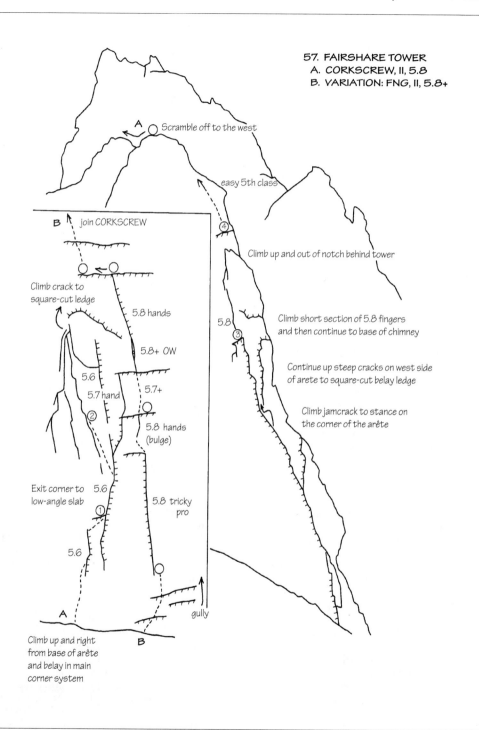

57. FAIRSHARE TOWER
A. CORKSCREW, II, 5.8
B. VARIATION: FNG, II, 5.8+

A ○ Scramble off to the west

easy 5th class

B ↑ join CORKSCREW

Climb up and out of notch behind tower

Climb crack to
square-cut ledge

5.8 hands

5.8+ OW

5.8   Climb short section of 5.8 fingers
③   and then continue to base of chimney

5.6

5.7 hand   5.7+

Continue up steep cracks on west side
of arete to square-cut belay ledge

②

5.8 hands
(bulge)

Climb jamcrack to stance on
the corner of the arête

Exit corner to   5.6
low-angle slab

①   5.8 tricky
pro

5.6

gully

A

B

Climb up and right
from base of arête
and belay in main
corner system

var: August 9, 1966, Sherman Lehman,
William Hooker, William Kirkpatrick
Irene's Arête: July 10, 1957, John Dietschy, Irene
Ortenburger
var: July 2, 1970, Jim Olson, Mark Chapman
Grunt Arête: July 23, 1957, John Dietschy, James
Langford
var: **South Face:** July 6, 1958, John Gill, Paul
Rieche
Open Book: August 21, 1963, Phil Jacobus, Steve
Larsen; first free ascent, June 26, 1977, Jim
Donini, Mike Munger
var: **Left of Open Book:** July 28, 1977, Mike
Munger, Ed Sessions
var: **Right of Open Book:** July 1983, Kim
Schmitz, Jim Donini
Caves Arête: August 7, 1957, John Dietschy, Robert
Larson
var: **West Face:** July 11, 1970, Thomas
Dunwiddie, Scott Stewart, Roger
Zimmerman
Almost Arête: July 15, 1958, John Gill, Fred
Truslow
var: **Gray Slab:** July 23, 1963, Richard Gold-
stone, Peter Gardiner, Steven Derenzo
var: **Almost Overhanging:** August 20, 1972,
Howard Friedman, Henry Mitchell
var: 1980, Andy Carson, Jim Evangelista
var: July 13, 1985, Steve Saez, Mark Golde
Fifth Column: July 17, 1958, John Gill, James
Langford
var: **The Knob:** July 25, 1958, John Gill, Yvon
Chouinard
var: **Hummingbird Face:** July 12, 1981, Rich
Perch, Mike Beiser
Beelzebub Arête: July 19, 1958, John Gill, Fred
Truslow
Lance's Arête: July 28, 1958, John Gill, Dave Jones
Satisfaction Buttress: July 28 and August 1, 1958,
Yvon Chouinard, Bob Kamps; first free ascent
July 15, 1977, Rich Perch, Mike Munger
Hidden Arête: July 31, 1958, John Gill, Bill Mason
Delicate Arête: August 16, 1958, John Gill, Fred
Wright
West Side Story: August 23, 1977, George
Montopoli, Keith Hadley
Whiton-Wiggins: September 19, 1981, Earl
Wiggins, Mark Whiton
var: **Sacco-Vanzetti Memorial:** Spring, 1992,
Jay Pistono, Keith Cattabriga, Ray
Warburton
Jern-Wiggins: September 11, 1983, Ken Jern, Earl
Wiggins
Yodel This: summer 1995 (unfinished), Mike
Fisher, Sam Lightner

ROUTE 1. West Side Story. II, 5.8. First ascent August 23, 1977, by George Montopoli and Keith Hadley. See *Topo 58* and *Photos 57* and *58*. This route lies on the west side of the southwest ridge of Disappointment Peak where a large di-hedral system begins about 600 feet past (north of) the base of the ridge. Take the Garnet Canyon trail from the Lupine Meadows trailhead, continuing on the trail past the Caves to a point from which it is possible to angle up into the large talus gully to the west of the southwest ridge of Disappoint-ment Peak. Proceed up this gully several hundred feet to the major right-facing corner or dihedral. This major dihe-dral is located down and to the south of the Great West Chimney route. The first two leads are to the right of the dihedral, first up a ramp, then in a crack system before traversing left back into the dihedral itself. The next two leads ascend the dihedral proper to the final pitch, which passes an overhang on the left, exiting on a 5.8 face to the top where the dihedral system intersects the upper south-west ridge and the summit plateau. For descent use the Southwest Couloir (*Disappointment Peak, Route 6*) to get back into Garnet Canyon or the Lake Ledges (*Disappoint-ment Peak, Route 10*) to Amphitheater Lake and the main trail back to Lupine Meadows. Some loose rock is to be expected on this route.

ROUTE 2. Whiton–Wiggins. II, 5.9. First ascent September 19, 1981, by Earl Wiggins and Mark Whiton. See *Photo 58*. High on the face to the right (south) of the West Side Story line is another large corner formation that is visible from be-low. This eight-pitch route ascends a crack system up to this corner. The climb starts from the vicinity of a very large right-facing corner that rises immediately above the talus a short distance up the Red Sentinel Gully. Ascend the talus of the gully and turn up the wall just past this corner. Sev-eral leads of 5.7 and 5.8 difficulty go mostly straight up toward the right-facing corner high on the face, with some angling left in steep cracks and past bulges. The two leads up the corner were the crux of the route. These pitches involve climbing a large black slot (5.8) and climbing left around a gray roof into a strenuous offwidth crack (5.9). One final pitch of easier rock then leads to the top of the route from which the upper plateau is easily reached. On the first ascent of this route the Great West Chimney (see *Dis-appointment Peak, Route 4*) was downclimbed with difficulty; one rappel was required to gain the talus of the Red Sentinel Gully.

Variation: Sacco–Vanzetti Memorial. II, 5.10. First as-cent spring 1992, by Jay Pistono, Keith Cattabriga, and Ray Warburton. See *Topo 59* and *Photo 58*. This six-pitch climb apparently started just to the right (south) of *Route 2*. The first two pitches went up the difficult (5.10) "very large right-facing corner" mentioned earlier and then joined *Route 2* for the middle three leads. At the gray roof on the final pitch this variation avoids the offwidth by face climb-ing out around to the right and then finishes with 5.9+ stemming up to the summit plateau.

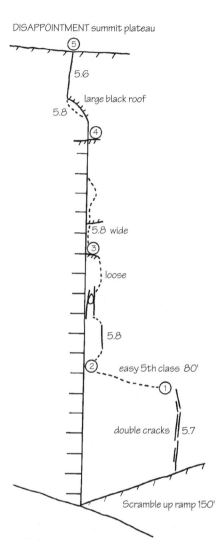

DISAPPOINTMENT summit plateau

⑤

5.6

large black roof

5.8

④

5.8 wide

③

loose

5.8

② easy 5th class 80'

①

double cracks 5.7

Scramble up ramp 150'

Take GARNET CANYON trail to CAVES;
several hundred feet up RED SENTINEL
gully to major right-facing corner

58. DISAPPOINTMENT PEAK
WEST SIDE STORY
II, 5.8

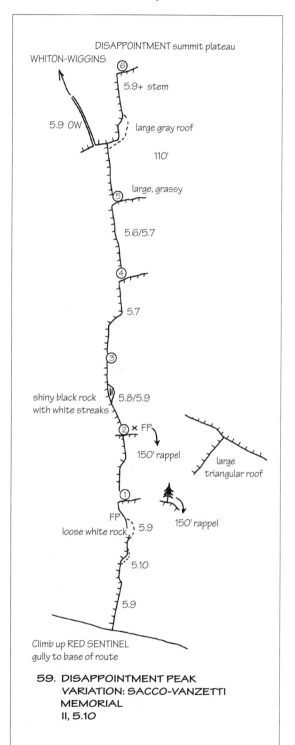

DISAPPOINTMENT summit plateau

WHITON-WIGGINS ⑥

5.9+ stem

5.9 OW

large gray roof

110'

⑤ large, grassy

5.6/5.7

④

5.7

③

shiny black rock 5.8/5.9
with white streaks

② × FP

150' rappel

large
triangular roof

①

FP 150' rappel

loose white rock 5.9

5.10

5.9

Climb up RED SENTINEL
gully to base of route

59. DISAPPOINTMENT PEAK
VARIATION: SACCO-VANZETTI
MEMORIAL
II, 5.10

ROUTE 3. Jern–Wiggins. II, 5.9. First ascent September 11, 1983, by Ken Jern and Earl Wiggins. See *Photo 58*. This five-pitch route on the west face of the southwest ridge is a short distance to the right (south and east) of the Whiton–Wiggins route (*Route 2*). From the Caves take the talus, or snow in early season, a short distance up into the Red Sentinel Gully. The start of this climb is found just to the right of a very large right-facing corner that rises immediately above the talus. The first pitch angles right, up toward but passing below a higher but equally large, overhanging right-facing corner. The roofs to the right of this corner are passed on the right to gain the steep wall above, which is then climbed more or less straight up. Near the top a band of light-colored rock between two sections of black rock is climbed via a good vertical crack near its center.

ROUTE 4. Caves Arête. II, 5.4. First ascent August 7, 1957, by John Dietschy and Robert Larson. See *Photos 59* and *60*. This ridge forms the right (east) edge of the southwest couloir of Disappointment Peak and lies west of the more distinct Irene's Arête. The lower 300 feet involves nothing more than scrambling. The upper portion includes three pitches, which, for the most part, stay near the crest and are steep and exposed. *Time: 3½ hours* from Garnet Canyon. See *American Alpine Journal*, 11, no. 1 (1958), pp. 85–88.

Variation: West Face. II, 5.6. First ascent July 11, 1970, by Thomas Dunwiddie, Scott Stewart, and Roger Zimmerman. Scramble up to the highest trees on the southwest corner of the arête. Now climb 40 feet and make a long 5.4 traverse into a grassy couloir. Follow this couloir for about 300 feet, staying next to the west face of the arête, to reach a platform with a small tree. Resume climbing directly up the face (5.6) with a long lead up a lieback crack, a slab, and a nose onto a grassy belay ledge. Continue up to a row of overhangs that guards the top of the face. Passing these overhangs is only of 5.6 difficulty. This indirect variation has little to recommend it.

ROUTE 5. Irene's Arête. III, 5.8. First ascent July 10, 1957, by John Dietschy and Irene Ortenburger. See *Topo 60* and *Photos 59* and *60*. This outstanding rock climb of a beautiful knife-edge ridge has become one of the most popular of the difficult rock climbs in the Tetons. Purity of line, excellence of rock, and ease of access contribute to its high regard. This ridge is the one seen in profile when looking east from the Caves. The route goes almost directly up the crest of the ridge for six or seven pitches. Many excellent variations are possible on this route and some are marked on the topo. Approach via the Garnet Canyon trail from the Lupine Meadows trailhead, continuing to the Caves; leave the trail here. Scramble up and to the east (4.0) to the base of the main part of the arête.

From the large ledge at the base of the ridge, climb shallow cracks to the right of the crest to a belay at a flake. The second lead up the hand crack above passes two fixed pitons to gain a belay ledge, still on the right side of the crest. The next pitch begins just left of the crest with 5.7 face climbing leading out east to a left-facing corner in a black-rock area. It then continues up and around to the west side of the arête to a good belay ledge. The fourth lead can be climbed on either side of the crest. The original line goes up and left (5.8 face) and then continues with easier climbing to an area of black rock. Climb up past an overhang (5.7) and face climb into and then up a steep groove (5.7) to a sloping belay ledge. The next pitch is normally climbed on the left of the crest via cracks and face climbing to gain the horizontal knife-edge section of the ridge; a more difficult variation can be taken directly upward (5.9 corner, short). The cleft separating this section from the final wall is now directly ahead. The usual scheme here is to descend 150 feet to the right (east) and climb a break (5.7) in the wall. However, the wall above can be attacked directly via 5.9+ climbing, or between these alternatives there is a 5.8 fist crack. Some 200 feet of additional but easier climbing now provide access to the summit plateau. For descent, scramble to the west, past one small gully, over to the first major gully, the Southwest Couloir (*Disappointment Peak, Route 6*), which is easily descended. Alternatively, one could descend the Southeast Ridge (*Disappointment Peak, Route 9*) to Amphitheater Lake and the trail. *Time: 10½ hours* from the Caves. See *American Alpine Journal,* 11, no. 1 (1958), pp. 85–88; *Harvard Mountaineering,* 16 (May 1963), pp. 82–83.

Variation: III, 5.7. First ascent July 2, 1970, by Jim Olson and Mark Chapman. This variation begins at the step in the ridge crest midway up the fourth pitch. Instead of traversing right to gain the 5.7 groove, move left on the west face of the arête and slightly down to a ledge system, past the beginning of some overhanging jam cracks. Continue north for two leads in shallow gullies to a rotten belay alcove. The final lead goes 10 feet above the alcove, right and slightly down past a downward mantle, climbs up past the right side of an overhang (5.7), and finishes with an exposed friction face up and right onto the ridge crest. This variation reaches the ridge crest about 300 feet east of the prominent tower at the summit plateau and so avoids the notch to the east.

ROUTE 6. Beelzebub Arête. II, 5.7. First ascent July 19, 1958, by John Gill and Fred Truslow. See *Photo 59*. This small ridge can be described as the second arête west of the large south central buttress and the second arête east of Irene's Arête. The route starts close to the crest and follows it to the top of the arête. A 5.7 overhang was climbed during the first ascent on the final summit pitch.

ROUTE 7. Delicate Arête. II, 5.9. First ascent August 16, 1958, by John Gill and Fred Wright. See *Photos 59* and *61*. This small ridge lies immediately west of the south central buttress and is separated from it by a large chute. Several ropelengths lead up the lower crest and then into and up a short section of this chute, which contains a large chockstone. After securing a belay stance (a bolt will be

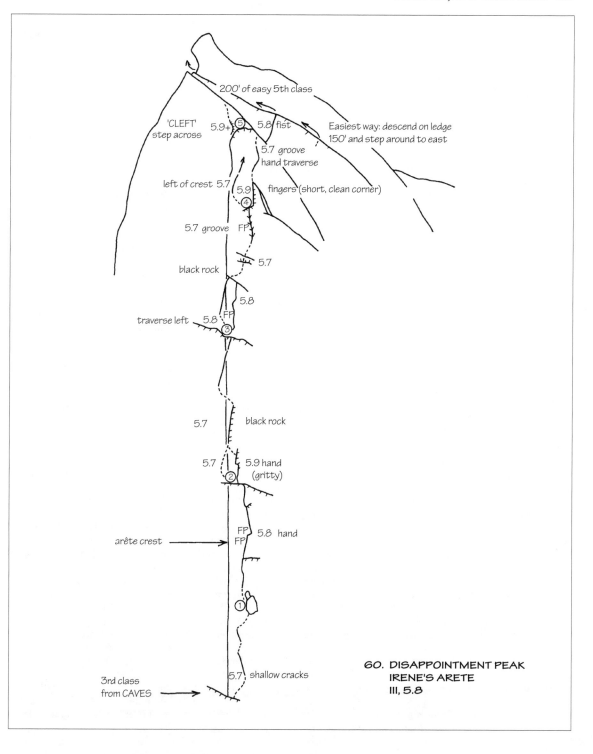

200' of easy 5th class

'CLEFT'
step across   5.9+ ⑤   5.8 fist

Easiest way: descend on ledge
150' and step around to east

5.7 groove
hand traverse

left of crest 5.7   5.9 ┃   fingers (short, clean corner)
④

5.7 groove   FP

5.7

black rock

5.8

traverse left   5.8 FP
③

5.7   black rock

5.7   5.9 hand
②   (gritty)

FP
arête crest   FP   5.8 hand

①

3rd class
from CAVES   5.7 shallow cracks

60. DISAPPOINTMENT PEAK
IRENE'S ARETE
III, 5.8

found here) at the base of the large slablike section of the crest above, avoid the temptation to move right onto easy rock and, instead, move a few feet left onto the eastern edge of this face, then around the corner continuing up with very little protection 120 feet to a large ledge. Easier climbing can be found in a crack system located even farther east. As done on the first ascent, however, this significant lead requires very difficult balance climbing on exposed and poorly protected rock. Above this crux pitch climb directly up the crest to the large roof that caps the arête. This can be passed on the right via a smooth face to the left of a slanting crack. A short scramble then leads to the top of the ridge. *Time: 6½ hours* from Jenny Lake.

ROUTE 8. South Central Buttress. II, 5.1. First ascent June 29, 1957, by William Cropper, Evelyn Cropper, and James Langford. See *Photos 59* and *61.* This route curves up from east to west and then, in the upper part, back to the crest of the ridge. Start from a large tree ledge, and climb up and west on the buttress to a steep section of smooth yellow rock. Traverse left (west) on easy slabs and then back to the crest for the final portion of the climb. There are about five pitches on this route. *Time: 9 hours* from Jenny Lake. See *American Alpine Journal,* 11, no. 1 (1958), pp. 85–88.

Variation: II, 5.4. First ascent July 22, 1957, by John Dietschy and James Langford. See *Photo 61.* This essentially distinct route on the south central buttress angles up from west to east, in the opposite direction from the first route, and hence crosses it. Begin roped climbing at the base of a steep gully just west of the buttress. After two pitches a large chockstone is passed, and the route leads onto the west face of the buttress for two more ropelengths. The crest is then reached. Make two leads in the section of smooth yellow slabs; then follow several small ledges around to the east side of the ridge and up to the top of the buttress. *Time: 5½ hours* from the Caves. See *American Alpine Journal,* 11, no. 1 (1958), pp. 85–88.

Variation: Direct East Corner. II, 5.7. First ascent August 5, 1958, by John Gill and Bill Mason. This route lies on the east edge of the broad central buttress, but west of the large chimney that separates the buttress from Grunt Arête. It is, in fact, almost completely distinct from either of the two routes described above. From the lower portions of this large chimney, traverse 100 feet to the west, and climb up and right (east) in a break in the smooth face above. The first-ascent party avoided the easy rock by climbing more or less straight up from this point. After several pitches, climb a 5.7 roof directly. Above this overhang, scrambling leads to the top of the buttress.

Variation: II, 5.4. First ascent August 9, 1966, by Sherman Lehman, William Hooker, and William Kirkpatrick. About eight pitches are involved in this variation, which is similar to the preceding *1957 variation.* From below the bottom of the Merriam Couloir (*Disappointment Peak, Route 8*), follow a red ledge leading left across the base

of the buttress until it ends near the left side of the buttress. Climb the red chimney above for two pitches to an area of small pine bushes. Avoid the gray gully above by climbing up and right to a small cave, then on to the right below a prominent yellow nose and across a horizontal section. The ridge of the Direct East Corner is now just to the east. The yellow tower above is passed on the left, a knife-edge ridge is gained, and finally a corner is turned to the left to the grassy slope leading to the main summit plateau.

ROUTE 9. Grunt Arête. II, 5.6, A1. First ascent July 23, 1957, by John Dietschy and James Langford. This route may have been climbed free in 1977 (see *Route 10, Left of Open Book variation*). See *Photos 59* and *62.* This is the first ridge east of the south central buttress and is easily viewed from the Garnet Canyon Meadows. It can also be located as the arête 100 feet left (west) of the Open Book. The lower portion of the arête is better described as a broad buttress. For the approach take the Garnet Canyon trail from the Lupine Meadows trailhead to a point just before the trail end at Garnet Creek. Grunt Arête is visible directly above. This route stays near the crest at the left (west) edge of the buttress. Three enjoyable and steep leads go directly up the crest of the ridge to an obvious overhang. The first pitch provides a 5.8 move only 20 feet off the ground. After reaching the first overhang, traverse onto the west wall and up for one pitch to meet a second overhang, which is passed using aid for about 15 feet. The next lead continues up the west wall and regains the crest at a belay position on a steep slab (fixed pins here). The first-ascent party climbed the start of the next lead by means of a tension traverse across a 10-foot overhanging wall. They then encountered a vertical section with downsloping holds. This 110-foot pitch finished with an upward traverse on a very steep, smooth, exposed slab to a small shelf. An easier lead around the corner to the east brings one to easy ground near the top of the ridge. The remainder of the climb is not difficult. The rock quality on this route varies, and the protection is sometimes poor. For descent from the top of the climb, traverse across a ledge system to the north until above Amphitheater Lake. Walk down the ridge to the east and drop into a large chimney system to the south. Downclimb and scramble around some large chockstones and eventually end up in the major drainage to the east of Grunt Arête. Alternatively, one could scramble down to Amphitheater Lake and walk down the trail. *Time: 5½ hours* from the Caves. See *American Alpine Journal,* 11, no. 1 (1958), pp. 85–88.

Variation: South Face. II, 5.7. First ascent July 6, 1958, by John Gill and Paul Rieche. This climb, starting several hundred feet east of the preceding route, is completely separate from the first climb on this ridge until the uppermost portions are reached. After two or three ropelengths up a large chimney, continue up a flakelike ridge to a belay stance. A diagonal traverse up and to the left under a large overhang leads to a belay position on a 2-foot downsloping ledge. Now climb the right side of this overhang until beneath a second large overhang where a hand traverse to the right leads to a detached nubbin. A 2-foot ledge now diagonals up to the right to a belay stance beneath the large black overhang that caps this entire portion of the face. After swinging directly up over this, climb a series of open chimneys and minor walls and rejoin the main route near the top of the arête.

ROUTE 10. Open Book. III, 5.8, A3, or III, 5.9. First ascent August 21, 1963, by Philip Jacobus and Steve Larsen; first free ascent June 26, 1977, by Jim Donini and Mike Munger. See *Topo 61* and *Photos 59* and *62.* This seven-pitch route is one of the finest of the difficult rock climbs in the Tetons. In the western third of the broad Grunt Arête is an obvious large open book, readily visible from the trail below, about midway between the two previous climbs. The approach is the same as for Grunt Arête (*Route 9*).

Proceed up easy ledges on the left (west) side of the face of Grunt Arête to the base of this book. While there is a more difficult (5.9) alternative to the left, start from a large flake at the base of an easy ramp leading up and left (west). Climb up past a tree to the belay under an overhang. The second lead goes straight up to a second overhang in gray rock, which is passed on its right side. Belay at the top of a large detached flake. Undercling out and around to the right using a flake (5.8) and then continue up the corner passing through a thin crack section (5.9) to a sloping belay ledge beneath the huge overhang visible from below. This overhang is normally passed on its right side via 5.8 face climbing; one can also go out to the west from the belay—either way this is a memorable pitch. The fifth lead can be taken off to the right on easy 5th-class rock, but one can also continue straight up the crack in a left-facing corner up to a roof requiring a 5.9+ move to escape out its left side. The next lead goes up from the large belay ledge on sloping holds (5.6 to 5.7) or escape is again possible out to the east. The final, optional pitch climbs the rotten left-facing corner (5.8) above to the top of the arête. For protection take a standard rack to 3 inches, mostly medium nuts. Descent from the top of the climb is the same as for Grunt Arête (*Route 9*). See *American Alpine Journal*, 14, no. 1 (1964), p. 188.

Variation: Left of Open Book. III, 5.8. First ascent July 28, 1977, by Mike Munger and Ed Sessions. The variation starts at the first obvious ramp to the left (west) of the Open Book, just left of some trees and bushes; this ramp diagonals up and left. Climb 100 feet (5.6) up this ramp and exit to the right to a belay. Make an easy traverse (loose) right and then up to gain the base of a corner. The third long lead goes up this corner, passes an awkward roof, then continues up a 5.8 crack in a steep face. The next pitch continues up easier (5.6) rock for 150 feet onto a belay ledge. Easy escape could be made to the right from this ledge, but this variation continued up one more pitch past two 5.8 roofs to easier 3rd- and 4th-class climbing and the top of the arête.

Variation: Right of Open Book. II, 5.10+. First ascent July 1983, by Kim Schmitz and Jim Donini. The variation goes up the obvious crack system to the right of the Open Book, starting with a steep 5.8 pitch. The second lead goes easily up to the overhang, which is turned on the left with difficulty (5.10+). Two more short pitches, containing overhangs, complete the variation. The difficult overhang lead was by far the hardest climbing encountered.

ROUTE 11. Almost Arête. II, 5.7. First ascent July 15, 1958, by John Gill and Fred Truslow. See *Photos 59* and *63.* This is the somewhat indistinct ridge between Satisfaction Arête and Grunt Arête; the upper portions ultimately taper to form a ridge crest. Satisfaction Crack is defined as the demarcation line between Almost and Satisfaction Arêtes. The lower portion of Almost Arête is split in half vertically by a prominent chimney; to the right (east) of this chimney is a rectangular region of yellow-white overhanging rock, the "Postage Stamp." The first few leads of this route go up the left wall of the chimney. A scramble up and right then leads to the base of the smooth, slablike, very steep upper crest. Start at the right side of this slab, and diagonal to the left underneath the overhang which caps the face. After the overhang has been climbed directly, the route stays within 10 feet of the crest to the top of the arête. One short pinnacle is climbed directly.

Variation: Gray Slab. II, 5.4. First ascent July 23, 1963, by Steven Derenzo, Peter Gardiner, and Richard Goldstone. See *Photos 59* and *63.* This variation of several pitches ascends the rock near the left (west) edge of the lower buttress of Almost Arête to gain the Gray Slab, an area of uniformly gray rock on the upper left shoulder of the arête. Hike up the talus, and scramble up the lowest broken rocks to the left of the central chimney until the rock steepens. At this point, follow for one ropelength a shallow depression diagonaling up and left on steep rock with rounded holds. Thirty feet beyond is a grassy platform at the west end of the first wide ramp that slopes back up to the right (east). Walk up the ramp for about 50 feet to the east end of a narrow ledge that leads back west above some overhangs. This ledge is traversed left for about 60 feet until it ends at a vertical chimney-crack. The next short lead first goes up the crack and then up the wall on the right to a comfortable belay ledge. After another 60 feet up broken, slightly overhanging rock, the second wide ramp cutting across the arête is reached. Scramble up, crossing the ramp, for about 150 feet onto the lower portion of the Gray Slab. Continue another 150 feet up the slab on small but adequate holds to a stance above some bushes at the lower end of a groove of white rock. Climb this easy groove up and right until it opens out into the third large ramp, which is followed back to what is now a well-defined ridge crest. At this point join the 1958 route and follow it for three leads over excellent exposed rock within inches of the crest to the top of the arête.

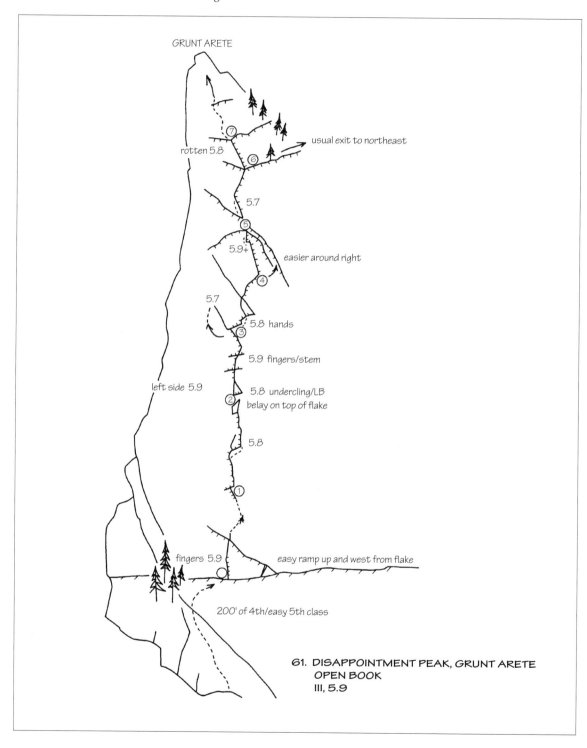

GRUNT ARETE

usual exit to northeast

rotten 5.8

⑦

⑥

5.7

⑤

5.9+

easier around right

④

5.7

⑬

5.8 hands

5.9 fingers/stem

left side 5.9

② 5.8 undercling/LB
belay on top of flake

5.8

①

fingers 5.9

easy ramp up and west from flake

200' of 4th/easy 5th class

61. DISAPPOINTMENT PEAK, GRUNT ARETE
    OPEN BOOK
    III, 5.9

Variation: Almost Overhanging. III, 5.8. First ascent August 20, 1972, by Howard Friedman and Henry Mitchell. See *Topo 62* and *Photo 63.* The lower half of Almost Arête is a buttress barred by overhangs and the rectangular yellow-white area known as the Postage Stamp. This variation is up the buttress just to the right (east) of the Postage Stamp and goes through the overhangs. A large chimney about 75 feet left (west) of Satisfaction Crack leads up through gray rock to a prominent triangular roof several hundred feet above the base. Scramble up this chimney until it steepens. The first 5.6 lead goes up this narrowing chimney, passing two overhanging sections, to a rock-strewn step. Next climb the jam crack above to a point where it forks, taking the left fork to the top of a block under a roof. Continue up via 5.5 face climbing to a jutting nose of yellow rock. The fourth and most difficult pitch starts with a lieback (5.7) under this nose to gain the left branch of the previous crack, then up over a smooth vertical area (5.8) to a belay position in a recess under a roof. Now pass this roof, climbing up the left wall to a sloping ledge. The next lead goes up the wall to the upper, exposed edge of the buttress, continuing to a stance in a niche. The final pitch goes up the awkward chimney in this niche and ends on a sloping face to a rocky bench with trees. An exit can now be made up a couloir to the southeast ridge of Disappointment above Surprise Lake. Or, if desired, there are a number of additional ropelengths of easy climbing to the extreme top of the arête. This route follows a logical line on predominantly sound rock.

Variation: II, 5.9. First ascent in 1980 by Andy Carson and Jim Evangelista. See *Photo 63.* This difficult variation provides a distinct three-pitch start to the left of the standard Almost Arête route. The initial lead goes up a large chimney capped by an overhang. The next pitch is up a steep wall to the right via a 5.9 crack. The easy third pitch is up and out to the right onto the steep red slab, containing a crack, on the ridge crest. One pitch up the crest completes the climb, as exit to the right is possible at this point.

Variation: II, 5.7. First ascent July 13, 1985, by Steve Saez and Mark Golde. See *Topo 62.* This variation provides two new pitches at the start of Almost Overhanging. Climb a large chimney to the left (west) of that described in Almost Overhanging for 80 feet of easy 5th class to a belay ledge. The second pitch (130 feet) continues up this chimney, with large loose blocks in its bottom, to an overhang that is passed on the right side (5.7) up to a belay ledge that contains a tree with rappel slings. The next lead joins the preceding *Almost Overhanging variation.* For protection bring a standard rack up to 3½ inches.

ROUTE 12. Satisfaction Crack. II, 5.6. First ascent August 19, 1956, by John Gill, Gene Davant, and Tom Clohessy. See *Photos 59* and *63.* This crack, actually a major chimney system, just left (west) of Satisfaction Arête, separates that ridge on the east from Almost Arête on the west. Six pitches are required to ascend this chimney, or crack. Difficulty will

be encountered in passing the chockstone capping the upper section of the crack. Descent from the top of the crack can be easily made to Surprise Lake and the trail.

ROUTE 13. Satisfaction Arête. II, 5.6. First ascent August 20, 1955, by Richard Pownall and Allen Steck. See *Photo 63.* The first ridge west of the Surprise Lake outlet stream, prominent from the Garnet Canyon trail, was named Satisfaction Arête by the first-ascent party. Although "arête" is a misnomer because the ridge is broad and not sharp, the name has been retained to distinguish this route from the more difficult later route, Satisfaction Buttress. Both routes, however, are on the same ridge. For the approach take the Garnet Canyon trail and cross the Surprise Lake outlet stream. Leave the trail around the next trail corner and scramble up the talus slope along the west side of the ridge to the beginning of the major chimney, Satisfaction Crack *(Route 12),* on the left side of this face. Start the climb here, well left (west) of the crest of the ridge, up and slightly right in a chimney system for three leads. Traverse right under a prominent overhang on a broken ledge that crosses the crest at a band of white rock. The only difficult lead of this indirect route is the last one, up over the white rock and around the corner to the right (east). From this point one can contour on around, reaching the outlet stream from Surprise Lake. The complete ridge, however, culminates at one of the towers south of Surprise and Amphitheater Lakes. Descent can be made easily either to Surprise Lake or back to Garnet Canyon. See *American Alpine Journal,* 10, no. 1 (1956), pp. 116–119.

ROUTE 14. Satisfaction Buttress. IV, 5.9, A2, or IV, 5.10-. First ascent July 28 and August 1, 1958, by Yvon Chouinard and Robert Kamps; first free ascent July 15, 1977, by Rich Perch and Mike Munger. See *Topo 63* and *Photos 59* and *63.* The first broad ridge west of the Surprise Lake outlet stream harbors both this Satisfaction Buttress route and Satisfaction Arête *(Route 13).* Instead of reaching the ridge crest from the west, as in *Route 13,* this route follows a line starting from the base of the ridge. This is a serious route with difficult climbing on loose rock on the first three pitches. It appears that more than one line on this buttress has been taken by climbers; the topo delineates one line. The first-ascent party used a different start for the first pitch. For the approach take the Garnet Canyon trail from the Lupine Meadows trailhead. Scramble up talus to the first buttress west of the Surprise Lake outlet stream.

Start at the left edge of the buttress in a rotten, black-rock area and climb this corner to a belay ledge. The second short lead is up rotten 5.8 rock, past an overhang to another ledge. The third difficult lead (5.9) starts with a 5.8 left-facing corner to a roof, which is passed on the left on decomposing white rock to a sling belay under a square-cut roof. Passing this roof on the left is the crux of the route (5.10-); this fourth pitch ends with a belay under the next roof. Turn this roof on the left to gain a 5.8 hand crack lead-

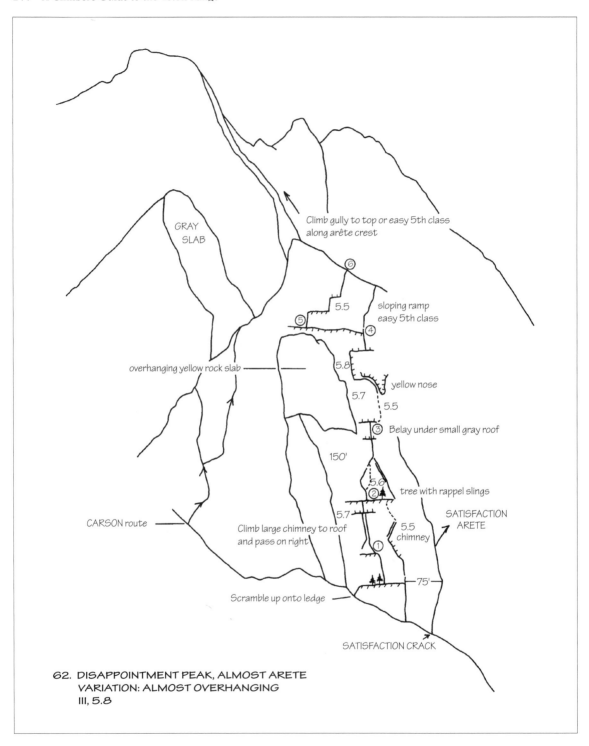

GRAY
SLAB

Climb gully to top or easy 5th class
along arête crest

⑥

5.5   sloping ramp
        easy 5th class

⑤   ④

overhanging yellow rock slab ⎯⎯   5.8

                              yellow nose
                    5.7
                        5.5

                    ③ Belay under small gray roof

150'
                    5.6
                    ② tree with rappel slings

                                    SATISFACTION
                    5.7   ARETE
CARSON route ⎯⎯
        Climb large chimney to roof   5.5
        and pass on right   ① chimney

                                    75'

Scramble up onto ledge ⎯⎯

            SATISFACTION CRACK

62. DISAPPOINTMENT PEAK, ALMOST ARETE
VARIATION: ALMOST OVERHANGING
III, 5.8

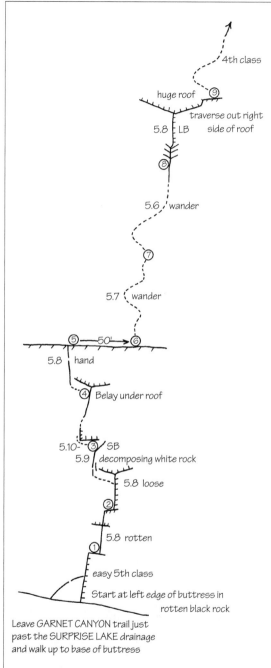

4th class

huge roof ⑨

traverse out right
5.8 ⌐ LB   side of roof

⑧

5.6 ⌐ wander

⑦

5.7 ⌐ wander

⑤ — 50' — ⑥

5.8 ⌐ hand

④ Belay under roof

5.10 ⌐③⌐ SB
5.9 ⌐ decomposing white rock

5.8 loose

②

5.8 rotten

①

easy 5th class

Start at left edge of buttress in
rotten black rock

Leave GARNET CANYON trail just
past the SURPRISE LAKE drainage
and walk up to base of buttress

**63. DISAPPOINTMENT PEAK
SATISFACTION BUTTRESS
IV, 5.10-**

ing onto a large belay ledge. Move right 50 feet on this ledge before starting up the face above. The next two leads wander up a steep face to the base of an inside corner below a huge roof. Climb this corner as a lieback to the roof, then traverse out to the right edge of the roof before turning up onto a belay ledge. From here the difficulty eases and the remainder of the route is 4th-class climbing to the top of the ridge. For protection take a standard rack to 4 inches with small nuts. For the descent scramble north down to Surprise Lake and take the trail back to Lupine Meadows, or the Surprise Lake outlet drainage can be used to get back into Garnet Canyon.

ROUTE 15. Yodel This. III, 5.12+ (unfinished). First ascent during the summers of 1995 and 1996 by Mike Fisher and Sam Lightner. See *Topo 64* and *Photo 59*. This route, most likely the hardest rock climb in the Tetons thus far, is presented here to its current high point as an example of determination, perseverance, and, above all, good style. It was established using ground-up tactics and all bolt placements were hand-drilled. Approach can be made as in *Route 16*. The climb is on the south side of the Fifth Column and is located 80 feet to the west of a large corner system. Begin by scrambling up to a ledge that is accessed from the left. The obvious corner, located 30 feet to the east, is loose and dangerous at the top and is 5.8 in difficulty. Pitch one consists of steep face climbing (5.10+) for 120 feet past four bolts, two fixed pitons, and a fixed #2½ Friend, and leads to a two-bolt belay anchor. The second pitch follows a crack up and left to a belay ledge with a fixed anchor (60 feet, 5.7, natural pro). The third and crux pitch is 80 feet in length and consists of steep face climbing past seven bolts. Begin by placing a large camming unit (#4 Friend) in a horizontal crack under a small right-facing corner. The most difficult climbing is getting past the first four bolts; it eases off to 5.11R after that! The anchor at the top of this pitch is also fixed.

ROUTE 16. Fifth Column. II, 5.9. First ascent July 17, 1958, by John Gill and James Langford. See *Topo 64* and *Photo 59*. This ridge, or rounded corner, just east of the Surprise Lake outlet, is climbed directly up its very steep crest to the giant flake at its top. From the intersection of the Garnet Canyon trail and the drainage from Surprise Lake, scramble up to the right to the base of this route. A total of six leads are required to reach the base of the summit flake. Climb the large overhanging flake, directly above, via balance holds on its east face. Scramble up and right for several hundred feet to the top of the buttress. Descent can be made easily to Surprise Lake. The rock is generally loose on this route and therefore it is not recommended. *Time: 5½ hours* from Jenny Lake.

Variation: The Knob. I, 5.9. First ascent July 25, 1958, by John Gill and Yvon Chouinard. See *Photo 59*. To the right (southeast) of the Fifth Column is a small tower, the "Knob," which can be approached via a 200-foot scramble from the Garnet Canyon trail. The route on the south face

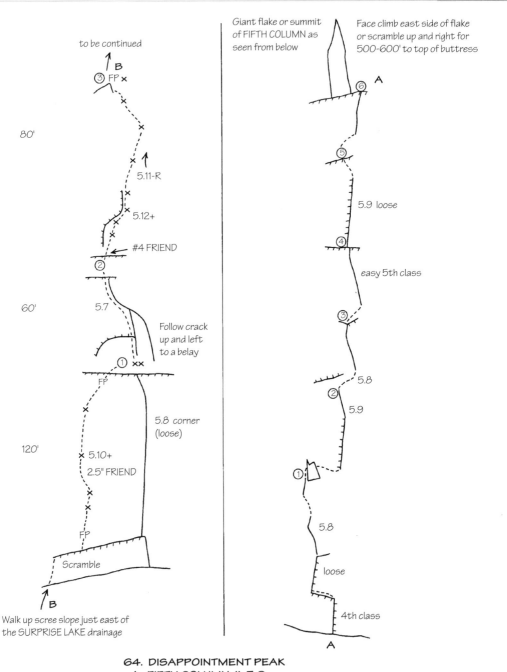

Giant flake or summit
of FIFTH COLUMN as
seen from below

Face climb east side of flake
or scramble up and right for
500-600' to top of buttress

to be continued

B
③ FP ✕

80'

✕

✕ ↑
5.11-R

✕
✕
5.12+
✕

← #4 FRIEND
②

60'   5.7

Follow crack
up and left
to a belay

① ✕✕
FP

5.8 corner
(loose)

120'   ✕ 5.10+
2.5" FRIEND
✕

✕

FP

Scramble

↑
B

Walk up scree slope just east of
the SURPRISE LAKE drainage

⑥ A

⑤

5.9 loose

④

easy 5th class

③

5.8
②
5.9

①

5.8

loose

4th class

A

64. DISAPPOINTMENT PEAK
A. FIFTH COLUMN, II, 5.9
B. YODEL THIS, III, 5.12+

moves from right to left, then up a very difficult open chimney to a short broken face that leads to the top. Protection in this last chimney is difficult to obtain.

Variation: Hummingbird Face. Rating unknown. First ascent July 12, 1981, by Rich Perch and Mike Beiser. This variation is east of the Fifth Column.

ROUTE 17. Lance's Arête. II, 5.6. First ascent July 28, 1958, by John Gill and Dave Jones. See *Photo 59.* This short ridge rises directly above the top corner of the first switchback in the Garnet Canyon trail and, hence, is immediately east of the Fifth Column. Scramble a few feet up a broken chimney and then move left and up a small face. Stay directly on the crest for the next move up a slab with a small overhang at the top. The next ropelength stays very nearly on the crest, to gain a level area. Here the route moves horizontally left across the crest, around a corner and up a slightly overhanging crack to a small notch in the crest. Continue to the top of the ridge. The route in general seeks out difficulty to provide interest; six pitches of 5.4 to 5.7 climbing can be found if one tries. *Time: 4 hours* from Jenny Lake.

ROUTE 18. Hidden Arête. II, 5.9. First ascent July 31, 1958, by John Gill and Bill Mason. See *Photo 59.* This ridge lies to the east of the Fifth Column and Lance's Arête, and its lower portion is not easily discerned. Hidden Arête is a 150-foot buttress with several overhanging steps, giving the appearance of an inverted staircase. The climbing begins on the steep, solid face of a short ridge immediately to the left (west) of the main mass of the ridge and to the right (east) of the upper switchback corner on the Garnet Canyon trail.

Climb directly up this face and the overhang at its top. Scramble, or climb by choosing short, interesting pitches, up and right (east) until reaching the base of the arête proper. Climb the overhangs on the buttress as directly as possible, even though easier rock can be found to the right or left.

PEAK 10,080+ *(0.8 mi ESE of Disappointment Peak)*

Map: Grand Teton

This minor summit is due south of the east end of Amphitheater Lake.

ROUTE 1. North Slope. I, 1.0. First ascent unknown, probably in the 1920s when the first trail to the lakes was completed. This high point is easily reached from the lake.

INSPIRATION PEAK (9,760+)
(1.0 mi ESE of Disappointment Peak)

Map: Grand Teton

The name, promoted in recent years by park trail publications, was intended to attract hikers who have ventured to Surprise Lake. Although Inspiration Peak rises only 200 feet above the lake, the view from the top is much more expansive than that obtained from the lakeshore, so the few minutes required to reach the top are well spent.

ROUTE 1. North Slope. I, 1.0. First ascent unknown, probably in the 1920s when the first trail to the lakes was completed. The summit is easily reached directly via its northwest side.

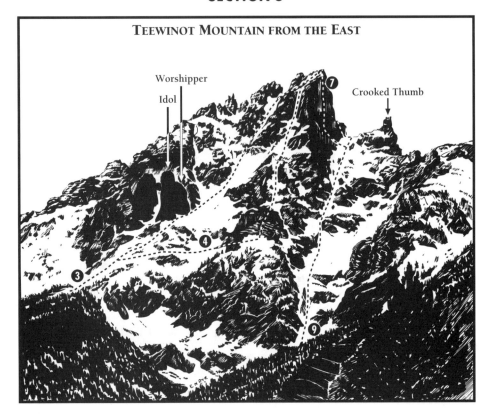

TEEWINOT MOUNTAIN FROM THE EAST

Worshipper

Idol

Crooked Thumb

Glacier Gulch to Cascade Canyon

GLACIER GULCH, SOUTH SIDE ROCK CLIMBS (CA. 9,800)

Map: Grand Teton

The lower section of Glacier Gulch contains significant buttresses on both the north and south sides, but only a single rock-climbing route has been worked out on the south walls.

ROUTE 1. Another Trailside Attraction. II, 5.8. First ascent August 24, 1986, by Yvon Chouinard, Roch Horton, and Alberto Bendinger. The approach to this route is from Amphitheater Lake. Take the small trail north from the lake over the saddle, as if heading to the Teton Glacier. The route ascends the wall just east of this trail down on the north side from the saddle. Four pitches of excellent climbing will be found, along with opportunities for spectacular photographs.

GLACIER GULCH, NORTH SIDE ROCK CLIMBS (CA. 10,200)

Map: Grand Teton

The terminus of the south ridge of Teewinot Mountain consists of a set of buttresses that rise above the west end of Delta Lake. The routes that have been worked out on these readily accessible rocks lie between about 9,500 and 10,200 feet. There are about five buttresses, sometimes referred to as arêtes, but these are not all well defined. The location is scenic, providing direct views of the north face of Disappointment Peak and the east ridge of the Grand Teton. The quality of the rock is not always good. See *Glacier Gulch* for the approach to these buttresses.

Red Arête: September 4, 1968, Ted Wilson,
   Dick Ream
      var: **Left Buttress:** August 1977, Yvon
      Chouinard, Steve Wunsch
      var: **Right Buttress:** August 1977, Jim Donini,
      Rick Black
Chouinard Buttress: September 4, 1972, Yvon
   Chouinard
Olson-Nelson Tower: August 14, 1974, Jim Olson,
   Doyle Nelson

ROUTE 1. Olson–Nelson Tower. II, 5.4. First ascent August 14, 1974, by Jim Olson and Doyle Nelson. This climb of four pitches goes up the small tower immediately to the right (east) of and below the westernmost of the arêtes. Scramble for 150 feet to the southeast base of the tower, which is just left of the prominent gully separating the tower from the large arête on the right (east). Continue past a steep section to sloping ramps at a small pine tree. Climb past loose blocks to a large sloping ramp beneath a large overhang. The last lead traverses left on a short wall around the overhang to the crest of the tower. An open book then leads to the summit. To descend, scramble down the back side of the tower to a notch separating it from the large arête on the left.

ROUTE 2. Chouinard Buttress. II, 5.7. First ascent September 4, 1972, by Yvon Chouinard. This buttress is the second from the left (west) and the fourth from the right of those above and north of Delta Lake. The original route followed the left skyline to the top of the buttress on excellent rock. Some 700 feet of climbing was involved.

ROUTE 3. Red Arête. II, 5.6. First ascent September 4, 1968, by Ted Wilson and Dick Ream. This arête is the easternmost of the small ridges at the base of the south ridge of Teewinot. Five pitches were found on this arête, which is quite distinct when viewed from Delta Lake. The first 150-foot lead, starting from a good belay ledge (with cairn) slightly left of the crest, goes up 5.1 cracks to a ledge from which grooves (5.6) lead to the next belay ledge. The main feature of the route, a red slab easily seen from the lake, constitutes the next pitch (150 feet). Climb a 5.6 crack, slightly right of the crest, then make a thin traverse left to a 5.4 crack ending at the top of the slab. The third pitch (150 feet) begins with a series of ledges (5.4) on the crest and then goes directly over an overhang (5.6). After 80 feet of exposed 4th-class rock, the finish involves easier climbing, ending with 300 feet of 4.0 or 5.1 rock.

   Variation: Left Buttress. III, 5.10. First ascent August 1977, by Yvon Chouinard and Steve Wunsch. This variation, also on the Red Arête, begins on the face that lies between the obvious large dihedral and the left (west) corner of the buttress. The initial lead up the left of two possible lines is 5.10 and can be well protected. The second lead goes over a difficult overhang and then straight up. The remainder of the climb is easier and the route is readily followed to the top of the buttress. Descent can be made to the right (east).

   Variation: Right Buttress. II, 5.9. First ascent August 1977, by Jim Donini and Rick Black. This variation, also on the Red Arête, parallels the *Left Buttress variation* and was climbed on the same day. It apparently took the right of the two possible lines and was slightly less difficult. This variation was probably that climbed on August 5, 1981, by Renny Jackson and Jim Olson. They reported four pitches, some of which were on poor rock.

WORSHIPPER (10,880+)
(0.4 mi ESE of Teewinot Mountain)

Map: Grand Teton

This is the lower and thinner of the two pinnacles about two-thirds of the way up the east face of Teewinot. The name, as Phil Smith has written, was suggested by the relative height and proportion of these two spires. Although very few of those who climb Teewinot notice it, the Worshipper has a large rectangular window just below the summit. This unique feature adds considerable interest to climbing the pinnacle. On August 21, 1934, during an ascent of Teewinot, Ernest Scheef climbed a tower that might have been the Worshipper.

East Ridge: August 8, 1936, Jack Durrance, Fred
   Ayres, Walter Spofford
West Face: July 16, 1953, Leigh Ortenburger, William Buckingham
Northeast Face: August 3, 1957, Yvon Chouinard,
   John Lowry

ROUTE 1. ☞ West Face. I, 5.4. First ascent July 16, 1953, by Leigh Ortenburger and William Buckingham. The Worshipper is separated from the Idol by a col that can be easily reached from the regular east face couloir of Teewinot. A slightly overhanging chimney leads up the west face from this col directly to the window. Climb through the window and reach the summit from the northeast.

ROUTE 2. East Ridge. I, 5.1. First ascent August 8, 1936, by Jack Durrance, Fred Ayres, and Walter Spofford. Follow the east ridge, which commences just south of the east face couloir of Teewinot. Near the summit traverse south to avoid loose blocks.

ROUTE 3. *Northeast Face.* II, 5.6, A1. First ascent August 3, 1957, by Yvon Chouinard and John Lowry. Start on the northeast face and climb easily about 150 feet to a belay ledge. After another 40 feet up to a small ledge, traverse up and right on more difficult rock to the north ridge and a belay spot under an overhang. Climb this overhang directly (A1).

IDOL (10,880+)   *(0.4 mi ESE of Teewinot Mountain)*

Map: Grand Teton

The Idol is the larger and higher of the two towers about two-thirds of the way up the broad east face of Teewinot Mountain. These two towers, the Idol and Worshipper, are passed on the north by every climber of the standard East Face route on the mountain. If time permits during the descent of that route, these towers make a pleasant addition to the day. The smaller pinnacles southwest of the Idol were climbed on August 3, 1957, by Yvon Chouinard and John Lowry.

CHRONOLOGY

Northwest Face: August 20, 1931, George
    Goldthwaite
South Face: July 3, 1982, Andy Carson, Jorge Colon

ROUTE 1. *South Face.* II, 5.8. First ascent July 3, 1982, by Andy Carson and Jorge Colon. This face of the Idol consists of a large mass of loose, white rock. The route of three pitches without an obvious line consists of face climbing on the left edge of the face, using discontinuous cracks.

ROUTE 2. ☞*Northwest Face.* I, 5.1. First ascent August 20, 1931, by George Goldthwaite. The chimney on the western portion of the north face is the natural route if the pinnacle is approached from the couloir of the East Face route on Teewinot. After one 30-foot 5.1 pitch up the chimney, climb down and around to the right (south) in order to make the second lead straight up the west face to the summit. An excellent view of the window in the Worshipper can be obtained from the summit of the Idol.

CROOKED THUMB (11,680+)
(0.15 mi NNE of Teewinot Mountain)

Map: Grand Teton

This is the spectacular pinnacle on the skyline ridge just north of the summit of Teewinot. From the summit an excellent view is obtained of the impressive north faces of Teewinot, Mount Owen, and the Grand Teton. Its overhanging northwest face is seen to best advantage from the northeast.

CHRONOLOGY

Southwest Ridge: [probable] July 26, 1935, William
    Loomis; [certain] July 30, 1936, Fred Ayres

var: August 17, 1944, John and Ruth
    Mendenhall
var: September 2, 1959, Robert Toepel, Ruth
    Kirtland
Direct North Face: August 11–13, 1966, Peter
    Cleveland, Donald Storjohann
West Ridge: July 28, 1981, Robert Irvine, Tom
    Kimbrough
North Ridge: September 1, 1991, Tom Turiano,
    Stephen Koch

ROUTE 1. *West Ridge.* III, 5.7. First ascent July 28, 1981, by Robert Irvine and Tom Kimbrough. See *Photo 68*. With an early start approach via the Teewinot–Owen cirque, scramble up the drainage of the couloir that separates the northwest ridge of Teewinot from the Crooked Thumb. A considerable distance of exposed 3rd-class scrambling leads to the start of the climb, a short distance above the base of the ridge itself. The first full ropelength on very steep and loose rock is unprotected and subject to some rockfall from the northwest face of Teewinot. The route improves with occasional difficult sections interspersed with more moderate climbing and even some occasional scrambling. The next-to-last pitch is continuous 5.6 for a full ropelength on steep, enjoyable rock; it is the best of the route. A total of nine pitches are involved in this route out of the beautiful and seldom-visited cirque.

ROUTE 2. ☞*Southwest Ridge.* II, 4.0. Probable first ascent July 26, 1935, by William Loomis; or July 30, 1936, by Fred Ayres (certain). This short ridge is climbed, via a short 4.0 southwest chimney, from the col between it and the north face of Teewinot. For the approach to this col see *Teewinot, Route 9*.

Variation: II, 4.0. First ascent August 17, 1944, by John and Ruth Mendenhall. The col between the Crooked Thumb and the summit of Teewinot can been reached directly from Cascade Canyon, but this has been done on very few occasions. A long approach on the northwest side in the loose rock couloirs from the Teewinot–Owen cirque is required.

Variation: II, 5.1. First ascent September 2, 1959, by Robert Toepel and Ruth Kirtland. The col between the Crooked Thumb and the upper north ridge of Teewinot can be reached from the north side of the Thumb. Approach the Thumb from the north (or east) and climb one small open-book pitch on the northeast corner onto a ledge on the north face. Traverse about 30 feet on the ledge and then ascend an easy rotten chimney, from which it is but a walk around the corner to the col and the Southwest Ridge route. *Time: 6 hours* from Jenny Lake.

ROUTE 3. *North Ridge.* II, 5.9+. First ascent September 1, 1991, by Tom Turiano and Stephen Koch. See *Topo 65* and *Photo 71*. Climb up the couloir that leads to the col between the Crooked Thumb and the upper north ridge of Teewinot and traverse out and right (north) early enough so as to

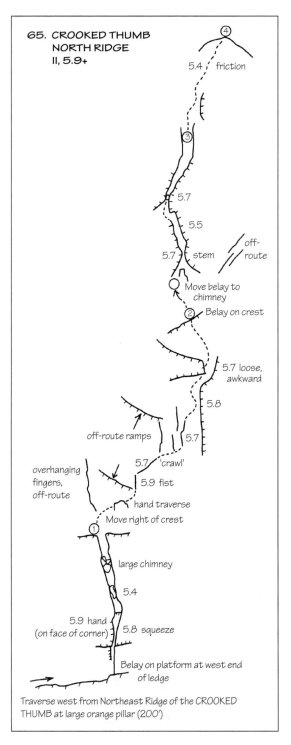

**65. CROOKED THUMB
NORTH RIDGE
II, 5.9+**

④

5.4 friction

③

5.7

5.5

5.7 stem   off-
                            route

○ Move belay to
   chimney

② Belay on crest

5.7 loose,
awkward

5.8

off-route ramps   5.7

5.7 'crawl'

overhanging
fingers,   5.9 fist
off-route
                  hand traverse

① Move right of crest

large chimney

5.4

5.9 hand
(on face of corner)   5.8 squeeze

Belay on platform at west end
of ledge

Traverse west from Northeast Ridge of the CROOKED
THUMB at large orange pillar (200')

reach the base of the northeast ridge of the Thumb. A ledge system on the north side leads to an "airy knob" from which the climb begins. The first pitch begins with 5.7 face climbing to reach a 6-foot ceiling with a slot on its left (east) side. This awkward slot (5.9+) is negotiated by hand jams, stemming, and eventually a squeeze chimney and finishes via a large 5.4 chimney (180 feet). The second pitch proceeds up just west of the crest and again begins with face climbing that leads right to a hand-traverse flake. Continue up and right to a 5.9 fist crack, across an awkward, 5.7 "crawl" section, and then farther right to a left-facing corner. Belay on the ridge crest. The fourth and final pitch ascends the large, classic chimney system directly above the belay and is 5.7 in difficulty. At the top of the chimney an unprotected 5.4 slab must be ascended that leads to the summit.

ROUTE 4. *Direct North Face.* V, 5.9, A3. First ascent August 11–13, 1966, by Peter Cleveland and Donald Storjohann. The first attempt on this imposing face, by Yvon Chouinard and Robert Kamps on August 9, 1959, ended with a 150-foot leader fall. This determined party returned three weeks later on September 2 and climbed the first 800 feet to the large ledge some 300 feet below the summit, only to be stopped again by the apparent lack of cracks in the overhanging upper wall. The face is divided into an upper third and lower two-thirds by a huge, horizontal ledge. The successful climb, considered by Cleveland as his most difficult Teton ascent, encompassed 18 pitches and spanned three days.

Approach via the Teewinot–Owen cirque (see *Mount Owen, Route 9*). When viewed from the west, two large black-stained overhangs, the key to the route, will be seen on the wall below the final, pointed section of the Thumb. Scramble up the main gully on the west and climb three pitches to the bottom of these black stains and the first overhang. After one pitch (100 feet) that traverses to the left, the next lead goes up a vertical crack to a downsloping ledge, which was traversed left on aid to a hanging belay. The third pitch continues left and then up into an open book under a small roof and then moves left around a bulge and up over an overhang (5.9) to a belay stance. Next go left up a gray face beneath a huge roof, passed by a hand traverse right until the crack runs out, where a pendulum is necessary to reach holds and a small ledge. Now continue slightly up and into a corner beneath an overhang to another hanging belay. The difficult overhang above is passed via aid using knifeblade pitons and RURPs. Mixed free and aid climbing then takes one across a sloping ledge to the base of a steep wall. An easier friction pitch then goes left 100 feet and up 20 feet to a small ledge. The tenth lead traverses right 20 feet and up 20 feet to a ledge that is followed up and right past wet, difficult rock to a belay ledge on black, water-stained rock. The next easy lead goes right and up, finally providing access to the huge, rock-strewn ledge beneath the final triangular face.

From the far side of this ledge the 12th lead starts up the middle of this face to a belay stance on a large black block beside a loosely attached flake. The next pitch ascends this flake, continuing up and right over enjoyable rock to a belay beside another large flake. Climb this flake and continue right into a steep open book, climbed with aid to a small roof that is passed on the left to a third hanging belay. The 15th lead traverses left (overhanging) toward the base of overhanging rock below a conspicuous chimney; continue up a lieback crack to a belay below and left of the severely overhung and fractured brown rock band. Climb this section on aid until it is possible to enter a deep, guano-filled chimney. The 17th pitch goes 10 feet up this chimney, then traverses out right and up a crawl ledge, then right into a deep chimney above. The final lead goes up this chimney and onto the west ridge about 50 feet below the summit, which is then easily reached. A total of 20 hours of climbing time was expended and 15 aid pitons were required to pass the difficulties of the upper face. Note that these pitches were defined in terms of the 120-foot ropes. With the longer ropes in use in recent years, the number of leads and the location of belay points will be different.

TEEWINOT MOUNTAIN (12,325)

Map: Grand Teton

The name for this salient peak was bestowed by the first-ascent party. *Tee-Win-At,* as it was originally spelled, is, according to the first-ascent party, a Shoshone word meaning "pinnacles." This peak is certainly one of the most important of the Teton peaks both in placement and in size. From the Jenny Lake campground, the original and best located of the campgrounds in the park, this mountain is the highest visible, and some visitors mistake it for the Grand Teton. Although a long climb of 5,600 feet, Teewinot is one of the more popular peaks. The routes on the east face can be studied at length from the highway with binoculars or telescope. The ascent of Teewinot, however, should be taken seriously because the moderately steep snow in the east face couloir has been the site of several accidents. Knowledge of use of the ice axe is essential for early and midseason climbs. The view from the summit of Teewinot is one of the finest in the park, as the north face of the Grand Teton and the northeast snowfields of Mount Owen are so near. The summit itself, a large monolith with room at its uppermost corner for only one person, is a spectacular place. From this airy summit the exposure down the northwest side of the mountain is sensational. Most of the routes on the mountain require one long day for the ascent.

In August 1980, the climbers' trail to the apex of the triangular, tree-covered east slope of Teewinot was completed. This Apex trail starts at the west edge of the parking area of the Lupine Meadows trailhead. It heads west through bushes and willows to the first rock band and then goes left and up a series of slabs (cairns) to a second rock band (adjacent to a waterfall), from where it goes 300 yards north before starting some 18 switchbacks leading to the Apex. Although not commonly used, an excellent but waterless campsite will be found on the crest near the tree line at the top of the Apex; water can be obtained from the main east snow couloir drainage.

CHRONOLOGY

East Face: August 14, 1929, Fritiof Fryxell, Phil Smith
    var: **Northern Approach:** July 4, 1931, S. John Ebert
    var: **Southeast Approach:** August 8, 1940, Paul Petzoldt, Elizabeth Cowles (Partridge)
    var: September 20, 1980, David and Jon Baddley
Southwest Couloirs: September 13, 1930, Paul Petzoldt, Maynard Barrows (descent); June 22, 1931, Fritiof Fryxell, Frank Smith (ascent)
Northwest Couloir: July 4, 1931, Fritiof Fryxell, Rudolph Edmund, Theodore Anderson, Harold Hendrickson (descent)
East Ridge: August 6, 1933, Angus Roy, Gordon Sutherland
    var: **Black Chimney:** [probable] July 22, 1939, Anne Sharples, Mary Whittemore, Philip Davis; [certain] July 10, 1940, Robert Bear, William Plumley
South Ridge: June 16, 1935, Malcolm Smith, Norman Dole
    var: **Southeast Couloir:** [possible] July 20, 1932, Glenn Exum, Edward Woolf, C. F. Jehlan; [possible] August 4, 1933, Floyd Wilson, Burl Bandel
Northeast Chimney: July 26, 1935, William Loomis (upper); July 30, 1936, Fred Ayres (complete)
Lower Northeast Ridge: July 14, 1938, Jack Durrance, Michael Davis, Harry Butterworth (to the Crooked Thumb Col)
    var: July 1, 1963, Tom Cochrane, Jim Mays
    var: **Ledger Book:** May 15, 1971, David Boyd, Chuck Schaap
Upper North Ridge: September 4, 1938, William Rice, Robert Bishop, Donald Grant
North Face: August 17, 1944, John and Ruth Mendenhall
    var: **Emerson's Chimney:** August 24, 1948, Richard Emerson, Pete Owen
    var: **Teewinot Tunnel:** August 30, 1948, Charles Crush, Graham McNear
    var: **Reese Arête:** July 28, 1965, Rick Reese, Mike Ermarth, Ralph Tingey

Northwest Ridge: September 7, 1954, John and Jean Fonda, Don Decker, Marty Benham
> *var:* **Direct Buttress:** July 29, 1967, Leigh Ortenburger, John Whitesel
> *var:* **Chockstone Chimney:** July 26, 1975, Tom Burns, Bill Katra

Northeast Face: July 13, 1957, John Dietschy, William and Evelyn Cropper

Direct North Ridge: July 28, 1957, John Breitenbach, Barry Corbet

Direct East Ridge: [probable] August 30, 1959, Rick Medrick, Sterling Neale; [certain] August 9, 1986, Renny Jackson, Leigh Ortenburger

Northwest Face: August 22–23, 1961, David Dornan, Barry Corbet, Richard Emerson

ROUTE 1. ☞*Southwest Couloirs.* II, 4.0. First descent September 13, 1930, by Paul Petzoldt and Maynard Barrows; first ascent June 22, 1931, by Fritiof Fryxell and Frank Smith. See *Photos 68* and *69.* The usual approach to this route is from Amphitheater Lake, but the direct route up Glacier Gulch can also be used. From the lower section of the Teton Glacier, climb out over the north edge of the terminal moraine where it abuts against the walls of Mount Owen. Contour east for several hundred feet before turning up to the high, flat plateau west and slightly south of the summit of Teewinot. Some of the couloirs leading to this plateau are difficult and require careful routefinding. Once the plateau is reached, climb the easy slopes to the northeast to reach the small west ridge of the first large tower south of the true summit. Some scrambling is necessary to cross this ridge to the north and to reach the couloir that leads east to the large main notch just south of the summit. Avoid turning up from the plateau too soon, that is, too far south, or else the south ridge of Teewinot will be reached south of the large tower. This final tower of the south ridge is separated from the summit by the large notch and is somewhat difficult. From the large main notch descend easily 100 feet down the east side and reach the summit as in *Route 3.* Or, instead of climbing all the way up to the large notch from the west, from slightly west of and below the notch climb northward to the summit ridge only a short distance east of the summit. The rock here is steep but not difficult. In early season the southwest couloirs provide a fast method of descent to Delta Lake, providing that one is knowledgeable in the art of glissading. *Time: 4 to 5¼ hours* from Amphitheater Lake. See *Appalachia,* 18, no. 4 (December 1931), pp. 388–408, illus.; *Chicago Mountaineering Club Newsletter,* 2, no. 5 (January–July 1948), pp. 5–7.

ROUTE 2. *South Ridge.* II, 5.4. First ascent June 16, 1935, by Malcolm Smith and Norman Dole; on July 20, 1933, W. T. Alleman climbed one of the towers on this ridge from the west. This route was first used as a substitute for the East Face route in early season to avoid that very long snow couloir, which involved tedious stepcutting at that time. To start the climb just north of Delta Lake, one approach to the ridge is from Glacier Gulch. Another more devious method is to take the standard Teewinot trail (see *Route 3*) to the Apex, and then cut left (south) across the large, open southern basin in the east face of Teewinot, crossing the stream, to reach the south ridge at a somewhat higher point. Either way the initial buttresses (see *Glacier Gulch, North Side Rock Climbs*) at the base of the ridge are avoided on the east. There are many towers on this ridge and some of these can be climbed directly, but most are bypassed on the east side. It is unlikely that any one party has climbed over all the towers and pinnacles. At the first main notch, just above a big monolith on the ridge crest, stay on the ridge using 5.4 crack and ledge systems on the northeast flank. Regain the crest and continue along the ridge, staying near the crest, zigging in and out of a half-dozen towers, eventually reaching the top of the final large tower immediately south of the main notch in the south ridge, just short of the summit of the mountain. Descent directly to the notch below requires a rappel, but one can go back down 150 feet to the south base of this tower and from there traverse around to the east to gain the notch. From the notch descend a short distance to the east and join the East Face *(Route 3),* to the summit. The rock on the ridge is mostly good and the views are excellent. *Time: 9 hours* from Lupine Meadows.

> *Variation: Southeast Couloir.* II, 5.1. First ascent uncertain, possibly July 20, 1932, by Glenn Exum, Edward Woolf, and C. F. Jehlan; or August 4, 1933, by Floyd Wilson and Burl Bandel; or it may have been used by Smith and Dole in 1935. This minor variation gains the south ridge via the obvious broad slope and couloir on the southeast side of the mountain, thereby avoiding the lower section of the ridge. This couloir is the upper extension of the southern basin on the east face, lying south of the Idol and Worshipper pinnacles. The couloir can be gained either by traversing around (east and north) from Delta Lake or going directly up from Lupine Meadows. It ends at the major notch in the lower South Ridge route, which is then followed to the summit.

ROUTE 3. ☞*East Face.* II, 4.0. First ascent August 14, 1929, by Fritiof Fryxell and Phil Smith. See *Photo 70.* From the vicinity of Jenny Lake the most prominent mountain of the Teton Range is Teewinot, and its east face is the most obvious route, attracting many climbers. For some this route serves as a good one-day conditioning climb, requiring the ascent and descent of 5,600 feet. In early season experience in the use of the ice axe is required to climb this route safely. From the Lupine Meadows trailhead take the Apex trail (unmaintained) leading west from near the north end of the parking area. This trail continues past slabs and through the trees, and after some 18 switchbacks it leads to the Apex, the top of the triangular, treed, lower east slope of Teewinot.

From the Apex the climbers' trail continues up and right (north) to get into the main couloir, passing first below and then on the north of the Idol and the Worshipper. Climb either up the snowfields, avoiding the center (where rockfall may occur), or up the rocks on either side of the couloir. In early season even this second alternative is mainly covered with snow and will involve stepkicking. In late season when the snow remnants can be avoided it is a scramble up scree and ledges with an occasional short chimney. During most of an ordinary season, the climb is somewhere between these extremes, but careful routefinding is essential. Keep in mind that the summit is to the right (north) as the main notch in the summit ridge is approached. About 100 feet below this notch, turn right up easy ledges to the summit. Cross a short knife-edge to the summit monolith. On the long descent continual care must be taken with the small, exposed scree-covered ledges on both sides of the main couloir. *Time: 6½ to 8 hours* from Lupine Meadows. See *Appalachia,* 18, no. 4 (December 1931), pp. 388–408, illus.; *Chicago Mountaineering Club Newsletter,* 2, no. 5 (January–July 1948), pp. 5–7; 2, no. 6 (July–December 1948), p. 5; *Trail and Timberline,* no. 148 (February 1931), pp. 22–24, illus.

Variation: Northern Approach. II, 4.0. First ascent July 4, 1931, by S. John Ebert. This variation essentially inverts the recommended approach to the Crooked Thumb Col; see *Route 9.* From Lupine Meadows ascend the large couloir on the right (north) of the wooded Apex; this open couloir leads to the col between the Crooked Thumb and the steep north face of Teewinot. Some bushwhacking is required in the lower reaches of the couloir, and in early season the upper portion will be largely a snow climb. From the Crooked Thumb Col it is possible to traverse almost horizontally left (east) across the bottom of the northeast face to the corner, which is the northeast ridge. This traverse is exposed but not difficult. Once around the corner traverse across the eastern slopes of the mountain until the regular East Face route couloir is reached.

Variation: Southeast Approach. II, 4.0. First ascent August 8, 1940, by Paul Petzoldt and Elizabeth Cowles (Partridge). The broad southeast side of Teewinot can be approached from the east or from the Amphitheater Lake area. From Amphitheater Lake drop down to the vicinity of Delta Lake. Then angle right (east) up to the south ridge and cross to the southeast side, which is an open talus and scree slope. From this slope there are several alternatives. Contour around the mountain at a level below the base of the Worshipper and reach the beginning of the east face couloir; or, a little more enterprising (the route of the 1935 party), ascend to a point near the upper right (northwest) corner of this slope and gain, via a couloir, the broad subsidiary ridge that connects the Idol and Worshipper with the main south ridge. It is possible then to climb this sub-

sidiary ridge to the south ridge and follow that route to the summit over the many towers that remain. Finally, if one climbs upward from the southeast slope, the south ridge is soon reached and can be followed north to the summit. See *Trail and Timberline,* no. 353 (May 1948), pp. 67–70, illus.

Variation: II, 5.6. First ascent September 20, 1980, by David and Jon Baddley. Between the upper narrow extension (a deep and wide chimney) of the east face snow couloir and the Black Chimney (see *Route 4*) is a small ridge ascending the summit mass. This variation goes up the right side of this small ridge but stays well left (south) of the Black Chimney. As the upper narrow extension is approached, a small notch will be seen on this small ridge to the right (north). Traverse over to this notch where the climbing begins. The first full lead (5.6) goes up first a crack, then a slab, to the base of a large overhanging block. The next pitch (5.4) passes this block on the right, goes around the corner onto the north face of the ridge, and then proceeds up two vertical sections to finish in a crack system angling up and right (west) to a belay just below an overhang. Traverse right below this overhang until it is possible to climb to the crest of the ridge. The summit of Teewinot is then but a scramble.

ROUTE 4. East Ridge. II, 5.4. First ascent August 6, 1933 (approximate), by Angus Roy and Gordon Sutherland; or August 24, 1933, by John McCrumm. After the first ascent of the mountain in 1929, several early climbs were described as "east ridge" rather than "east face." Because it is reasonably certain that none of these ascents followed the ridge directly, this terminology has resulted in serious confusion. It is likely that none of these ascents followed the same line. The ridge to the right (north) of the main couloir was probably followed for a portion of the ascent, while the easier ground to the south was ultimately gained. The prominent, very steep step in the ridge was avoided. See *Route 3* for the approach. After reaching the beginning of the main east couloir, traverse right (north) as soon as practicable onto the east ridge. The difficulty of the route depends on how closely the crest is followed. Shortly after roping up, a 30-foot pitch will be met on the crest; at a higher point some buttresses can be climbed or avoided as desired. Generally, however, the climbing is easy until the ridge steepens abruptly about 700 feet below the summit. Abandon the crest of the ridge here in order to get onto easier ground to the left (south) and join the regular East Face route to go to the summit. *Time: 6¾ to 9 hours* from Lupine Meadows.

Variation: Black Chimney. II, 5.6. Probable first ascent July 22, 1939, by Anne Sharples, Mary Whittemore, and Philip Davis; or July 10, 1940, by Robert Bear and William Plumley (certain); it is also possible that this chimney was climbed by one or more of the earlier parties who described their route as "east ridge." This distinctive chimney in the main summit mass of Teewinot lies to the right (north) of the standard east snow couloir but left (south) of the well-defined upper east ridge. It is easily seen from Lupine Meadows. Follow the general East Ridge route to the base of the steep section about 700 feet below the summit. Abandon the crest of the ridge here in order to get into the beginning of the Black Chimney 100 feet to the left (south) of the ridge. (This chimney leads to a small notch in the crest of the east ridge; the same notch is reached from the north via *Route 6*.) Above the two chockstones in the lower section of the Black Chimney is a steep rotten section that often has black ice in it. After three or four ropelengths, traverse left (south) out of the chimney onto the easier rock leading up to the summit. This route is not recommended for early season because running water converts the chockstones into waterfalls. At best, the Black Chimney is a treacherous place because of the rotten rock.

ROUTE 5. Direct East Ridge. III, 5.8. Probable first ascent August 30, 1959, by Rick Medrick and Sterling Neale; or August 9, 1986, by Renny Jackson and Leigh Ortenburger (certain). See *Photo 70*. The 1959 party found cairns and rusty pitons on this route, indicating that others had gone before but very likely had bypassed some or all of the more difficult climbing. This ridge can also be described as the east edge of the northeast face, when viewed from the north. In profile, the east ridge of Teewinot contains a prominent steep section of massive yellow rock a few hundred feet below the summit. The East Ridge route (*Route 4*) bypasses this section on the south. The lower ridge can be accessed from the north, as done in 1959, at a point below the steep section; for this approach, use the north couloir that leads to the Crooked Thumb Col (see *Route 9*). Or take the regular approach route to the Apex of the tree-covered slope on the east face of Teewinot and then traverse horizontally north to attain the extreme base of the direct east ridge. If this is done, the initial, smaller steep section of the ridge is climbed in two leads using cracks (5.8) on its left (south) side. A section of scrambling then provides access to the base of the main, steep rock section of the ridge which is broken by five cracks in the nearly vertical, yellow rock. Exactly how the 1959 party climbed this buttress has been lost in the mists of time. However, in 1986, the crack that was selected was the one nearest the nose of the ridge, the second from the right (north). From the end of this pitch two small steps broken by horizontal sections led to the final three towers that guard the summit. These were either climbed directly or passed on the right (north).

ROUTE 6. Northeast Chimney. II, 5.4. First ascent July 26, 1935, by William Loomis. The eastern facet of the north face of Teewinot holds, near its left (east) edge, a large chimney. This northeast chimney is the only large one that cuts up this face to a small notch in the uppermost east ridge. This climb is approached via the long couloir extending down from the col between the Crooked Thumb and the north face of Teewinot; see *Route 9* for the approach to this cou-

loir. Although for most of the season the upper part of this couloir is a snow climb, some bushwhacking is necessary in the lower part. One could climb directly from the upper couloir to the bottom of the obvious northeast chimney; however, it is better to proceed all the way to the col first. Once at the col, the Crooked Thumb can be climbed for an excellent view from the summit of this route and the rest of the northern aspect of Teewinot. It is a slightly upward traverse left (east) on ledges from this col to the middle of the northeast chimney. On July 30, 1936, Fred Ayres apparently took the other alternative, making a horizontal traverse with perhaps a slight descent, and reached the bottom of the chimney; this adds two or three additional pitches to the climb. Climb the chimney past the chockstone. Some loose rock will be encountered. The top of the chimney brings one out at a small notch above the steep section of the east ridge. A short scramble up and left (south) leads to the summit knife-edge. *Time: 5¾ hours* from Lupine Meadows.

ROUTE 7. Northeast Face. III, 5.7. First ascent July 13, 1957, by John Dietschy and William and Evelyn Cropper. See *Photo 71*. This fine route ascends the middle of the east facet of the north face of Teewinot between two overhanging bulges. Ascend the snow gully as in *Route 9* to the col between the Crooked Thumb and the north face of Teewinot. From a point about 200 feet short of the col, an obvious ledge leads diagonally about 200 feet onto the northeast face where a definite break in the wall above can be found. Climb two or three pitches almost straight up from this point, generally following a narrow crack. A prominent feature of this face is a giant flake or detached block about three-quarters of the way to the top, somewhat right of center. This route apparently goes up left (east) of this block, perhaps the right of the two overhanging bulges referred to by the 1957 first-ascent party. Other climbs of this face have attempted the small chimney behind the block unsuccessfully and have had to resort to a crack on the right to reach the top of the block. The route leaves the face just below its apex. This is a delightful climb on good rock. *Time: 10¾ hours* from Lupine Meadows. See *American Alpine Journal*, 11, no. 1 (1958), pp. 85–88.

ROUTE 8. Lower Northeast Ridge. II, 4.0. First ascent to the Crooked Thumb Col July 14, 1938, by Jack Durrance, Michael Davis, and Harry Butterworth; an earlier attempt the same year by Jack and Jim Durrance and George Kingsbury resulted in the first ascent of one of the towers on this ridge, Elizabeth's Needle. This very long, generally easy ridge rises from the mouth of Cascade Canyon and leads past the Crooked Thumb to the abrupt final north face of Teewinot. The climb starts from the Hidden Falls trail just south of the Cascade Creek crossing. Bushwhack directly up through trees onto the open ridge and over various pinnacles to a point just northeast of the Crooked Thumb. At this point the few parties who have climbed this ridge have scrambled up and across the eastern slopes of the Thumb to reach the col separating it from the north face of Teewinot. To reach the summit of Teewinot, one must take one of several routes that begin at the col (see *Routes 6, 7, 9,* and *10;* see also the *Crooked Thumb*). See *Harvard Mountaineering,* 16 (May 1963), pp. 83–84.

Variation: II, 5.7. First ascent July 1, 1963, by Tom Cochrane and Jim Mays. Little information is available concerning the exact location of this variation, but it is on a small arête or wall in Cascade Canyon about one-quarter of the way up the north side of Teewinot. It is on the west side of the lower northeast ridge. Cross Cascade Creek and bushwhack to the base of the arête or wall. Climb three pitches of 5.5, 5.6, and 5.7 to the top of the route. Descent was complicated by lack of usable cracks at the second rappel point.

Variation: Ledger Book. III, 5.6. First ascent May 15, 1971, by David Boyd and Chuck Schaap. The crest of the lower northeast ridge consists of tops of a series of steep buttresses rising from the base of its northwest face. From the Cascade Canyon trail just west of the cutoff to the west shore boat dock (the trail that leads past the Symmetry Couloir and Baxter's Pinnacle), two wide, parallel shelves at the bottom of the first buttress east of the Crooked Thumb will be seen angling up from left to right toward the col north of the Thumb. This variation, an early season snow-and-ice climb, ascends the left of these two shelves. Cross Cascade Creek and scramble or kick steps in the snow to the base of the left shelf. Climb directly up the shelf, at times only 15 feet wide, to the small notch at its head. Now traverse left across two ridges and gullies to a couloir leading back left to the northeast ridge crest only a short distance from the col north of the Crooked Thumb. Scramble to the col, traverse around the east side of the Crooked Thumb, and reach the Crooked Thumb Col, from which various routes lead to the summit. The climb is comparable to the Northwest Couloir of the Middle Teton or Northeast Snowfields of Mount Owen. Crampons for the ice are recommended.

ROUTE 9. *Upper North Ridge.* II, 5.6. First ascent September 4, 1938, by William Rice, Robert Bishop, and Donald Grant. As seen from the valley, this imposing high-angle ridge, which divides the north face of Teewinot into eastern and western facets, rises in three sections from the Crooked Thumb Col. The first shoulder is the top of the small Grandstand from which the north face routes lead out right (west) onto the west facet. At the top of the second section is a large scree-covered ledge that again provides access to the west facet of the north face. The final third section of the north ridge ends at a high point about 300 feet east of the summit. From Lupine Meadows take the Apex trail up toward the regular East Face (*Route 3*) and exit to the north in its upper reaches before reaching the Apex. Traverse across the basin and ascend the couloir to the Crooked Thumb Col. An ice axe will be required in early and midseason when the

couloir is snow-filled. Alternatively (and preferably) the Crooked Thumb Col can be reached from the Apex by taking the first part of the east face couloir to a point about 300 feet above the Idol and Worshipper and moving out to the right on ledges to a flat step in the east ridge. From the crest of the ridge a ledge system leads around to the north and gives access to the upper snow, or rocks in late season, just below the col. From the col gain the top of the Grandstand in two ropelengths of 5.6 climbing on its east side. The second section is more difficult and is climbed by staying left (east) of the crest in a series of cracks and open chimneys until the broad scree-covered ledge is reached. Follow this ledge to the right (west), out onto the west facet of the north face, where the rock is loose; the ledge narrows into a nearly horizontal crack. Climb along the crack, continue up, angling west past a steep V-shaped crack with a chockstone at its top. The final wide chimney, which is filled with loose rock, brings one out on the summit ridge only 100 feet east of the summit. *Time: 7¼ hours* from Lupine Meadows.

ROUTE 10. *Direct North Ridge.* III, 5.8. First ascent July 28, 1957, by John Breitenbach and Barry Corbet. See *Topo 66* and *Photo 71.* A splendid but strenuous climb is available on this excellent ridge if one stays very close, within 20 or 30 feet, of the actual crest of the ridge. In general, it is possible to find easier rock by climbing farther out to the left (east) during the second steep section and out to the right (west) above this section. Take the preceding route (*Route 9*) to reach the top of the Grandstand. This route begins from the top of the first step, the Grandstand, in a short (10-foot) right-facing corner slightly west of the crest; it then goes up to the left, about 20 feet east of the crest, to the edge of the first large overhang to a stance. At this point angle right and up a dihedral between two overhangs. Traverse west past a fixed piton around a small corner and then up two parallel cracks (5.8) to a piton belay on a slab. Climb out and west to a jam crack on the outside of the slab. This crack leads to a small overhang at the top of the second step. The route then traverses 25 feet west and up to an awkward chimney. Climb the chimney for 10 feet and then continue up through an overhang past easy ledges to a point where a traverse to the east is possible. Climb a large, right-facing corner above this traverse which leads to a few 5.8 exit moves and the summit ridge. This point is located about 300 to 400 feet east of the actual summit. Six pitches of excellent rock are found on this route and the trick is to stay as close as possible to the crest. *Time: 10½ hours* from Lupine Meadows. See *Dartmouth Mountaineering Club Journal,* 1958, pp. 7, 50, illus.

ROUTE 11. *North Face.* II, 5.6. First ascent August 17, 1944, by John and Ruth Mendenhall. This interesting route, which starts from the Crooked Thumb Col, traverses the west facet of the north face, reaching the northwest ridge not far below the summit. This col is most easily attained from the east (see *Route 9*) but can also be reached from

66. Disappointment Peak (North Aspect)
A. Upper North Face approach
B. Pownall-Unsoeld North Face

C. Chouinard-Frost Chimney
D. Kimbrough-Rickert

E. Direct North Face
F. Northwest Crack

67. Disappointment Peak and Red Sentinel (North Aspect)
A. Northwest Crack
B. Gran
C. Northwest Shelf
D. Red Sentinel

68. Teewinot Mountain and Crooked Thumb (West Aspect)

A. Crooked Thumb, West Ridge
B. Northwest Ridge; *var:* Direct Buttress
C. Northwest Ridge
D. Northwest Couloir
E. Southwest Couloirs

69. Teewinot Mountain (Southwest Aspect)
    A. Teton Glacier terminal moraine
    B. Southwest Couloirs

70. Teewinot Mountain (East Aspect)
    A. East Face
    B. Direct East Ridge

71. Teewinot Mountain and Crooked Thumb (North Aspect)

A. Northeast Face
B. Direct North Ridge

C. Emerson's Chimney
D. Crooked Thumb, North Ridge

72. Mount Owen, Northwest Aspect (Aerial)

A. Northwest Ridge
B. Great Yellow Tower, Western traverse
C. Northwest Face
D. Northwest Face; *var:* Gagner-Jackson, 1985
E. West Ledges (two alternatives)

73. Mount Owen, West Aspect (Aerial)

A. Northwest Ridge
B. Northwest Face
C. Northwest Face; *var:* Gagner-Jackson, 1985
D. Serendipity Arête

E. Mas Intrepido
F. Intrepidity Arête
G. West Ledges (two alternatives)

74. Mount Owen (Southwest Aspect)
   A. Intrepidity Arête

75. Mount Owen (South Aspect)

A. South Face
B. Fryxell
C. South Chimney
D Bunton
E Koven

76. Mount Owen (Northeast Aspect)

A. East Ridge; *var:* Unsoeld-Rickert, 1946
B. Northeast Snowfields; *var:* Larson-Quinlan, 1983
C. Northeast Snowfields; *var:* Montopoli, 1977
D. Northeast Snowfields

E. Crescent Arête
F. Run-Don't-Walk Couloir
G. North Ridge

77. Mount Owen (Northwest Aspect—Aerial)

A. North Face   B. North Face; *var:* Harrington-Larson, 1989   C. Northwest Ridge

78. Table Mountain (East Aspect)
A. Heartbreak Ridge
B. East Face, South Buttress

79. Table Mountain (Northeast Aspect)

80. Yosemite Peak (Northeast Aspect)

    A. Pensive

    B. East Face, Chouinard

    C. East Face, Weeks' Chimney

81. Fourteen-Hour Pinnacle, East Aspect
A. Direct South Ridge
B. East Face, Twenty-Four Hour Crack

82. Symmetry Crag 4 (South Aspect)
Cascade Canyon, North Side Rock Climbs
A. (A Climb on) Trinity Buttress

83. Storm Point, Lower Southwest Ridge (Southwest Aspect)
Cascade Canyon, North Side Rock Climbs

A. Guides' Wall

B. Vieux Guide start

C. Bat Attack Crack

D. Hot Dogs

84. Storm Point (Southwest Aspect)   *John Dietschy*

Cascade Canyon, North Side Rock Climbs

A. Guides' Wall
B. Vieux Guide
C. Bat Attack Crack
D. No Friends
E. Rags-to-Riches
F. Skinny Dip

85. Baxter's Pinnacle (Southeast Aspect) *James L. Olson*
    A. South Ridge, Upper South Face

86. Baxter's Pinnacle (North Aspect)
A. North Face   B. Northwest Corner

87. Cube Point (West Aspect)

A. West Chimney

88. Cube Point (Northeast Aspect)
   A. East Ridge

89. Symmetry Spire (East Aspect—Aerial)

A. Storm Point
B. Southwest Ridge
C. Durrance Ridge
D. Direct Jensen Ridge
E. The Jaw, East Face

F Lake of the Crags
G Cube Point
H East Cascade Buttresses, No Perches Necessary
I Baxter's Pinnacle, South Ridge, Upper South Face

90. Symmetry Spire (South Aspect)

- A. Southwest Couloir
- B. Southwest Ridge
- C. Direct South Face (modern version)
- D. South Face
- E. Durrance Ridge
- F. Direct Jensen Ridge

91. Rock of Ages (Northeast Aspect)
  A. Northeast Chimney
  B. Northeast Face
  C. Stettner

92. Mount St. John (Southeast Aspect—Aerial)

A. South Couloir start
B. Avocet Arête start

C. Ostrich Arête start
D. Peregrine Arête

93. Rockchuck Peak (Northwest Aspect—Aerial)

94. Mount Woodring (Southwest Aspect)
A. Southwest Slope
B. South Rib

95. Mount Moran, No Escape Buttress (South Aspect—Aerial)
Leigh Canyon, North Side Rock Climbs
A. No Escape Buttress, Direct South Face
B. No Escape Buttress, Direct South Face; *var:* Direct Finish
C. Gin and Tonic start
D. No Survivors start
E. No Escape Slabs

96. Albert Russel Ellingwood on the northeast ridge of Mount Moran, 1924 *Carl Blaurock*

97. On the first ascent of the West Horn *Fred Ayres*

98. West Horn (West Aspect)

99. Mount Moran, South Buttress (West Aspect)

A. Southwest Couloir
B. Fonda Ridge
C. Sandinista Couloir
D. Western Buttress
E. West Dihedrals
F. Revolutionary Crest
G. Direct South Buttress (traditional descent)
H. South Buttress, West Face

100. Mount Moran (Southwest Aspect—Aerial)

A. West Ridge
B. Southwest Couloir
C. Fonda Ridge
D. Sandinista Couloir

E. Western Buttress
F. West Dihedrals
G. Revolutionary Crest
H. Direct South Buttress (traditional descent)

101. Mount Moran, Lower South Buttress (South Aspect—Aerial)

A. Direct South Buttress
B. South Buttress Central
C. South Buttress Right

D. South Buttress Right; *var:* Deliverance
E. South Buttress Right; *var:* Habeler

102. Mount Moran, Lower South Buttress (South Aspect) *Steve Walker*

A. Direct South Buttress finish
B. South Buttress Central
C. South Buttress Right

D. South Buttress Right; *var:* Deliverance
E. South Buttress Right; *var:* Habeler

103. Mount Moran (Southeast Aspect—Aerial) *Leigh Canyon, North Side Rock Climbs*

A. Direct South Buttress
B. South Buttress Right
C. The Blackfin
D. Staircase Arête
E. Southeast Ridge
F. Traverse to CMC campsite

104. Mount Moran, Upper East Face (Southeast Aspect)
    A. CMC   B. CMC descent

105. Mount Moran (Northeast Aspect—Aerial)

A. East Horn, East Face
B. East Ridge
C. Skillet Glacier
D. Northeast Ridge

E. Northeast Ridge; *var:* Clark-Donald, 1939
F. Sickle Couloir
G. Pika Buttress
H. North Ridge

106. Mount Moran (North Aspect—Aerial)
A. Peak 11,795, North Prow Arête
B. North Buttress
C. North Face
D. Triple Glacier
E. Northwest Ridge

107. The Zebra, Peak 11,680+ (North Aspect)

108. Thor Peak (Southwest Aspect—Aerial)
   A. South Slope

109. Thor Peak (Southeast Aspect)

A East Face, South Chimney

B East Face, *var:* Boynton-Mahoney

C. East Face

D. Hidden Couloir

110. Cleaver Peak (West Aspect—Aerial)

111. Bivouac Peak (South Aspect—Aerial)

A. South Face II B. South Face III

112. Traverse Peak (Southwest Aspect—Aerial)

113. Rolling Thunder Mountain (Northeast Aspect) *Roald Fryxell*

115. William Unsoeld on the traverse into the "V" on the North Face of the Grand Teton   *Leigh Ortenburger*

114. Richard Emerson on the first free ascent of the Pendulum Pitch on the North Face of the Grand Teton   *Leigh Ortenburger*

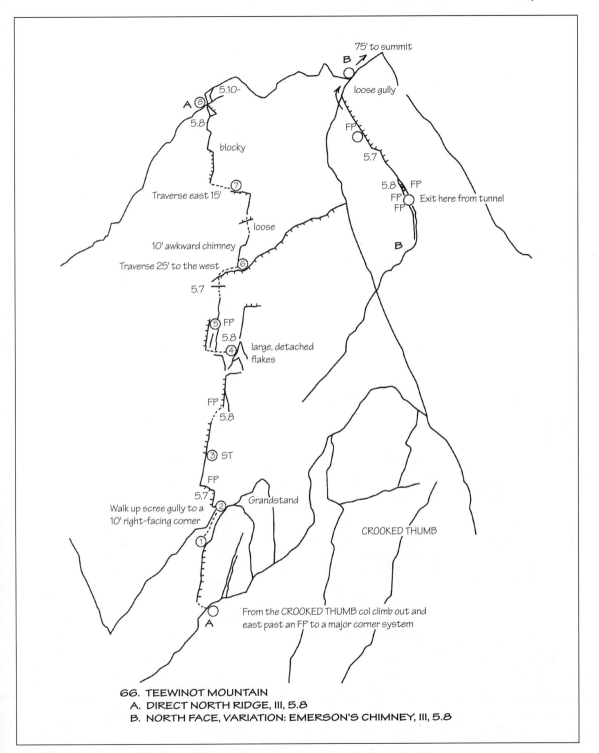

75' to summit

B

loose gully

A ⑧   5.10-

5.8

FP

blocky

5.7

5.8 FP

FP

Traverse east 15'   ⑦

FP   Exit here from tunnel

loose

10' awkward chimney

Traverse 25' to the west   ⑥

B

5.7

⑤ FP

5.8

④   large, detached
flakes

FP

5.8

③ ST

FP

5.7

Walk up scree gully to a   ②   Grandstand
10' right-facing corner

CROOKED THUMB

①

From the CROOKED THUMB col climb out and
A   east past an FP to a major corner system

66. TEEWINOT MOUNTAIN
    A. DIRECT NORTH RIDGE, III, 5.8
    B. NORTH FACE, VARIATION: EMERSON'S CHIMNEY, III, 5.8

Cascade Canyon to the west, as was done by the first-ascent party. These northwest couloirs leading to the col are long, contain much loose rock, and are not recommended. From the col one can reach the top of a shoulder, the Grandstand, which abuts against the north face, in two ropelengths of 5.6 climbing up the east side. From here three ledges can be seen leading up and to the right (west). Climb along this ledge system across the west facet all the way to its right (west) edge; there is some choice in this section, but with careful routefinding it should involve easy 5th-class climbing. Climb directly up the northwest ridge to the summit, which is then attained from the west.

Variation: Emerson's Chimney. III, 5.8. First ascent August 24, 1948, by Richard Emerson and Pete Owen. See *Topo 66* and *Photo 71*. This variation is perhaps done more often than all of the rest of the North Face routes. Emerson's Chimney is the second (westernmost) of the two left-slanting chimney-crack systems on the west facet of the north face. Proceed to the top of the Grandstand, which is reached as described under *Route 9,* and climb to the highest of the three ledges that lead to the right (west) across the west facet of the north face. Make a diagonal traverse out on this ledge past the first (eastern) of the left-slanting chimney systems. A total of three to four ropelengths of easy 5th-class climbing lead to the base of Emerson's Chimney. Start up the chimney. About halfway up one can see the remarkable tunnel that leads all the way through the peak and opens out on the south face. Continue up the chimney to a small ledge on its left (east) wall beneath the extremely narrow upper portion. On the face outside the chimney, up and to the left (east), is a shelf that leads diagonally up for 120 feet to the summit ridge. The problem is to reach this shelf. Make a strenuous and exposed move (5.8) onto the outside face, using some small chockstones as handholds to get up and out of the chimney onto the shelf. Once on the shelf, climb enjoyable but tricky slabs for 120 feet to a short, loose rock gully that leads to the summit knife-edge only a few feet east of the summit. The upper end of this shelf is the hardest. This entire climb from the Crooked Thumb Col is in the shadow and is likely to be cold. *Time: 10½ hours* from Lupine Meadows. See *American Alpine Journal,* 9, no. 2 (1955), pp. 147–149; *Stanford Alpine Club Journal,* 1955, pp. 48–50.

Variation: Teewinot Tunnel. II, 5.6. First ascent August 30, 1948, by Charles Crush and Graham McNear. It is possible to walk and crawl all the way through the tunnel from Emerson's Chimney on the north face and finish the climb by the easier south face. It is also possible to reverse this procedure (if one can find the tunnel), crawl from the sunny south side out to the belay below the crux of the Chimney, and finish by that route. This tunnel feature seems to be unique in the Teton Range.

Variation: Reese Arête. III, 5.7. First ascent July 28, 1965, by Rick Reese, Mike Ermarth, and Ralph Tingey. This variation is on a small arête on the north face of Teewinot about halfway between Emerson's Chimney and the north ridge crest. Some loose rock will be encountered. Approach as for Emerson's Chimney (see preceding variation) to a point about 125 feet short and northeast of the chimney. A chimney system that starts as a small couloir leads from here back toward the left (east), culminating in a very high-angle chimney. After 50 feet up this couloir, climb left onto the left (north) wall of the couloir. The first lead on this wall ascends an awkward jam crack (5.7) that slants up and left across the smooth face to a large chimney filled with loose blocks. The next lead goes 60 feet up this chimney before cutting right around a corner to large steep blocks. The final lead goes directly up over a small overhang onto the summit ridge, about 80 feet east of the summit itself.

ROUTE 12. *Northwest Face.* IV, 5.8, A3. First ascent August 22–23, 1961, by David Dornan, Barry Corbet, and Richard Emerson. This long and severe route of eight pitches surmounts the bulge of the lower portion of the west facet of the north face of Teewinot. One crack system, initially two parallel cracks, cuts through the bulge. This crack, which is partly wet and icy even at the end of a dry season, is easily distinguished from a distance. It slants up from right to left near the center of the northwest face and reaches the summit ridge about 300 feet to the left (east) of the summit. The upper face of Teewinot is composed of many bands of light and dark rock that dip slightly to the west and cross this main crack system. Some of the belays on this route are hanging belays.

Hike up the Cascade Canyon trail, cross the creek, and bushwhack into the cirque between Teewinot and Mount Owen (see *Mount Owen, Route 9*). The first task is to reach the base of the crack system described above. An obvious couloir leads to the col between the Crooked Thumb and the upper face of Teewinot. The ascent of this long, deep couloir involves nothing more than 3.0 or 4.0 climbing with the exception of an 80-foot 5.6 pitch (poorly protected) that leads past a chockstone on the left side about one-quarter of the way up the couloir. Leave the couloir to the right (south) before reaching the Crooked Thumb Col and wind back and forth on a series of easy ledges that leads to the plainly visible base of the cracks.

There are two parallel cracks at the start that join higher up. The right crack was the object of aid attempts in 1949 or 1950 by Richard Emerson and William Byrd (defeated by lack of knifeblades and bongs, neither of which were available at the time). This route utilizes the left crack. The first pitch is up a short chimney (5.4) at the beginning of the left crack to a belay position for the next lead, the most difficult of the route. This begins with a short aid ceiling above which is an inside corner that contains a moderate crack. Nail up as high as possible (about 30 feet) in order to make a difficult pendulum around the corner to the left; a knifeblade piton just before the corner will assist this move.

From this corner traverse left (5.8) for 10 feet to another aid crack. This 100-foot pitch was belayed during the first ascent from a bolt (not too good) about 30 feet up this crack. Above the bolt, knifeblade pitons allow progress on aid for 60 feet to a good belay ledge. The third pitch is free (5.8) for 80 feet up the rather smooth face on the left of the main crack or chimney. Once on a large ledge revert to aid climbing, using some bongs in the main crack, to reach a belay at a shaky flake. The final lead goes straight up free for 20 feet to the second bolt, used for aid, from which mixed 5.7 and A3 climbing in the main crack system leads to the end of the difficult climbing. One or two leads of 5.1 rock will now take you onto the easier ledges that diagonal up and right to the beginning of Emerson's Chimney (see *Route 11, 1948 variation*); climb this chimney to the summit.

From a high bivouac this route can perhaps be climbed in one day. The base of the cracks could also be approached by ascending to the Crooked Thumb Col from the east and then descending the upper portion of the northwest couloir to reach the ledges that lead to the cracks. It is worth noting that this route ascends the most difficult portion of the northwest face, the bulge, but the portion below the base of the two parallel cracks (which was the object of an attempt on August 2, 1960, by Gary Hemming, Rick Medrick, and Kenneth Weeks) and the final section of the crack system, above the diagonal ledges leading to Emerson's chimney, have not yet been climbed. The first of these is very steep and contains rotten rock, whereas the second should not prove very difficult.

ROUTE 13. *Northwest Couloir.* II, 5.1. First descent July 4, 1931, by Fritiof Fryxell, Rudolph Edmund, Theodore Anderson, and Harold Hendrickson. See *Photo 68*. This route, which starts from the Teewinot–Owen cirque, ascends the major wide couloir leading to the high plateau west of Teewinot's summit; the couloir is just to the right (west) of the northwest ridge of Teewinot. For the approach to the Teewinot–Owen cirque, see *Route 14*. Moderately steep scrambling is required to pass the lower portion of the couloir. During most of the season the upper portion will be steep snow. Edge left (east) as the plateau is approached; leave the couloir about 400 feet below the plateau level and enter a steep chimney, which is the beginning of the V-shaped couloir that descends west from the large main notch just south of the summit of Teewinot. Some difficulty should be expected initially in the chimney, but after two large chockstones it opens out into an easier couloir. Loose rock will be encountered as the main notch is approached. When about 200 feet short of the main notch, cut left (north) up the steep, but not difficult, rock leading to the ridge crest a few feet east of the summit monolith. See *Appalachia*, 18, no. 4 (December 1931), pp. 388–408, illus.

ROUTE 14. *Northwest Ridge.* III, 5.4. First ascent September 7, 1954, by John and Jean Fonda, Don Decker, and Marty Benham. See *Photo 68*. Follow the trail up Cascade Canyon and cross Cascade Creek where streams descending from the northeast snowfields of Mount Owen empty into the creek. Logs spanning the stream should be found in this area. Bushwhacking can be minimized by linking game and climbers' trails up the right (west) side of the drainage into the large basin that is enclosed by Mount Owen and Teewinot. Two parallel ridges descend into this basin from the main ridge connecting Teewinot and Mount Owen. Walk up the talus to the base of the western ridge, scramble up this ridge for about 500 feet, and then cross the couloir (*Route 12*) to the eastern ridge, which is the northwest ridge of Teewinot. In this lower part the climbing is easy but much of the rock is loose. Continue scrambling on poor rock until this ridge steepens and the nature of the rock abruptly changes for the better. At this point, where this ridge intersects the north and west faces, cut right (south) across the base of the west face on a series of ledges. The uppermost of these ledges terminates at the base of a chimney. Climb 200 feet up this chimney to a broad ledge; turn left (north) and climb directly up a rib for 300 feet to the small overhang near its top. The first-ascent party used a shoulder stand to surmount this overhang. At the top of this rib veer left again and climb over the top of the large chimney that separates the rib from the northwest ridge. After regaining the ridge follow it directly to the summit monolith. *Time: 11½ hours* from Jenny Lake. See *American Alpine Journal*, 9, no. 2 (1955), pp. 147–149.

Variation: Direct Buttress. III, 5.7. First ascent July 29, 1967, by Leigh Ortenburger and John Whitesel. See *Photo 68*. The initial ascent of the northwest ridge made a substantial horizontal traverse right (south) at the point where the steep section of the ridge with solid yellow rock was encountered. This variation continues directly up this steep section near the crest of the ridge, past a small tower, followed by a difficult (5.7) left-facing chimney. Three pitches of near-vertical, beautiful knobby rock (5.1) lead to the top of a second tower, which is separated from the remainder of the ridge by an impassable notch. At this point a descent of about 150 feet to the right, which includes a 30-foot rappel, permits access to a rib on the right (south) side of the main chimney, which leads back up to the aforementioned notch. This rib is then climbed to reach the summit from the northwest.

Variation: Chockstone Chimney. III, 5.8. First ascent July 26, 1975, Tom Burns and Bill Katra. During the horizontal traverse right (south) along the base of the west face, a deep, 10-foot-wide, vertical chimney containing a large chockstone will be found about 30 feet north of the shallower chimney of the original route. This variation follows this chimney, which is easily distinguished as the deepest break in the middle of the smoothest and most nearly vertical section of the west face. The top of the chimney breaks into two roughly parallel cracks that continue upward. The first 5.8 lead (130 feet) climbs past the chockstone on the left, going over a small overhang and up the left-hand crack of the chimney to a good belay. Then scramble for 80 feet to a good ledge about 40 feet below a huge, overhanging chimney. Go up this chimney and directly over the overhang. A step left provides access to face and crack climbing to a good belay stance. The fourth pitch continues up a 30-foot vertical lieback-jam crack combination (5.8) followed by easier climbing to the northwest ridge crest and a solid belay. From this point easier climbing leads to the summit.

PEAK 11,840+ *(0.3 mi WSW of Teewinot Mountain)*

Map: Grand Teton

This peak is the high point on the west end of the broad plateau due west of the summit of Teewinot Mountain. It is seldom visited except during a traverse from Teewinot to Mount Owen, or conversely. It does afford an excellent viewpoint of the impressive north precipice of the Grand Teton.

ROUTE 1. East Slope. II, 3.0. First ascent August 18, 1940, by Edward McNeill and Thomson Edwards; this ascent was made in the course of the first traverse from Teewinot to Owen. The high plateau to the east can be reached from the summit of Teewinot by descending the standard East Face route until the main notch in the ridge south of the summit can be reached from the east. From the notch one can easily descend 500 feet down onto the plateau. From the plateau it is but a scramble to the summit of this peak. The plateau, however, can also be reached directly from Glacier Gulch as in *Teewinot, Route 1.*

EAST PRONG (12,000+)

Map: Grand Teton

The East Prong is the first major tower east of Mount Owen on the ridge connecting with Teewinot. It is separated from the east ridge of Mount Owen by the East Prong Col. Although it provides an excellent viewpoint for all of the peaks and faces surrounding Glacier Gulch and the Teton Glacier, the East Prong is usually climbed only in conjunction with an ascent of Mount Owen or in the course of the ridge traverse between Mount Owen and Teewinot. It was the location of the widely published photograph, by Fritiof Fryxell, showing the young Paul Petzoldt in the foreground with the north face of the Grand Teton looming in the background.

CHRONOLOGY

South Couloir and East Ridge: August 1, 1927, Paul Petzoldt, Fritiof Fryxell, Robert Spahr

West Ridge: August 27, 1934, George Goldthwaite (descent); July 28, 1941, Orrin Bonney, Margaret Hawkes (ascent)

South Face: August 2, 1966, Peter Cleveland, Don Storjohann

ROUTE 1. West Ridge. II, 5.4. First descent August 27, 1934, by George Goldthwaite; first ascent July 28, 1941, by Orrin Bonney and Margaret Hawkes. Approach the East Prong Col as in *Mount Owen, Route 7.* Throughout most of the summer some ice climbing will be required to reach the summit of the Prong from the col. The steepest part can be avoided if one climbs onto the rocks of the west ridge about 100 feet below the summit. When using this route for descent, start by descending to the north for a short distance before turning west toward the col. See *Appalachia,* 20, no. 7 (November 1935), p. 421.

ROUTE 2. South Face. II, 5.8. First ascent August 2, 1966, by Peter Cleveland and Don Storjohann. This is a short straightforward climb with considerable exposure. Climb the initial face without great difficulty to the base of a large diamond-shaped face. The diagonal crack in this face is the one difficult pitch on the route. The top of the Prong is then reached easily.

ROUTE 3. South Couloir and East Ridge. II, 4.0. First ascent August 1, 1927, by Paul Petzoldt, Fritiof Fryxell, and Robert Spahr. From the northeastern edge of the Teton Glacier climb one of the couloirs that lead up to the east ridge of the East Prong. These couloirs are straightforward, and once one is on the ridge, no further difficulty will be experienced. See *Appalachia,* 18, no. 3 (June 1931), pp. 209–232, illus.

MOUNT OWEN (12,928)

Map: Grand Teton

Mount Owen is one of the greatest of the Teton peaks in height, beauty, and climbing interest. Named for William Owen, pioneer Wyoming surveyor and organizer of the 1898 ascent of the Grand Teton, it was one of the last of the high peaks to be ascended, resisting several early attempts. The first attempt was made on August 1, 1927, by Fritiof Fryxell, Paul Petzoldt, and Robert Spahr, but they chose the wrong couloir from Glacier Gulch and soon found themselves on the summit of the East Prong. Eight days later Phil Smith and Ben Lengel were stopped at about 11,500 feet. In the same week Albert R. Ellingwood and Robert Ormes also attempted the same peak. In 1928 Owen urged William Gilman, Fritiof Fryxell, and Phil Smith to try once again to reach the summit. On July 28 this trio attained the base of the summit knob only 100 feet below the summit, but they were unable to scale its smooth face; Gilman reached the high point about 50 feet up the face of the knob. The next year, on July 26, J. D. Hunter and Notsie Garnick made an attempt but apparently reached only the first bench on the south face. Not until 1930 did the very strong first-ascent party solve the problem of the summit knob. Even today there is no easy way to the summit, for every route requires mountaineering skill. Thus, Mount Owen is one of the most appealing goals in the range. The spectacular view of the north face of the Grand Teton from the summit of Mount Owen is most impressive.

Mount Owen can be climbed in one long day but this requires a strong, fast party and an early start. A high camp, usually at Surprise Lake, is desirable for any of the routes approached from east of southeast across the Teton Glacier. Similarly, a camp in Valhalla Canyon, either high or low, is recommended for the west and northwest routes; however, retrieval of this camp can be a problem, depending on one's itinerary. For the northeast routes, a camp in the Teewinot–Owen cirque is desirable. Note that all of the routes from the west, northwest, north, or northeast require crossing the swift and cold Cascade Creek. Climbers must expect some difficulty in this crossing, but with luck and some advance searching a log can often be located, permitting a dry crossing. Sometimes one must wade across the creek, which, in early season when the water is high, can be difficult and dangerous. If one wishes to make a north-side climb in one day, the crossing point should be reconnoitered in advance to avoid losing time on the climbing day.

CHRONOLOGY

East Ridge: July 16, 1930, Robert Underhill, Kenneth Henderson, Fritiof Fryxell, Phil Smith
   var: August 28, 1935, Paul Petzoldt, H. K. Hartline, A. Curtis Smith
   var: September 7, 1937, Joseph and Paul Stettner
   var: September 2, 1946, Willi Unsoeld, Herbert Rickert
Koven: July 20, 1931, Paul Petzoldt, Glenn Exum, Theodore and Gustav Koven
Northeast Snowfields: August 7, 1931, Paul Petzoldt
   var: **East Ridge Finish:** July 25, 1976, Rich Page, Corky Marshall, Phil Arnold
   var: September 1977, George Montopoli
   var: September 24, 1983, Norm Larson, Steve Quinlan
Fryxell: August 18, 1931, Fritiof Fryxell, Frank Smith
West Ledges: July 28, 1932, Paul Petzoldt, Edward Woolf
Southwest Ridge: September 3, 1937, Jack Durrance, George Sheldon, Percy Rideout
Northwest Ridge: August 5, 1941, Jack Durrance, Henry Coulter, Merrill McLane
North Face: August 21, 1945, Hans Kraus, Harrison Snyder
   var: July 16, 1989, Randy Harrington, Leo Larson
Bunton: August 16, 1949, C. A. Bunton, George Lucas
North Ridge: July 31, 1951, Richard Emerson, William Clayton
   var: **Crescent Arête Direct:** June 1994, Greg Collins, Stephen Koch

South Chimney: August 6, 1957, Yvon Chouinard, John Lowry, Tink Thompson
Serendipity Arête: August 8, 1959, William Buckingham, Frederick Medrick, Sterling Neale, Frank Magary
Crescent Arête: September 9, 1959, Fred Beckey, Yvon Chouinard
South Face: August 18, 1962, Ants Leemets, John Hudson
Northwest Face: August 4, 1965, Leigh Ortenburger, Herb Swedlund
   var: August 20–21, 1982, Rick Reese, David Susong
   var: August 9, 1985, Paul Gagner, Renny Jackson
Run-Don't-Walk Couloir: July 6, 1972, Stephen Arsenault, John Bouchard
Intrepidity Arête: August 18, 1990, Tom Turiano, Matthew Goewert
   var: **Mas Intrepido:** August 1994, Matthew Goewert, Mark Limage

ROUTE 1. West Ledges. II, 5.1. First ascent July 28, 1932, by Paul Petzoldt and Edward Woolf. See *Photos 72* and *73.* This long route was the first one to start from Valhalla Canyon, the beautiful high cirque lying beneath the west faces of the Grand Teton and Mount Owen. The west side of Mount Owen has a complex structure and is difficult to describe, but it has an obvious southern boundary at the long, straight snow couloir, the West Gunsight Couloir, leading to Gunsight Notch. The West Ledges route ascends the region just north (left) of this snow couloir. This region is a series of cliff bands, talus and scree slopes, and sloping ledges, containing a few ill-defined couloirs; it terminates at the crest of the southwest ridge of Mount Owen.

Approach via Cascade Canyon, cross Cascade Creek, and climb into the upper Valhalla Canyon. The initial cliff band just above the upper Valhalla bivouac site is easily passed by climbing near the West Gunsight Couloir or by ascending the couloir that begins just left (north) of the bivouac site. By either route the talus and scree slope leading to the second large, jumbled cliff band is reached and then climbed. Near the right (south) edge of this cliff band, just left of the West Gunsight Couloir, is a steep section of black rock capped by a vertical wall of light-colored rock. Climb the broken rock to the left of this wall to gain access to a section of moderate slabs. There are two alternatives at this point. One can make a lengthy scramble up and right (southeast) to the uppermost part of these slabs, skirting a cliff on the right, until a more broken area is found near the couloir. Climb for a hundred feet or more in this area before turning back left (north) to reach the lower southwest edge of the final large area of slabs and snow patches just below the southwest ridge. The second alternative is to move up and slightly left to the base of a smaller cliff; traverse left (north) under this wall until broken rock is reached just short (south) of a large couloir. Climb to reach the lower northwest edge of the same slab and snow patch area. Now scramble to the central, topmost point of these extensive slabs, beneath the cliffs that prevent easy access to the southwest ridge crest. Climb a short chimney, and traverse left and up to reach the prominent couloir forming the left (north) boundary of the west ledges region. Climb this couloir to the crest at a large notch between two of the largest towers on the southwest ridge; this is the distinctly U-shaped notch as seen from the east. At this point traverse around to the east side of the southwest ridge, and follow that route to the summit (see *Route 2*). Other routes can be worked out, for there are many possible variations. With either talent or luck in the routefinding, the West Ledges route provides both a relatively easy route of ascent and a fast means of descent because most of the route is scrambling.

When descending from the summit along the upper southwest ridge and looking for this route, remember that it strikes this ridge relatively low on the crest. It is important to avoid the temptation to turn off the ridge crest too early down to the west. Error slings for rappelling will be found in one or more notches too far to the north along the crest. Ignore these mistakes and continue downclimbing the ridge until there is a significant increase in the difficulty. At this point it is possible to downclimb onto the upper West Ledges route and no rappel is required; however, even here some may wish to commence the descent to the west by a rappel. For those skilled in the use of the ice axe there is an advantage in early or midseason in seeking out an early entry into the steep West Gunsight Couloir. If the snow is right, a fast descent can be made.

ROUTE 2. *Southwest Ridge.* III, 5.6. First ascent September 3, 1937, by Jack Durrance, George Sheldon, and Percy Rideout; while the ridge was climbed, electricity stopped them within "a short stone's throw of the summit." This is an excellent route containing some of the most enjoyable rock in the Tetons. The base of the southwest ridge of Mount Owen is in the spectacular Gunsight Notch. The recommended approach to the Gunsight is from the west, a straightforward but moderately steep snow-and-ice climb (see *Valhalla Canyon*). Rockfall, rotten rock, and wet and icy rock are good arguments against the direct approach up the East Gunsight Couloir to the notch; this was first done (circa August 22, 1936, by Fritz Wiessner, Paul Petzoldt, Brad Gilman, Beckett Howorth, William House, and Elizabeth Woolsey) by means of a three-person shoulder stand (Woolsey on Wiessner on House) to pass a large chockstone. The first-ascent party for this Southwest Ridge route, however, used another approach, a bit circuitous and difficult. From the upper Teton Glacier on the east, cross the *bergschrund* onto the Grandstand leading toward the north shoulder of the Grand Teton (see *Grand Teton, Route 34*) and

climb to the scree-covered second shelf, which diagonals up and right toward the Gunsight. Follow this shelf out to its upper end where the traverse can be continued for a pitch or two to a point where descent into the notch is possible. This approach, while feasible, makes a long day and some may wish to rappel in order to reach the notch.

From the notch the first pitch is 5.6, starting a few feet to the right of the nose. In the next few leads the route reaches the top of the first tower from the left (west) side of the crest over excellent rock. The sequence of towers leading to the junction with the Fryxell route (*Route 5*) can be climbed in various ways, but the most interesting is to keep as close as possible to the crest. At the north end of the first large horizontal step after passing these towers, *Route 5* is joined and followed to the summit. *Time: 8½ hours* from Valhalla Canyon. See *Dartmouth Mountaineering Club Journal*, 1938, pp. 37–41.

ROUTE 3. *South Face.* III, 5.6, A1. First ascent August 18, 1962, by Ants Leemets and John Hudson. See *Photo 75.* On the easily approached south or southeast face of Mount Owen there is an expanse of rock between the Southwest Ridge (*Route 2*) and the South Chimney (*Route 4*) that can be climbed more or less directly to the upper snowfield. Make the usual approach to the Teton Glacier, and climb above the crevassed section toward its extreme western extension in the East Gunsight Couloir. This route begins on broken rock in watercourses just to the right of a large buttress at the base of the rock wall on the right (north) of the East Gunsight Couloir; the exact start will vary according to the snow level on the glacier. The following leads to the first snowfield bench are all 120 to 140 feet in length.

The first lead bears slightly left on wet rock to a flake and then right and up to a belay under an obvious 15-foot corner. Climb this corner, and scramble up slabs, zigging left and zagging right, to a small belay ledge underneath a second corner of the same size. After ascending this, exit right, then scramble left to a watercourse that is followed by a wet corner. The fourth pitch starts with a 25-foot corner to the right of a large slab and leads, after zigzag scrambling, to a belay stance at the base of a slab capped by a small overhang. The next lead goes up to and diagonally left under the overhang, then up and right, past a small face to the left of a corner to a belay on large ledges. Walk right 70 feet and work up over some overhanging flakes to a scramble up to a large ledge. Two more scrambling pitches up and to the right under a vertical face lead to the lower snowfield on the Fryxell route bench. Scramble about 200 feet back to the left (west) on the bench, and then gain a smaller ledge above the bench. Climb the left of two corners above for 30 feet before scrambling right and up a large broken dihedral. An easy ledge now leads left and up for 60 feet to a large sloping ledge. After a slight downward traverse on this ledge, use some aid to climb an overhanging wall to the base of a chimney, which is climbed to a stance below an overhang. Move right to an easy chimney leading to a few hundred feet of 4.0 climbing in a shallow couloir that ends in the vicinity of the southwest ridge, at the upper snowfield of Mount Owen. Join the Koven route (see *Route 7*) at this point. For protection take a standard rack with some wide (3 to 4 inches) devices. See *American Alpine Journal*, 13, no. 2 (1963), pp. 487–489.

ROUTE 4. South Chimney. III, 5.6. First ascent August 6, 1957, by Yvon Chouinard, John Lowry, and Tink Thompson. See *Photo 75*. This route goes directly from the Teton Glacier to the upper snowfield of Mount Owen without touching the south ridge or the regular East Ridge route. Reach the lower portion of the Teton Glacier (see *Glacier Gulch*) and continue up the glacier beyond the crevassed section (crampons useful) until underneath the center of the south face, at the base of the prominent, large chimney containing a large chockstone about 150 feet above. Depending on the year, some difficulty should be expected in crossing the *randkluft* guarding the entrance to the chimney. Two 5.6 pitches lead to a belay point from which an exposed lead is made out of the chimney to the right and then back into it again above the chockstone. A short lead to the right brings one to easy ledges just below the Fryxell route bench, which is then crossed. After a slight traverse to the right, the route ascends the continuation of the chimney, which is now a deep chute that descends from the upper snowfield and forms a distinctive feature of the mountain. This chute can be climbed directly on steep snow, or else on the easy rock of the left wall. From the upper snowfield either the Koven route or the East Ridge route can be followed to the summit. See *American Alpine Journal*, 12, no. 1 (1960), pp. 125–127.

ROUTE 5. Fryxell. II, 5.4. First ascent August 18, 1931, by Fritiof Fryxell and Frank Smith. See *Photo 75*. This clever early route takes the lower broad bench and shelf on the south face of Mount Owen from the standard Koven Couloir on the east over to the southwest ridge on the west; it combines parts of *Route 2* and *Route 7* but is easier than either. From the Teton Glacier, climb the standard Koven Couloir (see *Route 7*) to the first broad bench. Instead of continuing up the couloir, turn left (west) and follow the bench itself, in early and midseason on a snow traverse. This bench soon ends at a slabby step that is passed via a chimney near the right edge to gain the wide shelf that now extends all the way to the south ridge. Follow the shelf west on snow or easy rock until the angle increases and downsloping slabs dominate; this is just past (west of) the point where the large chute of *Route 4* crosses the shelf. Climb this step on slabs about 150 feet out from the right corner. Continue out the slabs of the shelf on easier ground until the final steep section is encountered short of the southwest ridge. This step is climbed via a short face pitch about 50 feet left (south) of the chimney in the right corner. A short scramble brings one to the crest, which is attained

at a notch at the extreme right (north) end of the relatively level lower section of the southwest ridge. From this notch a single lead on the left (west) side of the tower above brings one to easier enjoyable climbing over, around, and through the various remaining towers on the ridge. Ultimately this ridge climb meets the Koven route, which crosses the southwest ridge very near its upper end above the upper snowfield at the summit knob. The summit is reached either by the west chimney or by the difficult chimney in the southwest corner of the summit knob (first climbed August 9, 1953, by William Buckingham and Rob Day). This is a pleasant mountaineering route, without great difficulty, in one of the most scenic areas in the range. With the north wall of the Grand Teton just across the glacier, which lies 1,000 feet below, it is a most interesting place to be. *Time: 10¼ hours* from Amphitheater Lake. See *Appalachia*, 19, no. 1 (June 1932), pp. 86–96; *Trail and Timberline*, no. 175 (May 1933), pp. 62–66, illus.

ROUTE 6. Bunton. II, 5.6. First ascent August 16, 1949, by C. A. Bunton and George Lucas. See *Photo 75*. This route, not well understood, reaches the upper snowfield without using the regular Koven Couloir to the East Prong Col. Take the Fryxell route (*Route 5*) to the bench above the glacier and out left to the vicinity of the first slabby step at the west end of the bench. At this point, about 300 feet west of the standard Koven Couloir and past a triangular wall, another smaller couloir, commonly snow-filled, leads up and right (northeast) back toward the East Prong Col. Take this couloir a short distance (apparently to the point where it forks) and then move left (west) to a "ledged rock wall" that, via a series of cracks on the right, leads toward the upper snowfield of the Koven route. This part of the route contains several pitches of 5.6 climbing on an open and comparatively exposed face. Easy slabs lead onto the snowfield from which either *Route 7* or *Route 8* can be followed to the summit. In early and midseason some snow and ice must be expected on this route, but when the regular Koven Couloir is dangerous because of poor snow conditions, this route may provide an accessible alternative.

ROUTE 7. ☞Koven. II, 5.4. First ascent July 20, 1931, by Paul Petzoldt, Glenn Exum, and Theodore and Gustav Koven. See *Photo 75*. This mountaineering route has become the most popular on the peak, because it is probably the least difficult climb from the east. However, before undertaking this climb, one should have knowledge of use of the ice axe. In late season, when most of the snow is gone, Mount Owen is much easier to climb. Follow the East Ridge route (*Route 8*) to the upper snowfield. Instead of cutting back onto the ridge crest when traversing the upper snowfield on the south side of the east ridge, continue west until due south of the summit. In early season this will be entirely an upward snow traverse, somewhat hazardous because the snowfield ends below with cliffs. In midseason or late season it is much easier to skirt the snow using bare rock ledges along its bottom edge. When directly south of the summit knob near the southwest ridge, one will see large easy chimneys leading up to the left (west) to a small notch in the uppermost southwest ridge just below the summit knob. Climb to this notch and then traverse north around the west side of the summit knob on an easy ledge until the big west chimney is seen. It is an easy climb up this chimney to the top. Do not turn up one of the smaller west chimneys. The proper one is several feet across, very deep, and due west of the summit. While this Koven route is the usual descent route on the mountain, it is not fast, as care must be taken, both on the traverse of the upper snowfield and in the Koven Couloir leading down to the glacier. Many parties will wish to remain roped during the majority of the climb. An early start will prevent potential time problems on this long climb. *Time: 6 to 7½ hours* from Amphitheater Lake; *7¾ to 9 hours* from Jenny Lake. See *Appalachia,* 19, no. 1 (June 1932), pp. 86–96; *Chicago Mountaineering Club Newsletter,* 2, no. 6 (July–December 1948), p. 9; *Trail and Timberline,* no. 175 (May 1933), pp. 62–66, illus.; no. 491 (November 1959), pp. 168, 171.

ROUTE 8. East Ridge. II, 5.6. First ascent July 16, 1930, by Robert Underhill, Kenneth Henderson, Fritiof Fryxell, and Phil Smith. The successful first ascent of Mount Owen by this route marked a major threshold in Teton climbing history. Not only was significant technical difficulty overcome but this was the last of the high peaks to be climbed. And this East Ridge route remains a fine mountaineering objective, combining excellent rock pitches with significant snow climbing. For the approach see *Glacier Gulch.* From the middle of the lower portion of the Teton Glacier, the Koven Couloir leading to the East Prong Col between the East Prong and Mount Owen is easily seen. About one-third of the way to the col, the two sections of this couloir are broken by a broad talus-and-scree bench that extends across the southeast flank of the mountain below the East Prong. This bench will be at least partially covered with snow in early and midseason. The first section of this couloir, containing rotten rock, is usually capped by a small waterfall from the melting snow on the bench. Climb to the waterfall and traverse left to easier ground on the left wall that takes one to the bench. Walk or kick steps up the bench, depending on the time of year. Ascend the upper section of the couloir for about 200 feet before turning left onto the rock forming its left (west) edge. Under good conditions late in the season, this rock is a scramble on small ledges all the way to the col. In early season, however, almost all this rock will be covered with snow, and many steps will have to be kicked in the steep upper part of the couloir in order to reach the col. Crampons can be useful here.

From the col turn abruptly left (west) up the ridge. The 120-foot band of rock that must be climbed in order to reach the upper snowfield can be passed in several places (from left to right): (1) From the crest of the ridge traverse left (south) around a corner just at the base of this rock band. Only a few feet around this corner, climb steep slabs to the snowfield in two ropelengths. This is one of the more difficult possibilities because the rock is commonly wet from the melting snow above. (2) The face directly above the crest of the ridge can be climbed, but this is even more difficult. (3) The standard scheme is to traverse 50 feet down to the right (north) of the ridge crest along the base of this rock band and enter a large chimney. The climbing is easy and the chockstone at the top is easily passed on either the right or left wall. In early season this chimney will be either wet or a snow climb. (4) Traverse even farther right to a series of ledges leading up to the base of the snowfield.

Two possibilities of about equal difficulty present themselves once the upper snowfield is reached. The east ridge, now directly above, ends in a vertical drop, so the object is to traverse around either the south or north side of this nose before turning up to gain the ridge crest again. *South side:* Traverse left (south), staying on the bare rock ledges at the lower edge of the snow if possible. If these rocks are covered with snow, cut diagonally up the snow until 200 or 300 feet past the nose of the ridge. A series of shallow chimneys and ledges will be seen leading back onto the ridge. If these are climbed at their left (west) edge, one will come out 100 feet below the ridge crest, where one climbs westward for two pitches to the base of the summit knob. If the chimneys and ledges are climbed at their right (east) edge, one will reach the actual crest of the ridge, which at this point is composed of smooth slabs. Climb these smooth slabs via cracks in the center for several ropelengths, angling slightly left (south) to the base of the summit knob. *North side:* Traverse right (north) around the nose, diagonaling up the snow about 200 feet past the nose until ledges lead back south to the ridge crest at the beginning of the aforementioned smooth slabs. In late season more rock will be exposed on this north side, increasing the difficulty somewhat.

Once the smooth and near-vertical east face of the summit knob is reached there are several ways to proceed: (1) The standard route is directly up the difficult face on small holds for about 25 feet. Once this somewhat runout section has been passed, climb upward a few feet before traversing left (south) to the easy rock at the summit. Little protection is available for this lead. (2) Traverse left (south) along the base of the knob to the southeast corner, where a large flake is detached from the knob itself. Climb the corner across from the flake using the crack. When the crack runs out, make a delicate traverse to the left (south) for 6 feet to gain a broad ledge just below the summit. This pitch is slightly less difficult than the standard direct route, and it has the advantage that some protection can be placed. (3) The devious route of the first ascent requires a 30-foot rappel to the north and then a traverse along a shelf extending clear around the summit knob to the west chimney. The great cleft of this chimney extends deep into the summit knob and is the only easy way to the summit.

The suggested route of descent is the Koven route, described earlier, or else rappel down the east ridge, which is more complicated. Caution must be exercised when climbing back down the main couloir, of course. *Time: 6 to 7¾ hours* from Amphitheater Lake. See *American Alpine Journal,* 1, no. 3 (1931), pp. 320–326, illus.; *Appalachia,* 18, no. 3 (June 1931), pp. 209–232, illus.; *Canadian Alpine Journal,* 19 (1930), pp. 84–91, illus.; *Trail and Timberline,* no. 447 (March 1956), pp. 47–48.

Variation: III, 5.6, A1. First ascent August 28, 1935, by Paul Petzoldt, H. K. Hartline, and A. Curtis Smith. From the East Prong Col traverse across the "bottom of snowfields to north ridge"; exactly how this was done is uncertain. There are several possibilities, but unless one wants to engage in long, steep horizontal snow traverses, this variation is probably best done in late season when more rock will be exposed. From the col one can descend a few feet and head northwest along the top edge of the steep snowfield past the initial wall to its right (north) edge where a snow chute, or rock ledge in late season, of moderate angle leads back due west to gain the edge of the next snowfield. This snowfield (sometimes ice in late season) must be crossed one way or another to reach the cliffs guarding, at this level, access to the north ridge. These cliffs, which appear difficult, form the east wall of the Great Yellow Tower of the north ridge. Once above this cliff band, which appears to harbor excellent but steep cracks or chimneys in good rock, the upper north ridge is at hand and is climbed to the summit knob, passing a moderately difficult chimney along the way. The summit can be attained by traversing to the right to gain the standard west chimney or a difficult chimney on the northwest corner of the knob can be climbed.

An almost completely different alternative is to start the traverse toward the north ridge from *above* the first cliff band above the East Prong Col. One could then traverse northwest along the bottom edge of the uppermost of the northeast snowfields. This scheme would also involve crossing some snow, perhaps ice in late season, to attain the north ridge at some point above the first step above the notch separating the Great Yellow Tower.

Variation: III, 5.6, A1. First ascent September 7, 1937, by Joseph and Paul Stettner; a similar route was climbed on August 19, 1952, by Willi Unsoeld, Ellis Blade, Steve Jervis, and Tom Klemens. It is possible to attack the nose at the end of the upper east ridge above the upper snowfield more or less directly. Ascend the snowfield directly to the extreme eastern point of the ridge. Climb broken ledges on the north side of the ridge for 20 to 50 feet (depending on the depth of the snow) to the big overhang that spans the entire width of the ridge. At the extreme north end of this overhang is a climbable corner reached by traversing about 12 feet to the right on a vertical face. At this corner aid was used to reach the ledge sloping up to the west just above the overhang. From this ledge climb a steep 30-foot wall to the block of rock at the top of the ridge, which is commonly used as a rappel point for the descent to the snowfield.

Variation: III, 5.6. First ascent September 2, 1946, by Willi Unsoeld and Herbert Rickert. See *Photo 76.* The low point (11,440+) of the ridge between Mount Owen and Teewinot Mountain can be reached directly from Cascade Canyon via a long, obvious snow couloir. In late season the upper portions of this couloir will be rock. Beware of falling rock here. To reach the east ridge of Mount Owen from this saddle, traverse west over the East Prong and descend to the East Prong Col, where *Route 7* or *Route 8* is joined.

ROUTE 9. *Northeast Snowfields.* III, 5.6. First ascent August 7, 1931, by Paul Petzoldt. See *Photo 76.* This very long and varied route provides one of the finest snow climbs in the range. The several early ascents of this route did not record their exact lines, so the history of the three significant variations of the main route is uncertain. It is difficult to say precisely when conditions on this route are the best. The right combination of conditions may exist during the late spring, well after the final avalanche cycle, and when low overnight temperatures allow for a hard freeze of the snow on this vast face. Because of the steepness and constant angle, there is some danger from rockfall on this route. Because the snow is likely to be hard in the early morning hours, when one is likely to be climbing this route, crampons are useful. Approach via the Cascade Canyon trail, continuing on past the point where the streams descending from the northeast snowfields of Mount Owen empty into the creek. Cross Cascade Creek in the vicinity of a very large boulder on the north side of the creek. Logs spanning the creek can sometimes be found in this area, but scouting the situation the day before the proposed ascent is recommended. The bushwhacking up into the Teewinot–Owen cirque is not easy, but one can often link up game trails and utilize the trees on the right (west) side of the drainage. Either way scramble up the talus below the first snowfield.

Proceed up the snow, keeping in mind that the obvious couloirs leading up from the upper southwest corner of this snowfield serve as funnels for falling rocks. It is recommended that this portion be passed very early in the morning before the sun starts melting the snow above. Avoid the easier climbing in these dangerous couloirs by accepting the increased difficulty of staying to the right to pass the initial cliffs. Some moderately difficult friction pitches will be met in this section. Proceed upward until one has a choice of routes for getting past the next vertical section of rock to the second major snowfield: (1) The most obvious and standard route is up to the right (west) over wet rock (some snow in early season) onto the lower right (west) corner of the second snowfield. Then climb up and slightly left (east) on this steep snowfield to the next and final rock band. (2) The other possibility is to climb the steep rock wall to the left (east) and thereby gain the small snowfield that descends from the East Prong Col. Climb along the right edge of this snowfield until above the initial wall and a large rock ledge (snow in early season) is reached, leading back right (west) to near the upper left corner of the second snowfield. Cross the upper portion of this snowfield to reach the same rock band as in option (1).

Cross this final rock band. Its difficulty depends on the quantity of snow present; in early season this may be completely covered by snow, simplifying matters. The third, last, and steepest snowfield is now at hand and is climbed diagonally right (west) up to the summit rock mass. From the highest point of the snow an interesting chimney leads up to the north ridge, ending at the base of the summit knob. The summit is then attained either directly from the northwest via a difficult chimney or, after a slight traverse to the right, via the large west chimney of the Koven route.

If the second major snowfield is reached, as in option (1), one can climb this snowfield, staying right (west) passing beneath a wall, the east face of the Great Yellow Tower. Then climb a steep crack or chimney near the left edge of this face to gain the extreme lower right corner of the third and final snowfield, which is then climbed to the summit rock mass.

It is also possible to bypass completely the first snowfield and initial rock band. This is accomplished by continuing up Cascade Canyon until under the main north walls of Mount Owen at about 7,600 feet, crossing Cascade Creek and bushwhacking up toward the base of the north ridge of Mount Owen. A continuous bench that diagonals up and left along the base of these cliffs is easily followed left (east) toward the bottom end of Crescent Arête (see *Route 10*). Some scrambling is required to continue this traverse east past the bottom of the arête. Ledges then take one into the main couloir system of the northeast face between the first and second major snowfields. *Time: 13¼ hours* from Cascade Canyon. See *Appalachia*, 19, no. 1 (June 1932), pp. 86–96; *Trail and Timberline*, no. 175 (May 1933), pp. 62–66, illus.

Variation: East Ridge Finish. III, 5.6. First ascent July 25, 1976, by Rich Page, Corky Marshall, and Phil Arnold. This variation follows the standard Northeast Snowfield route to the final snowfield. Instead of continuing up to the highest point (the upper right corner) of this snowfield, head for the lowest point of rock jutting down into the snowfield left of center. The initial rock lead (130 feet) is up an obvious crack to its end where a traverse right under an upside-down flake permits a move up to a small ledge. The next ropelength follows a line up and right, to and over a small bulge onto a grassy ledge for the belay. The third short lead (60 feet) goes up the rightmost groove above to a large

grassy ledge. Now scramble up and farther right to a large ledge with snow. The final lead goes up this section of snow and traverses left into an ice gully that is climbed onto the east ridge, apparently above the section of slabs. Follow the East Ridge route to the summit.

Variation: III, WI3+/4, 5.8. First ascent September 24, 1983, by Norm Larson and Steve Quinlan. See *Photo 76*. This difficult variation reaches the East Prong Col directly from the north. After climbing the first portion of the rock band above the first snowfield, move left to gain the leftmost narrow couloir leading up to the small snowfield below the East Prong Col. Two pitches of near-vertical ice climbing are climbed onto the snowfield, which is then taken to the col. It is possible that this section of ice forms only very late in the season.

Variation: III, 5.9. First ascent September 1977, by George Montopoli. See *Photo 76*. While the above variation follows primarily the ice line, this one links the various upper snowfields via the rock bands. After climbing up the narrow couloir mentioned earlier to a point just above the level of the base of Crescent Arête, traverse out and right to a cliff band. This is climbed via a corner system that was 5.6 in difficulty and nearly a ropelength in height. Traverse up and left across snow to a second small cliff band that was easy 5th class and that permits access to the snowfield directly below the East Prong Col. The third cliff band has a large overhang near its eastern end. This variation ascends a left-facing corner for two or three pitches (5.9) to the west of the overhang. The East Ridge route was then followed to the summit.

ROUTE 10. Crescent Arête. III, 5.7. First ascent September 9, 1959, by Fred Beckey and Yvon Chouinard. See *Photo 76*. Between the northeast snowfields and the true north ridge of Mount Owen is a prominent, well-defined subsidiary ridge. It is separated from the main north ridge to the west by a sharp steep couloir (Run-Don't-Walk Couloir). The upper end of this ridge curves west and joins the north ridge at the northeastern base of the Great Yellow Tower. The appropriate name of this ridge is derived from the combined appearance of this ridge and its lower extension, which also curves back to the west. The approach for this ridge is the same as that for the North Ridge route (*Route 12*). The route begins at the bottom end of Run-Don't-Walk Couloir. Several pitches of good rock are then climbed on or near the sometimes difficult crest until the north ridge is reached below the Great Yellow Tower. Then follow *Route 12* to the summit. There are apparently several ways to climb this arête since the difficulty reported by different parties has varied from 5.6 to aid; many climbers have encountered 5.8 pitches. Several recent parties have not continued from the top of the arête to the summit of Mount Owen and have descended to the east, down the lower northeast snowfields back to Cascade Canyon. *Time: 8 hours* from Jenny Lake. See *American Alpine Journal*, 12, no. 1 (1960), pp. 125–127.

ROUTE 11. Run-Don't-Walk Couloir. IV, 5.9, A3, WI4 (first ascent); IV, WI4, 5.4 (normal conditions with Koven finish). First ascent July 6, 1972, by Stephen Arsenault and John Bouchard. See *Photo 76.* This very steep, narrow ice couloir lies to the left (east) of the rather broad north ridge of Mount Owen, and is bounded on the left by the Crescent Arête *(Route 10).* The couloir provides three pitches of difficult ice climbing, but overall it is not a very safe route. Prospective climbers are warned that because of avalanche, icefall, and rockfall hazards they must be able to move rapidly on vertical ice. Conditions in the couloir can often be checked by spotting scope from the valley in the vicinity of the Cathedral Group turnout.

For the approach take the Cascade Canyon trail, cross the creek (logs can usually be found), and hike up into the Teewinot–Owen cirque where good camping spots can be found near its lower edge. Climb easily up the right side of the large snowfield below the main northeast face of Mount Owen until it is possible to traverse and climb up and right (west) to the base of Crescent Arête. Traverse farther west into the Run-Don't-Walk Couloir and climb a few hundred feet of steep snow to the base of the first ice bulge. The next three leads of difficult ice climbing with vertical sections on each pitch constitute the crux of the route. If the ice is not continuous, a very difficult rock pitch requiring aid will be encountered here. Continue up the couloir on moderate-angle snow for a few hundred feet, about six pitches, until the top of the arête is reached. From here there are four options: (1) traverse the northeast snowfields over to the East Ridge *(Route 8)* and follow that route to the summit; (2) climb the Northeast Snowfields *(Route 9)* to the summit; (3) join the North Ridge *(Route 12),* but this adds considerable climbing, including the Great Yellow Tower, before the summit is reached; or (4) downclimb the Northeast Snowfields *(Route 9)* as an escape route. A very early start is suggested for this route. Careful selection of conditions in the couloir is highly recommended in order to minimize the objective hazards. The best time to find good ice conditions seems to be in the late spring or very early summer when cold temperatures permit the ice sections to form but after the spring avalanche cycle.

ROUTE 12. North Ridge. IV, 5.9. First ascent July 31, 1951, by Richard Emerson and William Clayton. See *Photo 76.* The North Ridge, one of the finest routes on this major Teton peak, is a very long route and climbers must get an early start and move rapidly or expect to be benighted. The major feature on the route is a conspicuous 500-foot right-facing corner just left (east) of the crest of the ridge and just below the main tower on the ridge, the Great Yellow Tower (12,400+). This steep, right-facing corner is the key to the route. The several cliff bands that guard the access to this ramp are climbed on the left (east) side of the crest of the north ridge. From a point directly below the north face of Mount Owen (at about 7,600 feet) cross Cascade Creek,

either on a convenient log or by wading (dangerous when water in the creek is high), and bushwhack up the long slope to the base of the ridge. From here take the bench left (east) and up to the beginning of the serious portion of the Run-Don't-Walk Couloir. The initial problem is to get into the beginning of the upper corner system. A large ramp that is directly below a band of light-colored rock will be seen slanting up from the couloir to the right. Climb up to this ramp (or access it directly from the couloir) and proceed out to the end of it just slightly west of the bottom of the corner system above. Climb a short 5.6 section to a ledge. Follow the ledge back left (east) for 75 feet to a vertical wall with a crack and two fixed pitons. Climb up 20 feet (5.8), after which a pitch of easy 5th class leads to the bottom of the main corner. Once in the chimney, several pitches of enjoyable climbing (4th and easy 5th) lead to the small notch on the ridge at its head. Now climb easy ledges around on the west side until the crest is regained just short of the Great Yellow Tower.

There are two ways of attacking this formidable tower, which very effectively blocks further passage along the ridge: (1) See *Photo 72.* Traverse around and under the tower on the right (west) side on a sloping ramp beginning on easy ledges with great exposure. Continue along this ramp heading toward the notch separating the tower from the remainder of the ridge. An overhang 50 feet short of this notch can be passed by a very difficult lead to the right and then back left across its top up to the ridge crest on the tower side of the notch. Climb back down to the notch along the east side. Note that the notch cannot be reached directly from the west. (2) On the northwest corner of the tower is a very steep, narrow, and sometimes icy chimney or dihedral that extends upward for 150 to 200 feet. Climb the crack system in this 5.7 dihedral directly, exiting on the north face of the tower about 40 feet below the summit, where ledges will be found leading around the north and upper east wall of the tower to the sloping slabs that lead to the notch separating the tower from the ridge. The second is the recommended alternative.

The remainder of the ridge will usually involve a mixture of snow and rock climbing. Climb two ropelengths up toward the summit of Mount Owen on the left (east) flank of the ridge to a 100-foot chimney. From the chockstone at its top, continue for two more ropelengths and rejoin the ridge crest. Climb onto the summit of the final tower of the ridge, which is the apex of Serendipity Arête *(Route 16).* After descending about 50 feet to the col, one is confronted with a large, deep chimney. The initial moves in this chimney are probably the most difficult of the route (5.7, A0 or 5.9). From the top of the chimney one can then either climb several pitches directly up the ridge above and reach the summit from the northwest, or else traverse right (west) out onto the west face, and reach the summit via the large west Koven Chimney that splits the summit block. This is a climb of major proportions, containing a larger number of roped pitches than is usually the case for Teton climbing. *Time: 15½ hours* from Jenny Lake. See *American Alpine Journal,* 9, no. 2 (1955), pp. 147–149.

Variation: Crescent Arête Direct. IV, 510+R, A1. First ascent June 1994, by Greg Collins and Stephen Koch. This two-pitch climb is listed as a variation on *Route 12* simply because it provides an unusual means of accessing that route, that is, by climbing Crescent Arête initially and then continuing directly up the Great Yellow Tower. From the top of Crescent Arête, walk directly up to the base of a thin, black, left-facing corner on the northeast side of the Tower and belay on a grassy ledge. Climb the first portion of the corner (5.7) and then pass a block on the right (5.9). Continue up and over a bulge (5.10, A1) and belay in an alcove (anchor protection difficult). The second ropelength goes directly up the remainder of the dihedral (5.10+R) to a belay ledge. It is then 3.0 climbing to the top of the Great Yellow Tower. Follow *Route 12* to the summit. For protection take a regular rock rack with extra thin gear. Pitons may be useful for the first belay and the crux.

ROUTE 13. North Face. III, 5.6. First ascent August 21, 1945, by Hans Kraus and Harrison Snyder. See *Photo 77.* This triangular face lies between the North Ridge (*Route 12*) and the Northwest Ridge (*Route 14);* it starts from the 10,000-foot level and extends some 2,400 feet to its apex on the north ridge at the Great Yellow Tower. All three routes join here and follow the north ridge to the summit. The broad north face contains considerable rock that has been seldom explored and hence is not well known. The base of the face, which slants up from lower left to upper right, meets the upper end of the long talus slope east of the mouth of Valhalla Canyon.

For the approach to this route, take the Cascade Canyon trail and cross Cascade Creek at about the 7,600-foot level. Climb the talus, bearing right (west) of the north ridge until under the middle of the north face. Near the middle of the north face a large, gray, slabby triangular projection will be seen. The right side of this projection is a steep ramp clearly defined by a 200-foot large crack system or small couloir. The climbing begins in this crack-couloir; half scramble, half climb this couloir a total of about 400 feet until it is possible to move out left to the top of the triangular projection. At this point the scree bench that cuts across the upper face is still 800 feet above and it appears that there is more than one way to proceed. Two or three different possible routes can be seen.

The first-ascent route apparently went almost straight up for about 300 feet, then angled up and right in a succession of cracks for another 300 feet. They continued easy climbing up and slightly right for a few hundred feet to the upper scree bench. From the top of the triangular projection another party utilized the major crack system that can be seen angling up and right (west) across the face to a band

of black rock at the top of this first section of the north face. The major obstacles are two short, slightly overhanging jam cracks, separated by about 100 feet and also visible from the top of the projection. Climb a series of pitches angling up and right, past these jam cracks, and gain the scree bench.

This scree and talus bench is bounded on the right (south) by a small secondary ridge leading up to and joining the northwest ridge just below its final step to the base of the Great Yellow Tower. Scramble to the upper right corner of the bench and climb a shallow gully to the point where this ridge and the northwest ridge meet. Several pitches of easy climbing then take one to the sloping ramp at the west base of the Great Yellow Tower, which is climbed as in *Route 12.* For the route from here to the summit, also see *Route 12.* As with the other north-side routes of Mount Owen, this is a very long climb if pursued to the summit; the first-ascent party did not continue beyond the Great Yellow Tower. See *Appalachia,* 26, no. 1 (June 1946), pp. 105–108.

Variation: III, 5.8. First ascent July 16, 1989, by Randy Harrington and Leo Larson. See *Photo 77.* To the right (west) of the initial crack-couloir of the 1945 route is a steep wall bounded on the right by a steep indentation or near-vertical couloir. This five-pitch variation starts midway between these boundaries. The first lead is the most difficult, up a crack to and past a small roof (5.8) with an additional crack above leading to the belay. A pitch of scrambling up and left ends at the base of a second vertical crack in the wall above. The third and fourth leads go directly up this crack, past another small overhang (5.7). A final pitch of easier rock (4.0) moves up and left to join the original route in the diagonal scrambling up and right toward the northwest ridge.

ROUTE 14. Northwest Ridge. III, 5.7. First ascent August 5, 1941, by Jack Durrance, Henry Coulter, and Merrill McLane. See *Photos 72, 73,* and *77.* This stepped ridge leads from Valhalla Canyon east to the prominent Great Yellow Tower on the north ridge of Mount Owen. It forms the left (northern) boundary of the large but very steep couloir leading to the notch in the north ridge that separates the Great Yellow Tower from the remainder of the north ridge above; this couloir is at the north edge of the main west face of Mount Owen. Some upper sections of this ridge are rather broad and ill defined. The northeastern boundary of Valhalla Canyon, however, is a well-defined ridge starting from the final trees above Cascade Canyon and extending directly to the first tower or buttress of this northwest ridge. See *Valhalla Canyon* for the approach into the canyon.

From the floor of the canyon ascend several hundred feet of scree and talus to the base of the first tower on the ridge. The climb begins very near a small, fingerlike pinnacle that can be seen in profile from the Cascade Canyon trail. Scramble as high as possible and climb at least two pitches around the left side of the tower on ledges to reach the notch behind this tower. Bypass the initial blank wall of the second tower on the right to gain a crack-chimney leading in three pitches to the top of the second tower or buttress, which is the beginning of a major talus bench. Above this bench the rock is divided into two sections, one over to the left (apparently the third tower of the first-ascent party) and another on the right, more or less directly above. Four pitches suffice to climb this right section, containing two bands of black rock, first around to the right, then up the steep black rock wall of this section, and finally a long traverse back to the left toward a small saddle at the top of the third tower. From the saddle pass through a vertical window and traverse right to the beginning of a 120-foot difficult crack (5.7), one of the landmarks of this route. The remainder of the climbing to the base of the Great Yellow Tower is little more than scrambling. See *Route 12* for the passage of the Great Yellow Tower and the balance of the upper north ridge to the summit. *Time: 13¾ hours* from Valhalla Canyon. See *American Alpine Journal,* 5, no. 1 (1943), pp. 71–75. illus.

ROUTE 15. Northwest Face. III, 5.6. First ascent August 4, 1965, by Leigh Ortenburger and Herb Swedlund. See *Photos 72* and 73. This terraced face rises from the lower Valhalla Canyon to the last large tower on the north ridge of Mount Owen, the apex of Serendipity Arête. It is bounded on the right (south) by Serendipity Arête and on the left by the northwest couloir, the deep and near-vertical chute that defines the northwest ridge and separates the Great Yellow Tower from the remainder of the north ridge above. This is a broad face that supports more than a single route or line, as evidenced by the distinct variations taken by the first three parties on the face. The main steep portion of this face, which contains the primary climbing interest, lies above the upper of two huge horizontal talus and scree benches that extend across the entire western aspect of Mount Owen; two more scree ledge systems, smaller but prominent, are found in this upper portion.

From lower Valhalla Canyon take the obvious couloir (snow-filled in early season) through the initial broken cliff band. Head toward the black, water-streaked cliff band above, which may contain a small waterfall. If desired, suitable bivouac sites can be found here. Reach the second huge scree bench by scrambling to the left (north), between the waterfall and the northwest couloir itself. Continue scrambling for a few hundred feet in a zigzag, perhaps partially on snow, up and left to easy (5.1 to 5.6) rock that will lead onto the next large horizontal scree ledge (covered with snow in early or midseason) near its left (north) end.

The wall directly above this ledge is steep and cut by only a few cracks. Traverse right (south) along the ledge about 100 feet past an obvious jam crack until one can turn up the wall in a crack system for 75 feet and then cut back left (5.6 to 5.8) to easier rock. A second pitch, of similar difficulty, brings one to the large ledge just below the final huge open book of the upper face. An immense flake with

a chimney behind it will be seen above. Traverse right along this ledge to an area of black rock well to the right of the massive yellow rock containing the flake. There are several alternatives for climbing this section, depending on how far right one traverses. A chimney can be found leading upward, with strenuous 5.6 at the top. Continue for another 200 feet on the left (north) side of Serendipity Arête (see *Route 16*), finally joining that route near its last towers.

Variation: III, 5.8. First ascent August 20–21, 1982, by Rick Reese and David Susong. This variation used a different line up from the large horizontal scree ledge mentioned earlier. From this ledge one pitch leads up and right, then back left to the base of a steep, narrow, difficult ramp. After 40 feet this ramp turns into a chimney and finally a mere crack. Just below the crack stretch left across a face on small holds (5.8) and then up to a belay ledge. Easier rock then leads to a bivouac ledge from which a traverse right for some 250 feet provides access to an easy chimney. Climb this chimney and then 200 feet more to a rib from which Serendipity Arête is easily reached at the base of its third tower.

Variation: III, 5.9. First ascent August 9, 1985, by Paul Gagner and Renny Jackson. See *Photos 72* and 73. This variation attacked the final wall adjacent to (south of) the immense flake in a more direct and difficult manner. Traverse along the ledge only a short distance to the black-rock area, and then turn up a small dihedral (5.9). Two more leads (5.8 and 5.7) continue on the face itself, before finally joining Serendipity Arête only one pitch short of its top.

ROUTE 16. Serendipity Arête. IV, 5.6, A1, or IV, 5.7. First ascent August 8, 1959, by William Buckingham, Frederick Medrick, Sterling Neale, and Frank Magary; first free ascent July 14, 1965, by Henry Mitchell and George Griffin. See *Topo 67* and *Photo 73.* This is a very agreeable climb containing many fine sections with some enjoyable and unusual formations such as the knife-edge. The approach is via Cascade Canyon and Valhalla Canyon. The structure of the west side of Mount Owen as viewed from Valhalla Canyon is complex but must be understood to find this route. The west face is bounded on the south by the West Gunsight Couloir and on the north by the large couloir that separates the northwest ridge and the Great Yellow Tower from the principal mountain mass. Between these bounds and rising above the floor of Valhalla Canyon is a broad talus and scree slope that leads to the first cliff band. This initial cliff band attains maximum height at its northern extremity (north of the northwest ridge), forming the north face of Mount Owen. On the south this band narrows and ends at the West Gunsight Couloir. The major talus and scree bench above this cliff band lies about one-third the way up the west face from the bottom and can be reached easily from the vicinity of the Gunsight Couloir. It extends all the way across the face.

Serendipity Arête rises abruptly from this scree bench, just to the left (north) of a shallow drainage (both water and

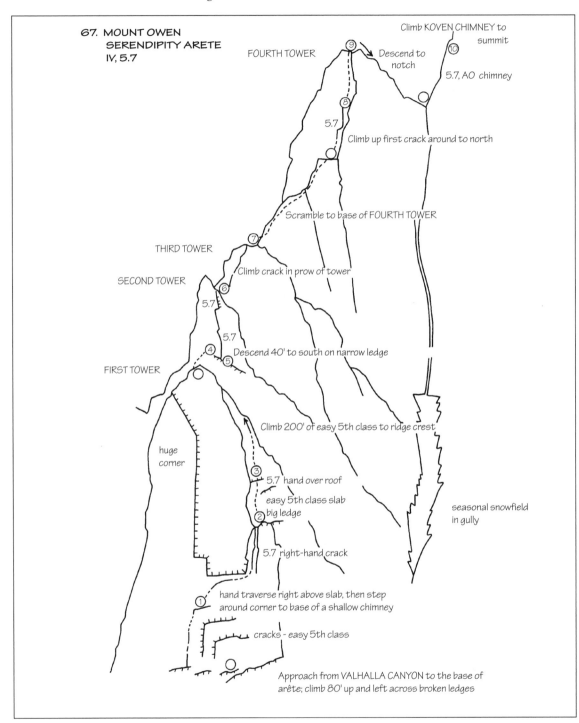

67. MOUNT OWEN
SERENDIPITY ARETE
IV, 5.7

Climb KOVEN CHIMNEY to summit

FOURTH TOWER

Descend to notch

5.7, AO chimney

5.7

Climb up first crack around to north

Scramble to base of FOURTH TOWER

THIRD TOWER

Climb crack in prow of tower

SECOND TOWER

5.7

5.7

Descend 40' to south on narrow ledge

FIRST TOWER

Climb 200' of easy 5th class to ridge crest

huge corner

5.7 hand over roof

easy 5th class slab

big ledge

seasonal snowfield in gully

5.7 right-hand crack

hand traverse right above slab, then step around corner to base of a shallow chimney

cracks - easy 5th class

Approach from VALHALLA CANYON to the base of arête; climb 80' up and left across broken ledges rock) gully, and leads diagonally upward to culminate at the last tower on the north ridge of Mount Owen. The arête can be identified by the huge, orange, left-facing dihedral on the left side of its initial steep section, the lowest of its four towers. This conspicuous dihedral has a square-cut ceiling on its lower left corner and the bottom of it is actually a great ceiling as well. While the bulk of the arête is recognizable, the beginnings are unfortunately somewhat indistinct.

Approach from the floor of Valhalla Canyon via scree and talus slopes, ledges, and gullies onto the major talus bench described above, starting with either the lowest portion of the West Gunsight Couloir or the next small gully to the north. Easy climbing and scrambling lead to the base of the first tower. Traverse slightly down and left for about 80 feet onto the west face of the tower before leading directly upward on steep rock for a long ropelength, bypassing a long, narrow, black overhang on the left. Now climb diagonally up to the right on steep slabs and across the crest to the right, using a hand traverse on the top of the slab to a belay point. The next pitch begins a few feet to the right and ascends an open-book chimney for 25 feet. Make an awkward step to the left and climb (originally with aid) a perfect crack to pass a difficult section of the chimney. A step to the right puts one back into the chimney, which is climbed past a small overhang to a belay point. The next lead, directly up the south side of the tower, brings one to the top of the tower, whence two pitches along the relatively level crest lead to the base of the second tower of the ridge; the first of these is one of the most spectacular knife-edges in the park. The final thin flake, which is passed à cheval, slightly overhangs 1,000 feet of space.

From the base of this second tower, descend diagonally to the right for 40 feet on a narrow ledge and belay at the base of a crack. Climb the crack (which at its end becomes a left-facing corner, 5.7) to reach the notch behind the second tower. To attain the summit of this tower climb the east side of a steep slab, where a cairn should be found. The third tower, about 80 feet high, is easily climbed directly up from the notch or by a zig out to the left and a zag back to the right. A couple of hundred feet of scrambling then leads to the base of the fourth and final tower on the ridge, whose crest here has a fearsome appearance. Proceed around to the left (north) and climb up the first crack system for 160 feet over loose flakes and blocks changing to more difficult (5.7) solid rock near the top. One more easy pitch brings one to the summit of the fourth and final tower on the route. Descend to the col and climb up to the base of the large chimney of the North Ridge. The most difficult moves of the climb (5.7, A0 or 5.9) are located a short distance up this chimney. From the top of this chimney climb up to the Koven Chimney, which leads, finally, to the summit. This long and enjoyable climb is consistently interesting and nowhere excessively difficult. For descent back into Valhalla Canyon, the recommended

route is the West Ledges (*Route 1*). *Time: 12 hours* from Valhalla Canyon. See *American Alpine Journal*, 12, no. 1 (1960), pp. 125–27; *Dartmouth Mountaineering Club Journal*, 1960, pp. 79–89, illus.

ROUTE 17. Intrepidity Arête. III, 5.10-. First ascent August 18, 1990, by Tom Turiano and Matthew Goewert. See *Topo 68* and *Photos 73* and *74*. According to the first-ascent party, as the leader proceeded up the crux pitch of the climb, a wild electric hail/rain storm blew in. The intrepid climber fought his way up the pitch and then belayed his second man from the summit of the "Electrode," with hair standing straight out and gear buzzing with electricity! Immediately to the right (south) of Serendipity Arête and slightly higher is an immense rock wall that culminates in the summit of Mount Owen. This route ascends the southern edge of this wall and, like its northern neighbor, passes four towers along the way. Use the same approach as outlined for Serendipity Arête (*Route 16*). From the base of that route cross the gully that descends from the notch behind the Great Yellow Tower of the North Ridge and climb up and to the south for approximately 400 to 500 vertical feet to the start of the climb. The first pitch begins on top of a huge block at the base of the arête and wanders back and forth across the crest. For specific route details refer to the topo. The "Electrode," or first tower, is four pitches up. Use the West Ledges (*Route 1*) for descent. The rock on this route is reported to be of exceptional quality and the climb was done in a 14½-hour round trip from Jenny Lake.

Variation: Mas Intrepido. III, 5.10-. First ascent August 1994, by Matthew Goewert and Mark Limage. See *Topo 68* and *Photo 73*. This is a three-pitch variation to *Route 17* and provides an alternate means of reaching the Electrode, also mentioned in *Route 17*. The first pitch begins 30 feet to the left (north) of the start of Intrepidity Arête and ascends a 130-foot, left-facing corner (5.10-). The first ascensionists noted that this particular pitch rates as "one of the ten best in the range." From a hanging belay, face climb up and left to a fist crack (5.9) that ends on a belay ledge. The third ropelength is a dirty, left-facing corner (5.8) that ends atop the Electrode. Continue on up *Route 17* to the summit.

RABBIT EARS (10,880+)
(0.7 mi WNW of Mount Owen)

Map: Grand Teton

These well-named twin pinnacles are on the northwest ridge of the Grand Teton, which forms the west boundary of Valhalla Canyon; they are almost due west of Mount Owen. Of the various peaks and towers on this ridge, these are the smallest, most difficult, and most distinctive. They are easily seen from the northern approach road to String Lake and from many other places in the valley.

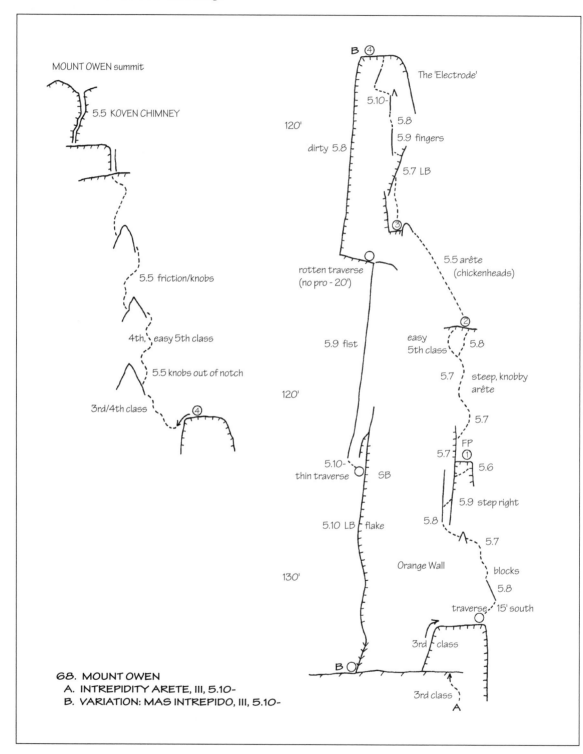

MOUNT OWEN summit

5.5 KOVEN CHIMNEY

5.5 friction/knobs

4th, easy 5th class

5.5 knobs out of notch

3rd/4th class   ④

B ④

The 'Electrode'

5.10-

5.8

120'   5.9 fingers

dirty 5.8

5.7 LB

③

5.5 arête
(chickenheads)

rotten traverse
(no pro - 20')

②

easy
5th class   5.8

5.9 fist   5.7   steep, knobby
arête

120'   5.7

FP
5.7 ①

5.10-   5.6
thin traverse   SB

5.9 step right

5.10 LB flake   5.8

5.7

Orange Wall   blocks
130'   5.8

traverse 15' south

3rd class

B

3rd class

A

68. MOUNT OWEN
   A. INTREPIDITY ARETE, III, 5.10-
   B. VARIATION: MAS INTREPIDO, III, 5.10-

North Ear (10,880+)

ROUTE 1. North Ridge. II, 5.4, A2, or II, 5.7. First ascent July 17, 1957, by Fred Ayres and Leigh and Irene Ortenburger; first free ascent July 31, 1968, by David Ingalls and Roy Kligfield. This remarkable pinnacle overhangs on all four sides. Approach from Valhalla Canyon through the col north of the North Ear. On the west side, a prominent downsloping shelf leading left to the north ridge is negotiated using aid. From the platform at its end, surmount the bulging overhang above to the sharp summit crest. A rappel is required for descent of the west face. See *American Alpine Journal*, 11, no. 1 (1958), pp. 85–88.

South Ear (10,880+)

ROUTE 1. South Ridge. II, 4.0. First ascent August 8–10, 1938, by Jack Durrance and Michael Davis. The easiest approach is by the same col north of the North Rabbit Ear reached from Valhalla Canyon. Bypassing the North Ear on the west leads to the west side of the South Ear. The last few feet to the summit are climbed via the south ridge. See *Dartmouth Mountaineering Club Journal*, 1938, pp. 29–36.

PEAK 10,640+   *(0.8 mi WNW of Mount Owen)*

Map: Mount Moran

ROUTE 1. North Ridge. II, 5.1. First ascent August 8, 1938, by Jack Durrance and Michael Davis. The col between this peak and the next peak to the north, Peak 10,405, can be reached via the couloir directly from the west after crossing the south fork of Cascade Creek or after descending from Peak 10,405 to the north. From the col the north ridge is climbed directly.

ROUTE 2. South Ridge. II, 3.0. First descent August 8, 1938, by Jack Durrance and Michael Davis. This ridge is easily descended during an ascent of the complete northwest ridge of the Enclosure.

PEAK 10,405   *(0.7 mi NW of Mount Owen)*

Map: Mount Moran

This easy peak, which rises on the southeast above the forks of Cascade Canyon, constitutes the extremity of the northwest ridge of the Enclosure. It apparently has been visited only in the course of the three complete ascents of that long ridge; even then one party bypassed it.

ROUTE 1. Northwest Ridge. II, 5.1. First ascent August 8, 1938, by Jack Durrance and Michael Davis. Cross the south fork of Cascade Creek to approach this ridge, which is then easily followed on loose rock to the summit of the peak.

ROUTE 2. South Ridge. II, 5.1. First descent August 8, 1938, by Jack Durrance and Michael Davis. This ridge is used to descend into the col between this peak and Peak 10,640+, which is the next tower on the northwest ridge of the Enclosure. No problems, other than loose rock, will be encountered.

ART-AND-BRENT PINNACLE (CA. 9,600)
(0.6 mi NE of Teewinot Mountain)

Map: Mount Moran

This obscure pinnacle, lately discovered on the south side of Cascade Canyon, is very difficult to find or even see. It is located on a lower north ridge of Teewinot Mountain, opposite Guides' Wall on the southwest ridge of Storm Point. The pinnacle is at about the same elevation as the Flake Pitch on that route.

ROUTE 1. North Face. II, 5.10-, A1. First ascent September 20, 1984, by Renny Jackson and Tom Kimbrough. Cross Cascade Creek just below the small pond (Perch Pond) formed by the rockslide from the southwest couloir of Storm Point. Hike up about 1,000 feet of scree toward a large ramp angling steeply upward, from which the pinnacle rises. The climb begins with a few aid moves on the northeast side of the pinnacle. Then climb up and left into a 5.9 groove on the east side to a belay below a small roof. The second short pitch goes up and over the roof (5.10-) and then follows good cracks to the summit. Two ropes are needed to rappel off the north side.

MCCAIN'S PILLAR (10,400+)
(0.55 mi NE of Mount Owen)

Map: Mount Moran

Near the base of the northeastern aspect of Mount Owen, this 150-foot black pinnacle lies on the ridge that forms the lower extension of Crescent Arête (see *Mount Owen, Route 10*). Approach via the Teewinot–Owen cirque, gaining the ridge about 1,000 feet north of the pinnacle. The pinnacle could also be approached by the couloir west of it or (best) from the first northeast snowfield on Mount Owen, from which it is clearly visible.

ROUTE 1. East Face and South Face. II, 5.7, A3. First ascent September 3, 1969, by Rick Reese and John Whitesel. Scramble to the vicinity of the base of the east face. Climb a series of furrows and cracks on the east face to a slanting shelf just below the final 70-foot vertical south face. Climb 20 feet up this wall to a small ledge where a protection bolt will be found. After another 10 feet, use aid on tied-off knifeblade pitons in a 25-foot crack to another small ledge. An overhanging face then leads free to the summit. The first-ascent party looped a sling carefully around the summit as a rappel anchor.

FAULTLINE (10,640+)   *(0.95 mi W of Middle Teton)*

Map: Grand Teton

Immediately west of and below Icefloe Lake in the upper south fork of Cascade Canyon is a prominent buttress with a sheer west wall. The wall is diamond-shaped and split by a huge vertical dihedral near its center. The base of the buttress is easily reached from the canyon via scree slopes.

ROUTE 1. West Face. II, 5.9. First ascent July 31, 1978, by Tom and Barry Rugo. Climb the lower third of the face via broken and somewhat loose rock (5.7), angling up and right to the large platform ledge to the left (north) of the huge dihedral. On the extreme right end of this ledge is a large left-facing corner that is part of the main dihedral; on the extreme left end a jam crack heads up and through an overhang. This route, however, climbs a 20-foot face to the start of another jam crack that lies in the middle between these extremes. Ascend this well-protected crack, which contains three strenuous 5.9 moves, for an entire ropelength to a good belay hole. Although the crack continues to the top of the buttress, the second lead (5.6) angles up and right to the dihedral, which is followed for 100 feet to the top. Descent can be easily made to the north. Take a good selection of nuts.

THE WALL (11,108)

Map: Grand Teton

Viewed from the east from one of the high central peaks of the range, the Wall appears as a sheer, 500-foot wall of sedimentary rock on the divide at the head of the north fork of Avalanche Canyon above Snowdrift Lake. The west side of the peak slopes off gently toward Sunset Lake, Alaska Basin, and the Teton Crest Trail. The original "Skyline Trail," constructed in the 1930s south from the Cascade–Avalanche divide, was built along the shelf at the base of the east cliffs and emerged onto the west side of the divide through the saddle (10,640+) separating the Wall from the northwest ridge of Veiled Peak. This trail was abandoned in 1950 when the magnitude of rockfall and rockslides from the cliffs immediately above became evident; the section of this trail leading to the Cascade–Avalanche divide is still intact. The cliff band can be seen to contain several indentations or caves, one of which extends for several hundred feet back into the Death Canyon Limestone. While not significant as a technical mountaineering objective, this minor sedimentary summit has the distinction of (probably) being the first Teton peak to be climbed. On an exploratory scouting trip prior to their ascent of, or attempt on, the Grand Teton on July 29, 1872, Nathaniel P. Langford and James Stevenson did reach the top of a peak on the divide, almost surely this one. It does provide an excellent vantage point for the three Tetons and is a recommended side trip for hikers of the Teton Crest Trail. Although it is not indicated on the map, there recently has been reported another bench mark (BM 10,953) located on top of the Wall, about 0.5 mile south of the highest point; this was probably placed by the Murphy topographic party in 1934 or 1935.

ROUTE 1. West Side. I, 1.0. Probable first ascent July 24, 1872, by Nathaniel P. Langford and James Stevenson; this peak was also presumably climbed by the Bannon topographic party in 1898, as their map indicates a bench mark on the summit. Although this peak is well guarded on the east by sedimentary cliffs, the ascent from the west from the trail in Alaska Basin is easy. The approach to all of these peaks along the divide is ordinarily made via the Teton Crest Trail, starting either at Jenny Lake and entering Cascade Canyon or starting at Death Canyon trailhead and entering Death Canyon.

PEAK 10,635   *(0.9 mi S of Table Mountain)*

Map: Grand Teton

This sedimentary ridge forms the divide on the west side of the south fork of Cascade Canyon. Rising only 300 feet above and immediately north of Hurricane Pass (10,320+) where the Teton Crest Trail crosses from Cascade Canyon to Alaska Basin, it is easily reached. This peak may have been the objective reached on July 28, 1872, by Robert Adams, Jr., and William R. Taggart, although another point on the divide, 10,800+, which is 0.6 mile southwest of the pass, is more likely the high point they climbed.

ROUTE 1. South Ridge. I, 1.0. First known descent late July 1958, by Howard R. Stagner, Jr., and Richard Byrd; first known ascent August 20, 1960, by Arthur J. Reyman. No difficulties will be encountered on this easy ridge.

ROUTE 2. North Ridge. I, 1.0. First known ascent late July 1958, by Howard R. Stagner, Jr., and Richard Byrd. This party found a hollow, circular 2-foot cairn on the summit.

TABLE MOUNTAIN (11,106)

Map: Grand Teton

This flat-topped summit is capped by only a thin layer of sedimentary rock; the excellent Precambrian rock is exposed down the 1,400-foot east face in the south fork of Cascade Canyon. One of the first peaks in the range to be ascended, Table Mountain has become famous as the viewpoint from which William H. Jackson, the pioneer photographer with the Hayden Surveys, obtained the first photographs of the Grand Teton in late July 1872. The peak is most easily reached from Teton Canyon to the west, where a popular USFS trail leads up the north fork of the canyon onto and up the long, gentle west ridge. The structure of the impressive east face needs description. It is divided into three main sections or buttresses. The southern section is the most prominent buttress looming over the Cascade Canyon trail. A large chimney or chute separates this buttress from the central section, which is somewhat inset and not clearly seen from some angles. From this main chimney a second couloir branches off to the right and separates the central and northern buttresses.

CHRONOLOGY

West Slope: ca. July 27, 1872, William H. Jackson, Charles Campbell, Philo J. Beveridge, Alexander Sibley, and perhaps John M. Coulter

South Ridge: July 23, 1934, Fritiof Fryxell, Reynold Holmen, Harry Thayer, Eugene Beattie

East Face, East Ledges: September 6, 1959, Steven Jervis, Robert Page

East Face, Central Buttress: September 7, 1959, Fred Beckey, Yvon Chouinard, Kenneth Weeks

East Face, South Buttress: June 15, 1961, M. E. Horn, Leon Sinclair

North Ridge: August 3, 1967, Leigh Ortenburger, John Lemon

Southeast Couloir: July 4, 1980, Jack Tackle, George Barnett

East Face, North Buttress: July 5, 1980, Jack Tackle, George Barnett

Heartbreak Ridge: July 28, 1995, Paul Horton, Jon Stuart

ROUTE 1. ☞*West Slope.* I, 1.0. First ascent about July 27, 1872, by William H. Jackson, Charles Campbell, Philo J. Beveridge, Alexander Sibley, and perhaps John M. Coulter; also in 1898 T. M. Bannon and party placed a bench mark on the summit, probably by some variation of this route. From the campground parking area at the (east) end of the road in Teton Canyon, a good trail leads northeast into the north fork of the canyon, ultimately turning south to gain the west end (9,900 feet) of the summit plateau, which is followed easily to the summit block. Since the time of Jackson, when pack animals were required to carry his heavy and bulky wet-plate photographic equipment to the summit plateau, horses have been used on this trail to the base of the summit block.

ROUTE 2. South Ridge. I, 2.0. First recorded ascent July 23, 1934, by Fritiof Fryxell, Reynold Holmen, Harry Thayer, and Eugene Beattie. This route is approached from Jenny Lake via the Cascade Canyon trail into the south fork of the canyon. Leave the trail at 9,000 feet, turning west up the open slope and drainage just past (south of) the southernmost east buttress. This drainage is easily followed to the saddle (10,120) south of Table Mountain. The broad ridge above is then easily followed to the summit plateau and final summit block. *Time: 5½ hours from Jenny Lake.*

ROUTE 3. Southeast Couloir. II, 5.8. First ascent July 4, 1980, by Jack Tackle and George Barnett. This large and distinct couloir, containing some snow in early season, lies on the left (west) side of the southernmost east buttress. Gain the base of the couloir (ca. 10,000) from the southeast, using the south fork of the Cascade Canyon trail for the approach. Six hundred feet of straightforward but sustained climbing is involved. The first and third leads require passing large chockstones on the right (east). The move past the second chockstone was the crux of the route because it was slippery from running water. Beyond the fourth pitch, snow was followed for 100 feet before moving right onto easier rock, which was followed up to a dropoff. From this point traverse left (west) for several hundred feet to gain the summit plateau.

ROUTE 4. Heartbreak Ridge. III, 5.7. First ascent July 28, 1995, by Paul Horton and Jon Stuart. See *Topo 69* and *Photo 78.* From the trail in the south fork of Cascade Canyon, below the impressive east face of Table Mountain, this route is visible as the left-hand skyline. This rib forms the left-hand (south) border of the southernmost buttress of the east face. It is distinguished by a veneer of golden rock along the crest of the lower ridge. For those seeking moderate routes containing excellent rock, both this ridge and *Route 5* are highly recommended. Start at the toe of the rib on golden rock by climbing 150 feet up a slab (5.6). Then ascend a ramp and corner on the left side of the crest or a 5.8 crack on the ridge crest itself. The third pitch initially goes up 5.7 cracks and then turns to 4th class up the crest. Another 4th-class section up the stepped crest leads to a 5.6 corner just to the right of the crest and a belay. Continue up the corner (5.6) and then more 4th-class leads, after another pitch, to a belay on a big ledge at the base of the steep section of the ridge. For the seventh pitch, ascend a crack and then traverse left across a black face to a belay on the prow immediately below a "nose." The next pitch either climbs the left side of the nose (5.7) or the right (5.9) and then regains the crest (150 feet). Continue on up and climb a short face (5.6) that leads to easier ground. Third- and 4th-class slabs lead to the top of the climb. To descend walk to the west a considerable distance until reaching a point where easy access down into the drainage to the south is possible.

ROUTE 5. East Face, South Buttress. III, 5.8+. First ascent June 15, 1961, by M. E. Horn and Leon Sinclair; the first portion of this route had been climbed on September 8, 1960, by M. E. Horn and Kenneth Weeks. See *Topo 69* and *Photo 78.* This imposing southernmost buttress contains the steepest rock on Table Mountain. The approach is the same as for the other eastern routes, via the trail in the south fork of Cascade Canyon.

The route starts from the north end of a wide bench at the base of the face, where 150 feet of easy face climbing on broken rock leads to a belay near a tree and boulder. The second pitch is a left-facing corner (5.6) that takes one to a tree for the next belay stance. More face climbing provides access to a wide diagonal ledge. The fourth lead starts a few feet to the left up 5.6 face climbing to a squeeze chimney (5.7) and an offwidth (5.8+) that ends at a narrow ledge.

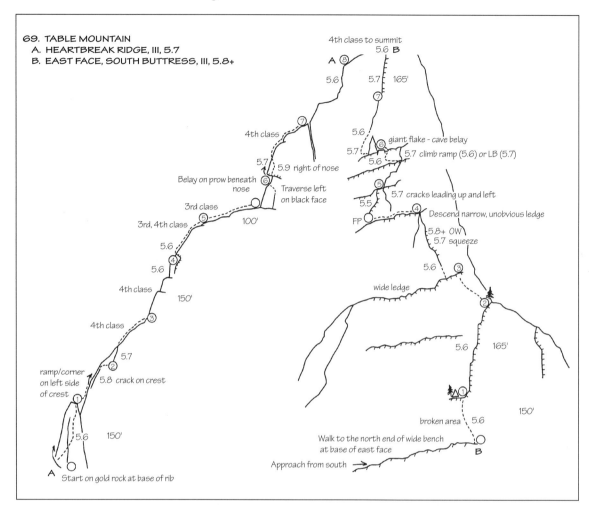

69. TABLE MOUNTAIN
  A. HEARTBREAK RIDGE, III, 5.7
  B. EAST FACE, SOUTH BUTTRESS, III, 5.8+

The fifth pitch begins with a traverse left and then continues up a face (5.6) to more difficult cracks leading up and left. The next lead continues in these cracks, which now angle back right to a wide, grassy ledge. Pass this ledge, using either a 5.6 ramp leading up and right or a 5.7 vertical lieback crack, to a ledge harboring a giant flake; move slightly left for a belay at a fixed piton behind the flake. From the far (south) side of the flake the seventh pitch descends slightly and goes up a face (5.7) and crack, angling slightly to the right. The final long lead (165 feet) starts up a 5.7 left-facing corner and ends by moving left up the face (5.6) on the left side of this corner. The summit is then reached by a scramble up and left. The upper part of the route has some spectacular exposure that is very enjoyable because the rock is good and the belay positions are secure. See *American Alpine Journal*, 13, no. 1 (1962), pp. 216–220.

ROUTE 6. East Face, Central Buttress. II, 5.6. First ascent September 7, 1959, by Fred Beckey, Yvon Chouinard, and Kenneth Weeks. Ascend the south fork of Cascade Canyon to the large chute that separates the south buttress from the central buttress. Climb this chute and begin the ascent of the second chute, which branches out to the right and separates the central from the north buttress. Traverse out on the first small sloping ledge leading left, onto the face of the central buttress. A prominent open book is encountered in the first pitch on the buttress. In general, the route from here stays in the middle of the face and consists of roped climbing all the way to the summit plateau. See *American Alpine Journal*, 12, no. 1 (1960), pp. 125–127.

ROUTE 7. East Face, East Ledges. II, 5.1. First ascent September 6, 1959, by Steven Jervis and Robert Page. This route ascends the left (south) edge of the north buttress. Walk up

2.0 miles in the south fork of Cascade Canyon, leaving the trail after one can clearly see that there are three buttresses; there appear to be only two until one is rather high up into the south fork. Angle up right to the first conspicuous tree-lined ledge at the base of the north buttress. Walk south along this ledge to within a few hundred feet of the large chute that separates the left (south) buttress from the central buttress. Follow up and right on more ledges to a broad sloping meadow. Ascend about 200 feet up the obvious chute separating the north and the central buttresses. At this point the chute steepens, so work up the right wall until a traverse to the left is possible. After about 50 more feet of climbing, simply follow the good rock on the right side of the chute all the way to the summit plateau. See *American Alpine Journal*, 12, no. 1 (1960), pp. 125–127.

ROUTE 8. East Face, North Buttress. II, 5.6. First ascent July 5, 1980, by Jack Tackle and George Barnett. Leave the trail in the south fork of Cascade Canyon when all three buttresses are clearly visible and angle up and right to the sloping meadow below the north buttress. Walk south along the tree-covered ledge to within about 200 feet of the large gully. Scramble up and right on diagonal ledges to some horizontal ledges with scattered trees. The route now ascends a prominent 5.6 corner to another ledge with a small clump of trees. The final section is 5.1 face climbing on good rock to the summit plateau.

ROUTE 9. North Ridge. II, 2.0. First ascent August 3, 1967, by Leigh Ortenburger and John Lemon. This ridge is encountered if one traverses along the main divide separating Teton Basin on the west from Jackson Hole on the east. From the east it is approached via Alpha-and-Omega Basin, just above the Cascade patrol cabin. One steep, shattered section of this ridge, between about 10,400 and 10,700 feet, must be negotiated. It is a dangerous undertaking and is not recommended. A snowfield lingers through most of the summer on the plateau just northeast of the summit and can provide sufficient water for an exposed bivouac on the plateau.

YOSEMITE PEAK (10,015)
(1.6 mi NE of Table Mountain)

Map: Mount Moran

This prominent point forms the northeast end of a long and nearly horizontal ridge extending out from the divide north of Table Mountain. It rises almost directly above the forks of Cascade Canyon. The steep but sloping east face, which resembles the granite rocks of Yosemite, suggested the name of this point. The diminutive north face is also impressive when viewed from the slopes above and north of the forks of the canyon. The highest point of the peak is not easy to find because the summit ridge is almost level. The rarely attained summit does provide a fine viewpoint of the west faces of Mount Owen and the Grand and Middle Tetons.

The peak is easily approached via the Cascade Canyon trail from Jenny Lake. For east face routes continue on the trail into the south fork of the canyon for 0.5 mile, leaving the trail at the north end of a small switchback where one can easily hike up the talus to the base of the face.

CHRONOLOGY

East Face, Weeks' Chimney: September 6, 1959, Fred Beckey, Kenneth Weeks
   var: August 19, 1974, Dave Anderson, Mark Jonas, Todd Chavez, Dale Tomrdle

East Face, Chouinard: September 4–5, 1961, Yvon Chouinard, Charles Ostin; first free ascent August 13, 1969, Steve Wunsch, Jim Erickson
   var: August 12, 1967, Jim Erickson, Sheldon Smith

North Face: August 4, 1963, Peter Koedt, Rich Kettler
   var: August 22, 1974, Rich Halgren, Jim Wheeler, Gene Francis

West Ledges: August 4, 1963, Peter Koedt, Rich Kettler (descent)

East Face, Tree Surgeon: July 27, 1974, Lincoln Freeze, Bob Horton

Pensive: August 1986, Dave Carman, Bill Givens

The Snake: August 31, 1988, Jim Woodmencey, John Carr

ROUTE 1. West Ledges. II, 2.0. First descent August 4, 1963, by Peter Koedt and Rich Kettler. From the patrol cabin near the forks of the Cascade Canyon trail, bushwhack southwest up into the drainage below Alpha-and-Omega Lakes. This attractive, small canyon opens out below the west slope of Yosemite Peak. Various routes are available on this slope to gain the nearly level summit ridge; the original line was described as a couloir. All will lead to the ridge crest somewhat south or southwest of the highest point, for which a diligent search must be made.

ROUTE 2. The Snake. III, 5.10. First ascent August 31, 1988, by Jim Woodmencey and John Carr. See *Topo 70.* Near the lower left (south) edge of the main east face is a horizontal inclusion of black rock that conveys the appearance of the head of a snake. It begins just to the right (north) of the gully forming the extreme south edge of the face. This route of four leads starts at the left (south) end of the "snake" with a 5.9 mantle move to get into a left-facing corner (5.10-); climb up and through the black rock to the upper edge of the snake for the belay. The second lead traverses right (5.6) to a right-facing dihedral and face that is climbed up to a belay ledge with a fixed piton. The next pitch starts with a 5.8 wide crack up to an overhanging block, which is passed on the left into a series of sloping ledges, cracks, and faces to a belay ledge below the upper left-facing corner system. The fourth pitch begins with a 5.7 hand crack which then leads up to a difficult undercling and lieback (5.10). If desired, a 5.5 escape is available at the right edge of the large sloping ledge, avoiding the difficult finish. For descent scramble up and left to tree ledges, cross the gully, and descend grassy slopes (with intermittent slabs) until you can cut back north to the bottom of the gully and the base of the route. The rock is very solid on this route, but expect some vegetation. For protection take a regular rack to 3½ inches with doubles of 2½ to 3 inches.

ROUTE 3. *East Face, Tree Surgeon.* II, 5.8. First ascent July 27, 1974, by Lincoln Freeze and Bob Horton. This route starts in a broken chimney in the main east face several hundred feet left (south) of the obvious chimney that cuts up through the entire face. Perhaps the best identifier of the route is a large cavelike overhang directly above, with some small trees and bushes to the left. Climb the chimney and move up into the cavelike structure for the belay. Now climb the face and around the corner to the left and then up cracks into a chimney, belaying as high up as possible. The third lead climbs up out of the chimney (5.6) and follows a crack up sloping slabs until directly beneath an overhang with a thin crack in it. From a belay under the overhang, move left 20 feet, then follow a corner and cracks above, ultimately climbing a crack on the left (5.8) to a ledge, then step right into a dirty chimney that is climbed up to trees. Climb over trees to a large ledge. From here scramble left up a corner to a second large ledge. Directly above is a 3rd-class gully that is easily climbed. For protection take a large selec-

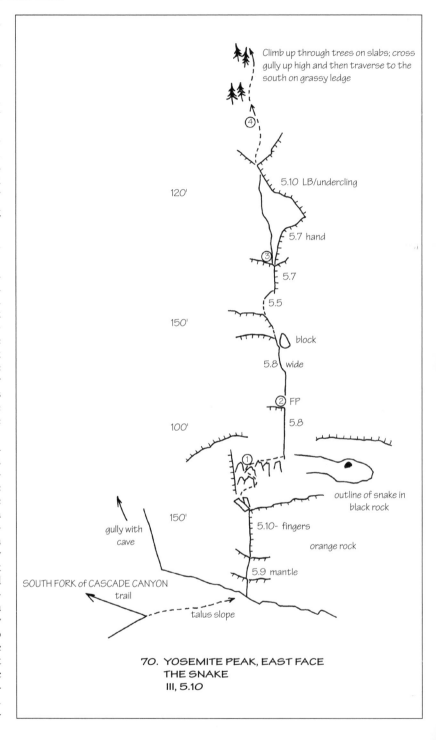

Climb up through trees on slabs; cross gully up high and then traverse to the south on grassy ledge

④

120'

5.10 LB/undercling

5.7 hand

③

5.7

5.5

150'

block

5.8 wide

② FP

5.8

100'

①

outline of snake in black rock

150'

gully with cave

5.10- fingers

orange rock

5.9 mantle

SOUTH FORK of CASCADE CANYON

trail

talus slope

70. YOSEMITE PEAK, EAST FACE
THE SNAKE
III, 5.10

tion of nuts and camming devices from very small to 4 inches.

ROUTE 4. Pensive. III, 5.10. First ascent August 1986, by Dave Carman and Bill Givens. See *Photo 80.* The name of this route adequately describes how others have felt on this particular wall while contemplating the upper overhangs. Begin by climbing a perfect lieback crack located left or south of a large left-facing corner. The lieback crack leads upward through some slightly loose blocks to a belay on a ledge left of a large flake. Traverse south (5.8, then 5.6) to a grassy ledge that leads up and right. Continue up and right and then straight up on grassy ledges. Move the belay up and left to a pillar that is situated below and left of a big roof. From the pillar climb up and left over a small roof and up a slab to a belay beneath a slot. The fifth and crux pitch goes up through this slot (5.9) and then up via 5.10 face climbing (protection described as marginal) to a very large, tree-covered ledge. For the descent proceed south along this ledge until easy scrambling takes one back to the trail in the south fork of Cascade Canyon.

ROUTE 5. East Face, Chouinard. IV, 5.9, A3, or IV, 5.10-. First ascent September 4–5, 1961, by Yvon Chouinard and Charles Ostin; first free ascent August 13, 1969, by Steve Wunsch and Jim Erickson. See *Topo 71* and *Photo 80.* The route can be found by looking for a gray right-facing corner just left of an orange pillar at the base of the face. A short pitch (5.6) angling left on ledges leads to the start of this 5.9 corner pitch. The third lead continues up the corner for 20 feet and then traverses right (5.8) and up across a face to a belay ledge. The next pitch goes up on face climbing to the left of and around to the right of (5.9) an amazing flake, finishing on a diagonal ramp sloping up and left. The fifth lead, the "Jungle Pitch," is very strenuous (5.10-) and at best unpleasant, up a right-facing dirt- and moss-filled corner past a fixed piton onto a belay ledge. Now climb left past a small corner and up a right-facing corner to a ledge and onto the top of a large block where a belay can be made. The seventh pitch angles right past another fixed piton up a left-facing corner and onto the first major horizontal ledge that extends all the way across the face. Climb a vertical hand crack above the ledge, using a hand traverse at its top to pass a small overhang to gain a belay ledge above, just below the second major horizontal ledge or terrace. The ninth lead goes up a large chimney above the terrace to a belay ledge. The final pitch goes up through a section of overhangs on poor rock, weaving right and then left to a right-facing corner; hand traverses are used to reach and then exit from this corner. The rock eases off at the top of this pitch and the climbing is much easier up and right to the summit. For descent, use the large couloir that cuts through the middle of the entire east face back down to the trail. See *American Alpine Journal,* 13, no. 1 (1962), pp. 216–220.

Variation: IV, 5.10-, A2. First ascent August 12, 1967, by Jim Erickson and Sheldon Smith. This major variation

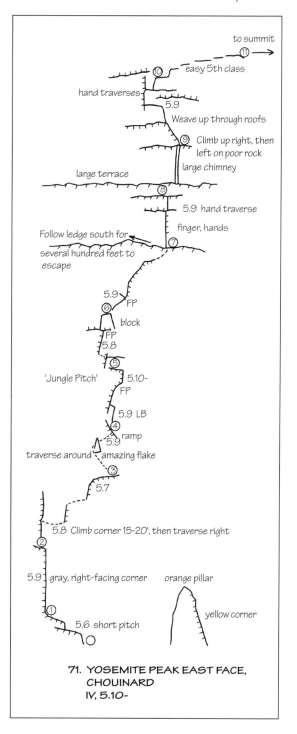

71. YOSEMITE PEAK EAST FACE, CHOUINARD
IV, 5.10-

of six pitches starts about 100 feet to the left (south) of the Chouinard Route, goes up to a huge impassable roof, and traverses 100 feet to the right to join the original 1961 route. The first lead (120 feet) begins with a short jam crack (5.7) up the left side of a large pillar on the face, leading into a dark overhanging chimney for the belay. The next pitch (90 feet) ascends two thin cracks (5.6) up and right until the chimney opens onto smooth low-angle slabs. The third lead (90 feet, 5.8) goes up the short, damp, overhanging cleft in the wall to the left and then traverses across slabs to a small belay stance. The next lead (60 feet) was severe, moving right and then up a very thin, poorly protected crack (5.10-) on small holds over a small overhang to a downsloping belay position under a wet roof. The roof and the dihedral above are then climbed (60 feet) on aid (A2) to a pitifully small belay stance just under the huge roof. The final exciting pitch (120 feet) traverses under the roof overhangs for 80 feet on very small holds (5.9) across wicked short slabs to a crack that leads up to a belay stance; protection on this lead is poor. From the end of this lead one can step around the corner to the right to join the Chouinard Route at an undetermined location (it is possible that this is at the base of the seventh pitch or simply on the first major ledge). Knifeblade pitons and very small nuts are useful on this climb.

ROUTE 6. East Face, Weeks' Chimney. III, 5.7. First ascent September 6, 1959, by Fred Beckey and Kenneth Weeks. See *Photo 80.* Two broad, tree-covered ledges divide the smooth east face of Yosemite Peak into three equal horizontal sections. Rising diagonally from lower left to upper right is a long chimney or crack that intersects both of these ledges; this chimney is a major feature of the right-hand (northern) portion of the east face. The first 100 feet of this chimney are 5.7. Follow the chimney to the second ledge, and then traverse out to the right on this ledge to the crest of the ridge that marks the extreme right edge of the east face. Follow this ridge to the summit. See *American Alpine Journal,* 12, no. 1 (1960), pp. 125–127.

Variation: III, 5.8, A1. First ascent August 19, 1974, by Dave Anderson, Mark Jonas, Todd Chavez, and Dale Tomrdle. The same major diagonal chimney is utilized in this variation. However, the first three pitches are on the ramp to the right, intersecting the chimney where it turns straight up the face. Here is the crux of the variation, which evidently required some A1 on the first and likely only ascent of this route. Two pitches go up the wall to the right of the chimney to the first large ledge. Then scramble up the northeast ridge to within two leads of the top. Climb this ridge (5.8) on the left side to the summit slabs. A wide selection of protection devices are needed on this climb.

ROUTE 7. North Face. II, 5.8. First ascent August 4, 1963, by Peter Koedt and Rich Kettler. From the trail in the vicin-

ity of the patrol cabin at the forks of the canyon, bushwhack up the drainage just north of Yosemite Peak toward the north face rising directly above, surmounting a broken abutment and the diagonal chimney system beyond, to reach a large tree below the middle of the face. The first 150-foot pitch starts 20 feet above, behind a large block-flake, and leads up an open book that has a jam crack in its right face. Climb this jam crack or the face to the left to some broken rock; bear slightly right to reach a belay stance on a large ledge. Proceed up a large, obvious open book for 20 feet, cut back slightly to the left, and then up a system of parallel jam cracks in high-angle rock for 20 feet until it is possible to traverse onto a small grassy ledge. After another 15 feet on easy broken rock, a large, grassy belay ledge is reached. From the left end of this ledge, climb directly up an obvious 90° open book to a large ledge, about 30 feet left of the large tree at the top of the face. From here, easy scrambling to the right along the ledge and then up will lead to the summit. For descent, the first-ascent party utilized a west couloir that heads a few hundred feet south of the summit. The couloir ends in a dropoff, which is avoided by taking a ledge back to the right (north), over to the base of the north face.

PEAK 10,650   *(0.9 mi N of Table Mountain)*

Map: Mount Moran

This easy sedimentary peak lies on the divide at the head of Alpha-and-Omega Basin. This name has been applied to the delightful upper canyon just south of the Wigwams that harbors the twin Alpha-and-Omega Lakes.

ROUTE 1. South Ridge. I, 1.0. First recorded descent August 3, 1967, by Leigh Ortenburger and John Lemon. An easy ridge.

ROUTE 2. North Ridge. I, 1.0. First recorded ascent August 3, 1967, by Leigh Ortenburger and John Lemon. An unusual cairn with no record was found on the summit.

SOUTH WIGWAM (10,840)

Map: Mount Moran

West of the Grand Teton on the ridge crest that forms the hydrographic divide between Jackson Hole and Teton Basin is a series of peaks (Mount Owen Quartz Monzonite formation) that have a conical or wigwam appearance when viewed from the east. These were named by Fritiof Fryxell in the first years of Grand Teton National Park. It is not known how many wigwams Fryxell had in mind, but two are listed in this book. This southern peak is in fact a double peak with a northern subsummit (10,800+).

ROUTE 1. South Ridge. I, 2.0. First recorded ascent August 3, 1967, by Leigh Ortenburger and John Lemon. This ridge is easier than the north ridge.

NORTH WIGWAM (10,855)
(2.0 mi N of Table Mountain)

Map: Mount Moran

This peak is the highest of the Wigwams, and, although records do not indicate an ascent prior to 1954, it offers little difficulty from either the west or south. There are two cairns on the summit. The east ridge is the most prominent feature of the peak, ending with a separate tower (10,480+) and a sharp dropoff into Cascade Canyon.

CHRONOLOGY

Northwest Ridge: [probable] August 3, 1954, Richard Armstrong, Hugh Rollins
East Ridge: [probable] August 3, 1954, Richard Armstrong, Hugh Rollins (descent); August 18, 1957, William and Evelyn Cropper (ascent)
    var: **East Tower:** July 28, 1947, E. W. Marshall, H. D. Holland
South Ridge: August 18, 1957, William and Evelyn Cropper (descent); [probable] 1958, Howard Stagner, Jr., Perkins (ascent)
West Slope: July 12, 1960, Arthur J. Reyman
Wigwam Buttress: July 23, 1990, Leo Larson, George Montopoli

ROUTE 1. West Slope. I, 2.0. First ascent July 12, 1960, by Arthur J. Reyman. This slope can be easily approached from the trail in the north fork of Teton Canyon.
ROUTE 2. South Ridge. I, 1.0. First descent August 18, 1957, by William and Evelyn Cropper; probable first ascent 1958, by Howard Stagner, Jr., and Perkins. This ridge provides no difficulties.
ROUTE 3. East Ridge. I, 3.0. Probable first descent August 3, 1954, by Richard Armstrong and Hugh Rollins; first ascent August 18, 1957, by William and Evelyn Cropper. The upper flat crest of this ridge can be easily attained either from Mica Lake to the north or from the basin to the south after an approach via the north fork of Cascade Canyon. It can also be reached from the north ridge by traversing around on a snowfield below the uppermost north face.
    Variation: East Tower. I, 4.0. First ascent July 28, 1947, by E. W. Marshall and H. D. Holland. This prominent tower is climbed from the notch separating it from the upper east ridge. There are minor towers both on the west of this East Tower and on the east.
ROUTE 4. Northwest Ridge. I, 3.0. Probable first ascent August 3, 1954, by Richard Armstrong and Hugh Rollins. This ridge must be negotiated if one traverses the divide between Littles Peak and Table Mountain. However, it consists of steep, shattered sedimentary rock and is not recommended.
ROUTE 5. Wigwam Buttress. III, 5.9. First ascent July 23, 1990, by Leo Larson and George Montopoli. This is the prominent buttress to the south when viewed from a point that is approximately 1.25 miles up into the north fork of Cascade Canyon (just after crossing the second foot bridge). Leave the trail and proceed up a talus field from which a tree-covered ledge is accessed; continue back east on this ledge until a dihedral is located (this dihedral is found just before reaching the corner of the buttress at a dead snag). Climb the dihedral and 5.6 cracks above to another tree-covered ledge. Walk right a short distance to a crack system that goes up and right. Climb this pitch, which ends with a 5.8 traverse back left (east) to a belay at a big flake. The third pitch continues straight up (5.5—no protection) to an alcove and then ends with a 5.7 traverse west below a number of overhangs. Now climb a corner that avoids two overhangs (the second one is large) on their eastern edges. The dihedral above is 5.9 (obvious from below) and this, the fourth pitch, is 160 feet in length. From the belay climb up and right on easy 5th class and then up via a 5.8 face to a belay on much easier ground. Scramble 50 feet to the east to a number of large flakes. The sixth and final pitch begins in a 5.8 jam crack, and then easier climbing leads to the top of "GeoLeo Pinnacle." From here a 50-foot rappel leads to a notch. Five hundred feet of easy to middle 5th-class scrambling provides access to the summit of the buttress. Exit to the south and descend the drainage to the east.

PEAK 10,720+   *(1.85 mi SW of Littles Peak)*

Map: Mount Moran
This unmarked high point due west of Mica Lake on the divide achieves peak status, while Point 10,686 just north does not.
ROUTE 1. South Ridge. I, 1.0. First recorded descent August 3, 1954, by Richard Armstrong and Hugh Rollins. This is an easy ridge.
ROUTE 2. North Ridge. I, 1.0. First recorded ascent August 3, 1954, by Richard Armstrong and Hugh Rollins. This ridge is easily climbed as one marches along the divide south of Littles Peak.

LITTLES PEAK (10,712)

Map: Mount Moran
This sedimentary peak, while minor in terms of its height and aspect, is a major Teton summit because of its location. Littles Peak is something of a landmark for traffic out of Cascade Canyon headed north on a high-level approach to the heads of Leigh Canyon, Moran Canyon, or even Moose Basin. Easily accessible from the west as well as from the popular Lake Solitude trail, it was one of the earlier high peaks in the range to be climbed. In more recent times, Littles Peak was ascended by Earl M. Buckingham on

October 16, 1931, who established the triangulation station, "Leigh Station," on the summit.

ROUTE 1. West Ridge. I, 1.0. Probable first ascent 1898, by T. M. Bannon and party, or August 24, 1912, by Eliot Blackwelder and Mack Lake. The original quadrangle map, issued in 1899, indicates a bench mark on the summit, so Bannon's topographic party must have climbed the peak. The geologist Blackwelder and his assistant also climbed the peak during the course of his geological study of the west slope of the Teton Range. The west ridge of this peak is easily reached and climbed from the trail in Granite Basin.

ROUTE 2. ☞East Ridge. I, 2.0. First recorded ascent September 1, 1933, by Dudley Hayden. This narrow and horizontal ridge connects the summit of Littles Peak with the extensive high flat plateau above and west of Lake Solitude. The plateau was reached in 1933 by the slopes due west of the lake to the saddle (10,320+) marking the south end of the plateau. It is now more commonly reached via the large couloir that leads northwest from the lake, providing a straightforward route past the headwall up onto the plateau, about 1.0 mile east of the summit. Proceed west to the summit along the slender but easy ridge. In descending from Littles Peak to the lake, remember that this couloir heads near the southeastern edge of the plateau. The portion of the headwall south of this couloir can be negotiated on either ascent or descent but requires adroit routefinding and some serious scrambling among the wet cliffs. *Time: 1 hour* from Lake Solitude.

ROUTE 3. North Ridge. I, 1.0. First descent September 1, 1933, by Dudley Hayden, who was on official duty as a park ranger to intercept a herd of sheep illegally crossing the divide into Leigh Canyon (it is felt by some that perhaps the sheep should be credited with this first!); first ascent September 1, 1941, by Fritiof Fryxell and Bob Crist, in one day after hiking up Moran Canyon from String Lake. This ridge has become the standard route for access into the south fork of Moran Canyon from the east side of the range. There are no difficulties and a semitrail can be found from the saddle (10,000+) at the head of Leigh Canyon.

PEAK 10,245   *(1.8 mi ESE of Littles Peak)*

Map: Mount Moran

This minor peak is a high point on the ridge between Littles Peak and the Paintbrush Divide north of Cascade Canyon. The higher point to the west, Point 10,538, was climbed on July 12, 1960, by Arthur Reyman.

CHRONOLOGY

West Ridge: July 11, 1960, Arthur J. Reyman
Northeast Chute: August 14, 1961, Ed Bellero, Ingmar Olafson, Rolf Schette
East Ridge: September 2, 1976, Leigh Ortenburger

ROUTE 1. West Ridge. I, 1.0. First known ascent July 11, 1960, by Arthur J. Reyman. The southwest slope leading to this ridge and the ridge itself are easily climbed directly from Lake Solitude.

ROUTE 2. East Ridge. I, 1.0. First ascent September 2, 1976, by Leigh Ortenburger. From the trail at the Paintbrush Divide proceed westward easily along this rocky ridge to the summit.

ROUTE 3. Northeast Chute. I, 2.0. First ascent August 14, 1961, by Ed Bellero, Ingmar Olafson, and Rolf Schette. Proceed from the high basin northwest of the Paintbrush Divide.

PEAK 10,880+   *(1.25 mi WSW of Mount Woodring)*

Map: Mount Moran

This easy summit lies but a short distance north of the Paintbrush Divide, which is reached by trail.

CHRONOLOGY

Northwest Slope: August 1, 1954, William Buckingham, Betty Bierer
South Ridge: August 23, 1958, Howard R. Stagner, Jr., Richard Byrd

Route 1. ☞South Ridge. I, 1.0. First recorded ascent about August 23, 1958, by Howard R. Stagner, Jr., and Richard Byrd. This is an easy hike from the trail, which is only 200 feet below the summit.

ROUTE 2. Northwest Slope. I, 1.0. First ascent August 1, 1954, by William Buckingham and Betty Bierer.

PEAK 11,270   *(1.5 mi NW of the Jaw)*

Map: Mount Moran

Although not usually an objective by itself, this high peak with a double summit does form a good viewpoint if one has time to spare while hiking the trail from Cascade Canyon to Paintbrush Canyon. It is also climbed by energetic climbers making the traverse from the Jaw at the head of Hanging Canyon to the Paintbrush Divide. An empty cairn was found on the point (10,960+) just northwest of the summit by William Buckingham and Betty Bierer on August 1, 1954; this was probably the summit reached by William Shand on August 4, 1943.

ROUTE 1. Southeast Ridge. I, 2.0. First descent August 1, 1954, by William Buckingham and Betty Bierer; first ascent August 2, 1958, by Paul Salstrom and Robert Marshall. The ridge from the saddle (10,480+) between this peak and Peak 10,960+ is straightforward. From this saddle the gully with the stream descending to the southwest toward the bridge over Cascade Creek makes a fast descent route. Stay west of the stream.

ROUTE 2. ☞*Northwest Ridge.* I, 2.0. First known ascent August 1, 1954, by William Buckingham and Betty Bierer. Take either the Cascade Canyon trail or the Indian Paintbrush Canyon trail to the Paintbrush Divide, from which this ridge is a straightforward scramble. A cairn but no record was found on the summit.

McCLINTOCK PEAK (10,960+)
(1.2 mi W of the Jaw)

Map: Mount Moran

The only intriguing feature of this otherwise undistinguished peak is its conspicuous rocky south ridge containing a number of small towers.

ROUTE 1. East Ridge. I, 2.0. First descent June 23, 1931, by H. L. and Frank McClintock, and Carl Sampson; first ascent August 2, 1958, by Paul Salstrom and Robert Marshall. Climb the easy ridge from the saddle (10,480+) separating this peak from Buckingham Palace.

ROUTE 2. North Ridge. I, 3.0. First ascent June 23, 1931, by H. L. and Frank McClintock and Carl Sampson. From Indian Paintbrush Canyon, ascend the gully leading to the saddle west of this peak. An ice axe will be useful in early season. From the saddle the summit is reached by ascending the easy ridge above.

BUCKINGHAM PALACE (11,097)
(0.7 mi W of the Jaw)

Map: Mount Moran

This peak, which apparently remained unclimbed until 1958, consists of three summits; the west summit is the highest.

ROUTE 1. East Ridge. I, 2.0. First ascent June 21, 1958, by William Buckingham and Margaret West. After climbing the Jaw from Hanging Canyon, continue traversing west, passing over Window Point (11,120+) on the way. The ridge itself from the high saddle (10,640+) to the east is an easy ridge scramble; the part between the central and the western summits is the most interesting. See *American Alpine Journal,* 11, no. 2 (1959), pp. 307–309.

ROUTE 2. Northwest Ridge. I, 3.0. First ascent August 1, 1958, by Paul Salstrom and Robert Marshall. Leave the Indian Paintbrush Canyon trail at about 9,500 feet and ascend the loose rock and steep snow to the col between McClintock Peak and Buckingham Palace. From the col walk up to the summit.

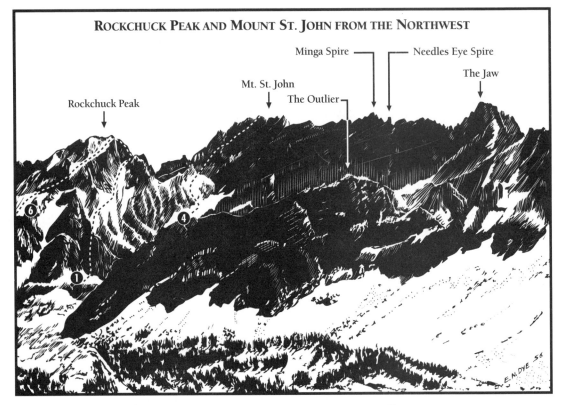

ROCKCHUCK PEAK AND MOUNT ST. JOHN FROM THE NORTHWEST

Minga Spire — ┌── Needles Eye Spire

The Jaw

Mt. St. John

Rockchuck Peak   The Outlier┐

Cascade Canyon to Leigh Canyon

FOURTEEN-HOUR PINNACLE (9,280+)
(0.95 mi SW of the Jaw)

Map: Mount Moran

Bracing the north side of Cascade Canyon, opposite the mouth of Valhalla Canyon lies this salient pinnacle or pillar. Located about 0.7 mile east of the trail junction in the canyon, Fourteen-Hour Pinnacle forms the extreme end of the south ridge of Buckingham Palace (11,097). From some angles, the notch separating the summit from the wall above cannot be seen, but the pillar still appears as a prominent buttress. Steep and rotten couloirs descend to the east and to the west from the notch. The name, given in advance, reflects the time required for the first ascent. The base of the pinnacle is easily approached via the Cascade Canyon trail.

CHRONOLOGY

Southeast Ridge: August 3, 1960, Jake Breitenbach, Sterling Neale

var: **Southeast Face:** August 11, 1960, Dick Bonker, William Crowther
Southwest Couloir: August 5, 1966, Alan Rubin, Dennis Memhet
Direct South Ridge: September 7, 1977, George Montopoli, Mugs Stump
Southeast Couloir: August 30, 1978, Keith Hadley, Lars Holbeck
East Face, Twenty-Four Hour Crack: August 11, 1983, by Peter Koedt, Kevin Dye

ROUTE 1. Southwest Couloir. II, 5.6. First ascent August 5, 1966, by Alan Rubin and Dennis Memhet. From the Cascade Canyon trail scramble up the gully to the left (west) of the pinnacle. At the first step, about one-third of the way up the couloir, rope up and climb (5.6) the center of the rock. Scramble up to the next step, and then climb the left corner and in the center for the next four and a half leads. This section contains occasional 5.6 climbing and is very rotten.

It leads to the ridge crest, from which one can scramble and climb left to the summit. This route contains much loose rock and is not recommended. There is natural rockfall on the right side of the gully.

ROUTE 2. *Direct South Ridge.* III, 5.9+. First ascent September 7, 1977, by George Montopoli and Mugs Stump. See *Photo 81.* This eight-pitch route follows the crest of the south ridge very closely. Start above huge boulders in a gully 150 feet west of the south ridge. The first pitch (100 feet) goes up slightly overhanging black rock to a crack system that is climbed to its top. Traverse right (east) for 30 feet past the crest to a crack system leading to a ramp that diagonals up and left to a belay at the base of a chimney. Climb the chimney past a 5.8 roof to a set of ledges. The fourth lead is difficult, up to orange blocky rock, then in obvious crack systems that turn into 5.9+ face climbing for 40 feet until a ledge is reached. After 10 feet to another ledge, the next pitch traverses 20 feet right (east) around a corner to another difficult but solid crack system, which is climbed for 30 feet until a difficult traverse left (15 feet, 5.9) leads onto easier ground. Cracks and dihedrals (5.7) continue upward for the next ropelength. The seventh lead passes a short roof and chimney and a crack, gaining the ridge crest at the end of the pitch. The final difficult lead goes up and left into a dihedral system that leads up and right. Some 200 feet of easier climbing then bring one to the summit.

ROUTE 3. *East Face, Twenty-Four Hour Crack.* II, 5.9. First ascent August 11, 1983, by Peter Koedt and Kevin Dye. See *Photo 81.* This entire route stays to the right or east of the south ridge. From the Cascade Canyon trail approach the pinnacle from the east to gain the bottom of the initial gray-white slabs at the base of this face. Proceed partway up these slabs to a belay "dish" at the right edge, just below the first wall. The first short lead (5.8) goes up and right to the top of a flake. Next pass two red roofs, the first on the right and the second on the left, via 5.8 climbing to the belay. The crux crack above ascends a section of polished white rock to the left of a dihedral; this polished white rock is separated from the south ridge by a section of red rock. This third pitch starts as 5.8 but becomes 5.9 above and is a sustained, hard-to-protect lead. The next lead after a short section of 5.8 becomes much easier (5.5) and angles up and left. Two more leads (5.6) bring one to a ledge. After belaying on this ledge, move out right and up for two more leads of similar difficulty to the summit.

ROUTE 4. *Southeast Ridge.* II, 5.6, A1. First ascent August 3, 1960, by Jake Breitenbach and Sterling Neale. Approach via the Cascade Canyon trail. This ridge is marked by three overhangs. The first is passed by climbing the white rock to the right. Then climb the crest to the base of the second overhang, which is passed around the corner to the left. The third overhang is also passed on the left. From here the crest of the ridge is followed to the summit. This route involves one direct-aid pitch. See *American Alpine Journal,* 12, no. 2 (1961), pp. 373–379.

Variation: Southeast Face. II, 5.6, A2. First ascent August 11, 1960, by Dick Bonker and William Crowther. After approaching via the Cascade Canyon trail, ascend the lower face and reach the large "pulpit" from the right. The face above is marked by two parallel cracks angling up to the right. Climb the lower crack and then up the overhanging face to a friction pitch. Three of the nine pitches required extensive use of aid. See *American Alpine Journal,* 12, no. 2 (1961), pp. 373–379.

ROUTE 5. *Southeast Couloir.* II, 5.6. First ascent August 30, 1978, by Keith Hadley and Lars Holbeck. The couloir on the east or southeast side leading to the notch behind the summit was apparently climbed by this party.

CASCADE CANYON, NORTH SIDE ROCK CLIMBS

Map: Mount Moran

Assembled here, from west to east, are routes that have been climbed on the walls on the north side of Cascade Canyon. The accessibility of these routes and the usually good rock make these climbs attractive to the rock climber. The lack of exact information concerning the numerous early climbs made in this area in the 1950s and 1960s implies that the attribution of first ascents is doubtful in many cases. As will be seen in the following descriptions, old pitons have been encountered on several of these "new" routes.

Ayres' Crag 5 (11,040+)   *(0.2 mi S of the Jaw)*

The south wall of this crag is the most imposing of those forming the north rim of Cascade Canyon. For the approach, hike up the Cascade Canyon trail to a point opposite the north face of Mount Owen. Above to the north is this nearly vertical face that starts at about 9,600 feet. It is bounded on the left (west) by the large open couloir that descends from the vicinity of the Jaw.

ROUTE 1. *South Face.* IV, 5.8, A4. First ascent June 23–26, 1963, by Fred Beckey and Steve Marts; attempted September 8, 1960, by Ed Cooper and Ron Niccoli. The original route follows approximately the left skyline of this face, as seen from the trail when the crag first comes into full view. The main south wall actually faces somewhat southwest and has two apparent summits; the left one is the highest. This somewhat dish-shaped wall has water stains down the middle; this route lies to the left (west) of these water stains. Ascend the talus directly beneath the highest summit. An overhanging band that bisects the face will be seen slanting upward from left to right. After the first two pitches, which go up and slightly to the right, make a very difficult aid lead, requiring three bolts to pass a slab and ending in a hanging belay. The fourth pitch takes one up to the overhang, which is attacked via an open book, both walls of which overhang. The one rotten piton crack ultimately bottoms out, and three more bolts are required to reach a small belay ledge. With inadequate protection, the next delicate lead works upward, free and slightly left, to a rocky ledge about half-way up the face. The route proceeds up and right again, using difficult cracks, to a second ample ledge about 200 feet below the upper rim of the face. A lead up steep but broken rock ends at a *cul-de-sac*, with vertical rotten rock on the left and a great overhanging wall on the right. Traverse right on pitons for about 60 feet (very exposed) until it is possible to pendulum into an open book. Climb about 100 feet of exposed slabs and flakes on the right side of this open book to the rim. See *American Alpine Journal*, 14, no. 1 (1964), pp. 184–185.

Variation: IV, 5.8. First ascent July 28–29, 1966, by Peter Cleveland and Don Storjohann. On this variation fewer difficulties were reported, partially because the third pitch and its bolts were avoided by climbing to the right of the aid crack. At the *cul-de-sac* at the top of the wall, instead of traversing right, climb directly up on 5.8 rock.

Variation: IV, 5.10. First ascent June 1979, by Ron Matous and Keith Hadley. While this climb was largely a free repetition of the 1963 route, its description differs in some regards and so will be given here. From the talus climb 200 feet of easy rock (5.1 to 5.4) to a ledge just right of a small overhang. The next lead (75 feet), up and slightly left toward the set of four bolts, is difficult (5.10). The third lead, equally difficult, passes these bolts and continues for 150 feet toward the base of an obvious dihedral below the main diagonal overhang of the face. Climbing this dihedral to and past the overhang to a bolt involves the third con-secutive 5.10 lead (150 feet). The fifth pitch (120 feet) is easier (5.6) but is unprotected, up and slightly left to a good belay ledge. Now continue up the face to a belay stance at the end of a long (165 feet) lead. The seventh pitch of 120 feet contains loose rock (5.6). The final short lead (75 feet) is again difficult (5.9) and brings one out at the top of the wall.

ROUTE 2. **South Face Dihedral.** IV, 5.8. First ascent August 4, 1979, by Peter Koedt and Kent Lugbill. This climb lies to the right (east) of the water stain in the middle of the main south face. In this area an obvious large dihedral that arches up from lower right to upper left is climbed (5.7). Some rotten rock will be found in this dihedral, but at its top there is good climbing, with considerable exposure while travers-ing out left over the face. The protection here is not good. From the top of the dihedral, climb straight up for 75 feet over good black rock, and then make a horizontal traverse up and right around the eastern edge of the face. There are about two pitches (5.8) from the dihedral to the top of the face; protection is again not good in this section.

Symmetry Crag 4 (10,720+)
(0.45 mi W of Symmetry Spire)

The southern battlements of the Symmetry Crags extend all the way down to the floor of Cascade Canyon. The most impressive of these is the sequence of steep cliffs forming the south buttress of Crag 4. Appropriately named Trinity Buttress in 1970, it is the first obvious wall beyond Storm Point and is divided horizontally into three sections by two large, prominent ledges with trees. It is located to the left (west) of the large rockslide issuing from the gully imme-diately west of the southwest ridge of Storm Point (and Guides' Wall). For the approach, hike up Cascade Canyon and leave the trail just beyond this rockslide, where the trees begin again.

ROUTE 1. **Lower South Buttress.** II, 5.8. First ascent Sep-tember 4, 1961, by Fred Beckey and John Hudson. From the trail climb into the gully along the left side of the first (low-est) buttress of the crag. Climb easily up the very steep rock on the nose that leads directly upward from the gully on the left (west) side of the buttress. From the first tree ledge, work left along a black dike chimney; then climb right and up, when the wall permits, to the second tree ledge. Traverse right (east) along the ledge (and slightly downhill) about 400 feet to the definite corner of the buttress. From this point the route goes directly upward, remaining slightly left of this corner. The first roped pitch leads up a crack system. A short overhang is encountered near the end of this pitch. Next work slightly right and up. The third pitch stays within a few feet of the corner, using an obvious 1-foot, slightly overhanging chimney, which is very strenuous. Work diagonally left on the next lead over an overhang and then up a difficult shallow groove, which contains nothing but rounded holds. The next pitch goes directly upward on very small holds to the obvious dead snag, which points about 45° to the right; this snag can be seen from the trail and marks the end of the technical climbing. Because the rock presents more than a single possibility at various points on the route, it is likely that the most difficult pitches can be avoided, if desired. This buttress ends about halfway to the summit of the crag from Cascade Canyon; the route was not pursued beyond the dead snag. See *American Alpine Journal*, 13, no. 1 (1962), pp. 216–220.

ROUTE 2. **Trinity Buttress.** III, 5.9. First ascent August 1, 1970, by Yvon Chouinard and T. M. Herbert. See *Topo 72* and *Photo 82*. This route, a fine climb on good rock with one of the shorter Teton approaches, stays more or less on the crest or nose of the three buttresses. Many variations are possible, with the most consistently hard climbing found on and to the left of the nose. Some eight pitches are involved. All three buttresses offer leads of 5.7 difficulty or above. The original climb found the most difficult section in a 150-foot lead of face climbing at the top of the second buttress. Other ascents indicate that the final pitch among the last flakes and towers is the most difficult. The topo illustrates only one of the route possibilities on this buttress. Descent is via a ledge system down to the east and into the same gully (see *Storm Point, Route 1*) as for the Guides' Wall descent.

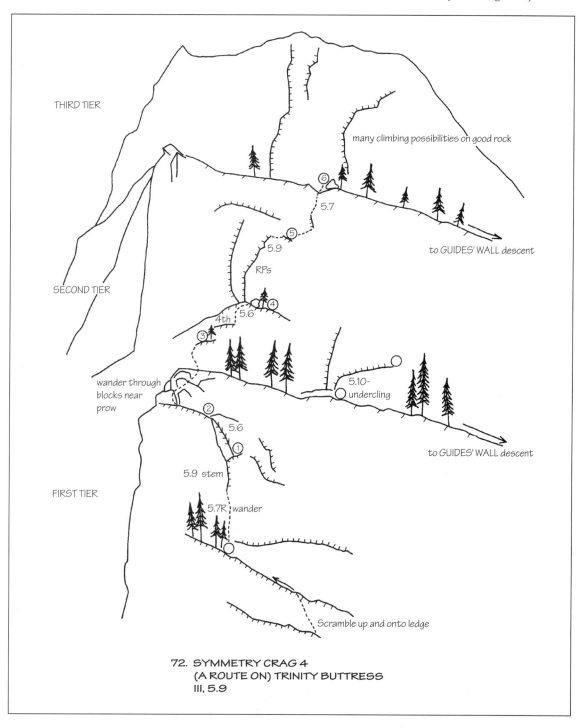

THIRD TIER

many climbing possibilities on good rock

⑥

5.7

⑤

5.9

to GUIDES' WALL descent

RPs

SECOND TIER

④ 5.6

4th

③

5.10-
undercling

wander through
blocks near
prow

② 5.6

① 5.9 stem

to GUIDES' WALL descent

FIRST TIER

5.7R wander

Scramble up and onto ledge

**72. SYMMETRY CRAG 4
(A ROUTE ON) TRINITY BUTTRESS
III, 5.9**

Storm Point (10,054)

Most of the rock climbing out of Cascade Canyon has been on the basal cliffs of Storm Point. Near the mouth of the canyon with one of the shortest of Teton approaches, this area has in recent years seen a flurry of climbing activity, both on the old routes and on new and difficult routes.

CHRONOLOGY

Guides' Wall: August 3, 1949, Richard Pownall,
　Art Gilkey
　var: Blobular Oscillations: August 25, 1984,
　　Renny Jackson, Larry Detrick
South Central Buttress: August 18, 1958, John Gill,
　Rick Lloyd
Bum's Wall: July 24, 1970, George Meyers,
　Andrew Cox
Picnic and Paranoia: August 29, 1970, Jeb Schenck,
　Mike Henderson, Fred Long
South Face of Guides' Wall: July 11, 1971, Yvon
　Chouinard, T. M. Herbert, Juris Krisjansons
No Friends: August 1979, Jim Williams, friend
Vieux Guide: July 22, 1980, Yvon Chouinard,
　Jim Donini
Morning Thunder: July 9, 1985, Paul Gagner,
　Dan Burgette
Bat Attack Crack: July 4, 1986, Paul Gagner,
　Renny Jackson
Hot Dogs: July 11, 1986, Paul Gagner,
　Jim Woodmencey
The Jones Sisters: August 13, 1987, Paul Gagner,
　Jim Woodmencey
No More Mr. Nice Guy: September 15, 1987, Paul
　Gagner, Jim Woodmencey
Skinny Dip: July 10, 1989, Dave Carman et al.
Rags-to-Riches: August 19, 1989, Tom Turiano,
　Harry Hollis

ROUTE 1. Guides' Wall. II, 5.8. First ascent August 3, 1949, by Richard Pownall and Art Gilkey. Forty years after this pioneering climb one cannot be certain whether all of the pitches of the current Guides' Wall were included in the 1949 ascent. Subsequent early climbs in this area were made on September 4, 1953, by Richard Emerson and Bill Wallace; on June 29, 1954, by William Buckingham and Gary Hemming; on August 16, 1954, by Steve Jervis, Mike Wortis, and John Mann; on July 30, 1955, by Bill Cropper, John Dietschy, Steve Jervis, and Mike Wortis; and on July 22, 1956, by Willi Unsoeld and R. L. Evans. During those years the present route was very likely worked out. The ascent that led to the current name, however, appears to have been made on September 5, 1959, by Barry Corbet, Jake Breitenbach, Sterling Neale, Carlos Plummer, Willi Unsoeld, and Fred Beckey. See *Topo 73* and *Photos 83* and *84.* The southwest ridge of Storm Point has the exceptionally attractive combination of easy

access and excellent rock. Guides' Wall, the first seven pitches of this ridge (although only six are now commonly done), has over the years become one of the most popular rock climbs in the park. Variations are possible, although any direct climb of the ridge must apparently funnel through the crux pitch described later. There are several possible escapes from this route into the southwest couloir to the left (north). During most of the climb this couloir is in sight; hence, the route is at or near the western edge of the main southwest buttress.

For the approach, take the boat across the lake and hike up the Cascade Canyon trail (beginning at Inspiration Point) about 1.5 miles until, past the southwest ridge, one can actually look up into the major southwest couloir immediately west of Storm Point. At this point there is in Cascade Canyon a small pond, known as Perch Pond, formed in recent years by a large rockslide from the north. A climbers' trail will be found leading north at this point through a scree slope, up across a small cliff band, and then west through large trees to the start of the climbing at the corner of the steep continuous section.

The first pitch starts right on the corner and ends at a bolted anchor (5.7). Take care climbing over the small tree at the base of this pitch. The next three ropelengths are most easily done on the ridge crest, but there are alternate routes on both sides. These pitches lead to the first broad ledge of the ridge just below a very large flake on the crest. The flake can be seen in profile from the trail. This ledge provides an escape route into the southwest couloir, if desired. Reach the top of the flake (5.7) by climbing a crack and flake system on the east side. Then move left (west) and up to a comfortable belay ledge at the base of the crux sixth pitch. Follow the obvious crack upward, face climbing at the top on very enjoyable rock (5.8). A bolted anchor at the top of this pitch currently marks the end of the Guides' Wall route as it is commonly done today. For protection on this route, take a standard rack to 2½ inches, with quickdraws.

For the walkoff descent, one must climb another easy pitch (5.5) to a ledge that leads out north and west into the southwest couloir. This ledge is easy, but caution is required because of the considerable exposure. The southwest couloir can then be taken back to the base of the climb by following a steep trail back down to the base, staying on the west side of the drainage. Parties nowadays usually rappel down, starting from the bolted anchors at the top of the sixth pitch. This initial rappel is 150 feet back down to the Flake Ledge. Two additional 150-foot rappels (from tree anchors) bring one down to the bolt anchors at the top of the first pitch, where another 150-foot rappel brings one to the starting point.

Variation: Blobular Oscillations. II, 5.10-. First ascent August 25, 1984, by Renny Jackson and Larry Detrick. See *Topo 73.* This variation provides a much more difficult start and finish for the Guides' Wall route. From the belay for the first pitch move up and right over an overhang (5.10-), then

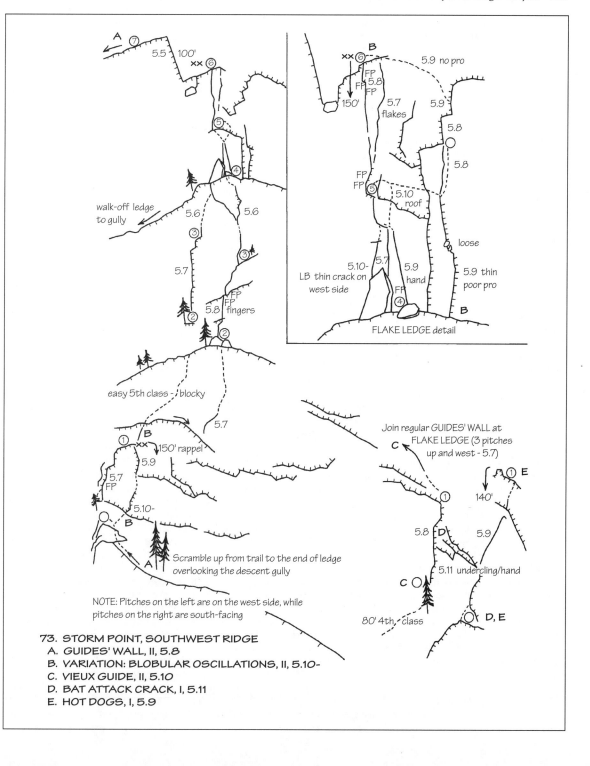

A   (7)
5.5   100'
xx (6)

B
xx (6)   5.9 no pro
FP 5.8
FP
150'   5.7   5.9
        flakes
                              5.8
(5)
                              5.8

(4)

walk-off ledge
to gully   FP (5)
        5.6   5.6   FP   5.10
                                       roof

(3)

(3)

5.7   5.10- 5.7 5.9   5.9 thin
                       LB thin crack on hand poor pro
(2) 5.8 fingers   west side   loose
FP   FP
FP   (4)
(2)   B

                            FLAKE LEDGE detail

easy 5th class - blocky

                    5.7   Join regular GUIDES' WALL at
                                       FLAKE LEDGE (3 pitches
(1) B   up and west - 5.7)
xx   150' rappel   C
5.9

5.7   (1) E
FP   (1)   140'
        5.10-   5.8 D   5.9
B
                                     5.11 undercling/hand
        A   Scramble up from trail to the end of ledge
             overlooking the descent gully   C ○

NOTE: Pitches on the left are on the west side, while
pitches on the right are south-facing   80' 4th class   D, E

73. STORM POINT, SOUTHWEST RIDGE
   A. GUIDES' WALL, II, 5.8
   B. VARIATION: BLOBULAR OSCILLATIONS, II, 5.10-
   C. VIEUX GUIDE, II, 5.10
   D. BAT ATTACK CRACK, I, 5.11
   E. HOT DOGS, I, 5.9

into and up a left-facing corner. Finish the lead via the left-facing corner (5.9), emerging at the rappel bolts at the top of the first pitch of Guides' Wall. Two pitches were climbed above and right (east) of the "Flake Ledge" on the first ascent. These are not really recommended, however.

ROUTE 2. Vieux Guide. II, 5.10. First ascent July 22, 1980, by Yvon Chouinard and Jim Donini. See *Topo 73* and *Photos 83* and *84*. The beginning of this route is marked by a prominent left-facing corner, 200 feet to the right (east) of the regular Guides' Wall start. Climb 80 feet (4.0) past a tree to reach the base of this corner, which is then climbed (5.8) to a belay to the right of some overhangs. From the top of this corner the route continues up and left for three pitches (5.7) to the Flake Ledge of the regular Guides' Wall route. The small roof directly above the 5.9 hand crack above the Flake Ledge was climbed on the first ascent of this route (5.10).

ROUTE 3. Bat Attack Crack. I, 5.11. First ascent July 4, 1986, by Paul Gagner and Renny Jackson. See *Topo 73* and *Photos 83* and *84*. Located to the right of the left-facing corner of Vieux Guide is a difficult ceiling or arching crack known as Bat Attack Crack. Scramble up and right on an easy ramp where a belay can be set just below the arch that forms the route. Very difficult jamming and the crux undercling then take one to the left, where a steep corner provides an exit at the top of the first pitch of Vieux Guide. Rappel anchors at the top of the pitch provide an escape from this one-pitch climb.

ROUTE 4. Hot Dogs. I, 5.9. First ascent ca. July 11, 1986, by Paul Gagner and Jim Woodmencey. See *Topo 73* and *Photo 83*. This excellent one-pitch climb begins at the same spot as Bat Attack Crack. Climb up to the beginning of the hard jamming and then exit out right (east) via a 5.9 jam crack.

ROUTE 5. Bum's Wall. III, 5.8, A3. First ascent July 24, 1970, by George Meyers and Andrew Cox. Start in the center of the broad face to the right of the Guides' Wall route and directly below a large right-facing corner. Work up to the start of this corner from the right; some aid will be needed in this section. Climb this corner until one can exit left below a chimney slot and follow a series of dihedrals to a large ledge. From here scramble 25 feet up to the right to the base of an obvious crack and corner system. Climb this corner and exit at the top, using pitons for aid (A3), to a ledge. The next pitch goes up pleasant rock for 80 feet to the large ledge that traverses the entire face. Take this ledge west to the regular Guides' Wall route.

ROUTE 6. Picnic and Paranoia. II, 5.8. First ascent August 29, 1970, by Jeb Schenck, Mike Henderson, and Fred Long. This route of six pitches ascends the first rock buttress to the right of the right end of Guides' Wall. It lies to the right (east) of a prominent left-arching black chimney. Start by scrambling up to a large chockstone for a belay stance. Climb loose blocks (5.6) and slabs until just left of a steep open-book chimney. Exit from the belay ledge to the right

(east) around an overhang. Now climb a chimney for 10 feet until a crack in the left face of the chimney is visible. Traverse to the crack and climb to a small ledge near the top of the chimney (5.7). Go back into the chimney, then right to a small ledge, and exit around a difficult block with poor protection to a belay ledge. Scramble up and right on easy holds to a large tree and then under the tree (left) to a large ledge. Now climb the nearly vertical slab above on small flakes and crystals for 20 unprotected feet (5.8). Directly above is a 40-foot corner with a large shifting flake on its right side. Climb about one-third of the corner on good protection, and then traverse right to the loose flake. Taking care not to dislodge it, jam up the flake to a ceiling, avoiding the loose blocks as handholds; protection is scarce on this lead. Traverse left to the opposite side of the ceiling. The next pitch is the crux, exiting left around "a horrifying holdless block," using only a hand jam up in the ceiling (5.8). Around the corner are good ledges and the next belay point. Now climb an easy corner and exit right then up to a left-slanting crack. Climb this lieback crack (5.6), then a very thin flake, and traverse right until directly above the belay. Continue up and right on the flake on chicken heads. Continue up and right of an overhanging block until directly right of the block. Climb to the right side on friction and knobs. Exit straight up (5.7) to the end of the climb. On the first ascent pitons were used extensively for protection, including thin horizontals. Descent is to the right (east) along the face.

ROUTE 7. South Face of Guides' Wall. III, 5.9. First ascent July 11, 1971, by Yvon Chouinard, T. M. Herbert, and Juris Krisjansons. This ten-pitch route is located east of Guides' Wall in the middle of the broad south face of Storm Point. It consists of a steep lower section, a middle easy ramp section, and a final very steep and overhanging wall. Start at the middle of the face under some overhangs and climb up and right on a hand traverse (5.7) to a grassy ramp that angles back to the left. From a belay at the end of this ramp, start up a corner and then cross over to the left to another corner and finish the lead (5.7) at an obvious ledge. The third short pitch goes up and right on easy broken rock (4.0). Now climb a shallow rounded crack straight up to an easy broken ledge system that permits access to the large ledges at the top of the steep lower section of the route. The next two pitches take easy ramps first to the right and then back left, passing a flat, blank alcove. The seventh lead (5.9), which was originally marked by a small cairn, goes up and over some overhangs and then angles right over another roof. Once over the top of this roof, traverse left under some more overhangs, and finish by climbing directly up a steep wall to a small belay stance. The next short pitch starts out to the right and goes up a shallow trough, ending on a large sloping ledge. The ninth lead (5.6) goes mostly straight up, following the easiest line to a good belay ledge. The final pitch begins slightly to the left, turns up over a small overhang, and finishes up and right in a broken section. Some 200 feet of scrambling take one to the end of the upper steep section of this route. On the original climb protection to 1½ inches was used. For the descent traverse over to the southwest couloir.

ROUTE 8. *No Friends*. II, 5.9+. First ascent August 1979, by Jim Williams and friend. See *Photo 84*. This route surmounts the initial south buttress of Storm Point well to the east of Guides' Wall. The start of the climb is about 400 feet from the ridge crest, below overhangs at the lower edge of a broad slabby region that is bordered on the left (west) by a large, right-facing corner formation. The first pitch, the most difficult, goes up toward and past these overhangs on the right, passing some small caves, to gain a shallow corner on the face above. Belay partway up this corner, which slants up and left. Climb to the top of the corner, and then cut back right up a major right-facing corner that diagonals up and right. The final lead continues up in cracks and chimneys to the broad ledge that is taken all the way west back onto the southwest ridge and the Guides' Wall route.

ROUTE 9. *South Central Buttress*. II, 5.7. First ascent August 18, 1958, by John Gill and Rick Lloyd. In the center of the basal buttress of the south face of Storm Point is the section directly beneath the large central gully between the southwest and southeast ridges. The upper portion of this section appears smooth and white and is capped by a large overhang. From the Cascade Canyon trail diagonal up tree-covered shelves from the east to the large gully just east of the base of this section of the buttress. An obvious jam crack facing east in the middle of the lower section is the key to this climb and should be located before starting. Traverse an obvious ledge out to a point about 80 feet beneath this crack. Climb directly up for one pitch, making one small zigzag before reaching a belay stance. Friction climb around the corner to the right for 30 feet, then ascend a jam crack. The next lead moves up the center of the face, passing to the right of a small tree, to a large ledge bisecting the buttress. Traverse left (west) on this ledge to a shallow chimney that is capped by an overhang centered 60 feet above in the smooth white face. Using a crack in this chimney, climb directly up to the overhang, and make a difficult traverse to the left (west) to gain a 40-foot crack. This crack leads to a belay ledge just above the overhang. The next ropelength goes directly up enjoyable rock, passing the first roof above on the left and climbing a thin and difficult 30-foot section to an open chimney beneath the large roof capping the buttress. After climbing several feet up from the belay stance, begin a 70-foot, very exposed and delicate hand traverse to the right across a vertical face to the east edge of the buttress wall; move up this edge to a belay. The final pitch zigzags first left, then right, then goes straight up over an overhang, finishing with some slabs to the top of the buttress. Now scramble easily up the central bowl or gully to the southwest ridge, which is followed to the

summit. The rock on this route is excellent.

ROUTE 10. *Rags-to-Riches*. II, 5.7, A1. First ascent August 19, 1989, by Tom Turiano and Harry Hollis. See *Photo 84*. This route on the lower south buttress of Storm Point (0.25 mile east of Guides' Wall) is approached via the Cascade Canyon trail. On the eastern portion of this buttress proceed north up the talus to an obvious gully system in the lower orangish section of the wall. The large triangular section of the wall above the grassy talus is attacked at the center of the base; the route is aimed at the huge black bulge at the top of the buttress. From the top of the gully the first lead goes up a sequence of open or flaring chimneys, past an overhang (5.7), past some trees and a final 5.6 loose wall, to a huge ledge. Walk left past another tree to the large chimney with chockstones that can be seen from the trail near Guides' Wall. Climb the left side of this chimney to the chockstone and fixed piton, then move out on the face to the left to belay at a tree. Next get back into the main chimney to the right and work upward, taking the left fork (5.7 stemming) when it narrows, to the belay above the end of the chimney. A large ledge is then gained and the belay is moved left past a tree. Do not take the obvious flake up from this ledge as it leads to dangerously loose blocks. Instead, climb the crack (5.7) in the wall to the left of a right-facing corner. Climb a 10-foot aid section (a knifeblade piton would be handy here) and on up the easier face above to gain the belay ledge. The fourth lead starts up a crack and continues up classic knobs (5.6) below and to the right of a triangular, right-facing roof and corner. Move on up and back toward this corner (fixed piton here), exiting past a small roof (5.7) onto the ledge near the top of the buttress. The end of this lead is a short distance to the right of the huge black bulge mentioned earlier. For descent hike east down the ramp at the top of the buttress. Rappels may be necessary if the ramp is followed and are certainly needed if one wishes to return to the base of the climb. Numerous trees are available for these rappels.

ROUTE 11. *Skinny Dip*. II, 5.7. First ascent July 10, 1989, by Dave Carman et al. See *Photo 84*. This route lies on the main buttress at the base of the south face of Storm Point, well east of Guides' Wall. Take the Cascade Canyon trail to a small gully about 300 feet past the end of the rapids of the stream and the beginning of the meandering section. Turn up here and scramble toward the start of the climb, on the right (east) of steep, rusty cliffs that appear rotten. Hike up the final scree, boulders, and bushes to the large tree ledge that diagonals up and left to the drainage just below the climb. Scramble up and right of the drainage on ledges with scattered trees, and then traverse left and up to the start of the first pitch. Begin to the right of a rock scar and climb 150 feet on 5.6 rock (two fixed pitons) past a very small tree to a small belay ledge. A short lead on broken and easier rock takes one to a large ledge. Move this belay about 30 feet left to start the third pitch (5.7, 150 feet) up to and beyond two

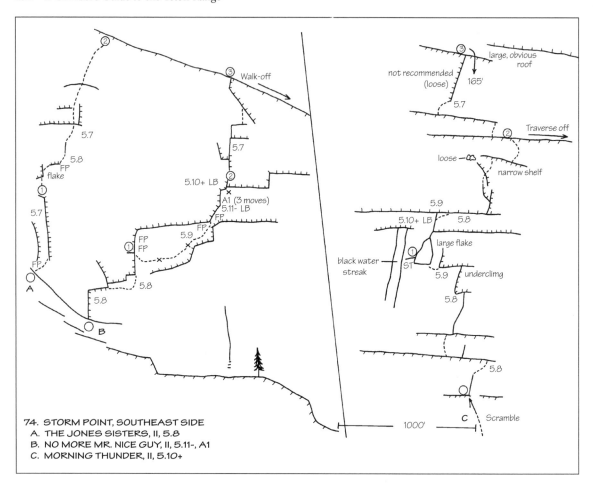

74. STORM POINT, SOUTHEAST SIDE
   A. THE JONES SISTERS, II, 5.8
   B. NO MORE MR. NICE GUY, II, 5.11-, A1
   C. MORNING THUNDER, II, 5.10+

left-facing corners (fixed piton) to a sloping ledge for the belay. The fourth and fifth leads are short (75 feet each) on broken rock (5.6) and lead to the large terrace, a major feature of this route. Move the belay up to a large tree and climb 150 feet on dark, classic Teton rock (5.6) past an old piton to a belay on a ledge sloping off to the right (east). Two hundred feet of easier rock (3.0 and 4.0) up and left takes one to the end of this pleasant route. Descent is made via downclimbing and rappels (75 feet) mostly to the right (east) of the ascent route.

ROUTE 12. The Jones Sisters. II, 5.8. First ascent August 13, 1987, by Paul Gagner and Jim Woodmencey. See *Topo 74*. There are three major ramps (see *Storm Point, Route 6*) that sweep up and left (west) to the crest of the southeast ridge of Storm Point. This two-pitch climb lies on the steep buttress between the middle and the third (most westerly) of these ramps. The top of the buttress, the end of the climb, is the edge of this middle ramp, which diagonals steeply

down to the right (east). From the talus slope with trees at the beginning of the first ramp, take this ramp up and left to the start of this route on the left edge of the buttress, past the left-facing corner of *Route 13*. The climb begins near an old fixed piton below a pair of left-facing corners. Move from the piton to the right to the second corner. Climb this corner (5.7, 160 feet) to a belay at its top. The second pitch goes up to and along the right side of a flake, then right past another fixed piton under a small roof, passing the roof on the right (5.8). Now climb the wall to and past two more overhangs (5.7); finally make an exit onto the ramp edge. For protection take a standard rack.

ROUTE 13. No More Mr. Nice Guy. II, 5.11-, A1. First ascent September 15, 1987, Paul Gagner and Jim Woodmencey. See *Topo 74*. This three-pitch route is located on the same buttress as *Route 12* and the approach is also the same. The climb starts with a left-facing corner (5.8) to a ledge. Move right along this ledge and under a roof to gain a right-facing corner. Belay from halfway up this corner, where two fixed pitons will be found. The wall to the right is undercut by an overhang, and the corner above converts into an overhang above this wall. The second intricate lead starts slightly down and across this wall to the right to a bolt and continues to a second bolt (5.9) and then on and up to the right edge of the overhang (two fixed pitons will be found here), which here converts to a right-facing corner again. Climb this corner (5.11-), using three points of aid (A1) to a third bolt below another overhang. The last part of the lead passes through this overhang, using a lieback (5.10+), to the belay on a small ledge. The final pitch, less difficult, goes up a left-facing corner past two small roofs to a diagonal, left-facing corner, which provides access to the edge of the major, middle ramp. For protection take RPs and camming devices up to 4 inches. Descent is easily made down to the ramp to the right (east).

ROUTE 14. *Morning Thunder.* II, 5.10+. First ascent July 9, 1985, by Paul Gagner and Dan Burgette. See *Topo 74.* As described under *Storm Point, Route 6,* there are three major ramps that sweep up and left (west) to the crest of the southeast ridge of Storm Point. This three-pitch route lies on the left half of the buttress between the first (most easterly) and second of these ramps. It can also be located just to the right of black water stains on the cliff. Approach via the Cascade Canyon trail and turn up just beyond the lowest rockslide coming down from the north. Scramble to the start of the first pitch, a short 5.8 wall leading up to a first ledge and then a second one that slant down from left (west) to right (east). From the second ledge climb into and up a left-facing corner that turns into a small roof. Climb over the roof and up the wall above to another overhang where 5.9 undercling holds permit one to move left to a belay stance on the left side of a large flake. Immediately above this block, the second lead must first pass a very difficult bulge (5.10+) using lieback holds, then continue on to a second overhang; move right along this overhang (5.9) to a break, then up the left-facing corner above, curving left to some loose blocks. This last section is sparsely protected. Finish the pitch by descending slightly to the right on a ledge, then up the face to belay on a large ledge, from which one could exit the route to the right. The third pitch, however, moves left along this ledge and then up to a second ledge to a sequence of two right-facing corners, which contain some loose rock, ending on another large ledge. For protection take devices up to 3½ inches. For descent make one long (165 feet) rappel to easier ground from which one can hike down to the trail.

East Cascade Buttresses (ca. 8,600)
(0.65 mi E of Symmetry Spire)

ROUTE 1. *No Perches Necessary.* I, 5.9. First ascent August 1989, by Renny Jackson and Evelyn Lees; partially climbed September 18, 1987, by Rich Perch and Jim Woodmencey,

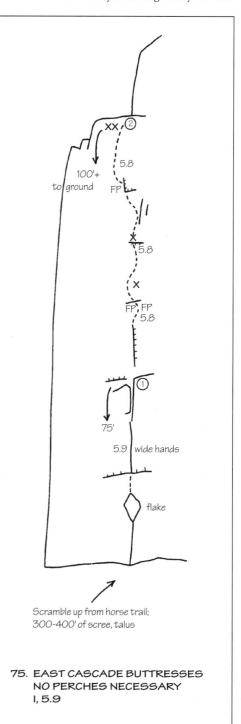

75. EAST CASCADE BUTTRESSES
NO PERCHES NECESSARY
I, 5.9

and in 1988 by Rich Perch, Renny Jackson, and Jim Woodmencey. See *Topo 75* and *Photo 89*. This climb is located on a small buttress up and left (west) of the southwest descent couloir of Baxter's Pinnacle. Leave the horse trail at the north end of the final switchback (just before the trail levels out and crosses the Symmetry Couloir drainage). Scramble up a short distance to the base of the first pitch, a prominent wide crack (5.9). The next pitch consists of excellent face climbing (5.8) past two bolts and a few fixed pitons. A 150-foot rappel from a two-bolt anchor at the top brings one back to the base. Protection to 3½ inches is necessary for the wide crack.

STORM POINT (10,054)

Map: Mount Moran

High above the mouth of Cascade Canyon, this small but conspicuous point gives the finest view in the park of the Cathedral Group—Teewinot, Grand Teton, and Mount Owen. The steep northwest face of Teewinot and the impressive northeast snowfields of Mount Owen are seen to close advantage from Storm Point. This magnificent summit view combined with the ease and shortness of the ascent makes Storm Point a preferred one-day climb from Jenny Lake. During the first ascent in 1931, the determined party started in a steady rain, climbing the Symmetry Couloir with 50 to 100 feet of visibility. By the time that the top of the couloir was reached the rain turned to snow and sleet and the wind was whipping over the divide "with gale velocity." The name, "Storm Point," was thus well earned. In recent years it has been the south side of this peak with its considerable expanse of excellent and challenging rock that has received the most attention. Much of this attention has concentrated on the lower portion of the southwest ridge, known as Guides' Wall, making it one of the most popular rock climbs in the range. In early season the south-facing routes on Storm Point are among the first to be clear of snow and so are especially attractive.

This side of Storm Point persists as something of an embarrassment for a Teton geographer, because in its entirety it still remains inadequately known even though it is almost the closest portion of the range to Jenny Lake, the epicenter of climbing activity. Knowledge seems to have advanced but little in the 33 years since the south side of Storm Point was described as "a real wilderness of broken walls, ridges which disappear, and gullies which lead nowhere" (Willi Unsoeld) and the impression was one of "bewildering confusion" (William Buckingham).

The complex structure of the south side of Storm Point is bounded by two ridges, the southwest and the southeast, both of which rise irregularly in a series of steps to the summit. Between these ridges is a large central gully or bowl; access to the bottom of this bowl is cut off by a con-

siderable wall that extends entirely across the base of the south face. The angle and height of this initial wall or buttress decreases from west to east. Near its eastern end it meets a steep chute that extends downward from the bowl toward the talus slope just above the Cascade Canyon trail. The southwest ridge is a large triangular facet bounded on the right by this central bowl and on the left by the west wall of Storm Point, which rises directly above the main southwest couloir. The crest of the southeast ridge is most easily reached from the east via one of the ramps or shelves that diagonal up to meet it. Above the basal south buttress, the upper west face of the southeast ridge drops very steeply into the large central gully or bowl. This central bowl, which apparently can be easily ascended past its trees and bushes once the lower end of it is gained, leads diagonally below the true upper south face of Storm Point onto the relatively flat section of the upper southwest ridge, several hundred feet below the summit. Between this flat section and the summit is the West Knob, defined by a distinct col on the southwest ridge.

The climbing history of this peak is especially difficult to convey because of the confused state of the terminology in the early years. The term "south face" was applied to various climbs on the southwest ridge and Guides' Wall, "south couloir" was sometimes used for the south bowl and sometimes for the southwest couloir, and by "west face" was at times meant the regular route via the Symmetry Couloir with the finish on the west face. Thus, one cannot at this late date be certain where some of the early climbs took place. Few of the many climbs made on the south side of the peak since 1937 have been carefully described, so not all of the many variations that have probably been climbed are listed here. Attributions of first ascents of routes or variations must be somewhat vague because some of the more recent routes may well have been first done in the enthusiasm of the two decades from 1945 to 1965; at least 65 climbs on the south side were made in those early years. The nonsummit rock climbs are listed separately; see *Cascade Canyon, North Side Rock Climbs*.

CHRONOLOGY

Symmetry Couloir and Upper West Face: August 13, 1931, Fritiof Fryxell, Frank Smith
Southwest Couloir: August 13, 1931, Fritiof Fryxell, Frank Smith (descent); August 1, 1940, C. Grove McCown, Thomson Edwards (ascent)
East Ridge, Symmetry Couloir: August 31, 1931, Arthur Kleinschmidt, or July 23, 1936, Jack Durrance, James Monroe
    var: **East Ridge, Southeast Couloir:** August 31, 1934, Whipple Andrews, Reynold Holmen
    var: **Direct East Ridge:** August 22, 1940, John and Elizabeth Buck

Southeast Ridge: August 17, 1938, Bert Jensen, William Rice, William Bigelow

West Face: June 26, 1948, William McMorris, James Colburn, or July 1, 1963, Peter Gardiner, Robert Williams

South Bowl: August 18, 1948, Martin Murie, Dick Nabors, Desmond Watt, George and John Bascom, or August 24, 1955, William Cropper, Richard Bonker, Brad Pearson, Tom McCalla, or July 31, 1958, Yvon Chouinard, Marliese Braitinger, or August 23, 1965, Richard Reese, Rich Ream

Southwest Ridge: August 3, 1949, Richard Pownall, Art Gilkey

West Ridge: June 30, 1963, Steven Derenzo, Peter Gardiner

ROUTE 1. West Ridge. II, 5.6. First ascent June 30, 1963, by Steven Derenzo and Peter Gardiner. This indistinct ridge is roughly due west of the summit of Storm Point and is separated from the west face (*Route 2*) by a steep couloir or two. It is on the right (south) side of the main southwest couloir (see *Route 3*), which is used to approach the base of this ridge. The climbing on the ridge itself contains little of interest with the exception of one 60-foot step of yellow rock. This is climbed by a very delicate lead on its northwest corner.

ROUTE 2. West Face. II, 5.6. Probable first ascent June 26, 1948, by William McMorris and James Colburn, or July 1, 1963, by Peter Gardiner and Robert Williams. There is a considerable quantity of rock rising above and east of the southwest couloir, which leads from Cascade Canyon to the Ice Point–Symmetry Spire col. Its features are equally obscure as those of the south face of Storm Point, but some general statements can be made. The principal face is the west face of the southwest ridge and culminates at the West Knob of that ridge a few hundred feet below the summit. To the left (north) of this steep face lie at least two ill-defined ridges and two steep couloirs leading up in the general direction of Ice Point. More than one climb has been made on the main west face, but detailed information is available only for the 1963 ascent described later.

In early season the lower end of the southwest couloir funnels into a series of vertical waterfalls a short distance above the Cascade Canyon trail. Avoid these by zigzagging up the slabby slope east of the falls, angling west to the top of the highest one. Hike about 300 feet up the couloir past a slimy vertical chimney that drains the shallow bowl underneath the west face. Continue about 100 feet up the couloir until an exposed ledge is found leading back south to the top of the slimy chimney. From this point climb a crumbly red-rock chute up and left. Continue in the same direction past the end of the chute, eventually reaching a grassy platform only 50 feet from the left (north) edge of the west face. After a 50-foot scramble upward, a full ropelength of steep rock gives access to a broad tree-covered ledge angling slightly back across the face to the south. Just above the right (south) end of the ledge, reached after some bushwhacking and a delicate traverse, a deep fissure angles up and back to the left (north). Follow this general line for about two pitches to the top of the face, and join one of the variations on the upper southwest ridge below the West Knob. Climb over the West Knob, staying on or near the crest, on enjoyable knobby rock, in places considerably exposed on either side.

ROUTE 3. Southwest Couloir. II, 4.0. First descent August 13, 1931, by Fritiof Fryxell and Frank Smith; first ascent August 1, 1940, by C. Grove McCown and Thomson Edwards. An alternative to the direct eastern approach to the Ice Point–Symmetry Spire saddle is the large southwest couloir, which leads to this same saddle from the west via Cascade Canyon. Hike into the canyon on the trail until a large talus fan issuing from the southwest couloir is reached. This talus fan is immediately west of the prominent southwest ridge of Storm Point. At the top of this talus fan, the bottom of the couloir is blocked by a short cliff band, which can be passed at its left edge by a series of ledges containing trees, bushes, and dirt. Once above this section, the couloir is followed without difficulty to the saddle. From the saddle, follow the upper part of *Route 10*.

ROUTE 4. Southwest Ridge. III, 5.8. First ascent August 3, 1949, by Richard Pownall and Art Gilkey. See *Topo 73* and *Photos 83* and *84*. The southwest ridge of Storm Point has the exceptionally attractive combination of easy access and excellent rock. These features have made the routes and variations on this ridge some of the most popular in the park. Although rarely done in its entirety, this 2,000-foot ridge is an enjoyable outing. The first six pitches, which surmount the difficult initial pyramidal buttress now known as Guides' Wall, are often done as a separate rock climb. The approach to and the description of this initial section are given above (see *Cascade Canyon, North Side Rock Climbs, Route 1*) and will not be repeated here.

From the top of Guides' Wall, at the end of the sixth pitch, it is still a long climb to the summit of Storm Point. Surmount the difficulties of the formidable wall above by using a series of downsloping slabs that cut across the face diagonally up to the right. After two pitches a Wall Street–type ledge leads around the corner to easy ground. From here to the summit the climbing is easier, and a route can be found along or beside the meandering crest. About 400 feet below the summit there is a pinnacle that is passed by a vertical 80-foot lead on the face to the left of the pinnacle. The uppermost portion of the ridge leads almost due east to the summit. *Time: 11½ to 12¼ hours from Jenny Lake.* See *American Alpine Journal*, 8, no. 1 (1951), pp. 176–181.

ROUTE 5. South Bowl. II, 5.1. First ascent uncertain, perhaps August 18, 1948, by Martin Murie, Dick Nabors, Desmond Watt, and George and John Bascom, or August 24, 1955, by William Cropper, Richard Bonker, Brad Pearson, and Tom McCalla, or July 31, 1958, by Yvon Chouinard and Marliese Braitinger, or August 23, 1965, by Richard Reese and Rich Ream. The main south bowl or gully in the upper south face of Storm Point is composed of two sections separated by some steep rock. The lower section is just above the initial rock buttress that extends along the base of the entire south face of Storm Point. The upper section holds a tree-covered shelf that diagonals from lower right to upper left to meet the upper end of the southwest ridge. Routes have been made in this region by climbing one or both of these sections. Access to the lower section of the gully apparently is possible via climbing the broken cliffs just below the lowest point of the gully near its eastern end. Once these cliffs have been passed and the lower section of the bowl has been gained, one can traverse left (west) all the way out to the crest of the southwest ridge.

However, to continue this route one must gain entry into the upper section of the bowl. This can apparently be done via either the left (west) edge of the lower section, or a large chimney in the right (east) edge, or more directly up a prominent, slanting chimney-crack system that leads all the way up the rock wall above. An alternative approach into this upper section is provided by the lowest of the three ramps that angle in from the east toward the crest of the southeast ridge. Once on the main shelf in this upper section one can scramble west and up along the shelf to its end at the uppermost southwest ridge. Follow that route to the summit.

ROUTE 6. Southeast Ridge. II, 5.6, A1. First ascent August 17, 1938, by Bert Jensen, William Rice, and William Bigelow. The length and difficulty of this route depend on both the point at which the crest is attained and the closeness with which it is followed to the summit. Many climbs have been made on the southeast side of Storm Point, but perhaps no two have been identical, and perhaps none has followed exactly the ridge crest from the base to the summit. It is not easy even to define the beginning of the ridge, which is lost in the basal buttress of the south side of Storm Point.

There are three major shelves or ramps that diagonal from lower right to upper left (west) across the southeast face to meet the southeast ridge. The southeast ridge can be said to have its true beginning just above the lowest and farthest west of these shelves. If followed westward, this lowest ramp gives access to the bottom of the gully in the central bowl. The next shelf up is easily gained from the talus above the Cascade Canyon trail, and, by moving up and out to the left (south) past a few trees, one can reach the ridge crest. However, this second ramp ends abruptly at the

west face of the southeast ridge. The difficulties of the steep step in the ridge above this bench are not known but are probably considerable. One can progress toward the summit by climbing out to the west, where apparently a narrow couloir will be found leading downward to the central tree gully or bowl, which is followed out to the upper part of the southwest ridge.

The third, highest, and largest of the ramps provides the access route most often used. The beginning of this shelf is just left (west) of a prominent black rock wall immediately above the talus slope above the trail. Follow this shelf west to the ridge crest, directly below a large overhang, which is avoided by traversing around the corner to the left on easy ledges. This traverse can be continued a considerable distance before one turns up to regain the ridge. Or, more directly, one can turn up after one traverse lead, regaining the ridge just above the overhang. If this alternative is chosen, continue up the ridge to the base of a pitch, the top of which overhangs; this is the most difficult pitch of the ridge. Aid climbing (A1) may be necessary to climb the first part of this pitch to the point where the overhang begins. Then traverse left 6 feet to a small ledge from which a traverse left on small holds around a corner leads to easier ground. Keep somewhat to the right (east) of the actual crest, and ascend the remainder of the ridge, scrambling most of the way. *Time: 6½ to 8¼ hours* from Jenny Lake. See *American Alpine Journal,* 3, no. 3 (1939), p. 363.

ROUTE 7. East Ridge, Symmetry Couloir. II, 4.0. First ascent August 31, 1931, by Arthur Kleinschmidt, or July 23, 1936, by Jack Durrance and James Monroe. See *Photo 89.* The east side of Storm Point is a hodgepodge of couloirs, cliffs, trees, and talus south of the standard Symmetry Couloir route (*Route 8*). To climb this side of the peak many variations are possible, and because there have been several climbs in this region in recent years, it is likely that most of these have been explored either intentionally or inadvertently; the route described here appears to have been the one followed by the first-ascent party. Take the standard route (see *Cascade Canyon*) to gain the Symmetry Couloir. Climb this couloir to the first large snowfield. Instead of continuing into the upper section of the main couloir and snowfield, cut out to the left (southwest) into one of two smaller, less well-defined couloirs. The first and larger couloir leads upward toward the Ice Point–Storm Point col from which the upper part of *Route 8* can be followed to the summit. This approach to the col is slightly more difficult than the standard route described below.

Variation: East Ridge, Southeast Couloir. II, 4.0. First ascent August 31, 1934, by Whipple Andrews and Reynold Holmen. The broad east side of Storm Point can also be reached using a major couloir on the southeast side of the peak. Hike up the Cascade Canyon trail about 0.3 mile above the top of Hidden Falls, beyond the usual turnoffs to the Symmetry Couloir, to a large, open talus slope leading up to the first cliffs of the southeast side of Storm Point. A small creek (may be dry in late season) forms the west edge of this sometimes bushy talus slope and leads directly to the large couloir that is utilized to pass this cliff band. Ascend this couloir, which is plainly visible from Jenny Lake, in a northwesterly direction for about 200 feet until it opens out to the left. (The narrow right-hand continuation of this couloir, walled vertically on the right [northeast], provides access to the bush- and tree-covered northeast slope of Storm Point utilized by *Route 7*.) Leave the couloir to the left and scramble up for several hundred feet until past a major eastern buttress. The original climb apparently cut back right (north) onto the upper eastern slope after passing to the south of this buttress. The summit is then attained directly from the east. One might also continue due west near the extreme south edge of the upper couloir to a small notch in the southeast ridge. If one proceeds all the way to this notch, some steep rock above the notch must be climbed in order to reach the summit.

Variation: Direct East Ridge. II, 5.1. First ascent August 22, 1940, by John and Elizabeth Buck. Both *Route 7* and the *East Ridge, Southeast Couloir variation* bypass the lower two-thirds of the east ridge of Storm Point. This lower section is unattractive, however, because it consists of trees interspersed with short, broad cliff bands, without anything like a clear line. It forms the left (south) boundary of the main Symmetry Couloir. The beginning of the ridge can be gained from the southeast or directly from the east by working up through the bushes, trees, and cliff bands south of the main stream draining the Symmetry Couloir. Scramble up, partly among the trees, and pass the head of the southeast couloir, mentioned in the preceding variation, still among trees, until the moderately steep rock due east of the summit is reached. Climb the center of this face to the summit.

ROUTE 8. ☞*Symmetry Couloir and Upper West Face.* II, 4.0. First ascent August 13, 1931, by Fritiof Fryxell and Frank Smith. For the route to the saddle between Symmetry Spire and Ice Point see *Cascade Canyon*. From the trees at the saddle, proceed around the right (west) side of Ice Point on a faint trail along some obvious ledges just below the cliffs of Ice Point. This will require a descent of a few feet from the level of the saddle. From the Ice Point–Storm Point col climb directly up the north ridge of Storm Point for about 50 feet to a very wide ledge that leads around to the right (west) side. After one mounts the 20-foot corner at the end of the ledge, the easiest way to the summit, now only about 200 feet above, is a zigzag route through the west chimneys. It is also possible to continue traversing around the peak and reach the summit from the south or even from the east. On descent inexperienced climbers may wish to make a short rappel. *Time: 4 to 6 hours* from Jenny Lake; *60*

to 90 minutes from the summit of Ice Point. See *Appalachia*, 18, no. 4 (December 1931), pp. 388–408, illus.

ICE POINT (9,920+)

Map: Mount Moran

This small pinnacle has an enjoyable, short, and exposed summit ridge, which, usually combined with a traverse to Storm Point or Symmetry Spire, or both, provides a pleasant conditioning climb at the beginning of a climbing season. The small summit affords an excellent closeup view of the south side of Symmetry Spire. Climbed on the same day as Storm Point, the names of these two peaks were given by the first-ascent party in recognition of the weather of the day—rain, wind, snow, and sleet—which made the ascent significantly more difficult than is normal in dry conditions. On July 23, 1931, an attempt by Anderson and Inez M. Hilding and David Tilderquist failed only 40 feet from the summit on the northwest ridge. The approach for Ice Point is the same as for the regular routes on Storm Point or Symmetry Spire; see *Cascade Canyon* for a description of the route to and up the Symmetry Couloir from Jenny Lake.

CHRONOLOGY

Northwest Ridge: August 13, 1931, Fritiof Fryxell, Frank Smith
Southwest Ridge: August 13, 1931, Fritiof Fryxell, Frank Smith (descent); August 30, 1948, John Holyoke, John Churchill, or June 21, 1949, Robert Brooke, Pete Brown (ascent)
    var: July 22, 1960, Bill Wentworth, Alan Feltman
North Face: August 8, 1952, Gary Driggs, David Sowles, Jim Fisk, Marcia Newell
East Chimney: August 12, 1952, William Byrd, S. Blain St. Clair
South Face: September 5, 1953, Dmitri Nabokov, Robert Kubie, Dave Arnold

ROUTE 1. *Southwest Ridge.* II, 4.0. First descent August 13, 1931, by Fritiof Fryxell and Frank Smith; first ascent either August 30, 1948, by John Holyoke and John Churchill, or June 21, 1949, by Robert Brooke and Pete Brown. From the Ice Point–Storm Point saddle a series of large downsloping steps leads up to the right directly to the summit. Some routefinding ability is required but the route is nowhere difficult.

Variation: II, 5.4. First ascent July 22, 1960, by Bill Wentworth and Alan Feltman. The southwest ridge can be attained from the east using the large eastern couloir. Follow the standard Symmetry Couloir approach up past the initial waterfall to the main snowfield in the couloir. Instead of proceeding up this snowfield (in late season, a loose scree slope with trail) toward the Ice Point–Symmetry saddle, cut left into the next large couloir to the south, which heads toward the Storm Point–Ice Point saddle. The talus and rock in the couloir are easily climbed for 300 feet until one can diagonal right onto a brushy ridge where the roped climbing begins. Climb this ridge to a platform, then right to and up an obvious jam crack, finishing at a tree on a second platform ledge. Move right and up along a ramp and then over a small overhang. One can now climb right along the southwest ridge to the summit.

ROUTE 2. South Face. II, 5.4, A1. First ascent September 5, 1953, by Dmitri Nabokov, Robert Kubie, and Dave Arnold. This route lies to the right (east) of the southwest ridge. The south face consists of downsloping slabs with some loose rock as well. One section involved a piton for aid.

ROUTE 3. East Chimney. II, 5.6. First ascent August 12, 1952, by William Byrd and S. Blain St. Clair. From the Ice Point–Symmetry Spire saddle, traverse out past the north face on the one large, obvious ledge to the base of the prominent east chimney, and climb this to the summit.

ROUTE 4. North Face. II, 5.4. First ascent August 8, 1952, by Gary Driggs, David Sowles, Jim Fisk, and Marcia Newell. This is an alternative route from the Ice Point–Symmetry Spire col. Traverse out on the large, obvious ledge near the base of the face to a point below and somewhat to the right (west) of the summit. Climb the face above, past a small tree, meeting the knife-edge northwest ridge only about 30 feet west of the summit block. The downsloping holds are intermixed with some vegetated sections.

ROUTE 5. ☞Northwest Ridge. II, 4.0. First ascent August 13, 1931, by Fritiof Fryxell and Frank Smith. For a description of the route to the Ice Point–Symmetry Spire saddle, see *Cascade Canyon.* From the saddle this route follows the obvious ridge curling upward to the summit of Ice Point. The first abrupt step in this ridge can be climbed via a small chimney just to the right (west) of the crest, but one can avoid this section by traversing out on a ledge on the left flank of the ridge to a series of easy ledges that lead back to the crest above this step. From this point to the summit closely follow the knife-edge crest. On descent no rappels are required. To climb Storm Point the same day, as is easily and commonly done, descend this ridge to the small notch where the ridge turns northward to the Ice Point–Symmetry Spire saddle. From this notch it is an easy matter to descend south to the Ice Point–Storm Point col via the southwest ridge. To approach the base of this ridge from Storm Point, a trail can be easily followed around the west base of Ice Point from the Storm Point–Ice Point saddle. *Time: 4½ to 5½ hours* from Jenny Lake; *75 minutes* from the summit of Storm Point. See *Appalachia,* 18, no. 4 (December 1931), pp. 388–408, illus.; *Trail and Timberline,* no. 447 (March 1956), pp. 47–48.

HANGOVER PINNACLE (CA. 8,800)
(0.3 mi SE of Symmetry)

Map: Mount Moran

This small but distinctive pinnacle is on the right (north) edge of the main east couloir that leads to the saddle between Ice Point and Symmetry Spire. Hangover Pinnacle is about one-quarter of the way up the couloir and is easily seen after one enters the area of the main snowfield above the initial shoulder, which is above the top edge of the waterfall. The pinnacle, composed of excellent solid rock, has significant overhangs on all sides except the north. It is easily approached via the Jenny Lake boat and a short hike and achieved considerable early popularity as a rock climb. More recently it has been eclipsed by Baxter's Pinnacle, which is an even shorter hike. With a top rope, various more difficult routes have been worked out starting on July 15, 1951 (Robert Merriam, Willi Unsoeld, Leigh Ortenburger); all four faces have yielded climbs of interest. For those interested in photographs, it is possible to establish an impressive Tyrolean traverse from the pinnacle to the slope of Symmetry Spire, rising above.

CHRONOLOGY

North Face: August 1948, Richard Pownall, Mickey Thomas, Leigh Ortenburger
Southwest Ridge: August 20, 1956, Richard Pownall, Marian Macy, Van Hellar

ROUTE 1. Southwest Ridge. II, 5.6, A2. First ascent August 20, 1956, by Richard Pownall, Marian Macy, and Van Hellar. Aid was used to lead and climb this overhanging ridge.

ROUTE 2. ☞North Face. I, 5.4. First ascent August 1948, by Richard Pownall, Mickey Thomas, and Leigh Ortenburger. From the main Symmetry Couloir some scrambling is required to reach the notch separating Hangover Pinnacle from the main mass of Symmetry Spire. From the notch the route lies up the downsloping slabs of the north face and angles left to reach the final summit block from the east. For descent, a rappel is necessary down either the regular route of ascent or the spectacular south face. *Time: 3 hours* from Jenny Lake.

BAXTER'S PINNACLE (CA. 8,000)
(0.65 mi E of Symmetry)

Map: Mount Moran

This minor spire has a history unique in the Tetons and perhaps in the United States. For ten years after its discovery and first ascent in 1947 by Baxter and Ramm-Ericson, it was lost. At the time of the first edition of this book, the note in the *Sierra Club Bulletin* concerning the first ascent was known among Teton climbers, and queries had been made of members of the first-ascent party as to its location. Several searching parties climbed some minor points in the area around Storm Point and Symmetry Spire, but it remained for John Gill, Frederick Lloyd, and Douglas Jefferson to rediscover the pinnacle on July 25, 1957. The second ascent was made a few days later on July 29 by Yvon Chouinard and John Lowry. Originally named in 1947 as Stanford Pinnacle, in honor of the school of the first-ascent party, the current name, while appropriate, was attached by editorial happenstance. The 1965 edition of this guidebook was published by the Sierra Club and a member of its editorial staff, a friend of Alfred Baxter, saw fit to change the name after the manuscript had been submitted for publication. Such is the crooked historical course of toponymy.

The approach to this small, distinctively yellow pinnacle requires so little time that any of its upper routes is entirely appropriate for an afternoon rock climb. It is an enjoyable, short, yet distinctly difficult climb to a genuine summit, which requires a rappel to leave. These features, together with the increased emphasis in recent years on rock climbing rather than mountaineering, has led Baxter's Pinnacle to become the third most popular climb in the Teton Range. The nearby small ridge east of Baxter's Pinnacle has also been climbed at least once.

Baxter's Pinnacle is located on the second lowest (counting from the east) of the south ridges of Cube Point, just above a large open talus slope that extends almost all the way down to the trail on the west side of Jenny Lake. For the approach, walk north from the west shore boat dock on the Valley Trail a short distance, about 0.25 mile, to the horse bypass trail (with sign) leading off to the west. Take this wide trail about 0.5 mile to a grove of trees where the trail makes a right-angle bend back to the left (south). From this point the south ridge of Baxter's Pinnacle can be seen rising above to the north. A climbers' trail turns off here and leads up through scree and talus to the start of the South Ridge route. The horse trail can also be reached by hiking south on the Valley Trail, starting at the south String Lake parking lot. The southwest couloir leading down from the notch behind the pinnacle is the standard route of descent. Great care must be taken in this couloir, because there are likely to be other climbers below in the couloir and much of the rock is loose. An alternative scheme for descent is to scramble a short distance up from the notch onto the ridge above and descend the far (northeast) side to a talus slope, which will bring one back to the horse trail.

CHRONOLOGY

Upper South Face: June 26, 1947, Alfred Baxter, Ulf Ramm-Ericson
Gill: July 10, 1958, John Gill, Gordon Sutton

East Face: July 18, 1958, Yvon Chouinard, David Craft; first free ascent ca. July 17, 1975, Jeb Schenck, partner
South Ridge: July 27, 1958, Barry Corbet, Robert French
   var: **Gray Ramp:** September 8, 1968, Peter Koedt, William Miller
   var: **Seizure Disorder:** September 5, 1989, Jim Springer, Lanny Johnson
Northwest Corner: August 7, 1958, Yvon Chouinard, Robert Kamps
North Face: August 11, 1958, Richard Pownall, Paul Kenworthy; July 19, 1960, Royal Robbins, Joe Fitschen, Robert Toepel, Kenneth Weeks (first free ascent)
Northeast Ridge: August 1959, Barry Corbet, Julie Peterson
Southwest Face: early July 1963, Rick Medrick, Barry Corbet, Sterling Neale
Howard: June 9, 1971, George Hurley, Dennis Wignall
West Face I: July 1971, Yvon Chouinard, Juris Krisjansons
West Face II: September 7, 1978, Yvon Chouinard, Mike Munger

ROUTE 1. West Face I. II, 5.8. First ascent July 1971, by Yvon Chouinard and Juris Krisjansons. The west face of Baxter's Pinnacle rises from the southwest gully, which is the standard, if unpleasant, descent route. From the col behind the pinnacle at the top of the gully a large ledge system cuts horizontally across this west face over to the base of the upper south face. From a point almost directly below the summit, a second ledge harboring a flake will be seen about halfway up from the gully to this ledge system. Climb directly up from the descent gully on a dark, high-angle face to this lower ledge, just to the right of this flake, and continue up the face (5.7) to gain the main ledge system. The second lead (5.8) goes slightly left and then up a 2½-inch slanting jam crack to the prominent horn on the northwest ridge; this same horn is attained from the col on the Northwest Corner route (see *Route 11,* later). From the horn climb directly up to the summit. For protection a device of 2½ inches width is useful.

ROUTE 2. West Face II. II, 5.10. First ascent September 7, 1978, by Yvon Chouinard and Mike Munger. This route starts in the southwest descent gully about 200 feet up from the base of the South Ridge route. Climb (4.0) up to the west base of an obvious fin on the crest of the south ridge. The first lead, on the left (west) side of the fin, goes up a left-facing corner (5.8) past some fixed pitons to a belay ledge. The second pitch moves left to a smooth right-facing corner, which is climbed (5.10) to its top. The next lead also stays out on the face to the left of the regular South Ridge route up to the crest of the ridge. An easier pitch takes one to the base of the upper south face where a descending traverse to the left of the summit block takes one to the west face crack (5.8) leading up toward the horn on the northwest ridge. From the horn and bolt (may have been removed) move out right and up to the summit instead of climbing straight up.

ROUTE 3. *Southwest Face.* II, 5.8. First ascent early July 1963, by Rick Medrick, Barry Corbet, and Sterling Neale. This three-pitch route starts out of the southwest descent gully, as do *Routes 1* and *2*, and ascends the southwest face of the south ridge. The first pitch begins in the first large open book to the west of the crest of the south ridge, proceeds up about 30 feet toward the large overhang that caps the book, and then traverses left 15 feet on thin holds (5.8) to a belay stance on a downsloping ledge where anchors are difficult. The next lead (5.8) goes up 20 feet to a loose block and then traverses slightly down and left for 15 feet around a bulge to a crack leading diagonally back up to the right for another 15 feet; now climb back left and up across the face, stepping around a corner to an easier crack that is followed, amid loose rock, for 40 feet to the belay. The final pitch turns left around a corner and continues up a short but strenuous overhang to the main west face ledge system at the base of the summit block. One can continue to the summit via *Route 1* or *5*.

ROUTE 4. *Gill.* II, 5.10-. First ascent July 10, 1958, by John Gill and Gordon Sutton. See *Topo 76*. This difficult variation of the regular route ascends the face to the *left* of the regular direct-aid crack of the south face of the final tower. Move up on thin holds about 20 feet, past a bolt, and then diagonal to the flake to the right. Follow the regular route to the summit.

ROUTE 5. *Upper South Face.* II, 5.6, A1, or II, 5.9. First ascent June 26, 1947, by Alfred Baxter and Ulf Ramm-Ericson; first free ascent August 1957, by John Gill and partner. See *Topo 76* and *Photos 85* and *89*. From the talus slope south of Baxter's Pinnacle, the notch separating the pinnacle from the remainder of the ridge above is reached by ascending the southwest couloir (loose rock) on the left (west) side of the pinnacle. From this notch a series of ledges leads without difficulty around the exposed west face to the small notch at the base of the upper south face of the final yellow tower.

The first- and second-ascent parties, and many parties since 1957, have used aid in the obvious crack in the wall above this notch in order to reach the easier rock leading to the large flake above and to the right and then the lieback that leads to the summit. The initial part of the first pitch is the most difficult, and most people find that dropping down to the right (east) a few feet and then climbing the wall directly up to the flake is the easiest way. It still requires

a few 5.9 moves, however. From the flake, climb up and left, liebacking up a steep ramp past old fixed pins, a maneuver that is fortunately somewhat easier than it appears. The final short vertical wall to the summit is exposed. For the descent, a summit tree furnishes a suitable point for rappelling (75 feet, partly free) into the notch on the north side. Descend the southwest couloir back to the base of the pinnacle. *Use great care* in this descent because there are likely to be other climbers below in the couloir and much of the rock is loose. *Time: 3¼ to 5 hours* from Jenny Lake. See *Sierra Club Bulletin,* 33, no. 3 (March 1948), p. 121.

ROUTE 6. *South Ridge.* II, 5.6. First ascent July 27, 1958, by Barry Corbet and Robert French. See *Topo 76* and *Photos 85* and *89*. This popular route is perhaps the most enjoyable climb on the pinnacle and certainly contains the most pitches. It starts at the base of the well-defined lower south ridge of the pinnacle at the upper end of the talus slope and stays on the crest for about five pitches, until the final tower is reached, at which point the Upper South Face route *(Route 5)*, is followed to the summit. Begin the route by climbing up from the base in a gully. From the top of the gully continue some 100 feet of 4.0 and 5.1 climbing to gain the ridge crest. The second pitch is usually climbed to the right of the crest, past some fixed pitons and up a small right-facing corner (5.6), or more difficult thin cracks (5.8) to the right of the crest can also be used to reach the belay on the crest. The third lead can now be made either directly up the very exposed crest (5.6) followed by a hand crack (5.6) or in the obvious chimney on the right (5.6, fixed pitons). The final lead to the base of the summit block is easier, either on the crest or scrambling along near the crest to the right. Climb the summit block as in *Route 5*.

Variation: Gray Ramp. II, 5.9. First ascent September 8, 1968, by Peter Koedt and William Miller. On the first pitch of the South Ridge route, follow a gray ramp below and to the left (west) of the blade of the ridge crest for one pitch.

Variation: Seizure Disorder. II, 5.10. First ascent September 5, 1989, by Jim Springer and Lanny Johnson. See *Topo 76*. After the first pitch up from the base of the south ridge in a gully, this difficult one-pitch variation starts on the southeast-facing wall to the right of the ridge crest near a large tree. Climb this wall to the left of a large detached pedestal toward and past a diagonal crack, moving right and up past two bolts (5.10) to a ledge. This brings one to the base of the third pitch of the standard South Ridge route.

ROUTE 7. *Howard.* II, 5.8. First ascent June 9, 1971, by George Hurley and Dennis Wignall. This route stays on the east side of the south ridge to the base of the summit block. The first pitch (130 feet, 5.1) starts below and to the right of the tree at the start of the South Ridge route. Follow an obvious lieback-jam crack for 30 feet; continue up, angling right to easy (4.0) ledges to belay at the base of a short headwall. The next lead (130 feet) proceeds up and slightly right in the obvious crack past a ledge with a large tree; go

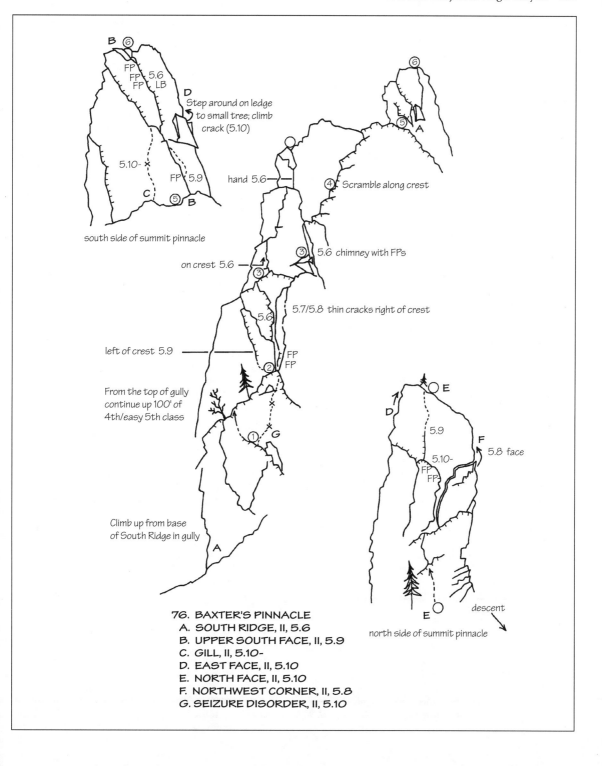

B ⑥
FP
FP 5.6
FP LB
D
Step around on ledge
to small tree; climb
crack (5.10)

5.10- ✗
FP 5.9
C
⑤
B
hand 5.6

south side of summit pinnacle

⑥
⑤
A
④ Scramble along crest

on crest 5.6
③
③ 5.6 chimney with FPs

5.6
5.7/5.8 thin cracks right of crest

left of crest 5.9

From the top of gully
continue up 100' of
4th/easy 5th class

②
FP
FP

① G

Climb up from base
of South Ridge in gully
A

D
E
5.9
F
5.8 face
5.10-
FP
FP

E

descent

north side of summit pinnacle

76. BAXTER'S PINNACLE
A. SOUTH RIDGE, II, 5.6
B. UPPER SOUTH FACE, II, 5.9
C. GILL, II, 5.10-
D. EAST FACE, II, 5.10
E. NORTH FACE, II, 5.10
F. NORTHWEST CORNER, II, 5.8
G. SEIZURE DISORDER, II, 5.10

right of the tree to and across more easy (4.0) ledges for the belay at another headwall. The third pitch (150 feet, 5.8) ascends the crack in this headwall into and up the rotten dihedral above to a large belay ledge. Next traverse left (west) for 20 feet to an obvious lieback-jam crack in the wall; climb this crack to easy ledges (4.0) and trees on the upper portion of the South Ridge route. The next two leads stay on the right side of the ridge crest up to the summit block. The summit is attained by the standard *Route 5*.

ROUTE 8. East Face. I, 5.6, A1, or II, 5.10. First ascent July 18, 1958, by Yvon Chouinard and David Craft; first free ascent about July 17, 1975, by Jeb Schenck and partner. See *Topo 76*. Start from the base of the south face of the final tower and climb to the flake, as in *Route 5*. From the flake, traverse around to the right to the east face and climb the steep, short face above. Small protection (RPs) devices are useful in the hard section.

ROUTE 9. Northeast Ridge. II, 5.9. First ascent August 1959, by Barry Corbet and Julie Peterson. Start as in *Route 8*, traversing around to the right (north) from the flake, but continue past the east face to the northeast ridge, which is climbed to the summit.

ROUTE 10. North Face. II, 5.6, A2, or II, 5.10. First ascent August 11, 1958, by Richard Pownall and Paul Kenworthy; first free ascent July 19, 1960, by Royal Robbins, Joe Fitschen, Robert Toepel, and Kenneth Weeks. See *Topo 76* and *Photo 86*. This route starts from the main col separating the pinnacle from the mountain and stays near the center, or slightly left of the center, of the north face. The obvious crack, which parallels *Route 11* and then cuts left into a right-angle alcove, is utilized for either aid or difficult free climbing. Leave the alcove to the right in order to reach easier free climbing above.

ROUTE 11. Northwest Corner. II, 5.8. First ascent August 7, 1958, by Yvon Chouinard and Robert Kamps. See *Topo 76* and *Photo 86*. Start from the main col at the base of the north face where a prominent, wide crack goes first up and then horizontally out to the right (northwest) corner. Climb this crack using jam holds and hand traverse out to the corner. Step up on top of the flake at the corner, and climb the face above (5.8); then angle slightly to the left and directly up the corner to the summit. A protection bolt for this lead may have been removed and/or replaced.

CUBE POINT (9,600+)*(0.4 mi E of Symmetry Spire)*

Map: Mount Moran

This is the prominent tower at the lower end of the east ridge of Symmetry Spire. See *Photo 89*. It is separated from the spire by a deep, sharp notch. Cube Point furnishes a fine summit and an interesting, easily approached, short one-day climb. The first climbs of this peak are a bit confused. The 1938 party (Fralick, Plumley, Plumley), after they found no evidence of a previous party, claimed the first

ascent. Originally it was thought that they had named the peak after the cubical shape of the summit block. However, after a more recent discussion with Jack Fralick, it has been determined that they were simply living on cube steaks purchased at the Jenny Lake store at the time. In the years since, however, a note has turned up among the summit register records: "August 5, 1937, Norton Nelson and Carroll Saffell. We came up the gully just to the south. . . ." This note, however, presumably was not found on the highest point, else the 1938 party would have reported it. The east ridge has become popular, especially for guided climbs, because it affords an enjoyable climb on moderate but exposed rock. To approach Cube Point, take the climbers' trail into Hanging Canyon. Just below Ribbon Cascade, the falls below Arrowhead Pool, cross the stream to the broad talus cone on the south side. Cube Point rises directly above.

CHRONOLOGY

East Couloir: June 25, 1938, Harold and William Plumley, Jack Fralick; (partial) August 5, 1937, Norton Nelson, Carroll Saffell
    var: [probable] June 29, 1957, Dean Millsap, M. W. Echo, Sam Mitchell, Anthony Lagani, S. Bostwick

West Chimney: 1939, John and George Holyoke (descent); July 6, 1940, Paul Petzoldt, Joseph Hawkes, Bernhard Nebel (ascent)
    var: [probable] July 12, 1960, Charles Sanders, Cora Sanders, A. Maram (descent)

East Ridge: [probable] August 17, 1945, Joseph and Edith Stettner, John Speck, Alan Stiles, Rex Parks, B. Hicks, Anna Gay, Betty Burno, Elv Bushman, Mary Tremaine, T. A. Campbell; [possible] July 1, 1938, Carl Heeschen, Clyde Havenstot, Robert Rynot

South Ridge: June 15, 1958, Walter Gove, Karl Ross, or July 16, 1959, Barry Corbet, Robert French
    var: September 4, 1966, Barry Corbet, Chuck Satterfield
    var: Wall of Leo: July 24 and August 10, 1990, Leo Larson, Jim Woodmencey, Brent Finley, George Montopoli

North Face: July 15, 1971, Mark Chapman, Bruce Patterson

ROUTE 1. West Chimney. II, 5.1. First descent in 1939, by John and George Holyoke; first ascent July 6, 1940, by Paul Petzoldt, Joseph Hawkes, and Bernhard Nebel. See *Photo 87*. From the vicinity of Arrowhead Pool, go to the notch between Cube Point and Symmetry Spire. Just left (north) of the notch is a steep-walled chimney or couloir that provides a chockstone route up through the first cliffs. From the top of this chimney, scramble along the narrow ridge to the summit. No rappel is actually needed to descend this chimney, although it may be desired.

Variation: II, 5.1. Probable first descent July 12, 1960, by Charles and Cora Sanders and A. Maram. The notch immediately west of Cube Point can also be reached from the south. To enter the couloir that leads to this notch, start the climb as in the usual route up the Symmetry Couloir (see *Cascade Canyon*). On the beginning of that route, after climbing the short cliff and cutting back left along the top of this cliff, cross a small stream. This stream drains the two couloirs. Ascend the left (western) of these two couloirs up to the notch in the ridge.

ROUTE 2. South Ridge. II, 5.4. First ascent June 15, 1958, by Walter Gove and Karl Ross, or July 16, 1959, by Barry Corbet and Robert French; on June 15, 1938, Jack Fralick, Harold and William Plumley attempted this side of the peak but retreated from a point on the lower east ridge. The main south ridge of Cube Point lies between the two couloirs drained by the stream that one crosses in the short traverse left at the top of the initial cliff of the regular route up the Symmetry Couloir. Several climbs have been made on the south side of the pinnacle, but the exact location of the routes is not accurately known. The 1959 ascent started by scrambling 500 feet up into a bowl of white rock on the right side of one of the south ridges; this ridge may have been the one described or the next one (southeast ridge) to the east. The bowl was abandoned when it became easier to climb the ridge itself. The top of the ridge ended at a south peak, separated from the main summit by the top of the east couloir (see *Route 3*). Scramble across this to the true summit.

Variation: II, 5.8, A2. First ascent September 4, 1966, by Barry Corbet and Chuck Satterfield. The start of this variation at the base of the south ridge is reached by scrambling up and to the far right side of the ridge toward a tree on a slanting apron. The first pitch starts up a 50-foot open book exiting to the left to a small ledge containing several blocks, then back to the right to a continuation of the open book; now move up and left over a 10-foot bulge (5.8) onto a downsloping ledge, the belay spot. The next short lead moves up and slightly left over slightly loose rock for 50 feet to a belay stance below a dark overhang. The third pitch, the crux, starts 10 feet left of the belay, goes up a difficult friction slab to the lower of two bulging troughs, and continues straight up the slab above to the slight bulge at its top; pass this bulge with aid to the belay stance. The next lead goes up a 20-foot tight chimney to the base of a ramp, where one continues left to the nose of the ridge, which is climbed on small delicate holds to the belay position. An easier pitch (4.0) leads after 100 feet to a smooth 30-foot face, which is climbed with some difficulty to a belay ledge. One more lead (4.0) allows exit from the ridge to the false summit, the southwest apex. From this point to the main summit is but a scramble.

Variation: Wall of Leo. II, 5.10-. First ascent (first pitch) by Jim Woodmencey and Leo Larson; (second and third pitch) by Brent Finley and George Montopoli. The southern side of Cube Point is an area that is complicated by numerous walls and smaller cliff bands. When one looks up the Symmetry Couloir a steep gully is seen dropping down from Cube Point. At the point where this gully intersects the Symmetry Couloir, an upward-slanting, continuous line of trees is apparent. The "Wall of Leo" is a smooth-looking wall directly above the highest of these trees. The belay for the first pitch (150 feet) is at the base of a left-facing corner. Climb the right-facing corner to the west past a bolt (5.10-) up to its top, past two fixed pitons, and then step over to the west (5.9) to another right-facing corner. Continue up a lieback crack (5.7 to 5.8) to a belay at another bolt. The second pitch ascends an easy face to a 5.8 finger crack and then proceeds up to a ledge for the belay. Diagonal right on a 6- to 12-inch ledge (5.7) and then climb a flaring crack that ends on a ramp that is the top of the climb. For the descent go up and east to a tree ledge that leads into the gully that comes down from Cube Point. Take a regular rack with several additional small camming devices.

ROUTE 3. ☞East Couloir. II, 4.0. First ascent June 25, 1938, by Harold and William Plumley and Jack Fralick, or August 5, 1937, by Norton Nelson, Carroll Saffell (probably partial). While this route can be used to climb Cube Point, it is more frequently used as the standard descent route. Cross the stream below Ribbon Cascade, the falls below Arrowhead Pool, and ascend the talus cone and obvious couloir east of the north face of Cube Point. A climbers' trail will be found in this region. After a few hundred feet, the couloir narrows a bit, changes direction from north–south to east–west, and parallels the distinct east ridge. Scramble up this couloir to the small col at its head, and turn right (north) to reach the summit block from the east. The summit "cube" can then be climbed either from the south or the west. Use caution with the loose rock in this couloir because other climbers may be below.

Variation: II, 4.0. Probable first ascent June 29, 1957, by Dean Millsap, M. W. Echo, Sam Mitchell, Anthony Lagani, and S. Bostwick. This east couloir can also be indirectly reached from the south. From the approach to the Symmetry Couloir take the main couloir leading onto the lower east ridge of Cube Point. It is located about halfway between Baxter's Pinnacle and the couloir (see *Route 1, 1960 variation*) that leads to the notch west of Cube Point. Once the east ridge is reached, one can contour around on the north side and scramble into the upper east couloir.

ROUTE 4. ☞East Ridge. II, 5.4. Probable first ascent August 17, 1945, by Joseph and Edith Stettner, John Speck, Alan Stiles, Rex Parks, B. Hicks, Anna Gay, Betty Burno, Elv Bushman, Mary Tremaine, and T. A. Campbell, or perhaps July 1, 1938, by Carl Heeschen, Clyde Havenstot, and Robert Rynot. See *Photo 88*. This airy ridge is now the popular route on this small peak, providing an enjoyable short day of rockwork. It has the advantage that the descent route, the East Couloir (see *Route 3*), passes by the start of the steep rock on the east ridge, so one can leave pack and hiking boots at the beginning of this climb. See the East Couloir (*Route 3*), for the approach from below Arrowhead Pool. Near the bend in the couloir, where it narrows and changes direction, scramble right onto the steep solid rock of the east ridge just above its lowest overhanging section. About five leads of enjoyable climbing on the narrow ridge crest lead to the summit "cube," which can be climbed from either the south or the west. Some fixed pitons will be encountered. Several small variations on the crest are possible. Descent is usually made down the east couloir by first scrambling down to the southeast a short distance to enter the upper section of this couloir. *Time: 5½ to 6 hours from Jenny Lake.*

ROUTE 5. North Face. II, 5.6. First ascent July 15, 1971, by Mark Chapman and Bruce Patterson. Approach this face from Arrowhead Pool and start the climb near the northeast corner. Climb toward the center of the face. In a few sections 5.6 rock will be encountered.

SYMMETRY SPIRE (10,560+)

Map: Mount Moran

Symmetry Spire, rising immediately above Jenny Lake, appears insignificant when the entire range is viewed from a distance, but this small peak has played a major role in the development and history of Teton mountaineering. Originally climbed in the opening wave of first ascents in the initial year of the new Grand Teton National Park, the peak became the locus of early difficult rock-climbing activity. The routes pioneered by Durrance and Jensen became early classics of the range and served as standard objectives for enterprising climbers who wished to apply their skill to Teton rock. This relatively insignificant little peak became more popular with the climbers who visited Grand Teton National Park than any other peak except the Grand Teton itself.

While this high level of popularity has declined in recent years, the south side routes remain fine climbs and even today can be recommended. In the 1950s the Direct Jensen Ridge route was one of the major test pieces of the range, and that impressive route attracted the best climbers of the day. With the advent of newer, more difficult rock climbs such as those in Death, Garnet, and Cascade Canyons, the Symmetry climbs have seen reduced activity, but they remain an enjoyable way to spend a day on a good training climb. As with all mountain routes, there is an occasional loose block here and there, but the rock is predominantly good with ample cracks available for protection. This peak is easily accessible from the Jenny Lake campground; only two hours are required to reach the base of the high-angle rock climbs on its south side. These south-side climbs also have the

advantage that climbers can easily see the approach of bad weather. Symmetry Spire also has the feature of a fast, easy route of descent in the event the summit is reached at a late hour. Although it is primarily a rock climber's peak, ice axes must usually be taken because of the moderately steep snow in the Symmetry Couloir in early season and in the upper couloir even in midseason.

The usual approach for the regular Southwest Couloir route or the south side climbs begins with an inexpensive boat ride across Jenny Lake. For those who wish a very early start, one can hike around either end of the lake to the Valley Trail on the west side. From the west shore boat dock on Jenny Lake, walk north on the Valley Trail about 0.25 mile to the horse bypass trail (small sign) leading off to the west. After passing through a considerable forest and past some bushes, this well-travelled trail levels out as it heads south back toward the Cascade Canyon creek and trail. On this section just before a small stream is crossed, a climbers' trail turns off uphill to the right (west). This trail parallels the streambed up a bushy talus slope toward the headwall guarding access to the Symmetry Couloir, the main drainage couloir between Symmetry Spire and Storm Point. Short of the headwall, however, bear right into a secondary *cul-de-sac* and exit up a 15-foot wall on the left (west) side to gain the top of the cliff band. Now move left (south) and zigzag up the open slopes above over ledges and slabs, using a faint climbers' trail that ultimately leads past a section of scrub pines near their left (south) edge up into the broad Symmetry Couloir.

In late season the main couloir above, narrowing at its top, is just talus and scree, but in early and midseason it will contain moderately steep snow and has been the scene of many accidents. A rope combined with an ice axe and knowledge of how to use it for a self-arrest are basic for safety in this heavily travelled couloir. The moats that open up in early season are commonly in the main fall line and are especially dangerous. Beware. In the cliff band above the snowfield a waterfall will be seen (except in very late season) descending from a shallow secondary gully (with loose rock) that leads up toward the main saddle. Depending on the season, hike up the talus and scree or climb the snow, bearing slightly left to the narrowing of the couloir until about even with the small waterfall, and then traverse over to the right into the secondary gully at the top of the waterfall. One can now proceed easily up to the saddle using the slope to the right (north) of the gully. The base of the south face and ridges is also readily reached by bearing right up past a few scattered trees.

The standard route of descent from the summit of Symmetry Spire is via the Southwest Couloir, *Route 3*.

CHRONOLOGY

East Ridge: August 20, 1929, Fritiof Fryxell, Phil Smith

var: [probable] July 30, 1935, M. N. Schell, R.
L. Harrington, P. E. Griffith

var: **Northern Couloir:** July 27, 1954, Bill
Cropper, Ellis Blade, Bob and Anne Larsen

var: August 16, 1955, Beatrice Burford, Gene
Schlichter

var: **Southern Couloir:** date and party
unknown

var: **Sam's Tower Ridge:** date uncertain, Barry
Corbet et al.

var: **Staircase Ridge:** July 5, 1963, Richard
Ream, Jr., J. Gully

Northwest Couloir and Ledges: July 13, 1931,
Fritiof Fryxell, Leland Horberg, Rudolph
Edmund, William Cederberg, Neuman Kerndt,
Elof Petersen

Southwest Couloir: July 8, 1935, Eldon Petzoldt

Durrance Ridge: August 7, 1936, Jack Durrance,
Walter Spofford

var: **South Face Start:** August 25, 1950, Leigh
Ortenburger, James Collison

var: **Traverse to Southwest Ridge:** June 30,
1952, Robert Merriam, Charles Wilder,
Roger Nichols, Ulrich Kruse

Jensen Couloir: July 28, 1938, Bert Jensen, Fred
Brown, David Davis (lower section); September
6, 1954, Gary Hemming, Leigh Ortenburger (upper section)

Direct Jensen Ridge: July 28, 1938, Bert Jensen,
Fred Brown, David Davis (upper portion from
east); August 5, 1952, Willi Unsoeld, Norman
Lee, Tony Mueller, Sandy Gregory (upper section
from west); August 14, 1953, Willi Unsoeld,
Norman Lee (lower portion); August 16, 1953,
Willi Unsoeld, Mary Sylvander, Steve Jervis (first
free complete ascent)

Southwest Ridge: July 30, 1938, Bert Jensen, Walter
Spofford

var: July 7, 1957, Al Read, Robert Kamps

Templeton's Crack: July 1943, Fritz Wiessner,
James Huidekoper, Hank Geering (attempt); July
18, 1946, Robin Hansen, Fritz Lippmann (partial); July 13, 1949, Lee Pedrick, Richard Pownall
(to bowl); July 24, 1949, Richard Pownall, Red
Austin, Harvey and Jewel Templeton (complete
to summit ridge)

var: **Lower Chimney:** August 30, 1951, Robert
and Doris Merriam, Leigh Ortenburger

var: August 17, 1961, Raymond Jacquot, Robert Scott

Northeast Chimney: July 19, 1949, Richard
Pownall, Art Gilkey, Red Austin

South Face: July 3, 1950, Richard Pownall, Leigh
Ortenburger

var: August 1, 1954, William Cropper,
Ellis Blade

var: June 25, 1962, Herb Swedlund, Mike
Borghoff

North Face: July 20, 1953, Roald Fryxell, Ronald
Cullen

var: **Cupa Kava:** August 1975, Bruce and Brent
Weide, Mark Sixel

var: August 28, 1989, Tom Turiano, Phil
McBride

West Face, North Edge: August 26, 1955, William
Cropper, Yves Ericksson, Ron Chapman

Direct South Face: August 8, 1956, Richard
Pownall, Willi Unsoeld, Norman Lee

var: August 30, 1958, William Buckingham,
Barry Corbet, Pete Sinclair

var: July 1978, Yvon Chouinard, T. M. Herbert

Northeast Face: July 24, 1957, John Dietschy, David
Dingman

Direct West Face: July 27, 1957, John Dietschy,
David Dingman

Dietschy Ridge: July 30, 1957, John Dietschy, David
Dingman, Karl Pfiffner

Northwest Face: July 15, 1974, John Cain, Tim East

ROUTE 1. West Face, North Edge. II, 5.1. First ascent August 26, 1955, by William Cropper, Yves Ericksson, and Ron
Chapman. The west face of Symmetry Spire rises above the
regular-route couloir that leads to the high col between the
peak and the first of the Symmetry Crags to the west. This
very short route starts on the face only a short distance
below (south of) the col. Two pitches lead easily to the top
of the wall, well north of the top of the southwest ridge.

ROUTE 2. Direct West Face. II, 5.6. First ascent July 27,
1957, by John Dietschy and David Dingman. This face is approached via the regular Symmetry Couloir to the saddle
connecting Ice Point with Symmetry Spire. From the saddle,
scramble north up the southwest couloir leading to the col
between Symmetry Spire and Symmetry Crag 1 until just
past the first pitch of the Southwest Ridge route. About nine
pitches, including two overhanging cracks, rise more or less
straight up to end at the apex of the face, about 200 feet left
(north) of the top of the southwest ridge (the Flake Pitch).

ROUTE 3. ☞Southwest Couloir. II, 4.0. First ascent July 8,
1935, by Eldon Petzoldt, who pieced together two earlier
routes of Fritiof Fryxell into what has become the regular
route on the peak. The Symmetry Spire–Ice Point saddle
was first reached by Fryxell and Frank Smith on August 13,
1931, in the course of their first ascents of Ice and Storm
Points. The higher col immediately west of the summit was
reached by Fryxell and his party on July 13, 1931, during
a west-to-east traverse of Symmetry and the pinnacles on
either side of it. See Photo 90. From Jenny Lake follow the
standard approach as given above to the saddle between

Symmetry Spire and Ice Point. The large southwest couloir below the west face of Symmetry Spire leads directly to the high col west of the summit; as already mentioned, the same col is reached from the north via Northwest Couloir and Ledges, *Route 16*. A substantial stream drains the southwest couloir, which harbors snow of moderate steepness during most of the summer. Climb this couloir to the high col at its head. The lower section is loose rubble and the upper portion is filled with snow during the first half of the climbing season. In late season and sometimes in midseason one can bypass the snow by using ledges on the left (west) side of the main couloir. From the col climb right (east) up the ridge for about 100 feet before following easy but sometimes exposed ledges out to the left (north) and up the northwest side of the peak to the summit. There is virtually a trail now, worn by the boots of climbers over the past 60 years.

As a descent route, scramble from the summit down the exposed north side, on the small path, angling west and down toward the col to the west. From the col descend the southwest couloir down to the main saddle between Symmetry Spire and Ice Point. Use care with the loose rock in the couloir because other climbers may be below and in the fall line. In early or midseason an ice axe will be needed for this descent, but by late season the snow in this upper couloir can usually be avoided by downclimbing on the ledges on the west side of the couloir. *Time: 5 to 5¼ hours* from Jenny Lake.

ROUTE 4. *Southwest Ridge*. II, 5.6. First ascent July 30, 1938, by Bert Jensen and Walter Spofford. See *Topo 77* and *Photos 89* and *90*. This beautifully direct and impressively steep route is probably the most pleasant climb on Symmetry Spire. Approach as already described to the col between Symmetry Spire and Ice Point, from which the spectacular southwest ridge is seen, forming the extreme left edge of the south face. The route contains five to eight leads depending on the starting point and the ropelength. The first pitch begins in the bushes at the very base of the ridge. After two ropelengths of easy 5th-class climbing (although quite steep), there is a nearly vertical wall. Climb it by means of the cracks on the right (east) side. Near its top, traverse out on easy rock to the right; then regain the ridge crest. The next 60-foot lead up a smooth band of yellow rock, the Nose Pitch, is considered the hardest of the climb. It can be attacked directly up the nose (5.7), moving up and around to the left past some fixed pitons, using difficult balance. Or one can traverse right a few feet across a small vertical face and descend a few feet around a small corner to the right to gain a steep shelf that leads up and left to the top of the pitch; this is the easier, but less obvious, alternative. The next ropelength leads more or less directly up, staying slightly left of the crest, and finishes on a face with good holds. One can now see a steep shelf slanting upward to the right. After descending left a few feet to gain access to this shelf, climb to its top on small holds. The Flake Pitch,

which is now directly above, starts with an awkward, broken face of black rock leading to a ledge below the obvious flake. Either the inside chimney or the exposed outside face of the flake can be climbed. This is the last major pitch of the climb. Follow the easier but still exposed ridge above to the summit, keeping usually on the right (east) of the crest. For descent, take the regular northwest ledges and Southwest Couloir (see *Route 3*) back to the Symmetry Spire–Ice Point saddle. *Time: 6¼ to 7¾ hours* from Jenny Lake. See *American Alpine Journal,* 3, no. 3 (1939), pp. 361–365; *Chicago Mountaineering Club Newsletter,* 5, no. 1 (January 1951), p. 5.

Variation: II, 5.7. First ascent July 7, 1957, by Al Read and Robert Kamps. A more difficult beginning of about two pitches can be made around the corner to the right (east). From the trees about 70 feet east of a small, shallow couloir on the south face that leads to the southwest ridge, climb slightly to the right over two black overhangs; the upper one is prominent. Now traverse left under a white wall to the slightly overhanging couloir, which is followed up to meet the ridge.

ROUTE 5. *Direct South Face*. III, 5.8, A2, or III, 5.9. First ascent August 8, 1956, by Richard Pownall, Willi Unsoeld, and Norman Lee. See *Topo 78* and *Photo 90*. The direct south face is defined to lie between the southwest ridge on the left (west) and the long left-facing corner of *Route 6* on the right (east). This readily identifiable corner is the line of the original 1950 South Face route. The considerable expanse of wall in this region has seen a number of early climbs that are, or have been claimed to be, distinct, but this 1956 route was the first. In addition to the *1958* and *1978 variations* listed under this Direct South Face route, there are also the *variations (1954, 1958, and 1962),* listed under the South Face route *(Route 6),* that merged with this 1956 route in their upper sections. Most recent climbs seem to be a combination of one or more of these variations and the topo attempts to depict one such composite.

The route starts in a prominent dihedral about halfway between the southwest ridge and the left-facing corner of the original South Face route. Angle up and slightly left on good rock for about two pitches to a belay platform. Now traverse up and right until one can turn straight up once more in the center of the face for two leads to a prominent 4-foot ceiling. This serious obstacle can be passed using a crack on the left or, as originally done, it can be climbed directly using aid. It is uncertain whether or not this ceiling has been free climbed via the original aid line. Now continue up the narrowing face to the traverse ledge (Durrance Ridge to the southwest ridge), and avoid being forced out to the right onto the Durrance Ridge. Just above is the large final overhang that extends across the top of the south face immediately left (west) of the final pitch of the Durrance Ridge. This overhang can also be surmounted directly using aid, as was done on the first climb in 1956.

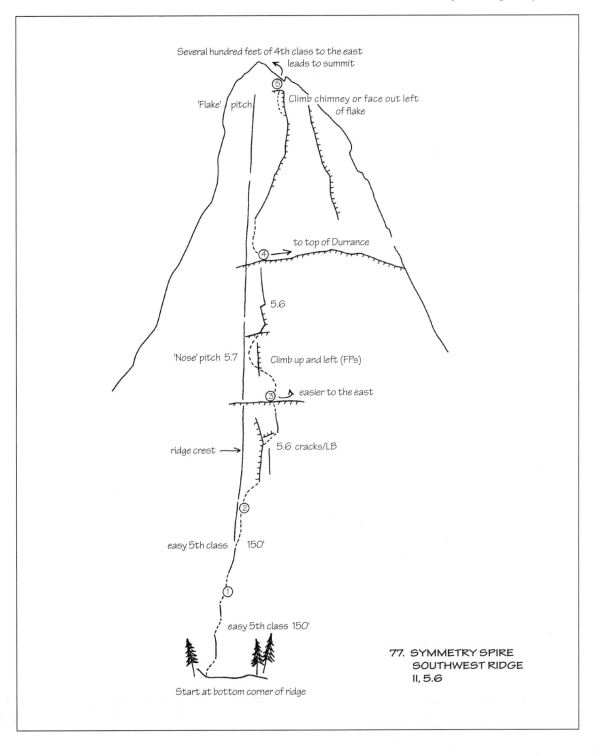

Several hundred feet of 4th class to the east
leads to summit

Climb chimney or face out left
of flake

⑤

'Flake' pitch

to top of Durrance

④

5.6

'Nose' pitch 5.7

Climb up and left (FPs)

③ easier to the east

ridge crest →

5.6 cracks/LB

②

easy 5th class   150'

①

easy 5th class 150'

77. SYMMETRY SPIRE
SOUTHWEST RIDGE
II, 5.6

Start at bottom corner of ridge

Time: 10 hours from Jenny Lake. See *American Alpine Journal*, 10, no. 2 (1957), pp. 148–149.

Variation: III, 5.9. First ascent August 30, 1958, by William Buckingham, Barry Corbet, and Pete Sinclair. Just above the traverse ledge (Durrance Ridge to the southwest ridge) is the large final overhang that extends across the top of the south face immediately left (west) of the final pitch of the Durrance Ridge. Pass this overhang on the left, up an obvious, large open-book chimney that faces left (west) and is some 60 feet to the east of the Flake Pitch of the Southwest Ridge. This is a difficult pitch involving many small overhangs, but does not require aid.

Variation: III, 5.8. First ascent July 1978, by Yvon Chouinard and T. M. Herbert. Starting at some small pine trees, this variation apparently begins and remains somewhat to the right (east) of the main route. Climb two pitches of excellent vertical rock (5.8), continue up to the traverse ledge, and finish using the *1958 variation*. The 4-foot ceiling of the main route is avoided using this variation.

ROUTE 6. South Face. II, 5.8. First ascent July 3, 1950, by Richard Pownall and Leigh Ortenburger. See *Topo 78* and *Photo 90.* The south face of Symmetry Spire extends from the southwest ridge to the Durrance Ridge. A prominent left-facing corner, curiously described in earlier editions of this book as a "vertical ledge," runs up the center of the face to an obvious overhang. This route follows the crack in the corner and sometimes uses the face to its left. The rock is steep and solid but belay positions are exposed, requiring good anchors for safety. To pass the overhang at the top of the corner, climb up and out on the face until even with its top, then make a spectacular step back to the right onto the top of the overhang. The line of least resistance now leads in one ropelength up to the right to join the Durrance Ridge, which is then followed to the summit. This is an enjoyable high-angle climb on good rock. *Time: 9 hours* from Jenny Lake. See *American Alpine Journal*, 9, no. 2 (1955), pp. 147–149.

Variation: II, 5.6. First ascent August 1, 1954, by William Cropper and Ellis Blade. From the top of the final overhang mentioned in the standard route, one can continue up without touching the Durrance Ridge. After traversing left (west) for about 60 feet from the top of the overhang to a roomy platform, go up and left in a band of broken rock to join the Southwest Ridge route. There seems to be more than one possible line, and the difficulty will vary depending on which is chosen.

Variation: II, 5.6. First ascent June 25, 1962, by Herb Swedlund and Mike Borghoff. (*Note:* This route is not well understood with respect to other routes in the immediate vicinity.) From the final overhang of the main route, continue up for 60 feet on steep rock to a small ledge. Start the next pitch on 5.6 rock, which is avoided after 20 feet by a traverse left on good handholds, then climb for 120 feet, easily bearing left to avoid the Durrance Ridge, until about

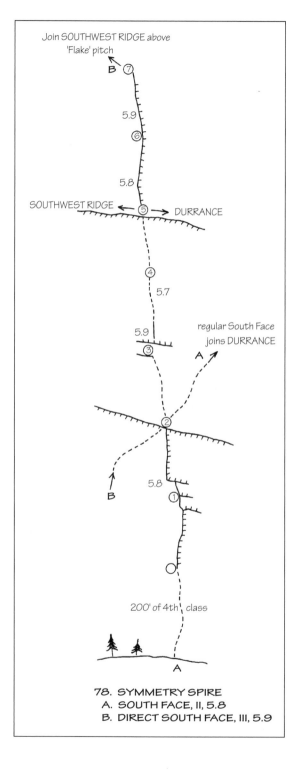

Join SOUTHWEST RIDGE above 'Flake' pitch

B ⑦

5.9

⑥

5.8

SOUTHWEST RIDGE ← ⑤ → DURRANCE

④

5.7

5.9

③

regular South Face joins DURRANCE

A

②

5.8

B

①

200' of 4th class

A

78. SYMMETRY SPIRE
A. SOUTH FACE, II, 5.8
B. DIRECT SOUTH FACE, III, 5.9

30 feet below a prominent roof. This roof apparently can be bypassed on the left by a difficult fingertip traverse or on the right (east). This is followed by a friction move and a strenuous move up a secondary overhang to a vertical crack with adequate holds. One full ropelength on steep, exposed rock then leads to a point below the final overhang where one can traverse either to the Durrance Ridge or to the Southwest Ridge, or finish by one of the methods described under *Route 5*.

ROUTE 7. *Durrance Ridge.* II, 5.6. First ascent August 7, 1936, by Jack Durrance and Walter Spofford, after climbing Storm and Ice Points earlier the same day. See *Photos 89* and *90*. The southeast side of Symmetry Spire is deeply cut by a great couloir (see *Templeton's Crack, Route 8*), and this, the first of the south side rock climbs, goes directly up the ridge forming its left (west) edge. The Durrance Ridge is a very enjoyable but relatively long climb on steep, solid rock. This route, which contains a total of eight or more pitches, can serve as an excellent introduction to Teton climbing. The base of the Durrance Ridge is easily reached from the slope just below the Symmetry Spire–Ice Point saddle. Many variations can be made, because one can climb almost anywhere on the ridge. The route is best initiated at the extreme toe of the ridge. Climb several ropelengths of easy rock until, about halfway up the ridge, all the variations seem to funnel into a vertical pitch, consisting of a crack in a very steep 20-foot wall. This is one of two "crux" pitches of the route; a fixed piton can be found here. Above, the climbing becomes easier and includes one 200-foot section of scrambling to reach the steeper upper section of the ridge. The final lead, which lies slightly left of the rounded ridge crest, is the most interesting and difficult but can be well protected; some fixed pitons will be found here. It consists of a 100-foot system of cracks and a small chimney that exits at the top of the ridge. This point is at the lower edge of the "Bowl" some 300 feet below the summit. The objective here is to scramble left (west) over to the crest of the upper southwest ridge. From the top of the ridge, climb one long or two short additional pitches up and left across a section of downsloping black slabs to gain the upper southwest ridge, which is followed to the summit, either on the crest itself or slightly on the right (east) side. For descent, see the Northwest Ledges, *Route 16. Time: 7 to 8½ hours* from Jenny Lake. See *Chicago Mountaineering Club Newsletter,* 15, no. 1 (February 1961), pp. 4–7.

Variation: South Face Start. II, 5.4. First ascent August 25, 1950, by Leigh Ortenburger and James Collison. Instead of starting directly from the bottom of the ridge, climb the south face between *Route 6* and the Durrance Ridge via a left-facing corner. After about three ropelengths, a smooth wall above forces one to traverse to the right to the Durrance Ridge.

Variation: Traverse to Southwest Ridge. II, 5.6. First ascent June 30, 1952, by Robert Merriam, Charles Wilder,

Roger Nichols, and Ulrich Kruse. Two pitches from the top of the ridge, a ledge below the overhang at the top of the south face diagonals up and to the left (west) across the south face all the way to the southwest ridge. Hence, this climb can be completed on the southwest ridge by following this ledge, which meets the ridge just below the Flake Pitch (see *Route 4*).

ROUTE 8. *Templeton's Crack.* II, 5.6. First ascent July 13, 1949, by Lee Pedrick and Richard Pownall. The first attempt on this prominent feature was made in July 1943, by Fritz Wiessner, James Huidekoper, and Hank Geering. On July 18, 1946, Robin Hansen and Fritz Lippmann made a partial ascent of this crack, bypassing one 300-foot section with a 150-foot traverse out to the left onto the Durrance Ridge. On July 13, 1949, Lee Pedrick and Richard Pownall climbed the crack directly to the bowl; the upper continuation of the crack to the summit ridge was first climbed July 24, 1949, by Richard Pownall, Red Austin, and Harvey and Jewel Templeton. This climb, consisting of a series of scree walks and difficult chockstones, goes up the great chimney that cuts the southeast face of Symmetry Spire. The usual approach is from the slope just below the Symmetry Spire–Ice Point saddle to the base of the Durrance Ridge, from which one can scramble down into the chimney and walk to the base of the first overhang. Climb the first three overhangs in the first ropelength, and pass the fourth overhang by climbing the right wall of the chimney. Another scree walk leads to an 80-foot chimney at the top of which is a small cave. The 100-foot difficult chimney above is known as the "Green Chimney" because of the slippery green slime on its walls in early season. Pass outside the chockstone at the top of this chimney, and after another scree walk ascend some 250 feet in moderate chimneys, climbing the vertical section on the right wall. Go up and to the right to a downsloping ledge. The 15-foot pitch directly off this ledge, the Harvey Pitch, is the most difficult of the route. The main chimney, which is 15 feet to the left of the Harvey Pitch, has also been climbed, but the rock is rotten, and it is not easier than the Harvey Pitch. Above this pitch, easier climbing leads to the "Bowl," from which most parties traverse left (west) to the Southwest Ridge and follow it to the summit. However, in order to finish the climb of the entire chimney, another two ropelengths of climbing must be made up the continuation of the chimney. On the right wall there are adequate holds on the downsloping, slabby rock. This section appears more difficult than it is and leads to the ridge about 50 feet west of the summit. *Time: 7½ to 9½ hours* from Jenny Lake. See *American Alpine Journal,* 8, no. 1 (1951), pp. 176–181; *Sierra Club Bulletin,* 32, no. 5 (May 1917), pp. 128–129.

Variation: Lower Chimney. II, 5.6. First ascent August 30, 1951, by Robert and Doris Merriam and Leigh Ortenburger. A longer climb can be obtained by beginning the climb in the lower extension of the chimney, which starts from the upper right corner of the snowfield in the Symmetry Couloir. In late season several ropelengths on rock of poor quality are required to reach the initial overhang of the regular Templeton's Crack route. In early season this 500-foot lower extension will be almost entirely snow.

Variation: II, 5.6. First ascent August 17, 1961, by Raymond Jacquot and Robert Scott. Above the scree above the Green Chimney, face climb out on the right (north) wall instead of staying in or near the main chimney. The sloping ledge at the base of the Harvey Pitch will be reached from the right instead of from the left.

ROUTE 9. *Direct Jensen Ridge.* III, 5.7. First complete ascent August 16, 1953, by Willi Unsoeld, Mary Sylvander, and Steve Jervis. The upper portion of this ridge, gained from the couloir to the right (east), was ascended July 28, 1938, by Bert Jensen, Fred Brown, and David Davis; this upper section, gained from Templeton's Crack on the west, was also climbed on August 5, 1952, by Willi Unsoeld, Norman Lee, Tony Mueller, and Sandy Gregory; the lower section was first climbed with aid on August 14, 1953, by Willi Unsoeld and Norman Lee. The complete climb two days later was done free. See *Topo 79* and *Photos 89* and *90*. The Jensen Ridge forms the right (eastern) boundary of Templeton's Crack. The ridge, very impressive when seen from any angle, was considered one of the better rock climbs of its day. It is a more difficult climb than either of the two Symmetry Spire standards, the Durrance Ridge and the Southwest Ridge. The base of the Jensen Ridge is approached by descending into Templeton's Crack from the base of the Durrance Ridge and then scrambling up the smooth slabby rock on the far (east) side. The lower section of this ridge rises at a very high angle and is capped by a large overhang. After ten pitches the standard traverse is then made west over to the Southwest Ridge, by which route the summit is attained. *Time: 7 to 10 hours* from Jenny Lake. See *American Alpine Journal,* 9, no. 1 (1954), pp. 172–184, illus.

ROUTE 10. *Jensen Couloir.* II, 5.6. First ascent July 28, 1938, by Bert Jensen, Fred Brown, and David Davis (lower section), and September 6, 1954, by Gary Hemming and Leigh Ortenburger (upper section). This distinct couloir is just to the right (east) of the Jensen Ridge, separating it from the next ridge to the east, the Dietschy Ridge. The difficult entrance to the Jensen Couloir was first climbed by the 1938 party, who traversed left onto the ridge after climbing only 200 feet up the couloir. From the roping-up place described under *Route 9,* climb up and to the right 80 feet to a poor belay position. The next pitch just left of the overhanging right wall of the couloir is difficult because of the smooth downsloping rock. Few, if any, cracks are available for protection. The upper portion of the couloir is just a scramble. See *American Alpine Journal,* 3, no. 3 (1939), pp. 361–365.

ROUTE 11. *Dietschy Ridge.* II, 5.6. First ascent July 30, 1957, by John Dietschy, David Dingman, and Karl Pfiffner.

See *Photo 90.* This ridge of good rock lies just east of the Jensen Ridge; the Jensen Couloir separates the upper portions of the two ridges. At the bottom all three of these features blend together where the lower portion of this southeast ridge is a 200-foot wall. This ridge is best approached the same way as the Jensen Ridge (see *Route 9*). The first lead traverses low across the broad nose of the ridge onto and up its right (east) flank. Three additional short pitches (4.0 to 5.6) of interesting climbing on good rock remain slightly on the right side of the crest. The fifth lead brings one back to the crest, which is followed to the knife-edge horizontal section which can be done *à cheval.* Immediately above the knife-edge is a 200-foot steep yellow step in the ridge that is visible from Jenny Lake. Although it is possible to traverse left into the top of the Jensen Couloir at this point, the step is usually passed on the right (east) side. A short lead around to the east brings one to easy ground, where steep scrambling leads directly up to the east ridge of Symmetry Spire, from which the nearby summit is easily attained.

ROUTE 12. *East Ridge.* II, 4.0. First ascent August 20, 1929, by Fritiof Fryxell and Phil Smith. This pleasant scrambling ridge is the most obvious route on the peak, especially when viewed from the north. It is not a difficult climb and can be enjoyed by almost any mountaineer seeking a pleasurable outing in the mountains. For those who have climbed the peak more than once, the east ridge can serve as an alternate route of descent. On its south side there is a considerable degree of complexity. In all there are five ridges and five couloirs between Templeton's Crack and Cube Point, exclusive. For the scenic approach to the north side of Symmetry Spire see *Hanging Canyon.* From Hanging Canyon cross the stream between Arrowhead Pool and Ramshead Lake, and follow a distinct grassy horizontal ledge on the northeast face of Symmetry Spire out to the east ridge. Between Cube Point, the peak on the lower end of this ridge, and the summit of Symmetry Spire, there is another large gendarme, Sam's Tower. This ledge brings one onto the ridge just above this tower. From this point to the summit the route requires little more than scrambling. Near the summit, a short knife-edge ridge adds interest to the route. *Time: 5 to 6½ hours* from Jenny Lake. See *Appalachia,* 18, no. 4 (December 1931), pp. 388–408, illus.; *Chicago Mountaineering Club Journal,* 2, no. 5 (January–July 1948), pp. 5–7.

Variation: II, 4.0. Probable first ascent July 30, 1935, by M. N. Schell, R. L. Harrington, and P. E. Griffith; it is possible that this party climbed one of the two couloirs to the east of the one described here. From the upper (west) end of the snowfield that persists throughout most of the summer in the Symmetry Couloir, a narrow couloir leads directly north to the crest of the east ridge, well to the west of Sam's Tower. This couloir begins very near the base of the lower extension of Templeton's Crack (see *Route 8, Lower Chimney variation*). For purposes of identification, the cor-

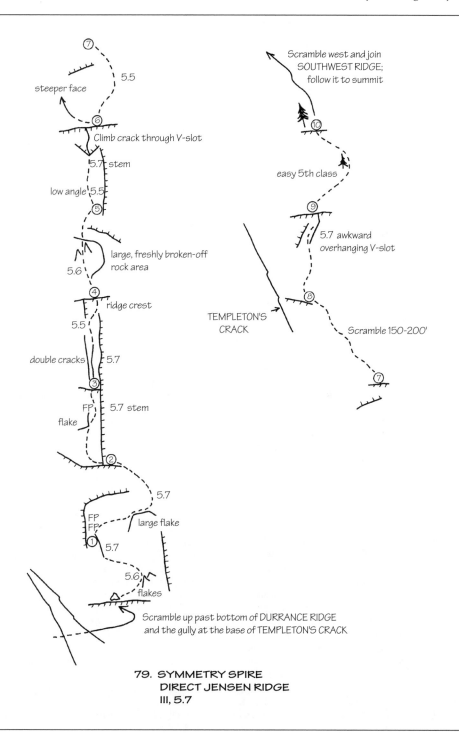

⑦

5.5

steeper face

⑥

Climb crack through V-slot

5.7 stem

low angle 5.5

⑤

large, freshly broken-off
rock area

5.6

④

ridge crest

5.5

double cracks   5.7

③

FP   5.7 stem

flake

②

5.7

FP
FP   large flake

①   5.7

5.6
flakes

Scramble up past bottom of DURRANCE RIDGE
and the gully at the base of TEMPLETON'S CRACK

Scramble west and join
SOUTHWEST RIDGE;
follow it to summit

⑩

easy 5th class

⑨

5.7 awkward
overhanging V-slot

TEMPLETON'S
CRACK

⑧

Scramble 150-200'

⑦

**79. SYMMETRY SPIRE
DIRECT JENSEN RIDGE
III, 5.7**

rect couloir is the first one west of the large couloir above Hangover Pinnacle. A short wall prevents easy access to the beginning of the couloir, but it can be climbed near its left end, which forms the north wall of the lower extension of Templeton's Crack. Once in the couloir, scramble to the east ridge; in early season snow will be encountered.

Variation: II, 5.1. First ascent August 16, 1955, by Beatrice Burford and Gene Schlichter. Leave the regular Symmetry Couloir at Hangover Pinnacle, which stands at the entrance to a large subsidiary couloir running north to the crest of the east ridge. This couloir can very likely be ascended without great difficulty all the way to the east ridge, but this party, after scrambling up three-quarters of the couloir, turned horizontally left (west) on a tree ledge for about 300 feet. This ledge widens out into a broad slope bounded on the right by an overhanging buttress. Three steep pitches somewhat to the right lead to a notch in the Staircase Ridge (see the *Staircase Ridge variation*) of which this buttress is a part. Traverse into the next couloir to the west (the preceding *1935 variation*), and climb to the east ridge, which leads to the summit.

Variation: Southern Couloir. II, 5.1. First ascent unknown. It is also possible to reach the east ridge via the southern couloir, which leads to the col immediately west of Cube Point. This large couloir is the first one east of Hangover Pinnacle and is easily reached by following up the main drainage of a small stream. This is the same stream ordinarily crossed (from north to south) just after scaling the short cliff on the west wall of the *cul-de-sac* on the approach to the regular Symmetry Couloir. There is little information available concerning this couloir, but it has very likely been ascended or descended and should not prove difficult. From the col, one will be faced with the task of passing the gendarme, Sam's Tower, between the col and the upper east ridge of Symmetry Spire; see the *Northern Couloir variation.*

Variation: Northern Couloir. II, 5.4. First ascent July 27, 1954, by Bill Cropper, Ellis Blade, and Bob and Anne Larsen. The crest of the east ridge can also be gained from the north at the col just west of Cube Point via a scree couloir. The traverse of Sam's Tower, referred to earlier, involves two awkward pitches including some 5.4 climbing and perhaps a rappel down its west face.

Variation: Sam's Tower Ridge. II, 5.8. First ascent uncertain, but it has been climbed by Barry Corbet and party. The large gendarme, Sam's Tower, on the east ridge of Symmetry Spire just west of Cube Point, has a south ridge that extends down toward the regular Symmetry Couloir. This ridge is the one immediately west of the large couloir that descends from the col separating this large tower from Cube Point. In the lower portion of the ridge, a 5.1 corner will be found on the second pitch. About halfway up the ridge a ledge 50 feet wide will be reached. Just above this ledge is an overhang with a chimney piercing it. This 20-foot pitch

is difficult, 5.8 or A1, and apparently cannot be bypassed on either side. The remainder of the climb can be as easy as desired because one can just scramble to the top of the tower by avoiding the exact crest, which contains the more interesting climbing.

Variation: Staircase Ridge. II, 5.4. First known ascent July 5, 1963, by Richard Ream, Jr., and J. Gully. Staircase Ridge is the second ridge east of the Dietschy Ridge and it rises immediately west of Hangover Pinnacle, leading north to the east ridge with one large, flat step approximately halfway up the ridge. The climbing is easy, the only difficulties being two short walls; the first is climbed up the middle and the second is climbed up the left (west) edge. This ridge climb can be very well combined with an ascent of Hangover Pinnacle at the base.

ROUTE 13. Northeast Chimney. II, 5.6. First ascent July 19, 1949, by Richard Pownall, Art Gilkey, and Red Austin. This deep chimney is as conspicuous from the northeast as Templeton's Crack is from the southeast. At its top it forms a small but distinct notch separating the north pinnacle of Symmetry Spire from the spire itself. Approach from Hanging Canyon and gain the base of the chimney by crossing the stream between Arrowhead Pool and Ramshead Lake. Scrambling and easy climbing take one about three-quarters of the way up the chimney, to the point where it narrows—the one difficult pitch of the climb. Climb perhaps 10 feet in the narrow section until it is possible to climb to the outside; then cross over to the right (north) wall. A 15-foot 5.6 chimney is then ascended to a wide ledge. The 30-foot step above the ledge is also difficult, but once above it just scramble to the notch at the top of the chimney. The first-ascent party climbed the north pinnacle, and most parties usually include it. From the notch scramble up and to the right (south and west) on easy ledges to the summit. *Time: 6 hours* from Jenny Lake. See *American Alpine Journal,* 8, no. 1 (1951), pp. 176–181.

ROUTE 14. Northeast Face. II, 5.7, A1, or II, 5.8. First ascent July 24, 1957, by John Dietschy and David Dingman. Just to the right (north) of the prominent northeast chimney is a face containing a light-colored bulge of rock about halfway up. Approach this route via Hanging Canyon. From the bottom of the face below the overhanging bulge, the first two pitches angle off to the west. The next pitch goes straight up for 40 feet to a shelf, from which a thin traverse back to the east leads to a good belay stance below the bulge. The overhanging corner that bisects the bulge is difficult and was first climbed by tension from three pitons; it has now been done free. An additional difficult pitch, followed by several easier leads, puts one on top of the north pinnacle of Symmetry Spire. Scramble down to the south and then up the north ledges to the main summit. This is an excellent, enjoyable rock climb of eight pitches, but the routefinding is not easy. See *American Alpine Journal,* 11, no. 1 (1958), pp. 85–88.

ROUTE 15. North Face. II, 5.1. First ascent July 20, 1953, by Roald Fryxell and Ronald Cullen. From Ramshead Lake in Hanging Canyon, scramble to the highest snow patch near the right (west) base of the face, where a wide ramp leads back left and upward across the wall. Rope up where this ledge narrows and continue 60 feet around a bulge in the face. Once past this bulge, the face slopes back, and easy climbing leads to a ledge system that can be followed diagonally up to the right (west) to the west ridge of the north pinnacle (10,400+) of Symmetry Spire. The short pitch up this ridge to the summit of the pinnacle is perhaps the most difficult of the climb. After descending into the cleft that isolates this small pinnacle, scramble easily up to the right (west) to the main summit.

Variation: Cupa Kava. II, 5.7. First ascent August 1975, by Bruce and Brent Weide and Mark Sixel. Instead of starting with the diagonal ledge leading left, make a direct ascent aiming at an overhanging point above. The first lead goes up a very shallow dihedral on small holds (5.7) over a bulge onto a ledge. Now angle slightly right and up either a chimney or the overhang at its left edge (5.7). A slightly overhanging lieback and jam crack lead onto big ledges with trees. After one easier pitch, climb the face above directly, passing a small, nearly holdless overhang; this takes one into the gully below the summit overhangs, the overhanging point seen from the beginning of the climb. Now climb over the point to the right and continue to the summit of the north pinnacle.

Variation: II, 5.7. First ascent August 28, 1989, by Tom Turiano and Phil McBride. This variation, while similar to Cupa Kava above, differs in that the north pinnacle of Symmetry Spire is reached more directly from its north face. From Arrowhead Lake hike to a large ramp under the base of the north face that leads from left (east) to right (west); this ramp narrows to a 2-foot width for a 20-foot section and then widens out again. Start this route at a small bush at the narrowest part of the ramp. The first short lead goes up and left over (5.4) rock to a belay ledge. The next pitch goes up between two overhangs, past a fixed piton into a lieback (5.7) with thin protection, from the top of which one continues up a 5.6 face to the right of some flakes and blocks, finishing on a short belay ledge just left of a small arête. Now climb a face (5.7) between two right-facing corners to the large ramp that diagonals down to the right (west) to the base of the face; one can escape the route easily here. Continue this third lead, moving up and left, passing two right-facing corners with a fine 5.7 face with edge holds between them, to a belay ledge where an old fixed piton will be found. The fourth pitch moves up the face (5.6) above the ledge, past a small overhang into a set of black-rock cracks that diagonal up and right to a sloping ledge that holds a large block; follow this ledge left past the block and climb the face above to a right-facing corner (5.7), which takes one to the belay at a broken mossy ledge. From here

one can scramble onto the left (east) ridge of the north pinnacle and follow it to the summit.

ROUTE 16. Northwest Couloir and Ledges. II, 4.0. First ascent July 13, 1931, by Fritiof Fryxell, Leland Horberg, Rudolph Edmund, William Cederberg, Neuman Kerndt, and Elof Petersen. Approach this route from Hanging Canyon. Cross the stream between Ramshead Lake and the Lake of the Crags and climb directly up the main couloir to the col between Symmetry Spire and the Symmetry Crags to the west. This is the same col as reached from the south via the Southwest Couloir (*Route 3*). During most of the summer this northwest couloir is filled with steep snow and sometimes ice, so knowledge of the use of an ice axe is essential. From the col climb left (east) up the ridge for about 100 feet before following easy but sometimes exposed ledges out to the left (north) and up the northwest side of the peak to the summit. There is almost a trail now in this final section of ledges. Given good snow conditions, this route also is useful for a descent into Hanging Canyon, but the uppermost snow is very steep indeed and should not be attempted unless one is experienced on such hazardous ground. *Time: 5¼ to 6¼ hours* from Jenny Lake. See *Appalachia*, 18, no. 4 (December 1931), pp. 388–408, illus.

ROUTE 17. Northwest Face. II, 5.6. First ascent July 15, 1974, by John Cain and Tim East. The route apparently ascended the face to the left (east) of the northwest couloir and below the final northwest ledges. From Hanging Canyon climb the snow and ice of the couloir for about 300 feet to an obvious point that provides access to this face. The first lead is face climbing to a grassy belay ledge. The next two pitches lead into a huge face of overhanging rock. Now traverse right and up for the next lead to a large belay ledge. The next pitch continues straight up to another belay ledge. Three pitches of scrambling then lead to the summit.

SYMMETRY CRAGS (10,320+ TO 10,400+)

Map: Mount Moran

All the pinnacles of the series extending west from Symmetry Spire to Rock of Ages have gentle east slopes and precipitous west faces. The exact number of summits depends on who is counting; the numbering from east to west, which is given here, is one approximation. However, the first pinnacle west of Symmetry Spire and the first two pinnacles east of Rock of Ages are quite distinct. Only these last two qualify as peaks and are treated separately. On the south slopes of the Symmetry Crags and west of the Symmetry Spire–Ice Point saddle are three small pinnacles that were climbed on July 22, 1957, by Fred Ayres and Ellis Blade, during the search for the lost Baxter's Pinnacle. The first is in the main couloir west of Storm Point, about 400 feet below the saddle, and the other two are on the crest of the next ridge to the west; all are short, easy climbs. Cutting across the lower southern slopes of the western crags is a line of weakness in the rocks, forming a wide and continuous shallow couloir running in a southwest–northeast direction. Although not specifically recognized as a fault, it forms a conspicuous feature from the proper viewpoint; it isolates the pinnacles climbed in 1957.

Crag 1. I, 3.0. First ascent July 13, 1931, by Fritiof Fryxell, Leland Horberg, Rudolph Edmund, William Cederberg, Neuman Kerndt, and Elof Petersen. This crag is climbed by its east ridge, a short scramble from the high col just west of Symmetry Spire, which is reached by *Route 3* for that peak.

Crag 2. I, 3.0. First ascent July 26, 1934, by Fred Ayres. This pinnacle is reached by dropping down from Crag 1 and climbing up a steep southern couloir to the east ridge, which is followed west to the summit. A climb of the north ridge of this crag, after an ascent of Crag 1, has been reported by Mark Chapman, July 26, 1971.

Crag 3. I, 3.0. First ascent July 26, 1934, by Fred Ayres. From Crag 2 drop down to the north on ledges to gain the notch between Crags 2 and 3, and then climb the east ridge to the summit. On August 8, 1973, Tom Kimbrough and Bob Greenspan climbed the north slope directly from Hanging Canyon onto the east ridge, which was followed to the summit.

SYMMETRY CRAG 4 (10,720+)
(0.45 mi W of Symmetry Spire)

Map: Mount Moran

Protected by crags on either side, this summit is seldom climbed even though it is readily accessible. Its west face, like the other crags of this series, is indeed steep, discouraging the casual climber.

CHRONOLOGY

East Ridge: July 26, 1934, Fred Ayres
Upper South Face: July 12, 1959, William Buckingham, Fred Wright

ROUTE 1. Upper South Face. II, 5.4. First ascent July 12, 1959, by William Buckingham and Fred Wright. From the Symmetry Spire–Ice Point saddle (see *Symmetry Spire, Route 3*), traverse west across several gullies to the long scree shelf that angles upward along the base of the nearly vertical, upper south face of Crag 4. Begin the ascent in the obvious line of weakness near the center of the face in a very shallow and deceptive gully. One ropelength up this depression leads to a grassy ledge. Traverse right on this ledge for about 200 feet to the point where it intersects another large ledge that diagonals upward to the left. Follow this ledge back for 150 feet to a point where two chimneys form a break in the wall above. Climb one of these chimneys for one ropelength; an easy pitch then leads to the summit ridge 200 feet east of the summit. See *American Alpine Journal,* 12, no. 1 (1960), pp. 125–127.

ROUTE 2. East Ridge. I, 3.0. First ascent July 26, 1934, by Fred Ayres. Crag 4 denotes the second summit east of Rock of Ages. As is the case for the crags to the east, there are no difficulties on this ridge once it is attained. One method is to start from the Symmetry Spire–Ice Point saddle, stay below (south of) the main ridge crest, and then gain the ridge just west of Crag 3. From the summit of Crag 3 the easiest method of reaching Crag 4 is to return to the notch between Crags 2 and 3, drop down around the south cliffs of Crag 3, regain the ridge crest at the notch between Crags 3 and 4, and continue on the east ridge to the summit of Crag 4. A direct descent of the west face of Crag 3 to reach the start of this ridge may involve rappelling.

SYMMETRY CRAG 5 (10,720+)
(0.55 mi W of Symmetry Spire)

Map: Mount Moran

Immediately to the east of Rock of Ages, Crag 5 presents a very steep west face with rock of dubious quality.

CHRONOLOGY

East Ridge: June 19, 1936, Fred and Irene Ayres
South Couloir: August 12, 1947, George Bell, Austen Riggs II, Rolfe Glover III, Wayland Griffith

ROUTE 1. South Couloir. II, 5.6. First ascent August 12, 1947, by George Bell, Austen Riggs II, Rolfe Glover III, and Wayland Griffith. This climb starts from Cascade Canyon and probably ascends the couloir located immediately beyond (west of) Trinity Buttress. At some point the shallow couloir below the upper south side of this crag must be crossed or ascended partway. The left (west) face of the couloir is climbed and a western branch is then followed to the summit, which is attained from the southeast.

ROUTE 2. East Ridge. I, 3.0. First ascent June 19, 1936, by Fred and Irene Ayres. Above and south of Lake of the Crags is a wide ledge that angles from lower left (east) to upper right (west) and joins the east ridge of Crag 5 immediately west of Crag 4. In early season this ledge will be covered with snow. The ridge itself offers no problems. The short east ridge can probably also be reached from the south, using the wide diagonal shelf that passes under the south face of Crag 4. This shelf can be gained from the Symmetry Spire–Ice Point saddle. To traverse west from Crag 4 will require a rappel down the steep west face of Crag 4.

ROCK OF AGES (10,895+)

Map: Mount Moran

This curiously flat-topped peak gained its maximum popularity 25 years ago or more, but it deserves more attention than it has received in recent years. Many of the routes are as challenging as those on the south side of Symmetry Spire and the approach is only a little longer. The nine routes range from easy to difficult, and, like Symmetry Spire, Rock of Ages has one easy descent route, the South Couloir (*Route 2*). The rock is usually sound and in places is outstanding. The features of the north face of Rock of Ages can be described in terms of two major indentations in the shape of Vs. The western V is larger, more distinct, lies directly below the summit, and contains prominent black water stains on the rock at its bottom. The eastern V is less distinct and begins just above a small Wall Street–like ledge that diagonals up across the face from left to right.

The best approach is from Hanging Canyon. Take the climbers' trail into the canyon and continue past the meadow on the west side of Lake of the Crags. Because the slopes and chutes leading up to the notches to the east and west of Rock of Ages are very rotten, there is a definite advantage in making the ascent in early season when the rubble is covered by snow, even though the snow is steep. In midseason or late season there are significant difficulties (5.4) in climbing the treacherous rock just below these notches.

It is also possible to approach Rock of Ages from Cascade Canyon, but the couloirs are long and not easy to find and steepen considerably in their upper reaches. Go up Cascade Canyon, past the drainage west of Trinity Buttress, to the next major stream draining a relatively narrow couloir; this couloir (with a short dogleg to the right) leads to the notch east of the peak. It is relatively free of loose rock and provides good rock scrambling. Near the notch the couloir narrows to a cleft 6 feet wide with multiple chockstones that are passed on the left wall. The next couloir to the west, also narrow, leads toward the notch west of Rock of Ages. About 200 feet short of the ridge crest the open couloir narrows and splits, the right branch leading up to the desired notch, while the left branch leads more easily to the col west of the Schoolhouse. Both of these couloirs are directly opposite the falls (on the opposite [south] side of the canyon) in the stream that drains the northeast snowfields of Mount Owen.

CHRONOLOGY

East Chimneys: August 14, 1934, Fred and Irene Ayres
Northwest Corner: July 23, 1935, Paul Petzoldt, Phil Smith, Herman Petzoldt
    var: **Northwest Face:** August 26, 1972, Tom Kreuzer, John Waldvogel
Stettner: August 21, 1941, Joseph and Paul Stettner
    var: August 8, 1949, Joseph Murphy, John Rouson
South Couloir: July 23, 1935, Paul Petzoldt, Phil Smith, Herman Petzoldt (descent); August 14, 1947, Ronald K. Smith, James T. Smith, Donald F. Smith, Bruce Edwards (ascent)

East Ridge: August 8, 1946, James T. Smith, Ronald K. Smith, Donald Caruthers
Southwest Couloir: August 14, 1947, George Bell, Rolfe Glover III
Northeast Face: August 25, 1949, William Primak, Reinhold Mankau, Peter Pfister
    var: July 24, 1951, Robert and Doris Merriam, Leigh Ortenburger
Northeast Chimney: July 30, 1951, Peter Robinson, Jim Cooke, Percy Crosby
Southeast Ridge: June 24, 1979, George Montopoli, Tim Hogan
    var: July 1993, Jim Howe, Mark Rump

ROUTE 1. Southwest Couloir. II, 5.4. First ascent August 14, 1947, by George Bell and Rolfe Glover III. This route ascends the westernmost couloir on the upper south side of Rock of Ages; this couloir leads to the west ridge just below the flat summit block. The base of this couloir can be reached via the long couloir extending upward from Cascade Canyon, or it can be gained by traversing other crags along the ridge to the west and passing the Schoolhouse on the south. If coming up from Cascade Canyon, take the last branch of the long couloir to the right (east) before attaining the notch west of Rock of Ages; this eastern branch is more of a broad ledge than a couloir. If starting from the notch west of Rock of Ages, climb down or rappel south down the very steep couloir and gain this same broad ledge system. Either way, climb up and east along the ledges to gain the west edge of the upper south face and climb directly upward to reach the uppermost west ridge of Rock of Ages. One 5.4 pitch is encountered just below the ridge crest. Follow the west ridge to the summit.

ROUTE 2. ☞ *South Couloir.* II, 4.0. First descent July 23, 1935, by Paul Petzoldt, Phil Smith, and Herman Petzoldt; first ascent August 14, 1947, by Ronald K. Smith, James T. Smith, Donald F. Smith, and Bruce Edwards. This short couloir is the one major break in the upper defenses of Rock of Ages. One can reach it via one of the long couloirs out of Cascade Canyon, but it is usually approached from the notch east of Rock of Ages after a Hanging Canyon approach. From this notch, traverse west underneath the south walls of Rock of Ages to the crest of the small south ridge. Climb the ridge until it is possible to work up and slightly to the right (east) over easy blocks and chimneys into the south couloir. Scramble up to its head; then climb easy slabs leading right (east) up to the sloping summit ridge, and follow this back (west) to the summit block. This south couloir is also the standard route of descent. To locate it from the summit, walk east down the broad summit ridge until just past the small evergreen bushes, then cut back downward south and west on the aforementioned slabs.

ROUTE 3. Southeast Ridge. III, 5.9. First ascent June 24, 1979, by George Montopoli and Tim Hogan. See *Topo 80*.

This route lies very close to the crest of the southeast ridge, which is left (south) of the notch east of Rock of Ages. Descend a short distance from the notch and climb the initial section, over a pointed flake that hangs down, and then up (5.4) to the first belay point at the base of a steep face. The second lead goes up a flake (5.6 hand crack) past a curious round, gray projection (1 foot in diameter) and into and up cracks (5.8) to the next belay stance located just to the right of a hollow flake. The third pitch starts by passing a roof on the right (5.6), and then a short, overhanging flake move (5.9) is followed by an unprotected friction traverse (15 feet) to the right to a shallow dihedral (5.7), which is climbed up and left to the next belay. The last lead climbs an overhanging crack (5.8) up onto an easier face that ends at the broad summit ridge. The route contains good, solid rock. For protection devices up to 4 inches are useful.

Variation: III, 5.9. First ascent July 1993 by Jim Howe and Mark Rump. This variation takes off from the second pitch of *Route 3*. The crux third pitch ascends a thin finger crack on excellent rock to a steep (vertical), blocky face.

ROUTE 4. ☞*East Chimneys*. II, 5.6. First ascent August 14, 1934, by Fred and Irene Ayres, from Cascade Canyon; attempted from Hanging Canyon on July 16, 1934, by Fred and Irene Ayres. This climb starts from the notch just east of Rock of Ages. Directly above the notch is the east ridge. An indentation containing a series of steep chimneys begins a little left (about 80 feet south) of the notch. Climb these chimneys on good rock (during the first ascent a *courte-échelle* was used at one overhang) for several pitches. (Note: The term *courte-échelle*

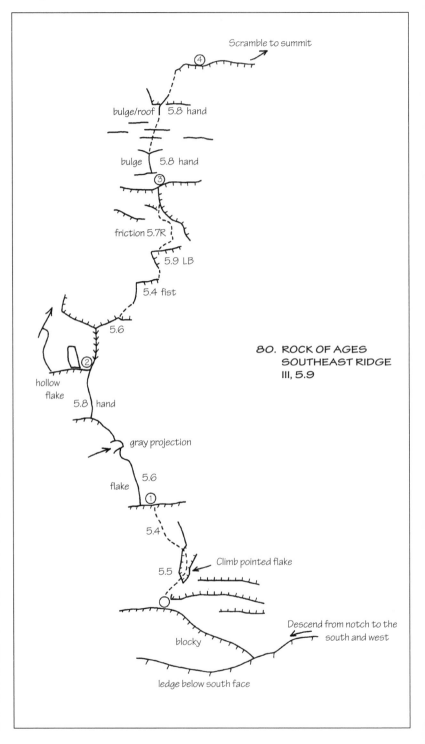

Scramble to summit

bulge/roof | 5.8 hand

bulge | 5.8 hand ③

friction 5.7R

5.9 LB

5.4 fist

5.6

② hollow flake

5.8 | hand

gray projection

5.6

flake ①

5.4

5.5 ← Climb pointed flake

Descend from notch to the south and west

blocky

ledge below south face

80. ROCK OF AGES
   SOUTHEAST RIDGE
   III, 5.9

refers to the once commonly accepted technique of a shoulder stand.) Near the top, traverse to the right on a ledge out onto the east face and climb the last few feet onto the gently sloping, grass-covered summit ridge. Stroll westward to the unusual flat summit block, which can be climbed via a crack near its north end or by a lieback on its east face (more difficult). Many variations are possible in the chimneys, and the climbing is steep and not too difficult. *Time: 7¾ hours* from Jenny Lake. See *Chicago Mountaineering Club Newsletter,* 2, no. 5 (January–July 1948), pp. 5–7; *Trail and Timberline,* no. 196 (February 1935), p. 18; no. 223 (May 1937), p. 56.

ROUTE 5. *East Ridge.* II, 5.8. First ascent August 8, 1946, by James T. Smith, Ronald K. Smith, and Donald Caruthers. From the col, one can stay directly on the east ridge and never enter the couloir or chimneys of the regular East Chimneys route, but this is significantly more difficult.

ROUTE 6. *Northeast Chimney.* II, 5.6. First ascent July 30, 1951, by Peter Robinson, Jim Cooke, and Percy Crosby. See *Photo 91.* From the meadow west of Lake of the Crags climb (snow in early season) toward the notch east of Rock of Ages; cut right (west) onto the north face by means of the small, Wall Street–like ledge that slopes up to the right and narrows at the end. From this point climb over an overhang to a shelf that leads steeply up to the right toward the bottom of the eastern V. Instead of following this shelf out to the right, climb 20 feet left (east) to a chimney. On the first ascent the next pitch began with a shoulder stand. Then climb 60 feet up this chimney past another overhang. Continue up the chimney to a large chockstone, which can be passed either by a steep ledge on the left side (this may be wet) or on the right wall. Climb left onto the summit ridge and follow it westward to the summit block. See *Dartmouth Mountaineering Club Journal,* 1951, pp. 11–15, illus.

ROUTE 7. *Northeast Face.* II, 5.6. First ascent August 25, 1949, by William Primak, Reinhold Mankau, and Peter Pfister. See *Photo 91.* This route utilizes the right (west) branch of the less distinct eastern V on the north face of Rock of Ages. The original climb reached the lower end of this V, which is about 300 feet above the slabs and snow at the base of the north face, via a series of chimneys well east of the water stains of *Route 8.* After three short leads, including the passage of a chockstone, a 10-foot wide grassy ledge was reached. From the broken rock of the V, a sequence of chimneys and ledges angles up slightly to the right (west). After five short leads the easy summit ridge is attained through a chimney near the right edge of the V. See *Chicago Mountaineering Club Newsletter,* 3, no. 6 (August 1949), pp. 26–27.

Variation: II, 5.6. First ascent July 24, 1951, by Robert and Doris Merriam and Leigh Ortenburger. This climb starts as in *Route 6,* using the same small, Wall Street–like ledge. At its west end climb over the same overhang to the same shelf, and follow it steeply up to the right toward the bottom of the eastern V. An awkward step with considerable exposure is required to complete the traverse into the V. This variation provides an alternate to the chimneys used by the 1949 party. *Time: 8½ hours* from Jenny Lake. See *Stanford Alpine Club Journal,* 1955, pp. 48–50.

ROUTE 8. *Stettner.* II, 5.7. First ascent August 21, 1941, by Joseph and Paul Stettner. See *Photo 91.* This route is perhaps unique in the Tetons in that its starting point was originally marked by a circular blaze of red paint on the rock; this circle was found in 1948 on the second ascent but has not been seen since. It was also an early scene of a 30-foot leader fall, successfully held by a sitting belay. This route goes up the western V. Below the bottom of this V are prominent black water stains on the rock. The climb starts in a narrow chimney about 50 feet to the right (west) of these black markings. Climb about 150 feet up this wet chimney on steep and exposed rock. Because the chimney terminates in an impossible-looking narrow crack that slants to the left, climb out about 15 feet on the difficult open wall to a grassy shelf at the bottom of the V. Follow the steep ledges of the right (west) section of the V and reach the summit ridge at a point north and west of the summit block. Traverse around underneath the summit block on the west, and climb to the summit from the south. Some rotten rock can be expected on this route.

Variation: II, 5.1. First ascent August 8, 1949, by Joseph Murphy and John Rouson. Instead of climbing up and to the right (west) from the bottom of the V, walk down and to the left (east) along an obvious ledge to join *Route 7* about two pitches above the first overhang. Follow that route to the summit.

ROUTE 9. *Northwest Corner.* II, 5.7. First ascent July 23, 1935, by Paul Petzoldt, Phil Smith, and Herman Petzoldt. From the meadow at the west end of Lake of the Crags, proceed up the talus and snow to the notch between the Schoolhouse and Rock of Ages. This is much more easily and safely done in early season when snow will extend all the way to the notch; otherwise, steep, loose, and hazardous rock must be negotiated. The first-ascent party climbed about 150 feet out to the left onto the north face in order to avoid the smooth face rising out of the notch. Once above this face, they cut back right (west) onto the northwest face, which was climbed up and left to a small platform on the northwest corner of the peak.

In recent years a more direct route has been taken out of and only a few feet left of the notch. From a belay at its base, climb the initial slightly overhanging section on small holds up and right past a small, strenuous, very awkward corner (5.7) onto easier rock that angles up and slightly left to a stance near the north edge of the main wall above the notch. Protection here is difficult to place, but a large camming device can be placed up and left of the awkward corner. An alternative to this corner is an overhanging crack (5.7) about 15 feet to the right (south).

The second pitch rejoins the original route, going up and right around the main corner of the ridge to a sequence of vertical jam cracks (5.6) that lead to the belay at the base of an outstanding steep, slabby wall of excellent rock. Climb directly up this wall (5.4) on good holds, even though the absence of cracks makes protection scarce. The fourth lead goes up and slightly left around an overhanging section to a belay well around on the north side. Next, continue in a crack up and left out to an exposed point at the upper end of the Stettner route. Easier climbing in cracks and blocks then takes one to within 100 feet of the summit. Scramble to the top via the northern break in the summit block. This six-pitch climb on uniformly excellent rock is recommended as an early-season climb for those who can pass the first lead safely. It is not as well protected as one might wish. See *Harvard Mountaineering*, 12 (May 1955), pp. 57–58.

Variation: Northwest Face. II, 5.8. First ascent August 26, 1972, by Tom Kreuzer and John Waldvogel. From the platform out on the northwest corner, one can climb straight up for 100 feet and then continue up and slightly right until the easier rock below the summit block is reached. Most of the climbing is 5.6, but two sections of 5.8 will be encountered below the final overhang of the summit block.

AYRES' CRAGS (10,640+ TO 10,720+)

Map: Mount Moran

This series of five pinnacles, numbered from east to west, on the ridge immediately west of Rock of Ages contains some of the better climbing around Lake of the Crags. All these pinnacles, as well as several others on the rim of Hanging Canyon, were first climbed by Fred Ayres, who modestly objected to the name, Ayres' Crags, saying it was "hardly euphonious." A traverse of these crags along with Rock of Ages provides a full day of good climbing, or ridge running as Ayres would say. All are normally reached from Hanging Canyon, but long couloirs from Cascade Canyon do provide direct access to Crags 4 and 5. The proper couloir, more open than those to the east, leads due north from the eastern edge of a barren talus slope just beyond (west of) a section of trees. The proper couloir lies just west of the falls (on the opposite [south] side of the canyon) in the stream that drains the northeast snowfields of Mount Owen. To reach Crag 1 or 2 from the south, take the next couloir to the east (see *Rock of Ages, Route 1*), which ends at the notch just west of Rock of Ages.

The Schoolhouse (Ayres' Crag 1) (10,640+)
(0.05 mi W of Rock of Ages)

The Schoolhouse, the smallest and sharpest of these crags, is the first pinnacle west of Rock of Ages. Originally called "The Old Setting Hen" in the 1930s, this pinnacle was renamed by Fred Ayres, who felt that the first name was

"hardly dignified enough for an official name." It is not easy to find today such a concern for dignity in nomenclature.

ROUTE 1. West Face. I, 5.4. First ascent July 8, 1940, by Fred and Irene Ayres and Margaret Smith; attempted July 22, 1936, by Fred Ayres solo. From the notch west of the Schoolhouse, first climb over the large boulder that rests directly on the ridge. The lower part of the west face, which is now directly above, is a very large detached slab. On the first ascent the high-angle outside face of the slab was climbed; the chimney between the slab and the face itself may possibly be climbable for a small person. The first part of this pitch is very exposed. From the top of the slab climb a series of cracks to the knife-edge summit. *Time: 4½ hours from Ramshead Lake.*

ROUTE 2. East Ridge. I, 5.6. First ascent June 17, 1958, by William Buckingham, Karl Ross, and Walter Gove. From the notch east of the Schoolhouse (and west of Rock of Ages) climb two pitches up the east ridge, the second of which is a pleasant jam crack, to the platform just south of the summit. One short, slightly overhanging pitch then leads to the summit. See *American Alpine Journal*, 11, no. 2 (1959), pp. 307–309.

ROUTE 3. The Windowsill. II, 5.6. First ascent August 12, 1966, by Robert Fenichel, Mary Louise Denman, and Robert Hoguet III. Beneath the large boulder at the base of the west face of the Schoolhouse is a tunnel or window some 12 feet in length; it is large enough for a crouching climber to pass through. This four-pitch route provides access to this window from the north, using the face just to the right of the extremely loose chute that leads to the notch between Rock of Ages and the Schoolhouse. The first pitch goes approximately straight up from the right of the chute for 100 feet on downsloping holds to a good ledge for a belay. Now move right from the ledge to an overhang, which is passed (5.6) through a V cleft in it, and finish the lead (140 feet) over very poor rock to a 20-square-foot square ledge. The third pitch (120 feet, 5.1) exits right from this ledge. Climb up to a long ledge and then go out to and up a short, steep open book near the right end of this ledge. From the top of this corner move right to an enormous detached block. The final lead (140 feet) starts left from the top of the block, goes up 12 feet, continues left to corner overlooking the original chute, and then ends with a scramble up to the Window.

Ayres' Crag 2 (10,720+)   *(0.15 mi W of Rock of Ages)*

This is the major summit between Rock of Ages and the Blockhouse, higher and larger than the smaller crags (1 and 3) to either side.

ROUTE 1. East Face. II, 3.0. First ascent July 22, 1936, by Fred Ayres. The ascent or descent of the sloping east face involves no difficulties.

ROUTE 2. West Face. II, 4.0. First descent July 22, 1936, by Fred Ayres; first ascent August 3, 1950, by Jiggs and Ted

Lewis and Jim Smith. This broad and slabby face can be readily climbed on good holds near its north edge.

Ayres' Crag 3 (10,640+)   (0.16 mi W of Rock of Ages)

ROUTE 1. West Ridge. I, 3.0. First ascent July 22, 1936, by Fred Ayres. From the notch west of this small pinnacle climb directly up the knife-edge west ridge leading to the summit until a traverse can be made to the right (south), down onto a shelf, which leads around the south side of the pinnacle. Continue along this shelf until due south of the summit; then climb blocks leading back to the west ridge and follow it to the summit. If approaching this pinnacle from the east, contour around its south ridge and reach the summit in a similar manner.

Blockhouse (Ayres' Crag 4) (10,720+)
(0.2 mi W of Rock of Ages)

This significant tower rises steeply on all sides, with the northeast face providing the only break in the otherwise serious defenses. It was first explored by Fred Ayres on July 22, 1936, who wisely decided that the climbing was too exposed for a solo climber. It provides an interesting multipitch climb worthy of the approach hike into Hanging Canyon.

CHRONOLOGY

Northeast Face: August 1, 1940, Fred Ayres, John
    Oberlin, Orrin Bonney, Margaret Smith
South Ridge: August 15, 1959, Barry Corbet,
    Frederick Medrick
Southwest Face: August 15, 1959, William
    Buckingham, Al Read, Frank Magary
West Face: July 8, 1960, Al Read, Sterling Neale

ROUTE 1. West Face. II, 5.6. First ascent July 8, 1960, by Al Read and Sterling Neale. Approach the saddle between the Blockhouse and the Canine Tooth via Hanging Canyon and Lake of the Crags. From the base of the west face of the Blockhouse, traverse right on easy rock around to the edge of the southwest face. Climb directly up and to the left until a ledge is reached about 80 feet above the belayer. Now move left and up for 15 feet on very small holds to a broad ledge. The second pitch goes directly up the corner formed by the west and south faces. After 100 feet one can scramble along the level ridge to the summit block; attain the summit from the north. See *American Alpine Journal,* 12, no. 2 (1961), pp. 373–379.

ROUTE 2. Southwest Face. II, 5.7. First ascent August 15, 1959, by William Buckingham, Al Read, and Frank Magary. This route ascends a crack system near the center of the face; the crack is reached by angling left from a point near the south edge of the face. This difficult pitch is nearly vertical and poorly protected. After 150 feet an adequate belay stance on a broad ledge is reached. The final 200-foot

section is moderate 4.0 climbing in a shallow couloir that leads right and up to the summit.

ROUTE 3. South Ridge. II, 5.6. First ascent August 15, 1959, by Barry Corbet and Frederick Medrick. The south face of the Blockhouse, which faces Cascade Canyon, is divided by the sharp south ridge containing a huge ceiling near the summit. This climb stays slightly left (west) of the ridge crest; a traverse to the left is required just below the ceiling. This enjoyable ridge can be approached directly from Cascade Canyon or from Hanging Canyon via a slight descent from the Canine Tooth–Blockhouse saddle.

ROUTE 4. ☞Northeast Face. II, 5.1. First ascent August 1, 1940, by Fred Ayres, John Oberlin, Orrin Bonney, and Margaret Smith; attempted on July 22, 1936, by Fred Ayres solo. From the notch east of this pinnacle, scramble up to a large black ledge where the climbing begins. Descend a few feet to the left (south) in order to reach a small chimney. Ascend this chimney and pass the chockstone; then use the face to the right to regain the east ridge. Scramble up some very large, loose blocks to a ledge containing a thin 5-foot flake set on edge. The next lead traverses about 50 feet out on the north face on a 2-foot ledge and then diagonals up to the right (west). The last ropelength that leads to the summit also angles up to the right on ledges and chimneys. Descend by several short rappels.

Ayres' Crag 5 (11,040+)   (0.2 mi S of the Jaw)

This solitary high point lies at the end of a ridge extending south of the rest of the pinnacles that surround Lake of the Crags. From Cascade Canyon, Ayres' Crag 5 is seen as a prominent buttress with a sheer south face (see *Cascade Canyon, North Side Rock Climbs*). From the summit, the major couloir west of this crag appears to offer a fast descent route down to Cascade Canyon. However, the bottom of it drops off, entailing at least one rappel, so it is preferable to cut left (east) out of the main couloir just below the imposing south face of the crag.

ROUTE 1. Northeast Ridge. I, 3.0. First ascent July 22, 1936, by Fred Ayres. This ridge connects with the east ridge of the Canine Tooth about halfway to its summit. Climb the slope from Hanging Canyon to the col west of the Blockhouse and ascend the east ridge of the Canine Tooth until it is easy to get onto the northeast ridge of Ayres' Crag 5. Follow this ridge to the summit, which consists of loose boulders.

JAW CRAGS (CA. 11,200+)
(0.8 mi WSW of St. John)

Map: Mount Moran

This group of pinnacles at the western end of Hanging Canyon extending west and north from the Ayres' Crags forms the south ridge of the Jaw. Together with the Jaw, which is the highest of the group, they present a profile for which the name is apt when viewed from Lake of the Crags.

The Grinders, although small, contain some difficult and exposed climbing. They are numbered from south to north. See *Dartmouth Mountaineering Club Journal,* 1952, pp. 45–46, illus.

Canine Tooth. I, 3.0. First ascent July 5, 1940, by Robert Bear and William Plumley. This is the first high point west of the Blockhouse. It is an easy climb from east or west.

Grinder 1. I, 3.0. First ascent July 4, 1952, by Peter Robinson, Brian Brett, Percy Crosby, and Bill and John Briggs. This easy climb from the north uses a series of ledges.

Grinder 2. I, 5.4. First ascent July 4, 1952, by Peter Robinson. Climb the chimney separating this pinnacle from Grinder 3 until it is possible to climb out on friction holds on the east face, which leads to the summit. Another route, first climbed on September 9, 1954, by Gary Hemming and Leigh Ortenburger, leads up the prominent shelf on the south face. From the exposed end of this shelf climb a crack to the summit.

Grinder 3. I, 5.1. First ascent September 9, 1954, by Leigh Ortenburger and Gary Hemming. This is climbed from Grinder 4 via the sharp north ridge.

Grinder 4. I, 5.1. First ascent September 9, 1954, by Gary Hemming and Leigh Ortenburger. Climb the north ridge from the notch between this pinnacle and Grinder 5. Descent can be made via Grinder 3.

Grinder 5. I, 4.0. First ascent July 5, 1940, by Robert Bear and William Plumley. This pinnacle was first climbed by the chimney in the middle of its east face. On July 4, 1952, Peter Robinson, Brian Brett, Percy Crosby, and Bill and John Briggs climbed this pinnacle by its easy north ridge.

THE JAW (11,400)

Map: Mount Moran

At the extreme west end of Hanging Canyon lies the Jaw, which is only 30 feet lower than Mount St. John, the highest point of those that surround this canyon. It is easily approached from Lake of the Crags. The summit of the Jaw affords an excellent view of the impressive north and northwest faces of Teewinot, Mount Owen, and the Grand Teton.

CHRONOLOGY

East Face: August 29, 1931, Frank Smith, Eccles Johnson
West Ridge: June 21, 1958, William Buckingham, Robert and Margaret West, Robert Keyes (descent); July 30, 1989, Susie Harrington (ascent)
North Ridge: August 21, 1960, Loring Woodman, Duncan Cameron

ROUTE 1. West Ridge. I, 5.6. First descent June 21, 1958, by William Buckingham, Robert and Margaret West, and

Robert Keyes; first ascent July 30, 1989, by Susie Harrington. This ridge begins just east of Buckingham Palace (11,097) at the saddle (10,640+), which can be reached either from the north via a snow slope from Paintbrush Canyon or from the south via a 3,000-foot couloir from Cascade Canyon. At the base of the north approach is an interesting example of a rock glacier, perhaps the most accessible example in the range. Scramble easily from the saddle to the first high point, Point 11,120+, which contains a natural window. The remainder of the pinnacle ridge consists of scrambling until the uppermost steep section is reached. If this is climbed directly (as on the first ascent), a dihedral (5.6) with very loose rock in places leads to the summit. This section can be bypassed (as on the first descent) on the south to a small notch between the Jaw and the Grinders; the summit is then easily attained. As a descent route for a traverse continuing to the west, the southern bypass is recommended. See *American Alpine Journal,* 11, no. 2 (1959), pp. 307–309.

ROUTE 2. ☞East Face. I, 2.0. First ascent August 29, 1931, by Frank Smith and Eccles Johnson. See *Photo 89.* From Lake of the Crags continue up the benches and talus slopes of western Hanging Canyon to the summit. No difficulties will be met except for some snow climbing early in the season. *Time:* 4½ hours from Ramshead Lake.

ROUTE 3. North Ridge. I, 4.0. First ascent August 21, 1960, by Loring Woodman and Duncan Cameron. Approach via Indian Paintbrush Canyon into the cirque between the Outlier (10,560+) and Mount St. John to the saddle separating the Outlier and the Jaw. Scramble up the north ridge to a col just below the steep section of the main west ridge. Climb the first nearly vertical 50 feet directly. Ninety feet of scrambling on loose rock brings one to the base of a slight overhang, which is climbed by a crack on the left. On the next pitch pass the "Man," a pinnacle (named for its appearance from the northeast) on the right. The final pitch follows the corner of the open chimney just to the right of the summit ridge; the jam crack on the left (the smaller of two) leads to a large depression just below the overhanging part of the chimney. A small horizontal ledge or crack then provides a hand traverse to the top of the chimney on the right. A short scramble then brings one to the top. See *American Alpine Journal,* 12, no. 2 (1961), pp. 373–379.

CAMELS HEAD (11,200+)

(0.7 mi WSW of Mount St. John)

Map: Mount Moran

This very small pinnacle (only about 60 feet high) is located a short distance east of the first saddle east of the Jaw. It is the only difficult part of the ridge between Needles Eye Spire and the Jaw and can be approached from the upper east slopes of the Jaw.

ROUTE 1. *East Face.* I, 5.4. First ascent September 9, 1954, by Gary Hemming and Leigh Ortenburger. The route starts on the left (south) edge of the smooth east face (5.4). Climb until the holds run out (about 20 feet), then traverse right (north) across the face and finish the short climb by the northeast ridge. The first-ascent party used interesting tactics to get off the pinnacle. One climber was belayed down, and then the rope was fixed and the second climber rappelled off the opposite side. There are no nubs or piton cracks at the summit.

NEEDLES EYE SPIRE (11,200+)
(0.6 mi WSW of Mount St. John)

Map: Mount Moran

This spectacular finger is immediately west of the window in the St. John–Jaw ridge. The direct southern approach from Hanging Canyon is guarded by a cliff band that extends across the south side of Minga Spire.

ROUTE 1. *East Face.* I, 5.4. First ascent August 7, 1946, by Fred Ayres and John Oberlin. Pass the series of cliffs, which prevents a direct approach to the spire from Hanging Canyon, by ascending the first (eastern) couloir of Minga Spire. Once past these cliffs, turn abruptly left (west) and scramble up and left along the top of the cliffs past the south buttress of Minga Spire. One can now climb a 120-foot, very steep chimney to reach the notch just east of Needles Eye Spire. An easier approach is to go first to the col west of Needles Eye Spire and then circle in back (north) of the spire to reach this same notch. The almost-vertical east face is climbed by a series of small ledges and large flakes. A 60-foot rappel is just adequate for descent.

MINGA SPIRE (11,360+)
(0.5 mi WSW of Mount St. John)

Map: Mount Moran

This is the most prominent high point on the ridge between Mount St. John and the Jaw; it lies immediately east of the window on that ridge. From the highway just south of the Jenny Lake campground, this section of ridge is seen as the skyline between Storm Point and Symmetry Spire.

ROUTE 1. *East Ridge.* I, 3.0. First ascent July 9, 1940, by Paul Petzoldt, Elizabeth Cowles, and Anthony Whittemore. From Hanging Canyon proceed west past Lake of the Crags and climb the couloir leading toward the low point in the flat east ridge; follow this easy ridge west to the summit.

ROUTE 2. *West Ridge.* II, 5.6. First descent September 9, 1954, by Gary Hemming and Leigh Ortenburger. In the course of a traverse west to the Jaw, the west ridge of Minga Spire was descended to the window, but a rappel was required.

MOUNT ST. JOHN (11,430)

Map: Mount Moran

This peak, the highest point among the numerous towers and pinnacles that surround the alpine lakes of the beautiful Hanging Canyon, was named after Orestes H. St. John, the geologist of the Teton Division of the Hayden Survey of 1877. The popular Mount St. John is one of the easier peaks in the park and only one short day is required for its ascent. In early season, however, some snow slopes must be negotiated and knowledge of use of the ice axe is advisable. Its long, serrated summit ridge contains several peaks, all very nearly the same altitude, making it difficult to select the proper couloir to ascend from Hanging Canyon. Efforts to reach the summit began in late September 1925 with a solo attempt by Phil Smith in which he reached the most easterly of the subsummits. Other easterly subsummits were reached on August 20, 1926, by H. C. Forman; on July 9, 1928, by Fritiof Fryxell and Floyd Steele; and on July 14, 1929, by Phil Smith and Arthur Montgomery. On the first ascent repeated sightings with a Brunton transit were required to verify that the highest point had finally been reached.

CHRONOLOGY

South Couloir, West Ridge: August 20, 1929, Fritiof Fryxell, Phil Smith
East Ridge: July 10, 1931, Robert L. M. Underhill (partial descent); June 16, 1934, Hans Fuhrer, Alfred Roovers (ascent, probably bypassed some subsummits)
South Couloir, East Ridge: unknown
North Ridge and North Face: July 2, 1936, Wayne Thompson, Ralph Sinsheimer; July 2, 1939, Francis Hendricks, Adam Koj, Stanley Grites (descent)
North Face, East Couloir: August 19, 1939, Arthur Guyer, C. Barber Moseley, or August 21, 1940, Bud Garnaas, Theodore Brandon, Robert Anderson, Tim Ramsland, Frank Blake

ROUTE 1. ☞*South Couloir, West Ridge.* I, 3.0. First ascent August 20, 1929, Fritiof Fryxell and Phil Smith. See *Photo 92.* The entire south side of Mount St. John, rising above Hanging Canyon, is covered with couloirs leading up to the summit ridge. For this route, one is attempting to find the couloir that emerges just west of the summit. Hike up Hanging Canyon, continuing past Lake of the Crags along its north shore. From the meadows at the west end of the lake, scramble due north, turning up either of the couloirs west of the prominent steep buttress in the lowest portion of the south face of St. John. In early season some steep snow must be expected in these couloirs; by midseason it is usually possible to avoid these snow patches. Depending on which couloir is chosen, one or more steps in the west ridge itself will have to be climbed. The major step rises about 250 feet, is steep and exposed on the north, and involves some 4.0 climbing. This west ridge is seldom intentionally climbed, because the east ridge alternative (see *Route 2*) has become the regular route. The ridge would be encountered, however, if one were traversing to St. John from the Jaw. For time and references, see *Route 2*.

ROUTE 2. ☞ *South Couloir, East Ridge.* I, 3.0. First ascent unknown. See *Photo 92*. As already noted, the entire south side of Mount St. John is covered with couloirs leading up to the summit ridge. The principal difficulty with this route is the selection of the proper couloir. Proceed up Hanging Canyon to Lake of the Crags. From the north shore of the lake start up the talus where the lake is the narrowest and proceed up toward the ridge, occasionally moving left (west) into the adjacent couloir when it becomes convenient. In early season some steep snow must be expected in these couloirs; by midseason it is usually possible to avoid these snow patches. If the proper couloir is followed—and there are several possibilities in the upper third of the peak—the summit ridge will be reached at a broad col from which it is but a short scramble east to the summit. If the next couloir east has been inadvertently taken, the first subsummit east of the true summit must be traversed, and this will involve some 4.0 climbing and perhaps a rappel. A combination of the second couloir east and its associated ridge, climbed on July 14, 1971, by John Kevin Fox and Steven Doyle, provides a long, mixed rock-and-snow climb that ends at the second eastern subsummit, requiring an even longer traverse west to the true summit. *Time: 5½ to 6¾ hours* from Jenny Lake. See *Appalachia*, 18, no. 4 (December 1931), pp. 388–408, illus.; *Chicago Mountaineering Club Newsletter*, 2, no. 5 (January–July 1948), pp. 5–7; 2, no. 6 (July–December 1948), pp. 4–5; *Trail and Timberline*, no. 491 (November 1959), pp. 153–156.

ROUTE 3. *East Ridge.* II, 5.1. First partial descent July 10, 1931, by Robert L. M. Underhill; first ascent June 16, 1934, by Hans Fuhrer and Alfred Roovers, although this climb apparently bypassed some of the subsummits. There are two approaches to the base of this ridge. One is to take the trail into the beginning of Hanging Canyon and cut north onto the broad east face or ridge as soon as convenient. Another less heavily travelled approach is to cross the bridge at the south end of String Lake and take the trail north around its west shore until the first open slope is reached only a short distance from the south end of the lake. A small trail heading upward through the low bushes of this slope will be found; it leads to the picturesque Laurel Lake (7,400+). From the lake take the long open couloir near the right (north) edge of the east face; this couloir ultimately blends in with the upper ridge, well short of the first subsummit. This couloir is discernible on the Grand Teton quadrangle map. There are five distinct subsummits on this ridge and

one deep notch between the first and second. If one follows the ridge closely, this is an enjoyable climb; one or more rappels may be desired, depending on one's downclimbing limits. It is easy enough to bypass the notch and most of the subsummits by climbing along the south side of this ridge. *Time: 6¾ to 8¾ hours* from Jenny Lake. See *Appalachia*, 18, no. 4 (December 1931), pp. 388–408, illus.

ROUTE 4. *North Ridge and North Face.* II, 5.1. First ascent July 2, 1936, by Wayne Thompson and Ralph Sinsheimer; first descent July 2, 1939, by Francis Hendricks, Adam Koj, and Stanley Grites. The structure of this face can be characterized as a sequence of diagonal benches or broad ledges, leading up from lower left to upper right, separated by very steep, commonly vertical walls. The climbs of Mount St. John from the north have perforce taken somewhat zigzag lines, moving upward from bench to bench whenever a break in the next wall permits. These benches harbor quantities of loose rock but in early season will be covered with snow. It also appears that every ascent of the north side of Mount St. John has utilized at least part of the north ridge that connects with Rockchuck Peak. The difficulty encountered is very sensitive to the routefinding. In recent years this route from the col separating Rockchuck Peak from Mount St. John has been used primarily in connection with the traverse from Rockchuck Peak. The first alternative described here approximates that of the first-ascent party; the last describes the traverse to the summit of St. John from the col. Descents of this face have been made (rarely) by rappel directly into Indian Paintbrush Canyon.

Hike to Laurel Lake from String Lake (see *Route 3*) and continue up the cirque between Rockchuck Peak and Mount St. John. Climb up and west out of the southwest corner of this cirque, usually on snow, onto a broad bench leading to the north ridge. Scramble up loose rock to the crest of the north ridge, and continue out to the west to a sequence of diagonal shelves that leads up toward the summit ridge of St. John. In early season these shelves will be covered with snow, in late season scree-covered. There is considerable exposure off the right (north) edge down into Indian Paintbrush Canyon. If the proper sequence is selected, one will emerge onto the summit ridge about 200 feet east of the summit.

A second alternative is to follow the route described above onto the north ridge and then to climb back up and left (east) over loose rock to the most westerly of the three slanting (from lower left to upper right) ledges that lead to the summit ridge of St. John. Climb this wide ledge to the ridge, where the one tower lying between the climber and the summit can be either climbed over or bypassed on the left (south). This alternative can be very difficult if the easiest line is not found.

The third alternative is to start the climb from the main col separating St. John from Rockchuck. This col will ordinarily be approached from the east via the same cirque described in the first alternative. Climb out of this col on the left (east) side on grassy ledges and then cut up onto the ridge crest over wet rock slabs. To reach the second notch, the large knoblike tower, clearly seen from the valley, can be either bypassed on the left (east) or climbed. The buttress on the far (south) side of this notch can be climbed directly (difficult) or passed on the left (wet, narrow, mossy ledges) or the right (recommended). After a few hundred feet along the base of the west side of this buttress, enter a narrow couloir angling up to the left. In early or midseason this couloir will be filled with snow. The large chockstone at the upper end of this couloir is passed by climbing a steep 40-foot pitch on the right (south) wall. One can now scramble up to the left (east) to a slanting ledge and follow it to the summit ridge. It should be noted that this variation also can be reached from the west via the Indian Paintbrush Canyon trail, which begins at the south end of String Lake. From about the 8,600-foot level, cross the stream and ascend the talus in the cirque below the north face of St. John and the west face of Rockchuck. Either proceed to the initial col or join the variation at the narrow diagonal couloir beyond the buttress; the latter would be the more obvious. Keep in mind that the summit of Mount St. John is just a short distance west of the ridge joining Rockchuck with St. John. The Jaw is misleading when seen from the north, as it appears higher than St. John.

ROUTE 5. *North Face, East Couloir*. II, 5.4. First ascent August 19, 1939, by Arthur Guyer and C. Barber Moseley, or August 21, 1940, by Bud Garnaas, Theodore Brandon, Robert Anderson, Tim Ramsland, and Frank Blake. The upper east ridge of Mount St. John apparently can be reached from the north, via the cirque between St. John and Rockchuck, without using the north ridge. Proceed as in *Route 4* up the cirque until past the first buttresses. Well before reaching the north ridge connecting St. John and Rockchuck, a large talus cone will be seen leading south toward the main notch in the east ridge. Climb this cone to its upper end where a cliff band will be encountered, guarding access to the notch and the three parallel shelves that slant up and right (west) to the summit ridge. The route ascended was one of these shelves, probably the most westerly one, although the notch itself might have been reached.

HANGING CANYON, NORTH SIDE ROCK CLIMBS (CA. 10,240+)

Map: Mount Moran

These rock climbs on the north side of lower Hanging Canyon are listed in order from west to east. While there is some good rock on these routes, the largely mediocre quality is perhaps compensated for by the relatively short Teton approach.

ROUTE 1. *Treeline*. II, 5.7, A1. First ascent September 8, 1968, by George Goedecke, Bill Hackett, Bill Cooper, and

Rick Thomas. This route is on one of the easterly south arêtes of Mount St. John, but apparently west of the "Bird Arêtes." Start from about the elevation of Arrowhead Pool and climb a 4.0 couloir to the left of the arête. Move right to start the climb at about the elevation of Cube Point. The first pitch (5.6), just left of an overhang, goes up to a belay below a second overhang that extends across the face of the arête. Move right and climb past this difficult overhang (5.7, A1) and again to the right to a belay from a tree. The next lead goes up and slightly right to another tree belay. The fourth pitch passes a second overhang (5.7) to a third tree on the right edge of the arête, from which two easy leads take one to the top of the arête. Descent is back to the east down to the lower Hanging Canyon.

ROUTE 2. *St. John's Wart*. II, 5.6. Probable first ascent July 17, 1980, by William Soller and Jonathan Hollin, or June 3, 1981, by Chuck Harris. This small, free-standing pinnacle at the base of a south ridge of Mount St. John is located about 0.3 mile north-northeast of the outlet of Ramshead Lake. Several routes are available on the pinnacle, ranging from 5.4 to 5.7.

ROUTE 3. *Avocet Arête*. II, 5.7. First ascent 1980, by unknown climbers; partial ascent 1977 by Al Read and Rod Newcomb. See *Topo 81* and *Photo 92*. Containing six pitches, Avocet Arête is the left-hand (western) of the Bird Arêtes, the three small ridges that are located on the southeast side of Mount St. John. For approach see *Route 5*, Peregrine Arête. The first pitch begins with a right-facing corner (5.7), which is ascended for 75 feet to a belay ledge. A ropelength of 4th-class climbing leads back to the left to a belay on the crest. The third pitch ascends the crest for 100 feet and consists of blocky corners. Pitch four consists of a 40-foot hand crack (5.7). Then wander up through ledges and trees and belay at the base of the final pitch, 50 feet of 5.6 climbing. Scrambling then leads to the top of the climb, which is situated at the base of a nice-looking wall.

ROUTE 4. *Ostrich Arête*. II, 5.8. First ascent June 5, 1981, by Chuck Harris and Steve Rickert. See *Topo 81* and *Photo 92*. This is the central, white arête of the three Bird Arêtes. For approach see *Route 5*, Peregrine Arête. The first pitch goes up steep cracks on the arête to a belay, which is moved up and left for the beginning of the second lead. Now climb a steep, overhanging corner, containing loose blocks, to the left of a chimney. The third lead moves up around to the left of a flake on a pedestal and then up a lieback crack to a belay. The final pitch is on a knobby face up and then left to finish the route. The climb is consistently in the 5.6 to 5.8 level, but a quantity of loose rock will be encountered. For the descent rappel 50 feet down to the notch to the north, then scramble down a gully and traverse east to the notch situated above the top of Peregrine Arête and continue down to Laurel and String Lakes.

ROUTE 5. *Peregrine Arête*. II, 5.7. First ascent July 1, 1981, by Chuck Harris and Leo Larson, and on July 26, 1981, by Jack Tackle, Jim Donini, and Yvon Chouinard, by a slightly

Rappel 50' to north side of notch; scramble down
gully and traverse east to notch above the top
of PEREGRINE

④ B

Scramble to top

↑ A

easy
5th

⑤

③

5.6 (50')

Traverse left to
chimney/crack

Descent from summit involves
5th class downclimb
into a gully

④ C

cracks on right
side of årete

5.7

easy 5th

Wander through
ledges, trees ④

③

Belay in chimney
below pinnacle
(visible from below)

②

hand 5.7 (40')

③

loose

corners left of årete 5.8

5.10-

5.5
right of crest

scary flake

5.6 (100')
blocky corners

②

②

②

①

Climb crack left
of alcove

alcove

①

B ○

crest →

5.7 (75')

gully

5.6

5.7

A ○

ramp, gullies
corners

steep face

low point of buttress

①

5.10- roof

easy 5th class

walk-up

5.9

C

○

81. MOUNT ST. JOHN, SOUTHEAST ARETES
A. AVOCET ARETE, II, 5.7
B. OSTRICH ARETE, II, 5.8
C. PEREGRINE ARETE, II, 5.7

different variation. See *Topo 81* and *Photo 92*. This is the right-hand (eastern) of the three arêtes on the southeast side of Mount St. John. It has developed into the most popular of these Bird Arêtes. Approach via Hanging Canyon to Arrowhead Pool. From Arrowhead Pool walk up scree slopes to the north onto the grassy talus bench from which this arête and the other two Bird Arêtes can be seen rising above. To start this route one has a choice of a 5.10 roof near the crest or 3rd-class scrambling up a ramp on the right (east) side of the arête. The next pitch starts either with a 5.7 left-facing corner or 5.6 face climbing. Both options lead to the crest, and the belay can be moved up to a ledge. From the ledge move right to a 5.5 chimney just east of the crest. Another pitch of similar difficulty on the crest leads to the top of the climb. There are more difficult variations possible on each of the pitches. The descent from the summit involves a 5.1 downclimb into a gully from which one can easily walk down to the northeast and back down to Hanging Canyon or Laurel and String Lakes.

ROUTE 6. Hawkeye. II, 5.9. First ascent September 5, 1980, by Leo Larson, Chuck Harris, and Mike Beiser. This three-pitch climb is on the south-facing buttress just below (east of) Peregrine Arête. The first 150-foot pitch (loose) starts to the right of a large snag with face climbing that leads to a left-facing corner. Continue past an overhang to a belay at a flake. The next lead begins in a right-facing corner to a roof that is passed on the right to a second roof; climb over this roof and left onto the ridge crest for the belay. The final 140-foot lead proceeds almost on the crest to the top of the buttress. Protection for the second lead is minimal, and large devices are useful.

ROCKCHUCK PEAK (11,144)

Map: Mount Moran

This inconspicuous peak has, reasonably enough, attracted little attention from mountaineers seeking technical routes. Readily accessible from String Lake, the eastern routes, however, do offer a pleasant and relatively short climb for climbers with modest ambitions. The traverse from Rockchuck to St. John, or *vice versa*, provides a longer and more challenging day. Rockchuck is separated from Mount St. John to the south by a cirque leading to a distinctive U-shaped col (10,560+). Surprisingly, this cirque and col were the location of one of the earliest penetrations, probably the second, into the Teton Range from the east. The col was apparently first reached on August 14, 1888, by Owen Wister, famous author of *The Virginian,* and George West, who visited Laurel Lake *en route.* However, the knoblike pinnacle south of this col, on the ridge connecting Rockchuck with Mount St. John, was not climbed until August 17, 1959, by William Cropper and Sam Tanner. A distraction for today's climbers, and a hindrance for Fritiof Fryxell attempting the first ascent in 1929, is the plentitude

of huckleberries available on the eastern slopes. Another feature of interest is the recent fault scarp that is passed early in the ascent from the east; it is readily seen at an elevation of about 7,200 feet as a brief steepening of the otherwise uniform slope. The scarp makes a step of about 65 feet, indicating movement along the main Teton fault within the last 15,000 years, since the underlying slope is of recent glacial origin. The eastern routes *(Routes 3, 4, and 5)* are all immediately available from the String Lake trailhead, whereas the approach for the western routes *(Routes 1 and 6)* is via Indian Paintbrush Canyon.

CHRONOLOGY

East Slopes: August 16, 1929, Fritiof Fryxell
Northwest Side: August 1, 1932, Fred Ayres (descent); August 6, 1952, Theodore Brandon, Clement Ramsland, Frederick Tillotson (ascent)
Northeast Ridge: June 27, 1933, Fritiof Fryxell, Frank Swenson
West Face: August 20, 1935, Phil Smith, Floyd Wilson
    var: July 7, 1960, Tim and Sally Bond
East Ridge: August 16, 1940, Judy Peterson, Beatrice Burford, Rick Hemmenway
    var: **Southeast Couloir:** August 28, 1941, Theodore Brandon, Robert Anderson, John Dewey
    var: **Southeast Face:** July 1987, George Montopoli, Leo Larson (descent)
South Ridge: August 11, 1946, Michael and John Ladd, Helen and Anne Pratt, Mary Bartlett (descent)

ROUTE 1. West Face. II, 5.4, A1. First ascent August 20, 1935, by Phil Smith and Floyd Wilson. See *Photo 93.* The first two-thirds of the route were climbed on August 13, 1935, by the same party; they returned to complete it a week later. From about 8,600 feet on the Indian Paintbrush trail, turn up past a small lake into the canyon on the west side of Rockchuck. The climb begins by ascending the smooth, downsloping rock of a wide couloir; at the top, 600 feet of talus lead to a dish-shaped 800-foot section of steep rock. This second wide couloir gradually narrows into the final 30-foot chimney. On the first ascent an aid piton was required to surmount the chimney. From this point it is possible to traverse up and right (south) to the southwest corner. The last portion ascends a broken ridge to the summit.

Variation: II, 5.1. First ascent July 7, 1960, by Tim and Sally Bond. From String Lake ascend the cirque above Laurel Lake to the col separating Mount St. John and Rockchuck Peak. Descend on the far (west) side of the col, traversing around to the second couloir north of the col. This couloir leads up on good rock to the southwest ridge, which is followed to the summit via *Route 1.*

ROUTE 2. South Ridge. II, 4.0. First descent August 11, 1946, by Michael and John Ladd, Helen and Anne Pratt, and Mary Bartlett. This ridge is ordinarily used only when traversing from Rockchuck to Mount St. John; the traverse in the other direction has apparently not been done. From the summit of Rockchuck, the objective is to reach the U-shaped col separating Rockchuck from St. John. This can probably be done in various ways, some of which will stay more nearly on the crest of the south ridge than the route described here. From the summit of Rockchuck descend the west side until a break in the ridge line to the left (south) is seen. This break is the top of a steep, rotten couloir about 150 feet below the summit; descend this couloir for about 250 feet, cutting out left on rotten ledges to a small notch. Some scrambling on the far side of the notch will bring the climber onto the south ridge proper. The U-shaped col is now reached by passing the first large step in the ridge on the left (east) and the second on the right (west). This notch can also be reached directly from String Lake by ascending the cirque separating Mount St. John from Rockchuck Peak. Others, to make the Rockchuck–St. John traverse, have descended from the summit down the west side for 400 feet and then traversed on easy ledges to the U-shaped col. For ascent either of these descent schemes would be reversed.

ROUTE 3. East Ridge. II, 5.1. First ascent August 16, 1940, by Beatrice Burford, Judy Peterson, and Rick Hemmenway. This major ridge forms the northern boundary of the prominent cirque that separates Mount St. John from Rockchuck Peak, and the southern boundary of the main east couloir used in *Route 4*. It provides an enjoyable day of rock scrambling, especially if one stays directly on the crest of the often sharp ridge. The ridge is not continuous and it does contain some loose rock, although it is mostly sound. Beware of the lichenous rock when it is wet. Some pinnacles will be found near the upper end of the ridge, which does not lead directly to the summit but intersects the main northeast ridge a few hundred feet north of the summit. The pinnacles provide the most interesting climbing on the ridge and one may wish to rappel for descent from their summits.

Variation: Southeast Couloir. I, 5.1. First ascent August 28, 1941, by Theodore Brandon, Robert Anderson, and John Dewey. From String Lake hike into the cirque between Mount St. John and Rockchuck Peak. After passing the large broad tower on the east ridge of Rockchuck, turn up the southeast wall of the peak to reach the east ridge just left (west) of the westernmost pinnacle of the ridge. Follow the upper east ridge to the main northeast ridge to the summit. This variation can also be used for the traverse from Rockchuck to Mount St. John.

Variation: Southeast Face. II, 5.1. First descent July 1987, by George Montopoli and Leo Larson. The southeast face, between the couloir described in the *Southeast Couloir variation* and the South Ridge route, can be used for the traverse from Rockchuck to Mount St. John. From the summit of Rockchuck descend this face, containing easy 5th-class rock, to a point below a shoulder on the Rockchuck side of the U-shaped notch. Climb back up to this shoulder and then descend a gully on the west side until one can traverse south over to the notch.

ROUTE 4. ☞*East Slopes.* I, 3.0. First ascent August 16, 1929, by Fritiof Fryxell. From the parking lot at the south end of String Lake, cross the bridge and continue along the trail on the west side of String Lake until the trail crosses the open slope that leads up into the broad east couloir of Rockchuck. Climb the couloir until it steepens, then angle slightly left onto the upper east ridge and follow it to its intersection with the main northeast ridge. Climb south along this bouldery ridge to the summit. Like Teewinot, in early season this climb is mostly on snow, but later it is mostly talus and scree. *Time: 4½ to 6 hours* from Jenny Lake. See *Appalachia,* 18, no. 4 (December 1931), pp. 388–408, illus.; *Chicago Mountaineering Club Newsletter,* 15, no. 5 (December 1961), pp. 6–8.

ROUTE 5. Northeast Ridge. I, 5.1. First ascent June 27, 1933, by Fritiof Fryxell and Frank Swenson; one of the high points on this ridge had been reached on July 28, 1931, by Ray King and Edna Olson. This prominent ridge is reached from the trail that leads around the west side of String Lake. The lower portion of this major ridge is easy, but higher up it flattens into a section containing many towers. Some difficulty will be experienced in passing these towers, some of which are turned on the left (east). *Time: 8¼ hours* from Jenny Lake.

ROUTE 6. Northwest Side. I, 3.0. First descent August 1, 1932, by Fred Ayres; first ascent August 6, 1952, by Theodore Brandon, Clement Ramsland, and Frederick Tillotson. See *Photo 93.* Follow the trail up Indian Paintbrush Canyon to about 8,600 feet, then turn south past a small lake into the canyon on the west side of Rockchuck. Climb over talus and boulders up the northwest side of the peak, working right (south) near the top to avoid some cliffs. It is probable that one could also turn sooner up the northwest slopes of Rockchuck Peak from the Indian Paintbrush trail and climb the peak by a parallel route to the left (north) of the route described here. Either route is recommended for those who desire a traverse of the mountain; using the trail in Indian Paintbrush Canyon, the descent of this route does not take much more time than *Route 4*.

THE OUTLIER (10,560+)

(0.8 mi W of Mount St. John)

Map: Mount Moran

Rising above Indian Paintbrush Canyon on the south is a salient ridge (running from the northeast to the southwest) that isolates the considerable cirque lying below the northwest face of Mount St. John. This ridge, named the Outlier because of its remote position, has the topographical prominence to justify its separate treatment even though it does not qualify as a peak. The lower reaches of the seldom-entered cirque contain an extended expanse of morainal debris, while a small glacial remnant clings to the upper portion below the north face of the Jaw. The approach for all the routes is via Indian Paintbrush Canyon, taking the trail to the vicinity of the forks (8,100 to 8,800 feet).

CHRONOLOGY

East Side: August 15, 1956, Roald and Redwood Fryxell, Julia Peterson (descent); July 27, 1958, Paul Salstrom, Robert Marshall (ascent)
Northwest Face: August 15, 1956, Roald and Redwood Fryxell, Julia Peterson
Southwest Ridge: July 16, 1966, Michael Petrilak, J. Curtiss Sinclear, Sherman Heller

ROUTE 1. Southwest Ridge. I, 2.0. First ascent July 16, 1966, by Michael Petrilak, J. Curtiss Sinclear, and Sherman Heller. From Indian Paintbrush Canyon ascend into the cirque between Mount St. John and the Outlier. Continue to the col (10,400+) at the upper west margin of the cirque. From the col climb the easy ridge, containing loose rock, to the summit.

ROUTE 2. East Side. I, 2.0. First descent August 15, 1956, by Roald and Redwood Fryxell and Julia Peterson; first ascent July 27, 1958, by Paul Salstrom and Robert Marshall. From Indian Paintbrush Canyon ascend into the cirque between Mount St. John and the Outlier. Scramble up the east side onto the ridge north of the summit. The summit is reached with no significant difficulties.

ROUTE 3. Northwest Face. I, 3.0. First ascent August 15, 1956, by Roald and Redwood Fryxell and Julia Peterson. From Indian Paintbrush Canyon ascend an easy diagonal ramp on the northwest face to the col (10,080+) between the lower northwest summit and the main summit. From the col the ridge is followed easily to the main summit as well as to the northwest summit if desired.

PEAK 10,919   *(0.8 mi NE of Mount Woodring)*

Map: Mount Moran

At the end of the east ridge of Mount Woodring lies this seldom-visited high point. From its summit a fine view of the entire southern battlements of Mount Moran is available.

ROUTE 1. Southeast Couloir. I, 2.0. First ascent June 25, 1939, by Francis Hendricks and Stanley Grites. Immediately after crossing the bridge over the main stream in Paintbrush Canyon head north up the drainage that leads to this peak.

MOUNT WOODRING (11,555)

Map: Mount Moran

This rounded peak is one possible objective for those who would like to reach a major Teton summit as easily as possible. While the regular route from the south, which consists of loose talus and scree, is perhaps not appealing to the discriminating mountaineer, the standard approach to Mount Woodring does provide a pleasant day's hike up through the attractive Indian Paintbrush Canyon. The view of Mount Moran and Thor Peak from the summit is especially good. This technically easy peak, like a few other summits in the range, was found to have a cairn on top when the "first-ascent" party arrived in 1929. This cairn was very likely built by members of the crew that constructed the trail in Indian Paintbrush Canyon in the mid-1920s for the U.S. Forest Service. For the topographically inquisitive, most of the north side of this peak remains to be explored, partly because of the loose rock that it appears to hold. For the approach to the north side of this mountain, see *Leigh Canyon.* On August 12, 1937, Edmund Lowe and Rainer Schickele descended from Mount Woodring via Grizzly Bear Lake into the "utterly wild and unspoiled" Leigh Canyon, where they found remnants of the old horse trail that had been built in the 1920s.

CHRONOLOGY

Southeast Slope: July 24, 1929, Fritiof Fryxell, Everett Norling, Kenneth Landon, Roland McCannon, Roy Swanberg
Southwest Slope: June 15, 1930, Fritiof Fryxell, Phil Smith
East Ridge: July 31, 1932, Phil Smith, William Rea; August 15, 1953, John Dorsey, Leigh Ortenburger (descent)
North Ridge: August 16, 1957, William Buckingham, Barry Corbet
West Ridge: September 24, 1960, Gordon Fish, Gordon Esden, or September 5, 1973, Ron and Gretchen Perla
North Face: August 5, 1963, John Reed, David Steller
North Couloir: June 1, 1985, Andy Carson, R. Harris, S. Beitzel
South Rib: September 14, 1989, Andy Carson, Paul Horton

ROUTE 1. West Ridge. II, 3.0. First ascent September 24, 1960, by Gordon Fish and Gordon Esden, or September 5, 1973, by Ron and Gretchen Perla. During the descent from the Paintbrush–Leigh Canyon divide toward the beautiful Grizzly Bear Lake, an initial plateau at about 9,700 feet must be crossed. The west ridges and couloirs rise above this plateau and are bounded on the right by the southwest ridge that forms the divide. One of these indistinct ridges was apparently climbed but is not recommended because of rotten rock.

ROUTE 2. ☞Southwest Slope. I, 2.0. First ascent June 15, 1930, by Fritiof Fryxell and Phil Smith. See Photo 94. This is the easiest route on the peak. Follow the Paintbrush Canyon trail to Holly Lake. Walk around the left (west) side of the lake and start up the talus and scree slope leading to the summit. Angle slightly right (east) to avoid the southwest ridge; this ridge can be followed but it is slightly harder. In early season some snow of moderate angle will be encountered and an ice axe will be needed. Time: 6 to 7¼ hours from String Lake; 2½ to 3¼ hours from Holly Lake. See Appalachia, 18, no. 4 (December 1931), pp. 388–408, illus.

ROUTE 3. Southeast Slope. I, 2.0. First ascent July 24, 1929, by Fritiof Fryxell, Everett Norling, Kenneth Landon, Roland McCannon, and Roy Swanberg, who found an empty cairn on the summit. From the trail in Indian Paintbrush Canyon, one can start climbing the southeast side of the peak at almost any place. One method is to follow the left (west) side of the main drainage on the southeast side that heads in a small permanent snowfield as shown on the map. Mount Woodring has three subsidiary east peaks, so head toward the highest peak, which is the one farthest west. See Appalachia, 18, no. 4 (December 1931), pp. 388–408, illus.

ROUTE 4. South Rib. II, 5.8. First ascent September 14, 1989, by Andy Carson and Paul Horton. See Photo 94. This well-defined, stepped rib of surprisingly good rock extends from just above the highest trees northeast of Holly Lake and ends about 300 feet below and southeast of the summit. From Holly Lake hike up talus and scree to the obvious ridge, past a small buttress and across a gully to the start of this route, which is about 100 feet above the very beginning of the rib. This eight-pitch climb stays on or near the crest of the rib following the line of least resistance. The first lead starts near the crest and moves right on a ledge to and up a chimney (5.6) to the belay. Now move left around the crest and climb cracks (5.6) and ledges, ending on the right side at a ledge with a large block. Walk 50 feet to begin the third pitch just left of the crest on poor rock (5.8); then continue out right and up good cracks (5.6) to an overhang that is passed on the right to reach the belay on the crest. Walk along the level crest here for 100 feet and climb the next step (40 feet). Again walk 100 feet to the start of the next step and climb up and onto a ramp on the left side of the ridge, exiting on cracks (5.4) to a belay ledge. The sixth lead climbs up to a crack or chimney that must be climbed (5.7) to get through a prominent overhang and then on up to complete the lead at the top of this step in the rib. Now scramble or walk for about 200 feet to the start of the next step, where a 40-foot open chimney with truly bad rock (5.6) and an additional short climb lead to the top of this

step. The final lead is easier climbing on the right side of the crest to the top of the rib. Scramble about 300 feet to the summit. A standard rack suffices for protection on this route.

ROUTE 5. East Ridge. I, 5.1. First ascent July 31, 1932, by Phil Smith and William Rea; first descent August 15, 1953, by John Dorsey and Leigh Ortenburger. This ridge contains one distinct peak (see Peak 10,919, earlier) and two major, separate subsummits and offers an interesting day of ridge scrambling. Where the Paintbrush Canyon trail crosses to the north side of the main stream, climb from the southeast directly up to Peak 10,919, the most easterly of the three high points on this ridge. From there the crest of the ridge can be followed all the way to the summit, although the first-ascent party apparently bypassed a direct descent of the second point (11,120+), reaching the col between the third subsummit (11,200+) and the main summit by contouring around the south side. The short steep section on the ridge crest above this final col was also avoided by the 1932 party by working out on the north slope of the mountain to the northwest corner and probably to the upper portion of the North Ridge (Route 8). A short, broad couloir led from this corner to the summit. On the east ridge itself the schistose rock of this last steep section is very rotten, although it is probably climbable; on descent a rappel is desirable.

ROUTE 6. North Couloir. II, 4.0. First ascent June 1, 1985, by Andy Carson, R. Harris, and S. Beitzel. This route leads from the far (west) end of the second lake (7,785) in Leigh Canyon to the saddle (10,480+) in the east ridge of Mount Woodring separating the peak from Peak 10,919. This couloir was climbed as a snow route, and as such it is a fine route. Later in the season there may be difficulties with what will probably prove to be loose rock in the couloir. The first-ascent party did not continue on the east ridge to the summit of the peak.

ROUTE 7. North Face. II, 3.0. First ascent August 5, 1963, by John Reed and David Steller. From the lower lake in Leigh Canyon, climb diagonally up to the first saddle east of the summit on the east ridge. Significant routefinding skill is needed in order to minimize the difficulties on the face. Depending on the time of year and the exact route selected, some snow climbing may be involved. The final ridge to the summit will involve the steep rotten section referred to in Route 5.

ROUTE 8. North Ridge. II, 5.6. First ascent August 16, 1957, by William Buckingham and Barry Corbet. From a half mile above the lakes in Leigh Canyon, Mount Woodring is seen to have two prominent faces, the concave north face and the northwest face. Both appear to contain much rotten rock. This route ascends the ridge that separates these two faces; it leads directly to the summit. The ridge, composed of good rock, rises in four steps from the canyon floor. The climbing is straightforward to the base of the third step, where there is a small but spectacular pinnacle (Corbuck Pinnacle). Scramble to the base of the chimney that separates the pinnacle from the ridge on the west side. Climb two pitches up this chimney to the notch. To climb the pinnacle, one enjoyable corkscrew pitch starts at the south side of the notch, circles around the east to the north, and finishes on the northwest corner. From the notch, more enjoyable climbing leads to the summit wall, which is climbed directly over steep slabs to the summit ridge. See *American Alpine Journal,* 11, no. 1 (1958), pp. 85–88; *Dartmouth Mountaineering Club Journal,* 1958, p. 21.

MOUNT KIMBURGER (10,080+)

(1.1 mi W of Mount Woodring)

Map: Mount Moran

Rising immediately above and west of Grizzly Bear Lake is an impressive and massive cliff band capped by a flat summit ridge with occasional pinnacles. Thought to be the last unclimbed peak in the Teton Range, this summit remained unvisited until 1986. It is surprisingly well protected on all sides from casual ascent; it appears to have no easy route to the summit. The north ridge rises in tiers for over 1,500 feet from Leigh Canyon, its east face is a substantial wall, and the southwest ridge is very sharp. Only its west face is accessible and broken. The peak is readily approached via the Paintbrush Canyon trail to the divide leading over to Grizzly Bear Lake and the Leigh Canyon drainage. The rounded point (10,240+) to the southwest was climbed on July 7, 1984, by William Dennis via the west slope.

ROUTE 1. West Face and North Ridge. II, 5.7. First ascent July 29, 1986, by Tom Kimbrough and Leigh Ortenburger. From the divide above Grizzly Bear Lake make a slight descent and climb loose scree to the saddle (9,920+) southwest of this point. Scramble directly up the ridge above the saddle for 100 feet on loose rock to a ledge system leading left (north) out onto the main west face of the peak. Belay from the end of this ledge for the lead, which zigs out and then zags back to gain an awkward, left-slanting squeeze chimney (5.7). From the top of this chimney continue up and left for two more pitches over easier but steep ground to gain the center of the summit ridge. Scramble along the narrow ridge past the "2001" monolith toward the north end of the ridge, where a short wall on the east side leads to the extreme northeast corner of the summit block. Climb this block (5.7) by small cracks and ledges on the face.

ROUTE 2. Northwest Ledges. I, 5.7. First ascent July 19, 1994, by Paul Horton and Jon Stuart. From the vicinity of Grizzly Bear Lake scramble onto the north ridge and continue to the base of the summit walls. Traverse via the highest ledge onto the west face. Zigzag up wooded ramps to the summit block. The only technical pitch of the route ascends this block from the north and west.

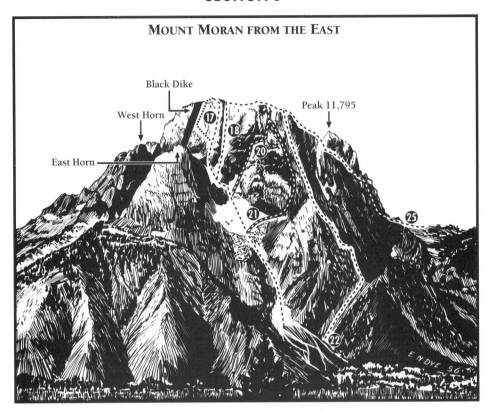

MOUNT MORAN FROM THE EAST

Black Dike

West Horn

East Horn

Peak 11,795

E N DVE 56

Leigh Canyon to Moran Canyon

LEIGH CANYON, NORTH SIDE ROCK CLIMBS

Map: Mount Moran

The entire collection of these routes out of Leigh Canyon, including the major southern routes on Mount Moran, contain many of the finest difficult rock climbs of the Teton Range. The rock is massive, generally of excellent quality, and commonly exceedingly steep. The earliest difficult routes on Mount Moran on the north side of Leigh Canyon were first done as summit climbs. These and the other summit routes are described later under *Mount Moran,* even though several, such as the Direct South Buttress of Moran, are now usually climbed just as rock routes with descent after the finish of the initial difficult sections. The imposing northern walls and ridges, listed here from west to east, do not lead to a summit in any direct fashion. The rock-climbing routes described here

have a relatively short approach and are sometimes done in a single day by a fast party with an early start. One can approach the mouth of Leigh Canyon partway on maintained trails to the south or north end of Leigh Lake, but either way the last 2.0 miles requires bushwhacking over remnants of trails that the National Park Service abandoned several years ago. The best scheme now is to take a canoe across Leigh Lake to a point just north of the mouth of the main stream in Leigh Canyon; campsite #14 is located here. A climbers' trail, sometimes hard to follow, will be found leaving the area of these shoreline campsites heading west into Leigh Canyon on the north side of the creek. Recent avalanche debris has seriously cluttered some of the upper portions of this small trail.

CHRONOLOGY

Southeast Ridge: July 6, 1957, John Dietschy, William Cropper

Staircase Arête: August 28, 1959, David Dornan, Al Read

No Escape Buttress, West Arête: August 21, 1960, Al Read, Peter Lev (lower half); September 11, 1960, Al Read, David Dornan (upper half)
> *var:* July 16, 1969, Rick Reese, Ted Wilson
> *var:* August 1, 1977, Buck Tilley, Ivan Rezucha

No Escape Buttress, Direct South Face: August 17, 1962, David Dornan, Yvon Chouinard, James McCarthy
> *var:* **Direct Finish:** July 30, 1977, Mike Munger, Rich Perch

No Escape Slabs: August 1970, Al Rubin, Charles Jackson (discovered); August 14, 1977, Mike Munger, Charlie Fowler (first friction climbs)

No Survivors: August 6, 1977, Mike Munger, Jim Donini, Steve Wunsch

Gin and Tonic: August 23, 1977, Mike Munger, Charlie Fowler

No Escape Buttress, East Edge: July 30, 1978, Andy Carson, Jorge Colon

Direct Avoidance: July 31, 1978, Dieter Klose, Mike Kehoe

Spreadeagle: August 1, 1978, Dieter Klose, Mike Kehoe

Irvine Arête: August 13, 1982, Leo Larson, Ed Thompson

ROUTE 1. Staircase Arête. III, 5.6, A1, or III, 5.8. First ascent August 28, 1959, by David Dornan and Al Read; the same party had attempted the route on July 21, 1957. See *Photo 103.* On the lower south side of Mount Moran, to the east of the south buttress, is a prominent waterfall that has been named "Laughing Lions Falls." This falls drains the bowl in the upper portion of the south face of the mountain, between the upper south ridge and Drizzlepuss. Immediately to the right of these falls, at an altitude of about 7,800 feet, the slender Staircase Arête begins. It ascends in three large steps and many smaller ones for about 1,000 feet and ends in a final steep wall, where it joins the long southeast ridge. Take the climbers' trail into Leigh Canyon for about 1.0 mile to the waterfalls. The route begins with a traverse to the right from the falls on an unobvious ledge to the face of the first step. (*Note:* An alternate start to the climb can be obtained by climbing corner systems on the south face of the first step. The rock is superb, and nearly tnree additional pitches of climbing can be done, generally 5.9 to 5.10 in difficulty.) At the end of this ledge, climb straight up the corner 120 feet over moderate rock and through a small V to a fine belay ledge. Continue up a crack system, but work right as soon as possible to gain the large chimney leading to the crest of the arête. From the top of the chimney, scramble 150 feet to the second great step. From a wide platform, traverse left a few feet, and turn up over an awk-

ward step at the obvious bush. The first-ascent party used aid for about 15 feet at this point to get up the steep, leaning corner (5.8). A short scramble leads to the third step. Climb a corner to the left of the crest by means of a 20-foot lieback. Complete this lead up a chimney with a difficult overhang at its top, which again required aid on the first ascent. The next pitch leads straight up smooth slabs in moderate cracks; after about 80 feet it is possible to exit to the right. At this point one can also scramble off to the left and traverse to the lower Blackfin rappels. This is most likely the easiest way off the climb. From the top of this fourth step, climb a series of slabs, liebacks, short steps, cracks, and one overhang on or near the crest for about 250 feet to a good belay position at the base of the last step. The final 150-foot wall of the arête is avoided by a traverse left on a large ledge allowing access to about 200 feet of easy climbing back toward the right to the very top of the arête, where a cairn should be found. Most of the southeast ridge lies above this junction point.

The descent from this point to Leigh Canyon is complex, requiring careful routefinding. From the cairn, descend the southeast couloir on the east side of the southeast ridge about 1,000 feet to a grass-covered slope that leads east above the lower cliff band. Follow this slope until an easy couloir leads down into Leigh Canyon. If the correct route is found, no rappels are required. See *American Alpine Journal,* 13, no. 2 (1963), pp. 487–489.

ROUTE 2. Irvine Arête. III, 5.9, A1. First ascent August 13, 1982, by Leo Larson and Ed Thompson. The initial 1957 ascent of the Southeast Ridge (see *Route 3*) stayed primarily on the east side of the crest to the end of the second step. This much more difficult route, containing interesting and tricky pitches, starts on the left (west) side of the crest and ends just above the junction of Staircase Arête (*Route 1*) with the southeast ridge. Approach from Leigh Canyon to a point due east of the base of Laughing Lions Falls, the prominent waterfall on the south side of Mount Moran east of the south buttress. Scramble up the rocky couloir between Staircase Arête and the southeast ridge to the chockstone where the couloir narrows. The first lead starts out to the right at a large tree in a difficult 50-foot jam crack to a ledge followed by a narrow chimney. At the top of this chimney a bulge forces a series of 5.9 moves on thin friction and loose blocks to a belay position. A chimney then leads to the next belay ledge. Continue up to a large ledge below a short vertical wall. Climb this wall using a fine parallel-sided jam crack to the next belay stance at a large tree. The sixth lead ascends the right side of the steep wall above on shallow cracks and thin flakes. Now move right from the small belay ledge over broken rock and short walls to a small belay tree. The steep, smooth wall above, broken by a thin, shallow crack, is climbed along the left side toward the tapering overhang at its top. At the overhang pendulum 10 feet to the right to easier ground and then up over loose rock with poor protection to yet another large tree. The final three pitches involve moderate scrambling to join the main Southeast Ridge route. This route could be followed to the summit of Drizzlepuss, or descent can be made down the large couloir (much loose rock) to the east, angling east from time to time, ultimately reaching the next crest, which is the first ridgelet west of No Escape Buttress. Downclimb this slender ridge to a tree from which three rappels of 75 feet suffice to reach the talus below.

ROUTE 3. *Southeast Ridge.* II, 5.4. First ascent July 6, 1957, by John Dietschy and William Cropper. See *Photo 103.* This long ridge leads directly to the summit of Drizzlepuss from Leigh Canyon. It is paralleled on the west by an equally long gully containing at least two waterfalls (one is Laughing Lions Falls) in the lower section and opening out in the upper section to form the main large bowl beneath the final south walls of Moran. The only other ridge of this length on the south side of Moran is the main south ridge (see *Mount Moran, Routes 9* and *10*). Take the climbers' trail into Leigh Canyon and approach the bottom of the ridge from the east along tree ledges. The ridge is easy scrambling to the first large step. Use a diagonal ledge on the east side of this step to pass this obstacle and regain the crest. Follow a knife-edge to the base of the second step. An unusual 300-foot horizontal cave on the west side provides an easy traverse into a gully, from which an easy walk leads back to the crest. Then scramble to the summit of Drizzlepuss, where the CMC route of Mount Moran (*Route 14*) is joined. See *American Alpine Journal,* 11, no. 1 (1958), pp. 85–88.

ROUTE 4. *No Escape Buttress, West Arête.* IV, 5.10-. See *Topo 82.* First ascent of the lower half August 21, 1960, by Al Read and Peter Lev; the upper half was completed September 11, 1960, by Al Read and David Dornan; first free ascent August 1, 1977, by Buck Tilley and Ivan Rezucha. This buttress is the first significant wall rising to the north from the mouth of Leigh Canyon; the route ascends the left (west) edge of the wall. The name was derived from the fact that a descent of the buttress could be difficult, the ceilings making rappelling uncertain. The approach is via the climbers' trail for 0.5 mile into Leigh Canyon. The climb begins at the base of the couloir immediately northwest of the buttress. Angle up and right to a very wide platform.

The objective is to reach an obvious jam crack that angles slightly left but begins above an overhang. The first-ascent party climbed a corner about 15 feet to the right of this crack for about 20 feet until a piton placed in a ceiling allowed a pendulum to the base of the jam crack. After about 30 feet up this crack they again used a pendulum to access the crescent-shaped crack beneath the small overhang to the left. Direct aid (pitons and one wooden wedge) was used to surmount difficulties on a few of the pitches above. Refer to the topo, which is a general representation of how the climb is done today. There are nearly 11 pitches of roped climbing to the top of the buttress. The grassy slopes on the eastern side of the buttress can be used for descent. See *American Alpine Journal,* 13, no. 2 (1963), pp. 487–489.

Variation: III, 5.8, A2. First ascent July 16, 1969, by Rick Reese and Ted Wilson. This variation is but one of several possibilities on this arête. To reach the "obvious jam crack" at the beginning of the route, the initial overhang was overcome by aid (overhanging) directly up the crack, rather than using a pendulum. When the edge of the arête is reached at the end of the second lead, continue directly up the crest instead of traversing out onto the face to the right (east). The first lead (5.7) up this crest (the third lead of the route) goes up 15 feet and then requires a hand traverse left for 8 feet to gain a slightly overhanging crack just left of the crest; climb this crack for 30 feet to a belay in easier rock. To regain the crest on the next pitch climb a 30-foot wall to the left of a chimney that has a large jam crack up one side; scrambling to the east through some trees puts one back on the crest at the end of the 1960 route. Continue a ropelength of scrambling on the crest over easy blocks and then low-angle slabs to the base of a steep wall. The route now goes up this wall, starting next to a dead gray tree, for 20 feet (5.7) until one can enter a very steep, left-leaning, wide crack. Climb this strenuous (5.8 or 5.9) crack for 30 feet and then traverse left across a smooth face on a small ledge. The arête continues from this point, but the 1969 party was deterred by the weather; the *1977 variation,* described next, probably climbed this last portion.

Variation: IV, 5.10-. First ascent August 1, 1977, by Buck Tilley and Ivan Rezucha. This variation extends the standard route by adding four additional pitches and is probably the free climb represented in *Topo 82.* From the end of the last pitch of the 1960 route at the top of a large step in the ridge, the first lead (100 feet, 5.7) of this variation starts from the right edge of the step, goes up a corner and a chimney to gain a ledge on the south face, and then moves right 15 feet and up 15 feet in steep cracks to a good ledge. The next pitch (140 feet) of similar difficulty continues up cracks for 15 feet, moves up and left on chicken heads to a notch in the skyline, and then on up the arête to a belay stance. The third long lead starts with a traverse down and right for 20 feet across a face to a chimney and then goes up this chimney to black ramps that lead to a large ledge. Now climb a corner behind a large chockstone and another corner above to a belay tree on the ridge crest. The final pitch traverses right around the crest up moderate slabs to finish with easy climbing.

ROUTE 5. *No Escape Buttress, Direct South Face.* IV, 5.9. First ascent August 17, 1962, by David Dornan, Yvon Chouinard, and James McCarthy. See *Topo 83* and *Photo 95.* This difficult rock climb goes more or less directly up the south face of No Escape Buttress (see *Route 4*). Because the approach is relatively short, the route has been climbed many times in recent years and now is well understood, but

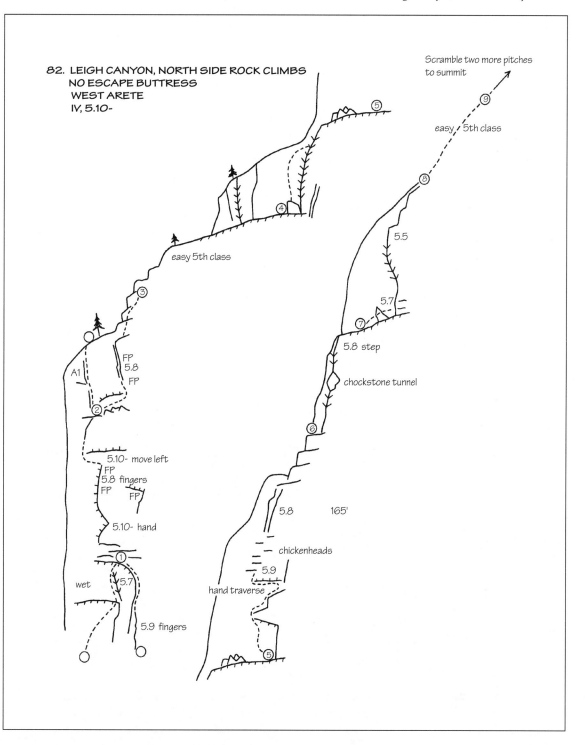

82. LEIGH CANYON, NORTH SIDE ROCK CLIMBS
    NO ESCAPE BUTTRESS
    WEST ARETE
    IV, 5.10-

Scramble two more pitches
to summit

⑨

easy   5th class

⑤

⑧

⑤

⑤

5.5

④

5.7

⑦

easy 5th class

5.8 step

③

chockstone tunnel

FP
5.8
FP

A1

②

⑥

5.10- move left
FP
5.8 fingers
FP   FP

5.8   165'

5.10- hand

chickenheads

①

5.9

wet   5.7

hand traverse

5.9 fingers

⑤

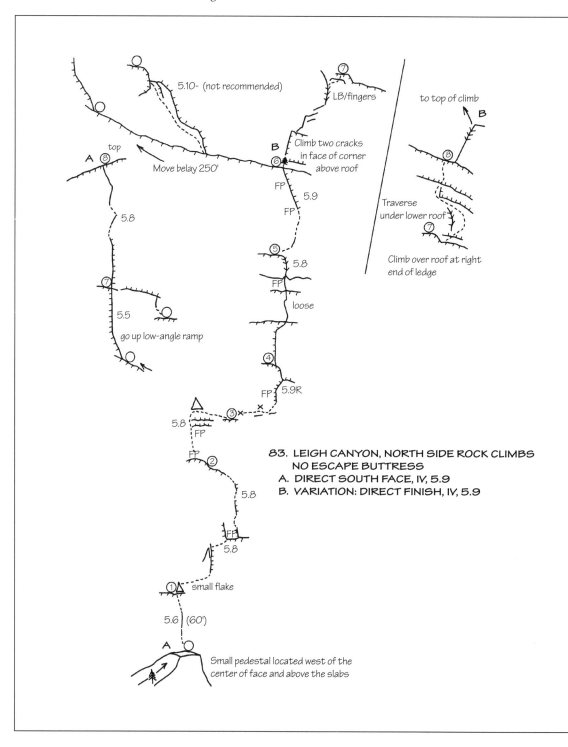

5.10- (not recommended)

LB/fingers

to top of climb

B

A ⑧ top

Move belay 250'

B
⑥
Climb two cracks
in face of corner
above roof

⑧

FP

5.9

FP

Traverse
under lower roof

⑦

5.8

⑤

5.8

FP

⑦

Climb over roof at right
end of ledge

5.5

go up low-angle ramp

loose

⑦

④

FP 5.9R

△

⑤×   ×

5.8

FP

FP

②

**83. LEIGH CANYON, NORTH SIDE ROCK CLIMBS
   NO ESCAPE BUTTRESS
A. DIRECT SOUTH FACE, IV, 5.9
B. VARIATION: DIRECT FINISH, IV, 5.9**

5.8

FP

5.8

①△ small flake

5.6 (60')

A

Small pedestal located west of the
center of face and above the slabs

climbers should appreciate that routefinding on this complex buttress is difficult. It is also important to note that the bolts that are now on the route were placed by others subsequent to the first ascent. This is a testament to the impressive abilities of McCarthy on the fourth lead. From the west shore of Leigh Lake take the climbers' trail about 0.5 mile into Leigh Canyon. No Escape Buttress, the first major rock feature on the southeast side of Mount Moran, and the slabs at its base will be seen rising above on the north. Walk up the boulder field to the base of the buttress.

The route begins from the top of the small pedestal located a bit left (west) of the center of the face. Approach and climb to the top of this pedestal from the west. The first short lead (60 feet) goes up to a small belay ledge (with a small flake) directly above the belayer. The complexities of the next five pitches leading to the broad ramp near the top of the climb are best presented in *Topo 83* and will be only briefly described here. The second pitch goes right and up, involving some tricky traverses and a small inside corner (5.8), to gain a ledge that is followed to its top. The next lead goes up past two fixed pitons around the left edge of a pair of small ceilings to a block and ends at a ledge and belay bolt. The fourth pitch moves right on friction past another bolt and then up a difficult corner (5.9). Continue up right-facing corners in dark broken rock using liebacks and stemming, finishing in a short steep slot (5.8) past a fixed piton onto the belay ledge. The final lead onto the ramp goes directly up the steep face into a steep slanting crack (5.9) containing flakes and chockstones and fixed pitons. Once on the broad ramp, walk up to the left (west) for about 200 or 250 feet and then climb a low-angle higher ramp that turns into a right-facing corner (150 feet). The eighth pitch (150 feet) continues up this corner over a difficult 5.8 bulge to the top of the buttress. Easy climbing now takes one up to the crest. An alternative finish or escape avoids these last two pitches and takes the broad ramp all the way left to the west corner of the face before turning up to reach the top of the buttress. To descend back to Leigh Lake from the top of the buttress, proceed down the grassy slopes to the east. See *American Alpine Journal*, 13, no. 2 (1963), pp. 410–420, illus.

Variation: Direct Finish. IV, 5.9. First ascent July 30, 1977, by Mike Munger and Rich Perch. See *Topo 83* and *Photo 95*. From the top of the sixth pitch, at the broad ramp, this variation continues straight up for three additional pitches instead of making the 250-foot traverse out to the left on the ramp. The first lead (140 feet) up from the ramp uses two cracks in the face of a dihedral above a roof and then moves right across a face to a corner, which is climbed using a thin lieback, exiting to the right at the top. The next pitch moves in a complex manner (see *Topo 83*) up past three roofs onto a big ledge. The final easier lead continues up a corner and then left to the top of the buttress.

ROUTE 6. Gin and Tonic. III, 5.9. First ascent August 23, 1977, by Mike Munger and Charlie Fowler. See *Topo 84* and

Photo 95. This route begins to the right (east) of the original 1962 Direct South Face (*Route 5*), but to the left (west) of the No Survivors route (*Route 7*). Because this route has apparently not been repeated, it may be difficult to locate and its ascent should be a challenge. The route starts up a corner, with the first long lead (170 feet) finishing with a difficult, unprotected 30-foot face; perhaps this pitch can be recognized by the old rappel anchor out to the right in a system of large cracks. Move the belay to the right to a pair of corners, either of which can be climbed straight up, and then right onto a belay ledge below a series of roofs. The third pitch goes up through the roofs at a huge overhanging block (5.9). The actual break through which one escapes through the roofs is difficult to find. The next lead starts with a crack (5.9) past the left edge of another roof to and up a sharp left-leaning corner ending at a belay ledge. The final difficult pitch, Charlie's Nightmare, is a full lead up a 5.9 left-facing corner. From the top of this corner, easier climbing goes up and right to the top of a tower and the end of the route.

ROUTE 7. No Survivors. III, 5.10R. First ascent August 6, 1977, by Mike Munger, Jim Donini, and Steve Wunsch. See *Topo 84* and *Photo 95*. This route begins to the right of the Gin and Tonic route (*Route 6*) but is also poorly understood, so finding and climbing this route will also be a challenge. This climb starts on a large square-cut ledge "with large blocks sitting on it." This ledge curves up at its left end, forming a left-facing corner that gets smaller as it goes up. Directly above the ledge are some roofs. The first pitch (crux 5.10R) goes up the corner at the left end of the ledge until it is possible to traverse right to a small right-facing corner. This is a very intimidating traverse, given the lack of protection and the large ledge above which one is climbing. Zig first up and right and then zag back left under a roof, passing it just left of a loose flake to a belay below a huge block. Next, climb to the top of the block and traverse right to a long roof, crossing it via an awkward move and continue right to a large easy dihedral with a ledge on the right. The third lead can be made up the corner, which angles left, or one can go left and cross a roof on bucket holds. Now move the belay up and right to the highest grassy terrace. The next pitch goes up to the left of a left-facing corner at the left edge of a white streak in the rock and past a loose flake to a ramp that leads up and left; follow this ramp until it is possible to climb to a large ledge for the belay. The fifth lead follows a dihedral above this ledge to another ledge below a ceiling; this ledge goes left around a corner and eventually up to a terrace. The final rock is easier and leads up and right to the top of the buttress.

ROUTE 8. No Escape Buttress, East Edge. III, 5.7. First ascent July 30, 1978, by Andy Carson and Jorge Colon. This route contains six pitches with rock of fair quality, sometimes wet and licheny. It starts from trees near the right (east) edge of the main face, going up a series of chimneys

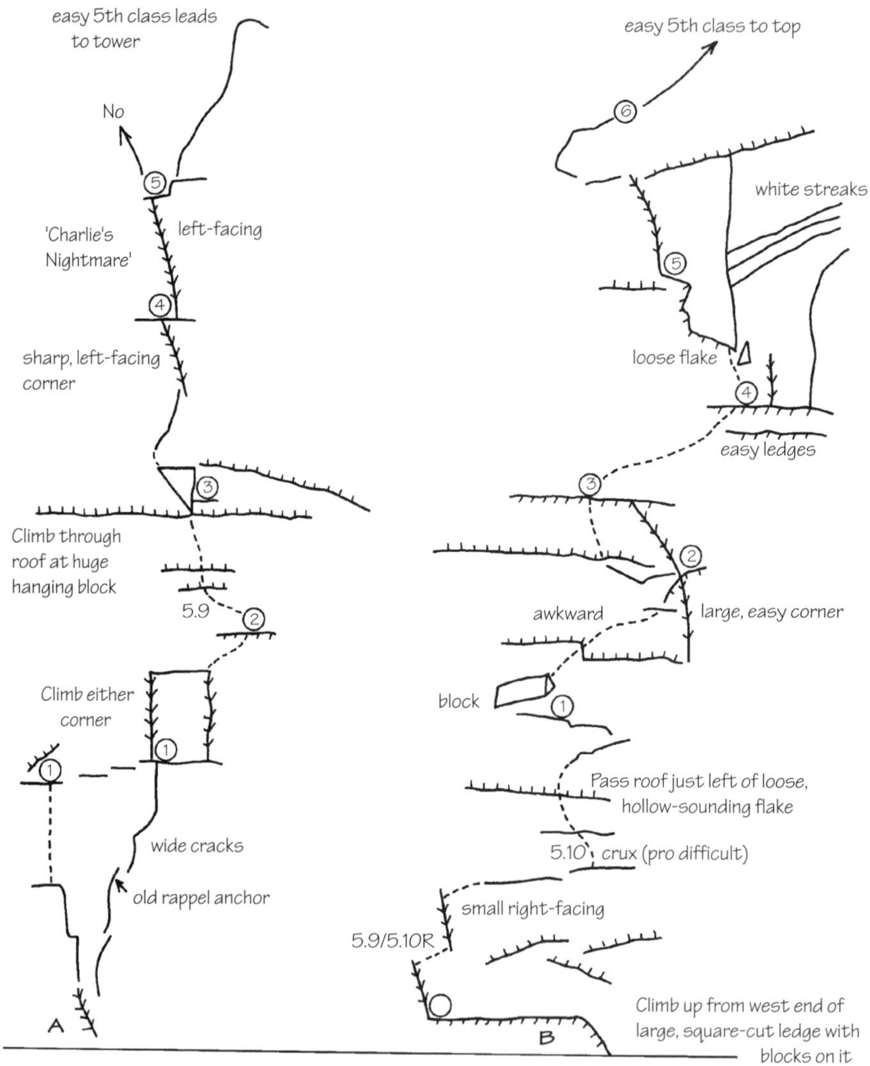

easy 5th class leads
to tower

easy 5th class to top

No

⑤

⑥

white streaks

left-facing

'Charlie's
Nightmare'

⑤

④

sharp, left-facing
corner

loose flake

④

③

easy ledges

Climb through
roof at huge
hanging block

③

②

5.9

②

large, easy corner

awkward

Climb either
corner

block

①

①

Pass roof just left of loose,
hollow-sounding flake

wide cracks

5.10 crux (pro difficult)

old rappel anchor

small right-facing

5.9/5.10R

A

B

Climb up from west end of
large, square-cut ledge with
blocks on it

84. LEIGH CANYON, NORTH SIDE ROCK CLIMBS
NO ESCAPE BUTTRESS
A. GIN AND TONIC, III, 5.9
B. NO SURVIVORS, III, 5.10R

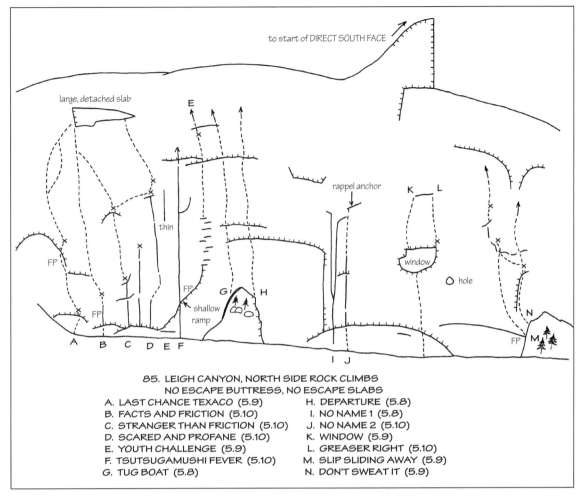

85. LEIGH CANYON, NORTH SIDE ROCK CLIMBS
NO ESCAPE BUTTRESS, NO ESCAPE SLABS

A. LAST CHANCE TEXACO (5.9)	H. DEPARTURE (5.8)
B. FACTS AND FRICTION (5.10)	I. NO NAME 1 (5.8)
C. STRANGER THAN FRICTION (5.10)	J. NO NAME 2 (5.10)
D. SCARED AND PROFANE (5.10)	K. WINDOW (5.9)
E. YOUTH CHALLENGE (5.9)	L. GREASER RIGHT (5.10)
F. TSUTSUGAMUSHI FEVER (5.10)	M. SLIP SLIDING AWAY (5.9)
G. TUG BOAT (5.8)	N. DON'T SWEAT IT (5.9)

and corners. One 5.7 chimney will be encountered near the beginning, prior to the traverse to the left (west) to gain the indentation, which is the only line of weakness in this part of the face. In a band of white rock higher on the route another chimney of similar difficulty must also be climbed. *ROUTE 9. Direct Avoidance.* III, 5.10. First ascent July 31, 1978, Dieter Klose and Mike Kehoe. The exact location of this route is uncertain, but it apparently starts 400 feet to the right of the Direct South Face (*Route 5*); the description has some similarity to the line of *Route 6*, which was climbed the day before. Perhaps it can be identified by the first lead, 5.10 on good granite. After two pitches up the wall, a traverse was made left (west) for 200 feet. Now climb a short offwidth crack and into a system of cracks. Next move left up to the crux overhang and then back right to a sloping ledge. Climb right up through the overhang and move left on the face above, finishing back to the right to a belay point. Now

descend 10 feet and climb 40 feet to the right, up through another overhang, and then move left to the belay. Two additional pitches lead to the top of the buttress. Because the rock was not good after the first pitch, this route is not greatly recommended.

ROUTE 10. Spreadeagle. II, 5.10. First ascent August 1, 1978, by Dieter Klose and Mike Kehoe. Rather little information is available on this route, which aims for a set of dihedrals on a prominent nose on the north side of Leigh Canyon. One such nose with dihedrals is located on the buttress to the right (east) of the large talus cone and stream draining the couloir system east of the Southeast Ridge (*Route 3*). Proceed up Leigh Canyon to this talus cone (about 0.25 mile east of Laughing Lions Falls) and scramble up for about 1,200 feet to the base of the nose. The first difficult lead (5.10) is up a large, left-facing, gray-and-orange corner to an overhanging jam crack; climb 10 feet up this crack to the belay. The next pitch, also 5.10, starts with a step 10 feet to the right and up the right-hand crack to the belay. The third lead (5.8) moves left and up a crack in the face above to the end of this route. (*Note:* This route may be the direct start mentioned in the description of Staircase Arête.)

ROUTE 11. No Escape Slabs. I, 5.7 to 5.10. The first climb on the beautiful slabs located immediately below No Escape Buttress appears to have been done by Al Rubin and Charles Jackson in August of 1970. This was most probably the 5.8 crack located in the center section. The name "Easy Escape Slabs" was applied to the area at that time. The pure friction climbing potential of the slabs was realized somewhat later on July 30, 1977, by Rich Perch and Mike Munger. See *Topo 85* and *Photo 95.* These slabs are a great place to spend a day of climbing on excellent rock in a scenic location. Pure friction climbing is a rarity in the Tetons. Some 14 different lines are available; however, many more possibilities exist. From the west shore of Leigh Lake take the climbers' trail about 0.5 mile into Leigh Canyon. No Escape Slabs will be seen at the base of No Escape Buttress, which is the first major rock feature on the southeast side of Mount Moran. Two ropes for top-roping are recommended for these climbs. Some routes can be led but top-roping first is strongly suggested because the protection for some routes is marginal or nonexistent. For descent walk back down around the sides to the base of the slabs.

EAST HORN (11,465)

Map: Mount Moran

The East Horn is more easily recognized as the northern of the two horns that flank the Falling Ice Glacier on the southeast side of Mount Moran. It also forms the southern boundary for the Skillet Glacier, and so separates the two major glaciers on the east side of Mount Moran. Although Teton glaciers normally lurk below dark north faces of the mountains, the Falling Ice Glacier, which faces southeast, is unique in the range and, as Fryxell noted, is able to persist because of the topography: " . . . so deep is the cleft in which it lies and so well do its two horns protect it that the sun reaches its surface only a few hours each day" (*The Tetons, Interpretations of a Mountain Landscape,* pp. 58–59). During his solo first ascent in 1931 Fryxell noted that on his approach hike he saw eight different types of ripe berries; mountaineering sometimes has unanticipated benefits. The summit of the East Horn offers a comprehensive view of the east faces of Moran, extending from the northeast ridge to the south edge of the CMC face. The eastern extension of the prominent black dike on the east face of Mount Moran passes along the base of the north face of the West Horn at the south edge of the Falling Ice Glacier and is then lost beneath the rubble below the snout of the glacier. It reappears below the southeast wall of the

East Horn and finally crosses the south ridge of Point 9,808 among the trees.

For approaches to the East Horn, see *Mount Moran,* later. The easiest method is from the southeast via the stream gully below the Falling Ice Glacier. Hike up the stream drainage to about 8,800 feet and cut north to the saddle (9,600+) that separates Point 9,808 to the east from the east slopes of the East Horn. Alternatively, one could use one of the northeastern approaches and hike and bushwhack up the stream drainage below the Skillet Glacier to reach the same saddle from the north.

CHRONOLOGY

East Face: July 30, 1931, Fritiof Fryxell
West Ridge: July 18, 1951, Peter Robinson, William Briggs, Brian Brett (descent); August 31, 1954, Stanley and Virginia Boucher, Sayre Rodman, Jean Winne (ascent)
South Face: November 14, 1976, Paul Horton, Hal Gribble
Southeast Buttress: July 25, 1978, Yvon Chouinard, Juris Krisjansons
North Face: August 9, 1984, Yvon Chouinard, Naoe Sakashita

ROUTE 1. West Ridge. II, 5.6. First descent July 18, 1951, by Peter Robinson, William Briggs, and Brian Brett; first ascent August 31, 1954, by Stanley and Virginia Boucher, Sayre Rodman, and Jean Winne. This sharp ridge is significantly more difficult than the East Face route. The route was first utilized for a traverse to the summit of Mount Moran via its east ridge. From the summit of the East Horn, climb down the ridge to a rotten pinnacle. Because a rappel is undesirable from here, descend about 200 feet down toward the Falling Ice Glacier, where a ledge system leads back and slightly up to the ridge crest. After a 60-foot rappel from this point, easy scrambling places one on the col between the Horn and the east ridge of Moran. To ascend this West Ridge route, the col can be reached from the north via the Skillet Glacier (see *Mount Moran, Route 18*). It is also possible to reach the col from the south via the Falling Ice Glacier through a chimney leading to the low point in the col, but getting onto the surface of the glacier is not a simple matter. Direct approach from the glacier snout is possible but very hazardous unless done when the ice blocks and rocks are frozen in place; steep ice requiring crampons is usually encountered. Descent from the Drizzlepuss notch (see *Mount Moran, Route 14*) down onto the glacier is also possible but not pleasant. See *Dartmouth Mountaineering Club Journal,* 1952, pp. 8–11, illus.

ROUTE 2. South Face. II, AI2+, 5.4. First ascent November 14, 1976, by Paul Horton and Hal Gribble. From Leigh Lake follow the main gully containing the stream draining the Falling Ice Glacier to the snout of the glacier. Attain the upper flat section of the glacier by four ice pitches near its right (north) edge. Discretion must be used here, because at times ice avalanches have occurred at the glacier snout; some years will be more dangerous than others. Just east of the summit of the East Horn is a sharp notch from which a large chimney extends down to the glacier below. This route generally follows the right (east) edge of the face to the left of this large chimney. This edge becomes a small ridge halfway up the face, curving slightly west and ending at the summit. Start a few hundred feet to the left of the chimney and diagonal right and up for one and a half pitches to reach the edge of the face, which is then followed to the summit in six pitches. Most of the climb is 4.0 on broken, blocky rock that, while somewhat loose, is not especially dangerous.

ROUTE 3. Southeast Buttress. III, 5.8. First ascent July 25, 1978, by Yvon Chouinard and Juris Krisjansons. This rock route starts at the lowest point of the southeast buttress to the right (east) of the snout of the Falling Ice Glacier. The initial lead passes some large overhangs along a break on the right (north) side. The second pitch goes up to the first diagonal ledge. A second diagonal ledge is reached after two more pitches up the nose of the buttress. Now traverse left on ledges for one and a half pitches, and then turn upward to finish the second of these two leads. From this point, near the center of the south face, climb up and slightly left to the southeast summit of the East Horn. This climb contains a total of 12 pitches on excellent rock.

ROUTE 4. ☞East Face. II, 3.0. First ascent July 30, 1931, by Fritiof Fryxell. See *Photo 105.* From the saddle (9,600+) to the east, separating Point 9,808 from the East Horn, the broad east face above can be climbed in various ways, all of which involve moving somewhat out to the right (north) from this saddle. Easy routes can be worked out linking together ledges intermixed with slabs in the middle of this face. If the south edge of the east face (this could be called the southeast ridge) is followed closely over the various gendarmes, interesting climbing of somewhat greater difficulty (5.1) will be found. *Time: 5½ hours* from the north end of Leigh Lake. See *Appalachia,* 18, no. 4 (December 1931), pp. 388–408, illus.

ROUTE 5. North Face. II, 5.4. First ascent August 9, 1984, by Yvon Chouinard and Naoe Sakashita. The climb, involving crampons and axe, started from the Skillet Glacier and reached the summit of the East Horn from the north.

WEST HORN (11,605)

Map: Mount Moran

This splendid pinnacle is the more southerly of the two that flank the Falling Ice Glacier. The north and south faces are remarkably sheer, the west ridge is a knife-edge, and the slightly broader east ridge harbors excellent rock. Although every party that climbs the popular CMC route on Mount Moran passes the base of this horn, it is seldom climbed,

very likely due to its forbidding appearance from the south or west. Its overall thinness, combined with the great overhang on its west ridge, leads one to believe that its ascent is a major undertaking. However, the West Horn is a short, exciting climb and is recommended as a viewpoint before or after a climb of the CMC route. The view of the east face of Mount Moran from the summit of the West Horn is especially impressive, the slabs of the CMC route appearing absolutely sheer and smooth. One can also look vertically down on the surface of the Falling Ice Glacier, for which Fryxell gave this apt description: "This glacier lies in its cleft [between the two horns] like a beast in its lair."

The pioneer Teton mountaineer, Fred Ayres, was especially intrigued by this region of the horns of Moran. On August 13, 1934, "a tremendous mass of ice" broke off the snout of the Falling Ice Glacier, leaving a trail of ice fragments 0.25 mile long. On August 18 and 19, Ayres twice explored this ice avalanche, climbing partway up the lower extension of the black dike on the south edge of the glacier. On June 29, 1936, he made a solo attempt on the west ridge of the West Horn, but without rope was stopped by the "terrific overhang" on the ridge crest. On July 10, 1936, he made the second ascent (solo) of the East Horn and on the same day attacked the West Horn again, this time by the east ridge, but retreated at the steep and exposed slabs about 400 feet below the summit. His third effort on August 28 via the west ridge with companions and rope was finally rewarded by success. He returned 15 years later, in 1951, to make the second (perhaps third) ascent of the West Horn by its west ridge and, on July 24, 1953, completed his explorations with the first ascent of the east ridge.

For the various approaches to the West Horn, see *Mount Moran,* later.

ROUTE 1. ☞West Ridge. II, 5.4. First ascent August 28, 1936, by Fred and Irene Ayres, Donald Grant, and J. Keith Anderson. See *Photo 98.* The west ridge of the West Horn is separated from the main col between the West Horn and Drizzlepuss by an incredible gendarme with a rock balanced on its top. Reach this col by scrambling from the CMC campsite as in the CMC route (see *Mount Moran, Route 14*). From the col climb along ledges on the right (south) side of this gendarme to the small notch between the gendarme and the spectacular overhang on the west ridge of the West Horn. Avoid this overhang by ascending a small, easy chimney on its right (south) flank for a ropelength before turning up ledges to the knife-edge west ridge, which is followed to the summit. Both the north and south faces drop off very steeply from this narrow ridge. On descent climb back down the west ridge until just above an overhang in the knife-edge, where old slings will be found. A full-length rappel down the south face is followed by exposed downclimbing and a second (and perhaps third) rappel, all the while angling west to minimize the distance to the talus. Once the talus is reached follow the usual climbers' trail back to the CMC campsite. *Time: 7½ hours* from the north end of Leigh Lake.

ROUTE 2. East Ridge. II, 5.6. First ascent July 24, 1953, by Fred Ayres and Alexander Creswell. From the CMC campsite climb the talus slope south of the West Horn until the big gash that slices across the east ridge in a north–south direction can be seen. This gash separates a distinct, eastern high point (10,560+) from the main West Horn summit. It is probably possible to go to the col at the head of this gash and start the east ridge of the West Horn by climbing up and out to the right on ledges with *krummholz* trees. A better scheme is to continue west 200 or 300 feet beyond this gash to a break in the wall, leading to a small notch in the ridge; a short 5.6 pitch is climbed to reach this notch. The ridge from here to the summit is enjoyable climbing of 5.4 difficulty, and there are a variety of ways to proceed, mostly edging right (north) when opportunity presents itself. Four or five pitches are involved, containing intervals of slabs and some excellent rock, especially in one knobby section. One eastern subsummit with a knife-edge is passed just before reaching the summit.

UNSOELD'S NEEDLE (11,680+)
(0.2 mi SE of Mount Moran)

Map: Mount Moran

This slender pinnacle stands at the left (south) edge of the east face of Mount Moran, south of the black dike. It is west of and about 100 feet above the notch behind (west of) Drizzlepuss. The approach is the same as for the CMC route (see *Mount Moran, Route 14*). This pinnacle, although difficult, can be ascended *en route* to the summit of Mount Moran via that route.

ROUTE 1. East Ridge. I, 5.4. First ascent July 31, 1952, by Willi Unsoeld, Robert Moffitt, Elias Gregory, and Gilbert Mueller. From the notch between Drizzlepuss and the beginning of the east face, climb about 50 feet up out of the notch. Now instead of traversing right (north), climb about 40 feet straight up the sharp east ridge of the Needle, now directly above, to a vertical, crackless band. Swing left (south) off the crest to climb around the band, up a 5.4 break and out onto the shoulder immediately below the summit. A 60-foot rappel reaches the notch to the west.

MOUNT MORAN (12,605)

Map: Mount Moran

Among all the peaks of the Teton Range, Mount Moran may justifiably be considered as second only to the Grand Teton. If the range is approached from the north or northeast, Mount Moran easily dominates the scene. The primary impression conveyed by the mountain is that of massiveness, and when one climbs on the mountain this impression is reinforced. The singular, nearly flat summit marks the boundary between the Precambrian crystalline gneiss rock of the mountain bulk and the thin sedimentary sandstone cap marking the highest rounded point; it measures some 600 by 1,600 feet, covering more than 15 acres. It is a big mountain in every respect and a most worthy objective for the Teton mountaineer. Like several other peaks in the range, Moran affords no really easy route to the summit; but there is a wide range of difficulty from the moderate northeast ridge to the very difficult routes from the south and north. The five glaciers of Mount Moran provide extensive opportunity for snow-and-ice climbing and, in combination with adjacent rock walls, for significant mixed routes. In addition to massive rock walls, the prolific mountain contains numerous ridges and couloirs, some of which have been investigated only in recent years, resulting in several routes of the first order. Many years still remain, however, before the last sector of Mount Moran will have been explored. A number of the recent routes on the south side of Moran have been rock climbs not leading to the summit. These rock climbs are described separately under *Leigh Canyon, North Side Rock Climbs,* earlier.

Mount Moran, named by members of the Hayden Survey for the famous landscape artist Thomas Moran, was the second great peak of the Tetons to attract the attention of mountaineers. Moran himself never saw his mountain from Jackson Hole but caught a brief glimpse from the west through smoky skies during his one visit to the range in late August of 1879. This view did provide the basis for his prophetic pronouncement: "The Tetons here loomed up grandly against the sky & from this point it is perhaps the finest pictorial range in the United States or even in N. America." As early as 1886 the north shoulder of the peak was reached by the geologist Joseph P. Iddings on a short side trip from the geologic mapping of Yellowstone National Park. In 1915 the first semiserious effort to attain the summit was made by John Shive, veteran of the 1898 ascent of the Grand Teton, with three others. They were turned back by lack of time at a point apparently above the Skillet Glacier some 600 feet below the summit. An outing to one of the eastern glaciers in August of 1917 by the manager of the Yellowstone Park Transportation Company, Harry Child, with a retinue of photographers and writers, resulted in an article in *Scientific American* ("The Jackson Hole Country of Wyoming," March 30, 1918, p. 272) with this tantalizing sentence: "The summit has never been attained and probably never will, as the last 3000 feet of the mountain are sheer perpendicular walls of rock." Almost surely inspired by this self-defeating prophecy, LeRoy Jeffers, a mountaineer well known in his day, on August 11, 1919, reached the lower north summit at 9 PM in a sleet storm, after a remarkable solo climb of a variant of the northeast ridge. There can be no doubt that he would have continued to the higher south summit had the weather been better and the day longer. With at least some competitive motivation, Dr. L. H.

Hardy and Ben C. Rich came to Jackson Hole in 1922 to climb the mountain and, after meeting Bennet McNulty, formed a party of three to attain the summit on July 27. Curiously, their summit note remained undiscovered until August 25, 1964, when it was found intact in its half-pint whiskey bottle by W. and J. Bousman. Jeffers returned with Warren Loyster only ten days later, on August 6, 1922, and this time reached the main south summit but was most disappointed to gain only the second ascent of the mountain.

The numerous distinctive features of the mountain deserve mention. On the north and south Mount Moran is confined by Moran and Leigh Canyons, but to the west there is a well-defined ridge that soon deteriorates into a sequence of complexities. About 2,500 feet above the floor of Moran Canyon, three large but seldom-visited glaciers sweep up to meet the complex west ridge. In contrast, above Leigh Canyon, the imposing south walls rise abruptly to provide very steep ground for some of the finest rock routes in the park. The southwest aspect of Mount Moran contains a very large expanse of rock forming the west face of the main south ridge as it rises from the initial buttress to the summit. Not visible from the valley floor and, hence, under-appreciated by many visiting climbers, this section contains several clearly defined ridges and steep couloirs between the southwest couloir on the north and the south buttress on the south. Extending eastward from the south ridge and above the major basal buttresses on the south is the con-siderable bowl of the upper south face. The right (east) edge of this rarely visited face is the left (south) edge of the east face.

The remarkable black dike that cleaves the east face into two unequal sections measures about 125 feet in width. This dike continues through the mountain to the west and can be traced for 7.0 miles all the way to the divide at the head of Moran Canyon. The two major glaciers below the east face, the Skillet Glacier and Falling Ice Glacier, are guarded by the salient East and West Horns. Around on the northeast side of the mountain, lying below the northeast ridge and the east face of the north ridge of Mount Moran, is a most interesting cirque seldom visited by mountaineers. From the snowfield and the expanse of morainal boulders in the cirque, rock walls cut by four large parallel couloirs diagonal up from east to west to join these ridges. The northwest aspect of Mount Moran encompasses both the west face of the north ridge and the north face and is bounded on the right by the upper snow arm of the eastern-most Triple Glacier. The north buttress or pillar is a prominent vertical feature in the center (southeast corner) of the face to the right (south) of the third couloir.

During the first quarter-century of climbing after the opening of Grand Teton National Park in 1929 Mount Moran was quite naturally one of the major objectives for mountaineers in the Teton Range. In more recent years it is

an unfortunate fact that the mountain is not frequently climbed. Its popularity has diminished as difficulties of access have increased. In the early years of the park, access was simplified by a road to the north end of Leigh Lake, but following complaints concerning noisy motorcycles on this near-wilderness road, it was closed by the National Park Service in 1953.

To approach the southeastern side of Mount Moran, as for an ascent of the CMC route (Route 14) or either the West or East Horn, there are three methods available. By far the best means of approach (in these days of minimal trail maintenance) is to take a canoe across Leigh Lake from the String Lake portage to the mouth of the stream draining the Falling Ice Glacier; this involves 3.1 miles of paddling plus the String Lake–Leigh Lake portage. Without canoe but with noticeably more exertion, one can hike on the Valley Trail from the String Lake trailhead to the north end of Leigh Lake, where, with some effort, the remnants of the once-good but now-abandoned trail around the northwest side of the lake can be followed with bushwhacking to the stream. It is also possible, but not recommended, to hike around the southwest side of Leigh Lake on yet another NPS-abandoned trail now nearly impassable with years of deadfall to the mouth of Leigh Canyon. Continue around the northwest shore of the lake to reach the same stream from the Falling Ice Glacier. Either way, from the lakeshore hike up the bouldery stream gully for some 2,500 feet to the open, semigrassy slope due east of and below the West Horn, just south of the glacier. A climbers' trail will be found on this slope leading up to the outstanding CMC campsite (ca. 10,000), located on the flat ridge up to the left (south) in the large trees, one step down (about 100 feet) from the last trees. Excellent flat areas will be found among the trees on the ridge crest, and except in the late season during dry years there is water in the boulder field 100 feet to the south.

To approach the northeastern side of Mount Moran, as for an ascent of the Skillet Glacier (Route 18) or Northeast Ridge (Route 22), there are also three methods available. The first is by canoe across Leigh Lake from the String Lake portage. One can head for the north shore of the lake (2.9 miles of paddling) and continue by hiking north on the final portion of the Valley Trail to Bearpaw Lake. To reach the northeastern base of the mountain or the mouth of Moran Canyon, fierce bushwhacking will be encountered not far beyond Bearpaw Lake. Maintenance of the trail that once led easily to the mouth of Moran Canyon was abandoned by the National Park Service about 25 years ago, and now the trail can scarcely be found among the avalanche debris. Instead of canoeing, one can hike around the east side of Leigh Lake on the Valley Trail to reach the north end of the lake in about the same amount of time but with noticeably greater exertion. The best approach to the northern or northeastern routes on the mountain is across Jackson Lake by power boat from Colter Bay or Signal Mountain Lodge or by canoe (4.0 miles of paddling) from Spalding Bay. All of these schemes are time consuming, so the first of two climbing days is normally devoted to packing in to a high camp. Compensating for the effort is the picturesque and remote setting of some of the high campsites.

CHRONOLOGY

Skillet Glacier: July 27, 1922, LeGrand Haven Hardy, Ben C. Rich, Bennet McNulty

Northeast Ridge: August 19, 1924, Albert R. Ellingwood, Carl Blaurock
   var: August 11, 1919, LeRoy Jeffers
   var: August 25, 1939, Earl Clark, Donald Grant
   var: **Northeast Buttress Couloir:** July 16, 1971, Gale Long, Robert Frisby

Dike: June 23, 1931, Hans Wittich, Otto Stegmaier
   var: August 14, 1946, Gerald Brandon, Theodore Brandon (descent); August 12, 1952, Theodore Brandon, Tim Ramsland, Willis Wood, Don and Ivan Zastrow (ascent)

East Ridge: July 24, 1931, Robert L. M. Underhill, Paul Petzoldt
   var: July 24, 1931, Paul Petzoldt, Robert Underhill (descent)
   var: July 18, 1951, Peter Robinson, William Briggs, Brian Brett

Upper South Ridge: June 30, 1935, Phil Smith, Eldon Petzoldt

West Ridge: August 26, 1935, Paul Petzoldt, H. K. Hartline

Triple Glacier: September 8, 1935, Malcolm Smith

North Ridge: July 5, 1939, Paul Petzoldt, William Ringler
   var: September 13, 1957, Bill Pope, Mary Kay Pottinger (complete), or September 10, 1960, Peter Gardiner, Frank Knight, Mihaly Csikszentmihalyi (complete), or July 27, 1956, Richard Emerson, Robert Bowen (partial)

CMC: July 14, 1935, Chris Scoredos, Joe Merhar (descent); June 25, 1941, Paul Petzoldt, Joseph Hawkes, Earl Clark, Harold Plumley
   var: July 23, 1952, Richard Emerson, Walt Sticker
   var: August 17, 1952, Martin Benham, Dmitri Nabokov (descent)

Direct South Buttress: August 29–30, 1953, Richard Emerson, Don Decker, Leigh Ortenburger; first free ascent July 3, 1979, Stan Mish, Hal Gribble
   var: September 9, 1958, Richard Sykes, William Briggs
   var: August 12–13, 1965, Peter Cleveland, Roland Fleck, Jack Stauffer

East Chimney: July 9, 1956, Robert Day, Peter Lipman, Alan Williamson

Fonda Ridge: August 22–23, 1957, John Fonda, David Dingman, Karl Pfiffner

The Blackfin: July 4–5, 1960, David Dornan, Leigh Ortenburger

South Buttress Right: July 25, 1961, David Dornan, Herb Swedlund; July 14, 1961, David Dornan, Peter Lev (attempt); (nail-up bypass) July 18, 1973, Steve Wunsch, Art Higbee (first free ascent); (original route) August 2, 1978, Buck Tilley, Jim Mullin (first free ascent)
   var: **Habeler:** July 13, 1969, Peter Habeler, Juris Krisjansons
   var: **Deliverance:** July 6, 1990, James Earl, Todd G. Cozzens

North Face: June 29, 1962, Pete Sinclair, Peter Lev, William Buckingham, Leigh Ortenburger

Skillet Glacier Headwall: July 27, 1962, Don Anderson, Larry Scott

Southwest Couloir: August 17, 1962, Ted Vaill, Stuart Kearns

South Buttress, West Face: August 25–26, 1962, Art Gran, John Hudson

Northeast Slabs: September 10, 1962, Fred Beckey, Dan Davis

Sickle Couloir: August 8, 1964, Gary Cole, Ray Jacquot

South Buttress Central: July 16, 1967, Peter Koedt, Keith Becker; summer 1984 by Eric Breitenberger and Bill Trull (first free ascent)

Pika Buttress: July 27–28, 1968, James Kanzler, Paul Myhre, John Neal

Western Buttress: August 6–7, 1968, Peter Cleveland, Bill Widule

North Buttress: July 18, 1969, Peter Habeler, George Lowe

Northwest Ridge: July 17, 1977, Paul Horton, Lew Hitchner

Skillet Chimney: October 13, 1978, Paul Horton, W. D. Horton

West Dihedrals: June 28, 1979, Jim Beyer

Revolutionary Crest: July 15, 1982, Jim Beyer, Dave Koch

Sandinista Couloir: late June 1983 (or 1984), Jim Beyer

ROUTE 1. West Ridge. III, 5.4. First ascent August 26, 1935, by Paul Petzoldt and H. K. Hartline. See *Photo 100.* This long ridge, one of the major but seldom seen features of the mountain, extends west from the summit to a point west of Peak 12,000+, where it splits into a northwest branch leading to the Rotten Thumb (11,658) and a southwest branch leading to Thor Peak. The first ascent commenced with the ascent of Thor Peak from which the ridge looks more fearsome than it actually is. There is, however, a certain unavoidable amount of loose rock. Descend from the summit of Thor toward the ridge and Peak 11,840+; avoid much of the worst section, which contains apparently unstable pinnacles, by following a ledge (apparently) on the left (northwest) side 50 to 100 feet below the crest until it seems wise to cut back up onto the crest. It appears that the 1935 party climbed over Peak 11,840+ along the way. In general, the route to Peak 12,000+ goes partly along the crest but mostly along ledges on the north side, and after crossing to the right (southeast) side, ultimately emerges on the broad east face of the peak. To reach the summit of Peak 12,000+ one must then backtrack slightly. Walk down to the saddle (11,680+) that separates Peak 12,000+ from Moran and climb the next portion of ridge that consists of dike rock and rises rather steeply; care must be taken with the loose rock here but it is not difficult. One is now on the broad, flat final portion of the west ridge, which is separated from the summit of Moran by a notch at the head of the Southwest Couloir (see *Route 2*). Descend to the notch, and climb the short, steep pitch on good rock to the summit.

In the event that one does not want to traverse the entire ridge, it is possible to attain the crest from either the north or south. From the north one can (1) start with an ascent of *Peak 12,000+* via its west or north ridge and then continue east toward the summit of Mount Moran or (2) reach the saddle between Peak 12,000+ and Moran directly from the central Triple Glacier. This second alternative, a route apparently not yet done, will require climbing a substantial, and probably unpleasantly loose, wall above the glacier. From the south there are three large couloirs providing access to the west ridge (from west to east): (1) the steep couloir (see *Thor Peak, Route 7*) that leads to the low point (11,600+) of the ridge connecting Peak 11,840+ with Peak 12,000+; (2) a couloir turning into a shelf that diagonals up from right to left (east to west) to meet the crest (and black dike) just west of Peak 12,000+; and (3) the main south couloir, the upper extension of the main drainage just west of the south ridge of Moran, which leads to the saddle (11,680+) between Peak 12,000+ and Moran. Only the third alternative is straightforward and even then some routefinding is required to find the easiest way up the drainage and couloir. In early or midseason all of these couloirs will contain moderately steep snow.

ROUTE 2. Southwest Couloir. II, 5.4. First ascent August 17, 1962, by Ted Vaill and Stuart Kearns. See *Photos 99* and *100*. Rising from the floor of Leigh Canyon, at a remarkable, nearly constant angle (36°), is a north–south side canyon that is bounded on the right (east) by the various western cliffs of the long south ridge of Mount Moran and on the left (west) by the impressive east side of Thor Peak. This side canyon contains two separate and parallel drainages. The western stream originates at the glacier below the east face of Thor Peak and the other (eastern) descends from the snows of the upper southwest couloir. To reach this well-defined couloir ascend Leigh Canyon to the huge talus cone that rises above the first lakes in the canyon. Hike north up the talus, passing the first cliff band by a rotten rock chute on the right (east) side. The side canyon then opens out, and just scrambling is involved all the way up to the point where it splits. About halfway up the couloir, at 10,000 feet, is an excellent bivouac spot on the left (west) side of the couloir in a wind and rainproof cave that is some 30 feet deep, providing ample space for five; the opening of the cave is easily seen as one ascends the open slopes. A V-shaped notch above and about 200 feet west of the cave assists in locating this cave.

At the point of bifurcation (about 11,000 feet), the main left branch goes north to meet the west ridge, and the other turns right (northeast) almost directly toward the summit of Moran. Both branches contain snow until late season. This route follows the right (northeast) branch, which is bounded on the right (south) by the Fonda Ridge. Do not turn up and right too soon; the correct couloir is the last possibility before reaching the west ridge. The black dike crosses the couloir near its top, having passed completely through the mountain from the east side where it is more familiar. Climb 1,000 feet or more of steep snow (35–55°) in this couloir to its upper end, which narrows to a small, steep, icy chimney only a short distance below the summit; climb the sometimes loose rock on the exposed left wall of this chimney to pass the first large chockstone. The two final chockstones are passed by stemming directly. Scramble to the notch in the west ridge above, and gain the summit plateau either by climbing the final step of the west ridge directly (5.4) or by working diagonally up the north slope left of the ridge. This southwest couloir, while requiring mountaineering skill, is nowhere very difficult and can serve satisfactorily for those experienced with an ice axe as a fast method of descent to Leigh Canyon as long as the snow remains in the upper couloir. Two rappels will probably be desired by most climbers in order to start the descent, one from the summit down the final step of the west ridge and a second down the uppermost chimney of the couloir. Because this is an enclosed, narrow, and steep couloir, there is some, but apparently not excessive, rockfall danger on this route. See *American Alpine Journal*, 13, no. 2 (1963), pp. 410–420, illus.

ROUTE 3. Fonda Ridge. III, 5.6. First ascent August 22–23, 1957, by John Fonda, David Dingman, and Karl Pfiffner. See *Photos 99* and *100*. The sector of Mount Moran that lies between the south ridge and the west ridge contains several ridges and buttresses, of which only one, the Fonda Ridge, leads directly to the summit plateau. The approach is the same as that described for *Route 2*. Because this is a long ridge (2,000 feet), a camp or bivouac is essential either at the cave in the side canyon (also described above for *Route 2*) or down in Leigh Canyon at the first lake. From the lake, climb the huge talus slope up into the north–south side canyon. A major problem now is the selection of the proper ridge. By moving to the left side of the drainage below the western buttresses of the south ridge of Moran, one obtains a better view of the complexities above. The Fonda Ridge can be identified by its solid midsection composed of lighter colored rock than either of the two flanking ridges. The high-angle flanking ridge on the right (south) ends on the main south ridge; the left (north) flanking ridge connects with the west ridge of Mount Moran.

There are many possible routes up the first 600-foot section of the Fonda Ridge. This section is very rotten and great caution must be exercised in climbing and in selecting belay positions under overhangs. Perhaps the least dangerous route lies up a small subsidiary abutment on the right (south) of the main base of the ridge. Climb directly up this abutment for about 500 feet to the large amphitheater that separates the Fonda Ridge from the ridge flanking it on the south. Regain the ridge proper here, and climb onto the second section of the ridge, which angles north toward the crest. This section is not as steep as the first section, and the rock is solid, comparable to the steeper parts of the Exum Ridge of the Grand Teton. After the crest is reached, the first towers and steps of the third and last section of the ridge are in sight. In general, these step-towers are most easily turned on the right (south). The final two or three steps, however, are passed on the left. A final pitch will place the party on the summit plateau. Two days were required by the first-ascent party. This ridge is primarily a mountaineering and routefinding problem.

ROUTE 4. *Sandinista Couloir*. II, 5.6. First ascent late June 1983 (or 1984), by Jim Beyer. See *Photos 99* and *100*. This short but well-defined couloir, which forms the right (south) boundary of the Fonda Ridge, ends at the last notch on the south ridge of Mount Moran 1,000 feet below the summit. One-third of the way up the couloir there is a split, the main left branch forming the base of the south face of the Fonda Ridge and the smaller right branch angling back to hit the south ridge crest several hundred feet lower. The route goes up the main left couloir branch, which is in its best climbing condition in early summer. The approach from Leigh Canyon into and up the north–south side canyon is described under *Route 2*. Just short (south) of the Fonda Ridge enter the initial narrow section of the Sandinista Couloir. Climb this section on snow that steepens to 80° or more for about 25 feet. It is an unusual fin of snow, free-standing from the sides of the couloir; it will disappear in midsummer or late summer. From the top of this fin make a 5.6 dogleg traverse left and gain the main couloir, which is followed all the way to the crest of the south ridge. This upper portion is straightforward 45° snow. Two final 5.6 rock pitches provide access to the south ridge, which is followed to the summit. It appears that there is less rockfall in this couloir than in the southwest couloir. For reasons that are not clear, near the bottom of the couloir the rock has been rent asunder by two bolts, placed by nameless, faceless climbers.

ROUTE 5. *Western Buttress*. IV, 5.8. First ascent August 6–7, 1968, by Peter Cleveland and Bill Widule. See *Photos 99* and *100*. The southwest aspect of Mount Moran contains a very large expanse of rock forming the west face of the main south ridge as it rises from the initial buttress to the summit. Clearly defined features include (from north to south) the following: the Southwest Couloir (*Route 2*), the Fonda Ridge (*Route 3*), and the Sandinista Couloir (*Route 4*). This Western Buttress route ascends the well-defined buttress forming the right (south) edge of the Sandinista Couloir described earlier, but little detailed information is available because the route diagram prepared at the time of the first ascent has apparently been lost. The top of this route meets the crest of the south ridge at the same point where the Blackfin joins the ridge from the other (east) side. The nature of the climb is sensitive to the exact route selected. The first-ascent party reported mostly face climbing of 5.8 difficulty on solid rock in about nine pitches up a series of steps. The second ascent in 1978 found moderate rock, 5.6 or perhaps 5.7, and 12 or 13 pitches.

ROUTE 6. *West Dihedrals*. IV, 5.9. First ascent June 28, 1979, by Jim Beyer. See *Photos 99* and *100*. The expanse of rock forming the upper west face of the main south ridge has already been described (see *Routes 3, 4,* and *5*). There are several important features in the central section between the Western Buttress on the left and the two parallel steep couloirs involved in the standard descent route for the Direct South Buttress (*Route 10*) in the lower right (south) portion of the face. Across the lower portion of this entire section is a major ramp or bench paralleling the base, slanting up from right (south) to left (north). In the wall immediately above the far (north) end of this major ramp is a conspicuous, huge, curving black arch contained within a second, smaller arch with a 40-foot roof. Above and to the right of these arches is an indentation containing two large left-facing dihedral formations, the left relatively clean, the right blocky, which reach the crest of the south ridge. This 13-pitch route begins below and right of the huge arch and ends with the left dihedral to gain the ridge.

From Leigh Canyon ascend the side canyon on the west side of the south ridge of Moran (see *Route 2*) to the last break in the wall short of the Western Buttress. This point is recognizable as a steep secondary ramp that leads from the talus up toward the midpoint of the huge arch. A bivouac site can be found near the trees just above the beginning of this ramp. The route should be scouted during the approach up the side canyon because most of it cannot be seen from the base of the secondary ramp where the climbing begins. The first two pitches up the ramp are easy climbing (4.0 and 5.1), using a dihedral that diagonals left to gain the main bench of orange rock, where one can contour left toward the huge arch. Traverse some tricky slabs and continue up to the base of the first left-facing dihedral to the right (south) of the huge arch. This 120-foot dihedral (5.6) is climbed to a ledge at its top, from which 5.6

cracks, first on the left and then on the right, lead to a be-lay at the top of a buttress. The next lead begins with an easy traverse down and right, before turning up to a cramped belay near the base of an obvious, black, left-facing dihedral. Climb the crack to the right over a 5.7 overhang up to the base of a short ramp diagonaling up and left. Go up this ramp to the next lead, the most difficult of this route. It does not go up to the roof in the dihedral (where a huge, loose flake will be seen) but instead climbs a face (5.9) on the slightly overhanging wall to the left. Traverse left, then di-agonal back right on easy rock to a belay below a small roof containing a hand crack.

Climb this roof and traverse right on an easy unpro-tected face to a dihedral that is climbed to a belay ledge below a large left-facing open book. The ninth lead (5.6) is liebacked and jammed up this open book. The next very long pitch wanders up and right, then back left into the dihedral, finally diagonaling up and right into an area of broken black rock, where a belay piton should be found. Climb the next dihedral, over a 5.8 roof, to the "Pillar of Fate," a precarious stack of loose blocks, passing to the left around the pillar to a belay 15 feet left of the dihedral crack. The 12th lead follows the left-angling, left-facing dihedral to its top, continuing up cracks and blocks to the belay. The final 40 feet up exposed 5.1 slabs take one onto the ridge crest, which is then followed to the summit as in *Route 9*. In addition to the usual set of nuts and devices to 3 inches, this very long climb may require pitons for adequate protection, as well as an ice axe for the convenient descent of the South-west Couloir (*Route 2*).

ROUTE 7. Revolutionary Crest. IV, 5.8, or V, 5.8 (to the sum-mit). First ascent July 15, 1982, by Jim Beyer and Dave Koch. See *Photos 99* and *100*. This is an exceptionally long climb, containing 16 pitches just to gain the crest of the south ridge about 2,000 feet below the summit. The Revo-lutionary Crest is the buttress to the right (south) of the indentation of the Western Dihedrals route (*Route 6*). The climb starts about halfway along the first broad wall past (north) the Direct South Buttress descent couloir and stays on the southwest aspect of the massive rock forming this part of the main south ridge of Moran. This initial wall separates the south buttress descent couloir from the con-spicuous curving black arch that dominates the beginning of the West Dihedrals route.

From Leigh Canyon use the same approach as for *Route 6*. Some easy climbing (5.1) is involved in reaching a suit-able bivouac spot for this route on a flat shoulder near the beginning of the major ramp that lies along the base of the west face of the south ridge of Mount Moran. The route begins a short distance up this ramp beyond the mouth of the Direct South Buttress descent couloir. The first two pitches (5.1) on the broken wall above the ramp angle up and right to a small ridge crest and a belay just right of a cluster of small roofs. Two moderate pitches then go straight up this ridge that forms the top edge of the initial wall. After

a lead (5.4) up and right to a belay below an overhanging block, the sixth pitch traverses horizontally right around the crest (5.6), then up and right to an overhang. Take a line to the right of this overhang, make a short hand traverse (5.6) right, and then climb left and straight up to the base of a long band of overhangs, finally traversing right across a slab to a belay ledge. To pass this band of overhangs, traverse right for 90 feet to the first non-overhanging dihe-dral and climb this left-facing, crackless dihedral (5.8) to easier ground. A ropelength on a 4th-class ramp now leads left. The tenth lead ascends a second left-facing, crackless dihedral (5.7) that angles left to a ridge crest. Climb 4th class to the col between the overhanging wall on the left and a pinnacle to the right (south). The 12th lead goes horizon-tally right to a belay in a chimney just right of an 8-inch crack. Climb a few feet to the right of this offwidth crack, then step into it at the first chockstone and continue up the chimney above. The next two moderate leads attain the ridge crest and continue along the crest. The final pitch (5.4) goes up, traversing right over a rib. One can unrope here, climbing the snow-and-rock gully on the right of the ridge, eventually regaining the crest. Now climb with an occasional bit of 5.4 to the summit. Water can usually be found 500 feet below the summit near the upper reaches of the main south ridge. To descend, the Southwest Couloir (*Route 2*) is a convenient route to return to the bivouac site. Although this route can be climbed in one extremely long day, two days will be preferred by many climbers.

ROUTE 8. South Buttress, West Face. IV, 5.7, A3. First as-cent August 25–26, 1962, by Art Gran and John Hudson. See *Photo 99*. This very long route, which lies well around on the west face of the south buttress, is continuously steep and difficult. Little is known about this climb other than what was reported by the first-ascent party, which is pre-sented here; a second ascent has probably not been done. From Leigh Canyon ascend the talus, go around left under the beginnings of the south buttress, and enter the north–south side canyon. Continue a few hundred feet up the gully to the second rotten inside corner, which is climbed for 30 feet to a belay position beneath a bulge on the left. This point marks the start of the climb, and unless it is found the following route description cannot be under-stood. The first pitch goes 140 feet up the inside corner to a belay on top of a capping chockstone. Now climb diago-nally up the right wall and around the corner to and past a large ledge, ending the ropelength on a higher ledge. The large ledge is the westward continuation of the first ledge of *Route 10*. Below this large ledge the rock is somewhat rot-ten, but it is noticeably better above. Climb the nose above, then a shallow groove to an overhang from which one exits to the right and up, to a belay ledge. The fourth pitch as-cends the inside corner above until it becomes overhanging, at which point the route moves left and up to a flake. From its top traverse 25 feet right and up to a ledge at the end of a 110-foot lead. The next long lead takes one up past another large ledge to the beginning of a small ramp leading left and up; this large ledge is the westward continuation of the second ledge of *Route 10*.

After 40 feet up this ramp climb up and right over a bulge, passing one ledge, and continue up and right to another at the end of 100 feet. Now gain the slab above, and ascend to a belay under an overhang. The eighth lead starts to the right, then goes up a steep wall, and finishes by moving left and up, first with a hand traverse and then with a crack and two inside corners, to the beginning of a second, large ramp. Climb up and left one long pitch on the ramp, past a short wall, ultimately going around the corner to a large block. The tenth lead continues up and left on the ramp, reaching a flake, from the top of which another ramp is gained and followed out left to its end. Now climb a steep corner and exit to the right to a nose; move up and left and climb another corner to a roof, where one exits to the left to a small ramp. The 12th pitch goes up over a bulge, left on a ramp, around a corner, then straight up to a bulge, where a traverse to the right leads to a large ledge. Scramble right on this ledge around the corner and then up to the right, entering a chimney. The final pitch goes up this long chimney all the way to the crest of a west spur of the south buttress. From this point one can traverse over to the uppermost part of the south buttress route on the level section at the top of the buttress. The ascent can be continued to the summit of Mount Moran via the upper south ridge, or one can descend via one of the two standard methods outlined under *Route 10*. This climb required knifeblade pitons and many angle pitons to 2 inches on the first ascent. Many parties will find two days necessary for this climb, especially if the ridge is completed to the summit. See *American Alpine Journal*, 13, no. 2 (1963), pp. 410–420, illus.

ROUTE 9. Upper South Ridge. II, 5.4. First ascent June 30, 1935, by Phil Smith and Eldon Petzoldt. The principal south ridge of Moran, as seen from the west or east in profile, has two distinct sections. The buttress forming the bottom 1,500 feet rises smoothly at a very high angle to its overhanging cap. The upper south ridge sweeps up to the summit in a series of giant steps, each adorned with pinnacles. This route avoids the lower buttress by contouring in above it from the east. From the usual CMC campsite (see *Route 14*) traverse left and up over grass- and tree-covered ledges along the south edge of the talus slope to the crest of the south ridge of Drizzlepuss. Climb down northward into the large bowl of the upper south face of Moran. Below, toward Leigh Canyon, this bowl funnels into the narrow and steep drainage of Laughing Lions Falls. Scramble west, crossing the bowl into and up a rotten gully leading to the notch in the upper Blackfin ridge; this is the same notch crossed from west to east during an escape from the top of the south buttress routes to the CMC campsite. From the notch descend slightly on the far (west) side to a grassy bench and continue on to the south ridge, which is then followed to the summit. Most parties stay somewhat on the right (east) side of the crest of the south ridge until the final step, leading onto the southwest corner of the summit plateau, is reached. This final step is steeper than those below and contains difficult rock that can be avoided by traversing left to the west side of the ridge, where two moderate pitches (5.4) lead to the summit plateau.

Although not difficult, this route is an interesting and challenging climb partly because much of the route cannot be seen at the start. The rock is solid and enjoyable and the terrain is not on the beaten path of the standard routes. During the traverse to gain the south ridge, rather than crossing the Blackfin one can climb its upper part and join the south ridge higher up. This alternative may have been selected by the first-ascent party, who indicated that they stayed somewhat on the left (west) of the crest of the south ridge rather than on right (east). *Time: 8 hours* from the CMC campsite.

ROUTE 10. Direct South Buttress. V, 5.8, A1, or V, 5.12-. (Note: The Grade V rating for this climb reflects the overall difficulty of the ascent if one goes to the summit; the climb was originally rated IV, 5.7, A3, due to the dubious quality of the piton used for the pendulums!). First ascent August 29–30, 1953, by Richard Emerson, Don Decker, and Leigh Ortenburger; previously attempted on August 14, 1953, by Richard Emerson and Don Decker, who climbed to the 4-inch ledge at the beginning of the pendulum pitch before retreating in a hailstorm; first free ascent July 3, 1979, by Stan Mish and Hal Gribble. See *Topo 86* and *Photos 99, 100, 101, 102,* and *103*. The Direct South Buttress of Mount Moran with its southern aspect, fine rock, and airy exposure has become one of the Teton classics over the course of the past nearly half-century. At the time of its first ascent, the route was one of the longest roped climbs in the country. The prospective climber now has the option of using the route as a rock climb, descending from the top of the buttress, or embarking on one of the longer Teton routes by continuing to the summit of Mount Moran. It attacks directly from Leigh Canyon the very high-angle buttress forming the lower 1,500 feet of the south ridge. As a rule, two days should be allowed for the complete ascent of the south buttress and ridge to the summit. It is useful to camp in Leigh Canyon at the base of the ridge the night before the climb in order to study the ridge from below and to get an early start. See *Leigh Canyon* for the approach into the canyon. Hike up into Leigh Canyon until reaching the stream below Laughing Lions Falls. One will see two conspicuous grassy ramps cutting across the lower part of the south buttress to the left of the falls. Hike up just west of this stream drainage for some 700 feet to gain access to the right (east) end of the first ramp. Climb up and west along the first ramp to a small group of trees at its far (western) end. Continue up and around the west side to the start of the roped climbing. The topo presents the technical details of

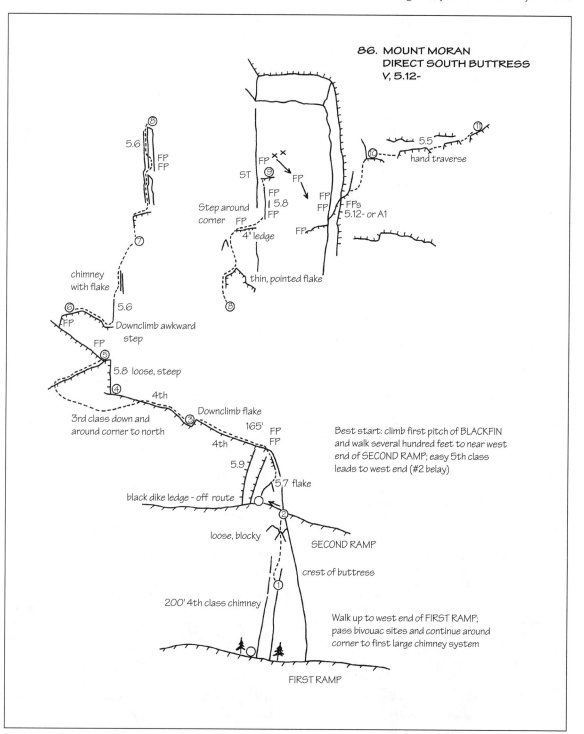

**86. MOUNT MORAN
DIRECT SOUTH BUTTRESS
V, 5.12-**

5.5
hand traverse

5.6
FP
FP

FP
ST
5.8
FP
FP
FP
FP
FPs
5.12- or A1
Step around
corner   FP
4" ledge
FP

chimney
with flake

thin, pointed flake

5.6
Downclimb awkward
FP   step
FP
5.8 loose, steep
4th
3rd class down and
around corner to north

Downclimb flake
165'
FP
FP

Best start: climb first pitch of BLACKFIN
and walk several hundred feet to near west
end of SECOND RAMP; easy 5th class
leads to west end (#2 belay)

4th
5.9
5.7 flake

black dike ledge - off route

loose, blocky
SECOND RAMP

crest of buttress

200' 4th class chimney

Walk up to west end of FIRST RAMP;
pass bivouac sites and continue around
corner to first large chimney system

FIRST RAMP

the route. For protection on this route take a standard rack to 3 inches, with small wireds and RPs.

Climb two pitches up a moderate chimney (with some loose rock) slightly on the west side of the ridge crest and gain the west end of the second ramp. (*Note:* By climbing the first pitch of the Blackfin one can gain access to the second ramp at its eastern end. Then several hundred feet of walking and a short, easy pitch bring one to this same point.) Move the belay a short distance up and to the left (west) to start the third long pitch, which heads up, right, and then back left onto a ledge system that curves up to the left (west) side of the crest. Climb out along this ledge for two ropelengths or at least 200 feet before looking up toward the ridge crest. Two large flakes will be seen, the lower gray and separated from the mountain by a fine chimney; the upper is capped by white rock and is to the right of the first. The topo shows two methods of reaching the fine chimney, but in general avoid turning up the wall too soon. The ninth lead as shown on the topo starts with a climb up to and then off of a remarkably thin flake. Proceed up to the 4-inch ledge from which one must traverse up and right via tricky balance moves to the very edge of the ridge crest. Step around the corner and continue up (5.8) to a stance for the belay. This spectacular position at the left edge of the now famous 80° face is located just below the large ceiling-like overhang that caps the initial 1,500-foot high-angle portion of the buttress. Across this face a beautiful thin crack will be seen leading up and over the overhanging corner at the right (east) edge of the face. The problem is to reach it.

One can tension traverse using an intermediate fixed piton down and over to the 3-inch ledge at the base of the thin crack, or, by dropping down lower, one can use holds at the lower edge of the undercut face to pull across onto the 3-inch ledge (reported to be 5.9 face climbing during the first free ascent). (*Note:* In 1953 this entire pendulum was done from a single, partially driven, wafer piton.) One may wish to bring the belayer over to the stance at the base of the 5.12- crack or simply continue on up if one decides that the crack is A1 on that particular day. Climb the crack up and around the overhang to the right (A1); four fixed pitons will be found. This pitch has now twice been done free at the 5.12- level. An exposed but comfortable 2-foot ledge is reached at the end of this lead. The last pitch of the difficult section of this route consists of a fun hand traverse out of sight around to the right (east). This finally puts one above the buttress in a large open bowl just below and east of the first level section of the ridge.

One now has the choice of three completely different methods of descending from this point, the top of the buttress, or one can continue to the summit of Mount Moran. In any case, if needed, an excellent bivouac can be made among the pine trees and needles across the slabs up and to the right, although water may be scarce in late season. The first option

for descent, recently developed, begins immediately after the hand-traverse pitch. Proceed several hundred feet up and to the eastern edge of the large open bowl. Several double-rope rappels from trees and other fixed anchors bring one to the usual multiple-rappel route for the South Buttress Right, down the Blackfin chimneys (see *Route 12*). A second, effective but seldom-used route of descent is to traverse (roughly horizontally) east crossing the notch in the Blackfin above the third tower, then across various gullies (which may contain snow) and the south ridge of Drizzlepuss, finally emerging on the southeast side of Drizzlepuss. This is initiated by walking 300 yards to the right along the ledge at the end of the hand-traverse pitch and rappelling to easier ground. From here continue contouring, with some up and down in crossing the intervening couloirs and ridges, around to the CMC campsite ridge. See *Photo 103*.

Alternatively, to continue to the summit or to find the traditional descent route, climb the rocks on the left (west) edge of the bowl and exit onto the horizontal ridge crest at the very top of the main buttress. If this is selected, almost the entire horizontal section must be negotiated, involving numerous pitches of enjoyable but sometimes exposed climbing over or around towers to reach the final sharp tower on the crest. From its summit a 60-foot rappel on the east side permits one to reach the notch beyond (north of) the tower. The standard method of descent starts here and involves two steep parallel couloirs or gullies that descend to the west from the ridge crest. See *Photos 99* and *100*. This notch is at the head of the first (the more southerly) of these couloirs. Do not continue along the crest and attempt to climb down directly into the second (the more northerly) of these couloirs. Instead, climb down into this first couloir for 200 to 300 feet until one can conveniently cross the separating rib into the more northerly couloir; from above, this part of the descent looks worse than it is. With adroit routefinding this main western couloir permits downclimbing and scrambling all the way down into the main drainage separating Mount Moran from Thor Peak. No rappels are required. No matter what, do *not* try to continue all the way down the first southern couloir, for it is blocked by huge overhanging chockstones, and terrifying rappels into outer space are required.

To proceed to the summit of Mount Moran from this point, which is just short of the next large steep step in the south ridge, traverse slightly to the right (east) and climb the long (2,200 feet) but easier ridge above, keeping generally on the right (east) side of the crest. The 1935 Upper South Ridge route (*Route 9*) is joined in this section and is followed to the summit. Combined with the buttress below, the complete south ridge does indeed provide a long climb. See *American Alpine Journal*, 9, no. 1 (1954), pp. 172–184, illus.; *Harvard Mountaineering*, 16 (May 1963), pp. 82–83; *Sierra Club Bulletin*, 39, no. 6 (June 1954), pp. 27–33.

Variation: IV, 5.7, A3, or IV, 5.10. First ascent September 9, 1958, by Richard Sykes and William Briggs. Near the top of the south buttress, from the 2-foot ledge at the end of the final aid crack, before making the final long hand traverse, one can turn directly upward and complete the climb in this slightly more direct manner. This lead goes up over a sequence of small bulges in difficult and uncompromising rock.

Variation: V, 5.9, A1. First ascent August 12–13, 1965, by Peter Cleveland, Roland Fleck, and Jack Stauffer. From the west end of the second grassy ledge, this variation, which is not well understood, found a line between the standard Direct South Buttress route and the South Buttress, West Face *(Route 8),* emerging at the top of the first step on the south ridge. At the west end of the second ledge, traverse west for one ropelength and then scramble farther west to the beginning of a gully. Climb half a lead up this gully and then one and a half leads up and left on a sloping ledge. The route now passes up and right over three steps of increasing difficulty, the last via a strenuous jam crack to a good belay ledge on the corner of the south face west of the south ridge. The next pitch traverses right for 20 feet and then diagonally up and right for 90 feet (5.9) over a thin face to a wall below a sloping ledge. Aid was used to pass this wall. Now traverse left 20 feet to a good belay ledge. After a small overhang, climb right to an open book well below a large black overhang. One more lead plus some scrambling places one on top of the

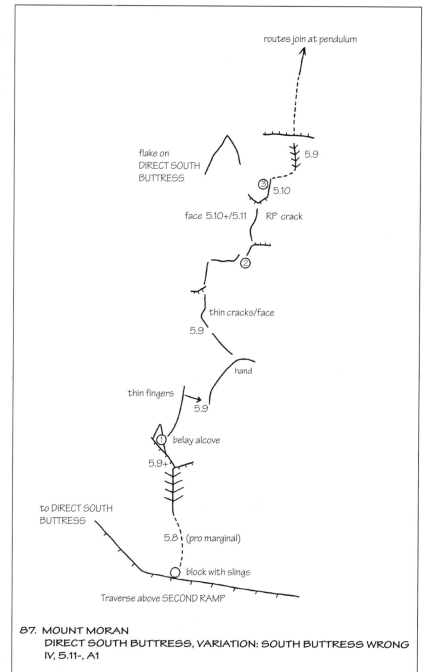

routes join at pendulum

flake on
DIRECT SOUTH
BUTTRESS

5.9

③ 5.10

face 5.10+/5.11   RP crack

②

thin cracks/face

5.9

hand

thin fingers

5.9

① belay alcove

5.9+

to DIRECT SOUTH
BUTTRESS

5.8 (pro marginal)

block with slings

Traverse above SECOND RAMP

87. MOUNT MORAN
    DIRECT SOUTH BUTTRESS, VARIATION: SOUTH BUTTRESS WRONG
    IV, 5.11-, A1

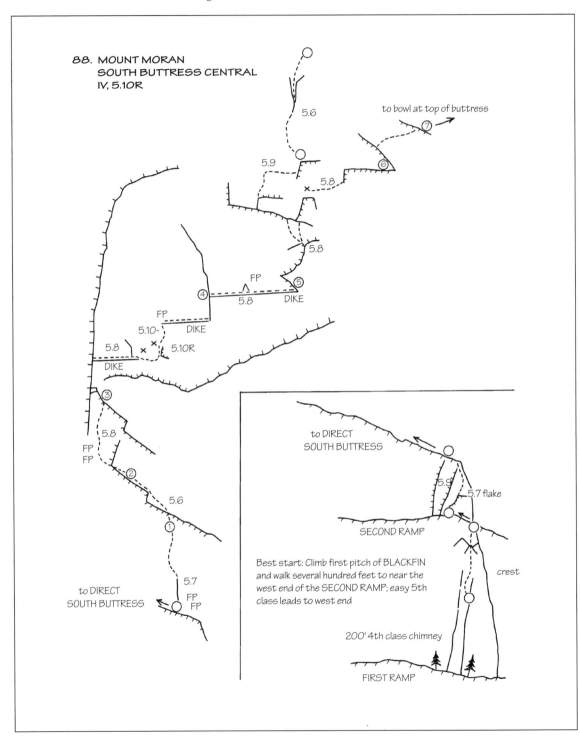

88. MOUNT MORAN
SOUTH BUTTRESS CENTRAL
IV, 5.10R

to bowl at top of buttress

5.6

5.9

5.8

5.8

FP

5.8   DIKE

FP

5.10-   DIKE

5.8   5.10R

DIKE

5.8

FP
FP

5.6

to DIRECT
SOUTH BUTTRESS

to DIRECT
SOUTH BUTTRESS

5.9

5.7 flake

SECOND RAMP

crest

Best start: Climb first pitch of BLACKFIN
and walk several hundred feet to near the
west end of the SECOND RAMP; easy 5th
class leads to west end

5.7

FP
FP

200' 4th class chimney

FIRST RAMP

first step of the south buttress. Two days were spent on this long climb to the summit of Moran.

Variation: IV, 5.11-, A1. First ascent by Ken Sims and Rick Reese. It is unclear exactly when this climb was done and whether or not the first ascentionists joined the Direct South Buttress route. However, a topographic record of the climb entitled "South Buttress Wrong" exists and is presented here as part of the historical record of ascents in *Topo 87.* The route is probably located between *Routes 10* and *11* and proceeds more or less up the prow of the buttress.

ROUTE 11. South Buttress Central. IV, 5.8, A3, or IV, 5.10R. First ascent July 16, 1967, by Peter Koedt and Keith Becker; three earlier attempts on this route had been made by Koedt in 1966: on June 19 with Ken Fisher and Lynn Swanson; on July 30 and 31, and on August 6 with Will Bassett; first free ascent summer 1984, by Eric Breitenberger and Bill Trull. See *Topo 88* and *Photos 101* and *102.* The South Buttress Central is flanked by the Direct South Buttress *(Route 10)* on the west and the South Buttress Right *(Route 12)* on the east. Regrettably overlooked for 20 years, this very difficult and daring route has finally taken its place in the front rank among major Teton routes along with the other south buttress lines on Moran. Major features of the route include three horizontal quartz dikes extending across the most spectacular "great smooth 300-foot slab." This slab is similar to but two or three times larger than the Great Traverse Slab of the South Buttress Right route. The technical details of the route are presented in the topo.

Proceed as in the Direct South Buttress route one pitch above the second ramp onto the main ledge system, which leads around on the west side of the buttress. As shown on the topo, three leads up and left take one to a belay just right of the huge overhang that arches up and to the right over the great, smooth slab cut by prominent horizontal quartz dikes. The next lead up to and across the first two dikes is the crux lead of the route. The passage between the first and second dikes is especially serious because if done with aid, as on the first ascent, the absence of cracks makes the aid difficult to place, and, if done free, for the same reason there is little protection available on the section of 5.10. This runout lead is a perilous undertaking, even though there are two bolts (dating from 1967) available. The fifth lead proceeds horizontally along the dike past a fixed piton to a belay at the end. From here to complete the route the topo shows different ways that were followed by the two recent climbs of the route. These last two leads initially go up a right-facing corner and face to gain a ledge, where one alternative moves left and up a 5.9 wall and finishes in a V slot; the other alternative moves up and right past a bolt along a system of ledges to gain the bowl at the top of the south buttresses. The original climb of the route apparently made yet a third finish, but its location is not clear.

ROUTE 12. South Buttress Right. IV, 5.8, A1, or IV, 5.11-. First ascent July 25, 1961, by David Dornan and Herb Swedlund; previously attempted on July 14, 1961, by David Dornan and Peter Lev; first complete free ascent (nail-up bypass) July 18, 1973, by Steve Wunsch and Art Higbee (although the individual pieces had all been done free by 1969), but the flake that permitted the free ascent via this alternative route has subsequently fallen off; first free ascent (original route) August 2, 1978, by Buck Tilley and Jim Mullin. See *Topo 89* and *Photos 101, 102,* and *103.* This major route reaches the top of the south buttress from the southeast rather than directly from the south as in the 1953 route. It is located to the right of a prominent set of water streaks on the buttress. The South Buttress Right is probably the finest pure rock climb in the Tetons and has justifiably achieved popularity among those seeking a difficult climb. The rock is splendid and some of the features of this route are unique. The Great Slab Traverse is an exciting place, and the exposure is most impressive.

The approach is the same as for the Direct South Buttress (see *Route 10*). The South Buttress Right proper begins at the second grassy ledge or ramp above the base of the buttress. The technical details of the route are presented in the topo. This ramp is usually gained by means of the first pitch of the Blackfin route, a chimney (5.8) in a right-facing corner just left (west) of Laughing Lions Falls. Scramble easily about 600 feet west along this terrace. Once past the Blackfin corner system (recognized as being a large, loose-looking, left-facing corner and chimney system) proceed up until just past three prominent, sharp, right-facing corners. The beginning of the route, which is just past these three nice corners, is marked by a sharply pointed flake about 10 feet high and 15 feet above the terrace. Do not continue left (west) too far on the sloping ledge at the top of the second lead, else unpleasant territory will be entered. The third pitch, commonly climbed with aid as on the first ascent, has been freed at 5.11-, after attempts spreading over several years; a number of fixed pitons and one bolt (placed by an unknown climber in recent years) will be found on this lead. Two pitches above is the spectacular Great Slab Traverse, which goes horizontally right across smooth slabs, using small flakes and hand traverses, for 100 feet to a good belay stance at a group of flakes. It is one of the memorable pitches in the Teton Range and is as exciting to follow as it is to lead. A slip would probably entail a dramatic pendulum with the unfortunate suspended in midair, an interesting situation to contemplate.

The seventh lead up from the end of the traverse originally used aid for 30 feet in a 1-inch crack with mixed aid and free climbing to turn the ceiling system above; this crack is now freed as a 5.10- hand jam/lieback. This pitch ends on a perfect, square-cut belay ledge, the first roomy and comfortable area on the climb. Follow this ledge to its right end and climb a thin crack to a blank wall (5.9), where a four-bolt ladder will be found. From the broad ledge at the end of this difficult lead many climbers make their descent

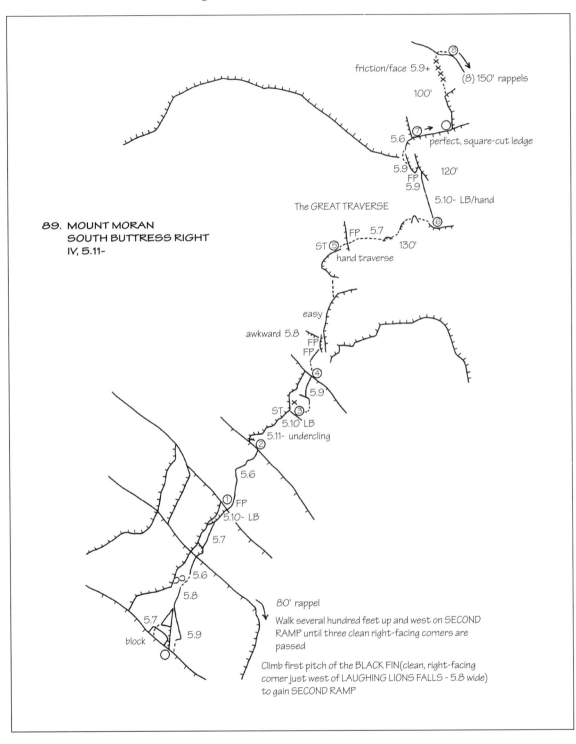

friction/face 5.9+

(8) 150' rappels

100'

5.6   perfect, square-cut ledge

5.9
FP
5.9

120'

5.10- LB/hand

The GREAT TRAVERSE

FP   5.7

ST ⑤   130'

hand traverse

**89. MOUNT MORAN
SOUTH BUTTRESS RIGHT
IV, 5.11-**

easy

awkward 5.8

FP
FP

④

5.9

ST ③

5.10 LB

5.11- undercling

②

5.6

① FP

5.10- LB

5.7

5.6

5.8

80' rappel

5.7   5.9

block

Walk several hundred feet up and west on SECOND
RAMP until three clean right-facing corners are
passed

Climb first pitch of the BLACK FIN(clean, right-facing
corner just west of LAUGHING LIONS FALLS - 5.8 wide)
to gain SECOND RAMP

to the right (east), as shown on the topo, but the original route continued on excellent rock mainly in cracks for four or five more pitches. One or two pitches bring one to the bottom of an arête that parallels the top of the Direct South Buttress route. Then climb the crest of the arête for about three more leads to finish at a tree-covered ledge, from which one can descend down to the right toward the Blackfin. This extension produces one of the longest rock climbs in the park. The now-standard descent from the top of the bolt ladder pitch leads off down to the east to the first of eight 150-foot rappels alongside the Blackfin route. Some scrambling and downclimbing are necessary to link them together. The lower rappels go down a left-facing chimney system (Blackfin route) and the final rappel is from a small tree on the ramp near the top of the first Blackfin pitch. For protection take a standard rack to 3 inches with small wireds and RPs. See *American Alpine Journal*, 13, no. 1 (1962), pp. 216–220.

Variation: Deliverance. IV, 5.10-, A3. First ascent July 6, 1990, by James Earl and Todd G. Cozzens. See *Topo 90* and *Photos 101* and *102*. The approach is the same as for the South Buttress Right route. The first pitch begins by climbing the first of the three square-cut, right-facing corners already mentioned (5.9 for 90 feet). Refer to *Topo 90* for the technical details of the route. Note that Deliverance joins the South Buttress Right at the end of the Great Slab Traverse. For protection the first-ascent party suggests a "standard clean aid rack," 6 copperheads, 4 KBs, several LAs, 2 RURPs, hooks including 1 large.

Variation: Habeler. IV, 5.7, A1. First ascent July 13, 1969, by Peter Habeler and Juris Krisjansons. See *Photos 101* and *102*. This variation goes up the obvious broken section just left of the Blackfin route (*Route 13*) below and terminates by means of a pendulum to the end of the Great Slab Traverse of the South Buttress Right. The approach and the descent are the same as for the South Buttress Right route. This is an enjoyable climb without severe difficulties. The route has apparently not been repeated in the last 20 years, so little information is available; the topo from the first ascent is presumed accurate but has not been verified (*Note:* An attempt at verification by the author resulted in not finding either the route depicted or the location of the pendulum allowing access to the end of the Great Slab Traverse.) A few loose rocks will be found but these are obvious and not a large problem. The aid on the fifth pitch can probably be eliminated by climbing up and to the right (east).

ROUTE 13. *The Blackfin.* IV, 5.8, A1, or IV, 5.8. First ascent July 4–5, 1960, by David Dornan and Leigh Ortenburger; previously attempted by Dave Dornan and Peter Lev. See *Photo 103*. This fine ridge, immediately to the right (east) of the main south ridge of Moran, is a very long route if continued to the summit. It begins with a tower of dark rock, which has been aptly named the Blackfin. This tower appears about 1,000 feet above the first grassy ledge of the

Direct South Buttress route and is the first of five on the distinct ridge that curves upward to the west to join the main south ridge about 1,000 feet below the summit. The initial major problem is to reach the base of the first tower. Climb the right-facing corner and chimney (5.8) immediately to the left (west) of the bottom section of Laughing Lions Falls. Now scramble left (west) along this large second ledge, past the tree, to the beginning of the obvious crack and chimney system. Four leads upward (one place originally passed using aid) bring one out on a large platform at the lower edge of the south face bowl. Scramble up and left to the beginning of a difficult friction pitch. Four 5th-class pitches, always bearing left (west) toward the Blackfin, which is now in full view above, lead to the area below the Blackfin itself. Pass the nose of the Blackfin on the left, and scramble up to a large, more or less horizontal quartz vein. Follow this vein, which lies in the west face of the Blackfin, back to the right (east) for two leads, to the top of the Blackfin.

The second tower, or more properly step, is climbed directly. The second lead is about 140 feet and of 5.6 difficulty. The third involves some scrambling to the summit of the tower. The buttress of the third tower begins with a crack system in a steep but short face. The top of this tower can very likely be attained directly, but, on the first ascent, a small detour was made to the left (west), from which side the top was reached. The descent to the notch is not difficult. In early season, the area near this notch makes a good bivouac spot, because there is water and some level ground. The escape route to the east from the south buttress crosses the Blackfin at this point (see *Photo 103*). The fourth tower starts with a small overhang and slabs for about 80 feet. Then a chimney must be climbed, perhaps most easily by the use of lieback technique. Moderate climbing leads to the top of this step. The fifth and final tower is even easier. The Blackfin joins the south ridge just after this last tower. This last 1,000 feet of the south ridge is climbed staying mostly on the right (east) side of the crest until the final steep section is reached. Bypass this section on the left (west) and reach the summit plateau from the west by climbing one pitch. This route is a long climb on rock that is good, once the initial chimney/corner system is passed. Two days are recommended for this climb. See *American Alpine Journal*, 12, no. 2 (1961), pp. 373–377.

ROUTE 14. ☞*CMC.* II, 5.5. First descent July 14, 1935, by Chris Scoredos and Joe Merhar; first ascent June 25, 1941, by Paul Petzoldt, Joseph Hawkes, Earl Clark, and Harold Plumley of the Chicago Mountaineering Club. See *Photo 104*. This pleasant climb, with one of the finest campsites in the range, has become the most commonly used route for reaching the summit of the mountain. It is a varied climb on good rock and, if one has a canoe, enjoys a relatively short approach with little bushwhacking. The ascent nevertheless will normally require two days.

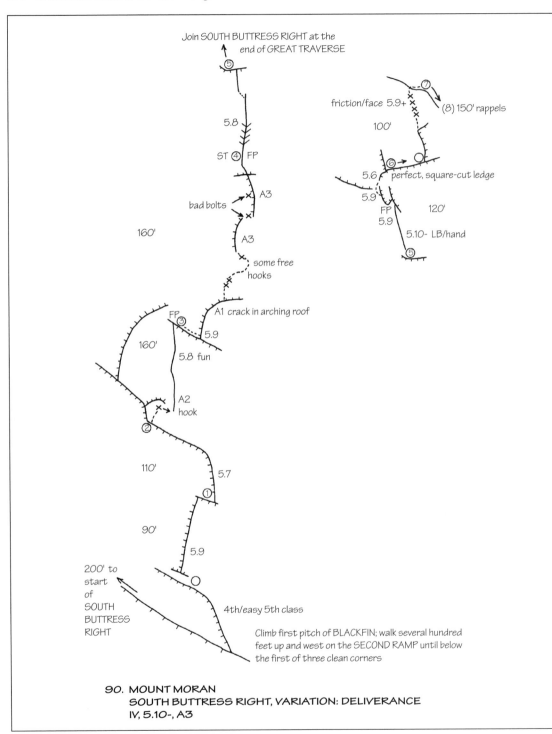

Join SOUTH BUTTRESS RIGHT at the
end of GREAT TRAVERSE

friction/face 5.9+

(8) 150' rappels

100'

5.8

ST ④ FP

perfect, square-cut ledge

5.6

5.9

bad bolts   A3

FP   120'
5.9

5.10- LB/hand

160'   A3

some free
hooks

A1 crack in arching roof

FP ③
5.9

160'
5.8 fun

A2
hook

②

110'

5.7

①

90'

5.9

200' to
start
of
SOUTH
BUTTRESS
RIGHT

4th/easy 5th class

Climb first pitch of BLACKFIN; walk several hundred
feet up and west on the SECOND RAMP until below
the first of three clean corners

90. MOUNT MORAN
SOUTH BUTTRESS RIGHT, VARIATION: DELIVERANCE
IV, 5.10-, A3

For the approach, if at all possible, take a canoe across Leigh Lake to the mouth of the stream descending from the Falling Ice Glacier. Or, with noticeably more exertion, one can hike the Valley Trail from the String Lake trailhead to the north end of Leigh Lake where, with some effort, the remnants of the NPS-abandoned trail around the northwest side of the lake can be followed to the stream. Ascend the bouldery stream gully for some 2,500 feet to the open semigrassy slope due east of and below the West Horn, just south of the glacier. A faint trail will be found on this slope leading up to the outstanding CMC campsite (ca. 10,000), located on the flat ridge up to the left (south) in the large trees, one step down (about 100 feet) from the last trees. Excellent flat areas will be found among the trees on the ridge crest, and there is water in the boulder field 100 feet to the south. During most of the summer a snow tongue extends up toward the col between the West Horn and Drizzlepuss, the large tower between the West Horn and the main east face of Mount Moran. This tower was so named as a result of the wet conditions encountered during the first ascent. One route follows up the ridge a short distance above the camping spot and then cuts left (south) to the bottom of the snow tongue, there following the small gully in which the snow tongue lies and continuing up toward the col east of Drizzlepuss. Another more direct method, which has the advantage of avoiding most of the snow if one does not want to carry an ice axe, is to follow the ridge up above the camping spot until it disappears and then cut slightly to the right (north) onto another smaller rocky ridge with some bushes. If the proper tricky route is selected, easy scrambling will bring one to the desired col. Do not get too close to the south cliffs of the West Horn. One does not have to proceed all the way to the col because the objective is the summit of Drizzlepuss, the tower on the west side of the col. Scramble easily up its east face to its top.

From here there is a terrifying view of the CMC route, which goes more or less up the middle of the face to the left (south) of the black dike; most of the slabs appear impossible. However, take heart and downclimb the very steep west face of Drizzlepuss toward the notch separating it from the main east face of Mount Moran. One may wish to rappel the final 25 feet into the notch (only 10 to 15 feet wide here); however, this will have to be ascended on the return trip. From the notch, climb about 50 feet up the left (south) edge of the main east face of the mountain, until it is possible to traverse 120 feet horizontally out to the middle of the face, using a little friction work. One can now see plainly the last remaining pinnacle, Unsoeld's Needle, on the south edge of the east face. Climb diagonally toward the notch between the Needle and the east face, but before reaching it traverse back out onto the face. From here to the summit not much description is needed. The climbing is exposed all the way because there are no very large ledges yet at no place

is there a shortage of holds. The last section of the face has a more gentle angle; if one moves somewhat closer to the dike than before, the climb can be easily completed to the rounded summit area. The highest point on the spacious summit plateau is a few hundred feet to the north and is easily recognized by its large cairn. The summit view is quite unlike that obtained from the more frequently trodden summits farther to the south.

For the descent one can simply retrace the ascent route all the way to the Drizzlepuss notch. One may wish to rappel in a number of places, depending on the downclimbing abilities of the party. It is easier to keep to the right (south) when descending from the plateau and stay near the south edge of the CMC face until just above Unsoeld's Needle; this section can usually be downclimbed, if the easiest route is found, without the need for rappels. The last portion of this descent is in a shallow couloir just off (south of) the edge of the face and will lead naturally to a mass of slings, from which two rappels down the main CMC face to the left (north) brings one to the vicinity of the Drizzlepuss notch; this section can also be downclimbed with effort and care. It is also marginally possible to reach the notch by bypassing the Needle on the south along small and exposed ledges. From the Drizzlepuss notch there are three possibilities: (1) The easiest scheme is to climb out of the notch to the right, traversing out on a ledge on the west wall of Drizzlepuss (5.5). Turn up to the next ledge at the first likely opportunity, as difficulties increase the farther out one traverses. From this second ledge ascend without difficulty the remainder of the steep ledges to the top of Drizzlepuss. (2) Another method is to climb directly up out of the notch. If this alternative is selected, it will be the most difficult (5.7) pitch of the climb, involving a few overhanging moves. (3) It is also possible, but not recommended, to follow down the steep couloir leading south from the Drizzlepuss notch toward Leigh Canyon. Because this ultimately leads to the south cliffs of Mount Moran, bear left (east) after about 300 feet, cross the south ridge of Drizzlepuss, and continue contouring to the vicinity of the CMC campsite, from which the rest of the descent is easy. *Time: 5½ to 6¾ hours from the CMC campsite.* See *Appalachia,* 25, no. 2 (December 1944), pp. 239–241, illus.; *Dartmouth Mountaineering Club Journal,* 1956, pp. 34–38; *Trail and Timberline,* no. 285 (September 1942), pp. 115–118, illus.

Variation: II, 5.5. First ascent July 23, 1952, by Richard Emerson and Walt Sticker. The notch between Drizzlepuss and the main east face of Mount Moran can also be reached from the CMC campsite by climbing up the snout of the Falling Ice Glacier. The difficulties depend on the year and the route is potentially threatened by serac fall. Ice-climbing equipment will also have to be carried. The final snow-and-ice chute leading to the notch from the main portion of the glacier is usually protected by a small *bergschrund.*

Variation: II, 5.6. First descent August 17, 1952, by Martin Benham and Dmitri Nabokov. From the col between Drizzlepuss and the West Horn it is possible, although difficult, to descend to the south edge of the Falling Ice Glacier and follow it to the Drizzlepuss notch, thereby bypassing Drizzlepuss on the north. This variation was originally used on descent to avoid the overhang out of the notch, but it is equally difficult from that direction.

ROUTE 15. *Dike.* II, 5.4. First ascent June 23, 1931, by Hans Wittich and Otto Stegmaier. This remarkable early route goes up the face of the black dike that cuts the east face of Mount Moran so prominently. The first problem is to reach the base of the dike where it meets the Falling Ice Glacier. The direct approach is to climb the snout of the glacier on its right (north) side to the flat section above. Depending on the year and the season, there may be both difficulty and danger associated with this part of the route. At the upper end of the glacier some difficulty can be expected crossing the *randkluft,* which widens as the season advances, between the rock and the ice. A more roundabout route used on the first ascent is to proceed as in *Route 9* up over Drizzlepuss (this was the first ascent of Drizzlepuss) and down into the notch; then traverse horizontally to the right (north) all the way over to the dike. The lower portion of the dike offers no great difficulty, although one must be on guard for loose rock. Because the dike is only about 125 feet wide, it is not possible to stray very far off the route. The final 200 to 300 feet of the dike stands away from the main face of the mountain and must be climbed with caution owing to the downsloping nature of the rock. See *American Alpine Journal,* 9, no. 2 (1955), pp. 147–149; *Appalachia,* 18, no. 4 (Dec. 1931), pp. 388–408, illus.; *The Nature Friend,* 25, no. 6 (June 1947), pp. 3–4.

Variation: II, 5.4. First descent August 14, 1946, by Gerald Brandon and Theodore Brandon; first ascent August 12, 1952, by Theodore Brandon, Tim Ramsland, Willis Wood, and Don and Ivan Zastrow. The flat portion of the Falling Ice Glacier can be reached by ascending a 200-foot chimney on the left (south) side of the snout of the glacier where the dike again outcrops. Because of its loose and rotten rock, this chimney is not recommended.

ROUTE 16. *East Chimney,* II, 5.4. First ascent July 9, 1956, by Robert Day, Peter Lipman, and Alan Williamson. From the usual campsite for the CMC route (see *Route 14*) climb onto the Falling Ice Glacier; this is discussed under *Route 15.* Ascend the glacier to its upper right (northwest) corner, and climb the large chimney or crack that leads from the glacier to the summit plateau. This chimney lies between the east ridge (which connects with the East Horn) and the black dike and consists of easy 5th-class climbing. It begins about 500 feet north of and is roughly parallel to the dike.

ROUTE 17. *East Ridge.* II, 4.0. First ascent July 24, 1931, by Robert L. M. Underhill and Paul Petzoldt. See *Photo 105.* This ridge forms the left (south) edge of the "handle" of the

Skillet Glacier; it begins at the notch separating the East Horn from the mountain and is reached from the north via the glacier. For the approach to the glacier see *Route 18.* From a campsite below the moraine of the Skillet Glacier, climb over the moraine onto the pan of the glacier. A *bergschrund* separates the lower and larger section from the upper section. During most of the summer the slabby rocks to the left (southeast) of the *bergschrund* are exposed and provide an easy but wet route past this obstacle. Above these rocks, continue up the snow, and climb onto the right (north) flank of the east ridge of Mount Moran (immediately south of the Skillet's handle) some 200 feet above the col between the East Horn and Moran. Some rotten rock will be met before one reaches the crest of the ridge, three ropelengths above the glacier. The ridge is straightforward climbing all the way to its top, which is only about 200 feet north of the summit. *Time: 5¾ hours* from camp below the glacier. See *Appalachia,* 18, no. 4 (December 1931), pp. 388–408, illus.

Variation: II, 4.0. First descent July 24, 1931, by Paul Petzoldt and Robert Underhill. After climbing up the ridge a short distance, cut left (south) across the slabby face, passing a chimney (see *Route 16*), and finish the climb on the rock near the black dike.

Variation: II, 4.0. First ascent July 18, 1951, by Peter Robinson, William Briggs, and Brian Brett. This longer variation combines the climb of the East Horn with the east ridge of Mount Moran. Ascend the east ridge of the East Horn to its summit, and then descend its west ridge to the col separating the Horn from the mountain; for route description see *East Horn, Route 1.* From the col ascend the east ridge of Mount Moran as already described. The summit of the East Horn can also be bypassed on the south; this unlikely and tricky maneuver was first done on September 15, 1954, by Craig Merrihue and William Hooker. Stay near the left (south) edge of the east ridge of the East Horn, and when confronted by a pinnacle move left on a ledge system across the south face of the East Horn to the vicinity of the col between the Horn and Moran. Near the beginning of the traverse, it may prove necessary to drop down a few feet onto a second set of ledges before continuing. See *Dartmouth Mountaineering Club Journal,* 1952, pp. 8–11, illus.

ROUTE 18. *Skillet Glacier.* II, AI2+, 5.4. First ascent July 27, 1922, by LeGrand Haven Hardy, Ben C. Rich, and Bennet McNulty. See *Photo 105.* The Skillet Glacier route is one of the few long snow-and-ice climbs in the Tetons and has been much climbed in recent years. As seen from the valley, this well-named glacier provides a very obvious line through the imposing precipices that protect the summit plateau from easy access. But the route has also produced a disproportionate number of serious accidents and fatalities, perhaps because of its deceptive appearance. This is *not* a route for beginning climbers inexperienced in the use of an ice axe and the rope. The handle of the glacier is very steep and must be ascended and descended with great care. Do *not* undertake a descent by glissade unless snow conditions are exactly right and you are truly expert in this demanding form of hazardous snow work. The large crevasse that opens at the lower end of the handle forms a great mouth ready to swallow any climber who slips on the snow above.

Two days are normally required to climb this long route and the approach to a campsite can be made by land, by water, or by a combination of the two. The traditional method is simply to hike from the String Lake trailhead around the east shore of Leigh Lake to Bearpaw Lake, which is the end of the maintained Valley Trail. Continue north past Trapper Lake around the east side of Mount Moran to the main creek descending from the Skillet Glacier; cross to the north side of the stream and cut left (west) up the timbered slope. This portion (1.0 mile) of the approach is neither easy nor pleasant because many years ago the National Park Service abandoned the maintenance of the once-good trail to Moran Creek and beyond, and winter avalanches have since left a broad area of flattened tree debris. No specific recommendation can be given to simplify this section, as serious bushwhacking has been impossible to avoid. Some game trails will usually be found, however, leading up to the morainal basin below the Skillet Glacier; even here some bushwhacking must be expected. The bouldery main streambed can then be followed to within 300 feet of the moraine. Another scheme to reach the Skillet Glacier, which minimizes the bushwhacking and might be better than these, is to canoe across Leigh Lake to the mouth of the stream from the Falling Ice Glacier, hike up the drainage of that stream, and cut right (north) to the broad saddle (9,600+) connecting the treed eastern Point 9,808 with the East Horn. From this saddle drop down on the north side only about 250 feet and contour around the eastern base of the East Horn to gain access to the moraine below the Skillet Glacier. Below the moraine and a short distance to the right (north) is a clump of trees that makes a suitable campsite for two.

Cross the moraine and ascend the glacier to the *bergschrund* that separates the lower and large portions of the pan of the skillet from the upper portion. This obstacle can be passed on the left (south), using the rock island of wet slabs that are exposed during most of the summer; it is also possible to use the rock on the right (north) end of the *bergschrund,* but this is more difficult. Now continue on the glacier, and proceed directly up the narrow handle to the summit plateau. This is a straightforward but steep snow-and-ice climb. Be constantly alert for falling rock while on the handle. Near the summit, steep snow in the left (south) fork of the upper handle couloir leads almost all the way to the flat summit. For competent and experienced mountaineers the Skillet Glacier can serve as a fast descent route in early season. It has the advantage of very simple route-finding and can be found even in the dark if absolutely

necessary. *Time: 6¾ hours* from camp below the glacier. See *Appalachia,* 18, no. 4 (December 1931), pp. 388–408, illus.; *Canadian Alpine Journal,* 19 (1930), pp. 84–91, illus.; *Chicago Mountaineering Club Newsletter,* 12, no. 6 (November 1958), pp. 5–9; *Sierra Club Bulletin,* 12, no. 4 (1927), pp. 356–364, illus.

ROUTE 19. Skillet Chimney. II, AI2+, 5.4. First ascent October 13, 1978, by Paul Horton and W. D. Horton. In the rock wall on the north side of the lower end of the handle of the Skillet Glacier is an indentation leading directly to the north summit. This becomes a well-defined chimney and this route follows the line of the chimney. Proceed to and up the Skillet Glacier as in *Route 18,* past the *bergschrund* to the narrowing at the beginning of the handle. Exit from the snow and ice onto the rock to the right (north) and start up the chimney. The rock is sound and the climbing is mainly on the left (west) side of the chimney, although much of the route is in the chimney itself. While there is a considerable extent of exposed climbing, the difficulty is never greater than 5.4 and much of it can be done by careful scrambling.

ROUTE 20. Northeast Slabs. III, AI2+, 5.7. First ascent September 10, 1962, by Fred Beckey and Dan Davis. This route starts well left of *Route 21,* makes a considerable horizontal traverse midway up the northeast face, and reaches the uppermost northeast ridge a short distance from the north summit in a manner similar to *Route 19.* Proceed to the lower portion of the Skillet Glacier as in *Route 18,* and ascend toward the handle in the upper left corner. Cross the *bergschrund,* and climb the snow and ice (crampons useful) to the highest point of the glacier to the right (north) of the handle proper, directly below a prominent vertical headwall a few hundred feet above. Climb a short, steep wall, and enter the obvious open gully, which is followed for about four leads up and slightly right (north) until a headwall blocks progress. It may be possible to continue directly at this point, but the first-ascent party angled up and left for about 160 feet before diagonaling back right. An exposed traverse of several leads, nearly horizontal and occasionally losing some altitude, to the north over very steep slabs beneath a series of overhangs is then made until it is possible to climb over a short overhang to the rock above. From this point climb nearly directly upward for four ropelengths on steep, smooth slabs, occasionally climbing some short overhangs formed by huge slabs overlapping those below. The final section is more broken, and a large chimney or gully will be found that leads easily to the ridge crest north of the north summit. See *American Alpine Journal,* 13, no. 2 (1963), pp. 410–420, illus.

ROUTE 21. Skillet Glacier Headwall. III, AI2+, 5.7, A1. First ascent July 27, 1962, by Don Anderson and Larry Scott. There is a considerable expanse of steep, slabby rock between the handle of the Skillet Glacier and the northeast ridge of Mount Moran. This long route, the first to penetrate this region, starts from the lower portion of the Skillet

Glacier (see *Route 18*) and ascends nearly a direct line to the uppermost crest of the northeast ridge, just short of the north summit. Leave the glacier near its upper right (northwest) margin, cross the *randkluft*, and climb the wall above, which is immediately left (south) of a prominent gully in the main headwall. When the wall steepens, traverse right into the gully, and follow it upward. A vertical wall will be met, where one traverses slightly left (south) and up to a belay on a steep slab. Now work back right (north) across a delicate, sometimes wet, slab to a deep crack, which leads to an awkward chimney. Climb easier rock above the chimney, keeping a large wall about 25 feet to the left (south). A difficult lieback crack in the steepening main wall above provides the most difficult pitch of the route. An overhanging wall higher up forces a slightly descending traverse 150 feet to the right (north). Climb out to a small rib on the skyline and then up until past the overhanging wall. Work back to the left to a gully that provides an easy upward route. Climb this gully and the slabs to the left, bypassing two bulging buttresses on the left (south). Several pitches (wet) on the left of the final buttress provide the concluding problems; the final pitch required aid. The crest is reached just 150 feet north of the north summit. See *American Alpine Journal*, 13, no. 2 (1963), pp. 410–420, illus.

ROUTE 22. ☞*Northeast Ridge.* II, 5.4. First complete ascent August 19, 1924, by Albert R. Ellingwood and Carl Blaurock; on August 11, 1919, LeRoy Jeffers climbed a variant of this ridge to the lower north summit. See *Photos 96 and 105*. Before the closing of the Leigh Lake road and the discovery of the CMC route, the Northeast Ridge was the popular route to the summit of Mount Moran. It is a pleasant climb on good rock of modest difficulty, but one should carefully consider the weather prior to starting for the summit because storms coming in from the west are not visible while climbing this route. The ridge is an exposed and fearful place during a thunderstorm. The approach alternatives for this route are about the same as described earlier for the Skillet Glacier (see *Route 18*). One way or another the stream descending from the Skillet Glacier must be reached at or near the shore of Jackson Lake. Stay out of the avalanche thickets. Much of the uphill bushwhacking can be avoided if one can piece together the game trails on the right (north) side of this stream. With skill or luck these can be followed to the open slope, which is then taken to the ridge crest. The usual camping spot for this climb is in or near the last trees on the ridge. Water is usually obtained from a nearby snowfield but may be difficult to find in late season.

The first and principal obstacle on the ridge is the Great Gendarme (10,230), which is easily reached a short distance above camp. It is usually bypassed on the right (north) using a broad but somewhat insecure ledge; one can also climb it directly and make a tricky rappel down the far (west) side. The route from the tower to the north summit of Mount Moran requires little description, as the ridge is well defined and the climbing is not difficult. A macabre point of interest partway up this ridge is the wreckage of the airplane crash that occurred on November 21, 1950. In general stay on the ridge, sometimes climbing on the slabs just left (south) of the crest, until the steep section below the north summit is reached. Although it is possible to climb this section directly, it is simpler to traverse left (south) for about 100 feet to a prominent chimney, which brings one out on the flat north summit; either way one pitch of 5.4 difficulty will be encountered. Traverse the narrow ridge leading to the south summit, which is about 150 feet higher and 0.25 mile away. This route offers few technical difficulties, but it is a long climb. Get an early start. *Time: 4 to 7⅓ hours from timberline camp on the ridge; 6¼ to 8½ hours from camp below the glacier; 8 to 11 hours from Leigh Lake.* See *American Alpine Journal*, 2, no. 3 (1935), pp. 312–314; *Appalachia*, 18, no. 4 (December 1931), pp. 388–408, illus.; *Canadian Alpine Journal*, 19 (1930), pp. 84–91, illus.; *Chicago Mountaineering Club Newsletter*, 12, no. 6 (November 1958), pp. 5–9; *Harvard Mountaineering*, 1 (June 1927), pp. 12–17; *Summit*, 6, no. 9 (September 1960), pp. 16–17, illus.; *Trail and Timberline*, no. 83 (August 1925), pp. 1–8, illus.

Variation: II, 5.4. First ascent August 11, 1919, by LeRoy Jeffers; an early descent in this region was made with difficulty on September 15, 1931, by Harvey Sethman and John Seerley. The crest of the northeast ridge can be gained from the south at a point above (west of) the Great Gendarme. Use the same approach as in *Route 18* to the area below the terminal moraine of the Skillet Glacier. To the right (north), on the eastern portion of the south face of the northeast ridge, one or more diagonal couloirs will be seen leading up to the ridge crest. One of these apparently provides a relatively easy but probably loose route; little information is available. In 1978 the gully and slabs immediately west of the Great Gendarme were descended by a competent party with no particular difficulties. See LeRoy Jeffers, *The Call of the Mountains*, chapter 2, 1922; *Appalachia*, 15, no. 1 (November 1920), pp. 108–109; 18, no. 4 (December 1931), pp. 388–408, illus.; *Canadian Alpine Journal*, 11 (1920), pp. 49–55, illus.; *Sierra Club Bulletin*, 11, no. 2 (January 1921), pp. 161–166, illus.; *Trail and Timberline*, no. 23 (August 1920), pp. 2–5, illus.; no. 148 (February 1931), pp. 16–20, illus.

Variation: II, 5.4. First ascent August 25, 1939, by Earl Clark and Donald Grant. See *Photo 105*. The upper northeast ridge can be reached via an interesting variation from the large cirque just north of the ridge. For the approach to this cirque see *Route 25;* a campsite is available to the north of the main snowfield in the cirque. Of the five snow couloirs that extend upward from the cirque, the first as described later, the most easterly, can be climbed to reach the crest of the northeast ridge a few hundred feet above the Great Gendarme. Entry into the couloir is gained from the upper left corner of the snow-filled cirque. It is probably best climbed in early or midseason, because in late season the floor of the cirque is filled with steep black ice and is swept by rockfall. While ascending the couloir under these conditions, one must stay high on the left (east) wall, which is composed of loose debris. The top of the couloir narrows, and after passing a moat climb a short awkward 5.1 corner to exit from the couloir. A few hundred feet of open slopes with ledges and scrambling leads onto the northeast ridge at the site of the airplane wreckage. This variation is the probable route used on November 25, 1950, by Paul Petzoldt and Blake Vandewater to investigate the airplane crash that occurred four days earlier; this climb in winter conditions was much more difficult than normal, needless to say.

Variation: Northeast Buttress Couloir. III, 5.4. First ascent July 16, 1971, by Gale Long and Robert Frisby. This variation begins in the first couloir to the right (north) of the Sickle Couloir (see *Route 23*). This is the third of the snow couloirs described under *Route 23,* and it leads to the notch that separates Peak 11,795 from the upper north ridge of Mount Moran. Climb this couloir to the large bench area about halfway up the buttress. From the bench angle almost horizontally left across early-season snowfields to gain the northeast ridge in the vicinity of the airplane wreckage. Later in the season the absence of these snowfields would make this traverse much more difficult. Follow the northeast ridge to the summit.

ROUTE 23. *Sickle Couloir.* III, 5.4. First ascent August 8, 1964, by Gary Cole and Ray Jacquot. See *Photo 105.* Between the northeast ridge and north ridge of Mount Moran is a significant but seldom-visited morainal cirque from which five major couloirs rise toward the ridges. These couloirs can be identified from left (south) to right (north). The first, *Route 22, 1939 variation,* leads to a point about halfway up the northeast ridge to the general vicinity of the airplane crash site. The second, the Sickle Couloir, is the major couloir, snow-filled except in late season, that ends at the last notch on the north ridge before its final rise to the north summit. The third follows a line to reach the first and main notch separating Peak 11,795 from the upper sections of the north ridge. The fourth is a minor couloir or chimney, disappearing in a face on the northeast ridge of Peak 11,795. The fifth is just a steep bench, mostly talus in the lower sections, ending low on the northeast ridge of Peak 11,795.

Extending for nearly 3,000 feet, the Sickle Couloir is one of the major Teton snow-and-ice climbs. The route is best done in early season while there is snow to cover the ice. It can be climbed by a fast party in a single day from the shore of Jackson Lake, or a high camp can be placed to the north of the snowfield in the cirque. The base of the Sickle Couloir is reached from the shore of Jackson Lake by bushwhacking through the timber to the talus slope leading into the cirque. Climb the southwest corner of the snowfield in the cirque up into the couloir and proceed directly up the cou-

loir. After a few hundred feet the couloir steepens and splits. Climb the wet chimney left of the rock bulge between the two branches. Re-enter the couloir and continue up past the bench area of the northeast buttress and climb another 1,500 feet to the notch in the north ridge. Follow that ridge (*Route 25*) to the summit.

ROUTE 24. *Pika Buttress.* III, 5.4. First ascent July 27–28, 1968, by James Kanzler, Paul Myhre, and John Neal. See *Photo 105.* This long route ascends the broad ridge or buttress separating the Sickle Couloir from the next couloir to the north. The approach is the same as for the Sickle (*Route 23*) to the base of the buttress. The route is nowhere difficult, with enjoyable climbing on easy but sometimes good rock pitches. The north ridge is joined just north of the Sickle notch and is followed to the summit. The buttress seems to be a haven for friendly pikas (*Ochotona princeps*). Two days may be desired for this route; the first-ascent party bivouacked on the bench about halfway up to the ridge.

ROUTE 25. *North Ridge.* III, 5.4. First ascent July 5, 1939, by Paul Petzoldt and William Ringler. See *Photos 105* and *106.* This ridge, a major feature of Mount Moran, rises at a steady angle from Moran Canyon until it passes over Peak 9,940 and flattens out at approximately 9,800 feet, forming a large shoulder or bench. The dominant steep section above this bench provides the standard north ridge ascent; the lower 3,000 feet has so far been ignored. The north ridge of Moran is a worthwhile mountaineering objective in a wild section of the park.

To approach this route one must first reach the northeast base of Mount Moran. This is done by one of the alternatives described earlier: hike from String Lake; canoe across Leigh Lake and hike and bushwhack the remainder of the distance; canoe on Jackson Lake from Spalding Bay; or take a power boat from Colter Bay or Signal Mountain Lodge. From the shore of Jackson Lake the starting point for uphill work is one of the streams (not shown on the map) draining the large open cirque on the north side of the northeast ridge of Moran. One must bushwhack directly up through the timber for an hour or more to gain the open slope leading to the talus bowl beneath the northeast ridge. Once through the trees the rest of the approach is one of the most attractive features of this climb. Follow along the right side of the small stream, through a sequence of superb alpine meadows with many exquisite flowers. Continue to the broad crest of the north shoulder of Moran and camp in the last trees, at about 9,800 feet. Melting snow will provide water during early season; later it may be necessary to camp somewhat lower in order to obtain water. This is a most scenic location, one of the finest in the range. Retrieval of this camp after the ascent, however, involves some problems because the ridge has never been directly descended. If the Northeast Ridge (*Route 22*) is used for descent, an alternative campsite is about 800 feet below the shoulder in the trees on the north margin of the talus bowl that lies at the northern base of the northeast ridge of Mount Moran. Camp retrieval then involves little or no uphill; descend the northeast ridge past the Great Gendarme until a couloir is reached leading down west into the talus bowl.

The northernmost point of the upper north ridge, Peak 11,795, is a distinct peak. This summit possesses a north-northwest face, the base of which is reached via a talus slope above the north shoulder. The north ridge is considered to be the left (east) edge of this face, separating it from the main east (or slightly northeast) face of the mountain. Start at the base of this edge; climb up and left on easy exposed ledges to a wide ledge. Three or four pitches then lead up and to the right, back toward the ridge crest. One can proceed to the crest, but the easiest route involves a long scramble up and diagonally left. There are many possibilities in this region that involve crossing couloirs, climbing ribs, and ultimately reaching the distinct couloir that contains snow most of the season and that leads to the first notch south of Peak 11,795. In the course of this easy upward diagonal traverse, the entire east face of Peak 11,795 will be skirted. Most parties bypass this summit but it can be bagged with only small additional effort during the course of this north ridge climb; see *Peak 11,795*, later, for further information on this peak and its routes.

From this first notch south of Peak 11,795, remain on the crest and climb a small gendarme, which is separated from the remainder of the ridge by a second notch at the head of large and prominent couloirs ascending from both east and west. The west couloir connects with the upper snow band of *Route 27*, and the east couloir is the Sickle Couloir that lies at the base of the north face of the northeast ridge. Descend to the second notch and climb two easy pitches on loose rock directly up out of the notch. After a section of scrambling, two somewhat more difficult pitches on good rock will put one well up the north ridge, where it levels off and joins the northeast ridge. The north summit is then reached by that route without further difficulty, and the usual traverse to the main south summit is made. This is a long and enjoyable climb on predominantly good rock, although there is one section of loose rock above the second notch. *Time: 7 hours* from timberline camp. See *Sierra Club Bulletin*, 32, no. 5 (May 1947), pp. 128–129; *Summit*, 6, no. 9 (September 1960), pp. 16–17, illus.; *Trail and Timberline*, no. 354 (June 1948), pp. 79–83, illus.

Variation: II, 5.6. First ascent September 13, 1957, by Bill Pope and Mary Kay Pottinger; a similar route was climbed on September 10, 1960, by Peter Gardiner, Frank Knight, and Mihaly Csikszentmihalyi. On July 27, 1956, Richard Emerson and Robert Bowen made the first climb of the difficult portion of this face but did not finish the last easy portion to the summit of Peak 11,795. The route described is that taken by the 1960 party. On the regular North Ridge route of Mount Moran, after the initial traverse left, climb up and back to the right (west) for about four pitches

all the way up to the ridge crest. Gain the ridge at the relatively level section below the final steep rise of the north ridge and northwest face, which culminates at the summit of Peak 11,795. This level section is somewhat more than halfway from the base of the ridge to the summit of Peak 11,795. From the point where the ridge meets the left edge of this final north face, a narrow diagonal ledge system of broken rock will be seen stretching up and right (west) across the entire face. Follow this delightfully exposed, but relatively easy, ledge system for three or four ropelengths until it begins to peter out at a point after the Triple Glaciers have come into clear view. Now turn straight up for two leads on very steep, solid rock to the top of this north face; the 1957 party encountered a large chockstone in this section. Scramble south to the base of a short headwall containing a 30-foot jam crack, which is easier than it appears. From the summit of Peak 11,795, a short distance above this headwall, descend easily to the col to rejoin the main route described earlier.

ROUTE 26. North Buttress. IV, 5.8. First ascent July 18, 1969, by Peter Habeler and George Lowe. See *Photo 106*. The northwest aspect of Mount Moran encompasses both the west face of the North Ridge (*Route 25*) and the North Face (*Route 27*) routes and is bounded on the right by the upper snow arm of the easternmost Triple Glacier (*Route 28*). Three couloirs cut the left (northern) half of the face below the north ridge. From north to south, the first, nearly vertical, descends from the notch immediately south of Peak 11,795, and the third (largest and snow-filled) descends diagonally to the right (south) from the notch at the head of the Sickle Couloir, just below the final rise to the north summit, to connect with the upper snow band above the eastern Triple Glacier. The second, at an intermediate angle, divides the face between the other two. The north buttress or pillar is the main prominent vertical feature in the center (southeast corner) of the face to the right (south) of the third couloir; it leads directly to the north summit of Mount Moran. Approach this route as in the North Face (*Route 27*) to the eastern Triple Glacier and on up to and across the upper snow band above the glacier proper. To reach the base of the north buttress above, climb in the general line of the main chimney system, which descends from the left (north) face of the buttress. This section is not easy. The main portion of the climb goes straight up the crack and chimney system on the left (north) side of the well-defined pillar. The climbing is fairly continuously difficult, requiring a mixture of techniques, but is mostly in cracks, including two 5.8 pitches. Some of the rock is not good. The route exits onto the flat summit by going left around the final bulge that separates the split in the uppermost end of the chimney system.

ROUTE 27. North Face. IV, 5.8. First ascent June 29, 1962, by Pete Sinclair, Peter Lev, William Buckingham, and Leigh Ortenburger. See *Photo 106*. Between the upper snow arm of the easternmost of the Triple Glaciers and the north ridge of Mount Moran lies a considerable face containing small ridges, snow chutes, and walls. This route, the first on this portion of the mountain, goes approximately up the center of the face that rises directly above the lower portion of the eastern Triple Glacier. The face could be approached directly up from Moran Canyon (see *Route 28*), but a far better method is to use the same approach as for the North Ridge (see *Route 25*) up to the north shoulder, where an excellent camp can be placed. From the shoulder it is an easy matter to descend about 100 feet onto the level of the lower eastern Triple Glacier. Ascend the glacier past the *bergschrund* toward the one crack in the first wall above; this crack diagonals up and left toward the upper snow band, which is completely separated from the main body of the glacier. In late season this snow band may disappear, leaving a sloping scree ledge. At the base of this crack traverse left (east) along a very wet ledge (in early season, through a waterfall) to its end, about 150 feet. Then turn up and right across difficult wet rock to reach the edge of the upper ledge, which parallels the smaller first ledge. Take this second ledge up and to the left until it is possible to scramble up to the edge of the snow band. Cut steps more or less straight up the snow band to reach the upper rock.

Cutting up through the entire face above, and diagonaling from lower right to upper left, is a prominent chimney with overhangs in the upper portions. Start on the rocks about 200 feet to the right of the chimney and traverse easily up and left toward the chimney. Moderate climbing for about three long ropelengths leads back to the chimney just beneath an overhanging section of the wall. Climb 150 feet up the rock to the left (north) of the chimney to a large area suitable for lunch. The next two pitches go up and right over difficult and somewhat loose rock. The climbing from here to the upper ramps becomes progressively steeper. At this point it appears that it should be possible to go up and left, but after about 80 feet in this direction the rock becomes excessively overhanging. Hence, one must make a difficult traverse to the right; a piton will be found at the beginning of this 25-foot traverse. There is some degree of commitment once this traverse has been made, because the face below and to the right of this traverse is overhanging; retreat would be difficult. Continue up and right to the end of the rope after negotiating the traverse. The next lead is also difficult, ascending an ill-defined chimney (an angle piton will be found here) for about 60 feet before continuing upward to the right to the end of the ropelength. Two more ropelengths diagonal out in the same direction. The first is moderate, but the end of the second is difficult. A wafer piton will be found in the belay position at the end of this pitch. The final pitch of 150 feet leads again up and to the right and is of sustained difficulty, consisting of a series of small, bulging overhangs before ending on the upper right edge of the face. Protection is difficult to obtain on this vertical and overhanging pitch,

because cracks are scarce. This pitch exits onto the upper ramps leading to the summit ridge; these ramps lie back at a much more reasonable angle, and three relatively easy ropelengths lead to the ridge connecting the north summit to the south summit. See *American Alpine Journal*, 13, no. 2 (1963), pp. 410–420, illus.

ROUTE 28. *Triple Glacier.* II, AI2+, 5.6. First ascent September 8, 1935, by Malcolm Smith. See *Photo 106*. This climb was an achievement, considering the fact that it was a solo ascent that required a variety of climbing skills on an unexplored section of a major Teton peak. In early season it is a moderate snow-and-ice climb, but in midseason and late season there is serious climbing in the wet, downsloping rocks that will be found between the main lower section and the upper arm of the glacier. The traditional approach to this route is from Moran Canyon; the mouth of the canyon is best reached by power boat from Colter Bay or Signal Mountain Lodge. About 1.0 mile up the canyon, where the streams descending from the Triple Glaciers meet the main Moran Creek, bushwhack up the talus to the terminal moraines of the three glaciers, and scramble up onto the easternmost glacier. The crossing of Moran Creek will present a problem best solved the night before the climb. A much better approach is from the east via the north shoulder of Moran, establishing a camp in the last trees on the shoulder (see *Route 25*). A descent of about 100 feet will then be required to reach the lower portion of the eastern Triple Glacier.

From the lower edge of the glacier the upper arm or snow tongue, which does not actually connect with the main lower glacier, will be seen leading to the west ridge of Mount Moran just a short distance from the summit. Climb directly up the snow toward this snow tongue. Crossing the *bergschrund* of this glacier is the first problem, the severity of which will depend on the season. In early season there is usually a bridge near the middle of the glacier, but in late season it may be necessary to climb onto the rocks at the left (east) edge of the glacier in order to pass the *bergschrund* and gain the upper ice. Crampons will be very useful. Climb to the steep upper right (southwest) corner of the glacier above the *bergschrund* and onto the rock band separating the glacier from the snow tongue. This rock is not overly difficult but is unpleasant, because it is all downsloping slabs, many of which are wet with running water. The snow tongue itself is straightforward but moderately steep snow climbing to the crest of the west ridge a short distance west of the notch at the head of the Southwest Couloir (see *Route 2*). Descend into the notch, and climb the pitch out of it onto the flat summit of Mount Moran.

ROUTE 29. *Northwest Ridge.* II, AI2, 5.1. First ascent July 17, 1977, by Paul Horton and Lew Hitchner. See *Photo 106*. Between the eastern and central Triple Glaciers lies this major ridge, which rises in a series of sloping shelves to the final broad portion of the west ridge of Moran. It is mostly easily approached from the east over the north shoulder of Mount Moran (see *Route 25*) and across the lower portion of the eastern Triple Glacier, although the base of the ridge could be reached by a 3,000-foot hike directly up from Moran Canyon. An excellent campsite can be found at the base of the ridge. The route stays on or near the crest, and most of it consists of exposed scrambling up very broken rock of generally poor quality. The first roped pitch occurs low on the route, where climbing out of a notch behind a small tower is steep and exposed. About two-thirds of the way up the ridge, two more pitches will be found on the face of a step where the rock quality is surprisingly good. After joining the west ridge, follow that route to the summit.

MOUNT MORAN, NORTH SUMMIT (12,400+)

Map: Mount Moran

Separated from the main summit of Mount Moran by a flat ridge 0.3 mile long, the north summit was one of the earliest Teton peaks to be ascended. The solo climb of LeRoy Jeffers on August 11, 1919, was widely publicized in several magazine articles that he wrote as well as in his book, *The Call of the Mountains*. Most of the routes on Mount Moran from the north or northeast pass across the top of this flat subsummit, and so no separate route descriptions will be given here.

PEAK 11,795   *(0.5 mi NNE of Mount Moran)*

Map: Mount Moran

This conspicuous subsummit high on the north ridge of Mount Moran is ordinarily climbed only during the course of an ascent of that ridge (see *Mount Moran, Route 25*). By chance, the first four ascents of the north ridge of Moran apparently bypassed the top of this peak on the east. A mapping curiosity is the large 167-foot change in elevation of this point between the 1948 and 1968 USGS maps, perhaps the largest such shift between the two editions. It would be of interest to know which map was in error, or was it both?

CHRONOLOGY

Upper East Face: July 13, 1957, Yvon Chouinard, Duane Ewers
North Face: September 13, 1957, Bill Pope, Mary Kay Pottinger (complete), or September 10, 1960, Peter Gardiner, Frank Knight, Mihaly Csikszentmihalyi (complete), or July 27, 1956, Richard Emerson, Robert Bowen (partial)
North Prow Arête: September 2, 1986, Steve Walker, Hugh Phillips, Bert Stolp
East Buttress: September 2, 1986, Steve Walker, Hugh Phillips, Bert Stolp (descent)

ROUTE 1. Upper East Face. II, 4.0. First ascent July 13, 1957, by Yvon Chouinard and Duane Ewers. On the usual

traverse around the east side of Peak 11,795 during an ascent of the North Ridge of Moran (see *Route 25*), one can scramble carefully upward and reach the summit of this peak. The difficulty is about the same whether one begins the traverse from the east, southeast, or even south. See *American Alpine Journal,* 11, no. 1 (1958), pp. 85–88.

ROUTE 2. East Buttress. II, 5.7. First descent September 2, 1986, by Steve Walker, Hugh Phillips, and Bert Stolp. The continuous couloir or chute that descends from the notch separating Peak 11,795 from the upper north ridge of Mount Moran forms the right (north) boundary of the Pika Buttress. To the right (north) of this couloir is a second well-defined buttress that was used as a direct route of descent from the summit of Peak 11,795. The complex and diverse terrain of this buttress require careful routefinding. One 150-foot rappel was required, so the difficulty of this buttress for ascent can only be estimated.

ROUTE 3. North Face. II, 5.6. First ascent September 13, 1957, by Bill Pope and Mary Kay Pottinger; a similar route was climbed on September 10, 1960, by Peter Gardiner, Frank Knight, and Mihaly Csikszentmihalyi. On July 27, 1956, Richard Emerson and Robert Bowen made the first climb of the difficult portion of this face but did not finish the last easy portion to the summit of Peak 11,795. This route is described under *Mount Moran, Route 25, 1957 variation*.

ROUTE 4. North Prow Arête. III, 5.8. First ascent September 2, 1986, by Steve Walker, Hugh Phillips, and Bert Stolp. When Peak 11,795 is viewed from the north, the steep north face or prow is seen to be bordered on the lower right by a subsidiary ridgelet or arête that leads south and terminates at the main arête forming the western edge of the main north face. From the north shoulder of Mount Moran, gain this initial subsidiary arête, which is then climbed easily (4.0) in several pitches to reach the main arête. Climb two pitches up this arête (5.6 and 5.7) to a belay stance from which one can go around the corner to the right. Climb the steep face (5.8) above for the third lead to gain a bowl. Several easier pitches up and slightly left lead to the top of the face or prow. After emerging north of the summit, scramble up along the crest of the ridge above to the top.

PEAK 9,940   *(2.0 mi NNE of Mount Moran)*

Map: Mount Moran

Rising 3,200 feet directly above the mouth of Moran Canyon is this high point at the end of the north shoulder of Mount Moran. It is well off the beaten path and has been visited very few times, perhaps only by one or two parties whose main objective was the north ridge of Mount Moran. The flat crest leading southwest to join that ridge is an attractive place to stroll, through a sparse grove of timberline trees. At the saddle (9,680+) a dike comes up from the west along the line of drainage and meets this ridge.

ROUTE 1. Southwest Ridge. I, 2.0. First recorded ascent July 19, 1962, by John C. Reed, Jr., who found a cairn but no record. The connecting ridge to Mount Moran is most directly approached from Jackson Lake up the main couloir leading to the base of the north ridge of Moran. The 1962 party, however, attained this ridge from the eastern Triple Glacier after hiking up from Moran Canyon. Either approach offers no technical difficulty, but some bushwhacking will be involved.

PEAK 12,000+   *(0.6 mi W of Mount Moran)*

Map: Mount Moran

This remote peak, which lies about halfway along the ridge connecting Mount Moran with Thor Peak, is unique in that it is composed largely of the black dike that extends from the east side of Moran all the way west to the divide. It is ordinarily climbed only in conjunction with the ascent of Mount Moran via its West Ridge; see *Mount Moran, Route 1.* The distance from the valley to this peak is sufficient to suggest a high camp prior to the ascent to the summit. See *Leigh Canyon* for the southern approach and *Moran Canyon* for the northern approach.

CHRONOLOGY

East Ridge: August 26, 1935, Paul Petzoldt, H. K. Hartline
West Ridge: August 24, 1964, Peter Cleveland, James Gregg
North Ridge: September 12, 1977, Norm Larson, Kevin Tischer

ROUTE 1. West Ridge. II, 5.1. First ascent August 24, 1964, by Peter Cleveland and James Gregg. From about 7,300 feet in Moran Canyon ascend the very long slope up to the middle Triple Glacier, passing the extensive moraines at the base of the glacier. This glacier could also be approached, perhaps with less effort, by hiking first to the north shoulder of Mount Moran, and then with a slight descent, contouring west across the eastern Triple Glacier and the intervening ridge. Once on the glacier climb to the highest point of the glacier at its left (east) side where a snow bridge can usually be found across the *bergschrund.* Ice axes will be necessary on the glacier and in late season crampons will be useful on the bare ice. Then gain a broad ledge, which traverses Peak 12,000+ from east to west. Take this ledge right (west) to emerge on the ridge (rotten rock) west of the summit. Climb the first blocky pinnacle, descend 200 feet to the right (south), and traverse east to a snow couloir leading back onto the ridge. Climb the couloir to the ridge and follow it east to the summit on a mixture of better rock (5.1) and easy scrambling.

ROUTE 2. East Ridge. II, 3.0. First ascent August 26, 1935, by Paul Petzoldt and H. K. Hartline. In the course of their long traverse from the summit of Thor Peak to Mount Moran via its west ridge, this party incidentally climbed Peak 12,000+. Approaching this peak along its west ridge,

this party contoured around the north side of the peak on ledges until the east ridge was reached. It was then an easy matter to scramble up the east ridge to the summit of the peak. More directly, from Leigh Canyon two separate drainages will be seen leading up into the large side canyon between Thor Peak and the south ridge of Mount Moran. Scramble up the right-hand (eastern) drainage toward the ridge connecting Mount Moran with Peak 12,000+. While this can be done without difficulty, some routefinding skills will be needed and an ice axe will be useful on some steep snow chutes during most of the season. The crest of the east ridge will be reached near its lowest point and then can be followed west to the summit. With an early start it is possible to reach the summit of this peak in one day, but a camp or bivouac will be required before the return.

ROUTE 3. North Ridge. II, 5.4. First ascent September 12, 1977, by Norm Larson and Kevin Tischer. The base of this major ridge, which separates the western and central Triple Glaciers, can be reached as already described for the West Ridge *(Route 1).* This ridge has an imposing appearance but contains some rock of less than high quality. The ridge begins between the considerable terminal moraines of the adjacent glaciers. Start this scenic climb on the crest of the ridge up to the first high point (10,640+). The significant sharp tower above, capped by good yellow rock, is bypassed on the left (east) until one can scramble back up to the crest south of its summit. The remainder of the climb to the summit of Peak 12,000+ is scrambling, largely up loose scree.

THE ZEBRA (11,680+)   *(0.45 mi N of Thor Peak)*

Map: Mount Moran

This remarkable and isolated peak lies on the northwest spur of the west ridge of Mount Moran. From a distance it appears as a group of unstable pinnacles, an impression based on the generally rotten nature of the rock in this area and the fact that there is an impressive hole or window in the ridge. The northeast and southwest faces of the peak are sheer and the northwest ridge connecting to the Rotten Thumb also has a vertical step. These conditions led the few mountaineers who had seen the peak to avoid an attempted ascent because it was believed that the towers would probably collapse if an ascent was attempted. It was indeed a surprise to find that the summit block of the peak is formed from the finest Teton crystalline rock, of the same nature as Cleaver Peak. The approach used for the first ascent is described later, but it is clear that in early season a better approach might be directly up the western Triple Glacier to the col just east of the summit of the Zebra. In late season, however, such an ascent of the glacier will be a serious undertaking, involving significant ice climbing and passage of large crevasses.

ROUTE 1. Southwest Couloir and Southeast Ridge. III, 5.4. First ascent July 26, 1989, by Leigh Ortenburger and Paul Horton. See *Photo 107.* From Leigh Canyon ascend the side canyon on the west side of Thor Peak. Before turning north up into this drainage, it is best to stay near the creek in Leigh Canyon until the stream from this drainage is met, else grievous bushwhacking will be encountered on an upward diagonal approach. In early season moderately steep snow will be encountered in some chutes before reaching the high plateau (ca. 10,800) just west of the summit of Thor Peak; ice axes and crampons will be required. Two cliff bands in this canyon are passed by some tricky routefinding on the left (west) side. The high plateau provides an adequate campsite with outstanding and unique views of the Teton Range. From this plateau ascend slightly to the upper left bounding ridge, from which a view can be had across the little-known cirque below the northwest face of Thor Peak. This cirque harbors a significant snowfield (see *Thor Peak*) that must be crossed to reach the Zebra. Descend from the ridge onto the snowfield, cross to the far northeast edge, pass the crest of the lateral moraine, and head toward one of the black rock couloirs descending from the northeast. Start in a couloir that leads toward the col to the right (east) of the summit of the Zebra, but switch when required to other subsidiary couloirs when the going becomes difficult or unpleasant. Some steep snow will be involved. If the correct route up the couloirs is found, the roped climbing does not begin until the col on the summit ridge is reached. Almost immediately the good yellow crystalline rock will be found, as one climbs northwest along the ridge crest toward the summit. Five leads are involved, some short, mostly staying on the right side of the crest on ledges. At times the top edge of the snowfield will be used. The final pitch to the small summit involves enjoyable friction. A rappel was needed for descent from the summit; an anchor will be found at the summit for the initial rappel back down the southeast ridge. A second rappel along the ridge leads to the initial small notch in the ridge. A long rappel straight down the southwest face takes one past the "stripes," 100 feet thick, of alternating white and black rock, which provided the name for the peak. Scrambling then permits a traverse left (east) to the couloirs used for the ascent.

ROTTEN THUMB (11,658)
(1.1 mi WNW of Mount Moran)

Map: Mount Moran

The vagaries of topographic mapping initially (1948) indicated that this prominent high point culminating the northwest spur of the west ridge of Mount Moran was indeed a peak, that is, it had five closed 50-foot contour lines. The newer map (1968) changed contour intervals and the Rotten Thumb lost its peak status while the more impressive neighbor, the Zebra, gained peak status by holding three closed 80-foot contour lines. In any event, this isolated point was a climbing objective in the early 1960s and

is even today not easily reached. Moran Canyon is the obvious method of approach, but an alternative worth considering is via Leigh Canyon and then up over the ridge into the largely unknown canyon west of Thor Peak and the Rotten Thumb. The only route that has been used to reach the summit by the three successful parties is probably neither the easiest nor the most pleasant. Consideration should be given to the west ridge, west slope, or the northwest ridge.

ROUTE 1. East Face. II, 5.1. First ascent August 31, 1962, by Ted Vaill, Stuart Kearns, and Ben Shapiro. From Moran Bay on Jackson Lake hike into Moran Canyon along the north side about 1.5 miles to the point where the stream draining the western Triple Glacier joins Moran Creek. On the first ascent the talus was ascended to the apex of the tree-covered triangle just below the third (most westerly) Triple Glacier, where a large boulder (visible from Moran Canyon) provides an adequate campsite for two. Above this camping area, the glacier was reached and climbed along its right side toward the east face of the Thumb.

A more recent ascent suggests proceeding up the same talus slope, keeping to the right (west) of this stream until the lowest edge of the lateral moraine from the glacier is encountered. It is possible to gain and stay on the crest of this moraine all the way to its upper end at a clearly evident cliff band. This is not recommended because this moraine crest is extremely sharp and, as with all moraines, is made of crumbly morainal dirt, scree, and rocks. Of all the glacial moraines in the park this is probably the sharpest and best defined, reminiscent of Andean moraines. It is better to keep to the slope to the right of this moraine until meeting the cliff band, where exit can be made onto the uppermost flat end of the moraine. A campsite can be found at this point. The difficulty of the remainder of the climb is somewhat dependent on the time of year. In early season snow will be available, requiring ice axes to ascend the relatively low-angle right (west) edge of the glacier to sneak around the south end of the cliff band. In late season this will be bare ice, requiring crampons as well. Some rockfall can be expected from the slabs above the glacier.

When convenient, leave the glacier onto the talus, scree, and downsloping slabs of the east face of the Rotten Thumb, and make an upward traverse toward the ridge just north of the summit block. This traverse is unpleasant going, loose, slippery, and exposed, on thin scree on downsloping slabs. The final ascent to the summit can be made in two ways. For the original route, traverse left (east) around to the east face and climb an exposed, rotten chimney to the top. More easily one can simply continue up the north ridge, bypassing the final steep step on the right (west) to gain the summit via a short chimney on the northwest side. See *American Alpine Journal*, 13, no. 2 (1963), pp. 487–489.

PEAK 11,840+   *(0.2 mi NE of Thor Peak)*

Map: Mount Moran

On the north ridge of Thor Peak rises this peak, about half-way toward the point at which this ridge joins the west ridge of Mount Moran. Not an objective in itself, this point is climbed only in the course of the rarely done traverse from Thor to Moran or *vice versa.* The rock is not solid.

ROUTE 1. South Ridge. II, 4.0. Probable first ascent August 26, 1935, by Paul Petzoldt and H. K. Hartline. This crumbly ridge has been gained only directly from the summit of Thor Peak and the connecting col (11,600+). There are blocky towers on this ridge that must be passed.

ROUTE 2. North Ridge. II, 4.0. Probable first descent August 26, 1935, by Paul Petzoldt and H. K. Hartline; possible first ascent June 30, 1966, by Don Storjohann, Pres Ellsworth, and Gunther Schlader. Similar to the South Ridge, this route is climbed only during a traverse, or attempted traverse, between Thor and Moran.

THOR PEAK (12,028)

Map: Mount Moran

This fine peak (one of the few in the park rising to more than 12,000 feet) has received little attention from climbers, largely because it is overshadowed by the massive Mount Moran. Thor Peak is one of the major Teton summits, harboring glaciers on both the east and the northwest sides. It is a challenging climb, and should not be overlooked by visiting mountaineers. Thor Peak is readily approached via Leigh Canyon, but one very long day must be allowed for the ascent of the mountain. Some climbing is involved in ascending the steep valley on the west side of the peak, and in early season ice axes and even crampons will be required. A campsite with an extensive view can be found on the high plateau (10,800) west of the summit. The eastern approach toward the glacier at the base of the east face is not as difficult, involving scrambling up the slope and talus near the stream from the bottom of Leigh Canyon.

The snowfield at the northwest base of the peak has ice, crevasses, moraines, and a *bergschrund,* but in 1963 no evidence of movement was found, so at present it apparently should not be called a glacier. This snowfield was first visited three years earlier, in 1960, and the remote and unnamed north–south canyon west of Thor Peak and Peak 11,126 was probably first entered at that time.

CHRONOLOGY

Northeast Couloir: late August 1930, Paul Petzoldt, Bruton Strange

South Slope: late August 1930, Paul Petzoldt, Bruton Strange (descent); August 26, 1935, Paul Petzoldt, H. K. Hartline (ascent)

East Face: July 22, 1950, Glenn Exum, Michael Brewer, Richard Pownall
   var: August 15, 1957, Yvon Chouinard, Kenneth Weeks
   var: August 1, 1994, Beverly Boynton, Rob Mahoney

Southeast Ridge: September 28, 1954, Keith Jones, Martin Benham

East Face, South Chimney: September 2, 1957, Kenneth Weeks, Curtis Butler

Northwest Face: August 13, 1960, Leigh and Irene Ortenburger, Leon Sinclair, Raymond Jacquot

East Face Arête: June 19, 1966, Don Storjohann, Pres Ellsworth

Hidden Couloir: September 6, 1975, Paul Horton, Renny Jackson

ROUTE 1. ☞*South Slope.* II, 4.0. First descent late August 1930, by Paul Petzoldt and Bruton Strange; first ascent August 26, 1935, by Paul Petzoldt and H. K. Hartline. See *Photo 108.* There are two principal southern approaches to the upper portions of Thor Peak. Both ultimately take the climber to a large talus couloir that leads in a southwest–northeast direction from the saddle between Thor and Peak 11,126 to the notch on the southeast ridge a few feet from the summit. The very steep, diagonal, east face snow chute leads to this same notch from the other side. This easy talus couloir, which does contain much loose rock, can be reached by first ascending Leigh Canyon past the side canyon between Mount Moran and Thor Peak, and past the southeast ridge of Thor. Then turn up and west to gain the main south talus and scree slope. Some cliff bands will be encountered on this slope and routefinding skill will be required while diagonaling up and west. This slope ultimately leads to the talus couloir already mentioned, which takes one almost directly to the summit.

To reach this couloir more directly, continue up Leigh Canyon until the stream descending from the steep valley between Thor Peak and Peak 11,126 is reached. In general, the route ascends this valley to the saddle and then cuts right (northeast) up the obvious couloir that leads to within a few feet of the summit. The first headwall in the valley can be passed near the stream or on the left (west) side; either way involves scrambling up a steep pitch or two. A second headwall blocks the valley about halfway up; it can be climbed to the left (west) of the stream or to the right (east). Some routefinding is necessary on both of these headwalls. To avoid having to rappel on descent, one should remember where these obstacles were passed on the ascent. Continue to the gentle saddle and then turn up the talus couloir that leads to a small notch in the southeast ridge; the summit is quickly reached from this notch by scrambling along the ridge. On descent from the summit take the talus couloir down to the saddle; if you try to descend more directly down to the southwest, cliffs requiring rappelling will be unavoidable.

ROUTE 2. *Southeast Ridge.* II, 5.4. First ascent September 28, 1954, by Keith Jones and Martin Benham. Bushwhack up Leigh Canyon somewhat more than 1.0 mile to the large talus fan on the north side of the canyon just west of the south buttress of Mount Moran. Ascend this fan, bearing left (west) toward Thor's southeast ridge, which forms the left edge of the prominent east face. Cross the creek from the east face glacier and climb a grassy slope and boulders to the point where the crest of the glacial moraine meets the southeast ridge. At this point the ridge broadens into a face bisected by a large crack. Climb a section of rotten rock, traversing left across the face to the large crack. Enter the crack and ascend it for about 150 feet, or use the slabs to the left (south) that are covered with loose scree. Continue to a small notch overlooking the steep snow couloir that leads upward from the left (south) edge of the east face glacier. A short traverse on a narrow ledge leads to the col at the head of this couloir. Now scramble over easy rocks up the remainder of the ridge to the summit. It would also be possible to traverse west to the main south scree slope.

ROUTE 3. *East Face, South Chimney.* II, 5.6. First ascent September 2, 1957, by Kenneth Weeks and Curtis Butler. See *Photo 109.* This route starts at the top of the east face glacier, as in *Route 4.* Near the beginning of the rock above the glacier, a difficult friction pitch must be negotiated in order to gain access to the large chimney leading upward and slightly left (south) to the southeast ridge. About one-third of the way up the chimney, climb out on the face to the right (north) for about one ropelength before returning to the chimney. Once the ridge (*Route 2*) is attained, follow it without difficulty to the summit.

ROUTE 4. *East Face.* IV, 5.8. First ascent July 22, 1950, by Glenn Exum, Michael Brewer, and Richard Pownall. See *Photo 109.* Proceed as in *Route 7* into the side canyon between Thor Peak and the south ridge of Mount Moran, and ascend to the apex of the small glacier at the base of the east face. The first lead from the top of the ice goes up rather smooth friction slabs to a broad belay ledge. After the second lead up a series of broken chimneys and slabs to a grassy ledge, a 100-foot chimney is climbed. The fourth pitch ascends a series of ledges, climaxed by a 50-foot chimney containing running water. A ropelength of friction slabs traverses slightly to the right (north). The sixth lead climbs short vertical faces up and slightly left (south) to a broad ledge from which the large open book, or V chimney, in orange rock can be seen above near the top of the face. The next portion of the route is an upward traverse to the left toward the bottom of this easily recognized V chimney. Scramble for a ropelength and then climb some broken faces including a difficult, crackless, 40-foot chimney. The ninth pitch ascends a 50-foot chimney, makes an upward

traverse to the right, and finishes with a 30-foot vertical chimney. The next short lead goes up a 15-foot chimney, traverses left (south) for 20 feet, and reaches a beautiful flower-covered grassy ledge after passing a 10-foot wall. Traverse up and left for about 150 feet toward the base of the V chimney, which the first-ascent party attempted but did not climb. Attack the nearly vertical 80-foot chimney, which is about 60 feet to the right of the main V chimney. The upper portion of this chimney is difficult as is the exit that is made to the right across a vertical face. After this traverse right, climb about 10 feet up on good rock to a good belay anchor ledge. Now climb 60 feet in a vertical chimney to a chockstone anchor. The next lead, a full ropelength, goes directly upward; the final 40 feet is on downsloping and loose rock to a perch beneath a band of overhanging yellow rock. The first 30 feet of this final pitch, directly up over several overhanging bulges in downsloping and loose rock, are the most difficult of the climb; the end of this lead is on the ridgelet (*Route 5*) that forms the outer border of the steep, diagonal snow couloir (*Route 6*) on the east face of Thor Peak. This ridgelet is followed easily up to the summit ridge from which the summit is gained. This long and complex route entails some rockfall danger in the lower sections, some loose rock, and very few cracks for protection. See *American Alpine Journal,* 8, no. 1 (1951), pp. 71–77.

Variation: IV, 5.8. First ascent August 15, 1957, by Yvon Chouinard and Kenneth Weeks. This variation differs mainly in the beginning. Instead of angling right from the start, climb two friction pitches on the left of the large chimney that angles slightly left. Three pitches then follow in this distinct chimney before a traverse to the right is made to easy scrambling on whitish rock. Then head for a point 200 feet below the open book or V chimney mentioned earlier; join the original route here.

Variation: IV, 5.9. First ascent August 1, 1994, by Beverly Boynton and Rob Mahoney. See *Photo 109.* This important variation marked the first time that the large upper dihedral, so conspicuous from down below, was climbed. The upper dihedral and its orange rock are easily visible from the cirque. Directly below this one can see a large, light-colored, dishlike area of rock. The main object in the lower portion of the route is to get to this dishlike area. From the upper left (west) portion of the glacier, this party went up the first pitch of *Route 3* and then traversed up and east for two ropelengths to join the original line (*Route 4*). Two pitches were climbed up and then back to the west into the dish. Scramble up for approximately 300 feet along the east side of the dish, heading for the upper dihedral and the large chimney to the right. Two roped pitches (5.6 to 5.7) lead up and left to the base of the dihedral. Three spectacular pitches (5.8 to 5.9) of 100 feet lead up the main corner system. The climbing consists of jamming and delicate stemming with good protection (except for a moderate runout on the final pitch). Easy climbing leads up the final portion of *Route 5* and the top of the Hidden Couloir to the summit of the peak.

ROUTE 5. East Face Arête. III, 5.6. First ascent June 19, 1966, by Don Storjohann and Pres Ellsworth. The major feature of the east face of Thor Peak is the Hidden Couloir (*Route 6*), which diagonals up from lower right to upper left, reaching the southeast ridge 100 feet short of the summit. This east face arête forms the left edge of this couloir; the uppermost part of this arête is used by the 1950 East Face route (*Route 4*). Approach the glacier lying at the east base of Thor Peak as in the Northeast Couloir route (*Route 7*). From the *bergschrund* continue up the couloir, either on snow (early season) or on steep slabs (5.6), for some 300 feet to reach the bowl at the beginning of the arête. The arête is then climbed on broken rock.

ROUTE 6. Hidden Couloir. III, AI3, 5.6. First ascent September 6, 1975, by Paul Horton and Renny Jackson. See *Photo 109*. This major, well-defined diagonal couloir is readily seen from the summit plateau of Mount Moran, but it is not visible from Jackson Hole. Entry to the couloir is gained in the same manner as the East Face Arête (*Route 5*), which forms the left edge of the couloir. The climbing in the couloir itself consists of eight or nine pitches (some 1,200 feet) of 40–50° snow and ice, the proportion of ice depending on the year and time of year. By climbing near the right side of the couloir, belay anchors can be placed in the sometimes poor-quality rock. While rockfall danger must exist in such a steep and narrow chute, very little has been observed in the ascents to date. An assortment of hardware, including nuts, pitons, and ice screws, was used on the first ascent.

ROUTE 7. Northeast Couloir. II, 5.6. First ascent in late August 1930, by Paul Petzoldt and Bruton Strange. The name of this route is somewhat misleading because the couloir faces southeast but reaches the summit ridge north or northeast of the summit. Proceed up Leigh Canyon for about 1.5 miles, past the south ridge of Mount Moran; then turn right (north) up into the side canyon between the east face of Thor and the south ridge of Mount Moran. From the vicinity of the glacier a shallow couloir (or a concave face) leads northwest up to the ridge that joins Thor with Mount Moran. This couloir is at the right (north) edge of the main east face and ends at the col (11,600+) between Thor and Peak 11,840+. Some 5.6 climbing leads to the ridge crest north of the summit of Thor. Follow the ridge south to the summit. See *Appalachia,* 18, no. 4 (December 1931), pp. 388–408, illus.

ROUTE 8. Northwest Face. III, 5.4. First ascent August 13, 1960, by Leigh and Irene Ortenburger, Leon Sinclair, and Raymond Jacquot. There are three possible approaches to the base of this obscure 1,200-foot face. More than one day will be required to reach and climb this face so a campsite must be selected. First one can ascend Moran Canyon and turn up the unnamed north–south subsidiary canyon that leads to this side of Thor Peak; this has not yet been done but should work well. Or one can ascend Leigh Canyon, climb its north slope between Peak 11,126 and Point 10,805, and drop down into the head of this unnamed canyon. For this alternative there is an excellent camping site at 9,400 feet in the highest trees on the north side of the 10,000+-foot col between the unnamed canyon and Leigh Canyon. From this site make a gradual upward traverse to reach the high plateau west of Thor, from which descent (400 feet) is made to the glacier at the base of the face. Ice axes are required in order to deal with the problems encountered in this descent. Finally, one can ascend Leigh Canyon and climb the steep valley between Thor and Peak 11,126 to the high plateau and then descend the far (north) side to the base of the northwest face. This alternative is most direct but will also require ice axes for the steep snow.

An obvious moraine leads around the left edge of the snowfield to the base of the face. From the top end of the moraine climb up and then slightly to the right, following a line of weakness to about 200 feet below the summit. This final portion could be climbed directly, but the first-ascent party veered slightly left here and reached the northeast ridge of Thor about 150 feet below the summit. A considerable quantity of rotten and loose rock must be expected on this climb, although this route, which actually stays generally left of center, does not seem to be subject to much falling rock. Routes farther to the right would be both more difficult and more dangerous. This climb is not to be recommended because of the unpleasant nature of the rock, even though it is a 1,200-foot high-angle face. See *American Alpine Journal,* 12, no. 2 (1961), pp. 373–379.

PEAK 11,126   *(0.8 mi SW of Thor Peak)*

Map: Mount Moran

Perhaps the least known of the Teton peaks in the formidable class, this peak is ringed with barriers of difficulty even after the considerable approach up Leigh Canyon is overcome. Only the side of the first ascent is moderate. From the west the summit block is seen as a solid wedge resting in a "V" of couloirs. The cliff band above these couloirs extends around the east side and rises above extensive downsloping slabs. The steep western couloir that bounds the block on the north forms a distinct notch on the north ridge and continues with equal clarity down the east face of the mountain. It appears to be an important line of weakness in the structure, if not a fault line.

ROUTE 1. Southwest Ridge. II, 5.1. First ascent June 28, 1953, by Leigh Ortenburger and William Buckingham. This peak was climbed from Cirque Lake via a traverse of its southwest ridge from Point 10,805. This ridge intersects the summit mass of Peak 11,126 about 400 feet below the top of the south ridge. From this point, contour around to the east side of the peak, crossing some small gullies and ridges before turning up toward the summit. It should be possible to reach this same place by approaching via Leigh Canyon and the steep side valley separating Peak 11,126 from Thor Peak (see *Thor Peak, Route 1* and *The Zebra* for information concerning this valley). From the upper east side an easy scramble will lead to the summit ridge just left (south) of the summit block. Traverse underneath the summit block on the west and reach the flat, slabby summit from the northwest. This route involves some tricky routefinding. For descent this route could be reversed, or a sequence of three rappels can be made onto and past the smooth slabs of the east face to reach the upper end of the valley separating this peak from Thor. One party reported a descent using a system of slabs toward the northeast.

Variation: II, 4.0. First ascent August 3, 1963, by John C. Reed, Jr., and David Steller, the second ascent of this peak. Gain the low point on the same southwest ridge directly from Leigh Canyon and follow it toward Peak 11,126. However, instead of traversing around to the east side, climb the last few hundred feet on the south face. This variation also involves tricky routefinding. Descent to Leigh Canyon was made via the south gully from the small 10,400+-foot col on the southwest ridge, traversing west out of the gully at about 9,000 feet to avoid a waterfall.

PEAK 10,952   *(1.2 mi E of Cleaver Peak)*

Map: Mount Moran

Between Cleaver Peak on the west and Mount Moran on the east lies this major north–south ridge, separating the relatively well-known Cirque Lake from the almost unknown side canyon to the east. Geological peculiarities mark this mountain. Just north of and only 300 feet lower than the summit are some curious depressions along the flat and broad ridge, perhaps attributable to the north–south fault in the region that crosses at right angles the east–west continuation of the black diabase dike of Mount Moran. The black dike here is offset some 0.2 mile from the east–west line of the dike to the east. The entire eastern side of this mountain is a dreadful continuous scree-and-talus slope, not to be considered for ascent and probably not pleasant even for descent. The small lake, Jipe Lake, at 9,840+ feet above Cirque Lake on the west slope of this peak makes a fine campsite.

ROUTE 1. South Ridge. I, 2.0. Probable first ascent in 1935 by T. F. Murphy and Mike Yokel, Jr.; first recorded ascent June 27, 1953, by Leigh Ortenburger and William Buckingham. From a camp at Cirque Lake, ascend the easy slope to the col between Peak 10,952 and Point 10,805. A short section of the south ridge above the col involves 3.0 scrambling and is climbed on the right (east) side. An alternative is to diagonal left (north) when approaching this col from Cirque Lake and to reach the ridge crest above (north of) this section. A cairn but no record was found on the plateau that is 200 yards south of the summit and a few feet lower.

ROUTE 2. North Ridge. II, 2.0. First ascent July 13, 1963, by John C. Reed, Jr., and David Steller. From Moran Canyon ascend into the unnamed canyon east of the peak to about 8,800 feet and then climb the easy but dreadful slope to the north ridge near the line of the dike. Follow the north ridge past the curious depressions to the summit.

PEAK 10,880+   *(0.5 mi E of Maidenform Peak)*

Map: Mount Moran

This is an unimportant high point on the ridge crest south of Cirque Lake.

ROUTE 1. West Ridge. I, 2.0. First ascent June 27, 1953, by Leigh Ortenburger and William Buckingham. This ridge is easily traversed from the summit of Maidenform Peak.

ROUTE 2. East Ridge. I, 2.0. First descent June 27, 1953, by Leigh Ortenburger and William Buckingham. The crest of this ridge is readily traversed to Point 10,805 at the southeast corner of the Cirque Lake region.

MAIDENFORM PEAK (11,137)

Map: Mount Moran

This easy but isolated peak affords one of the most comprehensive views in the range. With the exception of Mount Wister, Shadow Peak, Nez Perce, Cloudveil Dome, and Disappointment Peak, every peak from Buck Mountain to Eagles Rest Peak and beyond is visible. The name, given in 1955, is derived from the remarkable appearance of the peak as seen from the north. The rock unfortunately is not sound. The most common method of approach is circuitous, via the Cascade Canyon trail, over Littles Peak, and on north and east to the saddle at the head of the south fork of Moran Canyon; the route was discovered by Fred Ayres in the course of his first ascent. The direct but long approach via *Leigh Canyon* is fraught with bushwhacking.

CHRONOLOGY

North Ridge: August 7, 1941, Fred Ayres
East Ridge: June 27, 1953, Leigh Ortenburger, William Buckingham (descent); July 25, 1973, Jim Bruggeman, Don Thompson (ascent)
Southwest Ridge: August 7, 1941, Fred Ayres (descent); August 15, 1955, John and Jean Fonda, Roald Fryxell (ascent)

ROUTE 1. ☞*Southwest Ridge.* II, 3.0. First descent August 7, 1941, by Fred Ayres; first ascent August 15, 1955, by John and Jean Fonda and Roald Fryxell. From the saddle to the west separating the south fork of Moran Canyon from Leigh Canyon, scramble up this ridge to the summit. Of the three routes to the summit this is perhaps the most devious because one cannot easily stay directly on the ridge crest. The steeper and rotten sections are usually bypassed on the right (south).

ROUTE 2. East Ridge. II, 2.0. First descent June 27, 1953, by Leigh Ortenburger and William Buckingham; first ascent July 25, 1973, by Jim Bruggeman and Don Thompson. The entire ridge was descended over Peak 10,880+ to Point 10,805. This ridge has also been reached directly from the south by climbing the long slope out of upper Leigh Canyon.

ROUTE 3. North Ridge. II, 3.0. First ascent August 7, 1941, by Fred Ayres. This ridge can be easily reached from either the Cirque Lake side or the south fork of Moran Canyon. On the first ascent, this ridge was followed after a climb of Cleaver Peak.

CLEAVER PEAK (11,055)

Map: Mount Moran

The massive character of the rock makes this aptly named peak conspicuous from most points, including the summit of the Grand Teton. The attractiveness of this double summit stems from the sharpness of its end-on profile and partially from the remoteness from standard tourist traffic. Furthermore, the rock of the upper peak is of the finest Teton type, golden and solid, in sharp contrast to the crumbly dark rock surrounding its base. Cleaver Peak is actually two separate peaks of almost the same elevation; the U.S. Geological Survey strangely places the highest elevation, 11,055, on the south peak, which is the lower of the two. The first ascent was made somewhat unintentionally following the remarkable early attempt (1940) on the south face of Bivouac Peak.

From Jackson Hole there are three methods of approach, but all are long, requiring hours of hard work. The most obvious is the bushwhack directly up Moran Canyon from Moran Bay on Jackson Lake, as was done on the first ascent. Continue to the south fork to reach the west side of the peak or hike into the Cirque Lake basin for the eastern routes. One can also approach via Leigh Canyon, an equally difficult bushwhack, to the divide (9,920+) west of Maidenform Peak and thereby reach the upper south fork of Moran Canyon. Most commonly used, however, is the devious route that starts with the Cascade Canyon trail to Lake Solitude, up and over the top of Littles Peak, then along the main divide north (easy), turning right (east) to enter the uppermost south fork of Moran Canyon. A sneaky scheme (perhaps first utilized by Marty Thompson in the early 1970s) that requires less physical effort than any of the preceding ones, however, involves the trails of the Targhee National Forest west of the divide. From Driggs, Idaho, drive to the trailhead on North Leigh Creek at the edge of the USFS wilderness area on the west slope of the Teton Range (see Granite Basin quadrangle map). Take the Green Mountain trail to the basin above and beyond Green Lake, from which one can easily reach and cross the divide at the broad saddle (9,760+) due west of Cleaver Peak. The south fork of Moran Canyon is then easily crossed to reach the peak.

North Peak, Northwest Chimney: August 9, 1940, John McCown II, C. Grove McCown, Edward McNeill, Thomson Edwards

North Peak, Northeast Chimney: August 9, 1940, John McCown II, C. Grove McCown, Edward McNeill, Thomson Edwards (descent); August 22, 1969, Charles Bockes, Marvin Conway, Judy Horn and Rick Horn (ascent)

North Peak, West Chimney: August 7, 1941, Fred Ayres (first descent likely); August 1992, Jim Springer (first known ascent)

South Peak, Southeast Shoulder: August 7, 1941, Fred Ayres (first ascent, south peak)

South Peak, East Face–South Ridge: August 19, 1988, Jim and Kim Springer

North Peak, Annatia's: August 11, 1990, Paul Horton, Marianne Fraser

ROUTE 1. ☞North Peak, Northwest Chimney. II, 5.4. First ascent August 9, 1940, by John McCown II, C. Grove McCown, Edward McNeill, and Thomson Edwards. See *Photo 110.* The west side of the North Peak has two distinct features: a small, sharp notch that bisects the summit block and a larger, rounder notch farther north with a spire on its north side. From the west in the south fork of Moran Canyon, scramble up talus and ledges to a wide chimney leading to the large rounded notch. About 50 feet short of the notch one is forced out onto the left (north) face of the wide chimney, where small holds and a jam crack (5.4) permit passage. One can also climb up in the right corner and do a hand traverse left (5.6) to gain the notch. From the notch climb (south) using a vertical face left of some large cracks. Mantle onto a ledge, then climb a steep east-facing slab (5.4) and scramble south to the higher north peak. From the notch the small spire "Jipe Point" can be ascended (5.4) *en route* to the summit.

ROUTE 2. North Peak, West Chimney. II, 5.4. First descent August 7, 1941, by Fred Ayres; first known ascent August 1992, by Jim Springer. See *Photo 110.* From the base of the wide chimney described in *Route 1,* ascend a corner up and right to the sharp notch that bisects the main summit block. At two points one is forced to traverse out right onto the face and then back left to the corner. At the top of the second detour there are two options: continue straight up a chimney to the notch and the nearby summit (normal), or traverse left (north) behind a gigantic flake, then up a slab to join *Route 1* just above the rounded notch. This route can be descended with two single-rope rappels with an occasional section of easy downclimbing.

ROUTE 3. North Peak, Annatia's. II, 5.6. First ascent August 11, 1990, by Paul Horton and Marianne Fraser. See *Photo 110.* Scramble up the dark rock of the west face to the base of the gold rock. Traverse to a point above which a crack and chimney system leads up to the north end of the col between the peaks. The initial pitch ascends cracks (5.6). Climb to a broken area behind a large detached block. Take a narrowing ramp in the upper headwall out to and around a prow on the right, then immediately climb steep cracks to and above the headwall (5.6). Follow ledges and steps up to the col, then onto the face left of the steep south edge of the north peak (5.4). Trend left up the face to a large ledge at the base of the summit headwall (5.1). Scramble north on this ledge, eventually reaching the small, sharp notch and the nearby summit. One can also climb directly up to the summit (5.7, no protection) from the south end of this ledge (Richard DuMais, summer 1993).

ROUTE 4. *South Peak, Southeast Shoulder.* II, 5.4. First ascent August 7, 1941, by Fred D. Ayres. The ridge between Maidenform Peak and the south peak can easily be gained from the east or west at a point just south of the south peak. From the small final notch in the black rock, avoid the short vertical section of the south ridge of the south peak (*Route 5*) by climbing down on the right (east) shoulder of the ridge and climbing up and right over a series of diagonal, narrow ledges and onto the south summit from the east side. To traverse to the col between the south and north peaks keep on the east side of the connecting ridge. From the col traverse down and left (west) around the west side of the north peak on obvious ledges to the base of the large Northwest Chimney (*Routes 1* and *2*). Fred Ayres reported climbing to the north summit "from the south and west," a route that was perhaps distinct from *Route 2*. To descend the south ridge over the top of the south peak, a rappel will be needed to pass the vertical section on the south ridge of the south summit. *Time: 11½ hours* from Jenny Lake.

ROUTE 5. *South Peak, East Face–South Ridge.* III, 5.8. First ascent August 19, 1988, by Kim and Jim Springer. The east face of the south peak is bisected from the left at half-height by a tree-covered grassy ledge. Hike to the south end of this ledge from Cirque Lake and traverse out on it to its highest point at a shallow, low-angle V of rock where a chimney slants up and left. Climb the face to the right up to a tree, and then up to a steep flake (5.7), until above a promontory that juts out from the face on the right. After moving the belay up 30 feet, climb the obvious ramp up and left onto a second ramp also leading up and left to a corner directly above. Rather than climbing the corner, move down and left (5.7) from a flat edge to the left of the corner and then across and up loose holds into the large chimney above. A short scramble up the remainder of the chimney leads to the small final notch in the south ridge. Now climb straight up on the left of a small tower and then left under a roof until it is possible to mantle (5.8) via rounded holds onto a ledge. Easy scrambling then leads to the south summit.

ROUTE 6. *North Peak, Northeast Chimney.* II, 5.4. First descent August 9, 1940, by John McCown II, C. Grove McCown, Edward McNeill, and Thomson Edwards; first ascent August 22, 1969, by Charles Bockes, Marvin Conway and Judy and Rick Horn. The northeast ridge of Cleaver Peak is easily reached from Cirque Lake at the saddle connecting to Dragon Peak. From this saddle climb and scramble up slabs to reach the main notch on the north ridge, attained from the west by *Route 1*. The final pitches of that route on the ridge are then followed south to the summit.

DRAGON PEAK (10,465)

(0.4 mi NE of Cleaver Peak)

Map: Mount Moran

This thin peak, when viewed broadside from the west, has the appearance of a humpbacked monster, hence the name. The summit ridge crest is very narrow and at places composed of precariously positioned rock splinters. The exact location of the highest point is very difficult to determine; it behooves one to bring a hand level. Both the west and east faces of the peak are steep crystalline rock; the west face appears to be very rotten.

ROUTE 1. *Southwest Ridge.* II, 5.1. First ascent August 11, 1959, by W. V. Graham Matthews and Irene Ortenburger. The approach to the saddle separating Dragon Peak from Cleaver Peak can be made either from the northwest from Moran Canyon or from the southeast from Cirque Lake. The sharp southwest ridge provides an interesting, slightly crumbly, climb. Care must be taken as one proceeds along the crest because it is not obvious that all the rock splinters are solid. Parts of the crest can be bypassed on steep ledges on the left (west) side. See *American Alpine Journal,* 12, no. 1 (1960), pp. 125–127.

ROLLING THUNDER MOUNTAIN

Moran Canyon to Webb Canyon

PEAK 10,345   (1.5 mi N of Littles Peak)

Map: Mount Moran

This is the first rounded peak on the divide north of Littles Peak. The first ascent was inadvertent, made by a park ranger in the course of intercepting and ushering out of the park a band of sheep and their herder.

ROUTE 1. South Ridge. I, 1.0. First ascent September 1, 1933, by Dudley Hayden. This is an easy scramble from Littles Peak and is easily gained from Leigh Canyon or from the west.

ROUTE 2. North Ridge. I, 3.0. First descent September 1, 1933, by Dudley Hayden; first ascent August 8, 1963, by Leigh and Irene Ortenburger, Julie Peterson, and Dennis Wilson. This ridge contains a steep, slabby section that requires care because of the unsound rock.

PEAK 10,484   (1.1 mi S of Green Lakes Mountain)

Map: Granite Basin

According to the Grand Teton quadrangle map (1901), the Bannon topographic party in 1898 placed a bench mark on this peak, perhaps the most interesting of those on the northern divide. However, the bench mark found by a 1963 party seemed to date from the Murphy topographic party of the 1930s and was located on the central of five summits. It is believed that the highest point is the most northerly summit, although this is not known definitely; a hand level is necessary. However, the central summit is certainly not the highest point. The easiest approach for this peak is from the west via the Green Mountain trail in the Targhee National Forest (see *Cleaver Peak*).

371

Northeast Ridge: July 2, 1963, John C. Reed, Jr., David Steller, Alfred Chidester

North Ridge: August 7, 1963, Leigh and Irene Ortenburger, Julie Peterson, Dennis Wilson

South Ridge: August 14, 1954, Gene Balaz, Roald Fryxell (partial ascent, to south summit); August 7, 1963, Leigh and Irene Ortenburger, Julie Peterson, Dennis Wilson (complete descent)

ROUTE 1. South Ridge. II, 4.0. First partial ascent (to south summit) August 14, 1954, by Gene Balaz and Roald Fryxell; first complete descent August 7, 1963, by Leigh and Irene Ortenburger, Julie Peterson, and Dennis Wilson. Dudley Hayden may have also climbed this ridge on September 1, 1933. The ridge is easily climbed to the south summit from the broad expanse along the divide north of Littles Peak. The 1954 party found no cairn or record on the south summit. The traverse of the pinnacled summit ridge involves significant difficulties, because the ridge is sharp and contains some distinct notches between pinnacles, and in places the rock is unsound, although not sedimentary. Some of the problems could be avoided by dropping down from the crest to the east side.

ROUTE 2. Northeast Ridge. I, 3.0. First known ascent July 2, 1963, by John C. Reed, Jr., David Steller, and Alfred Chidester. This ridge, which connects with Window Peak (10,508), was climbed from a camp in Moran Canyon to the north summit only.

ROUTE 3. North Ridge. I, 3.0. First recorded ascent August 7, 1963, by Leigh and Irene Ortenburger, Julie Peterson, and Dennis Wilson. The northern summit was reached by traversing the ridge from Green Lakes Mountain. No cairn, bench mark, or record was found, although this summit was climbed a month earlier and may have been reached by either the Bannon party or the Murphy party or both. All five summits were traversed by the August 1963 party.

PEAK 10,300   *(0.6 mi SW of Window Peak)*

Map: Mount Moran

Separating this small high point from the divide is the western continuation of the main black dike of Mount Moran, which can be seen disappearing at the lake (9,680+) in the cirque to the northwest.

ROUTE 1. East Ridge. II, 3.0. First recorded ascent September 3, 1988, by Leigh Ortenburger. The saddle separating this peak from Window Peak can be reached from either fork of Moran Canyon, although some scrambling is involved. The ridge itself is interesting, involving some climbing usually slightly on the right (north) side of the crest. The left (south) side contains some smooth slabs.

WINDOW PEAK (10,508)

Map: Mount Moran

A worthwhile objective, this prominent peak divides upper Moran Canyon into the north and south forks. The name is derived from a natural window said to be in a subsidiary south ridge.

ROUTE 1. Southwest Ridge. II, 3.0. First recorded ascent August 10, 1959, by W. V. Graham Matthews and Irene Ortenburger, who found an empty cairn on the summit. From the south fork of Moran Canyon, climb past a very small lake (not shown on the map) to the saddle west of the peak where an interesting pinnacle will be found. Some scrambling, usually on the right (south) side of the crest, is required to negotiate the ridge to the large summit. See *American Alpine Journal,* 12, no. 1 (1960), pp. 125–127.

GREEN LAKES MOUNTAIN (10,240+)

Map: Granite Basin

Most easily approached via the USFS trail to the pass (9,480+) on the west, the main distinction of this peak is that it has been given a name, taken from the four lakes in the high cirque two miles to the southwest.

Northeast Ridge: [probable] July 1935, T. F. Murphy, Mike Yokel, Jr.

South Ridge: August 7, 1963, Leigh and Irene Ortenburger, Julie Peterson, Dennis Wilson (descent)

ROUTE 1. South Ridge. I, 1.0. First known descent August 7, 1963, by Leigh and Irene Ortenburger, Julie Peterson, and Dennis Wilson. There are no difficulties on this ridge.

ROUTE 2. Northeast Ridge. I, 1.0. Probable first ascent in July 1935, by T. F. Murphy and Mike Yokel, Jr. This is an easy ridge that is reached directly from the north fork of Moran Canyon or via a traverse from Dry Ridge Mountain.

DRY RIDGE MOUNTAIN (10,321)

Map: Mount Moran

The name for this mountain is taken, curiously, from the ridge to the west in Targhee National Forest, which actually meets the divide at Green Lakes Mountain. The Bannon topographic party presumably placed a bench mark on this summit in 1898. The 1952 party from the J Bar Y Ranch near Ashton, Idaho, built on the summit one of the largest cairns in the park.

ROUTE 1. Southeast Slope. I, 1.0. Probable first ascent in July, 1935, by T. F. Murphy and Mike Yokel, Jr.; first recorded ascent August 7, 1963, by Leigh and Irene Ortenburger, Julie Peterson, and Dennis Wilson. No problems will be found on this peak no matter which route is used from the north fork of Moran Canyon.

ROUTE 2. Northwest Ridge. I, 1.0. First known ascent August 11, 1952, by Jack and Frank Young, Henry Tausend, Roger Abelson, Richard Cohen, Kirby Orme, Frederick Berlinger, Richard Luria, and Roger and Peter Bensinger. This straightforward ridge is presumably the route used on the upper climb; the approach was made on horse to timberline, via Hidden Corral Basin in the south fork of Bitch Creek, to the ridge above Dead Horse Pass (9,376).

PEAK 10,160+ *(0.55 mi ENE of Dry Ridge Mountain)*

Map: Ranger Peak

This is a small high point on the divide between the north fork of Moran Canyon and the south fork of Bitch Creek. During an extended exploratory traverse of peaks in the north end of the range in 1963, this summit was bypassed via the bench to the south because on the old map (1948) it did not qualify as a peak. No information is available concerning ascents.

PEAK 10,474 *(1.1 mi ENE of Dry Ridge Mountain)*

Map: Ranger Peak

The main distinction of this peak above the north fork of Moran Canyon is that it is one of two enclosing the beautiful cirque containing the high lake (9,610), Dragon Lake. The U.S. Department of the Interior Board on Geographic Names regrettably rejected the proposal that this lake be named in honor of Leigh N. Ortenburger in 1993.

ROUTE 1. North Ridge. I, 2.0. First ascent August 7, 1963, by Leigh and Irene Ortenburger, Julie Peterson, and Dennis Wilson. From Lake 9,610, which makes an ideal campsite, proceed easily up the slope to the saddle on the divide north of this peak. Once on the ridge, only ten minutes are required to reach the summit.

DOUBTFUL PEAK (10,852)
(1.1 mi NW of Raynolds Peak)

Map: Ranger Peak

Named by the first-ascent party due to their uncertainty of finding the summit unclimbed, Doubtful Peak is one of the highest points of the divide. It also stands as the dividing point between the two branches of the south fork of Snowshoe Canyon. Composed of crystalline rock, most approaches to the summit are not difficult, except for one steep step on the southeast ridge. All approaches to this peak are long. The shortest is probably from the USFS

trailhead north of Badger Creek, up and over Dead Horse Pass and then cross-country over the intervening ridge to the basin just west of the peak. Coming directly up either Moran Canyon or Snowshoe Canyon will require considerable effort and heinous bushwhacking. Most of the rare climbs of Doubtful Peak have been made in the course of a north–south traverse of this part of the range—for example, from Berry Creek to Cascade Canyon, or conversely.

CHRONOLOGY

North Ridge: July 23, 1958, Jack Davis, Julie Peterson, Silvia Prodan

Southeast Ridge: July 23, 1958, Jack Davis, Julie Peterson, Silvia Prodan (descent)

West Ridge: July 27, 1975, Gary Kofinas, Amy Wilbur, John Polstein, Jim Siesfield, Paul Sachs, Matthew Rice, Gordon Anteil, Jeff Garbaty, David Rattray, Liz Ganfort, Jim Verdone, Andy Sebesta

ROUTE 1. West Ridge. I, 2.0. First ascent July 27, 1975, by Gary Kofinas, Amy Wilbur, John Polstein, Jim Siesfield, Paul Sachs, Matthew Rice, Gordon Anteil, Jeff Garbaty, David Rattray, Liz Ganfort, Jim Verdone, and Andy Sebesta. This ridge on the divide starts at the saddle (10,160+), which is crossed by an east-west–trending dike, and leads directly to the summit. The saddle can be easily reached from the south (Moran Canyon) or the north (South Bitch Creek).

ROUTE 2. Southeast Ridge. I, 4.0. First descent July 23, 1958, by Jack Davis, Julie Peterson, and Silvia Prodan. This ridge contains some of the excellent yellow Teton rock, much like that of the Exum Ridge of the Grand Teton or Cleaver Peak on the south side of Moran Canyon. Both of the parties that have descended this ridge bypassed the steep, difficult section that is about 150 feet long on the west, via a convenient gully. A dike crosses the base of this ridge at about 10,480+ feet, a situation similar to the west ridge. The 1958 party continued east to Point 10,214 (named Birthday Cake), where they built an elaborate cairn prior to descending north into Snowshoe Canyon.

ROUTE 3. North Ridge. I, 3.0. First ascent July 23, 1958, by Jack Davis, Julie Peterson, and Silvia Prodan. The saddle between Doubtful Peak and Peak 10,480+ is easily reached from Bitch Creek, but some 3rd-class gullies must be climbed to reach it from Snowshoe Canyon. Once on the ridge, many sharp pinnacles and steep rock restrict access to the west side of the ridge. Near the summit the slabs on the ridge provide enjoyable climbing. During the first ascent the entire ridge on the divide from Blackwelder Peak (10,822) was traversed south over all the intervening pinnacles. The most southerly of these was shown as Point 10,445 on the original Grand Teton quadrangle map (1901) and as Point 10,480+ on the Ranger Peak quadrangle (1968). The 1901 map indicated a bench mark on this point; the 1958 party found a cairn here, but a thorough search by the second-ascent party in 1963 failed to reveal any traces of it. It does seem likely that Bannon's topographic surveying party in 1898 very likely reached at least the saddle north of Doubtful Peak via horse from South Bitch Creek and probably hiked up to this easy Point 10,480+. See *American Alpine Journal*, 11, no. 2 (1959), pp. 307–309.

RAYNOLDS PEAK (10,910)

Map: Mount Moran

This fine, isolated peak is the highest point on the long ridge that extends west from Traverse Peak to the divide. It was named for Capt. William F. Raynolds, who in 1860 led the first scientifically oriented expedition of exploration into Jackson Hole. Raynolds, incidentally, had made the first ascent of Pico de Orizaba (18,750) in 1848 with some of his men while on duty in the Mexican-American War; this was very likely the American altitude record for the next half century. The general approach to this peak can be made from Moran Canyon, Snowshoe Canyon, or Cascade Canyon via Littles Peak. It is not clear that anyone has ever visited the three very small glaciers or snowfields that lie along the north base of the mountain.

CHRONOLOGY

Southwest Side: [probable] summer 1935, by T. F. Murphy's party, perhaps Frank Somner; [certain] August 15, 1954, Roald Fryxell, Gene Balaz
East Ridge: September 4, 1955, John Fonda, William Buckingham
West Ridge: August 6, 1963, Leigh and Irene Ortenburger, Julie Peterson, Dennis Wilson

ROUTE 1. West Ridge. II, 3.0. First ascent August 6, 1963, by Leigh and Irene Ortenburger, Julie Peterson, and Dennis Wilson. This is a long ridge containing many pinnacles, towers, and false summits, some of which can be avoided on the right (south), but it is usually simpler to climb over most of them.
ROUTE 2. Southwest Side. I, 2.0. Probable first ascent in summer 1935, by T. F. Murphy's surveying party, perhaps Frank Somner; first recorded ascent August 15, 1954, by Roald Fryxell and Gene Balaz. From the south base of the peak in Moran Canyon, obvious couloirs lead easily to the summit. This party discovered on the summit a large cairn composed half of white rocks and half of black rocks. Hence, it is reasonable to assume that the first ascent was actually made by surveyors; Frank Somner was working in this area as an assistant to T. F. Murphy.

The slender, fingerlike pinnacle standing just east of the summit was first climbed by Fryxell and Balaz. A climb of similar difficulty from the same direction, somewhat more on a ridge than in a couloir, was made on August 14, 1962, by J. H. Dieterich and T. B. Ranson. *Time: 4½ hours* from the forks of Moran Canyon.
ROUTE 3. East Ridge. II, 5.1. First ascent September 4, 1955, by John Fonda and William Buckingham. This ascent, the third of the peak, was made via the very long traverse of the entire ridge from Traverse Peak. This *tour-de-force* required a considerable amount of climbing effort and careful routefinding in order to climb all the many tall and impressive towers on the ridge. Several of the pinnacles near Traverse Peak are over 150 feet high. Many hours of 4.0 and 5.1 scrambling were involved. It is intriguing that a cairn was found on the summit of one of the towers. It should prove possible to gain this ridge from various points either in Moran Canyon or in Snowshoe Canyon. See *American Alpine Journal*, 10, no. 1 (1956), pp. 116–119.

IMAGE (10,750)   (1.0 mi E of Raynolds Peak)

Map: Mount Moran

This pinnacle, the higher of the Images, lies on the north side of the ridge extending from Raynolds Peak to Traverse Peak. The name is derived from the fact that these peaks are reflected in the still waters of Dudley Lake (8,243), which provides a nifty wilderness campsite for these peaks. Passing through the saddle (10,560+) to the south is an east-west–trending dike.

CHRONOLOGY

Northeast Face: August 20, 1957, Jack Davis, Redwood Fryxell, Nick Ellena, Julie Peterson
Southeast Face: August 15, 1962, John C. Reed, Jr.
North Ridge: July 31, 1983, Leigh Ortenburger, Roman Laba

ROUTE 1. Southeast Face. II, 3.0. First ascent August 15, 1962, by John C. Reed, Jr. From the upper part of the south fork of Snowshoe Canyon, ascend into the cirque between the Images and Raynolds Peak. Climb to the col south of the summit and then up the east face.
ROUTE 2. Northeast Face. II, 3.0. First ascent August 20, 1957, by Jack Davis, Redwood Fryxell, Nick Ellena, and Julie Peterson. From Dudley Lake bushwhack up into the cirque east of the summit and ascend the northeast couloir, then scramble up a series of ledges to the summit.
ROUTE 3. North Ridge. II, 4.0. First ascent July 31, 1983, by Leigh Ortenburger and Roman Laba. Reach the notch between the two Images from the east, and then climb the moderate north ridge to the summit.

COUNTERIMAGE (10,560+)

(1.0 mi E of Raynolds Peak)

Map: Mount Moran

This peak, the lower and northern Image, presents a striking appearance when seen from the west, as it is composed of a light-colored rock that contrasts with the black rock of the surrounding peaks. The name, in addition to its apparent meaning, also is a technical term in mathematical set theory, given appropriately by the first-ascent party, a mathematician and his wife.

CHRONOLOGY

Northeast Ridge: August 9, 1956, Sherman and Lillian Lehman
West Ledges: August 9, 1956, Sherman and Lillian Lehman (descent)
South Ridge: July 31, 1983, Leigh Ortenburger, Roman Laba

ROUTE 1. West Ledges. II, 4.0. First descent August 9, 1956 by Sherman and Lillian Lehman. This route is a comparatively easy rock climb, approached from the seldom-entered cirque between the Images and Raynolds Peak.

ROUTE 2. South Ridge. II, 5.1. First ascent July 31, 1983, by Leigh Ortenburger and Roman Laba. Climb this ridge directly from the notch between the two Images. It is an interesting climb on good rock.

ROUTE 3. Northeast Ridge. II, 4.0. First ascent August 9, 1956, by Sherman and Lillian Lehman. Approach via Snowshoe Canyon to the couloir that leads from the east to the notch between the two Images. At the level of the lower slope of the higher Image traverse right (north) to the northeast ridge. Follow this moderate ridge to the summit, staying mostly left of the crest. This is not the prominent north ridge seen in outline from Dudley Lake.

TRAVERSE PEAK (11,051)

Map: Mount Moran

This flat-topped peak was incorrectly named "Bivouac Peak" on the original USGS topographic map (1938) of Grand Teton National Park. The history of this error is worth noting. In 1916, A. C. Tate and Gibb Scott climbed the easy east slope and stopped on the first east summit, indicated by the 10,640-foot contour line on the current map (1968). Then, in 1930 Fritiof Fryxell and party repeated this climb but continued along the ridge leading west to the higher flat-topped summit, which is indicated by the 10,800-foot contour line on the map. Fryxell named this peak "Bivouac," because some of the party were benighted before returning to Jenny Lake. The highest point,

Traverse Peak, lies still farther west and was not climbed until 1934 (in one day from Leigh Lake and return) by Fred and Irene Ayres, who named the peak. This discrepancy in names was not noticed until 1953, when the second ascent of Traverse Peak was made. In the course of their ascent in 1934 the Ayreses witnessed the "heavy, jarring rumble" of the collapse of a crevasse on the small glacier on the northeast side of the peak. The southern aspect of this peak contains steep walls similar to but not as extensive as those on the neighboring Bivouac Peak. See *Moran Canyon* for the approach to the south side of Traverse Peak or *Snowshoe Canyon* for the north side of the mountain.

CHRONOLOGY

East Ridge: August 23, 1934, Fred and Irene Ayres
South Couloir: June 25, 1953, Leigh Ortenburger, William Buckingham
West Ridge: September 4, 1955, William Buckingham, John Fonda (descent); August 8, 1956, Redwood and Roald Fryxell (ascent)
var: **North Approach:** July 12, 1987, Doug Parker, Jim and Steve Herzog

ROUTE 1. West Ridge. II, 5.4. First descent September 4, 1955, by William Buckingham and John Fonda; first ascent August 8, 1956, by Redwood and Roald Fryxell. See *Photo 112.* This ridge consists of very steep and loose scrambling; the route must be chosen with care to avoid difficult and dangerous sections. See *American Alpine Journal,* 10, no. 1 (1956), pp. 116–119.

Variation: North Approach. II, 5.4. First ascent July 12, 1987, by Doug Parker and Jim and Steve Herzog. From the south fork of Snowshoe Canyon climb the snowfield at the base of the northwest face of Traverse Peak to gain the west ridge at a point 0.3 mile west of the summit. Pass over the top of a subsummit (10,880+), descend to the col, and continue up steep rock (5.4) to the main summit.

ROUTE 2. South Couloir. II, 3.0. First ascent June 25, 1953, by Leigh Ortenburger and William Buckingham. See *Photo 112.* Proceed up Moran Canyon about 1.5 miles to the streams descending from the Triple Glaciers. A large, obvious couloir descends from the col between Traverse Peak and Bivouac Peak. In early season this is a 3,500-foot snow chute, making a rapid and enjoyable route of descent (glissaded all the way in 1953). To ascend Traverse Peak, turn left (west up a subsidiary couloir) about 200 feet before the top of the couloir, thus avoiding the pinnacles on the ridge crest itself. The flat summit, unlike that of Bivouac Peak, has no bushes or trees.

ROUTE 3. ☞*East Ridge.* II, 3.0. First ascent August 23, 1934, by Fred and Irene Ayres. This route starts at the summit of Bivouac Peak, using the East Ridge (*Bivouac Peak,*

Route 6) to begin the ascent. From the Bivouac summit continue traversing west, "threading in and out through a long array of splintered pinnacles," to the flat summit of Traverse Peak. There is an excellent view of the northwest side of Mount Moran and the Triple Glaciers from the summit. *Time: 10¾ hours from Leigh Lake.*

PRIMROSE PEAK (10,800+)

(0.2 mi N of Traverse Peak)

Map: Mount Moran

Relatively small and obscure by most standards, this peak is prominent on the skyline as seen from the vicinity of Colter Bay. The notch separating Primrose Peak from the higher Traverse Peak is formed by an east–west black dike, which can be seen extending from the small glacier (or snowfield) on the east to the same feature on the west. The name arose from the astonishing multitude of the flower Parry's Primrose encountered on the slopes above Dudley Lake during the first ascent.

ROUTE 1. West Couloir and South Ridge. II, 2.0. First descent August 14, 1975, by Leigh and Carolyn Ortenburger. This rotten couloir follows the line of the black dike from the left (east) edge of the small glacier (or snowfield) lying at the northwest base of Traverse Peak. Take the couloir to the notch and then follow the south ridge to the summit.

ROUTE 2. East Face. II, 4.0. First ascent August 14, 1975, by Leigh and Carolyn Ortenburger. Climb directly up from Dudley Lake into the cirque east of this peak to gain the base of the east face well north of the summit. A few pitches in the chimney system in the slabs of the face are then climbed to reach the north ridge, which is followed to the summit. Some loose rock will be found on this route.

BIVOUAC PEAK (10,825)

Map: Mount Moran

Bivouac Peak on the north and Mount Woodring on the south provide a visual balance flanking the central bulk of Mount Moran. A lesser mountain than Moran, it shares the same unusual feature of a flat summit area. Bivouac Peak is not a difficult summit to attain and in June of 1972 a mountain sheep and three lambs were seen on the summit. It also is similar to Mount Moran in harboring significant south walls, which in this case rise above Moran Canyon. As a climbing objective, Bivouac Peak was surprisingly one of the first in the range to be attempted. The ascent in 1916 of the east peak ranks as one of the first successfully attained Teton summits following the 1898 climbs of the Grand Teton by Owen, Spalding, Peterson, and Shive. And even as there was an early attempt on the south ridge of Moran (1938), so the south face of Bivouac was nearly climbed at an early date. In early August of 1940, three-quarters of the face was climbed by a group of Philadelphia lawyers, John McCown II, C. Grove McCown, Edward McNeill, and Thomson Edwards; their remarkable attempt was stopped by lack of time and an understandable reluctance to spend the night on the face. This same party later continued up Moran Canyon to make the first ascent of Cleaver Peak.

The approach to Bivouac Peak begins at Moran Bay on Jackson Lake, but there are three ways to reach the shore of the bay. One is to hike in from String Lake: this is a long hike, and the trail, which has not been maintained by the National Park Service for several years, gives out after Trapper Lake is reached. Considerable deadfall will be encountered if one continues north to Moran Creek, but it can be done. An alternative from the vicinity of Bearpaw Lake, with less bushwhacking but much walking at an angle, is to head for the shore of Jackson Lake and follow that shoreline all the way west to Moran Bay. The second method is via canoe from a put-in at Spalding Bay. This is a fairly long paddle but will be preferred by some. For some reason, either obtuseness or error, the road to the Spalding Bay boat put-in has been omitted from the Jenny Lake quadrangle map but is shown on the overall Grand Teton National Park sheet. The third method, the easiest but most difficult to arrange, is to take a boat across Jackson Lake from Colter Bay.

For the south face routes, bushwhack from the lake shore up Moran Canyon on the north side of the creek for about 1.0 mile to the vicinity of the stream descending from the bench below the south face. Turn up here and hike up the long talus and scree slope to the base of the face.

CHRONOLOGY

East Ridge: July 12, 1930, Fritiof Fryxell, Theodore and Gustav Koven
　　var: August 3, 1948, Orrin and Roger Bonney
　　var: **Northeast Couloir:** July 29, 1956, Frank Ewing, Zach Stewart
West Ridge: August 23, 1934, Fred and Irene Ayres
　　var: **South Gully, West Ridge:** July 14, 1985, Jim Lemmon, Merle King, Mark Wilk
South Face I: August 19, 1947, Paul Kenworthy, Richard Pownall
　　var: August 22, 1981, Andy Carson, Jim Roscoe
North Slope: July 29, 1956, Frank Ewing, Zach Stewart (descent), or June 28, 1972, Doug Leen (descent)
South Face II: September 2, 1969, George Lowe, Juris Krisjansons
South Face III: July 24, 1970, Yvon Chouinard, Juris Krisjansons
East Couloir: June 19, 1994, Paul Horton, Cathy Mitchell (ascent); August 20, 1947, Paul Kenworthy, Richard Pownall (descent)

ROUTE 1. West Ridge. II, 4.0. First ascent August 23, 1934, by Fred and Irene Ayres. This ridge containing several shattered towers has been used principally for traversing to Bivouac Peak after an ascent of Traverse Peak or *vice versa.* The rock is not always trustworthy on this ridge.

Variation: South Gully, West Ridge. II, 4.0. First ascent July 14, 1985, by Jim Lemmon, Merle King, and Mark Wilk. From Moran Canyon take the second major drainage gully that meets Moran Creek at the same point as the stream descending from the easterly Triple Glacier on Mount Moran. Follow this gully, which contains a dogleg to the right, to its head at the crest of the west ridge. Some considerable scrambling will be involved in this gully and some moderately steep snow may be encountered. From the ridge crest it is only a short distance to the summit along the final west ridge.

ROUTE 2. South Face II. IV, 5.7. First ascent September 2, 1969, by George Lowe and Juris Krisjansons. See *Photo 111.* This long route can be recognized and located by three features on the main south face of Bivouac Peak. A large gray ceiling will be seen about 200 feet up and left of a small detached pillar at the base of the face. This small detached pillar is well left of the obvious black water streaks, where South Face III *(Route 3)* starts. The third feature is the large buttress or pillar in the center of the face; this route starts and remains to the left of this pillar.

The base of the climb is under the gray overhang (largest on the face), which has a large, deep chimney in its right side. A dihedral, which begins just left of the small detached pillar, leads up toward the base of the overhang. The first pitch goes up this dihedral (5.4) on poor rock toward the gray overhang (some 200 feet above) to an alcove. Scramble up easy rock to the next belay in the large chimney already mentioned. The third lead climbs the right wall of the chimney to avoid poor rock in the chimney itself. Next, climb the chimney to the top and crawl through a horizontal continuation to the right. This is followed by a slightly downward hand traverse, followed by chimneying up a large crack to the belay. The fifth pitch goes to the top of the flake forming the chimney and then moves left up a small gully and back right through overhangs to the belay. Next climb the chimney and then traverse left on easier rock. Now continue up and left almost on the crest of a small ridge. The eighth lead ascends a large lieback flake followed by difficult cracks left and up to the belay, staying near the crest. Two more leads permit one to reach an alcove, moving out and left to avoid some difficult cracks. After an 80-foot jam crack pitch leading to a large ledge, scramble up and right, then ascend some 200 feet off to the left on easier ground. Avoid the obvious chimneys above, climbing instead on the difficult crest to the left. The final lead is up a lieback chimney, followed by a crack to a ledge with a hole in it. The rock on this long route is not the best.

ROUTE 3. South Face III. IV, 5.9. First ascent July 24, 1970, by Yvon Chouinard and Juris Krisjansons. See *Photo 111.* Of the three south face routes on this peak, this was the last to be ascended but it has been the most frequently climbed. It is a long and serious climb of some 14 or 15 pitches. The main feature available to locate the route is the large central buttress or pillar about halfway up this part of the face. This route goes up the wall to the right (east) and below this buttress, staying just left (west) of black watermarks on the steep rock. From the talus slope at the base of the face, climb two 4th-class pitches up and right under a band of overhangs, angling toward the vertical black watermark that is between two overhangs. The next five leads zigzag upward to avoid overhangs, following the line of least resistance up the middle of the steep and at times slightly overhanging face, staying left of the vertical black watermarks. This section contains sustained 5.8 to 5.9 climbing on high-angle rock with good belay ledges, but several of the leads require long runouts. Anchors and protection are at times hard to place, and knifeblade pitons are useful, in addition to the standard rack. The last lead in this section, the seventh, moves out on white rock to the right (east) to the top of the black watermarks and then goes left up cracks to the first major feature of the route, a huge ledge leading left (west) to meet the large central pillar.

Above this main ledge is a loose and rotten-looking wall. Scramble left on this ledge (3rd class) to the pillar, then up the enjoyable chimney (5.6) behind the pillar. From the top of the pillar five or six more leads, somewhat less difficult than those below, are required to reach the top of the face. The first from the pillar moves up and right under an overhang to a belay in a crack. Next climb up and back left to a belay below a chimney. This general line is then followed for the next three leads. The top of this route is on the uppermost southeast ridge, which must be traversed to reach the flat summit of Bivouac Peak. For protection, take small nuts and pitons, including knifeblades. For descent, either take the East Ridge route or the east couloir that drops down to the east (slightly southeast) from the summit plateau. In early season this east couloir will contain snow, and there is a large chockstone that can be bypassed on its south side.

ROUTE 4. South Face I. III, 5.6. First ascent August 19, 1947, by Paul Kenworthy and Richard Pownall. From the vicinity of Moran Bay on Jackson Lake one can see on the southeast side of Bivouac Peak the large talus-filled couloir *(Route 5)* that separates a southeast pinnacle ridge from the higher, flat north summit. Approaching the south face of Bivouac from Moran Canyon, one will see a gendarme on the profile of the face. This route begins some 200 feet west of this gendarme and runs straight up to this southeast pinnacle ridge. Several overhangs will be encountered on this route and rotten rock must be expected for part of the climb. This route ends on this southeast pinnacle ridge from which the main summit is reached by first descending about 200 feet down into the upper end of the east couloir, and then climbing west and up to the summit. See *The Iowa Climber,* 2, no. 2 (Summer 1948), pp. 73–74, illus. (the photograph in this article is reversed).

Variation: III, 5.9. First ascent August 22, 1981, by Andy Carson and Jim Roscoe. This more recent climb has several similarities to the original 1947 South Face I route and so, given the uncertain location of that route, is listed as a variation; it may well be a separate route and it is very likely more difficult. This variation starts well east of the main face used by *Routes* 2 and 3. The initial climbing is 4th class up to the bench. Climb cracks above this bench. The second lead is a 5.9 crack. In all there are eight pitches of good rock on this route, with much continuous 5.7 and 5.8 climbing in cracks and corners. The variation ends about one-quarter of the way down from the top of the main face at the edge of the east couloir (see *Route 5*). The small ridge at the edge of the couloir here probably is the same as the "south pinnacle summit" referred to in the 1947 description. Descent was the same as in 1947, the east couloir, where two descent pitons were found in 1981.

ROUTE 5. East Couloir. II, 5.4. First ascent June 19, 1994, by Paul Horton and Cathy Mitchell; first descent August 20, 1947 by Paul Kenworthy and Richard Pownall. Although this route had been used as a descent route a number of times, it was curiously overlooked as a way up the peak until 1994. This is the main large couloir on the east (slightly southeast) side of the peak that leads from the flat summit area directly down toward Moran Bay. At the bottom, access to this couloir is blocked by a large chockstone and an overhang, so climb on the left (south) side (5.4) until it is possible to traverse right (northeast) into the couloir. Then scramble up the couloir, staying in the left branch, which goes in a straight line to the summit area. As a descent route, the chockstone and overhang must be avoided by moving right (south) out onto a ridge to the south of the couloir. Alternatively the chockstone can be passed by means of a 40-foot rappel. Much of the couloir during the late season consists of talus, excessive brush, and loose and rotten rock and is therefore not recommended. It would, however, be a good early-season snow climb were it not for the need to pass the chockstone. See *The Iowa Climber,* 2, no. 2 (Summer 1948), pp. 73–74, illus. (the photograph is reversed).

ROUTE 6. ☞*East Ridge.* II, 3.0. Partial first ascent 1916, by A. C. Tate and Bill Scott (to east peak only); first complete ascent July 12, 1930, by Fritiof Fryxell and Theodore and Gustav Koven. This is the standard route on an easy but seldom-climbed Teton peak. From the west end of Moran Bay ascend the open slope on the southeast side of the wooded east ridge of Bivouac Peak; this will minimize the bushwhacking. Once the east ridge itself is gained above, follow it by scrambling amongst some giant boulders on the crest to the summit of the east peak. A short, steep descent to the col to the west is most easily made by taking an exposed shelf (3.0) immediately below and south of the east peak summit. Now scramble along the remaining ridge (3.0), past some dwarfed trees, to the main flat summit and cairn. *Time: 4¾ hours* from Moran Bay. See *Appalachia,* 18, no. 4 (December 1931), pp. 388–408, illus.; *Chicago Mountaineering Club Newsletter,* 2, no. 6 (July–December 1948), p. 4; *Trail and Timberline,* no. 157 (November 1931), pp. 177–178, illus.

Variation: II, 3.0. First ascent August 3, 1948, by Orrin and Roger Bonney. Contour north from the east slope and bypass the east peak to reach the main summit from the north.

Variation: Northeast Couloir. II, 3.0. First ascent July 29, 1956, by Frank Ewing and Zach Stewart, or June 28, 1972, by Doug Leen. From Moran Bay proceed (with difficulty) up Snowshoe Canyon through the initial trees to the avalanche slope below this rocky couloir that extends in a southwesterly direction straight toward the east peak. In early season this couloir is snow-filled and provides a relatively fast route of ascent. Join the standard East Ridge route at or near the east summit.

ROUTE 7. North Slope. II, 4.0. First descent July 29, 1956, by Frank Ewing and Zach Stewart. This descent was made almost directly down the north side, utilizing snow in the couloirs. The best route is not obvious; hence, some routefinding skill will be useful. In early season good glissading will be found down to Dudley Lake, where one turns east out Snowshoe Canyon to Moran Bay.

MORAN CANYON, NORTH SIDE ROCK CLIMBS: BIVOUAC PEAK, SOUTH SHOULDER (CA. 9,200)
(0.35 mi SSE of Bivouac Peak)

Map: Mount Moran

Rising immediately above and north of the floor of Moran Canyon from 7,300 feet is this initial buttress of Bivouac Peak, which mirrors on a smaller scale the north shoulder of Mount Moran on the other side of the canyon. It lies separate from and south of the base of the main south faces of the peak.

ROUTE 1. Southwest Corner. II, 5.6. First ascent July 16, 1985, by Jim Lemmon, Merle King, and Mark Wilk. From Moran Canyon start by ascending the first (easternmost) drainage gully between Bivouac Peak and Traverse Peak. The protruding south shoulder of Bivouac Peak rises just above and to the right (east) of this gully. Take the talus slope east out of the gully onto a grassy slope just above a white rock ledge. Several initial pitches of 5.1 climbing were required, first up and right and then back left to the southwest corner. The more interesting final four short leads begin at some trees where a large flake will be found. From the flake move right into a narrow chimney. Then climb on ledges right and up toward the top of the shoulder. The final pitch goes up some slabs to the shoulder. Descent is made back to the southeast via the large scree slope at the base of the main south face of Bivouac Peak.

PEAK 10,625 (0.8 mi E of Rolling Thunder Mountain)

Map: Ranger Peak

Dividing the two forks of Snowshoe Canyon, this modest peak is the high point at the end of the east ridge of Rolling Thunder Mountain. Tracks of mountain sheep were found within 50 feet of the summit in 1983.

CHRONOLOGY

Southeast Ridge: August 22, 1957, Jack Davis, Redwood Fryxell, Julie Peterson
West Ridge: August 22, 1957, Jack Davis, Redwood Fryxell, Julie Peterson (descent)
South Couloirs: August 1, 1983, Leigh Ortenburger, Roman Laba

ROUTE 1. West Ridge. I, 3.0. First descent August 22, 1957, by Jack Davis, Redwood Fryxell, and Julie Peterson. This party traversed the entire ridge from the summit to Rolling Thunder Mountain.
ROUTE 2. South Couloirs. I, 3.0. First ascent August 1, 1983, by Leigh Ortenburger and Roman Laba. A pair of couloirs, one narrow, leads from about 8,100 feet in the south fork of Snowshoe Canyon to the col west of the summit. Some routefinding is required in these couloirs. From the col the ridge is easily followed to the summit.
ROUTE 3. Southeast Ridge. I, 3.0. First ascent August 22, 1957, by Jack Davis, Redwood Fryxell, and Julie Peterson, from a camp at Dudley Lake. This ridge, containing brush, scree, and talus, leads to the east ridge about 0.2 mile from the summit, which is then easily reached.

ROLLING THUNDER MOUNTAIN (10,908)

Map: Ranger Peak

Not only does this peak possess the finest name among the northern peaks, but it also presents the most alpine aspect. Except for the top 10 feet, the rock is crystalline. A genuine glacier survives at the northwest foot of the peak, and from the northeast Rolling Thunder appears astonishingly sharp. The cirque of lakes to the north and Dudley Lake to the southeast provide beautiful and pristine campsites. The approach, however, is long (see Snowshoe Canyon) and it appears that only the first-ascent party has made the ascent and return in one day. The wedge-shaped high point

(10,320+) at the end of the northeast ridge was first reached on August 5, 1963, by Leigh and Irene Ortenburger, Julie Peterson, and Dennis Wilson.

CHRONOLOGY

Southeast Ridge: August 15, 1933, Fritiof Fryxell, Phil Smith
Southwest Couloir: August 15, 1933, Fritiof Fryxell, Phil Smith (descent); August 21, 1970, Leigh, Irene, and Carolyn Ortenburger (ascent)
West Ridge: [probable] August 1935, T. F. Murphy, Mike Yokel, Jr.; August 25, 1954, Roald and Redwood Fryxell, Earle McBride (descent); August 5, 1963, Leigh and Irene Ortenburger, Julie Peterson, Dennis Wilson (ascent)
Northeast Ridge: [probable] August 30, 1967, Hugh Scott, Harold Woodham, or August 3, 1974, David Lowe, Leigh Ortenburger
Renny's Route: July 9, 1980, Anne MacQuarrie, George Montopoli

ROUTE 1. West Ridge. II, 5.1. Probable first ascent August 1935, by T. F. Murphy and Mike Yokel, Jr., or August 5, 1963, by Leigh and Irene Ortenburger, Julie Peterson, and Dennis Wilson; first descent August 25, 1954, by Roald and Redwood Fryxell and Earle McBride. Although there are several towers and notches, there is no great difficulty in traversing this ridge from Peak 10,894. It is easier to gain this ridge from the south than from the north where a glacier must be crossed and the couloirs are steep.
ROUTE 2. Southwest Couloir. II, 3.0. First descent August 15, 1933, by Fritiof Fryxell and Phil Smith; first ascent, August 21, 1970, by Leigh, Irene, and Carolyn Ortenburger. This couloir starts from the north branch of the south fork of Snowshoe Canyon at 9,100 feet and leads directly toward the summit. Some scrambling will be involved near the summit, but this is the easiest route on the peak. Numerous sheep beds will be passed along the way.
ROUTE 3. Southeast Ridge. II, 4.0. First ascent August 15, 1933, by Fritiof Fryxell and Phil Smith. Ascend the north fork of Snowshoe Canyon to the high cirque directly east of the summit. Various couloirs provide access from the cirque to the ridge, which is then followed to the summit knob. The difficulty and length of the climb depend on which couloir is selected. One must expect to encounter snow in getting onto the ridge during most of the season. On August 22, 1957, Jack Davis, Redwood Fryxell, and Julie Peterson climbed the entire southeast ridge, over all the intervening towers and subsummits. The two lakes in the cirque provide excellent campsites. Time: 3¼ hours from Talus Lake; 8¼ hours from Dudley Lake.
ROUTE 4. Northeast Ridge. II, 5.4. Probable first ascent August 30, 1967, by Hugh Scott and Harold Woodham, or

August 3, 1974, by David Lowe and Leigh Ortenburger. See *Photo 113.* This ridge is one of the major features of this isolated peak. Approach via Snowshoe Canyon to Talus Lake in the uppermost north fork, where campsites can be found. This splendid wilderness lake could also be reached from Moose Basin by passing over one of the ridges to the west or north. From Talus Lake, the saddle on the ridge connecting with Peak 10,320+ is reached via snowfields on the northwest side of Rolling Thunder and a diagonal couloir. Scrambling or easy 4.0 climbing along the ridge, which at times is very narrow, leads to the last step to the flat summit. This step is not as difficult as it appears from below. It appears that the 1967 party stayed on the right (west) side of the ridge using slabs and chimneys but found loose rock.

ROUTE 5. Renny's Route. III, 5.9. First ascent July 9, 1980, by Anne MacQuarrie and George Montopoli. Above Talus Lake in the north fork of Snowshoe Canyon on the north side of Rolling Thunder Mountain lies a considerable glacier bounded on the right by the west ridge of the mountain and on the left by the northeast ridge. This difficult route follows a crack system in the north wall of the mountain, just right (west) of the intersection of the north face and the northeast ridge. The first pitch (150 feet, 5.9) off the snow steps onto face holds just right of this crack system. Then move up and left into the crack, where two mantles left of the crack lead to a big ledge. This is followed by 30 feet of offwidth crack to a belay stance on small ledges and a chockstone. The next lead of equal difficulty and length ascends a lieback and a jam among loose flakes to a wet, mossy diagonal gully. Climb up and right along this gully for 30 feet, then straight up through a crack-dihedral system to a large platform belay. The next easy pitch goes straight up through loose blocks for 150 feet to the base of a 20-foot corner at the intersection of the northeast and north faces. Climb the corner and crack (which turns into a chimney) above, passing a chockstone to the end of the crack. Exit by a tricky move left onto a ledge, crawling until face holds are found that permit standing, to reach a belay at the base of a left-slanting dihedral. The final short lead goes up this dihedral for 30 feet until just below a roof. Step up and right on a brown wall to a ledge. Traverse right along this ledge past some blocks and then up a crack to the summit.

PEAK 10,880+
(0.8 mi NW of Rolling Thunder Mountain)

Map: Ranger Peak

Of all the crystalline peaks in the park, this long, nearly flat ridge is perhaps the least imposing in appearance. From almost any direction it presents no difficulties. In the course of their surveying in 1935 for the first USGS map of Grand Teton National Park, T. F. Murphy and Mike Yokel, Jr. probably ascended this peak.

East Ridge: August 25, 1954, Roald and Redwood Fryxell, Earle McBride
West Ridge: ca. August 15, 1960, Loring Woodman
South Slope: August 14, 1962, John C. Reed, Jr.

ROUTE 1. West Ridge. I, 1.0. First ascent about August 15, 1960, by Loring Woodman. The saddle west of the summit provides the principal route for passing between the south fork of Snowshoe Canyon and the head of Webb Canyon. It is easily reached from both north and south, and the ridge above is equally simple.

ROUTE 2. South Slope. I, 1.0. First ascent August 14, 1962, by John C. Reed, Jr. Approach via the north branch of the south fork of Snowshoe Canyon and turn north and climb the easy slope to the lower east summit; then follow the ridge to the west summit.

ROUTE 3. East Ridge. I, 2.0. First ascent August 25, 1954, by Roald and Redwood Fryxell and Earle McBride. This party traversed the entire ridge from the summit of Rolling Thunder Mountain.

BLACKWELDER PEAK (10,800+)
(0.55 mi SE of Glacier Peak)

Map: Ranger Peak

In 1912, during the course of his geological explorations of the west side of the Teton divide, Professor Eliot Blackwelder and his assistant ascended this point from South Bitch Creek. His field notes indicate: "From here we intended to climb the next peak north [Glacier Peak] but found the arête too dangerous." This arête and the east ridge both contain many towers and pinnacles. Besides being the intersection point of three canyons, Snowshoe, Webb, and the South Bitch Creek canyon, Blackwelder Peak has the added distinction of harboring one of the two remaining glaciers north of those on Mount Moran. The glacier has apparently receded in the past 30 years, as there is now a small lake at the snout.

ROUTE 1. South Ridge. I, 2.0. First ascent August 12, 1912, by Eliot Blackwelder and Mack Lake. From a camp in the South Bitch Creek canyon, the saddle immediately south of this peak was easily reached. The ridge itself offers no significant difficulties.

ROUTE 2. East Ridge. I, 3.0. First ascent July 23, 1958, by Jack Davis, Julie Peterson, and Silvia Prodan. Approach via the north fork of Snowshoe Canyon to the important 10,320+-foot saddle between this peak and Peak 10,894. Climb west from this saddle over the first peak, "Crocodile Crag," along the pinnacled ridge connecting with the summit. Some of these towers are most easily bypassed by utilizing the top edge of the glacier along the north side.

PEAK 10,880+   *(0.2 mi E of Eagles Rest Peak)*

Map: Ranger Peak

This east peak of Eagles Rest Peak provides an impressive view of the main peak. For unknown reasons two register bottles adorn this seldom-visited summit.

ROUTE 1. West Ridge. I, 1.0. First ascent September 4, 1962, by John C. Reed, Jr. From the vicinity of the Moran Bay patrol cabin, cross the creek that flows from Snowshoe Canyon just below the large swamp. Proceed up the southeast couloir of Eagles Rest Peak (see *Route 3* of that peak) to the saddle that separates the summits of Eagles Rest and Peak 10,880+. Turn east up to the summit, which can be reached in 30 minutes.

ROUTE 2. East Ridge. I, 1.0. First descent September 4, 1962, by John C. Reed, Jr. No significant obstacles were reported on this 4,000-foot ridge, which begins in the vicinity of North Moran Bay.

EAGLES REST PEAK (11,258)

Map: Ranger Peak

It is surprising that this attractive peak, which presents a double-summit skyline when viewed from Jenny Lake, has been climbed so seldom. Following the first ascent, 21 years passed before the second ascent was made. It is one of the northernmost crystalline peaks, and the summit view presents the Tetons from an angle rarely seen. The peak can be ascended by starting from String Lake, but far better is to approach via boat across Jackson Lake. The west summit, only a few feet lower than the main east summit, was first attained on June 25, 1957, by Leigh and Irene Ortenburger.

CHRONOLOGY

Northeast Chimney: August 30, 1932, Phil Smith, Walcott Watson, W. C. Lawrence

North Ridge: August 30, 1932, Phil Smith, Walcott Watson, W. C. Lawrence (descent); July 31, 1962, John C. Reed, Jr., T. B. Ranson, J. H. Dieterich (ascent)

Southeast Couloir and East Ridge: June 28, 1953, Fred Ayres, A. E. Creswell, Roald Fryxell

West Ridge: June 25, 1957, Leigh and Irene Ortenburger

    var: **North Couloir-West Ridge:** February 1991, Tom Turiano, Christoph Schork, Jim Schultz

South Ridge: September 10, 1976, Leigh Ortenburger

ROUTE 1. West Ridge. II, 5.1. First ascent June 25, 1957, by Leigh and Irene Ortenburger. The high ridge that connects Anniversary Peak with Eagles Rest Peak can be attained from either the south or the north via one of the several fairly steep couloirs. The first-ascent party traversed the entire ridge. The west summit was easily reached by scrambling. Descend to the col separating the two summits. From the col a chute filled with loose rocks will be seen somewhat to the left of the ridge crest. A pitch or two up this chute suffices to put one on the main summit. However, it is much easier (3.0) to traverse on the south side of the west ridge into a gully that leads to the summit. See *American Alpine Journal*, 11, no. 1 (1958), pp. 85–88.

    Variation: North Couloir–West Ridge. II, (50° snow). First descent February 1991, by Tom Turiano, Christoph Schork, and Jim Schultz. From the high cirque northwest of Eagles Rest Peak, climb 50° snow for approximately 900 feet to the notch between the east and west summits of the peak. Follow the west ridge to the summit.

ROUTE 2. South Ridge. II, 4.0. First ascent September 10, 1976, by Leigh Ortenburger. The south side of this peak contains several, somewhat indistinct ridges separated by somewhat indistinct couloirs. The final 1,000 feet funnel into a distinct south ridge that brings one onto the last short section of the west ridge. The climbing consists of 3.0 and 4.0 scrambling with considerable loose rock. The approach is similar to that for the Southeast Couloir and East Ridge route (see *Route 3*) except that one continues farther into Snowshoe Canyon before turning up the mountain.

ROUTE 3. ☞ *Southeast Couloir and East Ridge.* II, 3.0. First ascent June 28, 1953, by Fred Ayres, A. E. Creswell, and Roald Fryxell. This route uses the large couloir that descends the southeast side of the peak and ends at the saddle (10,640+) between the main summit and Peak 10,880+. The primary difficulty is locating the proper couloir, because the first portion of the ascent is made in the trees with little visibility. Take a good look before starting. The final 600 feet up the east ridge are enjoyable scrambling. This is a very long, one-day climb from String Lake. *Time: 12 hours from String Lake.*

ROUTE 4. Northeast Chimney. II, 4.0. First ascent August 30, 1932, by Phil Smith, Walcott Watson, and W. C. Lawrence. From Jackson Lake ascend Waterfalls Canyon about 1.5 miles before bearing left (southwest) up into the cirque northeast of the mountain. Ascend a scree slope that lies below the northeast face of the peak. Near the top of this slope a chimney, which is blocked at its base by a chockstone, leads to the north ridge just below the summit. A variation was climbed by Watson by moving left (east) from the chimney onto the upper east ridge, which was then followed to the summit.

ROUTE 5. North Ridge. II, 5.1. First descent (partial) August 30, 1932, by Phil Smith, Walcott Watson, and W. C. Lawrence; first ascent July 31, 1962, by John C. Reed, Jr., T. B. Ranson, and J. H. Dieterich. From a camp at the foot of

Wilderness Falls in Waterfalls Canyon, proceed up the east side of the rock glacier into the high valley northwest of the summit. Gain the notch (10,640+) in the north ridge from the west via a steep chimney, and then follow the ridge to the summit. Some exposed and loose climbing will be encountered. This same notch can also apparently be reached from the cirque to the east.

ANNIVERSARY PEAK (11,253)

(0.5 mi W of Eagles Rest Peak)

Map: Ranger Peak

Rising directly above the forks of Snowshoe Canyon, this high crystalline peak features a fine double summit.

ROUTE 1. East Ridge. I, 2.0. First descent June 25, 1957, by Leigh and Irene Ortenburger. Descent of this ridge was made to Eagles Rest Peak. The couloirs descending from this ridge to either the north or south are rather steep but should be entirely feasible.

ROUTE 2. Northwest Ridge. I, 2.0. First ascent June 25, 1957, by Leigh and Irene Ortenburger. This party traversed the easy ridge from Doane Peak to the double summit. No great difficulty should be experienced in reaching this ridge from either the north fork of Snowshoe Canyon or the south fork of Waterfalls Canyon.

PEAK 10,720+

(0.6 mi W of Doane Peak)

Map: Ranger Peak

The sedimentary capping of this peak forms a flat top, which makes the summit less than attractive, but the lower slopes are composed of crystalline rock possessing some interesting features. The long southeast ridge has an inviting profile, while the southwest ridge rising east of Talus Lake contains the most garnetiferous rock the author has seen in the park. The unnamed lake (just below the 9,200-foot contour line) at the base of this ridge is one of the more secluded and perhaps the most picturesque lake in the range.

CHRONOLOGY

West Ridge: August 26, 1954, Roald and Redwood Fryxell, Earle McBride

Northeast Ridge: August 26, 1954, Roald and Redwood Fryxell, Earle McBride (descent); August 7, 1962, John C. Reed, Jr., T. B. Ranson, J. H. Dieterich (ascent)

Southwest Ridge: August 5, 1963, Leigh and Irene Ortenburger

ROUTE 1. West Ridge. I, 1.0. First ascent August 26, 1954, by Roald and Redwood Fryxell and Earle McBride. From Talus Lake ascend the easy slope leading north and east to the summit. It is difficult to say where the highest point on

the long, flat summit is to be found, but it is perhaps at the location of the cairn.

ROUTE 2. Southwest Ridge. I, 2.0. First ascent August 5, 1963, by Leigh and Irene Ortenburger. This is the ridge that forms the eastern boundary of Talus Lake. Although somewhat steeper than the west ridge, it offers no difficulties if the small cliff sections are bypassed on the right (east). Garnetiferous rock is to be found on the ridge itself and in the talus slope just west of the crest. Once the plateau of sedimentary rock is reached, only a stroll is required to reach the summit.

ROUTE 3. Northeast Ridge. I, 1.0. First descent August 26, 1954, by Roald and Redwood Fryxell, and Earle McBride; first ascent August 7, 1962, by John C. Reed, Jr., T. B. Ranson, and J. H. Dieterich. From the north fork of Snowshoe Canyon, ascend into the hanging canyon that leads to the saddle between this peak and Doane Peak. From the saddle scramble easily west and then south up the ridge to the summit.

DOANE PEAK (11,355)

Map: Ranger Peak

The name for this summit, the highest point north of Mount Moran, was given by Fryxell in 1936 in recognition of the epic winter expedition led by Lt. Gustavus C. Doane, which passed along the mouth of Waterfalls Canyon to the east on November 24, 1876. It had earlier in 1931 been given a temporary name, "Moose Station," by Earl Buckingham. The 9-foot cairn that he built on its flat summit was to facilitate his triangulation work. As with several of the other peaks in the north end of the range, Doane Peak is most easily approached using a boat across Jackson Lake. Waterfalls Canyon provides the direct eastern approach. Perched above Moose Basin, the remote Lake 10,032, 0.5 mile west of Doane Peak, is one of the higher lakes in the range.

CHRONOLOGY

West Slope: September 10, 1931, by Earl M. Buckingham

North Ridge: July 22, 1956, Zach Stewart, Eleanor Page, Neil Penry, Frank Ewing, Cecile Hilding, Jack Walther

Southeast Ridge: June 25, 1957, Leigh and Irene Ortenburger

　　var: **Southeast Couloir:** February 1991, Tom Turiano, Christoph Schork, Jim Schultz

ROUTE 1. West Slope. I, 1.0. First ascent September 10, 1931, by Earl M. Buckingham; T. F. Murphy and Mike Yokel, Jr., also climbed this general route on August 21, 1935, during the course of their topographic work. On August 26, 1954, Roald and Redwood Fryxell and Earle McBride ascended the west ridge from Peak 10,720+; this may have been a new route, because the exact routes of 1931 and 1935 are not known. This mountain presents no difficulties from the Moose Basin side. The northwest ridge is also an easy hike.

ROUTE 2. Southeast Ridge. I, 2.0. First descent July 22, 1956, by Zach Stewart, Eleanor Page, Jack Walther, and Neil Penry, or June 25, 1957, by Leigh and Irene Ortenburger. Most of this easy ridge is sedimentary. The saddle (10,720+) at the base of the ridge can very likely be reached from either the east or west without great difficulty.

Variation: Southeast Couloir. First ascent February 1991, by Tom Turiano, Christoph Schork, and Jim Schultz. From the high cirque enclosed by Anniversary Peak and Doane Peak, climb directly toward the summit plateau via a 40° couloir.

ROUTE 3. North Ridge. I, 1.0. First ascent July 22, 1956, by Frank Ewing, Zach Stewart, Cecile Hilding, Eleanor Page, and Neil Penry. This broad ridge can easily be reached from the upper end of the north fork of Waterfalls Canyon.

PEAK 11,200+   *(0.8 mi WSW of Ranger Peak)*

Map: Ranger Peak
Lying west of Ranger Peak and north of Doane Peak is a connecting ridge composed of massive limestone with three distinct summits.

ROUTE 1. South Ridge. I, 1.0. First ascent June 26, 1957, by Leigh and Irene Ortenburger. From the small lake at 10,480+ feet in the north fork of Waterfalls Canyon, this ridge is easily climbed.

PEAK 11,238   *(0.5 mi W of Ranger Peak)*

Map: Ranger Peak
ROUTE 1. South Slope. I, 1.0. First descent June 24, 1957, by Leigh and Irene Ortenburger. There are no difficulties on this slope, which is easily approached via the north fork of Waterfalls Canyon.

ROUTE 2. North Ridge. I, 2.0. First ascent June 24, 1957, by Leigh and Irene Ortenburger. This long ridge extends without difficulties from the saddle (10,480+) at the head of Colter Canyon for almost 1.0 mile over two high points (10,852 and 10,960+). The Forellen Peak fault, one of the major faults in the range, passes in a southeast–northwest direction through this saddle.

MARMOT POINT (11,200+)
(0.35 mi W of Ranger Peak)

Map: Ranger Peak
While this is the most interesting point on the sedimentary Ranger–Doane ridge, it does not qualify as a peak. Near-vertical cliffs guard both the south and north faces and the west ridge is also steep and crumbly.

ROUTE 1. East Ridge. I, 4.0. First ascent June 24, 1957, by Leigh and Irene Ortenburger. This attractive little point lies immediately west of Ranger Peak and was climbed by the crumbly east ridge.

RANGER PEAK (11,355)

Map: Ranger Peak
This peak, which according to the topographers is the same elevation as Doane Peak, takes its name from the members of the first-ascent party, all of whom were park rangers at the time. The climbing history of this peak is murky, but the following chronology seems to be the most likely reconstruction of the original routes. By far the best approach for this peak is by boat across Jackson Lake from the Colter Bay area. Because it is capped by sedimentary rocks, Ranger Peak holds little interest for the technical climber, but the unspoiled region about it should attract the wilderness seeker. Worth quoting here is this striking phrase from the book *Mountaineering in the Tetons: The Pioneer Period 1898–1940,* by Fritiof Fryxell and Phil D. Smith, describing their first ascent:

> Our day seems memorable in retrospect chiefly by reason of the thrilling new country it revealed, a type of beauty in mountains and waterfalls very different from that of the severe alpine region to the south. It is the great matterhorn peaks that give distinction to the Teton Range, but one's appreciation of the major summits is broadened by acquaintance with the surrounding mountains from which they spring. Ventures afield, to outlying summits like Ranger Peak, never fail to make for new and richer understanding of these incomparable mountains.

CHRONOLOGY

Northeast Ridge: July 29, 1935, Fritiof Fryxell, Phil Smith, Allyn Hanks

South Ridge: July 29, 1935, Fritiof Fryxell, Phil Smith, Allyn Hanks (descent); August 26, 1955, Roald and Redwood Fryxell, Bob Perkins (ascent)

West Ridge: 1938 or 1939, Rudolph Edmund, or August 13, 1941, Fritiof Fryxell, Leland Horberg, Joe Hoare, Bob Crist

East Slope: August 26, 1955, Roald and Redwood Fryxell, Bob Perkins (descent); July 30, 1976, Ed Wilson, Elaine Gross (ascent)

Southeast Ridge: July 22, 1956, Frank Ewing, Cecile Hilding (partial); July 25, 1962, John C. Reed, Jr., T. B. Ranson, J. H. Dieterich (descent); September 9, 1976, Leigh Ortenburger, Patty McDonald (complete ascent)

ROUTE 1. West Ridge. I, 1.0. First ascent either in 1938 or 1939 by Rudolph Edmund, or on August 13, 1941, by

Fritiof Fryxell, Leland Horberg, Joe Hoare, and Bob Crist. This is an easy slope and a natural route from the upper part of the north fork of Waterfalls Canyon.

ROUTE 2. *South Ridge.* I, 2.0. First descent July 29, 1935, by Fritiof Fryxell, Phil Smith, and Allyn Hanks; first ascent August 26, 1955, by Roald and Redwood Fryxell and Bob Perkins. Follow a semi-trail in Waterfalls Canyon from Jackson Lake up past Wilderness Falls to the scenic lake (9,615) in the north fork of the canyon. The south ridge starts at the east shore of this lake and leads directly to the summit.

ROUTE 3. *Southeast Ridge.* I, 2.0. First ascent (partial) July 22, 1956, by Frank Ewing and Cecile Hilding; first descent July 25, 1962, John C. Reed, Jr., T. B. Ranson, and J. H. Dieterich; first complete ascent September 9, 1976, by Leigh Ortenburger and Patty McDonald. The easy southeast ridge begins at the 10,240+-foot saddle separating Peak 10,716 from the main Ranger Peak and joins the south ridge at the high south shoulder (11,000). This saddle is most enjoyably reached from the shore of Jackson Lake through the untrammeled Quartzite Canyon due east of Ranger Peak. It could also be attained from the vicinity of Columbine Cascade in Waterfalls Canyon, and it has also been reached more directly by traversing over the top of Peak 10,716 from the east.

ROUTE 4. *East Slope.* I, 2.0. First descent August 26, 1955, by Roald and Redwood Fryxell and Bob Perkins; first ascent July 30, 1976, by Ed Wilson and Elaine Gross. This route starts from Jackson Lake and enters Quartzite Canyon immediately east of Ranger Peak. This canyon has seldom been entered and contains a succession of small lakes; from the highest lake, one can climb directly to the summit or, by veering north or south, one can reach the northeast or southeast ridge and follow it to the summit.

ROUTE 5. *Northeast Ridge.* I, 2.0. First ascent July 29, 1935, by Fritiof Fryxell, Phil Smith, and Allyn Hanks. The first-ascent party gained the beginning of this ridge by first climbing over the top of Peak 10,732 and descending to the 10,560+-foot saddle. The easy crest of the ridge was then followed without difficulty to the summit. Of considerable interest is the high saddle (11,120+) just east of the summit, formed by weathering and erosion of the shattered rock of the Forellen Peak fault.

PEAK 10,716   *(0.85 mi ESE of Ranger Peak)*

Map: Colter Bay

This high point, the westerly of the two peaks on the southeast ridge of Ranger Peak, is normally approached only in the course of an ascent of that peak.

East Ridge: July 22, 1956, Frank Ewing, Cecile Hilding
West Ridge: July 25, 1962, John C. Reed, Jr., T. B. Ranson, J. H. Dieterich

ROUTE 1. *West Ridge.* I, 2.0. First ascent July 25, 1962, by John C. Reed, Jr., T. B. Ranson, and J. H. Dieterich. This ridge was first climbed via a descent of the southeast ridge of Ranger Peak.

ROUTE 2. *East Ridge.* I, 2.0. First ascent July 22, 1956, by Frank Ewing and Cecile Hilding. This ridge was reached via a traverse from Peak 10,686 toward the summit of Ranger Peak.

PEAK 10,686   *(1.2 mi ESE of Ranger Peak)*

Map: Colter Bay

While it is perhaps unimportant in itself, this peak does form the beginning of the long southeast ridge of Ranger Peak, whose traverse makes a pleasant day on easy ground.

ROUTE 1. *West Ridge.* I, 1.0. First descent July 22, 1956, by Frank Ewing and Cecile Hilding. There are no difficulties on the 500-foot descent to the saddle west of this peak.

ROUTE 2. *East Ridge.* I, 1.0. First ascent July 22, 1956, by Frank Ewing and Cecile Hilding. From Jackson Lake this ridge is a long 4,000-foot ascent with no difficulties. The lowest section above the shores of the lake shows the traces of the fire that burned from July to November in 1974.

PEAK 10,732   *(1.0 mi NE of Ranger Peak)*

Map: Colter Bay

On the ridge separating Quartzite Canyon on the south from Colter Canyon on the north, Peak 10,732 is the high point. Surprisingly in this northern region of easy sedimentary peaks there is a sequence of towers on the east ridge of Peak 10,732 that offer some technical difficulty. These towers were first climbed directly on the ridge crest, from west to east, on September 9, 1976, by Leigh Ortenburger and Patty McDonald; a rappel was used to descend the last of these towers.

ROUTE 1. *West Ridge.* I, 2.0. First descent July 29, 1935, by Fritiof Fryxell, Phil Smith, and Allyn Hanks; first ascent July 26, 1962, by John C. Reed, Jr., and J. H. Dieterich. From the saddle west of the peak, the ridge leads easily to the summit.

ROUTE 2. *East Ridge.* I, 2.0. First ascent July 29, 1935, by Fritiof Fryxell, Phil Smith, and Allyn Hanks. From Jackson Lake ascend into Quartzite Canyon following the slope just north of the stream until past (west of) the pinnacled section of the ridge. Turn north to the ridge crest just east of the first lake in the canyon. Scramble west to the summit.

MOUNT ROBIE (10,881) *(1.5 mi N of Ranger Peak)*

Map: Ranger Peak

This peak stands at the north end of the massif separating Moose Basin in Webb Canyon from Jackson Lake. It is probably most easily reached from Webb Canyon directly from the west, but this has perhaps not yet been done. Point 10,515, 0.5 mile to the east, was first climbed on August 23, 1953, by Roald Fryxell and Charles McCary from Webb Canyon. An attempted ascent on September 7, 1958, by Frank Ewing and Keith Jones via the long ridge from Webb Canyon leading toward Point 10,298 was stalled by too much loose rock and too many kinds of ripe berries along the way. The line of the Forellen Peak fault coincides with the drainage just west of Mount Robie from the saddle (10,480+) on the south ridge at the head of Colter Canyon all the way down to Moose Creek.

ROUTE 1. South Ridge. I, 2.0. First descent June 23, 1957, by Leigh and Irene Ortenburger. No difficulties were encountered in traversing this ridge to Peak 10,238 and beyond. It could undoubtedly be attained either from Colter Canyon or Webb Canyon.

ROUTE 2. East Ridge. I, 3.0. First known ascent June 23, 1957, by Leigh and Irene Ortenburger, who found on the summit a cairn but no record. From Jackson Lake ascend the entire east ridge directly over the top of Point 10,515. The summit is guarded by a sharp sedimentary tower (10,800+) immediately to the east. With rope and protection gear this tower could probably be climbed from the east. The first-ascent party, lacking proper equipment, contoured around the tower on the south (this involved a short rappel) in order to reach the notch that separates the tower from the flat summit area. The tower was climbed by a chute containing loose rock. The main summit is very easily reached from the notch. See *American Alpine Journal,* 11, no. 1 (1958), pp. 85–88.

NORTHERN TETON PEAKS FROM THE SUMMIT OF MOUNT MORAN

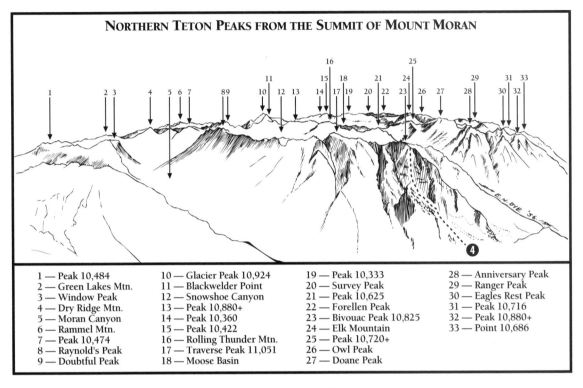

1 — Peak 10,484	10 — Glacier Peak 10,924	19 — Peak 10,333	28 — Anniversary Peak
2 — Green Lakes Mtn.	11 — Blackwelder Point	20 — Survey Peak	29 — Ranger Peak
3 — Window Peak	12 — Snowshoe Canyon	21 — Peak 10,625	30 — Eagles Rest Peak
4 — Dry Ridge Mtn.	13 — Peak 10,880+	22 — Forellen Peak	31 — Peak 10,716
5 — Moran Canyon	14 — Peak 10,360	23 — Bivouac Peak 10,825	32 — Peak 10,880+
6 — Rammel Mtn.	15 — Peak 10,422	24 — Elk Mountain	33 — Point 10,686
7 — Peak 10,474	16 — Rolling Thunder Mtn.	25 — Peak 10,720+	
8 — Raynold's Peak	17 — Traverse Peak 11,051	26 — Owl Peak	
9 — Doubtful Peak	18 — Moose Basin	27 — Doane Peak	

North of Webb Canyon

GLACIER PEAK (10,927)
(2 mi NW of Rolling Thunder Mountain)

Map: Ranger Peak
As the highest peak on the divide north of Table Mountain between Teton Basin and Jackson Hole, Glacier Peak is an outstanding viewpoint for the entire north end of the Teton Range. It was named "Glacier Station" in 1931 by Earl Buckingham, who occupied it as a triangulation point. Although the summit is graced by a large cairn, Buckingham placed the bench mark, which is not easily found, some 200 feet to the north. Just east of the summit at the extreme southwest head of Webb Canyon is the substantial glacier that gives rise to the name of the peak. A lake has formed at the snout of this glacier from either insufficient winter snow accumulation or general climatic warming in the past century, or both. This high peak was known to, but probably not climbed by, the various hunting parties in Moose Basin in the 1890s. Because it is on the northern section of the divide, Glacier Peak is a good ex-

ample of those peaks that are perhaps most easily approached from the west. From Teton Basin the closest approach appears to be from the USFS trailhead on the north side of Badger Creek. A trail then heads east up South Badger Creek with one branch turning north over Deadhorse Pass and dropping down into the head of South Bitch Creek at a point 1.1 miles west of Glacier Peak.
ROUTE 1. North Ridge. I, 2.0. First ascent September 9, 1931, by Earl M. Buckingham. This gentle ridge begins at the 9,600+-foot saddle and lake, which provides a good camping site, but it can be attained considerably higher from either side. Some scrambling is involved because the ridge consists of large blocks, but it is not difficult.

PEAK 10,010 *(1.8 mi NW of Rolling Thunder Mountain)*

Map: Ranger Peak
ROUTE 1. East Slope. I, 1.0. First known ascent August 4, 1963, by Dennis Wilson. This peak, perhaps the least important of the Teton peaks, was easily reached from the

small lake at 9,720+ feet. Some evidence of previous ascent was found.

PEAK 9,970   (0.6 mi SSE of Moose Mountain)

Map: Ranger Peak

This is the broad rounded knoll on the divide between Glacier Peak and Moose Mountain.

CHRONOLOGY

North Slope: [probable] August 1935, T. F. Murphy, Mike Yokel, Jr., or July 31, 1963, Loring Woodman

South Ridge: August 4, 1963, Leigh and Irene Ortenburger, Julie Peterson, Dennis Wilson

ROUTE 1. South Ridge. I, 2.0. First descent August 4, 1963, by Leigh and Irene Ortenburger, Julie Peterson, and Dennis Wilson. A sedimentary cliff band on this ridge can be bypassed by a couloir on the west side.

ROUTE 2. North Slope. I, 1.0. Probable first ascent August 1935, by T. F. Murphy and Mike Yokel, Jr. First known ascent July 31, 1963, by Loring Woodman, who found a cairn but no record on the flat, tree-covered summit.

MOOSE MOUNTAIN (10,054)

Map: Ranger Peak

About 0.3 mile to the north on the north ridge of this very easy peak are some interesting sedimentary pinnacles that rise 60 feet or more from their surroundings. Moose Mountain is easily approached from the USFS trail at Nord Pass, only 0.5 mile to the northwest.

CHRONOLOGY

North Slope: [probable] August 1935, T. F. Murphy, Mike Yokel, Jr.; [certain] July 31, 1963, Loring Woodman

South Slope: July 31, 1963, Loring Woodman (descent)

ROUTE 1. South Slope. I, 2.0. First known descent July 31, 1963, by Loring Woodman.

ROUTE 2. North Slope. I, 1.0. Probable first ascent August 1935, by T. F. Murphy and Mike Yokel, Jr.; first known ascent July 31, 1963, by Loring Woodman, who also first climbed the pinnacles to the north.

PEAK 10,360   (0.85 mi N of Moose Mountain)

Map: Ranger Peak

Lying on the main divide between Jackson Hole and Teton Basin, this peak forms a portion of the western boundary of Moose Basin.

ROUTE 1. South Ridge. I, 3.0. Probable first ascent August 1935, by T. F. Murphy and Mike Yokel, Jr.; first known ascent July 31, 1963, by Loring Woodman. This ridge can be gained from the west as done in 1963 or it can be easily reached from the Moose Basin Divide between Webb and Owl Canyons. However, if one starts at the saddle north of Moose Mountain, a cliff band will be encountered that can be passed on the east with a short exposed traverse on semistable rock.

PEAK 10,422   (1.3 mi N of Moose Mountain)

Map: Ranger Peak

This is one of the more challenging of the sedimentary peaks because it is ringed, almost without break, by a prominent cliff band.

ROUTE 1. East Ridge. I, 2.0. First ascent August 4, 1963, by Leigh and Irene Ortenburger and Dennis Wilson. The Moose Basin Divide, the important saddle just east of this peak, is easily reached by trail either from Owl Creek or from Webb Canyon. From this saddle, pass to the north (right) of the first buttress, which prevents a direct ascent of the east ridge. Gain the col behind this eastern buttress, and follow the rest of the ridge to the summit. The eastern buttress involves short sections of 3.0 climbing on its western side.

PEAK 10,333   (1.75 mi WSW of Elk Mountain)

Map: Ranger Peak

From the Moose Basin Divide an unbroken cliff band will be seen guarding this peak on the northwest and southwest. It should prove possible to climb past this obstacle (probably loose) at the nose where these two faces meet and then traverse the long ridge east to the summit.

ROUTE 1. East Ridge. I, 2.0. First ascent August 3, 1963, by Leigh and Irene Ortenburger, Julie Peterson, and Dennis Wilson. After ascending Elk Mountain (10,720+), descent was made along its south ridge and then west over Peak 9,924. At this point the east ridge was gained and followed without difficulty to the summit.

ROUTE 2. North Ridge. I, 3.0. First descent August 3, 1963, by Leigh and Irene Ortenburger, Julie Peterson, and Dennis Wilson. From Owl Canyon this ridge can be attained by following the trail to about the 9,000-foot level and then cutting east up one of the few breaks near the north end of the cliff band that protects this peak on the northwest. Once the plateau at about 9,300 feet is reached, no further problems will be met.

PEAK 9,924   (0.9 mi SW of Elk Mountain)

Map: Ranger Peak

This minor peak lies on the ridge connecting Elk Mountain and Moose Basin Divide.

ROUTE 1. *West Ridge.* I, 1.0. First descent August 3, 1963, by Leigh and Irene Ortenburger, Julie Peterson, and Dennis Wilson. This tree-covered bump is easily climbed from any direction.

ROUTE 2. *East Ridge.* I, 1.0. First ascent August 3, 1963, by Leigh and Irene Ortenburger, Julie Peterson, and Dennis Wilson.

ELK MOUNTAIN (10,720+)

Map: Ranger Peak

Of all the sedimentary peaks north of Webb Canyon, this is the highest and dominates the north end of the Teton Range. Protected on most sides by interminable sedimentary talus and scree slopes, Elk Mountain rises over 3,000 feet from either Owl Canyon to the north or Webb Canyon to the south. On August 23, 1955, the "Buster Point" triangulation station was established by Kenneth S. McLean on the summit. In 1963 the pole signal in the summit cairn was found, still held in place by the surveyors' wires. Elk Mountain actually has two distinct summits separated by a 0.3-mile ridge. When one is standing on the north summit, it seems to be several feet higher than the more easily reached south summit; the older USGS map indicated that the south summit was at least 8 feet higher. To be assured of success the cautious mountaineer was obliged to climb both. The major and readily visible Forellen Peak fault runs through the high saddle just to the east that separates Elk Mountain from Owl Peak.

CHRONOLOGY

Southeast Ridge: [probable] August 23, 1955, Kenneth McLean

Southwest Ridge: August 3, 1963, Leigh and Irene Ortenburger, Julie Peterson, Dennis Wilson

ROUTE 1. *Southwest Ridge.* I, 3.0. First ascent August 3, 1963, by Leigh and Irene Ortenburger, Julie Peterson, and Dennis Wilson. This route begins at the saddle (9,680+) in the Owl–Webb divide just west and south of Elk Mountain. This saddle can be reached from either north or south, using the Webb Canyon trail or the Owl Creek trail. Either way about 2,000 feet of uphill scrambling will be involved. The south end of this ridge is easily attained from the saddle. The upper, more or less horizontal, section of the ridge that leads to the south summit (10,720+) involves some scrambling, either on the crest or very slightly to the right (east) of the crest. This section is very sharp and exposed and contains some equally sharp, although small, notches. The traverse from the south summit to the north summit (perhaps higher) does not share these problems.

ROUTE 2. *Southeast Ridge.* I, 2.0. Probable first ascent August 23, 1955, by Kenneth S. McLean. This ridge leads directly up to the south summit of Elk Mountain from the

saddle that separates Elk Mountain and Owl Peak. The saddle is most easily reached from the south from Webb Canyon. The southern approach requires some adroit routefinding to avoid the sedimentary cliff bands that sweep in from the west. During most of the summer the direct northern approach from lower Berry Creek is complicated by the presence of a snow slope; an ice axe may be desirable. The ridge itself is loose and there is rather steep talus from the saddle to the south summit. From the south summit to the north summit (perhaps higher) is a pleasant ten-minute ridge walk.

OWL PEAK (10,612)

Map: Ranger Peak

The 1898 quadrangle map indicates that the Bannon topographic party placed a bench mark on this summit, although it appears that not always when the letters "BM" appear on a USGS map does this imply that the summit was actually reached and a bronze marker placed. Earl M. Buckingham named this peak "Owl Station" in the course of his triangulation work in 1931, but he did not occupy this site. T. F. Murphy may have been the first surveyor to visit the summit. The major Forellen Peak fault cuts through the saddle separating this peak from Elk Mountain. The dark crystalline rocks of this peak contrast strikingly with the lighter sedimentary rocks of Elk Mountain. Surveyors' paraphernalia, dating from the 1955 visit by Kenneth McLean, will be found on the summit.

CHRONOLOGY

South Slope, West Ridge: [probable] August 1935, T. F. Murphy, Mike Yokel, Jr.

North-Northeast Ridge: August 22, 1955, Kenneth McLean

East Ridge: July 8, 1963, John C. Reed, Jr., J. H. Dieterich

ROUTE 1. *South Slope, West Ridge.* I, 2.0. Probable first ascent in August 1935, by T. F. Murphy and Mike Yokel, Jr. If the main couloir, leading from Webb Canyon to the col west of the summit, is used, some routefinding will be required to avoid the sedimentary cliff bands that approach the couloir from the west. From the col, easy scrambling up the dark rocks of the moderately sharp west ridge takes one to the summit.

ROUTE 2. *East Ridge.* I, 2.0. First ascent July 8, 1963, by John C. Reed, Jr., and J. H. Dieterich. From Webb Canyon climb a large southern couloir to gain the east ridge about 0.5 mile east of the summit; the east ridge is then easily followed to the summit. The correct couloir can be identified as the one starting at the word "Webb" of "Webb Canyon Trail" on the Ranger Peak quadrangle map.

ROUTE 3. *North-Northeast Ridge.* I, 1.0. First known ascent August 22, 1955, by Kenneth McLean. Although most of the possible eastern approaches to this peak are far more straightforward, the following tedious route has actually been climbed. From the patrol cabin near Jackson Lake hike up the Berry Creek trail to approximately 0.5 mile below the junction of Berry Creek and Owl Creek. Cross to the south side of Berry Creek and ascend the long timbered ridge in a southwest direction to the bare, rocky, rounded summit of dark-colored rock. This creek-crossing point on lower Berry Creek can be reached via the trail directly from Jackson Lake (if one takes a boat or canoe across the lake) or via the connecting trail between upper Berry Creek and Owl Creek (if one hikes in from the trailhead on the Grassy Lake road around the north end of the range).

PEAK 8,602   (3.25 mi ENE of Owl Peak)

Map: Colter Bay

This tree-covered high point on the extreme end of the east ridge of Owl Peak separates the lower reaches of Berry Creek from Moose Creek. A north–south fault lies just east of the summit, aligned with the open couloir that descends toward Webb Canyon. No information is available regarding ascents. I, 1.0.

WEBB CANYON, NORTH SIDE ROCK CLIMBS (8,080+)

Map: Ranger Peak

ROUTE 1. All in a Day's Work. II, 5.9. First ascent August 20, 1984, by Todd Swain and Ralph Moore. On the north side of Webb Canyon, about 3.5 miles west along the trail from the patrol cabin at the mouth of Berry Creek, is the Webb Wall of crystalline rock. This route of seven pitches ascends this wall, passing trees and a midway terrace to a single tree marking the top of the climb. The location of this wall seems to be in the vicinity of the "C" of Moose Creek on either the Ranger Peak quadrangle or Grand Teton National Park maps. From the trail scramble up a talus slope and grassy ledges to a dead tree on the middle west part of the cliff where the route begins. The first pitch (150 feet) starts at the tree and goes straight up slabs (70 feet) to and up a small left-facing corner (5.4) to broken ledges; then traverse 20 feet right to the belay in a large left-facing corner. Next, climb the broken corner (5.2) left of the obvious buttress until one can traverse left and up toward three trees; belay at the highest tree just below two dihedrals. The third lead ascends either of the two dihedrals (right is better, 5.6) straight up to another tree belay at the end of 80 feet. Then climb the corner above the tree and take an obvious hand crack (5.7) out to the steep wall on the right to the belay on the midway terrace above. Move the belay about 100 feet out to the right to a point just uphill of an obvious right-facing corner. The next crux pitch starts about 30 feet left of the yellow left-facing corner and moves up a steep face to the right to a small left-facing corner. After placing high protection, downclimb and traverse right to an obvious crack system that leads to a chute. Climb the wall (5.9) to a beautiful 2-inch crack and then climb the crack (5.9) to the belay about 30 feet farther up on the left. The final lead goes easily up and left to a tree that marks the end of this route. For the descent make one 150-foot rappel from the tree down to the midway terrace, which is followed out and to the right (east) to regain the trail below.

PEAK 7,185T   (1.6 mi SE of Elk Ridge)

Map: Flagg Ranch (prov.)

Rising only about 300 feet above the mouth of Berry Creek, this small forested hill has, reasonably enough, not yet attracted the attention of climbers. No information is available regarding ascents. I, 1.0.

ELK RIDGE (8,451T)

Map: Survey Peak (prov.)

Elk Ridge is a relatively large, rounded formation separated from Owl Peak on the south by Owl Creek, from Forellen Peak on the west by the modern Berry Creek and from Peak 9,047 on the north by the ancient abandoned Berry Creek channel. It is awkwardly located at the intersection of four modern quadrangle sheets—Ranger Peak, Colter Bay, Flagg Ranch (prov.), and Survey Peak (prov.)—with the summit found on the last-mentioned map. This wooded ridge was apparently first climbed by the geologists Joseph P. Iddings and Walter H. Weed in late August or early September 1886 during the course of their pioneering work on the geology of the old Shoshone quadrangle; they provide a description of the summit rocks in their monograph. Except for the somewhat precipitous west side, Elk Ridge does not present difficulties for the prospective climber. I, 1.0.

FORELLEN PEAK (9,772)

Map: Survey Peak (prov.)

The first ascent was almost certainly made by Joseph P. Iddings and Walter H. Weed on September 4, 1886, while studying the geology of the old Shoshone quadrangle whose southern edge was 44° north latitude. The unusual name, the German word for "trout," was almost surely given by these geologists, because this peak was known as Forellen Peak at least as early as 1889. T. F. Murphy and Mike Yokel, Jr., in their topographic work in 1935, also very likely climbed the peak. Rudolph Edmund climbed the peak on August 11, 1938, and again in August of 1939 during fieldwork for his geological thesis. Before the expansion of the national park in 1950 to include the northern end of the Teton Range, Forellen Peak was within the Teton National Forest and for at least a few years in the 1940s was used as a fire lookout station. Dave Adams, who spent three summers on the summit during this period, was able to report by telephone to Moran. Until the middle of August, the southwest slope of this peak is covered with beautiful alpine flowers. A field identification guide is most useful when trying to decipher the many varieties.

ROUTE 1. Southwest Slope. I, 1.0. First ascent September 4, 1886, by Joseph P. Iddings and Walter H. Weed. The approach to the Berry–Owl divide (8,840+) west of Forellen Peak is best made using the trail from Berry Creek. South of the divide in Owl Creek the trail soon becomes difficult or impossible to follow although one can hike cross-country up from the main Owl Creek trail. As the Grassy Lake Reservoir quadrangle map shows, there was something of a trail that leads from the saddle to the summit and down the east ridge to Berry Creek; hence, there is no difficulty in climbing this route. This trail is no longer shown on the more recent Survey Peak (prov.) quadrangle map. The major north–south Forellen Peak fault crosses the line of ascent at about the 9,100-foot level.

ROUTE 2. East Ridge. I, 1.0. First ascent unknown, perhaps in 1935 by T. F. Murphy and Mike Yokel, Jr. The Grassy Lake Reservoir quadrangle indicated that the lower reaches of the Forellen Peak trail started at the base of this ridge, at the point where Berry Creek turns south to join Owl Creek. As an ascent route, this trail cannot be found. However, as a route of descent, the trail can be followed from the summit down to about 7,800 feet. The lower 400 feet of the ridge must be negotiated by bushwhacking through the timber. Just above the tiny lake at 8,364 feet a north–south fault crosses this trail.

RED MOUNTAIN (10,205 AND 10,177)

Map: Ranger Peak

Easily approached from the west and providing a good view of the region, this peak has long been a favorite of geologists. It is identifiable as "Station XXXII," established by Orestes St. John in 1877. The first-ascent party undoubtedly included others from the "Teton Section" of the Hayden Survey, specifically Gustavus R. Bechler, who, with Fred A. Clark, produced the first topographic (with contour lines) map of the Teton Range in 1878. The 19-year-old Stephen J. Kubel, who later figured in the controversy over the first ascent of the Grand Teton, was also probably on the ascent, as he served as one of Bechler's assistants in that summer of 1877. On September 3, 1886, Joseph Paxson Iddings and Walter Harvey Weed, in the course of their geological explorations of the old Shoshone quadrangle, reached the summit on horseback from Berry Creek. On August 14, 1912, the geologist Eliot Blackwelder and his assistant, Mack Lake, made the ascent by gaining the north ridge from the west. His description of the summit is worth repeating:

" . . . flat grassy top strewn with beautifully rounded cobbles of yellow quartzite, a most surprising occurrence on top of a high peak." It is a large bulky mountain with two summits connected by a 0.6-mile summit ridge.

The original name, Crimson Peak, was given by Iddings and Weed after the red color of the Late Mississippian shales that cap most of the peak and are interbedded with more resistant limestones. Unfortunately this splendid name has, over the years, been bowdlerized, largely by the U.S. Forest Service, into the prosaic "Red Mountain."

CHRONOLOGY

North Ridge: August 1, 1877, Orestes St. John, and [probable] Gustavus Bechler, Stephen Kubel
Southeast Slope: [probable] summer 1935, T. F. Murphy, Mike Yokel, Jr.

ROUTE 1. Southeast Slope. I, 1.0. Probable first ascent in 1935, by T. F. Murphy and Mike Yokel, Jr. The higher summit is easily and directly climbed via this slope from the Owl Creek trail.

ROUTE 2. North Ridge. I, 1.0. First ascent August 1, 1877, by Orestes St. John and probably Gustavus Bechler and Stephen Kubel. This very long ridge forms the divide between Berry Creek on the east and North Bitch Creek (and its tributaries) on the west. It starts from the pass (8,720+) marked on the current USGS and USFS maps as Conant Pass. This name, however, is very likely incorrectly placed, as the historic Conant Pass almost surely refers to the lower pass (8,440+) just southwest of Survey Peak. The exact route taken in 1877 is unknown and might have been some combination of the west and north ridges. The geologist Eliot Blackwelder in 1912 apparently reached only the northwest end of this summit ridge (10,177). The traverse between the two summits is a pleasant stroll.

PEAK 8,688T   *(1.65 mi SW of Survey Peak)*

Map: Survey Peak (prov.)

A small high point on the divide between Conant Pass and Jackass Pass, there is no record of ascents, but its easy summit was probably reached during the fur-trapper era prior to 1850. I, 1.0.

SURVEY PEAK (9,277)

Map: Survey Peak (prov.)

This easy, round-topped sedimentary peak may have been climbed in 1877 by the topographic unit of the Hayden Survey under Gustavus R. Bechler, but there appears to be no record of it. The origin of the name is not known, but this era of surveying and exploration seems to be a reasonable explanation. The geologists Joseph P. Iddings and Walter H.

Weed did apparently reach the summit on August 31, 1886, during the course of their work on the geology of the Shoshone quadrangle; it was already known to them by the name Survey Peak. When Earl M. Buckingham established a triangulation station on its summit on September 11, 1931, there was a wagon road from the west that crossed the divide at the southern foot of the peak and led to an old mine at the head of Berry Creek. Dave Adams built a cabin (1.0 mile east of the summit) and the trail between it and the summit when he served for four or five years (about 1939) as a fire lookout in this area for the U.S. Forest Service.

One can approach this peak from the west via the Grassy Lake road, which leads around the north end of the range between Grand Teton National Park and Yellowstone National Park and connects Jackson Hole with Teton Basin in Idaho. Before reaching Squirrel Meadows, a side road leads south to two trailheads, one at South Boone Creek and the other near the head of Jackass Creek. Either could be used for the hike into Survey Peak. To approach this part of the range from the east, the Berry Creek trail can be followed from the shore of Jackson Lake. The low pass (8,440+) just southwest of Survey Peak has the misnomer "Jackass Pass" marked on the current USGS and USFS maps. The correct name for this pass is almost surely Conant Pass, the historic pass of the fur trappers of the early 19th century.

ROUTE 1. Southwest Slope. I, 1.0. First ascent probably in 1877, by Gustavus Bechler and party. From Jackass Pass (8,440+) where the trail crosses the divide, this slope is an easy hike to the summit, where a quantity of surveyors' paraphernalia will be found.

ROUTE 2. Northeast Slope. I, 1.0. First ascent unknown, perhaps in 1886 by Joseph Iddings and Walter Weed. The old trail constructed on this slope served to ease Dave Adams' daily trip to the summit from the cabin he built at 8,400 feet about 1.0 mile east of the summit. This cabin, shown on the map as a patrol cabin, has now been completely eliminated by the National Park Service.

PEAK 8,803T   *(1.7 mi NE of Survey Peak)*

Map: Grassy Lake Reservoir
This heavily forested hill forms the north wall above upper Berry Creek immediately east of Survey Peak. No information is available regarding ascents, although it may have been visited by the geologists Joseph Iddings and Walter Weed in 1886. I, 1.0.

PEAK 8,582T   *(2.2 mi NE of Survey Peak)*

Map: Grassy Lake Reservoir
Near the extreme north boundary of Grand Teton National Park, this minor wooded peak is unknown to climbers. Con-siderable bushwhacking would be required to reach its flat summit. No information is available regarding ascents. I, 1.0.

MOUNT BERRY (8,971T)

Map: Survey Peak (prov.)
The original Grand Teton National Park map (1948) showed the summit of this tree-covered high point as outside the park boundary, but the more recent maps, Grassy Lake Reservoir (1956) and Survey Peak (1989 prov.), show the summit as 300 feet inside the park and with a different elevation. It appears that Earl M. Buckingham or some member of his triangulation party must have occupied this peak in 1931 because the records of the U.S. Geological Survey in Washington, D.C., mention a "pole and cloth signal" and "standard tablet reference, Berry 1931" as being on the summit.

ROUTE 1. South Ridge. I, 1.0. First ascent mid-September 1931, by members of the triangulation party of Earl M. Buckingham. This ridge is easily approached from the Berry Creek trail via the branch trail leading to Hechtman Lake, which is perched 400 feet above the swamps of Berry Creek Canyon. This route was also used by Leland Horberg and Bob Crist on August 5, 1941, during a reconnaissance trip for the Geological Society of America. Note that this trail is not shown on the most recent map, Survey Peak (1989 prov.).

ROUTE 2. North Ridge. I, 1.0. First descent August 5, 1941, by Leland Horberg and Robert Crist. This gentle but almost unknown ridge appears to consist of seemingly endless pine forest, extending for 5.0 miles to the Grassy Lake Reservoir road.

DAVE ADAMS HILL (9,047)

Map: Survey Peak (prov.)
As the highest point north of Berry Creek, this peak is well situated as a fire lookout station and may have been used for that purpose in the decades from 1930 to 1950. It forms the north wall of Berry Creek with clear views to the west up the canyon and south into the lower Owl Creek drainage. It is an easy, tree-covered summit. No information is available regarding ascents. I, 1.0.

HAREM HILL (7,330)

Map: Flagg Ranch (prov.)
The first ascent of this low wooded hill rising directly from the west shore of the northernmost part of Jackson Lake was apparently made in late August or early September 1886, by the geologists Joseph P. Iddings and Walter H. Weed, because they give a description of the summit rocks in their geological monograph. The name presumably derives from elk, not man. I, 1.0.

Rick Wyatt on the Run-Don't-Walk Couloir on Mount Owen in winter (Photo: David Jenkins)

Winter Climbing in the Teton Range

The Teton Range has long provided American mountaineers a convenient arena in which the skills and experience necessary for challenging ascents in the great mountain ranges of the world can be developed. But it is during the winter months, when these peaks appear so magnificently remote, that this opportunity is greatly expanded. Surprisingly, little winter mountaineering had been done here until recent years, considering the accessibility of the major peaks from the valley. Some climbers have doubtless been constrained by their distance from the rather isolated Tetons, and many do not have sufficient free time in the winter season for travel. The difficulty of hitting the weather and snow conditions just right also has been, and still is, an important contributing factor. Yet the Tetons offer one of the finest areas in the country for difficult winter ascents, both in major mountaineering routes and in frozen waterfall ice climbing. Because winter conditions in the Tetons have a deservedly harsh reputation, all but the most tenacious individuals may be deterred. Traditionally, the winter season has been defined as the period between December 20 or 21 (winter solstice) and March 20 or 21 (vernal equinox). However, conditions commonly referred to as *winter*, which require some means of over-snow transport for the approach portion of the climb (skis and, less commonly, snowshoes), may occur as soon as early November and extend until late April.

History of Winter Climbing

Through the centuries the severity of the Wyoming winter, the manifest difficulty of the enterprise, and the simple challenge of winter living in Jackson Hole kept the Teton peaks unmolested in the winter season. This changed in the 1930s, when enterprising rangers from the newly formed Grand Teton National Park initiated the winter exploration of the range. This generalization does neglect the probable prowling about the canyon entrances in near-winter conditions by the fur trappers in the 19th century. But the practical trappers had neither motivation nor time to explore the "useless" upper portions of the Teton Range.

To provide protection of game animals from winter poaching, the staff of the new national park instituted a policy of winter snowshoe patrols along the base of the range in Jackson Hole. This justification for winter trips was then extended to provide an excuse for winter exploration of the high country; illegal hunters might well be coming into the heads of the canyons from the west. The first reported winter trip (almost surely on snowshoes) into the high country apparently was made in 1933 by NPS rangers Allyn Hanks and Dudley Hayden, but no details are available. Such vigorous activity was not unnatural for the early NPS men, who commonly were skilled outdoorsmen.

The pioneering first winter ascent of the Grand Teton was made by Paul and Eldon Petzoldt and Fred Brown on December 17, 1935. They skied to the caves in Garnet Canyon the first day and then spent two days relaying loads to the Lower Saddle, from which they climbed via the Owen–Spalding route. It was a near-perfect day with a large temperature inversion, permitting shirtsleeves on the summit while it was -20° in Jackson. On March 5, 1949, Paul Petzoldt and John and Ted Lewis repeated this climb. This time they camped at the Platforms the first night and reached the Lower Saddle the second night. The third successful winter expedition (again on skis) was that of Leigh Ortenburger, William Dunmire, Richard Long, and Norman Goldstein, who on February 4, 1952, climbed the Middle Teton by the Southwest Couloir in a blizzard. The remainder of the 1950s saw very little winter activity in the Tetons. Two attempts on the Grand Teton were made, but neither came close to the summit or even to the Lower Saddle. However, success in these early years was gained on two lesser peaks at the extremes of the range, Survey Peak and Rendezvous Peak, by Frank Ewing and by Keith Jones and Rod Newcomb, respectively.

Extended ski traverses in the range were initiated early in the climbing history of the park, partly because of the influence of the Dartmouth mountaineers and skiers in the mid-1930s. The route of the first such traverse started from the old park headquarters at Beaver Creek, up Cascade Canyon, across Alaska Basin, down Granite Canyon, and then back to the starting point; it was carried out on skis from February 15 to 19, 1938, by Fred Brown of Dartmouth with NPS rangers Allyn Hanks and Howard Stagner. Food and equipment caches had been placed in the fall of 1937 at the forks of Cascade Canyon, Alaska Basin, and Marion Lake. The first known ski traverse of the crest of the range was done as a spring trip, from May 13 to 19, 1979, when

Jeff Crabtree, Owen Anderson, and Greg Lawley started from Teton Pass, stayed close to the divide, and exited Berry Creek Canyon to Huckleberry Hot Springs. This major undertaking has been repeated in both directions. As a solo winter trip, in late December 1985 Pete Koedt made the south–north traverse in five days, entering at Phillips Canyon and emerging at Berry Creek. The trip was repeated in the reverse direction, from April 2 to 6, 1987, by George Lowe, Rich Henke, and Tom Dickey, who started from Flagg Ranch, entered the range at Owl Creek, stayed close to the divide, and exited via Phillips Canyon to the Teton Pass road.

The recent era of winter mountaineering was ushered in by the climb on January 2, 1964, to the summit of the Grand Teton via the Owen–Spalding route; the party was composed of James Greig, Earl Lory, John Mugaas, Robert Napier, Rod Newcomb, and Heinie Nolden. Taking advantage of unusually light autumn and early-winter snowfalls, the party camped at the Meadows in Garnet Canyon after a seven-hour trip from the old Jenny Lake Store; four of the party used snowshoes. The second night was spent on the Lower Saddle in a severe wind, and the summit was reached at 2 PM the next day.

After 1964 the pace of winter mountaineering accelerated, with most of the original impetus coming from Utah climbers who had the privilege of living close enough to the Tetons to be able to take immediate advantage of a session of good weather. In 1965 the first winter ascent of the formidable Mount Owen was made by a party from Salt Lake City (George Lowe, Mike Lowe, John Marsh, Lenny Nelson, Tom Stevenson, and Steve Swanson) via the East Ridge and Koven routes. After three earlier failed attempts, success was finally gained on Mount Moran in 1966 by nine climbers from the Salt Lake area via the Northeast Ridge. The myths about inaccessibility began to break down. Then from February 28 to March 2, 1968, the North Face of the Grand Teton was climbed in one alpine-style push by Rick Horn, George Lowe, and Greg and Mike Lowe. This extraordinary climb shattered the psychological barriers. That same year first winter ascents were made of Teewinot and the South Teton, and the regular routes on the Middle and Grand Tetons were climbed again. These last climbs brought the final new element to the Teton winter mountaineering scene, local climbers from Jackson Hole, who were only minutes away from the base of the range. A new era in popularity of climbing, or at least attempting, the Grand Teton began in 1969, exemplified by the near-annual expeditions led by the patriarch Paul Petzoldt and his groups from the National Outdoor Leadership School.

The 1970s saw numerous new winter climbs, including major peaks such as Mount Wister, the North Face of Cloudveil Dome, Nez Perce, the Glacier and North Ridge of the Middle Teton, Teepe Pillar, Disappointment Peak, the West Horn, the CMC route on Mount Moran, and even Thor Peak. The prize of the Exum Ridge of the Grand Teton was climbed in 1972. But, perhaps more importantly, the North Face feat encouraged other ascents of similar challenge during the decade. Routes of great difficulty and commitment that were completed included the Black Ice–West Face to the Upper Saddle (1971), the West Face of the Grand Teton (1972), the East Ridge of the Grand Teton, the North Ridge of the Grand Teton (1975), the Lower Exum Ridge and Petzoldt Ridge of the Grand Teton (1976), and the Enclosure Ice Couloir (1977).

During this decade the search for short, nearby winter ice climbs in Death Canyon was started in 1973 by well-known Jackson climbers Pete and Dave Carman, Donnie Black, Jim Roscoe, Jay Wilson, and Chuck Schaap. Their creative climbs, such as 737 Earful, Prospectors Falls, and Dread Falls, introduced a new element that has expanded and now flourishes every winter. This ice-climbing tangent culminated with the three climbs on Laughing Lions Falls on the south wall of Mount Moran between 1983 and 1985, by Renny Jackson, Jim Woodmencey, Dan Burgette, Bill Pelander, Alex Lowe, Andy Carson, and Jack Tackle.

The last decade has seen more new winter ascents such as Buck, Prospectors, and Rolling Thunder Mountains; Mounts Hunt, Bannon, and Meek; and Static, Veiled, Shadow, Doane, and Forellen Peaks. These have been done by a variety of climbers, with important contributions from Bob Graham, Ron Matous, Tom Turiano, and Donnie Black. Two difficult ascents of the Grand Teton, the Otterbody Chimneys and Alberich's Alley, were first done in the winter by Renny Jackson with Dan Burgette and Jim Woodmencey. Jackson also climbed the summertime classic, Irene's Arête on Disappointment Peak, while the prolific winter climber and guide Andy Carson first did the winter traverse from Cloudveil Dome to the South Teton. Some of the major events in recent years have been carried out by Alex Lowe and Jack Tackle, who have made concentrated efforts on the hardest routes in the range, including the second winter ascents of the Grand Teton North Face and North Ridge and the first of the South Buttress Direct and South Buttress Right on Mount Moran.

Now, as the start of the next century approaches, we marvel at how winter Teton climbing has matured. The Grand Teton has seen more than 100 ascents, and the Middle Teton has now been climbed over 50 times. But, just as is seen in summer Teton ascents, most of the climbing is carried out on the standard routes and in the standard canyons. As an example, through all these years the summit of the relatively remote yet major Mount Moran has been visited less than ten times. A few difficult lines have been done, however. The foreboding Northwest Chimney on the Grand was climbed by Alex Lowe and Renny Jackson in 1991 and the Beyer East Face I by Jackson and Larry Detrick in 1993. Lander climbers Greg Collins and Dan Powers accomplished the impressive Cathedral Traverse in 1993, and this was repeated in an astonishing single day by Alex Lowe and

Andrew McLean. Lowe flashed the complete North Face of the Grand in an unbelievable 20-hour day from the valley in 1992. Serendipity Arête on Mount Owen was climbed solo by Jack Tackle in 1994. In February 1996, Mark Newcomb and Hans Johnstone made the first winter ascent of and then skied back down the Northeast Couloir (Hossack–MacGowan) route on the Grand Teton. In spite of all this outstanding activity, one can easily see, by examining the chronology of first winter ascents given later, that many obvious and important peaks and routes remain to be done. In some ways these winter climbs represent the future of major Teton mountaineering. See *American Alpine Journal*, 2, no. 4 (1936), pp. 543–545; 7, no. 4 (1950), pp. 506–507; *Appalachia*, 27, no. 4 (December 1949), p. 503, illus.; 28, no. 1 (June 1950), pp. 21–24, illus.; *Sierra Club Bulletin*, 38, no. 8 (October 1953), pp. 72–73; *Summit*, 10, no. 8 (October 1964), pp. 24–27, illus.; *Trail and Timberline*, no. 211 (May 1936), pp. 43–44, illus.

National Park Service Winter Policy

Winter climbing in the Teton Range is a physically demanding but mentally exhilarating experience. The additional challenges imposed by the severe environmental conditions result in some limitations and a few additional regulations imposed by Grand Teton National Park. These winter regulations will be outlined here. Because from time to time the park makes changes in the rules, it is advisable to make personal inquiry for updated details at the Visitor Center at Moose. In winter the ranger staff on hand to assist climbers and other park visitors is greatly reduced from that available in midsummer. Thus, there is unavoidably some minor inconvenience resulting from fewer ranger stations and reduced hours. The rationale behind regulations, which the park tries to keep to a minimum, should be recognized as primarily the protection of park resources and secondarily the safety of the climber. There is an extra beauty available in the winter to the hardy outdoor traveller, but this beauty is fragile. Winter places considerable stress on the climber and even more on the wildlife. View the winter animals from a distance and minimize their hardships.

General Regulations: Beginning in 1994 the regulations that required registration for all climbs and for any over-snow travel away from the plowed roads in the park were abolished (see *National Park Service Policy* in the introduction). Backcountry permits are required for any overnight use, but the rules are somewhat less restrictive than in the summer. These permits and climbing information may be obtained in person at the Moose Visitor Center. There are no designated sites, and one may camp at any location that is 1.0 mile or more from a plowed road. Campfires in the backcountry are prohibited, the same restriction as for summer. Pets, such as dogs, are permitted only on roads open to snowmobiles, but they must be either leashed or in harness at all times. Infor-

mational pamphlets available from the park are *Snowmobiling* and *Nordic Skiing and Snowshoeing*.

As a final note on winter rules, remember that garbage and human waste, which disappear so conveniently under a little blowing snow in the winter, reappear in full force in the heavily used summer Tetons. All garbage must be carried out of the mountains.

Winter Rescue: Climbers planning winter ascents in the Teton Range should understand that rescue by the National Park Service in this season should not be presumed. New powder snow and avalanche hazard may severely impede or prevent ground travel of the relatively few in Jackson Hole who are capable of handling severe winter conditions. Storms or strong winds aloft may well prevent helicopter flying. Even in the best of conditions wintertime rescue is more time-consuming than in the summer. Climbing parties who come to these mountains in the winter should be equipped to deal with the possibility of an avalanche accident and, hence, be a self-contained rescue team. Individuals should each carry avalanche transceivers, shovels, and collapsible probe poles and should be trained in the use of such specialized equipment. Your best protection, however, consists of a cautious attitude and good judgment; these are, by far, the most important things that one can carry into the mountains.

Snowmobiles: Snowmobiles may be operated in limited areas within Grand Teton National Park, but state registration is required. Snowmobile travel is allowed on the unplowed section of the Teton Park road and on the road to the String Lake trailhead, making the peaks north of Cascade Canyon somewhat more accessible than by overland ski travel. Snowmobile traffic is permitted on Jackson Lake, which, when feasible, will simplify access to the peaks on its west shore. However, because of frequent flooding of the ice surface, climbers using this form of access should beware. It is advisable to consult with the rangers at Colter Bay. For access to the northernmost peaks, snowmobile travel on the Grassy Lake road is legal and feasible. There are a few additional regulations that affect the use of snowmobiles in the park. Climbers visiting the park with snowmobiles should check at the Moose Visitor Center for current information.

Winter Access

Winter access to the mountains is necessarily more difficult than in the rest of the year when roads are not blocked by snow. The main eastside highway (US 26, 89, and 191) extending north from Jackson toward Yellowstone National Park is kept plowed as far as Flagg Ranch. The inner Teton Park road, which runs west from Moose and then north past Jenny Lake to the Jackson Lake Junction, is only partially plowed. From the Jackson Lake Junction it is plowed south only to Signal Mountain Lodge; from Moose north the plowed road ends at the Taggart Lake trailhead. The Moose–

Wilson road is also only partially plowed. From Wilson it is plowed north to the vicinity of the park boundary, about 1.0 mile past the Teton Village turnoff. South from Moose, it is plowed only to the end of the pavement near the JY Ranch.

For winter mountaineers the entry points into the range are usually the plowed-out parking areas associated with the open roadways. An exception is the top of the tram at the Jackson Hole Ski Area, which obviously represents a good starting point if one is interested in the southern peaks. Access from the tram, however, is under the control of the Jackson Hole Ski Corporation and permission must be arranged with the ski patrol; during high avalanche conditions permission will likely be denied. For winter ice climbs in or near Death Canyon a plowed parking area is available on the Moose–Wilson road just north of the turn-off to the Death Canyon trailhead. Most of the winter mountaineering, however, has utilized the Taggart Lake trailhead because this is the closest vehicular approach to the high central peaks of the range. Overnight winter parking is also available at parking areas at Signal Mountain Lodge, at Colter Bay, or at any of the plowed turnouts along the highway.

For the enterprising, the entire western slope of the Teton Range also offers access to the high peaks. The Grand Targhee Ski Area, almost due west of the Grand Teton, may be utilized, but the office of the Targhee National Forest, Teton Basin Ranger District in Driggs, Idaho, should be consulted for their advice and winter use regulations. Once one crosses the divide into the park, all of the NPS regulations apply.

Berry Creek is most commonly entered by skiing due west from the turnout just south of the Lizard Creek campground. Access to Mount Moran and other peaks of the north end of the range is also available directly across the ice of Jackson Lake. The advisability of lake crossing is left to the climbers' judgment, but anyone contemplating this route should check with the NPS ranger staff at Colter Bay for information on current ice conditions and known hazard areas. Jackson Lake "flooding" with a few inches of water on top of the ice is common, can be widespread, and is obviously hazardous. Special precautions also should be taken with the dangerous thin ice at the Snake River inlet at the north end of the lake and at the Moran Creek inlet at the mouth of Moran Canyon.

From the winter parking areas in Jackson Hole there are a few marked ski trails, but most of these are simply for nordic ski touring or snowshoeing, rather than winter climbing. These trails are defined by orange markers, either on trees or poles. The ski trails that are useful for mountaineers include the popular ski-touring route to Jenny Lake from the end of the plowed road at the Taggart Lake trailhead. Rather than following the road, which is frequented by noisy snowmobiles, this Jenny Lake ski trail proceeds north along the trees to the west of Cottonwood Creek.

Another marked trail, and perhaps the most useful, is the one that leads due west from the Taggart Lake trailhead. This ski trail soon turns north and heads up the moraine to a junction after about 1.0 mile. The left fork provides a loop tour of Taggart Lake. The right fork is more commonly used by climbers because it leads farther north to Bradley Lake. The main access route into Garnet Canyon is either directly across Bradley Lake (only when the ice is sufficiently thick) or on the north edge of the lake along the moraine. In winters with good weather and a volume of winter climbing, there may be a considerable ski trail from Bradley Lake up into the canyon. Note that the usual summer Garnet Canyon trail is not used in the winter. The preferred route into the canyon stays, with minor exceptions, on the south side of the creek.

A third standard winter trail of value to climbers is the one to the Phelps Lake Overlook from the parking area on the Moose–Wilson road. This trail leads easily for 2.0 miles to the end of the current summer road and then continues up the summer trail to the overlook. Continuing safely beyond the overlook requires an understanding of current avalanche hazards on the slopes that must be traversed to gain entrance into Death Canyon.

Additionally, some portions of the Berry Creek and Webb Canyon ski trails are marked.

Winter Hazards and Methods

Climbing in the Teton Range in the winter season exposes the climber to hazards beyond those normally encountered in the summer. The first is avalanche hazard. Knowledge of recent snow conditions is essential to estimate local avalanche potential. In addition to the recorded forecast available from the U.S. Forest Service at the Jackson Hole Ski Area [(307) 733-2664], advice based on experience combined with the latest snowfall data can be obtained from NPS ranger staff at the Moose Visitor Center. Mountaineering parties venturing into the Teton Range during the winter should be capable of doing their own avalanche hazard estimation and snow stability evaluation. Careful routefinding is perhaps the most essential component of travel within the range. A trip up any of the canyons, however, will necessarily include crossing many different slide paths, some of which are of immense proportions. A second major hazard consists of thin or breakable ice at the various stream inlets or outlets from the larger lakes, such as Phelps, Bradley, Taggart, Jenny, Leigh, and Jackson Lakes. Climbers should appreciate that any travel over lakes in wintertime is potentially hazardous. Better to go around than to risk your life on thin ice.

Methods that are successful in Teton winter climbing range from multiday tactics to light and fast trips on the highest peaks, up and down in a single day. The suitability of the selected method depends on the experience and strength of the climbing party, but the potential of weather changes to create major avalanche danger argues for as much speed as possible. Over the years there has been a trend toward light and fast to take full advantage of a spell of good weather. As one example, the West Face of the Grand Teton was done by two climbers in four days, valley to valley. Another is Alex Lowe's solo winter ascent of the North Face of the Grand in 20 hours. In addition it has been found that it is possible, but not pleasant, to climb in reasonably bad weather. The first winter ascent of the North Ridge of the Grand Teton was climbed during a continuous storm that shut down the Jackson Hole Ski Area. The trend lately has been toward one-day ascents of the major peaks, including St. John, Teewinot, South Teton, Middle Teton, Grand Teton, and even Mount Owen. There are both rewards and drawbacks of such exertions, however, as George Lowe has observed:

> [T]hese ascents have produced some of the most exhilarating times the writer has had in the mountains. It is difficult to top the sensation of moving rapidly in good weather amid the winterized peaks. But these efforts do tend to be physically exhausting!

Climbing conditions on the west and east sides of the peaks may differ dramatically due to the prevailing winds coming from the west and southwest. Typically, the west sides of the peaks are covered with 12 inches or more of rime, and slopes may be almost bare of snow due to the wind. This snow is, of course, deposited on the northeast-facing lee slopes, causing slab avalanche hazard that may persist for weeks. Snow conditions range from very hard slab high in the canyons to light powder at medium altitudes. Except for the northwest sides of the Grand Teton and Enclosure, little ice is to be found mixed with the rock, as it is rarely warm enough to allow the melting that is required. Additionally, much of the ice that is deposited disappears relatively quickly due to sublimation.

Winter Mountaineering Equipment

Equipment needed for winter climbing in the Tetons is generally equivalent to that required for Himalayan, Andean, or Alaskan conditions. An effective wind-protection shell, insulated clothing, and warm mitts are needed to counter the cold except on the very finest of winter days. Double mountaineering boots or double cross-country boots with effective, perhaps insulated, gaiters are recommended. After the skis are left behind and if technical climbing is encountered, crampons are frequently necessary, so the boots should be selected with this requirement in mind. Light touring skis and boots have also been used, but such equipment may involve carrying a second set of climbing boots.

A strong, lightweight tent is a necessity for multiday climbs because adequate snow for caves cannot always be counted on. The Lower Saddle, for example, quite frequently is completely blown free of snow all winter long. A sturdy snow shovel should be part of every winter mountaineer's avalanche rescue kit, and knowing how to dig a snow cave can provide that extra margin of safety even during the fast one-day trips that have become increasingly popular.

Metal-edged skis with mountaineering bindings or bindings that will accommodate touring boots have become the preferred means for approach. Climbing skins for the skis to supplement wax are strongly advised, as the slopes are steep and conditions may vary rapidly, especially in late winter. Most of the existing tracks that will be encountered will have been made by others using skins for climbing.

Ice screws are rarely needed, except for those routes that are ice climbs in the summer. The usual summer rack of rock protection, such as camming devices and chocks, works well for winter ascents. And while pitons are perhaps without honor in the summer, many times in winter conditions they will provide better anchors than chocks in the rime-filled cracks. An alpine hammer and an ice axe (or two ice tools) are useful for cleaning cracks and placing protection.

Chronology of First Winter Ascents

Note: *Ascents accomplished outside of the "official" winter season, that is, December 20 to March 20, are enclosed in brackets.*

Rendezvous Peak (10,927)
  West Ridge: January 25, 1961, Frank Ewing, Rod Newcomb
Housetop Mountain (10,537)
  Southeast Ridge: March 1967, Robbie Fuller, Juris Krisjansons, Robert Redmayne, Ray White, Bob Sartor
Mount Hunt (10,783)
  West Ridge: January 1972, Callum Mackay, George Colon
  East Ridge: January 12, 1986, Norm Larson, Martha Clark, Angus Thuermer, Linda Sternberg, George McClelland, Scott Berkenfield
Tukuarika Peak (10,988)
  Northeast Ridge: late February 1990, Christoph Schork
Prospectors Mountain (11,241)
  Southwest Ridge: January 17, 1990, Michael Best
Fossil Mountain (10,916)
  Southeast Side: January 1973, Callum Mackay, Ray White, Robbie Fuller
Mount Bannon (10,966)
  South Slope: January 28, 1989, Tom Turiano, Tom Bennett
Mount Meek (10,681)
  Southeast Slope: January 28, 1989, Tom Turiano, Tom Bennett

Albright Peak (Peak 10,552)
    East Slope: March 1974 or 1975, Steve Lundy, Dave Fox, Ed Lowton; March 15, 1979, John Connors, Larry Gilbert (first recorded ascent)
Static Peak (11,303)
    North Face: [October 27, 1976, Mike Volk, Dick Simmons]
    East Ridge: March 15, 1981, Steven Poole
    Southwest Ridge: [March 28, 1986, Chris Sabo, David Smith]
Peak 10,696
    East Ridge: late 1970s, Bill Barmore, Dean Millsap, Joe Gale, Bob Hammes; February 20, 1988, Jim Olson (first recorded ascent)
Point 9,975 (25-Short)
    East Slope: winter 1950s, NPS residents of Beaver Creek; 1960s, Barry Corbet; 1974–1977, Bill Barmore, Dean Millsap, Woody and Jim Barmore
Buck Mountain (11,938)
    East Face: winter 1972, Callum Mackay, George Colon
    North Face, East Couloir: January 9, 1981, Don Black, Scott Wade, Jim Humphries
    North Central Ridge: January 10, 1981, Norm Larson, Jack Clinton (to North Face, East Couloir)
    North Face, West Couloir: February 26, 1982, Lyle Dean
    East Ridge: February 29, 1984, Ron Matous, Martin Springer
Veiled Peak (11,330)
    Northeast Ledges: December 21, 1985, Bob Graham
Mount Wister (11,490)
    Northeast Couloir, var: 1928: March 3–4, 1973, Chuck Schaap, Art Becker, Bob Stevenson
    West Ridge: winter 1984 or 1985, Bob Graham
    South Couloir: January 3, 1985, Ron Matous
    North Face, West Chimney: January 19, 1997, Norm Larson, Callum Mackay
Shadow Peak (10,725)
    East Ridge: January 3, 1988, Bob Graham
Nez Perce Peak (11,901)
    Northwest Couloirs: February 6–8, 1972, George Lowe, David George
    Northwest Couloirs, var: 1952: [December 10, 1988, Norm Larson, Jack Clinton]
    South Face: February 9–10, 1980, Mark Whiton, John Ninenger
    Southeast Face: February 9–10, 1980, Mark Whiton, John Ninenger (descent)
Cloudveil Dome (12,026)
    North Face: March 8–10, 1972, Robert Redmayne, Ian Wade
    East Ridge: December 31, 1980, Rob Slater, Kirk Duffy
    West Ridge: [April 4–6, 1973, Vince Fayad, George

Hunker, Jans Lund, Landry Corkery]; February 24, 1988, Norm Larson, Lorna Corson (ascent); February 18, 1987, Andy Carson, Gary Patton (descent)
Spalding Peak (12,240+)
    Zorro Snowfield: December 26, 1985, Craig Patterson, Roger Millward
    East Ridge: February 18, 1987, Andy Carson, Gary Patton (ascent); February 24, 1988, Norm Larson, Lorna Corson (descent)
    West Ridge: February 18, 1987, Andy Carson, Gary Patton (descent); February 24, 1988, Norm Larson, Lorna Corson (ascent)
Gilkey Tower (12,320+)
    Sunrise Ridge: February 27, 1975, Pete Carman, Jim Roscoe, Mike Fitzpatrick
    East Face: February 18, 1987, Andy Carson, Gary Patton (ascent); February 24, 1988, Norm Larson, Lorna Corson (descent)
    West Ridge: February 18, 1987, Andy Carson, Gary Patton (descent); February 24, 1988, Norm Larson, Lorna Corson (ascent)
Icecream Cone (12,400+)
    East Face: February 18, 1987, Andy Carson, Gary Patton
South Teton (12,514)
    Northwest Couloir: January 22, 1968, Rick Horn, Gary Cole, Frank Ewing, Denny Becker, Greg Bourassa, Peter Koedt, Keith Becker, John Walker, Don Ryan, John Horn
    East Ridge: December 21, 1975, Jim Roscoe (ascent); February 25, 1988, Norm Larson, Lorna Corson (descent)
    South Ridge: December 21, 1977, William H. Barmore, Craig George
    West Ridge: [November 23, 1972, Tom Warren, Gene Forsythe, Boots and Charla Brown, Jim Huntly, Judy Fox, Pat Viani]; December 20, 1972, Tom Warren, Gene Forsythe, Dan Miller, Roger Pope, Scott Russell, Sam Evans, Georgia and Stewart Silk, Cliff Berger
Middle Teton (12,804)
    Southwest Couloir: February 4, 1952, Leigh Ortenburger, William Dunmire, Norman Goldstein, Richard Long
    Glacier: January 27, 1973, Tom Warren, Lorni Brown, Jack Cockran, Michael McGowan, John Kirk
    Northwest Ice Couloir: January 27, 1973, Tom Warren, Lorni Brown, Jack Cockran, Michael McGowan, John Kirk (descent); January 1, 1975, Dennis Turville, Dean Hannibal (ascent)
    Ellingwood Couloir: February 23, 1975, Bill Rosqvist, Dave Bjorkman, Melvin Davis
    Chouinard Ridge [?]: December 21, 1975, Glenn Milner, Joseph Costello, James Kilroy

North Ridge: [April 13–15, 1974, Pete Carman, Dave Carman]; February 7, 1976, Andy Carson, Swep Davis

Dike: December 28–31, 1977, Dennis Turville, Dean Hannibal (to Dike Pinnacle only)

Southeast Ridge: January 31, 1994, Greg Collins, Ron Matous

Grand Teton (13,770)

Owen–Spalding: [December 19, 1935, Paul and Eldon Petzoldt, Fred Brown]; March 3–6, 1949, Paul Petzoldt, John Lewis, Ted Lewis

North Face: February 28 to March 2, 1968, George Lowe, Mike and Greg Lowe, Rick Horn; January 1–3, 1987, Jack Tackle, Alex Lowe

Black Ice Couloir–West Face, var: Traverse to Upper Saddle: February 2–4, 1971, George and David Lowe, Greg and Jeff Lowe (to Upper Saddle only)

Exum Ridge: February 19–20, 1972, David Lowe, Jock Glidden, David Smith

West Face: February 19–24, 1972, George Lowe, Jeff Lowe

East Ridge: February 16–18, 1973, George and David Lowe, Jock Glidden

North Ridge: March 20–22, 1975, Dave Carman, George Lowe; January 3–4, 1985, Alex Lowe, Jack Tackle

Petzoldt Ridge: January 30, 1976, Glenn Milner, Don Black, Joseph Costello

Lower Exum Ridge: February 2, 1976, Tom Ballard, Tom Shreve, Daniel Winner, Gregory Lee (to summit)

Stettner Couloir: January 14, 1981, Bill Danford, Gene Forsythe

East Ridge, North Molar Tooth Couloir: January 31, 1984, Alex Lowe (to east ridge only)

Otterbody Chimneys: December 29, 1985, Renny Jackson, Dan Burgette

Northwest Chimney: December 21, 1991, Alex Lowe, Renny Jackson

Beyer East Face I: January 29, 1993, Renny Jackson, Larry Detrick (to top of climb)

Northeast Couloir: February 16, 1996, Mark Newcomb, Hans Johnstone (first winter ascent, first ski descent)

The Enclosure (13,280+)

South Couloir: January 21, 1989, Ron Matous (to summit)

Enclosure Ice Couloir: February 1977, Dennis Turville, Dean Hannibal (to top of climb only)

Black Ice Couloir: January 1, 1981, Mark Bennett, Dave Bjorkman, Kent Jamison (to top of climb only)

Alberich's Alley: February 28 to March 2, 1990, Renny Jackson, Jim Woodmencey (to summit)

Glencoe Spire (12,320+)

North and West Faces: January 29, 1973, Gene Forsythe, Stephen Bussell, Edwin Hinch, William McKinney

Teepe Pillar (12,266)

West Ridge: January 26, 1973, Tom Warren, Robert Gathercole

Fairshare Tower (11,520+)

South Ridge: February 8, 1976, Andy Carson, Swep Davis

Disappointment Peak (11,618)

West Face: January 25 to February 2, 1973, Gene Forsythe, Stephen Bussell, Rod Ewald, Richard Kroll, Edwin Hinch

Southwest Couloir: January 25 to February 2, 1973, Gene Forsythe, Stephen Bussell, Rod Ewald, Richard Kroll, Edwin Hinch (descent); January 29, 1976, Tom Milligan, Peter Hart, Jim Olson, Ralph Tingey, Bill Conrod

Southwest Ridge: March 11–12, 1973, Richard Taplin, Chris Latour, Cecelle Brumder, Davie Agnew; March 11–13, 1973, Andy Carson, Pete Carman; January 23, 1981, Jeff Lowe, Kerry Shroyer (possible new route on Southwest Ridge)

Merriam Couloir [?]: December 25, 1982, Snyder and three others

Lake Ledges: [November 26, 1972, Clinton Blair, Jim Miller]; January 24, 1985, Ray Warburton, John Jakubowski

Southeast Ridge: February 1985, Glenn Vitucci

East Snow Couloir: February 1985, Glenn Vitucci (descent)

Irene's Arête: March 14, 1985, Renny Jackson, Larry Detrick (to top of climb only)

Teewinot Mountain (12,325)

Southwest Couloirs: [November 3, 1965, Jim Gregg, Bernie Shanks]; March 1, 1968, Dennis Becker, Rex Alldredge

South Ridge: December 26, 1977, Darvin Vandegrift, Tom Deuchler

South Ridge, var: Southeast Couloir: [March 24, 1981, John Maniglia]; February 11, 1982, Hooman Aprin, John Callahan

East Face: February 11, 1982, Kitty Calhoun, Len Wechter

Northwest Ridge: [March 21, 1986, Andy Carson, Gary Patton] (via Teton Glacier)

East Prong (12,000+)

West Ridge: March 20, 1972, George Lowe

Mount Owen (12,928)

East Ridge: [December 19, 1965, George Lowe, Larry Nelson]; December 20, 1965, T. Q. Stevenson, Mike Lowe, Steve Swanson, John Marsh (direct east ridge except for summit block)

Koven: [December 19, 1965, Mike Lowe, Steve Nelson]

South Chimney: January 3–5, 1980, Jack Tackle, Pat Callis (to east ridge only)

Fryxell: February 26, 1988, Steve Quinlan, Jim Olson
Serendipity Arête: March 10 or 11, 1994, Jack Tackle
Cathedral Traverse (Teewinot, Mount Owen, Grand Teton): January 26–28, 1993, Greg Collins, Phil Powers, Gary Wilmot; February 4, 1993, Alex Lowe, Andrew McLean (one-day traverse)
Littles Peak (10,712)
   East Ridge: probably as early as 1947 by Grant Hagen, Grover Bassett during the first traverse of the crest of the Teton Range; [April 5, 1990, Tom Turiano, Tom Bennett, Gary Kofinas]
Baxter's Pinnacle (8,560+)
   South Ridge: [April 4, 1976, Andy Carson, Jan Olson, Jug Bacon, Ben Toland]; March 20, 1986, John and Bruce Spitler; December 29, 1986, Jed Flanagan, Chuck Odette
Symmetry Spire (10,560+)
   Southwest Couloir: [April 7, 1971, David Boyd, Owen Anderson]
The Jaw (11,400)
   East Face: March 17, 1990, Bob Graham
Mount St. John (11,430)
   South Couloir West/East Ridge: February 12, 1972, Dennis and Karen Caldwell, David Smith, Milt Hollander (and one other)
Mount Woodring (11,555)
   Southeast Slope: [April 20, 1991, Tom Turiano] (ski descent of Southwest Slope)
West Horn (11,605)
   West Ridge: December 25, 1975, Dave Carman, Charles Field
Mount Moran (12,605)
   Northeast Ridge: [December 19, 1966, Tom Stevenson, George Lowe, Mike Lowe, Dennis Caldwell, Tom Spencer, Court Richards, Bill Conrod]; December 20, 1966, George Lowe, Mike and Greg Lowe, George Gerhart
   CMC: December 25, 1975, Dave Carman, Bob Graham, Charles Field
   Staircase Arête: February 18, 1985, Jack Tackle, Alex Lowe (to top of climb only)
   South Buttress Right: December 16–22, 1985, Alex Lowe, Jack Tackle (to top of climb only)
   Skillet Glacier: February 1990, Keith Cattabriga
   Direct South Buttress: January 5, 1988, Jack Tackle, Alex Lowe (to top of climb only)
   Southwest Couloir: January 28, 1989, Ron Matous
Peak 12,000+
   East Ridge: February 22, 1988, Andy Carson, Gary Patton
Thor Peak (12,028)
   Southeast Ridge: January 21–23, 1976, Jan Olson, Andy Carson, Jim Roscoe
   South Slope: March 8, 1985, Andy Carson, Gary Patton

Maidenform Peak (11,137)
   East Ridge: [April 5–6, 1990, Tom Turiano, Tom Bennett, Gary Kofinas]
   South Couloir: [March 31, 1994, Christoph Schork]
Cleaver Peak (11,055)
   North Peak, Northwest Chimney: January 26, 1994, Tom Turiano, Wesley Bunch, David Bowers
Green Lakes Mountain (10,240+)
   Northeast Ridge: February 10, 1991, Tom Turiano, Tom Bennett
Doubtful Peak (10,852)
   South Couloirs: January 4, 1995, Tom Turiano, Wesley Bunch
Raynolds Peak (10,910)
   East Ridge: March 16, 1994, Tom Turiano, Wesley Bunch, Christoph Schork
   West Summit, Northwest Side: January 4, 1995, Tom Turiano, Wesley Bunch
Image (10,750)
   Southeast Face: March 15, 1994, Tom Turiano, Wesley Bunch, Christoph Schork, Scott McGee
Primrose Peak (10,800+)
   West Couloir and South Ridge: March 15, 1994, Tom Turiano, Wesley Bunch, Christoph Schork, Scott McGee
Bivouac Peak (10,825)
   East Ridge, var: Northeast Couloir: February 9, 1991, Tom Turiano, Tom Bennett; February 25, 1991, Michael Best
Rolling Thunder Mountain (10,908)
   North Snowfield to West Ridge: March 20, 1990, Tom Turiano, Tom Bennett
Eagles Rest Peak (11,258)
   North Ridge: February 27, 1991, Tom Turiano, Christoph Schork, Jim Schultz
   West Ridge: February 27, 1991, Tom Turiano, Christoph Schork, Jim Schultz (descent)
Doane Peak (11,355)
   North Ridge: March 1984, Peter Koedt, John Silverman
   South Couloirs: February 27, 1991, Tom Turiano, Christoph Schork, Jim Schultz
Ranger Peak (11,355)
   West Ridge: [March 27, 1992, Tom Turiano, Matthew Goewert, Michael Keating, Wesley Bunch]
   Southeast Ridge: February 3, 1991, Dave Moore, Bill Stanley
Glacier Peak (10,927)
   North Ridge: [April 4, 1974, John Carr, Susan Enger, Ted Shimo, George Bloom]; March 5, 1976, Bill Conrod, Jim Barmore
Moose Mountain (10,054)
   East Slopes: January 20, 1985, Norm Larson, Martha Clarke
   South Ridge: February 1986, Ron Matous

Peak 10,360
   South Ridge: [first recorded ascent April 7, 1993, Tom Turiano, John Fettig, Forrest McCarthy]
Peak 10,422
   South Ridge: January 20, 1985, Norm Larson, Martha Clarke
   East Ridge: [April 7, 1993, Tom Turiano, John Fettig, Forrest McCarthy]
Peak 10,270
   East Ridge: [April 14, 1994, Dave Moore, Tom Turiano, Mike Whitehead]
Peak 10,333
   West Ridge: [April 14, 1994, Dave Moore, Tom Turiano, Mike Whitehead]
Elk Mountain (10,720+)
   Southeast Ridge: [March 26, 1994, Dave Moore, Dave Coon]
Owl Peak (10,612)
   East Ridge: February 10, 1979, Robbie Fuller, Ray White, Marty Krautter, Ken Thomasma
Forellen Peak (9,772)
   Southwest Slope: [possible first winter ascent in 1957 or 1958, Frank Ewing, Keith Jones, Don Williams]; [probable ascent in early to mid-1980s, Steve Barnett]; February 10, 1989, John Carr, Chuck Schaap, Barbara Zimmer (first recorded winter ascent)
   East Ridge: February 10, 1989, John Carr, Chuck Schaap, Barbara Zimmer (descent)
Red Mountain (10,205 and 10,177)
   North Ridge: February 10, 1980, Bill and Woody Barmore, Mike Whitfield, Shari Gregory, Don Black; [10,205 summit, April 15, 1994, Tom Turiano, Dave Moore]
Survey Peak (9,277)
   Northeast Slope: December 1957, Frank Ewing, Keith Jones
   Southwest Slope: March 16–18, 1973, Doug Leen, Jim Olson

Winter Waterfall Ice

The discovery and climbing of winter waterfall ice in the Teton Range is a recent phenomenon. Through the first decades of winter climbing the existence and accessibility of frozen waterfalls remained unnoticed here. As interest in ice climbing developed in the United States in the 1970s, a few perceptive and energetic climbers who wintered in Jackson Hole saw that there were a number of opportunities for this type of climbing in their home range. In the years since, winter ice climbing has gained considerable popularity, with most of the activity occurring in Death Canyon because it is the most readily accessible and provides a variety of worthwhile routes. While many of these routes reappear every winter, others are the creatures of the specific weather conditions. In a given winter, some ice sections will not

form even once, while others will be suitable for climbing only for a few days or weeks. Local inquiry or telescopic viewing from the valley should precede the approach if one has a specific objective in mind. To be consistent with the summer Teton routes, the brief descriptions given here will be listed in each canyon from west to east.

Because most of these ice routes are of a high-angle nature, the risks associated with these climbs should be fully recognized by prospective climbers. Remember that it is frequently the case that ice protection, gained through screws or pitons, is not as reliable as rock protection. Hence, the implications of a leader fall can be more severe. Practice and experience may be safely obtained by use of a top rope. Rescue is necessarily less efficient in winter for many reasons listed earlier.

Death Canyon

For the approach to the ice climbs in Death Canyon, drive south from Moose on the Moose–Wilson road to a plowed turnout located just north of the spur road into the Death Canyon trailhead. (*Note:* The Moose–Wilson road is only plowed to the JY Ranch during the winter, and the road into the Death Canyon trailhead is not plowed at all.) From this turnout there is then a 3.5- to 4.5-mile ski-in to most of the Death Canyon ice climbs. Climbing skins are recommended for skiing upcanyon and for getting back up to the crest of the Phelps Lake moraine. Depending on snow conditions, allow two to three hours to approach these ice climbs and about the same for the return to the Moose–Wilson road.

The season for these climbs is, in most years, late November to early April. The ice usually forms from melting and refreezing of early-season snowfall (autumn). In an autumn drought these climbs may not form or can be marginal until a snowfall followed by a melt–freeze cycle occurs. The best conditions are usually from mid-December to mid-March. Prospectors Falls generally forms the earliest and stays the latest.

DEATH CANYON, SOUTH SIDE ICE CLIMBS (CA. 8,400)

Map: Grand Teton
ROUTE 1. Rimrock Falls. II, WI3–4. First ascent February 20, 1977, by Richard Rossiter and Jeff Splitgerber. This route ascends the ice formed by the outlet stream from Rimrock Lake. The climbing can be broken into two sections—the first is WI3 and consists of ice-covered slabs that are hard to protect. Then proceed up a long snow slope (400 yards; at times prone to avalanche) to the base of the second tier. This pitch is a 120-foot WI3+ to WI4 hose. To descend rappel from a tree near the top of the last pitch, walk down the middle section, and then rappel again from a tree on the west side of the first pitch. These are double-rope rappels.

ROUTE 2. *The Nugget.* I, WI4+. First ascent January 1983, by Rex Hong and Tony Tulip. Climb nearly 200 yards up the Apocalypse Couloir from the top of the talus cone. Bear left at a dogleg in the couloir and begin this ice climb on the left side of the couloir shortly thereafter. It involves 110 feet of vertical and just off-vertical climbing. Anchors at the top are marginal. Beware of avalanches coming down the formidable Apocalypse Couloir.

ROUTE 3. *Prospectors Falls.* II, WI3+. First ascent in March 1973, by Pete Carman and Dave Carman. This route, the most popular frozen waterfall climb in the canyon, was given the name Raven Falls by the first-ascent party. It is located immediately east of the northeast couloir of Prospectors Mountain. This major couloir lying at the base of the main north face of the mountain is the most prominent winter feature of Prospectors Mountain when viewed from Death Canyon. For the approach, leave the trail in the bottom of the canyon before starting up the lower switchbacks, cross the creek, and ascend the snow cone that forms at the base of the falls. The route contains two pitches of 70–80° ice with some vertical sections. During early season and/or some wetter winters, three additional pitches are available. The fifth and highest ropelength consists at times of a narrow smear that steepens to vertical ice at the very top. To descend, rappel from trees on the right (northwest) side using two ropes. The avalanche hazard consists of heavy spindrift from above with some potential for larger slides from the main northeast couloir, so cross the base of this couloir as rapidly as possible. Once on the climb itself, the main danger is from spindrift.

DEATH CANYON, NORTH SIDE ICE CLIMBS (CA. 8,000)

Map: Grand Teton

ROUTE 1. *Sentinel Winter Gully.* II, WI3+. First ascent winter 1978, by Norm Larson and Jack Clinton. This moderate climb of one and a half pitches in a very scenic location ascends a section of ice just west of Sentinel Turret. It should be recognized that the name of this winter route differs from the summer terminology, which applies this same name, "Sentinel Gully," to the large gully immediately east of Sentinel Turret. The first pitch on moderate-angle (60°) ice leads to the base of a short steep section. Climb about 20 feet of steep ice (80–85°) up into a small rock amphitheater containing a snowfield. Continue straight up the snow to the rock wall at the head of the amphitheater. Although fixed nuts and pitons can often be found here for rappelling (including an old Wort Hog pounded into the rock from the first-ascent party), bring some hardware just in case they are not found. One full-length rappel, that is, two ropes, will put you about 30 feet from the snow at the base of the gully. Set up a second short rappel on ice or rock to reach the base, or one may downclimb the lower-angle ice. The avalanche

potential is low because this is a well-protected route, with the only danger being a slide from the small snowfield at the top of the climb or during the canyon approach.

ROUTE 2. *Dread Falls.* III, WI3–4. Earlier referred to as the Curtain of Death, the name Dread Falls is derived from early attempts by Norm Larson, George Austigue, and Jack Clinton during which Clinton took a long fall. The successful first ascent was accomplished by Rex Hong and Tony Tulip in January of 1982, in which gear was recovered from the previous ill-fated attempt. This is the most prominent ice climb on the north side of Death Canyon, and it can be climbed in at least two ways. For either method approach along the trail until about 0.25 mile past the Bulge (*Route 4*). Minimal avalanche hazard exists on this climb besides that which is encountered on the approach.

(1) *Main falls.* This method is directed toward the climb of the upper section only, bypassing the lower section of mixed climbing. Approach by continuing upcanyon on the trail about 300 yards past Dread Falls, and then angle back right and up to the base of the main falls on a large ramp. This route consists of one and a half pitches on ice that can often be of the hollow and "chandelier" variety. There are two methods of descent. One may rappel from a tree to the right of the top of the falls, using two 165-foot ropes, which will just reach the ground at the base of the falls; then retrace the route back to the trail. The avalanche gully to the east may be taken back down to the base of the climb as an alternative.

(2) *Direct approach.* From the trail directly below the falls start the climb by working up smears of mostly low-angle ice (often thin) to the base of Dread Falls. This method adds about 300 feet of additional mixed climbing. Routefinding up these lower slabs can be interesting, and rock protection is desirable.

ROUTE 3. *The Three Stooges.* I, WI3. First ascent December 31, 1986, by Daniel Blumstein and Nancy Auerbach. Three prominent smears of moderate-angle ice form on the smooth rock slabs that are located about 150 feet left (west) of the Bulge. These smears are approximately 100 feet long with an angle of 60–70°. To descend, rappel from a small tree at the top of the center smear. The avalanche potential consists of some sloughing and icefall from the ledges and snowfield above, but the route is generally sheltered. Because this route can be top-roped, it is a good area for practice.

ROUTE 4. *The Bulge.* II, WI3–4. First ascent January 12, 1984, by Jim Woodmencey and Dan Burgette. This route is located on the south-facing side of Death Canyon just beyond the end of the first switchback as one goes upcanyon from Phelps Lake. The ice can be seen in a shallow right-facing corner. The first pitch has a 10-foot vertical section at the base, with lower-angle ice (often mixed) leading to the base of the Bulge itself, 150 feet. Bring some rock protection for this section. The second pitch surmounts a 12-foot bulge of vertical ice to the lower-angle ice above, exiting right to a large tree. Use this tree for the upper belay and as the rappel point, using two 165-foot ropes. The avalanche hazard is the same as for The Three Stooges.

ROUTE 5. 737 Earful. I, WI3–4. First ascent February 1973, by Pete and Dave Carman, Jim Roscoe, Jay Wilson, and Chuck Schaap. Located at the base of a long drainage chute on the southeast corner of Peak 10,552, this one-pitch climb was named for the excessive noise generated by jets departing from the Jackson Hole Airport (the only one inside a national park). Because of the proximity to the airport, the acoustics here are perfect to hear terrifying thunder, making one wonder whether it is a jet or an avalanche coming down the gully immediately above the climb.

The 737 Earful route is reached by descending the trail from the Phelps Lake Overlook to the end of the first switchback and then traversing to the west along the base of the south-facing rock. The main falls, containing 120 feet of 70–90° ice, can be hollow at times, with running water underneath. The ice that forms to the left of the main falls over steeper rock and out of the main gully is generally thicker and less hollow; however, this does not always touch down and become continuous until later in the winter. There are numerous other short, sometimes narrow, or mixed possibilities to the right of the main falls in rock chimneys. Descent off the main falls or the variations to the left is made by walking up and left (west) in a gully to trees and then continuing left (west) and down to the base. The avalanche potential is that of a southeast-facing slope at the base of a 3,000-foot slide path. Beware.

ROUTE 6. Sunrise Pillar. I, WI3–4. First ascent January 29, 1980, by Randy Harrington, Shad Dusseau, and Jan Schofield. Seen from the Death Canyon trail before the Phelps Lake Overlook is reached, this short ice climb is at the base of Albright Peak, facing east in the main gully coming down from the summit. It is approximately 40 feet high and contains some vertical ice. For the descent one can walk off up and left out of the gully, or a rappel can be made from a small tree, which is sometimes buried. The avalanche hazard is that of an east-facing slope at the base of a 3,000-foot slide path. In late winter this ice route is sometimes completely covered by avalanche debris.

Avalanche Canyon

Most of these little-known ice routes have been climbed only once, but they are readily accessible from the plowed parking area at the Taggart Lake trailhead.

ROUTE 1. Wistersheer Falls. I, WI3+. First ascent 1980 or 1981, by Rex Hong and Scott Lehman. This ice route of two pitches, one short (30 feet moderate angle) and one long (up to 80°), forms on the cliffs to the right of the large northwest couloir of Mount Wister; it is in the vicinity of the second line of drainage to the right of the couloir. Approach from Lake Taminah toward the left (southwest) edge of the headwall below Snowdrift Lake.

ROUTE 2. Mount Wister, North Face Ice. II, WI3–4. First ascent (probable) in the 1970s, by Jack Clinton, or on November 3, 1981, by Mike Fischer and Greg Miles. Information concerning the location of this two-pitch ice climb is sketchy. The first lead of 60 to 80 feet was strenuous. The second pitch of the same length goes up a narrow gully containing mixed climbing involving some rockwork. Exit by traversing on snow up and to the right to gain the crest of the east ridge of Wister. One may then descend into the north fork via the standard snow slope, the Northeast Couloir.

ROUTE 3. Shoshoko Falls. I, WI2+. First ascent in the 1970s by Jack Clinton (probable), or on November 11, 1981, by Doug Speirs and Roger McMurtrey. One short pitch of ice was climbed near the base of the summertime Shoshoko Falls. Exit was made off on snow to the right.

ROUTE 4. The Talon. III, WI3+. First ascent January 24, 1983, by Mark Whiton (Norm Larson may have preceded Mark at some earlier point in time). On the right (north) side of Avalanche Canyon, about 1.5 miles west of Taggart Lake, is a prominent ice formation (in some winters), starting as a single frozen waterfall and then splitting into three twisted ice runnels or "talons" at the top. All three were climbed. The first (easternmost) "talon" is the longest (350 feet total) and most exciting from a climbing standpoint. From the top traverse right to descend on snow (sometimes danger of avalanche) to a tree from which a rappel or two suffice to reach easier ground below.

Garnet Canyon

In such a major area as Garnet Canyon the climbs listed here, some not yet completed, probably represent only a portion of what is possible. There is little information available because these have seen only a single climb or attempt, and some are available only during brief intervals in a given winter.

ROUTE 1. Middle Teton, Right of Dike. II, WI3–4. First ascent about 1980, by Ron Matous and Mark Whiton. This climb is somewhat rare and forms at the base of the east ridge of the Middle Teton, just right of the black dike and to the left of the steep east buttress. Climb to the top of the snow cone at the base of the ice. The first ice pitch (80 feet) contains a 20-foot vertical section. The second lead is a full ropelength on reasonable 60–70° ice. From the top the party traversed left across slabs to gain the dike, which was followed to the top of the Dike Pinnacle. Descent was made by rappel into the Ellingwood Couloir and down into the south fork of Garnet Canyon.

ROUTE 2. Middle Teton, North Face. IV, WI4+. First ascent June 1978, by Steve Shea and David Breashears. This climb, referred to as the "Robbins Chimney," was likely the system on the eastern portion of this north face. Large icicles are often seen hanging in this chimney system during late spring, but they very rarely are continuous. The first-ascent party made their ascent during one of those rare years in which it was formed up.

ROUTE 3. Grand Teton, Lower Stettner Couloir Ice. First ascent June 1978, by Steve Shea and David Breashears (to the Black Dike only). In some years there is sufficient ice formed from the melting in the Stettner Couloir and refreezing on the cliffs below the Black Dike to provide an ice climb. The route starts from the vicinity of the Middle Teton Glacier moraine. Information concerning the difficulty of the climbing is not available.

ROUTE 4. Grand Teton, Lower Glencoe–Teepe Chute. First ascent in 1979 by Steve Shea and David Breashears (incomplete). The steep chute between Glencoe Spire and Teepe Pillar will in some years form with ice, providing a potential route. While very steep indeed, this ice climb is probably preferable to the rotten rock found here in the summer.

Teewinot Mountain

During the extremely dry winter of 1976–1977, Norm Larson and Forrest Rade climbed a few new routes on this peak that are normally covered with snow and avalanche debris. The first was the small waterfall in the drainage to the south of the Apex (40 to 50 feet, WI3). On the north side of the mountain, near the mouth of Cascade Canyon, three gullies were also climbed (300 to 500 feet, WI2+ or WI3). These are located just west of a rock outcrop (200 to 300 feet high and moss covered).

Cascade Canyon

Because of its relatively long approach and significant avalanche hazard, Cascade Canyon has not been carefully explored for winter ice climbs.

ROUTE 1. Left Pillar. II, WI5. First ascent December 1991, by Jack Tackle. The first pitch of this climb consists of 70 feet of vertical ice climbing on a prominent pillar. A section of mixed climbing is then encountered. A second pillar was then ascended that contained about 40 feet of vertical ice. Descent from both of these climbs was accomplished by means of rappel anchors from the ice.

ROUTE 2. Right Pillar. I, WI5. First ascent December 1991, by Jack Tackle. This route and its neighbor below are both located to the west of Gorbachev Falls on the steep section of rock to the east of Guides' Wall. The right pillar is a one-pitch climb that has a 40-foot vertical section.

ROUTE 3. Gorbachev Falls. II, WI3–4. First ascent December 24, 1991, by Jack Tackle. The name commemorates Gorbachev's fall from power. This climb of four or five pitches forms on the southeastern side of Storm Point near the eastern edge of the broad ledge on which one can traverse west all of the way over to the "Flake Pitch" of the summertime Guides' Wall rock climb. The first pitch begins with 25 feet of vertical ice and then eases off. The next pitch consists of snow- or ice-covered slabs for half a ropelength. Pitch three is a small curtain of ice that then continues off to the west where the climbing turns to thin ice-covered slabs. Pitch four begins with a vertical pillar and continues upward for 120 feet. Exit from the upper amphitheater via a chimney of ice. The first of the descent rappels (150 feet)

is from fixed pins. The following three rappels are from pitons and trees.

ROUTE 4. Lower Symmetry Couloir Ice. I, WI3. First ascent early December 1976, by Norm Larson and Forrest Rade. The route ascends the short (50 feet) ice section that forms from the small waterfall that one passes on the standard summertime approach to the Symmetry Couloir. Follow the usual approach from the Cascade Canyon trail up into the *cul-de-sac* below the short cliff band. This ice is immediately apparent on the wall to the left. In many years it will be covered with snow, but in dry winters it is bare ice. Note that this route is not in the main drainage from the Symmetry Couloir that separates Symmetry Spire from Storm Point.

Leigh Canyon

The approach to Leigh Canyon in winter is by usual standards long, requiring an 11.0-mile ski-in from the end of the plowed road at the Taggart Lake trailhead, or 4.0 miles if one uses a snowmobile to reach the String Lake trailhead.

ROUTE 1. Mount Woodring Ice. WI3+ or WI4. First ascent January 1977, by Norm Larson and Will Mylander. This climb is located on the lower north side of Mount Woodring opposite Staircase Arête. Two 100-foot pitches were climbed.

ROUTE 2. Laughing Lions Falls. IV, WI4. First ascent March 8, 1983, by Jim Woodmencey, Dan Burgette, and Bill Pelander (to top of first pitch only); January 5, 1985, by Dan Burgette, Renny Jackson, Jim Woodmencey, and Bill Pelander (to top of main icefall); February 19, 1985, by Jack Tackle, Alex Lowe, and Andy Carson (to top of climb). This major ice climb forms at the right (east) edge of the base of the south buttresses of Mount Moran. The first pitch consists of 150 feet of 70° ice (often thin) to a large snow ledge. The second and third pitches continue for 300 feet of 80–90° ice. This is the top of the main continuous ice section. However, it is possible to climb another 100 feet of ice in the center of the large gully above the third pitch, or skirt it to the left toward an upper curtain of ice that rarely, if ever, touches down. The route was extended in February of 1985 by using aid on the intervening rock to reach and then climb the final hanging ice section of 150 feet. The avalanche hazard on this climb can be significant and must be carefully evaluated before becoming enmeshed with this very serious route.

ROUTE 3. No Escape Ice. Three smears were climbed on the No Escape Slabs in January of 1977 by Norm Larson and Will Mylander.

Waterfalls Canyon

The winter approach to any of the northern canyons in the Teton Range requires the crossing of Jackson Lake. From the lakeshore one must then ski about 2.5 miles up the canyon to reach the main waterfalls.

ROUTE 1. Wilderness Falls. II, WI4. First ascent January 18, 1985, by Dan Burgette, John Carr, and Renny Jackson. Near the head of Waterfalls Canyon, this route ascends the summer waterfall, which is readily seen from the highway in the valley. The route is about 300 feet long. To descend from the top end of the ice, walk left (south) up to the top of the main cliff band and rappel, using two ropes, or walk off to the north and around the cliff band. The avalanche potential can be very high in the canyon on the approach but is greatly reduced once you are on the climb.

ROUTE 2. Darkness Falls. II, WI4+ or WI5. First ascent January 23, 1985, by Rex Hong and Jim Olson. Described as the "first thing you come to" (just south of Columbine Cascade), the route is reached by going up the canyon to the base of a large, mostly vertical falls on the left. This requires passing some steep rock. The route consists of two 80-foot pitches of steep ice climbing. To descend, walk off to the east and rappel.

Teton Canyon

During cold dry autumns, this west side canyon offers perhaps the most accessible array of ice climbs in the range. Numerous smears, curtains, hoses, fangs and gullies stretch along the canyon's north-facing limestone rim between the Treasure Mountain Boy Scout Camp and Teton campground. Nice top-rope routes may be found near the forks, and a few ice climbs have even been explored farther up the immense south fork canyon.

Depending on the intended ice route, climbers may park in one of several pullouts along Teton Canyon Road until the road closes in mid-November or early December. After the road closes, parking may be found in a large plowed-out area 100 yards down Teton Canyon Road from its junction with Freds Mountain Road, 1.0 mile east of Alta, Wyoming. Most climbers approach by skiing along the snowbound road, but many use snowshoes or snowmobiles, or simply walk.

Teton Canyon is a sensitive winter range for deer, elk, moose, and bighorn sheep. Stick to the road to minimize the impact of your passage.

TETON CANYON, SOUTH SIDE ICE CLIMBS (CA. 7,200)

Maps: Granite Basin and Mount Bannon

ROUTE 1. Boy Scout Falls. II, WI3+. First ascent unknown. This two- or three-pitch route lies in the obvious gully above the Treasure Mountain Boy Scout Camp. Pitch one (100 feet) ascends undulating moderate ice (40–80°) to a belay niche below a steep rock wall with some fixed pitons, bolts, and old slings. Bring some rock protection to back up this belay and to help protect the next pitch in early season. The remainder of the climb may be done in one long pitch or in two short pitches with an intermediate belay on a good ledge. The second pitch ascends an 80° ice tongue (crux), the width and thickness of which varies from year to year and month to month. The final 30-foot section ascends an 80° headwall to a large bush, which is suitable as a rappel

anchor. Descend in one full double-rope rappel, three single-rope rappels, or two single-rope rappels and some downclimbing. Avalanche danger is limited to the slope below the climb.

ROUTE 2. Reunion Falls. These three adjacent 70-foot ice curtains form on the same limestone cliff band as Boy Scout Falls approximately 1.0 mile to the east. Rappels may be made from bushes near the tops of the climbs. Potential avalanche danger exists on slopes above and below the climbs.

(1) *Left route.* I, WI4. First ascent February 1984, by Norm Larson and Andy Carson. Contains one 20-foot section of vertical ice. Rappel from a bush.

(2) *Center route.* WI4+. First ascent on December 14, 1993, by Tom Turiano and Stephen Koch. Ascends a rock overhang covered with thin ice in most years. Rock protection is useful. Rappel from a bush.

(3) *Right route.* WI5+. First ascent on December 14, 1993, by Stephen Koch and Tom Turiano. Forming irregularly, this difficult route ascends thin ice and a pair of icicles through a large rock overhang. TCUs and knifeblades help to protect the crux.

ROUTE 3. Right Ghost. I, WI5. First ascent late 1970s or early 1980s, by Steve Shea and Whitney Thurlow. Growing in a good year to 20 feet in diameter, this climb is reported to occasionally form a 110-foot, free-standing monolith. The approach can be arduous. Before embarking, scout the route with binoculars from just south of the practice rocks area to see if it is formed.

From the Teton campground, hike or ski to the first large meadow 0.25 mile up the south fork of Teton Canyon. Cross the meadow and Teton Creek and bushwhack and posthole 1,000 vertical feet up steep and forested northeast-facing slopes and gullies to the overhanging limestone cove that houses the climb.

The ice begins vertical, then steepens to overhanging, often with brittle or rotten chandeliers. The bulge at the top makes this one of the endurance test pieces of the range. Water flows consistently during the winter, so be sure to climb during a solid freeze to avoid getting soaked. A shorter and easier second pitch may be done if climbers are still game after the first. Rappel on double ropes from a tree. Beware of avalanche danger in the approach gullies and from the huge, steep, wind-loaded slopes above the climb.

ROUTE 4. Left Ghost. I, WI4. First ascent in the late 1970s, by Steve Shea, or during the winter of 1982, by Rex Hong and Tony Tulip. This 90-foot, nearly free-standing fang drips over a cove 200 yards to the south in the same cliff band as the Right Ghost. Ascend sustained near-vertical ice to the top section, which is often hollow. Belay and rappel from a tree at the top. Approach to either climb can be made via the forested ridges immediately below.

ROUTE 5. Birdbrains on Ice. II, WI4. First ascent winter 1982, by Rex Hong and Tony Tulip. This climb is located 1.0

mile or more farther up the canyon than the two Ghosts and forms as water flows over the same cliff band. The first pitch is lower angle and leads up to the second, which is a 120-foot pillar. The rappel from the top of the climb was made from pitons.

TETON CANYON, EAST SIDE ICE CLIMBS (CA. 7,000)

Maps: Granite Basin and Mount Bannon

Several excellent top-roping areas may be found at the western foot of Table Mountain between the practice rocks and the mouth of Roaring Creek. Easy to moderate practice climbs may be found at the bottom of the long treeless west draw of Table Mountain, while a small granite cove just to the north sports several more challenging options. Bring rock protection for the former area and long slings or a second anchor rope for the latter.

General References

Alpine Journal. London: The Alpine Club.

American Alpine Journal. Golden, Colorado: The American Alpine Club.

Appalachia. Boston: Appalachian Mountain Club.

Bartlett, Richard A. *Great Surveys of the American West.* Norman: University of Oklahoma Press, 1962.

Betts, Robert B. *Along the Ramparts of the Tetons: The Saga of Jackson Hole, Wyoming.* Niwot: University Press of Colorado, 1978.

Brower, David R., editor. *Manual of Ski Mountaineering.* San Francisco: Sierra Club, 1962.

Canadian Alpine Journal. Toronto: Alpine Club of Canada.

Climbing Magazine. Carbondale, Colorado: Michael Kennedy (publisher and editor).

Coulter, Henry, and Merrill F. McLane. *Mountain Climbing Guide to the Grand Tetons.* Hanover, New Hampshire: Dartmouth Mountaineering Club, 1947.

Dartmouth Mountaineering Club Journal. Hanover, New Hampshire: Dartmouth University.

Duffy, Katy, and Darwin Wile. *Teton Trails, a Hiker's Guide.* Moose, Wyoming: Grand Teton Natural History Association, 1995.

Farquhar, Francis. "Franklin Spencer Spalding and the Ascent of the Grand Teton in 1898." *American Alpine Journal,* III, no. 3 (1939), pp. 304–309, illus.

Fryxell, Fritiof M. *The Teton Peaks and Their Ascents.* Grand Teton National Park, Crandall Studio, 1932.

—. *The Tetons, Interpretations of a Mountain Landscape.* Berkeley: University of California Press, 1938. Reprint, Moose, Wyoming: Grand Teton Natural History Association, 1995.

Fryxell, Fritiof M., and Phil D. Smith. *Mountaineering in the Tetons: The Pioneer Period 1898–1940.* Moose, Wyoming: Grand Teton Natural History Association, 1995.

Grand Teton Natural History Association. *Campfire Tales of Jackson Hole,* rev. Moose, Wyoming: Grand Teton Natural History Association, 1990.

Grand Teton Nature Notes. Moose, Wyoming: Grand Teton National Park, 1935–1941.

Graydon, Don, editor. *Mountaineering: The Freedom of the Hills,* 5th ed. Seattle: The Mountaineers, 1992.

Harvard Mountaineering Club Journal. Cambridge, Massachusetts: Harvard University.

Hayden, Elizabeth Wied. *From Trapper to Tourist in Jackson Hole.* Moose, Wyoming: Grand Teton Natural History Association, 1992.

The Iowa Climber. Iowa City: State University of Iowa.

Jeffers, LeRoy. *The Call of the Mountains.* New York: Dodd, Mead and Company, 1922.

Langford, Nathaniel P. "The Ascent of Mount Hayden." *Scribner's Monthly,* VI, no. 3 (June 1873), pp. 129–157, illus.

Leonard, Richard M., et al. *Belaying the Leader: An Omnibus on Climbing Safety.* San Francisco: Sierra Club, 1956.

Love, J. D., and John C. Reed. *Creation of the Teton Landscape.* Moose, Wyoming: Grand Teton Natural History Association, 1968. Reprint, 1995.

Madsen, B. D. "History of the Upper Snake River Valley, 1807–1825." Unpublished M.A. thesis, University of California, Berkeley, 1940.

Mattes, Merrill J. *Behind the Legend of Colter's Hell.* Cheyenne: Wyoming State Historical Society, 1949.

—. *Colter's Hell and Jackson Hole.* Yellowstone Library and Museum Association, and Grand Teton Natural History Association in cooperation with the National Park Service U.S. Department of the Interior, 1962.

—. "Jackson Hole, Crossroads of the Western Fur Trade." *Pacific Northwest Quarterly,* XXXVII, no. 2 (April 1946), pp. 87–108; XXXIX, no. 1 (January 1948), pp. 3–32. Reprint, with permission by Jackson Hole Historical Society, 1987.

The Mazama. Portland, Oregon: The Mazamas.

Minnesota Naturalist. VIII, no. 2 (1957); XXII, no. 1 (1961).

The Mountaineer. Seattle: The Mountaineers.

Murie, Olaus J. *Jackson Hole with a Naturalist.* Jackson, Wyoming, 1963.

Nielsen, Cynthia, and Elizabeth Weid Hayden. *Origins, a Guide to the Place Names of Grand Teton National Park.* Moose, Wyoming: Grand Teton Natural History Association, 1988.

Petzoldt, Patricia. *On Top of the World.* New York: Thomas Y. Crowell Company, 1953.

Raynes, Bert. *Birds of Grand Teton National Park.* Moose, Wyoming: Grand Teton Natural History Association, 1989.

Righter, Robert W. *Crucible for Conservation, the Creation of Grand Teton National Park.* Boulder: Colorado Associated University Press, 1982.

Rock & Ice Magazine. Boulder, Colorado: George Bracksieck (publisher and editor-in-chief).

Scott, Doug and Souvi. *Wildlife of Yellowstone and Grand Teton National Parks.* Salt Lake City: Wheelright Lithographing Company, 1989.

Shaw, Richard J. *Wildflowers of Yellowstone and Grand Teton National Parks.* Salt Lake City: Wheelright Lithographing Company, 1992.

Sierra Club Bulletin. San Francisco: Sierra Club.

Sottile, Joe. *Jackson Hole—A Sport Climbing and Bouldering Guide.* Jackson Hole, Wyoming: Pingora Press. First edition, *Full Circle,* 1991.

Summit. Hood River, Oregon: Craig Sabina (publisher), David H. Swanson (executive publisher), and John Harlin III (editor).

Summit Magazine. Big Bear Lake, California: Jene M. Crenshaw and H.V. J. Kilness (co-publishers and editors).

Trail and Timberline. Denver: Colorado Mountain Club.

Watson, Walcott. "History of Jackson's Hole, Wyoming, before the Year 1907." Unpublished M.A. thesis, Columbia University, New York, 1935.

Index of Peaks, Routes, Topos, and Photographs

About the Authors

A CLIMBER WITH OVER 27 YEARS OF EXPERIENCE, Reynold Jackson has participated in five Himalayan climbing expeditions, including two on Mount Everest, as well as the first ascent of the North Face of Cholatse in Nepal. The recipient of two Department of the Interior Awards for Valor, Jackson has worked as a climbing ranger for 19 years for Denali and Grand Teton National Parks. He lives in Kelly, Wyoming.

LEIGH ORTENBURGER FIRST VISITED THE TETONS IN 1948 and immediately began compiling information for the first edition of *A Climber's Guide to the Teton Range*. For the next 40 years, he followed the growth of climbing and the addition of new routes in the area and conducted research on the early exploration of the range by European-Americans. Ortenburger did most of his climbing in the Tetons and the Cordillera Blanca in Peru, but he also took part in the 1961 Makalu expedition led by Sir Edmund Hillary. He passed away in 1991.

THE MOUNTAINEERS, founded in 1906, is a nonprofit outdoor activity and conservation club, whose mission is "to explore, study, preserve, and enjoy the natural beauty of the outdoors. . . . " Based in Seattle, Washington, the club is now the third-largest such organization in the United States, with 15,000 members and five branches throughout Washington State.

The Mountaineers sponsors both classes and year-round outdoor activities in the Pacific Northwest, which include hiking, mountain climbing, ski-touring, snowshoeing, bicycling, camping, kayaking and canoeing, nature study, sailing, and adventure travel. The club's conservation division supports environmental causes through educational activities, sponsoring legislation, and presenting informational programs. All club activities are led by skilled, experienced volunteers, who are dedicated to promoting safe and responsible enjoyment and preservation of the outdoors.

If you would like to participate in these organized outdoor activities or the club's programs, consider a membership in The Mountaineers. For information and an application, write or call The Mountaineers, Club Headquarters, 300 Third Avenue West, Seattle, WA 98119; (206) 284-6310; clubmail@mountaineers.org.

The Mountaineers Books, an active, nonprofit publishing program of the club, produces guidebooks, instructional texts, historical works, natural history guides, and works on environmental conservation. All books produced by The Mountaineers are aimed at fulfilling the club's mission.

Send or call for our catalog of more than 300 outdoor titles:

The Mountaineers Books
1001 SW Klickitat Way, Suite 201
Seattle, WA 98134
1-800-553-4453
e-mail: mbooks@mountaineers.org